D0193450

Roger Ebert's
Movie Yearbook
2001

Roger Ebert's Movie Yearbook 2001

Andrews McMeel Publishing

Kansas City

This book is dedicated
to Robert Zonka, 1928–1985.
God love ya.

Roger Ebert's Movie Yearbook 2001
copyright © 1998, 1999, 2000 Roger Ebert.
For information write
Andrews McMeel Publishing,
an Andrews McMeel Universal company,
4520 Main Street,
Kansas City, Missouri 64111.

ISBN 0-7407-1089-3

All the reviews in this book originally appeared
in the *Chicago Sun-Times.*

Contents

Introduction

And so here we are in the year 2001, which seemed so distant when I saw Stanley Kubrick's *2001: A Space Odyssey* in 1968. There was much talk in the months and years after the screening about how accurately Kubrick foretold the future. What no one foresaw was that the movie itself represented a dying breed. Consider how much luck a director would have today if he pitched a studio on a project that (1) was in 70mm wide screen; (2) was epic-length; (3) did not tell a conventional story; (4) did not move quickly; (5) did not contain any movie stars; (6) could not be easily summarized in the trailer; (7) had no hit songs on the sound track, only classical music; (8) had an ending that was frankly intended to be mystifying; (9) would be directed in total privacy by a director with complete control; and (10) would be premiered for the public before the studio had a chance to see it.

That movie could not be made today. And therefore *2001: A Space Odyssey* could not be made today. It is also depressing to reflect that if it *were* made, it would not survive to find an audience. *2001* opened to many negative reviews. Business was slow. Then it began to build. It played in some theaters more than a year, gradually finding its audience. Today, it would have had a bad opening Friday and be gone in a few weeks (sort of like Kubrick's final film, *Eyes Wide Shut*).

This 2001 edition of the *Movie Yearbook* includes both my original 1968 review of the film and my 1997 visit to it for the Great Movies series I write every other week. The 1997 review was written soon after seeing the movie once again in 70mm at Cyberfest at the University of Illinois at Urbana, during a celebration of HAL 9000's birthday.

* * *

This 2001 yearbook includes every review I've written in the thirty months since January 1, 1998, as well as the past year's Answer Man entries, film festival reports, interviews, essays, and glossary entries. My best guess is that about 60 percent of the book is new since last year.

This new format, introduced in 1999, replaces the long-running series of *Companions* in which I tried to do two things at once: Print most of my new reviews, and survey some of the 5,000 or so older reviews I have written. That format was frustrating. Reviews of lesser new movies had to be squeezed out, and the old reviews kept being culled until mostly the favorable ones were left.

Better, I thought, to choose a format in which every single review could be in print for at least a couple of years. I review a lot of movies (about 250 last year). Not only the major commercial releases but also foreign films, indie productions, documentaries, whatever. One of the purposes of this book is to draw attention to titles off the beaten path. By and large, if you avoid each week's most expensively promoted film, you will find, at year's end, that you have not missed many of the year's best films.

* * *

In April 2000, I held the second annual Roger Ebert's Overlooked Film Festival at the University of Illinois in Urbana-Champaign (my alma mater). The landmark Virginia Theater, a downtown vaudeville palace that once featured the Marx Brothers, was the venue. An article in the Film Festivals section of this yearbook describes the second year's selections. Included was a screening of Fred Zinnemann's *Oklahoma* in the rare thirty-frame-per-second ToddAO process. It was the first time most of the people in the audience had seen a film projected at more than twenty-four frames a second, and they were astonished by its clarity. Where did we find the ToddAO projector? Incredibly, it has been left behind in the Virginia's projection booth! Thus do we value cinema's history. (For a discussion of the forty-eight-frame-per-second MaxiVision48 process, which I support as far superior to digital projection, see an article elsewhere in this edition.)

* * *

Mention of MaxiVision provides a segue into the following paragraphs, which I want to hold over from last year's edition. Since I wrote more than a year ago about the threat of digital projection, much has changed. A year ago, digital seemed to own the future, and Dean Goodhill's struggling celluloid system seemed destined to be the better idea that failed. Today, disenchantment has set in about digital projection, and MaxiVision is attracting interest in influential quarters.

Here's what I wrote in 2000:

I believe the whole universe of film is at a dangerous crossroads.

It is taken as an accepted fact in some circles that film projection will be replaced in theaters by digital video projection, sometime in the next five years. Texas Instruments has the best projection system, and has won good reviews for its test screenings of *Phantom Menace*. Most viewers agree it is somewhere between 85 percent as good as film, and "about as good" as film.

Splendid, right? Especially since satellite delivery of movies would save the studios the cost of making and distributing prints?

Well, maybe not so good. Because satellite delivery would involve compression, so the picture quality might not be as high as in those *Phantom Menace* demos, when the projection booth was stuffed with Texas Instruments acolytes, fine-tuning their custom installation.

And maybe not so good for theaters, because satellite distribution might create the odd situation of low-paid projectionists being replaced in the booth by expensive computer systems engineers, who could expect salaries larger than the theater managers— or, in some cases, the owners.

And maybe not so good because this would further the tyranny of mass bookings. And because movies would start *exactly* on time, even if the lights were still on and the audience filing in.

And *especially* not so good because the movie industry has devoted zero research to the crucial question of whether film and video *are the same thing*. Some experts in the psychology of perception believe that film and video affect the mind in fundamentally different ways. Film creates an alpha, or reverie, state. Video creates a beta, or hypnotic, state. It may be that a video picture, no matter how "good," would not affect the subconscious in the same way—that a video movie in a theater would somehow subtly not reach us emotionally in the same way that film does. In that case, theatrical video projection could destroy the intangible relationship between the viewer and the screen.

Meanwhile, why settle for video "about as good" as film, when a new film projection system promises a picture more than twice as good? MaxiVision48 uses forty-eight frames a second, not twenty-four, and has a picture area 30 percent larger (it recaptures the unneeded space used by the analog sound track). It incorporates existing technology, so is much cheaper than video projection. I've seen MaxiVision and video projection and, believe me, there's no comparison.

For more info: www.mv48.com.

* * *

The *2001 Yearbook* also includes:

• All the new Answer Man entries that are still relevant, arranged by movie title or topic. A little pointing finger at the end of a review means there are Answer Man questions on the film. I also included a few dozen AM entries that got squeezed out of the biweekly column but are still relevant.

• Selections from my daily film festival coverage from Telluride, Toronto, Sundance, and Cannes, plus three articles from my visit to India for film events in Calcutta and Hyderabad.

• A selection of new Glossary Entries. *Ebert's Bigger Little Movie Glossary* was published in May 1999. But keep those new contributions coming in.

• Those interviews and "think pieces" I've done during the past twelve months. I don't attend as many junkets as I used to, because they're not a useful way of getting real information: They've been turned into assembly lines for sound bites, and cater to the "benevolent blurbsters" who can be counted on for burbles of ecstasy about every film they see.

My reviews and articles can be found on-line on CompuServe (the go-word is "Ebert") and the Web (www.suntimes.com/ebert). From the TV program, *Ebert & Roeper and the Movies,* audio is on-line at www.ebert-movies.com.

* * *

Where should you start in compiling a movie library? *For Keeps,* by Pauline Kael, brings together a generous selection from her many previous books of reviews, providing an overview of the career of the most influential of film critics. The greatly revised and expanded edition of David Thomson's *Biographical Dictionary of Film* is an opinionated, informed, concise summary of hundreds of key careers. The late Ephraim Katz's *Film Encyclopedia* is an invaluable one-volume survey of the world of film. And *Distinguishing Features,* by Stanley Kauffmann, is the latest collection of reviews by the critic whose superb writing and scholarship have distinguished the *New Republic* for decades. Jonathan Rosenbaum's recent book *Movies as Politics* showcases the work of one of the best contemporary critics. David Bordwell's *A History of Film Style* tells you more about how to look at a movie than any other book I have ever found.

For DVD fans, there is no better guide than *The DVD and Laserdisc Companion*, by Douglas Pratt. For the critics who shaped today's film criticism, I recommend the collected works of Kael, Kauffmann, Manny Farber, Andrew Sarris, Dwight Macdonald, James Agee, and Graham Greene.

On the Web, the best critics include James Berardinelli, Peter Brunette, Charles Taylor, Scott Renshaw, Damien Cannon, Harvey S. Karten, Edwin Jahiel, and the excellent writers at Mr. Showbiz and Film.com. For parents in search of *detailed* factual information about the contents of movies, supplied without a political or religious agenda, there is no better site than www.screenit.com. David Poland's Hot Button column at the TNT Rough Cut site is the best-informed daily report on the movie biz. To survey many different reviews of a movie, try Rotten Tomatoes (www.rottentomatoes.com) and the Movie Review Query Engine (www.mrqe.com). For gossip and insider scoops, Harry Knowles operates a clearinghouse at Ain't It Cool. The most valuable resource for finding material on the Web is the Internet Movie Database (http://us.imdb.com/search).

* * *

My muse is my wife, Chaz, who offers an atmosphere of love and encouragement, enriching my life and work. She is a movie lover like myself, attending most of the screenings and festivals, helping me plow through the mob scenes at Cannes, and survive the sneak previews. Chaz has a gift I can only wonder at: She remembers the names of all the characters. Not just Marsellus Wallace, but Doc Wallace. To her, my love and gratitude.

ROGER EBERT

Acknowledgments

My editor is Dorothy O'Brien, tireless, cheerful, all-noticing. She is assisted by the equally invaluable Julie Roberts. My friend and longtime editor, Donna Martin, suggested this new approach to the annual volume. The design is by Cameron Poulter, the typographical genius of Hyde Park. My thanks to production editor Christi Clemons-Hoffman, who renders Cameron's design into reality. I have been blessed with the expert and discriminating editorial direction of John Barron, Laura Emerick, Jeff Wisser, Marlene Gelfond, and Miriam DiNunzio, and the copyediting of Jeff Johnson, Paige Smoron, and Teresa Budasi at the *Chicago Sun-Times*; Sue Roush at Universal Press Syndicate; and Michelle Daniel at Andrews McMeel Publishing. Many thanks are also due to the production staff at *Ebert & Roeper,* and to Marsha Jordan at WLS-TV. My gratitude goes to Carol Iwata, my expert office assistant, and to Marlene Gelfond, at the *Sun-Times.* And special thanks and love to my wife, Chaz, for whom I can only say: If more film critics had a spouse just like her, the level of cheer in the field would rise dramatically.

ROGER EBERT

Key to Symbols

★★★★ A great film
★★★ A good film
★★ Fair
★ Poor

G, PG, PG-13, R, NC-17: Ratings of the Motion Picture Association of America

G   Indicates that the movie is suitable for general audiences

PG   Suitable for general audiences but parental guidance is suggested

PG-13   Recommended for viewers 13 years or above; may contain material inappropriate for younger children

R   Recommended for viewers 17 or older

NC-17   Intended for adults only

141 m.   Running time

1999   Year of theatrical release

☞   Refers to "Questions for the Movie Answer Man"

Reviews

A

The Adventures of Rocky & Bullwinkle ★ ★ ★
PG, 90 m., 2000

Rene Russo (Natasha), Jason Alexander (Boris), Piper Perabo (Karen Sympathy), Randy Quaid (Cappy Von Trapment), Robert De Niro (Fearless Leader), June Foray (Rocky [voice]), Keith Scott (Bullwinkle [voice]), Keith Scott (Narrator), Janeane Garofalo (Minnie Mogul). Directed by Des McAnuff and produced by Jane Rosenthal and Robert De Niro. Screenplay by Kenneth Lonegran, based on characters developed by Jay Ward.

The original *Rocky & Bullwinkle* TV show was smarter than it needed to be, and a lot of adults sneaked a look now and then. It helped point the way to today's crossover animated shows like *The Simpsons*. Now comes the movie version of the TV show (which was canceled in 1964), and it has the same mixture of dumb puns, corny sight gags and sly, even sophisticated in-jokes. It's a lot of fun.

The movie combines the animated moose and squirrel with live action—and even yanks three of the characters (Natasha, Boris, and Fearless Leader) out of the TV set and into the real world (where they're played by Rene Russo, Jason Alexander, and Robert De Niro, explaining, "We're attached to the project").

The breathless narrator portentously explains: "Expensive animation characters are converted to even more expensive movie stars!" The narrator (Keith Scott), of course, always seemed to stand outside the action and know that *R&B* was only a cartoon (at one point he complains he has been reduced to narrating the events of his own life). And the movie is also self-aware; when someone (I think maybe Fearless L) breathlessly announces, "There has never been a way to destroy a cartoon character until now!" he's asked, "What about Roger Rabbit?"

The plot involves a scheme by Fearless Leader to win world domination by hypnotizing everyone with RBTV (Really Bad TV). Only Rocky and Bullwinkle have long years of experience at foiling the evil schemes of Fearless, Natasha, and Boris, and as they fumble their way to a final confrontation we also get a coast-to-coast road movie (cheerfully acknowledged as a cliché by the narrator).

The movie has a lot of funny moments, which I could destroy by quoting, but will not. (Oh, all right: At one point Rocky cries, "We have to get out of here!" and Bullwinkle bellows: "Quick! Cut to a commercial!") As much fun as the wit is the film's overall sense of well-being; this is a *happy* movie and not the desperate sort of scratching for laughs we got in a cartoon retread like *The Flintstones in Viva Rock Vegas*. It's the sort of movie where De Niro parodies his famous "Are you talking to me?" speech with such good-natured fun that instead of groaning, we reflect—well, everyone else has ripped it off, so why shouldn't he get his own turn?

The movie is wall-to-wall with familiar faces, including Janeane Garofalo as a studio executive, Randy Quaid as the FBI chief, Whoopi Goldberg as a judge, John Goodman as a cop, Billy Crystal as a mattress salesman, James Rebhorn as the president, and Jonathan Winters in three roles. Rene Russo makes a persuasive Natasha, all red lipstick, seductive accent, and power high heels, and De Niro's patent leather hair and little round glasses will remind movie buffs of Donald Pleasance.

But the real discovery of the movie is its (human) lead, a twenty-three-year-old newcomer named Piper Perabo, who plays an FBI agent. She has fine comic timing, and is so fetching she sort of stops the clock. Like Renee Zellweger in *Jerry Maguire*, she comes more or less out of nowhere (well, a couple of obscure made-for-videos) and becomes a star right there before our eyes.

Comedy is such a fragile art form. *The Adventures of Rocky & Bullwinkle* isn't necessarily any more brilliant or witty or inventive than all the other recent retreads of classic cartoons and old sitcoms. But it feels like more fun. From time to time I'm reminded of George C. Scott's Rule No. 3 for judging movie acting: "Is there a joy of performance? Can you tell that

1

the actors are having fun?" This time, you can. There's a word for this movie, and that word is jolly.

The Adventures of Sebastian Cole ★ ★ ★
R, 99 m., 1999

Adrian Grenier (Sebastian Cole), Clark Gregg (Hank/Henrietta), Aleksa Palladino (Mary), Margaret Colin (Joan), Marni Lustig (Jessica), John Shea (Hartley). Directed by Tod Williams and produced by Karen Barber and Jasmine Kosovic. Screenplay by Williams.

The Adventures of Sebastian Cole is a coming-of-age movie that puts a new spin on some of the challenges faced by sensitive teenagers. It's not unusual to have problems with a stepfather—but it's fairly rare for the stepfather to announce he's decided to become a woman. It's also rare for a movie to show a teenager who needs guidance, and a parent willing to provide it. The fathers of most movie teenagers are absent, stupid, or cruel; Sebastian's is wise and loving, first as Hank, then as Henrietta.

Sebastian (Adrian Grenier) is an introverted, screwed-up member of a dysfunctional upper-class family. He wants to be a writer. He's good-looking, but with so little self-confidence that when a girl seriously likes him, he dumps her. We can guess from an early scene what a confusion his life has been. At a family holiday dinner, we meet his divorced parents, who are both with their new spouses, in one of those uneasy exercises designed to provide continuity for the children, who in fact only want to flee the table.

His mother, Joan (Margaret Colin), is bright, pretty, British, and usually drunk. She's married to a floppy-haired hulk named Hank (Clark Gregg). Sebastian's father, Hartley (John Shea), is an architect with a new Asian-American wife who hardly even seems to be there, so little does she ever say. Then there is Sebastian's sister, Jessica (Marni Lustig), who has a boyfriend on a motorcycle and yearns to climb on behind him and ride far, far away.

Soon after this tortured family event, Hank calls together his wife and stepchildren and calmly announces that he has decided to become a woman. This doesn't go over well. Jessica leaves on the boyfriend's motorcycle and enrolls at Stanford, which is more or less as far as you can get from Dutchess County in New York. Sebastian listens to Hank's news in stunned silence. Hank wants to remain married to Joan, but she pulls out and moves back to England. At first Sebastian lives with her, but as she recedes into heavier drinking he moves back in with Hank, who is the only parent who really cares for him. Hank is firm, with traditional values, and sets rules for Sebastian.

The Adventures of Sebastian Cole might have developed along predictable lines as a sitcom about coming of age with a transsexual as your parent. But the movie avoids easy and cheap shots, and actually grows more perceptive and thoughtful, until at last we're drawn in on the simple human level: These are people worth knowing.

Clark Gregg's performance as Hank and Henrietta is the most remarkable element of the movie. No matter what he does with clothing and hair, he looks like a large man in a dress. But there is no simpering, no coquetry, no going for laughs; in his heart he knows he is a woman, and he is true to that inner conviction with a courage that the movie doesn't need to underline because it permeates the performance. At one point, he has to hit someone to defend his honor; when Sebastian asks him, "Where'd you learn to fight like that?" his answer approaches perfection.

Sebastian is not thrilled by the emergence of Henrietta, and blames everything on his stepfather: "If you hadn't been so selfish and thought only of yourself, we'd all still be together and happy. Things were perfectly fine before." But they were not. Joan, the mother, was drifting into drunken passivity. And the biological father, Hartley, a famous architect, has a revealing talk with his son: "If you're serious about being a writer, you've got to sacrifice the people you love to your work." It's pretty clear that's what Hartley did.

Adrian Grenier, an actor previously unknown to me, at first appears to be just another movie hunk, but he reveals depths and quiet notes and by the end of the film has created a complex character. His Sebastian is uncertain about himself, without goals, afraid of emotional involvement, and yet with a certain cocky daring; faced with spending another year in school because of a missing P.E. requirement, he fakes proficiency at karate.

His relationship with a girl his age, Mary (Aleksa Palladino), seems truer to life than the simplified soap opera romances we often get in teenage movies. They're both uncertain about their emerging sexuality; she likes him, finds a charming way to let him know that, and has to wait a year for the lesson to take. And because he likes her so much, he breaks off communication. Why do guys do that? Girls have been asking that question for centuries.

The film, written and directed by Tod Williams, reminded me of *A Soldier's Daughter Never Cries* (1998), another movie about children emerging from an unconventional family. That one, based on a memoir by the daughter of the novelist James Jones, showed a happy family. Sebastian Cole comes from an unhappy one— but Hank/Henrietta makes it all right by being willing to invest time and trouble in caring about him. This movie, which must sound odd, is reassuring: A good kid can survive a lot and turn out all right, despite the pain along the way.

Affliction ★ ★ ★

R, 114 m., 1999

Nick Nolte (Wade Whitehouse), Sissy Spacek (Margie Fogg), James Coburn (Glen Whitehouse), Willem Dafoe (Rolfe Whitehouse), Mary Beth Hurt (Lillian), Jim True (Jack Hewitt), Marian Seldes (Alma Pittman), Holmes Osborne (Gordon LaRiviere). Directed by Paul Schrader and produced by Linda Reisman. Screenplay by Schrader, based on the novel by Russell Banks.

Nick Nolte is a big, shambling, confident male presence in the movies, and it is startling to see his cocksure presence change into fear in Paul Schrader's *Affliction*. Nolte plays Wade Whitehouse, the sheriff of a small New Hampshire town, whose uniform, gun, and stature do not make up for a deep feeling of worthlessness. He drinks, he smokes pot on the job, he walks with a sad weariness, he is hated by his ex-wife, and his young daughter looks at him as if he's crazy.

When we meet Glen, his father, we understand the source of his defeat. The older man (James Coburn) is a cauldron of alcoholic venom, a man whose consolation in life has been to dominate and terrorize his family. There are scenes where both men are on the screen together, and you can sense the sheriff shrinking, as if afraid of a sudden blow. The women in their lives have been an audience for cruelty; of the older man's wife, it is said, "Women like this, it's like they lived their lives with the sound turned off. And then they're gone."

Affliction is based on a novel by Russell Banks, whose work also inspired *The Sweet Hereafter*. Both films are set in bleak winter landscapes, and both involve a deep resentment of parental abuse—this one more obviously, since Sheriff Whitehouse's entire unhappy life has been, and still is, controlled by fear of his father. We're reminded of other films Schrader wrote (*Taxi Driver, Raging Bull, The Mosquito Coast*) or directed (*Mishima, Hardcore*), in which men's violence is churned up by feelings of inadequacy. (He also wrote *The Last Temptation of Christ*, in which at least one line applies: "Father, why hast thou forsaken me?")

Wade Whitehouse is a bad husband, a bad father, and a bad sheriff. He retains enough qualities to inspire the loyalty, or maybe the sympathy, of a girlfriend named Margie (Sissy Spacek), but his ex-wife (Mary Beth Hurt) looks at him in deep contempt, and his brother Rolfe (Willem Dafoe), the film's narrator, has been wise to clear out of the town and its poisons.

Early in the film, Wade decides to show a little enterprise on the job. A friend of his has gone out as a hunting guide for a rich man and returned with the man's expensive gun, some bloodstains, and a story of an accident. Wade doesn't believe it was an accident, and like a sleepwalker talking himself back to wakefulness, he begins an investigation that stirs up the stagnant town—and even rouses him into a state where he can be reached, for the first time in years, by fresh thoughts about how his life has gone wrong.

Because there are elements of a crime mystery in *Affliction*, it would be unwise to reveal too much about this side of the plot. It is interrupted, in any event, by another death: Wade and Margie go to the old man's house to find that Wade's mother, Glen's wife, lies dead upstairs and Glen is unable to acknowledge the situation. It is even possible that the sick woman crawled upstairs and was forgotten by a man whose inner eye has long been focused only on his own self-diagnosis: not drunk enough, drunk just right, or too drunk?

Rolfe returns to town for the funeral and to supply missing elements from the story of their childhood, and the film ends in an explosion that seems prepared even in the first frame. Its meaning is very clear: Cruelty to a child is not over in a moment or a day, but is like those medical capsules embedded in the flesh, which release their contents for years.

Nolte and Coburn are magnificent in this film, which is like an expiation for abusive men. It is revealing to watch them in their scenes together—to see how they're able to use physical presence to sketch the history of a relationship. Schrader says he cast Coburn because he needed an actor who was big enough, and had a "great iconic weight," to convincingly dominate Nolte. He found one. Coburn has spent a career largely in shallow entertainments, and here he rises to the occasion with a performance of power.

There is a story about that. "I met with Coburn before the picture began," Schrader told me, "and told him how carefully Nolte prepares for a role. I told Coburn that if he walked through the movie, Nolte might let him get away with it for a day, but on the second day all hell would break loose. Coburn said, 'Oh, you mean you want me to really act? I can do that. I haven't often been asked to, but I can.'" He can.

Afterglow ★ ★ ★
R, 113 m., 1998

Nick Nolte (Lucky Mann), Julie Christie (Phyllis Mann), Lara Flynn Boyle (Marianne Byron), Jonny Lee Miller (Jeffrey Byron), Jay Underwood (Donald Duncan), Domini Blythe (Helene Pelletier), Yves Corbeil (Bernard Ornay), Alan Fawcett (Count Falco/Jack Dana). Directed by Alan Rudolph and produced by Robert Altman. Screenplay by Rudolph.

Julie Christie has the kind of face you find on the covers of romance novels, and surely one of the reasons she was cast in *Dr. Zhivago* was that she would look so good on the poster. She projects the wounded perfection of a great beauty who has had the wrong sort of luck. In *Afterglow,*

only her third role in the 1990s, Alan Rudolph has given her the sort of character she knows inside out: bemused, sad, needful, mysterious.

She plays Phyllis Mann, a former B-movie actress specializing in horror roles, who now lives in Montreal with her husband, Lucky (Nick Nolte), a handyman equally at home with wrenches and wenches. Some great sadness from the past overshadows their marriage, and although Phyllis and Lucky are held together by love and understanding, he philanders, with her tacit permission, among the lonely housewives who phone for his services ("Plumbing and a woman's nature are both unpredictable, and filled with hidden mysteries," he philosophizes).

Nolte plays Lucky not as a sex machine, however, but as a tender, observant man who feels a certain sympathy with the women he has sex with. The deal with his wife is, he can fool around, as long as he doesn't get serious. One day seriousness threatens, when he meets Marianne Byron (Lara Flynn Boyle), a yuppie wife who yearns for the baby her husband will not, or cannot, give her. So deep is her need that she has hired Lucky Mann to convert an extra bedroom into a nursery, even as her cold, arrogant husband, Jeffrey (Jonny Lee Miller, Sick Boy in *Trainspotting*), vows he wants nothing to do with children.

The plot to this point could be the stuff of soap opera, but there's always something askew in an Alan Rudolph film, unexpected notes and touches that maintain a certain ironic distance while permitting painful flashes of human nature to burst through. Imagine a soap in which the characters subtly mock their roles while the actors occasionally break down in grief about their offscreen lives.

Afterglow has a script that permits coincidence and contrivance; like many of Rudolph's films (*Choose Me, Trouble in Mind*), it has characters who seem fated to share common destinies. As Lucky Mann falls into the pit created by Marianne's great need, Phyllis meets Jeffrey and allows herself to be drawn toward him in a mixture of curiosity and revenge.

Afterglow doesn't depend on a visible style as much as some of Rudolph's films; he seems so interested in the story, which he wrote himself, that he doesn't need to impose directorial distance. That may be because the characters are so poignant. Julie Christie, lounging on a sofa looking at her old horror films, has speeches in which she looks back on Hollywood with the fascination of an accident victim. Nolte's character is not a one-dimensional louse but a man whose sex life may reflect a deep sympathy for women—the same sympathy he feels for his wife, so steeped in sadness.

As for Christie, what's the story with her? She is so familiar a face from her early films *(Darling, McCabe and Mrs. Miller, Far from the Madding Crowd, Shampoo)*, but then her career drifted into unessential and forgettable films. Infrequent newspaper interviews reported on her happiness in solitude. Like the character Phyllis, she has a distance on her early career; unlike her, she uses it here to create something fresh and vulnerable. How mysterious and intriguing some performances can be.

After Life ★ ★ ★ ★
NO MPAA RATING, 118 m., 1999

Arata (Takashi Mochizuki), Taketoshi Naito (Ichiro Watanabe), Erika Oda (Shiori Satonaka), Susumu Terajima (Satoru Kawashima), Takashi Naito (Takuro Sugie), Hisako Hara (Kiyo Nishimura). Directed by Hirokazu Kore-eda and produced by Sato Shiho and Akieda Masayuki. Screenplay by Kore-eda.

The people materialize from out of clear white light as a bell tolls. Where are they? An ordinary building is surrounded by greenery and an indistinct space. They are greeted by staff members who explain, courteously, that they have died and are now at a way station before the next stage of their experience.

They will be here a week. Their assignment is to choose one memory, one only, from their lifetimes: one memory they want to save for eternity. Then a film will be made to reenact that memory, and they will move along, taking only that memory with them, forgetting everything else. They will spend eternity within their happiest memory.

That is the premise of Hirokazu Kore-eda's *After Life,* a film that reaches out gently to the audience and challenges us: What is the single moment in our own lives we treasure the most? One of the new arrivals says that he has only bad memories. The staff members urge him to

think more deeply. Surely spending eternity within a bad memory would be—well, literally, hell. And spending forever within our best memory would be, I suppose, as close as we should dare to come to heaven.

The film is completely matter-of-fact. No special effects, no celestial choirs, no angelic flimflam. The staff is hardworking; they have a lot of memories to process in a week, and a lot of production work to do on the individual films. There are pragmatic details to be worked out: Scripts have to be written, sets constructed, special effects improvised. This isn't all metaphysical work; a member of an earlier group, we learn, chose Disney World, singling out the Splash Mountain ride.

Kore-eda, with this film and the 1997 masterpiece *Maborosi,* has earned the right to be considered with Kurosawa, Bergman, and other great humanists of the cinema. His films embrace the mystery of life, and encourage us to think about why we are here and what makes us truly happy. At a time when so many movies feed on irony and cynicism, here is a man who hopes we will feel better and wiser when we leave his film.

The method of the film contributes to the impact. Some of these people, and some of their memories, are real (we are not told which). Kore-eda filmed hundreds of interviews with ordinary people in Japan. The faces on the screen are so alive, the characters seem to be recalling events they really lived through in a world of simplicity and wonder. Although there are a lot of characters in the movie, we have no trouble telling them apart because each is unique and irreplaceable.

The staff members offer a mystery of their own. Who are they, and why were they chosen to work here at the way station instead of moving on to the next stage like everybody else? The solution to that question is contained in revelations I will not discuss, because they emerge so naturally from the film.

One of the most emotional moments in *After Life* is when a young staff member discovers a connection between himself and an elderly new arrival. The new arrival is able to tell him something that changes his entire perception of his life. This revelation, of a young love long ago, has the same kind of deep, bittersweet resonance as the ending of *The Dead,* the James Joyce short story (and John Huston film) about a man who feels a sudden burst of identification with his wife's first lover, a young man now long dead.

After Life considers the kind of delicate material that could be destroyed by schmaltz. It's the kind of film that Hollywood likes to remake with vulgar, paint-by-the-numbers sentimentality. It is like a transcendent version of *Ghost,* evoking the same emotions, but deserving them. Knowing that his premise is supernatural and fantastical, Kore-eda makes everything else in the film quietly pragmatic. The staff labors against deadlines. The arrivals set to work on their memories. There will be a screening of the films on Saturday—and then Saturday, and everything else, will cease to exist. Except for the memories.

Which memory would I choose? I sit looking out the window as images play through my mind. There are so many moments to choose from. Just thinking about them makes me feel fortunate. I remember a line from Ingmar Bergman's film *Cries and Whispers.* After the older sister dies painfully of cancer, her diary is discovered. In it she remembers a day during her illness when she was feeling better. Her two sisters and her nurse join her in the garden, in the sunlight, and for a moment pain is forgotten and they are simply happy to be together. This woman who we have seen die a terrible death has written: "I feel a great gratitude to my life, which gives me so much." ☞

Agnes Browne ★ ★ ½
R, 92 m., 2000

Anjelica Huston (Agnes Browne), Marion O'Dwyer (Marion Monks), Ray Winstone (Mr. Billy), Arno Chevrier (Pierre), Niall O'Shea (Mark Browne), Ciaran Owens (Frankie Browne), Roxanna Williams (Cathy Browne), Carl Power (Simon Browne), Mark Power (Dermot Browne), Gareth O'Connor (Rory Browne). Directed by Anjelica Huston and produced by Jim Sheridan, Arthur Lappin, Huston, and Greg Smith. Screenplay by John Goldsmith and Brendan O'Carroll, based on the novel *The Mammy* by O'Carroll.

Agnes Browne is an Irish housewife with six sons and a daughter and her husband dead since ten minutes past four this afternoon, giving a piece of her mind to the government clerk who wants to see a certificate before paying out the poor man's death benefits. She doesn't make much money with her fruit and vegetable cart in a street market, but she's got her pride and her friends, and her children all wear matching sweaters to the funeral—even if they match because they all came from the same charity agency.

Agnes (Anjelica Huston) is like the lucky twin of Angela McCourt, the heroine of *Angela's Ashes.* Things are grim but not bleak, and at least there's no drunken husband in the picture (one of her youngest is so overcome at the funeral he holds two oranges up to block his eyes). She's best friends with Marion (Marion O'Dwyer), who runs the next cart in the market, and if she's not overly smart at least she's observant and thoughtful.

Anjelica Huston might seem like an unlikely actress to play her, and to direct *Agnes Browne,* but reflect that her father, the director John Huston, maintained a country home (almost a castle, really) in Ireland during her childhood, and that she grew up feeling as Irish as American. Her accent can't be faulted, and neither can her touch for detail: not the realistic details of *Angela's Ashes,* but the pop fiction details of what's essentially a warmhearted soap opera.

The supporting characters come on-screen all but wearing descriptive labels on cords around their necks. Consider Mister Billy, played by Ray Winstone, an actor so good at being mean that two of England's best actors (Tim Roth and Gary Oldman) both cast him as an abusive father in their first movies. Mister Billy is the neighborhood loan shark, a man who hands you the cash and expects you to pay interest on it for the rest of your life.

Agnes has to borrow from him to finance her husband's funeral, and when she's able to pay him back in a lump sum, his eyes narrow with disappointment. When her son Frankie finds a trade and needs to buy tools, Mister Billy is there with another loan, and sinister intentions.

Some days are sunny, some cloudy in Agnes's life. She is flattered to be asked out on a date by the French baker Pierre (Arno Chevrier), and saddened when Marion gets bad news about a medical exam. And always in the back of her head is a dream, which, her aim being modest, is to meet Tom Jones. Whether she marries Pierre or meets Jones, as well as the state of Marion's health and the outcome of Frankie's loan, I will leave you to discover.

This is a modest but likable film, and Anjelica Huston plays a heroine who makes us smile. But it's skimpy material, and I'm not sure why Huston was attracted to it; her first film as a director, *Bastard Out of Carolina* (1996), a story about child abuse, was fiercer and more passionate. *Agnes Browne* is not consequential enough to inspire a visit to a theater, but as a video rental it's not a bad idea.

Air Bud 2: Golden Receiver ★ ½
G, 91 m., 1998

Kevin Zegers (Josh Framm), Cynthia Stevenson (Jackie Framm), Gregory Harrison (Patrick Sullivan), Nora Dunn (Natalia), Perry Anzilotti (Popov), Shayn Solberg (Tom Stewart), Robert Costanzo (Coach Fanelli), Simon Isherwood (Ram's Coach). Directed by Richard Martin and produced by Robert Vince. Screenplay by Aaron Mendelsohn and Paul Tamasy.

Air Bud 2: Golden Receiver is a pale shadow of the entertaining 1997 family movie. It's a sequel that lacks the spirit and sweetness of the original. I went to the first *Air Bud* with a heavy heart, since movies about dogs that play basketball do not rank high on my wish list. But I was won over by the movie's charm, and its story about a new kid in town who is an outcast who practices basketball by himself until he realizes that his dog, Buddy, can play too.

There was some sadness in the setup; the boy, named Josh (Kevin Zegers), had just lost his dad, a test pilot killed in a crash. He and his mom and little sister had moved to a leafy Seattle coastal suburb. Josh was the manager of the school basketball team, and Buddy— well, Buddy hardly ever missed a shot, and eventually helped the school team win the big game.

Is it against the rules for dogs to play on school teams? The movie nimbly sidesteps that question, and this time Buddy turns his talents to football, trading in his little paw-sized basketball shoes for a jersey with padded shoul-

ders, which makes him look weirdly deformed. Buddy, catching the ball in his mouth, flawlessly executes plays. He's never offside, always runs the patterns, inspires fumbles, and can outrun anyone on the field.

The human story is not quite as simple. Josh's mom, Jackie (Cynthia Stevenson), has started to date again and falls in love with the local veterinarian, Patrick Sullivan (Gregory Harrison). Josh and his buddy don't like this and do what they can to prevent the romance. Meanwhile, in a total miscalculation, the movie unwisely adds a lamebrained subplot about a couple of Russian petnappers who apparently plan to steal a lot of animals and use them to set up a zoo.

The chief pet thief, played by Nora Dunn, runs through people's yards after Buddy, wearing a slinky black dress and waving a big butterfly net that would certainly not attract the attention of a town alerted to dognapping. She and her sidekick tool around town in an ice-cream truck with an annoying little jingling bell, which would also certainly not attract attention. She finds out about Buddy through TV coverage of the dog's brilliant play in the basketball finals, which in this town are apparently held the day before football season opens.

There are way too many heartfelt scenes between Mrs. Framm and her fiancé. And not enough stunts by the dog (perhaps because the original and great Buddy, who could allegedly actually shoot baskets, died of cancer soon after the first film was completed). I did like Robert Costanzo's performance as the football coach, a quaint creature who actually believes that schoolchildren should play sports for fun.

And there was another aspect of the film that amused me. Whenever Buddy scores a touchdown, he doesn't spike the ball (lacking the equipment to do so). Instead, he celebrates his score by rolling onto his back and luxuriously digging his shoulders into the turf.

Watching him do that, I was reminded of the classic dog novels of Albert Payson Terhune, which I read as a boy. He wrote about "Lad," as I recall, and revealed that when dogs don't like you, they engage in that shoulder behavior as a way of suggesting they're rolling in the putrefying flesh of their dead enemies.

Too bad the play-by-play announcer doesn't

pick up on that, but then the announcers are not real sharp in this town. The first time Buddy runs onto the field, the announcer shouts, "It's a dog!" Don't you kinda think a play-by-play announcer in a small suburban town would recognize the golden retriever that had just won the basketball championship? A dog like that, it attracts attention.

An Alan Smithee Film
Burn Hollywood Burn no stars
R, 86 m., 1998

Ryan O'Neal (James Edmunds), Coolio (Dion Brothers), Chuck D (Leon Brothers), Eric Idle (Alan Smithee), Richard Jeni (Jerry Glover), Leslie Stefanson (Michelle Rafferty), Sandra Bernhard (Ann Glover), Cherie Lunghi (Myrna Smithee). Directed by Alan Smithee and produced by Ben Myron. Screenplay by Joe Eszterhas.

An Alan Smithee Film Burn Hollywood Burn is a spectacularly bad film—incompetent, unfunny, ill-conceived, badly executed, lamely written, and acted by people who look trapped in the headlights.

The title provides clues to the film's misfortune. It was originally titled *An Alan Smithee Film.* Then *Burn, Hollywood, Burn!* Now its official title is *An Alan Smithee Film Burn Hollywood Burn*—just like that, with no punctuation. There's a rich irony connected with the title. "Alan Smithee," of course, is the pseudonym that Hollywood slaps on a film if the original director insists on having his name removed. The plot of *AASFBHB* involves a film so bad that the director wants his name removed, but since his *real* name is Alan Smithee, what can he do? Ho, ho.

Wait, it gets better. The movie was directed by Arthur Hiller, who hated the way the film was edited so much that, yes, he insisted his name be removed from the credits. So now it really *is* an Alan Smithee film. That leaves one mystery: Why didn't Joe Eszterhas, the film's writer, take off his name too?

I fear it is because this version of the film does indeed reflect his vision. Eszterhas is sometimes a good writer, but this time he has had a complete lapse of judgment. Even when he kids himself, he's wrong. "It's completely terrible!"

a character says of the film within the film. "It's worse than *Showgirls!*" Of course, Eszterhas wrote *Showgirls*, which got some bad reviews, but it wasn't completely terrible. I was looking forward to explaining that to him this week, but he canceled his visit to Chicago, reportedly because his voice gave out. Judging by this film, it was the last thing to go.

Have you ever been to one of those office parties where the PR department has put together a tribute to a retiring boss? That's how this film plays. It has no proper story line. No dramatic scenes. It's all done in documentary form, with people looking at the camera and relating the history of a doomed movie named *Trio*, which cost more than $200 million and stars Sylvester Stallone, Whoopi Goldberg, and Jackie Chan, who play themselves as if they are celebrity impersonators.

The film stars Eric Idle as Smithee, who eventually burns the print and checks into the Keith Moon Psychiatric Institute in England (ho, ho). Ryan O'Neal plays the film's producer. I love the way he's introduced. We see the back of a guy's head, and hear him saying, "Anything!" Then the chair swivels around and he says "anything!" again, and we see, *gasp!*—why, it's *Ryan O'Neal!* I was reminded of the moment in Mike Todd's *Around the World in 80 Days* when the piano player swivels around and, gasp!—it's *Frank Sinatra!*

These actors and others recount the history of the doomed film in unconvincing sound bites, which are edited together without wit or rhythm. One is accustomed to seeing bad movies, but not incompetent ones. Sophomores in a film class could make a better film than this. Hell, I have a movie here by Les Brown, a kid who looks about twelve and who filmed a thriller in his mother's basement, faking a fight scene by wrestling with a dummy. If I locked you in a room with both movies, you'd end up looking at the kid's.

In taking his name off the film, Arthur Hiller has wisely distanced himself from the disaster, but on the basis of what's on the screen I cannot, frankly, imagine any version of this film that I would want to see. The only way to save this film would be to trim eighty-six minutes.

Here's an interesting thing. The film is filled with celebrities playing themselves, and most of them manifestly have no idea who they are.

The only celebrity who emerges relatively intact is Harvey Weinstein, head of Miramax, who plays a private eye—but never mind the role, just listen to him. He could find success in voice-over work.

Now consider Stallone. He reappears in the outtakes over the closing credits. Such cookies are a treat for audiences after the film is over. Here they're as bad as the film, but notice a moment when Stallone thinks he's off camera, and asks someone about a Planet Hollywood shirt. *Then* he sounds like himself. A second later, playing himself, he sounds all wrong. Jackie Chan copes by acting like he's in a Jackie Chan movie, but Whoopi Goldberg mangles her scenes in a cigar bar, awkwardly trying to smoke a stogie. It's God's way of paying her back for telling Ted Danson it would be funny to wear blackface at the Friars' Club.

All About My Mother ★ ★ ★ ½
R, 101 m., 1999

Cecilia Roth (Manuela), Eloy Azorin (Esteban), Marisa Paredes (Huma Rojo), Candela Pena (Nina), Antonia San Juan (Agrado), Penelope Cruz (Sister Rosa), Rose Maria Sarda (Rosa's Mother), Fernando Fernan Gomez (Rosa's Father), Toni Canto (Lola). Directed by Pedro Almodovar and produced by Agustin Almodovar. Screenplay by Pedro Almodovar.

Pedro Almodovar's films are a struggle between real and fake heartbreak—between tragedy and soap opera. They're usually funny, too, which increases the tension. You don't know where to position yourself while you're watching a film like *All About My Mother*, and that's part of the appeal: Do you take it seriously, like the characters do, or do you notice the bright colors and flashy art decoration, the cheerful homages to Tennessee Williams and *All About Eve*, and see it as a parody? Even Almodovar's camera sometimes doesn't know where to stand: When the heroine's son writes in his journal, the camera looks at his pen from the point of view of the paper.

All About My Mother is one of the best films of the Spanish director, whose films present a Tennessee Williams sensibility in the visual style of a 1950s Universal-International tearjerker. Rock Hudson and Dorothy Malone

never seem very far offscreen. Bette Davis isn't offscreen at all: Almodovar's heroines seem to be playing her. Self-parody is part of Almodovar's approach, but *All About My Mother* is also sincere and heartfelt; though two of its characters are transvestite hookers, one is a pregnant nun, and two more are battling lesbians, this is a film that paradoxically expresses family values.

The movie opens in Madrid with a medical worker named Manuela (Cecilia Roth) and her teenage son, Esteban (Eloy Azorin). They've gone to see a performance of *A Streetcar Named Desire*, and now wait across the street from the stage door so Esteban can get an autograph from the famous actress Huma Rojo (Marisa Paredes). She jumps into a taxi (intercut with shots from *All About Eve* of Bette Davis eluding an autograph hound), and Esteban runs after her and is struck dead in the street. That sets up the story, as Manuela journeys to Barcelona to inform Esteban's father of the son's death.

There is irony as the film folds back on itself, because its opening scenes show Manuela, now a hospital coordinator but once an actress, performing in a video intended to promote organ transplants. In the film grieving relatives are asked to allow the organs of their loved ones to be used; later Manuela plays the same scene for real, as she's asked to donate her own son's heart.

The Barcelona scenes reflect Almodovar's long-standing interest in characters who cross the gender divide. Esteban's father is now a transvestite prostitute. In a scene worthy of Fellini, we visit a field in Barcelona where cars circle a lineup of flamboyant hookers of all sexes, and where Manuela, seeking her former lover, finds an old friend named Agrado (Antonia San Juan). The name means "agreeable," we're told, and Agrado is a person with endless troubles of her own who nevertheless enters every scene looking for the laugh. In one scene she dresses in a Chanel knockoff and is asked if it's real. As a street hooker she couldn't afford Chanel, but her answer is unexpected: "How could I buy a real Chanel with all the hunger in the world?"

There are unexpected connections between the characters, even between Esteban's father and Sister Rosa (Penelope Cruz), a nun who works in a shelter for battered prostitutes. And new connections are forged. We meet the actress Huma once again, and her girlfriend and costar Nina (Candela Pena): "She's hooked on junk and I'm hooked on her." When Nina flakes out, Manuela is actually able to understudy her role, having played it years ago. And Agrado finds a job as Huma's personal assistant. Meanwhile, the search goes on for the missing lover.

Manuela is the heroine of the film and its center, but Agrado is the source of life. There's an extraordinary scene in which she takes an empty stage against a hostile audience, and tries to improvise a one-woman show around the story of her life. Finally she starts an inventory of the plastic surgeries that assisted her in the journey from male to female, describing the pain, procedure, and cost of each, as if saying, "I've paid my dues to be who I am today. Have you?"

Almodovar's earlier films sometimes seemed to be manipulating the characters as an exercise. Here the plot does handstands in its eagerness to use coincidence, surprise, and melodrama. But the characters have a weight and reality, as if Almodovar has finally taken pity on them— has seen that although their plights may seem ludicrous, they're real enough to hurt. These are people that stand outside conventional life and its rules, and yet affirm them. Families are where you find them and how you make them, and home, it's said, is the place where, if you have to go there, they have to take you in.

All the Little Animals ★ ★ ★

R, 112 m., 1999

John Hurt (Mr. Summers), Christian Bale (Bobby), Daniel Benzali (De Winter), James Faulkner (Mr. Whiteside), John O'Toole (Lorry Driver), Amanda Boyle (Des), Amy Robbins (Bobby's Mother), John Higgins (Dean). Directed and produced by Jeremy Thomas. Screenplay by Eski Thomas, based on the novel by Walker Hamilton.

All the Little Animals is a particularly odd film that, despite its title, is not a children's movie, a cute animal movie, or the story of a veterinarian, but a dark and insinuating fable. Because it falls so far outside our ordinary story expectations it may frustrate some viewers, but it has a fearsome single-mindedness that suggests deep Jungian origins. Like the 1989 fantasy *Paperhouse*, it seems to be about more than we can see.

Its hero is a twenty-four-year-old named Bobby (Christian Bale), who sustained some brain damage in a childhood accident and is now slightly impaired and often fearful. Much of his fear is justified; his stepfather, De Winter (Daniel Benzali), killed Bobby's mother by "shouting her to death," and now threatens him with imprisonment in a mental home unless he signs over control of the family's London department store.

Bobby flees. He hitches a ride with a truck driver who gleefully aims to kill a fox on the road. Bobby wrestles for the wheel, the truck overturns, the driver is killed, and everything is witnessed by a man standing beside the road. This is Mr. Summers (John Hurt), a gentle and intelligent recluse who lives in a cottage in the woods and devotes his life to burying dead animals. "The car is a killing machine, pure and simple," Mr. Summers snaps; he is even offended by the insects that die on windshields.

Who is this man really? What's his story? Why does he seem to have plenty of money? The movie is all the more intriguing because it roots Mr. Summers in reality, instead of making him into some kind of fairy-tale creature. He heats Campbell's soup for Bobby, gives him a blanket, tells him he can stay the night. There is no suggestion of sexual motivation; Mr. Summers is matter-of-fact, reasonable, and motivated entirely by his feelings about dead animals.

Bobby follows the man on his rounds, and then asks to stay and share his work. Mr. Summers agrees. Sometimes they go on raids. One is a guerrilla attack on a lepidopterist, who has built a trap for moths in his backyard, and sips wine and listens to classical music while the helpless creatures flutter toward nets around a bright light. "Smash his light!" Mr. Summers spits, and Bobby runs awkwardly forward with a rock to startle the smug bug collector.

All goes well until De Winter comes back into the picture, and then Bobby and Mr. Summers tell each other their stories, and we learn that the movie is not a simple tale of good and evil, and that Mr. Summers is a great deal more complicated than we might have anticipated. When he's heard Bobby's story, he suggests they visit De Winter and simply sign over the store to gain Bobby's freedom—but De Winter doesn't see it that way, especially not after Summers (who looks a little shabby) sneezes and gets snot on De Winter's exquisite suit.

The performances are minutely observed, which enhances the movie's dreamlike quality. Hurt builds Mr. Summers out of realistic detail, and Benzali makes De Winter into a cold, hard-edged control freak; he's a villain that would distinguish any thriller and redeem not a few. What drives him? Why is he so hateful? Perhaps he's simply pure evil, and entertains himself by putting on a daily performance of malevolence. Of course, anyone so rigidly controlled is trembling with fear on the inside.

Here's an intriguing question: What is this movie about? It's not really about loving animals, and indeed it's creepy that Mr. Summers (and Bobby) focus more on dead ones than living specimens. Is it about death? About fear, and overcoming it? About revenge? The appeal of archetypal stories is that they seem like reflections of the real subject matter: Buried issues are being played out here at one remove.

Most movies are one-dimensional and gladly declare themselves. This movie, treated that way, would be about an insecure kid, a vicious stepfather, and a strange coot who lives in the woods. But *All the Little Animals* refuses to reduce its story to simple terms, and the visible story seems like a manifestation of dark and secret undercurrents. Even the ending, which some will no doubt consider routine revenge, has a certain subterranean irony.

The film is by a first-time director, Jeremy Thomas, a leading British producer who has worked with such directors as Bertolucci, Roeg, and Cronenberg. He says he was so struck (indeed, obsessed) by the original novel by Walker Hamilton that he felt compelled to film it. He has wisely not simplified his obsession or made it more accessible, but has allowed the film to linger in the shadow world of unconscious fears.

American Beauty ★ ★ ★ ★
R, 120 m., 1999

Kevin Spacey (Lester Burnham), Annette Bening (Carolyn Burnham), Thora Birch (Jane Burnham), Wes Bentley (Ricky Fitts), Mena Suvari (Angela Hayes), Chris Cooper (Colonel Fitts), Peter Gallagher (Buddy Kane), Allison Janney (Barbara Fitts). Directed by Sam Mendes and produced by Bruce Cohen and Dan Jinks. Screenplay by Alan Ball.

American Beauty is a comedy because we laugh at the absurdity of the hero's problems. And a tragedy because we can identify with his failure—not the specific details, but the general outline. The movie is about a man who fears growing older, losing the hope of true love, and not being respected by those who know him best. If you never experience those feelings, take out a classified ad. People want to take lessons from you.

Lester Burnham, the hero of *American Beauty*, is played by Kevin Spacey as a man who is unloved by his daughter, ignored by his wife, and unnecessary at work. "I'll be dead in a year," he tells us in almost the first words of the movie. "In a way, I'm dead already." The movie is the story of his rebellion.

We meet his wife, Carolyn (Annette Bening), so perfect her garden shears are coordinated with her clothing. We meet his daughter, Jane (Thora Birch), who is saving up for breast implants even though augmentation is clearly unnecessary; perhaps her motivation is not to become more desirable to men, but to make them miserable about what they can't have.

"Both my wife and daughter think I'm this chronic loser," Lester complains. He is right. But they are not without their reasons. At an agonizing family dinner, Carolyn plays Mantovanian music that mocks every mouthful; the music is lush and reassuring, and the family is angry and silent. When Lester criticizes his daughter's attitude, she points out correctly that he has hardly spoken to her in months.

Everything changes for Lester the night he is dragged along by his wife to see their daughter perform as a cheerleader. There on the floor, engrossed in a sub-Fosse pom-pom routine, he sees his angel: Angela (Mena Suvari), his daugh-

11

ter's sixteen-year-old classmate. Is it wrong for a man in his forties to lust after a teenage girl? Any honest man understands what a complicated question this is. Wrong morally, certainly, and legally. But as every woman knows, men are born with wiring that goes directly from their eyes to their genitals, bypassing the higher centers of thought. They can disapprove of their thoughts, but they cannot stop themselves from having them.

American Beauty is not about a Lolita relationship, anyway. It's about yearning after youth, respect, power, and, of course, beauty. The moment a man stops dreaming is the moment he petrifies inside, and starts writing snarfy letters disapproving of paragraphs like the one above. Lester's thoughts about Angela are impure, but not perverted; he wants to do what men are programmed to do, with the most beautiful woman he has ever seen.

Angela is not Lester's highway to bliss, but she is at least a catalyst for his freedom. His thoughts, and the discontent they engender, blast him free from years of emotional paralysis, and soon he makes a cheerful announcement at the funereal dinner table: "I quit my job, told my boss to go fuck himself, and blackmailed him for $60,000." Has he lost his mind? Not at all. The first thing he spends money on is perfectly reasonable: a bright red 1970 Pontiac Firebird.

Carolyn and Jane are going through their own romantic troubles. Lester finds out Carolyn is cheating when he sees her with her lover in the drive-thru lane of a fast-food restaurant (where he has a job he likes). Jane is being videotaped by Ricky (Wes Bentley), the boy next door, who has a strange light in his eyes. Ricky's dad (Chris Cooper) is an ex-Marine who tests him for drugs, taking a urine sample every six months; Ricky plays along to keep the peace until he can leave home.

All of these emotional threads come together during one dark and stormy night when there is a series of misunderstandings so bizarre they belong in a screwball comedy. And at the end, somehow, improbably, the film snatches victory from the jaws of defeat for Lester, its hero. Not the kind of victory you'd get in a feel-good movie, but the kind where you prove something important, if only to yourself.

American Beauty is not as dark or twisted as *Happiness*, 1998's attempt to shine a light under the rock of American society. It's more about sadness and loneliness than about cruelty or inhumanity. Nobody is really bad in this movie, just shaped by society in such a way that they can't be themselves, or feel joy. The performances all walk the line between parody and simple realism; Thora Birch and Wes Bentley are the most grounded, talking in the tense, flat voices of kids who can't wait to escape their homes. Bening's character, a Realtor who chants self-help mantras, confuses happiness with success—bad enough if you're successful, depressing if you're not.

And Spacey, an actor who embodies intelligence in his eyes and voice, is the right choice for Lester Burnham. He does reckless and foolish things in this movie, but he doesn't deceive himself; he knows he's running wild—and chooses to, burning up the future years of an empty lifetime for a few flashes of freedom. He may have lost everything by the end of the film, but he's no longer a loser.   ☞

American History X ★ ★ ★

R, 118 m., 1998

Edward Norton (Derek Vinyard), Edward Furlong (Danny Vinyard), Beverly D'Angelo (Doris Vinyard), Stacy Keach (Cameron Alexander), Jennifer Lien (Davina), Ethan Suplee (Seth), Fairuza Balk (Stacey), Avery Brooks (Bob Sweeney), Elliott Gould (Murray), Guy Torry (Lamont). Directed by Tony Kaye and produced by John Morrissey. Screenplay by David McKenna.

American History X shows how two Los Angeles brothers are drawn into a neo-Nazi skinhead gang, and why one decides to free himself. In telling their stories, the film employs the language of racism—the gutter variety, and more sophisticated variations. The film is always interesting and sometimes compelling, and it contains more actual provocative thought than any American film on race since *Do the Right Thing*. But in trying to resolve the events of four years in one day, it leaves its shortcuts showing.

The film stars Edward Norton as Derek, a bright kid who has become the leader of a skinhead pack in Venice Beach; he's the lieutenant of a shadowy adult neo-Nazi (Stacy Keach). One night two black kids attempt to steal Derek's car as the result of a playground feud, and he shoots them dead. He's convicted of murder and sent to Chico for three years.

His kid brother, Danny (Edward Furlong), idolizes him, and to some degree steps into his shoes—although he lacks Derek's intelligence and gift for rabble-rousing rhetoric. Then Derek gets out of prison and tries to find a new direction for himself and Danny. Their backdrop is a family that consists of a chronically sick mother (Beverly D'Angelo) and two sisters. Their father, a fireman, was shot and killed by blacks while fighting a fire in a crack house in a black neighborhood.

On a TV news show, the grief-stricken Derek blamed his father's death on a laundry list of far-right targets. Later we learn it wasn't just his father's death that shaped him, but his father's dinner table conversation; his father tutors him in racism, but the scene feels like tacked-on motivation, and the movie never convincingly charts Derek's path to race hatred.

The scariest and most convincing scenes are the ones in which we see the skinheads bonding. They're led by Derek's brilliant speech-making and fueled by drugs, beer, tattoos, heavy metal, and the need all insecure people feel to belong to a movement greater than themselves. It is assumed in their world (the beaches and playgrounds of the Venice area of L.A.) that all races stick together and are at undeclared war with all others. Indeed, the race hatred of the skinheads is mirrored (with different words and haircuts) by the other local ethnic groups. Hostile tribalism is an epidemic here.

The film, written by David McKenna and directed by Tony Kaye, uses black-and-white to show the recent past, and color to show the twenty-four-hour period after Derek is released from prison. In prison, we learn, Derek underwent a slow transition from a white zealot to a loner; a brutal rape helped speed the process. Meanwhile, young Danny and his friends (including a massive guy named Seth, played by Ethan Suplee) wreck a grocery run by immigrants. At school, Danny is a good student, as Derek was before him; both are taught by a black history teacher named Sweeney (Avery Brooks), who supplies the moral center of the film.

In the immediacy of its moments, in the photography (by Kaye) that makes Venice look like a training ground for the apocalypse, and in the strength of the performances, *American History X* is a well-made film. I kept hoping it would be more—that it would lift off and fly, as it might have with a director like Oliver Stone, Martin Scorsese, or Spike Lee. But it never quite does. Its underlying structure is too apparent, and there are scenes where we sense the movie hurrying to touch its bases.

One crucially underdeveloped area is Derek's prison experience. With a swastika tattooed on his chest, he fits in at first with the white power faction, but is disillusioned to find that all the major groups in prison (black, Hispanic, white) have a working agreement; that's too much cooperation for him. Fine, but is it that or a crucial basketball game that gets him into trouble? Not clear.

He's assigned to the laundry, where his black coworker (Guy Torry, in a wonderful performance) gradually—well, begins to seem human to him. But there's a strange imbalance in the conversion process. The movie's right-wing ideas are clearly articulated by Derek in forceful rhetoric, but are never answered except in weak liberal mumbles (by a Jewish teacher played by Elliott Gould, among others). And then the black laundry worker's big speech is not about ideas and feelings but about sex and how much he misses it. There is no effective spokesman for what we might still hopefully describe as American ideals. Well, maybe Derek wouldn't find one in his circles.

What we get, finally, is a series of well-drawn sketches and powerful scenes in search of an organizing principle. The movie needs sweep where it has only plot. And Norton, effective as he is, comes across more as a bright kid with bad ideas than as a racist burning with hate. (I am reminded of Tim Roth's truly satanic skinhead in *Made in Britain,* a 1982 film by Alan Clarke.)

Tony Kaye wanted to have his name removed as the film's director, arguing that it needs more work and that Norton re-edited some sequences. We will probably never know the truth behind the controversy. My guess is that the postproduction repairs were inspired by a screenplay that attempted to cover too much ground in too little time and yet still hasten to a conventional conclusion. Still, I must be clear: This is a good and powerful film. If I am dissatisfied, it is because it contains the promise of being more than it is.

American Movie ★ ★ ★

R, 104 m., 2000

Mark Borchardt (Filmmaker), Mike Schank (Friend/Musician), Uncle Bill (Mark's Uncle), Monica Borchardt (Mark's Mom), Cliff Borchardt (Mark's Dad), Chris Borchardt (Mark's Brother), Alex Borchardt (Mark's Brother), Ken Keen (Friend), Joan Petrie (Mark's Girlfriend). A documentary directed by Chris Smith and produced by Sarah Price.

If you've ever wanted to make a movie, see *American Movie*, which is about someone who wants to make a movie more than you do. Mark Borchardt may want to make a movie more than anyone else in the world. He is a thirty-year-old odd-job man from Menomonee Falls, Wisconsin, who has been making movies since he was a teenager, and dreams of an epic about his life, which will be titled *Northwestern*, and be about "rust and decay."

Mark Borchardt is a real person. I have met him. I admire his spirit, and I even admire certain shots in the only Borchardt film I have seen, *Coven*. I saw it at the 1999 Sundance Film Festival—not because it was invited there, but because after the midnight premiere of *American Movie* there wasn't a person in the theater who didn't want to stay and see Mark's thirty-five-minute horror film, which we see him making during the course of the documentary.

American Movie is a very funny, sometimes very sad, documentary directed by Chris Smith and produced by Sarah Price, about Mark's life, his friends, his family, his films, and his dreams. From one point of view, Mark is a loser, a man who has spent his adult life making unreleased and sometimes unfinished movies with titles like *The More the Scarier III*. He plunders the bank account of his elderly Uncle Bill for funds to continue, he uses his friends and hapless local amateur actors as his cast, he enlists his mother as his cinematographer, and his composer and best friend is a guy named Mike Schank who after one drug trip too many seems like the twin of Kevin Smith's Silent Bob.

Borchardt's life is a daily cliff-hanger involving poverty, desperation, discouragement, and die-hard ambition. He's behind on his child support payments, he drinks too much, he can't even convince his ancient Uncle Bill that he has a future as a moviemaker. Bill lives in a trailer surrounded by piles of magazines that he possibly subscribed to under the impression he would win the Publishers' Clearing House sweepstakes. He brightens slightly when Mark shows him the portrait of an actress. "She wants to be in your movie, Bill!" Bill studies the photo: "Oh, my gorsh!" But when Mark tells him about great cinema, what he hears is "cinnamon." And when Bill fumbles countless takes while trying to perform the ominous last line of *Coven* and Mark encourages him to say it like he believes it, Bill answers frankly, "I *don't* believe it."

Smith's camera follows Borchardt as he discusses his theories of cinema (his favorite films: *Night of the Living Dead* and *The Seventh Seal*). We watch as Mark and Bill go to the bank so Bill can grudgingly sign over some of his savings. He is at cast meetings, where one local actor (Robert Jorge) explains in a peeved British accent that *Coven* is correctly pronounced "CO-ven." Not according to Mark, who says *his* film is pronounced "COVE-n." "I don't want it to rhyme with 'oven'!"

Some of the scenes could work in a screwball comedy. One involves an actor being thrown headfirst through a kitchen cabinet. To capture the moment, Mark recruits his long-suffering Swedish-American mother, Monica, to operate the camera, even though she complains she has shopping to do. He gets on the floor behind his actor, who finds out belatedly that Mark's special-effects strategy is simply to ram the actor's head through the door. The first time, the actor's head bounces off. Mark prepares for take two. One reason to see *Coven* is to appreciate that shot knowing what we know now. For another shot, Mark lies flat on the frozen ground to get low-angle shots of his friends, dressed in black cloaks. "Look menacing!" he shouts. That's hard for them to do, since their faces are invisible.

If Mark's mother is supportive, his father

stays out of sight, sticking his head around a doorway occasionally to warn against bad language. Mark has two brothers, who are fed up with him; one says he would be "well suited to factory work," and the other observes, "His main asset is his mouth."

And yet Mark Borchardt is the embodiment of a lonely, rejected, dedicated artist. No poet in a Paris garret has ever been more determined to succeed. To find privacy while writing his screenplays, he drives his old beater to the parking lot of the local commuter airport, and composes on a yellow legal pad. To support himself, he delivers the *Wall Street Journal* before dawn and vacuums the carpets in a mausoleum. He has inspired the loyalty of his friends and crew members, and his girlfriend observes that if he accomplishes 25 percent of what he hopes to do, "that'll be more than most people do."

Every year at Sundance young filmmakers emerge from the woodwork, bearing the masterpieces they have somehow made for peanuts, enlisting volunteer cast and crew. Last year's discovery was not *Coven* but *The Blair Witch Project*. It cost $25,000 and so far has grossed $150 million. One day Mark Borchardt hopes for that kind of success. If it never comes, it won't be for lack of trying.

American Pie ★ ★ ★

R, 110 m., 1999

Jason Biggs (Jim), Jennifer Coolidge (Stifler's Mom), Shannon Elizabeth (Nadia), Alyson Hannigan (Michelle), Chris Klein (Oz), Clyde Kusatsu (English Teacher), Eugene Levy (Jim's Dad), Natasha Lyonne (Jessica). Directed by Paul Weitz and produced by Warren Zide, Craig Perry, Chris Moore, and Chris Weitz. Screenplay by Adam Herz.

American Pie is a comedy about four high school senior boys who make a pact to lose their virginity before the end of the school year. This alone makes it almost touchingly old-fashioned; I did not know Hollywood still permitted high school seniors to be virgins.

Real teenagers are no doubt approximately as inexperienced and unsure as they have always been, and many wisely avoid the emo-

tional and physical dangers of early sex, but in the movies the kids make the adults look backward. Teenagers used to go to the movies to see adults making love. Now adults go to the movies to see teenagers making love. I get letters from readers complaining that Clint Eastwood or Sean Connery are too old for steamy scenes, but never a word from anyone who thinks the kids played by Christina Ricci or Reese Witherspoon are too young.

American Pie was released in the middle of a summer when moviegoers were reeling at the level of sexuality, vulgarity, obscenity, and gross depravity in movies aimed at teenagers (and despite their R ratings, these movies obviously have kids under seventeen in their crosshairs). Consider that until a few years ago semen and other secretions and extrusions dare not speak their names in the movies. Then *There's Something About Mary* came along with its hair-gel joke. Very funny. Then came *Austin Powers* with its extra ingredient in the coffee. Then *South Park*, an anthology of cheerful scatology. Now *American Pie*, where semen has moved right onto the menu, not only as a drink additive but also as filling for a pie that is baked by the hero's mom. How long will it be before the money shot moves from porn to PG-13?

I say this not because I am shocked, but because I am a sociological observer and want to record that the summer of 1999 was the season when Hollywood's last standards of taste fell. Nothing is too gross for the new comedies. Grossness is the point. While newspapers and broadcast television continue to enforce certain standards of language and decorum, kids are going to movies that would make longshoremen blush. These movies don't merely contain terms I can't print in the paper—they contain terms I can't even describe in other words.

I rise to the challenge. I seek an underlying comic principle to apply. I find one. I discover that gross-out gags are not funny when their only purpose is to gross us out, but they can be funny when they emerge unwittingly from the action. It is not funny, for example, for a character to drink a beer that has something in it that is not beer. But it is funny in *There's Something About Mary* when the Ben Stiller character discovers he has the same substance dangling from his ear and Cameron Diaz mistakes it for hair gel.

It is funny because the characters aren't in on the joke. They are embarrassed. We share their embarrassment and, being human, find it funny. If Stiller were to greet Diaz *knowing* what was on his ear, that would not be funny. Humor happens when characters are victims, not when they are perpetrators. Humor is generated not by content but by context, which is why *Big Daddy* isn't funny. It's not funny because the Adam Sandler character knows what he is doing and wants to be doing it.

But back to *American Pie*. It involves a great deal of sexual content which in my opinion is too advanced for high school, and a lot of characters who are more casual about it than real teenagers might be. But it observes the rules of comedy. When the lucky hero gets the foreign exchange student into his bedroom and she turns out to be ready for a romp, it is funny that he has forgotten and left his CU-See Me software running, so that the entire Internet community can watch him be embarrassed. It would not be funny if he left it on deliberately.

The film is in the tradition of *Fast Times at Ridgemont High, National Lampoon's Animal House,* and all the more recent teen sex comedies. It is not inspired, but it's cheerful and hardworking and sometimes funny, and—here's the important thing—it's not mean. Its characters are sort of sweet and lovable. As I swim through the summer tide of vulgarity, I find that's what I'm looking for: Movies that at least feel affection for their characters. Raunchy is okay. Cruel is not.   ☞

American Psycho ★ ★ ★
R, 100 m., 2000

Christian Bale (Patrick Bateman), Willem Dafoe (Donald Kimball), Jared Leto (Paul Allen), Reese Witherspoon (Evelyn Williams), Samantha Mathis (Courtney Rawlinson), Chloe Sevigny (Jean), Justin Theroux (Timothy Price), Matt Ross (Luis Carruthers). Directed by Mary Harron and produced by Edward R. Pressman, Chris Hanley, and Christian Halsey Solomon. Screenplay by Guinevere Turner and Harron, based on the novel by Bret Easton Ellis.

It's just as well a woman directed *American Psycho.* She's transformed a novel about bloodlust into a movie about men's vanity. A male director might have thought Patrick Bateman, the hero of *American Psycho,* was a serial killer because of psychological twists, but Mary Harron sees him as a guy who's prey to the usual male drives and compulsions. He just acts out a little more.

Most men are not chain-saw killers; they only act that way while doing business. Look at the traders clawing each other on the floor of the stock exchange. Listen to used-car dealers trying to dump excess stock on one another. Consider the joy with which one megacorp raids another, and dumps its leaders. Study such films as *In the Company of Men, Glengarry Glen Ross, Boiler Room,* or *The Big Kahuna.* It's a dog-eat-dog world, and to survive you'd better be White Fang.

As a novel, Bret Easton Ellis's 1991 best-seller was passed from one publisher to another like a hot potato. As a film project, it has gone through screenplays, directors, and stars for years. It was snatched up for Oliver Stone, who planned to star Leonardo Di Caprio, before ending up back in Harron's arms with Christian Bale in the lead. (To imagine this material in Stone's hands, recall the scene in Ken Russell's *The Music Lovers* where Tchaikovsky's head explodes during the 1812 Overture, then spin it out to feature length.)

Harron is less impressed by the vile Patrick Bateman than a man might have been, perhaps because as a woman who directs movies she deals every day with guys who resemble Bateman in all but his body count. She senses the linkage between the time Bateman spends in the morning lovingly applying male facial products, and the way he blasts away people who annoy him, anger him, or simply have the misfortune to be within his field of view. He is a narcissist driven by ego and fueled by greed. Most of his victims are women, but in a pinch a man will do.

The film regards the male executive lifestyle with the devotion of a fetishist. There is a scene where a group of businessmen compare their business cards, discussing the wording, paper thickness, finish, embossing, engraving, and typefaces, and they might as well be discussing their phalli. Their sexual insecurity is manifested as card envy. They carry on grim rivalries expressed in clothes, offices, salaries, and being able to get good tables in important restaurants. It is their uneasy secret that they make enough money to afford to look important, but are not very important. One of the film's running jokes is that Patrick Bateman looks so much like one of his colleagues (Jared Leto) that they are mistaken for each other. (Their faces aren't really identical, but they occupy empty space in much the same way.)

The film and the book are notorious because Bateman murders a lot of people in nasty ways. I have overheard debates about whether some of the murders are fantasies ("Can a man really aim a chain saw that well?"). All of the murders are equally real or unreal, and that isn't the point: The function of the murders is to make visible the frenzy of the territorial male when his will is frustrated. The movie gives shape and form to road rage, golf course rage, family abuse, and some of the scarier behavior patterns of sports fans.

You see why Harron has called the film "feminist." So it is—and a libel against the many sane, calm, and civilized men it does not describe. But it's true to a type, all right. It sees Bateman in a clear, sharp, satiric light, and it despises him. Christian Bale is heroic in the way he allows the character to leap joyfully into despicableness; there is no instinct for self-preservation here, and that is one mark of a good actor. When Bateman kills, it is *not* with the zeal of a villain from a slasher movie. It is with the thoroughness of a hobbyist. Lives could have been saved if instead of living in a high-rise, Bateman had been supplied with a basement, a workbench, and a lot of nails to pound.

Among Giants ★ ★ ★
R, 94 m., 1999

Pete Postlethwaite (Ray), Rachel Griffiths (Gerry), James Thornton (Steve), Lennie James (Shovel), Andy Serkis (Bob), Rob Jarvis (Weasel), Alan Williams (Frank), Emma Cunniffe (Barmaid). Directed by Sam Miller and produced by Stephen Garrett. Screenplay by Simon Beaufoy.

Sometimes movies are simply about actors. There is a story, but only to give them something to talk about while being themselves. With the right actors, a film can essentially be about the way they talk, the look in their eye, their personal style and grace. *Among Giants* is a movie like that. It stars Pete Postlethwaite and Rachel Griffiths as an unlikely couple who fall in love, but mostly it just stars them being interesting.

Postlethwaite you may recall from *In the Name of the Father,* the 1994 Irish film where he won an Oscar nomination for playing the father of a man unjustly accused of being an IRA bomber. Griffiths was an Oscar nominee, playing the sister of a doomed musician in *Hilary and Jackie* (1998). I've seen them both several times; when you look at them you always know how their characters are feeling.

Among Giants was written by Simon Beaufoy, who also wrote *The Full Monty,* and once again combines working-class camaraderie and sex, this time in the same couple. Postlethwaite is Ray, the foreman of a freelance work gang that signs on to paint a long row of electrical power pylons that march across the British landscape. He's in his forties, wiry, ruddy, balding. Griffiths plays Gerry, a backpacker from Australia, making her way around the world and climbing peaks that interest her.

"How long you been out on the road?" he asks her when they meet.

"How long is a piece of string?"

"You get lonely?"

"Yeah, I do."

Something intangible passes between them, and soon she's back, asking for a job. Ray's gang is leery of a woman, but Gerry points out that she's a climber, not afraid of heights—or work. Ray hires her. It's the beginning of a long summer in which the men build campfires to brew their tea, and sleep in vans or tents, and spend their days high in the air with paint buckets (singing "Stand By Me" at one point).

Ray lives in a nearby town, and we learn that he has an estranged wife and kids. He considers himself divorced, but the formalities haven't taken place. Gerry lives in her tent. She is a strange, winsome loner: "All I've got is a whole bunch of people I'm never gonna see

17

again, and a whole lot of places I'm never gonna go back to." One night Ray kisses her. They fall in love.

The complications of their romance provide the main line of the story. The counterpoint comes from details about the other characters in the work gang, especially a young man who relates to Ray as a surrogate father. The film is thick with atmosphere, and knows its way around blue-collar pubs where everybody wears jeans and cowboy shirts on Friday nights, the band plays C&W, and (in a scene that will seem realistic to British viewers and unlikely to Americans) the customers are skillful line dancers.

We are aware at some level that the whole story is a contrivance. The logistics are murky: Who is the man who hires the work gang, and why does he treat them like illegals, and why exactly is the power off now but scheduled to be turned on at the end of the summer? (No prizes for guessing that the uncertainty about power is the setup for his dramatic scene.) Those are questions that can be asked, but the answer is that the whole reality of the film is simply a backdrop to the relationship of these two characters.

They make an odd match. They're probably twenty years apart in age. They're prideful loners. Yet they have a certainty about their physical styles that makes them a good match. They both like to climb, they both work hard, and there is a scene where they frolic, not under a waterfall, but under a falling sheet of water inside the cooling tower of a power plant. Haven't seen that before.

One of the gifts of the movies is to allow us to guess what it might be like to be somebody else. As actors, Postlethwaite and Griffiths have the ability to evoke people it might be interesting to be, or know. The director, Sam Miller, uses this gift in unexpected ways. There is a scene where Gerry uses her climbing skills to traverse entirely around the four walls of a pub without ever touching the floor. Haven't seen that before, either.

Analyze This ★ ★ ★
R, 106 m., 1999

Robert De Niro (Paul Vitti), Billy Crystal (Ben Sobol), Lisa Kudrow (Laura MacNamara), Chazz Palminteri (Primo Sindone), Joe Viterelli (Jelly), Richard Castellano (Jimmy), Molly Shannon (Caroline), Max Casella (Nicky Shivers). Directed by Harold Ramis and produced by Paula Weinstein and Jane Rosenthal. Screenplay by Peter Tolan, Ramis, and Kenneth Lonergan.

"Do you know who I am?" the mobster asks the shrink.

"Yes, I do."

"No, you don't."

"No, I don't."

The psychiatrist is only too happy to please Paul Vitti, the boss of the New York mob. But Vitti is in a vulnerable position: He's lost his nerve, he has panic attacks, he breaks out crying during sentimental TV commercials. If his rivals find out, he's dead.

A comic situation like this depends on casting to elevate it from the environs of sitcom, and *Analyze This* has Robert De Niro and Billy Crystal to bring richness to the characters. Also a large, phlegmatic man named Joe Viterelli, as a bodyguard named Jelly who tries dimly to understand why the most feared criminal in America needs help from this little head doctor.

Analyze This is funny partly because De Niro and Crystal do what we expect them to do, and partly because they don't. De Niro kids his screen image from all those mob movies by Scorsese and others, making the psychiatrist compliments he cannot refuse.

"You're good."

"Well, I . . ."

"No! You're good!"

"I'm good."

Crystal's character, named Ben Sobol, is the kind of guy who figures if he can just keep talking, sooner or later he'll say the right thing. What we don't expect is that the characters take on a certain human dimension, and we care for them a little. This isn't a deeply involving human drama, you understand, but attention is paid to personalities, and the movie isn't all gag lines.

Of course there has to be a Meet Cute to explain how Ben Sobol meets the mob, and it's handled in a funny setup scene where the shrink's car rams the back of a car with an extra passenger in the trunk. The gangsters are only too happy to forget the incident, even though Crystal wants to call the cops; eventually Jelly accepts the psychiatrist's card, and still has it in his pocket when Vitti needs help.

Vitti's archenemy is a mobster named Primo Sindone (Chazz Palminteri), who would strike if he had any suspicion of his rival's weaknesses. That's why utter secrecy is important, and why Sobol is horrified when he discovers his son eavesdropping on their sessions. "You cannot tell a single person!" he shouts at the kid. "You mean," says the kid, "take it off the Internet?" Sobol is a divorced man about to remarry (to Lisa Kudrow), but Jelly comes for him even in the middle of a wedding, and it begins to look to his fiancée's parents as if he's a mobster himself.

Crystal can go over the top when he needs to, but here he wisely restrains his manic side, and gets into a nice rhythm with De Niro's fearful gangster. The movie surrounds them with fairly lively violence (the shrink himself ends up in a shark tank at one point), but a lot of the mob scenes are satires of *The Godfather* and its clones. There's even a dream sequence where the psychiatrist imagines himself being shot in the street in exactly the same way Don Vito Corleone was in the movie, with Vitti too slow to save him. He describes the dream to Vitti. "I was Fredo?" Vitti says. "I don't think so."

The director and cowriter is Harold Ramis, whose work ranges from broad comedy like *Caddyshack* to the fine-tuned observation of *Groundhog Day*. Here he's presented with all sorts of temptations, I suppose, to overplay the De Niro character and turn the movie into an *Airplane!*-type satire of gangster movies. I think he finds the right path—allowing satire, referring to De Niro's screen past, and yet keeping the focus on the strange friendship between two men who speak entirely different languages. (When Sobol explains Freud's theory that some men subconsciously want to kill their fathers and marry their mothers, Vitti's response is to the point: "You ever seen my mother?")

A movie like this will be thought of almost entirely in terms of De Niro and Crystal, with a nod to Palminteri and Kudrow, and yet I think what holds the parts together is the unexpectedly likable character of Jelly. Joe Viterelli makes the bodyguard not just a mobster, not just a tough guy, but an older man who is weary after many years in service, but loyal and patient with his weirdo boss. As Jelly patiently pads about trying to deal with the disturbing news that his boss is cracking up and seeing a shrink, he lends a subtle dimension to the movie; he gives Vitti a context, and someone who understands him. The comedy here isn't all on the surface, and Viterelli is one reason why.

Angela's Ashes ★ ★ ½
R, 145 m., 2000

Emily Watson (Angela), Robert Carlyle (Malachy [Dad]), Michael Legge (Older Frank), Ciaran Owens (Middle Frank), Joe Breen (Young Frank), Ronnie Masterson (Grandma Sheehan), Pauline McLynn (Aunt Aggie), Liam Carney (Uncle Pa Keating), Eanna MacLiam (Uncle Pat), Andrew Bennett (Narrator). Directed by Alan Parker and produced by Parker, Scott Rudin, and David Brown. Screenplay by Parker and Laura Jones, based on the book by Frank McCourt.

Frank McCourt's book *Angela's Ashes* is, like so much of Irish verbal history, suffering recollected in hilarity. I call it verbal history because I know from a friend of his that the stories so unforgettably told in his autobiography were honed over years and decades, at bars and around dinner tables and in the ears of his friends. I could have guessed that anyway, from the easy familiarity you hear in his voice on the audiobook he recorded, the quickening rhythm of humor welling up from the description of grim memories. Some say audiobooks are not "real" books, but in the case of *Angela's Ashes* the sound of the author's voice transforms the material with fondness and nostalgia. McCourt may have had a miserable childhood, but he would not trade it in for another—or at least would not have missed the parts he retells in his memories.

That whole sense of humor is mostly missing from Alan Parker's film version of *Angela's Ashes*, which reminded me of Mark Twain's description of a woman trying to swear: "She knows the words, but not the music." The film is so faithful to the content of the book that it reproduces scenes that have already formed in my imagination. The flooded downstairs in the Limerick home, the wretched family waiting for a father who will never come home with money for eggs and bacon, the joy of flying down the street on a post office bicycle—all of these are just as I pictured them. What is missing is the tone. The movie is narrated by Andrew Bennett, who is no doubt a good actor and blameless here, but what can he do but reproduce the words from the page without McCourt's seasoning of nostalgia? McCourt's voice tells us things he has seen. Bennett's voice tells of things he has heard about.

The result is a movie of great craft and wonderful images, lacking a heart. There must have been thousands of childhoods more or less like Frank McCourt's, and thousands of families with too many children, many of them dying young, while the father drank up dinner down at the pub and the mother threw herself on the mercy of the sniffy local charities. What made McCourt's autobiography special was expressed somehow beneath the very words as he used them: These experiences, wretched as they were, were not wasted on a mere victim, but somehow shaped him into the man capable of writing a fine book about them. There is in *Angela's Ashes* a certain lack of complaint, a sense in which even misery is treasured, as a soldier will describe his worst day of battle with the unspoken subtext: "But I survived, and I love to tell the story, because it is the most interesting thing that has ever happened to me."

The movie stars Emily Watson and Robert Carlyle as Angela and Malachy McCourt, Frank's parents. It is impossible to conceive of better casting of Angela, and although other actors (Tim Roth, Gary Oldman) might have done about as good a job as Carlyle, how much can be done with that poor man who has been made shifty-eyed, lying, and guilty by the drink? We do not even blame him as he leaves his family to starve while he pours their money into the pockets of the manufacturers of Guinness Stout: Clearly, he would not drink if it were at all within his control. But he is powerless over alcoholism, and it has rendered him not a man but simply the focus of the family's bad luck.

What is touching is the way Frank, and soon his younger brother Malachy, treasure those few moments when Dad was too abashed or

impoverished to drink, and lavished some attention on them. Consider my favorite sequence, in which the boys' shoes are letting in the rain, and Dad nails tire rubber to the soles. At school, flopping along on their little Michelin snowshoes, they're laughed at by the other kids, until the Christian brother who teaches the class reprimands them all, and points up dramatically to the crucifix on the schoolroom wall: "You don't see our Blessed Savior sportin' shoes!"

It is the "sportin'" that does it, that makes it work, that reveals McCourt's touch. The possibility that the dying Christ would, could, or even desired to "sport" shoes turns the whole sentence and the whole anecdote around, and it becomes not the story of schoolroom humiliation, but a rebuke to those classmates so foolish as to be sportin' shoes themselves. In the mechanics of that episode is the secret of the whole book, and although it comes across well in the film, so many of the similar twists, ironies, and verbal revenges are missed. The film lacks the dark humor with which the Irish like to combine victory with misfortune (as in the story of the man who cleverly fed his horse less and less every day, until "just when he finally had the horse trained to eat nothing— the horse died!").

Frank is played at various ages by Joe Breen (young), Ciaran Owens (middle), and Michael Legge (older). He comes across as determined to make his own way and get out of Limerick and back to New York where he was born, and there are scenes of him picking up spilled coal from the road as a little boy, impressing the brothers with his essay "Jesus and the Weather," getting his first job, falling in love, and coming home drunk the first time ("Jesus!" cries his mother. "It's your father you've become!").

The grim poverty of the lane in Limerick where the family lived for much of the time is convincingly re-created by Parker and production designer Geoffrey Kirkland, although Parker is much too fond of a shot in which Frank and Malachy splash deliberately through every puddle they can find, indoors and out, season after season and year after year. Surely they would eventually learn to keep their feet dry? And although we know from the book that the flooded downstairs was "Ireland" and the dry upstairs was "Italy," was the family so entirely without resources that a plank could not be found to make a bridge from the door to the stairs?

What is wonderful about *Angela's Ashes* is Emily Watson's performance, and the other roles are convincingly cast. She has the kind of bitterness mixed with resignation that was forced on a woman in a country where marriage to a drunk was a life sentence, and it was a greater sin to desert him than to let him starve her children. At one point, Dad leaves to seek work in England, complaining that she has "refused her wifely duties." His husbandly duties, of course, consisted of fathering more children to starve and die, and buying rounds like a big shot down at the pub.

Anna and the King ★ ★
PG-13, 149 m., 1999

Jodie Foster (Anna), Chow Yun-Fat (King Mongkut), Bai Ling (Tuptim), Tom Felton (Louis), Syed Alwi (The Kralahome), Randall Duk Kim (General Alak), Lim Kay Siu (Prince Chowfa), Melissa Campbell (Princess Fa-Ying). Directed by Andy Tennant and produced by Lawrence Bender and Ed Elbert. Screenplay by Steve Meerson and Peter Krikes, based on the diaries of Anna Leonowens.

King Mongkut of Siam and Anna Leonowens, the English schoolmarm who tries to civilize him, make up one of the most dubious odd couples in pop culture. Here is a man with twenty-three wives and forty-two concubines, who allows one of his women and her lover to be put to death for exchanging a letter, and yet is seen as basically a good-hearted chap. And here is Anna, who spends her days in flirtation with the king, but won't sleep with him because—well, because he isn't white, I guess. Certainly not because he has countless other wives and is a murderer.

Why is she so attracted to the king in the first place? Henry Kissinger has helpfully explained that power is the ultimate aphrodisiac, and Mongkut has it—in Siam, anyway. Why is he attracted to her? Because she stands up to him and even tells him off. Inside every sadist is a masochist, cringing to taste his own medicine.

The unwholesome undercurrents of the story of Anna and the King of Siam have nagged at me for years, through many ordeals of sitting through the stage and screen versions of *The King and I*, which is surely the most cheerless of Rodgers and Hammerstein's musicals. The story is not intended to be thought about. It is an exotic, escapist entertainment for matinee ladies, who can fantasize about sex with that intriguing bald monster, and indulge their harem fantasies. There is no reason for any man to ever see the play.

Now here is a straight dramatic version of the material, named *Anna and the King*, and starring Jodie Foster opposite the Hong Kong action star Chow Yun-Fat. It is long and mostly told in the same flat monotone, but has one enormous advantage over the musical: It does not contain "I Whistle a Happy Tune." The screenplay has other wise improvements on the source material. The king, for example, says "and so on and so on" only once, and "et cetera" not at all. And there is only one occasion when he tells Anna her head cannot be higher than his. Productions of the musical belabor this last point so painfully they should be staged in front of one of those police lineups with feet and inches marked on it.

Jodie Foster's performance projects a strange aura. Here is an actress meant to play a woman who is in love, and she seems subtly uncomfortable with that fate. I think I know why. Foster is not only a wonderful actor but an intelligent one—one of our smartest. There are few things harder for actors to do than play beneath their intelligence. Oh, they can play dumb people who are supposed to be dumb. But it is almost impossible to play a dumb person who is supposed to be smart, and that's what she has to do as Anna.

She arrives in Siam, a widow with a young boy, and finds herself in the realm of this egotistical sexual monster with a palace full of women. Yes, he is charming; Hitler is said to have been charming, and so, of course, was Hannibal Lecter. She must try to educate the king's children (sixty-eight, I think I heard) and at the same time civilize him by the British standards of the time, which were racist, imperialist, and jingoistic, but frowned on such Siamese practices as chaining women for weeks outside the palace gates.

By the end of the movie, she has danced with

the king a couple of times, come tantalizingly close to kissing him, and civilized him a little, although he has not sold off his concubines. She now has memories that she can write in her journal for Rodgers and Hammerstein to plunder on Broadway, which never tires of romance novels set to music.

Foster, I believe, sees right through this material and out the other side, and doesn't believe in a bit of it. At times we aren't looking at a nineteenth-century schoolmarm, but a modern woman biting her tongue. Chow Yun-Fat is good enough as the king, and certainly less self-satisfied than Yul Brynner. There is a touching role for Bai Ling, as Tuptim, the beautiful girl who is given to the king as a bribe by her venal father, a tea merchant. She loves another, and that is fatal for them both. There is also the usual nonsense about the plot against the throne, which here causes Anna, the king, and the court to make an elaborate journey by elephant so that the king can pull off a military trick I doubt would be convincing even in a Looney Tune.

Credits at the end tell us Mongkut and his son, educated by Anna, led their country into the twentieth century, established democracy (up to a point), and so on. No mention is made of Bangkok's role as a world center of sex tourism, which also, of course, carries on traditions established by the good king. 🖎

Another Day in Paradise ★ ★ ★
R, 101 m., 1999

James Woods (Mel), Melanie Griffith (Sid), Vincent Kartheiser (Bobbie), Natasha Gregson Wagner (Rosie), James Otis (Reverend), Branden Williams (Danny), Brent Briscoe (Clem), Peter Sarsgaard (Ty), Lou Diamond Phillips (Gangster). Directed by Larry Clark and produced by Stephen Chin, Clark, and James Woods. Screenplay by Christopher Landon and Chin, based on the book by Eddie Little.

Another Day in Paradise is a lowlife, sleazeball, drugs-and-blood road movie, which means its basic materials will be familiar to audiences of the post–*Easy Rider* decades. There's not much new here, but then there's so rarely something new at the movies that we're sometimes grateful to see the familiar done well.

What brings the movie its special quality is the work of James Woods and Melanie Griffith and their mirror images, played by Vincent Kartheiser and Natasha Gregson Wagner. Woods and Griffith play types they've played before, but with a zest and style that brings the movie alive—especially in the earlier scenes, before everything gets clouded by doom. Woods plays Uncle Mel, who describes himself: "I'm just a junkie and a real good thief. Kind of go together." Griffith is his woman, Sid. They met because he was her drug dealer.

The movie opens with the younger couple, Bobbie and Rosie (Kartheiser and Wagner). He breaks into a junior college to burgle a vending machine, gets in a struggle with a security guard, is badly wounded, and stabs the guard to death. Soon he's being treated by Uncle Mel. "Are you a doctor?" he asks. "Yeah, sure. I'm a doctor shooting you up with heroin," says Mel sarcastically.

As Bobbie recovers, Mel spins visions of the four of them as a family, setting out on a glorious adventure on the road. He's a spieler, a fast-talking spinner of visions, and Sid backs him up with warmth and encouragement. As a sample of the paradise ahead, she takes them on a shopping spree and then to a nightclub (where the kids get drunk and have to be hauled home by the grown-ups).

We know the good times can't last. Mel needs money too badly because he needs drugs—and because he needs drugs, he's willing to get money in dangerous ways. Soon Bobbie has learned about concealing himself in crawl spaces, and Mel is masterminding a particularly inept crime. The arc of the story is preordained: Early glorious scenes of freedom on the road, followed by lowering clouds, gathering omens, and the closing net of fate.

They do a lot of drugs in the movie. There are five scenes of shooting up and one of snorting, according to the invaluable "Screen It" Website (which helpfully adds that the f-word is used "at least" 291 times). The writer-director is Larry Clark, whose *Kids* (1995) told the harrowing story of young street teenagers in Manhattan, playing with sex and drugs as if they were harmless toys. Clark is drawn to decadence and marginal lifestyles, and he finds special interest in the tension generated by kids in danger.

In Kartheiser and Wagner, he finds performers in the tradition of Juliette Lewis and Brad Pitt in *Kalifornia* (1993) or, indeed, Martin Sheen and Sissy Spacek all those years ago in *Badlands* (1973). The underlying story structure is from *Bonnie and Clyde*, which itself was inspired by earlier road movies. The road and crime and doom seem to fit together easily in the movies.

If there are no new insights in *Another Day in Paradise*, at least there are old arias powerfully sung. James Woods and Melanie Griffith enjoy the possibilities of their characters—they enjoy the supercharged scenes of speed, fear, fantasy, and crime. Woods has played variations on this character many times (how many times have we seen him driving a car, smoking, and talking like a demented con man?). Griffith is like the last rose of summer: still fragrant, but you can see her energy running out, until finally it is more important for her to escape Uncle Mel than to have access to his drugs.

A movie like this reminds me of what movie stars are for. We see them many times in many movies over a period of years, and grow used to their cadences and their range. We invest in them. Those that we like, we follow. James Woods is almost always interesting and often much more than that. Melanie Griffith has qualities that are right for the role she plays here. The kids, Kartheiser and Wagner, are talented but new. It's a sign that you're a movie lover and not just a fan when you start preferring the fine older vintages to the flavors of the month.

Antz ★ ★ ★ ½
PG, 83 m., 1998

With the voices of: Woody Allen (Z), Dan Aykroyd (Chip), Anne Bancroft (Queen), Jane Curtin (Muffy), Danny Glover (Barbatus), Gene Hackman (Mandible), Jennifer Lopez (Azteca), Sharon Stone (Bala), Christopher Walken (Cutter), Sylvester Stallone (Weaver). Directed by Eric Darnell and Tim Johnson and produced by Brad Lewis, Aron Warner, and Patty Wooton. Screenplay by Todd Alcott, Chris Weitz, and Paul Weitz.

Antz rejoices in the fact that a cartoon can show us anything. It's so free, it turns visual cart-

wheels. It enters into a microscopic world—an ant colony beneath Central Park—and makes it into a world so vast and threatening that comparisons with *Star Wars* are not unjustified.

And it's sharp and funny—not a children's movie, but one of those hybrids that works on different levels for different ages. The kids will enjoy it when the hero and his girl get stuck in some gum on the bottom of a running shoe. Older viewers will understand the hero's complaint that it's not easy "when you're the middle child in a family of 5 million."

The movie is the first animated feature from the DreamWorks Studio and benefits from the input of studio partners Jeffrey Katzenberg, who earlier oversaw the renaissance in Disney animation, and Steven Spielberg, whose *E.T.* seems to have inspired the look of the hero's eyes and a crucial scene where a kiss brings him back to life. The movie is entirely computer-generated, incorporating a clever software program that makes the mouths of the insects look a little, but not too much, like morphs of the actors who voice their dialogue: Woody Allen, Sharon Stone, Sylvester Stallone, Jennifer Lopez, Gene Hackman, Christopher Walken, and others.

The story mixes adventure with political parable. As it begins, every ant in the colony goes dutifully about its age-old assignment, never thinking to question why some are workers, some are warriors, and only one can be the queen. Then the little ant named Z (voice by Allen) develops that attribute which an ant colony has no room for, a mind of his own. "I'm supposed to do everything for the colony?" he asks on a psychiatrist's couch. "And what about *my* needs?"

This is no time for individualism. The colony is engaged in an emergency project to dig a giant tunnel (in ant-scale, it looks as daunting as the Chunnel). Militarists led by General Mandible (Hackman) and Colonel Cutter (Walken) want to divert all resources to war. They even invent false reports of an approaching termite invasion, and convince the queen (Anne Bancroft) that they must strike first. Meanwhile, in a bar, Z meets the beautiful Princess Bala (Sharon Stone). All the other ants "dance" with a rigid precision that looks, well, insectlike. But Z breaks loose, and Bala, intoxicated with the sudden freedom of movement, regrets her engagement to Mandible. Like all ants, her fiancé is . . . predictable.

Z meets a warrior ant (Stallone) and arranges to switch jobs, just so he can impress Bala. Bad timing. Z finds himself hurled into battle against the vastly superior termites, in a microscopic version of the beach massacre in DreamWorks' previous release, *Saving Private Ryan*. Surviving, he returns to the colony and is the seed for a virus of individualism. Eventually Z and Bala find themselves alone on the surface, in search of the legendary Insectopia (a picnic), and threatened by vast creatures of man and nature, which loom overhead like Darth Vader's Death Star.

I have an abiding love of animation, all kinds of animation. (As a child, I naively thought it was "more real" than live action because the edges were sharper and the characters did things I could understand.) Modern animation embodies a certain irony: Although cartoons can literally show any imaginable physical action in any conceivable artistic style, most of the successful ones are contained within the Disney studio style, as it has evolved over the years.

That isn't a bad thing for Disney movies, and I treasure most of them, especially the early ones and the modern renaissance. But there are other ways a cartoon can look. The Japanese master Hayao Miyazaki (*My Neighbor Totoro*, *Kiki's Delivery Service*) has developed a look with the fanciful style of great children's book illustration. *Toy Story*, by Disney and Pixar, used computer animation to create a new world with a fresh, exciting look. Japanese anime titles like *Akira* and *The Ghost in the Shell* move closer to hard-edged science fiction.

And now look at the panoramic overhead shots of the ant colony in *Antz*. We could be looking at an alien life form, or the headquarters of one of James Bond's megalomaniac enemies. The scale and detail are astonishing. And consider the imagination involved in a sequence where most of the ants in the colony gather themselves into a giant ball, helped by a string of other ants, so that millions of individuals can become one collective tool.

Facts about the lives of real ants provide inspiration for many sequences. There is a scene where an ant is decapitated, and Z has a conversation with his head. Scenes of nursemaids

in perpetual procession, as the queen delivers a newborn every five seconds. A funny scene where ants drink nectar from the hindquarters of aphids, and Z complains, "I may be crazy, but I have a thing about drinking from the anus of another creature." And a visually exciting sequence in which an ant is trapped inside a body of water, and struggles with the power of its surface tension.

The visuals are joined to a screenplay with wickedly amusing dialogue and lots of cross-references to current culture. ("All we are saying," chants an ant chorus, "is, give Z a chance!" And later the hero is told, "You de ant!") Eric Darnell and Tim Johnson, who codirected the film, and Todd Alcott, Chris Weitz, and Paul Weitz, who wrote it, lead a team of gifted animators in telling a fable with the resonance of *Animal Farm*. And we sense Woody Allen's satirical spirit sneaking through in some lines; instead of attacking the termites, he suggests, why not try subverting them with campaign contributions?

Any Given Sunday ★ ★ ★
R, 170 m., 1999

Al Pacino (Tony D'Amato), Cameron Diaz (Christina Pagniacci), Dennis Quaid (Jack "Cap" Rooney), James Woods (Dr. Harvey Mandrake), Jamie Foxx (Willie Beamen), LL Cool J (Julian Washington), Matthew Modine (Dr. Oliver Powers), Charlton Heston (The Commissioner), Ann-Margret (Margaret Pagniacci), Lawrence Taylor (Shark), Lauren Holly (Cindy Rooney). Directed by Oliver Stone and produced by Lauren Shuler Donner, Clayton Townsend, and Dan Halsted. Screenplay by Stone, John Logan, and Daniel Pyne.

Oliver Stone's *Any Given Sunday* is a smart sports movie almost swamped by production overkill. The movie alternates sharp and observant dramatic scenes with MTV-style montages and incomprehensible sports footage. It's a miracle the underlying story survives, but it does.

The story's expose of pro football will not come as news to anyone who follows the game. We learn that veteran quarterbacks sometimes doubt themselves, that injured players take risks to keep playing, that team doctors let them, that overnight stardom can turn a green kid into a jerk, that ESPN personalities are self-promoters, that owners' wives drink, that their daughters think they know all about football, and that coaches practice quiet wisdom in the midst of despair. We are also reminded that all big games are settled with a crucial play in the closing seconds.

These insights are not startling, but Stone and his actors give them a human face, and the film's dialogue scenes are effective. Al Pacino, comfortable and convincing as Tony D'Amato, a raspy-voiced curmudgeon, tries to coach the Miami Sharks past a losing streak and into the play-offs, and the movie surrounds him with first-rate performances. We're reminded that very little movie material is original until actors transform it from clichés into particulars.

Jamie Foxx joins Pacino in most of the heavy lifting as Willie Beamen, a third-string quarterback in a game where the two guys above him have been carried off on stretchers. He's so nervous he throws up in the huddle ("That's a first," D'Amato observes), but then catches fire and becomes an overnight sensation. In a broken-field role that requires him to be unsure and vulnerable, then cocky and insufferable, then political, then repentant, Foxx doesn't step wrong.

The team's original owner was a sports legend who had a handshake deal with D'Amato, but with the owner's death, control has passed to his daughter (Cameron Diaz), whose mother (Ann-Margret) is never far from a martini. These two characters are written as women who will never really be accepted in a man's game. The mother knows it, but her daughter still doesn't. Diaz hopes to get rich by moving the franchise; her mother has kept the world of pro football under close observation for many years, and not found much to inspire her.

Dennis Quaid plays the veteran quarterback whose injury sets the plot into motion—and he, too, is seen in an unexpected light, as an on-field leader privately haunted by insecurity. There's a stunning moment when he considers retirement and is slapped by his wife (Lauren Holly), who won't hear of it; he complains, "Ever since college people have been telling me what to do."

Even at 170 minutes, *Any Given Sunday* barely manages to find room for some of its large cast. James Woods and Matthew Modine clash as team doctors with different attitudes toward life-threatening conditions, and pro veteran Lawrence Taylor has a strong supporting role as a player who wants to keep playing long enough to earn his bonus, even at the risk of his life. And there are lots of other familiar faces: Charlton Heston, Aaron Ekhardt, Edward Burns, Bill Bellamy, Jim Brown, LL Cool J, John C. McGinley, Lela Rochon, even Johnny Unitas as an opposing coach.

The reason they aren't better developed is that so much of the film's running time is lost to smoke and mirrors. There isn't really a single sequence of sports action in which the strategy of a play can be observed and understood from beginning to end. Instead, Stone uses fancy editing on montage close-ups of colorful uniforms and violent action, with lots of crunching sound effects. Or he tilts his camera up to a football pass, spinning against the sky. This is razzle-dazzle in the editing; we don't get the feeling we're seeing a real game involving these characters.

There's a lot of music, though, and even a fairly unconvincing MTV music video for Jamie Foxx to star in. It's as if Stone wanted to pump up the volume to conceal the lack of on-field substance. In his films like *JFK* and *Nixon,* there was a feeling of urgent need to get everything in; we felt he had lots more to tell us, and would if he could. *Any Given Sunday* feels stretched out, as if the story needed window dressing. It's like the second unit came back with lots of full-frame shots of anonymous football players plowing into each other in close-up, and Stone and his editors thought they could use that to mask their lack of substantial, strategic, comprehensible sports action footage. Adding to the distraction is the fact that the outcome of every single play matches the dramatic needs of the script.

It's a close call here. I guess I recommend the movie because the dramatic scenes are worth it. Pacino, Quaid, and Foxx have some nice moments together, and the psychology of the veteran coach is nicely captured in the screenplay by Stone, John Logan, and Daniel Pyne. But if some studio executive came along and made Stone cut his movie down to two hours, I have the strangest feeling it wouldn't lose much of substance, and might even play better.

Anywhere But Here ★ ★ ★
PG-13, 114 m., 1999

Susan Sarandon (Adele August), Natalie Portman (Ann August), Shawn Hatosy (Cousin Benny), Eileen Ryan (Lillian), Corbin Allred (Peter), Caroline Aaron (Realtor), Ray Baker (Ted [Stepfather]), Hart Bochner (Josh Spritzer), Michael Milhoan (Cop). Directed by Wayne Wang and produced by Laurence Mark. Screenplay by Alvin Sargent, based on the novel by Mona Simpson.

Wayne Wang's *Anywhere But Here* is about a frustrated mother who believes she is rotting away in a small Wisconsin town. She buys a used Mercedes, shoves her teenage daughter inside, and drives them cross-country to Beverly Hills, where she will put her M.A. in early education to work, and her daughter will go to auditions and be discovered by the movies.

That is the plan, anyway. Her daughter, who has not been consulted, is angry and resentful at being yanked away from the family she loves, and doesn't share her mother's social-climbing obsessions (their first apartment isn't in "the posh part of Beverly Hills, but it's in the school district").

The affordable streets they live on reminded me of *The Slums of Beverly Hills*, the 1998 movie where jobless Alan Arkin steers his kids into the same school system, but *Anywhere But Here* isn't a rip-off of the earlier movie—it's more as if the mom saw it, and made up her mind to try the same thing. (For that matter, it's based on Mona Simpson's 1987 novel, so the inspiration may have traveled the other way.)

The mother is Adele August (Susan Sarandon), sexy, wildly optimistic, consumed by her visions. Her daughter Ann (Natalie Portman) is a serious kid, smart and observant, who is tired of her mom's sudden inspirations. I think there's a possibility that Adele is manic, but the movie doesn't go that route, preferring to see her as a dreamer who needs to grow up.

Adele is right and wrong about the small town. Wrong to leave the way she does, because going away to college might have provided a saner transition for her daughter. Right that her second husband, Ted, Ann's stepfather, "will always be an ice-skating instructor," and Ann's fate is not to be "a nothing girl in a nothing factory in a nothing town." Adele waited too long to make her own move, and doesn't want Ann to make the same mistake. Well, parents have been living through their children since the dawn of time.

Beverly Hills is a challenge to the two of them. Ann gets along fairly well at school, but her mother is insecure behind her brassy facade, and afraid to go to the posh holiday party she moved to California so they could be invited to. She deceives herself about one-night stands, like a pickup by Dr. Josh Spritzer (Hart Bochner), who is "more than just a dentist. He's writing a screenplay." Ann has seen enough of romance to be wary of it, even though she attracts the attention of a nice kid named Peter (Corbin Allred), who quotes T. S. Eliot's *Four Quartets* while jogging—always a good sign.

The movie's interest is not in the plot, which is episodic and "colorful," but in the performances. Sarandon bravely makes Adele into a person who is borderline insufferable. This isn't Auntie Mame, but someone with deep conflicts and inappropriate ways of addressing them. And Ann is complex too. The movie is narrated in her voice ("Mother made an amazing amount of noise when she ate, like she was trying to take on the whole world"), and her drift seems to be that her mother did the right thing in the wrong way for the wrong reason. (When a family tragedy brings them back to Wisconsin, "the streets weren't as wide, the trees seemed lower, the houses smaller.")

Sarandon's role is trickier and more difficult, but Portman gets your attention. Her big career break was in *The Phantom Menace*, where she played young Queen Amidala, but her talent first glowed in *Beautiful Girls* (1996), where she was just on the other side of the puberty line, and vibrated with . . . well, kindness and beauty, I'd say. In *Anywhere But Here*, she gets yanked along by her out-of-control mother, and her best scenes are when she fights back, not emotionally, but with incisive observations.

The screenplay is by Alvin Sargent, who is

gifted with stories of troubled kids *(The Sterile Cuckoo, Ordinary People)*. Here he has two good supporting characters: not only the poetry-quoting Peter, but also a cousin named Benny (Shawn Hatosy) back home, who is Ann's best friend and soul mate. These kids, and a richer high school classmate who is not, in fact, a snob, give the movie a reality; we sense teenagers trying to construct rational lives from the wreckage strewn by their parents.

The Apostle ★ ★ ★ ★
PG-13, 133 m., 1998

Robert Duvall (The Apostle E.F.), Farrah Fawcett (Jessie Dewey), Miranda Richardson (Toosie), Todd Allen (Horace), John Beasley (Brother Blackwell), June Carter Cash (Mrs. Dewey Sr.), Walter Goggins (Sam), Billy Joe Shaver (Joe), Billy Bob Thornton (Troublemaker). Directed by Robert Duvall and produced by Rob Carliner. Screenplay by Duvall.

There's a scene early in *The Apostle* where Robert Duvall, as a Pentecostal preacher from Texas, is having a talk with God, who has to do all of the listening. In an upstairs room at his mother's house, he rants and raves at the almighty, asking for a way to see reason in calamity: His cheating wife is stealing his church from him.

So far, the scene could be in a more conventional film. But then the phone rings, and it's a neighbor, complaining to his mother that someone is "carrying on like a wild man." The call establishes that the preacher lives in a real world, with real neighbors, and not on a sound stage where his life is lived in a self-contained drama. His mother tells the neighbor that her son has talked to God ever since he was a boy and she's not going to stop him now.

The Apostle sees its characters in an unusually perceptive light; they have the complexity and spontaneity of people in a documentary. Duvall, who not only plays the preacher but also wrote and directed the film, has seen this preacher—named Eulis "Sonny" Dewey—with great attention and sympathy.

Sonny is different from most movie preachers. He's not a fraud, for one thing; Hollywood tilts toward the Elmer Gantry stereotype. Sonny has a one-on-one relationship with God, takes his work seriously, and in the opening scene of the movie pauses at an auto accident to ask one of the victims to accept Jesus Christ, "who you're going to soon meet." He is flawed, with a quick temper, but he's a good man, and the film is about his struggle back to redemption after his anger explodes.

As the film opens, Sonny is spending a lot of time on the road at revivals (we see him at one of them, made convincing because Duvall cast all the extras from real congregations). His wife (Farrah Fawcett) has taken up with the youth minister, and one night, sitting in a motel room, Sonny figures that out, drives home through the darkness, finds her absent from her bed, and throws a baseball through the minister's bedroom window.

His wife wants out of the marriage. And through legal but shady maneuverings, she also deprives him of his church and his job. Sonny gets drunk, wades into a Little League game being coached by the youth minister, and bangs him on the head with a baseball bat. Then he flees town (there is an overhead shot of his car circling aimlessly around a rural intersection; he has no idea where to go). Eventually he ends up in a hamlet in the Louisiana bayou, where he spends his first night in a pup tent supplied by a man who wants to help him but isn't sure he trusts him.

Sonny changes his name to "The Apostle E.F.," and sets about rebuilding a small rural church given him by a retired black minister. His mostly black congregation is small at first, but grows as the result of broadcasts on the local forty-watt station. We see in countless little ways that Sonny is serious: He wants this church to work, he wants to save souls, he wants redemption. Like the documentary *Say Amen, Somebody,* the film spends enough time at the church services, listening to the music and the preaching, that we get into the spirit; we understand his feelings.

The Apostle became something of a legend in independent film circles, because Duvall was so long in getting it made. The major studios turned him down (of course; it's about something, which scares them). So did old associates who had always promised help, but didn't return his calls on this project. As he waited, Duvall must have rewritten the script many times, because it is astonishingly subtle. There isn't a canned and prefab story arc, with predictable stops along the way. Instead, the movie feels as alive as if it's a documentary of things happening right now.

Consider a sequence where the Apostle E.F., who is a man after all, asks the receptionist at the local radio station out on a date. How will he approach her? How does she see him? He wants to find a way to make his desires clear, without offending her. She knows this. As played by Duvall and Miranda Richardson, the sequence is a brilliant observation of social and sexual strategies.

Many of his scenes develop naturally, instead of along the lines of obligatory clichés. A confrontation with his wife, for example, doesn't end as we think it might. And a facedown with a redneck racist (Billy Bob Thornton) develops along completely unexpected lines. The Apostle E.F. is not easy to read; Duvall's screenplay does what great screenwriting is supposed to do and surprises us with additional observations and revelations in every scene.

Perhaps it's not unexpected that Duvall had to write, direct, and star in this film, and round up the financing himself. There aren't that many people in the film industry gifted enough to make such a film, and fewer still with the courage to deal honestly with a subject both spiritual and complex. (Simpleminded spirituality is no problem; consider the market for angels right now.) The Apostle is like a lesson in how movies can escape from convention and penetrate into the hearts of rare characters.

Apt Pupil ★ ★
R, 112 m., 1998

Ian McKellen (Kurt Dussander) Brad Renfro (Todd Bowden), Bruce Davison (Todd's father), Elias Koteas (Archie), Joe Morton (Dan Richler), David Schwimmer (Edward French). Directed by Bryan Singer and produced by Jane Hamsher, Don Murphy, and Singer. Screenplay by Brandon Boyce, based on the story by Stephen King.

Apt Pupil uses the horrors of the Holocaust as an atmospheric backdrop to the more conventional horror devices of a Stephen King story. It's not a pretty sight. By the end of the film, as a death camp survivor is quoting John Donne's poem about how no man is an island, we're wondering what island the filmmakers were inhabiting as they assembled this uneasy hybrid of the sacred and the profane.

The movie is well made by Bryan Singer *(The Usual Suspects)* and well acted, especially by Ian McKellen as Kurt Dussander, a Nazi war criminal who has been hiding in America for years. The theme is intriguing: A teenager discovers the old man's real identity and blackmails him into telling stories about his wartime experiences. But when bodies are buried in cellars and cats are thrown into lighted ovens, the film reveals itself as unworthy of its subject matter.

Brad Renfro is the costar, as Todd Bowden, a bright high school kid who after a week's study of the Holocaust notices a resemblance between a Nazi criminal and the old man down the street. Using Internet databases and dusting the old guy's mailbox for fingerprints, Todd determines that this is indeed a wanted man, and confronts him with a strange demand: "I want to hear all about it. The stories. Everything they were afraid to tell us in school. No one can tell it better than you."

The old man is outraged, but trapped. He shares his memories. And the film, to its shame, allows him to linger on details: "Although the gas came from the nozzles at the top, still they tried to climb. And climbing, they died in a mountain of themselves."

Soon the boy undergoes a transformation into a bit of a Nazi himself. He brings the old man a Nazi uniform, makes him put it on, and orders him to march around the kitchen: "Attention! March! Face right!" When the old man protests, young Todd barks: "What you've suffered with me is nothing compared to what the Israelis would do to you. Now move!"

The movie at least doesn't present the old man as repentant. Indeed, under the urging of the boy, he seems to regress to his earlier state, and there is the particularly nasty scene where he attempts to gas a neighbor's cat in his oven. (Does he succeed? The movie's shifty editing seems to permit two conclusions.) This scene is paired with another in which an injured bird is killed by a bouncing basketball.

Is there some kind of social message here? Some overarching purpose? If there were, then the material itself would not automatically be offensive. But the later scenes in the movie seem more, not less, exploitative. After the old Nazi tries to kill a spying bum and push him down the basement stairs, he calls on the kid to finish the job: "Now we see what you are made of!" We even get the tired cliché where a body seems to be dead and then rears up, alive. And of course victims being hit over the head with shovels.

All of this plays against a subplot where the kid tells lies at school, and even blackmails the old Nazi into posing as his grandfather at a counseling session. And at the end, after it is far too late for the film to change its nature, there is an attempt at moral balancing, including the poetry-quoting patient in the next hospital bed. That John Donne poem, about how no man is an island, about how we are all part of the larger humanity, ends with words that might profitably be considered by the filmmakers: "Never send to know for whom the bell tolls; it tolls for thee."

Arlington Road ★ ★
R, 117 m., 1999

Jeff Bridges (Michael Faraday), Tim Robbins (Oliver Lang), Joan Cusack (Cheryl Lang), Hope Davis (Brooke Wolfe), Robert Gossett (FBI Agent Carver), Mason Gamble (Brady Lang), Spencer Treat Clark (Grant Faraday), Stanley Anderson (Dr. Archer Scobee). Directed by Mark Pellington and produced by Peter Samuelson, Tom Gorai, and Marc Samuelson. Screenplay by Ehren Kruger.

Arlington Road is a conspiracy thriller that begins well and makes good points, but it flies off the rails in the last thirty minutes. The climax is so implausible we stop caring and start scratching our heads. Later, thinking back through the film, we realize it's not just the ending that's cuckoo. Given the logic of the ending, the entire film has to be rethought; this is one of those movies where the characters only seem to be living their own lives, when in fact they're strapped to the wheels of a labyrinthine hidden plot.

In the days when movies were made more carefully and were reluctant to insult the intelligence of their viewers, hard questions would

have been asked at the screenplay level and rewrites might have made this story more believable. But no. Watching *Arlington Road,* I got the uneasy feeling that the movie was made for (and by) people who live entirely in the moment—who gape at the energy of a scene without ever asking how it connects to what went before or comes after. It's a movie that could play in *Groundhog Day;* it exists in the eternal present.

Jeff Bridges stars as Faraday, a professor of terrorism (no smiles, please), whose late wife was an FBI agent shot dead in a botched raid. Hitchcock would have made him an ordinary guy and exploited the contrast with the weird plot he's trapped in, but making him a professor lets the movie shoehorn in lots of info as he lectures, narrates slide shows, and takes his students on field trips.

Faraday's key academic belief is that big terrorist events are not the work of isolated loners. We see photos of a federal building blown up in St. Louis and hear his doubts about the official theory that it was the work of one man, who acted alone and died in the blast. "We don't want others," he tells his students. "We want one man, and we want him fast—it gives us our security back."

As the film opens, Faraday sees an injured kid wandering down the street. He races him to an emergency room, and later finds he is the son of some folks who have moved in across the street—Oliver and Cheryl Lang (Tim Robbins and Joan Cusack). Faraday and his girlfriend, a graduate student with the wonderful movie name of Brooke Wolfe (Hope Davis), grow friendly with the Langs. But then Faraday, who like all terrorism professors, no doubt, has a streak of paranoia, begins to pick up little signals that the Langs are hiding something.

His investigation into Lang's background is hard to accept, depending as it does on vast coincidences. (After he finds an old newspaper article about Lang on the Internet, he journeys to a library and looks up the same material on old-fashioned microfilm, just so Lang can come up behind him and see what he's looking at.) To be fair, some of the implausibilities in this stage of the movie can be explained once the movie is over and we rethink the entire plot.

But leave the plot details aside for a second. What about the major physical details of the final thriller scenes? How can anyone, even skilled conspirators, predict with perfect accuracy the outcome of a car crash? How can they know in advance that a man will go to a certain pay phone at a certain time so that he can see a particular truck he needs to see? How can the actions of security guards be accurately anticipated? Isn't it risky to hinge an entire plan of action on the hope that the police won't stop a car speeding recklessly through a downtown area?

It's here that the movie completely breaks down. Yes, there's an ironic payoff, and yes, the underlying insights of the movie will make you think. But wasn't there a way to incorporate those insights and these well-drawn, well-acted characters into a movie that didn't force the audience to squirm in disbelief? *Arlington Road* is a thriller that contains ideas. Any movie with ideas is likely to attract audiences who have ideas of their own, but to think for a second about the logic of this plot is fatal.

Armageddon ★

PG-13, 150 m., 1998

Bruce Willis (Harry S. Stamper), Billy Bob Thornton (Dan Truman), Ben Affleck (A. J. Frost), Liv Tyler (Grace Stamper), Keith David (General Kimsey), Chris Ellis (Walter Clark), Jason Isaacs (Ronald Quincy), Will Patton ("Chick" Chapple). Directed by Michael Bay and produced by Jerry Bruckheimer, Gale Anne Hurd, and Bay. Screenplay by Jonathan Hensleigh and J. J. Abrams.

Here it is at last, the first 150-minute trailer. *Armageddon* is cut together like its own highlights. Take almost any thirty seconds at random and you'd have a TV ad. The movie is an assault on the eyes, the ears, the brain, common sense, and the human desire to be entertained. No matter what they're charging to get in, it's worth more to get out.

The plot covers many of the same bases as the recent *Deep Impact*, which, compared to *Armageddon*, belongs on the AFI list. The movie tells a similar story at fast-forward speed, with Bruce Willis as an oil driller who is recruited to lead two teams on an emergency shuttle mission to an asteroid "the size of Texas," which is about to crash into Earth and obliterate all

life—"even viruses!" Their job: Drill an 800-foot hole and stuff a bomb into it to blow up the asteroid before it kills us.

Okay, say you do succeed in blowing up an asteroid the size of Texas. What if a piece the size of Dallas is left? Wouldn't that be big enough to destroy life on Earth? What about a piece the size of Austin? Let's face it: Even an object the size of that big Wal-Mart outside Abilene would pretty much clean us out, if you count the parking lot.

Texas is a big state, but as a celestial object it wouldn't be able to generate much gravity. Yet when the astronauts get to the asteroid, they walk around on it as if the gravity is the same as on Earth. Sure, they're helped by back-mounted compressed-air nozzles, but how does that lunar buggy fly across a jagged canyon, Evel Knievel–style?

The movie begins with Charlton Heston telling us about the asteroid that wiped out the dinosaurs. Then we get the masterful title card, "65 Million Years Later." The next scenes show an amateur astronomer spotting the object. We see top-level meetings at the Pentagon and in the White House. We meet Billy Bob Thornton, head of Mission Control in Houston, which apparently functions like a sports bar with a big screen for the fans, but no booze. Then we see ordinary people whose lives will be Changed Forever by the events to come. This stuff is all off the shelf—there's hardly an original idea in the movie.

Armageddon reportedly used the services of nine writers. Why did it need any? The dialogue is either shouted one-liners or romantic drivel. "It's gonna blow!" is used so many times, I wonder if every single writer used it once, and then sat back from his word processor with a contented smile on his face, another day's work done.

Disaster movies always have little vignettes of everyday life. The dumbest in *Armageddon* involves two Japanese tourists in a New York taxi. After meteors turn an entire street into a flaming wasteland, the woman complains, "I want to go shopping!" I hope in Japan that line is redubbed as "Nothing can save us but Gamera!"

Meanwhile, we wade through a romantic subplot involving Liv Tyler and Ben Affleck. Liv is Bruce Willis's daughter. Ben is Willis's best driller (now, now). Bruce finds Liv in Ben's bunk on an oil platform and chases Ben all over the rig, trying to shoot him. (You would think the crew would be preoccupied by the semidestruction of Manhattan, but it's never mentioned after it happens.) Helicopters arrive to take Willis to the mainland, so he can head up the mission to save mankind, etc., and he insists on using only crews from his own rig—especially Affleck, who is "like a son."

That means Liv and Ben have a heartrending parting scene. What is it about cinematographers and Liv Tyler? She is a beautiful young woman, but she's always being photographed while flat on her back, with her brassiere riding up around her chin and lots of wrinkles in her neck from trying to see what some guy is doing. (In this case, Affleck is tickling her navel with animal crackers.) Tyler is obviously a beneficiary of Take Our Daughters to Work Day. She's not only on the oil rig, but she attends training sessions with her dad and her boyfriend, hangs out in Mission Control, and walks onto landing strips right next to guys wearing foil suits.

Characters in this movie actually say: "I wanted to say—that I'm sorry," "We're not leaving them behind!" "Guys—the clock is ticking!" and "This has turned into a surrealistic nightmare!" Steve Buscemi, a crew member who is diagnosed with "space dementia," looks at the asteroid's surface and adds, "This place is like Dr. Seuss's worst nightmare." Quick—which Seuss book is he thinking of?

There are several Red Digital Readout scenes, in which bombs tick down to zero. Do bomb designers do that for the convenience of interested onlookers who happen to be standing next to a bomb? There's even a retread of the classic scene where they're trying to disconnect the timer, and they have to decide whether to cut the red wire or the blue wire. The movie has forgotten that *this is not a terrorist bomb,* but a standard-issue U.S. military bomb, being defused by a military guy who is on board specifically because he knows about this bomb. A guy like that, the *first* thing he should know is, red, or blue?

Armageddon is loud, ugly, and fragmented. Action sequences are cut together at bewildering speed out of hundreds of short edits, so that we can't see for sure what's happening, or how, or why. Important special effects shots (like the asteroid) have a murkiness of detail, and the movie cuts away before we get a good look. The few "dramatic" scenes consist of the sonorous recitation of ancient clichés ("You're already heroes!"). Only near the end, when every second counts, does the movie slow down: Life on Earth is about to end, but the hero delays saving the planet in order to recite cornball farewell platitudes.

Staggering into the silence of the theater lobby after the ordeal was over, I found a big poster that was fresh off the presses with the quotes of junket blurbsters. "It will obliterate your senses!" reports David Gillin, who obviously writes autobiographically. "It will suck the air right out of your lungs!" vows Diane Kaminsky. If it does, consider it a mercy killing.

Artemisia ★ ★ ★
R, 96 m., 1998

Valentina Cervi (Artemisia), Michel Serrault (Orazio), Miki Manojlovic (Agostino), Luca Zingaretti (Cosimo), Emmanuelle Devos (Costanza), Frederic Pierrot (Roberto), Maurice Garrel (The Judge), Brigitte Catillon (Tuzia). Directed by Agnes Merlet and produced by Patrice Haddad. Screenplay by Merlet.

Most painters draw life studies while looking at nude models. In the secretive opening scenes of *Artemisia*, a young woman uses herself as a model, sketching by candlelight, looking at her own body in a mirror. This is Artemisia Gentileschi, who wants to be a painter but lives at a time when the profession is forbidden to women. She sketches anyway, and when her nude drawings are discovered by the nuns and shown to her father, he responds with pride: "You are the child of a painter."

He is Orazio (Michel Serrault), a professional painter of considerable skills, although his craft is a little behind the new work being done in Florence. It is 1670, the Italian Baroque is flourishing, and he allows his beloved daughter to study in his studio—although he draws the line at letting her view nude males. She is direct and determined, and bribes the fisherman Fulvio with a kiss for letting her draw him.

Artemisia is played by Valentina Cervi, who you may remember as the dark-haired, bright-eyed love child of John Malkovich and Barbara Hershey in *Portrait of a Lady*. She looks older here but is still a coltish teenager, with an eager stride and impulsive courage. You like her right away, because you sense there's no deceit in her: Like all true artists faced with the nude form, she sees not the naughty bits but the technical challenge.

The famous artist Agostino Tassi (Miki Manojlovic) joins her father in carrying out a papal commission. He is more advanced in his work with light and shadow, and she wants to study under him. Tassi wants nothing to do with her until he sees her work. Then he accepts her. "Someday you'll take lessons from me," she tells him. It is foreordained that they will fall in love—and rather touching, since he is a man of the world (she spies on him through a brothel window). He's attracted to her not just for sexual reasons, but because he has literally never met anyone like her before: a woman who thinks for herself, is as talented and ambitious as a man, and says what she believes.

The film follows through on the inevitable consequences of their romance. There is an ecclesiastical trial in which the cardinal in charge, bored with the conflicting testimony, simply has her fingers wound tight with a leather thong until either they are cut off or someone tells the truth. In a sense, she shares the same fate as her sister to the north in *Dangerous Beauty*, another 1998 movie set a century earlier, about a Venetian woman who can be independent only by becoming a courtesan. She can't be a modern woman without her world getting medieval on her.

The difference—and this is the most important difference in the world—is that Artemisia gains her freedom not by selling herself, but by selling her work. She seems to have been the first professional woman artist in the Western world, the first to be commissioned, the first to be admitted to the Academy in Florence, the first to travel to England for employment. Her paintings hang in the museums of Europe, and the critic Harvey Karten says of her painting *Judith Beheading Holofernes* in a Florence gallery: "You don't have to look closely at it to guess that it's the work of a woman painter. Two women are standing over the bearded, defeated general Holofernes, one holding a sword at his neck, the other helping to hold him down to a bed." Not a favorite baroque male fantasy.

Artemisia is as much about art as about sex, and it contains a lot of information about techniques, including the revolutionary idea of moving the easel outside and painting from nature. It lacks, however, detailed scenes showing drawings in the act of being created (for that you need *La Belle Noiseuse*, Jacques Rivette's 1991 movie that peers intimately over the shoulder of an artist in love). And it doesn't show a lot of Artemisia's work. What it does show is the gift of Valentina Cervi, who is another of those modern European actresses, like Juliette Binoche, Irene Jacob, Emmanuelle Béart, and Julie Delpy, whose intelligence, despite everything else, is the most attractive thing about her.

The Astronaut's Wife ★ ★ ½
R, 110 m., 1999

Johnny Depp (Spencer Armacost), Charlize Theron (Jillian Armacost), Joe Morton (Sherman Reese), Clea Duvall (Nan), Nick Cassavetes (Alex), Tom Noonan (Jackson McLaren). Directed by Rand Ravich and produced by Andrew Lazar. Screenplay by Ravich.

The Astronaut's Wife is a movie so effectively made that it's a shame the story finally isn't worthy of it. It builds suspense with exquisite care, only to release it with more or less exactly what we've been anticipating; it's one of those Peggy Lee movies where we leave the theater humming, "Is that all there is?" And yet the setup is an effective one, and there's a point about halfway through where you're still thinking it's really a pretty good film.

Johnny Depp stars as Spencer Armacost, a U.S. astronaut who's trapped in space outside the space shuttle, along with another crew member, for two agonizing minutes after an explosion. Charlize Theron is his wife, Jillian, who waits with dread on Earth for news: Is he dead or alive? He's alive, it turns out, and after a comatose stay in the hospital, he's released along with Alex, the other crew member (Nick Cassavetes).

But . . . something is wrong. Jillian finds him strangely changed. They've been happy living in Florida, where she teaches the second grade, but suddenly he announces he's taken a high-level executive position with a New York aerospace firm. "You always said you were a flyer," she says. "I'm done up there," he announces, while the score by George S. Clinton coils uneasily beneath the dialogue.

What happened in space to make him so odd? There's a NASA official (Joe Morton) who has a good idea, but the movie is more entertaining while it keeps us in suspense. There are lots of those scenes much beloved of movies set in the world of high finance, where the guests at black-tie charity benefits move easily through vast spaces, holding their champagne glasses, while wives look in concern across the room at their troubled husbands. There's even one of those moments where the husband is seen in distant conversation with the ominous head of the big corporation (Tom Noonan), who of course has a shaved head and looks like a very rich sadist.

Not all of those corporate-suspense scenes end, however, with the husband making urgent love to his wife while they're just out of sight on the balcony—but we somehow know it's not just a sex scene; there's more to it than that, and soon memories of *Rosemary's Baby* begin to coil down there with the music. More of the plot I must not reveal. I will say that the filmmakers do a good job of building us up for a movie with the weight of, say, *Contact,* only to finally give us a payoff more appropriate for one of those Michael Douglas thrillers about selfish adulterers.

Johnny Depp has a thankless role, as a man who must spend most of the movie withholding information and projecting ominous mystery. As the title character, Charlize Theron has more water to carry, and she's . . . well, okay, but remember Kathleen Quinlan as an astronaut's wife in *Apollo 13* and you'll see how the role could have more depth and dimension. Whenever a movie lingers on the details of a gynecological exam ("This will feel cold"), you know the heroine can't trust her husband.

There are a couple of shots in the movie that are simply wonderful. One comes after Jillian is taken into a large room at NASA headquarters and stands in front of a wall-size TV monitor that shows the pilot's-eye view of the shuttle landing. With gradually tighter framing, cinematographer Allen Daviau makes it look as if Jillian herself is racing toward Earth. I liked that, and I also liked the way a retirement party is given an edge of menace through the manipulation of points of view. But it's rarely effective when a movie resorts to a montage of earlier alarming events just when it should be showing us new ones.

The Astronaut's Wife didn't have good buzz. New Line Cinema, indeed, declined to hold advance critics' screenings—sometimes an ominous sign. In fact the movie is better than its rep; the setup is tantalizing, and if the payoff is a disappointment, it's not a disgrace. Many a worse movie has been previewed for the press. Maybe I felt let down because the earlier scenes led me to expect more. This is the kind of movie you wouldn't want to stop watching halfway through. Three-quarters, maybe. ☞

At First Sight ★ ★
PG-13, 124 m., 1999

Val Kilmer (Virgil Adamson), Mira Sorvino (Amy Benic), Kelly McGillis (Jennie Adamson), Steven Weber (Duncan Allanbrook), Bruce Davison (Dr. Charles Aaron), Nathan Lane (Phil Webster), Ken Howard (Virgil's Father), Laura Kirk (Betsy Ernst). Directed by Irwin Winkler and produced by Winkler and Rob Cowan. Screenplay by Steve Levitt, based on the story "To See and Not See" by Oliver Sacks, M.D.

The Oliver Sacks case study that inspired *At First Sight* tells the story of a man who has grown accustomed to blindness, and then is offered an operation that will restore sight. The moment when the bandages are removed all but cries out to be filmed. But to have sight suddenly thrust upon you can be a dismaying experience. Babies take months or years to develop mind-eye-hand coordination; here is an adult blind person expected to unlearn everything he knows and learn it again, differently.

The most striking moment in *At First Sight* is when the hero is able to see for the first time since he was three. "This isn't right," he says, frightened by the rush of images. "There's something wrong. This can't be seeing!" And then, desperately, "Give me something in my hands," so that he can associate a familiar touch with an unfamiliar sight.

If the movie had trusted the fascination of this scene, it might have really gone somewhere. Unfortunately, its moments of fascination and its good performances are mired in the morass of romance and melodrama that surrounds it. A blind man can see, and *still* he's trapped in a formulaic studio plot.

The buried inspiration for this film, I suspect, is not so much the article by Oliver Sacks as *Awakenings* (1990), another, much better movie based on another report by Sacks. Both films have similar arcs: A handicapped person is freed of the condition that traps him, is able to live a more normal life for a time, and then faces the possibility that the bars will slam shut again. *Charly* (1968), about a retarded man who gains and then loses normal intelligence, is the classic prototype.

In *Awakenings*, Robert De Niro played a man locked inside a rare form of Parkinson's disease. Under treatment by a brilliant doctor (Robin Williams), the disease goes into remission, and the man, who had not been able to speak or move for years, regains normal abilities. He even falls a little in love. Then the regression begins. In *At First Sight*, Val Kilmer plays a blind man who meets and falls in love with a woman (Mira Sorvino). She steers him to a doctor (Bruce Davison) whose surgical techniques may be able to restore his sight.

The woman, Amy, is a New York architect. She's left an unhappy relationship: "For the last five years I have lived with a man with the emotional content of a soap dish." She goes to a small resort town on vacation and sees a man skating all by himself on a forest pond. Later, she hires a massage therapist, who turns out to be the same person, a blind man named Virgil (Kilmer). The moment he touches her, she knows he is not a soap dish. She begins to cry as the tension drains from her.

Virgil knows his way everywhere in town, knows how many steps to take, is friendly with everybody. He is protected by a possessive older sister named Jennie (Kelly McGillis), who sees Amy as a threat: "We're very happy here, Amy. Virgil has everything he needs." But Amy and Virgil take walks, and talk, and make love, and soon Virgil wants to move to New York City, where Amy knows a doctor who may be able to reverse his condition.

The movie is best when it pays close attention to the details of blindness and the realities of the relationship. When the two of them take shelter from the rain in an old building, for example, he is able to sense the space around him by the sound of the rain outside. Some of his dialogue is sweetly ironic; when they meet for a second time, he says, "I was describing you to my dog, and how well you smelled."

All of this is just right, and Kilmer and Sorvino establish a convincing, intimate rapport—a private world in which they communicate easily. But the conventions of studio movies require false melodrama to be injected at every possible juncture, and so the movie manufactures a phony and unconvincing breakup, and throws in Virgil's long-lost father, whose presence is profoundly unnecessary for any reason other than to motivate scenes of soap-opera psychology.

The closing credits tell us the movie is based on the true story of "Shirl and Barbara Jennings, now living in Atlanta." My guess is that their story inspired the scenes that feel authentic, and that countless other movies inspired the rest. Certainly the material would speak for itself, if the screenplay would let it: Every single plot point is carefully recited and explained in the dialogue, lest we miss the significance. Seeing a movie like this, you wonder why the director, Irwin Winkler, didn't have more faith in the intelligence of his audience. The material deserves more than a disease-of-the-week docudrama simplicity.

Footnote: For a contrast to the simplified melodrama of At First Sight, *see* Hilary and Jackie, *which examines relationships and handicaps in a more challenging and adult way.*

Austin Powers: The Spy Who Shagged Me ★ ★ ½
PG-13, 95 m., 1999

Mike Myers (Austin Powers/Dr. Evil), Heather Graham (Felicity Shagwell), Elizabeth Hurley (Vanessa Kensington), Rob Lowe (Young Number Two), Michael York (Basil Exposition), Robert Wagner (Number Two 1999), Seth Green (Scott Evil), Gia Carides (Robin Swallows), Verne Troyer (Mini-Me). Directed by Jay Roach and produced by Suzanne Todd, Jennifer Todd,

Demi Moore, and Eric McLeod. Screenplay by Mike Myers and Michael McCullers.

There are some big laughs in *Austin Powers: The Spy Who Shagged Me,* but they're separated by uncertain passages of noodling. You can sense it when comedians know they have dead aim and are zeroing in for the kill. You can also sense it when they don't trust their material. The first *Austin Powers* movie burst with confidence: Mike Myers knew he was onto something. This time, too many scenes end on a flat note, like those *Saturday Night Live* sketches that run out of steam before they end. *SNL* cuts to music or commercials; *Austin Powers* cuts to song-and-dance interludes.

The key to a lot of the humor in the first film was that Austin Powers had been transported lock, stock, and barrel from the sixties to the nineties, where he was a sexist anachronism. The other satirical target was the James Bond series. This second film doesn't want to be a satire so much as just zany, raunchy slapstick.

The Spy Who Shagged Me seems to forget that Austin is a man out of his time; there are few laughs based on the fact that he's thirty years past his sell-by date, and there's so much time travel in this movie that half of the time he's back in the sixties again. Even when he's in the nineties, however, the women seem to take him on his own terms. Myers and his collaborators, flush with the victory of the first film, have forgotten that Austin is a misfit and not a hero.

The plot again involves Austin and his archenemy, Dr. Evil (both played by Myers). Thirsting for revenge after being exiled into Earth orbit, Evil wants to travel through time to when Powers was cryogenically frozen, and steal his mojo. (In case you were wondering, a beaker of mojo looks like Kool-Aid with licorice ropes floating in it.)

I didn't use a stopwatch, but my guess is that Evil has more screen time than Austin this time. There are several revelations. Early in the movie, in a funny sequence set on *The Jerry Springer Show,* Dr. Evil's son, Scott (Seth Green), appears, complaining that he hates his dad. Later a secret of parentage is revealed, *Star Wars*–style. And Evil acquires a midget double named Mini-Me,

played by Verne Troyer and inspired, Myers has said, by the miniature Marlon Brando in *The Island of Dr. Moreau.*

In a film with a lot of babes, Heather Graham plays the lead babe, Felicity Shagwell, a spy dedicated to her craft. In one scene that had the audience cringing when they should have been laughing, she goes to bed with a villain from Scotland named Fat Bastard, who wears a kilt, "weighs a metric ton," and is covered with greasy chicken bits. (Study the end credits for a surprise about the actor playing the F.B.)

There were some laughs (but more groans) during a scene where Austin mistakes a fecal brew for coffee; the movie is going for the kind of gross-out humor that distinguished *There's Something About Mary,* but what this sequence proves is that the grosser a scene is, the funnier it has to be to get away with it. I saw the movie with an audience recruited from the radio audience of Mancow Muller, Chicago's most cheerful vulgarian, and if *they* had a mixed reaction, middle America is likely to flee from the theater.

The movie succeeds, however, in topping one of the best elements in the first film, which was when Austin's private parts were obscured by a series of perfectly timed foreground objects. After Dr. Evil blasts off in a phallic spaceship, characters look up in the sky, see what the ship looks like, and begin sentences that are completed by quick cuts to other dialogue. (If I told you the names of some of the people you'd get the idea, but that wouldn't be fair to the movie.)

There is an underlying likability to Austin Powers that sort of carries us through the movie. He's such a feckless, joyful swinger that we enjoy his delight. Myers brings a kind of bliss to the Bond lifestyle. I also liked Seth Green as Evil's son, not least because he has obviously studied *Ebert's Bigger Little Movie Glossary* and knows all about the Fallacy of the Talking Killer (when Evil gets Powers in his grasp, Evil's son complains, "You never kill him when you have the chance to"). And the movie has fun by addressing the audience directly, as when Austin introduces Burt Bacharach and Elvis Costello, or later observes, during a scene set in the British countryside but shot in the

Los Angeles hills, "Funny how England looks in no way like Southern California." Oh, and the tradition of homage to *Beyond the Valley of the Dolls* continues with a bit part for the Russ Meyer superstar Charles Napier. ☞

Note: This film obtained a PG-13 rating—depressing evidence of how comfortable with vulgarity American teenagers are presumed to be. Apparently you can drink shit, just as long as you don't say it.

Autumn Tale ★ ★ ★

PG, 112 m., 1999

Marie Riviere (Isabelle), Beatrice Romand (Magali), Alain Libolt (Gerald), Didier Sandre (Etienne), Alexia Portal (Rosine), Stephane Darmon (Leo), Aurelia Alcais (Emilia), Matthieu Davette (Gregoire), Yves Alcais (Jean-Jacques). Directed by Eric Rohmer and produced by Francoise Etchegaray, Margaret Menegoz, and Rohmer. Screenplay by Rohmer.

It is hard not to fall a little in love with Magali. A woman in her late forties, heedless of makeup, dressed in jeans and a cotton shirt, forever pushing her unruly hair out of her eyes, she runs a vineyard in the Rhone district of southern France. She is a widow with a son and daughter, both grown. She loves her life and the wines she makes, but yes, sometimes she feels lonely. And how will the right man, or any man, find her while she lives in such splendid isolation?

Her friend Isabelle, happily married, takes Magali's plight to heart. One day, in an opening scene that effortlessly establishes the characters and their lives, they walk around Magali's land, talking of the similarities between weeds and flowers, and the aging of wines and women. Isabelle (Marie Riviere) asks Magali (Beatrice Romand) why she doesn't seek a man by placing a personal ad. Magali would rather die. So Isabelle places the ad herself. She will audition the candidates and arrange a meeting between Magali and the chosen man.

There are other characters, in particular young Rosine (Alexia Portal), who is currently the girlfriend of Magali's son, Leo, but used to date an older philosophy professor named Etienne (Didier Sandre). Rosine doesn't take Leo seriously ("He's just a filler"), but adores

Magali, and decides to fix her up with Etienne. Without suspecting it, Magali is headed for two possible romantic adventures.

Eric Rohmer's *Autumn Tale*, which tells this story, is the latest in a long, rich series of films by the perceptive French director, who tells stories about people we'd like to know, or be. His movies are about love, chance, life, and coincidence; he creates plots that unfold in a series of delights, surprises, and reversals. When there is a happy ending, it arrives as a relief, even a deliverance, for characters who spend much of the movie on the very edge of missing out on their chances for happiness.

Rohmer, now seventy-nine, was the editor of the famous French film magazine *Cahiers du Cinema* from 1956 to 1963. He was a founding member of the French New Wave, which includes Godard, Truffaut, Resnais, Malle, and Chabrol. He makes his movies in groups. *Six Moral Tales*, which he said was not so much about what people did as what they thought about while they were doing it, included three that made him famous: *My Night at Maud's* (1969), *Claire's Knee* (1971), and *Chloe in the Afternoon* (1972). Then came his *Comedies and Proverbs*, and now his current series, *Tales of the Four Seasons*.

His films are heavily, craftily plotted, and yet wear their plots so easily that we feel we're watching everyday life as it unfolds. Consider the complexities of *Autumn Tale*, as both Isabelle and Rosine maneuver to arrange meetings between Magali and the men they've chosen for her. There are complications and misunderstandings, and Isabelle is almost accused of being unfaithful to her own husband (whom she adores, she says, although we never see him because Rohmer wisely knows he's not needed).

Everything comes together at a virtuoso scene that Rohmer stages at a wedding party. Magali is present, reluctantly, and so are the men, and of course all three misunderstand almost everything that happens. Since we like Gerald (Alain Libolt), the guy who answered the personal ad, and think Etienne is a twerp, we know who we're cheering for, but Rohmer creates quiet suspense by elegantly choreographing the movements at the party—who is seen, and when, and why, and in what context—until finally a smile and a nod of approval are exchanged over a glass of wine, and we feel like cheering. (The approval is of the wine, not the characters, but from it all else will follow.)

Even though I enjoy Hollywood romantic comedies like *Notting Hill*, it's like they wear galoshes compared to the sly wit of a movie like *Autumn Tale*. They stomp squishy-footed through their clockwork plots, while Rohmer elegantly seduces us with people who have all of the alarming unpredictability of life. There's never a doubt that Julia Roberts will live happily ever after. But Magali, now: One wrong step, and she's alone with her vines forever.

B

Babe: Pig in the City ★ ★ ★ ★
G, 96 m., 1998

Magda Szubanski (Mrs. Hoggett), James Cromwell (Farmer Hoggett), Mary Stein (The Landlady), Mickey Rooney (Fugly Floom), Roscoe Lee Browne (Narrator). And the voices of: E. G. Daily (Babe), Danny Mann (Ferdinand), Glenne Headly (Zootie), James Cosmo (Thelonious), Stanley Ralph Ross (Bull Terrier). Directed by George Miller and produced by George Miller, Doug Mitchell, and Bill Miller. Screenplay by George Miller, Judy Morris, and Mark Lamprell.

"The first hazard for the returning hero is fame."

So we are assured by the narrator in the opening line of *Babe: Pig in the City*. And what is true of heroes is even more true of sequels. The original *Babe* was an astonishment, an unheralded family movie from Australia that was embraced and loved and nominated for an Oscar as Best Picture. Can the sequel possibly live up to it?

It can and does, and in many ways is more magical than the original. *Babe* was a film in which everything led up to the big sheepherding contest, in which a pig that worked like a dog turned out to be the best sheep-pig of them all. *Babe: Pig in the City* is not so plotbound, although it has the required assortment of villains, chases, and close calls. It is more of a wonderment, lolling in its enchanting images—original, delightful, and funny.

It doesn't make any of the mistakes it could have. It doesn't focus more on the human characters—it focuses less, and there are more animals on the screen. It doesn't recycle the first story. It introduces many new characters. It outdoes itself with the sets and special effects that make up "the city." And it is still literate, humane, and wicked. George Miller, who produced, directed, and cowrote the film, has improved and extended the ideas in *Babe* (1995), instead of being content to copy them.

The movie begins with Babe returning in triumph to the farm with his sheepdog trophy. Alas, he soon falls into the well, setting in motion a calamitous chain of events that ends with Farmer Hoggett (James Cromwell) laid up in bed, and Mrs. Hoggett (Magda Szubanski) forced to exhibit Babe at a state fair in order to save the farm from foreclosure. Alas again, Babe and Mrs. Hoggett miss their connecting flight (she is busted on suspicion of drug possession, that merry, apple-cheeked dumpling of a lady). And they are homeless in the cruel city, where hotels sniff at pigs.

What a city this is! I love imaginary cities in the movies, from *Metropolis* to *Dark City*, and here is one to set beside the great ones. Using elaborate sets that surround the buildings with a canal system, Miller uses f/x to create a skyline that impudently incorporates such landmarks as the Statue of Liberty, the Sydney Opera House, and the Hollywood sign. This is all cities. And in it, Babe finds himself at a boardinghouse whose landlady (Mary Stein) believes animals deserve rooms just like people do.

There is a large cast of animal characters, whose dialogue is lip-synched, and who are colorful and individual—not at all like silly talking animals. One of my favorite scenes involves Ferdinand the duck (voice by Danny Mann), attempting to keep up with the jet plane taking Babe to the city; the rear view of him flapping at breakneck speed is one of the funniest moments in the movie. (He's eventually given a lift by a pelican, who intones, "Go well, noble duck!")

In the boardinghouse, we meet chimpanzees, orangutans, cats, fish, and a dog paralyzed from the waist down, who propels himself on a little cart. Babe is tricked by some of his new housemates into distracting fierce dogs during a desperate raid for food; apparently facing doom, he turns, looks his enemy in the eye, and asks, "Why?" He has a close call with a bull terrier (voice by Stanley Ralph Ross, sounding like a Chicago gangster) who tries to kill him and ends up dangling headfirst in the canal. Babe saves him from drowning, and the dog becomes his fierce protector: "What the pig says, goes!"

The movie is filled with wonders large and small. Little gags at the side of the frame and big laughs in the center. It is in no way just a "children's movie," but one that extends the imagination of everyone who sees it, and there is a wise, grown-up sensibility to its narration, its characters, and a lot of the action. (Other action is cheerfully goofy, as when Mrs. Hoggett gets involved in a weird bungeelike session of chandelier swinging.)

Here is a movie that is all made up. The world and its characters materialize out of the abyss of the imagination, and in their impossibility they seem more real than the characters in many realistic movies. Their hearts are in the right places. And apart from what they do and say, there is the wonderment of the world they live in ("A place just a little to the left of the twentieth century"). I liked *Babe* for all the usual reasons, but I like *Babe: Pig in the City* more, and not for any of the usual reasons, because here is a movie utterly bereft of usual reasons.

Baby Geniuses ½★
PG, 94 m., 1999

Kathleen Turner (Elena) Christopher Lloyd (Heap), Miko Hughes (voice) (Sly), Kim Cattrall (Robin), Peter MacNicol (Dan), Dom DeLuise (Lenny), Ruby Dee (Margo). Directed by Bob Clark and produced by Steven Paul. Screenplay by Clark and Greg Michael, based on a story by Paul, Francisca Matos, and Robert Grasmere.

Bad films are easy to make, but a film as unpleasant as *Baby Geniuses* achieves a kind of grandeur. And it proves something I've long suspected: Babies are cute only when they're being babies. When they're presented as miniature adults (on greeting cards, in TV commercials, or especially in this movie), there is something so fundamentally *wrong* that our human instincts cry out in protest.

Oh, you can have fun with a baby as a movie character. *Look Who's Talking* (1989) was an entertaining movie in which we heard what the baby was thinking. *Baby's Day Out* (1994), with its fearless baby setting Joe Mantegna's pants on fire, had its defenders. But those at least were allegedly real babies. *Baby Geniuses* is about toddlers who speak, plot, scheme, disco dance, and beat up adults with karate kicks. This is not right.

The plot: Kathleen Turner plays a woman with a theory that babies can talk to each other.

She funds a secret underground lab run by Christopher Lloyd to crack the code. Her theory is based on the Tibetan belief that children have Universal Knowledge until they begin to speak—when their memories fade away.

This is an old idea, beautifully expressed by Wordsworth, who said that "heaven lies about us in our infancy." If I could quote the whole poem instead of completing this review, believe me, we'd all be happier. But I press on. The movie involves a genius baby named Sly, who escapes from the lab and tries to organize fellow babies in revolt. The nauseous sight of little Sly on a disco floor, dressed in the white suit from *Saturday Night Fever* and dancing to "Stayin' Alive" had me pawing under my seat for the bag my Subway Gardenburger came in, in case I felt the sudden need to recycle it.

Every time the babies talk to one another, something weird happens to make it look like their lips are in synch (think of talking frogs in TV commercials). And when the babies do things that babies don't do (hurl adults into the air, for example), we lose all track of the story while trying to spot the visual trick.

There's only one way the movie might have worked: If the babies had been really, really smart. After all, according to the theory, they come into this world "trailing clouds of glory" (Wordsworth again: the man can write). They possess Universal Knowledge. Wouldn't you expect them to sound a little like Jesus or Aristotle? Or at least Wayne Dyer? But no. They arrive to this mortal coil (Shakespeare) from that level "higher than the sphery chime" (Milton), and we expect their speech to flow in "heavenly eloquence" (Dryden). But when they open their little mouths, what do they say? "Diaper gravy"—a term used four times in the movie, according to a friend who counted (Cleland).

Yes, they talk like little wise guys, using insipid potty-mouth dialogue based on insult humor. This is still more evidence for my theory that the greatest single influence on modern American culture has been Don Rickles.

Bad Manners ★ ★ ★
R, 88 m., 1998

David Strathairn (Wes Westlund), Bonnie Bedelia (Nancy Westlund), Saul Rubinek (Matt Carroll), Caroleen Feeney (Kim Matthews), Julie Harris (Professor Harper). Directed by Jonathan Kaufer. Screenplay by David Gilman, based on his play *Ghost in the Machine.*

Is this a dream or a nightmare? A man programs a computer to compose music at random. The computer gives him what he has asked for. But in the middle of all the binary coin-tossing, he discovers several perfect bars of Martin Luther's "A Mighty Fortress is Our God." How could this be? Did the computer have a serendipitous accident? Or did God himself reach down a bemused finger and stir the zeroes and ones?

There is another possibility that does not occur to the musicologist, who is a self-important middle-aged man named Matt (Saul Rubinek). His latest girlfriend is a brainy temptress named Kim (Caroleen Feeney), who is a computer expert. Could she have meddled with his program, just as she has reprogrammed his life? Do not hasten to choose the third possibility. It seems likely only because Kim is such a game-player anyway, a woman who draws out the worst in everyone around her for her private delight.

As the wickedly funny *Bad Manners* opens, Kim and Matt arrive as the house guests of a longtime married couple named Wes and Nancy Westlund (David Strathairn and Bonnie Bedelia). She is a successful academic. He is not. He has, in fact, just been denied tenure at a second-tier school, which hurts for a lot of reasons, among them: (1) Nancy has tenure at Harvard, and (2) the overbearing, condescendingly successful Matt is Nancy's former lover.

Matt is full of himself. He believes his computer program will make him as famous as if he had intercepted messages from distant galaxies. Wes also takes himself very seriously. He is pompous and easily wounded, and the dark-haired, chain-smoking young Kim immediately singles him out as a target. She observes that Wes and Nancy have no children, and asks him, "Firing blanks?" She uses his antique bowl as an ashtray. She wanders about the house wearing less than she should, and she seduces Wes once in a fantasy sequence and probably again for real, although the truth is obscured by much game-playing.

Bad Manners is based on the play *Ghost in the Machine,* by David Gilman, first performed at Chicago's Steppenwolf theater in 1993. Like work by that other Chicagoan, David Mamet, it toys with the integrity of its characters by subjecting them to devious games. In *Bad Manners,* the key game is one only two of the characters are playing—and perhaps they are playing it only with themselves. Wes is powerfully attracted to Kim but denies it, and when he discovers that a $50 bill is missing, he tells Nancy that Kim is the thief. At his urging, Nancy searches Kim's luggage and does indeed find a $50 bill, which appears to be concealed. But is it the same bill? The bill is removed, replaced, and doubled, in a fiduciary version of "Who's on First?" Sounds silly, but there's a way in which smart people can get obsessed with tiny, goofy matters of principle and blow them all out of proportion—and Wes goes weird over that bill.

Meanwhile, in the movie's best single scene, the proud Matt goes to visit the editor of a respected academic journal (Julie Harris). He has submitted a paper describing his computer miracle to her, and she tells him what she thinks of it. The Harris character is like a visitor from another world; the four main characters are trapped inside their rigid little dance, and she is not. She handles the interview with brutal directness.

Bad Manners, directed by Jonathan Kaufer, will remind some of *Who's Afraid of Virginia Woolf,* and others of Tom Noonan's oddly involving, overlooked *The Wife.* Like them, it is about intellectuals who would rather verbalize about their problems than solve them. But it doesn't choose to cut to the bone; the visitors will eventually leave, and perhaps routine will reestablish itself; the movie is more about games than about psychological reality, and all the more fun because of that.

There is a masochistic sense in which all of the characters are enjoying themselves with their mind games, especially Wes. And at least Kim, before she leaves, is able to provide Nancy with a useful suggestion.

Barney's Great Adventure ★ ★ ★
(Star rating for kids six and under; adults: bring your Walkman)
G, 75 m., 1998

Trevor Morgan (Cody Newton), Diana Rice (Abby Newton), Kyla Pratt (Marcella), George Hearn (Grandpa Greenfield), Shirley Douglas (Grandma Greenfield). Directed by Steve Gomer and produced by Sheryl Leach and Dennis DeShazer. Screenplay by Stephen White.

Since *Barney's Great Adventure* is intended for children six and below, I am writing this review to be read aloud:

Barney has his own movie. Not one of those videos you've watched a hundred times, but a real movie, more than an hour long. If you like him on TV, you'll like him here, too, because it's more of the same stuff, only outdoors and with animals and shooting stars and the kinds of balloons people can go up in.

The main character in the story, after Barney, is a boy named Cody, who is in about the first or second grade. He's just at that age when kids start to have their doubts about dinosaurs who look like large purple stuffed toys. Along with his sister Abby and her best friend, Marcella, he goes to visit Grandpa and Grandma on their farm. Cody doesn't think he'll like the farm, because his grandparents don't have cable TV, so how can he watch Nickelodeon? Plus Grandpa's pigpen is directly below Cody's bedroom window.

But then Barney turns up. He starts as a little toy, and then he becomes about eight feet tall, but looking just the same. He sings a song named "Imagine" and tells Cody that it was Cody's own imagination that made the toy dinosaur become the real Barney.

Cody plays a trick. He stops believing in Barney. Barney disappears. Then Barney plays a trick. He appears again, because *he* believes in Cody! That sort of makes sense.

Barney shows Cody a special wishing star. The star deposits an egg in Grandpa's barn. This is a wishing egg. It has different colored stripes on it. When all the stripes glow, the egg is about to hatch. The kids take the egg to Miss Birdfinch to find out about it.

But the egg gets in a lot of trouble. It falls into the back of a birdseed truck and is hauled off to town. Cody, Abby, and Marcella chase it, and get to be in a parade and see the balloons go up. To get to town they ride a pony.

Barney must not know any new songs, because mostly he sings old ones, like "Twinkle, Twinkle Little Star" and "Old McDonald" and "Clap Your Hands." It's sweet when Grandpa sings "Let Me Call You Sweetheart" to Grandma. Even though this is probably the first time you've heard that song, it's not new, either.

By the end of the movie, Cody believes in Barney, because it's pretty hard not to believe in something that's purple and eight feet tall and standing right there in front of you. The egg hatches and helps everyone have their wishes. Baby Bop and B.J., Barney's friends on television, have small roles. Baby Bop is always looking for her yellow blanket, which she calls a "blan-kee." Don't you think it's time for Baby Bop to get serious about learning to say "blanket"?

BASEketball ★ ½
R, 98 m., 1998

Trey Parker (Coop), Matt Stone (Remer), Yasmine Bleeth (Jenna), Jenny McCarthy (Yvette), Robert Vaughn (Cain), Ernest Borgnine (Denslow), Dian Bachar (Squeak), Bob Costas (Himself), Al Michaels (Himself). Directed by David Zucker and produced by Zucker, Robert LoCash, and Gil Netter. Screenplay by Zucker, LoCash, Lewis Friedman, and Jeff Wright.

BASEketball is a major missed opportunity from the creators of the TV grosstoon *South Park*. It starts promisingly as an attack on modern commercialized sports, and then turns into just one more wheezy assembly-line story about slacker dudes versus rich old guys.

It does give you a taste, every now and then, of what a genuinely subversive, satiric comedy on pro sports would feel like. I laughed at an opening montage of sponsored sports domes ("Preparation H Arena"), and when the narrator talked about runaway sports teams and stars who care only about money, my ears perked up. But there's little follow-through, and the movie sinks quickly into sight gags about bodily functions.

Bodily functions can be funny. I recall with

great affection the gas attack in Eddie Murphy's *The Nutty Professor* and the famous opening sequence in *There's Something About Mary*. But *BASEketball* thinks the functions *themselves* are funny. There's an enormous gulf between a joke built on peeing (opening scene of *Mary*) and the belief that peeing is a joke (an early scene in this film).

Thinking it's funny simply to show something—that it's hilarious just to be getting away with it—is junior high school humor. Once you outgrow that age, you kinda like the material to be taken to another level. Too much of this film is pitched at the level of guys in the back row of home room, sticking their hands under their armpits and making farting noises.

The movie stars Trey Parker and Matt Stone, creators of Comedy Central's *South Park*, as a couple of high school buddies who get desperate during a basketball grudge game, and invent baseketball, which combines basketball, baseball, and volleyball (it's a real game that David Zucker, the film's director, invented in the 1980s). Soon they're playing it in their driveway; then they start to draw a crowd, and an aging sports zillionaire (Ernest Borgnine) takes them pro.

The ideals of the first baseketball league are high. Teams will not jump from town to town in search of the highest bidder, and the players will all be paid the same. The sport catches on, and soon Bob Costas and Al Michaels (playing themselves) are announcing the games. The playing field consists of a big mockup of the heroes' original garage and driveway. The sport rewards the art of trash-talking your opponents, and players try to distract shooters by grossing them out.

The performances of Parker and Stone, who are onscreen in almost every scene, are surprisingly good, especially considering these guys don't have a lot of acting experience. They're goofy in a *Wayne's World* kind of way, and use the word "dude" so much that one conversation is conducted entirely in "dudes." Their long wet kiss toward the end of the film is not as funny as the tongue work between the neighbor and her dog in *There's Something About Mary* but at least they tried.

I liked the personal sports museum of another team owner (Robert Vaughn), who pays sports legends like Kareem Abdul Jabbar to sit in a glass case as an exhibit. And I guess it's sort of funny when the guys both fall for the sexy head of the Dreams Come True Foundation (Yasmine Bleeth) and treat her sick kids to a day with their baseketball heroes (the high point: sitting in a bar watching Jerry Springer on TV). The preview audience laughed at a scene where the guys visit poor little Joey after his liver transplant, inadvertently sit on his air tube, and then fry him with defibrillators; the movie's jaundiced attitude toward the deaths of kids is lifted straight from *South Park*, where little Kenny, of course, dies weekly and has been consumed by scavengers right there on the screen.

Famous faces float through the film. Jenny McCarthy plays Borgnine's mistress ("I gave him the best three months of my life!"), Robert Stack kids his work on *Unsolved Mysteries*, and Reggie Jackson turns up at the end. All of the guest stars are required to use four-letter words, but that takes us back to the original problem: It's not funny just *because* they say them; it has to be funny for another reason too.

Some commentators will no doubt seize upon *BASEketball* as further evidence of the deterioration of standards in our society. They will attack it as vulgar, offensive, disgusting, etc. That's not what bothers me. I think the movie is evidence of deteriorating *comic* standards in our society. It's not very funny, and tries to buy laughs with puerile shocks. My theory: Those who find it funny haven't advanced a whole lot from the sneaky-fart-noise evolutionary stage.

Battlefield Earth ½★
PG-13, 117 m., 2000

John Travolta (Terl), Barry Pepper (Jonnie Goodboy Tyler), Forest Whitaker (Ker), Kim Coates (Carlo), Richard Tyson (Robert the Fox), Michael MacRae (District Manager Zete), Michael Byrne (Parson Staffer), Sean Hewitt (Heywood). Directed by Roger Christian and produced by Elie Samaha, Jonathan D. Krane, and John Travolta. Screenplay by Corey Mandell and J. D. Shapiro, based on the novel by L. Ron Hubbard.

Battlefield Earth is like taking a bus trip with someone who has needed a bath for a long time. It's not merely bad; it's unpleasant in a hostile way. The visuals are grubby and drab. The characters are unkempt and have rotten teeth. Breathing tubes hang from their noses like ropes of snot. The sound track sounds like the boom mike is being slammed against the inside of a fifty-five-gallon drum. The plot . . .

But let me catch my breath. This movie is awful in so many different ways. Even the opening titles are cheesy. Sci-fi epics usually begin with a stab at impressive titles, but this one just displays green letters on the screen in a type font that came with my Macintosh. Then the movie's subtitle unscrolls from left to right in the kind of "effect" you see in home movies.

It is the year 3000. The race of Psychlos have conquered Earth. Humans survive in scattered bands, living like actors auditioning for the sequel to *Quest for Fire*. Soon a few leave the wilderness and prowl through the ruins of theme parks and the city of Denver. The ruins have held up well after 1,000 years. (The books in the library are dusty but readable, and a flight simulator still works, although where it gets the electricity is a mystery.)

The hero, named Jonnie Goodboy Tyler, is played by Barry Pepper as a smart human who gets smarter thanks to a Psychlo gizmo that zaps his eyeballs with knowledge. He learns Euclidean geometry and how to fly a jet, and otherwise proves to be a quick learner for a caveman. The villains are two Psychlos named Terl (John Travolta) and Ker (Forest Whitaker).

Terl is head of security for the Psychlos, and has a secret scheme to use the humans as slaves to mine gold for him. He can't be reported to his superiors because (I am not making this up), he can blackmail his enemies with secret recordings that, in the event of his death, "would go straight to the home office!" Letterman fans laugh at that line; did the filmmakers know it was funny?

Jonnie Goodboy figures out a way to avoid slave labor in the gold mines. He and his men simply go to Fort Knox, break in, and steal it. Of course it's been waiting there for 1,000 years. What Terl says when his slaves hand him smelted bars of gold is beyond explanation. For stunning displays of stupidity, Terl takes the cake; as chief of security for the conquering aliens, he doesn't even know what hu-

mans eat, and devises an experiment: "Let it think it has escaped! We can sit back and watch it choose its food." Bad luck for the starving humans that they capture a rat. An experiment like that, you pray for a chicken.

Hiring Travolta and Whitaker was a waste of money, since we can't recognize them behind pounds of matted hair and gnarly makeup. Their costumes look purchased from the Goodwill store on Tatoine. Travolta can be charming, funny, touching, and brave in his best roles; why disguise him as a smelly alien creep? The Psychlos can fly between galaxies, but look at their nails: Their civilization has mastered the hyperdrive but not the manicure.

I am not against unclean characters—at least now that the threat of Smell-O-Vision no longer hangs over our heads. Lots of great movies have squalid heroes. But when the characters seem noxious on principle, we wonder if the art and costume departments were allowed to run wild.

Battlefield Earth was written in 1980 by L. Ron Hubbard, the founder of Scientology. The film contains no evidence of Scientology or any other system of thought; it is shapeless and senseless, without a compelling plot or characters we care for in the slightest. The director, Roger Christian, has learned from better films that directors sometimes tilt their cameras, but he has not learned why.

Some movies run off the rails. This one is like the train crash in *The Fugitive*. I watched it in mounting gloom, realizing I was witnessing something historic, a film that for decades to come will be the punch line of jokes about bad movies. There is a moment here when the Psychlos' entire planet (home office and all) is blown to smithereens, without the slightest impact on any member of the audience (or, for that matter, the cast). If the film had been destroyed in a similar cataclysm, there might have been a standing ovation.

The Beach ★ ★
R, 119 m., 2000

Leonardo DiCaprio (Richard), Tilda Swinton (Sal), Virginie Ledoyen (Françoise), Guillaume Canet (Etienne), Robert Carlyle (Daffy), Paterson Joseph (Keaty), Lars Arentz Hansen (Bugs). Directed by Danny Boyle and produced by Andrew MacDonald. Screenplay by John Hodge, based on the book by Alex Garland.

The Beach is a seriously confused film that makes three or four passes at being a better one, and doesn't complete any of them. Since Leonardo DiCaprio is required to embody all of its shifting moods and aims, it provides him with more of a test than a better film might have; it's like a triathlon where every time he sights the finish line, they put him on a bicycle and send him out for another fifty miles.

The early scenes deliberately evoke the opening of *Apocalypse Now*, with its sweaty close-ups, its revolving ceiling fans, and its voice-overs by DiCaprio trying to sound like Martin Sheen. In a fleabag hotel in Bangkok, a fellow traveler (Robert Carlyle) tells him of an island paradise, hard to find but worth the trip. Will his journey borrow from a Joseph Conrad novel (*Victory*, say) as *Apocalypse Now* borrowed from *Heart of Darkness*?

No such luck, DiCaprio's character, named Richard, recruits a French couple in the next room, and as they set out for the legendary island, the movie abandons Conrad and *Apocalypse* and borrows instead from *The Blue Lagoon* on its way to a pothead version of *Lord of the Flies*. This is the kind of movie where the heroes are threatened by heavily armed guards in a marijuana field, and that's less alarming than when they jump off a ledge into a deep pool. Later they'll go swimming in glowing clouds of plankton, and Richard will face a shark in one-on-one combat.

Many of the scenes look, frankly, like time-fillers. Richard and his new French friends Francoise (Virginie Ledoyen) and Etienne (Guillaume Canet) arrive safely at a sort of retro hippie commune, where the pot is free, the bongos beat every night, and all is blissful on the beach, watched over by the stern eye of Sal (Tilda Swinton), the community's leader. It's paradise, Richard tells us—except for his lust for Francoise. So will this become a love triangle? No, because Francoise, once enjoyed, is forgotten, and besides, Etienne only wants her to be happy. Those French. A later encounter with Sal is more like plumbing than passion, and both sex scenes are arbitrary—they aren't important to the characters or the movie.

But then many of the sequences fall under the heading of good ideas at the time. Consider, for example, a strange interlude in which Richard becomes the hero of a video game, stomping through the landscape in computerized graphics. There is an echo here from *Trainspotting*, a better film by the same director, Danny Boyle, in which special effects are used to send the hero on a plunge into the depths of the world's filthiest toilet. There the effects worked as comic exaggeration; here they're just goofy.

What is important, I guess, is Richard's evolution from an American drifter in the Orient into a kind of self-appointed Tarzan, who takes to the jungle and trains himself, well aware that a movie so pointless and meandering will need contrived violence to justify the obligatory ending. In a paroxysm of indecision, the film's conclusion mixes action, existential resignation, the paradise-lost syndrome, and memories of happier days, the last possibly put in for studio executives who are convinced that no matter how grim a movie's outcome, it must end on a final upbeat. Watching *The Beach* is like experiencing a script conference where only sequences are discussed—never the whole film.

What is it about, anyway? There are the elements here for a romantic triangle, for a man-against-the-jungle drama, for a microcosm-of-civilization parable, or for a cautionary lesson about trying to be innocent in a cruel world. The little society ruled over by Sal is a benevolent dictatorship—you can be happy as long as you follow the rules—and that's material for satire or insight, I guess, although the movie offers none.

There is one extraordinary development. One of the commune guys is bitten by a shark, and when his anguished screams disturb the island idyll of the others, Sal simply has him moved out of earshot. This event suggests the makings of another, darker movie, but it's not allowed to pay off or lead to anything big.

Maybe that's because the whole film is seen so resolutely through Richard's eyes, and the movie doesn't want to insult its target demographic group or dilute DiCaprio's stardom by showing the character as the twit that he is. In a smarter film Richard would have been revealed as a narcissistic kid out of his depth, and maybe he would have ended up out in the woods where his screams couldn't be heard.

Beautiful People ★ ★ ★
R, 107 m., 2000

Charlotte Coleman (Portia Thornton), Charles Kay (George Thornton), Rosalind Ayres (Nora Thornton), Roger Sloman (Roger Midge), Heather Tobias (Felicity Midge), Danny Nussbaum (Griffin Midge), Siobhan Redmond (Kate Higgins), Gilbert Martin (Jerry Higgins). Directed by Jasmin Dizdar and produced by Ben Woolford. Screenplay by Dizdar.

A man boards a London bus, locks eyes with another man, and immediately starts to fight with him. Thrown off the bus, they chase each other through the streets and eventually end up in adjacent hospital beds, still ready to fight. One is a Croat, one is a Serb, and so they hate each other.

Ah, but hate is not limited to Bosnians. In the next bed is the Welsh firebomber, a man who torched the holiday cottages of twenty English weekenders before burning himself on the face. Elsewhere in *Beautiful People* we see three skinheads attacking a black kid, and a foreigner who is mistaken for a thief while trying to return a wallet, and the beat goes on even at the breakfast tables of the ruling class: "God!" says the wife of a government official, "Antonia Fraser is so bloody Catholic."

Beautiful People, written and directed in London by the Bosnian filmmaker Jasmin Dizdar, is about people who hate because of tribal affiliation, which is a different thing than hating somebody you know personally and have good reasons to despise. One of its interlocking stories involves a pregnant Bosnian woman who wants an abortion because her baby, the product of a rape, "is my enemy."

The movie loops and doubles back among several stories and characters, like Robert Altman's *Short Cuts* or Paul Thomas Anderson's *Magnolia*. The insights in one story cast light on the problems of another, and sometimes the characters meet—as when a young woman doctor falls in love with a patient, and brings him home to meet her stuffy family. Nor are the moral judgments uncomplicated. Although she explodes when her family condescends to the man, the fact remains that he speaks only about six words of English, and so her own affection for him is condescending too.

The most involving story involves a young heroin addict named Griffin (Danny Nussbaum), who has always been a trial for his parents ("Remember sixth form," his father asks, "when all of the teachers went on strike because no one wanted to teach him?"). As part of an involved attempt to attend a football match, Griffin stumbles onto an airfield, falls asleep on an air freight pallet, and is dropped by parachute into Bosnia as part of an airlift of UN aid supplies.

This has the aroma of an urban legend to it, like the scuba diver who was scooped up by a fire-fighting airplane and dumped onto a forest fire. In *Beautiful People*, it works like one of those fairy tales where a naughty child gets his comeuppance by trading places with one less fortunate. Here what happens is that Griffin, dazed and withdrawing, stumbles around the war zone and ends up behaving rather well.

There is another character stumbling there, too: a BBC war correspondent who loses his mind in the chaos of blood and suffering. Shipped home, he tries to check himself into a hospital to have his leg amputated; he has "Bosnian Syndrome," a doctor whispers, and perhaps he feels guilty to have two legs when so many do not.

I have made the film sound grim. Actually it is fairly lighthearted, under the circumstances; like *Catch-22*, it enjoys the paradoxes that occur when you try to apply logic to war. Consider the sequence where the foreigner walks into a café, annoys a British woman with his friendliness, and then, after she stalks out, he sees she has forgotten her billfold. He runs after her, is mistaken for a madman, and is injured in traffic. Another urban legend? Not if you saw the story only last week about a black taxi passenger in Chicago whose innocent presence so terrified his immigrant driver that the cabbie careened at top speed down one-way streets looking for a cop.

Why are we so suspicious of one another? It may be a trait hard-wired by evolution: If you're not in my tribe, you may want to eat my dinner or steal my mate. The irony about those two Bosnian patients, fighting each other in the London hospital, is that they're the only two people in the building who speak the same language. So to speak.

Being John Malkovich ★ ★ ★ ★
R, 112 m., 1999

John Cusack (Craig Schwartz), Cameron Diaz (Lotte Schwartz), Catherine Keener (Maxine), John Malkovich (John Horatio Malkovich), Mary Kay Place (Floris), Orson Bean (Dr. Lester), Byrne Piven (Captain Mertin). Directed by Spike Jonze and produced by Michael Stipe, Sandy Stern, Steve Golin, and Vincent Landay. Screenplay by Charlie Kaufman.

What an endlessly inventive movie this is! Charlie Kaufman, the writer of *Being John Malkovich,* supplies a stream of dazzling inventions, twists, and wicked paradoxes. And the director, Spike Jonze, doesn't pounce on each one like fresh prey, but unveils it slyly, as if there's more where that came from. Rare is the movie where the last half-hour surprises you just as much as the first, and in ways you're not expecting. The movie has ideas enough for half a dozen films, but Jonze and his cast handle them so surely that we never feel hard-pressed; we're enchanted by one development after the next.

John Cusack stars as Craig, a street puppeteer. His puppets are dark and neurotic creatures, and the public doesn't much like them. Craig's wife, Lotte, runs a pet store, and their home is overrun with animal boarders, most of them deeply disturbed. Lotte is played by Cameron Diaz, one of the best-looking women in movies, who here looks so dowdy we hardly recognize her; Diaz has fun with her talent by taking it incognito to strange places and making it work for a living.

The puppeteer can't make ends meet in "today's wintry job climate." He answers a help-wanted ad and finds himself on floor 7½ of a building. This floor, and how it looks, and why it was built, would be inspiration enough for an entire film or a Monty Python sketch. It makes everything that happens on it funny in an additional way, on top of why it's funny in the first place.

The film is so rich, however, that the floor is merely the backdrop for more astonishments. Craig meets a coworker named Maxine (Catherine Keener) and lusts for her. She asks, "Are you married?" He says, "Yeah, but enough about me." They go out for a drink. He says, "I'm a puppeteer." She says, "Waiter? Check, please." Keener has this way of listening with her lips slightly parted, as if eager to interrupt by deconstructing what you just said and exposing you for the fool that you are.

Behind a filing cabinet on the 7½th floor, Craig finds a small doorway. He crawls through it, and is whisked through some kind of temporal-spatial portal, ending up inside the brain of the actor John Malkovich. Here he stays for exactly fifteen minutes, before falling from the sky next to the New Jersey Turnpike.

Whoa! What an experience. Maxine pressures him to turn it into a business, charging people to spend their fifteen minutes inside Malkovich. The movie handles this not as a gimmick but as the opportunity for material that is somehow funny and serious, sad and satirical, weird and touching, all at once. Malkovich himself is part of the magic. He is not playing himself here, but a version of his public image—distant, quiet, droll, as if musing about things that happened long ago and were only mildly interesting at the time. It took some courage for him to take this role, but it would have taken more courage to turn it down. It's a plum.

Why are people so eager to enter his brain? For the novelty, above all. Spend a lifetime being yourself and it would be worth money to spend fifteen minutes being almost anybody else. At one point, there's a bit of a traffic jam. Lotte finds herself inside his mind while Maxine is seducing him. Lotte enjoys this experience, and decides she wants to become a lesbian, or a man. Whatever it takes. This is hard to explain, but trust me.

The movie just keeps getting better. I don't want to steal the surprises and punch lines. Even the Charlie Sheen cameo is inspired. At one point Malkovich enters himself through his own portal, which is kind of like being pulled down into the black hole of your own personality, and that trip results in one of the most peculiar single scenes I've ever seen in the movies. Orchestrating all this, Cusack's character stays cool; to enter another man's mind is, of course, the ultimate puppeteering experience.

Every once in a long, long while a movie comes along that is like no other. A movie that creates a new world for us, and uses it to produce wonderful things. *Forrest Gump* was a movie like that, and so in their different ways were *M*A*S*H, This Is Spinal Tap, After Hours, Babe,* and *There's Something About Mary.* What do such films have in common? Nothing. That's the point. Each one stakes out a completely new place and colonizes it with limitless imagination. ☞

Beloved ★ ★ ★ ½
R, 175 m., 1998

Oprah Winfrey (Sethe), Danny Glover (Paul D), Thandie Newton (Beloved), Kimberly Elise (Denver), Beah Richards (Baby Suggs), Lisa Gay Hamilton (Younger Sethe), Albert Hall (Stamp Paid), Irma P. Hall (Ella). Directed by Jonathan Demme and produced by Edward Saxon, Demme, Gary Goetzman, Oprah Winfrey, and Kate Forte. Screenplay by Akosua Busia, Richard LaGravenese, and Adam Brooks, based on the novel by Toni Morrison.

The moment the man walks into the house, he senses that something is wrong: "Good God, girl, what kind of evil you got in there?" And she replies: "It ain't evil. Just sad." That explains the difference between *Beloved* and other stories of ghosts. The movie is not about the ghost, but about the feelings that bring it into existence.

The film tells the story of Sethe (Oprah Winfrey), who was a slave on a Kentucky plantation in the days before the Civil War. Now Sethe is free, and lives in a frame house on a few acres on the outskirts of Cincinnati—"124 Bluestone Road," the film informs us, as if it would be an ordinary house if it were not for the poltergeist that haunts it. When Paul D (Danny Glover), who knew Sethe years ago in Kentucky, enters the house, the air glows red and the walls and floor shake violently; the spirit resents this visitor.

But Paul D remains, and seems to quiet the poltergeist. Then the spirit appears again, waiting for them one day when they return to the house. It now manifests as a young woman in a black dress and (Paul makes note) shoes that don't look as if they've been walked in. Asked her name, she spells it out one painful letter at a time, in a gravelly voice that doesn't sound as if it's ever been used: B-E-L-O-V-E-D.

Thandie Newton, who plays Beloved, does an interesting thing with her performance. She inhabits her body as if she doesn't have the operating instructions. She walks unsteadily. She picks up things as if she doesn't quite command her grasp. She talks like a child. And indeed inside this young woman there is a child, the ghost of the young daughter that Sethe killed rather than have her returned to the plantation as a slave.

Like the Toni Morrison novel it is based on, *Beloved* does not tell this story in a straightforward manner. It coils through past and present, through memory and hallucination, giving us shards of events we are required to piece back together. It is not an easy film to follow. Director Jonathan Demme and his screenwriters have respected Morrison's labyrinthine structure—which does, I think, have a purpose. The complexity is not simply a stylistic device; it is built out of Sethe's memories, and the ones at the core are so painful that her mind circles them warily, afraid to touch. Sethe's life has not been a linear story, but a buildup to an event of unimaginable horror, and a long, sad unwinding afterward.

The film had a curious effect on me. I was sometimes confused about events as they happened, but all the pieces are there and the film creates an emotional whole. It's more effective when it's complete than during the unfolding experience. Seeing it more than once would be rewarding, I think, because knowing the general outline—having the road map—would deepen the effect of the story *and* increase our appreciation of the fractured structure.

The film, based on a true story, is about a woman who is raised as a slave and then tastes twenty-eight days of freedom before "on the 29th day, it was over." She has been beaten and raped by her employer, School Teacher, and boys under his care; there is a flashback in which the boys steal the milk from her breasts, and her chained husband looks on and goes mad. Faced with the prospect that her children will be returned to the degradation of slavery, she chooses to kill them—and is stopped only after she does kill the daughter now returned as Beloved.

Postwar life in Ohio contains its peaceful moments, of bringing in the laundry or shelling peas, but the house at 124 Bluestone Road is forever saddened by what Sethe did. Was it wrong? Yes, said the law: She was guilty of destroying property. The law did not see her or her child as human beings and thus did not consider the death to be murder. In a society with those values, to kill can be seen as life-affirming.

These are all feelings that churn up after the film. *Beloved,* film and novel, is not a genre ghost story but a work that uses the supernatural to touch on deep feelings. Like *The Turn of the Screw,* it has no final explanation. Spirit manifestations come from madness, and need not follow logical agendas. It is a remarkable and brave achievement for Demme and his producer and star, Winfrey, to face this difficult material head-on and not try to dumb it down into a more accessible, less evocative, form.

Winfrey plays Sethe as a woman who can sometimes brighten and relax, but whose spirit always returns to the sadness of what she did, and the hatred of those who forced her to it. It is a brave, deep performance. Supernatural events whirl around her, but she is accustomed to that: She's more afraid of her own memories. Thandie Newton, as Beloved, is like an alien (I was reminded of Jeff Bridges in *Starman*). She brings a difficult character to life by always remembering that the tortured spirit inside was still a baby when it died. Danny Glover, big and substantial, is the pool of caring that Sethe needs if she is ever to heal. And Kimberly Elise, as Sethe's grown daughter, plays the character as a battered child—battered not by her mother but by the emotional maelstrom of 124 Bluestone Road. And the legendary Beah Richards has an electric screen presence as Baby Suggs, Sethe's mother-in-law, who presides over haunting spiritualist ceremonies.

Demme's direction tells the story through mood and accumulation of incident, rather than through a traditional story line. His editor, Carol Littleton, takes on the difficult task of helping us find our way through the maze. Some audience members, I imagine, will not like it—will find it confusing or too convoluted. And it does not provide the kind of easy lift at the end that they might expect. Sethe's tragic story is the kind where the only happy ending is that it is over.

Besieged ★

R, 92 m., 1999

Thandie Newton (Shandurai), David Thewlis (Mr. Kinsky), Claudio Santamaria (Agostino). Directed by Bernardo Bertolucci and produced by Massimo Cortesi. Screenplay by Bertolucci and Clare Peploe, based on a story by James Lasdun.

Note: I've found it impossible to discuss this film without mentioning important plot points. Otherwise, as you will see, the review would be maddeningly vague.

Bernardo Bertolucci's *Besieged* is a movie about whether two people with nothing in common, who have no meaningful conversations, will have sex—even if that means dismissing everything we have learned about the woman. It is also about whether we will see her breasts. How can a director of such sophistication, in a film of such stylistic grace, tell such a shallow and evasive story?

But wait. The film also involves race, politics, and culture, and reduces them all to convenient plot points. The social values in this movie would not have been surprising in a film made forty years ago, but to see them seriously proposed today is astonishing. In a hasty moment I described the film as "racist," but it is not that so much as thoughtless and lacking in all empathy for its African characters, whose real feelings are at the mercy of the plot's sexual desires.

The film opens in Africa, with an old singer chanting a dirge under a tree. We see crippled children. A teacher in a schoolroom tries to lead his students, but troops burst in and drag him away. The young African woman Shandurai (Thandie Newton) sees this. The teacher is her husband. She wets herself. So much for the setup. The husband will never be given any weight or dimension.

Cut to Rome, where Shandurai is a medical student, employed as a maid in the house of Mr. Kinsky (David Thewlis). He will always remain "Mr. Kinsky" to her, even in a love note. He is a sardonic genius who plays beautifully upon the piano and occupies a vast apartment given him by his aunt and hung with rich tapestries and works of art. Given the size and location of the apartment, she was a very rich aunt indeed. The maid's quarters are spacious enough for a boutique, and Mr. Kinsky's rooms are reached by a spiral staircase to three or four levels.

Thandie Newton is a beautiful woman. She is photographed by Bertolucci in ways that make her beauty the subject of the shots. There's a soft-core undertone here: She does housework, the upper curves of her breasts swelling above her blouse. Little wisps of sweaty hair fall down in front of those wonderful eyes. There is a montage where she vacuums and Mr. Kinsky plays—a duet for piano and Hoover.

It is a big house for two people, very silent, and they move around it like stalkers. One day she drops a cleaning rag down the spiral staircase and it lands on Mr. Kinsky's head. He looks up. She looks down. Mr. Kinsky decides he loves her. There is a struggle. "Marry me! I'll do anything to make you love me!" She throws him a curve: "You get my husband out of jail!"

He didn't know she was married. Other things divide them, including their different tastes in music. He performs the classics, but one day plays rhythmic African rhythms for her. She smiles gratefully, in a reaction shot of such startling falseness that the editor should never have permitted it. Later Shandurai has a speech where she says how brave, how courageous, her husband is. Eventually we gather that Mr. Kinsky is selling his possessions to finance the legal defense of the husband. Even the piano goes.

All of this time the film has been performing a subtle striptease involving Shandurai, who has been seen in various stages of partial or suggested nudity. Now, at the end, we see her breasts as she lies alone in bed. I mention this because it is so transparently a payoff; Godard said the history of cinema is the history of boys photographing girls, and Bertolucci's recent films (like *Stealing Beauty*) underline that insight.

I am human. I am pleased to see Thandie Newton nude. In a film of no pretension, nudity would not even require any justification; beauty is beauty, as Keats did not quite say. But in *Besieged* we have troublesome buried issues. This woman is married to a brave freedom fighter. She says she loves and admires him. Now, because Mr. Kinsky has sold his piano to free her husband, she gets drunk and writes several drafts of a note before settling on one ("Mr. Kinsky, I love you"). She caresses herself and then steals upstairs and slips into his bed. Do they have sex? We don't know. In the morning, her freed husband stands outside the door of Mr. Kinsky's flat, ringing the bell again and again—ignored.

If a moral scale is at work here, who has done the better thing: A man who went to prison to protest an evil government, or a man who freed him by selling his piano? How can a woman betray the husband she loves and admires, and choose a man with whom she has had no meaningful communication?

To be fair, some feel the ending is open. I felt the husband's ring has gone unanswered. Some believe the ending leaves him in uncertain limbo. If this story had been by a writer with greater irony or insight, I can imagine a more shattering ending, in which Mr. Kinsky makes all of his sacrifices, and Shandurai leaves exactly the same note on his pillow—but is not there in the morning.

The film's need to have Shandurai choose Mr. Kinsky over her husband, which is what I think she does, is rotten at its heart. It turns the African man into a plot pawn, it robs him of his weight in the mind of his wife, and then leaves him standing in the street. *Besieged* is about an attractive young black woman choosing a white oddball over the brave husband she says she loves. What can her motive possibly be? I suggest the character is motivated primarily by the fact that the filmmakers are white.

Best Laid Plans ★
R, 90 m., 1999

Alessandro Nivola (Nick), Reese Witherspoon (Lissa), Josh Brolin (Bryce), Rocky Carroll (Bad Ass Dude), Michael G. Hagerty (Charlie), Terrence Howard (Jimmy), Jamie Marsh (Barry), Sean Nepita (Freddie). Directed by Mike Barker and produced by Alan Greenspan, Betsy Beers, Chris Moore, and Sean Bailey. Screenplay by Ted Griffin.

X-rays can pass through the human body in much the same way that certain movies can pass through my mind. Hold up a photographic plate on the other side, and all you'd see would be some kidneys and a paper clip. I went to see *The Usual Suspects* twice and could not persuade my mind to engage with it; *Best Laid Plans* is the same kind of experience.

I am prepared to concede that I missed the boat on *The Usual Suspects*. So many people like it so much that they must have their reasons. I will see it yet again one of these days. I vividly remember Kevin Spacey's performance, which I enjoyed for its energy and texture, but I remember him sort of floating through the movie without hitting anything. I do not feel the need to see *Best Laid Plans* again. It's not that I don't remember it. It's that I don't care.

There is a moment in a certain kind of movie when I realize I am being toyed with. That everything is Not As It Seems. That we're trapped in a labyrinth of betrayals, double-reverses, surprises, and astonishing revelations, and that whatever is being established in this scene will be destroyed in the next. It's not just that I don't care—it's that the movie doesn't either. Its characters are pawns in a chess game, and all the action is designed to reveal hidden traps and buried strategies.

There are some double-reverse movies that work. *Body Heat* comes to mind. But *Body Heat* was not an exercise. It was a conspiracy with a purpose, a motivation, and an outcome. At every moment I *cared* about the characters— I believed in them, and it made a difference what they'd do next. I was being toyed with, but not *merely* being toyed with.

Best Laid Plans is a movie with several surprises too many. It opens in a bar with two old friends, Nick and Bryce (Allesandro Nivola and Josh Brolin), having a drink after several years. A girl named Lissa (Reese Witherspoon) walks in. Flash cut to later that evening. It's Nick's place. There's a panic call from Bryce. He picked up Lissa, brought her home, thought things were proceeding on schedule, and then was accused of rape and assault. Bad news. There's worse. Currently he has Lissa chained to a pool table of the place where he's housesitting, so now it's also kidnapping, endangerment, who knows? What's next? Murder?

Nick hurries over to help bail out his old friend, and at this point I must not reveal any more of the plot because reality begins to shift beneath our feet and there are fundamental surprises, and then surprises about them. Give us a break, I'm thinking. Either cut through the funny stuff, or make it worth watching. But *Best Laid Plans*, directed by Mike Barker from a screenplay by Ted Griffin (who wrote *Ravenous*, much better), is so concerned with being a film that it forgets to be a movie.

This is cutting edge, film school, Sundance, indie flash. Wow, this guy can manhandle a camera. And we can picture the screenplay meetings—three-by-five cards manipulated like jigsaw pieces to make sure all the elements join up again at the end. By the conclusion of this movie, the characters have been put through so many changes they need name tags and cue cards just to know who they still are and what they still need to say.

Here's my question: Would the same story, told in a linear form, without the gimmicks and with more attention to the personalities and behavior of the characters, have been more entertaining than this funhouse mirror version? I say it's worth a try.

The Beyond ½★

NO MPAA RATING, 88 m., 1998

Catriona MacColl (Liza Merrill), David Warbeck (Dr. John McCabe), Sarah Keller (Emily), Antoine Saint John (Schweik), Veronica Lazar (Martha), Al Cliver (Dr. Harris), Anthony Flees (Larry [painter]), Giovanni de Nava (Joe the Plumber). Directed by Lucio Fulci and produced by Fabrizio De Angelis. Screenplay by Dardano Sacchetti.

The Beyond not only used to have another title, but its director used to have another name. First released in 1981 as *Seven Doors of Death*, directed by Louis Fuller, it now returns in an "uncut original version" as *The Beyond*, directed by Lucio Fulci.

Fulci, who died in 1996, was sort of an Italian Hershell Gordon Lewis. Neither name may mean much to you, but both are pronounced reverently wherever fans of zero-budget schlock horror films gather. Lewis was the Chicago-based director of such titles as *Two Thousand*

Maniacs, She-Devils on Wheels, and *The Gore-Gore Girls.* Fulci made *Zombie* and *Don't Torture the Duckling.* Maybe that was a temporary title too.

The Beyond opens in "Louisiana 1927," and has certain shots obviously filmed in New Orleans, but other locations are possibly Italian, as was (probably) the sign painter who created the big DO NOT ENTRY sign for a hospital scene. It's the kind of movie that alternates stupefyingly lame dialogue with special-effects scenes in which quicklime dissolves corpses and tarantulas eat lips and eyeballs.

The plot involves . . . excuse me for a moment while I laugh uncontrollably at having written the words "the plot involves." I'm back. The plot involves a mysterious painter in an upstairs room of a gloomy, Gothic Louisiana hotel. One night carloads and boatloads of torch-bearing vigilantes converge on the hotel and kill the painter while shouting, "You ungodly warlock!" Then they pour lots of quicklime on him, and we see a badly made model of his body dissolving.

Time passes. A woman named Liza (played by Catriona MacColl, who was named "Catherine" when the director was named "Louis") inherits the hotel, which needs a lot of work. Little does she suspect it is built over one of the Seven Doors of Evil that lead to hell. She hires a painter, who falls from a high scaffold and shouts, "The eyes! The eyes!" Liza's friend screams, "This man needs to get to a hospital!" Then there are ominous questions, like "How can you fall from a four-foot-wide scaffold?" Of course, one might reply, one can fall from anywhere, but why did he *have* a four-foot-wide scaffold?

Next Liza calls up Joe the Plumber (Giovanni de Nava), who plunges into the flooded basement, wades into the gloom, pounds away at a wall, and is grabbed by a horrible thing in the wall, which I believe is the quicklimed painter, although after fifty years it is hard to make a firm ID.

Let's see. Then there is a blind woman in the middle of a highway with a seeing-eye dog, which later attacks her (I believe this is the same woman who was in the hotel in 1927), and a scene in a morgue, where the wife of one of the victims (the house painter, I think, or maybe Joe) sobbingly dresses the corpse (in evening dress) before being attacked by acid from a self-spilling jar on a shelf.

But my favorite scene involves the quicklimed, decomposed corpse, which is now seen in a hospital next to an oscilloscope that flatlines, indicating death. Yes, the rotting cadaver is indeed dead—but why attach it, at this late date, to an oscilloscope? Could it be because we'll get a shot in which the scope screen suddenly indicates signs of life? I cannot lie to you. I live for moments like that.

Fulci was known for his gory special effects (the Boston critic Gerald Peary, who has seen several of his films, cites one in which a woman vomits up her intestines), and *The Beyond* does not disappoint. I have already mentioned the scene where the tarantulas eat eyeballs and lips. As the tarantulas tear away each morsel, we can clearly see the strands of latex and glue holding it to the model of a corpse's head. Strictly speaking, it is a scene of tarantulas eating makeup.

In a film filled with bad dialogue, it is hard to choose the most quotable line, but I think it may occur in Liza's conversations with Martin, the architect hired to renovate the hotel. "You have carte blanche," she tells him, "but not a blank check!"

Beyond Silence ★ ★ ★ ½
PG-13, 100 m., 1998

Sylvie Testud (Lara), Tatjana Trieb (Lara as a child), Howie Seago (Martin), Emmanuelle Laborit (Kai), Sibylle Canonica (Clarissa), Matthias Habich (Gregor), Alexandra Bolz (Marie), Hansa Czypionka (Tom). Directed by Caroline Link and produced by Thomas Wobke, Jacob Claussen, and Luggi Waldleitner. Screenplay by Link and Beth Serlin.

Beyond Silence is one of those films that helps us escape our box of time and space and understand what it might be like to live in someone else's. It tells the story of Lara, the child of deaf parents, who loves them and has been well raised by them, but must, as all children must sooner or later, leave her nest and fly on her own.

The movie isn't centered on a few manufactured plot points, but gives us a sense of the whole span of the family's life. It's not a sentimental docudrama but a hard and yet loving look at the way these people deal with their issues and incriminations. No one is the hero and no one is the villain; they are all doing the best they can, given the way life has made them.

Lara, played as a child by Tatjana Trieb and as a young woman by Sylvie Testud, moves effortlessly between the worlds of sound and sign. She sits beside the TV set, signing for her parents, and translates for them during a heated meeting with a banker. (At the end of the conference, when the banker says, "Thanks, Lara," she pointedly tells him, "My parents are your customers, not me.") She is not above mischief. At a parent-teacher conference, she shamelessly represses the teacher's critical observations about her schoolwork.

The crucial event in the film is a simple one: Lara's aunt, her father's sister, gives her a clarinet. This is a gift fraught with meaning. In a flashback, we see the father as a young deaf boy, watching as relatives crowd around to applaud his sister's first clarinet recital. Frustrated, he gives voice to a loud, painful noise, and is banished to a bedroom. It is the kind of exclusionary wound that shapes a lifetime, and although the father and sister as children communicated effortlessly, as adults they are cool and distant.

There is a ten-year gap (the actresses are so well matched we hardly notice it), and Lara, now nearly twenty, is encouraged by her aunt to attend music school. Her father is opposed, and there is a bitter argument. Lara, who is a gifted player, sits in with her aunt's group, takes classes, and one day sees a man signing to a boy in a park. She follows them, and is surprised to find that he is not deaf, but the child of a deaf father, and a teacher in a school for the deaf. They fall in love.

All of these events are seen with a particular clarity, as stages in Lara's discovery of herself. The opening shot of the movie places the camera underwater in a frozen pond, as skaters circle on the surface and muffled voices come from far away. The whole movie is a process of breaking through the ice into the air of communication.

Beyond Silence was one of the 1998 Academy Award nominees for Best Foreign Film, but I have not mentioned until now that this is a German film, because I know some readers have an irrational prejudice against sub-

titles. But, really, what language is this film in? The subtitles handle not only the spoken dialogue but also describe the music and the sound effects, like thunder; they are designed to be useful for deaf viewers. If the movie were in English, it would still be subtitled. So little does the movie depend on which language is spoken that Howie Seago, the actor playing the father, is an American (both he and Emmanuelle Laborit, as his wife, are hearing impaired).

The movie is alert to nuances of the politics of deafness. Characters talk about the historical prejudice against sign language in Germany, and Lara's grandmother frets that she was advised not to sign, in order to "force" her son to learn to talk: "If I hadn't listened to that pighead, my hands might be able to fly too."

But *Beyond Silence* is wise and complex about the limitless subject of deafness. It is about how hurts are formed in families and remain for decades. About how parents favor a hearing child over a deaf one. About how Lara and her parents have formed a symbiosis that must be interrupted if she is to have a life of her own. So much hinges on simple things, as when Lara wants her mother to ride a bicycle "like other mothers."

One night on TV, Tom Brokaw asked Harrison Ford if movies have grown mediocre because of their dependence on mindless action and special effects, and I raised up my hands in frustration. If such a question really mattered to Brokaw, he would do a segment about a film like *Beyond Silence*, instead of publicizing the latest mindless 'plex product. Of course, you have to be the kind of person to whom *Beyond Silence* just plain *sounds* more interesting than, say, *Godzilla*. Such people are rare, and to be valued.

Beyond the Mat ★ ★ ★
R, 92 m., 2000

With Mick "Mankind" Foley, Terry Funk, "Jake the Snake" Roberts, "Stone Cold" Steve Austin, Coco BWare, The Rock, Chyna, Vince McMahon, and others. A documentary directed by Barry Blaustein and produced by Brian Grazer, Ron Howard, Michael Rosenberg, Barry Bloom, and Blaustein. Screenplay by Blaustein.

Beyond the Mat is the wrestling documentary that Vince McMahon had barred from advertising on his World Wrestling Federation programs. Why? Because it shows an old pro maintaining on crack cocaine, and children weeping at ringside while their daddy is beaten bloody? Not at all. Because he doesn't have a cut of the profits.

Even if you've never watched a professional wrestling match on television, you've probably heard the words "Mr. McMahon" just while surfing past the channel. Here he explains why the WWF is like the Muppets: "They're both family owned, and they both have real human beings playing characters."

Uh-huh. We see him interviewing Darren Drozdov, a former pro football player who wants to wrestle and has a unique skill: He can vomit "on command." McMahon gives him a ring name, "Puke," and envisions a scenario: "After you've regurgitated on your opponent or the referee . . ." Drozdov is sent to the minor leagues for seasoning, and calls his mother with the good news.

Other subjects of the documentary have been around a long time. Terry Funk is over fifty, has been wrestling forever, and hears the doctor forecast a lifetime of pain from his wrecked knees. Then he climbs into the ring again. He can hardly walk, but during the match he seems to come to life, giving audiences the show they expect.

It is a show, yes. *Beyond the Mat* makes no secret of the fact that every match is scripted, and that the outcomes are not in doubt. But we knew that. What I didn't fully realize, until I saw this film, is how real the show is. Just because you script a guy being thrown out of the ring doesn't mean it's painless when he bounces off a table and onto the floor. You can't bleed unless you're cut. And sometimes things go wrong; a wire cage mesh breaks and a wrestler falls maybe twenty feet to the mat. That hurts. Last year a wrestler named Owen Hart fell seventy feet and was killed when his harness failed while he was being lowered into a ring.

Mick "Mankind" Foley comes across as one of the nicest guys in the film, a family man with small children who's a gentle teddy bear when he's not in the ring. He explains to his kids how it's all carefully planned, how his opponent doesn't really hate him, and then the two preschoolers sit at ringside as their daddy is handcuffed and beaten with a chair. He starts to bleed. They start to cry. "Close your eyes," their mother says, before finally taking them out of the room. They watch in the dressing room as a medic applies first aid to Foley's cuts and checks for a concussion.

Later, the filmmakers show Foley their footage of his kids crying, and he is sobered. He vows never to let them watch a fight again. We sense the care in his voice, but we also wonder: What were they doing ringside in the first place? What do kids know about scripts?

Beyond the Mat was written and directed by Barry Blaustein, a onetime *Saturday Night Live* writer and successful film producer, mostly of Eddie Murphy projects *(Coming to America, Boomerang, The Nutty Professor)*. He confesses to being a TV wrestling fan all his life. There's real pain when he meets one of his old heroes, "Jake the Snake" Roberts, once a superstar, now reduced to barnstorming the back roads for small change.

Roberts opens up in an extraordinary way to the camera. He talks about an unhappy childhood, a mother who was thirteen when she married. He has shaky relationships with his own family, and when Blaustein arranges a meeting with his estranged daughter at the Ramada, she's so nervous she wants to bring along two friends. A fight promoter says Jake demands crack before doing a show, and Jake agrees he's had drug problems.

What we wonder is, how can you be a pro wrestler and not use drugs? A working wrestler performs twenty-six to twenty-seven days in a month—twice on weekends. It's not all on TV. There are bus and plane trips to far-flung arenas, where even on a good day (no serious injuries) their bodies are slammed around in a way that might alarm a pro football player. Have you ever heard of a pro wrestler being suspended for drug use? Do they even check for drugs? Only asking.

Beyond the Mat isn't a slick documentary; some of it feels like Blaustein's home movie about being a wrestling fan. But it has a hypnotic quality. Those who oppose boxing because of its violence acknowledge that it is at least a supervised sport, with rules and safeguards. Wrestling is not a sport but a spectacle, in which weary and wounded men, some obviously not in the best of shape, injure each other for money.

At one point we see two wrestlers set each other on fire and then throw each other on barbed wire. There are ways to do this in which you do not get burned severely or lacerated—much. But it's not simple trickery, and what goes on in the ring clearly really does hurt, sometimes a lot. After a bloody match, two wrestlers slap each other on the back, and explain, "The more you hurt each other, the more money you make, so the more you like each other." Not capitalism's finest hour.

Bicentennial Man ★ ★
PG, 132 m., 1999

Robin Williams (Andrew), Embeth Davidtz (Little Miss/Portia), Sam Neill (Sir), Oliver Platt (Rupert Burns), Kiersten Warren (Galatea Robotic/Human), Wendy Crewson (Ma'am), Hallie Kate Eisenberg (Little Miss, seven years old), Lindze Letherman (Little Miss, nine years old). Directed by Chris Columbus and produced by Wolfgang Petersen, Gail Katz, Neal Miller, Laurence Mark, Chris Columbus, Mark Radcliffe, and Michael Barnathan. Screenplay by Nicholas Kazan, based on the short story by Isaac Asimov and the novel *The Positronic Man* by Asimov and Robert Silverberg.

Bicentennial Man begins with promise, proceeds in fits and starts, and finally sinks into a cornball drone of greeting-card sentiment. Robin Williams spends the first half of the film encased in a metallic robot suit, and when he emerges, the script turns robotic instead. What a letdown.

Williams plays a robobutler named Andrew, who arrives in a packing crate one day outside the home of a family that is destined to share him for four generations, each and every moment of which seems mercilessly chronicled. His first owner is Sir (Sam Neill), who introduces Andrew to a dubious wife (Wendy Crewson) and a daughter named Little Miss, who grows up to be played by Embeth Davidtz (she also plays her own granddaughter).

At first the robot is treated unkindly. "It is a household appliance, yet you treat it like it is a man," an associate frets to Sir. But he comes around. It's clear from the first that Andrew is some kind of variant, smarter and more "human" than your average robot, although just as literal. In the early scenes, which have a life of their own, Andrew jumps out a window when told to, and has a lot of trouble mastering the principle of the "knock knock" joke. He also demonstrates various consequences of the Three Laws of Robotics, which were obviously devised by Isaac Asimov so that men of the future will be able to shout "gotcha!" at their robots.

From the first moment we see Andrew, we're asking ourselves, is that really Robin Williams inside the polished aluminum shell? *USA Today* claims it is, although at times we may be looking at a model or a computer-generated graphic. The robot's body language is persuasive; it has that same subtle courtliness that Williams himself often uses. Andrew also has good timing, which is crucial, since many of the movie's payoffs depend on the robot expressing its feelings through body language. ("One would like to have more expression," Andrew complains at one point. "One has thoughts and feelings that presently do not show.")

Peter Weller, who starred in *RoboCop*, told me it was the most excruciating physical ordeal of his lifetime, spending weeks inside a heavy costume under movie lights that raised the temperature over 100 degrees. Williams must have undergone a similar ordeal. His performance depends on the comic principle that it's funny when a man is subjected to the rules of a machine; everything we see here has its mirror image in the assembly-line sequence at the beginning of Chaplin's *Modern Times*. Unfortunately for this movie, it's funnier when a man becomes a machine than when a machine becomes a man, because man's free will is being subverted, while the machine has none.

The plot is based on a story by Asimov and a novel by Asimov and Robert Silverberg. It deals with the poignancy of an android that has humanlike feelings, and must live indefinitely, whereas all the humans must die. There are consolations. Andrew is allowed to bank his own income, and compound interest can work wonders for an immortal being; eventually he is rich, and goes on an odyssey to find a soul mate.

His search leads to the shabby laboratory of Rupert Burns (Oliver Platt), who tinkers with used robots, and the two of them fashion a new body for Andrew that looks much like Robin Williams. There is also the problem of finding Andrew a soul mate; will it be an advanced robot, or will his own progress make it plausible for him to consider a relationship with a human? Andrew can't reproduce, of course, but logic suggests he might make a versatile and tireless lover.

The movie's buried themes have to do with self-determination and the rights of the individual. Like many of Asimov's robot stories, it deals with the enigma of having the intelligence of a man, without the rights or the feelings. *Bicentennial Man* could have been an intelligent, challenging science-fiction movie, but it's too timid, too eager to please. It wants us to like Andrew, but it is difficult at a human deathbed to identify with the aluminum mourner.

Strange, how definitely the film goes wrong. At the sixty-minute mark, I was really enjoying it. Then it slowly abandons its most promising themes and paradoxes and turns into a series of slow, soppy scenes involving love and death. And since the beloved woman is essentially always the same person (played by Davidtz), the movie begins to seem very long and very slow, and by the end, when Andrew hopefully says, "See you soon," we hope he is destined for Home Appliance Heaven.

Big Daddy ★ ½
PG-13, 95 m., 1999

Adam Sandler (Sonny Koufax), Joey Lauren Adams (Layla), Jon Stewart (Kevin Gerrity), Rob Schneider (Delivery Guy), Cole and Dylan Sprouse (Julian), Leslie Mann (Corinne), Allen Covert (Phil), Kristy Swanson (Vanessa), Josh Mostel (Arthur), Steve Buscemi (Homeless Guy). Directed by Dennis Dugan and produced by Sid Ganis and Jack Giarraputo. Screenplay by Steve Franks, Tim Herlihy, and Adam Sandler, based on a story by Franks.

Big Daddy is a film about a seriously disturbed slacker who adopts a five-year-old and tutors him in cynicism, cruel practical jokes, and antisocial behavior. It's not every film where an adult role model throws himself in front of a moving car just to cheer the kid up. "Man, this Yoo Hoo is good!" the adult tells the tyke. "You know what else is good? Smoking dope!"

On the way down in the elevator after the *Big Daddy* screening, a fellow critic speculated that the line about weed was intended not as a suggestion, but as a feeler: The hero was subtly trying to find out if the kid and his friends were into drugs. I submit that so few five-year-olds are into drugs that it's not a problem, and that some older kids in the audience will not interpret the line as a subtle feeler.

Big Daddy stars Adam Sandler as Sonny Koufax, a layabout who won $200,000 in a lawsuit after a cab ran over his foot, and now hangs around the Manhattan loft that he shares with his roommate, a lawyer played by Jon Stewart—who must be doing well, since the space they occupy would sell or rent for serious money. Sonny's girlfriend, Vanessa (Kristy Swanson), tells him to get a real job, but he says he has one: He's a toll-booth attendant, I guess, although the movie gives him nothing but days off.

Just after the roommate heads out of town, little Julian (played by twins Cole and Dylan Sprouse) is dropped at the door. He is allegedly the roommate's love child. Sonny tries to turn the kid over to Social Services, but they're closed for Columbus Day, and so he ends up taking Julian to Central Park for his favorite pastime, which is throwing tree branches in the paths of speeding in-line skaters. One middle-aged blader hits a branch, takes a nasty fall, and ends up in the lagoon. What fun.

The predictable story arc has Sonny and Julian bonding. This is not as easy as it sounds, since any Adam Sandler character is self-obsessed to such a degree that his conversations sound like interior monologues. It is supposed to be funny that Sonny has a pathological hostility against society; when McDonald's won't serve them breakfast, he throws another customer's fries on the floor, and when a restaurant won't let the kid use the rest room, he and the kid pee on the restaurant's side door.

The movie is filled to the limit with all the raunchy words allowed by the PG-13 rating, and you may be surprised how many and varied they are. There's a crisis when a social worker (Josh Mostel) turns up, and Sonny impersonates his roommate and claims to be the kid's dad. We're supposed to think it would be nice if Sonny could win custody of little Julian. I think it would be a tragedy. If the kid turns out like Sonny, he's probably looking at prison time or heavy-duty community service. Sonny is the first couch potato I've seen with road rage.

The film is chock-full of supporting characters. The most entertaining is Layla (Joey Lauren Adams), whose sister is engaged to Sonny's roommate. (The sister is an ex-Hooters girl, leading to more talk about hooters than a non-drug-using five-year-old is likely to require.) Adams, who was so good in *Chasing Amy*, is good here, too, bringing a certain sanity to the plot, although I don't know what a smart girl like Layla would see in this closed-off, angry creep. Even when Sonny tries to be nice, you can see the passive aggression peeking around his smile.

The final courtroom scene is one of those movie fantasies where the judge bangs her gavel while everyone in the movie grandstands—yes, even the homeless person (Steve Buscemi) who has tagged along for the ride, an old drunk from Sonny's local bar, and the gay lawyers Sonny knows from law school. (Like many gay characters in comedies, they kiss and hug at every opportunity; why don't they just wear signboards?)

There have been many, many movies using the story that *Big Daddy* recycles. Chaplin's *The Kid* used Jackie Coogan as the urchin; *Little Miss Marker* (versions by Shirley Temple and Walter Matthau) was about an innocent tyke and a bookie; James Belushi's *Curly Sue* has some of the same elements. What they had in common were adults who might have made good parents. *Big Daddy* should be reported to the child welfare office.

The Big Hit ★
R, 93 m., 1998

Mark Wahlberg (Melvin Smiley), Lou Diamond Phillips (Cisco), Christina Applegate (Pam Shulman), Avery Brooks (Paris), Bokeem Woodbine (Crunch), Antonio Sabato Jr. (Vince), China Chow (Keiko), Lela Rochon (Mistress), Lainie Kazan (Jeanne Shulman), Elliott Gould (Morton Shulman). Directed by Che-Kirk Wong and produced by Warren Zide and Wesley Snipes. Screenplay by Ben Ramsey.

Hollywood used to import movie stars from overseas. Then directors. Then they remade foreign films. Now the studios import entire genres. It's cheaper buying wholesale. *The Big Hit* is a Hong Kong action comedy, directed by Che-Kirk Wong (*Crime Story*), starring an American cast, and written by Ben Ramsey, an American who has apparently done as much time in the video stores as Quentin Tarantino.

The movie has the Hong Kong spirit right down to the deadpan dialogue. Sample:

Hit Man: "If you stay with me you have to understand I'm a contract killer. I murder people for a living. Mostly bad people, but ..."

Girl He Has Kidnapped: "I'm cool with that."

The characters in these movies exist in a twilight zone where thousands of rounds of ammunition are fired, but no one ever gets shot unless the plot requires him to. The bullets have read the screenplay.

As the film opens, we meet four buddies working out in a health club. They're played by Mark Wahlberg (of *Boogie Nights*), Lou Diamond Phillips, Bokeem Woodbine, and Antonio Sabato Jr. The guys are hunks with big muscles, which we can study during a locker-room scene where they stand around bare-bottomed while discussing Woodbine's recent discovery of masturbation, which he recommends as superior to intercourse, perhaps because it requires only one consenting adult.

Then they dress for work. They're all garbed as utilities workers, with hard hats, tool boxes, and wide leather belts holding wrenches and flashlights. As they saunter down the street to Graeme Revell's pumping sound track, they look like a downsized road company version of the Village People.

The plot: They attack the heavily defended high-rise stronghold of a rich pimp who has just purchased three new girls for $50,000 a head. They break in with guns blazing, and there's an extended action sequence ending with one of the heroes diving out of an upper floor on a bungee cord, just ahead of a shattering explosion. And so on.

They kidnap Keiko (China Chow), the daughter of a rich Japanese executive. Complications ensue, and she ends up in the hands, and later the car trunk, of the leader of the hit men, named Melvin Smiley (Wahlberg). This is most likely the first movie in which the hero hit man is named Melvin Smiley. But he does smile a lot, because his weakness is, "I can't stand the idea of people who don't like me." You would think a hit man would have a lot of people walking around not liking him, but not if he is a good enough shot.

Keiko falls in love with Melvin with astonishing rapidity. Sure, she tries to escape, but by the end she realizes her future lies with him. Will this complicate Melvin's life? Not any more than it already is.

He has a black mistress (Lela Rochon), who looks at a dismembered body in their bathtub and says, "He's kinda cute." And he has a Jewish fiancée (Christina Applegate), who is Jewish for the sole purpose of having two Jewish parents (Lainie Kazan and Elliott Gould) so they can appear in the middle of the movie like refugees from a Woody Allen picture and provide crudely stereotyped caricatures. Gould makes crass remarks about his wife's plastic surgery, gets drunk, and throws up on Lou Diamond Phillips, in a scene where both actors appear to be using the powers of visualization to imagine themselves in another movie.

Many more action scenes. Cars explode. Cars are shot at. Cars land in trees. They fall out of trees. Remember those old serials where someone got killed at the end of an installment, but at the beginning of the next installment you see him leap quickly to safety? That trick is played three times in this movie. Whenever anyone gets blowed up real good, you wait serenely for the instant replay.

I guess you could laugh at this. You would have to be seriously alienated from normal human values and be nursing a deep-seated anger against movies that make you think even a little, but you could laugh.

The Big Kahuna ★ ★ ★ ½
R, 90 m., 2000

Kevin Spacey (Larry), Danny DeVito (Phil), Peter Facinelli (Bob). Directed by John Swanbeck and produced by Elie Samaha, Kevin Spacey, and Andrew Stevens. Screenplay by Roger Rueff.

There are two religions in America, one spiritual, one secular. The first worships in churches, the second at business conventions. Clergy of both religions wear dark suits and ties (or roman collars). They exchange a lot of business cards. *The Big Kahuna* is about an uneasy confrontation between these two systems of faith.

True believers are similar whatever their religion. Their theology teaches: We know the right way. We are saved. We support one another and strive to convert the heathen. Those who come with us will know the kingdom of heaven—or will be using the best industrial lubricant. Adherents of both religions often meet in hotels, attend "mixers," and participate in "workshops" at which the buried message is: The truth is in this room.

The Big Kahuna is about a tool and die industry convention in a Wichita hotel. In a "hospitality suite" on an upper floor, three men wait uneasily. Their company sells industrial lubricants. Their entire convention depends on landing the account of a man named Dick Fuller, referred to as the Big Kahuna. The men are Larry (Kevin Spacey), Phil (Danny DeVito), and Bob (Peter Facinelli). Larry and Phil have been comrades for a long time—road warriors who do battle at conventions. Bob is a young man, new to the firm, at his first convention. Larry is edgy, sardonic, competitive. Phil is more easygoing. Phil is the backslapper; Larry is the closer. "I feel like I've been shaking somebody's hand one way or another all of my life," Phil says.

The film mostly takes place within that one hotel room. Yes, it is based on a play. I like that. I like the fact that it is mostly dialogue among three people on one set. That is the way to tell this story. Why does every filmed play trigger movie critics into a ritual discussion of whether (or how, or if) the play has been "opened up"? Who cares? What difference would it make if the movie set some scenes in the coffee shop and others in the park across the street? The story is about these three guys and what they say to one another. Keeping it in one room underlines their isolation: They are in the inner sanctum of their religion.

The movie, directed by John Swanbeck and written by Roger Rueff, is sharp-edged, perfectly timed, funny, and thoughtful. Spacey and DeVito are two of the smartest actors in the movies, filled with the joy of performance, and they exchange their dialogue with the precision of racquetball players, every volley redefining the game. They talk about business strategy, sales goals, the cutthroat world of industrial lubricants, the mystical power of the Big Kahuna to transform their lives. There is not one word about the technical side of lubricants; they couldn't care less. Lubricants are the Maguffin. They could be selling auto parts, ladies' ready-to-wear, or kitchen gizmos.

Bob, the kid, is softer and more unformed. He hasn't been broken in (or down) by life on the road. It appears that the Big Kahuna did not visit their suite. But in the small hours of the morning, during a postmortem, Larry and Phil discover that the great man was indeed in the room, wearing someone else's name tag—and that Bob talked to him for hours. What did they talk about? The Big Kahuna was depressed by the death of his dog.

That leads to a larger discussion, about a topic close to Bob's heart—his personal savior, Jesus Christ. Bob believes in Jesus like Larry and Phil believe in sales. "We talked about Christ," he says, quietly and simply, filled with enormous self-satisfaction. "About *Christ?*" screams Larry. "Did you mention what line of industrial lubricant Jesus uses?"

Those who are not true believers may be left cold by this film. For those who link their lives to a cause, it may have a real resonance. The tricky thing may be realizing that the two systems are interchangeable. If Larry and Phil believed in Jesus, and Bob wanted to land the big contract, the dialogue could stay about the same, because the story is about their personalities, not their products.

Now here's a funny thing. This movie premiered last January at Sundance. A lot has been written about it since then. You can read about the actors, the dialogue, the convention, the Kahuna, the industrial lubricants. But you can search the reviews in vain for any mention of Jesus Christ. Most of the reviewers seem to have forgotten that Bob is born-again. Maybe it never registered. From their secular viewpoint, what they remember is that Bob had the Kahuna in the palm of his hand and blew the deal, but they don't remember why.

That underlines how, once you sign onto a belief system, you see everything through that prism, and anything outside of it becomes invisible. *The Big Kahuna* is remarkable in the way it shows the two big systems in conflict. Of course, there is such a species as the Christian businessman, who has his roots in a strain of the Protestant ethic. He believes that prospering and being saved go hand in hand. Maybe Bob was onto something. Maybe he had the right approach to Dick Fuller. Maybe that's why Fuller is the Big Kahuna.

The Big Lebowski ★ ★ ★
R, 117 m., 1998

Jeff Bridges (The Dude), John Goodman (Walter Sobchak), Julianne Moore (Maude Lebowski), Steve Buscemi (Donny), David Huddleston (The Big Lebowski), Philip Seymour Hoffman (Brandt), Tara Reid (Bunny Lebowski), Ben Gazzara (Jackie Treehorn), John Turturro (Jesus), Sam Elliott (Narrator). Directed by Joel Coen and produced by Ethan Coen. Screenplay by Joel Coen and Ethan Coen.

The Coen brothers' *The Big Lebowski* is a genial, shambling comedy about a human train wreck, and should come with a warning like the one Mark Twain attached to *Huckleberry Finn:* "Persons attempting to find a plot in it will be shot." It's about a man named Jeff Lebowski, who calls himself The Dude, and is described by the narrator as "the laziest man in Los Angeles County." He lives only to go bowling, but is mistaken for a millionaire named The Big Lebowski, with dire consequences.

This is the first movie by Joel and Ethan Coen since *Fargo*. Few movies could equal that one, and this one doesn't—but it's weirdly engaging, like its hero. The Dude is played by Jeff Bridges with a goatee, a pot belly, a ponytail, and a pair of Bermuda shorts so large they may have been borrowed from his best friend and bowling teammate, Walter Sobchak (John Goodman). Their other teammate is Donny (Steve Buscemi), who may not be very bright, but it's hard to tell for sure since he is never allowed to complete a sentence.

Everybody knows somebody like The Dude—

and so, rumor has it, do the Coen brothers. They based the character on a movie producer and distributor named Jeff Dowd, a familiar figure at film festivals, who is tall, large, shaggy, and aboil with enthusiasm. Dowd is much more successful than Lebowski (he has played an important role in the Coens' careers as indie filmmakers), but no less a creature of the moment. Both dudes depend on improvisation and inspiration much more than organization.

In spirit, *The Big Lebowski* resembles the Coens' *Raising Arizona*, with its large cast of peculiar characters and its strangely wonderful dialogue. Here, in a film set at the time of the Gulf War, are characters whose speech was shaped by earlier times: Vietnam (Walter), the flower power era (The Dude), and *Twilight Zone* (Donny). Their very notion of reality may be shaped by the limited ways they have to describe it. One of the pleasures of *Fargo* was the way the Coens listened carefully to the way their characters spoke. Here, too, note that when the In & Out Burger shop is suggested for a rendezvous, The Dude supplies its address: That's the sort of precise information he would possess.

As the film opens, The Dude is visited by two enforcers for a porn king (Ben Gazzara) who is owed a lot of money by the Big Lebowski's wife. The goons, of course, have the wrong Lebowski, but before they figure that out one has already urinated on his rug, causing deep enmity: "That rug really tied the room together," The Dude mourns. Walter, the Vietnam vet, leads the charge for revenge. Borrowing lines directly from President Bush on TV, he vows that "this aggression will not stand," and urges The Dude to "draw a line in the sand."

The Dude visits the other Lebowski (David Huddleston), leaves with one of *his* rugs, and soon finds himself enlisted in the millionaire's schemes. The rich Lebowski, in a wheelchair and gazing into a fireplace like Major Amberson in *The Magnificent Ambersons,* tells The Dude that his wife, Bunny (Tara Reid), has been kidnapped. He wants The Dude to deliver the ransom money. This plan is opposed by Maude (Julianne Moore), the Big Lebowski's daughter from an earlier marriage. Moore, who played a porno actress in *Boogie Nights,*

here plays an altogether different kind of erotic artist; she covers her body with paint and hurls herself through the air in a leather harness.

Los Angeles in this film is a zoo of peculiar characters. One of the funniest is a Latino bowler named Jesus (John Turturro), who is seen going door to door in his neighborhood on the sort of mission you read about, but never picture anyone actually performing. The Dude tends to have colorful hallucinations when he's socked in the jaw or pounded on the head, which is a lot, and one of them involves a musical comedy sequence inspired by Busby Berkeley. (It includes the first point-of-view shot in history from inside a bowling ball.)

Some may complain that *The Big Lebowski* rushes in all directions and never ends up anywhere. That isn't the film's flaw, but its style. The Dude, who smokes a lot of pot and guzzles White Russians made with half-and-half, starts every day filled with resolve, but his plans gradually dissolve into a haze of missed opportunities and missed intentions. Most people lead lives with a third act. The Dude lives days without evenings. The spirit is established right at the outset, when the narrator (Sam Elliott) starts out well enough, but eventually confesses he's lost his train of thought.

Big Momma's House ★ ★
PG-13, 99 m., 2000

Martin Lawrence (Malcolm), Nia Long (Sherry), Paul Giamatti (John), Jascha Washington (Trent), Terrence Howard (Lester), Anthony Anderson (Nolan), Ella Mitchell (Big Momma). Directed by Raja Gosnell and produced by David T. Friendly and Michael Green. Screenplay by Darryl Quarles and Don Rhymer.

Any movie that employs an oven mitt and a plumber's friend in a childbirth scene cannot be all bad, and I laughed a lot during *Big Momma's House.* I also spent a certain amount of time staring at the screen in disbelief. While it's true that comedy can redeem bad taste, it can be appalling when bad taste thinks it is being redeemed by comedy and is wrong. The movie's opening toilet scene, featuring the biggest evacuation since we pulled out of Vietnam, is a grisly example.

Martin Lawrence stars in the movie as Malcolm, an FBI agent who is a master of disguise. A vicious bank robber named Lester (Terrence Howard) escapes from prison, and Malcolm and his partner John (Paul Giamatti) conduct a surveillance on Lester's girlfriend Sherry (Nia Long), who may know where $2 million in loot has been concealed. Sherry, afraid of Lester, flees with her child to the Georgia home of her grandmother, Big Momma (Ella Mitchell). And when Big Momma is called out of town, Malcolm disguises himself as the 350-pound juggernaut, deceives Sherry, and infiltrates the case from within, while his partner keeps watch from the house across the street.

This is all essentially an attempt by Lawrence to follow Eddie Murphy's disguise as a fat guy in *The Nutty Professor,* and credit should also go to Robin Williams in *Mrs. Doubtfire.* The whole enterprise has been ratcheted down several degrees in taste, however; while Murphy's funniest scene involves vast explusions of intestinal gas, Big Momma's noisy visit to the bathroom is scary, not funny.

Martin Lawrence is a gifted actor, and with clever makeup, padding, and sass he creates a fake Big Momma who doesn't look completely like a drag queen, although she comes close. It's doubtful her granddaughter, neighbors, and would-be boyfriend would be fooled. But we go along with the gag, since the plot is no more than a flimsy excuse for Big Momma to behave in a way that most 350-pound grandmothers in their sixties would find impossible.

We see Big Momma playing a pickup basketball game, including a reverse dunk that ends with her hanging from the hoop. Big Momma in karate class, throwing the instructor around the room. Big Momma in church, letting some four-letter words slip into her testimony and covering up with a quick segue to "Oh, Happy Day!"

The funniest scene involves a pregnant neighbor in the throes of childbirth—which is how Malcolm the FBI agent finds out Big Momma is a midwife. The zany editing of the childbirth scene makes it work, and the appearance of the oven mitt is the high point of the film. Other scenes are not handled so well; when Big Momma's sexy granddaughter climbs into bed with her, for example, Malcolm has a physiological reaction not entirely explained by his

flashlight. This is a recycling of the classic bed scene between Steve Martin and John Candy in *Planes, Trains and Automobiles* ("Those aren't pillows!"), not handled nearly as well.

The movie's one of those ideas that seems increasingly labored as the plot drags on. A little of Big Momma is funny enough, but eventually we realize Martin Lawrence is going to spend virtually the entire movie in drag (he appears as Malcolm only long enough to stir up a sweet romance with Sherry). The problem is that Lawrence's gifts come packaged with his face and voice: Present him as Big Momma all the time, and you lose his star power. It's the same problem John Travolta presents in *Battlefield Earth.* We don't go to a big star's movie to see him as an unrecognizable character. The movie has some big laughs, yes, but never reaches takeoff velocity.

The Big One ★ ★ ★
PG-13, 96 m., 1998

A documentary directed by Michael Moore and produced by Kathleen Glynn. Screenplay by Moore.

Americans are happy with the economy. Unemployment is at an all-time low. Clinton gets high approval ratings despite scandals because times are good and we don't want to rock the boat.

Swimming upstream against this conventional wisdom, here comes Michael Moore, the proletarian in the baseball cap. In his new documentary, *The Big One,* he crisscrosses the country on a book tour and finds factories closing, corporations shipping jobs overseas, and couples working extra jobs to make ends meet. "It's like being divorced," a mother with three jobs tells him in Centralia, Illinois. "I only see the kids on weekends." Many locals have lost their jobs with the closure of, ironically, the Payday candy bar factory.

Moore became famous overnight in 1989 with his hilarious documentary *Roger and Me,* in which he stalked Roger Smith, president of General Motors, in an attempt to find out why GM was closing its plants in Flint, Michigan, and moving production to Mexico. The movie was filled with cheap shots and media manipulation, and proud of it: Part of the fun was watching Moore turn the imagery of corporate America against itself.

In 1989, though, we were in a slump. Now times are good. Is Moore's message outdated? Not necessarily. If unemployment is low, that doesn't mean the mother in Centralia is prosperous. And what about the workers at Johnson Products in Milwaukee, which celebrated $500 million in profits by closing its factory and moving to Mexico? Moore visits their factory and tries to present them with a "Downsizer of the Year Award" along with his check for eighty cents: "The first hour's wage for a Mexican worker."

He likes to write checks. He creates fictitious committees to make donations to 1996 presidential candidates: Pat Buchanan's campaign cashes a $100 check from "Abortionists for Buchanan," and Moore also writes checks from "Satan Worshippers for Dole," "Pedophiles for Free Trade" (for Perot), and "Hemp Growers for Clinton." Watching Steven Forbes on TV, he notes that the candidate never blinks, and gets an NYU doctor to say, "That's not human."

The occasion for this documentary is Moore's forty-five-city tour to promote *Downsize This!* his best-seller about hard times in the midst of prosperity. We see him lecturing campus crowds, confronting security guards, sympathizing with the striking workers at a Borders bookstore. He's an unapologetic liberal, prounion, anti–fat cat; during an interview with Studs Terkel, he beams beatifically as Studs notes the sixtieth anniversary of the CIO's sit-down strikes against the carmakers.

The movie is smart, funny, and edited cleverly; that helps conceal the fact that it's mostly recycled information. There is little here that *Roger and Me* didn't say first and more memorably. But we get two docs for the price of one: The second one is about book tours, with Moore on a grueling schedule of one city a day, no sleep, endless talk shows and book signings, plus his guerrilla raids on downsizers.

He still wears the gimme caps and the blue jeans with the saggy seats, but the Moore of *Roger and Me* was an outsider, and the Moore of *The Big One* is a celebrity (flight attendants recognize him from his TV show, kids want his autograph). He's rueful about the "media escorts" hired by his publisher to accompany him in every city; at one point, he describes

one of his escorts to security guards as a "stalker." She's forcibly led outside the building before the "joke" is revealed; I didn't find it as funny as Moore did.

She is, after all, a working person, too—and so are the security guards Moore banters with as they eject him from factories. Most of them don't even work for the companies they guard, but for temp agencies, and one of the movie's startling statistics is that the largest employer in America is not AT&T, not GM—but Manpower, the hourly temp agency.

Moore's goal in the film is to get at least one corporate big shot to talk to him on camera. He finally lands Phil Knight, CEO of Nike, whose shoes are famously manufactured in Indonesia by workers paid a few dollars a day. Knight is in a no-win situation, but at least he's willing to talk. He doesn't hide behind corporate security.

His case: Shoe factories are good for the Indonesian economy, which in another generation could bootstrap itself into more prosperity. And, "I am convinced Americans do not want to make shoes." But what about Indonesia's genocidal practices against minority groups? Moore asks. "How many people died in the Cultural Revolution?" asks Knight. That's not an answer, but it is a response.

Do Americans want to make shoes? Moore returns to his hometown of Flint and asks citizens to rally if they want a shoe job. It's a cold day, which may have kept the turnout down, but Moore is forced to use low-angle shots to conceal the fact that the crowd of eager shoe workers is not very large. Maybe the issue isn't whether poor Americans want to make shoes, but why poor Americans are charged $150 for a pair of shoes that Indonesians are paid pennies to manufacture.

Moore's overall conclusion: Large American corporations care more for their stockholders than for their workers, and no profit level is high enough to satisfy them. If he'd been able to get more top executives on camera, I have a feeling their response would have been: "Yes. And?"

The Big Tease ★ ★
R, 86 m., 2000

Craig Ferguson (Crawford Mackenzie), Frances Fisher (Candy Harper), Mary McCormack (Monique Geingold), David Rasche (Stig Ludwiggssen), Chris Langham (Martin), Donal Logue (Eamonn), Isabella Aitken (Mrs. Beasie Mackenzie), Kevin Allen (Gareth Trundle). Directed by Kevin Allen and produced by Philip Rose. Screenplay by Sacha Gervasi and Craig Ferguson.

In the theory of comedy, more attention should be paid to the time between the laughs. It's easy enough to get a laugh in a movie, but tricky and difficult to build comic momentum, so that underlying hilarity rolls over from one laugh to the next and the audience senses it's looking at a funny movie instead of a movie with funny moments.

The Big Tease is a movie with a lot of laughs, but they come one at a time. It doesn't build, and by the time we get to the big payoff it's kind of dragging. I could describe moments and lines to you and you'd probably laugh, but sitting there in the audience, you want it to roll, and it meanders.

The film stars Craig Ferguson, a gifted comic actor from Glasgow (and *The Drew Carey Show*), as a gay hairdresser named Crawford Mackenzie—by his own admission the finest hairdresser, indeed, in Scotland. When an invitation arrives from the World Freestyle Hairdressing Championship in Los Angeles, he vibrates with excitement: Here at last is his chance to compete against the big names in hairdressing. Accompanied by a documentary film crew, he flies off to L.A., only to discover belatedly that he has been invited, not to compete, but to sit in the audience (between Daniel Day-Lewis and Carrot Top), and is expected to pay all his own bills.

He's crushed, but not defeated. With the now-desperate doc crew following him around and lending him that air of vague importance bestowed by any camera, he invades the sanctum of the legendary Stig Ludwiggssen (David Rasche), defending hairdressing champion, a Norwegian twit with an accent that casts doubt on his Norwegian or any other origins. Rasche is wonderful in the role, conveying that tower-ing self-importance so often displayed by the giants of inconsequential fields; having once overheard Jose Eber when he was mad at a rental car agent, I can even speculate that Rasche's portrait is not particularly exaggerated.

To be considered for the competition, Crawford needs a union card. His quest for one occupies the middle passages of the movie. At one point he is reduced to grooming the animal costumes at a theme park. He thinks his fellow Scotsman Sean Connery might come to the rescue (perhaps he will remember the time Crawford groomed his hairpiece), and confronts Connery's publicist, played by Frances Fisher with dead-on accuracy.

Whether he gets his card, and what happens at the bizarre hairdressing finals, I leave it to you to discover. I found Ferguson likable as the hairdresser out of water, and enjoyed Fisher, Rasche, and Mary McCormack as the head of the competition. But somehow *The Big Tease* never quite attains takeoff velocity. Maybe it needed to position itself a little closer to the ground and go for the comedy of observation rather than exaggeration. I trust, anyway, that the final competition is an exaggeration. If it is anywhere at all close to real life, just the telecast of the real thing would have been funny enough.

Billy's Hollywood Screen Kiss ★ ★
R, 92 m., 1998

Sean P. Hayes (Billy), Brad Rowe (Gabriel), Paul Bartel (Rex Webster), Carmine D. Giovinazzo (Gundy), Meredith Scott Lynn (Georgiana), Bonnie Biehl (Connie Rogers). Directed by Tommy O'Haver and produced by David Mosley. Screenplay by O'Haver.

We wouldn't be fascinated by a routine Hollywood love story simply because the leading characters were heterosexual; we'd want them to be something else besides, like interesting or funny. The same standard isn't always applied to gay-themed movies, which sometimes seem to believe that gayness itself is enough to make a character interesting. It isn't, and the best recent movies with gay characters (*High Art* and *The Opposite of Sex*) have demonstrated that.

Billy's Hollywood Screen Kiss seems besotted

by its sexuality, and wouldn't be able to pass this test: Would the film be interesting if it was about heteros? The story involves Billy (Sean P. Hayes), who announces at the outset, "My name is Billy, and I am a homosexual" (the movie misses its first gag when nobody replies, "Hi, Billy!"). Billy tells us he grew up in Indiana (montage of old snapshots of tousle-headed lad squinting into camera), and now lives in Los Angeles, where he rooms platonically with a gal-pal named George, for Georgiana (Meredith Scott Lynn).

Billy is a nice kid, well-played by Hayes, who never pushes the character further than the material will take him. Billy's got a cool, laid-back personality, is quietly bemused, goes everywhere with a Polaroid, and eventually works on a photo series re-creating famous Hollywood love scenes with drag queens.

One day a thunderbolt strikes. Billy meets the angelic Gabriel (Brad Rowe), an improbably handsome waiter, and falls in love with him. But Gabriel, alas, is straight—or says he is. Billy runs into him again at a party, and convinces him to pose in one of his re-creations of Hollywood's golden age. And after the plot does handstands and back flips to make it happen, the two men wind up spending the night in Billy's apartment. First Gabriel sleeps on the couch. Then it looks like it might be more comfortable in the bed. You know the drill.

Do they have sex? I would not dream of saying. Whatever they have, Gabriel is still not sure he is gay, and there's a heartfelt discussion of the Kinsey scale, which rates people from 1 to 6, 1 being completely hetero and 6 being completely gay. Billy is a perfect 6. If I were a judge, I'd hold up a card scoring Gabriel at 3.5.

The movie surrounds this plot with a lot of amusing window dressing, including celebrity walk-ons (director Paul Bartel is at a party accompanied by what seems to be his pet chortler, and Warhol superstar Holly Woodlawn plays herself—and Deborah Kerr). From time to time a chorus line of three drag queens appears to provide musical commentary, and one of them has a hilarious line, explaining that her earrings are miniatures of Milli Vanilli and John Tesh.

The will-he-or-won't-he plot spins out as long as the movie is able to sustain it, which is long after we have given up hoping that Billy

and Gabriel will find the happiness they so earnestly deserve. And then the ending is a giant, soggy, wet blanket. I can't discuss it without revealing it, but let me say this: Does it make the whole movie a lie, or is it simply a case of a character with an attention span of six seconds?

Black and White ★ ★ ★
R, 100 m., 2000

Bijou Phillips (Charlie), Power (Rich Bower), Scott Caan (Scotty), Ben Stiller (Mark Clear), Allan Houston (Dean), Claudia Schiffer (Greta), Mike Tyson (Himself), Brooke Shields (Sam), Robert Downey Jr. (Terry), Stacy Edwards (Sheila), Gaby Hoffmann (Raven), Jared Leto (Casey), Marla Maples (Muffy), Kim Matulova (Kim), Joe Pantoliano (Bill King). Directed by James Toback and produced by Michael Mailer, Daniel Bigel, and Ron Rotholz. Screenplay by Toback.

Like James Toback himself, his new film is in your face, overflowing with ideas, outrageous in its connections, maddening, illogical, and fascinating. Also like its author, it is never boring. Toback is the brilliant wild child of indie cinema, now a wild man in his fifties, whose films sometimes seem half-baked, but you like them that way: The agony of invention is there on the screen.

Black and White is one of those Manhattan stories where everyone knows each other: rich kids, ghetto kids, rappers, Brooke Shields, the district attorney, a rogue cop, a gambler, a basketball star, Mike Tyson, recording executives. They're all mixed up in a story about race, sex, music, bribery, fathers, sons, murder, and lifestyles. What's amazing is how it's been marketed as a film about white kids who identify with black lifestyles and want to be black themselves. There's a little of that, and a lot more other stuff. It's a crime movie as much as anything.

The sex has gotten the most attention; the opening scene, of a threesome in Central Park, had to be recut three times to avoid an NC-17 rating (you can see the original version, murkily, on the Web). We meet Charlie (Bijou Phillips), the rich girl who "wants to be black" and also adds, later: "I'm a little kid. Kids go through phases. When I grow up, I'll be over it. I'm a kid from America."

True, the racial divide of years ago is blurred and disappearing among the younger siblings of Generation X. The characters in this movie slide easily in and out of various roles, with sex as the lubricant. Toback's camera follows one character into a situation and another out of it, gradually building a mosaic in which we meet a black gangster named Rich (hip-hop producer Power), a rap group (Wu-Tang Clan), a basketball guard named Dean (real-life Knick Allan Houston), his faithless Ph.D. candidate girlfriend (Claudia Schiffer), a crooked cop (Ben Stiller), a documentary filmmaker (Brooke Shields), the husband everyone but she knows is gay (Robert Downey Jr.), and heavyweight champ Mike Tyson, playing himself, and improvising some of the best scenes.

The story, which involves bribery, murder, and blackmail, I will leave for you to discover. Consider the style. Toback has observed that for musicians like Wu-Tang Clan, their language is their art form, so he didn't write a lot of the dialogue in the movie. Instead, he plugged actors into situations, told them where they had to go, and let them improvise. This leads to an electrifying scene where Downey makes a sexual advance on Mike Tyson ("In the dream, you were holding me . . ."), and Tyson's reaction is quick and spontaneous.

But now compare that with another scene where Brooke Shields makes a pass at Tyson. Downey is one kind of an actor, Shields another. Downey is in character, Shields is to some degree playing herself, and Tyson is completely himself. What we are watching in the second scene is Brooke Shields the celebrity playing a character who is essentially herself, acting in an improvised scene. So the scene isn't drama; it's documentary: cinema verité of Shields and Tyson working at improvisation. It's too easy to say the scene doesn't work because Shields is not quite convincing: It *does* work because she's not quite convincing. Toback's films have that way of remaining alive and edgy, and letting their rough edges show.

The plot is sometimes maddening. Without revealing too much, I will say that a great deal hinges on the policeman (Stiller) being able to count on a chain of events he could not possibly have anticipated. He needs to know that the basketball player will tell his girlfriend something, that she will tell another person, and that the other person will eventually try to hire as a killer the very person who suits the cop's needs. Unlikely.

Against untidiness like that, Toback balances passages of wonderful invention. Downey has a scene where he tries to tell Shields he is gay. Tyson ("I'm a man who has made too many mistakes to be known for his wisdom") has a scene where he gives advice to a friend who wants to know if he should have someone killed. Toback plays the manager of a recording studio who brushes off a rap group that wants to hire space, but the next day is happy to talk to their white manager (wary of the shootings associated with some rap artists, he explains, "What I cannot afford is a corpse in my lobby"). And to balance Charlie's rich white girl play-acting ("I want to be black") is a more sensible black girl ("I'm from the 'hood and I don't want to live there. I go back and see my friends and they wanna get out").

Black and White is not smooth and well-oiled, not fish, not fowl, not documentary, not quite fiction, and not about any single theme you can pin down. Those points are all to its credit.

Blade ★ ★ ★
R, 120 m., 1998

Welsey Snipes (Blade), Kris Kristofferson (Whistler), Stephen Dorff (Deacon Frost), N'Bushe Wright (Dr. Karen Jensen), Donal Logue (Quinn), Udo Kier (Dragonetti), Traci Lords (Racquel), Kevin Patrick Walls (Krieger). Directed by Stephen Norrington and produced by Peter Frankfort, Wesley Snipes, and Robert Engelman. Screenplay by David S. Goyer.

At a time when too many movies are built from flat, TV-style visuals of people standing around talking, movies based on comic books represent one of the last best hopes for visionary filmmaking. It's ironic that the comics, which borrowed their early visual style from movies, should now be returning the favor.

Blade, starring Wesley Snipes as a killer of vampires who is engaged in an armageddon for possession of Earth, is a movie that relishes high visual style. It uses the extreme camera angles, the bizarre costumes and sets, the exaggerated shadows, the confident cutting between long shots and extreme close-ups. It slams ahead in pure, visceral imagery.

Of course, anyone patiently attending the film in the hopes of a reasoned story line is going to be disappointed. Better to see it in comic book terms, as an episode in a master-myth in which even the most cataclysmic confrontation is not quite the end of things because there has to be another issue next month. The story, like so many comic myths, involves ordinary people who are connected through a superhero to an occult universe that lurks beneath reality—or, as Blade tells a young human doctor, "The world you live in is just a sugarcoated topping. There is another world beneath it—the real world!"

Blade, based on a Marvel Comics hero, is played by Snipes as a man on the border between human and vampire. Blade's origination story: His mother was bitten by a vampire in childbirth, infecting her child, who lived in the streets until being adopted by a man named Whistler (Kris Kristofferson), who masterminds a lonely war against vampires. Now Blade, raised to manhood, is the spearhead of that battle, as vampires spread their influence through the major cities. One of their chief gathering grounds: secret after-hours dance clubs where victims are lured by the promise of forbidden thrills, only to be bitten and converted.

The movie is based around a series of major action scenes; the first one features an update of an old friend from 1970s Hong Kong movies, the flying guillotine. This is a knife-edged boomerang that spins, slices, and returns to its owner. Very neat.

Blade encounters Dr. Karen Jensen (N'Bushe Wright), a blood specialist who has been bitten by a badly burned vampire brought in for emergency treatment. Can she be saved? He returns her to Whistler's secret lab for an injection of liquid garlic, which will give her a fighting chance. Blade himself lives under a daily reprieve; Whistler's serum keeps him on the human side, although he may be building up a resistance to it.

Arrayed against Blade are the forces of vampirism, represented by his archenemy Deacon Frost (Stephen Dorff), also half-human, half-vampire, who dreams of a final vampire uprising against humans, and world conquest. His rival within the vampire world is Dragonetti (Udo Kier), a pure vampire who prefers the current arrangement under which vampires secretly control key organizations to safeguard their interests.

There is a lot of mythology underlying Frost's plans, including the evocation of an ancient vampire god who may return to lead the creatures in their final conquest. The setting for the climactic scene is a phantasmagoric vampire temple where Blade, of course, must risk everything in a titanic showdown.

The movie, directed by Stephen Norrington, is another in a recent group of New Line movies that combine comic book imagery, *noir* universes, and the visual heritage of German Expressionism; I'd rank it third after *Dark City* and *Spawn*. This material is obviously moving in the direction of pure animation, which is the look it often tries to evoke, and there are some shots here that use f/x to evoke animation's freedom from gravity and other physical laws: Notice, for example, an unbroken shot where Blade takes Dr. Jensen in his arms and makes an improbable leap from a high window to a far rooftop. Can't be done—especially not with them seemingly floating down in midair to a safe landing—but the dreamlike feel of escape is effective.

Wesley Snipes understands the material from the inside out and makes an effective Blade because he knows that the key ingredient in any interesting superhero is not omnipotence, but vulnerability. There is always a kind of sadness underlying the personalities of the great superheroes, who have been given great knowledge and gifts but few consolations in their battle against evil. The fun all seems to be on the villain's side. By embodying those feelings, Snipes as Blade gives the movie that edge of emotion without which it would simply be special effects. Of course, you have to bring something to it yourself, preferably a sympathy for the whole comic superhero ethos. This is the kind of movie that gets better the more you know about the genre.

The Blair Witch Project ★ ★ ★ ★
R, 88 m., 1999

Heather Donahue (Heather), Joshua Leonard (Josh), Michael Williams (Mike). Directed and edited by Eduardo Sanchez and Daniel Myrick. Screenplay by Sanchez and Myrick. Produced by Gregg Hale and Robin Cowie.

We're instinctively afraid of natural things (snakes, barking dogs, the dark), but have to be taught to fear walking into traffic or touching an electrical wire. Horror films that tap into our hard-wired instinctive fears probe a deeper place than movies with more sophisticated threats. A villain is only an actor, but a shark is more than a shark.

The Blair Witch Project, an extraordinarily effective horror film, knows this and uses it. It has no fancy special effects or digital monsters, but its characters get lost in the woods, hear noises in the night, and find disturbing stick figures hanging from trees. One of them discovers slime on his backpack. Because their imaginations have been inflamed by talk of witches, hermits, and child-murderers in the forest, because their food is running out and their smokes are gone, they (and we) are a lot more scared than if they were merely being chased by some guy in a ski mask.

The movie is like a celebration of rock-bottom production values—of how it doesn't take bells and whistles to scare us. It's presented in the form of a documentary. We learn from the opening titles that in 1994 three young filmmakers went into a wooded area in search of a legendary witch: "A year later, their footage was found." The film's style and even its production strategy enhance the illusion that it's a real documentary. The characters have the same names as the actors. All of the footage in the film was shot by two cameras—a color video camcorder operated by the director, Heather (Heather Donahue), and a 16mm black-and-white camera operated by the cameraman, Josh (Joshua Leonard). Mike (Michael Williams) does the sound. All three carry backpacks and are prepared for two or three nights of sleeping in tents in the woods. It doesn't work out that way.

The buried structure of the film, which was written and directed by Eduardo Sanchez and Daniel Myrick, is insidious in the way it introduces information without seeming to. Heather and her crew arrive in the small town of Burkittsville ("formerly Blair") and interview locals. Many have vaguely heard of the Blair witch and other ominous legends; one says, "I think I saw a documentary on the Discovery Channel or something."

We hear that children have been killed in the woods, that bodies have disappeared, that strange things happened at Coffin Rock. But the movie wisely doesn't present this information as if it can be trusted; it's gossip, legend and lore, passed along half-jokingly by local people, and Heather, Josh, and Mike view it as good footage, not a warning.

Once they get into the woods, the situation gradually turns ominous. They walk in circles. Something happens to their map. Nature itself begins to seem oppressive and dead. They find ominous signs. Bundles of twigs. Unsettling stick figures. These crude objects are scarier than more elaborate effects; they look like they were created by a being who haunts the woods, not by someone playing a practical joke. Much has been said about the realistic cinematography—how every shot looks like it was taken by a hand-held camera in the woods (as it was). But the visuals are not just a technique. By shooting in a chill season, by dampening the color palette, the movie makes the woods look unfriendly and desolate; nature is seen as a hiding place for dread secrets.

As fear and desperation grow, the personalities of the characters emerge. "We agreed to a scouted-out project!" one guy complains, and the other says, "Heather, this is *so* not cool!" Heather keeps up an optimistic front; the woods are not large enough to get lost in, she argues, because "this is America. We've destroyed most of our natural resources." Eventually her brave attitude disintegrates into a remarkable shot in which she films her own apology (I was reminded of Scott's notebook entries as he froze to death in Antarctica).

At a time when digital techniques can show us almost anything, *The Blair Witch Project* is a reminder that what really scares us is the stuff we can't see. The noise in the dark is almost always scarier than what makes the noise in the dark. Any kid can tell you that. Not that he believes it at the time. ☞

Blast From the Past ★ ★ ★
PG-13, 106 m., 1999

Brendan Fraser (Adam), Alicia Silverstone (Eve), Christopher Walken (Calvin), Sissy Spacek (Helen), Dave Foley (Troy), Joey Slotnick (Soda Jerk), Dale Raoul (Mom). Directed by Hugh Wilson and produced by Renny Harlin and Wilson. Screenplay by Bill Kelly and Wilson.

Blast From the Past opens with a cocktail party in 1962 at the home of Calvin and Helen Webber, where some of the guests whisper about how brilliant, but weird, Calvin is. Their host meanwhile mixes cocktails, tells bad jokes, and hints darkly that "I could take a simple yacht battery and rig it to last a year, easily."

Suddenly President Kennedy appears on TV to announce that Russian missiles in Cuba are aimed at targets in America. Calvin (Christopher Walken) hustles the guests out the door and hurries his pregnant wife (Sissy Spacek) into an elevator to take them down to his amazingly well-stocked bomb shelter, where fish grow in breeding tanks, and the decor of their surface home has been exactly reproduced—right down to the lawn furniture on the patio.

Calvin is a brain from Cal Tech who has been waiting for years for the big one to drop. His prudence is admirable but his luck is bad: There's no nuclear war, but a plane crashes on his house and sends a fireball down the elevator shaft, convincing him there is one. So he closes the heavy steel doors and informs Helen that the time locks won't open for thirty-five years—"to keep us from trying to leave."

That's the setup for Hugh Wilson's quirky comedy that turns the tables on *Pleasantville.* That was a movie about modern characters visiting the 1950s; this is about people emerging into the present from a thirty-five-year time warp. In the sealed atmosphere far below Los Angeles, nothing changes. Calvin and Helen watch kinescopes of old Jackie Gleason programs ("People will never get tired of watching these," Calvin smiles, while Helen's eyes roll up into her head). Tuna casserole is still on the menu. And unto them a son is born, named, of course, Adam, and played as an adult by Brendan Fraser.

Adam is trained by Calvin to speak several languages, and he masters science, math, and history, while his mother teaches him good manners and gives him a dance lesson every day. His dad even tries to explain the principles of baseball to him. Try it sometime. Calvin is pleased as punch with how well his shelter is functioning, but Helen grows quietly stir-crazy and starts to hit the cooking sherry. Her wish for her son: "I want you to marry a nice girl from Pasadena." His birthday wish for himself: "A girl. One who doesn't glow in the dark."

Eventually the locks open, and Adam is sent to the surface, where his family's pleasant neighborhood has been replaced by a ruined strip mall made of boarded-up storefronts and porno shops, and populated by drunks and transvestite hookers. "Subspecies mutants," he decides. Then he meets a real girl who doesn't glow in the dark, the inevitably named Eve (Alicia Silverstone). She can't believe his perfect manners, his strange clothes, his lapses of current knowledge, or his taste in music. But eventually, as is the custom in such movies, they fall in love.

Brendan Fraser has a way of suggesting he's only passing through our zone of time and space. He was the "Encino Man" and "George of the Jungle," and even in *Gods and Monsters* his haircut made him look a little like Frankenstein's creature. Here he fits easily into the role of a nice man who has a good education but is, to borrow the title of Silverstone's best movie, clueless.

Blast From the Past is the first screen credit for writer Bill Kelly, who coscripted with the director, Wilson *(The First Wives Club* and the overlooked *Guarding Tess).* It's a sophisticated and observant film that wears its social commentary lightly but never forgets it, as Adam wanders through a strange new world of burgeoning technology and decaying manners. His innocence has an infectious charm, although the worldly-wise Eve can hardly believe he doesn't know the value of his dad's baseball card collection (wait until she hears about his dad's stock portfolio).

The movie is funny and entertaining in all the usual ways, yes, but I was grateful that it tried for more: that it was actually about something, that it had an original premise, that it used satire and irony and had sly undercurrents. Even the set decoration is funny. I congratulate whoever had the idea of putting Reader's Digest Condensed Books on the shelves of the bomb shelter—the last place on Earth where you'd want to hurry through a book.

Blood Guts Bullets and Octane ★ ★ ½
NO MPAA RATING, 87 m., 1999

Joe Carnahan (Sid French), Dan Leis (Bob Melba), Ken Rudulph (FBI Agent Jared), Dan Harlan (Danny Woo), Kurt Johnson (Hillbilly Sniper), Mark S. Allen (FBI Agent Franks), Kellee Benedict (FBI Agent Little). Directed by Joe Carnahan and produced by Dan Leis, Leon Corcos, and Patrick M. Lynn. Screenplay by Carnahan.

I've had a busy day on the Tarantino beat. First I reviewed a movie named *Go* that seemed inspired by *Pulp Fiction,* then I had a cup of coffee, and here I am back at the keyboard reviewing *Blood Guts Bullets and Octane,* which is so indebted to QT's kinetic style that it doesn't even pause to put commas in its title. One thing you have to say about the long shadow of *Pulp Fiction:* In a season dominated by movies that end at the senior prom, at least the QT retreads are generally more energetic and inventive, and involve characters over seventeen.

The story behind *BGB&O* is an inspiring fable for would-be filmmakers. Its writer-director-editor-star, Joe Carnahan of Sacramento, shot it in three weeks for less than $8,000, and cheerfully let it be known at Sundance that his cast and crew were paid "partly in Doritos." Like Robert Rodriguez's *El Mariachi,* the bargain price was enough to make a video version for showing to distributors; Lions Gate ponied up a reported $100,000 in post-production sound and transfer work to get the movie into theaters in 35mm.

What Carnahan made for his money is a fabulous calling card: This movie shows that he can direct, can generate momentum even in the face of a problematic story, and knows how to find and cast natural actors, including himself. There is real talent here. The most engaging aspect of the film is its spoken dialogue, which largely involves used car salesmen and seems inspired by David Mamet's real estate

agents in *Glengarry Glen Ross.* (Consider this line: "The best in this business are, by virtue, fabulous salesmen." Using "by virtue" without explaining by virtue of *what* is prime Mamet.)

The movie opens in a torrent of words, as two desperate used car salesmen named Sid and Bob (Carnahan and Dan Leis) try to close a sale while screaming into the phone to a supplier who hasn't delivered the cars he promised. They're going under fast, swamped by the TV ads of their powerful competitor, Mr. Woo (Dan Harlan). Then they're offered $250,000 to simply hang onto a vintage Pontiac Le Mans for two days—to just park it on their lot.

This is a car with a lot of history. An FBI agent has traced it from South America to California, and reckons thirty-four dead bodies are associated with it. There's something in its trunk, but the trunk, Sid and Bob discover, is wired to a bomb and can't be opened. The locked trunk functions for much of the movie like the trunk in *Repo Man* and the briefcases in *Pulp Fiction* and *Ronin;* it contains the MacGuffin.

Carnahan is nothing if not stylistically open-minded. He uses color, black-and-white, flash frames, tilt shots, weird points of view, whatever. True to the QT tradition, he also fractures his time line and moves back and forth between elements of his story. He ends up with a lot of icing and very little cake, and his ending is an exercise in narrative desperation, but for most of the way he holds our attention, if not our interest: If he can do this with smoke and mirrors, think what he might be able to accomplish with a real budget.

Blues Brothers 2000 ★ ★
PG-13, 121 m., 1998

Dan Aykroyd (Elwood Blues), John Goodman (Mighty Mack McTeer), Joe Morton (Cabel Chamberlain), J. Even Bonifant (Buster), Frank Oz (Warden), Kathleen Freeman (Mother Mary Stigmata), B. B. King (Malvern Gasperon), Aretha Franklin (Mrs. Murphy). Directed by John Landis and produced by Landis, Dan Aykroyd, and Leslie Belzberg. Screenplay by Aykroyd and Landis.

Blues Brothers 2000 has a lot of good music in it. It would have had more if they'd left out the story, which would have been an excellent idea. The film is lame comedy surrounded by high-energy blues (and some pop, rock, and country and western). And don't stop watching: *after* the end credits James Brown does "Please, Please, Please."

It's as if director John Landis had such good James Brown footage he had to use it, even though there was no room in the main plot line, which mostly involves updates on characters in the original 1980 film. "I always thought there was another story to be told," Landis says in the film's notes. Fine; then tell one.

The first movie opened with Jake Blues (the late John Belushi) getting out of Joliet Prison and going with his brother Elwood (Dan Aykroyd) to the orphanage where they were raised, still presided over by the fearsome Sister Mary Stigmata. The new movie begins with Elwood getting out of prison and seeking out the aging nun, who still whacks Elwood when his manners stray.

Elwood wants to get the old band back together again. Sister Mary has another idea: He should do a little "mentoring" for Buster (J. Even Bonifant), a ten-year-old orphan. Buster gets his own Blues Brothers uniform, plays some harmonica, and gets Elwood charged with kidnapping—but what's he *doing* in this story? Apparently Landis originally conceived the role for Macaulay Culkin. Culkin outgrew it, and Landis should have too.

Seeking out old friends, Elwood goes to a strip joint where he encounters Mighty Mack (John Goodman), a bartender who has a good voice and is enlisted as Jake's replacement. Other band members are added along the way, during an interstate chase orchestrated by a state policeman (Joe Morton) who is more or less Elwood's stepbrother (the dialogue spends a lot of time explaining that "more or less").

The original (much better) film made great use of locations in the Blues Brothers' sweet home Chicago, but this one was shot mostly near Toronto and New Orleans, with a few shots of the Chicago skyline thrown in for effect. (Hint: Bars in Louisiana do not usually advertise that they are "licenced.")

The 1980 movie had neo-Nazi bad guys. This one has a right-wing militia group, with a leader whose pep talks are unnecessarily offensive. I've noticed a disturbing trend recently for lightweight comedies to toss in racist language under the guise of "establishing" the villains. Vile language doesn't require additional currency.

But I stray from the heart of the film, which is good blues music. Just as the 1980 film included show-stopping numbers by Aretha Franklin and Cab Calloway, this one has great musical segments by Aretha ("R.E.S.P.E.C.T."), Eddie Floyd ("634-5789"), John Popper and Blues Traveler ("Maybe I'm Wrong"), Lonnie Brooks and Junior Wells ("Checkin' Up On My Baby"), and the Paul Butterfield Blues Band version of "Born in Chicago."

What is amazing is that the numbers by the guest artists are outnumbered by the Blues Brothers (including little Bonifant), who are backed up by a terrific band. There is food for thought in the sight of the late, great Junior Wells playing backup to a couple of comedians. It's not so much that I didn't enjoy their numbers as that, let's face it, with backup like these guys get, Buddy Hacket and I could be the Blues Brothers.

Jonathan Eig wrote an article in *New Republic* that explains "How the Blues Brothers destroyed the Windy City's musical heritage." It opens in a smoky dive on the South Side where the true blues still live, and then sniffs at the upscale North Side clubs where suburbanites pay $8 entry fees to hear tarted-up and smoothed-down blues.

But surely it has always been thus? The true blues come from, and flourish in, a milieu of hard times—hard emotionally, economically, racially, and not infrequently in lifestyle and substance abuse choices. Move the music to an affluent, paying audience, contract the musicians to two shows a night, mix in some soul and r-&-b to lighten the blues' heavy load, and that's entertainment. The notion that a professional blues musician can be "authentic" on demand (i.e., depressed, angry, bereft, and forlorn) is amusing. It's like they say in the theater: The most important thing is sincerity, and if you can fake that, you've got it made.

What the Blues Brothers do is worse than Eig's complaint about the posh blues clubs. They take a musical tradition and dine out on it, throwing scraps to the real pros. If Junior Wells, Aretha Franklin, Wilson Pickett, John Popper, and James Brown want to sing in a

Hollywood musical, they've got to be supporting characters for the brothers.

I don't suggest that Aykroyd and Belushi, in the 1970s, were not providing entertaining musical performances. I do suggest that the Blues Brothers schtick has outlived its usefulness. Watching *Blues Brothers 2000*, I found I had lost all interest in the orphanage, orphans, police cars, nuns, and mentoring. I wanted more music.

It's said that the climactic sequence of *BB2000*, a talent contest assembling many legendary musicians (even an ill-at-ease Eric Clapton), was a legendary jam session. No doubt. I'd love to see it as a concert film. With no chase scenes and no little kids. And really shot in Chicago. Or New Orleans would be okay. Not Toronto. I've heard Toronto called a lot of things, but not the home of the blues.

Blue Streak ★ ★ ★
PG-13, 93 m., 1999

Martin Lawrence (Miles Logan), Luke Wilson (Detective Carlson), Peter Greene (Deacon), William Forsythe (Hardcastle), Dave Chappelle (Tulley), Tamala Jones (Janiece), Nicole Ari Parker (Melissa Green). Directed by Les Mayfield and produced by Toby Jaffe and Neal H. Moritz. Screenplay by Michael Berry, John Blumenthal, and Steve Carpenter.

Blue Streak ranks in the upper reaches of the cop buddy genre, up there in *Lethal Weapon* territory. It has the usual ingredients for a cop comedy, including the obligatory Dunkin' Donuts product placement, but it's assembled with style—and it's built around a Martin Lawrence performance that deserves comparison with Richard Pryor and Eddie Murphy, with a touch of Mel Gibson's zaniness in the midst of action.

The movie opens with a high-tech caper scene; jewel thief Miles Logan (Lawrence) and his team put together a complicated plan involving illegal entry, alarm system workarounds, and steel getaway cables. Everything goes wrong, alas, and Lawrence is cornered on a construction site with a $17 million diamond. He tapes it inside an air duct, is arrested, and goes to prison.

Two years pass. On the street again, he finds his old girlfriend isn't happy to see him ("I didn't come to visit you for two years. Isn't that a sign?"). There is worse news. The building under construction turns out to be a police station, and the diamond is hidden deep inside. How to get it? He tries to get to the burglary department on the third floor by impersonating a crazy pizza-delivery guy. That's not a great idea, but he keeps improvising, and is somehow mistaken for a real cop. Soon he's out on the street with a partner (Luke Wilson), who is from the traffic division and thrilled to be working with an ace like Miles.

It's pretty clear that Miles isn't a standard cop. It doesn't take long for his partners to discover his name and badge number don't check out. But he's so confident, and so ruthless in roughing up suspects, they assume he's a genuine law enforcement officer of some description, who has infiltrated the department. His superior (William Forsythe) admires everything about him, and engages in debates about his true identity. FBI? Internal Affairs? CIA?

The movie, directed by Les Mayfield *(Encino Man)*, doesn't settle for the gag that Miles is a thief impersonating a cop. It takes that as a starting point and wrings laughs out of it—for example, in a funny scene where Miles walks in on a convenience store holdup that's being pulled by an old criminal buddy of his. While the other cop covers them from a distance, Miles engages in a desperate and unorthodox form of plea bargaining. If the old buddy doesn't blow his cover, Miles will promise him $10,000 and only one night in jail. Okay, $20,000?

I've seen enough car chases to last several lifetimes, but I like a good one when it's handled well, and the action in the last act of this movie is not only high-style, but makes sense in terms of the plot. Good casting of villains is essential in action comedies (remember Joe Pesci in *Lethal Weapon 2*?), and here the sinister Peter Greene is a convincing counterpoint. The villain always has to be the thankless straight man in a plot like this; he's never in on the joke, which is the joke.

Martin Lawrence is a comic actor with real talent not always shown to best advantage. *Bad Boys*, his 1995 cop buddy movie with Will

Smith, was not a career high point, and it took a certain nerve to make another one. But *Blue Streak* works. Lawrence himself was in shaky condition at the time of its release, recovering from a nearly fatal case of heat exhaustion. A movie like this is evidence that in the right material, he has a real gift. But he should dial down on the jogging.

Body Shots ★ ★
R, 99 m., 1999

Sean Patrick Flanery (Rick Hamilton), Jerry O'Connell (Michael Penorisi), Amanda Peet (Jane Bannister), Tara Reid (Sara Olswang), Ron Livingston (Trent Barber), Emily Procter (Whitney Bryant), Brad Rowe (Shawn Denigan), Sybil Temchen (Emma Cooper). Directed by Michael Cristofer and produced by Harry Colomby and Jennifer Keohane. Screenplay by David McKenna.

Body Shots suffers from a fatal misapprehension. It thinks it is about date rape, when actually it is about alcoholism. That's why the ending is inconclusive and unsatisfactory; not only does it fail to find answers—but they would be to the wrong questions.

The movie is about dating values and practices among affluent thirty-something professionals in Los Angeles. Some scenes are played straight to the camera, as if the characters are in a documentary. The girls as well as the guys are mostly looking for sex, and a "meaningful relationship" would be an unexpected bonus. The facile dialogue can't disguise the shallowness, but why should these characters have original thoughts about sex when nothing else in their lives is carefully examined?

Separate groups of men and women end up at the same bar, go on to another club, and split up. A pro football hero named Michael (Jerry O'Connell) ends up with a cute blonde named Sara (Tara Reid). They are both drunk. She pays for the $25 cab ride to her place on the beach in Santa Monica. They make out on the beach, go inside, and have sex. He says it was consensual, that she hit her head on the bed and got mad at him when he forgot her name. She says it was rape.

Each character is talked to urgently and pri-

vately by friends. Rick (Sean Patrick Flanery) quizzes the defiant and angry Michael, who is sure Sara was coming on to him and wanted sex, but cannot remember exactly what happened in her apartment. Jane (Amanda Peet) questions Sara, who also does not remember, although she has given the police a complete account of the rape. "Do you ever have blackouts?" another friend, Whitney (Emily Procter), asks her. Sara says no. Whitney reminds Sara of a couple of dramatic blackouts all her friends witnessed. Of course, by definition you cannot remember a blackout (this is the Heineken Uncertainty Principle).

As the movie dribbles to its inconclusive conclusion, we are left with the notion that in this case date rape may be in the mind of the beholder. Men see things one way, women another. Both Sara and Michael make persuasive arguments for their versions of events, while the film, which takes no sides, carefully presents both versions of the sexual encounter. This is like soft porn with a choice of point of view: First we see Sara's bra taken off, then we see it ripped off.

None of the characters (and perhaps none of the filmmakers) are enlightened about alcoholism. One danger sign of alcoholism is when a guy uses a Magic Marker to write DO ME on your forehead during a party, and you don't notice, as Sara doesn't. And what about her friend Whitney, whose part-time job consists of passing out free shots for a brand promotion at a club and setting a good example by tossing them back herself. I'm not saying that the job brands Whitney as an alcoholic (everyone has to earn a living), but that moderate drinkers somehow rarely find themselves employed as the free-shot girl.

It isn't surprising that Rick and Jane, the best friends, don't notice their friends are drunks. The movie's opening shot shows Rick and Jane in bed, still dressed, and the first line of dialogue is more realistic than most waking-up lines in the movies: "Do you have any Tylenol, honey?"

Body Shots means well and has some pointed dialogue about legal pitfalls, but it's clueless about its real subject. My own theory of date rape is that if you think you had sex and you didn't want to, but you're not sure why or how (or if) it happened, it's probably a good idea to call AA before you call the cops.

Boiler Room ★ ★ ★ ½
R, 119 m., 2000

Giovanni Ribisi (Seth), Vin Diesel (Chris), Nia Long (Abby), Nicky Katt (Greg), Scott Caan (Richie), Ron Rifkin (Seth's Father [Marty]), Jamie Kennedy (Adam), Taylor Nichols (Harry Reynard), Ben Affleck (Jim). Directed by Ben Younger and produced by Suzanne Todd and Jennifer Todd. Screenplay by Younger.

Boiler Room tells the story of a nineteen-year-old named Seth who makes a nice income running an illegal casino in his apartment. His dad, a judge, finds out about it and raises holy hell. So the kid gets a daytime job as a broker with a Long Island bucket shop that sells worthless or dubious stock with high-pressure telephone tactics. When he was running his casino, Seth muses, at least he was providing a product that his customers wanted.

The movie is the writing and directing debut of Ben Younger, a twenty-nine-year-old who says he interviewed a lot of brokers while writing the screenplay. I believe him. The movie hums with authenticity, and knows a lot about the cultlike power of a company that promises to turn its trainees into millionaires, and certainly turns them into efficient phone salesmen.

No experience is necessary at J. P. Marlin: "We don't hire brokers here—we train new ones," snarls Jim (Ben Affleck), already a millionaire, who gives new recruits a hard-edged introductory lecture, crammed with obscenities and challenges to their manhood. "Did you see *Glengarry Glen Ross*?" he asks them. He certainly has. Mamet's portrait of high-pressure real-estate salesmen is like a bible in this culture, and a guy like Jim doesn't see the message, only the style. (Younger himself observes that Jim, giving his savage pep talks, not only learned his style from Alec Baldwin's scenes in *Glengarry* but also wants to *be* Baldwin.)

The film's narrator is Seth Davis (Giovanni Ribisi), an unprepossessing young man with a bad suit who learns in a short time to separate suckers from their money with telephone fantasies about hot stocks and IPOs. Everybody wants to be a millionaire *right now*, he observes. Ironically, the dream of wealth he's selling with his cold calls is the same one J. P. Marlin is selling him.

In the phone war room with Seth are several other brokers, including the successful Chris (Vin Diesel) and Greg (Nicky Katt), who exchange anti-Jewish and Italian slurs almost as if it's expected of them. At night the guys go out, get drunk, and sometimes get in fights with brokers from other houses. The kids gambling in Seth's apartment were better behaved. We observe that both gamblers and stockbrokers bet their money on a future outcome, but as a gambler you pay the house nut, while as a broker you collect the house nut. Professional gamblers claim they do not depend on luck but on an understanding of the odds and prudent money management. Investors believe much the same thing. Of course, nobody ever claims luck has nothing to do with it unless luck has something to do with it.

The movie has the high-octane feel of real life, closely observed. It's made more interesting because Seth isn't a slickster like Michael Douglas or Charlie Sheen in *Wall Street* (a movie these guys know by heart), but an uncertain, untested young man who stands in the shadow of his father the judge (Ron Rifkin) who, he thinks, is always judging him. The tension between Seth and the judge is one of the best things in the film—especially in Rifkin's quiet, clear power in scenes where he lays down the law. When Seth refers to their relationship, his dad says: "Relationship? What relationship? I'm not your girlfriend. Relationships are your mother's shtick. I'm your father."

A relationship does grow in the film, however, between Seth and Abby (Nia Long), the receptionist, and although it eventually has a lot to do with the plot, what I admired was the way Younger writes their scenes so that they actually share hopes, dreams, backgrounds, and insecurities instead of falling into automatic movie passion. When she touches his hand, it is at the end of a scene during which she empathizes with him.

Because of the routine racism at the firm, Seth observes it must not be a comfortable place for a black woman to work. Abby points out she makes $80,000 a year and is supporting a sick mother. Case closed, with no long, anguished dramaturgy over interracial dating;

they like each other, and have evolved beyond racial walls. Younger's handling of their scenes shames movies where the woman exists only to be the other person in the sex scene.

The acting is good all around. A few days ago I saw Vin Diesel as a vicious prisoner in the space opera *Pitch Black,* and now here he is, still tough, still with the shaved head, but now the only guy at the brokerage that Seth really likes and trusts enough to appeal to. Diesel is interesting. Something will come of him.

Boiler Room isn't perfect. The film's ending is a little too busy; it's too contrived the way Abby doesn't tell Seth something he needs to know; there's a scene where a man calls her by name and Seth leaps to a conclusion when in fact that man would have every reason to know her name; and I am still not sure exactly what kind of a deal Seth was trying to talk his father into in their crucial evening meeting. But those are all thoughts I had afterward. During the movie I was wound up with tension and involvement, all the more so because the characters are all complex and guilty, the good as well as the bad, and we can understand why everyone in the movie does what they do. Would we? Depends.

The Bone Collector ★ ★
R, 118 m., 1999

Denzel Washington (Lincoln Rhyme), Angelina Jolie (Amelia Donaghy), Queen Latifah (Thelma), Michael Rooker (Captain Howard Cheney), Mike McGlone (Detective Kenny Solomon), Luis Guzman (Eddie Ortiz), Ed O'Neill (Lieutenant Paulie Sellitto), Leland Orser (Richard Thompson), John Benjamin Hickey (Dr. Barry Lehman). Directed by Phillip Noyce and produced by Martin Bregman, Louis A. Stroller, and Michael Bregman. Screenplay by Jeremy Iacone, based on the book by Jeffery Deaver.

The Bone Collector is assembled from off-the-shelf thriller contrivances, likable characters, and utter absurdity, with one of those scores that's the musical equivalent of trying to scrape the burnt meat off the bottom of the pot: *Unnngh! Unnngh! Unnngh!* Its big romantic scene has the girl cop caressing the index finger of the boy cop, which is the only part of him below the neck that still has any feeling. Freud has a lot to atone for.

The movie is a peculiar experience to sit through, because the quality of the acting is so much better than the material deserves. Denzel Washington and Angelina Jolie create characters we really like; there's chemistry when they're together, and they're surrounded by the good energy of supporting players like Queen Latifah, Luis Guzman, and Ed O'Neill. It's sad watching them wade through one of those plots where a depraved serial killer leads everyone in a find-the-corpse version of "Where's Waldo?"

Washington plays Lincoln Rhyme, a hero cop who has written twelve books on crime-scene forensics. He is paralyzed by a falling beam on the job: "I have one finger, two shoulders, and a brain." He occupies a bed in his Manhattan loft, which is one of those rent-controlled movie apartments large enough to house an entire task force for a serial killer manhunt (which it does—his buddies move in with their desks and computers). Rhyme is tended by a nurse named Thelma (Queen Latifah), who slaps an oxygen mask on him and chants "now breathe with me" when he goes into spasms. He manipulates his bed, his TV, his computer, and various analytical devices with a remote-control breathing tube and an extremely versatile one-button mouse.

We meet a beat cop named Amelia Donaghy (Angelina Jolie). She is the first on the scene of a gruesome murder: A man buried in gravel, with only his hand showing. One finger is amputated; on its stump is his wife's wedding ring. We know right away the killer is a contestant in the ever-escalating Hollywood Serial Killer sweepstakes, in which villains don't simply kill, but spend the time and patience of a set decorator on arranging the crime scene. No six Agatha Christie mysteries contain as many clues, each one lovingly placed by hand, as this guy leaves.

Some of them are very, very easy to miss, consisting of microscopic bits of paper about the size of *this* word, which, when pieced together by the two cops, lead to a used-book store where, wouldn't you know, a lot of books tumble from a top shelf and Amelia is able to turn to the very page where the next murder is illustrated. Just think. If she hadn't stumbled over that rare volume, we might have been denied a scene where a father drowns but his young daughter is resuscitated—for no dramatic purpose, mind you, since she says nothing and is never seen again, but simply so sentimentalists in the audience can think, "Whew! At least she didn't drown!" In a movie where a man gets his face eaten off by rats, these humanitarian interludes are touching.

Most of the plot consists of a series of laboriously contrived setups requiring the young woman to enter dark, dangerous places all by herself, her flashlight penetrating a Spielbergian haze that makes its beam visible. She walks into subterranean rat holes and abandoned factories where the homicidal maniac is, hopefully, lurking. She goes in alone so as not to disturb the forensics of the crime scene. If she gets killed, I guess the next cop goes in alone, too, to preserve her scene.

These Women in Danger thriller units alternate with the obligatory Superior Officer Who Is Always Angry, Wrong, and a Pig. This thankless role is played by Michael Rooker, who is required to be mistaken about everything, and who keeps trying to put Amelia under arrest, apparently on charges of brilliant police work. He's the obvious suspect, which means—well, you know what it means. Most movies with a zillion clues have the good manners to supply a couple that are helpful. This movie's villain appears so arbitrarily he must have been a temp worker, in for the day.

The Borrowers ★ ★ ★
PG, 83 m., 1998

John Goodman (Ocious Potter), Jim Broadbent (Pod Clock), Celia Imrie (Homily Clock), Flora Newbigin (Arrietty Clock), Tom Felton (Peagreen Clock), Aden Gillett (Joe Lender), Mark Williams (Exterminator Jeff), Bradley Pierce (Pete Lender), Hugh Laurie (Officer Steady), Raymond Pickard (Spiller), Ruby Wax (Town Hall Clerk), Doon Mackichan (Victoria Lender). Directed by Peter Hewitt and produced by Tim Bevan, Eric Fellner, and Rachel Talalay. Screenplay by Gavin Scott and John Kamps, based on the novels by Mary Norton.

The Borrowers is a charming, whimsical family adventure about little people who live in the walls and under the floors of big people's houses, and support themselves by stealing— excuse me, "borrowing"—the necessities of life. Their needs are small: One pea is enough to make a cup of pea soup. They're the ones to blame for all those items that go missing: buttons, cuff links, salt shakers. Ever notice how ice cream disappears from the freezer?

Borrowing and Borrowers are the inventions of the British author Mary Norton, whose books have been adapted twice into TV movies, and now inspire this big-screen, big-budget version with special effects so amusing it's like *Toy Story* has come to life.

As the movie opens, two children of the tiny Clock family (average height: four inches) are on an expedition to the kitchen of the Lenders, the "beings" whose house they inhabit. The kids want ice cream, but things go wrong and one is trapped inside the freezing compartment. It's up to their dad, Pod Clock (Jim Broadbent), to rescue the kid with an emergency trip up the ice-cube chute—and when cubes come crashing down, they look like boulders.

The Lender family is in trouble. An aged aunt left them their house, but after her death the will is missing, and an evil lawyer (John Goodman) plans to destroy the house and build condos. But the Borrower kids get their hands on the will, and the lawyer comes after them with an exterminator.

The plot, and there's a lot more of it, is simply a way to lead us from one wonderfully imagined set after another. Like *The Incredible Shrinking Man* (and Lily Tomlin's shrinking woman), the Clocks live in a world where everyday items look gargantuan: A birthday candle is as big as a torch. Some of the effects will also remind you of *Honey, I Shrunk the Kids*, but the charm comes in the way *The Borrowers* makes its world look like a timeless storybook. The Lenders' new neighborhood looks like a British factory town, for example, but the skyline is an (obvious) matte painting of a metropolis of the future.

The humor is physical. Goodman, as the lawyer, gets a face full of insecticide, is nearly electrocuted, and has all kinds of things bounce off his head. Little Peagreen Clock (Tom Felton) has a harrowing time in a milk bottling plant (he's trapped in a bottle that's filled with milk and capped shut—a challenge for Houdini). Exterminator Jeff (Mark Williams) has a bloodhound that feeds on cheese and stinks up the place. And all of the Clocks face terrifying dangers, as when the kids fall out the bottom of a moving truck, and are almost sucked into a vacuum cleaner.

The film is wisely modest in its scope: It sets up the situation, involves us, has fun with the special effects and the cliffhanging adventures, and is over in eighty-three minutes. If the action and the physical humor are designed to appeal to kids, the look of the film will impress adults who know what to look for. The director, Peter Hewitt, made *Bill & Ted's Bogus Adventure* (1991) and exhibits the same wild visual imagination this time.

Consider the possibilities, for example, when little Peagreen is desperately clinging to a lightbulb, and the evil lawyer turns on the light. How long can he hang on before the bulb heats up? Can his sister rescue him with that spring-loaded retractable tape measure? There's something you don't see every day.

Bowfinger ★ ★ ★ ½
PG-13, 97 m., 1999

Steve Martin (Bowfinger), Eddie Murphy (Kit Ramsey), Eddie Murphy (Jiff), Heather Graham (Daisy), Christine Baranski (Carol), Jamie Kennedy (Dave), Barry Newman (Kit's Agent), Adam Alexi-Malle (Afrim). Directed by Frank Oz and produced by Brian Grazer. Screenplay by Steve Martin.

It is a plan of audacity and madness: Bowfinger, a low-rent movie producer, will make a film with a top Hollywood action star, and the star won't even know he's making the picture. "He doesn't like to see the camera, and he never talks to his fellow actors," Bowfinger (Steve Martin) tells his trusting crew. "We'll use a hidden camera." The movie, to be titled *Chubby Rain*, will be about aliens in raindrops.

The big star, named Kit Ramsey (Eddie Murphy), is an ideal choice for this strategy, because he's crazy enough to believe in strange encounters. He's a member of Mind Head, a cult that recruits insecure Hollywood types, gives them little white pyramid hats to wear, and pumps them full of New Age babble. And

Bowfinger's actors and crew want to believe him, because this is as close as they'll ever get to being in a movie.

Bowfinger, written by Martin and directed by Frank Oz *(Little Shop of Horrors),* understands how deeply people yearn to be in the movies, and how fame can make you peculiar. Like Mel Brooks's *The Producers,* it's about fringe players who strike out boldly for the big time. The shabby frame house on a dead-end street has a sign outside promoting glorious enterprises ("Bowfinger International Pictures"), but inside everything is debt, desperation, and dreams.

Bowfinger is a bottom-feeder with a coterie even more hapless than he is. His screenplay is by his Iranian accountant, Afrim (Adam Alexi-Malle). His flunky is Dave (Jaime Kennedy), who specializes in being deceived because otherwise he would have nothing at all to believe in. His leading actress, Carol (Christine Baranski), has been kept on hold for years. "We'll hire the best crew we can afford!" Bowfinger declares, backing his vehicle up to the Mexican border and loading four illegal immigrants. And straight off the bus, swinging her suitcase, her lips parted with desire, comes Daisy (Heather Graham), an Ohio girl who's prepared to sleep her way to the top but didn't realize she'd start so close to the bottom.

All these characters are like an accident waiting to happen to Kit Ramsey, hilariously played by Eddie Murphy in his third best comic performance of recent years. The second best was in *The Nutty Professor.* The best is a second role in this film: As Jiff, a hapless loser hired to be Kit's double, Murphy creates a character of such endearing cluelessness that even in a comedy he generates real affection from the audience.

Murphy makes Kit into a loudmouthed image-monger with a racial chip on his shoulder; complaining about Arnold's "I'll be back" and Clint's "Make my day," he says, "The white man gets all the best catchphrases." Terrified by the smallest detail of daily living, he has frequent sessions with his Mind Head guru (Terence Stamp), who leads him patiently through reminders of good and bad behavior (one of his problems is too funny for me to spoil with even a hint).

But it's as Jiff that Murphy gets his biggest

laughs. Here is a man so grateful to be in a film, so disbelieving that he has been singled out for stardom, that he dutifully risks his life to walk across a busy expressway. Murphy shows here, as he did in *The Nutty Professor* and on *Saturday Night Live,* a gift for creating new characters out of familiar materials. Yes, Jiff looks like Kit (that's why he got the job as a double), but the person inside is completely fresh and new, and has his own personality and appeal. Although Murphy is not usually referred to as a great actor (and comedians are never taken as seriously as they should be), how many other actors, however distinguished, could create Jiff out of whole cloth and make him such a convincing and funny original?

Martin is also at the top of his form, especially in an early scene where he pitches his project to a powerful producer (Robert Downey Jr.). Martin steals a suit and a car to make an impressive entrance at the restaurant where Downey is having a power lunch, but undercuts the effect a little by ripping out the car phone and trying to use it like a cell phone—staging a fake call for Downey to overhear. Downey handles this scene perfectly, right down to his subdued doubletake when he sees the cord dangling from the end of the phone. His performance is based on the truth that strange and desperate pitches are lobbed at producers every day, some of them no less bizarre than this one. Instead of overreacting to Martin's craziness, Downey plays the scene to humor this guy.

Bowfinger is one of those comedies where everything works, where the premise is not just a hook but the starting point for a story that keeps developing and revealing new surprises. Like a lot of Steve Martin's other writing, it is also gentle and good-natured: He isn't a savage ironist or a vulgarian, and when he makes us laugh, it's usually about things that are really funny. Shell-shocked by gross and grosser comedies, we can turn to *Bowfinger* with merciful relief.

The Boxer ★ ★ ★
R, 105 m., 1998

Daniel Day-Lewis (Danny Flynn), Emily Watson (Maggie), Brian Cox (Joe Hamill), Ken Stott (Ike Weir), Gerard McSorley (Harry), Eleanor Methven (Patsy), Ciaran Fitzgerald (Liam), Kenneth Cranham (Matt McGuire). Directed by Jim Sheridan and produced by Sheridan and Arthur Lappin. Screenplay by Sheridan and Terry George.

The Boxer is the latest of Jim Sheridan's six rich stories about Ireland, and in some ways the most unusual. Although it seems to borrow the pattern of the traditional boxing movie, the boxer here is not the usual self-destructive character, but the center of maturity and balance in a community in turmoil. And although the film's lovers are star-crossed, they are not blind; they're too old and scarred to throw all caution to the wind.

The film takes place in a Belfast hungering for peace. It stars Daniel Day-Lewis (also the star of Sheridan's *My Left Foot* and *In the Name of the Father*) as Danny Flynn, an IRA member who was a promising boxer until he was imprisoned at eighteen for terrorist associations. Refusing to name his fellow IRA men, he was held captive for fourteen years, and is now back on the streets in a city where Joe Hamill (Brian Cox), the ranking IRA man, is trying to negotiate a truce with the British.

Danny was in love as a young man with Maggie (Emily Watson), Hamill's daughter. After his imprisonment, she married another IRA man, who is now in prison. IRA rules threaten death for any man caught having an affair with a prisoner's wife; Danny and Maggie, who are still drawn to one another, are in danger—especially from the militant IRA faction led by Harry (Gerard McSorley), a hothead who hates Hamill, fears Danny, and sees the forbidden relationship as a way to destroy them both.

Danny Flynn is no longer interested in sectarian hatred. He joins his old boxing manager, an alcoholic named Ike (Ken Stott), in reopening a local gymnasium for young boxers of all faiths. And he goes into training for a series of bouts himself, becoming a figurehead for those in the community who want to heal old wounds and move ahead. The story, which is constructed in a solid, craftsmanlike way by Sheridan and his cowriter, Terry George, balances these three elements—the IRA, boxing, and romance—in such a way that if elements of one goes wrong the other two may fail as well.

Sheridan is a leading figure in the renaissance of Irish films. His directing credits include *My Left Foot* (1989), with Day-Lewis in an extraordinary performance as Christy Brown, the poet who was trapped inside a paralyzed body; *The Field* (1990), which won Richard Harris an Oscar nomination as a man who reclaims land from a rocky coast; and *In the Name of the Father* (1993), nominated for seven Oscars and starring Day-Lewis as a Belfast man wrongly accused of bombings. He also cowrote Mike Newell's comedy *Into the West* (1993) and Terry George's *Some Mother's Son* (1996), about the mothers of hunger strikers in the Maze prison. George is his frequent collaborator.

His films are never exercises in easy morality, and *The Boxer* is more complex than most. Apart from Danny and Maggie, the film's key figure is Joe Hamill, played with a quiet, sad, strong center by Brian Cox as a man who has, in his time, killed and ordered killings—but has the character to lead his organization toward peace. Harry, the bitter militant, lost a child to the British and accepts no compromise; if Danny and Maggie act on their love for one another, they may destroy the whole delicate balance.

Against the political material, the boxing acts as a setting more than a world. We see how hot passions are passed along to a younger generation, how boxing can be a substitute for warfare, and (in an almost surrealistic scene in a black-tie private club in London) how the rich pay the poor to bloody themselves.

What's fascinating is the delicacy of the relationship between Maggie and Danny. Played by two actors who have obviously given a lot of thought to the characters, they know that love is not always the most important thing in the world, that grand gestures can be futile ones, that more important things are at stake than their own gratification, that perhaps in the times they live in romance is not possible. And yet they hunger. Day-Lewis and Watson (from *Breaking the Waves*) are smart actors playing smart people; when they make reckless gestures, it is from despair or nihilism, not stupidity.

The film's weakness is in its ambition: It covers too much ground. Perhaps—I hate to say it—the boxing material is unnecessary,

and if the film had focused only on the newly released prisoner, his dangerous love, and the crisis in IRA politics, it might have been cleaner and stronger. There are three fights in the film, and the outcome of all three is really just a distraction from the much more important struggles going on outside the ring.

Boys and Girls ★ ★
PG-13, 100 m., 2000

Freddie Prinze Jr. (Ryan), Claire Forlani (Jennifer), Jason Biggs (Hunter), Heather Donahue (Megan), Amanda Detmer (Amy). Directed by Robert Iscove and produced by Sue Baden-Powell, Harvey Weinstein, and Bob Weinstein. Screenplay by the Drews (Andrew Lowery and Andrew Miller).

Boys and Girls is about a boy and a girl who meet when they are both about twelve and carry on a love-hate relationship for the next ten years, until they finally sleep with each other, with disastrous results. It is clear they're in love, but after that night of bliss a great chill forms between them, and she doesn't understand why.

I thought I did understand why. The other day on the radio, Terry Gross was interviewing Jeffrey Eugenides, the author of *The Virgin Suicides*. In that novel, now made into a movie by Sofia Coppola, a boy and a girl have sex in the middle of the football field on prom night—and the next morning, when she awakes, she is alone. Trip, the boy, is the narrator, and tells us: "I liked her a lot. But out there on the football field, it was different."

Terry Gross gently grilled Eugenides about that passage. She was interested, she said, because Trip's behavior was—well, not atypical of boys after sexual conquests, and a lot of women, courted and then dumped, were curious about that cruel male pattern. Eugenides declined to analyze Trip's behavior. He'd known people like Trip, he said, and he thought it was just the sort of thing Trip would do.

I have a theory to explain such postcoital disillusionment: Boys cannot deal with their dreams made flesh. He has idealized a woman who now turns out to be real, who engages in the same behavior as ordinary women, who allows herself to be despoiled (so he thinks) by his lust, which he has been taught to feel guilty about. He flees in shame and self-disgust. Boys get over this, which is the good news, but by losing their idealism about women, which is the bad news.

This is an excellent theory, but *Boys and Girls* does not use it. Instead, confusing the sexes, it supplies the boy with a motive for his behavior that in the real world would more likely come from a girl. He cut off contact between them, he says, because it was the greatest moment of his life, and he knew then that she was his true love, and when she said it had perhaps been "a mistake," and that they should move on and go back to being "best friends," nothing had ever hurt him more. Of course, she was just trying to say what she thought he wanted to hear, because she really loved him, but . . .

Their dilemma is fueled by the movie convention in which the characters say the wrong things and do not say the right things, and remain baffled by a situation long after it has become clear to us. But then Ryan and Jennifer (for those are their names) are not quick studies anyway. It takes them ten years and countless Meet Cutes before they finally break down and have their first kiss. They specialize in that form of sex most maddening for the audience, "coitus postponus."

They're both awfully nice people. They're played by Freddie Prinze Jr. and Claire Forlani as good and sweet and honest and sensitive, and we like them a lot. We also like his best friend (Jason Biggs) and hers (Amanda Detmer). Perky Heather Donahue, survivor of the *Blair Witch*, gets good screen time as his interim girlfriend. They are so lovable that we earnestly wish they'd grow up and develop more interesting and complex personalities. We are reminded of the theory that American society prolongs adolescence far beyond its natural life span. If these characters were French and engaging in the same dialogue and behavior, we would guess their age at about thirteen.

I was amused by their college majors. He is a structural engineer, as we can see in scenes that invariably show him studying balsa-wood models of bridges with a perplexed expression. After his junior year, the models do not collapse any more, so he must be learning something. She studies Latin. Why? "Because I plan to do postgraduate work in Italy." In the Vatican City, I hope.

Boys and Girls is soothing and harmless, gentle and interminable. It is about two people who might as well fall in love, since fate and the plot have given them nothing else to do and no one else to do it with. Compared to the wisdom and wickedness of *High Fidelity*, this is such a slight movie. It's not that I don't like it. It's that I don't care.

Boys Don't Cry ★ ★ ★ ★
R, 114 m., 1999

Hilary Swank (Brandon Teena), Chloe Sevigny (Lana), Alicia Goranson (Candace), Alison Folland (Kate), Peter Sarsgaard (John), Brendan Sexton III (Tom). Directed by Kimberly Peirce and produced by Eva Kolodner, Jeff Sharp, and John Hart. Screenplay by Peirce and Andy Bienen.

Sex was more interesting when we knew less about it, when we proceeded from murky impulses rather than easy familiarity. Consider the Victorians, slipping off to secret vices, and how much more fun they had than today's Jerry Springer guests ("My girlfriend is a dominatrix"). The intriguing border between the genders must have been more inviting to cross when that was seen as an opportunity rather than a pathology. One of the many virtues of *Boys Don't Cry*, one of the best films of 1999, is that never once does it supply the tiresome phrase, "I am a man trapped in a woman's body." Its motto instead could be, "Girls just wanna have fun."

Teena Brandon doesn't think of herself as a sexual case study; nothing in her background has given her that vocabulary. She is a lonely girl who would rather be a boy, and one day she gets a short haircut, sticks a sock down the front of her jeans, and goes into a bar to try her luck. She is not a transsexual, a lesbian, a cross-dresser, or a member of any other category on the laundry list of sexual identities; she is a girl who thinks of herself as a boy, and when she leaves Lincoln, Nebraska, and moves to the small town of Falls City in 1993, that is how she presents herself. By then she has become Brandon Teena, and we must use the male pronoun in describing him.

All of this is true. There is a documentary, *The Brandon Teena Story*, that came out earlier in 1999 and shows us photographs of Brandon, looking eerily like Hilary Swank, who plays the role in *Boys Don't Cry*. In that film we meet some of the women he dated ("Brandon knew how to treat a woman") and we see the two men later charged with Brandon's rape and, after the local law authorities didn't act seriously on that charge, murder a few days later. Like Matthew Shepard in Wyoming, Brandon died because some violent men are threatened by any challenge to their shaky self-confidence.

Boys Don't Cry is not sociology, however, but a romantic tragedy—a *Romeo and Juliet* set in a Nebraska trailer park. Brandon is not the smartest person on Earth, especially at judging which kinds of risks to take, but he is one of the nicest, and soon he has fallen in love with a Falls City girl named Lana (Chloe Sevigny). For Lana, Brandon is arguably the first nice boy she has ever dated. We meet two of the other local studs, John (Peter Sarsgaard) and Tom (Brendan Sexton III), neither gifted with intelligence, both violent products of brutal backgrounds. They have the same attitude toward women that the gun nut has about prying his dying fingers off the revolver.

The film is about hanging out in gas stations and roller rinks, and lying sprawled on a couch looking with dulled eyes at television, and working at soul-crushing jobs, and about six-packs and country bars and Marlboros. There is a reason country music is sad. Into this wasteland, which is all Lana knows, comes Brandon, who brings her a flower.

The Lana character is crucial to the movie, and although Hilary Swank deserves all praise for her performance as Brandon, it is Chloe Sevigny who provides our entrance into the story. Representing the several women the real Brandon dated, she sees him as a warm, gentle, romantic lover. Does Lana know Brandon is a girl? At some point, certainly. But at what point exactly? There is a stretch when she knows, and yet she doesn't know, because she doesn't want to know; romance is built on illusion, and when we love someone, we love the illusion they have created for us.

Kimberly Peirce, who directed this movie and cowrote it with Andy Bienen, was faced with a project that could have gone wrong in countless ways. She finds the right note. She never cranks the story up above the level it's comfortable with; she doesn't underline the stupidity of the local law-enforcement officials because that's not necessary; she sees Tom and John not as simple killers but as the instruments of deep ignorance and inherited antisocial pathology. (Tom knows he's trouble; he holds his hand in a flame and then cuts himself, explaining, "This helps control the thing inside of me so I don't snap out at people.")

The whole story can be explained this way: Most everybody in it behaves exactly according to their natures. The first time I saw the movie, I was completely absorbed in the characters— the deception, the romance, the betrayal. Only later did I fully realize what a great film it is, a worthy companion to those other masterpieces of death on the prairie, *Badlands* and *In Cold Blood*. This could have been a clinical Movie of the Week, but instead it's a sad song about a free spirit who tried to fly a little too close to the flame.

The Brandon Teena Story ★ ★ ★
NO MPAA RATING, 90 m., 1999

A documentary directed and produced by Susan Muska and Greta Olafsdottir.

Brandon Teena was a "good kisser" and "knew how to treat a woman," we are told, and even after Brandon's secret was revealed—"he" was a biological female born Teena Brandon— there is a certain wistfulness in the memories of her girlfriends. None of the women who dated Brandon seem particularly angry about the deception, and after we've spent some time in the world where they all lived, we begin to understand why: Most of the biological men in *The Brandon Teena Story* are crippled by a vast, stultifying ignorance. No wonder a girl liked a date who sent her flowers and little love notes.

Consider, for example, the sheriff in the rural area where Brandon Teena and two bystanders were shot dead. We hear his words on tape as he interviews Brandon, who was raped by those who would commit the murders a few days later. To hear the interrogation is to hear words shaped by prejudice, hatred, deep sexual incomprehension, and ignorance. I cannot quote most of what the sheriff says—his words are too cruel and graphic—but consider that he is interviewing, not a rapist, but a victim, and you will get some notion of the atmosphere in some corners of the remote Nebraska district where the murders occurred.

The sheriff did not like it one bit that a woman was pretending to be a man. There is the hint that a woman who behaves like this deserves whatever she gets; that it is natural for a red-blooded man to resent any poaching on his phallic preserve. The tapes also preserve the voice of Brandon, who was twenty or twenty-one at the time and sounds very young, insecure, and confused. "I have a sexual identity crisis," we hear at one point.

The documentary includes photos of Brandon, or Teena, at various ages, and although the clothing gradually becomes masculine and the haircut gets shorter, I must say that I never really felt I was looking at a man. Perhaps the deception would have worked only in a rural and small-town world far removed from the idea of gender transitions. The two men who were convicted of the murders were apparently deceived; they considered Brandon a friend, before growing suspicious and brutally stripping their victim of her clothes and, apparently, virginity.

But what about the women Brandon dated? Their testimony remains vague and affectionate. They were not lesbians (and neither was Brandon—who firmly identified with a male identity), but they were responsive to tenderness and caring and "good kissing." One woman in the film dated both one of the murderers and Brandon; given a choice between the narrow-minded dimness of the man and the imagination of someone prepared to cross gender lines, the more attractive choice was obviously Brandon.

The film itself is not slick and accomplished. It plays at times like home video footage, edited together on someone's computer. There are awkward passages of inappropriate music, and repeated shots of the barren winter landscape. Oddly enough, this is an effective style for this material; it captures the banality of the world in which individuality is seen as a threat. The testimony in the film is often flat and colorless (the killers are maddeningly passive and detached). Even the hero, Brandon Teena, was only slowly coming to an understanding of identity and sexuality.

Watching the film, I realized something. It is fashionable to deride TV shows like *Jerry Springer* for their sensational guests ("My boyfriend is really a girl!"). But as I watched *The Brandon Teena Story*, I realized that Brandon lived in a world of extremely limited sexual information, among people who assumed that men are men and women are women, and any violation of that rule calls for the death penalty. To the degree that they have absorbed anything at all from church or society, it is that homosexuals are to be hated. If tabloid TV contains the message that everyone has to make his or her own accommodation with life, sex, and self-image, then it's performing a service. It helps people get used to the idea that some people are different. With a little luck, Jerry Springer might have saved Brandon Teena's life.

Bringing Out the Dead ★ ★ ★ ★
R, 118 m., 1999

Nicolas Cage (Frank), Patricia Arquette (Mary), John Goodman (Larry), Ving Rhames (Marcus), Tom Sizemore (Walls), Marc Anthony (Noel), Cliff Curtis (Cy Coates), Mary Beth Hurt (Nurse Constance). Directed by Martin Scorsese and produced by Scott Rudin and Barbara De Fina. Screenplay by Paul Schrader, based on the novel by Joe Connelly.

"I came to realize that my work was less about saving lives than about bearing witness. I was a grief mop."

The speaker is Frank, a paramedic whose journeys into the abyss of human misery provide the canvas for Martin Scorsese's *Bringing Out the Dead*. There may be happiness somewhere in the city, but the barking voice on Frank's radio doesn't dispatch him there. His job is to arrive at a scene of violence or collapse, and try to bring not only help but encouragement.

"Do you have any music?" he asks the family of a man who seems dead of a heart attack. "I think it helps if you play something he liked." As the old man's Sinatra album plays in the background, he applies the defibrillator to his chest and shouts, "Clear!" The corpse jumps into life like a movie monster. The psychology is sound: Sinatra may not bring the dead to life, but he will give the family something to do, and the song will remind them of their dad's happier times.

Frank is played by Nicolas Cage, seen in the movie's close-up with his eyes narrowed in pain. He cruises the streets of Hell's Kitchen with a series of three copilots, in a three-day stretch during which he drifts in and out of sanity; he has hallucinations of an eighteen-year-old homeless girl named Rose, whose life he failed to save, whose death he wants to redeem. Like Travis Bickle, the hero of Scorsese's *Taxi Driver* (1976), Frank travels the night streets like a boatman on the River Styx, while steam rises from manholes as if from the fires below. Travis wanted to save those who did not want saving. Frank finds those who desperately want help, but usually he is powerless.

The movie is based on a novel by Joe Connelly, himself once a New York paramedic. The screenplay by Paul Schrader is another chapter in the most fruitful writer-director collaboration of the quarter-century *(Taxi Driver, Raging Bull, The Last Temptation of Christ)*. The film wisely has no real plot, because the ambulance driver's days have no beginning or goal, but are a limbo of extended horror. At one point he hallucinates that he is helping pull people's bodies up out of the pavement, freeing them.

To look at *Bringing Out the Dead*—to look, indeed, at almost any Scorsese film—is to be reminded that film can touch us urgently and deeply. Scorsese is never on autopilot, never panders, never sells out, always goes for broke; to watch his films is to see a man risking his talent, not simply exercising it. He makes movies as well as they can be made, and I agree with an observation on the Harry Knowles Web site: You can enjoy a Scorsese film with the sound off, or with the sound on and the picture off.

Now look at *Bringing Out the Dead.* Three days in Frank's life. The first day his copilot is Larry (John Goodman), who deals with the grief by focusing on where his next meal is coming from. To Larry, it's a job, and you can't let it get to you. Day two, Larry works with Marcus (Ving Rhames), who is a gospel Christian and uses emergencies as an opportunity to demonstrate the power of Jesus; bringing one

man back to life, he presents it as a miracle. On the third day, the day Christ rose from the dead, Frank's partner is Walls (Tom Sizemore), who is coming apart at the seams and wreaks havoc on hapless patients.

Haunting Frank's thoughts as he cruises with these guys are two women. One is Rose, whose face peers up at him from every street corner. The other is Mary (Patricia Arquette), the daughter of the man who liked Sinatra. After her dad is transferred to an intensive care unit, his life, such as it is, consists of dying and being shocked back to life, fourteen times one day, until Frank asks, "If he gets out, are you gonna follow him around with a defibrillator?" Mary is a former druggie, now clean and straight, and Frank—well, I was going to say he loves her, but this isn't one of those autopilot movies where the action hero has a romance in between the bloodshed. No, it's not love; it's need. He thinks they can save each other.

Scorsese assembles the film as levels in an inferno. It contains some of his most brilliant sequences, particularly two visits to a high-rise drug house named the Oasis, where a dealer named Cy (Cliff Curtis) offers relief and surcease. Mary goes there one night when she cannot stand any more pain, and Frank follows to save her; that sets up a later sequence in which Frank treats Cy while he is dangling near death.

All suffering ends at the same place, the emergency room of the hospital nicknamed Our Lady of Perpetual Misery, where the receiving nurse (Mary Beth Hurt) knows most of the regulars by name. She dispenses the same advice in many forms: Stop what you're doing. But they don't listen, and will be back again. Noel (Marc Anthony) stands for many street people, tied to a gurney, screaming for a glass of water, hour after hour, while the ER team labors to plug the leaks, gaps, and wounds of a night in the city. They make long stories short: "This guy's plant food."

Nicolas Cage is an actor of great style and heedless emotional availability: He will go anywhere for a role, and this film is his best since *Leaving Las Vegas.* I like the subtle way he and Scorsese embody what Frank has learned on the job, the little verbal formulas and quiet asides that help the bystanders at suffering. He embodies the tragedy of a man who has necessary work and is good at it, but in a job that is never, ever over.

Bringing Out the Dead is an antidote to the immature intoxication with violence in a film like *Fight Club.* It is not fun to get hit, it is not redeeming to cause pain, it does not make you a man when you fight, because fights are an admission that you are not smart enough to survive by your wits. *Fight Club* makes a cartoon of the mean streets that Scorsese sees unblinkingly.

Brokedown Palace ★ ★ ★
PG-13, 100 m., 1999

Claire Danes (Alice), Kate Beckinsale (Darlene), Bill Pullman (Yankee Hank), Daniel Lapaine (Nick Parks), Lou Diamond Phillips (U.S. Official), Jacqui Kim (Yon Green). Directed by Jonathan Kaplan and produced by Adam Fields and A. Kitman Ho. Screenplay by Fields and David Arata.

Brokedown Palace tells the story of two American teenage girls who are sentenced to spend most of their lives in a Thai prison. Their crimes are apparently harmless: being silly and naive. Yet it is a fact that they had drugs in their possession when they passed through Thai customs on their way to Hong Kong, and that is a practice the Thai authorities do not find amusing.

The girls are Alice (Claire Danes) and Darlene (Kate Beckinsale). They're high school buddies who plan a graduation trip to Hawaii, and then secretly change their designation to the more exotic Thailand without telling their parents. Once there, they find a $6 guest house and sneak into a luxury hotel to sip expensive drinks at poolside. They get caught trying to charge the bill to the wrong room, but they are saved from trouble by a friendly Australian, Nick (Daniel Lapaine), who takes care of the bill and makes smooth romantic moves, first toward Alice, then toward Darlene.

By now alarm bells are going off among moviegoers who have seen *Return to Paradise* (1998), not to mention *Midnight Express* (1978). A lot of foreign countries sentence drug traffickers to life, or death, and trusting Americans are sitting ducks for smooth-talking smugglers who take advantage of them.

Return to Paradise posed a fascinating moral dilemma, since three friends went to Malaysia but two were already safe back in the United States when the third was busted for possession of hashish. The deal: He'll get death, because of the amount in his possession. But if both friends return to share the blame, they'll all get three years. If one returns, he and the prisoner will get six years. If you're selfish but don't want your friend to die, obviously the best deal for you is if the other guy goes back while you stay at home.

Brokedown Palace doesn't offer a simple moral equation like that—at least not at first, although the ending sets a challenge for the audience. The two girls are sentenced to thirty-three years, and in desperation find a local American lawyer named Yankee Hank (Bill Pullman) who agrees to take their case. (As he's on the phone with one of their fathers, he doodles how much money he can ask for. $40,000? $30,000?) He's greedy but honest, and doubtful about a lot of things, including the story the girls tell about the friendly Australian.

The heart of the film is in the performances of Danes and Beckinsale after they're sent to prison. Consider. One moment your entire life is ahead of you: college, marriage, kids, a career, a home, middle age, fulfillment. The next moment all of that has been taken away. Your future has been locked in a foreign prison. One poignant scene shows the girls shouting across an open space to visitors—friends and relatives from home, whose lives continue while theirs are on hold.

The movie, directed by Jonathan Kaplan *(Over the Edge, The Accused)* plays the material straight, to great effect. There are no sneaky plot tricks or grandstand plays, and the reasoning of a Thai judge, during an appeal hearing, is devastating in its logic. There is, however, an interesting development at the end, which I will not even hint at, which requires the audience to decide whether or not something can be believed, and what exactly are the motives behind it.

Claire Danes, clear-eyed and straightforward, plays Alice as just a little more complex than her friend. She comes from a poorer background, has a reputation for getting into trouble, and doesn't seem trustworthy to Darlene's dad. Pullman, weighing the pros and cons, dealing with a cynical and unhelpful U.S. embassy official (Lou Diamond Phillips), has seen cases like this before. The girls should have known not to trust strangers, to be suspicious of a free trip to Hong Kong, to never let their luggage out of the sight of both of them. Should have. Now they have a lot of time to think about that.

Broken Vessels ★ ★ ★
R, 90 m., 1999

Todd Field (Jimmy), Jason London (Tom), Susan Traylor (Susy), James Hong (Mr. Chen), Patrick Cranshaw (Gramps), Roxana Zal (Elizabeth). Directed by Scott Ziehl and produced by Ziehl and Roxana Zal. Screenplay by Ziehl, David Baer, and John McMahon.

"I could have gotten off the train before it left the station," Tom muses early in *Broken Vessels*. "There were plenty of warnings." He has moved from Altoona to Los Angeles and taken a job as a rescue squad member, touring the city in an ambulance with his new partner, Jimmy— who, it is said, is a gifted paramedic but has gone through a lot of partners.

The two men are like freelance pirates, sailing the city streets, grabbing bodies instead of plunder. Jimmy "has his own system," Tom learns. It includes rest stops in topless bars, sex in the back of the ambulance, buys from street-corner cocaine dealers, and direct methods with unruly clients (one injured man who goes berserk in the back of the ambulance gets a jolt to the head from a fibrillator).

Tom is played by Jason London as a man who wants to do right but lacks the will or the knack. He's swept into the world of Jimmy (Todd Field), who is smart, competent, and has the tunnel vision of the addict. Everything he does falls into two categories: pre-using and post-using. Working on the rescue squad gives him a free pass to roam the city streets, and a certain invulnerability. And he knows the places to hide the ambulance, like culverts and cemeteries. Work is the price he has to pay for the use of the job.

The film, tightly wound and convincing, was directed, coproduced, and cowritten by Scott Ziehl. It has passages of dark humor, but life in the ambulance is not zany; even when

Tom and Jimmy do funny or crazy things, it's because of a desperation that begins as a sort of thrumming beneath the action, and ends as raw desperation. Jimmy has a twisted view of drugs and honor, as if it's his duty to use. The symbol of his addiction is Gramps (Patrick Cranshaw), an old man who has needed his daily fix of heroin since long before Jimmy was born. For Gramps, the ambulance makes house calls. And it is perhaps no accident that the heroin intended for Gramps's last fix becomes Jimmy's first.

If cocaine makes life unmanageable, heroin is no improvement, and soon Jimmy and Tom need more money than they have. Their daily lives are disintegrating around them. Tom's gay roommate throws him out after he throws up in the goldfish tank. He moves in with Jimmy. His next-door neighbor is a speed freak named Susy (Susan Traylor, in a performance beautifully edged with hysteria). Soon she has an occupant for the shed behind her house: a weird little guy and his drug factory. The job meanwhile comes down to futile threats from their boss (James Hong) and police questioning about property stolen from patients. The police don't seem very curious.

Susy has a roommate named Elizabeth (Roxana Zal) for about five minutes, before Elizabeth sizes up the situation and moves out. Tom likes Elizabeth, dates her a little, forgets her in the confusion of drugs, calls her in need and desperation. He feels so abandoned and lonely in the middle of the night, alone and with the sick feeling of needing drugs. Elizabeth sensibly tells him he needs help. He does, but the only help he can imagine is to find more drugs. This is like treating a cold with virus injections.

The story arc of *Broken Vessels* is familiar from a lot of other movies about drug users who crash and burn. They don't use to feel good. They use to stop feeling awful. Relief is a window that opens briefly after using, and then slams shut again. What makes the movie special is the way both lead actors find the right quiet notes for their performances. No prizes here for chewing the wallpaper; they're ordinary, quiet, smart guys whose best thinking can't get them out of the trap they've laid for themselves.

Buena Vista Social Club ★ ★
NO MPAA RATING, 101 m., 1999

A documentary featuring Ibrahim Ferrer, Compay Segundo, Ruben Gonzalez, Omara Portuondo, Luis Barzaga, Joachim Cooder, Ry Cooder, Pio Leyva, Manuel "Puntillita" Licea, Eliades Ochoa, and others. Directed by Wim Wenders and produced by Ulrich Felsberg and Deepak Nayar.

There's an overwhelming temptation to praise *Buena Vista Social Club* simply because it is about legendary performers and wonderful music. But that praise should really go to the Grammy-winning 1997 album of the same name, produced by Ry Cooder, who rediscovered an almost vanished generation of Cuban musicians in Havana and assembled them for a last hurrah. It is a touching story, and the musicians (some more than ninety years old) still have fire and grace onstage, but, man, does the style of this documentary get in the way.

Wim Wenders, who directed it, seems to have given his cameramen a few basic instructions that they follow over and over again for the entire movie. One shot of a camera circling a musician on a chair in a big room would have been splendid—especially since the interiors in the movie are of beautiful, decaying Havana locations. But the camera circles obsessively. In big empty rooms, in bars, on verandahs, in rehearsal halls, in a recording studio, it circles and circles annoyingly.

When it isn't circling, there's another problem. The credits say the film was made on two digital cameras; one seems to have been handheld by a cameraman with the shakes. One camera is level, smooth, and confident. The other has the jitters so badly that you can sense the editor cutting away from it as much as he can. The unstable handheld look can be an interesting choice in certain situations. As a style, it becomes a problem.

Then there is the question of how to show Ry Cooder in the film. Yes, he is the godfather of this project, and there would be no film and no Buena Vista Social Club without him. But the filmmakers seem too much in awe of him. When the musicians give concerts in Amsterdam and at Carnegie Hall, the onstage footage keeps returning to a single repetitive camera move: focus on musician, then pan up to Ry Cooder smiling benevolently. He is positioned in the top row of the onstage musicians, on the strong visual axis just to the right of center, and the camera keeps glancing up at him as if for approval from the teacher.

Then there's the problem of presenting the music. I didn't expect a concert film, but I did expect that I might be allowed to hear one song all the way through, with the cutting dictated by the music. No luck. The songs are intercut with biographical testaments from the veteran musicians. These in themselves are splendid: The stories of how these performers grew up, learned their music, flourished, were forgotten, and then rediscovered are sometimes amazing, always moving (as when we reflect that the singer Ibrahim Ferrer, "the Cuban Nat King Cole," dominating the orchestra and the audience at Carnegie Hall, was shining shoes when Cooder found him). But the movie's strategy is to show them in performance, then cut away to their story, leaving the songs stranded.

When the Social Club gets to New York, the Carnegie Hall concert should have been the climax. (Consider the emotional payoff of the not dissimilar *The Weavers: Wasn't That a Time!* Consider, too, Terry Zwigoff's magical documentary *Louie Bluie*, about Martin, Bogan, and the Armstrongs—also elderly musicians who were belatedly rediscovered.) Instead of pausing sometimes to simply listen to the music, Wenders intercuts Carnegie Hall with shots of the musicians visiting the Empire State Building and Times Square, looking in souvenir shop windows, talking about how wonderful it all is, as if they were on a school trip. This is condescending. The movie reminded me of a concert where somebody behind me is talking and moving around all the time. Let them play.

When they do, it is magical. We meet not only Ferrer, who has all of the ease and charisma of a born star, but a pianist named Ruben Gonzalez, who is eighty years old and complains of arthritis but has a strong and unmistakable piano style; Compay Segundo, a guitarist and singer, over ninety; and Omara Portuondo, "the Cuban Edith Piaf," luxuriating in the joy of the music. And many more; the faces become familiar, the music becomes seductive.

Wenders's visual texture for the film is interesting. He overexposes slightly with moderately high contrasts and then washes the picture out a little; it's like the watercolor technique where you finish the painting, let it dry, and then let it soak briefly in a pan of water so that the strong colors remain and others become more faded. It's a nice surface for the film, and appropriate.

But there's that constant humming undercurrent of adulation for Ry Cooder—who I am sure is a good man and a gifted musician and does not need to be shown so constantly that his presence becomes like product placement. I was reminded uncannily of those old *Amateur Hour* programs on TV, where the emcee beamed benevolently on one act after another. The musicians of the Buena Vista Social Club needed to be rediscovered, but that's all they needed: They came ready to play. I bought the album. You should, too. If this movie comes out on DVD, I hope the other side contains bonus concert footage.

Buffalo '66 ★ ★ ★
NO MPAA RATING, 110 m., 1998

Vincent Gallo (Billy Brown), Christina Ricci (Layla), Anjelica Huston (Janet Brown), Ben Gazzara (Jimmy Brown), Kevin Corrigan (Goon), Mickey Rourke (Bookie), Roseanna Arquette (Wendy), Jan-Michael Vincent (Sonny). Directed by Vincent Gallo and produced by Chris Hanley. Screenplay by Gallo.

Vincent Gallo's *Buffalo '66* plays like a collision between a lot of half-baked visual ideas, and a deep and urgent need. That makes it interesting. Most movies don't bake their visual ideas at all, nor do we sense that their makers have had to choose between filming them or imploding. Oh, and the film contains an astonishing performance by Christina Ricci, who seems to have been assigned a portion of the screen where she can do whatever she wants.

Gallo plays Billy Brown, who is being released from prison when we first see him. He waits outside a long time, and then knocks on the gates, asking a guard if he can come back in to use the john. Turned away, urgently needing to pee, he takes a bus into town, is turned away at the bus station and the restaurant, and then barges into a tap-dancing class. While he's there, he grabs one of the students, drags her out, tells her she's being kidnapped, and says she has to pretend to be his wife when he goes to visit his parents.

This is Layla (Christina Ricci), who is dressed like Barbie as a hooker, and takes the kidnapping in stride: "Are your parents vegetarians? I hope so, because I don't eat meat—ever!" At Billy's house, we meet the parents. Dad (Ben Gazzara) glowers but doesn't speak. Mom (Anjelica Huston) has her eyes glued to the TV, where a tape of an old Buffalo Bills game is playing. She named her son for the team. The display of family photos includes Jack Kemp and O. J. Simpson. Eventually Dad warms up to Layla, grabbing her clumsily and cooing, "I love my little daughter. Daddy loves his daughter." Later, he mimes to a record by a Sinatra soundalike (actually, we learn from the end titles, Gallo's father).

Gallo shot these scenes in his childhood home in Buffalo, and has said the parents are based on his own. His memories are like an open wound. Consider, for example, a flashback where his mother *knows* he's allergic to chocolate doughnuts and feeds him some anyway, and his face swells up like the Pillsbury doughboy. The movie plays like revenge time.

But that's not all. Gallo, an angular and unshaven man with a haunted look, has acted for such offbeat and experimental directors as Abel Ferrara *(The Funeral)*, Bille August *(The House of the Spirits)*, Mika Kaurismaki *(L.A. Without a Map)*, Emir Kusturica *(Arizona Dream)*, Claire Denis *(Nenette and Boni)*, Mira Nair *(The Perez Family)*, and Kiefer Sutherland *(Truth or Consequences, N.M.)*. His career is proof that it is possible to work steadily and well in challenging and original films by gifted directors and remain almost completely unknown. Now, directing his own film at last, he seems filled with ideas that he wants to realize—sequences that spring to life even though they may have precarious attachments to the rest of the film.

Consider his visit to the local bowling alley, still with Ricci as his hostage (he has named her "Wendy Balsam" and explained that they met "while overseas on assignment for the CIA"). Although he was in prison for six or seven years, his old locker is still waiting for him (when they don't change your lock after you're sent to the Big House, that's a bowling alley with a heart). He bowls, brilliantly. She, dressed like a finalist for Little Miss Sunbeam, does a tap-dance routine right there on the hardwood, while a spotlight follows her. What's this scene doing in *Buffalo '66*? Maybe Gallo didn't have any other movie he could put it in.

We gradually learn a little of Billy's story, although nothing of Layla's. Carried away by the family obsession with the Buffalo Bills, he bet $10,000 he didn't have and lost it on a crucial missed field goal. His bookie (Mickey Rourke) forgave the debt on the condition he do the prison time for another guy. Now he wants revenge. Not on the bookie—on the placekicker.

There's probably a dark and violent ending looming for the film, although there's a good chance, we think, that it may avoid it: The movie has stepped nimbly around all sorts of other obligatory scenes. *Buffalo '66* isn't really about endings, anyway. Endings are about conclusions and statements, and Gallo is obviously too much in a turmoil about this material to organize it into a payoff.

What we get is more like improvisational jazz, in which themes are introduced from other movies, and this one does riffs on them. Christina Ricci is like a soloist who occasionally stands up and takes the spotlight while the other players recede into the shadows, nodding and smoking. Why does her character go along with the kidnapping? Why does she throw herself into the role of "wife" with such zeal—and invention? Well, it's more interesting than if she was merely frightened and trying to escape. That would be the conventional approach. There's not a thing conventional about this movie.

A Bug's Life ★ ★ ★ ½
G, 94 m., 1998

With the voices of: Dave Foley (Flik), Kevin Spacey (Hopper), Julia Louis-Dreyfus (Princess Atta), Hayden Panettiere (Dot), Phyllis Diller (Queen), Richard Kind (Molt), David Hyde Pierce (Slim), Joe Ranft (Heimlich), Denis Leary (Francis), Jonathan Harris (Manny), Bonnie Hunt (Rosie). Directed by John Lasseter and produced by Darla K. Anderson and Kevin Reher. Screenplay by Andrew Stanton, Donald McEnery, and Bob Shaw, based on the original story by Lasseter, Stanton, and Joe Ranft.

As ants struggle to gather morsels of food, a leaf falls and interrupts their procession. "I'm lost!" screams a worker in panic. "Where's the line?" Rescue workers quickly arrive: "We are going around to the *left!*" The harvest continues. "This is nothing compared to the twig of '93," an ant observes.

Enjoying this, I enjoyed too the use of animation to visualize a world that could not be seen in live action and could not be created with special effects. Animation contains enormous promise for a new kind of storytelling, freed from reality and gravity, but although the Japanese have exploited that freedom, too, many American feature cartoons follow the Disney formula of plucky young heroes and heroines and comic sidekicks.

It's a formula that has produced wonderful movies. But the Pixar computer animation studio, a Disney coproducer, broke new ground with *Toy Story* in 1995, and again in *A Bug's Life* it runs free. The story, about an ant colony that frees itself from slavery to grasshoppers, is similar in some ways to the autumn's other big animated release, *Antz*, but aimed at a broader audience and without the in-jokes.

The film's hero is Flik (voice by Dave Foley), the smartest ant in the colony (the competition is not fierce). As the other ants labor to pile up "the Offering," a mountain of food for tyrannical grasshoppers, Flik perfects an invention to harvest grain more quickly; he's the Cyrus McCormick of the hymenopterous Formicidae. But he's still basically just an ant; the film is more about the fate of the colony and not so much about individuals like the Woody Allen hero of *Antz*.

There is a crisis. Flik spills the Offering, and Hopper (Kevin Spacey), the leader of the grasshoppers, is not pleased. Hopper has the kind of personality that makes him talk with his hands, and since he has four, Flik gets the message: Rebuild the Offering or face unspeakable consequences. What to do? Flik feels terrible because his clumsiness caused the trouble; he apologizes to the queen (Phyllis Diller), is encouraged by Princess Atta (Julia Louis-Dreyfus) and resolves to fight back.

Flik uses a dandelion pod as a sort of aircraft, and flies off on a hopeful quest to find mercenaries he can hire to defend the colony. He finds nine, including a walking stick named Slim (David Hyde Pierce), a praying mantis (Jonathan Harris), a caterpillar that looks military and sounds like a Nazi (Joe Ranft), a black widow (Bonnie Hunt), and others. How is he to know they aren't really warrior insects, but simply discontented performers from P. T. Flea's Circus?

The animators, led by director John Lasseter, provide rich images. A rainstorm feels like the colony is being water-bombed. A circus trick involves matches and flypaper. There are sneaky throwaway lines (when Flik visits a city, he encounters a beggar who explains, "A kid pulled my wings off").

Will *A Bug's Life* suffer by coming out so soon after *Antz*? Not any more than one thriller hurts the chances for the next one. *Antz* may even help business for *A Bug's Life* by demonstrating how many dramatic and comedic possibilities can be found in an anthill. And the Pixar animators, using later generations of the software that created such a fresh look in *Toy Story*, have made a movie that is always a pleasure to look at: There are glistening rounded surfaces, the sense of three dimensions, an eye for detail. And big laughs at the end, when the credits are interrupted by animated "outtakes" that satirize the blown lines and missed cues in live-action credit cookies.

Antz has a more sophisticated sensibility, and could play for adults attending by themselves. *A Bug's Life* is more clearly intended as a family film. Smaller children will respond to the threat from the Hoppers and the zaniness of the weird assortment of mercenaries hired by Flik.

Note: After seeing A Bug's Life, *you might want to rent that French documentary* Microcosmos, *which uses enormously magnified images to show us the insect kingdom. There's a whole other world down there. Be careful where you step.*

Bulworth ★ ★ ★ ½
R, 108 m., 1998

Warren Beatty (Jay Bulworth), Halle Berry (Nina), Don Cheadle (L.D.), Paul Sorvino (Graham Crockett), Jack Warden (Eddie Davers), Sean Astin (Gary), Nora Dunn (Missy Berliner), Laurie Metcalf (Mimi), Oliver Platt (Dennis). Directed by Warren Beatty and produced by Beatty and Pieter Jan Brugge. Screenplay by Beatty.

What it comes down to is a politician who can no longer bring himself to recite the words, "America is standing on the doorstep of a new millennium." Over and over and over again he has repeated the same mindless platitudes, the same meaningless baloney, the same hot air. Now he sits in his office, playing one of his stupid TV commercials on an endless loop. He has not eaten or slept in three days. He is sick to the soul of the American political process.

These do not seem to be the makings of a comedy, but Warren Beatty's *Bulworth* made me laugh, and wince. You realize that if all politicians were as outspoken as Bulworth, the fragile structure of our system would collapse, and we would have to start all over again. The movie suggests that virtually everything said in public by a politician is spin. "Spin control" is merely the name for spin they don't get away with.

Bulworth is a onetime Kennedy liberal (like Beatty himself), an incumbent senator from California who is accused by an opponent of being "old liberal wine trying to pour himself into a new conservative bottle." The joke to Bulworth is that liberal and conservative, Democrat and Republican, are no longer labels that mean much: When it comes to national health care, for example, the insurance companies have both parties in their pockets (and both parties have their hands in the companies' pockets).

Bulworth is in trouble. He hates his job and his life, and has just lost millions in the market. So he puts out a contract on his own life and flies back to California thinking he has three days to live. His impending death fills him with a sense of freedom: At last he is free to say exactly what he thinks, and that's what he does. In a black church, he observes, "We all come down here, get our pictures taken—forget about it." Blacks will never have power within the establishment, he says, until they've spent the money to buy it like the whites do.

Bulworth's campaign manager (Oliver Platt)

goes ballistic and hits a fire alarm to end the church service. But an hour later in Beverly Hills Beatty is insulting a mostly Jewish audience of movie moguls: "How much money do you guys really need?" he asks, observing that they produce "mostly crap." And so it goes. "That was good. Really good," he says. He's enjoying political speechmaking for the first time in his life.

Following Bulworth through his conversion is a posse of foxy young black women who pile into his limousine and direct him to an after-hours club, where he samples hip-hop and drugs. Lingering always nearby in the background is an attractive woman named Nina (Halle Berry), who eventually takes him home to her neighborhood, where he sees grade-school kids selling crack, and is treated to the truth of families where everybody has lost someone to gunfire.

Bulworth doesn't consist simply of the candidate making insults like a radical Don Rickles. There's substance in a lot of the dialogue, written by Beatty with a debt to the critiques of American society by such as Noam Chomsky. Beatty zeroes in on the myth that government is wasteful and industry is efficient by claiming that government runs Medicare for a fourth of the overhead raked off by insurance companies for equivalent health care. But why don't we have national health care like every other First World country? Because of insurance payoffs, Bulworth is only too happy to explain.

The movie fires shots in all directions. Some of them hit, some of them miss. When Bulworth asks Nina where all the black leaders have gone, her answer is as intelligent and plausible as a year's worth of op-ed columns. But when the movie presents black culture as automatically more authentic and truthful than white, that's a leftover knee-jerk; the use of blacks as repositories of truth and virtue is a worn-out convention in white liberal breast-beating. (There is even a mysterious old black man who follows Bulworth around reciting incantations that are meant, I guess, to be encoded universal truths.) It's better when Bulworth simply abandons political correctness and says what he thinks, however reckless, as when he theorizes that the solution to racial

difficulties is for everybody to bleep everybody else until we're all the same color.

Bulworth seems to reflect a rising tide of discontent with current American political discourse. Like *Wag the Dog* and *Primary Colors*, it's disenchanted with the state of the system. No wonder. I can remember listening, as a child, to radio debates between those two old warhorses of Illinois politics, Paul Douglas and Everett Dirksen. They simply had at each other, like two opinionated guys talking off the tops of their heads. Now debates, like campaigns, are carefully hedged with rules and regulations designed to ensure that everyone stays timidly within the tradition of "doorsteps of the new millennium," etc.

Bulworth is not a perfect movie, nor could it be. It's too messy and takes too many risks. I didn't buy the romance between Bulworth and Nina; it's a recycling of the tired movie convention that a man in a fight for his life can always find time, in three days, to fall in love with a woman half his age. And I didn't much like the movie's ending—not the false ending, and not the real one that follows, either.

But those are minor complaints. *Bulworth* plays like a cry of frustrated comic rage. It's about an archetypal character who increasingly seems to stand for our national mood: the guy who's fed up and isn't going to take it anymore. Funny how in the twenty-two years since we heard those words in *Network*, we've kept right on taking it.

The Butcher Boy ★ ★ ½
R, 105 m., 1998

Stephen Rea (Da Brady), Fiona Shaw (Mrs. Nugent), Eamonn Owens (Francie Brady), Alan Boyle (Joe Purcell), Aisling O'Sullivan (Annie Brady), Sinead O'Connor (Virgin Mary). Directed by Neil Jordan and produced by Redmond Morris and Stephen Woolley. Screenplay by Jordan and Patrick McCabe, based on the novel by McCabe.

Neil Jordan's *The Butcher Boy* tells the story of a young Irish boy who turns violent and insane under the pressure of a tragic childhood and a sense of betrayal. By the end of the film, when he acts out his murderous fantasies, I was thinking, of course, about the shooting spree by the two young boys in Jonesboro.

This film is, in a sense, optimistic. It suggests that children must undergo years of horrible experiences before they turn into killers. The Jonesboro shooters were apparently more fortunate: more or less normal kids raised with guns, and unable to understand the consequences of their actions. We want to believe violent kids have undergone emotional torments like Francie Brady, the young hero of *The Butcher Boy*. If they haven't, then the abyss is closer than we think.

The film takes place in the early 1960s, in a small town in the west of Ireland. It is narrated by Francie, who is played by the newcomer Eamonn Owens in one of the cockiest and most confident performances I've seen by a young actor. Francie's home life is not happy. His father (Stephen Rea) is a drunk who turns violent, who kicks in the TV, who weeps for the lost innocence of his days before whiskey. His mother (Aisling O'Sullivan) is suicidal; one day Francie comes home from school to find a chair on the kitchen table, and his ma preparing to hang herself.

She has a "breakdown," and is sent to a mental institution, which Francie calls a "garage," because that's where you usually go with a breakdown. He meanwhile clings to the islands of reassurance in his fragile universe, especially his best friend, Joe (Alan Boyle). They hide out in a playhouse near the river, they live in the fantasies of comic books, and Francie feels a fierce, possessive pride in his friend.

Francie's archenemy is the hated Mrs. Nugent (Fiona Shaw), who speaks with an English accent and is a snob and a scold, and seems to delight in persecuting Francie. It's she who turns in Francie and Joe for stealing apples. Francie in his fantasies imagines dire consequences, and is occasionally comforted by the appearance of the Virgin Mary (Sinead O'Connor), who sometimes turns up on TV and is not above using the f-word (although always, to be sure, in a lilting Irish context).

Things fall apart. He's sent to a youth home, where the priest dresses him in girl's clothes before being caught and whisked away to another garage. Francie returns to a job as a butcher boy, cutting up pig carcasses. He has

fantasies of nuclear disaster, of humans turned into beasts, of charred corpses. His dad dies, and Francie leaves him in his favorite chair for a long time, until the authorities break in. Joe betrays him and becomes the friend of Mrs. Nugent's hated son.

The closing passages of the film, which is based on a novel by Patrick McCabe, are the logical outcome of what has come before. Jordan doesn't exploit; his tone is one of sad regarding, in which Francie's defiant voice sounds brave and forlorn. This is a kid who keeps up a front while his heart is breaking.

Neil Jordan *(The Crying Game, Michael Collins)* is a strong, passionate director, and *The Butcher Boy* is original work, an attempt to combine magic realism with everyday reality and tie it together with Francie's own brash, defiant personal style (he is not a dumb kid). Yet in some way the movie held me outside; I didn't connect in the way I wanted to, and by the end I was out of sympathy with the material.

Why was this? I can see, objectively, that this is a film of weight, daring, and visual invention. I was in a little awe of young Eamonn Owens's performance. I can understand any praise this film receives, but I cannot feel it. *The Butcher Boy* has been compared to Kubrick's *A Clockwork Orange,* an acknowledged masterpiece that I have also found myself standing outside of. Rationalize as I will, revisit the film as I have, I cannot feel the emotional shift that would involve me in the material: It remains for me an exercise, not an experience (odd that his detached, cerebral *2001* sweeps me so easily into its spell).

Am I simply out of sympathy with Francie? Would I have been more moved by a more realistic approach (like the treatment of the reform school boy in *The Loneliness of the Long-Distance Runner*), rather than this film with miracles and horrific mirages? I can't say. I know there is something substantial here. I can't recommend the film, and yet if it sounds intriguing to you, I certainly think you should see it.

Butterfly ★ ★ ★
R, 97 m., 2000

Fernando Fernan Gomez (Don Gregorio), Manuel Lozano (Moncho), Uxia Blanco (Rosa), Gonzalo Uriarte (Ramon), Alexis De Los Santos (Andres), Jesus Castejon (D. Avelino), Guillermo Toledo (Otis), Elena Fernandez (Carmina), Tamar Novas (Roque). Directed by Jose Luis Cuerda. Screenplay by Rafael Azcona, based on the collection of short stories *Que Me Quieres, Amor* by Manuel Rivas.

Butterfly takes place during that brief moment in Spain between the formation of the Republic and the civil war. A history lesson will be necessary for most viewers, and the movie provides it, explaining that the old order of church, military, and monarchy was overthrown by a new leftist government, legally elected, which was then challenged by the right.

The war that followed was like a rehearsal for World War II, with Hitler testing his Luftwaffe and Russia supplying the communist side. The story was more complicated, because the Russians also fought for control of the left against the democratic socialists and the anarchists; Orwell's *Homage to Catalonia* tells the whole story from the point of view of an observer who was left-wing but anticommunist.

The point is that freedom flickered briefly before being crushed by big players on the world stage, who ushered in Franco and decades of dictatorship. People dared to admit their real religious beliefs (or lack of them), and to prefer democracy to the king. And in a village in Galicia, a seven-year-old boy is preparing for his first day of school.

His name is Moncho (Manuel Lozano), and he is frightened because his older brother sometimes comes home after being beaten. In class, when the teacher calls him to the front of the room, Moncho pees his pants and flees. But then the teacher comes calling. He is a kindly old man named Don Gregorio (Fernando Fernan Gomez), who explains he would never beat anyone. He coaxes the boy back into class, and gently introduces him to the world and its wonders. He gives him two presents in particular: *Treasure Island,* by Stevenson, and a butterfly net. Together, the old man and the boy study nature.

The boy's father is a tailor. Moncho's home life is happy, and enlivened by his older brother's enthusiastic interest in the opposite sex. There are, however, scandalous secrets in the village, which lend an ironic twist to one of the subplots. But in general, life is good—until the fascist uprising changes their lives forever.

Butterfly is based on the short stories of Manuel Rivas, and indeed ends like a short story, with a single word that colors everything that went before. Because the film marches so inexorably toward its conclusion, it would be unfair to hint at what happens, except to say that it provides a heartbreaking insight into the way that fear creates cowards.

Fernando Fernan Gomez, who plays the teacher, had the title role in *The Grandfather,* a 1998 Spanish film that got an Oscar nomination and won Gomez the Goya Award as Spain's best actor of the year. I found it a little too sentimental; *Butterfly,* while not lacking in sentiment, excuses it by being seen through the eyes of a naive child, and dilutes it with nostalgia and regret. The film's ending poses a hard question for the viewer: Would we behave more bravely than the characters on the screen do? We are fortunate to live in easy times.

C

Cabaret Balkan ★ ★ ★ ★
NO MPAA RATING, 100 m., 1999

Nikola Ristanovski (Boris), Nebojsa Glogovac (Taxi Driver), Miki Manojlovic (Michael), Marko Urosevic (Alex), Bogdan Diklic (John), Dragan Nikolic (John's Boxer Friend), Mira Banjac (Bosnian Serb Mother), Danil Bata Stojkovic (Viktor). Directed by Goran Paskaljevic and produced by Antoine de Clermont-Tonnerre and Paskaljevic. Screenplay by Dejan Dukovski and Paskaljevic, based on Dukovski's play *Bure Baruta*.

Cabaret Balkan is a scream of agony over the madness in Kosovo and the neighboring lands where blood feuds run deep and the macho virus is a killer epidemic. It's a film about violence, sadism, brutality, and the hatred of women, which seems to go hand in hand with those pastimes. The director, Goran Paskaljevic, opens his film with a taxi driver telling a returning citizen: "This is a goddamned lousy country; why would anyone want to come back?" The film shows us nothing to contradict his statement.

Yes, I know, the "former Yugoslavia," as we now wistfully refer to it, contains beauty and greatness. But what is going on there now, the film argues, is ugliness. The dark side has taken over and decent citizens on both sides flee for their lives, or choose the lesser of evils. It's hard at times to tell which side the characters are on, a New York critic complains. Yes, this film might reply, but what difference does it make? They're all doomed.

The movie's device is a series of interlocking, self-contained stories. Some of the same characters turn up from time to time, like haunting reminders. After a while many of the dominant males seem to blur together into one composite: an alcoholic middle-aged man with an absurd mustache, lurching through the world killing, vomiting, urinating, bleeding, belching, swearing, and entertaining himself by terrorizing women.

Some of the episodes end with surprises—not because we don't see them coming, but because we can't believe that the characters are complete monsters. We are inevitably dis-

appointed: None of the men in this movie are nice, except for a few bewildered older men (one of whom crushes a lout's skull and then cradles him, sobbing, "My boy, my boy"). Small events escalate into exercises in terror, and the men in the film seem to be consumed by violence. None of the killings in the film are overtly political; *Cabaret Balkan* seems to argue that monstrous behavior is so ingrained in a sick culture that ethnic cleansing is just an organized form of everyday behavior.

Example: Bus passengers are terrorized by a cretin who hijacks the bus. The elderly driver eventually kills him. A woman passenger, the target of the hijacker's sexual rage, stumbles out of the bus and into the car of her boyfriend, who instantly flies into a jealous rage and accuses her of encouraging the other man. As the two argue, two other men approach, hold them both at gunpoint, and start the next act. Or consider an ordinary traffic accident that escalates: The wronged driver finds the apartment of the other driver's parents and breaks everything in sight. (The other driver got into the crash in the first place because he was cruising the streets harassing single women.)

The most harrowing episode, which starts quietly and escalates, involves a war widow traveling on a train. A large menacing man comes in, sits down, wants her to smoke and drink with him, forces his conversation on her, orders another passenger out of the compartment, and begins the preliminaries to rape. She breaks free and desperately grabs a grenade from her bag. He wrenches the grenade away from her and contemptuously pulls the pin, holding the grenade with one hand as he holds her with the other.

The buried argument of *Cabaret Balkan* seems to be that violence and macho sexual insecurity are closely linked. I was reminded of *Savior* (1998), the film where Dennis Quaid plays a mercenary fighting for the Serbs; he finds himself protecting a woman who has been raped, and whose father and brother want to kill her—because, you see, she has therefore brought dishonor on her family. It is not a crime to rape, but to be raped. Such diseased values, *Cabaret Balkan* seems to suggest, almost inevitably lead to savagery, and indeed the intimidation of women is the primary way the men in this movie express their manhood.

Amazingly, *Cabaret Balkan* is an enormous hit in its homeland, no doubt among the many good citizens who are fed up. Societies can rip themselves to pieces only so long before they are forced to wonder how their values could possibly survive the cost of fighting for them. When war leaves no ideals worth defending, there is only the consolation of depriving the other side of any shreds of remaining standards. Of all the movies about all the tragic places where old hatreds fester over ethnic, racial, and religious animosity, this is the angriest, and therefore possibly the bravest.

Note: The film was released "unrated." Of course, no film that considers violence this unblinkingly and bravely can qualify for an R; that rating is more hospitable toward films that make it look like fun.

Can't Hardly Wait ★ ½
PG-13, 98 m., 1998

Ethan Embry (Preston Meyers), Jennifer Love Hewitt (Amanda Beckett), Lauren Ambrose (Denise Fleming), Peter Facinelli (Mike Dexter), Seth Green (Kenny Fisher), Charlie Korsmo (William Lichter), Jenna Elfman (The Angel), Jerry O'Connell (Trip McNeely). Directed by Deborah Kaplan and Harry Elfont and produced by Jenno Topping and Betty Thomas. Screenplay by Kaplan and Elfont.

There's one character in *Can't Hardly Wait* who is interesting and funny. Maybe it was a mistake to write her in; she makes the other characters look like gnat-brained bozos. Her name is Denise, she is played by Lauren Ambrose, and she has a merry face, a biting tongue, and a sardonic angle on high school. Her classmates look like candidates for *Starship Troopers* or the *Sports Illustrated* swimsuit pictorial.

The early days of June seem to bring a movie like this every year, celebrating the graduation of the senior class and its ejection onto the conveyor belt of life. *Can't Hardly Wait* is a lesser example of the genre, which includes (in descending order of accomplishment) *Say Anything, American Graffiti, Dazed and Confused, Fast Times at Ridgemont High,* and *Porky's.*

The movie lumbers gracelessly from romantic showdowns to deep conversations to bathroom humor. The hero is Preston (Ethan Embry), a would-be writer who has lusted for four years after the class sexpot, Amanda (Jennifer Love Hewitt). He knew their destinies were entertwined when they both ate strawberry Pop Tarts during their first freshman class. But the class jock, Mike (Peter Facinelli), won her instead.

Now it is the night of graduation day, and Mike has dumped Amanda because he plans to move up from high school *girls* to college *women.* At a long (some would say endless) keg party, Preston tries to give Amanda a letter he has written, spilling out his innermost thoughts. This must be some letter. We never get to see what it says, no doubt because a letter good enough to win Amanda would have to be better than anything the screenwriters are capable of writing.

Meanwhile, Mike learns from last year's high school make-out champ, Trip McNeely (Jerry O'Connell), that college women are always talking about serious stuff and dating older guys. Bummer. So he tries to win Amanda back in a scene played before a hushed crowd, but is rejected. That's even though Amanda has earlier wailed, "If I'm not Mike's girlfriend, who am I? Nobody knows me as anything else. I don't even know me as anyone else."

Real poignancy there. My own rule of thumb, in high school and ever after, is that if a woman has little of interest to say, she is likely, over a span of time, to have less and less to say, until finally she will drive you mad. That is true even though she may, as Amanda does, have awesome boobs.

Now take Denise, on the other hand. She gets accidentally locked into the bathroom with Kenny (Seth Green), who talks like a black rap artist even though he's white, and wears goggles and thinks he's cool and will someday no doubt be a radio talk jock. Denise is cute and plucky, and has intelligent lips (don't pretend you don't know what I mean), and kids Kenny's affectations, and remembers that they were best pals until the sixth grade, when he dropped her because, she says, "I was in all the smart classes, and my parents didn't make a lot of money, and you desperately needed to sit at the popular table in the lunchroom."

Denise is the only person in this senior class that anyone of any taste would want to be friends with. Why don't the filmmakers know that? Why do they go through the tired old motions of making Denise the comic relief, and assigning the romantic leads to a couple of clueless rubber stamps?

You tell me. *Can't Hardly Wait* is the kind of movie that somehow succeeds in moving very, very slowly even while proceeding at a breakneck pace. It cuts quickly back and forth between nothing and nothing. It underlines every single scene with a pop song that tells us what the scene is about. It doesn't have the zing of life and subversion that the best high school movies always have. Or, if they don't have them, like *Porky's* didn't, at least they have mercy on us and throw in a shower scene.

The Castle ★ ★ ★
R, 85 m., 1999

Michael Caton (Darryl Kerrigan), Anne Tenney (Sal Kerrigan), Stephen Curry (Dale Kerrigan), Anthony Simcoe (Steve Kerrigan), Sophie Lee (Tracey Kerrigan), Wayne Hope (Wayne Kerrigan), Tiriel Mora (Dennis Denuto), Eric Bana (Con Petropoulous), Charles "Bud" Tingwell (Lawrence Hammill). Directed by Rob Sitch and produced by Debra Choate. Screenplay by Santo Cilauro, Tom Gleisner, Jane Kennedy, and Sitch.

Early in *The Castle*, the happy Kerrigan family is served a chicken dinner by Sal, wife of proud Darryl and mother of daughter Tracey and three sons Dale, Steve, and Wayne; Wayne, currently in prison, is the only one missing from the table. Dad (Michael Caton) observes something on the chicken and asks his wife (Anne Tenney) what it is. "Seasoning," she says proudly. Dad beams: "Seasoning! Looks like everybody's kicked a goal."

And so life spins along at 3 Highview Crescent in Melbourne, where the Kerrigan home sits surrounded by its built-on rooms, screened-in porch, greyhound kennel, big-dish satellite, and carport. For Darryl, it is not so much a house as a shrine to one of the best darn families in the universe, and he proudly points out the plastic Victorian gingerbread trim and the fake chimney to an inspector—who is there,

as it turns out, to condemn the property under the laws of public domain.

The Kerrigans don't want to move. They've been told that the three most important words in real estate are "location, location, location"— and how could they improve on their home's convenient location, so close to the airport? So close, indeed, that jumbo jets pass within inches of the property line and the house trembles when they take off.

The Castle, directed by Rob Sitch, is one of those comic treasures like *The Full Monty* and *Waking Ned Devine* that shows its characters in the full bloom of glorious eccentricity. The Kerrigans may be the proudest and happiest family you've ever met, what with Dad's prosperous tow-truck business, and the inventions of Steve (Anthony Simcoe), the "idea man," who specializes in fitting tools together so they can do two jobs equally badly. Tracey (Sophie Lee) is the only college graduate (from beauty school), and Dale (Stephen Curry) is the narrator, frequently quoting his dad, who observes, as he gazes up at pylons towering over the home, that "power lines are a reminder of man's ability to generate electricity."

Dad is a bit of an idea man himself, taking advantage of a narrow room by building an even narrower pool table for it. Meanwhile, Steve searches the *Trader* ad paper for bargains, making sudden discoveries: "Jousting sticks! Make us an offer!" So tightly knit is the family that Dale proudly reports that during mealtimes, "the television is definitely turned down." So it is with a real sense of loss that the Kerrigans discover they may be evicted from their castle, a fate they share with their neighbors Jack and Farouk.

The movie's comic foundation is the cozy if spectacularly insular family life of the Kerrigans. They think almost as one: When Darryl rises to offer the toast at his daughter's wedding, he begins expansively with, "Speaking as the bride's parents . . ." Australia seems to abound with peculiar households, and the Kerrigans are wholesome, positive-thinking versions of such strange samples of Aussie family life as the dysfunctional weirdos in *Muriel's Wedding* and the sisters in *Love Serenade*, who date a disk jockey who is a fish. I can picture them in the audience to view the finals in *Strictly Ballroom*.

The film develops suspense with a big (or, actually, a very small) courtroom finale. The Kerrigans determine to mount a legal battle against eviction and hire an attorney named Dennis Denuto (Tiriel Mora) to represent them, against his own advice (he specializes in repossessions). When he approaches the bench, it is to ask the judge, "How am I doing?" or to whisper urgently, "Can you give me an angle?" He gives the case his best shot (Dale informs us he "even learned Roman numerals" for the appeal), but it isn't until a kindly old expert in constitutional law (Charles "Bud" Tingwell) comes on board that they have a prayer.

This is the sort of movie the British used to make in black-and-white, starring Peter Sellers, Alec Guinness, Terry-Thomas, and Ian Carmichael. It's about characters who have a rock-solid view of the universe and their place in it, and gaze out upon the world from the high vantage point of the home that is their castle. The movie is not shocking or daring or vulgar, but sublimely content—as content as the Kerrigans when Mom not only serves pound cake for dessert but is so creative she actually tops it with icing sugar. At a time like that, she doesn't need to be told she's kicked a goal.

Caught Up ★ ★
R, 95 m., 1998

Bokeem Woodbine (Daryl), Cynda Williams (Vanessa), Joseph Lindsey (Billy Grimm), Clifton Powell (Herbert/Frank Lowden), Basil Wallace (Ahmad), Snoop Doggy Dogg (Kool Kitty Kat), LL Cool J (Roger), Tony Todd (Jake). Directed by Darin Scott and produced by Peter Heller. Screenplay by Scott.

Caught Up is the first movie directed by Darin Scott, who has written three earlier movies and has produced eight. I suspect he spent those years impatiently stashing away ideas and images for his own first film; *Caught Up* plays like Fibber McGee's closet—it opens and everything but the kitchen sink comes tumbling out. Scott is ambitious and not without talent, but he ought to ration his material a little; there's so much plot it's dizzying.

Caught Up stars Bokeem Woodbine as Daryl, a man who dreams of opening his own club to support his girlfriend and their son. He needs

$10,000, and a friend offers to get it at the bank. Daryl realizes too late that the withdrawal is a robbery. In prison, Daryl reads Greek philosophy. "You wanna know what those five years were like?" he asks. And when he answers, "Hell!" Scott has flames shoot up from the bottom of the screen. It's that kind of film.

On the outside again, Daryl meets a woman named Vanessa (Cynda Williams, from *One False Move*), who looks uncannily like his former girlfriend (who he is "staying away from" until he has his act together). She tells his fortune (tarot cards are superimposed on the screen) and gets him a job as a limo driver, ferrying dubious people to unsavory destinations.

And then—well, at some point I have to bail out of the plot description because it begins to appear that Daryl is caught in an elaborate web of betrayal and deception, and nobody is quite who or what they seem. We get the rug pulled out from beneath us so many times we stop caring: What's the use of trying to figure things out when the story is toying with us?

Yet the film has qualities. I liked the stylized way the story was told, with narration and flashbacks, visual overlays and special effects. Even those phony flames from hell were entertaining just because the movie was trying something. You could sense the enthusiasm of the director.

What I didn't much like was the device of a mysterious man in black, his face concealed, who follows Daryl and tries to kill him. I didn't like him as a gimmick, and I liked him even less when I heard the ludicrous explanation of who he was and why he was mad. And my patience was running a little thin by the time a body was hurled through a glass window perfectly on cue—timed to be the punch line for dialogue that, of course, no one on the other side of the window could hear. I sort of liked the sulfuric acid scene, though.

Caught Up is a film by a man who wanted to make a movie more than he wanted to tell a story. The story is the excuse for visual gizmos and directorial virtuosity. It makes me curious to see Scott's next film, but next time he should remember that if the audience can't care about the characters it has a hard time caring about the style.

The Celebration ★ ★ ★
R, 105 m., 1998

Ulrich Thomsen (Christian), Henning Moritzen (Helge), Thomas Bo Larsen (Michael), Paprika Steen (Helene), Birthe Neumann (Elsa), Trine Dyrholm (Pia), Helle Dolleris (Mette), Therese Glahn (Michelle). Directed by Thomas Vinterberg and produced by Birgitte Hald. Screenplay by Vinterberg and Mogens Rukov.

Thomas Vinterberg's *The Celebration* mixes farce and tragedy so completely that it challenges us to respond at all. There are moments when a small, choked laugh begins in the audience, and is then instantly stifled, as we realize a scene is not intended to be funny. Or is it? Imagine Eugene O'Neill and Woody Allen collaborating on a screenplay about a family reunion. Now let Luis Buñuel direct it.

The story involves a sixtieth birthday party at which all of a family's corrupt and painful secrets are revealed at last. To the family's country inn in Denmark come the surviving children of Helge (Henning Moritzen) and his wife, Elsa (Birthe Neumann). We meet the eldest son, Christian (Ulrich Thomsen), his younger brother, Michael (Thomas Bo Larsen), and their sister Helene (Paprika Steen). Christian's twin sister has recently committed suicide. Also gathering around the table for the patriarch's birthday are assorted spouses, relations, and friends.

The film opens with a family in turmoil. The drunk and furious Michael careens his car down a country road while blaming his wife for everything. He comes across Christian, walking, and stops to give him a lift (throwing out his wife and children, who must walk the rest of the way). In their room, Michael starts berating his wife again (she has not packed some of his clothing) before they have rough sex; we assume this vaudeville is the centerpiece of their marriage.

At the birthday banquet, Christian raps his spoon against a glass and rises to calmly accuse his father of having raped his children. The gathering tries to ignore these remarks; Helene says they are not true. In the kitchen, the drunken chef gleefully observes that he has been waiting for this day for a long time and dispatches his waitresses to steal every-

one's car keys from their rooms, so they won't be able to escape. Christian rises again and accuses his father of essentially murdering the sister who killed herself.

The evening spins down into a long night of revelation and accusation. The father at first tries to ignore his son's performance. The mother demands an apology, only to have Christian remind her she witnessed her husband raping him. Helene's boyfriend, an African-American anthropologist, arrives late and is the target of Michael's drunken racist comments. The family joins in a racist Danish song. A servant accuses a family member of having impregnated her; she had an abortion, but still loves him. And on and on, including fights and scuffles and an interlude when Christian is tied to a tree in the woods.

Vinterberg handles his material so cannily that we must always look for clues to the intended tone. Yes, the family history is ugly and tragic. But the chef, hiding the keys and intercepting calls for taxis, is out of French farce. The fact that the family even stays in the same room is a comic artifice (in farce, you can never just walk away). That nearly everyone is drunk doesn't explain everything, but that many of them are chronic alcoholics may explain more: This is a chapter in a long-running family saga.

Vinterberg shot the film on video, then blew it up to 35mm film. He joined with Lars von Trier *(Breaking the Waves)* and two other Danish directors in signing a document named "Dogma 95," which was unveiled at the 1998 Cannes Film Festival and pledged them all to shoot on location, using only natural sounds and props discovered on the site, using no special effects, using no music, using only hand-held cameras. *The Celebration* and Von Trier's *The Idiots* are the first two, and may be the last two, films shot in this style. It would be tiresome if enforced in the long run, but the style does work for this film, and suits it, as a similar style is at the heart of John Cassavetes's work.

It's a tribute to *The Celebration* that the style and the story don't stumble over one another. The script is well planned, the actors are skilled at deploying their emotions, and the long day's journey into night is fraught with wounds that the farcical elements only help to keep open. Comes the dawn, and we can only shake our heads in disbelief when we see the family straggling back into the same room for breakfast.

Celebrity ★ ★ ½
R, 113 m., 1998

Kenneth Branagh (Lee Simon), Judy Davis (Robin Simon), Leonardo DiCaprio (Brandon Darrow), Melanie Griffith (Nicole Oliver), Famke Janssen (Bonnie), Michael Lerner (Dr. Lupus), Joe Mantegna (Tony Gardella), Hank Azaria (David), Charlize Theron (Model), Gretchen Mol (Girlfriend), Winona Ryder (Nola). Directed by Woody Allen and produced by Jean Doumanian. Screenplay by Allen.

Celebrity plays oddly like the loose ends and unused inspirations of other Woody Allen movies; it's sort of a revue format in which a lot of famous people appear on-screen, perform in the sketch Woody devises for them, and disappear. Some of the moments are very funny. More are only smile material, and a few don't work at all. Like all of Allen's films, it's smart and quirky enough that we're not bored, but we're not much delighted, either. All of his films can't be as good as *Everyone Says I Love You*, and this one proves it.

The film stars Kenneth Branagh as—there is only one way to put this—Woody Allen. The character is named Lee Simon, but Branagh has all the Allen vocal mannerisms and the body language of comic uncertainty. He does Allen so carefully, indeed, that you wonder why Allen didn't just play the character himself. Lee Simon is supposed to be a celebrity journalist, and Branagh might have been more useful and amusing if he'd used another real-life legend as his model: Perhaps the indestructible Anthony Hayden-Guest, who has been playing a Lee Simon–like role so long he even inspired a character in *Bonfire of the Vanities*.

Simon is a thirty-fivish man on the make with a precious antique Aston-Martin and the touching belief that his car can help him pick up chicks. The chicks he wants to pick up, he'd have to give the car to, and that would only get his foot in the door. In a flashback, we see him divorcing his wife (Judy Davis) for reasons that he tries to explain in sentences that never quite arrive at a subject or an object.

As the movie opens, he's doing a profile of a movie star played by Melanie Griffith, who takes him on a visit to her childhood home and in her old bedroom performs an act we suspect she rehearsed there many times in her imagination, in the years before stardom. Is it unethical for a journalist to have sex with the person he is interviewing? Yes, but not as unethical as what he does next, which is to pitch her his screenplay. That's getting too personal.

The film is filled with cameos (Donald Trump buying St. Patrick's Cathedral as a tear-down, Isaac Mizrahi as a painter who fears that fame will cut into his success). The best of the self-contained sequences stars Leonardo DiCaprio as a spoiled young movie star who beats up his girlfriend (Gretchen Mol), trashes his hotel room, and offers Lee Simon a leftover groupie when the journalist arrives (once again, to pitch his script).

As in *Deconstructing Harry,* his 1997 film, Allen seems fascinated by the mechanics of sex. Charlize Theron plays a model who informs the writer that she is polymorphously perverse, and has orgasms when touched on any part of her body. Simon's fingers flutter near her like a man about to test a hot stove.

Simon is also bewitched throughout the movie by the reappearances of a bright, pretty young thing played by Winona Ryder, who actually even likes him. They might have had a future together, but the message is that Simon uses women like stepping-stones, landing on one only long enough to launch himself toward the next.

The movie's shot in black and white; Allen is one of the rare and valuable directors who sometimes insists in working in the format that is the soul of cinema. It has a nice, crisp look, and the b + w places the emphasis on the body language and dialogue, instead of allowing too much of incidental atmosphere in. But the screenplay isn't as sharp as the movie's visuals. As the movie careens from one of Simon's quarries to the next, Allen pauses on most scenes only long enough to extract the joke, and the film begins to seem as desperately promiscuous as its hero. The words "The End" no longer appear at the ends of most films, but *Celebrity* ends (and begins) on a note that seems about right: An airplane skywriting the word "HELP!"

Center Stage ★ ★ ★
PG-13, 113 m., 2000

Amanda Schull (Jody), Ethan Stiefel (Cooper Neilson), Peter Gallagher (Jonathan Reeves), Sascha Radetsky (Charlie), Shakiem Evans (Erik), Zoe Saldana (Eva Rodriguez), Donna Murphy (Juliette [Teacher]), Susan Mary Pratt (Maureen), Ilia Kulik (Sergei). Directed by Nicholas Hytner and produced by Laurence Mark. Screenplay by Carol Heikkinen.

Center Stage follows a group of young ballet students through their first year of advanced training at the fictional American Ballet Academy in New York. They had to be very good to get in. Only three will be chosen at the end of the year to join the company. They work hard, but when they are not actually dancing, they are a lot like freshmen in any college; they survive romances, they party, they gossip, they despair and dream, and they smoke too much.

Dancers do tend to smoke a lot. It's bad for their wind, but they think it helps them to lose weight. The movie knows that and a lot of other things about the world of ballet; it feels like an inside job. It isn't so perceptive about its characters, who tend to fall into recognizable types (the ingenue, the rebel, the girl who's too fat, the girl who is pushed by her mother). Here it's similar to Fame, but not as electrifying. But if you look at Center Stage as another example of the school movie of the week, with auditions taking the place of the senior prom, you realize it's a lot smarter and more perceptive—and it's about something.

It is about the union of hard work and artistic success. To be a world-class ballet dancer is to be an athlete of the highest order, and if you look at ballet as a sport, it has many Michael Jordans and the NBA had only one. The movie casts real dancers in many of the roles, and that provides an obvious standard of excellence that gives the movie an underlying authenticity.

Ethan Stiefel, considered by many to be the best male dancer in the world, plays Cooper, the lead—the star of the company, who has just lost his girlfriend to Jonathan (Peter Gallagher), the company's head. He becomes attracted to Jody (Amanda Schull), one of the new students, and in a predictable progression invites her into his bed and into the new ballet he is creating.

Predictable, yes, but not with all the soap-opera payoffs we might fear. The movie uses the materials of melodrama, but is gentle with them; it's oriented more in the real world, and doesn't jack up every conflict and love story into an overwrought crisis. That restraint is especially useful in creating the character Eva Rodriguez (Zoe Saldana), the class rebel, who talks back to the teacher (Donna Murphy), comes late to rehearsals, has a bad attitude—and yet actually has the best attitude of all, because she dances out of her love for dance, not because of ambition or duty.

Some of the other students are not so lucky. One has been pushed into dancing by her mother. One has a body-image problem. And so on. But a lot of these kids are pretty normal, apart from their demanding profession. In a dance club, Sergei (Ilia Kulik), from Russia, tries to pick up two women. They both want to know what he does. He says he's a ballet dancer, and they turn away. With the next woman, he has more luck. "Mafia," he explains.

The movie doesn't force it, but it has the pleasures of a musical. It ends with two big ballet numbers, wonderfully staged and danced, and along the way there are rehearsals and scenes in a Broadway popular dance studio that have a joy and freedom. Film is a wonderful way to look at dance, because it gets you closer and varies the point of view, but since the death of the Hollywood musical there hasn't been enough of it. Center Stage has moments of joy and moments of insight, and is about both human nature and the inhuman demands of ballet.

Central Station ★ ★ ★
R, 115 m., 1998

Fernanda Montenegro (Dora), Marilia Pera (Irene), Vinicius De Oliveira (Josue), Soia Lira (Ana), Othon Bastos (Cesar), Otavio Augusto (Pedrao), Stela Freitas (Yolanda), Matheus Nachtergaele (Isaias). Directed by Walter Salles and produced by Arthur Cohn and Martine De Clermont-Tonnerre. Screenplay by Joao Emanuel Carneiro and Marcos Bernstein, based on an original idea by Salles.

The tone of life in Rio is established in an early scene in Walter Salles's *Central Station,* as a train pulls into the platform and passengers crawl through the windows to grab seats ahead of the people who enter through the doors. In this dog-eat-dog world, Dora (Fernanda Montenegro) has a little stand in the rail station where she writes letters for people who are illiterate.

A cynic, she destroys most of the letters. One day a mother and son use her services to dictate a letter to the woman's missing husband. Soon after, the mother is struck and killed by a bus. The kid knows one person in Rio: Dora. He approaches her for help, and her response is brief: "Scram!"

The key to the power of *Central Station* is in the way that word echoes down through most of the film. This is not a heartwarming movie about a woman trying to help a pathetic orphan, but a hard-edged film about a woman who thinks only of her own needs. After various attempts to rid herself of young Josue (Vinicius De Oliveira), she finally sells him to an adoption agency and uses the money to buy herself a new TV set.

There's not a shred of doubt or remorse as she settles down before the new set. But the whole story is known by her friend Irene (Marilia Pera, who played the prostitute who adopts the street kid in *Pixote*). "Those children aren't adopted!" she cries. "They're killed, and their organs are sold!" As if it is a great deal of trouble to go to, Dora now steals Josue back from the "orphanage" and finds herself, against her will and beyond her comprehension, trying to help him find his father, who lives far away in an interior city.

Central Station then settles into the pleasures of a road movie, in which we see modern Brazil through the eyes of the characters: the long-haul trucks that are the lifeline of commerce, the sprawling new housing developments, the hybrid religious ceremonies, the blend of old ways and the twentieth century. Whether they find the father is not really the point; the film is about their journey, and relationship.

The movie's success rests largely on the shoulders of Fernanda Montenegro, an actress who successfully defeats any temptation to allow sentimentality to wreck her relationship with the child. She understands that the film is not really about the boy's search for his father, but about her own reawakening. This process is measured out so carefully that we don't even notice the point at which she crosses over into a gentler person.

The boy, ten-year-old De Oliveira, was discovered by the director in an airport, shining shoes. He asked Walter Salles for the price of a sandwich, and Salles, who had been trying for months to cast this role, looked at him thoughtfully and saw young Josue. Whether he is an actor or not I cannot say. He plays Josue so well the performance is transparent. I hope he avoids the fate of Fernando Ramos da Silva, the young orphan who was picked off the streets to star in *Pixote*, later returned to them, and was murdered. I met De Oliveira at the Toronto Film Festival, where, barbered and in a new suit, he looked like a Rotarian's nephew.

It's strange about a movie like this. The structure intends us to be moved by the conclusion, but the conclusion is in many (not all) ways easy to anticipate. What moved me was the process, the journey, the change in the woman, the subtlety of sequences like the one where she falls for a truck driver who doesn't fall for her. It's in such moments that the film has its magic. The ending can take care of itself.

Character ★ ★ ★ ½
R, 114 m., 1998

Fedja van Huet (Katadreuffe), Jan Decleir (Dreverhaven), Betty Schuurman (Joba [mother]), Victor Low (De Gankelaar), Tamar van den Dop (Lorna Te George), Hans Kesting (Jan Maan), Lou Landre (Retenstein), Bernhard Droog (Stroomkoning). Directed by Mike van Diem and produced by Laurens Geels. Screenplay by van Diem.

Character oozes with feelings of spite and revenge that grow up between a father and the son he had out of wedlock. It is dark, bitter, and fascinating, as all family feuds are—about hatred so deep that it can only be ended with a knife.

The Dutch winner of this year's Academy Award as Best Foreign Film, it involves the character of Dreverhaven (Jan Decleir), a lone and stony bailiff who exacts stern measures on the poor. One day, and one day only, he enters the room of his housekeeper, Joba (Betty Schuurman). That visit leads to a pregnancy. The man doesn't send his housekeeper into disgrace and abandonment, as we might expect; she freely chooses such a state, preferring it to the prospect of becoming Dreverhaven's wife. "When is our wedding?" the stern man demands of her, from time to time, but she does not answer.

The boy is named Katadreuffe (Fedja van Huet). In school he is taunted as a bastard, and his mother is shouted at in the streets. He grows up with a deep hatred for his father. We learn all of this in flashbacks; the film opens with a confrontation between father and son, and with reasons to suspect that the boy is guilty of his father's murder.

The film is based on a 1938 novel by Ferdinand Bordewijk. It evokes some of the darker episodes of Dickens, and also, in its focus on the grind of poverty and illegitimacy, reflects the twisted stories of family secrets by that grim Victorian, George Gissing. It is essentially the story of a young man growing up and making good, by pluck and intelligence, but all of his success comes out of the desire to spite his father.

"Today, I have been made a lawyer. You no longer exist for me! You have worked against me all my life," the son tells his father in the opening scene. "Or for you," the father replies. For reasons concealed in his own past, he believes that to spare the rod is to spoil the child, and indeed calls in a loan just three days before the son's final examinations, apparently hoping to cause him to fail. "Why don't you leave our boy in peace?" Joba asks Dreverhaven in one of their rare meetings. "I'll strangle him for nine-tenths, and the last tenth will make him strong," the old man replies, carrying Tough Love a shade too far.

The film is set in Rotterdam, in sets and streets suggesting its gloomy turn-of-the-century shadows; I was reminded of *M* and other German Expressionist films in which the architecture sneers at the characters. The boy finds work in a law firm, rises to the post of office manager, and even falls in love, with Lorna Te George (Tamar van den Dop). She perhaps likes him, too, but he is so mired in self-abasement that he cannot declare his love, and he bitterly looks on as she keeps company with another man from the office. When he encounters her in a park some years later, he tells her, "I shall never marry anyone else. I have never forgotten you." For a man like him, masochistic denial is preferable to happiness.

The film is filled with sharply seen characters, including Katadreuffe's friend, an odd-looking man with an overshot lower jaw, who tries to feed him common sense. There are scenes of truly Dickensian detail, as when the father evicts a family from quarters where the rent has not been paid—going so far as to carry their dying mother into the streets himself. (He says she's faking it; he has a good eye.)

The opening scenes, which seem to show a murder, provide the frame, as the young man is cross-examined by the police. The closing scenes provide all the answers, in a way, although there is a lot more about old Dreverhaven we would like to know, including how any shreds of goodness and decency can survive in the harsh ground of his soul.

Chicago Cab ★ ★ ★
R, 96 m., 1998

Paul Dillon (Cab Driver), John Cusack (Scary Man), Gillian Anderson (South Side Girl), Laurie Metcalf (Female Ad Exec), Michael Ironside (Al), Moira Harris (Religious Mother). Directed by Mary Cybulski and John Tintori and produced by Paul Dillon and Suzanne De Walt. Screenplay by Will Kern, based on his play *Hellcab*.

Chicago Cab has received reviews complaining that every single one of the taxi driver's passengers is a colorful character with a story. True, the movie seems to be mixing the paint a bit thick—but would the film improve with the substitution of boring passengers who just want to go to the Wrigley Building and leave a nice tip? Drama is always made of the emotional high points.

The film, based on Will Kern's play *Hellcab*, stars Paul Dillon of TV's *Pretender* as a taxi driver whose job makes him confessor to some, target of others, witness to the misery of the city. I was reminded of the Fritz Leiber story about the man who could read minds and went crazy because of all the unhappiness he picked up. The driver works from early in the morning until late at night, North Side, Loop, South Side, O'Hare, his direction and ultimately his destiny determined by who happens to get into his cab.

There are more than thirty different fares (played by such as John Cusack, Laurie Metcalf, Gillian Anderson, and Michael Ironside). The first passengers of the day are churchgoers who prompt their sullen young daughter to assist in saving the driver for Jesus. The last passenger is a quiet black man who listens to the driver's sad story of the rape victim he has just taken home.

In between he races a pregnant woman to the hospital, is tricked by a couple who pretend to have sex, witnesses a drug deal, gives legal advice to a man cheated by a used car lot, gets into what looks like a stickup situation, has a girl say, "I wish you were my boyfriend," and listens silently to some New Yorkers insulting Chicago (he speaks only when they bring up the Bulls, warning them ominously, "Leave Michael out of this").

The driver, whose name is not established, is a weird-looking duck, with a bald head but sideburns. He smokes, drinks coffee, is made obscurely miserable because an arm rest in the backseat has fallen off (he tries to fix it with Elmer's Glue, an excellent product that is nevertheless somehow rarely quite strong enough for the uses you want to put it to).

At O'Hare he gets a snack from the stainless steel food truck. He observes Muslim drivers on the side of the parking area, facing Mecca for their prayers. In a hotel cab stand he gets in a discussion about the ancient topic of giving rides to dangerous-looking black guys. He gives rides to everyone. The most alarming guys he meets are the white kids looking for drugs on the South Side; they leave a girl in the cab, and he drives off with her—saving them both, maybe, from something bad.

There is the seed of a savior in him. A guy drops off his date and then tells the guy all about her: what a slut she is, how he's mistreating her, how he lies to her. "Should I tell her what he said?" the driver asks himself. He does. Then he is furious at himself for handling the situation so badly.

Dillon plays the role properly by giving us

very little of this driver: no name, no background, just a few insights when he talks to himself in the empty cab. Essentially he is a witness. I have had friends who drove cabs part-time. "You wouldn't believe some of the stories," they say. When you do it full-time, for years and years, I suppose you have two choices: Become a saint, or tune out. Here is a cab driver who doesn't know which way to turn.

Chicken Run ★ ★ ★ ½
G, 85 m., 2000

Mel Gibson (Rocky), Miranda Richardson (Mrs. Tweedy), Tony Haygarth (Mr. Tweedy), Julia Sawalha (Ginger), Jane Horrocks (Babs), Lynn Ferguson (Mac), Imelda Staunton (Bunty), Benjamin Whitrow (Fowler), Timothy Spall (Nick), Phil Daniels (Fetcher). Directed by Peter Lord and Nick Park and produced by Lord, Park, and David Sproxton. Screenplay by Karey Kirkpatrick.

Mrs. Tweedy isn't fooling. Despite her twee British name, she's not a nice little old lady chicken farmer. She means business. Early in *Chicken Run*, she singles out a chicken who hasn't been laying its daily egg, and condemns it to the chopping block. Since this is an animated film, we expect a joke and a close escape. Not a chance. The chicken gets its head chopped off, the other chickens hear the sickening thud of the ax—and later, in case there's the slightest shred of doubt about what happened, we see chicken bones.

So it truly is a matter of life and death for the chickens to escape from the Tweedy Chicken Farm in *Chicken Run*, a magical new animated film that looks and sounds like no other. Like the otherwise completely different *Babe*, this is a movie that uses animals as surrogates for our hopes and fears, and as their chickens run through one failed escape attempt after another, the charm of the movie wins us over.

The film opens as a spoof on the World War II prison pictures like *The Great Escape* and *Stalag 17* (the most important location in the movie is Hut 17). Most of the chickens are happy with captivity and free meals ("Chicken feed! My favorite!"), but one named Ginger has pluck, and tries one escape attempt after another, always being hurled into the coal-hole for a week as her punishment. Her cause grows more urgent when Mrs. Tweedy (voice by Miranda Richardson) decides to phase out the egg operation and turn all of her chickens into chicken pies.

Ginger (voice by Julia Sawalha) has tried everything: tunnels, catapults, disguises, deceptions. Mr. Tweedy (Tony Haygarth) is sure the chickens are mapping intelligent escape plans, but can't convince his wife, who is sure they are too stupid. Then a godsend arrives: Rocky the Flying Rooster (Mel Gibson), an American bird who is on the run from a circus. Surely he can teach the chickens to fly and they can escape that way?

Maybe, maybe not. There are many adventures before we discover the answer, and the most thrilling follows Ginger and Rocky through the bowels of the chicken pie machine, in an action sequence that owes a little something to the runaway mine train in *Indiana Jones and the Temple of Doom*. There are tests of daring and skill in the escape plan, but also tests of character, as the birds look into their souls and discover hidden convictions.

In a more conventional movie, the plot would proceed on autopilot. Not in *Chicken Run*, which has a whimsical and sometimes darker view of the possibilities. One of the movie's charms is the way it lets many of the characters be true eccentrics (it's set in England in the 1950s and sometimes offers a taste of those sly old Alec Guinness comedies). Characters like the Royal Air Force veteran rooster with a sneaky secret exist not to nudge the plot along but to add color and texture: This movie about chickens is more human than many formula comedies.

The movie is the first feature-length work by the team of Peter Lord and Nick Park, who've won three Oscars (Park) and two Oscar nominations (Lord) for the work in Claymation, a stop-action technique in which Plasticine is minutely changed from shot to shot to give the illusion of 3-D movement. Park is the creator of the immortal Wallace and Gromit, the man and his dog who star in *The Wrong Trousers* and *A Close Shave*.

Here, they bring a startling new smoothness and fluid quality to their art. Traditional Claymation tweaks and prods the clay between every shot; you can almost see the thumb-prints. Their more sophisticated approach here is to start with Plasticine modeled on articulated skeletons, and clothe the models with a "skin" that gives them smoothness and consistency from shot to shot. The final effect is more like *Toy Story* than traditional Claymation.

What I like best about the movie is that it's not simply a plot puzzle to be solved with a clever escape at the end. It is observant about human (or chicken) nature. A recent movie like *Gone in 60 Seconds* is the complete slave of its dim-witted plot and fears to pause for character development, lest the audience find the dialogue slows down the action. *Chicken Run*, on the other hand, is not only funny and wicked, clever and visually inventive, but . . . kind and sweet. Tender and touching. It's a movie made by men, not machines, and at the end you don't feel wrung out or manipulated, but cheerful and (I know this sounds strange) more hopeful.

Children of Heaven ★ ★ ★ ★
PG, 87 m., 1999

Amir Naji (Ali's Father), Amir Farrokh Hashemian (Ali), Bahare Seddiqi (Zahra), Nafise Jafar-Mohammadi (Roya), Fereshte Sarabandi (Ali's Mother), Kamal Mir Karimi (Assistant), Behzad Rafiee (Trainer), Dariush Mokhtari (Ali's Teacher). Directed by Majid Majidi and produced by the Institute for the Intellectual Development of Children and Young Adults. Screenplay by Majidi.

Children of Heaven is very nearly a perfect movie for children, and of course that means adults will like it too. It lacks the cynicism and smart-mouth attitudes of so much American entertainment for kids, and glows with a kind of good-hearted purity. To see this movie is to be reminded of a time when the children in movies were children, and not miniature stand-up comics.

The movie is from Iran. Immediately you think kids would not be interested in such a movie. It has subtitles. Good lord!—kids will have to read them! But its subtitles are easy for eight- or nine-year-olds, who can whisper them to their siblings, and maybe this is their perfect introduction to subtitles. As for Iran: The theme of this movie is so universal there is not a child who will not be wide-eyed with interest and suspense.

The film is about a boy who loses his sister's shoes. He takes them to the cobbler for repairs, and on the way home, when he stops to pick up vegetables for his mother, a blind trash-collector accidentally carries them away. Of course the boy, named Ali, is afraid to tell his parents. Of course his sister, named Zahra, wants to know how she is supposed to go to school without shoes. The children feverishly write notes to each other, right under their parents' noses.

The answer is simple: Zahra will wear Ali's sneakers to school every morning, and then run home so that Ali can put them on for his school in the afternoon. But Zahra cannot always run fast enough, and Ali, who is a good student, gets in trouble for being late to class. And there is a heartbreaking scene where Zahra solemnly regards her own precious lost shoes, now on the feet of the ragpicker's daughter.

I submit that this situation is scarier and more absorbing for children than a movie about Godzilla or other manufactured entertainments. When you're a kid, you know you're not likely to be squished by a giant lizard, but losing something that has been entrusted to you? And getting in trouble at school? That's big time.

Majid Majidi's film has a wonderful scene where Ali and his father bicycle from the almost medieval streets and alleys of the old town to the high-rises and luxury homes where the rich people live. The father hopes for work as a gardener, but he is intimidated by the challenge of speaking into the intercoms on the gates of the wealthy. His son jumps in with offers of pruning, weeding, spraying, and trimming. It is a great triumph.

And then there is a footrace for the poor children of the quarter. The winner gets two weeks in a summer camp and other prizes. Ali doesn't care. He wants to place third, because the prize is a new pair of sneakers, which he can give to his sister. My guess is that the race and its outcome will be as exciting for many kids as anything they've seen at the movies.

Children of Heaven is about a home without unhappiness. About a brother and sister who love one another, instead of fighting. About situations any child can identify with. In this film from Iran, I found a sweetness and innocence that shames the land of Mutant Turtles, Power Rangers, and violent video games. Why do we teach our kids to see through things before they even learn to see them?

Chill Factor ★ ★
R, 105 m., 1999

Cuba Gooding Jr. (Arlo), Skeet Ulrich (Tim Mason), Peter Firth (Captain Andrew Brynner), David Paymer (Dr. Richard Long), Hudson Leick (Vaughn), Daniel Hugh Kelly (Colonel Leo Vitelli), Kevin J. O'Connor (Telstar), Judson Mills (Dennis). Directed by Hugh Johnson and produced by James G. Robinson. Screenplay by Drew Gitlin and Mike Cheda.

In April 1999 at the University of Colorado, wounded by students who jeered at my affectionate review of *Speed 2*, I recklessly announced a contest to make a film named *Speed 3*. Entries couldn't be more than five minutes long and had to be about something that couldn't go slower than fifty miles an hour.

Chill Factor looks exactly like the first entry in my contest, but I have reluctantly had to disqualify it because it exceeds the time limit by 100 minutes, and it's not about speed but temperature. With just a tweak here and there, however, it could qualify as a parody of *Speed*—one of those *Airplane!*-type spoofs by Zucker-Abrahams-Zucker. Where are the ZAZ boys when we need them?

I promise you the movie is played straight. It is really supposed to be a thriller and we are really supposed to be thrilled. I explain that to prepare the ground for the information that the story involves a chemical weapon that cannot be allowed to grow warmer than fifty degrees, and about two brave citizens who try to keep it away from evil terrorists by keeping it in the back of a speeding ice-cream truck. Yes. There is also a sequence where they use an aluminum rowboat as a toboggan, sliding down a steep hill into a river, where the dangerous substance can be dragged behind the boat because the stream is "fed by glaciers."

The heroes are played by Skeet Ulrich, who thinks he is in a Jerry Bruckheimer production, and Cuba Gooding Jr., who has been in *Jerry Maguire* for the last four years, including

Oscar appearances. The biological weapon has been developed by Dr. Richard Long (David Paymer), whose dialogue seems to have been phoned in by the team of Carl Sagan and Mephistopheles. Early on he announces an "epiphany" about a "new molecular configuration," in which, as I murkily recall, he plans to remove atoms from one side of his molecules and stick them on the other side instead. He discovers that his plan is flawed when a test goes wrong, defoliating not 200 yards of a remote island, but five miles. Eighteen soldiers die, their flesh erupting like cheese on a burnt pizza. "Oh, my God!" he cries. "I am become Death—the destroyer of worlds."

Usually a line like that sets up a mournful aria, but in *Chill Factor* it simply results in a ten-year prison sentence for Brynner (Peter Firth), the U.S. military man in charge of the operation. Embittered, and who wouldn't be, he gets out of prison and comes looking for Dr. Long and his magic formula. Follow this closely: Because Brynner believes the United States does things it condemns other nations for doing, he therefore plans to sell the deadly poison to the terrorists with the most money.

Nobody questions this logic, but then there are a lot of logical gaps in this movie. How, for example, does a short-order clerk on the run in a stolen ice-cream truck find a hardware store with the precise materials necessary to contrive a fake version of the poison vials in the refrigerated cannister? How can you blow up both ends of a tunnel and not cut off the electricity inside? How can you be shot in the leg with a high-powered rifle and then run with only sort of a limp?

The movie is abundantly stocked with items borrowed from *Ebert's Bigger Little Movie Glossary*. The red digital readout is handy, of course, distracting from the question of what kind of chemical compound explodes at fifty degrees. The Talking Killer Syndrome sinks two scenes. So eager is *Chill Factor* to include every possible cliché, indeed, that it even keeps one as a spare: An amusement park turns up complete with Ferris wheel and merry-go-round, and then is completely forgotten, leaving us longing for the missing scenes of screaming children tumbling off their wooden horses and running through the funhouse. ☞

The Cider House Rules ★ ★

PG-13, 129 m., 1999

Tobey Maguire (Homer Wells), Charlize Theron (Candy Kendall), Delroy Lindo (Mr. Rose), Erykah Badu (Rose Rose), Paul Rudd (Wally Worthington), Michael Caine (Dr. Wilbur Larch), Jane Alexander (Nurse Edna), Kathy Baker (Nurse Angela). Directed by Lasse Hallstrom and produced by Richard N. Gladstein. Screenplay by John Irving, based on his novel.

The Cider House Rules tells the story of an orphan who is adopted by his own orphanage and raised by the doctor in charge—who sees him as a successor. At one point he runs away to pick apples and fall in love, but his fate awaits him and has been sealed at his birth.

At least, I think that's what the story is about. Other critics have zeroed in on the movie's treatment of abortion. Dr. Larch (Michael Caine), in charge of the orphanage, will provide abortions without question because, in the 1930s and 1940s, he wants to save young women from the coat hook artists of the back alleys. He has taught Homer (Tobey Maguire), his protégé, everything he knows about medicine, but Homer is opposed to abortion.

This results in a "controversial pro-choice stance on abortion" (David Rooney, *Variety*), or "it makes men the arbiters of what happens to a woman's body" (Amy Taubin, *Village Voice*). James Berardinelli, a leading Web critic, thinks it provides a "reasonably balanced perspective" on the debate, but Peter Brunette, another leading Web critic, doesn't even mention Homer's doubts. Nor does the *New York Times*.

If I had to choose, I'd vote with Taubin, who notes that Dr. Larch will perform an abortion on request, but Homer believes it is justified only in cases of rape or incest (not unknown in this movie). A larger question remains: Why is there such a muddle about the movie's subject? I left the theater wondering what the movie thought it was about, and was unable to say. It's almost deliberately unfocused; it shows us many events without guiding them to add up to anything definite.

The story begins at an orphanage in St. Cloud's, Maine, where you go to "add a child to your life, or leave one behind." Dr. Larch, who rules benevolently, is beloved by his staff and orphans. At lights-out he salutes them: "Good night, you princes of Maine—you kings of New England!" Larch is an old-fashioned progressive who would be a secular saint were it not for a few flaws, such as snuggling with his nurses and addicting himself to ether.

He names the baby Homer Wells, and essentially adopts the kid himself, teaching him everything he knows about medicine and grooming him to take over the institution. (If forged papers are necessary, no problem.) Homer, meanwhile, wonders if he might not be allowed to choose his own path in life.

Candy (Charlize Theron) and her boyfriend Wally (Paul Rudd) arrive at the orphanage for an abortion. Homer becomes their friend and follows them to Wally's family farm, where he joins an apple-picking crew headed by Mr. Rose (Delroy Lindo) and including his daughter, Rose Rose (Erykah Badu). Manual labor clears Homer's head and fresh air delights him; he embraces this world, and after Wally goes off to fight in World War II, Homer and Candy fall in love. Eventually it becomes clear that Rose is an incest victim, and Homer must decide whether to offer her an abortion.

All of this somehow sounds more dramatic than it plays. The *Cider House Rules* has been adapted by John Irving from his own novel, and we learn from his book *My Movie Business: A Memoir*, that he wrote the first draft thirteen years ago, and has seen the project through four directors, finally settling on Lasse Hallstrom *(My Life as a Dog, What's Eating Gilbert Grape)*. An author, of course, treasures all the episodes in his stories, and perhaps there was a tendency to keep in as much as possible without marshaling it toward a payoff. The result is a film that plays like a Victorian serial—*David Copperfield*, for example, which is read to the orphans—in which the ending must not come before the contracted number of installments have been delivered.

The Cider House Rules is often absorbing or enchanting in its parts. Michael Caine's performance is one of his best, and Charlize Theron is sweet and direct as the girl. But Tobey Maguire is almost maddeningly monotone as Homer (is his performance inspired by Benjamin in *The Graduate*?) and the movie never does resolve its ambiguity toward Mr. Rose, who is guilty of incest and yet—somehow,

murkily—not entirely a monster. The story touches many themes, lingers with some of them, moves on, and arrives at nowhere in particular. It's not a story so much as a reverie about possible stories.

City of Angels ★ ★ ★
PG-13, 116 m., 1998

Nicolas Cage (Seth), Meg Ryan (Dr. Maggie Rice), Dennis Franz (Nathaniel Messinger), Andre Braugher (Cassiel). Directed by Brad Silberling and produced by Dawn Steel and Charles Roven. Screenplay by Dana Stevens.

Angels are big right now in pop entertainment, no doubt because everybody gets one. New Age spirituality is Me-oriented, and gives its followers top billing in the soap operas of their own lives. People like to believe they've had lots of previous incarnations, get messages in their dreams, and are psychic. According to the theory of karma, however, if you were Joan of Arc in a past life and are currently reduced to studying Marianne Williamson paperbacks, you must have made a wrong turn.

When there's a trend toward humility and selflessness, then we'll know we're getting somewhere on the spiritual front. That time is not yet. *City of Angels* hits the crest of the boom in angel movies—and like most of them, it's a love story. Hollywood is interested in priests and nuns only when they break the vow of chastity, and with angels only when they get the hots for humans. Can you imagine a movie where a human renounces sexuality and hopes to become an angel?

Still, as angel movies go, this is one of the better ones, not least because Meg Ryan is so sunny and persuasive as a heart surgeon who falls in love with an angel. This is one of her best performances, as Dr. Maggie Rice, who loses a patient early in the film and then, in despair, finds herself being comforted by an angel named Seth (Nicolas Cage). The amazing thing is that she can see him. Angels are supposed to be invisible and hang around in long black coats, looking over people's shoulders and comparing notes at dawn and dusk.

Seth is deeply moved that he is visible to Maggie. He has wondered for a while (which in his case could be millions of years) what it would be like to have a physical body. "Do you ever wonder what that would be like—touching?" he asks another angel. Maggie has a patient named Nathaniel Messinger (Dennis Franz) who is due for a heart operation, and as she operates on him she tips her hand: "No dying, now, Mr. Messinger—not until you give me Seth's phone number."

She knows Seth is special: "Those eyes. The way he looked right down into me." Soon she has him over for dinner, where he slices his finger, but does not bleed. She feels betrayed, and cuts him again. Still no blood. She slaps him: "You freak! Just get out! Get out!" This is jarringly the wrong note, forced and artificial, but required by modern screenplay formulas, which specify that the loving couple must fight and break up so that later they can get back together again.

There are revelations in the story, involving Mr. Messinger and others, that I will leave you to discover. And a surprise development toward the end that the movie sets up so mechanically that it comes as an anticlimax. It's not a perfect movie, and there are times when Cage seems more soppy and dewy-eyed than necessary. But it has a heart, and Meg Ryan convincingly plays a woman who has met the perfect soul mate (as, indeed, she has).

The movie is based on *Wings of Desire*, the great 1988 film by Wim Wenders. But it's not really a remake. It's more of a formula story that benefits from some of Wenders's imagery (solitary angels standing in high places, solemnly regarding humanity) and his central story idea (in his film, an angel played by Bruno Ganz falls in love with a trapeze artist and chooses to become human, with the guidance of a former angel played by Peter Falk).

The Wenders film is more about spirituality. The decision to fall to Earth comes toward the end. In *City of Angels* the angel's decision to fall is, of course, only the necessary theological prelude to the big scene in front of the fireplace ("Do you feel that? And that?"). To compare the two films is really beside the point, since *Wings of Desire* exists on its own level as a visionary and original film, and *City of Angels* exists squarely in the pop mainstream. Using Dwight Macdonald's invaluable system of cultural classification, *Paradise Lost* would

be high cult, *Wings of Desire*, would be mid-cult, and *City of Angels* would be masscult.

Example of the difference: In *Wings of Desire*, an angel simply says, "I learned amazement last night." In *City of Angels*, Seth says: "I would rather have had one breath of her hair, one kiss from her mouth, one touch of her hand, than eternity without it. One." That's too much icing on the cake. Much more effective would have been simply, "I would rather have had one breath of her hair." Period. And then give the audience the pleasure of mentally completing the implications of that statement. By spelling it all out, the dialogue keeps the emotion on the screen, instead of allowing it to unfold in the viewer's imagination.

What I did appreciate is that *City of Angels* is one of the few angel movies that knows one essential fact about angels: They are not former people. "Angels aren't human. We were never human," observes Seth. This is quite true. Angels are purely spiritual beings who predate the creation of the physical universe. That leaves us with the problem of why Seth is male, and attracted to a female, when angels are without gender. But Maggie doesn't seem to have any complaints there in front of the fireplace.

A Civil Action ★ ★ ★ ½
PG-13, 118 m., 1999

John Travolta (Jan Schlichtmann), Robert Duvall (Jerome Facher), Tony Shalhoub (Kevin Conway), William H. Macy (James Gordon), Zeljko Ivanek (Bill Crowley), Bruce Norris (William Cheeseman), John Lithgow (Judge Skinner), Kathleen Quinlan (Anne Anderson), David Thornton (Richard Aufiero). Directed by Steven Zaillian and produced by Scott Rudin, Robert Redford, and Rachel Pfeffer. Screenplay by Zaillian based on the book by Jonathan Harr.

A Civil Action is like John Grisham for grown-ups. Watching it, we realize that Grisham's lawyers are romanticized hotshots living in a cowboy universe with John Wayne values. The real world of the law, this movie argues, has less to do with justice than with strategy, and doesn't necessarily arrive at truth. The law is about who wins, not about who should win.

The movie costars John Travolta and Robert

Duvall as the leaders of two opposing legal teams. At issue are the deaths by leukemia of twelve children. Travolta's argument is that the deaths were the result of pollution by two large corporations, W. R. Grace and Beatrice. Duvall, working for Beatrice, argues that neither the pollution nor its results can be proven. He also angles to separate Beatrice from its bedmate, Grace, correctly perceiving that the Grace legal strategy is unpromising.

Beatrice and Grace are real companies, and *A Civil Action* is based on a nonfiction best-seller by Jonathan Harr, which won the National Book Award. But the movie takes fictional liberties, which have been much discussed in the financial press. In particular, the Grace lawyer, William Cheeseman (Bruce Norris), is said not to be a doofus in real life. For the facts, read the book or study the case; the movie is more concerned with how the law works, and how perhaps the last thing you want is a lawyer who is committed heart and soul to your cause. What you want is a superb technician.

Duvall plays Jerome Facher, brilliant and experienced, who hides his knowledge behind a facade of eccentricity. He knows more or less what is going to happen at every stage of the case. He reads the facts, the witnesses, the court, and his opposition. There is a moment at which he offers the plaintiffs a $20 million settlement, and an argument can be made, I think, that in the deepest recesses of his mind he knows it will not be necessary. He makes the offer in the same spirit that Vegas blackjack tables offer "insurance"—he thinks he'll win, but is guarding the downside. His style is indirection; his carefully nurtured idiosyncrasies conceal his hand.

Travolta plays Jan Schlichtmann, the head of a small firm of personal injury attorneys who take on cases they believe they can win. Often their clients are too poor to pay legal fees, but Schlichtmann's firm eats the legal costs itself, hoping for a rich slice of an eventual settlement. Essentially, he's gambling with the firm's money every time he accepts a case. That's why he turns down the delegation of parents who tell about the deaths of their children: He doesn't see enough money in it to justify the risk. (The movie has a hard-boiled discussion of how much various victims are "worth." A white male professional struck down in his prime gives the biggest payoff; a dead child is worth the least of all.)

From the point of view of his financial well-being, Schlichtmann makes two mistakes. First, he decides the parents have a moral case. Second, he begins to care too much about justice for them and loses his strategic bearings. (Of course, all follows from his discovery that the polluters, whom he thought were small, shabby local firms, are actually owned by rich corporations.)

The movie, written and directed by Steven Zaillian, doesn't simplify the issues and make Schlichtmann into a romantic hero. He's more the kind of guy you refer to affectionately as "that poor sap." We hear what he hears: the emotion in the voice of one of the mothers (Kathleen Quinlan) who asks him to take the case because "all we want is somebody to apologize to us." And the heartrending story of how one of the boys died, told by his father (David Thornton) in details so sad that Schlichtmann is very deeply moved—which is, perhaps, not the best thing for his clients.

Zaillian is clear about his movie's approach. This is not a film in which a hero attorney beats up the bad guys in a climactic courtroom scene. The movie doesn't even end with its courtroom scene, but has a wry aftermath. No major characters are painted in black-and-white terms, least of all Duvall's; he is not a man without emotions and sympathies, we sense, but simply a man whose long and wise experience of the law has positioned him above the fray. He's fascinated by the law, by its opportunities and maneuverings, by its realities. Like a chess player, he knows that to win a tournament it is sometimes wise to offer a draw even when you think you can win it.

Some of the film's tension comes not from the battle between good and evil, but from the struggle between Schlichtmann's firm and its creditors. The small firm eventually sinks $1.4 million into the case, the homes of all the partners are mortgaged, and in the background during some scenes their furniture is being removed. William H. Macy plays their accountant, whose function is to announce steady progress toward professional and personal bankruptcy.

This is Zaillian's second film. His first was *Searching for Bobby Fischer* (1993), one of the most absorbing films of recent years, about a child chess prodigy whose great gift might take him to the top of the game—but at what personal price? *A Civil Action* is also about the gulf between skill and justice. In the law as in chess, the better player usually wins. It has nothing to do with which is the better person. The theme of Zaillian's first film, I wrote, was: "What makes us men is that we can think logically. What makes us human is that we sometimes choose not to." That's the message this time too. There's a subtext: When hiring an attorney, go for the logician.

Claire Dolan ★ ★ ★ ½
NO MPAA RATING, 95 m., 2000

Katrin Cartlidge (Claire), Colm Meaney (Roland), Vincent D'Onofrio (Elton). Directed by Lodge Kerrigan and produced by Ann Ruark. Screenplay by Kerrigan.

"I'm here for you," Claire Dolan tells one of her clients. "I can't get you out of my head," she whispers to another over the telephone. "You're not like other men," she tells a third. He is exactly like other men. All men are like other men when they visit a prostitute. "What do you want?" she says. "You can tell me."

Lodge Kerrigan's *Claire Dolan* is a film about a woman whose knowledge about men encompasses everything except how to trust them and find happiness with them. She is a Manhattan prostitute, mid-priced, who presents herself as a quiet, almost shy woman dressed in understated good taste. She has none of the flamboyance of the typical movie hooker, is not voluptuous, looks her clients straight in the eye while lying to them about how much she's missed them. Some guys like that. Makes them think they're doing the poor deprived girl a favor.

Claire is played by Katrin Cartlidge (the sister-in-law in *Breaking the Waves*) as a woman whose profession has given her an instinctive knowledge about how to deal with some men. There is a scene in the movie where she is seated in a bar, bothering no one, not looking for attention. Two men walk up. "I'm not looking for company," she says. "That's not your decision," says the first man, who is aggressive and menacing. She seems in danger. She looks

up at the man who is looming over her, his aggression pulsing in his face. Then she looks at his sidekick, who hangs back. "I prefer him," she says. "He's better-looking than you. Would you let him go first?"

The scene is no longer than my description of it. It is just about perfect. She has changed the subject. She understands the tension that must exist between two men who have agreed to harass a woman. Beneath their relationship is a fear of women, which links to sexual insecurity; she has castrated the first by preferring the second, and called the bluff of the second by depriving him of his leader. The men are stopped cold, and skulk away.

Much of the movie consists of Claire Dolan's business dealings. Her clients are white-collar guys in offices and hotel rooms. They believe her praise. Maybe it's what they're really paying her for. She isn't very enthusiastic during sex— sometimes she seems repelled or indifferent— but the men don't notice or care. When she doesn't follow the script, though, they have a way of turning vicious.

Her pimp, who has known her since she was a child in Dublin, is Roland (Colm Meaney, his neat little lips swimming in a face so broad he looks like Humpty-Dumpty). He addresses her with formal politeness. We see he is strong and vicious, but with Claire he has an enigmatic relationship based on buried mutual history, which perhaps involves her dying mother, and perhaps involves money he has loaned her for the mother's care (the movie is wisely vague). They work well together, Roland tells a taxi driver who thinks he loves her, because she was born to be a prostitute, likes it, and will always be one.

Whether that statement is true is the movie's central question. The taxi driver is named Elton (Vincent D'Onofrio). They spend some monosyllabic time together, make love successfully and then unsuccessfully, and agree to have a child. "We can make this work," she says. "All right," he says. They cannot make it work, because he cannot understand her profession or her pimp; he shadows her, and even goes to the extreme of hiring a new girl in the pimp's stable in order to vicariously understand how it might be between Claire and a client.

If a movie like this had a neat ending, the

ending would be a lie. We do not want answers, but questions and observations. The film is bleak about sex. It avoids the common Hollywood assumption that hookers love sex (many producers apparently believe the same lies Claire tells her clients). It is the second film by writer-director Lodge Kerrigan, whose *Clean, Shaven* was a portrait of a schizophrenic. In both films he accepts the challenge of central characters who do not let us know what they're thinking. We have to look and listen and decide for ourselves. I think Claire Dolan will make a good mother. I think she can make it work. Not with Elton, but by herself, which is the only way she can live and not have to lie.

Clay Pigeons ★ ★ ½

R, 104 m., 1998

Joaquin Phoenix (Clay), Janeane Garofalo (Agent Shelby), Vince Vaughn (Lester), Scott Wilson (Sheriff Mooney), Georgina Cates (Amanda), Vince Vieluf (Barney). Directed by David Dobkin and produced by Ridley Scott and Chris Zarpas. Screenplay by Matthew Healy.

Clay Pigeons allows the wheels of its story to spin a little too long. Creation takes two steps. First you put in. Then you take out. Many first-time filmmakers leave in too much, maybe because they don't want to take any chances, maybe because they worked so hard on their film that every shot has become a treasure for them. Within *Clay Pigeons* is a smaller story that might have involved us more, but it's buried by overkill.

The film is one of those macabre comedies where the body count steadily rises while a (possibly) innocent man looks guilty. It's set in a small Montana town where everybody knows everybody else, you can find your friends if you look in the saloon, and the deputy sheriff is named Barney.

Joaquin Phoenix stars as Clay, who has been having an affair with his best friend's wife. The best friend kills himself in an opening scene, setting it up to look like Clay killed him. Terrified, Clay tries to make the death look like a suicide, and this mistake compounds itself until he looks exactly like a serial murderer. His wife, Amanda (Georgina Cates), isn't

much help at first, and even less later. A friendly local waitress also comes to an unfortunate end.

A lot of people die in *Clay Pigeons*. If Clay isn't the serial killer, someone certainly is. But to FBI Agent Shelby (Janeane Garofalo), Clay seems like a logical suspect: "You're dating one victim, you're having an affair with another, and you find the body of the third. Kind of a coincidence, wouldn't you say?"

The Garofalo character, obviously inspired by Chief Marge Gunderson (Frances McDormand) in *Fargo*, is one of the best things in the movie. She's smart, direct, sarcastic, a wise guy. She even knows how to handle approaches in bars from tall strangers in ten-gallon hats, although her confidence is shaken somewhat when she discovers, after he leaves, that he was probably the killer.

Another important character is Lester Long (Vince Vaughn), a stranger in town who forces his way into Clay's life and soon seems like the only person who knows all his secrets. Lester has the kind of high-pitched laugh that, when you hear it, makes it seem prudent to stop whatever you're doing and move to another state. And there's Sheriff Mooney (Scott Wilson), who is none too thrilled to have the FBI butting into his jurisdiction, but realizes he needs help every time he observes Deputy Barney (Vince Vieluf), a borderline narcoleptic.

The plot cannot really be described without going into the setups and payoffs of a great many crimes, alibis, suspicions, appearances, and investigations. Director David Dobkin and writer Matthew Healy find the right tone and many individual moments spring alive, but I think they go around the track a couple of extra times.

Once we get the notion that poor Clay is digging himself deeper and deeper, once we understand that the body count will multiply, that's the moment to stop with the digging and the counting. When it comes to the use of repetition in comedy, a curious math takes place. Twice may be funnier than once and three times may be funnier than twice, but four times is about as funny as the first time and then you get into negative numbers.

What I liked were the performances, all of them, not neglecting Scott Wilson's solid work as the sheriff; he correctly understands that his character is not supposed to be funny, but to ground the others. Vince Vaughn, who is in a lot of movies these days, relishes this role and it's fun to watch him relish it. Janeane Garofalo stands there and belts out zingers and is a delight. You don't dislike the movie, but it just unwinds on you.

And at the end the plot abandons all common sense. Isn't jailbreak a crime even if you're innocent? And how is that whole business with the racehorse and the hitchhiker going to work? And is it necessary? And in an area that flat, how far away would police cars have to be before a jumpy serial killer couldn't see them?

Clockwatchers ★ ★ ★ ½
PG-13, 96 m., 1998

Toni Collette (Iris), Parker Posey (Margaret), Lisa Kudrow (Paula), Alanna Ubach (Jane). Directed by Jill Sprecher and produced by Gina Resnick. Screenplay by Jill Sprecher and Karen Sprecher.

Clockwatchers is a wicked, subversive comedy about the hell on earth occupied by temporary office workers. Hired by the day, fired on whims, they're victims of corporate apartheid: They have no rights or benefits and can't even call their desks their own. They're always looking at Polaroids of someone else's family.

This is a rare film about the way people actually live. It's about the new world of security cameras, Muzak, cubicle life, and hoarding office supplies. "Try not to make too many mistakes," a new temp worker is told. "These forms are expensive." When she botches some forms, she throws them out in the ladies' room to hide her crime. The toilet, indeed, is the only sanctuary in a big office: the refuge, the retreat, the confessional. Only when your underwear is off can you find a space to call your own.

Clockwatchers was written by two sisters, Jill and Karen Sprecher, and directed by Jill. I don't have to be psychic to know they've worked as office temps. The Coen, Hughes, and Wachowski brothers make movies about crime and passion, and so do the Sprecher sisters, but their violence is more brutal and direct, like stealing the precious rubber-band ball of Art, the anal-retentive guy in charge of the office supplies.

The movie stars Toni Collette as Iris, the new temp. Frightened and insecure, blinded by the buzzing overhead fixtures like a rabbit in the headlights, she's taken under the wing of Margaret (Parker Posey), a temp who knows the ropes and has a healthy contempt for the office, her bosses, and temp life in general. When she answers someone else's phone, she doesn't take a message, she just leaves the caller on hold until they get bored and hang up: "By the time they find out, you're long gone."

At lunchtime, Margaret leads Iris to the lonely Formica tables in the corner of the cafeteria, where the temps sit huddled together. None of the permanent workers mix with them; it's like they have a disease. Jane (Alanna Ubach) tells Iris: "I used to work in a bank. There was this button on the desk and I kept looking at it every day for a month and finally I just pushed it. It was the alarm. They never tell you anything because they're afraid you'll take their stupid jobs."

Boredom hangs low over the office like a poisonous fog. It's the kind of place where you carve I WAS HERE into the desk, but don't sign your name. Paula (Lisa Kudrow), another temp, is given a business card by a male coworker and it's the same card she's always finding left in the ladies' room, as if the guy's pathetic title and embossed little name would make him sexually irresistible. A new girl is hired, and the temps try to figure out how she got the job as the boss's new permanent assistant. At quitting time, every eye is riveted to the wall clock: They're like third-graders, waiting to be dismissed, so they can go to nearby bars, smoke cigarettes, and be lied to by half-looped junior executives.

Something interesting happens. There is a crime wave. Office supplies and little doodads are missing from people's desks. Who is the thief? Eyes narrow. There's lots of whispering at lunchtime. Security cameras are pointed directly at the desks of the temps: Yeah, like they're going to steal from themselves. One of the girls is fired and gets the last word: "How can you fire me? You don't even know my name!"

I take hope when I see a movie like this, because it means somebody is still listening and watching. Most new movies are about old movies; this one is about the way we live now.

109

Clockwatchers is the kind of movie that can change lives by articulating anger; a few of the people who see it are going to make basic changes because of it—they're going to revolt—and ten years from now the Sprecher sisters will get a letter from one of them, thanking them.

There's that, and then there's also the way the movie is so mercilessly funny, because it sees stupidity so clearly. Take Iris's first day on the job, where she's told to sit in a chair and wait, and sits there for hours, until the office manager says, "Why didn't you tell me you were here?" Like it's her fault. Like Iris knew who the stupid office manager was. Like it's not the office manager's job to see if anyone is sitting in the stupid chair. Like at the salary level of a temp, it makes any difference how long she sits there. Like maybe someday, with hard work, good luck, patience, and timing, she can be a big shot like Art, and have her own stupid rubber-band ball.

The Closer You Get ★ ★
PG-13, 92 m., 2000

Niamh Cusack (Kate), Sean McGinley (Ian), Ian Hart (Kieran), Ewan Stewart (Pat), Sean McDonagh (Sean), Cathleen Bradley (Siobhan), Pat Shortt (Ollie), Deborah Barnett (Ella). Directed by Aileen Ritchie and produced by Uberto Pasolini. Screenplay by William Ivory, based on a story by Herbie Wave.

See enough of its movies and a nation's cinema can tell you something about the nation involved. It may be right, it may be wrong, but there it is. I now assume, for example, that everyone in Australia is a little strange, and half of them are bizarre eccentrics. The French, they are worried all the time. Americans live trapped inside the clichés of genre fiction, and so do the Canadians, only they are nicer, unless they are in David Cronenberg films.

And the Irish are sweet, cheerful folk who live in each other's pockets, settle things by communitywide debate, gang up men against women, and visit home briefly between pubs. They are also blessed with great verbal alacrity, and there would be a great many more of them if the women were not so opinionated and the men so baffled by women with opinions.

This picture has nothing to do with the Irish I have met during half a dozen visits to the Emerald Isle, who are likely to be successful professionals benefiting from a booming economy and a standard of living higher than England's. But the Irish have no one but themselves to blame for their screen image, except in the case of *The Closer You Get,* which was produced by an Italian.

Umberto Pasolini earlier made *The Full Monty,* which made millions of dollars with its heartfelt and bawdy comedy about six unemployed Englishmen who became male strippers. Now he has moved to the west of Ireland, to county Donegal, upon whose sainted strands late one night I once kissed a publican's red-haired daughter.

She was, I must admit, a good deal like Siobhan (Cathleen Bradley), the heroine of *The Closer You Get,* who will stand for no nonsense from Kieran (Ian Hart), the local butcher—who is both her employer and her obvious mate, if he were not so daft he doesn't realize it. "Siobhan is a hard case," Kieran laments, by which he means that she is disinclined to conduct both sides of their courtship while he slips out for a few pints with his mates.

This is a town starved for entertainment. The priest livens things up by mounting loudspeakers on the bell tower and playing tapes of the bells from St. Peter's in Rome. (Then he starts a film society and books *The Ten Commandments,* but is sent 10 instead.) The local lads, despairing of the standoffish women in town, chip in to buy an ad in the *Miami Herald* to invite American women to their annual dance. The local women retaliate by inviting a band of alarmingly swarthy and hirsute Spaniards, who make the pale Donegal locals look like they've spent too much time in the cellar counting the root vegetables.

Everyone in *The Closer You Get* is nice, and Ian Hart's butcher is especially likable, with his brown hair dyed platinum in a failed attempt to look hip. But the movie is too thin and low-key to generate much comic energy. Compared to *Waking Ned Devine,* it's dilute and transparent. And I doubt many contemporary Irish young people are this naive and shy. It's a sweet film, mildly pleasant to watch, but it's not worth the trip or even a detour.

The Color of Paradise ★ ★ ★ ½
PG, 90 m., 2000

Mohsen Ramezani (Mohammad), Hossein Mahjub (Hashem), Salime Feizi (Granny). Directed by Majid Majidi and produced by Mehdi Karimi. Screenplay by Majidi.

Words appear on a black screen: "To the glory of God." I was reminded of Catholic grade school, where every page of homework began at the top with our childish handwriting: "JMJ"—for Jesus, Mary, and Joseph. Was I dedicating my arithmetic to heaven, or requesting a miracle?

There is no doubt in the mind of Majid Majidi, the Iranian writer and director of *The Color of Paradise*. His work feels truly intended for God's glory, unlike so much "religious art" that is intended merely to propagandize for one view of God over another. His film looks up, not sideways. In this and his previous film, the luminous Oscar nominee *Children of Heaven,* he provides a quiet rebuke to the materialist consumerism in Western films about children. (Both films have subtitles, but they're not too difficult for any child who can read.)

The Color of Paradise is about a blind boy. Quick and gentle, in love with knowledge, acutely attuned to the world around him, Mohammad loves his lessons at a school for the blind. He is loved at home by his grandmother and his two sisters. But his father, Hashem, does not love him. Hashem is a widower, ambitious to marry into a prosperous family, and he fears the possession of a blind son will devalue him in the marriage market.

As the film opens, the school term is over, and the other boys have been picked up by their parents. Mohammad waits alone outside his school, for a father who does not come. There is a remarkable sequence in which he hears the peep of a chick that has fallen from its nest. The boy finds the chick, gently takes it in his hand, and then climbs a tree, listening for the cries of the lost one's nest-mates. He replaces the bird in its nest. God, who knows when a sparrow falls, has had help this time from a little blind boy.

The father finally arrives, and asks the headmaster if Mohammad can stay at the school over the vacation term. The answer is no. Hashem reluctantly brings the boy home with him, where his grandmother and sisters welcome him. Mohammad is under no illusions about his father's love. Local children attend a school. Mohammad has all the same books, in Braille, and begs to be allowed to attend. In class, he knows the answers—but his father forbids him to continue at the school, possibly hoping to keep his existence a secret. Eventually the boy is apprenticed to a blind carpenter, who will teach him how to build cabinets by touch. This might be a good job for some, but not for Mohammad, who is eager to compete in the world of the seeing.

For all of its apparent melodrama, *The Color of Paradise* is not an obvious or manipulative film. It is too deliberately simple. And it is made with delicacy and beauty. The sound track is alive with natural sounds of woodpeckers, songbirds, insects and nature, voices and footfalls. A blind person would get a good idea of the locations and what is happening—as Mohammad does. The performance by young Mohsen Ramezani, as the boy, is without guile; when he cries once in frustration, we do not see acting, but raw grief.

The ending, after a sequence in which the boy is in great danger, will strike some as contrived. Certainly it is not subtle by our cynical Western standards. If Hollywood told this story, the father would have a change of heart. In Iran, heaven intervenes more directly—as if God, having tested Mohammad as much as he dares, has the change of heart Himself.

The Color of Paradise is a family film that shames the facile commercialism of a product like *Pokemon* and its value system based on power and greed. Because they do not condescend to young audiences, Majidi's films, of course, are absorbing for adults as well, and there is a lesson here: Any family film not good enough for grown-ups is certainly not good enough for children.

Conspirators of Pleasure ★ ★ ★
NO MPAA RATING, 83 m., 1998

Petr Meissel (Peony), Anna Wetlinska (Mrs. Beltinska), Gabriela Wilhelmova (Mrs. Loubalova), Jifi Labus (Kula), Barbora Hrzanova (Mrs. Malkova), Pavel Novy

(Beltinsky). Directed by Jan Svankmajer and produced by Jaromir Kallista. Screenplay by Svankmajer.

The opening scene of *Conspirators of Pleasure* shows a man examining the skin magazines in a porno shop and finally selecting one. This will be the most normal moment of sexual behavior in the movie. At home, paging through the magazine, the man's attention is distracted by a large cabinet standing by the wall. The busty girls in the magazine are no competition for whatever it contains. As the man eyes the cabinet's keyhole and nervously licks his lips, we meet some of his neighbors.

His landlady, for example, is involved in stealing straw from a mattress to construct a large dummy. The man who owns the magazine store is building an apparatus that will embrace and caress him while he watches tapes of a pretty newscaster. The newscaster, while she is broadcasting, keeps her feet in a tank so catfish can nibble her toes. Out in the garage, her husband is building devices that will roll up and down his body, alternating nail heads with tickly fluff. Then there is the postwoman, who rolls a loaf of bread into little round balls that she pokes into her nose and ears.

These pastimes reminded me of the films of Luis Buñuel, the great Spanish filmmaker whose characters pleasured themselves in strange ways (a bishop got off by pretending to be a gardener, a man constructed wax dolls and put them into furnaces, and in *Belle de Jour* there was that strange client with his little box; we never saw what was in it, but the women in the brothel wanted nothing to do with it).

Conspirators of Pleasure is a film about lonely people who apply the "do-it-yourself" approach to previously unimagined possibilities. By the end of the film, when the first little man has pulped his porno magazines to construct a papier-mâché chicken head, and is flapping about the garden with wings made of old umbrellas, we realize our notions of kinky behavior are seriously deficient. Whether the movie is serious or funny depends, I suppose, on whether you're the toes or the fish.

This is the third feature film by Jan Svankmajer, a Czech who gets around the problem of subtitles by the simple device of having no dialogue in his movie. There are sound effects

and music, but no conversations, because these six people are in isolation chambers of their own making. As they tinker busily in their solitary rooms and garages, constructing devices that will give them pleasure, I thought of the great crushing loneliness that must have descended on creatures like Jeffrey Dahmer, who literally stood outside the ordinary consolations of the human race.

And yet *Conspirators of Pleasure* is not an angry or tragic film. It's too matter-of-fact for that. It's not even overtly sexual, because its eroticism takes place inside the imaginations of its characters. It doesn't have an MPAA rating, but I'd love to see how the ratings board would deal with a film that is entirely about masturbation, but has no explicit nudity, no "language," no contact between two people and no intimate touching. Would they rate it "R" because we can see some breasts in the skin mags at the beginning? Films like this subvert the whole notion of ratings by showing that pornography exists in the unseen places of the individual mind.

Svankmajer up until now has been mostly an animator; his short films are seen all over the world. Here he's used living actors, but treats them like the subjects of animation: caricatures whose thoughts are conveyed in broad physical terms. There is a little stop-action animation in the film, but essentially it's as unadorned and straightforward as porno, with people in their rooms, absorbed in their activities. Its lesson, I suppose, is that in the absence of love one turns to technology, which is a small consolation; the characters seem to derive more pleasure out of constructing their toys than using them.

In his end credits, Svankmajer acknowledges the "technical expertise" of a number of people, including de Sade, Sader-Masoch, Freud, and, of course, Buñuel—whose *Un Chien Andalou*, made with Salvador Dali, must have helped inspire *Conspirators of Pleasure*. Svankmajer calls himself a radical surrealist, and like the original surrealists he gains his effects not by abstract fantasies but by taking a skewed new look at everyday reality. So much of this film is practical: how to keep the fish alive under the bed, or what to do with little bread balls after you've used them (the postwoman mails them to the newscaster to feed the fish).

All of this ingenuity reminded me of a college friend, the late novelist Paul Tyner, who was studying ads for electric sexual aids when he hit upon the ultimate perversion: plug them in, fit them together, and watch them.

Cookie's Fortune ★ ★ ★ ★
PG-13, 118 m., 1999

Glenn Close (Camille Dixon), Julianne Moore (Cora Duvall), Liv Tyler (Emma Duvall), Chris O'Donnell (Jason Brown), Charles S. Dutton (Willis Richland), Patricia Neal (Cookie Orcutt), Ned Beatty (Lester Boyle), Niecy Nash (Deputy Wanda), Lyle Lovett (Manny Hood), Donald Moffat (Jack Palmer), Courtney B. Vance (Otis Tucker), Ruby Wilson (Josie Martin). Directed by Robert Altman and produced by Altman and Etchie Stroh. Screenplay by Anne Rapp.

Cookie's Fortune is Robert Altman's sunniest film, a warmhearted comedy that somehow manages to deal with death and murder charges without even containing a real villain. True, the Glenn Close character comes close to villainy by falsifying a death scene, but since she's in the middle of directing the Easter play at her church, maybe it's partly a case of runaway theatrical zeal.

The movie takes place in the small town of Holly Springs, Mississippi, where Altman assembles a large cast of lovable characters. He's a master of stories that interconnect a lot of people (*M*A*S*H, Nashville, The Player, Short Cuts*), and here one of the pleasures is discovering the hidden connections.

The film begins with a false alarm. A black man named Willis (Charles S. Dutton) wanders out of a bar, seems to break into a home, and studies the guns displayed in a cabinet. An elderly white woman (Patricia Neal) comes downstairs and finds him, and then we discover they're best friends. Neal plays Cookie, a rich widow who misses her husband fiercely. Glenn Close is Camille Dixon, her niece, who before long discovers Cookie's dead body and rearranges the death scene to make it look like a break-in and a murder.

Meanwhile, Altman's camera strolls comfortably around town, introducing us to Cora (Julianne Moore), Camille's dim sister; Emma (Liv Tyler), Cora's daughter, who takes a pass

on genteel society and works at the catfish house; and the forces down at the police station, including the veteran officer Lester (Ned Beatty), Jason the doofus rookie (Chris O'Donnell), and Wanda the deputy (Niecy Nash). Some of these people have roles in the Easter play, which is *Salome* (the letterboard in front of the church says it's "by Oscar Wilde and Camille Dixon").

The key dramatic event in the film is the arrest of Willis on suspicion of murder, even though everyone in the town is convinced he could not have committed such a crime. His fingerprints are indeed on the guns in Cookie's house, but no wonder, since he just finished cleaning them.

"He's innocent. You can trust me on that," declares Lester the cop.

"What makes you so sure of that?"

"Because—I fish with him."

Emma also believes he's innocent, and demonstrates her confidence by moving into his jail cell. The cell door is kept open, which is convenient for Emma and Jason the doofus deputy, since they are desperately in love and sneak off behind the Coke machine for rumpy-pumpy whenever possible.

"They read you your rights?" the lawyer (Donald Moffat) asks Willis. "Yeah, and gave me a cup of coffee and an issue of *Field and Stream*." Also a Scrabble board. Meanwhile, Camille and Cora (who has been sworn to secrecy about the falsified death scene) are beside themselves: They like Willis and are horrified he's under arrest, but to free him would involve incriminating themselves.

Altman and his writer, Anne Rapp, use the crime story as a way to reveal connections of one sort or another between almost everyone in the movie. They also show a small southern town that is not seething with racism, classism, and ignorance, but is in fact a sort of heavenly place where most people know and like one another, and are long accustomed to each other's peculiarities. (There's a lovely scene where the bar owner tries to explain to the cops, without really saying so, that it is Willis's custom to steal a half-pint of Southern Comfort when he's broke, and return it when he's in funds.)

Altman has always been good with sly humor at the edges of his frame. He doesn't only focus on the foreground action, but allows supporting characters to lead their own lives on the edges. Notice in particular the delightful character of Wanda (Niecy Nash), the African-American deputy, who wields a tape recorder with great drama. There's a scene where a state investigator arrives from Jackson to look into the case, and is a handsome black man (Courtney B. Vance). He interviews the blues singer at the bar (Ruby Wilson), while Wanda mans the tape recorder, and both women subtly but shamelessly flirt with him.

Cookie's Fortune is the kind of comedy with a lot of laughs, and even more smiles. The cast blends so smoothly you can believe they all live in the same town. There is a great warmth at the center of the story, in the performance by Charles S. Dutton, who is one of the most likable characters in any Altman film (his scenes with Liv Tyler include some very tricky revelations, which they both handle with perfect simplicity). Glenn Close has the richest comedy in the film, as the meddling, stage-struck director ("The two of you keep forgetting this is ancient Galilee!"). Patricia Neal's role is brief, but crucial and touching. Ned Beatty's sheriff uses fishing as his metaphor for life.

Altman's films are sometimes criticized for being needlessly enigmatic and elliptical, for ending at quixotic moments, for getting too cute with the asides. He does sometimes commit those sins, if sins they are, but in the service of creating movies that are fresh and original. *Cookie's Fortune* has no ragged edges or bothersome detours, and flows from surprise to delight. At the end, when just deserts are handed out, it arrives at a kind of perfection.

The Corruptor ★ ½

R, 111 m., 1999

Chow Yun-Fat (Nick Chen), Mark Wahlberg (Danny Wallace), Ric Young (Henry Lee), Elizabeth Lindsey (Louise Deng), Paul Ben-Victor (Schabacker), Jon Kit Lee (Jack), Andrew Pang (Willy Ung), Brian Cox (Sean Wallace), Kim Chan (Uncle Benny). Directed by James Foley and produced by Dan Halsted. Screenplay by Robert Pucci.

Even when it's transplanted to the streets of New York's Chinatown, as *The Corruptor* is, the Hong Kong action genre has certain obligatory requirements. Low-angle shots of bad guys looming over the camera, for example. And the sound of a metallic whoosh when there's a quick cut from one scene to the next. And what seems like more dialogue during action scenes than before and after them.

The Corruptor touches these bases, and has an icon as its lead: Chow Yun-Fat, who has made almost seventy films and has recently followed Jackie Chan into the American market (*Replacement Killers*, with Mira Sorvino, in 1998). His *Hard Boiled* (1992), directed by the master of the genre, John Woo, is a cult favorite. *The Corruptor* isn't in that league.

Chow Yun-Fat plays Nick Chen, a tough cop in an all-Asian station house in Chinatown. A white cop named Danny (Mark Wahlberg) is assigned to the precinct, and greeted with much suspicion: He will stand out, he won't be trusted, he doesn't understand the Chinese, etc. This is a setup for one of the weariest of all cop formulas, the cop-buddy movie, in which opposites first repel and then attract. Will Nick and Danny be friends by the end of the movie? What do you think?

But there are a couple of fundamental twists I dare not reveal, involving secrets held by both men—a secret, in Danny's case, that makes you wonder how his superiors could possibly have hoped for him to operate effectively in an Asian environment. No matter; the plot chugs along as the cops get involved in a scheme involving the boss of Chinatown, Uncle Benny (Kim Chan, who according to the Internet Movie Database played a character with exactly the same name in *Lethal Weapon 4*—is this trivia, or homage?).

Everybody in Chinatown is more or less on the take, but there are degrees of immorality, and Nick is the kind of cop who tries to be realistic and principled at the same time. As for Danny: Well, I just never believed he was a cop at all. Mark Wahlberg was effective in a much more difficult role in *Boogie Nights*, but he's not an action star and he never feels at home in the role.

There's an opportunity for some kind of love or human interest with another cop in the precinct, played by Elizabeth Lindsey; she's set up as a major character, but given a role so underwritten (or badly edited) that she spends a lot of time just standing in the backgrounds of other people's shots. The problem with relationships is that they involve personalities and dialogue, and there's not much time for those in an action picture.

The director is James Foley, who is obviously not right for this material. It's a shame, actually, that he's even working in the genre, since his gift is with the intense study of human behavior, and his best films include *Glengarry Glen Ross, At Close Range,* and *After Dark, My Sweet.* John Woo, who might have brought crackling energy to this material (especially if he nixed the casting of Wahlberg), wouldn't be right for *Glengarry.* So there you are.

Cotton Mary ★ ★
R, 125 m., 2000

Greta Scacchi (Lily MacIntosh), Madhur Jaffrey (Cotton Mary), Sakina Jaffrey (Rosie), James Wilby (John MacIntosh), Prayag Raaj (Abraham), Laura Lumley (Theresa), Sarah Badel (Mrs. Evans), Joanna David (Mrs. Smythe), Gemma Jones (Mrs. Davids), Neena Gupta (Blossom). Directed by Ismail Merchant and produced by Nayeem Hafizka and Richard Hawley. Screenplay by Alexandra Viets.

Ismail Merchant's *Cotton Mary* centers on the stories of two women: an Anglo-Indian who wants to be white, and a white British woman who wants to brood and sulk and be left alone. We don't like either character, but what we can't understand is the British woman's sullen passivity and indifference to her household; a faithful servant is fired, her husband has an affair, a crazy woman takes charge of her new baby, and she hardly seems to notice. The film wants to make larger points, but succeeds only in being a story of derangement.

The British Raj shut down in 1947, and Indians took over their own country for the first time in centuries. But many people of British descent, born there, considered it home and stayed after independence. The best portrait of that time I've read is Paul Scott's *Staying On,* the novel that followed his masterful *Raj Quartet. Cotton Mary* is like a lurid reduction of material set in a similar time and place, without the human insights—either in the story or between the characters.

As the story opens, a British woman named Lily (Greta Scacchi) has given birth, but has no milk. Mary (Madhur Jaffrey), a nurse at the hospital, takes the sickly child to her sister Blossom (Neena Gupta), who lives in a poorhouse and serves as a wet nurse. Lily hardly seems to notice. When she finally asks, "Mary, how do you feed the baby?" and is told, "Mother's milk, madam," that seems to satisfy her. She is maddeningly incurious.

Mary insinuates herself into the household, which is run by the aged family servant Abraham (Prayag Raaj). Soon she plots to convince Lily to fire Abraham (who can clearly see Cotton Mary is mad) and replace him with her own candidate, the cousin of a cousin. Abraham is the most convincing and touching character in the movie; when Lily tells him to go home, he protests, "But madam, this is my home." The newly hired cousin is a drunk; Lily sees him staggering around the garden, pulling up plants, and does nothing.

Lily's husband, John (James Wilby), a reporter for the BBC World Service, is absent much of the time covering alarming portents, and when he returns it is to have an affair with Mary's shapely friend Rosie (Sakina Jaffrey). But this affair is more obligatory than necessary, and supplies little more than a perfunctory sex interest. Meanwhile, the household goes to pieces while Cotton Mary dreams ominously of having white babies.

What is the point of this movie? To show that some Anglo-Indians identified with the departing British? Of course they did. When British men first arrived in India as soldiers and traders, they engaged in widespread liaisons and marriages with Indian women, and that custom ended only with the arrival of large numbers of British women, who introduced racism into the mix; similar feelings were mirrored on the Indian side. The Raj provided a privileged place for Anglo-Indians, but when the British departed, mixed-race people like Cotton Mary were left without a safety net. This story could be told more poignantly if Mary were not so clearly bonkers that her race is beside the point.

As for Lily, is she suffering from postpartum depression, or is she so clueless because the story requires her to notice almost nothing around her? A competent person would have treasured Abraham and left instructions for Mary to be barred from the house, and then there would have been no story. I think of the old couple in *Staying On,* and their life-long loyalty to one another—their friendship with the manager of the nearby hotel, and their clockwork firing of their faithful servant (who refuses to be fired), and the loneliness of the local Anglican church, surrounded by the gravestones of ghosts whose descendants have all gone back to England. That is a story. *Cotton Mary* is a soap opera.

Cousin Bette ★ ★ ★
R, 108 m., 1998

Jessica Lange (Cousin Bette), Bob Hoskins (Mayor Crevel), Elisabeth Shue (Jenny Cadine), Hugh Laurie (Baron Hulot), Kelly MacDonald (Hortense), Aden Young (Wenceslas), Geraldine Chaplin (Adeline). Directed by Des McAnuff and produced by Sarah Radclyffe. Screenplay by Lynn Siefert and Susan Tarr, based on the novel by Honoré de Balzac.

Characters motivated by money are always more interesting than characters motivated by love, because you don't know what they'll do next. Tom Wolfe knew that when he wrote *The Bonfire of the Vanities,* still an accurate satire of the way we live now. Maybe that's why writers from India, where marriages are often arranged, are the most interesting new novelists in English.

The Victorians knew how important money was. The plots of Dickens and Trollope wallowed in it, and Henry James created exquisite punishments for his naively romantic Americans caught in the nets of needy Europeans. And now consider *Cousin Bette,* a film based on one of Balzac's best-known novels, in which France of the mid-nineteenth century is unable to supply a single person who is not motivated more or less exclusively by greed. Wolfe said his *Bonfire* was inspired by Balzac, and he must have had this novel in mind.

The title character, played by Jessica Lange with the gravity of a governess in Victorian pornography, is a spinster of about forty. Her life was sacrificed, she believes, because her family had sufficient resources to dress, groom, and train only one of the girls—her cousin (Geraldine Chaplin). Bette was sent to work in the garden, and the lucky cousin, on her deathbed, nostalgically recalls the dirt under Bette's nails. When the lucky cousin dies, Bette fully expects to marry the widower, Baron Hulot (Hugh Laurie). But the baron offers her only a housekeeper's position.

Refusing the humiliating post, Bette returns to her shabby hotel on one of the jumbled back streets of Paris, circa 1846, where the population consists mostly of desperate prostitutes, starving artists, and concierges with arms like hams. Bette is not a woman it is safe to offend. She works as a seamstress in a bawdy theater, where the star is the baron's mistress, Jenny Cadine (Elisabeth Shue). The rich playboys of Paris queue up every night outside Jenny's dressing room, their arms filled with gifts. Baron Hulot does not own her, but rents her, and the rent is coming due. Bette knows exactly how Jenny works, and uses her access as a useful weapon ("You will be the ax—and I will be the hand that wields you!").

Every night, pretending to sleep, Bette watches as Wenceslas (Aden Young), the handsome young Polish artist who lives upstairs, sneaks into her room to steal the cheese from her mousetrap and a swig of wine from her jug. She offers to support him from her savings (as a loan, with interest, of course), and falls in love with him, only to learn that he has fallen in love with Jenny. ("They say," Jenny unwisely tells Bette, "that he lives with a hag. A fierce-eyed dragon who won't let him out of her sight.")

Meanwhile, the baron is bankrupt and in hock to the moneylenders. His son fires the family servants in desperation. Nucingen, a familiar figure from many of Balzac's novels, lends money at ruinous interest. And the baron's daughter Hortense (Kelly MacDonald) unexpectedly weds Wenceslas, who unwisely allows love to temporarily blind him to Jenny's more sophisticated appeals. Also lurking about is the rich lord mayor of Paris, Crevel (Bob Hoskins), who once offered Hortense 200,000 francs for a look at her body, and is now, because of her desperation, offered a 50 percent discount.

All of these people are hypocrites, not least Wenceslas, who designs small metal decorations and poses as a great sculptor. When the baron, now his father-in-law, underwrites the purchase of a huge block of marble, Wenceslas's greatest gift is describing what he plans to do with it.

This is a plot worthy of *Dynasty*, told by the first-time director Des McAnuff with an appreciation for Balzac's droll storytelling; he treats the novel not as great literature but as merciless social satire, and it is perhaps not a coincidence that for his cinematographer he chose Andrzej Sekula *(Pulp Fiction)*, achieving a modern look and pace. The movie is not respectful like a literary adaptation, but wicked with gossip and social satire. ("The nineteenth century as we know it was invented by Balzac," Oscar Wilde said.)

Between 1846, when the movie opens, and 1848, when it reaches a climax, popular unrest breaks out in Paris. Angry proletarians pursue the carriages of the rich down the streets, and mobs tear up cobblestones and build barricades. Balzac's point is that history has dropped an anvil on his spoiled degenerates. But the plot stays resolutely at the level of avarice, and it is fascinating to watch Cousin Bette as she lies to everyone, pulls the strings of her puppets, and distributes justice and revenge like an angry god. By the end, as she smiles upon an infant and the child gurgles back, the movie has earned the monstrous irony of this image.

Cradle Will Rock ★ ★ ★
R, 132 m., 1999

Hank Azaria (Marc Blitzstein), Emily Watson (Olive Stanton), Rubén Blades (Diego Rivera), Joan Cusack (Hazel Huffman), John Cusack (Nelson Rockefeller), Angus MacFadyen (Orson Welles), Cary Elwes (John Houseman), Philip Baker Hall (Gray Mathers), Cherry Jones (Hallie Flanagan), Bill Murray (Tommy Crickshaw), John Carpenter (William Randolph Hearst), Vanessa Redgrave (Comtesse LaGrange), Susan Sarandon (Margherita Sarfati), John Turturro (Aldo Silvano). Directed by Tim Robbins and produced by Robbins, Jon Kilik, and Lydia Dean Pilcher. Screenplay by Robbins.

It was a time when the rich flirted with communists and fascists, when the poor stood in breadlines, when the class divide in America came closer to the boil than ever before or since. The 1930s were a decade when the Depression put millions out of work and government programs were started to create jobs. One of them was the Federal Theater Project, which funded "free theater for the people" all over the country, but was suspected by Congressman Martin Dies of harboring left-wing influences. Since the last right-wing theater was in ancient Greece, his was a reasonable suspicion.

Tim Robbins's sweeping, ambitious film, *Cradle Will Rock*, is a chronicle of that time, knitting together stories and characters both real and fictional, in a way similar to John Dos Passos's novel *USA*. It tells the story of the production of Marc Blitzstein's class-conscious musical *The Cradle Will Rock;* its opening has been called the most extraordinary night in the history of American theater.

Intercut with that production are stories about Nelson Rockefeller (John Cusack), the millionaire's son who partied with the Mexican communist painter Diego Riviera (Rubén Blades) and commissioned his mural for Rockefeller Center; and the newspaper publisher William Randolph Hearst (John Carpenter) and fictional steel tycoon Gray Mathers (Philip Baker Hall), who bought Renaissance masterpieces secretly from Mussolini, helping to finance Italian fascism. We meet theatrical giants such as Orson Welles (Angus MacFadyen) and John Houseman (Cary Elwes). And little people like the homeless Olive Stanton (Emily Watson), who eventually sang the opening song in *Cradle*, and Tommy Crickshaw (Bill Murray), a ventriloquist so conflicted that he helps a young clerk (Joan Cusack) rehearse her red-baiting testimony, while his dummy sings "The Internationale," apparently on its own.

There is a lot of material to cover here, and Robbins covers it in a way that will be fascinating to people who know the period—to whom names like Welles, Rockefeller, Hearst, and Rivera mean something. For those who don't have some notion of the background, the film may be confusing and some of its characters murky. It needs a study guide, and viewing *Citizen Kane* might be a good place to start.

The film's anger is founded in the way Dies and his congressional red-hunters brought the full wrath of the government down on poverty-stricken theater people whose new musical might be a little pink, while ignoring fat cats like Hearst, who not only bought paintings from Mussolini for bags full of cash, but whose newspapers published flattering stories about the dictator from his former mistress Margherita Sarfatti (played by Susan Sarandon).

Nelson Rockefeller's flip-flops provide in some ways the best material in the film. Swept up in the heady art currents of the time, Rockefeller commissioned Rivera to paint a mural—and then, while the painter and his assistant were busy covering a huge wall of Rockefeller Center, was unhappy to learn the amorphous blobs hovering above portraits of the rich were molecules of syphilis and bubonic plague. The last straw was Rivera's addition of a portrait of Lenin. Rocky ordered the mural sledgehammered to dust, and its destruction is intercut with the crisis in the *Cradle Will Rock* production (one syphilis molecule escapes the hammers and clings to the wall in defiance).

Cradle Will Rock was produced under the aegis of Welles and Houseman, whose Mercury Theater then dominated radio drama, and whose *Citizen Kane* was only a few years in the future. Welles was a golden boy, only twenty-one, flamboyant and cocky. When union actors declare a rest break during a rehearsal, he thunders, "You're not actors! You're smokers!" Then he limousines off to "21" for oysters and champagne. Welles comes across as an obnoxious and often drunken genius in a performance by MacFadyen that doesn't look or sound much like the familiar original (ironically, Tim Robbins would make an ideal Welles).

Houseman is more admirable, especially after Federal Theater funds are cut off and the army padlocks the theater where *Cradle Will Rock* is set to open. He and Welles lead a defiant march uptown to another theater, and when Actors' Equity forbids its members to step foot on stage, composer Blitzstein (Hank Azaria) plays his score on a piano, and the cast members stand up in the audience to perform their roles.

The power of the Bliztstein play itself never really comes across in the film. It's too fragmented, and its meaning seems less political than theatrical. It's not what the play says that matters, so much as the fact that it was per-formed despite attempts to silence it. Its opening night was, in a way, an end of an era. Welles and Houseman soon went off to Hollywood and America went off to war, and it was thirty years before young Americans felt revolutionary again. Nelson Rockefeller went on to portray a "moderate" Republican, Hearst retired to San Simeon, and Rockefeller Center lost a tourist draw. Think how amusing the Lenin portrait would seem today, and imagine the tour guides pointing out the molecules of bubonic plague.   ☞

Crazy in Alabama ★ ★

PG-13, 104 m., 1999

Melanie Griffith (Lucille), David Morse (Dove), Lucas Black (Peejoe), Cathy Moriarty (Earlene), Meat Loaf Aday (Sheriff John Doggett), Louis Miller (Taylor Jackson), Rod Steiger (Judge Mead), Richard Schiff (Norman), John Beasley (Nehemiah), Robert Wagner (Harry Hall). Directed by Antonio Banderas and produced by Debra Hill. Screenplay by Mark Childress.

Crazy in Alabama is an ungainly fit of three stories that have no business being shoehorned into the same movie. The first one is familiar: events seen through the eyes of a young boy in a small town, who recalls, "And after that day nothing was ever the same again." This point of view could have worked with either of the other two stories, but not both at once: (1) ditzy dame snaps after years of cruel husband, leaves for Hollywood to find fame and fortune; and (2) local black boy becomes the focus of a civil rights crusade.

It is a symptom of the movie's confused agenda that although the outcome produces two trials, it is the ditzy dame whose fate is settled on-screen, and not the man charged with the death of a black boy. One wonders whether the eccentric local judge, who has such sympathy for a sexy brunette who chops off her husband's head, will be such a humanitarian when it comes to judging a racist white sheriff in a town with no black voters.

The head-chopping is announced almost in the first scene. Melanie Griffith plays Lucille, a woman who is clearly insane, and who kills her husband, decapitates him to be sure he is dead, and leaves for Hollywood to be discovered. She takes his head along, and frequently hears his voice, in scenes that are like a comic reprise of Peckinpah's *Bring Me the Head of Alfredo Garcia*. Her journey takes her through New Orleans and the Southwest, where she slinks and flirts her way out of arrests, and finally to Hollywood, where her career takes an unexpected turn.

Meanwhile, through the eyes of young Peejoe (Lucas Black), we see not only his loony Aunt Lucille but also the story of Taylor Jackson (Louis Miller), a black boy about his same age, who wants to swim in the segregated local pool and is warned off by the sheriff (Meat Loaf Aday) with the thought-provoking line, "You are trespassing on public property!" His determination leads to a local civil rights struggle, a death, and a visit from Martin Luther King Jr., and for young Peejoe, yes, after that summer nothing would ever be the same again.

The film is the directorial debut of the actor Antonio Banderas, Melanie Griffith's husband, who does a competent, professional job, although at the outset they should have realized that each of their main stories would curdle the other one. When a boy is dead in a civil rights case, that kind of takes the comedy out of the sexy nutcase defending herself in court. Nor is her self-justification very persuasive: "You spend all day making a beautiful meal for your husband, and he comes home and gobbles it down, and a little piece of you dies." Yeah, and a big piece of him.

Croupier ★ ★ ★
NO MPAA RATING, 91 m., 2000

Clive Owen (Jack Manfred), Kate Hardie (Bella), Alex Kingston (Jani de Villiers), Gina McKee (Marion), Nicholas Ball (Jack's Father). Directed by Mike Hodges and produced by Jonathan Cavendish. Screenplay by Paul Mayersberg.

You have to make a choice in life: Be a gambler or a croupier.

So believes Jack Manfred, the hero of *Croupier*, whose casino job places him halfway between the bosses and the bettors, so he can keep an eye on both. He is a cold, controlled man, at pains to tell us, "I do not gamble." True enough, he does not gamble at casino games of chance, but in his personal life he places appalling bets, and by the end of the film is involved with three women and a scheme to defraud the casino.

Manfred (Clive Owen) wants to be a writer, and narrates his own story in the third person, as if he's writing it. With his slicked-back black hair, symmetrical good looks, and cold detachment, he's a reminder of Alain Delon's professional killer in *Le Samourai*—a man who wants to stay aloof and calculate the odds, but finds himself up to the neck in trouble anyway. There's the hint that this is a pattern, and that at one time he did gamble, obsessively.

The key figure in Jack's life is his father (Nicholas Ball), who was indeed a gambler, a Jack-the-lad who womanized, drank, gambled, and ran roughshod over Jack's early years. Jack's secret is that his hard, calculating facade has been hammered together as a shield over the little boy inside.

Jack's father, now in South Africa, lines up a job for him at the roulette wheels of a London casino. Jack never gambles, but he does deal, and is a skilled card manipulator (we imagine his dad teaching the boy to shuffle). The movie knows its way around casinos, and particularly observes how the dealers, with their strange hours and surreal jobs, tend to date each other instead of outsiders ("incest," the screenplay calls it). He observes dispassionately as punters line up to try their luck, and the movie notices what complete indifference the dealers have for their clients: Whether they win or lose, the work shift is exactly as long.

Jack has a girlfriend named Marion (Gina McKee), who is a store detective. "I want to marry a writer, not a (bleeping) croupier," she tells him. During the course of the story he also has liaisons with a dealer named Bella (Kate Hardie) who works on his shift. And he meets the glamorous Jani de Villiers (Alex Kingston), a casino client from South Africa— wild, reckless, in debt, a sexual predator who wants to hook him on a scheme to cheat the casino. Jack is just detached enough from his job, just enough of a mechanic intrigued by the intricacies of the plot, to be interested.

The movie was directed by Mike Hodges,

whose *Get Carter* (1971) is one of the best of the hard-boiled British crime movies. It was written by Paul Mayersburg *(The Man Who Fell to Earth, Eureka),* who must have done his research, since the casino scenes feel real: This isn't an unconvincing movie casino (even though it was built on a set in Germany), but a convincing portrayal of one of those smaller London operations where the plush and the gilt and the tuxedos on the gorillas at the door don't quite cover the tarnish.

The plot is more than we bargained for. I will not hint at the details, which lead to an unexpected and satisfactory but not entirely convincing ending. The point of the movie is not the plot but the character and the atmosphere; Hodges is bemused by Jack Manfred, who thinks he can stand outside his own life, control it, figure the odds, and turn it into a novel.

The choice of Clive Owen as the star is a good one. He's got the same sort of physical reserve as Sean Connery in the *Bond* pictures; he doesn't give himself wholly to the action, but seems to be keeping a part of his mind outside of it, measuring and calculating. This is not just a strategy but essential to his personality. We sense that his father had a way of catching him off balance, and that he vowed that when he grew up he would never be fooled again. If he ever did grow up.

Cruel Intentions ★ ★ ★
R, 97 m., 1999

Sarah Michelle Gellar (Kathryn Merteuil), Ryan Phillippe (Sebastian Valmont), Reese Witherspoon (Annette Hargrove), Selma Blair (Cecile Caldwell), Louise Fletcher (Helen Rosemond), Joshua Jackson (Blaine Tuttle), Eric Mabius (Greg McConnell), Sean Patrick Thomas (Ronald Clifford). Directed by Roger Kumble and produced by Neal H. Moritz. Screenplay by Kumble.

Teenagers once went to the movies to see adults making love. Now adults go to the movies to see teenagers making love. *Cruel Intentions* is a modern-day version of *Dangerous Liaisons,* with rich kids in a prep school playing roles that were written for jaded French aristocrats in the wicked 1782 novel by Choderlos De Laclos. He created a world of depraved amorality, in which the only goal was to indulge one's selfishness. It's refreshing, after the sponge-brained teenage romances of recent months, to see this movie reflecting that cynicism—up to a point. It crash-lands with an ending of soppy moralizing, but until the end, it's smart and merciless in the tradition of the original story.

The film stars Ryan Phillippe, a slinky schemer in the tradition of James Spader, as Sebastian Valmont, a rich kid who lives in a Manhattan mansion with his stepsister Kathryn Merteuil (Sarah Michelle Gellar). He's known as an unprincipled seducer who "has never uttered a single word without dishonorable intentions." She's a minx who's angered when her current boyfriend dumps her for the sweeter Cecile (Selma Blair), and in revenge she urges Sebastian to conquer Cecile and destroy her reputation.

Agreed, says Sebastian, but soon he finds a greater challenge—the virginal Annette (Reese Witherspoon), daughter of the new headmaster at their expensive school. She's written an article for *Seventeen* magazine praising premarital virginity, and Sebastian bets Kathryn he can deflower her. The wager: If he loses, his stepsister gets his classic sports car. If he wins, he gets his stepsister.

Sebastian pulls heartstrings, tells lies, and employs devious seductive strategies, and the movie is startling in its frank language and forthright approach to sex; it's like a throwback to the 1970s. The plot's Machiavellian emotional strategies remind us of the same story as it was told in Stephen Frears's *Dangerous Liaisons* (1988) and Milos Forman's *Valmont* (1989), but the much younger actors create the uncanny illusion of a high school production of a grown-up play. Are teenagers capable of sexual strategies this devious and sophisticated? I doubt it; few adults are, and even those who qualify may simply lack the energy.

The movie's at its best in the scenes between Gellar and Phillippe, who develop a convincing emotional charge, and whose wickedness seems to work as a sexual stimulant. There's one scene where she persuades him, emotionally and physically, to do what she wants, and we are reminded that slow, subtle eroticism is, after all, possible in the movies—even though recently it has been replaced by calisthenics. Gellar is effective as a bright girl who knows exactly how to use her act as a tramp, and Phillippe seems cold and detached enough to make it interesting when he finally gets skewered by the arrow of true love.

The best parts of the movie allow us to see how good it might all have been, with a little more care. It steps wrong in three ways. The first is with the ending, which lacks the courage to take the story to its logical conclusion, and instead contrives a series of moralistic payoffs that are false and boring. The second is with the treatment of some gay characters; surely kids as sophisticated as those in this story would be less homophobic. The third is with the use of a black character (Sean Patrick Thomas), Cecile's cello instructor, whose race is uneasily employed in awkwardly written scenes.

Still, overall, the film at least has style and wit, and a lot of devious fun with its plot. Compared to the sluggish *Jawbreaker*, it's a wake-up call. I almost hesitate to repeat my usual complaint about movies where twentysomethings play teenagers. Yes, the characters in this movie look too old to be sixteen or seventeen, but on the other hand, if actors are too young to attend R-rated movies, should they be making them? Only kidding.

The Cruise ★ ★ ★

NO MPAA RATING, 76 m., 1998

A documentary directed and produced by Bennett Miller. Featuring Timothy (Speed) Levitch.

"Right now you are six and a half blocks from where Thomas Paine died!" Speed Levitch announces breathlessly. The necks of the tourists on the Gray Line bus swivel uncertainly. Where are they supposed to be looking? "O. Henry lived and wrote near here! You are five blocks from where Dorothy Parker wrestles with alcoholism, and fails!"

It is like taking a virtual bus tour. You are here and the sights are there. Levitch never pauses for breath, rattling ahead in his adenoidal voice: "There are 2.4 million people in Manhattan!" He adds beneath his breath, "I heard 1.7 the other day, but I don't care."

This is Manhattan's most famous tour bus guide, a man for whom the island is not just the backdrop to his needs and dreams, but their very embodiment: "The anger, the inferiority that some of the smaller buildings feel—I feel." Tourists from Omaha, Altoona, and Cincinnati blink their eyes uncertainly as he tells him how close they are at this very moment to the Greenwich Village home of the poet e. e. cummings. He may be moving too fast for them, but maybe not: "I expect the total transformation of their lives the moment they get on the bus."

Timothy (Speed) Levitch is the star and subject of *The Cruise*, a loopy documentary about a man who literally lives by his wits. Levitch is a 1992 college graduate who has lived in Manhattan ever since without ever having a permanent home. He sleeps over at the houses of friends and depends on the kindnesses of strangers. He calls it "couch surfing." He made $9 an hour plus tips from the Gray Line, better than the $7 paid by Big Apple tours, but still he is winsome: "Big Apple was *Spartacus*. Gray Line is *Willy Wonka*." His tendency to personalize inanimate objects reaches some sort of apex when he emerges from his bus to gaze up at an early skyscraper and suggests that a terra-cotta frieze is the structure's orgasm.

I get letters from people who would like to make a movie. My advice could be, find a subject like Speed Levitch and follow him around with a video camera. That's what Bennett Miller did—directing, producing, and photographing *The Cruise*. Levitch (who has now retired and gives private tours) became a legend in the New York bus tour universe in the mid-1990s; customers, far from being confused by his curious rants, recommended his tours to one another. That makes a kind of sense. You can see buildings anywhere, but Levitch is the kind of sight perhaps only New York could engender.

"I went to double-decker buses to meet and seduce women," he says. It didn't work (maybe because of homelessness, a Goodwill wardrobe, and a flat-footed duckwalk?). Now he sees that "every double-decker loop is a loop toward my death." He's not just a cheerful clown; there's a strange, dark undertow that we sense beneath lines like: "Eleven people have jumped off this bridge and survived. One of my cruising dreams would be to get those people together on a cruise."

Around and around the city he cruises by land, driven mad by the repetition of the spiel, but not as mad as some guides, since he feels free to comment at length on sights the passengers cannot even see. There is something more to him, we feel, and deeper than this colorful showoff. A story not told. Like Tiny Tim, he gives the sense of a man whose only home is his personality. "I was reemerged into my own naïveté," he explains.

The Cup ★ ★ ★
G, 94 m., 2000

Orgyen Tobgyal (Geko), Neten Chokling (Lodo), Jamyang Lodro (Orgyen), Lama Chonjor (Abbot), Godu Lama (Old Lama), Thinley Nudi (Tibetan Layman), Kunsang (Cook Monk), Kunsang Nyima (Palden), Pema Tshundup (Nyima), Dzigar Kongtrul (Vajra Master). Directed by Khyentse Norbu and produced by Malcolm Watson and Raymond Steiner. Screenplay by Norbu.

In the courtyard of their monastery, dressed in traditional robes, their heads shaven, young monks play a game of soccer, kicking around a Coke can. This image, near the beginning of *The Cup*, symbolizes its cheerful truce between the sacred and the mundane. The movie is a lighthearted comedy with serious undertones about the Chinese campaign against the traditions of Tibet.

The film takes place at a Tibetan monastery in exile in India, which from time to time receives Tibetan children whose parents have smuggled them past the border guards so that they can be raised in the ancient Buddhist teachings. And so they are, in a monastery which seems a little like any boarding school for irrepressible kids. "We shave our heads so that girls will not find us attractive," one explains to another, sighing that it doesn't work in the opposite direction.

The monastery is overseen by an abbot (Lama Chonjor), who is old and holy and deep and revered, and human, with a twinkle in his eye. He knows that the ancient ways in which he was raised are now in collision with the modern world, and so he is not altogether astonished when a fourteen-year-old student named Orgyen (Jamyang Lodro) stirs up desire among his fellow students to watch the World Cup finals on TV.

Why is this match so important? Because the World Cup itself is an obsession for most males in most of the world, of course, but especially because the final is between France and Brazil, "and France supports the cause of Tibet."

The abbot's assistant (Orgyen Tobgyal) is not an unreasonable man, and agrees to take the request to the holy man, who after due thought agrees. But official permission is only the first of many hurdles for the young monks, who now must raise the money to rent a television set and a satellite dish, and transport both to the monastery. Their attempts are told against a backdrop of daily life and human (and sacred) comedy in the monastery.

In addition to the Coke can, we see a lot of soccer magazines, studied by the students at least as intently as their sacred texts. And we get a real sense for these monks as human beings whose calling does not set them aside from contemporary society so much as give them a distinctive position in it. Often Tibetan monks are portrayed in the movies as distant and almost inhuman: automatons of worship. These are men and boys for whom Buddhism is a religion, a calling, a profession, and a reasonable way to live. Perhaps Westerners are too much in awe of the spirituality they encounter, and it took an insider to see the humanity involved.

The Cup, which is the first feature film ever made in Bhutan, was directed by Khyentse Norbu, a lama who must have learned a lot about filmmaking while serving as Bernardo Bertolucci's assistant during the filming of *Little Buddha*. The film has a distinctly Western feel in its timing and character development; it's not an inaccessible exercise in impenetrable mysteries, but a delightful demonstration of how spirituality can coexist quite happily with an intense desire for France to defeat Brazil.

The movie was a runner-up for the Audience Award at the Toronto Film Festival in 1999, and was also a hit at Sundance in 2000, where I met Khyentse Norbu, and was struck by his poise and a certain distance he kept from those around him; his body language seemed to suggest he was interested in more evolved questions than what films Miramax was picking up. Then I learned that in addition to being a lama and a director, he is also considered to be the incarnation of the nineteenth-century saint Jamyang Khyentse Wangpo. And I thought: Of course. So many sinners have directed films that it is only fair for a saint to have a chance.

D

Dance With Me ★ ★ ★
PG, 126 m., 1998

Vanessa L. Williams (Ruby Sinclair), Chaynne (Rafael Infante), Kris Kristofferson (John Burnett), Joan Plowright (Bea Johnson), Rick Valenzuela (Julian Marshall), Jane Krakowski (Patricia), Beth Grant (Lovejoy), William Marquez (Stefano), Harry Groener (Michael). Directed by Randa Haines and produced by Shinya Egawa, Haines, and Lauren Weissman. Screenplay by Daryl Matthews.

Dance With Me is romance and intrigue in a shabby Houston dance studio, where pro dancers are in training for the World Open Dance Championship in Las Vegas. A lot of the plot is standard, but a lot of it isn't, including the relationship between a young man from Cuba (the Puerto Rican singing star Chayanne) and a gifted dancer (Vanessa L. Williams), who says, "I don't want to be in love."

It goes without saying that these two people are destined to fall in love. But the movie sees Ruby, the Williams character, clearly and with surprising truthfulness; she has a depth associated with more serious movies. And there's another convincing character, grizzled old John Burnett (Kris Kristofferson), who runs the studio but would much rather be standing on the end of a Gulf pier fishing.

The movie opens in Cuba, where the young and handsome Rafael Infante (Chayanne) buries his mother and then accepts an invitation to visit her old friend Burnett in Texas. At the bus station he's greeted not by Burnett but by Ruby Sinclair, who is pointedly standoffish. So is Burnett, who gives the newcomer a place to live over his garage, but doesn't warm up to him.

It's thirty days until the Vegas championships, and Ruby is having trouble with her partner. So is Burnett, whose heart is no longer in dancing. Rafael, pleasant and helpful, begins as a handyman and scores his first success by decorating the studio for a party by using every single decoration he can find—Christmas and Halloween stuff included. Before long, he's dancing.

It's clear to the audience from the first scene that Burnett is Rafael's father. But this is not clear to Burnett, or at least he won't admit it. It's also clear that Ruby and Rafael are powerfully attracted to one another, but Ruby has issues, including her child by her former partner Julian (Rick Valenzuela). She doesn't want love, and eventually she decides to rejoin Julian for the championships, and leave Rafael and Houston for good.

The director, Randa Haines (*Children of a Lesser God*), says she is a fan of ballroom dancing herself, and makes it clear that relationships off and on the floor are two different things. Ruby needs money and success, and dancing is what she's best at. She's been hurt by men and is single-minded. Yes, she's attracted to Rafael, and sometimes her heart melts, but then she pulls away again. Julian can help her win.

Ruby is the most interesting character in the movie. Williams, who, by the way, is a spectacularly good dancer, plays Ruby as a woman struggling to retain control of her life. There's steel and rigidity in her, and that's how she dances too. Watching her do technical exercises, Rafael asks her, "How do you dance without music? Dancing *comes* from the music. That's why you look so stiff." The first time they dance together, he's clumsy, because he doesn't understand her instructions. But "I'm Cuban, and so of course I can dance," he says, and he can. Even when drenched by sprinklers.

Chayanne is famous in Latin music circles, not so well known in the mainstream. He's good-looking and can dance, but, more important, he's got a pleasing personality, and he doesn't overplay the schmaltz. By the end we're invested in wanting Rafael and Ruby to be together, and a movie that has achieved that has done its job.

I liked Kristofferson as a man tired and lonely. And I liked the other dance studio regulars, including Joan Plowright, an unlikely but inspiring casting choice, as a competitor in the seniors division. I also liked the big dance sequences at the end. Rick Valenzuela is a world-class dancing star whose character treats Ruby like his puppet. (He hisses criticisms even during dance numbers.) Their dance style is like a violent quarrel between two people who have long and bitterly hated and loved one another—perfect, of course, for the tango, but also perfect as a contrast to Rafael's looser and more spontaneous style.

Like *Strictly Ballroom* and *Shall We Dance, Dance With Me* uses the dance scenes as a way to sneak musical numbers into a film that is technically not a musical. It sneaks in a lot more, too, and I was surprised by how much humanity Vanessa L. Williams brings to a character that could have been a cliché. This is a movie of predictable pleasures, and then it has those surprises.

Dancing at Lughnasa ★ ★ ½
PG, 94 m., 1998

Meryl Streep (Kate Mundy), Michael Gambon (Father Jack Mundy), Catherine McCormack (Christina Mundy), Kathy Burke (Maggie Mundy), Sophie Thompson (Rose Mundy), Brid Brennan (Agnes Mundy), Rhys Ifans (Gerry Evans), Darrell Johnston (Michael Mundy). Directed by Pat O'Connor and produced by Noel Pearson. Screenplay by Frank McGuinness, based on the play by Brian Friel.

Why did *Dancing at Lughnasa* affect me so much more deeply on the stage than it does on film? Was it the physical presence of the actors? No, I think just the opposite: It was their distance. Up *there* on the stage, they took on allegorical dimensions, while in the close-ups of film they are too present, too close, too specific. The closer you get to these characters, the less you sympathize with their plight and the more you grow impatient with them.

The story, based on an award-winning play by Brian Friel, tells of the five Mundy sisters, who live in a cottage in rural Ireland in the 1930s. One has an out-of-wedlock son, Michael. As the film opens, they receive a visitor: their older brother, Father Jack, who has returned in retirement after years in Africa. He is not quite all there; his eyes wander and he loses the drift. The equatorial sun and the lure of African customs (shown in the opening credits) have worn down his Catholic beliefs, and

after inquiring about his young nephew's father and discovering there is none of record, he suggests cheerfully, "I'd like you all to have a love child!"

This does not go down well with Kate Mundy (Meryl Streep), a local schoolteacher, firm and unyielding. It becomes apparent that the five women and the boy have been living in such close quarters for so long that only silence and routine make it bearable. One sister smokes all the time. Rose (Sophie Thompson), simpleminded, moons for a married man. Christina (Catherine McCormack), Michael's mother, waits (too) patiently for periodic visits from her dashing lover, Gerry (Rhys Ifans). He roars up on a motorcycle, charms her, dazzles his son (Darrell Johnston), and then roars off again—to fight against Franco in Spain, he explains.

The story is narrated, years later, by the adult Michael. He sees the surfaces, and we are meant to see beneath them. We see that Rose yearns to lead a life of her own, that Christina can feed for months on the memory of a kiss, that survival for Kate consists of keeping everyone's real feelings under her fearful discipline. The arrival of Father Jack disturbs this delicate balance, ending the past and beginning the present.

Played with sad charm by Michael Gambon in a performance deliberately vague and well-meaning, Father Jack is a man whose mind, long baked by the sun and cured by alcohol, has brought Christian and pagan ideas together into peaceful harmony. And indeed the Africans dancing around their tribal fires in the opening credits are mirrored, in Ireland, by the annual pagan festival of Lughnasa, held up in the hills, also with bonfires. Rose runs off with her fellow for a night of freedom, and we suspect she finds the courage because Father Jack has somehow set her free. He's in the old dramatic convention of the madman who speaks the truth.

At the end of the film, everyone dances. This time it is to the radio and the dancing is more sedate, but the suggestion is that the Mundy sisters have somehow been able to let out their breath at last, to end the fearful, rigid stillness that enveloped their cottage. Michael, the young narrator, remembers that time of the dancing many years later, and it is his memory that drives the story. But it is all memory and no drama. On stage, they dance and they are dancing now. On film, somehow, they are dancing then. It is not enough.

Dangerous Beauty ★ ★ ★ ½
R, 115 m., 1998

Catherine McCormack (Veronica Franco), Rufus Sewell (Marco Venier), Oliver Platt (Maffio), Moira Kelly (Beatrice), Fred Ward (Domenico Venier), Jacqueline Bisset (Paola Franco). Directed by Marshall Herskovitz and produced by Herskovitz, Ed Zwick, Arnon Milchan, and Sarah Caplan. Screenplay by Jeannine Dominy.

"The life you lead, the freedom you have—will you deny my daughters the same chance?" Not the request every mother would address to a prostitute, but *Dangerous Beauty* makes a persuasive case for the life of a courtesan in sixteenth-century Venice. At a time when Europeans are bemused by our naïveté about dalliance in high places, this is, I suppose, the film we should study. It's based on the true story of Veronica Franco, a well-born Venetian beauty who deliberately chose the life of a courtesan because it seemed a better choice than poverty or an arranged marriage to a decayed nobleman.

Veronica, played by Catherine McCormack with cool insight into the ways of men, is a woman who becomes the lover of many because she cannot be the lover of one. She is in love with the curly-headed Marco (Rufus Sewell), and he with her, but they cannot wed; "I must marry," he tells her, "according to my station and my family's will." Veronica knows this is true, and knows, too, that because her father has squandered the family fortune, she is also expected to marry money.

Shall they then become unmarried lovers? Marco persuasively argues, "God made sin that we might know his mercy." But then Veronica, her virginity lost, could never make a good marriage. Her mother (Jacqueline Bisset) has a better idea. "You cannot marry Marco, but you shall have him! You'll become a courtesan—like your mother used to be."

Veronica's eyes widen, but her mother's logic prevails, and the daughter is launched on a training course in grooming, fashion, and deportment. Her mother even shows her a great Venetian library, off limits to women, but not to Veronica ("Courtesans are the most educated women in the world"). For a courtesan, as for an army recruit, the goal is to be all that she can be. And indeed Veronica is soon the most popular and respected fallen woman in Venice, sought by princes, generals, and merchants, and even dandled on the knee of the cardinal.

The film, directed with great zest by Marshall Herskovitz, positions this story somewhere between a romance novel and a biopic. It looks like Merchant-Ivory but plays like *Dynasty*. And it's set in a breathtakingly lovely Venice, where special effects have been used to empty the Grand Canal of motorboats and fill it with regattas and gondolas. No city is more sensuous, more suited to intrigue, more saturated with secrets.

McCormack plays Veronica as a woman not averse to physical pleasure (the morning after her initiation, she smiles dreamily and asks, "Who's next?"). But sex is not really the point with a courtesan. She provides intellectual companionship for her powerful clients; through her connections she can share valuable pillow talk. And there is high entertainment as she uses poetry for verbal duels with noblemen. Her lover Marco, by contrast, is doomed to marriage with a rich girl who, like all wives of the time, is sheltered and illiterate. "Do you like poetry?" he asks her hopefully on their wedding night. "I know the psalms," she replies.

Veronica's great moment comes when the Turkish fleet seizes Venetian territory and prepares an assault on the city itself. Everything depends on the French king: Will he supply ships for the Venetian cause? The king, young and with a reputation for depravity, visits Venice and singles out Veronica for his night's pleasure. The screenplay, by Jeanine Dominey, who brings a woman's realism to matters of the heart, is pointed.

"What do you yearn for, King Henry?" asks Veronica. "Your tears," he says, pressing a knife to her throat. "I don't think so," she says, and a shadow of doubt crosses his face. "Then what do I yearn for?" he asks. She graces him with a cold smile: "Why don't we find out?" Cut to the next morning, as the doge and other nobles nervously await the king's reappearance. He emerges, settles himself somewhat painfully on a cushion, and says, "You'll get your ships."

Veronica saves the city, but is herself condemned when the plague strikes Venice and the Inquisition blames it on women and heresy. Obviously a woman with so much power must be a witch. In a courtroom scene that I somehow doubt played out quite this way in real life, she defends herself and the life of a courtesan. It is better, she argues, to prostitute herself willingly, for her own gain, than to do so unwillingly in an arranged marriage: "No biblical hell could be worse than a state of perpetual inconsequence."

I am not surprised, as I said, that the screenwriter is a woman. Few movies have been so deliberately told from a woman's point of view. We are informed in all those best-sellers about Mars and Venus, that a man looks for beauty and a woman for security. But a man also looks for autonomy, power, independence, and authority, and a woman in sixteenth-century Venice (and even today) is expected to surrender those attributes to her husband. The woman regains her power through an understanding of the male libido: A man in a state of lust is to all intents and purposes hypnotized. Most movies are made by males, and show women enthralled by men. This movie knows better.

Dark City ★ ★ ★ ★
R, 103 m., 1998

Rufus Sewell (John Murdoch), William Hurt (Inspector Bumstead), Kiefer Sutherland (Dr. Daniel Schreber), Jennifer Connelly (Emma Murdoch), Richard O'Brien (Mr. Hand), Ian Richardson (Mr. Book), Bruce Spence (Mr. Wall), Colin Friels (Walenski). Directed by Alex Proyas and produced by Andrew Mason and Proyas. Screenplay by Proyas, Lem Dobbs, and David S. Goyer.

Dark City by Alex Proyas is a great visionary achievement, a film so original and exciting it stirred my imagination like Lang's *Metropolis* or Kubrick's *2001.* If it is true, as the German director Werner Herzog believes, that we live in an age starved of new images, then *Dark City* is a film to nourish us. Not a story so much as an experience, it is a triumph of art direction, set design, cinematography, special effects—and imagination.

Like *Blade Runner,* it imagines a city of the future. But while *Blade Runner* extended existing trends, *Dark City* leaps into the unknown. Its vast *noir* metropolis seems to exist in an alternative time line, with elements of our present and past combined with visions from a futuristic comic book. Like the first *Batman,* it presents a city of night and shadows, but it goes far beyond *Batman* in a richness of ominous, stylized sets, streets, skylines, and cityscapes. For once a movie city is the equal of any city we could picture in our minds; this is the city *The Fifth Element* teased us with, without coming through.

The story combines science fiction with *film noir*—in more ways than we realize and more surprising ways than I will reveal. Its villains, in their homburgs and flapping overcoats, look like a nightmare inspired by the thugs in *M,* but their pale faces would look more at home in *The Cabinet of Dr. Caligari*—and, frighteningly, one of them is a child. They are the Strangers, shape-changers from another solar system, and we are told they came to Earth when their own world was dying. (They create, in the process, the first space vessel since *Star Wars* that is newly conceived—not a clone of that looming mechanical vision.)

They inhabit a city of rumbling, elevated, streamlined trains, dank flophouses, scurrying crowds, and store windows that owe something to Edward Hopper's *Night Owls.* In this city lives John Murdoch (Rufus Sewell), who awakens in a strange bathtub beneath a swinging ceiling lamp, to blood, fear, and guilt. The telephone rings; it is Dr. Schreber (Kiefer Sutherland), gasping out two or three words at a time, as if the need to speak is all that gives him breath. He warns Murdoch to flee, and indeed three Strangers are at the end of the corridor and coming for him.

The film will be the story of Murdoch's flight into the mean streets, and his gradual discovery of the nature of the city and the Strangers. Like many science-fiction heroes, he has a memory shattered into pieces that do not fit. But he remembers the woman he loves, or loved—his wife, Emma (Jennifer Connelly), who is a torch singer with sad eyes and wounded lips. And he remembers . . . Shell Beach? Where was that? He sees it on a billboard and old longings stir.

There is a detective after him, Inspector Bumstead (William Hurt). Murdoch is wanted in connection with the murders of six prostitutes. Did he kill them? Like the hero of Kafka's *The Trial,* he feels so paranoid he hardly knows. Rufus Sewell plays Murdoch like a man caught in a pinball machine, flipped back into danger every time it looks like the game is over.

The story has familiar elements made new. Even the hard-boiled detective, his eyes shaded by the brim of his fedora, seems less like a figure from *film noir* than like a projection of an alien idea of *noir.* Proyas and his co-screenwriters, Lem Dobbs and David S. Goyer, use dream logic to pursue their hero through the mystery of his own life. Along the way, Murdoch discovers that he alone, among humans, has the power of the Strangers—an ability to use his mind in order to shape the physical universe. (This power is expressed in the film as a sort of transparent shimmering projection aimed from Murdoch's forehead into the world, and as klutzy as that sounds, I found myself enjoying its very audacity: What else would mind power look like?)

Murdoch's problem is that he has no way of knowing if his memories are real, if his past actually happened, if the woman he loves ever existed. Those who offer to help him cannot be trusted. Even his enemies may not be real. The movie teasingly explores the question that babies first ask in peek-a-boo: When I can't see you, are you there? It's through that game that we learn the difference between ourselves and others. But what if *we're* not there, either?

The movie is a glorious marriage of existential dread and slam-bang action. Toward the end, there is a thrilling apocalyptic battle that nearly destroys the city, and I scribbled in my notes: "For once, a sequence where the fire and explosions really work, and don't play just as effects." Proyas and his cinematographer, Dariusz Wolski, capture the kinetic energy of

great comic books; their framing and foreshortening and tilt shots and distorting lenses shake the images and splash them on the screen, and it's not "action" but more like action painting.

Proyas was the director of *The Crow* (1994), the visually inspired film that was almost doomed when its star, Brandon Lee, was killed in an accident. I called that film "the best version of a comic book universe I've seen," but *Dark City* is miles beyond it. Proyas's background was in music videos, usually an ominous sign, but not here: His film shows the obsessive concentration on visual detail that's the hallmark of directors who make films that are short and expensive. There's such a wealth on the screen, such an overflowing of imagination and energy, of sets and effects. Often in f/x movies the camera doesn't feel free because it must remain within the confines of what has been created for it to see. Here we feel there's no limit.

Is the film for teenage boys and comic book fans? Not at all, although that's the marketing pitch. It's for anyone who still has a sense of wonder and a feeling for great visual style. This is a film containing ideas and true poignancy, a story that has been all thought out and has surprises right up to the end. It's romantic and exhilarating. Watching it, I thought of the last dozen films I'd seen and realized they were all essentially about people standing around and talking to one another. *Dark City* has been created and imagined as a new visual *place* for us to inhabit. It adds treasure to our notions of what can be imagined.

Deceiver ★ ★
R, 102 m., 1998

Chris Penn (Braxton), Ellen Burstyn (Mook), Tim Roth (Wayland), Renee Zellweger (Elizabeth), Michael Rooker (Kennesaw), Rosanna Arquette (Mrs. Kennesaw). Directed by Josh Pate and Jonas Pate and produced by Peter Glatzer. Screenplay by Josh Pate and Jonas Pate.

Deceiver is a Chinese box of a movie, in which we learn less and less about more and more. It's centered in a police interrogation room, where a rich kid undergoes a lie detector test in connection with the murder of a prostitute. Did he do it? At first it seems he did. Then he turns the tables on the two cops running the polygraph exam, and by the end of the film everyone is a suspect.

Tim Roth stars as Wayland, a Princeton grad and the son of a textile magnate, but currently unemployed. There's no doubt he knew the prostitute, named Elizabeth (Renee Zellweger, from *Jerry Maguire*): He even took her to a black-tie party at his parents' home, and got disowned in the process. But did he cut her into pieces and distribute her throughout Charleston, South Carolina?

The cops are Braxton (Chris Penn) and Kennesaw (Michael Rooker). Their methods are a little crude; they seem intent on helping Wayland fail the test with intimidation and hints he isn't doing too well. Wayland responds with all the cockiness and self-assurance of a man who knows he's not so much a suspect as a character in a movie, taunting the cops with inside information about their private lives.

Deceiver has similarities to *Usual Suspects* in the way it coils around its central facts, looking at them first one way and then another. It also has a less obvious parallel with Quentin Tarantino's practice of working arcane knowledge into the dialogue of his characters. Carefully polished little set-pieces are spotted through the film; the action stops for well-informed discussions about Vincent van Gogh, the dangers of absinthe, the symptoms of epilepsy, and the relative intelligence of the two cops.

There wasn't much I could believe. The movie is basically about behavior—about acting, rather than about characters. The three leads and some supporting characters get big scenes and angry speeches, and the plot manufactures big moments of crisis and then slips away from them. It feels more like a play than a movie.

One of the ways it undermines its characters is by upstaging them with the plot. We get several theories about the death of the prostitute, and lots of flashbacks in which Wayland's tortured childhood offers explanations for actions he may or may not have taken. Facts are established, only to be shot down. Having seen the film twice, I am prepared to accept that its paradoxes are all answered and its puzzles solved, although unless you look closely and remember the face of an ambulance driver, you may miss the explanation for one of the big surprises.

The thing is, even after you figure it all out, a movie like this offers few rewards. It's well acted, and you can admire that on a technical level, but the plot is such a puzzle it shuts us out: How can we care about events that the movie itself constantly undercuts and revises? By the time the final twist comes along, it's as if we've seen a clever show in which the only purpose, alas, was to demonstrate the cleverness.

Deep Blue Sea ★ ★ ★
R, 106 m., 1999

Saffron Burrows (Dr. Susan McAlester), Samuel L. Jackson (Russell Franklin), Thomas Jane (Carter Blake), LL Cool J/James Todd Smith ("Preacher" Dudley), Jacqueline McKenzie (Janice Higgins), Michael Rapaport (Tom Scoggins), Stellan Skarsgard (Jim Whitlock). Directed by Renny Harlin and produced by Akiva Goldsman, Tony Ludwig, and Alan Riche. Screenplay by Duncan Kennedy, Donna Powers, and Wayne Powers.

Sharks, it is said, are all teeth and muscle, and have been doing two things very efficiently for millions of years: moving and eating. *Deep Blue Sea* resembles a shark. It moves ceaselessly, and someone gets eaten from time to time.

The movie is a skillful thriller by Renny Harlin, who made *Die Hard 2* and *Cutthroat Island*, and here assembles a neat package of terror, sharks, and special effects. That isn't as easy as it sounds. After slogging through the predictability of countless would-be action thrillers, I admired the sheer professionalism of this one, which doesn't transcend its genre, but at least honors it.

The premise: A scientist (Saffron Burrows) has devised a way to use the brain tissue of sharks to cultivate a substance that might be useful in fighting Alzheimer's. A big corporation underwrites the research and maintains a deep-sea station with shark corrals and underwater living and research areas. One of the

129

sharks escapes and tries to eat a boat. The head of the corporation (Samuel L. Jackson) pays a visit to the station and meets the other key characters, including a shark wrangler (Thomas Jane), a Bible-quoting cook (LL Cool J), and crew members including Jacqueline McKenzie, Michael Rapaport, Stellan Skarsgard, and Aida Turturro.

Some of these characters turn up on the shark menu, although the timing and manner of their ingestion is often so unexpected that I'll say nothing more. The shark attacks are intercut with a desperate escape plot, after storms and explosions incapacitate the station and the characters are trapped below the waterline in areas threatened by water pressure and sharks.

Common sense, of course, has nothing to do with the screenplay, ingeniously devised by Duncan Kennedy, Donna Powers, and Wayne Powers. Its premise is that the sharks' brains have been increased fivefold, with a corresponding increase in intelligence, so that the sharks can figure out the layout of the station and work together to batter down watertight doors, swim down corridors, etc. The most obvious problem with this premise is that just because a shark is smarter doesn't mean it has more information; the smartest shark in the world would only know how to be a smart shark if it had a way to learn.

But never mind. The sharks exist in *Deep Blue Sea* as the McGuffins, creating situations that require the characters to think fast, fight bravely, improvise their way out of tight spots, dangle between flames and teeth, etc. There's a little perfunctory scientist-bashing, but not much (the Burrows character violates ethical guidelines, but, hey, it's for a good cause—fighting Alzheimer's).

Jackson is more or less the straight man in the cast. Jane handles most of the action duties, convincingly if, of course, not plausibly (in other words, he looks like he can hold his breath underwater indefinitely even though we know it's impossible). The surprise in the cast is LL Cool J, who has a kind of Cuba Gooding Jr. quality as a cook whose best friend is a parrot, and who hides from the shark in an oven, which the shark cleverly sets to five hundred degrees.

The movie is essentially one well-done ac-tion sequence after another. It involves all the usual situations in movies where fierce creatures chase victims through the bowels of a ship/space craft/building (the *Alien* movies, *Deep Rising*, etc). It's just that it does them well. It doesn't linger on the special effects (some of the sharks look like cartoons), but it knows how to use timing, suspense, quick movement, and surprise.

Especially surprise. There is a moment in this movie when something happens that is completely unexpected, and it's over in a flash—a done deal—and the audience laughs in delight because it was so successfully surprised. In a genre where a lot of movies are retreads of the predictable, *Deep Blue Sea* keeps you guessing.

Deep Crimson ★ ★ ★ ½
NO MPAA RATING, 109 m., 1998

Regina Orozco (Coral Fabre), Daniel Gimenez Cacho (Nicolas Estrella), Marisa Paredes (Irene Gallardo), Patricia Reyes Espindola (The Widow Ruelas), Julieta Egurrola (Juanita Norton), Rosa Furman (The Widow Morrison), Veronica Merchant (Rebecca San Pedro), Sherlyn Gonzales (Teresa). Directed by Arturo Ripstein and produced by Miguel Necoechea and Paolo Barbachano. Screenplay by Paz Alicia Garciadiego.

Deep Crimson, macabre and perverse, is based on a true story from the 1940s, about the "Lonely Hearts Killers"—a couple who posed as brother and sister, victimized lonely widows, and then killed them. Their story was told in a 1970 American film, *The Honeymoon Killers*, but now here is Arturo Ripstein with a Mexican version that combines black comedy with horrifying heartlessness. There were walkouts when I saw the film; those who stay will not easily forget it.

The movie opens like a dark comedy by Pedro Almodovar or Luis Buñuel (who Ripstein once worked for as an assistant director). We meet Coral Fabre, played by the opera singer Regina Orozco; she is a sometime embalmer, now caring for an old man and raising two children haphazardly. My diagnosis: hysteria and manic-depression. She answers a lonely hearts' ad from a "Charles Boyer type," and soon meets Nicolas Estrella (Daniel Gimenez Cacho), a vain, bald gigolo who spends hours adjusting his hairpiece before putting on his trench coat, snapping the brim of his fedora, and sailing out to defraud lonely women.

She has sent him a picture of herself when slim. She is fat. "I lose weight when I want to," she tells him. "How lucky to be able to control your body like that!" he says, before trying to flee. She begs him to stay, blaming his distaste on the smell of formaldehyde from her undertaking duties. "I've never been with a gentleman," she weeps. "Do it to me. Just do it—as a favor!" He does, but not as a favor; as she sleeps, he steals the money from her purse and creeps out.

But Coral has seen him from beneath lowered lids. The next day she arrives at Nicolas's apartment with her two children in tow. "I saw you robbing me," she tells him. "Maybe you were charging for excess fat. I came to stay with you. We're made for each other." He demurs, and so she takes decisive action: dumps her kids at an orphanage, enters his apartment when he's not there, reads his phony letters to lonely hearts victims, and when he returns offers him a partnership. They'll pose as brother and sister, and she'll select the victims.

Nicolas, who is as stupid as he is vain, is flattered. ("You gave up your kids for me! Nobody's ever done anything like that before.") Soon they are choosing their victims, but there's a hitch: Coral is not content to simply defraud and rob them. When she eavesdrops as Nicolas makes love to them, or even talks sweet, she grows jealous, and soon they're leaving a trail of corpses behind.

Deep Crimson sinks easily into the swamp of human depravity. Coral and Nicolas are demented even when apart; together, they create an amoral composite personality, a world in which soap opera clichés about love are used to excuse unspeakable sins. Ripstein leads us into this world with the seduction of deadpan black humor, and then pulls out the rug in the final scenes, which are truly horrific. As a study in abnormal psychology, *Deep Crimson* would make his master, Buñuel, proud.

The film has a strong effect on its viewers. When I saw it, there was a scene of harm toward a child that sent many audience members racing for the exits. Others feel betrayed because they laughed along with the earlier scenes, only to be blindsided by the cruelty and dark despair of the conclusion.

One thing that engages some viewers is Coral's weight. It is an unspoken rule of female killers in movies that they be thin. "While Coral's plight calls out for some sympathy from the audience, her loathsome obesity prevents us from commiseration," writes Harvey Karten, an Internet critic. Yet here is Ruthe Stein from the *San Francisco Chronicle,* who cites the slender killers played by Faye Dunaway and Linda Fiorentino and then adds of this one: "Anyone in Hollywood who thinks large women can't be sexy should get a load of her."

This disagreement is revealing. Karten is obviously a candidate for urgent briefings by the Fat Acceptance lobby. Stein may find Coral sexy for politically correct reasons, but Nicolas certainly doesn't. The film isn't about appearances at all, but about the way Coral and Nicolas see what they need to see. She sees not a pathetic, toupee-wearing fraud, but Charles Boyer. He sees not a fat embalmer who has dumped her children, but a woman who would make any sacrifice for him. Their mutual weakness is vanity: She can feel she has Charles Boyer as a lover, and he can feel that she sees Boyer when she looks at him. As long as these mutual fantasies are reinforced, the deaths of a few unfortunate widows can be excused.

Ripstein, not well-known in America, is Mexico's most respected director, and in *Deep Crimson* he creates the kind of dangerous film that Americans made more freely in the 1970s (when *The Honeymoon Killers* got reviews similar to this one's). He is unafraid of offending his audience. He is going for hard truths, and approaching them through humor and a willingness to offend. His purpose is to undercut the way that movies glamorize legendary criminals like Coral and Nicolas. Anyone who thought *Bonnie and Clyde* romanticized its killers is likely to feel that the heroes of *Deep Crimson* get what they have coming, without mercy.

The Deep End of the Ocean ★ ½
PG-13, 108 m., 1999

Michelle Pfeiffer (Beth), Treat Williams (Pat), Whoopi Goldberg (Candy), Jonathan Jackson (Vincent [sixteen]), John Kapelos (George Karras), Cory Buck (Vincent [seven]), Ryan Merriman (Sam). Directed by Ulu Grosbard and produced by Kate Guinzberg and Steve Nicolaides. Screenplay by Stephen Schiff, based on the novel by Jacquelyn Mitchard.

Ulu Grosbard's *The Deep End of the Ocean* is a painfully stolid movie that lumbers past emotional issues like a wrestler in a cafeteria line, putting a little of everything on its plate. It provides big roles for Michelle Pfeiffer and Treat Williams, but doesn't provide them with the screenplay support they need; the result is awkwardness when characters express emotions the audience doesn't share.

(There's no way I can discuss the failure of the movie without revealing details, so if you plan to see it, I'd suggest reading this review later to preserve the surprises.)

Pfeiffer and Williams play the parents of a three-year-old boy who is kidnapped from a hotel lobby during a class reunion. They are befriended by a detective (Whoopi Goldberg), who reveals she is gay, for no other reason than to provide a politically correct line, since her sexuality is utterly irrelevant to the story. Nine years pass, they move to Chicago, and then the boy is found again—mowing their lawn. He was kidnapped by a neurotic classmate of Pfeiffer's, who later married and then committed suicide. So the child has been raised by an adoptive father who of course had no idea he was kidnapped.

The film's most crippling failure is in the treatment of the father, who is played with gentleness and great strength by John Kapelos. The audience knows, but the movie apparently doesn't, that the real drama in the later stages is in the father's story. We suffer with Pfeiffer and Williams as they grieve their lost child and fight over the blame, but after nine years their life has fallen into a rhythm, and it is the other family that is ripped apart when the boy's true identity is revealed.

Consider. You raise a son from infancy in a happy household, only to have him snatched

away from you, just like that. (The movie doesn't even supply the usual hearings, social workers, etc.) There is a scene at the other home, with Kapelos protesting his innocence to dozens of cops, and then an awkward scene in which the story of the kidnapping is explained in snappy dialogue. (This scene feels suspiciously as if it were slapped in as a replacement for cuts.)

And then . . . well, the boy is back with his birth family eating pizza. And then there is a scene at night, with an older brother curling up on the floor next to his bed. And then the family goes to church, where the priest welcomes him back to his birth family—with no mention of or reference to the adoptive father, who is sitting in another pew. And then a scene in the Italian restaurant that Williams owns; the kid is recruited for an Italian dance, but prefers a Greek dance he learned from his father.

All of this time, all of these scenes are undermined by our concern for the father. How does he feel? The film eventually allots him one brief but telling speech ("This was my wife and my son. This wasn't some lunatic and the boy she kidnapped. Not to me.") The weight it is given is suggested by Treat Williams's question to his wife after the man's visit: "So, what happened?"

The boy misses his adoptive father and the only home he has ever known, but he's almost too articulate about it ("[My mom] didn't mean to be sick. So why am I being punished?"). Oh, there's a scene where the boy and his new family fight over where he's going to spend Thanksgiving. But we never see the outcome. Where *did* he spend Thanksgiving and how did it go? And the film's ending, when it comes, feels unconvincingly neat. King Solomon could not have divided the child with more skill.

The movie's background details feel shoveled in for effect, instead of growing organically from the story. Consider that Treat Williams is said to run an Italian restaurant. The character talks, acts, and moves like no Italian-American restaurant owner I have ever encountered. He projects the aura of a Kinko's franchisee. There is a scene on a Saturday morning where the guy is in his workshop building *birdhouses,* for cripe's sake.

(These are Screenplay Birdhouses—provided by the prop department to give him something to hold in his hands.) Eventually he says, "I've got to go to work." At noon on a Saturday? Any Italian restaurant owner worth his oregano would have been up before dawn, visiting the produce market and supervising the marinara.

Such lapses wouldn't be fatal in a better movie, but *The Deep End of the Ocean* is unconvincing from start to finish. One can see that Pfeiffer's performance would have adorned a better screenplay, and that Jonathan Jackson, as the family's older son, has a convincing screen presence. But the film curiously seems to be long and slow, and yet missing large chunks of the story (it runs 108 minutes, but early press material clocks it at 148). My best guess: It was filmed before it was adequately written.

Deep Impact ★ ★ ½
PG-13, 115 m., 1998

Robert Duvall (Spurgeon Tanner), Tea Leoni (Jenny Lerner), Morgan Freeman (President Beck), Elijah Wood (Leo Biederman), Vanessa Redgrave (Robin Lerner), Maximilian Schell (Jason Lerner), Leelee Sobieski (Sarah Hotchner), James Cromwell (Alan Rittenhouse). Directed by Mimi Leder and produced by Richard D. Zanuck and David Brown. Screenplay by Michael Tolkin and Bruce Joel Rubin.

Early in *Deep Impact* we learn that a comet "the size of Mt. Everest" is on a collision course for Earth. There would seem to be two possible outcomes: (1) The comet hits Earth, destroying it, or (2) the comet does not hit Earth, in which case humanity is spared but the audience is denied the sight of lots of special effects. In the first scenario you don't get the obligatory happy ending, and in the second one everyone leaves feeling cheated.

Most doomsday movies avoid this choice by prudently choosing less than apocalyptic events. A volcano, a twister, or a tidal wave can supply lots of terrifying special effects and still leave a lot of people standing. But *Deep Impact* seems to back itself into a corner, and maybe that's why the producers hired not one but two of the brightest writers in Hollywood to work on the project: Bruce Joel Rubin *(Ghost)* and Michael Tolkin *(The Player)*. Together, they've figured out how to have their cake and eat it too.

How do they do this? I would not dream of revealing their inspiration, although you may be able to figure it out yourself. Meanwhile, you can enjoy the way they create little flashes of wit in the dialogue, which enlivens what is, after all, a formula disaster movie. What's the formula? Assorted archetypal characters are introduced, they're assigned personal problems, and the story cuts between them as the moment of disaster grows closer. I always think it's more interesting if they know from the start that there's a big problem; I get tired of scenes in which they live blissfully unaware of the catastrophe unfolding beneath their feet, or above their heads, or wherever.

Deep Impact begins with the obligatory opening precatastrophe, in this case a runaway semi that mows down a Jeep and kills the astronomer who is bringing news of the approaching comet. (The other movie I saw on the same day, *The Horse Whisperer,* also opened with a runaway semi, and indeed I cannot recall a single movie in which a semi on a two-lane road does not career out of control.)

Then there's a little ritual media-bashing; Tea Leoni plays a reporter for MSNBC who suspects there's more to the story of a cabinet official's resignation. She accuses him of having an affair with a woman named "Ellie," and he gets to say, "I know you're just a reporter, but you used to be a person." (The approved media response to this is, "Look who's talking! A cabinet member!")

Soon she discovers her error; he is resigning not because of Ellie but because of an E.L.E., which is jargon for "Extinction Level Event." He wants to spend more time with his family, and has stocked a yacht with dozens of cases of vitamin-rich Sustain. He must not have been invited to the briefing where it was explained that all surface life would be destroyed by the comet, or the other briefing about the 1,000-foot-tall tidal wave. My guess is the president wanted him out of the cabinet.

The president, played convincingly by Morgan Freeman, goes on TV to break the bad news to the world, and talks of the *Messiah* Project, which will send a manned U.S.-Russian spacecraft to plant nuclear bombs in the comet and blow it up. We meet the *Messiah* crew members, including old Spurgeon Tanner (Robert Duvall), called out of retirement because he once landed on the Moon and might be able to land on the comet.

The younger crew members resent him, we are told, although dissension onboard is never followed up on. The veteran has a nice line about the youngsters: "They're not scared of dying. They're just scared of looking bad on TV." There's another good line at the high school assembly where the kid (Elijah Wood) who codiscovered the comet is honored. A friend tells him, "You're gonna have a lot more sex starting now. Famous people always get more sex." And I liked a line from late in the movie when one hero tells another, "Look on the bright side. We'll all have high schools named for us."

But the movie as a whole is pretty routine. There's a laborious subplot in which Tea Leoni resents her father (Maximilian Schell) for divorcing her mother (Vanessa Redgrave) and marrying a bimbo, and while Redgrave brings a nice sad quality to her scenes, the rest of the subplot plays out suspiciously like a scheme to place two humans in front of a big special effect. There are also some fairly unconvincing scenes in which millions of people try to flee from a city, and all of them are trapped in gridlock except, of course, for the two who are required by the plot to get somewhere fast.

Whether Earth is saved or doomed or neither, I will leave you to discover for yourself. I personally found it easier to believe that Earth could survive this doomsday scenario than that the *Messiah* spacecraft could fly at thousands of miles an hour through the comet's tail, which contains rocks the size of two-car garages, without serious consequences. On the disaster epic scale, on which *Titanic* gets four stars and *Volcano* gets one and a half, *Deep Impact* gets two and a half—the same as *Dante's Peak*, even though it lacks a dog that gets left behind.

Deep Rising ★ ½
R, 106 m., 1998

Treat Williams (Finnegan), Famke Janssen (Trillian), Anthony Heald (Carlton), Kevin J. O'Connor (Pantucci), Wes Studi (Hanover), Derrick O'Connor (Captain), Jason Flemyng (Mulligan), Cliff Curtis (Mamooli). Directed by Stephen Sommers and produced by Laurence Mark and John Baldecchi. Screenplay by Sommers.

Deep Rising could also have been titled *Eat the Titanic!* It's about a giant squid that attacks a luxurious cruise ship in the South China Sea. Like all movie monsters, the squid has perfect timing and always bursts into the frame just when the characters are least expecting it. And it has an unsavory way of dining. "They eat you?" asks one of the survivors. "No—they drink you."

The mechanics for a movie like this were well established in the *Alien* pictures, and *Deep Rising* clones the same formula: Survivors are trapped inside giant vessel. Creature finds its way around air ducts and sewer pipes, popping out of shaft openings to gobble up minor characters (the first victim is sucked down the toilet).

D'ya think they have meetings out in Hollywood to share the latest twists? I've been seeing the same gimmicks in a lot of different pictures. Evidence: No sooner does the snake in *Anaconda* release a slimy survivor from its innards than the squid in *Deep Rising* does the same thing. No sooner is there an indoor Jet Ski chase in *Hard Rain* than there's one in *Deep Rising*. No sooner does a horrible monster crawl out of the air ducts in *Alien Resurrection* than it does so in *Deep Rising*. And last week I saw *Phantoms*, which was sort of *Deep Rising Meets Alien and Goes West*. In that one, the creature emerged from the depths of the earth rather than the sea, but had the same nasty practice of living behind piles of undigested remains.

An effort has been made by Stephen Sommers, writer-director of *Deep Rising*, to add humor to his story, although not even the presence of Leslie Nielsen could help this picture. The hero, Treat Williams, is a freelance power cruiser skipper who hires his craft out to a gang of vile and reprehensible bad guys, led by Wes Studi. They want to hijack a new casino ship on its maiden voyage. The owner of the ship (Anthony Heald) makes several speeches boasting about how stable it is; it can stay level in the water even during a raging tempest. I wonder if those speeches were inserted after the filmmakers realized how phony their special effects look. Every time we see the ship, it's absolutely immobile in the midst of churning waves.

No matter; the creature from the deep attacks the ship, and by the time Williams delivers the pirates, it seems to be deserted. All except for the evil owner, of course, and also a jewel thief (Famke Janssen) who was locked in the brig and survived the carnage.

A movie like this depends much upon the appearance of the monster, which has been designed by f/x wizard Rob Bottin. There is a vast evil squid head, and lots of tentacles (which seem to have minds of their own, and lots of mouths with many teeth). So vicious is the squid, indeed, that only the cynical will ask how it can survive for long periods out of water, or how and why it emits its piercing howl, which goes reverberating through the air shafts.

There's comic relief from Williams's engine room man, Pantucci (Kevin J. O'Connor), who plays the Donald O'Connor role and is always wisecracking in the face of adversity. And an effective supporting performance by Djimon Hounsou, as one of the more fanatic members of the pirate gang (he played Cinque in *Amistad,* and shows a powerful screen presence once again, although on the whole I'll bet he wishes the giant squid movie had come out *before* the Spielberg film).

Bemusing, how much money and effort goes into the making of a movie like this, and how little thought. It's months of hard work—for what? The movie is essentially an *Alien* clone with a fresh paint job. You know something's wrong when a fearsome tentacle rears up out of the water and opens its mouth, and there are lots of little tentacles inside with their own ugly mouths, all filled with nasty teeth, and all you can think is, been there, seen that.

Deja Vu ★ ★ ★ ½
PG-13, 116 m., 1998

Victoria Foyt (Dana), Vanessa Redgrave (Skelly), Stephen Dillane (Sean), Michael Brandon (Alex), Glynis Barber (Claire), Noel Harrison (John Stoner), Anna Massey (Fern Stoner). Directed by Henry Jaglom and produced by John Goldstone. Screenplay by Jaglom and Victoria Foyt.

We all look for love like the love in *Deja Vu.* We hardly ever find it. That's why there are movies. We want a love that spans the generations and conquers time, a love so large that only the supernatural can contain it. Here is a movie about a love like that. It makes *City of Angels* look timid.

The story involves an American woman named Dana (Victoria Foyt) on a buying trip to Jerusalem when she is approached by a mysterious older blonde who engages her in conversation. Soon she is revealing all her secrets: Yes, she is engaged, because "being engaged has become a condition of my life," but after six years and no marriage she is not very happy.

The other woman tells her about the love of her life. It was a wartime romance. She was a French Jewish woman; he was an American GI. They planned to wed. He went home "to tell his girlfriend" and never returned. Eventually she got a letter with a photo of the man's first child.

Perhaps, Dana says, he could not find you. The woman smiles sadly. "He knew where to find me. Life had got hold of us." She pauses. "Nothing seemed so real again. In fact, all my life since then has been like a dream." The woman gives her a piece of jewelry—a clip—and disappears, after mentioning that the clip was a gift from the GI, who kept the other one.

Dana heads toward home. When the Chunnel train stops briefly at Dover, she inexplicably gets off instead of going on to London. Above the white cliffs of Dover, she meets a painter named Sean (Stephen Dillane). "Have we met before?" she asks him. He says, "It feels like one of those moments where if you turn the wrong way you regret it forever." It's love at first sight, but they fight it. She's engaged, after all. But then they meet again, by coincidence, at the house of British friends. She discovers he is married.

Her fiancé is Alex (Michael Brandon). His wife is Claire (Glynis Barber). It becomes clear that Dana and Sean are helplessly in love, and their partners react in disbelief and anger, but with a certain civilized restraint. I must not reveal any more. I must say instead that old songs like "The White Cliffs of Dover" and "We'll Meet Again" and "These Foolish Things" are like time machines that can carry love down through the years and can leap from mind to mind, spreading their foolishness and dreams.

Deja Vu is not a weepy romantic melodrama, but a sophisticated film about smart people. Foyt and Dillane make convincing lovers not because they are swept away, but because they regard what has happened to them and accept it. When they fall in love, there is a lot at risk: jobs, businesses, which country they live in, the people they're committed to. It takes no trouble at all to fall in love when you're twenty and single. But Dana and Sean must look in their hearts and be sure they cannot live without one another.

The film was directed by Henry Jaglom and written by Jaglom and his star, Victoria Foyt, who is also his wife. Ah-ha, you think, guessing the connection, especially since the movie is dedicated "to the love of my life." But there is another connection coiling down through the years. The trademark of Jaglom's film company is a brief moment of time, showing Orson Welles producing a rainbow out of thin air. Jaglom was one of Welles's close confidants and friends.

In *Citizen Kane*, which Welles made in 1941, there occurs my favorite passage of movie dialogue. Old Mr. Bernstein is talking about the peculiarities of time. "A fellow will remember a lot of things you wouldn't think he'd remember," he says. "You take me. One day, back in 1896, I was crossing over to Jersey on the ferry, and as we pulled out, there was another ferry pulling in, and on it there was a girl waiting to get off. A white dress she had on. She was carrying a white parasol. I only saw her for one second. She didn't see me at all, but I'll bet a month hasn't gone by since that I haven't thought of that girl."

Late in *Deja Vu*, a character tells a similar story, about a woman he once met: "A week hasn't gone by since I last saw her that I haven't thought of her. She was the love of my life."

Yes. And can you, dear reader, think of such a moment too? Perfect love is almost always unrealized. It has to be. What makes those memories perfect is that they produce no history. The woman with the white parasol remains always frozen in an old man's memory. She never grows old, is never out of temper, never loses interest in him, never dies. She exists forever as a promise, like the green light at the end of Gatsby's pier.

Only rarely does the universe wheel around to bring two hearts once again into communion. That's what *Deja Vu* is about. And that explains the two most curious characters in it. They are the old couple (Anna Massey and Noel Harrison) who own the house where Dana and Sean meet by accident. They have been married a very long time, and like to read in bed and eat Mars bars at the same time and be happy to be together. At first you wonder what their scenes mean. Then you understand.

Desert Blue ★ ★ ★
R, 93 m., 1999

Brendan Sexton III (Blue), Kate Hudson (Skye), Christina Ricci (Ely), Casey Affleck (Pete), Sara Gilbert (Sandy), Ethan Suplee (Cale), John Heard (Lance), Isidra Vega (Haley), Lucinda Jenney (Caroline). Directed by Morgan J. Freeman and produced by Andrea Sperling, Nadia Leonelli, and Michael Burns. Screenplay by Freeman.

Imagine the town in *The Last Picture Show* after thirty more years of shrinking and loneliness, and you'd have the town in *Desert Blue*. Both movies are about teenage friends with not much to do, but the kids in *Desert Blue* are more resigned; there's a kind of sweet sadness to their exile—all except for Ely (Christina Ricci), who entertains herself by blowing things up.

Baxter, California ("pop. 89," according to the shot-up sign outside town), is known for one thing: the world's largest ice-cream cone, a forlorn structure that sits in the desert like a god on Easter Island. The cone was built by the late father of Blue (Brendan Sexton III). At the time of his suicide, the father was working on a water park, but then the Empire Cola company grabbed all the water, and now the park is just a shabby relic of water slides, picnic tables, and rowboats with no place to float.

Into this town one day comes a professor of roadside culture (John Heard), who wants to research the ice-cream cone. He's traveling with his daughter, Skye (Kate Hudson), a TV starlet who has an audition tomorrow in L.A. A truck overturns outside town, spilling the secret ingredient of Empire Cola (or whatever it is they really manufacture in that sinister plant outside town), and the authorities throw up roadblocks. Skye and her dad are trapped in the town. He welcomes the chance to research rural culture. She's a snob and thinks the local kids are hayseeds.

They're not. Most of them plan to leave Baxter (Ricci plans to do it by blowing herself up), but in the meantime they enjoy each other's company. They're gentle with one another, as if they deserve a certain pity just because they live here, and *Desert Blue*, in its sweet and unaffected way, succeeds in making a convincing movie about eccentrics without their performances obstructing the view.

The movie was written and directed by Morgan J. Freeman (not the actor), whose *Hurricane Streets* (1997) was a Sundance winner about young teenagers who are petty thieves on the Lower East Side of New York. I like *Desert Blue* more, but in both films I like the way Freeman doesn't pump up the volume. The overturned trailer, the arrival of the FBI, the mystery of a motel fire, and even Ricci's enthusiastic dynamitings are all played in a kind of bemused detachment. This is the herbal tea version of Oliver Stone's *U Turn*. Even when the FBI shoots at someone, it's handled as a terrible mistake, not an action scene.

Skye can't believe it at first when they're trapped in the town. She's an ambitious little number, worried about her audition, but soon the understated acceptance of the local kids begins to get to her, and she pairs off with Blue and begins to hear about his father's dreams of a water park and a better life. Perhaps they have a future together: Skye and Blue, get it?

A movie like this depends on tone more than anything else. Moviegoers who don't like the rhythm may grow impatient. It's not a romance, a drama, or an adventure, but the evocation of a time and place. The characters are odd because they grew up that way. Even Ricci's love of dynamite is inspired not by hostility but by skill and boredom: One of her early targets is chosen because it was "just sitting there." We are no doubt expected to reflect that the same words could describe the whole town.

Desperate Measures ★ ★
R, 100 m., 1998

Michael Keaton (Peter McCabe), Andy Garcia (Frank Connor), Brian Cox (Jeremiah Cassidy), Marcia Gay Harden (Samantha Hawkins), Erik King (Nate Oliver), Efrain Figueroa (Vargus), Joseph Cross (Matthew Connor), Janel Maloney (Sarah Davis). Directed by Barbet Schroeder and produced by Schroeder, Susan Hoffman, Gary Foster, and Lee Rich. Screenplay by David Klass, Henry Bean, and Neal Jimenez.

Desperate Measures opens with the same hook as *Hard Rain:* What looks like a robbery turns out to be an action by the good guys. *Hard Rain* really cheated (hey—they're not robbers; they're armored car drivers!). *Desperate Measures*, which is a better movie, has a better gimmick. A raid is staged on government computers in order to search for the perfect DNA match for a kid who is dying and needs a bone marrow transplant.

Andy Garcia plays a cop named Connor, the father who will do anything to save his son's life. Searching a national database, he discovers that only one man has the proper DNA. He's Peter McCabe (Michael Keaton), a psychopath now in prison after killing four people, including a fellow inmate. Will McCabe agree to become a bone marrow donor? Why should he? Offered the opportunity, he reflects on the alternative: "After all these years of being locked up, I'm given the opportunity to kill again."

But McCabe eventually caves in, after a laundry list of demands including better prison quarters and all the cigarettes he wants. Turns out it's all a trick. Using blueprints available (of course) on the Internet, he plans an elaborate escape from the hospital where he's taken to have the tricky operation. How does he get out of the handcuffs? How does he ward off the effects of anesthesia? It's all here. It's not convincing, but it's here.

All of this is prelude to the movie's real plot, which centers on the fact that McCabe must remain alive in order for his bone marrow to be of any use to little Matthew, the dying kid. McCabe sets people on fire during his escape attempt and uses violence as he flees a police dragnet. And Connor finds himself in the curious position of trying to shield this vicious killer, sometimes with his own body, against fellow policemen who might kill him.

What is the proper morality here? Or, as a police official (Brian Cox) succinctly asks, "How many people are gonna have to die here tonight so that kid of yours can live?" It's a good question, and explored a different way in a more thoughtful movie, it might have generated some genuine drama.

Desperate Measures is, unfortunately, only masquerading as a thoughtful movie that's really about something. At heart, it's an action thriller—a chase picture. It has all the usual implausible or impossible stunts, the highway carnage, the jumps off bridges, the slides down laundry chutes, and other feats that make it more of a video game than a drama.

Too bad, because the actors could have brought class to better material. Michael Keaton, an actor who can convincingly project intelligence, is intriguing as McCabe, a thinker who likes to toy with people he can control. Garcia's dilemma as a cop and a father is handled well in a handful of quiet scenes (especially in conversations with pediatrician Marcia Gay Harden), and his son (Joseph Cross) is a smart kid who asks all the right questions at the wrong times.

But the movie would rather jolly along an action audience than play fair with its material, and so we're treated to the usual, standard, obligatory bankrupt action dreck: kinetic energy on autopilot. Too bad. The director, Barbet Schroeder, has made some good movies *(Barfly, Reversal of Fortune, Single White Female)*. This time he's a hired gun. He could have made a better movie, I imagine, if the producers had wanted him to, but sometimes that's just not the way it works.

Destiny ★ ★ ½
NO MPAA RATING, 135 m., 1999

Nour el-Cherif (Averroes), Laila Eloui (Gypsy Woman), Mahmoud Hemeida (Al Mansour [Caliph]), Safia el-Emary (Averroes's Wife), Mohamed Mounir (The Bard), Khaled el-Nabaoui (Nasser [Crown Prince]), Abdallah Mahmoud (Borhan), Ahmed Fouad Selim (Cheikh Riad). Directed by Youssef Chahine and produced by Humbert Balsan and Gabriel Khoury. Screenplay by Chahine and Khaled Youssef.

Destiny takes place in twelfth-century Spain, but could take place today. It is an odd, brave film, part impassioned melodrama, part musical, taking a broad popular approach to questions of religious belief. It was directed by an Egyptian, financed from France, set in the Spanish province of Andalusia, and photographed in Lebanon and Syria. It's completely off the map for most American moviegoers, which is one of its charms.

The story involves an Arabic philosopher named Averroes, who believed that the Koran was open to interpretation. Yes, he taught, the book is the word of God, but God gave us intelligence so that we might reason about his words and not blindly follow their literal meanings. After all, to assume that the mind of God can be reduced to ordinary human language and contained in mere words is itself a kind of heresy. And those who oppose the interpretation of the Koran are of course imposing their own interpretation upon it.

As the film opens, one of Averroes's followers is being burned at the stake, the bonfire fed by his writings. The burning man calls out to his son to seek out the philosopher, and the main story takes place in Andalusia, where Averroes has gathered a group of disciples who study his books and copy them out by hand. Ah, but that gives a wrong idea of the film, which is not about scholars in their cells, but about politics, sexual passion, jealousy, and romance, and contains several song and dance numbers. Imagine *My Dinner with André* as a musical.

Andalusia is ruled by a caliph who has two sons, one a follower of Averroes, the other a party animal who is lured into the camp of

fundamentalists. One feels of these fundamentalists, as one often does about the type in
general, that they're driven not so much by
what they believe, as by their fear or envy of
those who do not agree. The movie argues
that a belief that cannot stand up to free debate is not a belief worth holding.

Political intrigue is rife in the area. The
caliph supports Averroes, but is opposed by a
cult that hopes to overthrow him. Meanwhile,
his oldest son is concealing a forbidden love
with a gypsy woman, and his trusted adviser is
working both sides of the street. A secret project is set in motion, to copy out the writings of
Averroes and spirit them far away, in case the
tide turns and his books are burned again (a
good possibility).

Much of the film's interest comes from historical details. We hear of the great Arabic
contributions to mathematics, and we see a
fascinating invention, a telescope that uses the
magnifying power of water in order to work.
We see a society that is part European, part
Arabic, in which Islam is as much a political
movement as a religious one. And then there
is the uncanny way the characters have of
looking toward the camera and simply breaking out into song. (I was reminded of Woody
Allen's *Everyone Says I Love You,* which was
equally direct in the way ordinary people
moved from speech to singing.)

There are places in the world where *Destiny,*
directed by the veteran Egyptian filmmaker
Youssef Chahine, would be controversial—
even dangerous. In those places, the music
and romance will help find a wider audience
for a charged message. The interest in this
country is more indirect. The film is naive and
simple at times, even clumsy in its musical sequences, and yet lurking beneath its story is a
conflict between rationalism and fundamentalism that is as fraught today as it ever was.

As I write these words, Serbs are slaughter-
ing ethnic Albanians and we are bombing
Serbs, all because of religious and ethnic
differences that date back almost to the period
of this film. At the end of *Destiny,* Chahine
quotes Averroes: "Ideas have wings. No one
can stop their flight." Heartening words. But
are they flying or fleeing?

Deterrence ★ ★ ★
R, 101 m., 2000

Kevin Pollak (Walter Emerson), Timothy Hutton
(Marshall Thompson), Sheryl Lee Ralph (Gayle
Redford), Sean Astin (Ralph), Bajda Djola
(Harvey), Mark Thompson (Gerald Irving),
Michael Mantell (Taylor Woods), Kathryn
Morris (Lizzie Woods), Clotilde Courau (Katie).
Directed by Rod Lurie and produced by Marc
Frydman and James Spies. Screenplay by Lurie.

Not long before election day 2008, the president of the United States is making a campaign tour through Colorado when a sudden
snowstorm traps him in a roadside diner.
Alarming news arrives: Saddam Hussein's son
has sent Iraqi troops into Kuwait, and 80 percent of America's troops are far away, committed in the Sea of Japan. What to do? Drop the
bomb, obviously.

Or at least threaten to. That's the strategic
tactic tried by President Walter Emerson, played
by Kevin Pollak as a man who wasn't elected
to the highest office but got there through a
combination of unforeseen events. He doesn't
look very presidential, and he's not terrifically
popular with the voters, but the office makes
the man, they say, and Emerson rises to the
occasion with terrifying certitude: Yes, he is
quite prepared to drop the first nuclear weapon
since Nagasaki.

This story unfolds in a classic closed-room
scenario. The storm rages outside, no one can
come or go, and the customers and staff who
were already in the diner get a front-row seat
for the most momentous decision in modern
times. Although the president cannot move
because of the weather, he can communicate,
and he negotiates by telephone and speaks to
the nation via a camera from the cable news
crew that's following him around.

Watching the film, I found a curious thing
happening. My awareness of the artifice
dropped away, and the film began working on
me. The situation, it is true, has been contrived out of the clichés of doomsday fiction.
The human relationships inside the diner are
telegraphed with broad strokes (and besides,
wouldn't the Secret Service clear the room of
onlookers while the president was conducting
secret negotiations with heads of state?). There

is a ludicrous moment when the president steps outside into the storm with his advisers to tell them something we're not allowed to hear. And the ending is more or less inexcusable.

And yet the film works. It really does. I got caught up in the global chess game, in the bluffing and the dares, the dangerous strategy of using nuclear blackmail against a fanatic who might call the bluff. With one set and low-rent props (is that an ordinary laptop inside the nuclear briefcase "football"?), *Deterrence* manufactures real suspense and considers real issues.

The movie was written and directed by Rod Lurie, the sometime film critic of *Los Angeles* magazine. On the basis of this debut, he can give up the day job. He knows how to direct, although he could learn more about rewriting. What saves him from the screenplay's implausibilities and dubious manipulation is the strength of the performances.

Kevin Pollak makes a curiously convincing third-string president—a man not elected to the office, but determined to fill it. He is a Jew, which complicates his Middle East negotiations and produced a priceless theological discussion with the waitress (Clotilde Courau). He is advised by a chief of staff (Timothy Hutton) and his national security adviser (Sheryl Lee Ralph), who are appalled by his nuclear brinkmanship, and who are both completely convincing in their roles. The screenplay gives them dialogue of substance; the situation may be contrived, but we're absorbed in the urgent debate that it inspires.

I mentioned the ending. I will offer no hints, except to say that it raises more questions than it answers—questions not just about the president's decisions, but about the screenwriter's sanity. *Deterrence* is the kind of movie that leaves you with fundamental objections. But that's after it's over. While it's playing, it's surprisingly good.

Deuce Bigalow: Male Gigolo ★ ½
R, 84 m., 1999

Rob Schneider (Deuce Bigalow), William Forsythe (Detective Chuck Fowler), Eddie Griffin (T. J. Hicks), Arija Bareikis (Kate), Oded Fehr (Antoine Laconte), Gail O'Grady (Claire), Richard Riehle (Bob Bigalow), Jacqueline Obrador (Elaine Fowler). Directed by Mike Mitchell and produced by Sid Ganis and Barry Bernardi. Screenplay by Haris Goldberg and Rob Schneider.

I laughed, yes, I did, several times during *Deuce Bigalow: Male Gigolo*. That's proof, if any is required, that I still possess streaks of immaturity and vulgarity. May I never lose them. There is a scene where Deuce the gigolo dates a woman so gigantic that her feet are almost too large for him to massage. I mean these are seriously large feet. Very funny.

There is a scene, too, where a pimp lectures Deuce on his place in the gigolo food chain. It is an illustrated lecture, with three varieties of tropical fish as the visual aids. Deuce is not like the rare imported fish, or even the beautiful domestic fish, but the bottom-feeder, down there with the plastic scuba diver. Very funny, especially the way the actor Eddie Griffin handles the explanation.

I laughed enough toward the beginning of *Deuce Bigalow*, indeed, that my hopes began to rise: Would this be that hardest of all films to pull off, a really funny comedy? I hoped, and then my hopes began to flag, and by the end I was hunkered down in my seat, depressed, waiting for the misery to end. It's like someone let all the air out after about the twenty-five-minute mark.

The movie stars Rob Schneider, from *Saturday Night Live*, as a tropical fish tank cleaner. He's so luckless in love that he has to buy sea snails just in the hopes that the girl behind the counter at the fish store will dip her T-shirt into the tank. When he sees a handsome stud (Oded Fehr from *The Mummy*) with a pretty babe, he is filled with envy—especially when he finds out the babe is paying the stud, who is a gigolo.

Many plot complications result. The fearsome gigolo hires the innocuous tank cleaner to baby-sit his valuable fish while he goes to Switzerland. And then, when Deuce desperately needs to raise money and the phone starts to ring, he finds himself backing into the gigolo racket, so to speak. He is well advised by the pimp, who is an expert on what the movie calls (about a million times) man-whores.

So of course we get a series of dates that

Deuce goes out on, and a romantic plot about Kate (Arija Bareikis), the one girl he really likes. (What would you guess the chances are that she finds out he was paid for their first date and gets mad at him?) Deuce works his way through a series of dates with problems: Tina with the big feet, who is about eight feet tall; the Jabba Lady, who is very large; Ruth, who has Tourette's syndrome; and other women who are missing a limb or suffer from narcolepsy or blindness. (His date with the Tourette's victim is creative; he takes her to a baseball game, where everything she shouts sounds appropriate.)

The movie also has a police detective (William Forsythe) who is a compulsive exhibitionist, and in general alternates vulgarity, obscenity, scatology, and cruelty. Not for nothing is Deuce's dad a washroom attendant (and don't get me started on his mother, Bangkok Betty). After the early flashes of humor, the material settles down into a long, dull slog. The plot demonstrates what people will do for money, and so does the movie. It's the kind of picture those View 'n' Brew theaters were made for, as long as you don't View.

Diamonds ★
PG-13, 89 m., 2000

Kirk Douglas (Harry), Dan Aykroyd (Lance), Corbin Allred (Michael), Lauren Bacall (Sin-Dee), Kurt Fuller (Moses), Jenny McCarthy (Sugar), Mariah O'Brien (Tiffany), June Chadwick (Roseanne). Directed by John Asher and produced by Patricia T. Green. Screenplay by Allan Aaron Katz.

Diamonds is a very bad movie and a genuinely moving experience. As the story of three generations of menfolk who go looking for long-lost diamonds and find hookers with hearts of gold, it is unbearable dreck. As a demonstration of Kirk Douglas's heart and determination, it is inspiring.

Douglas suffered a stroke years ago, which left his speech impaired, a problem which the film addresses directly by showing him, in his first scene, doing speech therapy with a videotape. This therapy (or other therapy and a lot of determination) must have worked, because Douglas's speech is easily understandable (as clear, indeed, as Robert De Niro's stroke victim in *Flawless*). And the Kirk Douglas personal style is unaffected: He was always one of the cocky, high-energy stars, the life force made lithe and springy.

Diamonds feels like it was conceived as a showcase for Douglas at eighty-three, and so it is, but what a dreary story and unconvincing characters he has been surrounded with. Dan Aykroyd plays his son, and Corbin Allred plays his fifteen-year-old grandson. We get phoned-in scenes involving a lack of communication between them and learn that Aykroyd believes it's time for his old man to give up his independence and move into a retirement home.

Nothing doing! says Douglas, playing a former boxing champion named Harry who still likes to duke it out (there are flashbacks of him in the ring, lifted from his 1949 film *Champion*). He wants to live independently, and tells his son and grandson about some diamonds that he was given decades ago to throw a fight in Reno. The diamonds are still hidden inside the walls of the house of a man named Duff the Muff, he says, and they should all three go to Nevada and recover them. As a plot premise, this would look thin in an Adam Sandler movie.

The men travel south from Canada in the obligatory vintage convertible, its top down to make it easier to shoot all three passengers. Harry might get pneumonia in the winter weather, but nobody thinks of that—and besides, the old guy is feisty enough to get smart with the border guards. In Nevada, when their diamond search experiences a setback, they all end up at a brothel, where the young grandson draws Jenny McCarthy and Kirk Douglas gets the warmhearted madam, played by Lauren Bacall, who seems right at home as the nurturing angel, as indeed she should, having nursed the ailing John Wayne character back to life, so to speak, in *The Shootist* twenty-five years ago.

The scenes in the brothel are mostly unforgivable, especially the byplay between Allred and McCarthy, who is reminded of the high school sweetheart she left behind. The climax involving the diamonds is so wheezy that we could meet during our lunch hours and pep it up. Characters so simple in plots so tired with dialogue so banal are not easily found; it is painful to watch actors speaking dialogue that is clearly inferior to the thoughts that must be running through their minds at the very same time.

But tribute must be paid to Kirk Douglas. I remember meeting him over several days in 1969, while writing a profile for *Esquire* magazine. I was almost bowled over by his energy, his zest for life, his superb physical condition. He could hardly sit still. He bounded from his chair to the side of a desk to a yoga position on the floor, talking rapid-fire about his career and hopes, and I have never forgotten what determination and joy he seemed to gather into every day of living. You can see that same quality in *Diamonds,* and seeing it is a way to enjoy the film—alas, the only way.

Dick ★ ★ ★ ½

PG-13, 90 m., 1999

Kirsten Dunst (Betsy Jobs), Michelle Williams (Arlene Lorenzo), Dan Hedaya (Dick), Will Ferrell (Bob Woodward), Bruce McCulloch (Carl Bernstein), Saul Rubinek (Henry Kissinger), Teri Garr (Helen Lorenzo), Dave Foley (Bob Haldeman), Jim Breuer (John Dean), Harry Shearer (G. Gordon Liddy). Directed by Andrew Fleming. Produced by Gale Anne Hurd. Screenplay by Fleming and Sheryl Longin.

Dick is the flip side of *All the President's Men,* explaining at last all of the loose ends of the Watergate scandal—how the duct tape got on the Watergate lock, who Deep Throat really was, and why the 18½–minute gap appeared on the White House tapes. We also learn that Richard M. Nixon resented the fact that his dog didn't follow him around adoringly, like the Kennedy and Johnson dogs; at one point, he snarls, "Checkers—shut up! I'll feed you to the Chinese!"

The movie is a bright and sassy comedy, seeing Watergate entirely through the eyes of its prime movers, who are revealed to be two fifteen-year-old girls. Betsy Jobs (Kirsten Dunst) and Arlene Lorenzo (Michelle Williams) are best friends who live in the Watergate complex, and one night they sneak downstairs to mail a letter to the Bobby Sherman Fan Club;

they slap the tape on the door lock, it's discovered by a security guard, and the White House burglars are busted inside Democratic National Headquarters.

Ah, but it doesn't end there. The girls are on a class trip to the White House when they spot a man they'd seen in the Watergate. He's G. Gordon Liddy (Harry Shearer), but they don't know that; they get separated from their group and wander the White House corridors, stumbling upon shredding operations and cash rooms, and overhearing crucial conversations in the Oval Office itself.

President Nixon (Dan Hedaya, very funny) grows concerned over how much they may have heard and puts on a show of false good cheer: "How would you young ladies like to be the White House dog walkers?" Calling every day to walk Checkers, they dimly perceive that all is not as it should be in the Oval Office, and the plot reveals how they became Deep Throat, why John Dean had an attack of conscience, and why their rendition of Olivia Newton-John's "I Love You" appeared on a tape in the desk drawer of Rosemary Woods.

Yes, Arlene, the apple-cheeked one with the merry smile, gets a crush on Nixon. There's a funny dream sequence in which he appears to her riding a white charger on the beach, but even funnier is the classroom scene where, like millions of teenage girls before her, she tries out a married name by writing it in her notebook: "Mrs. Arlene Nixon."

Dick, directed by Andrew Fleming and written by Fleming and Sheryl Longin, finds just the right tone for its merciless satire: not strident, not wacky, but kind of earnest and intent, as the girls, who are not geniuses, blunder onto one incriminating secret after another. Their motivation seems to stem from ordinary teenage attributes, like curiosity, idealism, and romance.

The crusading reporters Woodward and Bernstein (Will Ferrell and Bruce McCulloch), on the other hand, are played more broadly—Woodward as a self-important totem pole, Bernstein as an insecure runt. They're always trying to grab the phone away from each other, and their Watergate coverage, so majestic when seen from the outside, is portrayed as the work of a couple of ambitious reporters on a power trip, believing everything the teenage ditzos tell them. (Of course, everything the girls tell them turns out to be correct.)

Comedy like this depends on timing, invention, and a cheerful cynicism about human nature. It's wiser and more wicked than the gross-out insult humor of many of the summer's other comedies. Consider the scene where the girls accidentally bake cookies with a secret herbal ingredient from their brother's stash and take them to Nixon, who offers one to Leonid Brezhnev. His mood is so altered that Nixon tells them, "You know, girls, I think your cookies just saved the world from nuclear catastrophe."

Dan Hedaya's president looks a little like the real Nixon, and the match of the public persona is uncanny, as he complains to Henry Kissinger (Saul Rubinek) about his enemies, his insecurities, and his dog. He grows bitter as his administration collapses around him, eventually retreating to bourbon and recrimination, while even the faithful Arlene grows disenchanted ("You're prejudiced and you have a potty mouth").

Will the movie play for audiences who don't remember Watergate—for teenage Kirsten Dunst fans? I think so, because it contains all the information the audience really needs to know, although older viewers will enjoy the wealth of cross-references, as when the Plumbers offer Nixon menus of dirty tricks. *Dick* is a sly little comic treasure.

Dinosaur ★ ★ ★
PG, 84 m., 2000

Voices of: Alfre Woodard (Plio), Ossie Davis (Yar), Max Casella (Zini), Hayden Panettiere (Suri), D. B. Sweeney (Aladar), Samuel E. Wright (Kron), Peter Siragusa (Bruton), Julianna Margulies (Neera), Joan Plowright (Baylene), Della Reese (Eema). Directed by Ralph Zondag and Eric Leighton and produced by Pam Marsden. Screenplay by John Harrison and Robert Nelson Jacobs, based on an original screenplay by Walon Green.

If a film had been made in the Jurassic age, it might have looked a lot like *Dinosaur*. The movie is startling in its impact. Against a backdrop of nature that is clearly real, we see dinosaurs that are scarcely less real. We feel the same sense of wonder that was stirred by *Jurassic Park*. These great beasts ruled the earth much longer than we have, their unlikely bodies sketched out in exaggerated Darwinian strokes.

The visual look of *Dinosaur* is a glimpse of wonders to come. The movie sends the message that computer animation is now sophisticated enough to mimic life itself in full motion, with such detail that the texture of reptilian skin seems as real as a photograph in *National Geographic*. The problem, as always, is to match the artistry with the technique.

The film opens with a little short story about an egg. The egg is first glimpsed in the nest of an iguanodon, which is fairly friendly looking, as dinosaurs go. Predators attack the parents and disturb the nest, and then the egg is snatched by a scampering little critter that runs away with it. There's a fight for possession, the egg drops into a stream, is swallowed and then disgorged by a river monster, is snatched up by a flying creature, and finally dropped from the sky to land in the habitat of lemurs.

Lemurs are, of course, about as cute as mammals can get. There were not any lemurs looking like this at the time of the dinosaurs, but never mind: The movie does a little overlapping of its eras to expand the cast, and to give the mammals in the audience a point of identification. The egg hatches, a mother lemur takes the baby iguanodon into its arms, and then . . . she speaks.

I can't tell you how disappointed I was to hear that voice. I guess I had forgotten that this movie wasn't going to be a reckless leap into the distant past, but a fairy tale in which the dinosaurs are human in all but outer form. They not only talk, they also have personalities, and they argue, plan, scheme, and philosophize, just like humans. They even have human values; when one of the leaders says it's going to be "survival of the fittest" on a long desert trek, he comes across as cold and heartless. If there is one thing I think I know about dinosaurs, it's that sentimentality for the underdog played no part in their decision making.

I wonder why I was disturbed by the sound of dinosaurs with human voices. I know that cartoons can speak. I expect them to. When the dinosaurs spoke in *The Land Before Time*, that was fine with me. But *Dinosaur* looked so real that it didn't play like an animated film for me—it felt more like a nature documentary. There is a continuum reaching from Mickey Mouse to *Jurassic Park*, and at some point on that continuum the animals stop wisecracking and start eating one another. *Dinosaur* feels too evolved for cute dialogue.

Why are we as a species so determined to impose our behavior on creatures that are manifestly not human, and all the more wondrous for not being so? Why must we make the past more "accessible" by translating it into the terms of the present? At one point during the desert trek, simians climb aboard a dinosaur for a free ride, and it complains, "Just what I need—a monkey on my back." A dinosaur, even one that spoke English, would be unlikely to know what that line implied—and so will the kids in today's audience.

I don't know if Disney has a house rule about which animals can speak and which cannot, but guidelines seem to be emerging. The rule is, if you are a predatory carnivore, you don't talk, but if you are a pacifist, a vegetarian, or cute, you do. In *Tarzan* the apes spoke, but the leopards didn't. In *Dinosaur*, all of the creatures speak except for the vicious carnotaurs. A Faustian bargain seems to be at work: If you are an animal in a Disney picture, you can speak, but only if you are willing to sacrifice your essential nature.

All of this is of limited interest, I know, to the hordes clamoring to see this movie. Most younger kids probably assume that dinosaurs *can* speak, because they hear them speaking on TV every day. Even adults will probably not wonder if dinosaurs really roared. I enjoyed the movie as sheer visual spectacle, and I felt a certain awe at sequences like the meteor shower or the discovery of water beneath a parched lake bed. I was entertained, and yet I felt a little empty-handed at the end, as if an enormous effort had been spent on making these dinosaurs seem real, and then an even greater effort was spent on undermining the illusion.

Disturbing Behavior ★ ★

R, 83 m., 1998

James Marsden (Steve Clark), Nick Stahl (Gavin Strick), Katie Holmes (Rachel Wagner), Bruce Greenwood (Dr. Caldicott), Steve Railsback (Officer Cox), William Sadler (Dorian Newberry). Directed by David Nutter and produced by Armyan Bernstein and Jon Shestack. Screenplay by Scott Rosenberg.

Disturbing Behavior is a small-town horror movie with an ironic flip-flop: This time, a sinister local cult takes rebels and delinquents and turns them into clean-cut models of deportment. "You still think this is about blood drives and bake sales?" one of the kids whispers fearfully, as they eavesdrop on a secret meeting where citizens are planning bake sales and blood drives.

The kid is named Gavin, and he's the whistle-blower, the one kid in school who knows what's going on. In the movie's best scene, he gives Steve, the newcomer, a guided tour of the various factions in the lunchroom: the dopers, the brains, the car crowd, and the Blue Ribbons, who wear letter jackets and have trim haircuts and always exhibit exemplary behavior.

It's the Blue Ribbons who are the dangerous ones, Gavin knows. Smoking some weed in the forest by the hydroelectric plant, he witnessed one of them break a girl's neck and shoot a cop—and then saw the cop's partner let the killer go. From his vantage point, Gavin was unable to see the evil red glow in the killer kid's eyes, but obviously, these are dangerous people.

The cult members hate all forms of rebellion. The reason the girl had to die was that she had a tattoo. "Self-mutilation," says her killer, who refuses sex because he has to "conserve his fluids" for the big game, and later utters the very worst line in the movie: "Self-mutilate this, fluid girl!"

Gavin is played by Nick Stahl. James Marsden is Steve, the newcomer, and Katie Holmes (from *Dawson's Creek*) is Rachel, who dresses in black and likes to strike poses on the beds of pickup trucks and is a bad girl who is in great danger of becoming a very good one. Meanwhile, down in the school basement, the janitor (William Sadler) has what Gavin describes as "the village idiot, Quasimodo thing going." But is the janitor quite what he seems?

Teenage horror movies are a popular genre after *Scream* and *Scream 2*, but this one doesn't make it. It's too murky and disorganized. The director, David Nutter, has done some *X-Files* episodes, and is great at suggesting conspiracies but not so good at payoffs. It's like he wants to postpone the answers to the end of the season.

But we catch on fairly quickly that this is, as the advance buzz has it, a teenage version of *The Stepford Wives.* The Blue Ribbons, with their Weekend Enlightenment Seminars, are, as Gavin says, "hypnotized, lobotomized, and brainwashed." And there's the obligatory element of scheming parents who double-cross their kids: They'd rather have a polite zombie than a sullen rebel.

Unlike *Scream 2*, which kids the horror clichés, *Disturbing Behavior* pretends they still hold power. But the movie is light on shocks and not ever scary. It does, however, find a great way to illustrate Pink Floyd's immortal line, "Hey! Teacher! Leave those kids alone!"

Doctor Dolittle ★ ★ ★
PG-13, 90 m., 1998

Eddie Murphy (Dr. John Dolittle), Ossie Davis (Archer Dolittle), Oliver Platt (Dr. Mark Weller), Peter Boyle (Calloway), Richard Schiff (Dr. Gene Reiss), Kristen Wilson (Lisa), Jeffrey Tambor (Dr. Fish), Kyla Pratt (Maya). Directed by Betty Thomas and produced by John Davis, David T. Friendly, and Joseph M. Singer. Screenplay by Nat Mauldin and Larry Levin.

Doctor Dolittle is a gross-out movie, yes, and it's going to be criticized by those who can't believe it got a PG-13 rating. Like Eddie Murphy's previous film, *The Nutty Professor*, it has a lot of jokes about bodily functions. It breaks some new ground, with a scene where the Murphy character gives the kiss of life to a rat, and when a pigeon makes a low-level bombing run at Oliver Platt's nostrils. And of course, there's the scene where the Murphy character, as a little boy, learns from his dog why dogs sniff each other's behinds, and then tries the same tactic in checking out the new school principal.

Is this material a mistake? I don't think so. Kids have a healthy interest in bodily functions, and if you don't believe me, ask Captain Mike, who runs a kiddie playland in Sawyer, Michigan, and gives away an amazing number of Whoopee Cushions as free prizes. Too many adults have a tendency to confuse bad taste with evil influences; it's hard for them to see that the activities in *Doctor Dolittle*, while rude and vulgar, are not violent or antisocial. The movie will not harm anyone, and in the audience I saw it with, lots of parents and kids seemed to be laughing together.

The movie stars Murphy as John Dolittle, who as a child could talk to the animals (there's a gem of an opening scene in which he chats matter-of-factly with his dog, whose voice is by Ellen DeGeneres, about what dogs think about people). The boy grows out of this stage, however, and even goes through an animal-hating phase before he knocks his head in a car accident and regains his inner ear for animals.

By now Murphy is grown up, a famous doctor whose partner (Platt) is in a lather to sell out their medical operation to an HMO. But Murphy gets seriously distracted by his new insights into animals, and on the night of a big business meeting he's more interested in emergency treatment for an ailing tiger from the zoo. There's also trouble with his despairing family, which has him committed to a mental institution.

Murphy is essentially the straight man in the movie; most of the laughs belong to the animals, who are brash and outspoken—especially Rodney the guinea pig, voiced by Chris Rock. Albert Brooks finds a nice long-suffering note as the ailing tiger, and Reni Santoni and John Leguizamo have some nice zingers as the laboratory rats who are brought back to life by Dolittle's first aid: "You want gratitude? Get a hamster." Some of the animals are real. Most of them are creations of the Jim Henson muppet builders. All of them look real enough, and there's some nice physical humor in a scene where Rodney gets drenched, dries itself out under a blower, and then enjoys a quick massage.

Murphy, I think, finds the right strategy in acting opposite this menagerie: He's mostly quiet, calm, not trying too hard for laughs; the overall tone of the movie, despite the gross material, is one of sweetness and gentleness. Sure, a lot of the stuff is in bad taste, but I'll never forget Mel Brooks's defense of one of his movies: "Vulgar? It rises *below* vulgarity."

Dogma ★ ★ ★ ½
R, 125 m., 1999

Ben Affleck (Bartleby), Matt Damon (Loki), Linda Fiorentino (Bethany), Salma Hayek (Serendipity), Jason Lee (Azrael), Alan Rickman (Metatron), Chris Rock (Rufus), Janeane Garofalo (Clinic Girl), George Carlin (Cardinal Glick), Jason Mewes (Jay), Kevin Smith (Silent Bob). Directed by Kevin Smith and produced by Scott Mosier. Screenplay by Smith.

Kevin Smith's *Dogma* grows out of an irreverent modern Catholic sensibility, a by-product of parochial schools, where the underlying faith is taken seriously but the visible church is fair game for kidding. For those raised in such traditions, it's no reach at all to imagine two fallen angels finding a loophole to get back into heaven. I can remember passionate debates during religion class about whether, if you missed your Easter duty, you could double back across the International Date Line and cover yourself.

Of course, the faith itself does not depend on temporal rules, and *Dogma* knows it. Catholicism, like all religions, is founded on deeper mysteries than whether you will go to hell if you eat meat on Friday. I am reminded of the wonderful play *Sister Mary Ignatius Explains It All for You,* in which a pre–Vatican II nun tries to cope with changes in church law; as I recall, her advice was to eat meat *once* on a Friday, to show you know the pope is right—and then never eat it again.

As someone who values his parochial school education and still gets into interminable debates about church teachings, I enjoyed *Dogma*'s approach, which takes church teaching jokingly and very seriously indeed—both at the same time. It reflects a mentality I'm familiar with. (For example, it's a sin to harbor an impure thought, but how many seconds counts as harboring?) I am also familiar with the types at William Donohue's small but loud

Catholic League, which protested this film as blasphemous.

Every church has that crowd—the holier-than-thous who want to be your moral traffic cop; when they run meetings, they drive you crazy with Robert's Rules of Order. It's interesting that no official church spokesman has seconded them. You'd think the church might tell the league to stop embarrassing it, but no, that would be no better than the league attacking Smith. We are actually free in this country to disagree about religion, and blasphemy is not a crime.

What's more, I think a Catholic God might plausibly enjoy a movie like *Dogma,* or at least understand the human impulses that made it, as he made them. ("He's lonely—but he's funny," an angel says in the movie.) After all, it takes Catholic theology absolutely literally, and in such detail that non-Catholics may need to be issued catechisms on their way into the theater (not everybody knows what a plenary indulgence is). Sure, it contains a lot of four-letter words, because it has characters who use them as punctuation. But, hey, they're vulgarities, not blasphemies. Venial, not mortal. Sure, it has a flawed prophet who never gives up trying to get into the heroine's pants, but even Saint Augustine has been there, done that.

The story: Matt Damon and Ben Affleck play Loki and Bartleby, two angels cast out of heaven and exiled for all eternity in Wisconsin. They hear about a trendy bishop (George Carlin) who wants to give the church an upbeat new image. He's rededicating a cathedral in New Jersey in the image of Buddy Jesus, a Christ who blesses his followers with the A-OK sign. Anyone entering the cathedral will get a plenary indulgence (which means that if you are in a state of grace, all temporal punishment for sin is remitted, and you can enter directly into heaven). Bartleby and Loki see the loophole: Walk through the church doors, and they qualify again for heaven.

There is a problem with this plan (apart from the obvious one, which is that church rules govern men, not angels). The problem is explained by Metatron (Alan Rickman), an angel who appears inside a pillar of fire in the bedroom of Bethany (Linda Fiorentino). After she douses him with a fire extinguisher, he explains that if the angels reenter heaven, God will be proven fallible—and all existence will therefore end. He tells Bethany that she is the last surviving relative of Jesus on Earth, that two prophets will appear to her, and that she must follow them in order to stop the angels and save the universe.

Fiorentino is a laconic, edgy actress with an attitude. That makes her perfect for this role. In an earlier draft of Smith's screenplay, the character was a bimbo, but she's much better like this, grown-up and sardonic. It's fun to watch her handle the prophets, who turn out to be a couple of slacker mall rats (Jason Mewes and Smith himself). Later she meets Rufus, the thirteenth apostle (Chris Rock), who has a grievance about why he was left out of the New Testament.

If the film is less than perfect, it is because Smith is too much in love with his dialogue. Like George Bernard Shaw, he loves to involve his characters in long, witty conversations about matters of religion, sexuality, and politics. *Dogma* is one of those rare screenplays, like a Shaw playscript, that might actually read better than it plays; Smith is a gifted comic writer who loves paradox, rhetoric, and unexpected zingers from the blind side.

There is a long tradition that commercial American movies challenge conventional piety at great risk. For a long time, any movie dealing with religion had to be run past Hollywood's resident monsignors, ministers, and rabbis for approval (the habits of actual orders of nuns could not even be portrayed, which led to great ingenuity in the costume department). On the other hand, nobody has any problem with a movie that treats spiritual matters on the level of the supernatural. This has led to an emerging antireligion based on magic, ghosts, mediums, and other New Age voodoo. Talk shows allow "psychics" to answer your questions over the phone, but God forbid they would put on a clergyman to supply thoughtful spiritual advice. And if a movie dares to deal with what people actually believe, all hell, so to speak, breaks loose.

Kevin Smith has made a movie that reflects the spirit in which many Catholics regard their church. He has positioned his comedy on the balance line between theological rigidity and secular reality, which is where so many Catholics find themselves. He deals with eternal questions in terms of flawed characters who live now, today, in an imperfect world. Those whose approach to religion is spiritual will have little trouble with *Dogma*, because they will understand the characters as imperfect, sincere, clumsy seekers trying to do the right thing. Those who see religion more as a team, a club, a hobby, or a pressure group are upset. This movie takes theological matters out of the hands of "spokesmen" and entrusts it to—well, the unwashed. And goes so far as to suggest that God loves them. And is a Canadian. ☞

Don't Look Back ★ ★ ★
NO MPAA RATING, 96 m., 1967 (rereleased 1998)

A documentary directed by D. A. Pennebaker and produced by Albert Grossman, John Court, and Leacock-Pennebaker Inc. With Bob Dylan, Joan Baez, Bob Neuwirth, Donovan, Tito Burns, and Albert Grossman.

What a jerk Bob Dylan was in 1965. What an immature, self-important, inflated, cruel, shallow little creature, lacking in empathy and contemptuous of anyone who was not himself or his lackey. Did we actually once take this twerp as our folk god?

I scribbled down these and other observations as I watched the newly restored print of *Don't Look Back*, the 1967 documentary about Dylan's 1965 concert tour of England. And I was asking myself: Surely I didn't fall for this at the time? I tried to remember the review I wrote when the movie was new. Was I so much under the Dylan spell that I couldn't see his weakness of character?

Take the two scenes, for example, where he mercilessly puts down a couple of hardworking interviewers who are only trying to do their job (i.e., give Dylan more publicity), while a roomful of Dylan yes-men, groupies, and foot-kissers join in the jeers. I was chilled by the possibility that I reacted to these scenes differently the first time around, falling for Dylan's rude and nearly illiterate word games as he pontificates about "truth."

I hurried home and burrowed into my files

for the 1967 review of *Don't Look Back,* and was relieved to discover that, even then, I had my senses about me. "Those who consider Dylan a lone, ethical figure standing up against the phonies will discover after seeing this film," I wrote, "that they have lost their hero. Dylan reveals himself, alas, to have clay feet like all the rest of us. He is immature, petty, vindictive, lacking a sense of humor, overly impressed with his own importance and not very bright." Thank God I was not deceived. I gave the movie three stars, and still do, for its alarming insights.

Of course there is the music. Always the music. I'm listening to "Highway 61 Revisited" as I write these words. I like his music, and I like his whiny, nasal delivery of it; it speaks to the eternal misunderstood complainer in all of us. I remember the thrill we all felt as undergraduates when we first heard "Blowin' in the Wind." Of course, at the time we thought *we* were the answer, my friends, but we were young and hadn't seen this movie.

As a musician, Dylan has endured and triumphed. Perhaps he has also grown and matured as a human being, and is today a nice guy with an infectious sense of humor and a certain soft-spoken modesty. Or maybe not. I don't know. What I do know is that D. A. Pennebaker's 1967 film, which invented the rock documentary, is like a time capsule from just that period when Sgt. Pepper was steamrollering Mr. Tambourine Man. "You don't ask the Beatles those questions, do you?" Dylan says to one reporter. To which the only possible answer was, Bob, you just don't know the half of it.

Another irony is that a true folk goddess, Joan Baez, with her remarkable voice, presence, and soul, tags along during the early scenes, barely acknowledged by Dylan. She brings a glow to the film by singing "Love Is a Four-Letter Word" in a hotel room one night, and then disappears from the film, unremarked. My guess is that she'd had enough.

The movie is like a low-rent version of the rock concert documentaries that would follow. Dylan is badgered by a room full of journalists at a press conference—but it's a small room, with only half a dozen reporters. He insults them, lacking the Beatles' saving grace of

wit. He's mobbed by fans—hundreds, not thousands. He fills Royal Albert Hall, not Wembley Stadium. He reminds me of that mouse floating down the Chicago River on its back, signaling for the drawbridge to be raised.

Sometimes you simply cannot imagine what he, or the filmmakers, were thinking. "How did you start?" he's asked at a press conference. Cut to a scene in a southern cotton field. Dylan stands in front of a pickup truck with some old black field hands sitting on it. He sings a song. Are we supposed to think he rode the rails and bummed in hobo jungles and felt proletarian solidarity with the workers, like Woody Guthrie, Pete Seeger, or Ramblin' Jack Elliott? I was reminded of Steve Martin in *The Jerk* saying, "I was born a poor black child." The field hands break into grateful applause, as the scene dissolves into a thunderous London concert ovation. Give us a break.

If Dylan sees this rerelease, I hope he cringes. We were all callow once, but it is a curable condition. A guy from *Time* magazine comes to interview him. "I know more about what you do just by looking at you than you'll ever be able to know about me," Dylan tells him, little suspecting how much we know just by looking at him. He suggests that the magazine try printing the truth. And what would that be? "A photo of a tramp vomiting into a sewer, and next to it a picture of Rockefeller," suggests the man described in a recent review as "one of the most significant artists of the second half of the twentieth century." Significance I will grant him. More than we knew.

Double Jeopardy ★ ★ ½
R, 105 m., 1999

Tommy Lee Jones (Travis Lehman), Ashley Judd (Libby Parsons), Bruce Greenwood (Nick Parsons), Annabeth Gish (Angie), Roma Maffia (Margaret Skolowski), Davenia McFadden (Evelyn Lake). Directed by Bruce Beresford and produced by Leonard Goldberg. Screenplay by David Weisberg and Douglas S. Cook.

Some jerk sent me an e-mail revealing the secret of *Double Jeopardy.* It's a secret the movie's publicity is also at pains to reveal. I know it's an academic question, but I'll ask it anyway: Why go to the trouble of constructing a screenplay that conceals information if you reveal it in the ads? Once tipped off, are we expected to enjoy how the film tells us what we already know?

If through some miracle you have managed to avoid learning anything about *Double Jeopardy,* you might want to stop reading after my next sentence. This is the sentence, and it advises you: not a successful thriller but with some nice dramatic scenes along with the dumb mystery and contrived conclusion.

Now that the idealists have bailed out, the rest of us can consider *Double Jeopardy,* which stars Ashley Judd as a woman named Libby, who thinks she is happily married until, and I quote from the *first* sentence of the Paramount press release, she is "framed for the murder of her husband." This is, come to think of it, not such a surprise anyway, considering that Judd is pure-faced and clear-eyed, and her husband is played as a weasel. When they go sailing and the Coast Guard finds her in a blood-soaked nightgown on a blood-smeared deck with a knife in her hand, we make an intuitive leap that she isn't a slasher. (The movie's trailer provides a helpful hint: "Libby Parsons is in prison for a crime she didn't commit!")

The whole business of how she was framed, and how she tries to find her husband and regain custody of her child, is basically just red meat the director throws to the carnivores in the audience. You know and I know and anyone over the age of ten knows that the movie is not going to end without that kid back in Libby's arms, probably with some heartrending music. What makes the film interesting isn't the story, but a prison sequence and a relationship.

Libby in prison is befriended by a couple of women prisoners who killed their husbands but are otherwise the salt of the earth. They create a nice dynamic. Not as realistic and evolved as Sigourney Weaver's startling jail scenes in *A Map of the World,* but not bad for a genre picture. One of the prisoners gives her an interesting piece of legal advice: Since she has already been tried and convicted for the murder of her husband, she cannot be tried for the same crime twice. Therefore, "You can

walk right up to him in Times Square and pull the (I must have missed a word here) trigger and there's nothing anybody can do about it."

Caution, convicted killers: I am not sure this is sound legal advice. I believe the constitutional protection against double jeopardy has a couple of footnotes, and I urge you to seek legal advice before reopening fire. It's good enough for Libby, however, and when she gets out of prison she determines to find her betraying louse of an ex-husband and their child.

She's assigned to a halfway house, where her parole officer is a hard-bitten man of few and succinct words played by Tommy Lee Jones. And their scenes together are good ones. When she feeds him the same heartfelt lines that worked with the parole board, he barks, as only Tommy Lee Jones can bark, "I'm not interested in your contrition. I'm interested in your behavior. Get out of here and behave yourself."

How Jones and Judd find themselves underwater is a little unlikely, but so what. As you know from the ads, at one point she's handcuffed to a sinking car. At another point, a terrifying thing happens to her in a New Orleans cemetery. And there is a charity auction of society bachelors at which she makes some Hitchcockian moves. You may have to play the video at slo-mo to figure out how everything happens in the big climax, but by then the movie is basically just housekeeping anyway.

Double Jeopardy was directed by Bruce Beresford. He and Ashley Judd and Tommy Lee Jones have all been involved in wonderful films in the past—films that expand and inspire, like *Tender Mercies* and *Driving Miss Daisy* (Beresford), *Ruby in Paradise* and *Normal Life* (Judd), and *The Executioner's Song* and *JFK* (Jones). This movie was made primarily in the hopes that it would gross millions and millions of dollars, which probably explains most of the things that are wrong with it. ☞

Doug's 1st Movie ★ ½
G, 77 m., 1999

Directed by Maurice Joyce and produced by Jim Jinkins, David Campbell, Melanie Grisanti, and Jack Spillum. Screenplay by Ken Scarborough. With the voices of: Thomas McHugh (Doug

Funnie, Lincoln), Fred Newman (Skeeter Valentine, Mr. Dink, Porkchop, Ned), Constance Shulman (Patti Mayonnaise), Chris Phillips (Roger Koltz, Boomer, Larry, Mr. Chiminy), Gay Hadley (Guy Graham), Doug Preis (Bill Bluff, Doug's Dad, Secret Agent).

Doug's 1st Movie is a thin and less-than-thrilling feature-length version of a Saturday morning animated series, unseen by me. Chatter on the Web suggests it was originally intended to go straight to video, but was rechanneled into theaters after the startling success of *The Rugrats Movie*. Since Doug originally started on Nickelodeon, where *Rugrats* resides, the decision made sense—or would have if this had been a better movie.

The plot: Skeeter, the best pal of twelve-year-old Doug, finds a polluted pond and is about to take a photo when a nasty trick is played on him by some schoolmates who pretend to be a monster. Then a real monster emerges from the waters behind him.

This creature, which serves as proof that the lake is polluted, is actually such a nice monster that it argues for, not against, pollution. It borrows the name Herman Melville from the cover of the book it's reading *(Moby-Dick)*, and becomes a secret friend of Doug and Skeeter's, in *E.T.* fashion.

The plot thickens: The lake is being polluted by the evil Bill Bluff, a local industrialist. Bluff's spy at the school is Guy Graham, editor of the school paper. Guy is also Doug's rival for the love of Patti Mayonnaise, whom Doug wants to take to the prom. Patti grows convinced that Doug is cheating on her with an exchange student, who is actually the monster in drag.

Meanwhile . . . but is the plot of any importance? I think not. It is the vehicle for some fairly routine animation, and characters who may inspire Saturday morning TV watchers but left me indifferent. They have a kind of joy in stupidity. I did like one sequence in the film, involving the ultimate in virtual reality: a VR experience in which everything is exactly as it is in real life, except more expensive.

Will kids like this movie? Who can say? *Rugrats* it ain't.

Down in the Delta ★ ★ ★ ½

PG-13, 111 m., 1998

Alfre Woodard (Loretta), Al Freeman Jr. (Earl), Mary Alice (Rosa Lynn), Esther Rolle (Annie), Loretta Devine (Zenia), Wesley Snipes (Will), Mpho Koaho (Thomas), Kulani Hassen (Tracy). Directed by Maya Angelou and produced by Rick Rosenberg, Bob Christiansen, Victor McGauley, Wesley Snipes, and Reuben Cannon. Screenplay by Myron Goble.

There is a moment in Maya Angelou's *Down in the Delta* when a Chicago woman applies for a job in a supermarket and cannot pass a math test. Turned down, she leaves the store and buys a bottle. Her feelings of inadequacy and worthlessness come through so painfully that we understand, with a surge of empathy, why her life has grown so complicated: She has experienced versions of this rejection for years, and booze or reefer at least offers a brief oblivion.

The woman is named Loretta, and she is played by Alfre Woodard in a performance that is like an act of sympathy with the character. Loretta lives in the Chicago projects with her mother, Rosa Lynn (Mary Alice), and her two children. Thomas (Mpho Koaho) is bright and hard-driving, taking Polaroids of tourists on Rush Street for $5 to make money. Tracy (Kulani Hassen), the baby, is autistic. For years Rosa Lynn has watched her daughter sleep late, sleep around, get drunk, and keep her life on hold. In an early scene, we see Rosa telephone Loretta to wake her up in the morning. She reminds Loretta to feed the baby. Loretta puts some Coca-Cola in a baby bottle.

Rosa Lynn decides things have to change. She delivers an ultimatum: Either Loretta agrees to take her children and spend the summer in the family home on the Mississippi Delta, or Rosa Lynn calls in the child welfare people to take the kids. Loretta has to agree. Rosa Lynn pawns an 1852 silver candelabra, a family heirloom, to finance the trip, which places Loretta and her kids in the hands of her brother-in-law Earl (Al Freeman Jr.).

Uncle Earl runs a diner and employs a local woman (Loretta Devine) to care for his wife, Annie (Esther Rolle), who has Alzheimer's. He's not crazy about taking in three visitors for the summer—especially since he and his sister Rosa have been arguing over that candelabra for years. Loretta doesn't fit in well at first, and her city son doesn't immediately take to the country. But eventually family feelings and values begin to take hold.

If this sounds perhaps like a morality play, it's because no summary can explain the effect of the details in the film. Woodard's performance as Loretta is good at illustrating her problems without ever making her pathetic. Al Freeman, recently seen in *Once Upon a Time . . . When We Were Colored,* is one of the most convincing and natural of actors. And the atmosphere of the Delta is evoked in side stories involving the closure of a chicken plant and the visit of Earl's son (Wesley Snipes), a lawyer from Atlanta.

Angelou is famous as a writer, but she didn't write this movie. It's based on a screenplay by a Georgian named Myron Goble, which won a contest. It illustrates that a strong story, deeply felt and engendered outside the Hollywood assembly line, is likely to get its effects from observation, instead of by following the lazy outlines of formulas from the screenwriting tutors. Study this film side by side with *Patch Adams,* the Robin Williams vehicle, and you will see the contrast between characters who are alive and those who are puppets.

Angelou's first-time direction stays out of its own way; she doesn't call attention to herself with unnecessary visual touches, but focuses on the business at hand. She and Goble are interested in what might happen in a situation like this, not in how they can manipulate the audience with phony crises. When Annie wanders away from the home, for example, it's handled in the way it might really be handled, instead of being turned into a set-piece.

Year after year, in film after film, I've seen Alfre Woodard at work. She is on that very short list of people who rarely seem to appear in anything unworthy. Films may work or they may not, but you don't sense cynicism in her choices. She looks for roles that look like they need to be played.

Woodard says she was more interested in the "early" Loretta than in the later one. Success has many parents, but failure has none, and the early Loretta, going to buy a bottle, is all alone and has little help. But she's not a bad

person. Perhaps she was failed by a school system that didn't take care to teach her. Or by a community with few role models. Or by herself. When you are young, you can carelessly take a path that branches far off from where you thought you were headed. Woodard plays her without turning her into a case study.

I liked the symbolism of the antique candelabra. I won't reveal its history. I will observe that in a poetic and unexpected way, it shows how Loretta's great-great-grandfather buys her out of slavery.

Dr. Akagi ★ ★ ★
NO MPAA RATING, 128 m., 1999

Akira Emoto (Dr. Akagi), Kumiko Aso (Sonoko), Jyuro Kara (Umemoto), Jacques Gamblin (Piet), Masanori Sera (Toriumi). Directed by Shohei Imamura and produced by Hisa Ino and Koji Matsuda. Screenplay by Imamura and Daisuke Tengan.

Dr. Akagi is the kind of family doctor that Spencer Tracy might have played in a 1940s Hollywood film—if Hollywood doctors in those days had lived with prostitutes, befriended morphine addicts, sheltered escaped prisoners of war, and dug up bodies to remove their livers. But I make him sound like a wild man, and in fact he is a gentle, driven soul—more an absentminded professor than a mad scientist.

The doctor (Akira Emoto) is the subject of the new film by Shohei Imamura, the Japanese director who makes films along the fault line between everyday life and outlaw human behavior. "I am interested in the relationship between the lower part of the human body and the lower part of the social structure," he has said. His previous film, *The Eel,* which won the Palme d'Or at the 1997 Cannes festival, was about a wife-murderer who is released from prison and sets up a barbershop in a remote area. Now here is *Dr. Akagi,* set during the last days of World War II.

Because of the war, its hero is the only family doctor for miles around, and in the first shot we see him running to a bedside. "Being a family doctor is all legs," he says. He is known locally as "Dr. Liver," because his diagnosis is invariably the same: hepatitis, treated with an injection of glucose. Sometimes he doubles as a social worker, as when a mother moans to him that her son, a respectable clerk at city hall, has taken up with a prostitute. He is not much shocked, not even when he finds the clerk has embezzled funds to pay the woman. Her name is Sonoko (Kumiko Aso) and she eventually falls in love with Dr. Akagi. How much in love? She was raised in a red-light district, where her mother lectured her, "No freebies!" But for Akagi, it's free—or would be, if he didn't reject her enthusiastic assaults.

He's too busy. He has a theory about why hepatitis cases are spreading so quickly, and experiments with new kinds of microscopes, borrowing an arc lamp from a movie projector to see the little microbes more clearly. Sonoko, peering over his shoulder, asks if there are male and female bacteria, and is shocked to learn there are not: "You mean there is no prostitution in nature?" She moves in and becomes the doctor's housekeeper. His laboratory assistant is another doctor, addicted to drugs. An oddly secular monk joins the household. When a Dutch POW escapes from a torture chamber, Akagi takes him in, too, treating his wounds and letting him help with the research.

Imamura's work reflects on Japanese life as it has changed in his lifetime (he is seventy-two). His best film is *Vengeance Is Mine* (1979), based on the true story of a serial killer who travels the countryside, hunted and hunting. In 1989, he made *Black Rain,* about the aftermath of radioactive fallout in a village near Hiroshima. I will never forget his famous *Ballad of Narayama,* the 1983 Cannes grand prize winner, based on a Japanese legend about a village that takes its old people up onto the mountain to die when they outlive their usefulness.

Dr. Akagi is more matter-of-fact. It is about a busy middle-aged man who treats all manner of illness, physical and mental, while obsessing over hepatitis. At one point he literally does dig up a corpse to dissect a fresh liver (the mourners find it curious that the doctor specifies the abdomen be kept iced after death). There is a war going on all during the movie, and indeed Akagi's son dies, but daily life in the village bumbles along, punctuated only by air raids and announcements of smaller rice rations.

Imamura allows himself poetic touches, sparingly. When the telegram arrives telling Akagi that his son is dead, he shreds it into tiny pieces and throws it into the air; countless more little paper scraps float down like snow, a reminder of how many telegrams the war has inspired. And at the end, Akagi and the former prostitute are out in a boat when an atomic bomb falls. He looks at the mushroom cloud and observes that it resembles a hypertrophied liver.

The Dreamlife of Angels ★ ★ ★ ½
R, 113 m., 1999

Elodie Bouchez (Isa), Natacha Regnier (Marie), Gregoire Colin (Chris), Jo Prestia (Fredo), Patrick Mercado (Charly). Directed by Erick Zonca and produced by Francois Marquis. Screenplay by Zonca and Roger Bohbot.

The French believe that most of the characters in American movies, no matter what their ages, act like teenagers. I believe that the teenagers in most French movies seem old, wise, and sad. There is a lesson here, perhaps that most American movies are about plots, and most French movies are about people.

The Dreamlife of Angels serves as an example. It is about two twenty-year-olds who are already marked by the hard edges of life. They meet, they become friends, and then they find themselves pulled apart by sexuality, which one of them sees as a way to escape a lifetime of hourly wages. This is a movie about a world where young people have to work for a living. Most twenty-year-old Americans in the movies receive invisible monthly support payments from God.

We meet Isa (Elodie Bouchez), a tough little nut with a scar over one eye and a gift of gab. She's a backpacker who cuts photos out of magazines, pastes them to cardboard squares, and peddles them in bars as "tourist views." She doesn't really expect to support herself that way, but it's a device to strike up conversations, and sure enough she meets a guy who offers her a job—as a seamstress in a sweatshop.

At work, she meets Marie (Natacha Regnier). The two women become friends, and Isa moves in with Marie. They hang out in malls and on the streets, smoking, kidding, playing at picking up guys. They aren't hookers; that would take a degree of calculation and planning ability that they lack—and, besides, they still dream of true romance. Isa tells Marie about one guy she met when she was part of a remodeling crew working on his house. They slept together, but when the job was over, she left, and he let her leave. She wonders if maybe she missed a good chance. Unlikely, Marie advises.

Marie steals a jacket and is seen by Chris (Gregoire Colin). He owns a club, and asks them to drop in one night. They already know the bouncers, and Marie has slept with one of them. Soon it comes down to this: Chris has money, Marie has none, and although her friendship with Isa is the most important relationship in her life, she is willing to abandon it in order to share Chris's bed and wealth. Isa, who in the beginning looked like a mental lightweight, has the wisdom and insight to see how this choice will eventually hurt Marie. But Marie will not listen.

The movie understands what few American movies admit: Not everyone can afford the luxury of following their hearts. Marie has already lost the idealism that would let her choose the bouncer (whom she likes) rather than the owner (whom she likes too, but not for the same reasons). The story is played out against the backdrop of Lille, not the first French city you think of when you think of romance. In this movie it is a city of gray streets and tired people, and there is some kind of symbolism in the fact that Marie is house-sitting her apartment for a girl in a coma.

The movie was directed and cowritten by Erick Zonca, a forty-three-year-old Parisian who lived in New York from the age of twenty, worked at odd jobs for ten years, then became the director of TV commercials. He returned to France to make his features; this is his third. He creates an easy familiarity with Isa and Marie. The story is about their conversation, their haphazard progress from day to day; it doesn't have contrived plot points.

I can't easily imagine Isa and Marie in Los Angeles, nor can I imagine an American indie director making this film, which contains no guy-talk in diners, no topless clubs, no drug dealers in bathrobes, no cigars. This year's Critics Week at Cannes has just announced that it was unable to find a single American film it admired enough to program. *The Dreamlife of Angels* shared the Best Actress Award between Bouchez and Regnier last year in the Cannes main competition. There you have it.

Drifting Clouds ★ ★ ★ ½
NO MPAA RATING, 96 m., 1998

Kati Outinen (Ilona), Kari Vaananen (Lauri), Sakari Kuosmanen (Melartin), Shelley Fisher (Pianist), Tero Jartti (Tax Inspector), Aarre Karen (Bank Director). Directed by Aki Kaurismaki and produced by Erkki Astala and Kaurismaki. Screenplay by Kaurismaki.

Aki Kaurismaki is the fortyish Finnish director of strange and quirky comedies, in which little people are crushed by vast economic systems, but they keep on truckin'. In *Drifting Clouds*, a woman loses her job at a bankrupt restaurant, her husband is laid off by the transport system, the TV is repossessed, she pays her savings to an employment agency for another job, she isn't paid, and when her husband tries to collect he gets beaten up. But there's a happy ending.

Kaurismaki has enormous love for these characters. He embraces their comic pathos and rejoices that they do not surrender. It's all done with such subtle irony that critics use words like "minimalist" to describe him— even though his screen is saturated with images and ideas, and true minimalism is more easily seen in something like *Armageddon*, which has half an idea and spreads it thinly over 144 minutes.

The heroine of *Drifting Clouds* is Ilona (Kati Outinen), a wan, sweet blonde with a dour expression, who works as the manager of a failing restaurant. The movie opens with a pianist singing of "the wonderful girl I love," and then there's a long shot of the interior, with customers seated at their tables like mourners at a wake. Lighting is used to highlight Ilona at her perch in the back of the shot, and after she seats a customer, there's a zoom in to her sad, thoughtful face.

There's a crisis in the kitchen. The cook is

drunk again, and brandishing a knife. After an offscreen struggle, the headwaiter returns to view with a bleeding wrist. Then Ilona disappears from the screen, there is a loud thud, she returns, and then we see the chef again, disconsolate. Kaurismaki loves to keep the action offscreen and focus on the reaction shots.

After closing, Ilona boards a streetcar and kisses the driver—her husband, Lauri (Kari Vaananen). At home, he covers her eyes to spring a surprise: a new TV set, bought on time. Of course they can't afford it (you can sense that in the haunted way they look at it), but as they sit side by side on a couch that's too small, we feel curious tenderness for them.

The couch is too small because Kaurismaki insists on bargain-basement sets; he wants his characters to always seem a little too large for their rooms and furniture, and the result is cartoonlike. Consider, for example, Ilona's interview with an employment agency; the interviewer's chair squeaks loudly as he confronts her across a desk that seems scaled for a grade-school classroom.

One misfortune follows another. The restaurant closes. The husband loses his job by drawing the wrong card in an office lottery. Ilona gets another job in a restaurant whose owner is a tax cheat. Desperate to keep up appearances, she calls each order loudly into the kitchen before sneaking around a corner to cook it herself. The cook from the former restaurant appears, announcing, "I am on a journey to the end of vodka." And then, improbably, there is a happy ending, which I will not reveal except to observe that it involves a reservation for thirty from the perfectly titled Helsinki Workers' Wrestlers.

Like Godard, Jarmusch, and Mark Rappaport, Kaurismaki pays great attention to the frame around his characters. Their costumes, their props, their sets, and the colors all conspire to make each shot look deliberately composed, as if we're being asked to contemplate people trapped by, and defined by, their environment. Ilona always seems self-conscious, as if she's posing for her photo. There's a shot at a time when things are going badly; she stands next to the bookcases they've bought on credit, and her face remains impassive—but her earrings vibrate, and that's the giveaway that she's trembling.

Kaurismaki himself is a jovial, self-deprecating sort, reportedly hard drinking; he said once that he doesn't move his camera a lot because "that's a nuisance when you have a hangover" (actually, his setups show infinite thought and patience). "I'm just a medium class of director," he told Jonathan Romney of *Sight & Sound* magazine. "I may never make a masterpiece, but if I make many quite good films, together they're something." That statement, which describes many of the most successful directors working today, would never be made by any of them; that Kaurismaki can look at his work so objectively helps to explain why it has such a dry, deadpan appeal.

Drive Me Crazy ★ ★ ½
PG-13, 94 m., 1999

Melissa Joan Hart (Nicole Maris), Adrian Grenier (Chase Hammond), Stephen Collins (Mr. Maris), Susan May Pratt (Alicia), Mark Webber (Dave), Kris Park (Ray Neeley), Gabriel Carpenter (Brad), Lourdes Benedicto (Chloe Frost). Directed by John Schultz and produced by Amy Robinson. Screenplay by Rob Thomas.

Drive Me Crazy is maybe the eighth movie of 1999 to hinge on a date to the big high school dance. The basic plot has three variations: (1) Will the heroine go with the guy she really likes? (2) Will the guy have sex for the first time? and (3) Will anyone be killed by a mad slasher? Like the Sammy Sosa of movie critics, I will clear the bases by giving away all three endings at once: The answer is always "yes."

What distinguishes *Drive Me Crazy* from your average prom movie is that the characters are more intelligent, and have dialogue written with a certain wit and insight. They're not the victims of the plot but its controllers, consciously taking charge of events. And here's a switch: None of them believes the world will end if they go to the dance with the wrong person. The movie is about kids who are as smart as real high school students, while most prom movies have characters who are no smarter than their parents.

The movie stars Melissa Joan Hart, who is "Sabrina, the Teenage Witch" on TV but here comes across perky and wholesome, a Doris Day for our time. She's Nicole, the chairman not of the prom but of the big high school Centennial Dance. She wants to go to the dance with a basketball star, but he strays out of her grasp. Then her thoughtful eye falls on her next-door neighbor, Chase (Adrian Grenier), who has just been dumped by a brunette vixen. He's a member of the outsider crowd at high school, given to commenting on the "fascist nature of pep rallies," but she takes him to the Gap, gets him a haircut, and he cleans up well. By pretending to be dating, they can both save face. Nicole and Chase are obviously right for one another, but have to make that discovery slowly, through many difficulties, including heartrending misunderstandings when she sees him kissing the bad girl. You know the drill.

There are some serious notes. His mom died a few years ago, and that led to tension between Chase and Nicole when they were in junior high—tension she analyzes in a scene not only touching but, for some audience members, probably helpful. Her parents are divorced, and her dad is the kind of guy who turns up unpredictably and stages father-daughter moments in which he takes her up in a hot-air balloon and hands her *Zen and the Art of Motorcycle Maintenance,* suggesting it might help her understand him. She throws it overboard. I felt like cheering.

Drive Me Crazy is slight and sweet, not a great high school movie but kinda nice, with appealing performances by Hart and Grenier. I remember him with respect from *The Adventures of Sebastian Cole,* in which his stepfather wanted to have a sex change. That was a much better movie, which suffered because audiences are shy about stories that take more than a sentence to summarize.

Despite my affection, I can't quite recommend *Drive Me Crazy.* The good stuff needs more energy behind it. John Schultz's direction is lackadaisical. Scenes arrive without feeling necessary. Plot points are belabored. These characters deserve a quicker pace; sometimes they feel ahead of the movie. Still, there's this: Although *Drive Me Crazy* is indeed based on one of the three basic prom plots, it isn't based on the other two.

Drop Dead Gorgeous ★ ★
PG-13, 97 m., 1999

Kirstie Alley (Gladys Leeman), Ellen Barkin (Annette), Kirsten Dunst (Amber), Denise Richards (Becky), Brittany Murphy (Lisa Swenson), Allison Janney (Loretta), Will Sasso (Hank Vilmes), Amy Adams (Leslie Miller). Directed by Michael Patrick Jann and produced by Gavin Polone and Judy Hofflund. Screenplay by Lona Williams.

Sometimes I wonder how anyone could have thought a screenplay was funny enough to film. The script for *Drop Dead Gorgeous,* on the other hand, must have been a funny read. It's the movie that somehow never achieves takeoff speed. Subtle miscalculations of production and performance are probably responsible; comedy is a fragile rose, eager to wilt.

The movie takes place in Mount Rose, Minnesota, a setting created after long study of *Fargo.* The fiftieth anniversary of the Miss Teen Princess America contest is approaching, and the local chairwoman is former winner Gladys Leeman (Kirstie Alley), whose daughter Becky (Denise Richards) is a leading contender. Her big competition: trailer-park cutie Amber (Kirsten Dunst), whose alcoholic mother, Annette (Ellen Barkin), is burned in a fire and spends much of the movie with a beer can permanently fused to the flesh of her hand.

Now there's an example of how a mental image can be funnier than a real one—how a screenplay can fail to translate. You possibly smiled as you read about Annette's hand being fused to a beer can. I did as I wrote the words. But the image of the charred can embedded in scarred flesh is not funny, and every time it turns up it casts its little pall.

Another example. One of the contestants has put herself on a four-hundred-calorie-a-day diet and is a patient at a recovery center for anorexics. Nevertheless, she's determined to compete in the pageant, and arrives onstage in a wheelchair. Funny as a satirical concept? Yes. Funny as a sight? No, because the concept, not the image, contains the joke.

The movie was written by Lona Williams, who is herself a beauty pageant survivor. She understands the backstage politics of such events, especially at the local level, where almost everyone has a buried agenda. Some of the mothers are using their daughters as surrogate reminders of their own faded beauty. Some of the daughters are compensating for insecurity; they think a crown will affirm their worth. Other daughters are resentful puppets. Some of the older men enjoy the proximity to nubile contestants. Some of the women may too.

I sometimes wonder if anybody involved in beauty pageants at the administrative level is completely without motivations they would rather not discuss. The idea of devoting your life to running an event at which young women are judged on the basis of their beauty and personality—as evaluated in a game show format—gets creepier the more you think about it.

As the title of *Drop Dead Gorgeous* suggests, some of the characters turn up dead or injured. The ferocious intensity of the parents is a reminder of *The Positively True Adventures of the Alleged Texas Cheerleader-Murdering Mom*, a made-for-cable movie that's one of the great buried comic treasures of recent years, with a Holly Hunter performance that would have been Oscar material if the movie had opened in theaters. Both films are savage, but *Cheerleader-Murdering Mom* was rich in human nature, while *Drop Dead Gorgeous* simply manipulates the ideas of satire without connecting to the underlying truth. I believed the Holly Hunter character would do what she did for the reasons she had; I felt the Kirstie Alley character was generated by a screenplay.

There is, however, a lot of funny stuff in *Drop Dead Gorgeous*, and Lona Williams has a future as a comedy writer—maybe in the Dave Barry/Molly Ivins tradition, since her ideas seem more literary than cinematic. I liked the idea of a contestant's dramatic reading being from *Soylent Green*. And the way another contestant kills two birds with one stone in the talent section of the contest by singing "I Love You, Baby" to Jesus. The notion that Mount Rose is famous as the "home of the oldest living Lutheran" (recently deceased) is worthy of Garrison Keillor's Lake Wobegon.

The attempt to link Lutherans with gun nuts is less successful; Becky belongs to the Lutheran Sisterhood Gun Club, but this doesn't ring true because, well, it doesn't fit with the general notion of Lutherans as pretty peaceable folks. For satire to work, it has to contain a kernel of truth. What made *Fargo* brilliant was the way it combined satire with affection and accuracy.

The climax of *Drop Dead Gorgeous* contains a few cheerfully disgusting scenes that qualify it to open in this Summer of Raunch. But once again, the ideas are funnier than the images. Contestants get food poisoning during their trip to the finals, and vomit into the atrium lobby of the host hotel. Funny to read about? You bet. To see? Judge for yourself.

Drowning Mona ★ ★
PG-13, 91 m., 2000

Danny DeVito (Chief Rash), Bette Midler (Mona Dearly), Neve Campbell (Ellen), Jamie Lee Curtis (Rona), Casey Affleck (Bobby), William Fichtner (Phil Dearly), Marcus Thomas (Jeff Dearly), Kathleen Wilhoite (Lucinda), Peter Dobson (Feege). Directed by Nick Gomez and produced by Al Corley, Bart Rosenblatt, and Eugene Musso. Screenplay by Peter Steinfeld.

Everyone in Verplanck, New York, drives a Yugo. An older Yugo, since the car hasn't been manufactured since its country went out of business. We learn that Verplanck was selected as a test market when the Yugo was being introduced to the United States. That explains why everyone was driving them then. After we meet the local residents, we understand why they're driving them now: They can't afford to replace them.

As the movie opens, a local woman named Mona Dearly (Bette Midler) speeds down a country road and directly into the Hudson River when her brakes fail. It is a measure of the local intelligence that when the car and driver are dragged to shore some hours later, the doctor checks her pulse. "She's dead," he confirms to Chief Rash (Danny DeVito), who nods grimly and begins a murder investigation.

Lucinda (Kathleen Wilhoite), the local garage mechanic, checks out the death vehicle and confirms his suspicions: The car was rigged. All four brake drums were tampered with, the brake fluid was drained, and the perp also drained some other fluids just to be on the safe side. Now Rash has to decide who killed Mona Dearly.

Almost everyone in town is a suspect. As played in flashbacks by Midler, Mona is a ferocious harridan who may have hacked off her own son's hand just because he was trying to snatch her beer. There are, to be fair, other theories about how Jeff (Marcus Thomas) lost his hand, although in every scenario he was reaching for a beer. Jeff might have wanted to kill her. Or perhaps the murderer was her husband, Phil (William Fichtner), who is having an affair with Rona (Jamie Lee Curtis), a waitress at the local diner (who is also having an affair with Jeff, so maybe she killed Mona just because she was tired of hearing about her from both men).

Or maybe Bobby (Casey Affleck), Jeff's landscaping partner, killed her to save the embarrassment of having her create a scene at his wedding to Ellen (Neve Campbell), Chief Rash's daughter. The possibility upsets Ellen, who explains, in some of the movie's best dialogue: "I can't marry a murderer. That's not who I am. That's not what I'm about."

It helps to understand that everyone in Verplanck is dim to one degree or another, except for the Rash family. The chief is not rash, but fairly levelheaded as he patiently sorts his way through a case that seems to reduce itself to a series of bar fights dimly remembered by drunks. No one in the movie is particularly vicious (well, Jeff's no prize), and the urgency of the case is undermined by the general agreement that Verplanck is calmer and happier now that Mona's gone.

The movie was directed by Nick Gomez, who in *Laws of Gravity* and *New Jersey Drive* brought a Cassavetes touch to working-class crime and confusion. The characters this time could be lightened up and dumbed-down versions of the confused drunks in *Laws of Gravity,* their social lives centered on bars, their center of gravity the bartender. These are the kind of people who don't like to be thrown out of bars because it's a loss of valuable drinking time.

My problem was that I didn't care who killed Mona Dearly, or why, and didn't want to know anyone in town except for Chief Rash and his daughter. The Jamie Lee Curtis character looks like she has some colorful insights to share, but isn't given the dialogue to do it—she's more of a plot marker than a person.

She does figure, however, in a quiet little in-joke. Ever notice how a lot of movie smokers seem to have just lighted their cigarettes? Hers are always burned down precisely half an inch, and then we see her lighting a new one from the old one, and realize, yeah, she only smokes them for the first two puffs. A very quiet little in-joke indeed, but I mention it anyway, so the filmmakers will know their work was not in vain.

Dudley Do-Right ★ ★ ½
PG, 75 m., 1999

Brendan Fraser (Dudley Do-Right), Sarah Jessica Parker (Nell Fenwick), Alfred Molina (Snidley Whiplash), Eric Idle (The Prospector), Robert Prosky (Inspector Fenwick), Alex Rocco (The Chief), Corey Burton (Announcer's Voice), Jack Kehler (Howard). Directed by Hugh Wilson and produced by John Davis, Joseph M. Singer, and J. Todd Harris. Screenplay by Wilson, based on characters developed by Jay Ward.

Dudley Do-Right is a genial live-action version of the old cartoon, with a lot of broad slapstick humor that kids like and adults wince at. I did a little wincing the ninth or tenth time Dudley stepped on a loose plank and it slammed him in the head, but I enjoyed the film more than I expected to. It's harmless, simpleminded, and has a couple of sequences that are better than Dudley really deserves.

The hero is a square-jawed Canadian Mountie who lives in Semi-Happy Valley and combats wrongdoing in his own dim way. He's played by Brendan Fraser, who, after great success in making a live-action character out of a cartoon figure in *George of the Jungle,* has less to work with this time. But work with it he does, dreaming sadly of his lost horse (named Horse) and pining for Nell Fenwick (Sarah Jessica Parker), his childhood sweetheart. He's joyous when Nell returns to the little town, having capped a brilliant academic career with the U.S. ambassadorship to Guam.

His other childhood playmate was Snidley K. Whiplash (Alfred Molina), who dressed in black even as a tot, and has grown up into a

157

mustache-twirling villain who likes his role because "the bad guy has more fun." (Whiplash ties a banker to the railroad tracks, in a nod to the cartoon's tradition, but spares Nell, which will offend traditionalists.)

The plot: Snidley devises a scheme to frighten away all the residents of Semi-Happy Valley with rumors of vampires and replace them with the 999 members of his gang. Then he salts the local streams with gold nuggets, to inspire a Gold Rush (we see Canadian border posts flattened by a stampede of what the TV news calls "Yuppie wetbacks"). He'll fleece the newcomers and get rich.

Dudley is the only lawman standing in his way (until, that is, Nell's father, a veteran inspector, strips him of his authority). His closest ally is the chief (Alex Rocco), head of the local Kumquat tribe, which stages a Corn Festival that looks a lot like a Vegas dance revue. The festival is the funniest thing in the movie (except perhaps for the use of the "Indian Love Song"), although the chief makes little pretense of ethnic authenticity: "Indians? This is basically a dinner theater we're running here."

The Corn Festival sets up one of those moments that, even in a so-so comedy, can blindside us with surprise laughter. As Dudley and Nell leave the festival, rowing across a lake in a canoe, Nell sighs, "I wish we could have stayed for the fireworks." I'd spoil the joke by explaining why this line is so funny, but you'll see. There are also some nice quasi-*Star Wars* scenes involving the prospector (Eric Idle), who tutors Dudley in a Semi-Happy version of the Force.

Fraser is stalwart and credulous as Dudley, Parker is wide-eyed and easily astonished as Nell, and Molina plays Whiplash so broadly he almost needs to stand sideways. Viewers below a certain age (nine?) will probably find the movie enormously entertaining, and truth to tell, I kinda sorta liked it myself. Not enough to recommend it to those in the upper grades, but enough to remember parts with a smile.

E

Earth ★ ★ ★
NO MPAA RATING, 104 m., 1999

Aamir Khan (Dil Navaz, Ice Candy Man), Nandita Das (Shanta, the Ayah), Rahul Khanna (Hasan, the Masseur), Kitu Gidwani (Bunty Sethna), Maia Sethna (Lenny Sethna), Kulbushan Kharbanda (Imam Din), Gulshan Grover (Mr. Singh). Directed by Deepa Mehta and produced by Mehta and Anne Masson. Screenplay by Mehta, based on the novel *Cracking India* by Bapsi Sidhwa.

England, having colonized India at its leisure, granted it independence with unseemly haste. Even its most outspoken nationalists were taken aback when Lord Mountbatten, the British viceroy, unexpectedly announced that the date for independence was a few months, not a few years, in the future. The British decision to pull out by August 15, 1947, left a country with no orderly way to deal with the rivalries between Hindus and Muslims, and the partition of India and Pakistan along religious lines led to bloodshed, massacres, and, as this film calls it, "the largest and most terrible exchange of population in history."

Earth is a film that sees that tragedy through the eyes of a group of friends in Lahore, then in India, now in Pakistan. There are Muslims, Hindus, Sikhs, Parsis, even a Christian or two. They have lived side by side since time immemorial, and the more idealistic think that situation can continue. But as India has proven, along with Northern Ireland, the Middle East, and Yugoslavia, many members of all faiths consider it no sin to murder a nonbeliever.

The film is told as a melodrama and romance, not docudrama, and that makes it all the more effective. It sees much of the action through the eyes of a little brace-legged Parsi girl named Lenny, whose beautiful Hindu nanny, or "ayah," is admired by all the men in a circle of friends. The ayah is Shanta (Nandita Das), with glowing eyes and a warm smile. She slowly comes to love Hasan, a masseur (Rahul Khanna), who is Muslim. She likes, but does not love, Dil, known as "Ice Candy Man" and played by the Indian star Aamir Khan. Her life is pleasant in a wealthy Parsi household ruled by Lenny's kind mother and officious father.

The friends meet in a nearby park for talk that sometimes grows political. They all agree they are above hatreds based on religion. The little girl looks and listens. Often she is present when Hasan courts the shy Shanta, and even watches as they share their first bashful kiss—just before the screen turns black and ominous music introduces shots of Hindu refugees treking from the new Pakistan to India, and Muslims making the opposite journey.

It is hard for us to imagine the upheaval and suffering unleashed when the British washed their hands of the jewel in their crown. Imagine a United States in which those with a last name beginning with a vowel had to leave their homes and belongings and trek north, while those with a consonant had to leave everything behind and trek south. Now add bloodthirsty mobs of zealots on all sides, with rumors of atrocities spreading like wildfire.

The film is based on the novel *Cracking India* by Bapsi Sidhwa. It is said to be partly autobiographical. She remembers the last moments of harmony between the groups, in particular a day spent on rooftops flying brightly colored kites. A few weeks later, from the same rooftops, some of the same people watch Hindu tenements in flames (the "firemen" spray gasoline on them) and a Muslim man torn in two by a mob that ties his arms to two automobiles. At home, little Lenny and her brother tear her favorite doll in two, and the ayah tearfully tries to stitch it back together.

The closing scenes must have been repeated a thousand times over, as a mob tries to find a hidden person of the wrong religion, and good-hearted people try to offer protection. There is a kind of inevitable logic involved in the way a child would view such a situation and cause harm while trying to help. This is the kind of film that makes you question any religion that does not have as a basic tenet the tolerance of other religions. If God allows men to worship him in many forms, who are we to kill them in his name?

Earth was written and directed by Deepa Mehta, a Canadian whose previous film, *Fire* (1997), was the first serious Indian film to deal with lesbianism. After sex and Partition, she plans to move on to *Water,* about "what happens when Hinduism comes in direct conflict with conscience." In a society still touchy about these subjects, she is nothing if not courageous. (Although the Sidhwa novel won the top literary award in Pakistan, *Earth* has been banned there; in India, censors cut out the gentle, sweet sex scene and made five other cuts.)

The fact is, many Americans do not know India and Pakistan were once one country, and few could provide an explanation of Partition. *Earth* is effective because it doesn't require much history from its viewers, explains what needs to be known, and has a universal message, which is that when a mob forms in the name of a religion, its first casualty is usually the teachings of that religion.

East Is East ★ ★ ★
R, 96 m., 2000

Om Puri (George Khan), Linda Bassett (Ella Khan), Jordan Routledge (Sajid Khan), Archie Panjabi (Meenah Khan), Emil Marwa (Maneer Khan), Chris Bisson (Saleem Khan), Jimi Mistry (Tariq Khan), Raji James (Abdul Khan). Directed by Damien O'Donnell and produced by Leslee Udwin. Screenplay by Ayub Khan-Din, based on his play.

George Khan is like that performer on the old Ed Sullivan show, who tried to keep plates spinning simultaneously on top of a dozen poles. He runs from one crisis to another, desperately trying to defend his Muslim worldview in a world that has other views. George is a Pakistani immigrant to England, living in Manchester in 1971 with his British wife and their unruly herd of seven children, and his plates keep falling off the poles.

As the movie opens, George glows proudly as his oldest son goes through the opening stages of an arranged marriage ceremony. The bride enters, veiled, and as she reveals herself to her future husband we see that she is quite pretty—and that the would-be husband is terrified. "I can't do this, Dad!" he shouts, bolting from the hall. George is humiliated.

George is played by Om Puri, as a mixture of paternal bombast and hidebound conserva-

tism. His wife, Ella (Linda Bassett), has worked by his side for years in the fish-and-chips shop at the corner of their street of brick working-class row houses. After their oldest son flees, they are left with a houseful, including a neighborhood ladies' man, a shy son, a would-be artistic type, a jolly daughter, and little Sajid, the youngest, who never, ever takes off his jacket with its fur-trimmed parka. There is even a son who agrees with his father's values.

Puri plays George Kahn as the Ralph Cramden of Manchester. He is bluff, tough, big, loud, and issues ultimatums and pronouncements, while his long-suffering wife holds the family together and practices the art of compromise. His own moral high ground is questionable: He upholds the values of the old country, yet has moved to a new one, taken a British wife although he left a Muslim wife behind in Pakistan, and is trying to raise multiracial children through monoracial eyes.

There's rich humor in his juggling act. His family is so large, so rambunctious, and so clearly beyond his control that it has entirely escaped his attention that little Sajid has never been circumcised. When this lapse is discovered, he determines it is never too late to right a wrong, and schedules the operation despite the doubts of his wife and the screams of Sajid. And then there is the matter of the marriages he is trying to arrange for his No. 2 and No. 3 sons—oblivious of the fact that one of the boys is deeply in love with the blond daughter of a racist neighbor who is an admirer of Enoch ("Rivers of blood") Powell, the anti-immigration figurehead (who has been confused in some reviews, perhaps understandably, with the 1930s fascist leader Oswald Mosley).

Of course the neighbor would have apoplexy if he discovered his daughter was dating a brown boy. And George would have similar feelings, although more for religious reasons. One purpose of the rules and regulations of religions is to create in their followers a sense of isolation from nonbelievers, and what George is fighting, in 1971 Britain, is the seduction of his children by the secular religion of pop music and fashion.

East Is East is related in some ways to *My Son, the Fanatic,* another recent film starring Om Puri as an immigrant from Pakistan. In that one, the tables are turned: Puri plays a taxi driver who has drifted away from his religion and falls in love with a prostitute, while his son becomes the follower of a cult leader and invites the man into their home.

In both films, the tilt is against religion and in favor of romance on its own terms, but then all movie love stories argue for the lovers. Two Oscar winners, *Titanic* and *Shakespeare in Love*, were both stories of romance across class lines, and *American Beauty* and *Boys Don't Cry* were about violating taboos; it could be that movie love stories are the most consistently subversive genre in the cinema, arguing always for personal choice over the disapproval of parents, church, ethnic groups, or society itself.

If there is a weakness in *East Is East*, it's that Om Puri's character is a little too serious for the comedy surrounding him. He is a figure of deep contradictions, trying to hold his children to a standard he has eluded his entire life. Perhaps the real love story in the movie is the one we overlook, between George and his wife, Ella, who has stood by him through good times and bad, running the fish shop and putting up with his nonsense. When he blusters that he will bring over his first wife, who understands his thinking, Ella tells him, "I'm off if she steps foot in this country!" But he's bluffing. His own life has pointed the way for his children. It's just that he can't admit it, to them or himself.

Note: This is a provocative film for useful discussions between parents and children. The "R" rating is inexplicable.

East-West ★ ★ ½
PG-13, 121 m., 2000

Sandrine Bonnaire (Marie), Oleg Menchikov (Alexei), Catherine Deneuve (Gabrielle), Sergei Bodrov Jr. (Sacha), Ruben Tapiero (Serioja [Seven]), Erwan Baynaud (Serioja [Fourteen]). Directed by Regis Wargnier and produced by Yves Marmion. Screenplay by Rustam Ibragimbekov, Sergei Bodrov, Louis Gardel, and Wargnier.

If the Soviet Union had made honorable use of the idealism it inspired in the West, it might have survived and been a happier place today. Marxism seduced and betrayed some of the best minds of its time. The executioner was Stalin. One of his cruel tricks, after the end of World War II, was to invite Russians in exile to return to the motherland—and then execute many of them, keeping the rest as virtual prisoners of the state.

East-West tells the fictional story of one couple who returned. Marie (Sandrine Bonnaire) is French; she married Alexei (Oleg Menchikov), a doctor, in Paris. He is eager to return and help in the rebuilding of Russia, and she loves him and comes along. Their disillusionment is swift and brutal. They see arriving passengers treated like criminals, sorted into groups, and shipped away into a void where many disappeared.

Alexei is spared because the state needs doctors, but the couple is lodged in a boarding-house where the walls are thin and many of their neighbors seem to be, in one way or another, informers. Marie is suspect because she speaks French and therefore, given the logic of the times, could be a spy. The old woman who once owned the house also speaks French, comforts Marie, is informed on, and dies—possibly not of natural causes.

The film, directed by Regis Wargnier (*Indochine*), tells its story not in stark, simple images, but with the kind of production values we associate with historical epics. The music by Patrick Doyle is big and sweeping, as if both the score and the visuals are trying to elevate a small story to the stature of, say, *Dr. Zhivago*. But Marie is not Lara Zhivago. She is a materialist Parisian who isn't a good sport about sharing spartan facilities, who complains to a husband who is doing his best, who unilaterally does things that endanger them both.

Not that she is a bad woman. She has the kind of strong-willed independence that would be safe enough, and effective, in the West. She is simply slow or reluctant to see that such behavior in Russia is suicidal. Her husband, born and raised in Russia, preaches patience and stealth, not techniques she is familiar with.

East-West shows physical deprivation, but makes it clear that its characters are starving mostly for the clear air of freedom. It shows a system that is unjust and brutal, but made barely livable because the ordinary humans who enforce it are prey to universal human feelings. Good people tend to want to do good things no matter what their duty commands them. Both Marie and Alexei find friends in the bureaucracy, and both find romantic friends, too; Marie's is a swimmer whose ability may be the key to their freedom.

Toward the end of the film there is a set piece worthy of a vintage thriller. A famous left-wing French actress named Gabrielle (Catherine Deneuve) arrives on tour, is made aware of the plight of the couple, and tries to help them. Her plan depends on an intuitive knowledge of how Soviet guards will react to foreign visitors; the payoff is suspenseful.

And yet the movie as a whole lacks the conviction of a real story. It is more like a lush morality play, too leisurely in its storytelling, too sure of its morality. I remember *The Inner Circle* (1992), by Andrei Konchalovsky, which starred Tom Hulce as Stalin's movie projectionist, a nonentity who through his job was able to see the dark side of the great man. It is told matter-of-factly, more in everyday detail and less in grand gestures. *East-West* has too large a canvas for its figures.

Edge of 17 ★ ★

NO MPAA RATING, 100 m., 1999

Chris Stafford (Eric), Tina Holmes (Maggie), Andersen Gabrych (Rod), Stephanie McVay (Mom), Lea DeLaria (Angie), John Eby (Dad), Antonio Carriero (Andy), Jason Sheingross (Steve). Directed by David Moreton and produced by Moreton and Todd Stephens. Screenplay by Stephens.

Edge of 17 is more about sex and less about love than most coming-out movies; its young hero, Eric, seems to aim directly for gay bars and empty promiscuity without going through intermediate stages of self-discovery, idealism, or the qualities encompassed in the code word *pride*. He cheerfully wants to become a slut. This doesn't make him unusual; the libido is stronger than the intelligence in many teenagers. He'll grow up eventually.

The movie is set in Sandusky, Ohio, in 1984, and said to be based in part on the memories of its writer, Todd Stephens. It was an era when flamboyantly gay pop acts were highly visible, and the film cites Boy George and the Bronski Beat. It's about a summer of sexual initiation for Eric (Chris Stafford), a spacy teenager who seems a little dazed a lot of the time; later he'll learn to mask his cluelessness with cool detachment.

Eric gets a summer job in the restaurant of an amusement park. Also on the staff: his best friend Maggie (Tina Holmes), a lesbian manager named Angie (Lea DeLaria), and a blond guy named, inevitably, Rod (Andersen Gabrych), who wants to seduce him. Eric doesn't have the usual tumultuous struggle against his emerging gay identity; Rod smiles at him, Eric gets the idea, and in a relatively short while they're sharing quality time in the meat locker. It's obvious to Angie, and even in an unacknowledged way to Maggie, that they're an item.

We see a little of Eric's home life. His dad (John Eby) is a salt-of-the-earth type, and his mom (Stephanie McVay), a much more fully developed character, is a former musician who put her career on hold for marriage and motherhood, but takes pride in the New Age compositions Eric pieces together on his electronic keyboard. As Eric's hairstyle morphs from moptop to David Bowie and his eyeliner consumption goes up, she begins to worry—especially when he starts staying out all night and (although not enough is made of this) coming home drunk.

Rod turns out to be a disappointment as a first love; he quickly disappears back into "the gay dorm at OSU." He makes a poor role model. "Don't call me again," he tells the lonely Eric on the phone one night. Depressed, Eric heads for the Universal Fruit and Nut Co., Sandusky's only gay bar, where the manager is, inevitably, Angie from the summer restaurant job. Angie welcomes him joyfully, reassures him there is life after coming out, and introduces him to three aging queens, one in drag, who become his buddies.

It is enormously helpful of Angie not to card Eric, who she knows is four years underage, since the gay bar will play such a central role in the plot. Soon Eric has his second sexual experience, a quickie in the parking lot with another guy who likes him only for his body. "Uh, wouldn't you like my phone number?" Eric offers. Depressed by his experiences as a mindless sex object, he turns for consolation to Maggie, who helps him find out if he likes straight sex (he doesn't). Maggie, Eric's mother, and Angie the manager are the most fully realized characters in the movie, which doesn't offer a single positively drawn male homosexual.

Watching the movie, I thought, yes, for a lot of people straight and gay, the initiation to sexuality is like this: awkward physical couplings, loneliness, misunderstanding, angst, and then finally you grow interested in the person attached to the sexual organs and not the other way around. *Edge of 17* may be more realistic, if less encouraging, than a more sensitive gay coming-out story like the British film *Get Real*. It deals with physical details with almost startling frankness, and doesn't sentimentalize.

If it seems to introduce Eric directly into the world of gay clichés (drag queens and strangers in the night), perhaps in Sandusky in 1984 that was the only visible gay culture, and more substantial relationships were low-profile. My hope for Eric is not merely that he grows comfortable with his sexuality, but that he becomes a more interesting conversationalist, hopefully before I see him in another movie.

The Edge of the World ★ ★ ★
NO MPAA RATING, 81 m., 1937 (rereleased 2000)

John Laurie (Peter Manson), Belle Chrystall (Ruth Manson), Eric Berry (Robbie Manson), Kitty Kirwan (Jean Manson), Finlay Currie (James Gray), Niall MacGinnis (Andrew Gray), Grant Sutherland (The Catechist), Campbell Robson (The Laird). Directed by Michael Powell and produced by Joe Rock. Screenplay by Powell.

Michael Powell was one of the greatest British directors—the best in the land after Alfred Hitchcock decamped to Hollywood—and his major films stand like bedrock in film history: *The Red Shoes, The Life and Death of Colonel Blimp, Black Narcissus, The Thief of Bagdad, A Matter of Life and Death, Peeping Tom.*

Powell was a quixotic individualist whose works also include films far from the mainstream, strange works like *A Canterbury Tale,* about a pervert who takes advantage of wartime blackouts to pour glue into women's hair. When I taught a class on Powell at the Univer-

sity of Chicago, the students applauded all of his films but one, *Tales of Hoffmann,* a mannered operatic production they found unbearable, walking out to discuss it mournfully in the hallway.

His two-volume autobiography is the best ever written by a director: *A Life in Movies* and *Million Dollar Movie.* His life paralleled the development of the cinema. Born in 1905, he died in 1990 still deeply involved in the cinema as a consultant to Scorsese, Coppola, and other successors. He began in silent films, made talkie thrillers he was indifferent to, and reached "the turning point of my life in art" with *The Edge of the World* (1937), the first of his films that he "wanted to make." It has long been unavailable, but has now returned in a restored 35mm print which made its way through art theaters on its way to video.

It is a strange, haunting, beautiful film, shot on location on the spare Scottish island of Foula, in the cold North Sea. Like Robert Flaherty's documentary of Irish islanders, *Man of Aran,* made three years earlier, it tells the story of a dying way of life. But it was risky to mention Flaherty's film to Powell, who rejected comparisons: "He hasn't got a story," he tells a friend in his autobiography, "just a lot of waves and seaweed and pretty pictures. This is a *drama!* An *epic!* About people!"

The inhabitants of Foula have supported themselves since time immemorial by fishing, and by the wool from their prized sheep herds. Now modern trawlers are grabbing the fishing market, and it is time for these rugged islanders to weigh their future—should they move to the mainland? The story involves two young men, Andrew and Robbie, and Robbie's twin sister, Ruth. Ruth and Andrew are engaged to be wed. The two men and their fathers stand on opposite sides of the question of evacuating the island, and there is a "parliament" at which all the island men sit in a circle and discuss the issue. Andrew and Robbie decide to settle it more simply: They will have a race to the top of a 1,300-foot sea cliff.

One is killed, which leads to the estrangement of the two families and more complications when it becomes evident that Ruth is pregnant. But the story is not told as hamhanded melodrama; all of the characters respect one another, and the daily struggle to

163

win a living from the hard land has made them stalwart and brave.

Watching the movie, I made a note about Powell's extraordinary close-ups of faces. Then in his book I found he went to extraordinary lengths, when money and time were running out, to get those close-ups, many shot from small boats in rising seas: "Why didn't I trick these shots in the studio? It was the faces. Islanders have an inner strength and repose that other men and women do not have, and it shows in their faces."

The film's location shooting creates a palpable sense of the time and place. No set designer would dare build a church as small as the one on Foula, where the congregation crams in shoulder-to-shoulder, and inches separate the first pew from the pulpit (one parishioner tells the dour preacher about his sermon, "One hour and fifteen minutes. Let them beat that in Edinburgh if they can!"). Small touches, like a kitten in an old lady's lap, and chickens foraging for their dinner in farmyards, seem unplanned.

The reception of this film allowed Powell to sign a contract with Alexander Korda, then the most powerful British producer, and soon he would begin his long association with the screenwriter Emeric Pressburger (they signed their productions "The Archers," and their trademark was an arrow striking a bull's-eye). Their films together made glorious use of Technicolor and theatricality, so striking that the opening credits of Kenneth Branagh's new *Love's Labour's Lost* pay obvious homage to them.

This first "serious" film by Powell doesn't seem to predict his career. You can't imagine the maker of this film going on to make *The Red Shoes*. What it does show, though, is a voluptuous regard for visual images. The cliff-climbing scenes are especially dramatic, and, watching them, I realized that in most climbing scenes the climbers seem heroic. Here they seem tiny and endangered. It is the cliff that seems heroic, and that is probably the right way around.

EDtv ★ ★ ½
PG-13, 122 m., 1999

Matthew McConaughey (Ed Pekurny), Jenna Elfman (Shari), Woody Harrelson (Ray Pekurny), Sally Kirkland (Jeanette), Martin Landau (Al), Ellen DeGeneres (Cynthia Topping), Rob Reiner (Whitaker), Dennis Hopper (Hank), Elizabeth Hurley (Jill), Adam Goldberg (John), Viveka Davis (Marcia), Clint Howard (Ken). Directed by Ron Howard and produced by Brian Grazer and Howard. Screenplay by Lowell Ganz and Babaloo Mandel, based on the film *Louis XIX: Le Roi des Ondes*.

Now that two movies have been made about a man living twenty-four hours a day on television, how long until TV actually tries this as a programming idea? *EDtv* arrives less than a year after *The Truman Show*, and although the two films have different approaches (*Truman* is a parable; *EDtv* is an ambitious sitcom), they're both convinced that enormous audiences would watch intently as a man brushes his teeth, clips his nails, and is deceived by a wicked woman.

Is this true? Would they? Much would depend on the nature of the experiment, of course. *The Truman Show* gathered its poignancy from the fact that its hero didn't know he was on TV. *EDtv* is about a man who auditions for the job; as his brother points out, "How many chances do guys like us get?" The two movies offer us a choice: Would you rather be a hidden voyeur, or watch an exhibitionist?

I'd rather be a voyeur. The star of a TV show like this is likely to show me more about human nature if he doesn't know I'm watching. The kind of guy who would agree to having his whole life televised, on the other hand, is essentially just a long-form Jerry Springer guest. Anyone who would agree to such a deal is a loser, painfully needy, or nuts. And since the hero of Ron Howard's *EDtv* isn't really any of those things, the film never quite feels convincing.

The film stars Matthew McConaughey as Ed Pekurny, a Texas charmer who is discovered during auditions by a desperate cable channel. He can talk "regular" or he can talk Texan, he says, demonstrating accents as a TV executive (Ellen DeGeneres) watches, enraptured. Televising Ed's life is her idea; her boss (Rob Reiner) has his doubts at first, until she points out their current ratings are lower than the Gardening Channel ("People would rather watch soil").

Ed is signed by the channel, which also gets releases from the people in his world, including his brother Ray (Woody Harrelson), Ray's girlfriend, Shari (Jenna Elfman), his mother (Sally Kirkland), and his stepfather (Martin Landau). The first hours of the new show are slow-going (including the toenail-clipping demonstration), but things pick up after it's revealed that Ed and Shari are poised to start cheating on Ray ("I just kissed my boyfriend's brother on television!").

The movie strikes an uneasy bargain between being about television, and just being a straightforward romantic comedy. After a few setup scenes, we never have the notion that Ed's *whole* life is being shown on TV; the alleged *cinema verité* approach has an uncanny way of always being there for the right moments, with the right camera angles. And when they're needed for story conflict, new characters arrive; Ed's birth father (Dennis Hopper) appears for some touching confessions, and when a *USA Today* poll shows that viewers are bored with Shari, the producers arrange for a British sex bomb (Elizabeth Hurley) to appear on Ed's viewfinder.

The juiciest character is Ray, played by Woody Harrelson as a man always on the edge of someone else's success. After it's announced on TV that he's a lousy lover, he actually produces a defense witness—a former girlfriend who testifies, "I've had worse." The character I never quite understood was Shari, who becomes totally disillusioned with the idea of having her romance telecast, even though she's so oblivious to the cameras that she dumps Ray and embraces Ed in full view of millions during the first few days.

The movie has a lot of TV lore, including programming meetings presided over by Reiner, whose enthusiasm for EDtv grows as DeGeneres loses hers. The story arc is obvious: TV is bad for invading the privacy of these lives, and we're bad for watching. Still, Ray was right: The brothers had nothing going for them before, and now Ed is rich and famous. If he doesn't have the girl he loves, at least he has Elizabeth Hurley as a consolation prize. The story keeps undercutting its own conviction that TV is evil.

I enjoyed a lot of the movie in a relaxed sort of way; it's not essential or original in the way *The Truman Show* was, and it hasn't done any really hard thinking about the ways we interact with TV. It's a businesslike job, made to seem special at times because of the skill of the actors—especially Martin Landau, who gets a laugh with almost every line as a man who is wryly reconciled to very shaky health ("I'd yell for her, but I'd die"). After it's over, we've laughed some, smiled a little, and cared not really very much.

The Education of Little Tree ★ ★ ★
PG, 117 m., 1998

Joseph Ashton (Little Tree), Graham Greene (Willow John), James Cromwell (Granpa), Tantoo Cardinal (Granma), Mika Boorem (Little Girl), Leni Parker (Martha), Rebecca Dewey (Dolly), William Rowat (Henry). Directed by Richard Friedenberg and produced by Jake Eberts. Screenplay by Friedenberg, based on the novel by Forrest Carter.

The Education of Little Tree is another fine family movie that will no doubt be ignored by the fine families of America. The notion that there is a hungry audience for good family entertainment, nurtured by such dreamers as the critic Michael Medved, is a touching mirage. American families made it a point to avoid *The Secret Garden, The Little Princess, Shiloh,* and even *Rocket Man,* and I fear they'll also shield their offspring from *The Education of Little Tree.* Too bad. If children still exist whose imaginations have not been hammered into pulp by R-rated mayhem like *Starship Troopers,* this film will play as a magical experience.

The film tells the story of a half-Cherokee orphan who eludes the clutches of his prim white aunt and is raised in the wilderness of the Great Smoky Mountains by his grandparents. Granma (Tantoo Cardinal) is Cherokee; Granpa (James Cromwell) was "born white, but learned to see through Cherokee eyes." In a series of vignettes that add up to life's lessons, they teach Little Tree (Joseph Ashton) his school lessons, the poetry of nature, and a lot of common sense.

The film, set in the 1930s, of course sentimentalizes the wisdom of Native Americans—who, after decades in which they could do no right in the movies, now can do no wrong. Even Granpa's occupation—distilling and selling moonshine—is seen as a sort of public service for the local population, who don't have the money for store-bought booze. But for Little Tree, life in his grandparents' small cabin is an idyll: He learns of nature, of the seasons, of dogs and frogs, and the mysteries of life and death. More insights are provided by an Indian neighbor, played by Graham Greene.

The movie has its share of suspense and action, especially when "revenooers" come tramping through the woods looking for the still (the loyal dog Blue Boy holds them at bay while the boy crashes through the undergrowth rescuing a sack of granpa's equipment). And when the grandparents lose custody of the boy because of the moonshine business, there is a sequence set in a place called the Notched Gap Indian School, which is less a school than a reformatory, trying to cure its students of the notion that they are Indians. Little Tree looks through a window at the star that Granma told him to keep in sight, and knows that it looks down on her too. Granpa takes more direct action.

The film is quietly well acted. James Cromwell, as Granpa, proves here, as he did as the farmer in *Babe* and the police chief in *L.A. Confidential*, that despite his unmistakable physical presence he can play characters who are completely different from one another. What I liked here was the way Granpa is allowed to be sweet and light from the start; the movie avoids the usual cliché in which the older man is stiff and unbending, and only gradually yields. There is a touching sequence where we fear deeply for him. Tantoo Cardinal, as Granma, has a presence and conviction that gives freshness to her dialogue, which on the page might have looked rather simplistic. And Joseph Ashton, as Little Tree, is another of those young actors who is fresh and natural on camera; I believed in his character.

The movie arrives with some baggage. It is based on a book by Forrest Carter, which was first identified as autobiographical, and then, after a literary scandal, moved across the page from the *New York Times* nonfiction best-seller list to the "fiction" column. In the process it was revealed that Carter was in fact a man named Asa Carter, who had links to white supremacist groups and wrote speeches for George Wallace in his preenlightened days. What journey Asa made on his way to becoming Forrest might make a good movie, too; in *The Education of Little Tree* he wrote a story that has the elements in it for a strong, unusual, affecting drama. Anyone can find redemption.

I began on a note of pessimism, fearing that families will not embrace this wholesome PG-rated film. That would be a shame. My best guess is that more nine-year-olds will see *Scream 2* than *Little Tree*. The loud, violent, cartoonish entertainment that's pumped into the minds of kids cannot be creating much room for thought and values. It's all sensation. Movies like *Little Tree* are the kinds that families can discuss afterward. There are truths to be found in them. And questions. Somehow the noisy action junk never leaves any questions (except about the future of our civilization).

The Eel ★ ★ ★

NO MPAA RATING, 117 m., 1998

Koji Yakusho (Takuro Yamashita), Misa Shimizu (Keiko Hattori), Fujio Tsuneta (Jiro Nakajima), Mitsuko Baisho (Misako Nakajima), Akira Emoto (Tamotsu Takasaki), Sho Aikawa (Yuji Nozawa), Ken Kobayashi (Masaki Saito), Sabu Kawara (Seitaro Misato). Directed by Shohei Imamura and produced by Hisa Iino. Screenplay by Motofumi Tomikawa, Daisuke Tengan, and Imamura, based on a story by Akira Yoshimura.

The Eel opens with a shocking sequence in which a man stabs his wife to death, and the screen is stained red with blood splashed on the lens. We spend the rest of the film in uneasy anticipation that the bloodshed will be repeated; the fact that the man is capable of such an act lurks quietly beneath the everyday life that follows, and prevents us from ever being sure what tone the movie is finally taking.

The man's name is Yamashita, and he is played by Koji Yakusho, the man who took the ballroom lessons in *Shall We Dance*. He's an office worker as the film opens. Receiving an anonymous letter telling him his wife has taken a lover, he arrives home early, finds them in bed, stabs her, and turns himself in to the police. Eight years pass, he is released from prison, and he settles in a rural backwater close to the Buddhist priest who is his parole officer. He opens a barbershop. One day he saves a young woman from suicide; the priest suggests he give her a job in his shop, and . . .

And we're wrong if we think we know what happens then. The movie doesn't fall into easy generic developments, but stubbornly focuses on the oddness of human nature. Yamashita is not a good candidate for redemption, but neither is he necessarily a dangerous man. The film seems to be about a lot of things (it is filled with colorful local characters, with a subplot about the young woman's problems), but in a way they all merely whirl about the still center, which is the enigma of Yamashita.

Why, for example, did he spend his prison years never speaking, except to an eel? And why does the pet eel remain so important to him? (He almost left it behind in prison, so we suspect it is not this eel so much as the idea of the eel that obsesses him.) He says he wants nothing to do with women, and little enough to do with men; his barbershop is not a center for happy chatter. When the woman comes to work for him, she brings her own damaged past, and when she tries to be friends—bringing him lunch while he fishes—he holds himself aloof. All around are people who are easily read (an angry former fellow inmate, a nutty mother, a man who thinks UFOs are landing), and here is Yamashita, in a zone of his own.

The Eel, which shared the grand prize at Cannes in 1997, is by Shohei Imamura. Born in 1927, he began as an assistant director for the great and poetic director Yasujiro Ozu but has never been attracted to his domestic stories. Instead, Imamura is drawn to the strangeness of the violent; he is interested in people who are not violent as a profession (as criminals are), but whose inner violence leaps out and shows us how wounded they are. His *Vengeance Is Mine* (1979), the story of a serial killer, is not only about the man's crimes but about his utter loneliness. *The Ballad of Narayama* (1983) is about the custom of leaving old people exposed on a mountain to die

when they grow too old to live comfortably. It is quietly, unblinkingly cruel, and yet told in terms of domestic details (one old woman does not want to die until she has married off all of her children).

The portrait of everyday Japan in *The Eel* is intriguing; the quiet area where the story is set is filled with people who take a lively interest in each other's business, while all the time seeming to keep their distance. There are conventional plot elements (will the fellow ex-con tell the woman that Yamashita murdered his wife?). There's comic relief from the local oddballs. And yet always thrumming beneath everything else is the possibility that Yamashita is a time bomb, that he may kill again. Or perhaps not. Perhaps the eel could tell us.

8½ Women ★ ★ ★
R, 120 m., 2000

John Standing (Philip Emmenthal), Matthew Delamere (Storey Emmenthal), Vivian Wu (Kito), Shizuka Inoh (Simato), Barbara Sarafian (Clothilde), Kirina Mano (Mio), Toni Collette (Griselda), Amanda Plummer (Beryl). Directed by Peter Greenaway and produced by Kees Kasander. Screenplay by Greenaway.

Having met Peter Greenaway, I find it easier to understand the tone of his films. Not a lighthearted man, he is cerebral, controlled, so precise in his speech he seems to be dictating. "He talks like a university lecturer," I wrote after meeting him in 1991, "and gives the impression he would rather dine alone than suffer bores at his table." Yet there is an aggressive, almost violent, streak of comedy in his makeup; one can imagine him, like Hitchcock, springing practical jokes.

Consider a scene in *8½ Women*, his new film. It takes place in a staid Swiss cemetery. His hero, Philip Emmenthal (John Standing), is a billionaire who has just lost his beloved wife. He arrives at the services dressed in a white summer suit, because his wife disliked dark clothing. He is informed that a black suit is absolutely required by the bylaws.

Enraged, defiant, stubborn, Philip grimly strips down until he is standing naked on the gravel; observing the letter of the law, he demands even black underwear. He is surrounded by minions who lend him their own clothing—a black shirt, black tie, pants, coat, even underwear ("it looks like a swimming suit," its wearer explains, "and I was hoping to go swimming later"). His decision has forced his employees to strip as well, and now, dressed in black, he walks a few feet to one side and we see what we could not see before—that the preacher and all of the mourners were waiting nearby, in full view of everything.

Now how is this funny? Trying to imagine other kinds of comedies handling the material, I ran it through Monty Python, Steve Martin, and Woody Allen before realizing it has its roots in Buster Keaton—whose favorite comic ploy was to overcome obstacles by applying pure logic and ignoring social conventions or taboos. Keaton would have tilted it more toward laughs, to be sure; Greenaway's humor always seems dour, and masks (not very well) a lot of hostility. But, yes, Keaton.

One possible approach to *8½ Women*, I think, is to view it as a slowed-down, mannered, tongue-in-cheek silent comedy, skewed by Greenaway's anger and desire to manipulate. The movie's title evokes memories of the ways Greenaway numbers, categorizes, sorts, and orders the characters in his other films. His titles *Drowning by Numbers* and *A Zed and Two Noughts* show the same sensibility; he distances himself from the humanity of his characters by treating them like inventory.

Here, however, real emotion is allowed to fight its way onto the screen. Philip is in genuine mourning for his dead wife ("Who will hold and comfort me now she's gone?"), and his hopelessness moves his son, Storey (Matthew Delamere). There is a scene, offscreen but unmistakably implied, in which they have incestuous sex, perhaps as a form of mutual comfort, and many scenes in which Greenaway, so interested in male nudity, has them naked in front of mirrors and each other. This is not the nudity of sexuality, but of disclosure; a billionaire stripped of his clothes (and his Rolls-Royces and chateaus and servants) is just, after all, a naked man with flat feet and a belly.

Father and son have been involved in a scheme to take over a series of pachinko parlors in Kyoto, Japan. Pachinko is an addictive form of pinball, much prized by the Japanese.

They meet a woman who has gambled away most of her family's money on pachinko, and are surprised to discover that her father and her fiancé both suggest she sleep with Storey (or Philip) to work off the debt. (This does not represent a loss of honor, the translator explains, because the Emmenthals are not Japanese, thus do not count.)

This woman becomes one of the first of eight and a half women the father and son move into their Geneva mansion, in an attempt to slake their grief with the pleasures of the flesh. All of the women are willing participants, for reasons of their own—the one in the bizarre body brace, the one unhappy unless she is pregnant, an amputee who only counts as a half, and so on. Greenaway deliberately does not build or shoot any of the movie's many sex scenes in a revealing or erotic way; they are always about power, manipulation, control.

Apart from the father's real scenes of grief, the film is cold and distant. It shows its bones as well as its skin; some of its shots are superimposed on pages from the screenplay that describes them. It is not possible to "like" this film, although one admires it, and is intrigued. Greenaway does not much require to be liked (is my guess), and what he is doing here has links to deep feelings he reveals only indirectly. At two times in the film, father and son watch Fellini's *8½*, particularly the scene where the hero gathers all of the women in his life into the same room and tries to tame and placate them. After the second viewing, the father asks the son, "How many film directors make films to satisfy their sexual fantasies?" "Most of them," his son replies. This one for sure.

8MM ★ ★ ★
R, 123 m., 1999

Nicolas Cage (Tom Welles), Joaquin Phoenix (Max California), James Gandolfini (Eddie Poole), Peter Stormare (Dino Velvet), Anthony Heald (Longdale), Chris Bauer (Machine), Catherine Keener (Amy Welles), Amy Morton (Mrs. Mathews). Directed by Joel Schumacher and produced by Gavin Polone, Judy Hofflund, and Schumacher. Screenplay by Andrew Kevin Walker.

Joel Schumacher's *8MM* is a dark, dank journey into the underworld of snuff films undertaken by a private investigator who is appalled and changed by what he finds. It deals with the materials of violent exploitation films, but in a nonpornographic way; it would rather horrify than thrill. The writer is Andrew Kevin Walker, who wrote *Seven,* and once again creates a character who looks at evil and asks (indeed, screams) "Why?"

The answer comes almost at the end of the film, from its most vicious character: "The things I do—I do them because I like them. Because I want to." There is no comfort there, and the final shots, of an exchange of smiles, are ironic; Walker accepts that pure evil can exist, and that there are people who are simply bad; one of his killers even taunts the hero: "I wasn't beaten as a child. I didn't hate my parents."

The movie stars Nicolas Cage as an enigmatic family man named Tom Welles, who works as a private investigator and comes home to a good marriage with his wife (Catherine Keener) and baby. He specializes in top-level clients and total discretion. He's hired by the lawyer for a rich widow who has found what appears to be a snuff film in the safe of her late husband; she wants reassurance that the girl in the film didn't really die, and Welles tells her snuff films are "basically an urban legend—makeup, special effects, you know."

The film follows Welles as he identifies the young woman in the film, meets her mother, follows her movements, and eventually descends into the world of vicious pornographers for hire, who create films to order for a twisted clientele. Joel Schumacher has an affinity for dark atmosphere (he made *The Lost Boys, Flatliners,* and two of the Batman pictures). Here, with Mychael Danna's mournful music and Robert Elswit's squinting camera, he creates a sense of foreboding even in an opening shot of passengers walking through an airport.

The purpose of the film is to take a fairly ordinary character and bring him into such a disturbing confrontation with evil that he is driven to kill someone. Tom Welles, we learn, went to a good school on an academic scholarship, but although his peers "went into law and finance," the rich widow's attorney muses, "you chose surveillance." Yes, says Welles: "I thought it was the future." Mostly his work consists of tailing adulterers, but this case is different. He meets and talks with the mother of the girl in the film, traces her journey to Hollywood, and then enlists a guide to help him explore the hidden world of the sex business.

This is Max California (Joaquin Phoenix), who once aimed high but now works in porno retail; the film suggests that the Los Angeles economy takes hopeful young job-seekers and channels them directly into the sex trades. Through Max, Welles meets Eddie Poole (James Gandolfini), the kind of guy who means it when he says he can get you whatever you're looking for. And through Eddie, they meet Dino Velvet, a vicious porn director played by Peter Stormare—who was the killer who said almost nothing in *Fargo,* and here creates a frightening set of weirdo verbal affectations. The star of some of his films is Machine (Chris Bauer), who doesn't like to remove his mask.

We expect Welles to get into danger with these men, and he does, but *8MM* doesn't treat the trouble simply as an occasion for action scenes. There is a moment here when Welles has the opportunity to get revenge, but lacks the will (he is not a killer), and he actually telephones a victim and asks to be talked into it. I haven't seen that before in a movie, and it raises moral questions that the audience has to deal with, one way or another.

I know some audience members will be appalled by this film, as many were by *Seven.* It is a very hard R that would doubtless have been NC-17 if it had come from an indie instead of a big studio with clout. But it is a real film. Not a slick exploitation exercise with all the trappings of depravity but none of the consequences. Not a film where moral issues are forgotten in the excitement of an action climax. Yes, the hero is an ordinary man who finds himself able to handle violent situations, but that's not the movie's point. The last two words of the screenplay are "save me," and by the time they're said, we know what they mean.

Election ★ ★ ★ ½
R, 104 m., 1999

Matthew Broderick (Jim McAllister), Reese Witherspoon (Tracy Flick), Chris Klein (Paul Metzler), Phil Reeves (Walt Hendricks), Mark Harelik (Dave Novotny), Delaney Driscoll (Linda Novotny), Jessica Campbell (Tammy), Molly Hagan (Diane McAllister), Colleen Camp (Judith R. Flick). Directed by Alexander Payne and produced by Albert Berger, Ron Yerxa, David Gale, and Keith Samples. Screenplay by Payne and Jim Taylor, based on the novel by Tom Perrotta.

I remember students like Tracy Flick, the know-it-all who always has her hand in the air while the teacher desperately looks for someone else to call on. In fact, I *was* a student like Tracy Flick. "A legend in his own mind," they wrote under my photo in the Urbana High School yearbook. I remember informing an English teacher that I didn't know why we were wasting time on the short stories of Eudora Welty when I could write better ones myself.

Tracy is smarter than that, and would never occupy such an exposed position. She's the subject of Alexander Payne's *Election,* a wicked satire about an election for student government president, a post Tracy wants to win to go along with her collection of every other prize in school. What sets this film aside from all the other recent high school movies is that it doesn't limit itself to the worldview of teenagers, but sees Tracy mostly through the eyes of a teacher who has had more than enough of her.

Tracy is embodied by Reese Witherspoon, an actress I've admired since she had her first kiss in *The Man in the Moon* (1991), and who moved up to adult roles in *Freeway* (1997), a harrowing retelling of "Little Red Riding Hood" with Kiefer Sutherland as the wolf. She was a virginal headmaster's daughter in *Cruel Intentions,* which opened last month, but she hits her full stride in *Election* as an aggressive, manipulative vixen who informs a teacher she hopes they can work together "harmoniously" in the coming school year.

The teacher is Jim McAllister (Matthew Broderick), the kind of man who turns up for an adulterous liaison and succeeds only in getting a bee sting on his eyelid. He thinks he knows what she means about "harmoniously," since last year she seduced a faculty member who was one of his best friends. Much as McAllister detests her, he also lusts after her; talking another student into running against her is his version of a cold shower. His recruit is a slow-witted jock named Paul (Chris Klein), and the race gets complicated when Paul's lesbian sister, Tammy (Jessica Campbell), jumps into the race on a platform of dismantling the student government "so we'll never have to sit through one of these stupid elections again."

Election is not really about high school, but about personality types. If the John Travolta character in *Primary Colors* reminded me of Bill Clinton, Tracy Flick puts me in mind of Elizabeth Dole: a person who always seems to be setting you a logical puzzle for which she is the answer. What is Tracy Flick's platform? That she should win simply because she is the school's (self-)designated winner. When a candidate turns up on election day having baked 480 customized cupcakes for the voters, doesn't she seem kind of inevitable?

For Jim McAllister, the Tracy Flicks have to be stopped before they do damage to themselves and others. She is always perfectly dressed and groomed, and is usually able to conceal her hot temper behind a facade of maddening cheerfulness. But she is ruthless. She reminds me of a saying attributed to David Merrick: "It is not enough for me to win. My enemies must lose."

The story, based on a novel by Tom Perrotta, shows McAllister as a dedicated teacher who is simply steamrollered by Tracy Flick. He narrates the film in a tone balanced between wonder and horror, and Broderick's performance does a good job of keeping that balance. Whatever else, he is fascinated by the phenomenon of Tracy Flick. We're inevitably reminded of Sammy Glick, the hero of Budd Schulberg's Hollywood classic *What Makes Sammy Run?* who had his eye on the prize and his feet on the shoulders of the little people he climbed over on his way to the top. *Election* makes the useful observation that although troublemakers cause problems for teachers, it's the compulsive overachievers who can drive them mad.

Alexander Payne is a director whose satire is omnidirectional. He doesn't choose an easy target and march on it. He stands in the middle of his story and attacks in all directions. His first film was *Citizen Ruth* (1996), starring Laura Dern as a pregnant, glue-sniffing young woman who was a moronic loser, but inspired a focus for a court battle between pro-choice and antiabortion forces. What was astonishing about his film (and probably damaged it at the box office) was that he didn't choose sides, but satirized both sides with cheerful open-mindedness.

Now here is a movie that is not simply about an obnoxious student, but also about an imperfect teacher, a lockstep administration, and a student body that is mostly just marking time until it can go out into the world and occupy valuable space. The movie is not mean-spirited about any of its characters; I kind of liked Tracy Flick some of the time, and even felt a little sorry for her. Payne doesn't enjoy easy targets and cheap shots. What he's aiming for, I think, is a parable for elections in general—in which the voters have to choose from among the kinds of people who have been running for office ever since high school.

Elizabeth ★ ★ ★ ½
R, 124 m., 1998

Cate Blanchett (Elizabeth I), Geoffrey Rush (Sir Francis Walsingham), Christopher Eccleston (Duke of Norfolk), Joseph Fiennes (Robert Dudley, Earl of Leicester), Richard Attenborough (Sir William Cecil), Fanny Ardant (Mary of Guise), John Gielgud (The Pope), Kathy Burke (Queen Mary Tudor), Vincent Cassel (Duke of Anjou). Directed by Shekhar Kapur and produced by Alison Owen. Screenplay by Michael Hirst.

The England of the first Elizabeth is a dark and sensuous place; the court lives intimately with treachery, and cloaks itself in shadows and rude luxury. As seen through the fresh eyes of an Indian director, Shekhar Kapur, *Elizabeth* is not a light *Masterpiece Theater* production, but one steeped in rich, saturated colors and emotions. The texture of the film is enough to recommend it, even apart from the story.

Cate Blanchett stars as Elizabeth I, who in 1558, at the age of twenty-five, took the throne of a Catholic country, declared it Protestant, fought off assassination by the French, the Spanish, her rivals, and the pope, and ruled for forty-five years. She succeeded, the film demonstrates, by learning on the job, growing from a naive girl to a willful strategist who picked her advisers well, and ignored them when they urgently advised her to marry: "I will have one mistress here! And no master!"

She was known as the Virgin Queen. Virginity for her, as for so many, was something she grew into. As the film opens, she frolics with her lover, Robert Dudley (Joseph Fiennes), and her ardor only subsides as she realizes no man loves the queen of England only for herself. She is contemptuous of such other suitors as the duke of Anjou (Vincent Cassel), who sees marriage as a social move and is surprised while frolicking in a frock. And her eyes narrow as she listens to proposals couriered in by various rulers who want to marry her as a sort of mergers-and-acquisitions deal.

The screenplay provides a series of hard-edged conversations in which Elizabeth's enemies conspire against her and her friends urgently counsel her, while she teaches herself to tell true allies from false ones. She is much helped in the beginning by white-bearded old Sir William Cecil (Richard Attenborough), although there comes a time when he must be put to pasture, and Attenborough's character accepts this news with humility that is truly touching.

Then the lurking, sinister Sir Francis Walsingham (Geoffrey Rush) moves to her side, and brilliantly helps guide her to triumph. He's instrumental to the plot, even though his role is at first murky. After Elizabeth's archrival Mary of Guise (Fanny Ardant) sends her a poisoned dress, which luckily claims the life of another, it is Sir Francis who adroitly convinces Mary he will betray Elizabeth. Francis and Mary spend a night together, and in the morning Mary is dead. It didn't happen like that in history, but it should have.

The movie, indeed, compresses and rewrites history at its own convenience, which is the rule anyway with English historical romances. What it gets right is the performance by Cate Blanchett, who was so good as the poker-playing glass manufacturer in *Oscar and Lucinda* (1997) and here uncannily comes to resemble the great monarch. She is saucy and heedless at the first, headstrong when she shouldn't be, but smart and able to learn. By the end she has outsmarted everyone and become one of the rare early female heads of state to rule successfully without an alliance with a man.

Shekhar Kapur, who directed *The Bandit Queen* (1995), about a fierce modern Indian Robin Hood, here clothes Elizabeth, her court, and her architecture in the colors and texture of medieval India. The film is largely set in vast, echoing halls, their pillars reaching up into the shadows. He is attentive to the rustle of dresses and the clank of armor, gives us a barge on the Thames like a houseboat on a lake in Kashmir. Action is glimpsed through iron filigree screens, dresses are rich with embroidery, hairstyles are ornately elaborate, and yet there is the feeling that just out of sight of these riches are the rats in the kitchen and the slop pots in the halls. This is not the Ye Olde approach, but a society still inventing gentility; sex is so linked with politics that old Sir William demands to inspect Elizabeth's sheets every morning to keep tabs on possibly alarming developments in her private life.

At the end of the film, Elizabeth announces, "I have become a virgin." And so she remained, ruling over and in some sense creating the England that gave us Shakespeare. Think what a play he might have written about her if commoners had been allowed to create characters out of reigning monarchs. No doubt he retired in sheer frustration.

The Emperor's Shadow ★ ★ ★
NO MPAA RATING, 116 m., 1999

Ge You (Composer Gao Jianli), Jiang Wen (Emperor Ying Sheng), Xu Qing (His Daughter, Yueyang). Directed by Zhou Xiaowen and produced by Tong Gang, Hu Yuesheng, and Cai Huansong. Screenplay by Lu Wei. In Mandarin with English subtitles.

The Emperor's Shadow tells the story of two boys raised at the same breast as foster brothers. One becomes emperor—the founder of China's Qin dynasty, circa 200 B.C. The other becomes his court composer, more or less over his own dead body. The film, which has caused some alarm in China because it may be read as an argument against government interference in the arts, is filmed as a large-scale costume epic, with countless extras, rivers running with blood, and dramatic readings of lines like, "You are the only man with the right to call me brother."

Once you accept the likelihood that no subtle emotional nuances are going to be examined in the course of the film, it's absorbing. The same story told today might seem a tad melodramatic, but the magnificent settings and the exotic world of the Chinese court inspire a certain awe. The director, Zhou Xiaowen, has possibly studied such Japanese epics as *Ran* and *Kagemusha,* and uses the Kurosawa-style telephoto lens to compress armies of men into faceless patterns moving on a plain; our first sight of imperial style comes when horses draw up with the emperor's carriage, which is about the same size and design as the location office on a construction site.

The emperor is named Ying Sheng (Jiang Wen). Although his predecessor ordered, "After my death, execute anyone who supports musicians," Ying is a music lover, and that causes a lifetime of agony for the composer Gao Jianli (Ge You), who lives in a neighboring province and wants to be left alone to pluck his gin (an instrument that looks like the ancestor of Chet Atkins's flatbed steel guitar).

Ying conquers Gao's province, has the composer hauled before him, and orders him to compose an anthem. His first effort ("10,000 men must suffer so that one may reach heaven") strikes the emperor as just possibly a veiled criticism of his reign. When Gao demurs at his request for a rewrite, Ying starts beheading slaves, which seems to confirm the accuracy of the first version, but eventually persuades Gao.

Meanwhile, Gao has fallen in love with Yueyang (Ying Zheng), the emperor's daughter, whose legs are paralyzed. Her form of locomotion is to be passed from arm to arm by the (remaining) slaves, her head above the crowd like a Super Bowl hero. Yueyang has been betrothed to a famous general, but likes Gao, and they make love, after which she discovers she can walk. Gao asks Ying if he can marry Yueyang, but Ying refuses. Still, moved by the miracle, he tries to be reasonable: "Look, her general will certainly die in battle within the next five years, and after a year of mourning, she can marry you. Can't you wait?"

The interesting dynamic in the film is that Ying, an absolute ruler who can enforce his will on anyone, is utterly baffled by Gao's independent spirit. Their arguments sometimes sound more like sibling quarrels than master and servant. Ying is forever ordering fearsome punishments against Gao and then repenting, sometimes too late (he doesn't mind having the musician blinded by the fumes of horse urine thrown into a coal fire, but is outraged to discover that it hurts).

The movie is not subtle or especially insightful, but it is intrinsically interesting (when have you seen these characters or situations before?), and sumptuously mounted and photographed. One of its closing images, of Ying mounting a pyramid, provides the closest thing to a message: It's lonely at the top. (On the other hand, as Mel Brooks reminds us, "It's *good* to be the king.") The end titles provide information about the Qin dynasty that adds a nice wry zinger.

Encounter in the Third Dimension ★ ★
NO MPAA RATING, 45 m., 1999

Stuart Pankin (Professor), Stuart Pankin (Voice of M.A.X.), Cassandra Peterson (Elvira, Mistress of the Dark), Harry Shearer (Narrator), Andrea Thompson (Ruth in the Booth). Directed by Ben Stassen and produced by Charlotte Clay Huggins. Screenplay by Kurt Frey and Stassen.

Encounter in the Third Dimension resembles several other giant-screen IMAX releases in being interesting primarily because of the size of the screen. The movie packages a lot of information about 3-D movies into a goofy story about a scientist who wants to demonstrate his latest 3-D invention.

The story is pretty lame, and the info is familiar. Is there likely to be anyone in the audience who isn't familiar with the 3-D effect of the Stereopticon? (Children know it as the familiar ViewMaster.)

Still, no doubt about it, the 3-D effect in IMAX and its cousin, Omnimax, is the best I've seen. That's because of the huge screen, which covers peripheral vision, and the oversize projectors that pump out a lot of brightness. The glasses, which resemble science-fiction headsets, contain shutters that separate the images for each eye. The result is truly three-dimensional, all right. There was an undersea IMAX film shot in 3-D that I really enjoyed.

But the underlying problem with 3-D remains exactly the same as when *Bwana Devil* and *House of Wax* first hit the screen in the 1950s: It's unnecessary most of the time, and distracting the rest of the time. The ordinary 2-D illusion of movies has long been accepted all over the world as an acceptable illusion of reality. The 3-D illusion seems used mostly to throw things at the audience. That gets old after a while. If the purpose of a movie's story is to absorb us, every exaggerated 3-D effect breaks our reverie and calls attention to the technique itself.

In *Encounter in the Third Dimension*, we meet a professor (Stuart Pankin) who hopes to unveil his new gimmick, Real-O-Vision. He has enlisted Elvira ("Mistress of the Dark," the credits remind us) to sing a song in this new process, but she keeps getting interrupted as the machinery breaks down, and so the professor dispatches a flying robot named M.A.X. (voice also by Pankin) to entertain us while he works on his invention.

The primary function of M.A.X., it goes without saying, is to zoom toward the audience and hang in midair, seemingly inches from our faces. Dr. Johnson once said of a dog standing on its hind legs: "It is not done well, but one is surprised to find it done at all." Watching M.A.X. whizzing about, I reflected that it was done well, but, alas, I did not want it done at all.

End of Days ★ ★
R, 118 m., 1999

Arnold Schwarzenegger (Jericho Cane), Gabriel Byrne (The Man), Kevin Pollack (Chicago), Robin

Tunney (Christine York), Rod Steiger (Father Kovak). Directed by Peter Hyams and produced by Armyan Bernstein and Bill Borden. Screenplay by Andrew W. Marlowe.

"There are forces here you couldn't possibly comprehend."

—dialogue

You can say that again. *End of Days* opens with a priest gazing out his window at the Vatican City and seeing a comet arching above the moon like an eyebrow. He races to an old wooden box, snatches up a silver canister, pulls out an ancient scroll, unrolls it and sees—yes! A drawing of a comet arching above the moon like an eyebrow! For verily this is the dreaded celestial display known as the "Eye of God."

The priest bursts into an inner chamber of the Vatican where the pope sits surrounded by advisers. "The child will be born today!" he gasps. Then we cut to "New York City, 1979" and a live childbirth scene, including, of course, the obligatory dialogue, "Push!" A baby girl is born, and a nurse takes the infant in its swaddling clothes and races to a basement room of the hospital, where the child is anointed with the blood of a freshly killed rattlesnake before being returned to the arms of its mother.

Already I am asking myself, where is William Donohue when we need him? Why does his Catholic League attack a sweet comedy like *Dogma* but give a pass to *End of Days,* in which we learn that once every 1,000 years a woman is born who, if she is impregnated twenty years later by the Prince of Darkness during the hour from 11 to 12 P.M. on the last day of the millennium, will give birth to the anti-Christ, who will bring about, yes, the end of days? Meanwhile an internal Vatican battle rages between those who want to murder the woman, and the pope, who says we must put our faith in God.

The murder of the woman would, of course, be a sin, but perhaps justifiable under the circumstances, especially since the humble instrument chosen by God to save the universe is an alcoholic bodyguard named Jericho Cane, played by Arnold Schwarzenegger. Jericho and his partner (Kevin Pollack) find themselves investigating a puzzling series of events, including a man with his tongue cut out who nevertheless screams a warning and is later nailed to the ceiling of his hospital room.

Movies like this are particularly vulnerable to logic, and *End of Days* even has a little fun trying to sort out the reasoning behind the satanic timetable. When Jericho has the Millennium Eve timetable explained to him, including the requirement that the Prince of Darkness do his dirty deed precisely between 11 P.M. and midnight, he asks the very question I was asking myself: "Eastern Standard Time?"

The answer, Jericho is told, is that the exact timing was meticulously worked out centuries ago by the Gregorian monks, and indeed their work on this project included, as a bonus spin-off, the invention of the Gregorian calendar. Let's see. Rome is six hours ahead of New York. In other words, those clever monks said, "The baby will be conceived between 5 and 6 A.M. on January 1, Rome time, but that will be between 11 P.M. and 12 A.M. in a city that does not yet exist, on a continent we have no knowledge of, assuming the world is round and there are different times in different places as it revolves around the Sun, which of course it would be a heresy to suggest." With headaches like this, no wonder they invented Gregorian chant to take the load off.

End of Days involves a head-on collision between the ludicrous and the absurd, in which a supernatural being with the outward appearance of Gabriel Byrne pursues a twenty-year-old woman named Christine (Robin Tunney) around Manhattan, while Jericho tries to protect her. This being a theological struggle Schwarzenegger style, the battle to save Christine involves a scene where a man dangles from a helicopter while chasing another man across a rooftop, and a scene in which a character clings by his fingertips to a high window ledge, and a scene in which a runaway subway train explodes, and a scene in which fireballs consume square blocks of Manhattan, and a scene in which someone is stabbed with a crucifix, and . . .

But the violence raises another question. How exactly do the laws of physics apply to the Byrne character? Called "The Man" in the credits, he is Satan himself, for my money, yet seems to have variable powers. Jericho shoots him, but he pulls up his shirt so we can see the bullet holes healing. Then Jericho switches to a machine gun, and the bullets hurl The Man backward and put him out of commission for a time, before he attacks again. What are the rules here? Is he issued only so much anti-injury mojo per millennium?

The movie's final confrontation is a counterpoint to the Times Square countdown toward the year 2000. Only a churl would point out that the new millennium actually begins a year later, on the last day of 2000. Even then, *End of Days* would find a loophole. This is the first movie to seriously argue that "666," the numerical sign of Satan, is actually "999" upside down, so that all you have to do is add a "1" and, whoa! You get "1999." ☞

The End of the Affair ★ ★ ½
R, 105 m., 1999

Ralph Fiennes (Maurice Bendrix), Stephen Rea (Henry Miles), Julianne Moore (Sarah Miles), Heather Jay Jones (Henry's Maid), James Bolam (Mr. Savage), Ian Hart (Mr. Parkis), Samuel Bould (Lance Parkis), Cyril Shaps (Waiter), Penny Morrell (Bendrix's Landlady). Directed by Neil Jordan and produced by Stephen Woolley and Jordan. Screenplay by Jordan, based on the novel by Graham Greene.

It is raining much of the time in *The End of the Affair*, and that is as it should be. The film is about love and adultery in cold, dark, wartime London—when sex was a moment of stolen warmth, an interlude between the air raids and the daily grind of rationing and restrictions. In the opening scene, two men meet on Clapham Common in the rain, and we can almost smell their damp, fungoid woolen suits, cut with the smoke of their cigarettes.

One is a government official named Henry Miles (Stephen Rea). The other is a novelist named Maurice Bendrix (Ralph Fiennes). Henry is married to Sarah (Julianne Moore). Maurice was her lover. Now both men are out in the rain and Sarah is apparently meeting secretly with a new friend. That's what Henry wants to talk to Maurice about. He doesn't suspect Maurice of adultery: He simply wants his help, as a friend, in hiring a private detective to follow Sarah.

This story and milieu are from a 1951 novel by Graham Greene, said to be based on his own wartime love affair and drenched with the Catholicism that was central to his work at that time. The engine of the story could come from melodrama or a thriller: A man unwittingly asks his wife's former lover for help in identifying her present lover. But in Greene, and in this adaptation by Neil Jordan, it is all so much more worldly, weary, and bittersweet than that, because Maurice feels he is being cheated on too. The new lover, if there is one, has made two cuckolds.

Maurice and Sarah met at a party just before the war, we learn. Henry was even then a sad sack with his attention always on his work. The two fell instantly in love and carried on a passionate affair until one day during their lovemaking the earth literally shook, and it appeared that Maurice had been killed in a German raid. We see all of this in flashback, and how when the dust cleared and Maurice crept slowly back to consciousness, Sarah was on her knees in prayer. Afterward things were never the same. Sarah withdrew from Maurice, turned cold and unavailable, and eventually he retreated into a long bitterness. Now we are back up to the meeting of the two men in the rain.

All of this makes an intriguing novel, and *The End of the Affair* is Greene dancing on the divide between the rules of religion and the lusts of the flesh. His adulterous husbands and sinning priests have to deal not only with built-in guilt but with the rules of the Church, which they never believe in more than while breaking them. The novel is a largely interior affair, existing inside Maurice's mind as he ponders again and again how a woman could seem so close and then suddenly be so far away.

The film, on the other hand, is as hangdog as Stephen Rea's face in the first scene. It is the story of characters who desperately require more lightness and folly; one can be grim in the confessional and yet be permitted a skip in the step on leaving the church. The characters seem too glum. We see release but miss joy. Sarah and Maurice meet for energetic sex, but their conversation doesn't suggest the kind of idealism required by great love. For a novelist, Maurice is surprisingly pedestrian in his speech, and we have to hear him telling Sarah he is jealous of her shoes, "because they will take you away from me." Not impossible dialogue (we are reminded of Prince Charles's fantasies involving feminine hygiene products), but we expect better from a novelist.

Greene has a good feel for muted low comedy in his supporting characters, and the best turn in *The End of the Affair* is by Ian Hart, as Mr. Parkis, the detective hired by Maurice to follow Sarah. Parkis brings along his boy, Lance (Samuel Bould), an earnest little fellow with a bold birthmark on his cheek and hair brilliantined flat like his dad's. Lance can hardly understand adultery, but joins in the game of following, snooping, and spying, as Parkis beams with pride. Nothing belittles a man more than suspicion of the woman he loves, and somehow a private detective is always able to choose just those words to make the man feel even shabbier and sneakier.

If the movie were not so downbeat and its literary pedigree so distinguished, the resolution would be soap opera. The outcome, indeed, would be right at home on a religious cable station (although the sex would have to be handled more disapprovingly). Without revealing the outcome I cannot express my doubts about it, but if I could have drawn Sarah aside before her fateful turning point, I would have told her the following parable. A woman tumbles out of the choir loft of a church and her dress catches in the chandelier. She swings above the congregation with her bloomers exposed. The priest in the pulpit thunders, "He who looks shall be stricken blind!" One altar boy claps a hand to his face and whispers to the other: "I'm going to risk one eye."

Endurance ★ ★ ★

G, 83 m., 1999

Himself (Haile Gebrselassie), Bekele Gebrselassie (Haile's Father), Shawananness Gebrselassie (Haile's Mother), Yonas Zergaw (Young Haile), Assefa Gebrselassie (Haile's Brother), Alem Tellahun (Haile's Wife), Tizazu Mashresha (Haile's Police Trainer). Directed by Leslie Woodhead and produced by Edward R. Pressman, Terrence Malick, and Max Palevsky. Screenplay by Woodhead.

The sound of the runner's breathing is like a percussion instrument made of wind. Each exhalation is a thrum of effort. He runs as if he has been running since time immemorial. His name is Haile Gebrselassie, and after he set a new record at the Atlanta Olympics in 1996, *Runner's World* magazine described him as "the greatest distance runner of all time."

Endurance is a film about Gebrselassie, his early life on an Ethiopian farm, his training, his shy courtship, and his Olympic triumph. It is not a documentary, exactly; scenes are written and staged, and actors play him at younger ages. But it is drawn from his life. His father, brother, and wife play themselves, and the footage of his triumph at Atlanta is real. So, I think, is the sound of his breathing.

The runner was raised in a rural area, where his father wanted him to stay and work on the farm. But in 1980, when the Ethiopian runner Miruts Yifter won the 10,000-meter race at the Moscow Olympics running barefoot, young Haile, like all of his countrymen, was stirred to hear the Ethiopian national anthem played after his victory. He determined to become a runner, and we see him as a boy (played by his nephew, Yonas Zergaw), running everywhere on the farm where his family of twelve lived in a mud hut.

Gebrselassie himself takes over the role as a teenager, and there is a scene where he and his father stand on a hilltop, the landscape unfolding below them, as he explains his plans to go to Addis Ababa to go into serious training for the Olympics. His father prefers him to stay on the farm. There is a stilted, formal quality to their conversation that oddly enough gives it more force: We are not seeing actors, but the real people somewhat self-consciously re-creating a conversation they actually had.

The British director, Leslie Woodhead, uses title cards to separate the sections of his film and provide information about Gebrselassie. "Finished 99th in first marathon," we read, and then a little later, "Two years of hard training." As we see marathon runners winding their way through the city streets: "A thousand others with the same dream." Gebrselassie doesn't fit the stereotype of the long-distance runner, tall and long-limbed. He is compact, wiry, muscular. The secret of his greatness, we gather, is that he ran and ran, longer and harder than anyone else, until in his big race he was simply the best prepared.

There are glimpses of his personal life. A shy date with a girl named Alem (who plays herself, and became his wife). One has coffee, the other a Fanta orange drink. Later, he has a heart-to-heart talk with her about his father's disappointment. The father's feelings are understandable: He has lost a strong son to help on the farm, so that the boy can move to the city and . . . run?

The footage of the race itself is never less than thrilling, as such races always are; the close-up lens lets us see the pain of the runners, who by the end are relying mostly on will and endurance. John Powell's music is not exhilarating boilerplate, as scores often are during films about athletics. Instead, it is brooding, introspective, almost sad, suggesting how the runners must look within themselves and endure their burning lungs in a race of such length and difficulty. There is a lot of time to be by yourself in a 10,000-meter race.

I learn from the *Variety* review of the film that the filmmakers had the eight leading contenders under contract, so that they were almost assured of being able to tell the story of the winner. Fair enough, but in Haile Gebrselassie they surely got the most interesting of subjects, a runner whose triumph must be explained almost entirely from within his own determination. He didn't come from a background of training, coaching, and determination, but from the rural hills, where we see him running to school, running to the water well, running to the fields, always with that stoic thrumming of his breath.

Enemy of the State ★ ★ ★
R, 128 m., 1998

Will Smith (Robert Dean), Gene Hackman (Brill), Jon Voight (Reynolds), Lisa Bonet (Rachel Banks), Regina King (Carla Dean), Loren Dean (Hicks), Jason Robards (Hammersly). Directed by Tony Scott and produced by Jerry Bruckheimer. Screenplay by David Marconi.

Enemy of the State uses the thriller genre to attack what it calls "the surveillance society," an America in which underground computers at Fort Meade monitor our phone calls for trigger words like "bomb," "president," and "Allah." It stars Will Smith as a Washington, D.C., lawyer whose life is dismantled bit by bit (and byte by byte) because he possesses proof that a congressman was murdered for opposing a bill that would make government snooping easier.

For much of the movie, the lawyer doesn't even know he has the evidence, a videotape showing the congressman's suicide being faked while a high government official looks on. The official, named Reynolds and played by Jon Voight with glasses and a haircut that make him uncannily resemble Robert McNamara, directs a vendetta against the lawyer that includes planting sexual gossip in the paper, canceling his credit cards, getting him fired, and eventually even trying to frame him for the murder.

Paranoid? Exaggerated? No doubt, although the movie reminded me of that scary recent Anthony Lewis column in the *New York Times* about Julie Hiatt Steele, an innocent bystander in the Kenneth Starr investigation who had her tax returns audited, her neighbors and employers questioned, and her adoption of a war orphan threatened—all because she testified that Kathleen Willey asked her to lie about a meeting with President Clinton.

It's not the government that is the enemy, this movie argues, so much as bureaucrats and demagogues who use the power of the government to gain their own ends and cover their own tracks. Voight's character is really acting on his own behalf: He wants a communications bill passed because it will make his job easier (and perhaps make him richer). He has the congressman (Jason Robards) killed because he's the key opponent of the bill. Everything else follows from the cover-up of the murder.

The movie was directed by Tony Scott (*Top Gun*), who films technology the way the *National Geographic* films wetlands. As the Will Smith character dodges around Washington, trying to figure out who's after him and why, the story is told with footage from spy satellites, surveillance cameras, listening devices, bugs, wiretaps, and database searches. The first time I saw a movie where a satellite was able to zoom in on a car license plate, I snickered. Recently I was able to log onto a Website (www.terraserver.microsoft.com/) and see the roof of my house—or yours. If Microsoft gives that away for free, I believe the National Security Agency can read license plates.

The fugitive lawyer's only friend is a shadowy underground figure named Brill (Gene Hackman), who was a U.S. spy until 1980, and since then has lived an invisible life as a hired gun in the outlands of intelligence and communications. His headquarters: a high-tech hideaway in an old warehouse building, with his equipment fenced in by copper mesh to stop the snoopers. (There is an echo here of Francis Coppola's 1974 film *The Conversation*, which also starred Hackman as a paranoid high-tech eavesdropper; the workplaces in the two movies resemble each other—deliberately, I assume.)

It's Brill who briefs the lawyer on what the government can do. I don't believe him when he says the feds have computers at Fort Meade monitoring our phone calls; I read that as a screenwriter's invention. But I do believe the government can listen to any phone call it wants to, and does so much more often than the law suggests it should.

The movie is fast-paced, centered around two big chase scenes, and ends in a clever double-cross that leads to a big shoot-out. In its action and violence it shows us how the movies have changed since 1974; *The Conversation* is a similar story that depended only on its intelligence and paranoia for appeal. *Enemy of the State* shoehorns in brief scenes between the lawyer and his wife (Regina King) and former girlfriend (Lisa Bonet), but is in too much of a hurry to be much of a people picture. And the standoff at the end edges perilously close to the ridiculous for a movie that's tried so hard to be plausible.

But by and large the movie works. Smith is credible as a good lawyer who is blindsided by the misused power of the state. Gene Hackman, with a bristly haircut and horn-rimmed nerd glasses, seems utterly confident of everything he says. Jon Voight's bureaucrat seems convinced that his job somehow places him above the law. "We are at war twenty-four hours a day," he barks out near the beginning of the film. It was Pogo who said, "We have met the enemy, and he is us."

Entrapment ★ ★ ★
PG-13, 113 m., 1999

Sean Connery (Mac), Catherine Zeta-Jones (Gin), Ving Rhames (Thibadeaux), Will Patton (Cruz), Maury Chaykin (Conrad Greene), Kevin McNally (Haas), Terry O'Neill (Quinn), Madhav Sharma (Security Chief). Directed by Jon Amiel and produced by Sean Connery, Michael Hertzberg, and Rhonda Tollefson. Screenplay by Ron Bass and William Broyles.

Entrapment is the very embodiment of a star vehicle: a movie with a preposterous plot, exotic locations, absurd action sequences, and so much chemistry between attractive actors that we don't care. It stars Sean Connery and Catherine Zeta-Jones in a caper that reminded me of *To Catch a Thief, Charade, Topkapi,* and the stunt sequences in Bond pictures. I didn't believe a second of it, and I didn't care that I didn't.

The film is about thieves. Connery plays a man named Mac, who is getting along in years but is still respected as the most resourceful master thief in the world. Jones plays Gin, who in the early scenes is established as an insurance investigator who sets an elaborate trap for Mac. I will be revealing little about the plot if I say that neither of these people is precisely as they seem.

Watching the film, I imagined the trailer. Not the movie's real trailer, which I haven't seen, but one of those great 1950s trailers where big words in fancy typefaces come spinning out of the screen, asking us to Thrill! to risks atop the world's tallest building, and Gasp! at a daring bank robbery, and Cheer! as towering adventure takes us from New York to Scotland to Malaysia.

A trailer like that would only be telling the simple truth. It would also perhaps include a few tantalizing shots of Zeta-Jones lifting her leather-clad legs in an athletic ballet designed to avoid the invisible beams of security systems. And shots of a thief hanging upside down from a seventy-story building. And an audacious raid through an underwater tunnel. And a priceless Rembrandt. And a way to steal $8 billion because of the Y2K bug. And so on.

It works because it is made stylishly, because Connery and Zeta-Jones are enormously attractive actors, and because of the romantic tension between them. I got a letter the other day complaining about the age differences between the male and female leads in several recent pictures—and, to be sure, Connery at sixty-nine and Zeta-Jones at twenty-nine remember different wars. But the movie cannily establishes ground rules (Mac lectures that thievery is a business that permits no personal relationships), and so instead of questioning why they're erotically involved, we wish they would be.

The plot, by Ron Bass and William Broyles, is put together like a Swiss watch that keeps changing time zones: It is accurate and misleading at once. The film consists of one elaborate caper sequence after another, and it rivals the Bond films in its climactic action sequence, which has Mac and Gin hanging from a string of holiday bulbs beneath the walkway linking the two towers of the Petronas Twin Towers in Kuala Lumpur. The stunt and f/x work here do a good job of convincing us that human beings are actually dangling precariously seventy stories in the air, and I for one am convinced that Zeta-Jones personally performs an earlier stunt, in which she treats an old wooden beam in Mac's Scottish castle as if it were a parallel bar at the Olympics. Most of the movie's action is just that—action—and not extreme violence.

Watching Connery negotiate the nonsense of the plot is an education in acting: He treats every situation as if it is plausible but not that big of a deal, and that sets the right tone. He avoids the smile in the voice that would give away the silliness of the plot. When he says, "I'm never late. If I'm late, it's because I'm dead," we reflect that some actors can get away with lines like that and others can't, and Connery is the leader of the first group.

As for Catherine Zeta-Jones, I can only reflect, as I did while watching her in *The Mask of Zorro*, that while beautiful women are a dime a dozen in the movies, those with fire, flash, and humor are a good deal more scarce. Taking her cue perhaps from Connery, she also plays a preposterous role absolutely straight. The costars and Jon Amiel, the director, respect the movie tradition they're working in, instead of condescending to it. There are scenes in this film when astounding revelations are made, and although I didn't believe them, I accepted them, which is more difficult and enjoyable. ☞

Erin Brockovich ★ ★
R, 126 m., 2000

Julia Roberts (Erin Brockovich), Albert Finney (Ed Masry), Aaron Eckhart (George), Marg Helgenberger (Donna Jensen), Cherry Jones (Pamela Duncan), Peter Coyote (Kurt Potter), Scotty Leavenworth (Matthew), Gemmenne De La Pena (Katie). Directed by Steven Soderbergh and produced by Danny DeVito, Michael Shamberg, and Stacey Sher. Screenplay by Susannah Grant.

Erin Brockovich is *Silkwood* (Meryl Streep fighting nuclear wastes) crossed with *A Civil Action* (John Travolta against pollution), plus Julia Roberts in a plunging neckline. Roberts plays a real-life heroine who helped uncover one of the biggest environmental crimes in history. But her performance upstages the story; this is always Roberts, not Brockovich, and unwise wardrobe decisions position her character somewhere between a caricature and a distraction.

I know all about the real Erin Brockovich because I saw her on *Oprah*, where she cried at just the right moment in a filmed recap of her life. She was a divorced mom of three with few employment prospects, who talked her way into a job at a law firm, began an investigation on her own initiative, and played a key role in a pollution suit that cost Pacific Gas and Electric a $333 million settlement.

There is obviously a story here, but *Erin Brockovich* doesn't make it compelling. The film lacks focus and energy, the character development is facile and thin, and what about those necklines? I know that the real Brockovich liked to dress provocatively; that's her personal style and she's welcome to it. But the Hollywood version makes her look like a miniskirted hooker, with her bras that peek cheerfully above her necklines.

Oh, the movie tries to deal with the clothes. "You might want to rethink your wardrobe a little," her boss (Albert Finney) tells her. She inelegantly replies, "I think I look nice, and as long as I have one ass instead of two, I'll wear what I like." Yeah, fine, after she's already lost her own personal injury suit by flashing cleavage on the witness stand and firing off four-letter words. When she dresses the same way to go door-to-door in a working-class neighborhood where industrial chemicals have caused illness, we have to wonder whether, in real life, she was hassled or mistrusted.

Whether she was or wasn't, the costume design sinks this movie. Julia Roberts is a sensational-looking woman, and dressed so provocatively, in every single scene, she upstages the material. If the medium is the message, the message in this movie is sex.

That's all the more true because the supporting characters are not vivid or convincing. Albert Finney is one of the most robust and powerful actors in the movies, but here, as a personal injury lawyer named Ed Masry, he comes across like an office manager at H & R Block. He's dampened; there's no fire in his performance, and when he complains that the cost of the lawsuit may bankrupt him, all we can think about is the infinitely greater impact of John Travolta's similar dialogue in *A Civil Action*.

Erin has a kind of relationship with her next-door neighbor, George, a Harley fan who becomes a baby-sitter for her children. George is played by Aaron Eckhart, who was so dominant in *In the Company of Men*, but here, wearing a twirpy John Ritter beard that he doesn't seem comfortable with, he's a shallow cipher. The couple can't even have convincing arguments because there's not enough between them in the first place.

Seeing the details of Brockovich's home life, her relationship with her kids and friends, the way she talks, the way she postures, we're always aware that there's a performance going on. Streep was so much more convincing in the somewhat similar role of Karen Silkwood.

We understand that Pacific Gas and Electric has polluted groundwater and is apparently responsible for death and disease, but it never emerges as much of a villain, and in the pallid confrontations with their attorneys there's none of the juice that Robert Duvall's company attorney brought to *A Civil Action*.

Steven Soderbergh, who directed, has blown a great opportunity to make the movie that the real Erin Brockovich calls for. Susannah Grant's by-the-numbers screenplay sees the characters as markers on a storyboard rather than flesh-and-blood humans. Scenes with members of the suffering families genuflect in the direction of pathos, but are cut and dried. It doesn't feel like we're seeing Erin Brockovich share the pain, but like we're seeing Julia Roberts paying a house call (again, we remember the power of *A Civil Action*).

Erin Brockovich has a screenplay with the depth and insight of a cable-TV docudrama, and that won't do for a 126-minute "major production." Maybe it's not that the necklines are distracting. Maybe it's just that the movie gives us so little to focus on that they win by default. ☞

Ever After ★ ★ ★
PG-13, 121 m., 1998

Drew Barrymore (Danielle), Anjelica Huston (Rodmilla), Dougray Scott (Prince Henry), Patrick Godfrey (Leonardo), Megan Dodds (Marguerite), Melanie Lynskey (Jacqueline), Timothy West (King Francis), Judy Parfitt (Queen Marie), Jeanne Moreau (Old Woman), Jeroen Krabbe (Auguste). Directed by Andy Tennant and produced by Mireille Soria and Tracey Trench. Screenplay by Susannah Grant, Tennant, and Rick Parks.

Ever After opens with an old lady offering to tell the true story of "the little cinder girl," who was, she says, a real person long before she was immortalized by the Brothers Grimm in the Cinderella myth: "Her name was Danielle. And this . . . was her glass slipper."

The movie that follows is one of surprises, not least that the old tale still has life and passion in it. I went to the screening expecting some sort of soppy children's picture, and found myself in a costume romance with some of the same energy and zest as *The Mask of Zorro*. And I was reminded again that Drew Barrymore can hold the screen and involve us in her characters.

The movie takes place in sixteenth-century Europe, although it is a Europe more like a theme park than a real place, and that accounts for Danielle's remarkable ability to encounter the rich and famous—not only Prince Henry of France, but even Leonardo da Vinci, who functions as sort of a fairy godfather. It's a Europe of remarkable beauty (magnificent castles and châteaus are used as locations), in which a young girl with spunk and luck has a chance even against a wicked stepmother.

Not that the stepmother is merely wicked. *Ever After* brings a human dimension to the story, which begins with Danielle living happily with her father (Jeroen Krabbe). He springs a surprise: He is to marry Rodmilla (Anjelica Huston), who will bring her daughters, Jacqueline and Marguerite (Melanie Lynskey and Megan Dodds), to live with them. Soon after the marriage, alas, the father drops from his horse, dead, and life changes abruptly for Danielle.

"To be raised by a man!" exclaims Rodmilla. "No wonder you're built for hard labor." She puts Danielle to work as the family maid—swabbing floors, cooking and doing the dishes, tending the barnyard. Meanwhile, she grooms the beautiful Jacqueline for marriage in high places.

But Rodmilla sometimes allows herself a certain sympathy for Danielle; it's not that she's cruel to the girl, so much as that she must look out for her own daughters. The older woman has had problems of her own. "Did you love my father?" Danielle asks her. Rodmilla conceals much in her answer: "I barely knew him. Now, go away—I'm tired."

Danielle's entry into the life of Prince Henry is handled through a series of coincidental encounters after a Meet Cute in which she bops him with an apple. And there is a false crisis after Danielle pretends to be a countess (but only to help a friend) and Henry falls in love with her. She is afraid that when her masquerade is exposed, he will scorn her, and she is very nearly right, but Danielle's attitude toward her dilemma is closer to modern feminism than to the cheerful sexism of the Brothers Grimm.

Henry is played by Dougray Scott with a certain complexity; he is not simply a shining knight. His parents, the king and queen of France, are, however, improbably benign, and lack the ruthlessness one might expect from historical figures. They're more like Madame Harriet and Monsieur Ozzie. Further intrigue comes from the fact that Marguerite, the younger and darker of Rodmilla's two daughters, is not at all a bad sort herself.

Drew Barrymore has been in the movies for nineteen years now (she was in *Altered States* when she was four, and starred in *E.T.* at the age of seven). I seem to have known of her for decades, and she's still only twenty-three. Child stars have a hard time of it, convincing us to forget their cherubic little faces, and there is usually a period of trouble along the way. Now her adult career is safely launched.

Barrymore has had no big hits as an adult (well, *Batman Forever*, but it wasn't exactly her picture). But she has put together a series of sound, interesting performances: as a runaway teenager on a shooting spree in *Guncrazy* (1992), as a druggie's abused girlfriend in *Boys on the Side* (1995), as an unstable teenager in love in *Mad Love* (1995, still her best film), and as the waitress who falls in love with *The Wedding Singer* (1998—not a good movie, but she was okay). Here, as the little cinder girl, she is able at last to put aside her bedraggled losers and flower as a fresh young beauty, and she brings poignancy and fire to the role.

Ever After has been directed by Andy Tennant, whose *Fools Rush In* (1997) was also a Cinderella story of sorts, about a rich developer (Matthew Perry) who falls in love with a poor little Mexican-American camera girl (Salma Hayek) at Caesars Palace in Vegas. I liked that movie for its human comedy and romantic energy, and the same qualities are abundant in *Ever After*—along with lush scenery, astounding locations, and luxuriant costumes. Also Leonardo da Vinci, who functions like a cross between a wise old saint and the kind of artist who sketches the guests at a wedding.

eXistenZ ★ ★ ★
R, 97 m., 1999

Jennifer Jason Leigh (Allegra Geller), Jude Law (Ted Pikul), Willem Dafoe (Gas), Ian Holm (Kiri Vinokur), Don McKellar (Yevgeny Nourish), Callum Keith Rennie (Hugo Carlaw), Sarah Polley (Merle), Christopher Eccleston (Levi). Directed by David Cronenberg and produced by Robert Lantos, Andras Hamori, and Cronenberg. Screenplay by Cronenberg.

Guys are always using the same lame excuses. First Ted licks Allegra's bio-port. Then he says, "That wasn't me—it was my game character!" Allegra is the world's leading designer of virtual reality games. Her newest game is named eXistenZ, and the bio-port plugs directly into the lower spine and connects to the game's control pod via an "umbrycord." When you're hooked up, you can't tell the game from reality. Not even if you designed the game.

eXistenZ is the new film from David Cronenberg, the Canadian director who must be a thorn in the side of the MPAA ratings board. He's always filming activities that look like sex, but don't employ any of the appurtenances associated with that pastime. In his previous film, *Crash*, the characters exhibited an unhealthy interest in wounds. This time it's bio-ports. And what about those "MetaFlesh Game Pods," input devices that combine the attributes of a joystick, a touch pad, and a kidney? They pulse with a life of their own, and Allegra holds hers as if it's a baby, or a battery-powered shiatsu machine.

eXistenZ arrived a few weeks after *The Matrix*, another science-fiction movie about characters who find themselves inside a universe created by virtual reality. *The Matrix* is mainstream sci-fi, but *eXistenZ*, written by Cronenberg, is much stranger; it creates a world where organic and inorganic are not separate states, but kind of chummy. Consider the scene where an oil-stained grease monkey implants a bio-port in the hero, using a piece of equipment that seems designed to give a lube job to a PeterBilt.

Jennifer Jason Leigh, that fearless adventurer in extreme roles, plays Allegra, whose new game is being marketed by Antenna Research. Jude Law is Ted, the company's mar-keting trainee. She barely misses being killed during a demonstration of eXistenZ, when an assassin slips past the metal detectors at the door with a gun made of flesh and blood. Ted helps her escape, and later, when he cuts the bullet out of her shoulder, he discovers it's not a bullet but a . . . hmmm, this is interesting . . . a human tooth. She decides Ted needs his own bio-port, and looks for a "country gas station." When she finds one (with a sign that says Country Gas Station) we assume they're inside the game, which is why she knows the station's name: She wrote it, and maybe also created its owner, named Gas (Willem Dafoe).

She knows her way around this world, and isn't surprised when they're told, "Look for a Chinese restaurant in the forest—and order the special." The owner rattles off the chef's daily selection, explaining that "mutant reptiles and amphibians produce previously unknown taste sensations." But Ted insists on *the* daily special and gets a dish that's really bony. No wonder. The bones click together into a gun. And soon they visit the Trout Farm, where organic game pods are grown, and come up against Kiri Vinokur (Ian Holm), owner of Cortical Systematics, a rival game firm.

Cronenberg's film is as loaded with special effects as *The Matrix*, but they're on a different scale. Many of his best effects are gooey, indescribable organic things, and some of the most memorable scenes involve characters eating things that surgeons handle with gloves on. He places his characters in a back-woods world that looks like it was ordered over the phone from L.L. Bean. Then he frames them with visuals where half the screen is a flat foreground that seems to push them toward us, while the other half is a diagonal sliding off alarmingly into the background.

eXistenZ is likely to appeal especially to computer game players, since it's familiar with that world and speculates on its future development. Allegra explains to Ted such phenomena as "genuine game urges"—"something your game character was born to do." She regards her programming handiwork with musings like, "I've devoted five of my most passionate years to this strange little creature." At one point she's alarmed to discover, "I'm locked outside my own $38 million game!"

And without the password, it looks like neither she nor anyone else can get back inside. What? You mean she didn't back up her disk?

Eye of God ★ ★ ★
R, 84 m., 1998

Martha Plimpton (Ainsley Dupree), Kevin Anderson (Jack), Hal Holbrook (Sheriff Rogers), Nick Stahl (Tommy Spencer), Mary Kay Place (Clair Spencer), Chris Freihofer (Les Hector), Woody Watson (Glen Briggs), Richard Jenkins (Parole Officer). Directed by Tim Blake Nelson and produced by Michael Nelson and Wendy Ettinger. Screenplay by Tim Blake Nelson.

Rural Oklahoma. Town named Kingfisher. Ainsley sits in the convenience store by the road, watching strangers on their way through. She works in a hamburger shop. She's lonely. Through a magazine, she gets into correspondence with a prisoner, and when he gets out he comes to see her. They get married.

This time and place are evoked with quiet, atmospheric shots in Tim Blake Nelson's *Eye of God,* a film in which dreams seem to yearn toward a place where they can grow. Kingfisher is a boring place which is a boring drive from other places just as boring. Ainsley (Martha Plimpton) likes people and would like to know more of them, but her opportunities are limited and her desperation makes her see the ex-convict as salvation.

Well, he looks wholesome enough. Jack (Kevin Anderson) is straightforward and sincere, looks her in the eye, tells her how he found Jesus in prison. At first their marriage looks like it will work. Then his controlling side takes over. He doesn't want her working. Doesn't want her hanging out at the truck stop. Doesn't want her to leave the house, indeed, except to go to church with him on Sunday. It's ironic: Her life was empty and barren before, and by marrying him, she's losing what little variety she was able to find.

The film tells this story in flashes of action, intercut with another story involving a local fourteen-year-old named Tommy (Nick Stahl) whose mother gassed herself. Now he lives with an aunt who can't control him. He's trapped in the town too. *Eye of God* works in a fractured

style, telling both films out of chronological order, cutting between them in a way that's disorienting at first, as it's meant to be.

Perhaps there's a clue to the editing in the title. The eyes of god exist outside time and don't need to see stories in chronological order, because they know the beginning, middle, and end before the story begins or the characters even exist. *Eye of God* sees its story in the same way: as events that are so interlocked by fate that, in a way, they don't have to happen one after another because they will all happen eventually.

Continuity of sorts is supplied by the sheriff (Hal Holbrook), who provides a narration of sorts, beginning with the story of Abraham and Isaac: How did the son feel as he saw his father poised to kill him? He finds Tommy wandering by the roadside, covered with blood, in one of the first shots of the film. It's not his blood, but whose is it? He doesn't seem able to talk.

Another outside observer is Jack's parole officer (Richard Jenkins), who tells Ainsley something she should have known before she got married: Jack was in prison for beating a woman nearly to death—a woman who was carrying his child, as, before long, Ainsley is.

Martha Plimpton's performance is the center of the movie, quiet and strong. She plays a capable woman for whom life has not supplied a role. I've often seen her playing bright, glib city girls (that was her first big role, in *Shy People*). As Ainsley, she isn't tragically shy and lonely; it's more that she's waiting patiently for her life to begin, with less and less evidence that it's about to.

The villain in the film is not exactly Jack. Like an animal, he behaves according to his nature, and the way to deal with him is to stay away from him. The movie is more about Ainsley's luck than Jack's behavior. Somebody always marries these jerks, but you gotta hope it's not you.

Eyes Wide Shut ★ ★ ★ ½
R, 159 m., 1999

Tom Cruise (Dr. William Harford), Nicole Kidman (Alice Harford), Sydney Pollack (Victor Ziegler), Marie Richardson (Marion), Rade Sherbedgia (Milich), Thomas Gibson (Carl),

Vinessa Shaw (Domino), Todd Field (Nick Nightingale), Alan Cumming (Desk Clerk), Leelee Sobieski (Milich's daugher), Carmela Marner (Waitress). Produced and directed by Stanley Kubrick. Screenplay by Kubrick and Frederic Raphael. Inspired by *Traumnovelle,* a novel by Arthur Schnitzler.

Stanley Kubrick's *Eyes Wide Shut* is like an erotic daydream about chances missed and opportunities avoided. For its hero, who spends two nights wandering in the sexual underworld, it's all foreplay. He never actually has sex, but he dances close and holds his hand in the flame. Why does he do this? The easy answer is that his wife has made him jealous. Another possibility is that the story she tells inflames his rather torpid imagination.

The film has the structure of a thriller, with the possibility that conspiracies and murders have taken place. It also resembles a nightmare; a series of strange characters drift in and out of focus, puzzling the hero with unexplained details of their lives. The reconciliation at the end of the film is the one scene that doesn't work; a film that intrigues us because of its loose ends shouldn't try to tidy up.

Tom Cruise and Nicole Kidman star as Dr. Bill and Alice Harford, a married couple who move in rich Manhattan society. In a long, languorous opening sequence, they attend a society ball where a tall Hungarian, a parody of a suave seducer, tries to honey-talk Alice ("Did you ever read the Latin poet Ovid on the art of love?"). Meanwhile, Bill gets a come-on from two aggressive women, before being called to the upstairs bathroom, where Victor, the millionaire who is giving the party (Sydney Pollack), has an overdosed hooker who needs a doctor's help.

At the party, Bill meets an old friend from medical school, now a pianist. The next night, at home, Alice and Bill get stoned on pot (apparently very good pot, considering how zonked they seem) and she describes a fantasy she had about a young naval officer she saw last summer on Cape Cod: "At no time was he ever out of my mind. And I thought if he wanted me, only for one night, I was ready to give up everything."

There is a fight. Bill leaves the house and wanders the streets, his mind inflamed by im-

ages of Alice making love with the officer. And now begins his long adventure, which has parallels with Joyce's "Nighttown" section of *Ulysses* and Scorsese's *After Hours,* as one sexual situation after another swims into view. The film has two running jokes, both quiet ones: Almost everyone who sees Bill, both male and female, reacts to him sexually. And he is forever identifying himself as a doctor, as if to reassure himself that he exists at all.

Kubrick's great achievement in the film is to find and hold an odd, unsettling, sometimes erotic tone for the doctor's strange encounters. Shooting in a grainy high-contrast style, using lots of backlighting, underlighting, and strong primary colors, setting the film at Christmas to take advantage of the holiday lights, he makes it all a little garish, like an urban sideshow. Dr. Bill is not really the protagonist but the acted-upon, careening from one situation to another, out of his depth.

Kubrick pays special attention to each individual scene. He makes a deliberate choice, I think, not to roll them together into an ongoing story, but to make each one a destination—to give each encounter the intensity of a dream in which *this* moment is clear but it's hard to remember where we've come from or guess what comes next.

The film pays extraordinary attention to the supporting actors, even cheating camera angles to give them the emphasis on two-shots; in several scenes, Cruise is like the straight man. Sydney Pollack is the key supporting player, as a confident, sinister man of the world, living in old-style luxury, deep-voiced, experienced, decadent. Todd Field plays Nick, the society piano player who sets up Bill's visit to a secret orgy. And there is also a wonderful role for Vinessa Shaw as a hooker who picks up Dr. Bill and shares some surprisingly sweet time with him.

The movie's funniest scene takes place in a hotel where Bill questions a desk clerk, played by Alan Cumming as a cheerful queen who makes it pretty clear he's interested. Rade Sherbedgia, a gravel-voiced, bearded patriarch, plays a costume dealer who may also be retailing the favors of his young daughter. Carmela Marner is a waitress who seems to have learned her trade by watching sitcoms. And Marie Richardson is the daughter of a dead man, who wants to seduce Dr. Bill almost literally on her father's deathbed.

All of these scenes have their own focus and intensity; each sequence has its own dramatic arc. They all lead up to and away from the extraordinary orgy sequence in a country estate, where Dr. Bill gate-crashes and wanders among scenes of Sadeian sexual ritual and writhings worthy of Bosch. The masked figure who rules over the proceedings has ominous presence, as does the masked woman who warns Dr. Bill he is in danger. This sequence has hypnotic intensity.

The orgy, alas, has famously undergone digital alterations to obscure some of the more energetic rumpy-pumpy. A shame. The events in question are seen at a certain distance, without visible genitalia, and are more atmosphere than action, but to get the R rating the studio has had to block them with digitally generated figures (two nude women arm in arm, and some cloaked men).

In rough draft form, this masking evoked Austin Powers's famous genital hide-and-seek sequence. Later I saw the polished version of the technique and will say it is done well, even though it should not have been done at all. The joke is that *Eyes Wide Shut* is an adult film in every atom of its being. With or without those digital effects, it is inappropriate for younger viewers. It's symbolic of the moral hypocrisy of the rating system that it would force a great director to compromise his vision, while by the same process making his adult film more accessible to young viewers.

Kubrick died in March. It is hard to believe he would have accepted the digital hocus-pocus. *Eyes Wide Shut* should have been released as he made it, either "unrated" or NC-17. For adult audiences, it creates a mesmerizing daydream of sexual fantasy. The final scene, in the toy store, strikes me as conventional moralizing—an obligatory happy resolution of all problems—but the deep mystery of the film remains. To begin with, can Dr. Bill believe Victor's version of the events of the past few days? I would have enjoyed a final shot in a hospital corridor, with Dr. Bill doing a double take as a gurney wheels past carrying the corpse of the piano player.   ☞

F

Fallen ★ ★ ½
R, 120 m., 1998

Denzel Washington (John Hobbes), John Goodman (Jonesy), Donald Sutherland (Lieutenant Stanton), Embeth Davidtz (Gretta Milano), James Gandolfini (Lou), Elias Koteas (Edgar Reese). Directed by Gregory Hoblit and produced by Charles Roven and Dawn Steel. Screenplay by Nicholas Kazan.

Fallen is the kind of horror story I most enjoy, set in ordinary and realistic circumstances, with a villain who lives mostly in our minds. Movies like this play with our apprehensions, instead of slamming us with freaky special effects. By suggesting that the evil resides in the real world, they make everything scary; one of the movie's best moments is supplied by a pop machine.

Denzel Washington stars as John Hobbes, a detective who works with his partner, good old Jonesy (John Goodman), on murder cases. The film opens with a flashback ("I want to tell you about the time I almost died"), and then cuts to Death Row, where a vicious killer (Elias Koteas) faces the gas chamber. Hobbes is among the witnesses as the poison capsule drops, and the killer uses his dying breath to sing "Time Is on My Side." And then, this is curious, there is a POV shot from above the dead man's head, and we wonder whose point of view it could possibly be.

Having established the possibility of the supernatural, *Fallen* is at pains to center Hobbes firmly in a real world. The screenplay, by Oscar nominee Nicholas Kazan *(Reversal of Fortune),* shows us Hobbes at home (he lives with his brother and nephew) and at work (Jonsey is a good pal, but a lieutenant played by Donald Sutherland seems to know more than he says). The story develops along the lines of a police procedural, with the cops investigating some strange murders, including a corpse left in a bathtub while the killer apparently enjoyed a leisurely breakfast.

Hobbes notices an incredible coincidence: The dead man in the bathtub is the same man who walked past him last night, drawing his attention by his singular manner. Now that's strange. And strange, too, are other developments, including the verdict of a linguist that the gas chamber victim's words, on a videotape, were spoken in ancient Aramaic, a language he had no way of knowing.

There is a connection between all these threads, which we discover along with Hobbes. (The audience, indeed, discovers it before Hobbes—but we have the advantage, because we know he's in a horror movie and he doesn't.) Among the characters Hobbes encounters on his search for missing threads, the most interesting is the daughter (Embeth Davidtz) of a cop who committed suicide after being accused of the kinds of offenses that Hobbes himself now seems to face. "If you value your life, if there's even one human being you care about," she tells him, "walk away from this case." Did her father leave a warning behind? What is the meaning of the word *Alazel,* scrawled on the wall of the basement where he killed himself?

Denzel Washington is convincing as a cop, but perhaps not the best choice for the role of Hobbes, which requires more of a *noir* personality. There's something essentially hopeful and sunny about Washington, and the best *noir* heroes encounter grim news as if they were expecting it. There should be, at the core of the protagonist in any *noir* story, guilt and shame, as if they feel they deserve what's happening to them. Washington plays Hobbes more like a conventional hero, and doesn't internalize the evil.

As for the rest of the characters, perhaps they are as they seem, perhaps not, at any given time. The evil presence in the film moves from person to person, and there is a chase scene in a crowd that is eerily effective, because there's no way to tell who the pursuer is. See the film, and you'll understand.

Fallen was directed by Gregory Hoblit, who also made *Primal Fear* (1996). Both films contain characters who are not as they seem, and leads who are blindsided by them. *Fallen* reaches further, but doesn't achieve as much; the idea is better than the execution, and by the end, the surprises become too mechanical and inevitable. Still, for an hour *Fallen* develops quietly and convincingly, and it never slips down into easy shock tactics. Kazan writes plausible, literate dialogue and Hoblit creates a realistic world, so that the horror never seems, as it does in less ambitious thrillers, to feel at home.

Fallen Angels ★ ★ ★
NO MPAA RATING, 96 m., 1998

Leon Lai (Wong Chi-Ming, the killer), Takeshi Kaneshiro (He Zhiwu), Charlie Young (Cherry), Michele Reis (The Agent), Karen Mok (Baby), Toru Saito (Sato, the manager), Chen Wanlei (Father), Kong To-Hoi (Ah-Hoi). Directed by Wong Kar-Wai and produced by Kar-Wai and Jeff Lau. Screenplay by Kar-Wai.

Fallen Angels is the latest work from the Hong Kong wild man Wong Kar-Wai, whose films give the same effect as leafing through hip photo magazines very quickly. It's a riff on some of the same material as his *Chungking Express* (1996), about which I wrote, "You enjoy it because of what you know about film, not because of what it knows about life."

I felt transported back to the 1960s films of Godard. I was watching a film that was not afraid of its audience. Almost all films, even the best ones, are made with a certain anxiety about what the audience will think: Will it like it? Get it? Be bored by it? Wong Kar-Wai, like Godard, is oblivious to such questions and plunges into his weird, hyper style without a moment's hesitation.

To describe the plot is to miss the point. *Fallen Angels* takes the materials of the plot—the characters and what they do—and assembles them like a photo montage. At the end, you have impressions, not conclusions. His influences aren't other filmmakers, but still photographers and video artists—the kinds of artists who do to images what rap artists are doing to music when they move the vinyl back and forth under the needle.

The people in his films are not characters but ingredients, or subjects. They include a hit man and his female "manager," who share separate dayparts in a hotel room that seems only precariously separate from the train tracks outside. (She scrubs the place down before her shift, kneeling on the floor in her leather minidress and mesh stockings.) There is also a man who stopped speaking after eating a can of outdated pineapple slices (pineapple sell-by dates were also a theme in *Chungking Express*). He makes a living by "reopening" stores that are closed for the night, and has an uncertain relationship with a young woman who acts out her emotions theatrically. There is another woman wandering about in a blond wig, for no better purpose, I suspect, than that *Chungking Express* also contained such a character.

Does it matter what these people do? Not much. It is the texture of their lives that Wong is interested in, not the outcome. He records the frenetic, manic pace of the city, exaggerating everything with wide-angle lenses, handheld cameras, quick cutting, slow motion, fast motion, freeze frames, black and white, tilt shots, color filters, neon-sign lighting, and occasionally a camera that pauses, exhausted, and just stares.

That exhausted camera supplies the movie's best moment. The hit man (Leon Lai) has just wiped out a roomful of gamblers. He runs into the street and boards a commuter train. The man behind him is—good God!—a junior high school classmate, now an insurance salesman. The classmate chatters about insurance policies and his own impending marriage, handing the killer an invitation ("fill in your name"). The camera framing holds the killer in left foreground, his face frozen into a rictus of unease and dislike, his eyes turned away, as the classmate rattles on and on.

Finally the classmate asks for the hit man's card, which he supplies ("Ah! You have your own business!"). Then he asks to see a photo of his wife. The hit man supplies a photo of a black woman and a child. On the sound track, narration tells us he paid the woman five dollars to pose with him, and bought the kid an ice cream. The scene is telling us, I think, that in this society even a hit man feels obligated to be able to produce a business card and family photos on request.

A structure emerges uneasily from the film's unceasing movement. We watch the "midnight shopper" as he visits his old father and videotapes him cooking a steak. We see an inflatable doll being slammed in a refrigerator door. We see all-night cafés and hurtling traffic and a man riding a dead pig.

It's kind of exhausting and kind of exhilarating. It will appeal to the kinds of people you see in the Japanese animation section of the video store, with their sleeves cut off so you can see their tattoos. And to those who subscribe to more than three film magazines. And to members of garage bands. And to art students. It's not for your average moviegoers—unless, of course, they want to see something new.

Family Name ★ ★ ★
NO MPAA RATING, 89 m., 1998

A documentary directed by Macky Alston and produced by Selina Lewis. Screenplay by Alston and Kay Gayner.

Family Name tells a story that could have been written by Faulkner. It coils back through the secrets of the South to find if there is a connection between two large families with the uncommon name of Alston. One family is white, the other black. As the film opens, both are having their family reunions only a week and a few miles apart in North Carolina. Neither family knows about the other reunion.

"When I was growing up in Durham," remembers Macky Alston, who is white, "I noticed that many of my black schoolmates had the same last name that I did." When Macky is thirty, living in New York, he decides to make a documentary about what that might mean. He finds two other Alston families, both black, living not far away, and his investigation begins with them and then moves south.

Slavery is the great shame of the nation, and like all shameful things it is not much talked about within families touched by it. The Alstons, Macky finds, "were one of the largest slaveholding families in the state." But the time itself is on the edge of living memory. His father's grandfather owned slaves. There are two very old sisters, light-skinned enough to pass as white, whose family name is also Alston, and who remember their grandparents, who were slaves.

Are the Alstons related by blood? "In slave time," one of the black Alstons tells him, "they knew everything that happened, and they never talked about it." Whose children were whose, even across racial lines, was known but not recorded, and the tombstones of old family cemeteries contain tantalizing hints but never the facts.

Family Name, which begins like a family album, develops into a fascinating detective story as Macky follows leads. He discovers old courthouse records, visits cemeteries, finds documents in unexpected places. He begins to focus on a great-great-great-great-grand-uncle named Chatham Jack, who may have had mixed children, and who in his old age, it was said, always "kept a couple of little black children around to sit on his feet when they got cold." Is Jack's blood in both branches of the Alston family?

Tracing descendants down through the years, Macky finds black Alstons of distinction. One, Spinky Alston, was a well-known painter during the Harlem Renaissance. His father, Primus, was a light-skinned man—and not a slave. Was Primus descended from Chatham Jack? Amazingly, Macky finds that Spinky's sister, Rousmaniere, is still alive. But what does she remember?

Another African-American branch includes a professional storyteller named Charlotte, whose ex-husband, Fred, is a classical musician. Coincidentally, Fred and their son Jeff are also interested in traveling south to explore their roots. In living rooms and on front porches, in old baptismal records and birth certificates and wills, there are possibilities and conjectures but no facts. Macky tries to narrow down the possibilities—to see if only one scenario will fit his findings.

But there is much more going on here. For one thing, Macky is gay, and this fact has been withheld from his own grandmother. So in his own life he has experienced the way that secrets work. Must he tell her? And Macky's parents? What secrets do they hide? The trails seem to grow warmer, and a chance remark by an ancient survivor might provide the crucial clue. By the end of the film, we sit in astonishment at the unexpected turn the story has taken. *Family Name* begins by seeking the secrets of a family, and the secrets it discovers cause us to question the very definition of a family. If blood is thicker than water, then perhaps love is thicker even than blood.

Fantasia 2000 ★ ★ ★
G, 75 m., 1999

Featuring Steve Martin, Bette Midler, James Levine, Itzhak Perlman, James Earl Jones, Angela Lansbury, Quincy Jones, and Penn and Teller. Directed by Pixote Hunt, Hendel Butoy, Eric Goldberg, James Algar, Francis Glebas, Gaetan Brizzi, and Paul Brizzi and produced by Donald W. Ernst.

After the worldwide acclaim that greeted his *Snow White and the Seven Dwarfs*, the first full-length color animated feature, Walt Disney's imagination soared. He had been assured by no less than the great Soviet director Sergei Eisenstein that *Snow White* was the greatest film ever made, and he saw no boundaries for the infant art of feature animation. In 1940, he produced *Fantasia*, a marriage of animation and classical music, and insisted it be shown only in his new process, Fantasound, which used an assembly of sixty-four speakers that gave audiences their first experience of what is now familiar as "surround sound."

The experiment was a disaster. Most exhibitors refused to install the speakers. Audiences, distracted by the gathering clouds of World War II, were not in a fanciful mood. And critics who praised Disney's earlier effort as art, now slapped him down to earth again, accusing him of being too pretentious. The critic Ernest Rister writes that Disney was personally embittered by the reception given his brainchild, and determined to stick to more commercial projects in the future. He remained fascinated by technical innovations (Rister points out that he shot the TV show *Davy Crockett* in color even when TV was all black-and-white, because he knew color was inevitable). But after *Fantasia* he never again crawled out so far on an artistic limb.

His original plan for *Fantasia* was to constantly renew the film, adding fresh segments, warehousing old ones, showing it in Fantasound as a sort of classical repertory for moviegoers. Now comes *Fantasia 2000*, produced by his nephew Roy, to continue that vision more than thirty years after Walt's death. Walt the tinkerer, who designed sound systems and movie cameras and got personally involved in designing the sights and sounds of the attractions at Disneyland, would have appreciated his nephew's boldness in shooting the film in the IMAX high-resolution, giant-screen process.

IMAX has even more than Walt's sixty-four speakers, and a five-story screen that literally envelops the audience in the experience. Mind-expanding audiences in 1968 went to the revival of *Fantasia* and sat in the front row (or even stretched out on the floor in front of the screen). Now the whole audience gets the same total immersion, in the images and the music by the Chicago Symphony Orchestra conducted by James Levine. Movies like this renew my faith that the future of the cinema lies not in the compromises of digital projection, but by leaping over the limitations of digital into the next generation of film technology.

Fantasia 2000 as a film is not the equal of the original *Fantasia*, maybe because it aims a little lower, for broader appeal. Some of the animation is powerful, including a closing segment with a theme of ecological healing. Other sections, including the opening abstraction of triangles dancing to Beethoven's "Fifth Symphony," seem a little pedestrian. Computer-animated experiments such as those shown on *The Mind's Eye* videos are more daring than anything in *Fantasia 2000*.

Still, as exactly what it is, *Fantasia 2000* is splendid entertainment, and the IMAX system is an impressive costar. My favorite sequence is the closing one, in which Stravinsky's Firebird Suite is illustrated by a blasted landscape that slowly renews itself. I also admired animator Eric Goldberg's interlocking New York stories, which accompanied Gershwin's "Rhapsody in Blue." The artistic inspiration for this section is said to be the great caricaturist Al Hirschfeld, but, curiously, I thought the style owed more to Ludwig Bemelmans and his "Madeleine" drawings. Certainly it has a different look than anything previously signed by the Disney studios, which has always specialized in the "clear line" style.

One section suited to the towering IMAX screen is Ottorino Respighi's music "Pines of Rome," illustrated by Hendel Butoy as a fantasy involving whales who gambol in the sea, in the sky, and eventually even in space. One effective sequence shows them moving through vast underwater ice caverns; I was reminded of the IMAX film *Antarctica*, with its footage of scuba divers inside glacial caverns.

Hendel Butoy's animation in the segment devoted to Shostakovich's Piano Concerto No. 2 plays wonderfully as a self-contained film. Based on Hans Christian Andersen's fable *The Steadfast Tin Soldier*, it's a three-way struggle in which a broken toy soldier, with only one leg, falls in love with a toy ballerina and protects her from a Jack-in-the-Box with evil designs.

Mickey Mouse's famous "Sorcerer's Apprentice" section, everyone's favorite from the 1940 film, is the only segment repeated here. Even though it's been carefully restored and subjected to a "degraining" process to help it play better in IMAX, it's not as visually sharp as the rest of the film. That's not a criticism of the source material but a demonstration of how breathtakingly detailed the IMAX picture is. The older film offers a retro look appropriate to a sequence nearly sixty years old, and then Mickey's stable mate Donald Duck leaps onscreen in the next section, helping Noah on his ark to Elgar's "Pomp and Circumstance." One animal missed by Noah turns up in Goldberg's animation for Saint-Saens's "Carnival of the Animals." It's a yo-yoing flamingo.

The segments are separated by guest hosts whose contributions seem rather labored; we see Steve Martin, Bette Midler, Itzhak Perlman, James Earl Jones, Angela Lansbury, Quincy Jones, and Penn and Teller. The original film used Deems Taylor, a famed radio commentator, to add an elevated and slightly wry tone; the new approach assumes an audience that needs a laugh break after each exhausting foray into the highbrow.

IMAX films are usually limited to forty-five minutes because of the huge size of the film reels (the projection booth looks like the *Starship Enterprise*). Only *Fantasia 2000* and the Rolling Stones documentary *At the Max* have exceeded that length. *Fantasia 2000* will eventually of course immigrate to home video. But IMAX is the way to see it—not just as a film, but as an event.

Fear and Loathing in Las Vegas ★
R, 128 m., 1998

Johnny Depp (Raoul Duke), Benicio Del Toro (Dr. Gonzo), Ellen Barkin (Waitress), Gary Busey (Highway Patrolman), Cameron Diaz (Blond TV Reporter), Lyle Lovett (Musician at Matrix Club), Flea (Musician). Directed by Terry Gilliam and produced by Laila Nabulsi, Patrick Cassavetti, and Stephen Nemeth. Screenplay by Gilliam, Tony Grisoni, Tod Davies, and Alex Cox, based on the book by Hunter S. Thompson.

Hunter S. Thompson's *Fear and Loathing in Las Vegas* is a funny book by a gifted writer, who seems gifted and funny no longer. He coined the term "gonzo journalism" to describe his guerrilla approach to reporting, which consisted of getting stoned out of his mind, hurling himself at a story, and recording it in frenzied hyperbole.

Thompson's early book on the Hells Angels described motorcyclists who liked to ride as close to the line as they could without losing control. At some point after writing that book, and books on Vegas and the 1972 presidential campaign, Thompson apparently crossed his own personal line. His work became increasingly incoherent and meandering, and reports from his refuge in Woody Creek, Colorado, depicted a man lost in the gloom of his pleasures.

Ah, but he was funny before he flamed out. *Fear and Loathing in Las Vegas* is a film based on the book of the same name, a stream-of-altered-consciousness report of his trip to Vegas with his allegedly Samoan attorney. In the trunk of their car they carried an inventory of grass, mescaline, acid, cocaine, uppers, booze, and ether.

That ether, it's a wicked high. Hurtling through the desert in a gas-guzzling convertible, they hallucinated attacks by giant bats, and "speaking as your attorney," the lawyer advised him on drug ingestion.

The relationship of Thompson and his attorney was the basis of *Where the Buffalo Roam*, an unsuccessful 1980 movie starring Bill Murray as the writer and Peter Boyle as his attorney. Now comes *Fear and Loathing in Las Vegas*, with Johnny Depp and Benicio Del Toro. The hero here is named Duke, which was his name in the original Thompson book and is also the name of the Thompson clone in the *Doonesbury* comic strip. The attorney is Dr. Gonzo. Both Duke and the Doctor are one-dimensional walking chemistry sets, lacking the perspective on themselves that they have in both the book and the strip.

The result is a horrible mess of a movie, without shape, trajectory, or purpose—a one-joke movie, if it had one joke. The two characters wander witlessly past the bizarre backdrops of Las Vegas (some real, some hallucinated, all interchangeable) while zonked out of their minds. Humor depends on attitude. Beyond a certain point, you don't have an attitude; you simply inhabit a state. I've heard a lot of funny jokes about drunks and druggies, but these guys are stoned beyond comprehension, to the point where most of their dialogue could be paraphrased as "eh?"

The story: Thompson has been sent to Vegas to cover the Mint 400, a desert motorcycle race, and stays to report on a convention of district attorneys. Both of these events are dimly visible in the background; the foreground is occupied by Duke and Gonzo, staggering through increasingly hazy days. One of Duke's most incisive interviews is with the maid who arrives to clean the room he's trashed: "You must know what's going on in this hotel! What do you think's going on?"

Johnny Depp has been a gifted and inventive actor in films like *Benny and Joon* and *Ed Wood*. Here he's given a character with no nuances, a man whose only variable is the current degree he's out of it. He plays Duke in disguise, behind strange hats, big shades, and the ever-present cigarette holder. The decision to *always* use the cigarette holder was no doubt inspired by the Duke character in the comic strip, who invariably has one—but a prop in a comic is not the same thing as a prop in a movie, and here it becomes not only an affectation but a handicap: Duke isn't easy to understand at the best of times, and talking through clenched teeth doesn't help. That may explain the narration, in which Duke comments on events that are apparently incomprehensible to himself on screen.

The movie goes on and on, repeating the same setup and the same payoff: Duke and Gonzo take drugs, stagger into new situations, blunder, fall about, wreak havoc, and retreat to their hotel suite. The movie itself has an alcoholic and addict mind-set, in which there is no ability to step outside the need to use and the attempt to function. If you encountered characters like these on an elevator, you'd push a button and get off at the next floor. Here the elevator is trapped between floors for 128 minutes.

The movie's original director was Alex Cox, whose brilliant *Sid & Nancy* showed insight into the world of addiction. Maybe too much insight—he was replaced by Terry Gilliam *(Brazil, Time Bandits)*, whose input is hard to gauge; this is not his proudest moment. Who was the driving force behind the project? Maybe Depp, who doesn't look unlike the young Hunter Thompson but can't communicate the genius beneath the madness.

Thompson may have plowed through Vegas like a madman, but he wrote about his experiences later, in a state which, for him, approached sobriety. You have to stand outside the chaos to see its humor, which is why people remembering the funny things they did when they were drunk are always funnier than drunks doing them.

As for Depp, what was he thinking when he made this movie? He was once in trouble for trashing a New York hotel room, just like the heroes of *Fear and Loathing in Las Vegas*. What was that? Research? After River Phoenix died of an overdose outside Depp's club, you wouldn't think Depp would see much humor in this story—but then, of course, there *isn't* much humor in this story.

Felicia's Journey ★ ★ ★ ½
PG-13, 114 m., 1999

Bob Hoskins (Hilditch), Elaine Cassidy (Felicia), Arsinee Khanjian (Gala), Peter McDonald (Johnny Lysaght), Gerard McSorley (Felicia's Father), Brid Brennan (Mrs. Lysaght), Claire Benedict (Miss Calligary), Danny Turner (Young Hilditch). Directed by Atom Egoyan and produced by Bruce Davey. Screenplay by Egoyan, based on the novel by William Trevor.

Atom Egoyan's *Felicia's Journey* tells the story of two children escaping from their parents. One of the children is middle-aged now, an executive chef for a factory lunchroom. The other is a young Irish girl, in England to seek the boy who said he would write her every day, and then never wrote at all. It is their misfortune that the paths of these two children cross.

The man is named Hilditch. He is played by Bob Hoskins, that sturdy, redoubtable fireplug. At work his staff is in thrall to his verdict. He sips a soup and disapproves: "It starts with the stock!" He lives alone in a huge house where nothing seems to have changed since the 1950s. He spends his evenings cooking ambitious dinners like a saddle of lamb, and eating them all by himself, listening to Mantovani on a record player. His drives a Morris Mini-Minor, a bulbous little car designed along the same lines as its driver.

The girl is named Felicia (Elaine Cassidy). She is sweet and bewildered. She gave her love to Johnny (Peter McDonald), who left for England—to work in a lawn-mower factory, he said. She is pregnant. Johnny has not written. Her father (Gerard McSorley) is a rabid Irish nationalist who is convinced Johnny has gone to join the British Army. He is offended by his daughter's pregnancy not on moral but political grounds: "You are carrying the enemy within you!"

Felicia takes the ferry to England and goes looking for Johnny's lawn-mower factory. Kindly Mr. Hilditch sees her wandering the streets and offers her guidance, and even a ride to a nearby town where Johnny might be working. Hilditch explains that his wife is a patient in the hospital there. We slowly gather that Mr. Hilditch is not a nice man, that he has no wife, that Felicia is in some kind of danger. The look of the film, wet, green, brown, cool, dark, underlines the danger.

The key to *Felicia's Journey* is that it has understanding for both characters—for Felicia, who is innocent, and for Hilditch, who is the product of a childhood that turned him out very wrong. Atom Egoyan is drawn to stories like this, stories about the lasting injuries of childhood, and in one way or another both his *The Sweet Hereafter* and *Exotica* are about damaged girls and predatory men. *Felicia's Journey* is based on a novel by William Trevor, and when he read it, Egoyan must have felt an instant sympathy with the material.

Trevor is one of the greatest living writers, and one who approaches his characters with the belief that to understand all is to forgive all. There are no villains in his work, only deserving and undeserving victims. The story of Felicia is not uncommon: Johnny loved her and left her. If there were more about Johnny in Trevor's story, we would know why. The glimpses we have of Johnny make him seem thoughtless and heartless, but then we see his mother, and get a hint of what he is escaping from.

What we gather about Hilditch, on the other hand, is that as a child he was not mistreated, so much as smothered. Anything is toxic in large enough quantities, even love. We eventually understand his connection to the old videotapes of a French cookery program, which he watches while he prepares food, and we find out why one room of his house is filled with cooking appliances. Hilditch is a real piece of work. We see him mostly as an adult, and then in flashbacks as a child. In both manifestations he reminded me of Alfred Hitchcock, who wanted his tombstone to read: "You see what can happen if you are not a good boy." Hilditch has grown into a bad boy who knows how to seem like a good one, seeking out young and helpless girls and offering them his aid. Naming some of his "lost girls" to Felicia, he says, "I was the world to them. In their time of need, they counted on me."

Some will find the ending of the film, with its door-to-door evangelist (Claire Benedict) unlikely. True, Miss Calligary is a *deus ex machina,* but I prefer her intervention to a more conventional thriller ending. Irony is usually more satisfying than action. And as Hilditch kneels on the wet grass next to a grave, there is pathos and at the same time that cold Hitchcockian humor.

Egoyan is such a devious director, achieving his effects at a level below the surface. He never settles for just telling a story. He shows people trapped in a matrix of their past and their needs. He embraces coincidences and weird lurches in his plots, because he doesn't want us to grow too confident that we know how things must turn out. He almost never provides a tear-jerking scene, an emotional climax, a catharsis. It's as if his films inject materials into our subconscious, and hours later, like a slow reaction in a laboratory retort, they heat up and bubble over. You leave *Felicia's Journey* appreciating it. A week later, you're astounded by it.

Fight Club ★ ★
R, 139 m., 1999

Brad Pitt (Tyler Durden), Edward Norton (Narrator), Helena Bonham Carter (Marla Singer), Meat Loaf Aday (Robert Paulsen), Jared Leto (Angel Face). Directed by David Fincher and produced by Art Linson, Cean Chaffin, and Ross Grayson Bell. Screenplay by Jim Uhls, based on the novel by Chuck Palahniuk.

Fight Club is the most frankly and cheerfully fascist big-star movie since *Death Wish,* a celebration of violence in which the heroes write themselves a license to drink, smoke, screw, and beat each other up. Sometimes, for variety, they beat themselves up. It's macho porn—the sex movie Hollywood has been moving toward for years, in which eroticism between the sexes is replaced by all-guy locker-room fights. Women, who have had a lifetime of practice at dealing with little-boy posturing, will instinctively see through it; men may get off on the testosterone rush. The fact that it is very well made and has a great first act certainly clouds the issue.

Ed Norton stars as a depressed urban loner filled up to here with angst. He describes his world in dialogue of sardonic social satire. His life and job are driving him crazy. As a means of dealing with his pain, he seeks out twelve-step meetings, where he can hug those less fortunate than himself and find catharsis in their suffering. It is not without irony that the first meeting he attends is for postsurgical victims of testicular cancer, since the whole movie is about guys afraid of losing their balls.

These early scenes have a nice sly tone; they're narrated by the Norton character in the kind of voice Nathanael West used in *Miss Lonelyhearts.* He's known only as the Narrator, for reasons later clear. The meetings are working as sedative and his life is marginally manageable when tragedy strikes: He begins to notice Marla (Helena Bonham Carter) at meetings. She's a "tourist" like himself—someone not addicted to anything but meetings. She spoils

it for him. He knows he's a faker, but wants to believe everyone else's pain is real.

On an airplane, he has another key encounter, with Tyler Durden (Brad Pitt), a man whose manner cuts through the fog. He seems able to see right into the Narrator's soul, and shortly after, when the Narrator's high-rise apartment turns into a fireball, he turns to Tyler for shelter. He gets more than that. He gets in on the ground floor of Fight Club, a secret society of men who meet in order to find freedom and self-realization through beating each other into pulp.

It's at about this point that the movie stops being smart and savage and witty, and turns to some of the most brutal, unremitting, nonstop violence ever filmed. Although sensible people know that if you hit someone with an ungloved hand hard enough, you're going to end up with broken bones, the guys in *Fight Club* have fists of steel, and hammer one another while the sound-effects guys beat the hell out of Naugahyde sofas with Ping-Pong paddles. Later, the movie takes still another turn. A lot of recent films seem unsatisfied unless they can add final scenes that redefine the reality of everything that has gone before; call it the Keyser Soze syndrome.

What is all this about? According to Durden, it is about freeing yourself from the shackles of modern life, which imprisons and emasculates men. By being willing to give and receive pain and risk death, Fight Club members find freedom. Movies like *Crash* must play like cartoons for Durden. He's a shadowy, charismatic figure, able to inspire a legion of (white) men in big cities to descend into the secret cellars of Fight Club and beat each other up. Only gradually are the final outlines of his master plan revealed. Is Tyler Durden in fact a leader of men with a useful philosophy? "It's only after we've lost everything that we're free to do anything," he says, sounding like a man who tripped over the Nietzsche display on his way to the coffee bar in Borders. In my opinion, he has no useful truths. He's a bully—Werner Erhard plus S&M, a leather club operator without the decor. None of the Fight Club members grow stronger or freer because of their membership; they're reduced to pathetic cult members. Issue them black shirts and sign them up as skinheads. Whether Durden represents hidden aspects of the male psyche is a question the movie uses as a loophole—but is not able to escape through, because *Fight Club* is not about its ending but about its action.

Of course, *Fight Club* itself does not advocate Durden's philosophy. It is a warning against it, I guess; one critic I like says it makes "a telling point about the bestial nature of man and what can happen when the numbing effects of day-to-day drudgery cause people to go a little crazy." I think it's the numbing effects of movies like this that cause people to go a little crazy. Although sophisticates will be able to rationalize the movie as an argument against the behavior it shows, my guess is that audiences will like the behavior but not the argument. Certainly they'll buy tickets because they can see Pitt and Norton pounding on each other; a lot more people will leave this movie and get in fights than will leave it discussing Tyler Durden's moral philosophy. The images in movies like this argue for themselves, and it takes a lot of narration (or Narration) to argue against them.

Lord knows the actors work hard enough. Norton and Pitt go through almost as much physical suffering in this movie as Demi Moore endured in *G.I. Jane,* and Helena Bonham Carter creates a feisty chain-smoking hellcat who is probably so angry because none of the guys think having sex with her is as much fun as a broken nose. When you see good actors in a project like this, you wonder if they signed up as an alternative to canyoneering.

The movie was directed by David Fincher, and written by Jim Uhls, who adapted the novel by Chuck Palahniuk. In many ways it's like Fincher's movie *The Game* (1997), with the violence cranked up for teenage boys of all ages. That film was also about a testing process in which a man drowning in capitalism (Michael Douglas) has the rug of his life pulled out from under him, and has to learn to fight for survival. I admired *The Game* much more than *Fight Club* because it was really about its theme, while the message in *Fight Club* is like bleeding scraps of Socially Redeeming Content thrown to the howling mob.

Fincher is a good director (his work includes *Alien 3,* one of the best-looking bad movies I have ever seen, and *Seven,* the grisly and intel-ligent thriller). With *Fight Club* he seems to be setting himself some kind of a test—how far over the top can he go? The movie is visceral and hard-edged, with levels of irony and commentary above and below the action. If it had all continued in the vein explored in the first act, it might have become a great film. But the second act is pandering and the third is trickery, and whatever Fincher thinks the message is, that's not what most audiences members will get. *Fight Club* is a thrill ride masquerading as philosophy—the kind of ride where some people puke and others can't wait to get on again.   ☞

The Filth and the Fury ★ ★ ★ ½
R, 105 m., 2000

A documentary directed by Julien Temple and produced by Anita Camarata and Amanda Temple.

At the height of their fame, the Sex Pistols inspired a London city councilor to observe, "Most of these guys would be much improved by sudden death." In a decade when England was racked by unemployment, strikes, and unrest, its season of discontent had a sound track by the Pistols. They sang of "Anarchy in the U.K.," and their song "God Save the Queen (She Ain't No Human Being)" rose to No. 1 on the hit charts—but the record industry refused to name it. In *The Filth and the Fury,* a hard-edged new documentary about the Pistols, we see a Top 10 chart with a blank space for No. 1. Better than being listed, Johnny Rotten grinned.

The saga of the Sex Pistols is told for the third time in *The Filth and the Fury.* Not bad for a band that symbolized punk rock but lasted less than two years, fought constantly, insulted the press, spit on their fans, were banned from TV, were fired by one record company twenty-four hours after being signed, released only one album, pushed safety pins through noses and earlobes to more or less invent body piercing, broke up during a tour of the United States, and saw front man Sid Vicious accused of murdering his girlfriend and dying of a drug overdose.

Director Julien Temple based his *Great Rock*

and Roll Swindle (1980) on a version of the Pistols story supplied by Malcolm McLaren, their infamously self-promoting manager, and now, twenty years later, Temple tells the story through the eyes and in the words of the band members themselves. In between came Alex Cox's *Sid & Nancy* (1986), with Gary Oldman's shattering performance as the self-destructive Sid Vicious.

It wasn't what the band stood for. It was what they stood against. "Attack, attack, attack," says lead singer Johnny Rotten in the film. Now once again John Lydon, he appears along with guitarist Steve Jones, drummer Paul Cook, McLaren, original band member Glen Matlock (deposed by Vicious), and even Vicious himself, in an interview filmed a year before his death. The surviving members are backlit so we cannot see their faces, which would have provided a middle-aged contrast to the savage young men on the screen; McLaren talks from behind a rubber bondage mask like those he and girlfriend Vivienne Westwood sold in their boutique Sex, on Kings' Road.

McLaren claimed the Sex Pistols were entirely his invention, and painted himself as a puppet master. Lydon, who calls him "the manager" throughout the film, says, "There was never a relationship between the manager and me except he stole my ideas and used them as his own." The truth probably resides in between.

I had a glimpse of the Sex Pistols in 1977, when McLaren hired Russ Meyer to direct them in a movie, and Meyer hired me to write it (McLaren and Rotten were fans of our *Beyond the Valley of the Dolls*). I wrote a screenplay in Los Angeles with McLaren feeding me background and ideas. Then Meyer and I flew to London to meet with Rotten, Vicious, Cook, and Jones. (Meyer, wary of McLaren's trademark bondage pants, insisted on sitting on the aisle: "If we have to evacuate, he'll get those goddamned straps tangled up in the seats.")

I remember a surrealistic dinner involving Rotten, Meyer, and myself ("We won the Battle of Britain for you," Meyer sternly lectured Rotten, while I mused that America was not involved in the Battle of Britain and Rotten was Irish). Rotten seemed amused by the fact that Meyer was unintimidated by his fearsomely safety-pinned facade. As we drove him home, he complained bitterly that McLaren had the band on a salary of £8 a week, borrowed £5 from Meyer, and had us stop at an all-night store so he could buy a six-pack of lager and cans of pork and beans.

The truth is, no one made much money off the Pistols, although McLaren made the most. The plug was pulled on our film, *Who Killed Bambi?* after a day and a half of shooting, when the electricians walked off the set after McLaren couldn't pay them. Meyer had presciently demanded his own weekly pay in advance every Monday morning.

The catch-22 with punk rock, and indeed with all forms of entertainment designed to shock and offend the bourgeoisie, is that if your act is *too* convincing, you put yourself out of business, a fact carefully noted by today's rappers as they go as far as they can without going too far.

The Sex Pistols went too far. They never had a period that could be described as actual success. Even touring England at the height of their fame, they were booked into clubs under false names. They were hated by the establishment, shut down by the police, and pilloried by the press ("The Filth and the Fury" was a banner headline occupying a full front page of the *Daily Mirror*). That was bad enough. Worse was that their own fans sometimes attacked them, lashed into a frenzy by the front line of Rotten and Vicious, who were sometimes performers, sometimes bearbaiters.

Rotten was the victim of a razor attack while walking the streets of London; McLaren not only failed to provide security, he wouldn't pay taxi fares. Vicious was his own worst enemy, and if there was one thing that united the other three band members and McLaren, it was hatred for Sid's girlfriend, Nancy Spungen, who they felt was instrumental in his drug addiction. "Poor sod," today's John Lydon says of his dead bandmate.

To see this film's footage from the '70s is to see the beginning of much of pop and fashion iconography for the next two decades. After the premiere of *The Filth and the Fury* at Sundance, I ran into Temple, who observed: "In the scenes where they're being interviewed on television, they look normal. It's the interviewers who look like freaks." Normal, no. But in torn black T-shirts and punk haircuts, they look contemporary, unlike the dated poly-estered, wide-lapeled, and blow-dried crea-tures interviewing them.

England survived the Sex Pistols, and they mostly survived England, although Lydon still feels it is unsafe for him to return there. He now has an interview program on VH-1 and the Web. Cook and Jones lead settled lives. McLaren still has bright ideas. Vivienne West-wood has emerged as one of Britain's most successful designers, and poses for photographs in which she has a perfect resemblance to Mrs. Thatcher. And as for Sid, my notes from the movie say that while the Pistols were signing a record deal in front of Buckingham Palace and insulting the queen, Sid's father was a Grena-dier Guard on duty in front of the palace. Surely I heard that wrong?

Final Destination ★ ★ ★
R, 90 m., 2000

Devon Sawa (Alex Browning), Ali Larter (Clear Rivers), Kerr Smith (Carter Horton), Kristen Cloke (Valerie Lewton), Daniel Roebuck (Agent Weine), Chad E. Donella (Tod Waggner), Seann William Scott (Billy Hitchcock). Directed by James Wong and produced by Glen Morgan, Warren Zide, and Craig Perry. Screenplay by Jeffrey Reddick, Morgan, and Wong.

Final Destination observes the time-honored formula of the Dead Teenager Movie: It be-gins with a lot of living teenagers, and dooms them. But the movie, made by two veterans of *The X Files* TV series, is smarter and more original than most DTMs. It has mordant humor, Rube Goldberg death traps, and sophomoric but earnest discussions of fate. Also an opening sequence that assures this film will never, ever, be shown on an airplane.

The movie begins with a high school class boarding a plane for a class trip to Paris. Alex (Devon Sawa), one of the students, has a vi-sion, vivid and terrifying, of the plane explod-ing in flight. He jumps up to get off, has a fight with another student, and ends up being ejected along with five other students and a teacher. Then the airplane takes off and, you guessed it, explodes in midair.

This scenario is, of course, in the worst pos-sible taste in view of the real-life fate of TWA flight 800, also bound for Paris with students aboard. I will observe that and not belabor it. The explosion is a setup for the rest of the movie, in which it appears that the survivors may also be marked for death—and that Alex is psychic and can foresee their deaths.

Can he really? That's where the movie gets interesting, since instead of using his eerie precognitions as a gimmick, the movie allows the characters to talk urgently about their feel-ings of doom and helplessness. The film in its own way is biblical in its dilemma, although the students use the code word "fate" when what they are really talking about is God. In their own terms, in their own way, using teen-age vernacular, the students have existential discussions.

Final Destination isn't all dialogue, however, and there's a weird disconnection between the words and the action. One after another, the characters die, almost always because of a bizarre chain of connected events. To describe them would be to spoil the fun—if that's what it is—as lightning, natural gas, knives, trains, laundry cords, power lines, and flying metal shards are choreographed by fate (or You Know Who).

Why must these students die? Well, every-body does. Why should they be the exception? As the movie opens, they're filled like most teenagers with a sense of their own immortal-ity, and gradually their dilemma wears them down.

The movie is neither quite serious nor quite ironic; sometimes it's funny, but in a creepy way rather than in the breezier style of the *Scream* movies. The very last shot, set in Paris but filmed in Canada (during a last-minute reshoot in January), is a shaggy dog trick. I laughed, I guess, but the movie really deserves better. My guess is the original ending was more considered, but New Line was afraid of it.

The director is James Wong. He and cowriter Glen Morgan worked on *The X-Files, 21 Jump Street,* and *Millennium.* They haven't made a great or distinguished film, but, working within a tired genre with a talented cast, they've brought unusual substance and impact to the DTM. The vision of the airplane crash is re-markably scary, and other scenes, like a car stopped on railroad tracks, work even though they're clichés—because of the dialogue and the motivations of the characters.

Final Destination will no doubt be a hit and inspire the obligatory sequels. Like the original *Scream*, this movie is too good to be the end of the road. I have visions of my own. I foresee poor Alex making new friends and then envisioning *their* deaths as they embark on ocean liners, trains, buses, and dirigibles. It's a funny thing about Hollywood: It can't seem to get enough of dead teenagers. Talk about biting the hand that feeds you. ☞

Fireworks ★ ★ ★

NO MPAA RATING, 103 m., 1998

Takeshi Kitano (Yoshitaka Nishi), Kayoko Kishimoto (Miyuki [Nishi's wife]), Ren Osugi (Horibe), Susumu Terajima (Nakamura), Tetsu Watanabe (Junkyard Owner), Hakuryu (Yakuza Hitman), Yasuei Yakushiji (Criminal). Directed by Takeshi Kitano and produced by Masayuki Mori, Yasushi Tsuge, and Takio Yoshida. Screenplay by Kitano.

It has been said that Western art is the art of putting in, and Oriental art is the art of leaving out. The Japanese film *Fireworks* is like a Charles Bronson *Death Wish* movie so drained of story, cliché, convention, and plot that nothing is left except pure form and impulse. Not a frame, not a word, is excess. Takeshi Kitano, who made it, must be very serene or very angry; only extreme states allow such a narrow focus.

Kitano, who wrote, directed, and edited the film, stars in it as Nishi, a man whose only two emotional states are agony and ecstasy. As the film opens, he is a policeman whose young daughter died not long ago; now his wife is dying of leukemia. During a stakeout, his partner Horibe (Ron Osugi) suggests he go visit his wife in the hospital. He does, and while he is gone another cop is killed and Horibe is so badly wounded that he will spend his life in a wheelchair.

A cop movie would have dwelled on the action. *Fireworks* reveals what happened only gradually, and at first we even misunderstand the source of the bullets. The movie is not about action, but about consequences and states of mind. Nishi leaves the police force, and we learn, abruptly, that he is deep in debt to yakuza loan sharks. How? Why? Unimportant. All of those scenes that other films find so urgent are swept away here. When punk yakuza collectors arrive in a noodle shop to try to get money from Nishi, he stabs one in the eyeball with a chopstick so suddenly and in a shot so brief that we can hardly believe our eyes.

Nishi cares deeply for his wife, Miyuki (Kayoko Kishimoto), and wants to spend time with her. He robs a bank to raise the necessary cash. They do childish things together, like playing with the kite of a girl they meet on the beach. Sometimes they dissolve in laughter. But when a stranger laughs at Miyuki for trying to water dead flowers, Nishi brutally beats him. And when more collectors arrive from the yakuza, Nishi explodes again.

The pattern of the movie is: ordinary casual life, punctuated by sharp, clinical episodes of violence. Nishi hardly speaks (there is little dialogue in the film), and his face shows almost no expression (reportedly because of injuries to Kitano in a motorcycle crash). He is like a blank slate that absorbs the events in the film without giving any sign that he has registered them. When he attacks, he gives no warning; the wrong trigger word releases his rage.

Nishi is therefore, I suppose, psychotic, a dangerous madman. To read his behavior any other way, as "protecting his wife," say, would be childish. Sane people do not behave like this. And his wife, who hardly says six words in the movie, and who seems unaffected by his brutal behavior, shares the family madness. But that isn't really the point: This is not a clinical study, but a distillation of attitudes. In Kitano's bipolar universe, you are happy when the world leaves you alone, and when it doesn't, you strike back.

Against this swing of yin and yang there is a steadying character: Horibe, the man in the wheelchair. He paints naive and yet colorful and disturbing pictures of people with the faces of flowers. At one point his wheelchair is at the edge of the sea, and we anticipate suicide as the tide washes in, but he is a man who has found some accommodation with life, and will endure. Nishi, on the other hand, has adopted such an inflexible and uncompromising attitude toward the world that it will, we feel, sooner or later destroy him.

The film is an odd viewing experience. It lacks all of the narrative cushions and hand-holding that we have come to expect. It doesn't explain, because an explanation, after all, is simply something arbitrary the story has invented. *Fireworks* is a demonstration of what a story like this is *really* about, fundamentally, after you cut out the background noise.

Flawless ★ ★ ★
R, 111 m., 1999

Robert De Niro (Walt Koontz), Philip Seymour Hoffman (Rusty), Barry Miller (Leonard Wilcox), Wanda De Jesus (Karen), Chris Bauer (Jacko), Daphne Rubin-Vega (Tia), Skipp Sudduth (Tommy), Wilson Jermaine Heredia (Cha-Cha), Nashom Benjamin (Amazing Grace), Scott Allen Cooper (Ivana), Rory Cochrane (Pogo). Directed by Joel Schumacher and produced by Schumacher and Jane Rosenthal. Screenplay by Schumacher.

I don't know if worlds really exist like the one in *Flawless*. I don't know if there are still dance halls in New York where you pay by the dance, although I see them from time to time in the movies. Or rooming houses where everyone is a character out of Tennessee Williams. Or stories that can involve, at the same time, hero cops, drag queens, two-bit drug dealers, and gay Republicans.

I don't know, and I don't much care, because Joel Schumacher's *Flawless* is more fable than slice-of-life, and all these people and props give Robert De Niro and Philip Seymour Hoffman their opening to create two screwy characters from opposite ends of the great personality divide. The only reason you can't say they deserve each other is that nobody deserves Walt Koontz.

Koontz is the De Niro character, a security guard who was a hero back in 1988 during a hostage crisis. Now he's getting too old for the work. One night he gets involved in a disturbance in the flophouse where he lives. A stroke leaves him partially paralyzed; his speech is slurred and his walk is a lurch from one handhold to the next. His life seems over. It looked pretty drab to begin with. One night a week he went to a dance hall and paid for dances with

Karen (Wanda De Jesus), and we sense the screenplay using heroic restraint to avoid the words, "Come on, big boy—10 cents a dance."

Walt's reaction to the stroke is despair, which he presents as anger. His buddies from work come to see him, but he's not interested. He retreats inside a shell. This is a man who had few enough resources for keeping himself amused before the stroke, and now his pastime of choice is sitting and brooding. Nor can he get to know his neighbors, since most of the other residents of the flophouse seem to be hookers, drag queens, or both, and he makes no secret of his distaste for homosexuals.

One of the neighbors is a drag artist named Rusty (Philip Seymour Hoffman). Some men can transform themselves into pretty women; they study *Vogue* magazine. Others do not make pretty women and study the works of Sophie Tucker. Rusty is in the second category—a good soul stuck in a completely impractical lifestyle that involves trying to pay the rent with one-liners instead of cash.

Walt contemplates suicide. Rehabilitation therapy is suggested—singing lessons, for example, to help his speech. Rusty has a piano, and Walt swallows his fierce pride and asks for lessons. Rusty needs the money, and agrees. They make a touching couple, there on the piano bench. Walt probably figures taking singing lessons from a drag queen is marginally preferable to sticking his gun into his mouth and pulling the trigger.

The plot of *Flawless* is too busy and sometimes strays into fictional hinterlands; Rusty's posse of drag friends has a way of turning up on cue, like the factory workers in *Carmen*. The subplot about hidden drug money is a creaky distraction. But when the movie involves Walt and Rusty, it has a wacky charm. De Niro spends most of the movie locked inside a stroke-induced slur, but somehow manages to communicate despite his character's difficult speech (Rusty observes he has no troubles with the f-sound). He's a pathetic coot who begins to grow on us, and for Rusty, who is a soft touch anyway, he's an opportunity for the mother hen routine.

There's also intrigue involving two women from the dance hall—not only the money-minded Karen, but also the younger, gentler

Tia (Daphne Rubin-Vega), who has one of the movie's most touching moments. When she comes to visit Walt, he says he's sure his buddy paid her to do it: "I get it. Harvey paid you. He felt sorry for me." Tia replies quietly, "Feel sorry for you? I never felt sorry for you, Walt, until now."

De Niro is a great technical actor who may have been attracted to this material because of the chance to play a stroke victim. His performance not only gets Walt's symptoms right, but also shows sympathy for the man inside. Hoffman, who played the pathetic man who made dirty phone calls in *Happiness,* shows he's one of the best new character actors, able to take a flamboyant role and find the quiet details in it. Too bad they're stuck in a jumbled plot, but as an odd couple, they work.

The Flintstones in
Viva Rock Vegas ½★
PG, 90 m., 2000

Mark Addy (Fred Flintstone), Stephen Baldwin (Barney Rubble), Kristen Johnston (Wilma Slaghoople), Jane Krakowski (Betty O'Shale), Thomas Gibson (Chip Rockefeller), Joan Collins (Pearl Slaghoople), Alex Meneses (Roxie), Alan Cumming (Gazoo/Mike Jagged). Directed by Brian Levant and produced by Bruce Cohen. Screenplay by Deborah Kaplan, Harry Elfont, Jim Cash, and Jack Epps Jr.

The Flintstones in Viva Rock Vegas has dinosaurs that lumber along crushing everything in their path. The movie's screenplay works sort of the same way. Think of every possible pun involving stones, rocks, and prehistoric times, and link them to a pea-brained story that creaks and groans on its laborious march through unspeakably obvious, labored, and idiotic humor.

This is an ideal first movie for infants, who can enjoy the bright colors on the screen and wave their tiny hands to the music. Children may like it because they just plain like going to the movies. But it's not delightful or funny or exciting, and for long stretches it looks exactly like hapless actors standing in front of big rocks and reciting sitcom dialogue.

The story isn't a sequel to *The Flintstones* (1994) but a prequel, recalling those youthful days when Fred and Wilma Flintstone first met and fell in love. Fred is portrayed this time by Mark Addy, the beefiest of the guys in *The Full Monty.* His best pal, Barney Rubble, is played by Stephen Baldwin, who recites his lines as if he hopes Fred will ask him to come out and play, but is afraid he won't. As the movie opens Fred and Barney have gotten jobs at the rock quarry, and have settled down to a lifetime of quarrying rocks, which their world does not seem to need any more of, but never mind.

Meanwhile, in a parallel plot, Wilma Slaghoople (Kristen Johnston) resists the schemes of her mother (Joan Collins) to get her to marry the millionaire Chip Rockefeller (get it?). Fleeing the rich neighborhood, she ends up working in a drive-in restaurant ("Bronto King") with Betty O'Shale (Jane Krakowski), and soon the two of them have met Fred and Barney. There's instant chemistry, and the two couples grind off to a weekend in Rock Vegas. The jealous Chip (Thomas Gibson) is waiting there to foil romance and get his hands on the Slaghoople fortune. His conspirator is a chorusline beauty named Roxie (Second City grad Alex Meneses), whose boulders are second to none. The Vegas sequence is livened by a soundtrack rendition of "Viva Las (and/or Rock) Vegas" by Ann-Margret.

Another story line involves Gazoo (Alan Cumming), an alien who arrives in a flying saucer. He looks exactly like a desperate measure to flesh out an uninteresting plot with an uninteresting character. The movie would be no better and no worse without Gazoo, which is a commentary on both Gazoo and the movie, I think.

The pun, it has been theorized, is the lowest form of humor. This movie proves that theory wrong. There is a lower form of humor: jokes about dinosaur farts. The pun is the second lowest form of humor. The third lowest form is laborious plays on words, as when we learn that the Rock Vegas headliners include Mick Jagged and the Stones.

Minute by weary minute the movie wends its weary way toward its joyless conclusion, as if everyone in it is wearing concrete overshoes, which, come to think of it, they may be. The first film was no masterpiece, but it was a lot better than this. Its slot for an aging but glamorous beauty queen was filled by Elizabeth Taylor. This time it is Joan Collins. As Joan Collins is to Elizabeth Taylor, so *The Flintstones in Viva Rock Vegas* is to *The Flintstones*. ☞

Follow Me Home ★ ★ ★

NO MPAA RATING, 102 m., 1998

Alfre Woodard (Evey), Benjamin Bratt (Abel), Jesse Borrego (Tudee), Steve Reevis (Freddy), Calvin Levels (Kaz), Tom Bower (Larry), John Allen Nelson (Perry). Directed by Peter Bratt and produced by Bratt, Irene Romero, and Alan Renshaw. Screenplay by Bratt.

After *Follow Me Home* was turned down by every mainstream distributor in America, a new distribution plan was conceived: It would be booked one theater at a time around the country, with a discussion scheduled after almost every screening. For the last year this difficult, challenging film has found audiences in that way. There is a lot to discuss afterward.

The film is about four graffiti mural artists who pile into a van and head cross-country from Los Angeles to Washington with a plan to cover the White House with their paintings. In an age when Cristo wraps up buildings, this is perhaps not as far-fetched as it sounds, although I imagine they'll have trouble getting a National Endowment grant through Congress.

The artists include an African-American, an American Indian, and two Chicanos; on their odyssey most of the people they meet are white weirdos. One is reminded of the ominous rednecks encountered by the hippie motorcyclists in *Easy Rider*. The whites are stereotyped in broad, unfair strokes, but then the movie throws you off balance by throwing in one decent white guy and one redeemable one, and by making one of the painters into a fulminating cauldron of prejudice. By the end, you realize *Follow Me Home* isn't making a tidy statement about anything, but is challenging the audience to make up its own mind: to view racial attitudes and decide where they come from and what lies beneath them.

The writer-director, Peter Bratt, might almost have taken *Easy Rider* as his model—the parts that work, and the other parts too. Some of his dialogue scenes are too long and disorganized, but then suddenly everything snaps together in a scene of real power.

Consider, for example, a scene in a diner where a waitress feels she's been mistreated by one of the men (she is right). The owner comes out, lays a shotgun on the table, and delivers a lecture about their right to free speech and his right to bear arms. What is this scene about? A racist gun owner? Not necessarily, or entirely. The four men in the booth have different ways of seeing the situation, and the scene is about styles of intimidation.

Along the road, the men encounter whites wearing various costumes. There's a white guy who dresses like an Indian; they steal his antique tomahawk. Later, they encounter three white guys dressed in uniform for a U.S. Cavalry reenactment. Are they so inflamed they mistake the men of color for savage redskins? The development and outcome of this scene is hard to believe, but since it builds into magic realism, belief isn't the point. It's about a battle between two myths: the white myth of taming the West, and the black/Indian myth of soul power.

A key character in the film, encountered midway, is an African-American woman played by Alfre Woodard. She takes a lift from the guys, and gets angry when one of them can think of no words for a woman except "whore" and "bitch." Her powerful speech ("Look at me! I am a woman!") quiets him, and later woman power saves them all.

The personal styles of the four painters are all different. The black guy (Calvin Levels) is an intellectual, vegetarian, and pacifist, who uses terms like "patriarchal theocracy." The Indian guy (Steve Reevis) is a recovering alcoholic (a little stereotyping there?). The leader of the expedition, Tudee (Jesse Borrego), is the idealist whose vision brought them together. His cousin Abel (Benjamin Bratt) is angry at everyone, especially women. Are they a cross section? No, just a collection.

Watching the film, I resented the broad caricatures of whites. Then I reflected that broad caricatures of blacks were a feature of movies for decades and decades; just their luck that when a generation of black filmmakers arrives, stereotyping has gone out of style. I don't think Bratt is a racist, however: He's an instigator. He's putting highly charged material on the screen and standing back to see what happens. Most movies are too timid to deal in such controversy.

Follow Me Home is being shown in just the right way. It needs that discussion afterward. It doesn't come as a package that you can wrap up and take home. It's open-ended. It shows how films can cut, probe, and wound. It can awaken a sense of fair play in the audience. And in its fantasy and symbolism, it evokes a mystery level, beneath explanation. Most movies are over when they're over. This one is only beginning.

Forces of Nature ★
PG-13, 103 m., 1999

Sandra Bullock (Sarah), Ben Affleck (Ben), Maura Tierney (Bridget), Steve Zahn (Alan), Blythe Danner (Virginia Cahill), Ronny Cox (Hadley Cahill), David Strickland (Steve), Meredith Scott Lynn (Debbie). Directed by Bronwen Hughes and produced by Susan Arnold, Ian Bryce, and Donna Roth. Screenplay by Marc Lawrence.

So I'm sitting there, looking in disbelief at the ending of *Forces of Nature,* and asking myself— if this is how the movie ends, *then what was it about?* We spend two endless hours slogging through a series of natural and man-made disasters with Sandra Bullock and Ben Affleck, and then . . . that's it?

Bronwen Hughes's *Forces of Nature* is a romantic shaggy dog story, a movie that leads us down the garden path of romance, only to abandon us by the compost heap of uplifting endings. And it's not even clever enough to give us the right happy ending. It gives us the *wrong* happy ending.

By then, of course, any ending is good news. The movie is a dead zone of boring conversations, contrived emergencies, unbelievable characters, and lame storytelling. Even then it might have worked at times if it had generated the slightest chemistry between Ben Affleck and Sandra Bullock, but it doesn't. She remains winsome and fetching, but he acts like he's chaperoning his best friend's sister as a favor.

The movie combines at least five formulas, and probably more: the Meet Cute, the Road Movie, the Odd Couple, Opposites Attract, and Getting to Know Yourself. It also cuts back and forth between a journey and the preparations for a marriage, and it tries to keep two sets of parents in play. With so much happening it's surprising that the movie finds a way to be boring, but it does, by cross-cutting between one leaden scene and another.

Affleck stars as an ad man who is flying from New York to Savannah, Georgia, for his wedding. On the plane, he's strapped in next to Bullock, who has held a lot of jobs in her time: flight attendant, wedding photographer, exotic dancer, auto show hostess. The flight crashes on takeoff, and they end up driving to Georgia together amid weather reports of an approaching hurricane.

Of course, circumstances conspire to make him pretend to be a doctor, and them to pretend they're married, and a motel to put them in the same room, and his best man to see him with this strange woman even though he tries to hide by holding his breath in a swimming pool, and so on. Rarely does the artificial contrivance of a bad screenplay reveal itself so starkly on the screen. And when the contrivances stop the revelations begin, and we learn sad things about Bullock's past that feel exactly as if Marc Lawrence, the writer, supplied them at random.

They have a lot of adventures. Arrests, crashes, trees falling on their car, hospitalizations. They take a train for a while (standing on top of one of the cars in a shamelessly pandering shot). And they take a bus (with condo-shopping oldsters). And a Spinning Sombrero ride. At one point they both find themselves performing onstage in a strip club—not quite the kind of club you have in mind. This scene would seem to be foolproof comedy, but the timing is off and it sinks.

Despite my opening comments, I have not actually revealed the ending of the movie, and I won't, although I will express outrage about it. This movie hasn't paid enough dues to get away with such a smarmy payoff. I will say, however, that if the weatherman has been warning for three days that a hurricane is headed thisaway, and the skies are black and the wind is high and it's raining, few people in formal dress for a wedding would stand out in the yard while umbrellas, tables, and trees are flying past. And if they did, their hair would blow around a little, don't you think?

For Love of the Game ★ ½
PG-13, 128 m., 1999

Kevin Costner (Billy Chapel), Kelly Preston (Jane Aubrey), John C. Reilly (Gus Sinski), Jena Malone (Heather), Brian Cox (Gary Wheeler), J. K. Simmons (Frank Perry), Vin Scully (Himself), Steve Lyons (Himself). Directed by Sam Raimi and produced by Armyan Bernstein and Amy Robinson. Screenplay by Dana Stevens, based on the novel by Michael Shaara.

You know those quizzes they run in women's magazines about testing your relationship? *For Love of the Game* is about the kinds of people who give the wrong answers. It's the most lugubrious and soppy love story in many a moon, a step backward for director Sam Raimi after *A Simple Plan,* and yet another movie in which Kevin Costner plays a character who has all the right window dressing but is neither juicy nor interesting.

Costner plays Billy Chapel, a forty-year-old pitcher for the Detroit Tigers, facing retirement at the end of a mediocre season. As the film opens, he's set the stage for a candlelit dinner in his New York hotel, but his date never arrives, he drinks the champagne and all the booze in the minibar, and next day he wakes up with a hangover and learns (a) crusty old Mr. Wheeler is selling the team because his sons don't want it, (b) he's being traded, and (c) Jane, the girl he was waiting for, is leaving him and taking a job in London because "you don't need me—you're perfect with you and the ball and the diamond." Not what you want to hear when you're facing retirement.

The movie has a screenplay that lumbers between past and present like regret on a death march. Billy suits up for his final game of the season, and as he starts pitching we get the "Five Years Earlier" card, and the movie cuts back and forth between his quest to pitch a perfect game, and his memories of his love affair with Jane. Will he pitch the perfect game and save the relationship? Or will he throw a home-run pitch in the bottom of the ninth,

while the girl disappears? What's your best guess?

Five Years Earlier, he first encountered Jane (Kelly Preston) in a Meet Cute, when he saw her kicking her rented VW by the side of the expressway. He's able to get the car running again, and likes her at first sight—even though she doesn't know who he is until the tow-truck guy says, "Hey—you're Billy Chapel!" He is indeed a baseball great, and soon she's complaining, "I need a regular guy. Not the guy in the Old Spice commercials." "It was Right Guard," he says. "I was being metaphorical," she says. She's also not thrilled by kids who collect his picture on bubble-gum cards. "They buy them for the gum," he says, revealing he's seriously out of touch. Today's wise child preserves the original wrappers, and finances his college education by selling them on eBay.

The rhythm of their relationship quickly grows sour. She keeps turning up, and he keeps pushing her away and then needing her when she's gone. She weeps when they're together, he weeps when they're apart. Typical crisis: One winter weekend, he's unwisely sawing some lumber with a rotary saw and cuts his hand. She packs it in snow, but isn't allowed on the medevac helicopter, is dissed by the obligatory rude nurse in the ER ("Are you his wife?"), and is crushed when Billy tells her the team trainer is "the most important person for me right now."

Another crisis. He's in Boston for a game and gets a panic call: Her daughter has run away from home and gone to Boston to seek her dad, who wasn't at home, so now she's alone in the big city. Billy didn't know she had a daughter. "What's her name?" he asks. "Freedom," she says. "Scared you, didn't I? It's Heather." Just the sort of quip a mother would make during a panic call. (In a wittier movie, she would have said, "Heather. Scared you, didn't I? It's Freedom.")

The screenplay, written by Dana Stevens and based on a novel by Michael Shaara, includes getting-to-know-you stuff ("Do you like white meat or dark?"), jealousy ("She's my masseuse."), and sports lore ("All the guys are here for you, Billy."). Some of the sports scenes consist of Costner on the mound, lost in thought (at one point the catcher is concerned because he's staring at clouds), but there are some nice details when he shuts out all the crowd noises, and when he directs a running monologue at each batter he faces. And of course no sports movie has any trouble building suspense at the end of the big game.

The ending is routine: false crisis, false dawn, real crisis, real dawn. Only a logician would wonder why two people meet in a place where neither one would have the slightest reason to be. Thinking back through the movie, I cannot recall a single thing either character said that was worth hearing in its own right, apart from the requirements of the plot. No, wait: She asks him, "What if my face was all scraped off and I was basically disfigured and had no arms and legs and no (something else, can't read my handwriting). Would you still love me?" And he replies, "No. But we could still be friends."

42 Up ★ ★ ★ ★
NO MPAA RATING, 139 m., 2000

A documentary series directed and produced by Michael Apted.

"Give me the child until he is seven, and I will show you the man."
—Jesuit saying

In 1964, a British television network began an intriguing experiment. They would interview a group of seven-year-olds, asking them what they wanted to do in life and what kind of a future they envisioned. Then these same subjects would be revisited every seven years to see how their lives were turning out. It was an intriguing experiment, using film's unique ability to act as a time machine—"the most remarkable nonfiction film project in the history of the medium," wrote Andrew Sarris.

Now here is *42 Up*, the sixth installment in the series. I have seen them all since *14 Up*, and every seven years the series measures out my own life too. It is impossible to see the films without asking yourself the same questions—without remembering yourself as a child and a teenager, and evaluating the progress of your life.

I feel as if I know these subjects, and indeed I do know them better than many of the people I work with every day, because I know what they dreamed of at seven, their hopes at fourteen, the problems they faced in their early twenties, and their marriages, their jobs, their children, even their adulteries.

When I am asked for career advice, I tell students that they should spend more time preparing than planning. Life is so ruled by luck and chance, I say, that you may end up doing a job that doesn't even exist yet. Don't think you can map your life, but do pack for the journey. Good advice, I think, and yet I look at *42 Up* and I wonder if our fates are sealed at an early age. Many of the subjects of the series seemed to know at seven what they wanted to do and what their aptitudes were, and they were mostly right. Others produce surprises, and keep on producing them right into middle age.

Michael Apted could not have predicted that his future would include a lifelong commitment to this series. He was a young man at the beginning of his career when he worked as a researcher on *7 Up*, choosing the fourteen subjects who would be followed. He became the director of *14 Up*, and has guided the series ever since, taking time off from a busy career as the director of feature films (*Coal Miner's Daughter, Gorillas in the Mist*). In his introduction to a new book about the series, he says he does not envy his subjects: "They do get notoriety and it's the worst kind of fame—without power or money. They're out in the street getting on with their lives and people stop them and say, 'Aren't you that girl?' or 'Don't I know you?' or 'You're the one,' and most of them hate that."

The series hasn't itself changed their lives, he believes. "They haven't got jobs or found partners because of the film, except in one case when a friendship developed with dramatic results."

That case involves Neil, who for most long-time followers of the series has emerged as the most compelling character. He was a brilliant but pensive boy, who at seven said he wanted to be a bus driver, so he could tell the passengers what to look for out the windows; he saw himself in the driver's seat, a tour guide for the lives of others. What career would you guess for him? An educator? A politician?

In later films he seemed to drift, unhappy and without direction. He fell into confusion.

At twenty-eight, he was homeless in the Highlands of Scotland, and I remember him sitting outside his shabby house trailer on the rocky shore of a loch, looking forlornly across the water. He won't be around for the next film, I thought: Neil has lost his way. He survived, and at thirty-five was living in poverty on the rough Shetland Islands, where he had just been deposed as the (unpaid) director of the village pageant; he felt the pageant would be going better if he were still in charge.

The latest chapter in Neil's story is the most encouraging of all the episodes in *42 Up*, and part of the change is because of his fellow film subject Bruce, who was a boarding school boy, studied math at Oxford, and then gave up a career in the insurance industry to become a teacher in London inner-city schools. Bruce has always seemed one of the happiest of the subjects. At forty, he got married. Neil moved to London at about that time, was invited to the wedding, found a job through Bruce, and today—well, I would not want to spoil your surprise when you find the unlikely turn his life has taken.

Apted says in his introduction to the book *42 Up* (The New Press, $16.95) that if he had the project to do again, he would have chosen more middle-class subjects (his sample was weighted toward the upper and working classes), and more women. He had a reason, though, for choosing high and low: The original question asked by the series was whether Britain's class system was eroding. The answer seems to be: yes, but slowly. Sarris, writing in the *New York Observer*, delivers this verdict: "At one point, I noted that the upper-class kids, who sounded like twits at 7 compared to the more spontaneous and more lovable lower-class kids, became more interesting and self-confident as they raced past their social inferiors. It was like shooting fish in a barrel. Class, wealth, and social position did matter, alas, and there was no getting around it."

None of the fourteen have died yet, although three have dropped out of the project (some drop out for a film and are back for the next one). By now many have buried their parents. Forced to confront themselves at seven, fourteen, twenty-one, twenty-eight, and thirty-five, they seem mostly content with the way things have turned out. Will they all live to forty-nine? Will the series continue until none are alive? This series should be sealed in a time capsule. It is on my list of the ten greatest films of all time, and is a noble use of the medium.

☞

Four Days in September ★ ★
R, 113 m., 1998

Alan Arkin (Charles Burke Elbrick), Pedro Cardoso (Fernando/Paulo), Fernanda Torres (Maria), Luiz Fernando Guimaraes (Marcao), Claudia Abreu (Renee), Nelson Dantas (Toledo), Matheus Nachtergaele (Jonas), Marco Ricca (Henrique). Directed by Bruno Barreto and produced by Lucy Barreto. Screenplay by Leopoldo Serran.

A quiet sadness hovers over *Four Days in September*, the story of young Brazilian revolutionaries who are described even by a government torturer as "innocent kids with big dreams." Based on a memoir by one of a group who kidnapped the American ambassador in 1969, the film examines the way that naive idealists took on more than they could handle.

The movie opens with newsreel footage of demonstrations against a military junta that overthrew the democratic government of Brazil, suspended freedoms, and ran a reign of terror. After the free press was shut down, a group of students decided that kidnapping the ambassador would be one way to get attention for their demands to release political prisoners.

In most movies about political terrorists, the characters are hard-edged and desperate, and the planning is incisive. Not here. The October 8 Revolutionary Movement uses the time-tested system of being sure no one in a cell knows the names of the others (that's also a way of concealing how few cells there may be). But two of the members conceal their friendship, and when one is captured by the police, it doesn't take long to make him talk.

Meanwhile, Paulo (Pedro Cardoso), the most intelligent and uncertain of the kidnappers, forms a bond with the kidnapped American (Alan Arkin). Guarding him for long hours, Paulo feels a certain gentleness toward the older man, who maintains his own dignity.

Since Paulo may be called on to shoot the ambassador, this leads to an impossible situation.

The movie cuts between the kidnappers and the police, showing both sides more or less aware of the other's moves. Indeed, there's an amateurish air about the whole situation. As the terrorists wait to intercept the ambassador's Cadillac, a woman looking out her window finds them suspicious and tries to warn the police, who ignore her. And, incredibly, after two cops knock on the gang's hideout, Paulo is able to follow them back to headquarters and eavesdrop at a window to find out how much they know.

These are not brilliant revolutionaries. They're found by the cops because of their large orders of take-out food ("If only they had learned to cook!" a cop says), and at one point, as they wait uneasily inside the house where they're holding the ambassador, the sound track is filled with the same mournful passage from Mascagni's "Cavalleria Rusticana" that opens Scorsese's *Raging Bull*. The tone is not one of determination, but of regret.

I suppose the purpose of the film is to humanize both sides. It succeeds only to a degree. We can sense what the film wants to say better than the film can say it. Political terrorism may be justified in some situations (when it's your revolution, you call it heroism), but these callow students are in over their heads. And making the police and torturers into more human characters doesn't excuse them. Although the kidnapping did result in the release of some political prisoners, it's unclear whether it sped the day of Brazil's return to democracy. And for the participants, in retrospect, it may have been an unwise strategy.

Four Days in September was directed by Bruno Barreto, best known in America for *Dona Flor and Her Two Husbands*. Its screenplay, by Leopoldo Serran, is based on the book by Fernando Gabeira (who took the revolutionary name Paulo). He is now an elected official, and we sense a mixture of pride and regret in his memories. Films of the 1960s (*Z, The Battle of Algiers*) were sure of their sympathies. Costa-Gavras's *State of Siege* (1973), about the kidnapping and killing of an American official in Uruguay, was uncompromising in its portrait of U.S. interference in another country's politics.

It was also more clear in its consideration of the choice facing the kidnappers, who stood to lose whether they killed the official or not. This film is more muddled, and by the end we are not quite sure what we feel—or, in the final scene, what the young revolutionaries feel, either. The point of view is that of a middle-aged man who no longer quite understands why, as a youth, he was so sure of things that now seem so puzzling.

Frequency ★ ★ ★ ½
PG-13, 117 m., 2000

Dennis Quaid (Frank Sullivan), Jim Caviezel (John Sullivan), Andre Braugher (Satch DeLeon), Elizabeth Mitchell (Julia Sullivan), Noah Emmerich (Gordo Hersch), Shawn Doyle (Jack Shepard), Jordan Bridges (Graham Gibson), Melissa Errico (Samantha Thomas), Daniel Henson (Johnny Sullivan [Six]). Directed by Gregory Hoblit and produced by Hawk Koch, Hoblit, Bill Carraro, and Toby Emmerich. Screenplay by Emmerich.

I know exactly where the tape is, in which box, on which shelf. It's an old reel-to-reel tape I used with the tape recorder my dad bought me in grade school. It has his voice on it. The box has moved around with me for a long time, but I have never listened to the tape since my dad died. I don't think I could stand it. It would be too heartbreaking.

I thought about the tape as I was watching Gregory Hoblit's *Frequency*. Here is a movie that uses the notion of time travel to set up a situation where a man in 1999 is able to talk to his father in 1969, even though his father died when the man was six. The movie harnesses this notion to a lot of nonsense, including a double showdown with a killer, but the central idea is strong and carries us along. There must be something universal about our desire to defeat time, which in the end defeats us.

The father in 1969 is named Frank Sullivan (Dennis Quaid). He is a fireman, and he dies heroically while trying to save a life in a warehouse fire. The son in 1999 is named John Sullivan (Jim Caviezel), and he has broken with three generations of family tradition to become a policeman instead of a fireman. One night he's rummaging under the stairs of the family house where he still lives, and finds a trunk containing his dad's old ham radio. The plot provides some nonsense about sunspots and the northern lights, but never mind: What matters is that the father and the son can speak to each other across a gap of thirty years.

The paradox of time travel is familiar. If you could travel back in time to change the past in order to change the future, you would already have done so, and therefore the changes would have resulted in the present that you now occupy. Of course, the latest theories of quantum physics speculate that time may be a malleable dimension, and that countless new universes are splitting off from countless old ones all the time—we can't see them because we're always on the train, not in the station, and the view out the window is of this and this and this, not that and that.

But *Frequency* is not about physics, and the heroes are as baffled as we are by the paradoxes they get involved in. Consider a scene where the father uses a soldering iron to burn into a desk the message: "I'm still here, Chief." His son sees the letters literally appearing in 1999 as they are written in 1969. How can this be? If they were written in 1969, wouldn't they have already been on the desk for thirty years? Not at all, the movie argues, because every action in the past *changes* the future into a world in which that action has taken place.

Therefore—and here is the heart of the story—the son, knowing what he knows now, can reach back in time and save his father's life by telling him what he did wrong during that fatal fire. And the father and son can exchange information that will help each one fight a serial killer who, in various time-line configurations, is active now, then, and in between, and threatens both men and, in some configurations, the fireman's wife. How do the voices know they can trust each other? The voice in the future can tell the voice in the past exactly what's going to happen with the Amazing Mets in the '69 Series.

Are you following this? Neither did I, half the time. At one point both the father and the son are fighting the same man at points thirty years separated, and when the father shoots off the 1969 man's hand, it disappears from the 1999 version of the man. But then the 1999 man would remember how he lost the hand,

right? And therefore would know—but, no, not in this time line he wouldn't.

There may be holes and inconsistencies in the plot. I was too confused to be sure. And I don't much care, anyway, because the underlying idea is so appealing—that a son who doesn't remember his father could talk to him by shortwave and they could try to help each other. This notion is fleshed out by the father's wife (Elizabeth Mitchell), who must also be saved by the time-talkers, by partners in the fire and police department, and so on. By the end of the movie, the villain (Shawn Doyle) is fighting father and son simultaneously, and there is only one way to watch the movie, and that is with complete and unquestioning credulity. To attempt to unravel the plot leads to frustration if not madness.

Moviegoers seem to like supernatural stories that promise some kind of escape from our mutual doom. *Frequency* is likely to appeal to the fans of *The Sixth Sense, Ghost,* and other movies where the characters find a loophole in reality. What it also has in common with those two movies is warmth and emotion. Quaid and Caviezel bond over the radio, and we believe the feelings they share. The ending of the movie is contrived, but then of course it is: The whole movie is contrived. The screenplay conferences on *Frequency* must have gone on and on, as writer Toby Emmerich and the filmmakers tried to fight their way through the maze they were creating. The result, however, appeals to us for reasons as simple as hearing the voice of a father you thought you would never hear again. ☞

Friends & Lovers ½★
NO MPAA RATING, 102 m., 1999

Stephen Baldwin (Jon), Danny Nucci (David), George Newbern (Ian), Alison Eastwood (Lisa), Claudia Schiffer (Carla), Suzanne Cryer (Jane), David Rasche (Richard), Neill Barry (Keaton), Robert Downey Jr. (Hans). Directed by George Haas and produced by Josi W. Konski. Screenplay by Haas.

I don't want to review *Friends & Lovers;* I want to flunk it. This movie is not merely bad, but incompetent. I get tapes in the mail from tenth-graders that are better made than this.

Recently I hosted the first Overlooked Film Festival at the University of Illinois, for films that have been unfairly overlooked. If I ever do a festival of films that deserve to be overlooked, here is my opening night selection. The only possible explanation for the film being released is that there are stars in the cast (Stephen Baldwin, Claudia Schiffer, Alison Eastwood, Robert Downey Jr). They should sue their agents.

The story involves a group of friends spending the holidays in a Park City ski chalet. They're involved in what an adolescent might think were adult relationships. Much time is spent in meaningless small talk. We also get the ultimate sign of writer desperation: characters introducing themselves to each other.

If I were marking this as a paper, I would note:

—Director George Haas often lines up actors so they awkwardly face the camera and have to talk sideways to one another.

—Much of the dialogue is handled by cutting to each character as he speaks. This is jarring because it reveals that the movie knows when each character will speak. Professional movies overlap sound and image so that dialogue begins offscreen, before a cut to the speaker.

—The characters frequently propose toasts, as if the movie is a social occasion.

—Pregnant girl looks like she has a pillow stuffed down her dress. Self-consciously holds her belly with both hands in many scenes.

—Dad puts tin can in microwave. Can explodes, and whole chalet is plunged into darkness. I am not surprised that a character in this movie would be stupid enough to microwave an unopened can, but why would the explosion blow every fuse?

—Characters gossip that one character has a big penis. Everyone strips for the Jacuzzi. Movie supplies close-up of penis. Since this is the first nudity of any kind in the movie, audience is jolted. In a light comedy, a close-up of a penis strikes a jarring note. An amazed reaction shot might work, but represents a level of sophistication beyond the reach of this film.

—The general preoccupation with sex and size reminds me of conversations I had when I was eleven. One guy says a female character has two-inch nipples. No one questions this theory. I say two-inch nipples are extremely rare among bipeds.

—Dad says, "My generation thought that working was the best way to support a family." Dad doesn't even know what generation he belongs to. Dad is in his fifties, so is a member of the sixties generation. He is thinking of his parents' generation.

—All dialogue on ski slopes involves ludicrous echoing effects. Yes, a yodel will echo in the Alps. No, conversational levels will not echo in Utah.

—David seems to be a virgin. Friend asks, "You have never done the dirty deed?" David asks, "How exactly would you define that?" Friend makes circle with thumb and finger, sticks another finger through it. Most twentysomething movie characters have advanced beyond this stage.

—Automobile scenes are inept. One "crash" is obviously faked to avoid damaging either vehicle. In a scene that cuts between girl walking by road while a guy drives beside her and talks through open window, the girl is walking at a slower rate of speed than car.

I have often asked myself, "What would it look like if the characters in a movie were animatronic puppets created by aliens with an imperfect mastery of human behavior?" Now I know.

Frogs for Snakes no stars
R, 98 m., 1999

Barbara Hershey (Eva), Robbie Coltrane (Al), Harry Hamlin (Klench), Ian Hart (Quint), David Deblinger (UB), John Leguizamo (Zip), Ron Perlman (Gascone), Lisa Marie (Myrna), Debi Mazar (Simone). Directed by Amos Poe and produced by Phyllis Freed Kaufman. Screenplay by Poe.

Amos Poe's *Frogs for Snakes* is not a film so much as a filmed idea. That could be interesting, but alas, it is a very bad idea. The film is about a group of Manhattan actors who support themselves between roles by acting as gangsters and hit men, and as the film opens they turn their guns on one another. This is a movie that gives new meaning to the notion of being willing to kill for a role.

Barbara Hershey stars, as a waitress and

debt collector who used to be married to crime kingpin Al (Robbie Coltrane), who doubles as a theater producer and is preparing a production of Mamet's *American Buffalo*. She and several other characters spend much of their time hanging out in a diner and talking about absent friends. So much time is spent in the diner, indeed, that *Frogs for Snakes* begins to resemble a one-set play, until there are excursions to pool halls, apartments, and even a theater.

Sample dialogue from a pool hall:

"What are you doing here?"

"We heard you were doing *True West*."

"Well, you heard wrong. We're doing *American Buffalo*."

(Shoots him)

Not a single one of the characters is even slightly convincing as anything other than an artificial theatrical construction. Is that the point? I haven't a clue. Much of their dialogue is lifted intact from other movies, sometimes inappropriately (Lisa Marie plays a buxom sex bomb who recites Harry Lime's speech about cuckoo clocks from *The Third Man*). Other speeches come from *Night and the City, Sex, Drugs and Rock 'n' Roll, The Hustler, The Apartment, Repo Man, I Am a Fugitive from a Chain Gang,* and several more. (The film ends by crediting the screenplays, just as most films end with a scroll of the songs on the sound track.)

"Today they write dialogue about cheeseburgers and big special effects," one of the characters says, contrasting the quoted classics with *Pulp Fiction*. Yes, but Tarantino's cheeseburger dialogue is wonderful comic writing, with an evil undercurrent as the hit men talk while approaching a dangerous meeting; no dialogue in this movie tries anything a fraction as ambitious, or risks anything.

Seeing the cast of familiar actors (not only Hershey and Coltrane but Harry Hamlin, Ian Hart, Debi Mazar, John Leguizamo, and Ron Perlman), I was reminded of *Mad Dog Time* (1996), another movie in which well-known actors engaged in laughable dialogue while shooting one another. Of that one, I wrote: "*Mad Dog Time* is the first movie I have seen that does not improve on the sight of a blank screen viewed for the same length of time." Now comes *Frogs for Snakes,* the first movie I have seen that does not improve on the sight of *Mad Dog Time.*

G

Galaxy Quest ★ ★ ★
PG, 102 m., 1999

Tim Allen (Nesmith/Taggart), Sigourney Weaver (Gwen DeMarco/Tawny Madison), Alan Rickman (Alexander Dane/Dr. Lazarus), Tony Shalhoub (Fred Kwan/Tech Sergeant Chen), Sam Rockwell (Guy Fleegman), Daryl Mitchell (Tommy Webber/ Laredo), Enrico Colantoni (Mathesar), Robin Sacgs (Sarris). Directed by Dan Parisot and produced by Mark Johnson and Charles Newirth. Screenplay by David Howard
and Robert Gordon.

One of my favorite moments in *Galaxy Quest* takes place as a red digital readout is ticking off the seconds until a spaceship is blown to smithereens. The only person who can save it is a teenage science-fiction fan far away on Earth—and he has just been ordered by his mother to take out the garbage. But then the ship is saved! How? I won't spoil the moment, except to say the ship is modeled in every possible respect on a ship that appears on a TV show, and that includes a digital readout that is also consistent with TV clichés.

Galaxy Quest begins at a convention for the fans of a cult TV program not a million light years removed from *Star Trek*. Anyone who has seen *Trekkies*, the documentary about *Star Trek* fans, will recognize this world at once—a world of fanatics who take the show very seriously indeed, packing hotel ballrooms to screen classic episodes of the show and get autographs from its now aging cast members.

Backstage in a dressing room, Alexander Dane (Alan Rickman), who played an alien who was a doctor on the show, vows, "I won't say that stupid line one more time." Other cast members are enraged that the show's star is late as usual. He is Jason Nesmith (Tim Allen), who plays Commander Peter Quincy Taggart and is not a million light years removed from William Shatner. The heroine is Gwen De-Marco (Sigourney Weaver), who plays Lieutenant Tawny Madison and complains that *TV Guide* interviewed her only about her boobs.

Something strange is about to happen. A race of aliens, who have intercepted broad-casts of the show in outer space and mistaken them for "historical documents," arrives on Earth and transports the entire crew into space, placing them on board a spaceship that has been carefully modeled on the sets of the show. Taggart, who is hung over and thinks he's at another fan event, is impressed by the ship: "Usually it's just something made out of cardboard in someone's garage."

The plot: A race of enemy aliens has attacked the home of the friendly aliens, who are led by Mathesar (Enrico Colantoni). The good guys actually look like many-tentacled octopi, but have a gizmo that gives them human form and even translates their speech. (One of their females and a human cast member fall in love, and a necking session gets interesting when she relapses into a few friendly tentacles.)

The original TV show of course looks cheesy, and the spaceship *Protector* looks as unconvincing as the command deck of the original *Enterprise*. But the enemy aliens, designed by Stan Winston, look fearsomely good, and no wonder: They're supposed to be real, not clones of TV aliens. Of course, all of the cast members turn out to be able to command and operate the ship the aliens have built for them, since it works just like the one on TV. And they find themselves repeating their familiar roles. When the onboard computer speaks, Tawny Madison (Weaver) repeats the words. It's not necessary, but: "That's my one job on the show!" Like any actor she's not about to cut her lines.

The movie's humor works best when the illogic of the TV show gets in the way. There is onboard, for example, a passageway blocked by alternating vertical and horizontal clappers that smash back and forth across the passageway. Negotiating it could be fatal. Why are they there? No reason. Just because they look good on TV.

The General ★ ★ ★ ½
R, 129 m., 1999

Brendan Gleeson (Martin Cahill), Jon Voight (Inspector Ned Kenny), Adrian Dunbar (Noel Curley), Sean McGinley (Gary), Maria Doyle Kennedy (Frances), Angeline Ball (Tina), Eanna

McLiam (Jimmy), Tom Murphy (Willie Byrne). Directed by and produced John Boorman. Screenplay by Boorman.

There is a certain honor in sticking to your guns, even if they are the wrong guns. Martin Cahill, the subject of John Boorman's *The General,* was for many years the most famous professional criminal in Ireland, a man who copied Robin Hood, up to a point: He stole from the rich and gave to himself. He was as stubborn a man as ever was born, and so clever that even though he was a villain, he inspired grudging admiration even from the police. He was shot dead in 1994 by the IRA, after getting involved in politics, the one thing in Ireland more dangerous than crime.

Boorman, whose films have ranged from *Deliverance* to *Excaliber,* had one close brush with Cahill, who broke into his house and stole the gold record he was awarded for "Dueling Banjos." The movie includes that episode; when Cahill gets the record home and finds it is not really made of gold, it confirms his low regard for straight society. Most of the time he was more lucky; his lifetime haul is estimated at $60 million.

Cahill is played in *The General* by Brendan Gleeson, an expert Irish actor (he was Hamish, Mel Gibson's sidekick, in *Braveheart*) who succeeds in doing two things not easy for an actor: He creates the illusion that we are looking at Cahill himself, and he makes us admit we like him even despite his vicious streak. Gleeson and Boorman, who wrote his own screenplay, look unblinkingly at horrors, and then find the other side of the coin.

Consider, for example, a scene where Cahill suspects a longtime partner of ratting to the cops. To get a confession out of him, he nails him to a snooker table. The man protests his innocence. Finally Cahill pulls out the nails, observing, "No one can stand that much pain without talking." Then he personally takes him to the hospital, reassuring him, "You came through with flying colors." Look on the positive side: Cahill at least has the integrity to pound the nails himself and not leave it to a flunky. And he's man enough to admit his mistake.

Cahill is, in fact, a charming rogue, able to bestir shreds of admiration even in the heart of his archenemy, police inspector Ned Kenny (Jon Voight). He embodies a certain style in his planning. Trying to buy a house, for example, he is told the agent cannot accept cash. So he takes 80,000 pounds to the bank and purchases a bank draft. He puts the draft in his pocket and walks across the street to the police station, where he is in conversation with Inspector Kenny at the very moment when, wouldn't you know, two masked men approach the very same teller and rob her of all the money in her drawer.

The General opens with Cahill as a young boy, stealing from a local merchant and being sent to reform school (where he socks a would-be molester). As an adult, he was a man who attracted enormous publicity even while obsessively guarding his privacy (he hides his face inside hooded sweatshirts, and invariably holds a hand over his face, peering out from between the fingers). His jobs included knocking over Dublin's largest jewelers, and stealing Old Masters from an Irish country house. In both cases, he uses a devious plan rather than a frontal assault.

Boorman finds subtle humor in Cahill's domestic arrangements; he was married to one woman (Maria Doyle Kennedy) but also shared his bed with her sister (Angeline Ball) and had children by both—apparently a satisfactory arrangement, perhaps because if you were going to be Cahill's sister-in-law you were in bed with him anyway, in one way or another. With his son he shares a delight in pigeons, and one of the low blows struck him by the Dublin police involves setting a ferret loose to kill his prized birds.

Cahill was not a political man, and the way he runs afoul of the IRA is presented in the movie as a lapse of strategy: He did a deal he shouldn't have. In real life, I learn, Cahill's problems came when he interfered in the IRA's drug trade, but such an inference is no doubt still too hot a potato for a director who hopes to film again in Ireland.

Boorman's film is shot in wide-screen black and white, and as it often does, black and white emphasizes the characters and the story, instead of setting them awash in atmosphere. And Boorman's narrative style has a nice offhand feel about it. Instead of explaining everything in neat little simpleminded setups, he lets us discover for ourselves that Cahill is living with both women. As the general unfolds his devious criminal schemes, we see them as they develop, instead of getting those clichéd crime movie chalk talks.

Part of Cahill's charm comes in the way he insists that crime is not his vice, but his occupation. After his neighborhood is torn down by city planners (over his stubborn protests), he demands to be relocated to "a nice neighborhood." A public official sneers: "Wouldn't you sooner live closer to your own kind?" Cahill replies, "No, I'd sooner live closer to my work." ☞

The General's Daughter ★ ★ ½
R, 115 m., 1999

John Travolta (Paul Brenner), Madeleine Stowe (Sarah Sunhill), James Cromwell (General Joe Campbell), Timothy Hutton (Colonel William Kent), James Woods (Colonel Robert Moore), Clarence Williams III (Colonel Fowler), Leslie Stefanson (Captain Elisabeth Campbell), Daniel Van Bargen (Chief Yardley). Directed by Simon West and produced by Mace Neufeld. Screenplay by William Goldman and Christopher Bertolini, based on the novel by Nelson DeMille.

"Elisabeth once told me she was conducting a field investigation in psychological warfare, and the enemy was Daddy."

So speaks one of the friends of the late Captain Elisabeth Campbell, whose bizarre death is the centerpiece of *The General's Daughter*. Her army job is to teach "psychological operations"—or, as she explains to a guy whose tire she helps to change, to mess with people's minds. Nobody's mind has been messed with more than her own.

The friendly guy is Warrant Officer Paul Brenner, played by John Travolta—first as a slow-talking redneck, and then, after he drops the undercover masquerade, as an aggressive army cop. He meets Elisabeth Campbell (Leslie Stefanson) just that once before her naked corpse is found staked spread-eagled to the ground, having been strangled. And if you

blinked at that description of her dead body, well, so did I. The circumstances of the victim's death are so bizarre and unlikely that they derail most of the scenes they involve.

The General's Daughter is a well-made thriller with a lot of good acting, but the death of Elisabeth Campbell is so unnecessarily graphic and gruesome that by the end I felt sort of unclean. If this had been a documentary, or even a fiction film with serious intentions, I would have accepted it. But does entertainment have to go this far just to shake us up?

The movie is based on a page-turner by Nelson DeMille, adapted for the screen by William Goldman and Christopher Bertolini, who along the way provide a dialogue scene for Travolta and James Woods that's sharpedged and crisply delivered; one-on-one, they fence with words and the theater grows as quiet as if it were a sex scene. Simon West, the director, creates a gloomy southern Gothic atmosphere for his film, which is set at an "urban warfare center," an army base that includes mock-ups of civilian architecture, and an antebellum mansion for the general to occupy.

The general (James Cromwell) seems to have lived there quite some time, judging by the furnishings, which make the interiors look like pages from *Architectural Digest*. General Campbell occupies rooms filled with wood, leather, brass, crystal, weapons, and flags, and is doted on by his loyal aide-de-camp, Colonel Fowler (Clarence Williams III). Campbell is a war hero now considered vice-presidential timber, although of course the messy murder of his daughter may put an end to that, especially if he had anything to do with it.

He is not the only suspect. With the efficiency of all good police procedurals, every single main character is a suspect, except for those deployed for local color and comic effect (and you can never be sure about them). Travolta's warrant officer is assigned to the case and partnered with another army cop, Sarah Sunhill (Madeleine Stowe); they had an affair once in Brussels, which gives them something to talk about—just as well, since the primary function of her character is to wait around in hopes that the screenplay will hurl her into a dangerous and threatening situation.

211

They quiz Captain Moore (Woods), who describes himself as Elisabeth's mentor in psychological warfare, and Colonel Kent (Timothy Hutton), the provost marshal, who seems awfully nosy if he has nothing to hide. The local police chief insulted Travolta while he was undercover, and now Travolta insults him back, and finds out that the chief's son and deputy was dating the dead woman.

He had a lot of company. Travolta finds a secret room in the woman's basement that contains S&M props and equipment, an automatic video system, and lots of incriminating tapes. The sweet blonde who changed Travolta's tire apparently spent her evenings tightening more than lugs. Travolta finds out from the tapes (and from gossip universally offered) that the general's daughter had apparently slept with more or less everyone on the general's staff.

We know from long experience with other thrillers that present problems always have their explanations in lurid flashbacks. Travolta discovers that something unspeakable happened to Captain Campbell during her third year at West Point. What that is, and how it leads to the death of the general's daughter, I leave to you to discover. The explanation does not speak highly for the psych courses at the Point, however, since Elisabeth apparently learned that the way to exorcise a traumatic memory is to reenact the events that produced it.

The General's Daughter is, as I have said, a well-made film. It is populated by edgy performances, and we get a real feeling for the characters played by Woods, as a career man with a secret to hide, Cromwell, as an unbending officer and father, and Williams, as a man who hero-worships the general to a fault. Travolta demonstrates again, as he did in *A Civil Action* and *Primary Colors*, that he has developed into a fine actor.

I also admired the darkly atmospheric look of the film, and the way it sustains its creepy mood. But I cringed when the death of the general's daughter was played out. Did the details have to be so graphic? Did we need to linger on the sight of a terrified woman? Did the filmmakers hesitate before supplying actual shots of her being strangled? Can anything be left to the imagination? I believe that

any subject matter is legitimate for artistic purposes, but this isn't art. It's a thriller that could have spared us the details of that woman's horrible death.   ☞

Genghis Blues ★ ★ ★ ½
NO MPAA RATING, 88 m., 1999

A documentary featuring Paul Pena and Kongar-ol Ondar. Directed by Roko Belic and produced by Roko Belic and Adrian Belic. Screenplay by Roko Belic.

This is the kind of story that has to be true because no novelist would dare to dream it up. In San Francisco lives a blind blues singer named Paul Pena. He plays and sings backup for such legends as Muddy Waters and B. B. King. Late at night when he cannot sleep, he listens to the world on a shortwave radio. We see his fingers delicately touching the dial, rotating it just a little at a time, seeking stations hidden in the bandwidth.

One night he hears strange, haunting music on Radio Moscow. He tracks it down. It is called "khoomei," or "throat-singing," and is practiced in the tiny Republic of Tuva, which you can find on the map between Mongolia and Siberia. Tuvan throat-singing, he learns, involves creating an eerie sound that combines different and distinct notes at the same time.

For years Paul Pena studies throat-singing, just for the love of it. He translates the lyrics using two Braille dictionaries, one to get them from Tuvan to Russian, and the other from Russian to English (we are not amazed to learn there are no Tuvan-English dictionaries in Braille). He becomes possibly the only throat singer not born in Tuva, all this time without ever meeting anyone else who knows what he is doing.

Now it is 1993. A touring group from Tuva performs in San Francisco. He visits them backstage, and sings their songs—in their style, in their language. They are thunderstruck. In 1995, Pena is invited to Tuva for the annual khoomei competition. He is accompanied by the sound engineer Lemon DeGeorge ("I am basically a tree-trimmer"), a San Francisco deejay named Mario Casetta, and Roko and Adrian Belic, from Evanston, Illinois, who are documentarians. They return with this film.

But so far we have touched only on the amazing facts of *Genghis Blues*. If the film were only about Pena learning throat-singing and going to Tuva, it would be a travelogue. It is about much more. About the way we communicate with music. About the way Paul Pena is clearly an extraordinary person—warm, funny, beset by the demon of depression but singing his way free of it. And about the friend he makes in Tuva, a man named Kongar-ol Ondar, who is the leading throat singer and becomes Paul Pena's close friend in no time at all.

The Tuvans have not had an easy time of it, with the Soviets trying their best to dismantle the national customs, music, and costumes. Now communism has collapsed, and in Tuva they are returning to the old customs with a fierce joy. To think that a man in San Francisco was listening to them on the radio! That he has written a throat-song about friendship in the Tuvan language!

Things happen along the way. Torrential rains. Illness. Competitions. Parades. Feasts. The peculiar way that the legendary physicist Richard Feynman was involved in this Tuvan story. They are all incidents, many colorful, that would be just as interesting in any other film. The heart of *Genghis Blues* is in the music and its singers. Throat-singing sounds as if it were discovered and perfected by musicians like Paul Pena, awake in the middle of the night, searching the dials of their minds for the stations between the numbers.

Get Bruce ★ ★ ★
R, 72 m., 1999

Appearing as themselves: Bruce Vilanch, Whoopi Goldberg, Billy Crystal, Bette Midler, Robin Williams, Nathan Lane, Lily Tomlin, Raquel Welch, Michael Feinstein, and Shirley MacLaine. Directed and produced by Andrew J. Kuehn.

Get Bruce is exactly the kind of documentary we all want to have made about ourselves, in which it is revealed that we are funny, smart, beloved, the trusted confidant of famous people, the power behind the scenes at great events, and the apple of our mother's eye. That all of these things are true of Bruce Vilanch only adds to the piquancy. I have known him for

thirty years. If there is a dark side to his nature, I believe it shows itself mostly when he can't decide which T-shirt to wear.

Vilanch writes "specialized material" for Hollywood stars. When Whoopi emcees, when Billy does the Oscars, when Better Midler opens a new show at Radio City Music Hall, much of what they say (and most of the funniest stuff) has passed through Bruce's laptop computer. He has written the recent Oscarcasts, and can be found backstage at almost every big Hollywood awards show or charity benefit, suggesting "improvised" one-liners as the host dashes onstage between acts. His greatest triumph was arguably the night Jack Palance did the one-armed push-ups, and Billy Crystal milked it for the whole evening.

It is not that Billy, Robin, Whoopi, Bette, and the others are idiots who need Vilanch to put words in their mouths. Quite the opposite, as this film shows in some fascinating footage of them at work. Vilanch is a foil, a collaborator, a dueling partner, a lateral thinker able to help them move in the direction they want to go. Only when some clients are insecure or truly at sea does he become a ventriloquist.

I knew him a long time ago in Chicago when he worked for the *Tribune*, the film says, although I recall, perhaps imperfectly, that it was *Chicago Today*. He was very funny then. He looked about the same: large, always wearing a well-stretched T-shirt, his face a cartoon made of a mass of hair, a Santa beard, and glasses. He wrote wonderful celebrity profiles, and that's how he met Bette Midler at Mister Kelly's and went from rags to riches.

I may not have actually been present when they met, but I was there at Kelly's one night at about the same time. Mort Sahl was on the stage. I was in the booth next to the runway to the dressing rooms. I heard a voice. "Why do I have to open for this guy?" It was Bette Midler. Another voice. "Why do I have to be your piano player?" Her piano player was Barry Manilow.

The world was young then and Bruce flirted briefly with the possibility that he could build a performing career of his own. He actually opened at Kelly's as a stand-up comic. This was in the days before comedy clubs, and it took nerve to stand up in front of a room of friends and critics (the friends were more frightening) and try to be funny. I do not recall that he was a hit. I can see from *Get Bruce*, however, that he's good in front of a crowd these days, no doubt because he has a lot more confidence and because his persona is familiar to his audiences.

"There isn't a show in town that can be held without him," says one of the subjects of *Get Bruce*. He recalls, usually with the perpetrators, how specific material was generated. Not just the triumphs (Palance's push-ups) but the disasters like Ted Danson's appearance in blackface at the Friar's Club roast for Whoopi Goldberg. Vilanch wrote a lot of Danson's material, which went over so badly it occupied the entire front page of the *New York Daily News* the next day, but Goldberg defends him: "It was my idea. All my idea."

I remember when he left for the coast. There was a farewell party at Larry Dieckhaus's and we all sat on the floor around a coffee table, eating pizza and weeping with laughter. At first it was slow going in L.A. He got a job on the *Brady Bunch Variety Hour*, and then interviewed with Donny and Marie. What he said to Donny during their unsuccessful meeting cannot be quoted here, but will be much quoted elsewhere. He also recalls some of the people he did not write for; he is well paid, we learn, and Barbra Streisand's offer was so low he told her, "Jim Bailey offered me more to write the drag version of this act."

Some of the film's best sequences have Vilanch bouncing lines back and forth with Crystal and Williams. He works differently with each client. With some he's a counselor, a source of calm reassurance. With others he's a competitor, a one-upper. Lots of funny lines are generated, and he remembers a few that went too far and were wisely left out of the script.

Where does he get his humor? Maybe from his mother back on Long Island, whose every statement is hilarious—apparently unintentionally, although we sense she knows exactly what she's doing. Bruce was adopted, she confides, but "he's more like me than any child who was ever naturally born." High praise. Deserved.

Get Real ★ ★ ★
R, 110 m., 1999

Ben Silverstone (Steven Carter), Brad Gorton (John Dixon), Charlotte Brittain (Linda), Stacy A. Hart (Jessica), Kate McEnery (Wendy), Patrick Nielsen (Mark), Tim Harris (Kevin), James D. White (Dave). Directed by Simon Shore and produced by Stephen Taylor. Screenplay by Patrick Wilde, based on the play *What's Wrong with Angry?* by Wilde.

Get Real tells the story of a teenage boy who has become sexually active at sixteen. That is, of course, the fodder for countless teenage sexcoms, in which the young heroes raid the brothels of Tijuana, are seduced by their French governesses, or have affairs with their teachers. The difference is that the hero in *Get Real* is gay, and so no doubt some critics will be offended by the film's assumptions.

I am thinking, for example, of a columnist for my own newspaper who doesn't think gays should be allowed into the Boy Scouts. His opposition to abortion clinics is matched only by his outrage at the birth control information supplied on a Planned Parenthood Web page; the logical result of his arguments is teenage childbearing. While it may be true that in his ideal world everyone is straight and they never have sex until they have been united by clergy, the real world is filled with young people who must deal every day with strong emotional and sexual feelings. Some of them have sex. This is a fact of life.

Such a person is Steven Carter (Ben Silverstone), the young British student who is the subject of *Get Real*. He has known he was gay since he was eleven. He keeps it a secret because in his school, you can be beaten for being gay. He's picked on anyway by insecure kids who deal with their own sexual anxiety by punishing it in others. The cards are stacked against him, he tells a girl who's his best friend: "I don't smoke or play football, and I have an IQ over 25."

One day Steven visits a local park where gays are known to meet, and is surprised to find that John Dixon (Brad Gorton), an athletic hero at his school, is hanging out there, too—and apparently for the same reason. John is far from out of the closet. He's attracted to Steven, and then runs away, and then comes creeping curiously back, and then denies his feelings. There is a heartbreaking scene (after they have become lovers) where he beats up Steven in the locker room, just to keep his cover in front of a gang of gay-bashers.

The movie deals with this material in a straightforward way, but is not sexually graphic and it somehow finds humor and warmth even while it shows Steven's lonely, secretive existence. In its general outlines, it's a typical teenage comedy like the ones that have been opening every weekend all spring, where the shy outsider is surprised to attract the most popular boy in class. This time the outsider is not played by Drew Barrymore, Rachel Leigh Cook, or Reese Witherspoon. And when Steven and John go to the school dance, they both dance with girls, while their eyes meet in hopeless longing.

Much of the humor in the film comes from Linda (Charlotte Brittain), Steven's plump best friend and for a long time the only one who knows he is gay. She acts as a confidante and cover, and even obligingly faints at a wedding when he needs to make a quick getaway. He's known her since the early days when everything he knew about sex was learned from his dad's hidden porno tapes ("I thought babies were made when two women tie a man to a bed and cover his willy with ice cream").

There is also Jessica (Stacy A. Hart), an editor on the school magazine, who likes Steven a lot and wants to be his girlfriend. He would like to tell her the truth, but nobody guesses it, certainly not his parents, and he lacks the courage. Then the relationship with John helps him to see his life more clearly, to grow tired of lying, and he writes an anonymous article for the magazine that is not (as he must have known) destined to remain anonymous for long.

The film takes a bit long to arrive at its obligatory points, and Steven's brave decision at the end is probably unlikely—he acts not as a high school boy probably would, but as a screenwriter requires him to. But the movie is sound in all the right ways; it argues that we are as we are, and the best thing to do is accept that. I doubt if movies have much influence on behavior, but I hope they can help us empathize with those who are not like us. There were stories that the Colorado shooters were taunted (inaccurately, apparently) for being gay. Movies like *Get Real* might help homophobic teenagers and adults become more accepting of differences. Certainly this film has deeper values than the mainstream teenage comedies that retail aggressive materialism, soft-core sex, and shallow ideas about "popularity."

Ghost Dog: The Way of the Samurai ★ ★ ★
R, 116 m., 2000

Forest Whitaker (Ghost Dog), Henry Silva (Ray Vargo), Richard Portnow (Handsome Frank), Tricia Vessey (Louise Vargo), John Tormey (Louie), Cliff Gorman (Sonny Valerio), Victor Argo (Vinny). Directed by Jim Jarmusch and produced by Jarmusch and Richard Guay. Screenplay by Jarmusch.

It helps to understand that the hero of *Ghost Dog* is crazy. Well, of course he is. He lives in a shack on a rooftop with his pigeons. He dresses like a homeless man. "He has no friends and never talks to anybody," according to the mother of the little girl in the movie. Actually, he does talk: to the little girl and to a Haitian ice-cream man. The Haitian speaks no English and Ghost Dog speaks no French, so they simply speak in their own languages and are satisfied with that. What's your diagnosis?

Ghost Dog (Forest Whitaker) is a killer for the mob. He got into this business because one day a mobster saved his life—and so, since he follows "The Way of the Samurai," he must dedicate his life to his master. The mobster is named Louie (John Tormey). He orders hits by sending Ghost Dog messages by carrier pigeon. The Dog insists on being paid once a year, on the first day of autumn. When the mob bosses want Ghost Dog rubbed out, they're startled to discover that Louie doesn't know his name or where he lives; their only contact is the pigeons.

It seems strange that a black man would devote his life to doing hired killing for a group of Italian-American gangsters after having met only one of them. But then it's strange, too, that Ghost Dog lives like a medieval Japanese samurai. The whole story is so strange, indeed, that I've read some of the other reviews in disbelief. Are movie critics so hammered by absurd plots that they can't see how truly, profoundly weird *Ghost Dog* is? The reviews treat it matter-of-factly: Yeah, here's this hit man, he lives like a samurai, he gets his instructions by pigeon, blah, blah . . . and then they start talking about the performances and how the director, Jim Jarmusch, is paying homage to Kurosawa and *High Noon*.

But the man is insane! In a quiet, sweet way, he is totally unhinged and has lost all touch with reality. His profound sadness, which permeates the touching Whitaker performance, comes from his alienation from human society, his loneliness, his attempt to justify inhuman behavior (murder) with a belief system (the samurai code) that has no connection with his life or his world. Despite the years he's spent studying "The Way of the Samurai," he doesn't even reflect that since his master doesn't subscribe to it, their relationship is meaningless.

I make this argument because I've seen *Ghost Dog* twice, and admired it more after I focused on the hero's insanity. The first time I saw it, at Cannes, I thought it was a little too precious, an exercise in ironic style, not substance. But look more deeply, and you see the self-destructive impulse that guides Ghost Dog in the closing scenes, as he sadly marches forth to practice his code in the face of people who only want to kill him (whether he survives is not the point).

Jarmusch is mixing styles here almost recklessly, and I like the chances he takes. The gangsters (played by colorful character actors like Henry Silva, Richard Portnow, Cliff Gorman, and Victor Argo), sit in their clubhouse doing sub-Scorsese while the Louie character tries to explain to them how he uses an invisible hit man. Ghost Dog meanwhile mopes sadly around the neighborhood, solemnly recommending *Rashomon* to a little girl ("you may want to wait and read it when you're a little older"), and miscommunicating with the ice-cream man. By the end, Whitaker's character has generated true poignance.

If the mobsters are on one level of reality and Ghost Dog on another, then how do we interpret some of the Dog's killings, particularly the one where he shoots a man by sneaking under his house and firing up through the lavatory pipe while the guy is shaving? This is a murder that demands Inspector Clouseau as its investigator. Jarmusch seems to have di-

rected with his tongue in his cheek, his hand over his heart, and his head in the clouds. The result is weirdly intriguing. ☞

The Gingerbread Man ★ ★ ★
R, 115 m., 1998

Kenneth Branagh (Rick Magruder), Embeth Davidtz (Mallory Doss), Robert Downey Jr. (Clyde Pell), Daryl Hannah (Lois Harlan), Tom Berenger (Pete Randle), Famke Janssen (Leeanne), Mae Whitman (Libby), Jesse James (Jeff), Robert Duvall (Dixon Doss). Directed by Robert Altman and produced by Jeremy Tannenbaum. Screenplay by Al Hayes, based on an original story by John Grisham.

The ominous approach of Hurricane Geraldo drenches the opening scenes of Robert Altman's *The Gingerbread Man* in sheets of rain and darkness at noon. John Grisham, who wrote the story, named the hurricane well, for like a week's episodes of the television program, the movie features divorce, adultery, kooky fringe groups, kidnapped children, hotshot lawyers, drug addiction, and family tragedy. That it seems a step up from sensationalism is because Grisham has a sure sense of time and place, and Altman and his actors invest the material with a kind of lurid sincerity.

As the film opens, a lawyer named Magruder (Kenneth Branagh, Georgia accent well in hand) has won a big case and driven back to his Savannah law offices for a celebration. Awaiting him in Georgia are his faithful assistant Lois (Daryl Hannah), his faithless estranged wife, Leeanne (Famke Janssen), and his office staff, not excepting the muddled private investigator Clyde (Robert Downey Jr.). After a catered office party at which he drinks too much, Magruder leaves for his car, only to find a woman outside in the rain, screaming after her own departing car. This is Mallory Doss (Embeth Davidtz), who was a waitress at the party, and now believes her car to be stolen.

Magruder offers her his cell phone and then a ride home, where, to their amazement, they find her stolen car. Her door is unlocked, the lights are on, a TV is playing, and she hints darkly that this sort of thing has happened before. It may be the work of her father, who belongs to a "group." Weeping and lashing out at her absent parent, Mallory absentmindedly undresses in front of Magruder, and as thunder and lightning tear through the sky they engage in what is categorically and unequivocally a sexual relationship.

Neat touch in the morning: Magruder prods Mallory's prone body and, getting no response, dresses and leaves, while we wonder if she's dead and he will be framed with the crime. Not at all. A much more complex plot is afoot, and only after the movie is over do we think back through the plot, trying to figure out what the characters planned in advance, and what was improvised on the spot.

Grisham's story line resembles one of those Ross Macdonald novels from thirty years ago, in which old sins beget new ones, and the sins of the fathers are visited on the children. Altman's contribution is to tell the story in a fresh and spontaneous way, to use Branagh's quickness as an actor to make scenes seem fresh. Consider the scene where Magruder, tired and hung over, returns to his office the next morning, marches grimly past his staff toward his office, and asks for "Some of that . . . you know." As his door closes, one secretary turns to another: "Coffee." It's just right: Hangovers cause sufferers to lose track of common words, and office workers complete the boss's thoughts. Lois, the Hannah character, is especially effective in the way she cares for a boss who should, if he had an ounce of sense, accept her safe harbor instead of seeking out danger.

Grisham's works are filled with neo-Nazis, but when we meet Mallory's dad he's hard to classify. Dixon Doss (Robert Duvall) is a stringy, unlovely coot, and his "group" seems to be made up of unwashed and unbarbered old codgers, who hang around ominously in a clubhouse that looks like it needs the Orkin man. In a cartoon they'd have flies buzzing about their heads. In a perhaps unintentional touch of humor, the codgers can be mobilized instantly to speed out on sinister missions for old Doss; they're like the Legion of Justice crossed with Klan pensioners.

Magruder has lots on his hands. He feels protective toward Mallory and assigns Clyde (Downey) to her case; Clyde's method of stumbling over evidence is to stumble all the

time and hope some evidence turns up. Magruder's almost ex-wife, who is dating his divorce lawyer, is in a struggle with him over custody, and Magruder finds it necessary to snatch his kids from their school, after which the kids are snatched again, from a hideaway motel, by persons unknown, while the winds pick up and walls of rain lash Savannah.

It's all atmospheric, quirky, and entertaining: the kind of neo-*noir* in which old-fashioned characters have updated problems. There is something about the South that seems to breed eccentric characters in the minds of writers and directors; the women there are more lush and conniving, the men heroic and yet temptable, and the villains Shakespearean in their depravity. Duvall, who can be a subtle and controlled actor (see *The Apostle*), can also sink his fangs into a role like this one and shake it by its neck until dead. And then there's Tom Berenger as Mallory's former husband, who seems to have nothing to do with the case, although students of the Law of Economy of Characters will know that no unnecessary characters are ever inserted into a movie—certainly not name players like Berenger.

From Robert Altman we expect a certain improvisational freedom, a plot that finds its way down unexpected channels and depends on coincidence and serendipity. Here he seems content to follow the tightly plotted maze mapped out by Grisham; the Altman touches are more in dialogue and personal style than in construction. He gives the actors freedom to move around in their roles. Instead of the tunnel vision of most Grisham movies, in which every line of dialogue relentlessly hammers down the next plot development, *The Gingerbread Man* has space for quirky behavior, kidding around, and murky atmosphere. The hurricane is not just window dressing, but an effective touch: It adds a subtle pressure beneath the surface, lending tension to ordinary scenes with its promise of violence to come.

Girl, Interrupted ★ ★ ½
R, 125 m., 2000

Winona Ryder (Susanna), Angelina Jolie (Lisa), Clea Duvall (Georgina), Brittany Murphy (Daisy),

Elisabeth Moss (Polly), Jared Leto (Tobias Jacobs), Whoopi Goldberg (Valerie [nurse]), Jeffrey Tambor (Dr. Potts), Vanessa Redgrave (Dr. Wick). Directed by James Mangold and produced by Douglas Wick and Cathy Konrad. Screenplay by Mangold, Lisa Loomer, and Anna Hamilton Phelan, based on the book by Susanna Kaysen.

In the spring of 1967, while everyone else in her senior class seems to be making plans for college, Susanna consumes a bottle of aspirin and a bottle of vodka. "My hands have no bones," she observes. Soon, with a push from her family, she has committed herself to Claymoore, an upscale psychiatric institution. The diagnosis? "Borderline personality disorder," say the shrinks. A supervising nurse played by Whoopi Goldberg offers her own diagnosis: "You are a lazy, self-indulgent little girl who is driving herself crazy."

Winona Ryder plays Susanna Kaysen, whose real-life memoir tells of how she lost two years of her life by stumbling onto the psychiatric conveyor belt. Although mental illness is real and terrifying, the movie argues that perfectly sane people like Susanna can become institutionalized simply because once they're inside the system there is the assumption that something must be wrong with them. Goldberg's nurse has seen this process at work and warns Susanna: "Do not drop anchor here."

But Susanna fits easily into the cocoon of Claymoore, where the other women include a rebel misfit named Lisa (Angelina Jolie), a roommate named Georgina (Clea Duvall) who would like to live in the land of Oz, the burn victim Polly (Elisabeth Moss), and the deeply troubled Daisy (Brittany Murphy). The staff is headed by a bureaucrat (Jeffrey Tambor) and an intelligent but detached psychiatrist (Vanessa Redgrave).

The film unfolds in an episodic way, like the journal it's based on. Themes make an appearance from time to time, but not consistently; the film is mostly about character and behavior, and although there are individual scenes of powerful acting, there doesn't seem to be a destination. That's why the conclusion is so unsatisfying: The story, having failed to provide itself with character conflicts that can be resolved with drama, turns to melodrama instead.

One problem is the ambivalent nature of Susanna's condition ("ambivalent" is one of her favorite words). She isn't disturbed enough to require treatment, but she becomes strangely absorbed inside Claymoore, as if it provides structure and entertainment she misses on the outside. Certainly Lisa is an inspiration, with her cool self-confidence masking deep wounds. Instead of being in a women's dorm at college, Susanna is in a women's dorm at Claymoore, where her subject of study is herself. Susanna is not therefore a captive of an evil system, but someone seduced by a careless one, and there is the temptation to suspect she deserves what she gets.

Even a feminist argument with her psychiatrist (Redgrave) lacks power. They argue over the definition of promiscuity; Susanna points out that women are labeled promiscuous after much less sexual experience than men. Susanna has indeed slept in one day with both her boyfriend and an orderly, but under the circumstances is that promiscuity or opportunism?

Jared Leto plays her boyfriend, Toby, whose number is up in the draft lottery. He wants them to run away to Canada. She is no longer much interested in steering her future into their relationship, and prefers her new friends in Claymoore. "Them?" says Toby. "They're eating grapes off of the wallpaper." Susanna chooses solidarity: "If they're insane, I'm insane." Wrong. They're insane and she isn't, and that deprives the film of the kind of subterranean energy that fueled its obvious inspiration, *One Flew Over the Cuckoo's Nest*.

Two reasons to see the film: Winona Ryder and Angelina Jolie. Their characters never really get a plot to engage them, and are subjected to a silly ending, but moment to moment they are intriguing and watchable. Jolie is emerging as one of the great wild spirits of current movies, a loose cannon who somehow has deadly aim. Ryder shows again her skill at projecting mental states; one of her gifts is to let us know exactly what she's thinking, without seeming to. Their work here deserves a movie with more reason for existing.

Gladiator ★ ★
R, 150 m., 2000

Russell Crowe (Maximus), Joaquin Phoenix (Commodus), Connie Nielsen (Lucilla), Oliver Reed (Proximo), Richard Harris (Marcus Aurelius), Derek Jacobi (Gracchus), Djimon Hounsou (Juba), David Schofield (Falco). Directed by Ridley Scott and produced by Douglas Wick, David Franzoni, and Branko Lustig. Screenplay by Franzoni, John Logan, and William Nicholson.

Maximus: I'm required to kill—so I kill. That's enough.

Proximo: That's enough for the provinces, but not for Rome.

A foolish choice in art direction casts a pall over Ridley Scott's *Gladiator* that no swordplay can cut through. The film looks muddy, fuzzy, and indistinct. Its colors are mud tones at the drab end of the palate, and it seems to have been filmed on grim and overcast days. This darkness and a lack of detail in the long shots helps obscure shabby special effects (the Coliseum in Rome looks like a set from a computer game), and the characters bring no cheer: They're bitter, vengeful, depressed. By the end of this long film, I would have traded any given gladiatorial victory for just one shot of blue skies. (There are blue skies in the hero's dreams of long-ago happiness, but that proves the point.)

The story line is *Rocky* on downers. The hero, a general from Spain named Maximus (Russell Crowe), is a favorite of emperor Marcus Aurelius (Richard Harris). After Maximus defeats the barbarians, Marcus names him protector of Rome. But he is left for dead by Marcus's son, a bitter rival named Commodus (the name comes from the Latin for "convenient" and not what you're thinking). After escaping and finding that his wife and son have been murdered, Maximus finds his way to the deserts of North Africa, where he is sold as a slave to Proximo (the late Oliver Reed), a manager of gladiators. When Commodus lifts his father's ban on gladiators in Rome, in an attempt to distract the people from hunger and plagues, Maximus slashes his way to the top, and the movie ends, of course, with the Big Fight.

This same story could have been rousing entertainment; I have just revisited the wonderful *Raiders of the Lost Ark,* which is just as dim-witted but twelve times more fun. But *Gladiator* lacks joy. It employs depression as a substitute for personality, and believes that if the characters are bitter and morose enough, we won't notice how dull they are.

Commodus (Joaquin Phoenix) is one of those spoiled, self-indulgent, petulant Roman emperors made famous in the age of great Roman epics, which ended with *Spartacus* (1963). Watching him in his snits, I recalled Peter Ustinov's great Nero, in *Quo Vadis* (1951), collecting his tears for posterity in tiny crystal goblets. Commodus has unusual vices even for a Caesar; he wants to become the lover of his older sister Lucilla (Connie Nielsen), whose son he is raising as his heir.

The ethical backbone of the story is easily mastered. Commodus wants to be a dictator, but is opposed by the Senate, led by such as Gracchus (Derek Jacobi). The senators want him to provide sewers for the city's Greek district, where the plague is raging, but Commodus decides instead on a season of games. Proximo arrives with his seasoned gladiators from Africa, who prove nearly invincible, and threaten the emperor's popularity. The moral lesson: It is good when gladiators slaughter everyone in sight, and then turn over power to the politicians.

The Coliseum productions play like professional wrestling. Events are staged to re-create famous battles, and after the visitors wipe out the home team, a puzzled Commodus tells his aide, "My history's a little hazy—but shouldn't the barbarians *lose* the battle of Carthage?" Later, an announcer literally addresses the crowd in these words: "Caesar is pleased to bring you the only undefeated champion in Roman history—the legendary Tiger!"

The battle sequences are a pale shadow of the lucidly choreographed swordplay in *Rob Roy* (1995); instead of moves we can follow and strategy we can appreciate, Scott goes for muddled close-ups of fearsome but indistinct events. The crowd cheers, although those in the cheaper seats are impossible to see because of the murky special effects.

When Maximus wins his first big fight, it's up to Commodus to decide whether he will live or die. "Live! Live!" the fans chant, and Commodus, bowing to their will, signals with a "thumbs up." This demonstrates that Commodus was not paying attention in Caesar School, since the practice at the Coliseum at that time was to close the thumb in the fist to signal life; an extended thumb meant death. Luckily, no one else in the Coliseum knows this either.

Russell Crowe is efficient as Maximus; bearded, taciturn, brooding. His closest friend among the gladiators is played by Djimon Hounsou, who played the passionate slave in *Amistad*. Since protocol requires him to speak less than Maximus, he mostly looks ferocious, effectively. Connie Nielsen shows the film's most depth as the sister. Phoenix is passable as Commodus, but a quirkier actor could have had more fun in the role. Old pros Harris, Jacobi, and Reed are reliable; Scott does some fancy editing and a little digital work to fill the gaps left when Reed died during the production.

Gladiator is being hailed by those with short memories as the equal of *Spartacus* and *Ben Hur*. This is more like *Spartacus Lite*. Or dark. It's only necessary to think back a few months to Julie Taymor's *Titus* for a film set in ancient Rome that's immeasurably better to look at. The visual accomplishment of *Titus* shames *Gladiator*, and its story is a whole heck of a lot better than the *Gladiator* screenplay, even if Shakespeare didn't make Titus the only undefeated champion in Roman history. ☞

Go ★ ★ ★

R, 100 m., 1999

Katie Holmes (Claire Montgomery), Sarah Polley (Ronna Martin), William Fichtner (Burke), Desmond Askew (Simon Baines), Taye Diggs (Marcus), Scott Wolf (Adam), Jay Mohr (Zack), Timothy Olyphant (Todd Gaines), Jane Krakowski (Irene). Directed by Doug Liman and produced by Paul Rosenberg, Mickey Liddell, and Matt Freeman. Screenplay by John August.

Sooner or later the statute of limitations has to run out on comparisons between new movies and *Pulp Fiction*. Quentin Tarantino's 1994 film mesmerized the Sundance generation, who have been doing riffs ever since on its in-terlocking time lines, its quirky sex and violence, its pop culture expertise, its familiarity with drugs, its squirmy comedy, its black-white friendships, its ironic profundity, and its revelations in all-night diners. Those who haven't seen it must wonder why it's cited in so many movie reviews; has no other movie been made in the interim?

Well, no, not one that staked out the territory so firmly. Consider, for example, Doug Liman's *Go*. This is an entertaining, clever black comedy that takes place entirely in Tarantino-land. Liman is a talented director who works as his own cinematographer and finds a nice off-center humor. His *Swingers* (1996) was an accomplished debut film, and here, with a screenplay by John August, he does more, and better, and yet the shadow of QT falls on many scenes.

When his characters deliberately create a flesh wound with a gunshot, for example, the setup and payoff reminds us of the needle plunging into the heart in *Pulp Fiction* (and of the deliberate blade wound in *Gridlock'd*). And when two of his characters sit in a diner and have a conversation about the comic strip *Family Circus*, we think of Uma Thurman and John Travolta sharing pop lore over their milk shakes in *PF*. We're also reminded of *Pulp* in scenes involving a laconic drug dealer, a crisis involving body disposal, an unintended drug overdose, the way its story lines branch off and then join up again, and even in an unusual character name, Zack.

Tarantino has created a generation of footnoters and cross-referencers. I'm not saying *Go* couldn't have been made without the example of *Pulp Fiction*, but it can't be seen without thinking of it. What it adds is a grittier feel; Liman's characters are closer to ground level.

The story begins in a supermarket, where Ronna the checkout girl (Sarah Polley) takes a shift for her friend Simon (Desmond Askew), a part-time drug dealer who wants to go to Vegas. She needs rent money. When two customers named Adam and Zack (Scott Wolf and Jay Mohr) want to score some ecstasy, she goes to Simon's usual dealer (Timothy Olyphant) to get twenty hits. Olyphant, lounging bare-chested in his apartment hideaway, stroking his girlfriend and his cat, working the phone, supplies the legal expertise such stories always require: "Twenty hits! The magic number where intent to sell becomes trafficking."

Without revealing too much of the plot, which depends on surprises and connections, I can say that the other main stories involve (1) Simon's adventures in Las Vegas, where he and his black friend Marcus (Taye Diggs) get into big trouble with the owners of a topless bar, and (2) the relationship between Adam, Zack, and a cop named Burke (William Fichtner), who invites the two men over to Christmas dinner with his wife (Jane Krakowski). This couple is extremely open to sexual adventures with strangers, but turns out to have another even stronger obsession; there is nothing like a pyramid scheme to bring out fanaticism.

Trouble in Vegas leads to more trouble in Los Angeles, where the stories of the checkout clerk and the two young men also meet again, unexpectedly. The plot, of course, is a complete contrivance, but Liman and August have a lot of fun with the details, including a "Macarena" dance in an unlikely setting, a telepathic cat, and a scene with echoes of *Blood Simple,* in which some characters try to leave a hotel room while others are trying to break in.

Go has energy and wit, and the performances are right for the material—especially Sarah Polley, who thinks fast and survives harrowing experiences, and Fichtner, the cop who is so remarkably open to new experiences. The movie is ruthless in its attitude toward the apparently dead or dying, but then grisly indifference is central to the self-centered values without which these characters would have no values at all. Liman shows here, as he did in *Swingers,* that he has a good eye and can create screwy characters. Can he break out of QT-land?

God Said, 'Ha!' ★ ★ ★ ½
PG-13, 85 m., 1999

Directed and performed by Julia Sweeney and produced by Rana Joy Glickman. Screenplay by Sweeney, based on the stage play directed by Greg Kachel.

There is a kind of luminous quality in the way Julia Sweeney talks about her life and family in *God Said, 'Ha!'* She wanders the stage for an hour and a half, talking about a year in her life when her brother, Mike, was dying of cancer. This is a sad subject, painful to her, and yet she makes humor of it. She is a comedian, and, like the hero of *Life Is Beautiful,* she deals with life with the gifts at her command.

What she weaves out of her memories is a funny love poem to Mike and her parents—who all moved into her small house for the duration of the crisis. She sees their human weaknesses, she smiles at their goofy logic, she lets their habits get on her nerves, but above all she embraces them. And when, midway through the year, even more bad news descends upon her, she is able to transform that, too, into truth and fond humor.

Sweeney may be familiar to you as a former cast member of *Saturday Night Live.* Her androgynous character "Pat" was a regular on the show, and later appeared in a movie. She began in show business as an accountant, keeping the books for *Rainman,* and edged into performance through local comedy clubs. After the *SNL* gig was over, she moved to Los Angeles, looking for work in movies and sitcoms, and bought her own house. Soon she was sharing it with her parents and Mike, and "the lines started to cross about whose house it really was."

Mike had lymphoma. He got worse and then he got better and then he got even worse, and then he got a little bit better—she charts the progress of an implacable foe. But there is laughter, too, especially from Mike, who found wry material in the doctor's decision to administer chemotherapy by inserting a permanent "shunt" into his body: Should it be called a faucet? A spigot? Where should it go? The possibilities were endless.

Sweeney's parents come across as nice people who, in their well-meaning attempts to stay out of the way, are usually in the way. When a light goes out in the bathroom, her mother reports, "I found a bulb—but I didn't know if there was some special way to screw it in."

During Mike's illness, Sweeney began talking about what she was going through as part of her act. "It must be hard," Mike joked, "you being an actress, and me in the cancer spotlight." It was hard for Mike, too—who now spent much of his time in a bed in her living room, and who as a child so valued his privacy that he installed a doorbell on his bedroom door.

Sweeney and other family members would take him to the UCLA Medical Center several times a week for chemotherapy, and as they met patients with many kinds of cancer, they began to muse on why cancer only seemed to strike vital organs. "Why can't there be cancer of the fat?" she wondered, only to find out that there was—and that you don't want it, either.

Watching God Said, 'Ha!', I wished that I could show it to people who wondered why I didn't approve of Patch Adams. This film has a dignity, an underlying taste, in the way it deals with subjects like cancer and dying. It doesn't simply use the subjects as an occasion for manipulative sentiment. At the end of the film, we feel we've been through a lot with Julia and Mike Sweeney and their family. We're sad, but we're smiling. I was thinking: Life's like that.

Gods and Monsters ★ ★ ★
NO MPAA RATING, 105 m., 1998

Ian McKellen (James Whale), Brendan Fraser (Clayton Boone), Lynn Redgrave (Whale's Housekeeper), Lolita Davidovich (Boone's Girlfriend). Directed by Bill Condon and produced by Paul Colichman, Gregg Fienberg, and Mark R. Harris. Screenplay by Condon, based on the novel Father of Frankenstein, by Christopher Bram.

The yard man looks a little like Frankenstein's monster, with his hulky body and flat-top haircut. Of course, he's more handsome. The old man sizes him up, invites him to tea, is friendly: "Feel free to use the pool. We're quite informal here—no need to use a bathing suit." We are listening to the last hopeful sigh of a dying romantic, an aging homosexual who is still cheered by the presence of beauty.

Gods and Monsters is a speculation about the last days of the director James Whale, who was open about his sexuality in an era when most homosexuals in Hollywood stayed prudently in the closet. Whale (1889–1957) directed some twenty-one films, but is best remembered for seven made between 1931 and

1939: Frankenstein, The Old Dark House, The Invisible Man, Bride of Frankenstein, Show Boat, The Great Garrick, and The Man in the Iron Mask. At the time of his death he had not made a movie in sixteen years, but still lived comfortably, dabbling at a little painting and a little lusting.

He made some good movies (Frankenstein placed eighty-seventh on the AFI's list of great American films, although Bride of Frankenstein is by far the better of the two pictures). He began as an actor, lost his first love in World War I, and joined the exodus to Hollywood, where he made a lot of money and never quite realized his potential. He must have seemed an attractive challenge to Ian McKellen, the gifted British Shakespearean who in this film and Apt Pupil is belatedly flourishing in the movies after much distinction on the stage.

McKellen playing Whale makes sense, but is it ideal casting to use Brendan Fraser (George of the Jungle) as Clayton Boone, the young man who comes to cut the grass? Fraser is subtle and attuned to the role, but doesn't project strong sexuality; shouldn't the yard man be not simply attractive but potentially exciting to the old man? We never ever believe there's a possibility that anything physical will occur between them—and we should, I think.

Of course, Whale's ambitions in that direction are mostly daydreams, and finally he's more interested in simply regarding the young man. He asks Clayton to be his artist's model, a request that essentially translates as, "Will you take off your clothes and stand there while I look at you?"

Clayton is slow to understand that Whale is gay. Well, in 1957 a lot of people might not have understood. When he figures it out, he isn't angered, and there's no painful and predictable scene of violence. Instead, the film proceeds on a bittersweet course in which a young and not terribly bright man grows to like an old and very intelligent man, and to pity him a little. The film is a biopic leading toward a graceful elegy.

Similar material was dealt with earlier this year in Love and Death on Long Island, starring John Hurt as an aging British writer who develops a crush on an American teen heartthrob (Jason Priestley). That was a funnier movie, and also more elusive, since the Hurt character is not an active homosexual (indeed, hardly seems sexual at all) and barely understands the nature of his own obsession. Levels of irony were possible. In *Gods and Monsters*, on the other hand, both the director and the yard man are pretty much kept at the service of the film's sentimental vision.

Directed by Bill Condon, who based his screenplay on the novel *Father of Frankenstein* by Christopher Bram, the movie has flashbacks to the making of Whale's classics, scenes where Clayton and his girlfriend (Lolita Davidovich) watch some of them, and memories of the pool parties that the closeted director George Cukor held every Sunday at his mansion above Sunset. (I once interviewed Cukor at the very poolside. A venerable and beloved figure in a liberated age, he was still prudent about his revelations; he remembered Katharine Hepburn swimming in the pool, but of course there was no whisper about the Sunday skinny-dips.)

In *Gods and Monsters*, Whale knows his health is failing. He lives alone except for a cheerless housekeeper (Lynn Redgrave, very good) who lectures him on bad behavior and tells him he will go to hell. She sizes up Clayton and knows the whole story instantly—has no doubt seen the same scenario enacted many times. But this time, because Clayton feels empathy and because Whale feels the chill of approaching death, the seduction strategies are pro forma. What the man most needs to do is talk, and Clayton lets him, as he slips between the present and his vivid memories.

Gods and Monsters is not a deep or powerful film, but it is a good-hearted one, in which we sense the depth of early loss that helped to shape Whale's protective style, and the California openness that allows Clayton Boone to care for a man he has nothing in common with. The film includes a clip from *Bride of Frankenstein* of a toast to "gods and monsters." By creating a wife for Frankenstein's monster out of base materials, Dr. Praetorious of course was the god. Now James Whale finds he no longer has the strength or the impulse to create a lover for himself. At the end there are neither gods nor monsters, only memories.

Godzilla ★ ½
PG-13, 138 m., 1998

Matthew Broderick (Dr. Niko Tatopoulos), Jean Reno (Philippe Roche), Maria Pitillo (Audrey Timmonds), Hank Azaria (Victor [Animal] Palotti), Kevin Dunn (Colonel Hicks), Michael Lerner (Mayor Ebert), Harry Shearer (Charles Caiman), Arabella Field (Lucy Palotti), Vicki Lewis (Dr. Elsie Chapman), Doug Savant (Sergeant O'Neal), Malcolm Danare (Dr. Mendel Craven). Directed by Roland Emmerich and produced by Dean Devlin. Screenplay by Devlin and Emmerich, based on the character Godzilla in films by Toho Co. Ltd.

CANNES, France—Going to see *Godzilla* at the Palais of the Cannes Film Festival is like attending a satanic ritual in St. Peter's Basilica. It's a rebuke to the faith that the building represents. Cannes touchingly adheres to a belief that film can be intelligent, moving, and grand. *Godzilla* is a big, ugly, ungainly device designed to give teenagers the impression they are seeing a movie. It was the festival's closing film, coming at the end like the horses in a parade, perhaps for the same reason.

It rains all through *Godzilla,* and it's usually night. Well, of course it is: That makes the special effects easier to obscure. If you never get a clear look at the monster, you can't see how shoddy it is. Steven Spielberg opened *Jurassic Park* by giving us a good, long look at the dinosaurs in full sunlight, and our imaginations leapt up. *Godzilla* hops out of sight like a camera-shy kangaroo.

The makers of the film, director Roland Emmerich and writer Dean Devlin, follow the timeless outlines of many other movies about Godzilla, Rodan, Mothra, Gamera, and their radioactive kin. There are ominous attacks on ships at sea, alarming blips on radar screens, and a scientist who speculates that nuclear tests may have spawned a mutant creature. A cast of stereotyped stock characters is introduced and made to say lines like, "I don't understand—how could something so big just disappear?" Or, "Many people have had their lives changed forever!" And then there are the big special effects sequences, as Godzilla terrorizes New York.

One must carefully repress intelligent

thought while watching such a film. The movie makes no sense at all except as a careless pastiche of its betters (and, yes, the Japanese *Godzilla* movies are, in their way, better—if only because they embrace dreck instead of condescending to it). You have to absorb such a film, not consider it. But my brain rebelled and insisted on applying logic where it was not welcome.

How, for example, does a 300-foot-tall creature fit inside a subway tunnel? How come it's sometimes only as tall as the tunnel, and at other times taller than high-rise office buildings? How big is it, anyway? Why can it breathe fire but hardly ever makes use of this ability? Why, when the heroes hide inside the Park Avenue tunnel, is this tunnel too small for Godzilla to enter, even though it is larger than a subway tunnel? And why doesn't Godzilla just snort some flames down there and broil them?

Most monster movies have at least one bleeding-heart environmentalist to argue the case of the monstrous beast, but here we get only Niko Tatopoulos (Matthew Broderick), an expert on the mutant earthworms of Chernobyl, who seems less like a scientist than like a placeholder waiting for a rewrite ("insert more interesting character here"). It is he who intuits that Godzilla is a female. (You would think that if a 300-foot monster were male, that would be hard to miss, but never mind.) The military in all movies about monsters and aliens from outer space always automatically attempts to kill them, and here they fire lots of wimpy missiles and torpedoes at Godzilla, which have so little effect we wonder how our tax dollars are being spent. (Just once, I'd like a movie where they train Godzilla to do useful tasks, like pulling a coaxial cable across the ocean floor, or pushing stuck trains out of tunnels.)

In addition to the trigger-happy Americans, there is a French force, too, led by Jean Reno, a good actor who plays this role as if he got on the plane shouting, "I'm going to Disneyland!" All humans in monster movies have simpleminded little character traits, and Reno's obsession is with getting a decent cup of coffee. Other characters include a TV newswoman (Maria Pitillo) who used to be the worm man's girlfriend, a determined camera-

man (Hank Azaria), a grim-jawed military leader (Kevin Dunn), and a simpering anchorman (Harry Shearer). None of these characters emerges as anything more than a source of obligatory dialogue.

Oh, and then there are New York's Mayor Ebert (gamely played by Michael Lerner) and his adviser, Gene (Lorry Goldman). The mayor, of course, makes every possible wrong decision (he is against evacuating Manhattan, etc.), and the adviser eventually gives thumbs-down to his reelection campaign. These characters are a reaction by Emmerich and Devlin to negative Siskel and Ebert reviews of their earlier movies *(Stargate, Independence Day)*, but they let us off lightly; I fully expected to be squished like a bug by Godzilla. Now that I've inspired a character in a Godzilla movie, all I really still desire is for several Ingmar Bergman characters to sit in a circle and read my reviews to one another in hushed tones.

There is a way to make material like *Godzilla* work. It can be campy fun, like the recent *Gamera, Guardian of the Universe.* Or hallucinatory, like *Infra-Man.* Or awesome, like *Jurassic Park.* Or it can tap a certain elemental dread, like the original *King Kong.* But all of those approaches demand a certain sympathy with the material, a zest that rises to the occasion.

In Howard Hawks's *The Thing,* there is a great scene where scientists in the Arctic spread out to trace the outlines of something mysterious that is buried in the ice, and the camera slowly pulls back to reveal that it is circular— a saucer. In *Godzilla,* the worm expert is standing in a deep depression, and the camera pulls back to reveal that he is standing in a footprint—which he would obviously already have known. There might be a way to reveal the astonishing footprint to the character and the audience at the same time, but that would involve a sense of style and timing, and some thought about the function of the scene.

There is nothing wrong with making a *Godzilla* movie and nothing wrong with special effects. But don't the filmmakers have some obligation to provide pop entertainment that at least lifts the spirits? There is real feeling in King Kong fighting off the planes that attack him, or the pathos of the monster in *Bride of Frankenstein,* who was so misunderstood. There is a true sense of wonder in *Jurassic Park.*

Godzilla, by contrast, offers nothing but soulless technique: A big lizard is created by special effects, wreaks havoc, and is destroyed. What a coldhearted, mechanistic vision, so starved for emotion or wit. The primary audience for *Godzilla* is children and teenagers, and the filmmakers have given them a sterile exercise when they hunger for dreams.

Gone in 60 Seconds ★ ★
PG-13, 119 m., 2000

Nicolas Cage (Memphis Raines), Delroy Lindo (Detective), Giovanni Ribisi (Kip Raines), Robert Duvall (Otto Halliwell), Angelina Jolie ("Sway" Wayland), Christopher Eccleston (Raymond Calitri), T. J. Cross (Mirror Man), William Lee Scott (Toby), Scott Caan (Tumbler), James Duval (Freb), Will Patton (Atley Jackson). Directed by Dominic Sena and produced by Jerry Bruckheimer and Mike Stenson. Screenplay by Scott Rosenberg.

Gone in 60 Seconds is like a practice game between the varsity and the reserves. Everybody plays pretty well, but they're saving up for Saturday. First team is Nicolas Cage, Delroy Lindo, and Robert Duvall. Second team is Giovanni Ribisi, Will Patton, and Angelina Jolie, who gets second billing but not much playing time. There are lots of subs who come off the bench for a play or two. This is the kind of movie that ends up playing on the TV set over the bar in a better movie.

Nicolas Cage plays Memphis Raines, who used to be the greatest car thief in Los Angeles ("I didn't do it for the money. I did it for the cars"). Now he has retired to the desert to run a gas station and go-cart track. He retired because his mom asked him to. She was afraid his younger brother Kip (Ribisi) would become a thief too. Kip became a thief anyway. Kip steals a car, recklessly leads the cops to a chop shop, and angers a vile crime lord named Raymond (Christopher Eccleston), who, according to a line Robert Duvall successfully says out loud without laughing, is "a jackal tearing at the soft belly of our fair city."

Memphis learns about Kip's screwup from one of his old crew members. He visits Ray-

mond to try to set things right, but Raymond has Kip handcuffed inside a car and threatens to crush him and sell him as scrap metal. Memphis can save him by stealing fifty hard-to-find cars. Memphis recruits an old pal (Duvall); together they assemble a very large team in a very long and boring sequence that produces so many car thieves we can't keep them all straight. It looks like they sent out contracts to a lot of actors and were surprised when they all said yes.

The pros try to steal the fifty cars. Delroy Lindo, as the cop, knows who they are and what they plan to do, but wants to catch them at it. He intuits that the key theft will be of a 1967 Shelby GT 350 Mustang, a car Memphis both loves and fears. "He'll save that for the last," says Lindo, planning to nab him in the act. This decision means that forty-nine cars will *already* have been stolen before Memphis moves on the Mustang. I am reminded of the line from *Fargo* when Marge tells her deputy, "I'm not sure I agree with you a hundred percent on your police work there, Lou."

There isn't much time for character development. Cage walks on-screen with his character already established from *The Rock* and *Con Air.* Duvall is . . . Duvall. Angelina Jolie's rare appearances are reminders she is still in the picture. After the confusions of the recruitment scenes and the puzzlement about who all these guys are, it's a relief when the movie goes on autopilot with a fabulous chase sequence and an obligatory final confrontation inside a flame and steam factory.

We have discussed flame and steam factories before. They are cavernous industrial locations with flame and steam in the background and no people around. The moment I saw the first shower of sparks, I predicted that Memphis and Raymond would eventually be climbing around on high catwalks while shooting at one another, that Memphis would inevitably cling to a catwalk by his fingers, and that Raymond would fall to his death. See how well your own predictions turn out.

The chase sequence is fine. Memphis hurtles the Mustang down city streets and alleys and hits 160 mph in a drainage ditch, outsmarting a police helicopter by taking the tunnel under the airport while the copter is waved away from commercial airspace. There is a stunt jump that would have made Evel Knievel famous, and dead. All of this is done in weirdly underlit, saturated dark colors; the movie desperately yearns to be in sepiatone, and some of its skies are so dark you're looking for the twister.

Movies like this are what they are. *Gone in 60 Seconds* is a prodigious use of money and human effort to make a movie of no significance whatever, in which the talents of the artists are subordinated to the requirements of the craftsmen. Witnessing it, you get some thrills, some chuckles, a few good one-liners, and after 119 minutes are regurgitated by the theater not much the worse for wear.

Goodbye, Lover ★
R, 102 m., 1999

Patricia Arquette (Sandra), Dermot Mulroney (Jake), Don Johnson (Ben), Mary-Louise Parker (Peggy), Ellen DeGeneres (Detective Rita Pompano), Ray McKinnon (Detective Rollins). Directed by Roland Joffe and produced by Arnon Milchan. Screenplay by Ron Peer, Joel Cohen, and Alec Sokolow.

I've just transcribed no less than eleven pages of notes I scribbled during *Goodbye, Lover,* and my mind boggles. The plot is so labyrinthine that I'd completely forgotten the serial killer named The Doctor, who murders young women by injecting curare into their veins with a syringe. When a character like The Doctor is an insignificant supporting character, a movie's plate is a little too full, don't you think?

Goodbye, Lover is not so much a story as some kind of a board game, with too many pieces and not enough rules. The characters careen through the requirements of the plot, which has so many double-reverses that the real danger isn't murder, it's being disemboweled by G-forces. There's no way to care about the characters, because their fates are arbitrary—determined not by character, not by personality, but by the jigsaw puzzle constructed by the screenwriters (there are three of them—which, for this material, represents a skeleton crew).

And yet the film does have a certain audacity. It contains a character played by Patricia Arquette who is the most enthusiastic sexual being since Emmanuelle, and another, played by Don Johnson, who just plain gets tuckered out by her demands. (At one point, they've taken the collection in church and are walking down the aisle with the offering, and she's whispering that he should meet her for sex tomorrow, or else.) There's also a droll supporting role for Ellen DeGeneres, as a police detective who keeps picking on her partner, a Mormon man who doesn't, I hope, understand most of her jokes. One of her key clues comes with the discovery of a *Sound of Music* tape, which arouses her suspicions: "I don't trust anybody over the age of ten who listens to 'The Sound of Music.'"

The movie opens with phone sex and never looks back. We meet Sandra (Arquette), a Realtor who memorizes Tony Robbins self-help tapes, treasures *The Sound of Music* as her favorite movie, and likes to whisper, "I'm not wearing any underwear." She is having an affair with Ben (Johnson), and at one point handcuffs him with some sex toys she finds in a house she's selling. When the clients return unexpectedly, poor Ben barely has time to release himself and hide the cuffs in his pants pocket. (The Foley artists, concerned that we may have missed the point, cause the cuffs to rattle deafeningly, as if Ben had a tambourine concealed in his underwear.)

Sandra is married to Jake (Dermot Mulroney), who is Ben's brother. Ben is the straight arrow who runs an ad agency, and Jake is the unkempt alcoholic who nevertheless is a brilliant copywriter. Why is Sandra cheating on Jake? The answer is not only more complicated than you might think—it's not even the real answer. This is one of those plots where you might want to take a night school class about double-indemnity clauses in insurance policies before you even think about buying a ticket.

My space is limited, but I must also mention the GOP senator who is caught with a transvestite hustler; the struggle on the condo balcony; the motorcycle-car chase; the sex scene in a church's organ loft; the black leather mask; the Vegas wedding chapel ploy; Mike, the professional killer (not to be confused with The Doctor); and Peggy, Ben's secretary, who is played by Mary-Louise Parker as the kind of woman who would be a nymphomaniac in any other movie, but compared to Sandra is relatively abstentious.

There is a part of me that knows this movie is very, very bad. And another part of me that takes a guilty pleasure in it. Too bad I saw it at a critic's screening, where professional courtesy requires a certain decorum. This is the kind of movie that might be materially improved by frequent hoots of derision. All bad movies have good twins, and the good version of *Goodbye, Lover* is *The Hot Spot* (1990), which also starred Don Johnson, along with Virginia Madsen and Jennifer Connelly, in a thriller that was equally lurid but less hyperkinetic. *Goodbye, Lover* is so overwrought it reminds me of the limerick about that couple from Khartoum, who argued all night, about who had the right, to do what, and with which, and to whom.

Gossip ★ ★
R, 90 m., 2000

James Marsden (Derrick), Lena Headey (Jones), Norman Reedus (Travis), Kate Hudson (Naomi Preston), Joshua Jackson (Beau Edson), Marisa Coughlan (Sheila), Edward James Olmos (Detective Curtis), Sharon Lawrence (Detective Kelly), Eric Bogosian (Professor Goodwin). Directed by Davis Guggenheim and produced by Jeffrey Silver and Bobby Newmyer. Screenplay by Gregory Poirier and Theresa Rebeck.

Gossip stays in the game until the bottom of the ninth, and then blows it. The trick ending is a kick in the teeth. The movie tells a story worth telling, and then cops out with an ironic gimmick that's like a sneer at the craft of storytelling. *Usual Suspects* had the grace to earn its surprise ending, but *Gossip* pulls a 180 just for the hell of it. Chop off the last two or three minutes, fade to black, and you have a decent film.

The premise is promising. We meet three college roommates who decide to start a rumor just to see how far it will go. They spread the news that a couple had sex in an upstairs bed-room at an off-campus party. Problem is, the rich girl in the bedroom was drunk and passed out. She hears the gossip, assumes it's true, and brings rape charges against her date. And then it gets a lot more complicated than that, until simply telling the truth won't mend things anymore.

The story takes place on the kind of campus that would be designed by the ad agency for Bennetton. The roommates are Jones (Lena Headey), independent and smart, who seems to cast herself in a real-time version of *Murder, She Wrote*, Derrick (James Marsden), a ladies' man with easy charm and something wrong inside, and Travis (Norman Reedus), who creates strange art out of graphics and photographs, and has trouble expressing himself. The roomies share a luxurious loft, where they spend more time drinking than Nick and Nora Charles in the *Thin Man* movies. My guess is that less booze and at least some drugs would be involved with characters like these, but it's glug, glug, glug, scene after scene.

The film is heavy on style, and knows what it's doing. Cinematographer Andrzej Bartkowiak *(Speed, Species)* deepens the colors and photographs the actors like models, which works because great though he makes them look, they can still act. Jones is the catalyst. She agrees to spread the rumor, and then develops a conscience when the gossip goes wrong. She also gets to perform the obligatory high school yearbook scene, in which secrets from the past are obligingly revealed.

As the seriousness of the situation escalates, the student charged with rape (Joshua Jackson) is led away in handcuffs, and his date (Kate Hudson) hits the bottle as if she were Dorothy Malone in a 1950s weeper. Edward James Olmos knocks on the door and introduces himself as the detective on the case, and he's good at his role, brushing aside Derrick's alibis and self-assurance as if shooing a fly. Eric Bogosian has a juicy role as one of those showboat professors who conducts lectures like a talk show and is filled with a deep appreciation of himself.

And then the movie self-destructs. The material was here, in Gregory Poirier and Theresa Rebeck's screenplay, for a movie that had something interesting to say about date rape and gossip. But it all derails in a self-indulgent exercise, as director Davis Guggenheim ducks responsibility to the story and gives us a cop-out instead. I really got into this film. If I hadn't, maybe the ending wouldn't have annoyed me so much.

The Governess ★ ★ ★
R, 114 m., 1998

Minnie Driver (Rosina da Silva), Tom Wilkinson (Charles Cavendish), Florence Hoath (Clementina), Jonathan Rhys Meyers (Henry), Harriet Walter (Mrs. Cavendish), Arlene Cockburn (Lily Milk). Directed by Sandra Goldbacher and produced by Sarah Curtis. Screenplay by Goldbacher.

The Governess could be an illustration of the ideas in Virginia Woolf's *A Room of One's Own,* in which she marvels at how necessary it is for men to have women to feel superior to. The film tells the story of an educated, spirited Jewish girl from London who, in the 1840s, finds work as a governess on a remote Scottish island to support her family. She enters a household where she is clearly the intellectual equal of the father, and that is more than he can take—although he gives it a good try.

Minnie Driver, grave and thoughtful between moments of high spirits and passion, plays Rosina, who grew up in a Sephardic Jewish community in London. Her family life is richly cultured, but almost entirely cut off from the gentile world around her, and anti-Semitism is a fact of life. When her father dies, she hopes to help her mother and sister, but there are few professions open to her; it was a truism much beloved of Victorian novelists that a single woman in her position had three choices: marriage, domestic service, or prostitution.

She takes the middle choice, and to sidestep discrimination renames herself Mary Blackchurch, a Protestant whose part-Italian ancestry explains her olive skin. She is hired by the Cavendish family of Scotland as a governess for their unpleasant little girl Clementina. The father (Tom Wilkinson) is a man obsessed with the new science of photography, and spends long hours in his studio and darkroom, as indeed anyone married to his ignorant and controlling wife (Harriet Walter)

would have great inspiration to do. There is also a teenage boy, Henry (Jonathan Rhys Meyers), who falls instantly into lust for "Mary," perhaps the first attractive girl he has seen.

The governess is fascinated by Cavendish's photography—both the artistic side and the technical problem of fixing images so they do not fade. She spends long hours in his company and they are drawn together, she by a healthy interest in a smart and virile man, he struggling with the mossy ropes of Protestant guilt. Photography is the instrument of their mutual seduction; she insists on posing for him, her image on the negative a way of forcing him to see her as a woman and not just a servant.

The film was written and directed by Sarah Goldbacher, who is, I understand, the child of an Italian Jewish father and a mother born on the very island where the film was shot. Although she sets the story at an earlier time in which all tensions and questions would have been heightened, there is no doubt some autobiography here, especially in her character's determination to remain privately true to her Jewish heritage. Her affair with Cavendish is given additional irony by the likelihood that he would scorn her if he knew she was Jewish.

Minnie Driver is an actress who creates the illusion of eroticism, not through appearance but through behavior. She is of course physically attractive, but that isn't the point: Her characters have a way of focusing on men, on paying them observant attention that causes them to grow a little squirmy, and that's a sexy phenomenon. Many male actors feel that their task in romantic scenes is to seem powerful, attractive, and in charge, when in fact those are precisely the qualities that obscure what effect, if any, the woman has on them. Tom Wilkinson (the proud foreman in *The Full Monty* and the outraged Marquese of Queensbury in *Wilde*) shows Cavendish attracted to this young woman despite his own best efforts, and that is ever so much more erotic than a confident seduction.

Photography provides the counterpoint: Their dance of attraction begins at arm's length through the pictures they take of one another. The claustrophobic, isolated Victorian household is a stage on which every nuance, however small, is noticed. And there are rich underlying ironies, not least that by denying their assigned places in society (he as a husband, she as a Jew), they are able for a time to function freely just as two people happy to be together in mind and body.

Grass ★ ★
R, 80 m., 2000

A documentary directed and produced by Ron Mann. Narrated by Woody Harrelson. Screenplay by Solomon Vesta.

It is agreed by reasonable people that one of the results of antidrug laws is to support the price of drugs and make their sale lucrative. If drugs were legalized, the price would fall, and the motive to promote them would fade away. Since anyone who wants drugs can already get them, usage would be unlikely to increase. Crime would go down when addicts didn't have to steal to support their habits, and law enforcement would benefit from the disappearance of drug-financed bribery, payoffs, and corruption.

All of this is so obvious that the opposition to the legalization of drugs seems inexplicable—unless you ask who would be hurt the most by the repeal of drug laws. The international drug cartels would be put out of business. Drug enforcement agencies would be unnecessary. Drug wholesalers and retailers would have to seek other employment. If it is true (as often charged) that the CIA has raised money by dealing in drugs, it would lose this source of funds free from congressional accounting. Who would *benefit* if drugs were legalized? The public—because both drug usage and its associated crimes would diminish.

Despite the logic of this argument, few political candidates have had the nerve to question the way that our drug laws act as a price support system, and encourage drug usage. *Grass,* a new documentary by Ron Mann, traces the history of the laws against one drug—marijuana—back to their origins in anti-Mexican prejudice at the turn of the century, and forward through periods when marijuana was seen as part of the Red conspiracy. When New York Mayor Fiorello LaGuardia commissioned a study of the weed, his commission found the "sociological, psychological, and medical" threat of the substance was "exaggerated." He called for its decriminalization. So, many years later, did President Jimmy Carter—until he had to lay low after an aide was nabbed on cocaine charges.

Other presidents, of course, have enthusiastically supported antidrug laws (Nixon going so far as to swear in Elvis Presley in the war against narcotics). *Grass* traces much of our national drug policy to one man, Harry J. Anslinger, the first drug czar, who like J. Edgar Hoover, created a fiefdom that was immune to congressional criticism.

Grass is not much as a documentary. It's a cut-and-paste job, assembling clips from old and new antidrug films, and alternating them with prodrug footage from the Beats, the flower power era, and so on. The narration by prohemp campaigner Woody Harrelson is underlined by the kind of lurid graphics usually seen on 1940s coming attractions trailers.

The film is unlikely to tell many of its viewers anything they don't already know, and unlikely to change our national drug policy. The situation will continue indefinitely, corrupting politicians and whole nations with billions of dollars of illegal profits. Those who use drugs will continue to do so. Others will abstain, die, or find a way to stop, just as they do now. Prohibition proved that when the government tries to come between the people and what the people want to do, laws are not effective; statistically, Prohibition coincided with a considerable increase in drinking.

Am I in favor of drugs? Not at all. Drug abuse has led to an epidemic of human suffering. Grass seems relatively harmless, but I have not known anyone who used hard drugs and emerged undamaged. Still, in most societies throughout human history, drug use has been treated realistically—as a health problem, not a moral problem. Have our drug laws prevented anyone from using drugs? Apparently not. Have they given us the world's largest prison population, cost us billions of dollars, and helped create the most violent society in the First World? Yes. From an objective point of view—what's the point?

Grease ★ ★ ★
PG, 112 m., 1978 (rereleased 1998)

John Travolta (Danny), Olivia Newton-John (Sandy), Stockard Channing (Rizzo), Jeff Conaway (Kenickie), Barry Pearl (Doody), Michael Tucci (Sonny), Kelly Ward (Putzie), Didi Conn (Frenchy). Directed by Randal Kleiser and produced by Robert Stigwood and Allan Carr. Screenplay by Bronte Woodard, based on the original musical by Jim Jacobs and Warren Casey.

Grease, a 1970s celebration of nostalgia for the 1950s, is now being resurrected as 1970s nostalgia. But no revival, however joyously promoted, can conceal the fact that this is just an average musical, pleasant and upbeat and plastic.

The musical is being revived not because it is invaluable, but because it contains an invaluable cultural icon: the singing, dancing performance of John Travolta. It is now clear that, slumps or not, comebacks or not, Travolta is an important and enduring movie star whose presence can redeem even a compromised *Grease*. This is not one of his great films, and lacks the electricity of *Saturday Night Fever* or the quirky genius of *Pulp Fiction*, but it has charm. If Travolta lacks the voltage of Elvis Presley (his obvious role model for this film), at least he's in the same ballpark, and Elvis didn't make such great movies, either.

The story, smoothed out and set in southern California, involves a greaser named Danny (Travolta) who has a sweet summertime romance with Sandy, an Australian girl (Olivia Newton-John; making her character Australian was easier than coaching her American accent). When summer ends, they part forever, they think, only to find themselves at the same school, where Danny's tough-guy image makes it hard for him to acknowledge the squeaky-clean Sandy.

The film re-creates a 1950s that exists mostly in idyllic memory (for an alternative version, see *Rebel Without a Cause*). There are hot rods, malt shops, school dances, songs from the original Jim Jacobs and Warren Casey musical, and new songs, written to fit the characters. It's fun, yes, but it doesn't lift off the screen; the only element that bears comparison with the musicals of the Golden Age is Travolta's performance, although in the 1950s at MGM he would have been best friend, not star.

One problem I always have watching the movie is that all the students look too old. They're supposed to be sixteen or seventeen, I guess, but they look in their late twenties, and don't seem comfortable as teenagers. One of my favorite performances is by Stockard Channing, as Rizzo, the tough girl who forges ahead heedlessly after the condom breaks. She's fun, but were there sixteen-year-old girls like that in the 1950s? Call me a dreamer, but I don't think so.

The movie's worth seeing for nostalgia, or for a look at vintage Travolta, but its underlying problem is that it sees the material as silly camp: It neuters it. Romance and breaking up are matters of life and death for teenagers, and a crisis of self-esteem can be a crushing burden. *Grease* doesn't seem to remember that. *Saturday Night Fever* does.

Great Expectations ★ ★ ★
R, 111 m., 1998

Ethan Hawke (Finnegan Bell), Gwyneth Paltrow (Estella), Anne Bancroft (Ms. Dinsmoor), Hank Azaria (Walter Plane), Chris Cooper (Joe), Robert De Niro (Prisoner/Lustig), Josh Mostel (Jerry Ragno). Directed by Alfonso Cuaron and produced by Art Linson. Screenplay by Mitch Glazer, based on a novel by Charles Dickens.

This is not, says Finn, the way the story really happened, but the way he remembers it. That is how everyone tells the stories that matter to them: Through their own eyes, rewritten by their own memories, with bold underscores for the parts that hurt. Finn's story is the life of a poor boy who falls in love with a rich girl who has been trained since childhood to break the hearts of men.

This tale has been borrowed from Charles Dickens's *Great Expectations*, where it is told in less lurid images and language, to be sure, but with the same sense of an innocent boy being lured into the lair of two dangerous women. That the women are lonely, sad, and good at heart makes it bittersweet. "What is it like not to feel anything?" Finn shouts at Estella after she has abandoned him. Of course, if you cannot feel anything, that is exactly the question you cannot answer.

The story has been updated by director Alfonso Cuaron, who moves it from Victorian England to a crumbling neo-Gothic mansion in Florida. It stars Ethan Hawke as Finn (Pip in the book), and Gwyneth Paltrow as Estella, the beautiful niece of the eccentric millionairess Ms. Dinsmoor (Anne Bancroft). Their paths cross in one of those backwaters of Florida that have been immortalized by writers like Elmore Leonard and John D. MacDonald, where creeping condos from the north have not yet dislodged small fishing shacks and the huge masonry pile of Paradiso Perduto, which once was a glittering showplace but is now engulfed in trees and creepers, and falling into decay.

Finn lives with his sister Maggie and "her man," Joe (Chris Cooper), who raises him after Maggie disappears. One day he is seen by Ms. Dinsmoor, who invites him to Paradiso Perduto to play with her niece. The two children are about ten. Finn is a gifted artist, and as he sketches the young girl, the old crone perceives that he will eventually fall in love with the girl, and sees her chance for revenge against men.

The original of Ms. Dinsmoor is, of course, Dickens's Miss Havisham, one of the most colorful and pathetic characters in Dickens, who was left stranded on her wedding day by a faithless lover. This version of *Great Expectations* spares us the sight of her wedding cake, covered in cobwebs after the decades (in Florida, tiny visitors would make short work of that feast). But it succeeds in making Ms. Dinsmore equally sad and venomous, and Anne Bancroft's performance is interesting: Despite the weird eye makeup and the cigarettes, despite the flamboyant clothing, she is human, and not without humor. "That's the biggest cat I've ever seen," Finn says on his first visit. "What do you feed it?" She waits for a beat. "Other cats," she says.

Paradiso Perduto and its inhabitants reminded me of *Grey Gardens,* the 1976 documentary about two relatives of Jackie Onassis, who lived in a decaying mansion in East Hampton with countless cats. There is the same sense of defiance: If I was once young, rich, and beautiful, these women say to the world, see what you have made of me! Cuaron, whose previous film was *The Little Princess,* brings a touch of magic realism to the setting, with weeping willows, skies filled with seabirds, and a scene where Finn and Estella dance to "Besame Mucho" while Ms. Dinsmore looks on, cold-eyed.

Time passes. The young actors who played Finn and Estella are replaced by Hawke and Paltrow, who meet again at the mansion after several years, and share a sudden kiss at a water fountain, which is cut between backlit shots from moving cameras so that it seems more orgiastic than most sex scenes. After this romantic spark Estella again dances away, and the story continues some years later in New York, where a mysterious benefactor offers to bankroll Finn's show at an important gallery, and Estella again appears on the scene, this time with a hapless fiancé/victim named Walter in tow.

Great Expectations begins as a great movie (I was spellbound by the first thirty minutes), but ends as only a good one, and I think that's because the screenplay, by Mitch Glazer, too closely follows the romantic line. Dickens, who of course had more time and space to move around in, made it the story of a young man's coming of age, and the colorful characters he encountered—from the escaped prisoner of the opening scenes (played here by Robert De Niro) to good old, proud old Joe. The moment this movie declares itself as being mostly about affairs of the heart, it limits its potential.

And yet the film is a successful translation of the basic material from one period and approach to another. Especially in the early Florida scenes, it seems timeless. Hawke and Paltrow project that uneasy alertness of two people who know they like one another and suspect they'll regret it. But the subplot involving the escaped prisoner doesn't really pay off (it feels more like a bone thrown to Dickens than a necessity of the plot). And I am not quite sure that any good artist can create only when he's in sync with the girl of his dreams: Some artists paint best when their hearts are broken, and most artists paint no matter what, because they have to.

Great Expectations doesn't finish at the same high level that it begins (if it did, it would be one of the year's best films), but it's visually enchanted; the cinematographer, Emmanuel Lubezki, uses lighting and backlighting like a painter. And the characters have more depth and feeling than we might expect in what is, underneath everything, a fantasy. There's great joy in a scene where Finn sweeps Estella out of a restaurant and asks her to dance. And sadness later as she observes that Ms. Dinsmore's obsessions have become her own.

The Green Mile ★ ★ ★ ½
R, 182 m., 1999

Tom Hanks (Paul Edgecomb), David Morse (Brutus "Brutal" Howell), Michael Clarke Duncan (John Coffey), Doug Hutchison (Percy Wetmore), Michael Jeter (Eduard Delacroix), Sam Rockwell (William Wharton), Bonnie Hunt (Jan Edgecomb), James Cromwell (Warden Hal Moores), Graham Greene (Arlen Bitterbuck), Patricia Clarkson (Melinda Moores). Directed by Frank Darabont and produced by David Valdes and Darabont. Screenplay by Darabont, based on the novel by Stephen King.

"We think of this place like an intensive care ward of a hospital." So says Paul Edgecomb, who is in charge of death row in a Louisiana penitentiary during the Depression. Paul (Tom Hanks) is a nice man, probably nicer than your average Louisiana death row guard, and his staff is competent and humane—all except for the loathsome Percy, whose aunt is married to the governor, and who could have any state job he wants, but likes it here because "he wants to see one cook up close."

One day a new prisoner arrives. He is a gigantic black man, framed by the low-angle camera to loom over the guards and duck under doorways. This is John Coffey ("like the drink, only not spelled the same"), and he has been convicted of molesting and killing two little white girls. From the start it is clear he is not what he seems. He is afraid of the dark, for one thing. He is straightforward in shaking Paul's hand—not like a man with anything to be ashamed of.

This is not a good summer for Paul. He is suffering from a painful infection, and suffer-

ing, too, because Percy (Doug Hutchison) is like an infection in the ward: "The man is mean, careless, and stupid—that's a bad combination in a place like this." Paul sees his duty as regulating a calm and decent atmosphere in which men prepare to die.

The Green Mile (so called because this death row has a green floor) is based on a novel by Stephen King, and has been written and directed by Frank Darabont. It is Darabont's first film since the great *Shawshank Redemption* in 1994. That, too, was based on a King prison story, but this one is very different. It involves the supernatural, for one thing—in a spiritual, not creepy, way.

Both movies center on relationships between a white man and a black man. In *Shawshank* the black man was the witness to a white man's dogged determination, and here the black man's function is to absorb the pain of whites—to redeem and forgive them. By the end, when he is asked to forgive them for sending him to the electric chair, the story has so well prepared us that the key scenes play like drama, not metaphor, and that is not an easy thing to achieve.

The movie is told in flashback as the memories of Paul as an old man, now in a retirement home. "The math doesn't quite work out," he admits at one point, and we find out why. The story is in no haste to get to the sensational and supernatural; it takes at least an hour simply to create the relationships in the prison, where Paul's lieutenant (David Morse) is rock-solid and dependable, where the warden (James Cromwell) is good and fair; and where the prisoners include a balmy coot named Delacroix (Michael Jeter) and a taunting monster named Wharton (Sam Rockwell).

Looming over all is the presence of John Coffey (Michael Clarke Duncan), a man whose own lawyer says he seems to have "dropped out of the sky." Coffey cannot read or write, seems simpleminded, causes no trouble, and exudes goodness. The reason Paul consults the lawyer is because he comes to doubt this prisoner could have killed the little girls. Yet Coffey was found with their broken bodies in his huge arms. And in Louisiana in the 1930s a black man with such evidence against him is not likely to be acquitted by a jury. (We might indeed question whether a Louisiana death row in the 1930s would be so fair and hospitable to a convicted child molester, but the story carries its own conviction, and we go along with it.)

There are several sequences of powerful emotion in the film. Some of them involve the grisly details of the death chamber, and the process by which the state makes sure that a condemned man will actually die (Harry Dean Stanton has an amusing scene as a stand-in at a dress rehearsal with the electric chair). One execution is particularly gruesome, and seen in some detail; the R rating is earned here despite the film's generally benevolent tone. Other moments of great impact involve a tame mouse that Delacroix adopts, a violent struggle with Wharton (and his obscene attempts at rabble-rousing), and subplots involving the wives of Paul (Bonnie Hunt) and the warden (Patricia Clarkson).

But the center of the movie is the relationship between Paul and his huge prisoner, Coffey. Without describing the supernatural mechanism that is involved, I can explain in Coffey's own words what he does with the suffering he encounters: "I just took it back, is all." How he does that, and what the results are, all set up the film's ending—in which we are reminded of another execution some 2,000 years ago.

I have started to suspect that when we talk about "good acting" in the movies, we are really discussing two other things: good casting, and the creation of characters we react to strongly. Much of a performance is created in the filmmaking itself, in photography and editing and the emotional cues of music. But an actor must have the technical and emotional mastery to embody a character and evoke him persuasively, and the film must give him a character worth portraying. Tom Hanks is our movie everyman, and his Paul is able to win our sympathy with his level eyes and calm, decent voice. We get a real sense of his efficient staff, of the vile natures of Percy and Wharton, and of the goodness of Coffey—who is embodied by Duncan in a performance that is both acting and being.

The movie is a shade over three hours long. I appreciated the extra time, which allows us to feel the passage of prison months and years. Stephen King, sometimes dismissed as merely a best-seller, has in his best novels some of the power of Dickens, who created worlds that enveloped us, and populated them with colorful, peculiar, sharply seen characters. King in his strongest work is a storyteller likely to survive as Dickens has, despite the sniffs of the litcrit establishment.

By taking the extra time, Darabont has made King's *The Green Mile* into a story that develops and unfolds, that has detail and space. The movie would have been much diminished at two hours—it would have been a series of episodes without context. As Darabont directs it, it tells a story with beginning, middle, end, vivid characters, humor, outrage, and emotional release. Dickensian.

Groove ★ ★
R, 86 m., 2000

Lola Glaudini (Leyla), Hamish Linklater (David), Denny Kirkwood (Colin), MacKenzie Firgens (Harmony), Vince Riverside (Anthony), Rachel True (Beth), Steve Van Wormer (Ernie), Nick Offerman (Sergeant), Ari Gold (Cliff). Directed by Greg Harrison and produced by Danielle Renfrew. Screenplay by Harrison.

Groove provides a cleaned-up, innocuous version of the rave scene, showing it as a life-affirming voyage of discovery instead of what it often is, a stop-and-shop ticket to troubles with Ecstasy. Like drug movies from the 1960s, it's naive, believing that the problems of the straight life can be solved by dropping out and tuning in. It somehow manages not to have any of its characters actually say, "After that night, nothing was ever the same again," but I have a feeling they're thinking it.

The movie opens with a raid on an abandoned warehouse by the rave-master Ernie (Steve Van Wormer), who is seeking a venue for his next rave. Ernie sees himself as a sort of public servant; he charges only $2 a head because he *believes* in raves. When he is asked, toward dawn, why he risks arrest on all sorts of charges, he explains he does it for "the nod." The nod? Yes, the nod he gets at least once every party from someone who tells him, "Thanks, man. I feel like I really needed this."

If that's a tad simpleminded as a rationale for the zealous promotion of a drug-soaked venue, consider one of the film's self-proclaimed amateur narcotics experts, who offers advice like, "Never take drugs on an empty stomach." These characters are living in a neverland of idealism and bliss, and I look forward to other rave movies to document what must be the underside of their dream.

The movie's characters are barely sketched. We meet an experienced raver named Colin (Denny Kirkwood), who convinces his straight-arrow brother David (Hamish Linklater) to attend a rave against his own better judgment. David meets a woman named Leyla (Lola Glaudini) at the party and gets past her somewhat forbidding exterior to discover he likes her. She gives him Ecstasy and advises him to "drink a lot of water," although I am not sure if the water intake is associated with the drug use, or is simply her ingrained mantra (she seems like one of those women who never goes anywhere without two liters of Evian, and lectures you on the ominous threat of dehydration). By dawn David and Leyla have arrived at an understanding that, I hope for their sake, will allow them to move in together and quit the rave singles scene.

What is a rave, anyway, but an all-night party where you get high and dance? And what is very new about that? What sets raves apart from disco parties, be-ins, beer blasts, and all the earlier manifestations of the same thing is that they've become professionalized; word is spread on the Internet, and with his $2 admissions Ernie has somehow been able to afford a series of famous DJs, who trundle their turntables and vinyl on and off the scene without ever inspiring the curiosity of the filmmaker, Greg Harrison. We see a lot of them, but learn little about them—but then the film itself is very thin, with dance and music sequences stretched out to cover the lack of dramatic substance.

I liked the music. I would rather have the movie's sound track than see it again—or at all. I know that every generation goes through its rites of passage, and having partied until the dawn more than a time or two myself, I am in sympathy. But the filmmaker has a different responsibility than his subjects. While their job is to be young, get high, meet a sexual partner, and possibly find someone they can stand to live with, the job of the director is to see beyond these immediate goals. I don't ask

that he take a long-term view. Even a taste of the middle distance would do.

Guinevere ★ ★ ★ ½
R, 107 m., 1999

Sarah Polley (Harper Sloane), Stephen Rea (Connie Fitzpatrick), Carrie Preston (Patty), Tracy Letts (Zack), Gina Gershon (Billie), Jean Smart (Deborah Sloane), Emily Procter (Susan), Sharon McNight (Leslie). Directed by Audrey Wells and produced by Jonathan King and Brad Weston. Screenplay by Wells.

Despite all the piety of conventional opinion, people will insist sometimes on falling in love with inappropriate partners. No thoughtful person is ever looking for an appropriate partner in the first place—they're looking for the solution to their own needs and dreams. If you find who you need, then that's the partner you want, no matter what your parents or society tell you. Heaven help the spouse who has been chosen for appropriateness.

Guinevere is a love story involving a twenty-one-year-old woman who is fresh, blond, and vulnerable, and a man in his fifties who is a wet-eyed, hangdog drunk. "He was the worst man I ever met—or maybe the best," she remembers four years after their affair ended. "If you're supposed to learn from your mistakes, then he was the best mistake I ever made." They are not a good match or even a reasonable one, but at that time, and for her needs, he was a better choice than some college boy.

The woman's name is not Guinevere but Harper. He calls all of his women Guinevere. His name is Connie Fitzpatrick, and he's a talented but alcoholic photographer who lives in a loft in San Francisco and specializes in mentoring young women. He also sleeps with them, but we sense that the sex is secondary to the need for protégés. Harper arrives at his loft as the previous Guinevere is tearfully leaving, and later in the film Connie is presented with a group portrait of five of his former lovers: "Your life work," they tell him.

Harper (Sarah Polley) meets Connie at a particular time in her life. Her family is rich and cold. She is on track for Harvard but feels no calling to go there. There is no boy in her life. Anger, irony, and cynicism circle the family dining table. She wants to break with this and find a partner who allows her to express her idealism. Writing those words, I realized that *Guinevere* tells the same story as *American Beauty,* with the ages and sexes reversed: The middle-aged Kevin Spacey character lusts for a high school cheerleader for the same reason that Harper knocks on the photographer's door; what they both seek is affirmation that they are good, unique, and treasured. If you can find that in a lover, you can put up with a lot.

Connie (Stephen Rea) is, we are told, a great photographer. We are told by him. We see a few of his pictures, which are good enough, and we hear some of his beliefs, such as, "Take a picture when it hurts so bad you can't stand it." Well, that's easy enough to say. He supports himself as a wedding photographer, which would seem to contradict his rule, but since it hurts really bad when he doesn't have enough money to buy booze, maybe the rule applies.

Connie's need is to find unformed young women and teach them. "You have to create something," he tells Harper when she moves in. He makes her read. And she is included in his boozy philosophical roundtable at the neighborhood tavern. His tragedy is that when his Guineveres learn enough, they know enough to leave. There is a horrible, perfect, brilliant moment in this film when Harper's society-bitch mother (Jean Smart) finds out about their relationship, and comes to call. She stalks the shabby loft in her expensive clothes, she smokes a cigarette with such style that he puts his own out, and in icy disdain she says, "What do you have against women your own age?" And answers her own question: "I know exactly what she has that I haven't got. Awe."

She's right, but can you blame him? To be regarded with awe can be a wondrous aphrodisiac. And he does care, really care, for her—for all the Guineveres. In her first night at his place, he lets her have the sleeping loft and he sleeps on the floor of his darkroom. "There's lots of reading matter here," he says. The book on top of the stack is the photography of Alfred Steiglitz. It falls open to a page. "That's Georgia O'Keeffe," she says. He tells her: "When they met, he was a famous photographer, and

she was about your age." If the movie had been fifteen seconds longer, there could have been a scene showing him placing that educational volume on top of the reading matter.

The film was written and directed by Audrey Wells, who wrote the inspired romantic comedy *The Truth About Cats and Dogs.* She does not cast stones or lay blame. Wells is far beyond judging this relationship on grounds of conventional morality; it would be less moral for either one of them to settle for whoever society puts in their path.

Sarah Polley played the teenage girl in *The Sweet Hereafter* who surprised everyone with her testimony. She contains depths of feeling. She does not use cheap effects. There is a moment in *Guinevere* when Connie calls her his "good girl," and I was fascinated by the subtle play of emotions on her face. The words mean a lot to her, not altogether pleasant. She is tired of being a good girl at home. Tired of being condescended to. He uses the words in a different context. She is not sure she likes that context, either, but she understands why he has to say them. There is a one-act play in the way she uses her face in that scene.

Stephen Rea, from *The Crying Game,* has a more thankless role, because he is shabby and sad. His Connie is never going to be happy (or sober), but he knows how to give a push to a shy girl with low self-esteem. One of his most touching scenes involves a carefree moment cut short by a catastrophe: His false teeth break loose. On any scale of male vanity, this ranks well above impotence. He has another scene, at the end of a disastrous trip to Los Angeles, that ranks in poignancy with some of the moments in *Leaving Las Vegas.*

Guinevere is not perfect. Like many serious modern movies, it lacks the courage to use the sad ending it has earned. There is an absurd final fantasy scene that undoes a lot of hard work. But the movie's heart is in the right place. This movie isn't really about an old man and a younger woman at all. It's about everyone's dream of finding a person who, in the words of the old British beer commercial, refreshes the parts the others do not reach.

H

Halloween: H2O ★ ★
R, 92 m., 1998

Jamie Lee Curtis (Laurie/Keri), Michelle Williams (Molly Cartwell), Josh Hartnett (John Tate), Adam Arkin (Will Brennan), Jodi Lyn O'Keefe (Sarah), LL Cool J (Ronnie Jones), Adam Hann-Byrd (Charlie), Joseph Gordon-Levitt (Jimmy Howell), Janet Leigh (Norma), Chris Durand (The Shape). Directed by Steve Miner and produced by John Carpenter, Paul Freeman, and Debra Hill. Screenplay by Robert Zappia and Matt Greenberg.

Notes jotted down while watching *Halloween H2O:*

—Medical science should study Michael Myers, the monster who has made the last two decades a living hell for Laurie Strode. Here is a man who feels no pain. He can take a licking and keep on slicing. In the latest *Halloween* movie he absorbs a blow from an ax, several knife slashes, a rock pounded on the skull, a fall down a steep hillside, and being crushed against a tree by a truck. Whatever he's got, mankind needs it.

—How does Michael Myers support himself in the long years between his slashing outbreaks? I picture him working in a fast-food joint. "He never spoke much, but boy, could he dice those onions!"

—I have often wondered why we hate mimes so much. Many people have such an irrational dislike for them that they will cross the street rather than watch some guy in whiteface pretending to sew his hands together. Examining Michael Myers's makeup in *Halloween H2O,* I realized he looks so much like Marcel Marceau as to make no difference. Maybe he is a mime when he's not slashing. Maybe what drove him mad was years and years of trying to make a living in malls while little kids kicked him to see if he was real. This would also explain his ability to seem to walk while somehow staying in the same place.

—I happen to know Jamie Lee Curtis is one of the smartest people in Hollywood. I cannot wait for the chapter on horror movies in her autobiography.

—There is a scene in the movie where a kid drops a corkscrew down a garbage disposal. Then the camera goes *inside* the garbage disposal to watch while he fishes around for it. Then the camera cuts to the electric switch on the wall, which would turn the disposal on. I am thinking, if this kid doesn't lose his hand, I want my money back.

—Michael Myers may also have skills as an electrician. All of the lights and appliances in every structure in this movie go on or off whenever the plot requires them to. I can imagine Myers down in the basement by the fuse box, thinking, "Gotta slash somebody. But first . . . geez, whoever filled in the chart on the inside of this fuse box had lousy handwriting! I can't tell the garage door from the garbage disposal!"

—I think Jamie Lee Curtis shouts, "Do as I say!" twice in the movie. I could be low by one.

—Yes, the movie contains the line "They never found a body."

—Michael Myers, described in the credits as "The Shape," is played by Chris Durand. There is hope. Steve McQueen started his career in (but not as) *The Blob.*

—Half of the movie takes place in an exclusive private school, yet there is not a single shower scene.

—Speaking of shower scenes: Janet Leigh, Jamie Lee's mother, turns up in a cameo role here, and she started me thinking about what a rotten crock it is that they're remaking *Psycho.* I imagined Miss Leigh telling her friends, "They wanted me to do a cameo in the remake of *Psycho,* but I said, 'Hell, I'd do *Halloween H2O* before I'd lower myself to that.'"

Hamlet ★ ★ ★
R, 111 m., 2000

Ethan Hawke (Hamlet), Kyle McLachlan (Claudius), Diane Venora (Gertrude), Sam Shepard (Ghost), Bill Murray (Polonius), Liev Schreiber (Laertes), Julia Stiles (Ophelia), Karl Geary (Horatio), Steve Zahn (Rosencrantz), Dechen Thurman (Guildenstern). Directed by Michael Almereyda and produced by Andrew Fierberg and Amy Hobby. Screenplay by

Almereyda, based on the play by William Shakespeare.

"I've seen Hamlet as an intellectual,
"And I've seen Hamlet as an ineffectual,
"And I've seen Hamlet as a homosexual,
"And I've seen Hamlet ev'ry way but textual. . . ."
—"I've Seen Shakespeare," by Weeden,
Finkle, and Fay

And now the melancholy Dane is a Manhattan techno-nerd, closeted with his computers, his video-editing gear, and his bitter thoughts. His father's company, the Denmark Corp., has made the front page of *USA Today* after a boardroom takeover by the scheming Claudius. Hamlet's mother has married the usurper. And the ghost of Hamlet's father appears on security cameras and materializes in a form transparent enough for Hamlet to see the Pepsi machine behind him.

Michael Almereyda's *Hamlet*, with Ethan Hawke as the prince and Bill Murray as Polonius, is both a distraction and a revelation. Sometimes the modern setting works against the material, sometimes it underlines it, and at all times it proves that *Hamlet* no more belongs in medieval Denmark than anywhere else. However it is staged, wherever it is set, it takes place within Hamlet's mind.

There are few thoughts worth having about life, death, and existence that *Hamlet* does not express in the fewest and most memorable words. "To be, or not to be" is the central question of human life, and Shakespeare asked it 400 years before the existentialists, and better than the Greeks. If man is the only animal that knows he must die, *Hamlet* is the distillation of that knowledge. This twenty-first-century *Hamlet*, with its concealed microphones, answering machines, videotapes, and laptops, is as much Shakespeare's as Olivier's in medieval dress was, or Burton's in business suits, or Branagh's in nineteenth-century Blenheim Castle, or Mel Gibson's in a Scottish castle. It is Shakespeare because it respects his language, just as Baz Luhrmann's *Romeo + Juliet* (1996) was not because it did not.

Ethan Hawke plays Hamlet as a restless, bitter neurotic, replaying his memories on video machines and doing dry runs of his big speeches on a PixelVision camera he aims at himself. "To be, or not to be" is sketchily seen on Hamlet's own video, and finally reaches its full ironic flower in the "Action" corridor of a Blockbuster store. When Polonius (Murray) asks his daughter Ophelia (Julia Stiles) to sound out Hamlet, he supplies her with a concealed tape recorder—and Hamlet discovers the bug. When Hamlet denounces Ophelia, there is a reprise on her answering machine. The play within a play is Hamlet's own video production, presented in a screening room.

Kyle McLachlan and Diane Venora play Claudius and Gertrude, as reasonable as any modern materialist parents or stepparents (indeed, Gertrude is so modern she might be literature's first corporate wife). They are a couple comfortable in their affluence, content in their compromises, annoyed as much as disturbed by Hamlet's whingeing. He has had every opportunity, and now look at him, holed up with his resentments and driving his girlfriend crazy. Even Hawke's wardrobe strikes the right note: He wears an ugly knit ski hat that looks a little like a Norse helmet and a lot like the deliberately gauche clothes that teenagers choose to show they reject such middleclass affectations as taste.

Bill Murray is a good choice as Polonius, although Almereyda should have simply let him deliver his great speech to Laertes ("Neither a borrower nor a lender be . . .") without so much unnecessary business on the sound track. Liev Schreiber, as Laertes, is the wellmeaning brother of Ophelia, helpless to intervene because his common sense provides no strategy for dealing with madness. Steve Zahn and Dechen Thurman, as Rosencrantz and Guildenstern, are the neighborhood layabouts, and it is a nice touch when Hamlet hacks into their laptop, changing their instructions so they, not he, will be murdered.

I like the way the material has truly been "adapted" to its modern setting without the language being adulterated. Yes, the play has been shortened (Branagh's *Hamlet* is one of the rare uncut versions, and runs 238 minutes). But it demonstrates how Shakespeare, who in a way invented modern English, has so dominated it ever since that his meanings are always broadly clear to us, even despite unfamiliar usages.

The purpose of this staging of the play is not simply to tart up *Hamlet* in modern dress, but to see him as the young man he was (younger than almost all of the great actors who have played him)—a seething bed of insecurities, guilt, unformed resolution, lust, introspection, and self-loathing. It was his misfortune that he was able to express his feelings so clearly that, once stated, they could not be evaded.

He marches here as he marched in Shakespeare's mind, toward an ending to life that settles nothing, that answers no questions, that contains victory for no one and confusion for all. The ultimate irony of Shakespeare's final scene, in which the dead king's successor steps over the bloody corpses and prepares for business as usual, is richly ironic in this modern corporate setting. Executives are eviscerated, their wives go down with them, their children die in grand, senseless gestures, new management comes in, and the stock price goes up. It happens every day.

The Hanging Garden ★ ★ ★
R, 98 m., 1998

Chris Leavins (Sweet William), Troy Veinotte (Teenage Sweet William), Kerry Fox (Rosemary), Sarah Polley (Teenage Rosemary), Seana McKenna (Iris), Peter MacNeill (Whiskey Mac), Joe S. Keller (Fletcher), Joan Orenstein (Grace). Directed by Thom Fitzgerald and produced by Louise Garfield, Arnie Gelbart, and Fitzgerald. Screenplay by Fitzgerald.

There is a character named William who appears in *The Hanging Garden* at three different ages: as an eight-year-old who is terrified of his father; as a fat fifteen-year-old; and as a twenty-five-year-old, now thin, who has returned for his sister's wedding. The peculiar thing is that the characters sometimes appear on the screen at the same time, and the dead body of the fifteen-year-old hangs from a tree during many of the scenes.

Well, why not? It may be magic realism, but isn't it also the simple truth? Don't the ghosts of our former selves attend family events right along with our current manifestations? Don't parents still sometimes relate to us as if we were children, don't siblings still carry old resentments, aren't old friends still stuck on who we used to be? And don't we sometimes resurrect old personas and dust them off for a return engagement? Aren't all of those selves stored away inside somewhere?

The movie opens on a wedding day. Rosemary (Kerry Fox, from *An Angel at My Table*), who has already started drinking, struggles with her wedding dress and vows she won't show herself until her brother arrives. Her brother, Sweet William (Chris Leavins), does eventually arrive, late, and is about 150 pounds too light to fit into the tux his mother has rented for him. He was fat when he left home. Now he is thin, and gay. We learn that his first homosexual experience was with Fletcher (Joe S. Keller), the very person Rosemary is planning to marry.

The family also includes Whiskey Mac (Peter MacNeill), the alcoholic patriarch, and Iris (Seana McKenna), the mother, who seems like a rock of stability. It's no accident that all the family members are named for flowers; Whiskey Mac poured all of his love and care into his garden, while brutalizing his family. His treatment of his overweight, gay son led the boy to hang himself in one version of reality, and to run away in another, so that when the twenty-five-year-old returns home the body of the fifteen-year-old is still hanging in the garden.

But I am not capturing the tone of the movie, which is not as macabre and gloomy as this makes it sound, but filled with eccentricity. The family members, who live in Canada's Maritime provinces, have survived by becoming defiantly individual. This is going to be one of those weddings where the guests look on in amazement.

The writer-director, Thom Fitzgerald, moves easily through time, and we meet the teenage version of Sweet William (Troy Veinotte) and Rosemary (Sarah Polley, from *The Sweet Hereafter*) as they form a bond against their father. Fitzgerald never pauses to explain his time-shifts and overlaps, and doesn't need to. Somehow we understand why a 300-pound body could be left hanging from a tree for ten years. It isn't really there, although in another sense, of course, it is.

Like many movies about dysfunctional families, *The Hanging Garden* involves more dysfunction than is perhaps necessary. There is the grandmother, who is senile but still has good enough timing to shout "I do!" out the window at the crucial moment in the marriage. And the tomboy little sister, Violet, who bitterly resents having to be the flower girl. And for all the secrets I have suggested, there are others that will surprise you even at the end—including a great big one that I doubt really proves anything.

The heart of the movie is its insight into the way families are haunted by their own history. How the memory of early unhappiness colors later relationships, and how Sweet William's persecution at the hands of his father hangs in the air as visibly as the corpse in the garden.

The movie is Canadian, and joins a list of other recent Canadian films about dread secrets, including *Exotica, The Sweet Hereafter,* and *Kissed.* Although there's a tendency to lump Canadian and American films together into the same cultural pool, the personal, independent films from Canada have a distinctive flavor. If Americans are in your face, Canadians are more reticent. If a lot of American movies are about wackos who turn out to share conventional values at the core, Canadian characters tend to be normal and pleasant on the surface, and keep their darker thoughts to themselves. I don't know which I prefer, but I know the Canadians usually supply more surprises.

Hanging Up ★ ★
PG-13, 99 m., 2000

Meg Ryan (Eve), Diane Keaton (Georgia), Lisa Kudrow (Maddy), Walter Matthau (Lou), Adam Arkin (Joe), Cloris Leachman (Pat). Directed by Diane Keaton and produced by Laurence Mark and Nora Ephron. Screenplay by Delia and Nora Ephron, based on the book by Delia Ephron.

"I live half my life in the real world and half on the telephone," Delia Ephron's father once told her. He was Henry Ephron (1911–1992), the successful writer of such comedies as *Desk Set* and *Daddy Longlegs.* He was always on the phone with his daughters, and they were always on the phone with one another, and now we have *Hanging Up,* a movie inspired by his last days, in which Walter Matthau plays the

father as a man who probably should have lived more of his life in the real world.

The movie is based on Delia's 1995 novel, has been adapted by Delia and her sister Nora, and directed by Diane Keaton, who stars with Meg Ryan and Lisa Kudrow. It is so blonde and brittle, so pumped up with cheerful chatter and quality time, so relentless in the way it wants to be bright about sisterhood and death, that you want to stick a star on its forehead and send it home with a fever.

Lou, the Matthau character, is in the hospital dying of one of those diseases that only leaves you with enough strength for one-liners. He's been in show business for centuries. He wants constant reassurance from his daughters, who are racing in three different directions and keep in touch through an amazing number of telephones. The oldest, Georgia (Diane Keaton), runs her own magazine, which is named *Georgia* and is apparently a cross between *George* and *Lear.* The middle daughter, Eve (Meg Ryan), is a party planner and mother. The youngest, Maddy (Lisa Kudrow), is an actress on a soap opera that she takes at least as seriously as any of its fans. They love telephone round-robins, where one will tell something to the second, who immediately has to tell the third.

The film is really more about the lifestyles of the women than about their parting from their father, and he sort of understands this; this family has been raised as if it's on a stage, putting on a performance for the world, and the show must go on. There is a moment when Eve recruits Georgia to speak at an event she is coordinating, and Georgia starts talking about her sick father, and does something that can only be described as faking real tears. Yes, she is snuffling on demand, for dramatic purpose, at a key moment in her remarks—but just because you can turn an emotion on and off at will doesn't mean it isn't real. Of course, the attitudes she is expressing are really Eve's ("You take my life and you use it"), but borrowed real emotion is still real, right?

Delia Ephron and her sister Nora have lived in worlds not unlike this film, and so, of course, have Keaton, Ryan, and Kudrow. There are moments of sharp observation, as when we sense that these pretty, chic women dress for their meetings with one another at least as carefully as a boxer tapes his wrists. The best scenes are the ones in which the daughters are performing as themselves—projecting the images they use in order to carve out psychic space within the family. Georgia must be dominant because oldest. Eve must be accommodating and commonsensical because middle. Maddy must be dotty because youngest. If the movie hadn't been based on *Hanging Up*, it could have been based on Gail Sheehy's *Passages*.

The peculiar thing about the Matthau character is that he doesn't seem to be sick so much as waiting in a hospital bed for his dialogue to arrive. This is not a movie about true dying heartbreak (for that, see *Unstrung Heroes*, Keaton's wonderful 1995 film, much wiser about death and about the children it leaves behind). *Hanging Up* is more about continuing the legend of the irascible but lovable old man into the grave, if necessary.

Matthau is of course an invaluable actor, lined and weathered, a perfect fit, a catcher's mitt that has seen us through many a good season. Matthau has himself been very ill, and could no doubt have drawn on that experience for enough cries and whispers to furnish a Bergman movie. But he's read the script and understands it, and doesn't embarrass himself by providing more authenticity than the material can carry.

And the movie doesn't really want to be all that heartbreakingly true. It's a facile comedy of manners, a story in which the three daughters have somehow been taught by their upbringing to put a consistent face on everything. Their incessant telephoning is like a way of staying in tune. There are a couple of other characters in the film, an Iranian doctor and his salt-of-the-earth mother, who at first seem inexplicable, until you realize they function as a reality check. They're phoning in from the real world.

Happiness ★ ★ ★

NO MPAA RATING, 140 m., 1998

Jane Adams (Joy Jordan), Lara Flynn Boyle (Helen Jordan), Cynthia Stevenson (Trish Maplewood), Dylan Baker (Bill Maplewood), Philip Seymour Hoffman (Allen), Camryn Manheim (Kristina), Louise Lasser (Mona Jordan), Ben Gazzara (Lenny Jordan), Rufus Read (Billy Maplewood), Jared Harris (Vlad), Jon Lovitz (Andy Kornbluth), Elizabeth Ashley (Diane Freed), Marla Maples (Ann Chambeau). Directed by Todd Solondz and produced by Ted Hope and Christine Vachon. Screenplay by Solondz.

Todd Solondz's *Happiness* is a film that perplexes its viewers, even those who admire it, because it challenges the ways we attempt to respond to it. Is it a portrait of desperate human sadness? Then why are we laughing? Is it an ironic comedy? Then why its tenderness with these lonely people? Is it about depravity? Yes, but why does it make us suspect, uneasily, that the depraved are only seeking what we all seek, but with a lack of ordinary moral vision?

In a film that looks into the abyss of human despair, there is the horrifying suggestion that these characters may *not* be grotesque exceptions, but may in fact be part of the stream of humanity. Whenever a serial killer or a sex predator is arrested, we turn to the paper to find his neighbors saying that the monster "seemed just like anyone else."

Happiness is a movie about closed doors—apartment doors, bedroom doors, and the doors of the unconscious. It moves back and forth between several stories, which often link up. It shows us people who want to be loved, and who never will be—because of their emotional incompetence and arrested development. There are lots of people who do find love and fulfillment, but they are not in this movie.

We meet Joy (Jane Adams), who has just broken up with the loser she's been dating (Jon Lovitz). He gives her a present, an engraved reproduction ashtray he got through mail order, but after she thanks him ("It almost makes me want to learn to smoke"), he viciously grabs it back: "This is for the girl who loves me for who I am."

We meet Allen (Philip Seymour Hoffman), who describes pornographic sexual fantasies to his psychiatrist (Dylan Baker) and then concludes that he will never realize them because he is too boring. The psychiatrist, named Bill, is indeed bored. Later he buys a teen-idol magazine and masturbates while looking at the photos.

We meet Joy's two sisters, Trish (Cynthia Stevenson) and Helen (Lara Flynn Boyle). Trish is a chirpy housewife, who is married to Bill the psychiatrist but knows nothing of his pedophilia. Helen is a poet who drops names ("Salman is on the line") and describes the countless men who lust for her. The parents of the three sisters, Mona and Lenny (Louise Lasser and Ben Gazzara), have been married for years, but now Lenny wants to leave. Not to fool around. Just to be alone.

We meet Kristina (Camryn Manheim), a fat girl who lives down the hall from the solitary Allen, and knocks on his door to announce that Pedro, the doorman, has been murdered. (His body has been dismembered and put in plastic bags: "Everyone uses Baggies. That's why we can relate to this crime.") Allen doesn't want to know. He leafs through porno magazines, gets drunk, and makes obscene phone calls. One of his calls goes to the woman he fantasizes about. It is Helen, the "popular" sister, who enjoys his heavy breathing and calls him back.

We get the sense of warehouses of strangers—of people stacked into the sky in lonely apartments, each one hiding secrets. We watch in sadness and unease as Bill the shrink attends his son Billy's Little League game and becomes enraptured by one of his teammates. When the other boy has a "sleepover" with Billy, Bill drugs his family and molests the young boy (not on-screen).

Later, there is a heartbreaking conversation between Billy and his father. (Billy is isolated in close-up and we assume the young actor is reading the lines without knowing what the older actor is saying.) Their talk lingers in uneasy memory. The boy has been told at school that his father is a molester. He asks his dad if it is true. His father says it is. In a scene of pain and sadness, the boy asks more questions and the father answers simply, briefly, and completely honestly. A friend who saw the movie told me, "Instead of lying, he kept telling him the truth, regardless of how hard that was for both of them. The honesty may be the one thing that saves the son from the immense damage done by the father." Well, I hope so.

Happiness belongs to the emerging genre of the New Geek Cinema, films that occupy the shadowland between tragedy and irony. Todd

Solondz also made *Welcome to the Dollhouse* (1996), about an unpopular eleven-year-old girl who defiantly improvises survival tactics. *Happiness* is harder to take, and yet equally attentive to the suffering of characters who see themselves outside the mainstream—geeks, if you will, whose self-images are formed by the conviction that the more people know about them, the less people will like them.

Why see the film? *Happiness* is *about* its unhappy characters in a way that helps us see them a little more clearly, to feel sorry for them, and at the same time to see how closely tragedy and farce come together in the messiness of sexuality. Does *Happiness* exploit its controversial subjects? Finally, no: It sees them as symptoms of desperation and sadness. It is more exploitative to create a child molester as a convenient villain, as many movies do; by disregarding his humanity and seeing him as an object, such movies do the same thing that a molester does.

These are the kinds of thoughts *Happiness* inspires. It is not a film for most people. It is certainly for adults only. But it shows Todd Solondz as a filmmaker who deserves attention, who hears the unhappiness in the air and seeks its sources.

Happy, Texas ★ ★ ★
PG-13, 104 m., 1999

Jeremy Northam (Harry Sawyer), Steve Zahn (Wayne Wayne Wayne Jr.), William H. Macy (Sheriff Chappy Dent), Ally Walker (Josephine McLintock), Illeana Douglas (Ms. Schaefer), M. C. Gainey (Bob), Ron Perlman (Nalhober), Tim Bagley (David), Michael Hitchcock (Steven), Paul Dooley (Judge). Directed and produced by Mark Illsley. Screenplay by Ed Stone, Illsley, and Phil Reeves.

There is a moment early in *Happy, Texas* when an escaped convict looks at a roomful of five-year-old beauty pageant contestants and asks them if they know the words to "Ninety-nine Bottles of Beer on the Wall." They look at him with curiosity. After all, he is the out-of-town pageant consultant, hired to prepare them for the Little Miss Fresh-Squeezed Pre-Teen Beauty Pageant.

The convict's name is Wayne Wayne Wayne

Jr. (Steve Zahn). He and Harry Sawyer (Jeremy Northam) have escaped from an overturned prison van, cut through their handcuffs, and stolen a van at a gas station. What they discover belatedly is that the van belongs to two gay men who travel around Texas consulting on beauty contests. "Lots of folks are looking for you," says Happy's sheriff Chappy Dent (William H. Macy) as he stops them outside of town.

They think they're being arrested. Not at all. They're being hired. And they decide to stay in the town after they meet the local bank president (Ally Walker) and realize a bank heist might be a pushover. That requires them to impersonate pageant consultants, in a plot that brings together three of the oldest dodges in the screenwriter's arsenal (Fish Out of Water, Mistaken Identities, Love Under False Pretenses). What saves the movie is that it doesn't really depend on the plot wheezes. They're taken for granted, in a comedy that's really about human nature.

Since Wayne and Harry are assumed by everyone in town to be a gay couple, that makes them safe "friends" for two local women—Walker, as Jo the bank president, and Illeana Douglas, as Ms. Schaefer, the teacher in charge of the little contestants. We get the obligatory dialogue passages in which the women are talking about one thing and the men about another, but we don't care, because the actors sell the situation so amusingly—and warmly. Zahn's performance is especially funny; he's rough-hewn, unsophisticated, and not very bright, and he quickly falls desperately in love with "Ms. Schaefer." The hurdle of his sexual orientation? No problem: "That whole gay thing is just like a hobby."

Harry quickly sees that pretending to be gay is a way to get close to Jo, but there's another complication: Sheriff Chappy Dent has a crush on Harry and asks him out for a date, leading to an evening in a cowboy gay bar, where Harry follows and Chappy leads ("Now I'm gonna spin ya!").

Macy's performance as the quietly, earnestly in love sheriff is the most touching in the movie, another role in which he gets laughs by finding the truth beneath the humor. Steve Zahn's work gets the loud laughs. In the division of labor between the two escaped cons,

Harry takes over the bank job and Wayne's task is to pose as a choreographer. Completely without a clue, he studies videotapes and then tries to teach the same steps to the dutiful little girls, and discovers, amazingly, that he is not without talent at the pageant business. ("I'm trying to figure out if slip-stitching or basting is the best way to sew on a sparkly heart.")

There's boundless good nature in the work by Douglas and Zahn. Macy lets his eyes carry scenes where no dialogue would have worked. And watching Jeremy Northam is a revelation: Here is the slick, urbane British gentleman of *Emma*, *The Winslow Boy*, and *An Ideal Husband*, playing a Texas convict and not missing a beat. Mark Illsley, who produced, directed, and cowrote the script, had his choice of two endings: the big pageant or the bank job. I would have liked more pageant and less of the bank, but the movie is so good-humored it hardly matters. This is one of those comedies that doesn't pound us on the head with the obvious, but simply lets us share vast amusement.

Hard Rain ★
R, 98 m., 1998

Morgan Freeman (Jim), Christian Slater (Tom), Randy Quaid (Sheriff), Minnie Driver (Karen), Ed Asner (Charlie), Michael Goorjian (Kenny), Dann Florek (Mr. Mehlor), Ricky Harris (Ray). Directed by Mikael Salomon and produced by Mark Gordon, Gary Levinsohn, and Ian Bryce. Screenplay by Graham Yost.

Hard Rain is one of those movies that never convince you their stories are really happening. From beginning to end, I was acutely aware of actors being paid to stand in cold water. Suspension of my disbelief in this case would have required psychotropic medications.

Oh, the film is well made from a technical viewpoint. The opening shot is a humdinger, starting out with a vast flood plain, zooming above houses surrounded by water, and then ending with a close-up of a cop's narrowing eyes. But even then, I was trying to spot the effects—to catch how they created the flood effect, and how they got from the flood to the eyes.

Funny how some movies will seduce you into their stories while others remain at arm's length. *Titanic* was just as artificial and effects-driven as *Hard Rain,* and yet I was spellbound. Maybe it was because the people on the doomed ship had no choice: The *Titanic* was sinking, and that was that.

In *Hard Rain,* there is a bad guy (Morgan Freeman) who *has* a choice. He wants to steal some money, but all during the film I kept wondering why he didn't just give up and head for dry ground. How much of this ordeal was he foolish enough to put up with? Water, cold, rain, electrocutions, murders, shotguns, jet ski attacks, drownings, betrayals, collisions, leaky boats, stupid and incompetent partners, and your fingertips shrivel up: Is it worth it?

The film opens in a town being evacuated because of rising flood waters. There's a sequence involving a bank. At first we think we're witnessing a robbery, and then we realize we are witnessing a pickup by an armored car. What's the point? Since the bankers don't think they're being robbed and the armored truck drivers don't think they're robbing them, the sequence means only that the director has gone to great difficulty to fool us. Why? So we can slap our palms against our brows and admit we were big stupes?

By the time we finally arrived at the story, I was essentially watching a documentary about wet actors at work. Christian Slater stars as one of the armored truck crew. Randy Quaid is the ambiguous sheriff. Morgan Freeman is the leader of the would-be thieves, who have commandeered a power boat. Ah, but, I hear you asking, why was it so important for the armored car to move the cash out of the bank before the flood? So Freeman's gang could steal it, of course. Otherwise, if it got wet, hey, what's the Federal Reserve for?

Minnie Driver plays a local woman who teams up with Slater so that they can fall in love while saving each other from drowning. First Slater is in a jail cell that's about to flood, and then Driver is handcuffed to a staircase that's about to flood, and both times I was thinking what rotten luck it was that *Hard Rain* came so soon after the scene in *Titanic* where Kate Winslet saved Leonardo DiCaprio from drowning after he was handcuffed on the sinking ship. It's bad news when a big action scene plays like a demonstration of recent generic techniques.

Meanwhile, Morgan Freeman's character is too darned nice. He keeps trying to avoid violence while still trying to steal the money. This plot requires a mad dog like Dennis Hopper. Freeman's character specializes in popping up suddenly from the edge of the screen and scaring the other characters, even though it is probably pretty hard to sneak up on somebody in a powerboat. Freeman is good at looking wise and insightful, but the wiser and more insightful he looked, the more I wanted him to check into a motel and order himself some hot chocolate.

Hard Rain must have been awesomely difficult to make. Water is hard to film around, and here were whole city streets awash, at night and in the rain. The director is Mikael Salomon, a former cameraman, who along with cinematographer Peter Menzies Jr. does a good job of making everything look convincingly wet. And they stage a jet ski chase through school corridors that's an impressive action sequence, unlikely though it may be.

I was in Los Angeles the weekend *Hard Rain* had its preview, and went to talk to the cast. I found myself asking: Wasn't there a danger of electrocution when you were standing for weeks in all that water with electrical cables everywhere? That's not the sort of question you even think about if the story is working. Hey, how about this for a story idea? An actor signs up for a movie about a flood, little realizing that a celebrity stalker, who hates him, has been hired as an electrician on the same picture.

The Harmonists ★ ★ ★
R, 115 m., 1999

Ben Becker (Robert Biberti), Heino Ferch (Roman Cycowski), Ulrich Noethen (Harry Frommermann), Heinrich Schafmeister (Erich A. Collin), Max Tidof (Ari Leschnikoff), Kai Wiesinger (Erwin Bootz), Meret Becker (Erna Eggstein), Katja Riemann (Mary Cycowski). Directed by Joseph Vilsmaier and produced by Reinhard Kloos, Hanno Huth, and Danny Krausz. Screenplay by Klaus Richter.

The Harmonists tells the story of the rise and fall of a vocal group that was wildly popular in Germany before it was disbanded in 1934 as part of the mounting persecution of Jews. The Comedian Harmonists, who did comic and romantic songs in intricate harmony, were popular and beloved. Even members of the Nazi hierarchy were among their fans. But eventually they were forbidden to sing songs by Jewish composers—and finally, because three of their members were Jewish, they were banned from performing in public.

Given the suffering created by the Nazis, the fate of the Harmonists ranks low on the scale. But as one of the countless little stories that add up to the plague of Nazism, they deserve an entry in the chronicle of despair. And it is revealing how, like many of their countrymen both Jewish and gentile, they were blind until the last moment to the actual intentions of the Nazis. There is a moment in the film when the Harmonists are performing in New York and consider staying in America. But they do not. The handwriting was on the wall, but it was not yet sufficiently clear.

The arc of the film leads from early cheerfulness to eventual defeat, but for much of the time *The Harmonists* plays like a standard showbiz biopic. We meet the founder of the group, Harry Frommermann (Ulrich Noethen), who in 1927 hears a record by a black American jazz group named the Revellers. Entranced by the beauty of their close harmony, he determines to start a German group that would sing in the same style. It's slow-going at first, but after the brash, confident Robert Biberti (Ben Becker) joins him, they find the other recruits and end up with five singers and a piano player.

The first agent they audition for tells them their music sounds "funereal." That night, the pianist plays around with a faster tempo, and they find their style. I've never heard the Revellers, but the Harmonists remind me of the Mills Brothers, and they do something the Mills Brothers also did: They use their voices, hands, and breath control to imitate the sound of musical instruments. There's an instrumental solo in the film done entirely without instruments.

As the six men work and travel together, tensions of course develop, and the most delicate involves the fact that Harry and Robert are both in love with the same woman, a comely music store clerk named Erna (Meret Becker). She likes Harry (indeed, she makes sure she's up on a ladder with a little of her slip and a lot of her leg showing when he enters the store). He likes her, too, enough to propose marriage even though he's Jewish and she isn't. (He visits his parents' grave to tell them, "God will forgive me—after all; it's his job.")

But Harry is a complicated man—distracted, driven, inattentive, forgetful, maddening. Robert, on the other hand, is as solid as a Teutonic rock, and looks a little like Mencken with the stogie he keeps planted in his mouth. Robert is not Jewish, but he's not a Nazi, either, and his decency helps hold the Harmonists together.

There are a lot of entertaining musical numbers in the film, and an ominous low-key, background treatment of the way that Nazism and anti-Semitism change the fabric of German society even while many of the characters are busy denying it. (When ugly slogans are painted on the window of the music store, the grandmotherly owner says it's "just kids.")

Eventually the situation can no longer be ignored. There's an electrifying scene just before the group sails for New York; a high Nazi official asks them to perform at his home, which they do, but when he requests a German folk song with Nazi associations, Harry says he "just cannot sing it." Their fate as a group is sealed at that moment, although it would have been sealed sooner or later anyway. Roman Cycowski (Heino Ferch), another Jewish member, announces eventually, "No power on Earth can force me to sing in this country again."

After they break up, the three Jewish Harmonists regroup outside Germany, and the three Germans start a new group at home. But what made them special fades away, and their music somehow seems like a reproach to the rising tide of war. An epilogue reveals what eventually happened to all the Harmonists. One moved to California and became the oldest active cantor in America. Others did not end so happily.

The Haunting ★ ★ ★
PG-13, 113 m., 1999

Lili Taylor (Nell), Liam Neeson (Dr. David Marrow), Catherine Zeta-Jones (Theo),

Owen Wilson (Luke Sanderson), Bruce Dern (Mr. Dudley), Marian Seldes (Mrs. Dudley), Alix Koromzay (Mary Lambetta), Todd Field (Todd Hackett), Virginia Madsen (Jane). Directed by Jan De Bont and produced by Susan Arnold, Donna Arkoff Roth, and Colin Wilson. Screenplay by David Self, based on a novel by Shirley Jackson.

To my surprise, I find myself recommending *The Haunting* on the basis of its locations, its sets, its art direction, its sound design, and the overall splendor of its visuals. The story is a mess, but for long periods of time that hardly matters. It's beside the point, as we enter one of the most striking spaces I've ever seen in a film.

That space is Hill House, the haunted manor selected by a psychology professor (Liam Neeson) for an experiment in the mechanics of fear. He recruits three people who are told they'll get help for insomnia, and installs them in the ornate and gloomy Gothic pile, where alarming things start to happen immediately. We assume the frightening manifestations are manufactured by the professor (last name: Marrow), but perhaps not.

The three patients are played by Lili Taylor, Catherine Zeta-Jones, and Owen Wilson. Professor Marrow is joined by two assistants, but in one of the screenplay's several clumsy moves, one of them is injured the first night, the other takes her to the hospital, and that's the last we ever see of them. Taylor's character, named Nell, is the key figure in the film, a woman whose life has been on hold until the ghosts of Hill House start to tell their story.

The exteriors of Hill House were shot at Harlaxton Manor in Nottinghamshire. Its architectural details look like a shriek from hell; now I know what a building looks like with its hair standing on end. (It's a bit of an anticlimax to discover that the building is currently used as a foreign campus of the University of Evansville, Indiana.) The interiors I gather are mostly sets, although some of them are inspired by Harlaxton and Belvoir Castle in Leicestershire.

The production design is by Eugenio Zanetti (*What Dreams May Come, Restoration*) and he has done a masterful job of creating interiors that seem to be alive with menace. One of the great moments in the film comes when Taylor and Zeta-Jones explore their bedrooms, which are so rich with detail that you want to wallow in them. The great hall of the house features a walk-in fireplace not unlike the one in *Citizen Kane*'s Xanadu, and indeed when Zeta-Jones first enters Hill House, she murmurs, "It's like Charles Foster Kane meets the Munsters."

The horror story itself is based on things that go thump (and bang and wheeze) in the night. The cavernous halls and ominous corridors reverberate with great groaning, echoing noises, as if the house has gas pains. Doors are hammered on. Ghostly manifestations appear. One or two moments are truly scary, including a recycled version of the classic *Carrie* end shot. We enter this space and feel enclosed by it; it's not like a set, but more like a virtual reality.

Lili Taylor struggles valiantly with her character, the movie's juiciest, and has some effective scenes, mostly by herself. "I can be a victim or I can be a volunteer," she tells herself when the going gets really rough. The rest of the characters are underwritten, including Catherine Zeta-Jones's beautiful Theo, who does some bisexual lip-smacking at the outset but never follows up, and spends most of her time running to the rescue. Owen Wilson, as the guy, asks obvious questions and helps tug open doors, etc., but is not made much of, and neither is Liam Neeson's professor, whose motivations are explained in some flat opening scenes, and who then goes adrift in the plot ("All right, you two! Enough about pharmaceuticals!").

But the special effects are original and effective, evoking a haunted house in unexpected ways. A floor-level gliding camera is insinuating. Scenes set in a huge old conservatory are creepy in the way they use dead vegetation, and there's a nice scene on a shaky spiral staircase. To enter these rooms, to move among them, to feel their weight and personality, is an experience. I am reminded of the abandoned subway station in *The Mimic* (1997), another space with a personality of its own.

The movie often edges so close to being truly scary that you wonder why they didn't try just a little harder to write more dimensional characters and add the edge of almost plausible realism that distinguished Shirley Jackson's original novel. The movie does not, alas, succeed as a horror film. But it succeeds as a film worth watching anyway, and that is no small achievement.

Hav Plenty ★ ½
R, 92 m., 1998

Christopher Scott Cherot (Lee Plenty), Chenoa Maxwell (Havilland Savage), Hill Harper (Michael Simmons), Tammi Katherine Jones (Caroline Gooden), Robinne Lee (Leigh Darling), Reginald James (Felix Darling). Directed by Christopher Scott Cherot and produced by Cherot and Robyn M. Greene. Screenplay by Cherot.

I've grown immune to the information that a movie is "a true story," but when a movie begins with that promise *and* a quote from the Bible, I get an uneasy feeling. And when it starts with a "true story," a Bible quote *and* clips from home movies, *and* photos of several main characters, I wonder if I'm watching a movie or a research project. Amateur writers love to precede their own prose with quotations. I don't know whether they think it's a warm-up or a good luck charm.

Hav Plenty is basically an amateur movie, with some of the good things and many of the bad that go along with first-time efforts. Set in a comfortable milieu of affluent African-Americans, it's ostensibly the autobiographical story of its writer-director, Christopher Scott Cherot, who plays a homeless writer named Lee Plenty. As the movie opens, he's cat-sitting for a woman named Havilland Savage (Chenoa Maxwell), who has just broken up with a famous musician. She's with her family in Washington, D.C., for New Year's Eve, and invites him to come down and join them, and he does. (So much for the cat.) At the end of the movie, there's a thank-you to "the real Havilland Savage," and I gather most of the things in the movie actually happened, in one way or another. How else to account for an episode involving the offscreen explosion of a toilet?

Cherot plays Lee Plenty as a smart young man of maddening passivity. The plot essentially consists of scenes in which Havilland's best friend Caroline throws herself at Plenty,

who rebuffs her. Then Havilland's sister, who has only been married for a month, throws herself at Plenty, but he rebuffs her too. Then Havilland herself throws herself at Plenty, and he does his best to rebuff her. Although we see the beginning of a sex scene, he eventually eludes her too. The movie ends with a scene at a film festival at which Plenty speaks after the premiere of a film that is a great deal like this one.

As a young man I would have been quite capable of writing and starring in a movie in which three beautiful women threw themselves at me. I would have considered this so logical that I would not have bothered, as Cherot does not bother, to write myself any dialogue establishing myself as intelligent, charming, seductive, etc. I would assume that the audience could take one look at me and simply intuit that I had all of those qualities. So I can accept that the homeless Lee Plenty character is irresistible, even to a newlywed and to a beautiful, rich ex-fiancée of a big star. What I cannot accept is that he fights them all off with vague excuses and evasions. "He's not gay," the women assure each other. That I believe. But either he's asexual, or exhibiting the symptoms of chronic fatigue syndrome.

Hav Plenty is not a film without charm, but, boy, does it need to tighten the screws on its screenplay. The movie's dialogue is mostly strained, artificial small talk, delivered unevenly by the actors, who at times seem limited to one take (how else to account for fluffed lines?). There are big setups without payoffs, as when Hav's grandmother insists, "You're going to marry him!" And nightmare dream sequences without motivation or purpose. And awkward scenes like the one where the newlywed sister tells her husband that something went on between her and Plenty. The husband enters the room, removes his jacket to reveal bulging muscles, and socks poor Plenty in the stomach. This scene illustrates two of my favorite obligatory cliches: (1) The husband is told only enough of the story to draw exactly the wrong conclusion, and (2) all muscular characters in movies always take off outer garments to reveal their muscles before hitting someone.

Hav Plenty is basically a three-actress movie; Cherot, as the male lead, is so vague and passive he barely has a personality (listen to his rambling explanations about why he "doesn't date"). All three actresses (Chenoa Maxwell as Hav, Tammi Katherine Jones as Hav's best friend, and Robinne Lee as the married sister) have strong energy and look good on the screen. With better direction and more takes, I suspect they'd seem more accomplished in their performances. But *Hav Plenty* is more of a first draft than a finished product.

He Got Game ★ ★ ★ ½
R, 131 m., 1998

Denzel Washington (Jake Shuttlesworth), Ray Allen (Jesus Shuttlesworth), Milla Jovovich (Dakota Burns), Rosario Dawson (Lala Bonilla), Hill Harper (Coleman "Booger" Sykes), Zelda Harris (Mary Shuttlesworth), Ned Beatty (Warden Wyatt), Jim Brown (Spivey). Directed by Spike Lee and produced by Jon Kilik and Lee. Screenplay by Lee.

Spike Lee brings the spirit of a poet to his films about everyday reality. *He Got Game,* the story of the pressures on the nation's best high school basketball player, could have been a gritty docudrama, but it's really more of a heartbreaker about a father and his son.

Lee uses visual imagination to lift his material into the realms of hopes and dreams. Consider his opening sequence, where he wants to establish the power of basketball as a sport and an obsession. He could have given us a montage of hot NBA action, but no: He uses the music of Aaron Copland to score a series of scenes in which American kids—boys, girls, rich, poor, black, white, in school and on playgrounds—play the game. All it needs is a ball and a hoop; compared to this simplicity, Jerry Seinfeld observes, when we attend other sports we're cheering laundry.

This opening evocation is matched by the closing shots of *He Got Game,* in which Lee goes beyond reality to find the perfect way to end his film: His final image is simple and very daring, and goes beyond words or plot to summarize the heart of the story. Seeing his films, I am saddened by how many filmmakers allow themselves to fall into the lazy rhythms of TV, where groups of people exchange dialogue. Movies are not just conversations on film; they can give us images that transform.

He Got Game is Lee's best film since *Malcolm X* (1982). It stars Denzel Washington as Jake, a man in prison for the manslaughter of his wife (we learn in a flashback that the event was a lot more complicated than that). His son, Jesus (Ray Allen), is the nation's top prospect. The state governor makes Jake an offer: He'll release him for a week, and if he can talk his son into signing a letter of intent to attend Big State University, the governor will reduce Jake's sentence.

The son is not happy to see Jake ("I don't have a father. Why is there a stranger in the house?"). He still harbors deep resentment, although his sister, Mary (Zelda Harris), has understood and forgiven. Jesus (named not after Christ but after a basketball player) is under incredible pressure. Recruiting offers arrive daily from colleges, and even his girlfriend Lala (Rosario Dawson) is involved; aware that she's likely to be dropped when Jesus goes on to stardom, she's working with a sports agent who wants the kid to turn pro ("He's a friend of the family," she keeps saying, as if her family would just happen to have a high-powered agent as a pal).

Spike Lee's connections with pro ball have no doubt given him a lot of insight into what talented high school players go through. There's a scene in *Hoop Dreams* where he exhorts all-stars at a summer basketball camp to be aware of how they're being used. In *He Got Game,* the temptations come thick and fast: job offers, a new Lexus, $10,000 from his own coach, even a couple of busty "students" who greet him in a dorm room with their own recruiting techniques.

Jake, on the other hand, faces bleak prospects. He moves into a flophouse next door to a hooker (Milla Jovovich) who is beaten by her pimp. Gradually they become friends, and he tries to help her. He also tries to reach his son, and it's interesting the way Lee and Washington let Jake use silence, tact, and patience in the process. Jake doesn't try a frontal assault, maybe because he knows his son too well. Finally it all comes down to a one-on-one confrontation in which the son is given the opportunity to understand and even pity his father.

This is not so much a movie about sports as about capitalism. It doesn't end, as the formula requires, with a big game. In fact, it never creates artificial drama with game sequences, even though Ray Allen, who plays for the Milwaukee Bucks, is that rarity, an athlete who can act. It's about the real stakes, which involve money more than final scores, and showmanship as much as athletics.

For many years in America, sports and big business have shared the same rules and strategies. One reason so many powerful people are seen in the stands at NBA games is that the modern game objectifies the same kind of warfare that takes place in high finance; while "fans" think it's all about sportsmanship and winning, the insiders are thinking in corporate and marketing metaphors.

He Got Game sees this clearly and unsentimentally (the sentiment is reserved for the father and son). There is a scene on a bench between Jesus and his girlfriend in which she states, directly and honestly, what her motivations are, and they are the same motivations that shape all of professional sports: It's not going to last forever, so you have to look out for yourself and make all the money you can. Of course, Spike Lee still cheers for the Knicks, and I cheer for the Bulls, but it's good to know what you're cheering for. At the end of *He Got Game,* the father and son win, but so does the system.

Henry Fool ★ ★ ½
R, 138 m., 1998

Thomas Jay Ryan (Henry Fool), James Urbaniak (Simon Grim), Parker Posey (Fay), Maria Porter (Mary), James Saito (Deng), Kevin Corrigan (Warren). Directed and produced by Hal Hartley. Screenplay by Hartley.

Simon is a garbage man who approaches the world at an angle. Literally. In Hal Hartley's new film *Henry Fool,* Simon is almost always shot with his head tilted down and cocked to one side, with the rims of his glasses positioned right above his eyes, which regard us sideways. He is a man so beaten down by life that he cannot look at anything straight on. Then Henry arrives to save him.

Simon Grim (James Urbaniak) has just been savagely beaten by a motorcyclist and his girlfriend. Like everyone else in the neighborhood, they treat Simon like a punching bag. Henry Fool (Thomas Jay Ryan) is a homeless drifter with a deep, wise voice. He moves into Simon's basement, where the flames from the furnace reinforce his Satanic undertones. His mission is to lift Simon to his feet, apparently, and instill a sense of mission in him.

Simon's family includes his mother, Mary (Maria Porter), who is on a lot of pills, and a chain-smoking sister named Fay (Parker Posey), who is an idle slattern quickly attracted to Henry. But Henry makes an unexpected choice and confesses to Simon: "I made love to your mother half an hour ago, and I'm beginning to think it wasn't such a good idea, because it makes Fay jealous." Simon looks at this statement as he looks at everything, askance.

Henry is working on his "Confessions," a vast opus. He claims to have connections at a publishing house. He gives Simon a journal with large blank pages and encourages him to write down everything that happens to him. Simon's thoughts flow out effortlessly in iambic pentameter, and when they are posted on the Web they make him world famous. Meanwhile, nobody much likes Henry's confessions, and it turns out his connection to the publisher is as a janitor, not an editor. There is also the matter of his conviction for child molestation.

What are we to make of all this? That is always the question with a Hal Hartley film, and I wish I were more sure of the answer. He works in a style of his own devising, he has an image of the world that is developing in a series of films, he seems to regard his characters in the same way Simon regards the world—obliquely, quizzically, without commitment. Sometimes he has a character do something odd and unexpected, and you think of a chess player making an unorthodox move just to make the game a little more interesting.

I wonder if the fault is in myself. I don't think this is a bad film, but after seeing it twice I'm unable to respond to it in any clear way. Things happen, and I don't know what they mean, and I have a feeling that in Hartley's view they need not mean anything. Henry

Fool lives in the basement and is illuminated by flames, but is not Mephistopheles; he is finally revealed as not as bright as he seems. Simon writes a famous poem but develops, not into a genius or into a savior, but simply into the semblance of a reasonable, successful man. Mary and Fay both go into orbit around Henry, but to what consequence?

Hartley is a gifted filmmaker (this time he wrote, produced, directed, and composed), and he has a precise visual style that develops themes over a series of scenes (notice the gradual shift in the relative balance of the body language between Simon and Henry). He has actors who evoke more than they reveal, although with the Henry Fool character I was never able to fit the child molestation into anything else, and wondered if Hartley added it capriciously. And what about the protracted, studiously graphic scenes of vomiting and defecation? What are they for? They break the frame of the picture. They're like fingers in the eyeballs of the film's style.

You watch, you are absorbed, and from scene to scene *Henry Fool* seems to be adding up, but then your hand closes on air. I am left unsure of my response—of any response. I want to see Hartley's next film. I always do. I sense he is headed somewhere, and perhaps his next work will provide the key allowing me to enter this one.

Here on Earth ★ ★
PG-13, 97 m., 2000

Chris Klein (Kelley), Leelee Sobieski (Samantha), Josh Hartnett (Jasper), Bruce Greenwood (Earl Cavanaugh), Annette O'Toole (Jo Cavanaugh), Michael Rooker (Malcolm Arnold), Annie Corley (Betsy Arnold). Directed by Mark Piznarkski and produced by David T. Friendly. Screenplay by Michael Seitzman.

When we see the sweet advertising art for *Here on Earth,* we suspect this may be another movie about angels walking among us, and it is—but these are human angels, not heavenly ones. It is about characters so generous, understanding, forgiving, and just doggone nice that they could have been created by Norman Rockwell, just as their town seems to have been.

The movie begins, however, on a sour note, as a snotty prep school boy named Kelley (Chris Klein) gets a new Mercedes convertible from his rich dad, and takes some friends slumming at the diner in the nearby small town. He gets smart with Samantha, the waitress (Leelee Sobieski), and has words with her boyfriend, Jasper (Josh Hartnett). That leads to a drag race during which Kelley and Jasper crash their cars into a gas pump and burn down the gas station and the diner, which are owned by Samantha's parents.

Kelley has come across up until this point as an arrogant brat. Sure, he's the class valedictorian, but he doesn't care about stuff like that. All he cares about is expanding the family fortune. So maybe it will teach him a lesson when the judge orders Kelley and Jasper to help rebuild the diner during the summer ahead. And maybe Samantha is right to see something good hidden beneath his cynical defiance. Consider the scene where he sneaks through the woods to eavesdrop on the substitute valedictorian's speech (he's been banned from graduation), and she tiptoes behind him and watches as he gives his own speech to the trees and the birds. It's a sweet scene. Unlikely in its logistics, but sweet.

Kelley isn't easy to like ("My probation doesn't say anything about sitting around and spitting out watermelon seeds with you people"). But as the summer meanders along, the boys get tans and develop muscles, and Samantha and Kelley fall in love, while good-hearted Jasper looks on helplessly. Read no further if you don't want to know . . . that Samantha, alas, has received bad news from her doctor. The cancer has spread from her knee to her liver, nothing can be done, and besides, "So I lived another year or two. It's not worth it."

Not worth it? When you're young and smart and in love? I would personally endure a good deal of pain just to live long enough to read tomorrow's newspaper. But Samantha fades away, another victim of Ali MacGraw's Disease (first identified many years ago in *Love Story*), which makes you more beautiful the sicker you get.

By now the film has become fairly unbelievable. Jasper is telling Kelley that although it kills him to see the woman he loves in the arms of another man, whatever makes her happy is all he wants for her. And Kelley is softening up and telling his rich dad that money isn't the only thing in life, and that you can be just as happy with a poor girl as a rich one.

But then comes a scene that clangs with a harsh false note. (Once again: Spoiler warning.) While Samantha bravely faces death and nobly smiles upon all around her, Kelley, the rat, suddenly announces he "has a life to get back to," and leaves town. This seems to be an utterly unmotivated act, but actually it has a splendid motivation: He has to leave so that he can come back. The plot requires a crisis before the dawn. The fact that his action is unconvincing and inexplicable doesn't bother the filmmakers, any more than it bothers the saintly and forgiving Samantha.

Leelee Sobieski is really very good in this movie. Still only nineteen, she was wonderful in *A Soldier's Daughter Never Cries* and *Eyes Wide Shut,* and in lesser movies like *Deep Impact* and *Never Been Kissed.* I didn't see her TV version of *Joan of Arc,* but with her deep, grave voice and unforced presence, I have a feeling she was equal to the role. The cast is filled with other winning actors: Klein and Hartnett, and Bruce Greenwood and the undervalued Annette O'Toole as Samantha's parents. But they need a little more reality to kick against. *Here on Earth* slides too easily into its sentimentality; the characters should have put up more of a struggle.

Hideous Kinky ★ ★ ★
R, 99 m., 1999

Kate Winslet (Julia), Said Taghmaoui (Bilal), Bella Riza (Bea), Carrie Mullan (Lucy), Pierre Clementi (Santoni), Abigail Cruttenden (Charlotte), Ahmed Boulane (Ben Said), Sira Stampe (Eva). Directed by Gillies MacKinnon and produced by Ann Scott. Screenplay by Billy MacKinnon, based on the novel by Esther Freud.

In the 1970s there were movies about the carefree lives of hippies and flower people, and on the screen you could see their children, longhaired, sunburned, and barefoot, solemn witnesses at rock concerts and magical mystery tours. Remember the commune in *Easy Rider.*

Now it is the 1990s and those children have grown up to make their own movies and tell their side of the story. *A Soldier's Daughter Never Cries* (1998) was based on an autobiographical novel by Kaylie Jones, whose novelist father, James, raised his family in bohemian freedom as exiles in Paris. Now here is *Hideous Kinky,* based on an autobiographical novel by Esther Freud, whose father is the British painter Lucien Freud. I'm not sure how much of the story is based on fact, but presumably the feelings are accurately reflected, as when a child tells her hippie mother: "I don't need another adventure, Mom! I need to go to school. I want a satchel!"

The film stars Kate Winslet, in an about-face after *Titanic,* as a thirtyish British mom named Julia, who has journeyed to Marrakech in 1972 with her two young daughters, Bea (Bella Riza) and Lucy (Carrie Mullan). She is seeking the truth, she says, or perhaps she is making a grand gesture against her husband, a London poet whom she caught cheating. Well, actually, he's not officially her husband, although he is the father of the children, and is sending them packages and checks from time to time, although sometimes they get packages intended for his other family, and the bank doesn't often receive the checks.

Julia is not a bad woman—just reckless, naive, foolishly trusting, and seeking truth in the wrong places, times, and ways. She doesn't do drugs to speak of, drinks little, wants to study Sufi philosophy. Her children, like most children, are profoundly conservative in the face of anarchy. They want a home, school, "real shirts." They're tired of Julia's quest, and ask, "Mom, when can we have rice pudding again?" The movie's tension comes from our own uneasiness about the mother, who with the best intentions seems to be blundering into trouble.

The film, directed by Gillies MacKinnon, fills its canvas with details about expatriate life in the time of flower power. Moroccan music blends with psychedelic rock, and they meet a teacher from the School of the Annihilation of the Ego. The expatriate American novelist Paul Bowles is presumably lurking about somewhere, writing his novel *The Sheltering Sky,* which is about characters not unlike these. One day in the bazaar the family encounters Bilal (Said Taghmaoui), a street performer who possibly has some disagreements with the police, but is humorous and friendly, and is soon Julia's lover.

Bilal is not a bad man, either. *Hideous Kinky* is not a melodrama or a thriller, and doesn't need villains; it's the record of a time when idealism led good-hearted seekers into danger. Some of the time Julia doesn't have enough food for her children, or a place for them to stay, and her idea for raising money is pathetic: She has them all making dolls to sell in the marketplace. Their trip to the desert leads to a nearly fatal ride with a sleepy truck driver, and to an uneasy meeting with a woman who may or may not be Bilal's wife.

In Marrakech, invitations come easily. They meet a Frenchman (Pierre Clementi, who played young hippies himself in the 1960s and 1970s) who invites them to his house: "I have lots of rooms." There they get involved in a strange ménage. Later, incredibly, Julia leaves Bea with them for safekeeping, only to discover that the household has broken up and her child has disappeared. She finds Bea in the keeping of an earnest Christian woman who runs an orphanage and doesn't seem inclined to surrender the child. "It's what Bea always wanted," she tells Julia. "To be an orphan?" "To be normal."

The movie is episodic and sometimes repetitive; dramatic scenes alternate with music and local color, and then the process repeats itself. What makes it work is Winslet's performance, as a sincere, good person, not terrifically smart, who doggedly pursues her dream and drags along her unwilling children. Parents, even flower-child moms, always think they know what's best for their kids. Maybe they do. Look at it this way: To the degree that this story really is autobiographical, Julia raised a daughter who wrote a novel and had it made into a movie. Bea might not have turned out quite so splendidly by eating rice pudding and carrying a satchel to school.

High Art ★ ★ ★ ½
R, 101 m., 1998

Ally Sheedy (Lucy Berliner), Radha Mitchell (Syd), Patricia Clarkson (Greta), Gabriel Mann (James, Syd's Boyfriend), Bill Sage (Arnie), Anh Duong (Dominique [The Editor]), Tammy Grimes (Vera, Lucy's Mother), David Thornton (Harry, Syd's Boss). Directed by Lisa Cholodenko and produced by Dolly Hall, Jeff Levy-Hinte, and Susan A. Stover. Screenplay by Cholodenko.

To explain the special strength of *High Art*, it is necessary to begin with the people who live in the apartment above Syd and James. There's a shifting population in the upstairs flat, since drugs are involved, but the permanent inhabitants are Lucy, who was a famous photographer ten years ago; Greta, who once starred in Fassbinder films; and Arnie, an unfocused layabout who's along for the ride and the heroin.

Syd has just been made an associate editor of a New York photo magazine—the kind with big pages, where you have to read the small print to tell the features from the ads. She goes upstairs because there's a leak coming through the ceiling, and walks into the sad, closed, claustrophobic life of the heroin users. And now here is my point: Those people really seem to be living there. They suggest a past, a present, a history, a pattern that has been going on for years. Their apartment, and how they live in it, is as convincing as a documentary could make it.

In other words, they aren't "characters." They don't feel like actors waiting for the camera to roll. And by giving them texture and complexity, writer-director Lisa Cholodenko has the key to her whole movie. The couple downstairs, Syd (Radha Mitchell) and her boyfriend, James (Gabriel Mann), are conventional movie characters—Manhattan yuppies. It's not that they seem false in the movie; it's that their lives are borrowed from media. Then Syd senses something upstairs that stirs her.

To begin with, she sees some photographs taken by Lucy (Ally Sheedy). They're good. She tells her so. "I haven't been deconstructed in a long time," Lucy says. Lucy is thin, a chain-smoker, projecting a kind of masochistic devotion to the older Greta (Patricia Clarkson). Both are deeply into drugs. Greta seems to drift between lassitude and oblivion; she's like a Fassbinder movie so drained of life it doesn't move anymore. She falls asleep during sex with Lucy. She nods off in a restaurant, and the waiter tells Lucy: "You know this restaurant has a policy about sleeping in here."

Syd is on the make. She wants to move up at her magazine. Her editor, the often hungover Dominique (Anh Duong), started as a receptionist at *Interview*—so all things are possible. Syd pitches Lucy's photos to Dominique. "She was so belligerent when she left New York," Dominique muses. They set up a luncheon. "I made it impossible for myself to continue," Lucy explains about her dead career. "I stopped showing up."

Dominique asks Lucy to do a shoot for the magazine. Lucy insists on Syd being her editor. Gradually, by almost imperceptible degrees, the two women are drawn toward one another. Greta sees what is happening, but her hold on Lucy is strong: a triangulation of drugs, exploited guilt, and domination. She knows what buttons to push.

High Art is masterful in the little details. It knows how these people might talk, how they might respond. It knows that Lucy, Greta, and the almost otherworldly Arnie might use heroin and then play Scrabble. It is so boring, being high in an empty life. The movie knows how career ambition and office politics can work together to motivate Syd: She wants Lucy to get the job because she's falling for Lucy, but also because she knows Lucy is her ticket to a promotion at the magazine.

Finally, at what seems like the emotionally inevitable moment, Syd and Lucy sleep together. This is one of the most observant sex scenes I have seen, involving a lot of worried, insecure dialogue; Syd feels awkward and inadequate, and wants reassurance, and Lucy provides it from long experience, mixed with a sudden rediscovery of the new. They talk a lot. Lucy is like ground control, talking a new pilot through her first landing.

The movie is wise about drug addiction. There are well-written scenes between Lucy and her mother (Tammy Grimes), who keeps her distance from her daughter. Lucy looks at her life and decides, "I can't do this anymore." She tries to open up with her mother: "I have a love issue and a drug problem." Her mother closes her off: "I can't help you with that." Lucy is tired of Greta, tired of drugs, tired of not working, tired of boredom. Greta's final, best

weapon is heroin: Can she keep Lucy with that? Or will Lucy be able to see that Greta is only the human face of her addiction?

High Art is so perceptive and mature it makes similar films seem flippant. The performances are on just the right note, scene after scene, for what needs to be done. The reviews keep mentioning that Ally Sheedy has outgrown her Brat Pack days. Well, of course she has. (She'd done that by the time of *Heart of Dixie*, in 1989.) Patricia Clarkson succeeds in creating a complete, complex character without ever overplaying the stoned behavior (she's like Fassbinder's Petra von Kant on heroin instead of booze). Radha Mitchell is successful at suggesting the interaction of several motives: love, lust, curiosity, ambition, admiration. And the movie's ending does not cheat. Just the opposite.

High Fidelity ★ ★ ★ ★
R, 120 m., 2000

John Cusack (Rob), Iben Hjejle (Laura), Todd Louiso (Dick), Jack Black (Barry), Lisa Bonet (Marie), Catherine Zeta-Jones (Charlie), Joan Cusack (Liz), Tim Robbins (Ian). Directed by Stephen Frears and produced by Tim Bevan and Rudd Simmons. Screenplay by D. V. Devincentis, Steve Pink, John Cusack, and Scott Rosenberg, based on the book by Nick Hornby.

In its unforced, whimsical, quirky, obsessive way, *High Fidelity* is a comedy about real people in real lives. The movie looks like it was easy to make—but it must not have been, because movies this wry and likable hardly ever get made. Usually a clunky plot gets in the way, or the filmmakers are afraid to let their characters seem too smart. Watching *High Fidelity*, I had the feeling I could walk out of the theater and meet the same people on the street—and want to, which is an even higher compliment.

John Cusack stars as Rob, who owns a used-record store in Chicago and has just broken up with Laura, his latest girlfriend. He breaks up a lot. Still hurting, he makes a list of the top five girls he's broken up with, and cackles that Laura didn't make it. Later he stands forlornly on a bridge overlooking the Chicago River and makes lists of the top five reasons he misses her.

The key design elements in Rob's apartment are the lumber bookshelves for his alphabetized vinyl albums. He has two guys working for him in his store. Each was hired for three days a week, but both come in six days a week, maybe because they have no place else to go. These guys are the shy, sideways Dick (Todd Louiso) and the ultraconfident Barry (Jack Black). They are both experts on everything, brains stocked with nuggets of information about popular culture.

Rob is the movie's narrator, guiding us through his world, talking directly to the camera, soliloquizing on his plight—which is that he seems unable to connect permanently with a girl, maybe because his attention is elsewhere. But on what? He isn't obsessed with his business, he isn't as crazy about music as Dick and Barry, and he isn't thinking about his next girl—he's usually moping about the last one. He seems stuck in the role of rejected lover, and never likes a girl quite as much when she's with him as after she's left.

Laura (Iben Hjejle) was kind of special. Now she has taken up with an unbearably supercilious, ponytailed brainiac named Ian (Tim Robbins), who comes into the store to "talk things over" and inspires fantasies in which Rob, Dick, and Barry dream of kicking him senseless. "Conflict resolution is my job," he offers helpfully. Whether Ian is nice or not is of no consequence to Rob; he simply wants Laura back.

The story unspools in an unforced way. Barry and Dick involve Rob in elaborate debates about music minutiae. They take him to a nightclub to hear a new singer (Lisa Bonet). Rob gets advice from Laura's best friend (Joan Cusack), who likes him but is fed up with his emotional dithering. Rob seeks out former girlfriends like Charlie (Catherine Zeta-Jones), who tells him why she left him in more detail than he really wants to hear. Rob decides that his ideal girl would be a singer who would "write songs at home and ask me what I thought of them—and maybe even include one of our private little jokes in the liner notes."

High Fidelity is based on a 1995 novel by Nick Hornby, a London writer, and has been directed by Stephen Frears, also British. Frears and his screenwriters (D. V. Devincentis, Steve Pink, Cusack, and Scott Rosenberg) have transplanted the story to Chicago so successfully that it feels like it grew organically out of the funky soil of Lincoln Avenue and Halsted, Old Town and New Town, Rogers Park and Hyde Park, and Wicker Park, where it was shot—those neighborhoods where the workers in the alternative lifestyle industry live, love, and labor.

This is a film about, and also for, not only obsessed clerks in record stores, but the video store clerks who have seen all the movies, and the bookstore employees who have read all the books. Also for bartenders, waitresses, greengrocers in health food stores, kitchen slaves at vegetarian restaurants, the people at GNC who know all the herbs, writers for alternative weeklies, disc jockeys on college stations, salespeople in retro-clothing shops, tattoo artists and those they tattoo, poets, artists, musicians, novelists, and the hip, the pierced, and the lonely. They may not see themselves, but they will recognize people they know.

The Cusack character is someone I have known all my life. He is assembled out of my college friends, the guys at work, people I used to drink with. I also recognize Barry, the character played by Jack Black; he's a type so universal it's a wonder he hasn't been pinned down in a movie before: a blowhard, a self-appointed expert on all matters of musical taste, a monologuist, a guy who would rather tell you his opinion than take your money. Jack Black is himself from this world; he's the lead singer of the group Tenacious D, and it is a measure of his acting ability that when he does finally sing in this movie, we are surprised that he can.

The women I recognize too. They're more casual about romance than most movie characters, maybe because most movies are simpleminded and pretend it is earthshakingly important whether this boy and this girl mate forever, when a lot of young romance is just window-shopping and role-playing, and everyone knows it. You break up, you sigh, you move on. The process is so universal that with some people, you sigh as you meet them, in anticipation.

I am meandering. All I want to say is that *High Fidelity* has no deep significance, does not grow exercised over stupid plot points, savors the rhythms of these lives, sees how pop music is a sound track for everyone's autobiography, introduces us to Rob and makes us hope that he finds happiness, and causes us to leave the theater quite unreasonably happy.

☞

Hilary and Jackie ★ ★ ★ ½

R, 121 m., 1998

Emily Watson (Jacqueline du Pre), Rachel Griffiths (Hilary du Pre), David Morrissey (Kiffer Finzi), James Frain (Daniel Barenboim), Charles Dance (Derek du Pre), Celia Imrie (Iris du Pre), Rupert Penry-Jones (Piers du Pre), Bill Paterson (Jackie's Cello Teacher). Directed by Anand Tucker and produced by Andy Paterson and Nicolas Kent. Screenplay by Frank Cottrell-Boyce, based on the book *A Genius in the Family* by Hilary and Piers Du Pre.

Jackie to Hilary: "The truth is, you're not special."

Hilary to Jackie: "If you think that being an ordinary person is any easier than being an extraordinary one, you're wrong. If you didn't have that cello to prop you up, you'd be nothing."

And yet the two sisters love each other with a fierceness that stands beside their lifelong rivalry. *Hilary and Jackie* is the story of two gifted musicians, who in a way were always playing for (or against) each other, and how one of them was struck down by disease. "I have a fatal illness," Jackie says, "but the good news is, I have a very mild case."

Jacqueline du Pre (Emily Watson) was one of the most gifted cellists of her time, and her brilliant marriage to the pianist and conductor Daniel Barenboim was a celebrated musical and romantic liaison. Hilary du Pre (Rachel Griffiths), her older sister, played the flute and might perhaps have been as gifted as her sister. But that we will never know, because a music teacher beat down her talent and crushed her spirit. Perhaps she had a happier life as a result.

Hilary and Jackie is an extraordinary film about riding the tiger of genius, and how that cuts through conventional rules and invests the rider with special license. That Jackie's long illness and too-young death was tragic there is no doubt, but she played such beautiful music that it is our tragedy as well as hers. And yet to those close to the story, there is always another side and more personal feelings.

Hilary and Jackie, directed by Anand Tucker, is based on a memoir written by Hilary and her brother, Piers du Pre, and it is unusually knowing for a biopic.

It opens with a long section seen from Hilary's point of view. We see the two young sisters playing at the beach and practicing their instruments. Hilary is the talented one, applauded at family gatherings, while Jackie smolders ignored in the corner. But when Hilary is asked to play on a BBC children's concert, she won't go without Jackie. And when Jackie is not very good, they're told by their mother: "If you want to be together, you've got to be as good as each other."

That line of instruction may have been the turning point in Jacqueline du Pre's musical career, inspiring her to practice obsessively until she was not only as good as Hilary, but better. It was her fortune to find teachers who supported her, while Hilary was driven off the stage by pressures mostly engendered by her teacher. Both young women moved freely while playing; Jackie's onstage enthusiasm helped make her famous, but Hilary was ordered to stand still: "It is impossible to produce a proper tone without proper deportment."

She freezes during an audition and abandons any hope of a concert career. Luckily, she finds a man who believes in her: Kiffer Finzi (David Morrissey). Jackie also finds love with "Danny" (James Frain), and they are happy, but there comes a time when Jackie walks off a concert stage and goes to Hilary's farm and demands to be allowed to make love to her husband: "You don't mind, do you, Sis?"

Her arrival, her demand, and her behavior ("bonkers") are all seen from Hilary's point of view. Then the film's next section, seen through Jackie's eyes, details the early warning signs of multiple sclerosis. The film follows through to the unhappy end, showing the destruction of a career, a personality, and a life. It stays tactfully at arm's-length in the way it handles Jacqueline's troubled relationship with Barenboim, and looks mostly through Hilary's eyes as the sad story unfolds.

A film like this lives in its performances. Emily Watson is fiery and strong willed as Jackie; we see the fierce stubbornness of her character in *Breaking the Waves* now wedded to talent and neurosis. The key performance, however, is Rachel Griffiths's, as Hilary, the witness, the person who senses on an almost telepathic level what her sister thinks and feels. Griffiths, not yet well known, is able to convey penetrating intelligence in a look; in a film named *My Son the Fanatic,* she plays a prostitute whose sense of herself and her occupation is almost scarily perceptive.

The film has details that only a family member could supply, such as the few but significant scenes involving the parents: the mother who engenders competition, the father (Charles Dance) who doesn't want his girls living near Soho for fear they will be snatched for the white slave trade. Although the brother, Piers, is coauthor of the book, he has hardly any dialogue in the movie; it is the sisters' story.

The movie makes no attempt to soften the material or make it comforting through the clichés of melodrama; it is instructive to see it side by side with *At First Sight.* One takes true experience and masks it with scenes that could literally be in any romantic melodrama; *Hilary and Jackie* feels as if every scene was newly drawn out of the sharp memories of actual lifetimes.

There is, of course, a lot of music in the film, and the sound track will be good to have; but it is not a film about performances, it is a film about performing: about how physically and emotionally difficult it is to travel from city to city, adored by strangers, far from friends, and find every night the ability to play the cello as well as it can be played. "Would you still love me if I couldn't play?" Jacqueline asks her husband. "You wouldn't be you if you didn't play," he replies, and that is the simple truth made clear by this film. We are what we do.

The Hi-Lo Country ★ ★
R, 114 m., 1999

Billy Crudup (Pete Calder), Woody Harrelson (Big Boy Matson), Patricia Arquette (Mona), Penelope Cruz (Josepha O'Neil), Sam Elliott (Jim Ed Love), Cole Hauser (Little Boy Matson), James Gammon (Hoover Young), Lane Smith (Steve Shaw), Katy Jurado (Meesa), Don Walser (Singer). Directed by Stephen Frears and produced by Barbara De Fina, Martin Scorsese, Eric Fellner, and Tim Bevan. Screenplay by Walon Green.

When poker players want to make the game a little more interesting, they either raise the stakes or declare a wild card. Woody Harrelson has the same effect on a movie. He has a reckless, risky air; he walks into a scene and you can't be sure what he'll do. He plays characters who are a challenge to their friends, let alone their enemies.

In Stephen Frears's *The Hi-Lo Country,* Harrelson has an energy the rest of the film lacks. He plays a variation on that old theme, the Last of the Cowboys, but does it with a modern irony. Watching his character tame unruly horses and strut into bars, I was reminded of a line from a completely different kind of movie, *A New Leaf,* where the aging playboy is told, "You are carrying on in your own lifetime a way of life that was dead before you were born."

Harrelson plays Big Boy Matson, a man's man in the arid Hi-Lo country of New Mexico. He's seen through the eyes of the film's narrator and nominal hero, Pete Calder (Billy Crudup), who returns to the area after serving in World War II and plans to raise cattle. He's advised against it by the rich local rancher Jim Ed Love (Sam Elliott), who says the days of the independent herds are over and gone. "People still drive cattle to railheads," Pete tells him. "Only in the movies," Jim Ed says.

The movie evokes the open space of New Mexico with a bright, dusty grandeur; Oliver Stapleton's camera places the characters in a wide-screen landscape of weathered buildings, lonesome windmills, and distant mountains. There do not seem to be enough people around; the inhabitants of the small town live in each other's pockets, and there are no secrets.

One secret that would be hard to keep is the allure of Mona (Patricia Arquette), a local man's wife who dances on Saturday nights at the tavern as if she might go home with the next man who takes her out on the floor. Mona likes Pete. Indeed, the first time she sees him after the war, at the tavern, she all but propositions him: "Am I keepin' you from something? Or someone? You look good, Pete.

Real good." Pete dances with her, and confides in a voice-over, "She was right. I was lookin' for someone. She came up against me like silver foil, all fragrance and warm pressure."

That's not the sort of line a New Mexico cowboy is likely to use in 1946, but there's a kind of distance between the hard-boiled life of the Hi-Lo country and the poetry of the film, which wants the characters steeped in nostalgia and standing for a vanishing way of life. The screenplay is by Walon Green, who also wrote *The Wild Bunch*, which was more hard-boiled about nostalgia.

Mona's problem is, as good as Pete looks to her, Big Boy looks better. That's who she really loves, and who really loves her. But Big Boy is untamed, just like Old Sorrel, the unruly horse he bought from Pete. And Big Boy is incautious in his remarks. Even though Mona is married to a man with friends who have guns, Big Boy makes reckless announcements for the whole bar to hear, like "A good woman's like a good horse—she's got bottom. Mona's gonna make me a partner to go along with Old Sorrel."

The romantic lines grow even more tangled because there is, as there always is in a Western, a Good Woman who steadfastly stands by the hero even while he hangs out with the boys and the bad girls. This is Josepha (Penelope Cruz), a Mexican-American Pete was seeing before the war. She loves Pete, and Pete says he loves her (he lies), and she knows about Mona: "She's a cheap ex-prostitute and a phony."

Mona may be, but she's sincere in her love for Big Boy, and in one way or another that drives most of the plot. The underlying psychology of the film is in the tradition of those Freudian Westerns of the 1950s, in which a man was a man but a gun was sometimes not simply a gun. There's a buried attraction between Big Boy and Pete, who not only sleep with the same woman (and know they do) but engage in roughhouse and camaraderie in a way that suggests that no woman is ever going to be as important to them as a good buddy (or a horse). Jim Ed Love, of course, represents patriarchal authority: He stands for wisdom, experience, and money, and for telling boys to stop that fooling around and grow up.

Stephen Frears is an Irish director who therefore grew up steeped in the lore of the American West (country-and-western music is more popular in Irish pubs than in some states of the union). He's seen a lot of revisionist modern Westerns (especially *Giant*), and he gets the right look and feel for his film. But I think he brings a little too much taste and restraint to it. If he'd turned up the heat under the other characters, they could have matched Big Boy's energy, and the movie could have involved us in the way a good Western can.

Instead, *The Hi-Lo Country* is reserved and even elegiac. It's about itself, rather than about its story. The voice-over narration insists on that: It stands outside and above the story, and elevates it with self-conscious prose. By the end, we could be looking at Greek tragedy. Maybe that's the idea. But Harrelson suggests another way the movie could have gone. With his heedless energy and his sense of complete relaxation before the camera (he glides through scenes as easily as a Cary Grant), he shows how the movie might have been better off staying at ground level and forgetting about the mythological cloud's-eye view.

Note: Two small scenes deserve special mention. One involves the legendary Mexican-American actress Katy Jurado, as a fortune-teller. When the boys visit her, she's asked if "all of us who are here will be alive and prosperous next year." They get their money's worth: "No." The other showstopper is a C&W singer named Don Walser, whose high, sweet voice provides a moment when the movie forgets everything and just listens to him.

Holy Man ★ ★
PG, 113 m., 1998

Eddie Murphy ("G"), Jeff Goldblum (Ricky), Kelly Preston (Kate), Robert Loggia (McBainbridge), Jon Cryer (Barry), Eric McCormack (Scoot Hawkes), Sam Kitchin (Director), Robert Small (Assistant Director). Directed by Stephen Herek and produced by Roger Birnbaum and Herek. Screenplay by Tom Schulman.

Holy Man is a love story about two people with no apparent chemistry, whose lives are changed by a stranger who remains an uninteresting enigma. No wonder it just sits there on the screen. This screenplay was in no shape to be filmed; perhaps the filmmakers assumed that the mere presence of Eddie Murphy would repair its wrongs and give them a big opening weekend.

Murphy is a charismatic star in the right material. Give him *The Nutty Professor* and he sparkles. Put him in a half-digested formula, and he sinks as quickly as a mortal would. Examine his flops and you can almost hear the executives reassuring each other, "We don't need a rewrite; we have Eddie!"

In *Holy Man,* Murphy plays a man in Indian garb who wanders through life on his "pilgrimage" while reciting platitudes recycled from twelve-step programs. His story is counterpoint to a romance between two executives for a TV shopping network, whose relationship rigidly follows the conventional outline: They dislike each other on sight, they become rivals at work, then mutual respect flowers in a difficult situation, they fall in love, and then (of course) she is disillusioned when he sells out, and then (of course) he does what he knows is right, and she comes flying back into his arms. It helps if the final embrace can be broadcast on live TV.

The Murphy character, named simply "G," materializes while walking down the median strip of a Miami expressway. He spots TV executives Ricky and Kate (Jeff Goldblum and Kelly Preston) with a flat tire, and offers to help them. He looks like a loony. Then he walks calmly across four lanes of the expressway while every speeding car misses him. (The flaw in this computer-assisted effect is that none of the oncoming cars slows down or swerves.)

"G" becomes a part of their lives. He has no history, no story, no philosophy except for boilerplate advice like "Be careful what you wish for—you may get it." Opportunities for satire are lost because "G" is presented not only as a straight holy man, but as a boring one.

At a party of TV executives at Ricky's house, he confronts an obnoxious guest, borrows his Rolex, wraps it in a hanky and pounds it with a shoe. Then the Rolex disappears. "Give me back my goddamn watch!" shouts the guest, only to find it has been returned to his arm.

Proof that "G" has miraculous powers? Only if you have not seen this trick done by countless magicians. (Ah, but did "G" perhaps perform it by miraculous means? If he did, I have advice for him: It's counterproductive to perform miracles that duplicate magic tricks.)

Ricky and Kate work for a TV shopping network run by Robert Loggia. The movie, credulous and soppy in its story of "G" and the romance, tries uneasily to convert itself into sketch comedy in portraying the network. We see a lot of celebs hawking their wares ("The James Brown Soul Survival System," etc.). Then "G" wanders onto a live set and begins to speak the truth, and sales shoot up. He quickly becomes a superstar salesman and gets his own show, inevitably named *The G Spot.*

Holy Man's director, Stephen Herek, and his editor, Trudy Ship, fall into a tiresome editing pattern in showing "G" on the air. First "G" says something. Then we cut to counterpoint from the control booth. Then "G." Then the booth. There's editing Ping-Pong for seven or eight rounds, and the same formula is repeated every time "G" goes on the air. This is fatal to comedy, which must seem spontaneously generated and not timed according to a system imposed from above.

Goldblum and Preston don't convince us they're really in love, although perhaps sincerity is impossible to find in this story. Robert Loggia supplies the standard apoplectic executive without the quirks and eccentricities that would have elevated the character above the cookie-cutter level.

And as for Murphy, the movie seems to think its task was completed when it put Eddie in a holy man uniform. Consider his lengthiest parable. He was walking along the beach, he says, when he saw thousands of starfish washed ashore. Then he saw a girl throwing as many as she could back into the sea. "You are wasting your time," the holy man tells her, "because there are just too many starfish." The girl holds up the starfish she is holding. "To this one," she says, "it makes a difference."

You've heard it a thousand times. So have I. Let's deconstruct it. The first error is for "G" to claim the story happened to him. It is such an ancient parable that he is obviously lying. Second error: The girl teaches him the lesson. As a self-respecting guru, he should be throwing in the starfish and explaining it to her. Third error: The movie has him tell the story to listeners whose mouths gape open in astonishment at his wisdom. A smart screenplay would have had someone interrupt him: "Yeah, yeah, I know—it makes a difference to *this* starfish! Everybody's heard that story." If "G" has a comeback to that line, then he's a guru and not just another underwritten character.

Holy Smoke! ★ ★ ½
R, 114 m., 2000

Kate Winslet (Ruth Barron), Harvey Keitel (P. J. Waters), Julie Hamilton (Miriam [Mum]), Tim Robertson (Gilbert [Dad]), Sophie Lee (Yvonne), Dan Wyllie (Robbie), Paul Goddard (Tim), George Mangos (Yani), Pam Grier (Carol). Directed by Jane Campion and produced by Jan Chapman. Screenplay by Anna and Jane Campion.

Holy Smoke! begins as a movie about the deprogramming of a cult member and ends with the deprogramming of the deprogrammer. It's not even a close call. The cult member is Ruth (Kate Winslet), an Australian who has gone to India and allied herself with a guru. And the deprogrammer is Harvey Keitel, summoned by Ruth's parents; he stalks off the plane like his no-nonsense fix-it man in *Pulp Fiction* and then starts falling to pieces. The movie leaves us wondering why the guru didn't become Ruth's follower too.

The film isn't really about cults at all, but about the struggle between men and women, and it's a little surprising, although not boring, when it turns from a mystic travelogue into a feminist parable. The director is Jane Campion *(The Piano),* who wrote the screenplay with her sister Anna. Like so many Australian films (perhaps even a majority), *Holy Smoke!* suggests that everyone in Australia falls somewhere on the spectrum between goofy and eccentric, none more than characters invariably named Mum and Dad. Parents are totally unhinged beneath a facade of middle-class conventionality; their children seem crazy but like many movie mad people are se-

cretly saner than anyone else. Campion's first film, *Sweetie,* was an extreme example; *Holy Smoke!* reins in the strangeness a little, although to be sure there's a scene where Keitel wanders the Outback wearing a dress and lipstick, like a passenger who fell off *Priscilla, Queen of the Desert.*

Ruth, the Winslet character, journeys to India and falls under the sway of a mystic guru. Her parents trick her into returning, and hire P. J. Waters (Keitel) to fly over from America and deprogram her. At this point I was hoping perhaps for something like *Ticket to Heaven* (1981), the powerful Canadian film about the struggle for a cult member's mind. But no. The moment Ruth and P.J. face off against each other, their struggle is not over cult beliefs but about the battle between men and women. And P.J., with his obsolete vocabulary of sexual references, is no match for the strong-willed young woman who overwhelms him mentally, physically, and sexually.

Winslet and Keitel are both interesting in the film, and indeed Winslet seems to be following Keitel's long-standing career plan, which is to go with intriguing screenplays and directors and let stardom take care of itself. That may mean he doesn't get paid $20 million a picture, but $20 million roles, with rare exceptions, are dog's bones anyway—because they've been chewed over and regurgitated by too many timid executives. A smaller picture like this, shot out of the mainstream, has a better chance of being quirky and original.

And quirky it is, even if not successful. Maybe it's the setup that threw me off. Ruth comes onscreen as one kind of person—dreamy, escapist, a volunteer for mind-controlling beliefs—and then turns into an articulate spokeswoman for Jane and Anna Campion's ideas. It's also a little disappointing that the film didn't penetrate more deeply into the Indian scenes, instead of using them mostly just as setup for the feminist payoff. And it's difficult to see how the Ruth at the end of the film could have fallen under the sway of the guru at the beginning. Not many radical feminists seek out male gurus in patriarchal cultures.

Home Fries ★ ★ ★
PG-13, 92 m., 1998

Drew Barrymore (Sally), Catherine O'Hara (Mrs. Lever), Luke Wilson (Dorian), Jake Busey (Angus), Shelley Duvall (Mrs. Jackson), Kim Robillard (Billy), Daryl Mitchell (Roy), Lanny Flaherty (Red). Directed by Dean Parisot and produced by Mark Johnson, Barry Levinson, Lawrence Kasdan, and Charles Newirth. Screenplay by Vince Gilligan.

Home Fries is the kind of movie where a man is frightened to death by a helicopter, dies sitting bolt upright on a park bench, and one of his killers wants to pose with him. What kind of movie does that make it? I'm not sure. It has elements of sweet romance and elements of macabre humor, and divides its characters between the two—except for a performance by Catherine O'Hara that seems serenely astride both worlds.

The movie stars Drew Barrymore, perky and plucky, as Sally, a drive-thru clerk at the Burger-Matic. We see her in the opening scene, serving a vanilla shake to a middle-aged man who whispers that he has finally told his wife he was having an affair. "Did you tell her about this?" asks Sally, standing up tall so the creep can see how pregnant she is. He offers her a ride home and hints at other pastimes. "I don't need a ride home," she snaps. "I need a father for my baby."

It is all going to get a lot more complicated. Later that night, the man will be frightened to death. We'll meet the two helicopter pilots: Dorian (Luke Wilson) and Angus (Jake Busey). The police will break the news to the man's widow, Mrs. Lever (O'Hara). And then (spoiler warning) we discover that Dorian and Angus are her sons by an earlier marriage, that the dead man was her current husband, and that she encouraged them to scare him.

The sons have reason to suspect that their radio conversations in the helicopter were overheard by Sally on her Burger-Matic headphones, so Dorian gets a job in the drive-in to spy on her, and falls in love with her, little realizing that he is the killer of the father of her unborn child. Are you following this? They begin to fall in love, but as the full implica-

tions of their romance start to emerge, Sally tells Dorian, "You can't be the father and the brother at the same time. That's the kind of thing that messes kids up."

The movie requires Barrymore and Wilson to play their characters straight most of the time, while Catherine O'Hara mixes sweetness with irony and Jake Busey chews the scenery with those marvelous teeth. Seeing the movie for the first time at the Toronto Film Festival in September, I found parts of it amusing but doubted the whole. I wanted to see it again before writing this review, and was surprised to find I liked it better the second time. I suspect the barrage of twists and revelations was off-putting at Toronto, distracting from the wit in O'Hara's performance and the sweetness in Barrymore's. The first time, you think the movie is about the plot, and the second time you realize it's about the characters.

This is one of O'Hara's best screen performances. The former Second City star is sweetness and reason as she manipulates her two luggy sons and brazenly acts her way through meetings with the cops and her late husband's young lover. She is so calm, so cool, she implies scary depths that she never has to reveal.

Barrymore, who is emerging this year as a versatile star (there's a big distance between this and *Ever After*), is wise to play Sally on a more or less realistic level, focusing on her pregnancy and newfound romance, and remaining oblivious (when possible) to the web of intrigue around her. She avoids the actor's mistake of knowing more about the screenplay than her character would know.

The movie is the feature debut of Dean Parisot, based on a screenplay that I gather Vince Gilligan found in his bottom drawer after *The X-Files* made him bankable. It might have seemed fresher ten years ago, before this kind of ironic labyrinthine plotting became common, but he has a sharp eye for characters, and introduces Sally's parents (Shelley Duvall and Lanny Flaherty) during an apparent fast-food hostage crisis that dissolves into a marital spat before our eyes.

Home Fries is not a great movie, and as much as I finally enjoyed it, I'm not sure it's worth seeing two times just to get into the rhythm. More character and less plot might have been a good idea. But the actors are tickled by their characters and have fun with them, and so I did too.

And I liked the wicked human comedy in scenes like the one where the blustering, dopey Angus (Busey) asks O'Hara, "Mom, what'd you mean when you said Dorian was your favorite?"

"Oh, Angus," she says, with fondness and exasperation, "I love you both. A difference of this much." She holds her thumb and forefinger two inches apart, knowing that when your mother likes your brother more, an inch is as good as a mile.

Hope Floats ★ ★
PG-13, 114 m., 1998

Sandra Bullock (Birdee Pruitt), Harry Connick Jr. (Justin Matisse), Gena Rowlands (Ramona Calvert), Mae Whitman (Bernice Pruitt), Michael Pare (Bill Pruitt), Cameron Finley (Travis), Kathy Najimy (Toni Post). Directed by Forest Whitaker and produced by Lynda Obst. Screenplay by Steven Rogers.

Hope Floats begins with a talk show where a woman learns that her husband and her best friend are having an affair. Devastated, she flees from Chicago with her young daughter, and moves back in with her mother in Smithville, Texas. Everybody in Smithville (and the world), of course, witnessed her public humiliation. "Why did you go on that show in the first place?" her mother asks. "Because I wanted a free makeover," she says. "Well, you got one."

The victim's name is Birdee Pruitt (Sandra Bullock), and she was three-time Queen of Corn in Smithville. But she doesn't type and she doesn't compute, and her catty former classmate, who runs the local employment agency, tells her, "I don't see a listing here for prom queen." Birdee finally gets a job in a photo developing lab, where the owner asks her to make extra prints of any "interesting" snapshots.

This material could obviously lead in a lot of different directions. It seems most promising as comedy or satire, but no: *Hope Floats* is a turgid melodrama with the emotional range of a sympathy card.

Consider the cast of characters in Smithville.

Birdee is played by Bullock as bewildered by her husband's betrayal (even though he's such a pig that she must have had hints over the years). Birdee's mother, Ramona (Gena Rowlands), is a salt-of-the-earth type who's able to live in a rambling Victorian mansion *and* keep her husband in a luxurious retirement home, despite having no apparent income. Birdee's daughter, Bernice (Mae Whitman), is a little drip who keeps whining that she wants to live with Daddy, despite overwhelming evidence that Daddy is a cretin. And then there's Justin (Harry Connick Jr.), the old boyfriend Birdee left behind, who's still in love with her and spends his free time restoring big old homes. (There is no more reliable indicator of a male character's domestic intentions than when he invites the woman of his dreams to touch his newly installed pine.)

Hope Floats is one of those screenplays where everything that will happen is instantly obvious, and yet the characters are forced to occupy a state of oblivion, acting as if it's all a mystery to them. It is obvious that Birdee's first husband is a worthless creep. And that Justin and Birdee will fall in love once again. And that Bernice will not go home to live with Daddy and his new girlfriend. And that the creeps who are still jealous of the onetime Corn Queen will get their comeuppance. The only real mystery in the movie is how Birdee keeps her job at Snappy Snaps despite apparently ruining every roll of film she attempts to process (the only photo she successfully develops during the entire movie is apparently done by magic realism).

I grow restless when I sense a screenplay following a schedule so faithfully that it's like a train conductor with a stopwatch. Consider, for example, the evening of tender romance and passion between Birdee and Justin. What comes next? A fight, of course. There's a grim dinner scene at which everyone stares unhappily at their plates, no doubt thinking they would be having a wonderful time—if only the screenwriter hadn't required an obligatory emotional slump between the false dawn and the real dawn.

I watch these formulas unfold, and I reflect that the gurus who teach those Hollywood screenwriting classes have a lot to answer for. They claim their formulas are based on analysis of successful movies. But since so many movies have been written according to their formulas, there's a kind of self-fulfilling prophecy going on here. Isn't it at least theoretically possible that after a man and a woman spend an evening in glorious romantic bliss, they could still be glowing the next day?

Hope Floats was written by Steven Rogers and directed by Forest Whitaker *(Waiting to Exhale)*. It shows evidence of still containing shreds of earlier drafts. At one point, for example, Birdee accuses her mother of embarrassing her as a child with her "roadkill hat and freshly skinned purse." Well, it's a good line, and it suggests that Gena Rowlands will be developed as one of the ditzy eccentrics she plays so well. But actually she's pretty sensible in this movie, and the line doesn't seem to apply.

There's also the problem that the sweet romantic stuff coexists uneasily with harsher scenes, as when little Bernice discovers her daddy doesn't want her to move back in with him. The whole TV talk show setup, indeed, deals the movie a blow from which it never recovers: No film that starts so weirdly should develop so conventionally. Sandra Bullock seems to sense that in her performance; her character wanders through the whole movie like a person who senses that no matter what Harry Connick thinks, she will always be known as the Corn Queen who got dumped on TV.

The Horse Whisperer ★ ★ ★
PG-13, 160 m., 1998

Robert Redford (Tom Booker), Kristin Scott Thomas (Annie MacLean), Scarlett Johansson (Grace MacLean), Sam Neill (Robert MacLean), Dianne Wiest (Diane Booker), Chris Cooper (Frank Booker), Cherry Jones (Liz Hammond), Ty Hillman (Joe Booker). Directed by Robert Redford and produced by Redford and Patrick Markey. Screenplay by Eric Roth and Richard LaGravenese, based on the novel by Nicholas Evans.

The Horse Whisperer is about a man of great patience faced with a woman, a child, and a horse in great need of it. It evokes the healing serenity of the wide-open spaces, and while I suspect that an unhappy New Yorker who moves to Montana is likely to become an unhappy Montanan, I concede that the myth is comforting. In films going back to *Jeremiah Johnson,* Robert Redford has shown that he has a real feeling for the West—he's not a movie tourist—and there is a magnificence in his treatment here that dignifies what is essentially a soap opera.

The story, from the best-selling novel by Nicholas Evans, involves a riding accident that leaves a horse named Pilgrim crippled, and a girl named Grace (Scarlett Johansson) so badly injured that part of her leg must be amputated. The girl's parents are high-powered Manhattanites: The father (Sam Neill) is a lawyer, and the mother, Annie (Kristin Scott Thomas), is clearly modeled on editor Tina Brown.

Their farm workers believe the horse should be put down (it's fearful and skittish), but Annie reads about a famed "horse whisperer" named Tom Booker who heals troubled animals. Booker (Redford) turns her down over the phone, but she's a type-A compulsive who decides to drive both the horse and her daughter to Montana and confront him directly. Her daughter fears "no one will ever want me" with only one leg; if the horse heals, Annie thinks, maybe Grace will heal too.

That's the setup. The heart of the film is in Big Sky country, where Tom Booker runs a cattle ranch with his brother Frank (Chris Cooper) and Frank's wife, Diane (Dianne Wiest). Tom was married once; it was love at first sight, but it didn't last because his city-born wife found the ranch had "too much space for her." Now he's famed for using patience and a gentle touch with difficult horses.

How does horse whispering work? As nearly as I could tell, Tom stares at the horse until the horse gets the idea. Eventually the horse succumbs to its need for love and acceptance. These methods work equally well with women, as both Grace and Annie discover; the girl's anger dissolves, and her mother, a brittle workaholic, finds her hyper personality dissolving in the mountain air—as she falls in love with Tom.

To describe the plot in this way makes it sound cornier than it feels. The elements are borrowed from elsewhere; there's a touch of

The Bridges of Madison County in the married woman's love for a man who represents freedom, and a touch of *My Friend Flicka* and its sequel, *Thunderhead*, in the treatment of a rebellious horse.

But Redford, as director and star, relates to the underlying themes of the story, which is about city versus country, and responsibility versus passion. The very lifestyle of Redford's ranch is a character in the movie; his plump, cheerful sister-in-law is a contented contrast to Annie, the rail-thin New Yorker who tries to control everything (fretting about her daughter's hospital care, she vows, "I'm going to get to know all the nurses' names"). There are big meals, long hours, and head-clearing rides on the range.

This life has imbued Tom Booker with an empathy that allows him to identify with pain, and for me the best scenes in the movie involved his careful touch with Grace. She's sullen and withdrawn at first, but he insists that Pilgrim will be ridden again—and Grace will ride him. He handles her with respect, and there's a nice moment when he asks her to drive the ranch pickup. She can't drive, she says. "No time like the present to start," he says.

The scenes between Tom and Annie are more problematic. Both adults begin to see the other as the ideal mate they've always been looking for. Love grows between them in unspoken words and quick glances, and eventually it appears that Annie is destined to leave her husband and stay on the ranch with the Bookers. She has fallen so much under the spell of the West that when she's fired from her magazine job, she hardly seems to notice. And Tom sees in her what he needs to see in a woman—what he saw in his wife, until she left.

"This is me," Tom tells her, looking around at the ranch. "This is where I belong. Could you live here?" Yes, says Annie, she could. Maybe that's because she sees the West in terms of a Redford film. Before she burns her bridges, I'd advise her to see *City Slickers*. I never felt much chemistry between Scott Thomas and Redford; their characters are in love with the idea of one another, not with each other's bodies and souls. And so Redford and his writers, Eric Roth and Richard La-Gravenese, were correct to supply their story

with a different ending than Nicholas Evans's climax.

What works is the beauty of the western country, the tactful way Tom deals with Grace, and the touching scenes in which the damaged horse is healed. The story moves a little too slowly, but it respects its characters, and even the lawyer from New York, when he finally arrives out west, turns out to be a person of insight and intelligence (his confession to his wife is really more touching than anything Tom says to her). *The Horse Whisperer* treads on the brink of contrivance, but the honesty of its feelings pulls it through.

How Stella Got Her Groove Back ★ ★ ½
R, 116 m., 1998

Angela Bassett (Stella), Whoopi Goldberg (Delilah), Taye Diggs (Winston), Regina King (Vanessa), Suzzanne Douglas (Angela), Michael J. Pagan (Quincy). Directed by Kevin Rodney Sullivan and produced by Deborah Schindler. Screenplay by Ron Bass and Terry McMillan.

How Stella Got Her Groove Back tries its best to turn a paperback romance into a relationship worth making a movie about, but fails. At the end of the movie we're prepared to concede that Stella may indeed have her groove back, but at a considerable price, and maybe not for long. If a romantic couple feels wrong to the audience, no plot gymnastics can convince us.

The movie stars Angela Bassett as Stella, a divorced mom and high-powered San Francisco trader who, as the movie opens, is promising a client a guaranteed 65 percent return on some Russian bonds. Her personal life is lonely, and her sisters advise her to find a man. I'm thinking—if those returns are real, the man will find you.

Stella's best friend, Delilah (Whoopi Goldberg), lays down the law: It's time for them to fly to Jamaica for some R&R. Her first morning, Stella finds herself at breakfast with an improbably handsome young man (Taye Diggs) who introduces himself as Winston Shakespeare. Delilah has lined up a couple of football players for them to party with, but Winston keeps coming around and being sincere and catching at corners of her heart, until Stella realizes she has a problem on her hands: There is the danger they will actually fall in love.

But she is forty and he is twenty and, as Winston's mother says when Stella eventually meets her, "You ought to be ashamed of yourself!" That's about all Winston's mother says. She's trundled onstage for her obligatory line and disappears, along with Winston's father, who doesn't even get a line. At least we got to see what a nice home Winston was raised in. The movie doesn't really care about the parents; it just needs them for a plot point. In a different kind of movie, the parents would have been dealt with, not just put on exhibit.

Meanwhile (spoiler coming up), Delilah is revealed as dying of cancer. It's one of those deaths that makes you cringe, because its only function in the plot is to provide a deathbed scene and a funeral scene (at which, yes, inevitably, Winston arrives late and stands silhouetted in the church doorway just as Stella is delivering her remarks. Has the key person at such a movie event ever arrived on time?). Goldberg and Bassett are fine actors, and the deathbed scene is indeed effective—funny and then sad. But that doesn't make it necessary. (During the course of the film, Stella also goes though two major changes involving employment, both of which seem unnecessary except to establish her professional status.)

Winston moves in with Stella while they test their relationship and the age gap between them. I had problems with those passages because, frankly, I couldn't find any genuine common ground for the two of them, except for physical passion, which can be wonderfully entertaining, yes, but is not invariably the best reason to get married. Stella sometimes has similar doubts, and has a good line: "He's never done anything, he's never been anyplace, he hasn't even had his heart broken. This morning I found Cocoa Puffs in the bed."

Is a twenty-year age difference surmountable? Sure, but maybe not when the man is still unformed (he says he wants to be a doctor). What about Stella? Will she return to her first love, woodworking? In ten years, young Dr. Shakespeare will be introducing his fifty-year-old wife, the cabinetmaker. Maybe she'd be better off looking for somebody like Marvin, the handyman in *Waiting to Exhale*.

Both that movie and this one are based on novels by Terry McMillan, with screenplays by Ron Bass. This time, though, the material is thinner and less convincing, and the movie is slow moving as Stella and Winston go through the routine of fighting and making up until we want to advise them: Look, try shacking up for a year or two and see how things work out.

Angela Bassett is an actress with aggressive intelligence, and when she plays a capable, smart woman, she can be fascinating. See her in *Malcolm X*, *What's Love Got to Do With It*, and *Strange Days*. The problem with *Stella* is that she has been given a woman who the screenplay *says* is smart, but whose intelligence doesn't come into play; if it did, Stella's relationship with Winston would be either briefer or much more complex. Instead, it's been smoothed down into manufactured suspense about whether these two nice people will find true love.

That's where I began. If a couple feels right to an audience, then we cheer for their romance and allow ourselves to care—if only for the length of a silly movie. In *The Parent Trap*, a silly movie if ever there was one, there's genuine chemistry between Dennis Quaid and Natasha Richardson, and so in a dumb way we're cheered by their happiness. In *Stella Got Her Groove Back*, I never felt Stella and Winston were on the same wavelength, that they could share their lives, that it would be a good idea for them to try. Oh, I believed Winston was blinded by her. But I couldn't believe in Stella's feelings. Even at the end, as they embrace, I was giving them three weeks, tops.

Human Traffic ★ ★
R, 84 m., 2000

John Simm (Jip), Lorraine Pilkington (LuLu), Shaun Parkes (Koop), Nicola Reynolds (Nina), Danny Dyer (Moff), Dean Davies (Lee). Directed by Justin Kerrigan and produced by Allan Niblo and Emer McCourt. Screenplay by Kerrigan.

"Act like an adult. Be fake."

So says one of the feckless heroes of *Human Traffic*, a sad comedy about druggies in Wales. This movie is about how he and his friends are already acting like adults. They're right that many adults are fakes, but some adults at least know when they're faking it. These kids are clueless.

They know how to take drugs and feel good. That doesn't require cleverness. When they don't take drugs they don't feel good, partly because of withdrawal, partly because they lack any other avenue to happiness. They possess, for the time being, youth. It is their only capital, and when it is spent, they will lead the rest of their lives empty-handed. They're sheep marching into the slaughter of middle age.

The film takes place in Cardiff, and is mostly about five friends who have jobs of stultifying boredom. They live for the weekends, when they can go out to rave clubs, use ecstasy, heroin, and whatever else they can get their hands on, and pretend for forty-eight hours that they are free. They have high spirits, and their speech possesses the style and wit that can still be heard in those pockets of verbal invention (Ireland is another) where conversation is an art form.

They are, in fact, likable. That's why their comedy is so sad. There must, we think, be something more for them than this dead-end lifestyle. The movie remembers how at a certain age, hanging out with your friends, feeling solidarity against the nine-to-five world, creates a fierce inner joy. They laugh at each other's self-destructiveness. It is funny to get wasted, to almost overdose, to do reckless things, to live dangerously, to flirt with crime and drugs. Why is it funny? Because they're getting away with it. The odds don't apply to them. They're immune. Fate has said they can put unknown substances into their systems and survive. Fate, of course, is a practical joker with a nasty streak, but tell them that.

The director of the film, Justin Kerrigan, is twenty-five. He sees his story from the inside. It's based on his friends. There is no perspective, no angle: He sympathizes with his characters. But he's already escaped their fate. He isn't working in a fast-food outlet at minimum wage. He's a movie director.

I was reminded of Mark Borchardt, the subject of the tragicomic documentary *American Movie*, who dropped out at thirteen or fourteen and started drinking with his friends in the basements of their houses. "I was always watching them, always fascinated by them," he

remembers, and today, at thirty-four, while he still plays the same role, he does it on the *Letterman* show, while his friends are still in the basement, or the ground.

Human Traffic is narrated as a pseudo-documentary; the characters take us on a tour of their world, but the real narrator is the director, who could not make the film if he lived as his heroes do. The characters have names, and there is a plot—a plot and a half, in fact. I could name them (all right: Jip, Lulu, Koop, Nina, and Moff). I could describe the plot. But every weekend has its own plot, and every plot has its own unhappy ending, which is known as Monday morning.

Stories like this can transcend. *Trainspotting* had a certain charm. *SLC Punk* had more wit and fewer drugs. *Kicking and Screaming* was enlightening because it showed that kids of about the same age, given a chance at a decent education, were more interesting and better at entertaining themselves. For the characters in *Human Traffic*, these weekends are as good as it's going to get.

"There is definitely more to their relationships than just going out, taking drugs, and having a good time," says Nicola Reynolds, an actress in the film. "They are strong, strong friendships. The more you go through things together, the more you bond those relationships." Uh-huh. You know the difference between a real friend and a party friend? You have a flat tire. The real friend goes outside in the rain and helps you change it. The party friend says, "Bummer," and buys you a drink.

Hurlyburly ★ ★ ★
R, 122 m., 1998

Sean Penn (Eddie), Kevin Spacey (Mickey), Robin Wright Penn (Darlene), Chazz Palminteri (Phil), Garry Shandling (Artie), Anna Paquin (Donna), Meg Ryan (Bonnie). Directed by Anthony Drazan and produced by Drazan, Richard N. Gladstein, and David S. Hamburger. Screenplay by David Rabe.

First witch: *When shall we three meet again? In thunder, lightning, or in rain?*
Second witch: *When the hurlyburly's done, When the battle's lost and won.*

—Macbeth

The philosopher William James thought that addiction expressed a yearning for the divine. While the characters in *Hurlyburly* have probably never heard of him (or Henry James or Harry James, for that matter—maybe no James but Etta), there is a real sense that Eddie, the most perpetually stoned character, is using drugs to escape from his hell on Earth. His hell has been created by the drugs he employs to escape it, an irony too simple for a mind that hurls challenges at the universe.

Eddie (Sean Penn) is a Hollywood casting agent who must be doing okay, judging by the house he has up in the Hollywood Hills. His roommate for the time being is Mickey (Kevin Spacey), who is on leave from wife and kids and bemused by the menagerie in Eddie's living room. Phil (Chazz Palminteri) is a frequent visitor, an actor with a sinister emotional underside. He turns up from time to time, and so does Artie (Garry Shandling), who materializes with a "CARE package"—an underage drifter (Anna Paquin) who is ready to trade sex for just about anything.

The major presence in Eddie's life is Darlene (Robin Wright Penn), his girlfriend, who likes him but has her eyes open and sees that Eddie is so far gone into cocaine that she'd better start looking around for another port in the storm. Mickey, maybe? And then there's a stripper named Bonnie (Meg Ryan), who sometimes goes out with Phil. Some of these gender couplings are entirely sex-based, while others append the illusion of meaning; Eddie, for example, is convinced he loves Darlene, although his love is expressed less by communicating with Darlene than by monologues about her that he delivers to his own drug-crazed brain.

The movie follows the loop-the-loops of habitual drug users. The rhythm of a day takes its shape from the availability of drugs and the degree and timing of usage. This is an important insight, because in David Rabe's perceptive screenplay there is no attempt to fashion the usual sort of dramatic give and take. Among characters who are in control of their lives, a dramatic piece takes form based on what they do and say. Among characters who are heavy into drugs, more depends on what is done and said to them.

There is a convention that booze and drugs bring truth. "In vino veritas," the Romans said, and Eugene O'Neill wrote his best plays about boozers who pursued truth into the night. Eddie, the Sean Penn character, is a bruised romantic with a good mind, who is as unhappy as a person can be, and in a remarkable scene uses cocaine to take him to a place of raw emotional pain. It is a remarkable performance.

The others talk, talk, talk. The most amusing is Spacey, who likes to hold himself a little aloof from a scene, as if he were the teacher. His sardonic intelligence aims a zinger here and there; we get the sense that he's only visiting, while the others live in this purgatory. We see that ordinary human judgment has been eroded by cocaine, that people use sex as a way of paying for it (or as a way of having something they can pay for), that if you tape-recorded the talk in this living room for a year it would all just go around and around and around.

There are times, indeed, when *Hurlyburly* feels like a year on a merry-go-round. There are brief excursions to the outside world, but the attention of the characters is always focused on the source of the drugs. They must, essentially, renew contact with the life in this room at regular intervals, or detox, or die, or kill themselves. Drugs make them talk but give them nothing to say. Eddie senses that. He wants to break out. He's digging himself in deeper, but at least his instinct is sound.

The Hurricane ★ ★ ★ ½
R, 125 m., 2000

Denzel Washington (Rubin Carter), Vicellous Reon Shannon (Lesera Martin), Deborah Kara Unger (Lisa Peters), Liev Schreiber (Sam Chaiton), John Hannah (Terry Swinton), Dan Hedaya (Della Pesca), Debbie Morgan (Mae Thelma), Clancy Brown (Lieutenant Jimmy Williams), David Paymer (Myron Beldock), Harris Yulin (Leon Friedman), Rod Steiger (Judge Sarokin), Garland Whitt (John Artis). Directed by Norman Jewison and produced by Armyan Bernstein, John Ketcham, and Jewison. Screenplay by Bernstein and Dan Gordon, based on *The 16th Round* by Rubin "Hurricane" Carter and *Lazarus and the Hurricane* by Sam Chaiton and Terry Swinton.

The key moment in *The Hurricane,* which tells the story of a boxer framed for murder, takes place not in a prison cell but at a used-book sale in Toronto. A fifteen-year-old boy named Lesera spends twenty-five cents to buy his first book, the autobiography of the boxer Rubin "Hurricane" Carter. As he reads it, he becomes determined to meet the boxer and support his fight for freedom, and that decision leads to redemption.

The case and cause of Hurricane Carter are well known; Bob Dylan wrote a song named "The Hurricane," and I remember Nelson Algren's house sale when the Chicago novelist moved to New Jersey to write a book about Carter. Movie stars and political candidates made the pilgrimage to Carter's prison, but his appeals were rejected and finally his case seemed hopeless.

This film tells his story—the story of a gifted boxer (Denzel Washington) who was framed for three murders in Patterson, New Jersey, and lost nineteen years of his life because of racism, corruption, and—perhaps most wounding—indifference. In the film, the teenage boy (Vicellous Reon Shannon), who is from New Jersey, enlists his Canadian foster family to help Carter, and they find new evidence for his defense attorneys that eventually leads to his release. The villain is a cop named Pesca (Dan Hedaya), who essentially makes it his lifelong business to harm Carter.

Norman Jewison's film starts slowly, with Carter's early years and his run-ins with Pesca. In my notes I wrote: "If this is going to be the story of a persecuting cop, we need to know him as more than simply the instrument of evil"—as a human being rather than a plot convenience. We never do. Pesca from beginning to end is there simply to cause trouble for Carter. Fortunately, *The Hurricane* gathers force in scenes where Carter refuses to wear prison clothing, and learns to separate himself mentally from his condition. Then young Lesera enters the picture, and two people who might seem to be without hope find it from one another.

This is one of Denzel Washington's great performances, on a par with his work in *Malcolm X.* I wonder if *The Hurricane* is not Jewison's indirect response to an earlier controversy. Jewison was preparing *Malcolm X* with Washington when Spike Lee argued that a white

man should not direct that film. Jewison stepped aside, Lee made a powerful film with Washington—and now Jewison has made another. Washington as Hurricane Carter is spare, focused, filled with anger and pride. There is enormous force when he tells his teenage visitor and his friends, "Do not write me. Do not visit me. Find it in your hearts to not weaken me with your love."

But the Canadians don't obey. They move near to Trenton State Prison, they meet with his lead defense attorneys (David Paymer and Harris Yulin), they become amateur sleuths who help take the case to the New Jersey Supreme Court in a do-or-die strategy. It always remains a little unclear, however, just exactly who the Canadians are, or what their relationship is. They're played by Deborah Kara Unger, Liev Schreiber, and John Hannah, they share a household, they provide a home for Lesera, a poor African-American kid from a troubled background, and we wonder: Are they a political group? An unconventional sexual arrangement?

I learn from an article by Selwyn Raab, who covered the case for the *New York Times,* that they were in fact a commune. Raab's article, which appeared the day before the film's New York opening, finds many faults with the facts in *The Hurricane.* He says Carter's defense attorneys deserve much more credit than the Canadians. That Carter was not framed by one cop with a vendetta, but victimized by the entire system. That Carter's codefendant, John Artis (Garland Whitt), was a more considerable person than he seems in the film. That events involving the crime and the evidence have been fictionalized in the film. That Carter later married the Unger character, then divorced her. That Lesera broke with the commune when it tried for too much control of his life.

News travels fast. Several people have told me dubiously that they heard the movie was "fictionalized." Well, of course it was. Those who seek the truth about a man from the film of his life might as well seek it from his loving grandmother. Most biopics, like most grandmothers, see the good in a man and demonize his enemies. They pass silently over his imprudent romances. In dramatizing his victories, they simplify them. And they provide the best roles to the most interesting characters. If they didn't, we wouldn't pay to see them.

The Hurricane is not a documentary but a parable, in which two lives are saved by the power of the written word. We see Carter's concern early in the film that the manuscript of his book may be taken from his cell (it is protected by one of several guards who develop respect for him). We see how his own reading strengthens him; his inspirations include Malcolm X. And we see how his book, which he hoped would win his freedom, does so—not because of its initial sales, readers, and reviews, but because one kid with a quarter is attracted to Hurricane's photo on the cover. And then the book wins Lesera's freedom too.

This is strong stuff, and I was amazed, after feeling some impatience in the earlier reaches of the film, to find myself so deeply absorbed in its second and third acts, until at the end I was blinking at tears. What affects me emotionally at the movies is never sadness, but goodness. I am not a weeper, and have only really lost it at one film *(Do the Right Thing)*, but when I get a knot in my throat it is not because Hurricane Carter is framed, or loses two decades in prison, but that he continues to hope, and that his suffering is the cause for Lesera's redemption.

That is the parable Norman Jewison has told, aiming for it with a sure storyteller's art and instinct. The experts will always tell you how a movie got its facts wrong (Walter Cronkite is no doubt correct that Oliver Stone's *JFK* is a fable). But can they tell you how they would have made the movie better? Would *The Hurricane* have been stronger as the story of two selfless lawyers doing pro bono work for years? And a complex network of legal injustice? And a freed prisoner and a kid disillusioned with a commune? Maybe. Probably not.
☞

Hurricane Streets ★ ★
R, 88 m., 1998

Brendan Sexton III (Marcus), Isidra Vega (Melena), Carlo Alban (Benny), David Roland Frank (Chip), Antoine McLean (Harold), Lynn Cohen (Lucy), Damian Corrente (Justin), L. M. Kit Carson (Mack), Jose Zuniga (Kramer). Directed by Morgan J. Freeman and produced by Galt Niederhoffer, Gill Holland, and Freeman.

Hurricane Streets takes place on the Lower East Side of New York, where its five characters, all fourteen or fifteen, commute to their crimes on bicycles. They're petty thieves who hang out in a secret clubroom and earn spending money by shoplifting CDs and athletic shoes, which they sell at a discount on playgrounds. It's only a matter of time until they graduate to more serious and dangerous things (indeed, it's a little hard to believe, in today's world, that they're not already drug couriers).

The group is racially mixed. The story mostly concerns a white kid, Marcus (Brendan Sexton III), whose mother is in prison and whose grandmother is raising him, after a fashion (she owns a bar, and that's where she holds his birthday party). Marcus dreams of someday moving to New Mexico with his mother, after she gets out on probation, but he doesn't have all the information about when that will be. Meanwhile, he meets a Latina girl named Melena (Isidra Vega) and dates her despite the opposition of her father.

The kids are on the brink of big trouble. The cops know who they are and what they're doing. They're ready to graduate to auto theft and burglary, and their days of stealing food from convenience stores are soon going to resemble a time of innocence. Their story may sound similar to *Kids, Fresh, Straight Out of Brooklyn,* and other films about tough street kids, but *Hurricane Streets* is mild by comparison—more of a love story than a sociological drama. The kids seem relatively harmless and normal, and the plot depends not on impending tragedy but on unlikely coincidences, including one that leads to a very unlikely death.

If you saw *Welcome to the Dollhouse,* the wonderful film about a junior high school girl in the midst of unpopular geekhood, you may remember Brendan Sexton III, the actor who plays Marcus here. In that film he tormented the heroine; that was his way of showing affection, and when he makes a date to "rape" her, she shows up for it—although clearly neither one knows exactly what to do then. Here he's an unlikely hero, a sad sack who drifts through a fairly clueless existence with little of the intelligence that made the characters in *Fresh* and those other films so interesting. His story is sad, yes, but he is not very compelling as its hero.

There was a time, I suppose, when *Hurricane Streets* would have been seen as a harrowing slice of life. So many better films have told the stories of alienated young street kids, alas, that this one seems relatively superficial. The dialogue sounds written, not said, and the twists in the plot are unconvincing (the characters are always able to turn up where and when they're needed).

Hurricane Streets won the Best Director and Best Cinematography at the 1997 Sundance Film Festival. And the "Audience Award." That means the audience preferred it to *In the Company of Men, Chasing Amy, Kissed, Suburbia,* and *love jones.* Strange.

Hush ★ ★
PG-13, 95 m., 1998

Jessica Lange (Martha), Gwyneth Paltrow (Helen), Johnathon Schaech (Jackson), Nina Foch (Alice Baring), Debi Mazar (Lisa), Kaiulani Lee (Sister O'Shaughnessy), David Thornton (Gavin), Hal Holbrook (Dr. Hill). Directed by Jonathan Darby and produced by Douglas Wick. Screenplay by Darby and Jane Rusconi.

Hush is the kind of movie where you walk in, watch the first ten minutes, know exactly where it's going, and hope devoutly that you're wrong. It's one of those Devouring Woman movies where the villainess never plays a scene without a drink and a cigarette, and the hero is inattentive to the victim to the point of dementia.

Gwyneth Paltrow stars as Helen, a New York career woman who's in love with Jackson (Johnathon Schaech). He takes her home to Virginia to meet his mother, Martha (Jessica Lange), and see the family spread, named Kilronan—a famous horse farm with a main house that looks like Thomas Jefferson either designed it or meant to. The house is large, elaborately decorated, and eerie, but then we knew it would be eerie because the music over the opening titles is "Hush, Little Baby," and that's a song used only in horror films.

Martha is a controlling woman, possessive about her beloved son. She prepares separate bedrooms for them. "It's a Catholic thing," Jackson explains, but when Martha accidentally finds the naked Helen in her son's bed she doesn't seem very perturbed, and I suspect the Catholic theme is there only because Hollywood traditionally depends on the church for props and atmosphere whenever true evil needs to be evoked.

It's a big house, with no servants. "She can't keep 'em," sniffs feisty old Alice (Nina Foch), Jackson's paternal grandmother, who lives in a nursing home and is prepared to talk to anyone, anytime, about Martha's devious ways. The youngsters are deep into lust, which seizes them at inopportune moments, so that they make love on the floor of the entry hall one night, while Martha observes from a shadowed landing.

Is Martha jealous of Helen's sexual relationship with her son? Not at all. She's a horse woman. "Started as a stable girl," Alice tells Helen, supplying a graphic explanation of the ways in which a woman like Martha not only breeds horses in the figurative sense, but is right there in the middle of the fray when a mare needs calming or a stallion needs guidance. Martha devises a way to inspire the young couple to leave New York and move to Kilronan, and we gather she hopes to breed a male heir to Kilronan by Jackson, out of Helen. Once she has one, of course, Helen may become unnecessary.

The general outlines of this scheme are visible early in the film, and the details grow more graphic, right up until a "push! push!" childbirth scene that is given a whole new spin. What's frustrating is that little of the evildoing would be possible if Jackson behaved at any moment like a normal, intelligent person. He consistently does the wrong thing just because the film needs him to.

The plot lumbers on its way to setting up the finale. Martha deviously tells Helen one thing and Jackson another, and we can hear the screenplay creaking in her dialogue. She spreads rumors that could be corrected in an instant if anyone bothered. The old family doctor (Hal Holbrook) is called upon for specialized information that is so transparently dangerous that the audience snickers.

And then credulity breaks down totally. I

will step carefully here, to preserve some secrets. I was amazed by the sequence of events after Jackson leaves the big horse race and speeds home to the rescue, only to never go near his possibly dying wife. I was astonished by her miraculous recovery, so that she could preside over a denouement that's not only wildly implausible but probably medically impossible.

The film's most intriguing element is the performance by Jessica Lange, who by *not* going over the top provides Martha with a little pathos to leaven the psychopathology. That side of her doesn't seem consistent with her demented behavior at a crucial moment, but then consistency is not the film's strong point.

I

An Ideal Husband ★ ★ ★
PG-13, 97 m., 1999

Cate Blanchett (Gertrude Chiltern), Minnie Driver (Mabel Chiltern), Rupert Everett (Lord Goring), Julianne Moore (Mrs. Cheveley), Jeremy Northam (Sir Robert Chiltern), John Wood (Lord Caversham), Lindsay Duncan (Lady Markby), Peter Vaughan (Phipps). Directed by Oliver Parker and produced by Barnaby Thompson, Uri Fruchtmann, and Bruce Davey. Screenplay by Parker, based on the play by Oscar Wilde.

A play like Oscar Wilde's *An Ideal Husband* works because it takes place in a society bound by inflexible rules and social inhibitions. Here is a story in which a marriage, a romance, a fortune, and government policy all rest on such foundations as a man's obligation to act like a gentleman. (Of course, he doesn't need to *be* a gentleman—that's where the story comes in.)

In the play, an incriminating letter is sent in the belief that it will never be revealed. Suspicions are aroused, but they don't inspire questions—because they involve matters it would be unseemly to ask a gentleman about. As long as everyone plays by the rules in public, they can be broken in private. But then an entire society is threatened by the willingness of one character to act as she should not.

The play tells the story of Sir Robert Chiltern (Jeremy Northam), a rising parliamentary star who has been a paragon of honesty all of his career—except right at the first, when he shopped some secret government information to a baron, who paid him handsomely. Sir Robert is adored by his wife (Cate Blanchett), whose high standards would not permit her to be married to a cheat and liar. An old acquaintance of theirs reappears in London: Mrs. Cheveley (Julianne Moore), who was once married to the baron and possesses the letter in which Chiltern leaked the information. She blackmails him. Either he will change his position on an upcoming piece of legislation, thus protecting her investments, or she will reveal him as a fraud.

It is even more complicated than that. Chiltern's best friend is Lord Goring (Rupert Everett), a rich and idle bachelor. Chiltern begs him to subtly prepare Lady Chiltern for bad news: to help her understand, in a general way, how a chap could do a bad thing and then lead a spotless life ever since. In the course of the plot machinations, romance appears: Goring falls in love with Chiltern's younger sister Mabel (Minnie Driver), and Mrs. Cheveley decides that Goring would be a splendid choice for her own third husband.

Would a man marry a woman he did not love simply to protect a friend or keep a confidence? Today that would be unlikely, but for the original audiences of *An Ideal Husband* it was plausible enough to keep the entire plot suspended over an abyss of misunderstandings.

In another sense, of course, neither Wilde nor his audience cared a fig about the letter, the bribe, the blackmail, or the romance. They were all just cogs in a complicated windup mechanism to keep several charming people on stage for three hours, and provide them with an excuse for saying witty things (this is the play where Goring observes, "To love oneself is the beginning of a lifelong romance"). I do not know if the British upper classes of a century ago were actually capable of standing handsomely in drawing rooms while trading elegant epigrams, and I suspect many of them were not, but I don't care—just so they do it on the stage.

An Ideal Husband works because Wilde created an expert mechanism (kind of slow-motion, serious screwball comedy) for manipulating the plot and characters. But of course the actors are indispensable: They have to make characters plausible while negotiating a plot of pure contrivance, and they have to be charming even while lying, scheming, and blackmailing. The two leading men, Northam and Everett, are smooth and charming—Northam's Sir Robert more realistic and serious about his life, Everett's Lord Goring like a Wildean visitor from outside the plot, who sees everything clearly, is amused, and hardly believes it when Mrs. Cheveley almost snares him in her net.

Women in the plays of a century ago were technically powerless; they lived through their husbands, and spent much of their time speculating on what the men were really up to or waiting for news. At the same time, the plays were really about them, and everything the men did was designed to win their love, admiration, or forgiveness. It is important that we believe Lady Chiltern (Blanchett) loves her husband but loves his upright character even more, and will leave him if she discovers his sins. And important to believe that Mabel (Driver), Sir Robert's sister, could fall in love with Goring in an instant. Well, of course she could. Modern critics who complain they fall in love too suddenly have forgotten that she would have spent months or years making up her mind about every eligible man in her universe.

As we leave the twentieth century there seems to be a powerful nostalgia for the British nineteenth. Every year brings three or four of these literate comedies (or melodramas) set in London. Life was more exciting when you were the entertainment in your own living room and didn't have to watch it on TV.

Idle Hands ★ ★ ½
R, 92 m., 1999

Devon Sawa (Anton), Seth Green (Mick), Elden Henson (Pnub), Jessica Alba (Molly), Christopher Hart (The Hand), Vivica A. Fox (Debi), Jack Noseworthy (Randy), Katie Wright (Tanya). Directed by Rodman Flender and produced by Suzanne Todd, Jennifer Todd, Andrew Licht, and Jeffrey A. Mueller. Screenplay by Terri Hughes and Ron Milbauer.

Idle Hands samples other teen horror movies like a video DJ with a tape deck, exhibiting high spirits and a crazed comic energy. It doesn't quite work, but it goes down swinging—with a disembodied hand. The hand, which has a mind of its own, is chopped off the arm of a teenage kid who is the victim of some kind of weird Halloween demonic possession.

The film involves the adventures of Anton (Devon Sawa), a pothead so addled he doesn't notice for a few days that his parents are dead—the victims of an evil power that writes, "I'm under the bed," on the ceiling of their bedroom, and is. Anton's chief occupations are getting high and hanging out with his friends Mick and Pnub, who live in a nearby basement. The three of them are dropouts

from all possible societies, and their world is like a cross between *SLC Punk* and *Evil Dead 2.* (If neither one of those titles rings a bell, the movie undoubtedly won't, either.)

The possessed killer hand is, of course, lifted from *Evil Dead 2,* but it wasn't original there, and has its origins in such films as *The Hand* and *The Beast with Five Fingers.* Rodman Flender, who directed this film, has fun with it in a scene where Anton is on a date with the babe of his dreams, Molly (Jessica Alba), and tries to fight down the hand as it tries to throttle her. Finally, he ties it to the bed. Molly, who is not very observant, translates this as kinky.

Anton finally rids himself of the hand (it's chopped off in the kitchen, with the wound cauterized by an iron). His pals Mick (Seth Green) and Pnub (Elden Henson, from *The Mighty*) have worse luck. Mick is taken out by a beer bottle, which remains embedded in his skull for the rest of the movie. Pnub loses his head altogether, and carries it in his hands until Anton figures out how to mount it on his shoulders using a barbecue fork. Don't ask. Both of them continue through the entire film as the living dead.

Vivica A. Fox plays the demonbuster, tracking down alarming manifestations and delivering the single best line of dialogue: "Well, my work here is done. Time for the ritualistic sex." The plot involves her pursuit only absentmindedly, however, since most of the big scenes involve comic gore: disembodied eyeballs, unusual biological processes, body parts discovered in unexpected ways, etc. There's no really convincing comic inspiration behind the f/x scenes, however, and although we might laugh at some of the goofiness, a movie like this works best when the effects are a means, not an end.

The movie has energy and is probably going to attract a young audience, especially on video, since the R rating will keep away some viewers in its target audience, which is junior high school boys. After the Colorado tragedy, some commentators have wondered if movies like this aren't partly responsible. I don't think we have to worry about *Idle Hands.* Kids understand this kind of macabre comedy, which is in the ancient horror spoof tradition, and don't take it seriously; any viewer capable of being influenced by such silly gags would have to be deeply disturbed already. The only thing this movie is likely to inspire a kid to do is study *Fangoria* magazine to find out how the special effects were achieved.

I Dreamed of Africa ★ ★
PG-13, 112 m., 2000

Kim Basinger (Kuki Gallmann), Vincent Perez (Paolo Gallmann), Liam Aiken (Emanuele [Seven]), Garrett Strommen (Emanuele [Seventeen]), Eva Marie Saint (Franca), Daniel Craig (Declan Fielding), Lance Reddick (Simon), Connie Chiume (Wanjiku). Directed by Hugh Hudson and produced by Stanley R. Jaffe and Allyn Stewart. Screenplay by Paula Milne and Susan Shilliday, based on the book by Kuki Gallmann.

It's strange to see *I Dreamed of Africa* at a time when the papers are filled with stories of white farmers being murdered in Zimbabwe. Here is the story of an Italian couple who move to the highlands of Kenya in 1972, buy a ranch near the Great Rift Valley, and lead lives in which the Africans drift about in the background, vaguely, like unpaid extras. Is it really as simple as that? The realities of contemporary Africa are simply not dealt with.

A shame, since Kuki Gallmann is a real woman and still lives on Ol Ari Nyiro, a 100,000-acre ranch in Kenya that she has made into a showcase farm and a wildlife conservancy. I know this because of her Web page (www.gallmannkenya.org); the movie never makes it very clear how the Gallmanns support themselves—it's not by working, apparently. Paolo is away for days at a time, hunting and fishing with his friends, and Kuki doesn't seem deeply engaged with the land, either (her attempt to create a dirt dam begins when she inadvertently pulls down a barn, and ends with the tractor stuck in the mud).

The real Kuki Gallmann must have arrived at an accommodation with Africa and Africans, and with the Kenyan government. The Kuki in the movie has a few brief conversations in Swahili with her farm foreman and laborers, but devotes most of her attention to the landscape, which is indeed breathtaking (the film was shot on the ranch and in South African game preserves). The only social commentary we get, repeated three times, is, "Things have a different rhythm here."

Kuki is played by Kim Basinger, who is ready to do more than the screenplay allows. She is convincing throughout, especially in a scene where trouble strikes her son, Emanuele (Garrett Strommen)—her panic is real, but so is her competence as she tries to deal with the emergency. Her frustration with her husband, Paolo (Vincent Perez), is also real, but mundane (frustrated at his extended hunting trips and general irresponsibility, she throws a handful of pasta at him).

Her life is interrupted from time to time by visits from her mother (Eva Marie Saint), who begs her to return to Italy, but no, she belongs to the land, learns from experience, and tries to bring good out of the tragedies in her life by becoming a conservationist and a leader in the fight against poaching.

All admirable. But Hugh Hudson's film plays curiously like a friendly documentary of her life, especially with the voice-over narration that sounds like it belongs in an idealistic travelogue. There is a lack of drama and telling detail. When events happen, they seem more like set pieces than part of the flow. Consider the big storm that blows up, toppling the windmill and blowing the thatch from the ranch house roof. It strikes, it is loud and fierce, and then it is over, and after one more shot, it is forgotten. An entry in a diary, growing from nothing, leading to nothing, but occupying screen time. As is the scene where Kuki, Paolo, and her mother drive a Range Rover down a rough road and it gets stuck in the mud (that happens to her a lot). What to do? They get out and walk home. The film doesn't even show them arriving there.

Watching *I Dreamed of Africa,* I was reminded that one often meets people who have led fascinating lives, but only rarely people who can tell fascinating stories. The events don't make the story; the storytelling does. Russell Baker or Frank McCourt can make human sagas out of everyday memories. Generals who have led thousands into battle can write memoirs of stultifying dullness. Kuki Gallmann has led a fascinating life, yes, but either she's not remembering the whole truth, or she should have made up more. The film doesn't sing with urgency and excitement, and we attend it in the same way we listen politely to the stories of a hostess who must have really been something in her day.

I'll Be Home for Christmas ★

PG, 86 m., 1998

Jonathan Taylor Thomas (Jake), Jessica Biel (Allie), Adam Lavorgna (Eddie), Gary Cole (Jake's Dad), Eve Gordon (Carolyn), Lauran Maltby (Tracey), Andrew Lauer (Nolan), Sean O'Bryan (Max). Directed by Arlene Sanford and produced by David Hoberman and Tracey Trench. Screenplay by Harris Goldberg and Tom Nursall.

Pleasantville is a movie about a bland 1950s world in which lives go around in circles until time travelers break in with the virus of change. Some writers have attacked the movie, arguing that things were better in the 1950s than they are now. They might enjoy *I'll Be Home for Christmas,* an exercise in cinematic Ovaltine.

The movie takes place in the present, I guess, but it feels like a 1950s sitcom. The characters have much in common with old (not new) Archie and Jughead comics. The sound track includes Gene Autry tunes, not selected for ironic purposes. It's the kind of movie that just misses a G rating and gets slapped with a PG for rudeness.

Oh, it'll have its fans. The star is Jonathan Taylor Thomas, from TV's *Home Improvement,* who is an immensely likable actor. But even his easy grin seems to weary a little by the later stretches of the film, which is unrelentingly corny.

The plot: Thomas plays Jake, a student at Palisades University, a campus on the Pacific Coast that, in this film, looks like a high school where Our Miss Brooks would still be on the faculty. His dad has sent him a ticket to fly home to Larchmont for Christmas, but his devious plan is to cash it in for two tickets to a beach resort, and convince his girlfriend Allie (Jessica Biel) to go along. Then Jake's dad bribes him with a restored '57 Porsche if he'll come home for Christmas.

Jake's rival for Allie's affections is Eddie (Adam Lavorgna), but this is the kind of movie where Allie is such a nice girl she doesn't even consider Eddie—no, not even when she drives cross-country with him, which she does because she is convinced Jake has stood her up. Jake was actually the victim of a practical joke, in which Eddie and his pals dressed him in a Santa suit and dumped him in the desert, where turkey vultures eye him beadily, ho, ho.

Jake wears the Santa suit for the rest of the movie, as he desperately tries to get home to Larchmont, rescue Allie from Eddie, etc. As you can imagine, the Santa costume inspires countless wheezy attempts at humor. It even gets him entered in a Santa 5K Charity Run, where all the contestants are dressed as Santa. (In a heartrending finale, he beats the loyal mayor, but still allows the mayor to donate the cash prize to buy turkeys for those without a bird on the table for the holidays.) Of course, Jake steals a sleigh for the big climax.

There is possibly an audience for this movie, but I have the oddest feeling that on opening night the people in the theater will all be in black and white. See *Pleasantville* if you wonder what I mean. In fact, see *Pleasantville* anyway. *I'll Be Home for Christmas* will appeal to people who don't care if nothing good happens in a movie, just so long as nothing bad happens in it.

The Impostors ★ ★

R, 102 m., 1998

Oliver Platt (Maurice), Stanley Tucci (Arthur), Lili Taylor (Lily), Campbell Scott (Meistrich), Alfred Molina (Jeremy Burtom), Steve Buscemi (Happy Franks), Isabella Rossellini (Ex-Queen), Billy Connolly (Sparks), Tony Shalhoub (First Mate), Hope Davis (Emily). Directed by Stanley Tucci and produced by Beth Alexander and Tucci. Screenplay by Tucci.

I'll bet when Stanley Tucci has a party he invites all of his friends over. His movies reflect a personality that opens wide and embraces the crowd. He likes big casts and complicated plots that involve them in interlocking intrigues. When that works, as it did in *Big Night* (1996), his movie about a doomed Italian restaurant, the result was a comic masterpiece—and one with a real feeling for people.

When it doesn't, as in *The Impostors*, it's more like a traffic jam.

The movie stars Tucci and Oliver Platt as Arthur and Maurice, best friends and fellow actors, who are out of work and starving. They're a little like Laurel and Hardy. They bunk together in a single room, and stage impromptu scenes in public. But nobody hires them, and Arthur says quietly, "I'm going to die if I don't get work."

The opening sequence, which is the movie's best, is played as silent film, and the silent spirit permeates the whole work. Maurice and Arthur attend a performance of *Hamlet* starring the inept Jeremy Burtom (Alfred Molina), insult him in a bar, flee from his wrath, and end up stowing away on the very ocean liner that he has booked passage on.

What to do? Burtom spots them and raises the alarm, and the chase is directed by Meistrich (Campbell Scott), a Nazi steward with tight lips and patent leather hair. Meistrich is in love with Lily (Lili Taylor), the social director, but she despises him and helps protect the stowaways, in a plot that also involves a first mate (Tony Shalhoub) who is a mad bomber, a tennis pro (Billy Connolly) who is flamboyantly gay, an ex-queen (Isabella Rossellini) in exile, a lounge singer (Steve Buscemi) who is suicidal, and all sorts of other passengers.

The movie has lots of long corridors and lots of doors that characters are forever popping into and out of; in that respect it mirrors screwball comedies like Bogdanovich's *What's Up, Doc?* The ocean liner reminds us of the Marx Brothers in *A Night at the Opera*, and Preston Sturges's great *The Lady Eve*. But the energy level in *The Impostors* is too laid-back for screwball. The movie is gentle and whimsical, not manic, and there are times when Tucci seems to be chewing more than he has bit off.

I liked the way the two lead characters, Maurice and Arthur, share a deep friendship and finish each other's sentences. I liked the way Lily, the social director, feels an instant sympathy for them. But the mad bomber plot and the other intrigues require characters at a boil, and everyone in this movie just sort of simmers sweetly.

There are laughs, but they are quiet chuckles. I found myself smiling a lot. I felt fond of the characters. There is the same warmth that permeated *Big Night*. But there is also the same impulse to bring people on board who don't seem to have a reason for being in the plot. Rossellini's sad queen, for example, signifies a great deal but reveals little; her character feels more like Tucci said he'd write a role for her than like the character needed to exist and she was the perfect person to play it.

There are movies that work, and then movies like *The Impostors* that don't really work but are pleasant all the same. There was nothing I actively disliked about the film. But my affection was more polite than impassioned. If this had been a first draft, I would have advised throwing some characters overboard and turning up the heat under the others.

In Dreams ★ ½
R, 100 m., 1999

Annette Bening (Claire Cooper), Robert Downey Jr. (Vivian), Aidan Quinn (Paul Cooper), Stephen Rea (Dr. Silverman), Paul Guilfoyle (Detective Jack Kay), Dennis Boutsikaris (Dr. Stevens), Katie Sagona (Rebecca Cooper), Krystal Benn (Ruby). Directed by Neil Jordan and produced by Stephen Woolley and Redmond Morris. Screenplay by Bruce Robinson and Jordan, based on the novel *Doll's Eyes*, by Bari Wood.

In Dreams is the silliest thriller in many a moon, and the only one in which the heroine is endangered by apples. She also survives three falls from very high places (two into a lake, one onto apples), escapes from a hospital and a madhouse, has the most clever dog since Lassie, and causes a traffic pileup involving a truck and a dozen cars. With that much plot, does this movie really need the drowned ghost town, the husband's affair with an Australian woman, the flashbacks to the dominatrix mom, and the garbage disposal that spews apple juice?

All of this goofiness is delivered with style and care by a first-rate team; this is a well-made bad movie. The heroine, named Claire, is portrayed by Annette Bening as a woman in torment. She begins to dream of horrible things, and realizes an evil killer is causing her nightmares ("He's inside my head!"). Her husband (Aidan Quinn) goes to the cops with her premonitions, but gets the brush-off. A frequent dream involves harm to a child; it turns out to be her own.

Eventually she falls into the hands of a psychiatrist (Stephen Rea) who is wise, kindly, and patient, and locks her up in two cruel institutions. One has a padded cell and is guarded by a Nurse Ratchet clone. The other looks like the original snake pit crossed with a dorm at summer camp. The psychiatrist isn't even the villain.

In Dreams is the kind of movie where children's nursery rhymes and sayings are underscored like evil omens. "Mirror, mirror, on the wall . . ." we hear, while the sound track vibrates with menace, and a mother, a daughter, and their dog walk on the banks of a reservoir that was, we learn, created in 1965 by flooding a village that still lurks beneath the waters, a ghost town. Scuba divers explore it, and we see that the napkin dispensers are still on the counters in the diner, while holy statues float around the church.

Was the villain (Robert Downey Jr.) drowned in this town? It's not that simple. The explanation of this movie contains more puzzles than the plot itself. Let's say we grant the premise that the villain can indeed project his dreams into the mind of poor Claire. In addition to being clairvoyant, is he also telekinetic? Can he make children's swings move on their own, and turn on boom boxes at a distance, and project words onto a computer screen, and control garbage disposals?

And does he control the family dog, which has an uncanny ability to find its masters anywhere, anytime? (This is such a clever dog it should know better than to lure Claire into the middle of that highway—unless, of course, its dreams are also under remote control.) And what does the buried village have to do with anything? And although the killer was abused as a child by his mother, whose high heels supply a central image, what does that have to do with the nursery rhyme about how "My father was a dollar"?

I dunno. The movie was directed by Neil Jordan, who has done a whole lot better (*Mona Lisa, The Crying Game, Interview With the Vampire*). Here he navigates uncertainly through a script that is far too large for its container. Whole subplots could have been dumped; why even bother with the other woman in Australia? Although the drowned village supplies some vivid images, wasn't it a huge expense just for some atmosphere? And how many viewers will be able to follow the time-shifted parallels as Claire's escape from a hospital is intercut with the killer's?

In *my* dreams, I'm picturing Tony Lawson's first day on the job. He was the editor of this picture. His survey of the unassembled footage must have been a real horror story.

Inside/Out ★ ★ ½
NO MPAA RATING, 115 m., 1999

Berangere Allaux (Monica), Tom Gilroy (Priest), Stefania Rocca (Organist), Frederic Pierrot (Jean), Steven Watkin (Roger). Directed by Rob Tregenza and produced by Gill Holland. Screenplay by Tregenza.

It happens that within two days I've seen a 52-minute film that seemed bursting with content, and now a 115-minute film that inspires admiration, but also restlessness. The shorter film (*See the Sea*), played just long enough to deliver its horrifying punch line. The longer one (*Inside/Out*) has no punch line, and indeed not much of a plot; it's about the arid passage of time in a mental hospital. A director approaching such a subject can either suggest the emptiness and ennui, or attempt to reproduce it. Rob Tregenza, who wrote, directed, photographed, and edited *Inside/Out*, chooses the second approach.

His film takes place in the late 1950s, in a cold and lifeless autumn or early spring, in a mental hospital of whitewashed walls and barren interiors. The institution isn't on the cutting edge of treatment; it's more like a holding cell for patients, a waiting room before death. The patients wander the grounds, sometimes try to run away, line up for their pills, are angry or morose, mill about aimlessly at a dance, attend religious services, and stand stock-still as if lost in thought.

Their actions are watched by Tregenza on the Cinemascope screen, the widest gauge available. The film covers an enormous expanse of screen, and is often photographed in

275

long shots, so that the characters seem isolated within vast, empty spaces. In one sequence two men shoot some baskets (one is completely uninvolved), and in the background there is a man dressed in black who simply stands, swaying slightly, the whole time.

One point of the wide screen may be to emphasize how little contact these people have with one another. They're looked over by nuns (Episcopalian, I gather) who give them their pills, issue instructions ("No sitting on the tables!"), and enforce standards (a female character undresses and tries to snuggle up to another inmate, only to be yanked away by a nun hissing, "You little whore!"). The lives of the people on the screen—patients and caretakers—seem bereft of happiness.

Dialogue is heard only in snatches. There are no word-driven relationships. Visuals make the point. The institution's priest works in a plain little chapel that reminded me of the church in Bergman's *Winter Light*, in the feeling that it was a place little frequented by God.

Some of the scenes have the same kind of deadpan visual punning we find, in another tone, in the films of Jacques Tati. Two men struggle on a train track, and we hear the whistle and roar of the approaching train—which arrives, passes, and disappears, invisibly. In an opening shot, two patients run across the crest of a hill, we hear dogs barking, and they reappear chased by the dogs—and by figures on horseback. It is a hunt.

Tregenza's handling of a "party" scene makes full use of his wide-screen camera. In a barren, low-ceilinged room, too big for the people in it, volunteers arrange clusters of balloons. Crepe paper hangs thinly from beams. An inept rock band sets up. Patients mill about endlessly (one darts across screen and up some stairs). The band starts playing and is accompanied by a patient who rhythmically bangs a folding chair open and closed. Finally, incongruously, a harpist begins to play, and the camera circles the room, which is stilled by the quiet music.

I admired *Inside/Out* in its moments, in individual scenes. I would recommend the party scene to film students, who could learn from it. But I was kept outside the film by the distanced, closed-off characters. That's the idea, I know—but Tregenza succeeds all too well

with it. Seeing the movie is like paying dues to his vision. We are witnesses that he accomplished what he set out to do. He does it in his own time and space. He's as little interested in us as his characters would be. We're like guests on visiting day, sitting restlessly on chairs along the side of the room. If anyone asked us, we'd say we were having a good time. But we're thinking restlessly of how long we have to stay, and where we can go next.

The Insider ★ ★ ★ ½
R, 148 m., 1999

Al Pacino (Lowell Bergman), Russell Crowe (Jeffrey Wigand), Christopher Plummer (Mike Wallace), Diane Venora (Liane Wigand), Philip Baker Hall (Don Hewitt), Lindsay Crouse (Sharon Tiller), Debi Mazar (Debbie De Luca), Stephen Tobolowsky (Eric Kluster), Gina Gershon (Helen Caperelli). Directed by Michael Mann and produced by Mann and Pieter Jan Brugge. Screenplay by Eric Roth and Mann, based on the *Vanity Fair* article "The Man Who Knew Too Much" by Marie Brenner.

Michael Mann's *The Insider* makes a thriller and exposé out of how big tobacco's long-running tissue of lies was finally exposed by investigative journalism. At its center stands Lowell Bergman, a producer for *60 Minutes*, the CBS News program where a former tobacco scientist named Jeffrey Wigand spilled the beans. First Bergman coaxes Wigand to talk. Then he works with reporter Mike Wallace to get the story. Then he battles with CBS executives who are afraid to run it—because a lawsuit could destroy the network. He's a modern investigative hero, Woodward and Bernstein rolled into one.

Or so the film tells it. The film is accurate in its broad strokes. Wigand did indeed reveal secrets from the Brown and Williamson laboratories that eventually led to a $246 billion settlement of suits brought against the tobacco industry by all fifty states. *60 Minutes* did eventually air the story, after delays and soul-searching. And reporting by the *Wall Street Journal* was instrumental in easing the network's decision to air the piece.

But there are ways in which the film is misleading, according to a helpful article in *Brill's*

Content. Mike Wallace was more of a fighter, less Bergman's puppet. *60 Minutes* producer Don Hewitt didn't willingly cave in to corporate pressure, but was powerless. The *Wall Street Journal*'s coverage was not manipulated by Bergman, but was independent (and won a Pulitzer Prize). Bergman didn't mastermind a key Mississippi lawsuit, or leak a crucial deposition. And the tobacco industry did not necessarily make death threats against Wigand (his former wife believes he put a bullet in his mailbox himself).

Do these objections invalidate the message of the film? Not at all. And they have no effect on its power to absorb, entertain, and anger. They go with the territory in a docudrama like this, in which characters and narrative are manipulated to make the story stronger. The *Brill's Content* piece, useful as it is, makes a fundamental mistake: It thinks that Lowell Bergman is the hero of *The Insider* because he fed his version of events to Mann and his cowriter, Eric Roth. In fact, Bergman is the hero because he is played by Al Pacino, the star of the film, and thus must be the hero. A movie like this demands only one protagonist. If Pacino had played Mike Wallace instead, then Wallace would have been the hero.

The decision to center on a producer, to go behind the scenes, is a good one, because it allows the story to stand outside Wallace and Hewitt and consider larger questions than tobacco. The movie switches horses in midstream, moving from the story of a tobacco cover-up to a crisis in journalistic ethics. Did CBS oppose the story only because it feared a lawsuit, or were other factors involved, such as the desire of executives to protect the price of their stock as CBS was groomed for sale to Westinghouse?

The movie is constructed like a jigsaw puzzle in which various pieces keep disappearing from the table. It begins when Bergman hires Jeffrey Wigand (Russell Crowe) as a consultant on another tobacco story. He learns that Wigand possesses information from the tobacco industry not only proving that nicotine is addictive (which the presidents of seven cigarette companies had denied under oath before Congress), but that additives were used to make it more addictive—and one of the additives was a known carcinogen! Wigand has signed a confidentiality agreement with B&W, and Bergman somehow has to get around that promise if the truth is going to be revealed.

Mann is able to build suspense while suggesting what a long, slow, frustrating process investigative journalism can be. Wigand dances toward a disclosure, then away. Bergman works behind the scenes to manipulate lawsuits and the coverage of the *Wall Street Journal* (these scenes are mostly fictional, we learn). He hopes to leak parts of the story in truncated form so that he's free to expose its full glory. Mike Wallace (Christopher Plummer) is beside him all the way, finally zeroing in on Wigand in one of those interviews where shocking statements are given little pools of silence to glisten in. Then a corporate lawyer (Gina Gershon) explains the law to the *60 Minutes* gang: The more truthful Wigand's statements, the more damaging in a lawsuit. *60 Minutes* boss Don Hewitt (Philip Baker Hall) sides with the network, and Bergman is blindsided when Wallace at first sides with Hewitt.

It's then that Bergman goes to work behind the scenes, leaking information and making calls to competitors to blast the story loose from legal constraints. And these are the scenes that owe the most to Hollywood invention; the chronology is manipulated, and actions of key players get confused. There is an underlying truth, however: *60 Minutes* did eventually find a way to air its original story, through the device of reporting about how it couldn't—a report that had the effect of breaking the logjam.

Hewitt, one of the patron saints of investigative journalism, is portrayed as too much of a corporate lackey, but Wallace's image emerges intact in a wonderful scene where Hewitt says the whole matter will blow over in fifteen minutes, and Wallace says, "No, that's fame. You get fifteen minutes of fame. Infamy lasts a little longer."

Pacino's performance underlies everything. He makes Bergman hoarse, overworked, stubborn, and a master of psychological manipulation who inexorably draws Wigand toward the moment of truth. Pacino can be flashy, mannered, over the top, in roles that call for it; this role calls for a dogged crusader, and he supplies a character who is always convincing.

There is, I admit, a contradiction in a film

277

about journalism that itself manipulates the facts. My notion has always been that movies are not the first place you look for facts anyway. You attend a movie for psychological truth, for emotion, for the heart of a story and not its footnotes. In its broad strokes, *The Insider* is perfectly accurate: Big tobacco lied, one man had damning information, skilled journalism developed the story, intrigue helped blast it free. *The Insider* had a greater impact on me than *All the President's Men,* because you know what? Watergate didn't kill my parents. Cigarettes did. ☞

Insomnia ★ ★ ★ ½
NO MPAA RATING, 97 m., 1998

Stellan Skarsgard (Jonas Engstrom), Sverre Anker Ousdal (Erik Vik), Maria Bonnevie (Ane), Bjorn Floberg (Jon Holt), Gisken Armand (Hilde Hagen), Marianne O. Ulrichsen (Froya).
Directed by Erik Skjoldbjaerg and produced by Anne Frilseth. Screenplay by Nikolaj Frobenius and Skjoldbjaerg. In Norwegian with English subtitles.

In northern Norway in the summer, the night is a brief finger of dusk drawn between the day and the dawn. In his hotel room, Jonas the chief investigator struggles for sleep. He tugs at the blackout curtains, but the sunlight streams in at 2 A.M. and he is haunted by unease. He is a veteran Swedish policeman in exile, working out of Oslo after, in a previous case, being discovered in "intimate conversation" with a witness.

His record is not clean, but he is considered a brilliant investigator, and now he is hunting for a killer who leaves no traces—who even washed the hair of his victim, an attractive young woman. After Jonas discovers the woman's knapsack in a shed on the beach, he sets a trap for the killer. He announces on TV that the knapsack is the key to the investigation, trusting that the killer will return to retrieve it.

And so the killer does—falling into Jonas's ambush. But there is a way out of the shed that the police do not know about, and the killer flees. Chasing him in a thick, muggy morning fog, Jonas sees a figure raise a gun, and

shoots. Then he discovers he has killed his own colleague.

Jonas is played by Skellan Skarsgard, the tall, thoughtful Scandinavian who first drew attention as the oil-rig worker in *Breaking the Waves* and the math professor in *Good Will Hunting.* Here he looks thinner, haunted, unsure of himself. Working under the protective blanket of fog, he fakes evidence to make it look as if the other policeman was shot by the escaping killer.

So now we have a police procedural turned in upon itself. Jonas is leading the investigation while at the same time struggling with the guilty knowledge of his cover-up. His queries take him to a writer named Holt, very full of himself, who had a relationship with the dead woman. And to the woman's best friend Froya, whom he is attracted to. He takes her for a drive, and slips his hand between her legs; will this be another intimate conversation with a witness?

His key adversary is a fellow police officer, Ane (Maria Bonnevie). He is able to distract the other cops with routine and exhortation, but Ane doesn't just look, she sees. She senses there is something off about Jonas after the death of the other cop: a certain wariness, a way of changing the subject. Some of her questions do not get good answers. She looks him in the face, and he doesn't like that.

The movie is not a thriller or an action picture, but a psychological study. *Crime and Punishment* comes to mind, with its theme of a man who believes he stands outside the rules that apply to other people. It is not that Jonas is a murderer—he made an honest mistake—but that he does not see himself as an honest man and cannot trust that others would believe him.

It's easy to make movies with external action, chases, and shoot-outs. It is much harder to make a film in which many of the important events take place inside the minds of the characters. Much depends simply on where the actors are arranged in the frame, so that we can see one face and not another. Jonas is sleepless and anguished. Ane is nagged by doubts she cannot silence.

The look of the film is almost a character in itself. The director, Erik Skjoldbjaerg, looks for grays and browns, dark greens and a washed-out drabness. The midnight sun casts an unremitting bright light, like the eye of God that will not blink. There is no place to hide, not even in sleep. And all the time, of course, there is the killer, who is the real villain, but figures for Jonas more like a distraction from his shame.

Inspector Gadget ★ ½
PG, 80 m., 1999

Matthew Broderick (Brown/Gadget/ RoboGadget), Rupert Everett (Scolex/Claw), Joely Fisher (Brenda/RoboBrenda), Michelle Trachtenberg (Penny), Andy Dick (Kramer), Cheri Oteri (Mayor Wilson), Michael G. Hagerty (Sikes), Dabney Coleman (Chief Quimby). Directed by David Kellogg and produced by Jordan Kerner, Roger Birnbaum, and Andy Heyward. Screenplay by Kerry Ehrin and Zak Penn, based on a story by Dana Olsen and Ehrin.

Inspector Gadget was an afternoon TV cartoon in the 1980s, much-loved by some, unseen by me, which has now inspired a high-tech live-action retread that has *Gadget* fans on the Internet furious because, apparently, they do not want to see the face of Dr. Claw. If Dr. Claw went unseen in the cartoon, their reasoning goes, it is no consolation that he is brought to life here by Rupert Everett. One person who might agree with them is Rupert Everett himself, who was on a winning streak until this movie came along.

Matthew Broderick stars, first as a security guard named John Brown, then as a bionic supercop named Inspector Gadget: "Colombo and Nintendo all rolled into one," quips Police Chief Quimby (Dabney Coleman). Broderick also plays an anti-Gadget look-alike, the bad guy RoboGadget, who impersonates the inspector and sets half the city on fire in an attempt to discredit him.

The gimmick with Gadget is that he has been equipped with a body, a suit, and (especially) a hat that are all stuffed with gadgets. All he has to say is, "Go-go gadget," and then name the gadget he wants, and it materializes, although it can be difficult remembering the

right go-go word while falling from the top of a skyscraper. His gadgets include hands that spray toothpaste (Gadget) and fire (RoboGadget), a hat that turns into a helicopter, and legs that extend into long steel stilts, allowing him to leapfrog traffic and cover a lot of ground in a hurry. Also about a zillion other gadgets.

His partner in the movie, Brenda (Joely Fisher), is the daughter of an inventor who figured out how to join flesh and technology. The enemy, Claw, wants to steal the technology for himself. Local officials get involved when the warfare escalates into a safety hazard, and there are also key roles for cats, mayors, and nieces.

Obviously I would be better armed to deal with this stuff had I ever seen an *Inspector Gadget* cartoon. I could discuss how the movie does or doesn't live up to, or down to, the original. As it is I'm stuck with the movie as a stand-alone, and I'm pretty underwhelmed. Perhaps younger kids will like it more. I didn't care about the action because it made no difference to me who won or lost. The plot was an arbitrary concoction. The bad guy is played by Everett as a man fastidiously keeping a certain distance from the jokes. There are all sorts of pop culture references, but so what? There are admittedly some individual funny lines. (When the Dabney Coleman character sees John Brown in a head-to-toe body cast, he calls him "The English Patient.")

The funniest moment in the movie comes at the end, as a credit cookie during the closing titles. It's a shot of a "Minion Support Group," showing Claw's sidekick twelve-stepping with other famous evil minions (I spotted Richard Kiel's "Jaws" and perhaps Odd Job). Now *that* is an idea for a comedy.

Question: Since the movie is only eighty minutes long, would it have killed them to add a real *Inspector Gadget* cartoon to the program as a warm-up and scene-setter?

Instinct ★ ½
R, 124 m., 1999

Anthony Hopkins (Ethan Powell), Cuba Gooding Jr. (Theo Caulder), Donald Sutherland (Ben Hillard), Maura Tierney (Lyn Powell), George Dzundza (Dr. John Murray), John

Ashton (Guard Dacks), John Aylward (Warden Keefer), Thomas Q. Morris (Pete). Directed by Jon Turteltaub and produced by Michael Taylor and Barbara Boyle. Screenplay by Gerald Di Pego, suggested by the novel *Ishmael* by Daniel Quinn.

If there's anything worse than a movie hammered together out of pieces of bad screenplays, it's a movie made from the scraps of good ones. At least with the trash we don't have to suffer through the noble intentions. *Instinct* is a film with not one but four worthy themes. It has pious good thoughts about all of them, but undermines them by slapping on obligatory plot requirements, thick. Nothing happens in this movie that has not been sanctioned by long usage in better films.

This is a film about (1) why Man should learn to live in harmony with Nature; (2) how prison reform is necessary; (3) how fathers can learn to love their children; (4) why it is wrong to imprison animals in zoos. The film doesn't free the beasts from their cages, but it's able to resolve the other three issues—unconvincingly, in a rush of hokey final scenes.

Instinct, directed by John Turteltaub *(Phenomenon),* is all echoes. It gives us Anthony Hopkins playing a toned-down version of Hannibal Lector, Cuba Gooding Jr., reprising his nice-guy professional from *As Good As It Gets,* Donald Sutherland once again as the wise and weary sage, and John Ashton (you'll recognize him) as a man who is hateful for no better reason than that the plot so desperately needs him to be.

Oh, and the settings are borrowed from *Gorillas in the Mist* and *One Flew Over the Cuckoo's Nest.*

The movie's just so darned uplifting and clunky as it shifts from one of its big themes to another while groaning under the weight of heartfelt speeches. The photography labors to make it look big and important, and the music wants to be sad and uplifting at the same time, as if to say it's a cruel world but that's not entirely our fault.

Hopkins stars as Ethan Powell, an anthropologist who went missing in 1994 in an African jungle and surfaced two years later while murdering two rangers and injuring three others. After a year in chains, he's returned to the

United States and locked up in a brutal psycho ward. His interrogation is set to be conducted by an eminent psychiatrist (Donald Sutherland), who instead assigns his famous prisoner to Theo Caulder (Gooding), a student just completing his final year of residency. Why give this juicy patient to a kid who admits he wants to write a best-seller about him? Because Cuba Gooding is the star of the movie, that's why, and Donald Sutherland, who cannot utter a word that doesn't sound like God's truth, always has to play the expert who waits in an oak-paneled study, passing around epigrams and brandy.

Powell's hair and beard make him look like the wild man of Borneo—with reason, since he lived with a family of gorillas in the jungle. He has been mute since the murders, but Caulder thinks he can get him to talk—and can he ever. Hopkins faces one of his greatest acting challenges, portraying a character who must seem reluctant to utter a single word while nevertheless issuing regular philosophical lectures. "I lived as humans lived 10,000 years ago," he explains. "Humans knew how to live then." Even 10,000 years ago, don't you suppose humans were giving gorillas lots of room?

Caulder believes that if he can get Powell to talk about what he did, and why, he can "get him out of there." No matter that Powell *did* kill two men; to understand is to forgive. In his struggle to comprehend his patient, Caulder meets Powell's bitter daughter (Maura Tierney, in a good performance). She is angry with her father. Her father doesn't want to talk about her. "Leave it," he snaps, menacingly. What dire issues stand between them? The movie disappoints us with a reconciliation that plays like a happy ending on the Family Channel. One should always have time for one's children, Powell learned (from the gorillas).

The prison is a snake pit of brutality, run by cruel guards and presided over by a sadistic warden and a weak psychiatrist. Each man is supposed to get thirty minutes a day outdoors. Because this is too much trouble, the guards hand out cards, and the man with the ace of diamonds gets to go outside. The toughest prisoner beats up anyone who won't give him the card. Dr. Caulder sees that this is wrong, and institutes a fair lottery, over the objections of the sadistic guards, but with the prisoners chanting their support. The entire business of the ace of diamonds, which occupies perhaps twenty minutes, is agonizingly obvious, contrived, and manipulative; the prison population, colorful weirdos of the *Cuckoo's Nest* variety, responds with enthusiastic overacting.

Ethan Powell, of course, sees through the entire system. Superhumanly strong and violent, he puts Caulder through a brief but painful education in the laws of the wild. What he is able to do at the end of the film, and where he is finally able to do it, I leave you to explain, since the film certainly cannot. I also have the gravest doubts about the thank-you note from Powell, which reads not like something that would be written by a man who had lived with the gorillas and killed two men, but by a marketing expert concerned that audiences feel real good when they leave the theater.

The Iron Giant ★ ★ ★ ½
PG, 81 m., 1999

Voices of: Jennifer Aniston (Annie Hughes), Eli Marienthal (Hogarth Hughes), Harry Connick Jr. (Dean McCoppin), Vin Diesel (The Iron Giant), James Gammon (Marv and Floyd), Cloris Leachman (Mrs. Tensedge), Christopher McDonald (Kent Mansley), John Mahoney (General Rogard), M. Emmet Walsh (Earl Stutz). Directed by Brad Bird and produced by Allison Abbate and Des McAnuff. Screenplay by Tim McCanlies and Bird, based on the book *The Iron Giant* by Ted Hughes.

Imagine *E.T.* as a towering metal man and you have some of the appeal of *The Iron Giant,* an enchanting animated feature about a boy who makes friends with a robot from outer space. The giant crash-lands on a 1957 night when America is peering up at the speck of *Sputnik* in the sky, and munches his way through a Maine village, eating TV antennas and cars, until he finds a power plant. That's where young Hogarth Hughes finds him.

Hogarth, with a voice by Eli Marienthal, is a nine-year-old who lives with his single mom (Jennifer Aniston) and dreams of having a pet. His mom says they make too much of a mess around the house, little dreaming what a 100-foot robot can get into. One night Hogarth discovers their TV antenna is missing and fol-

lows the Iron Giant's trail to the power plant, where he saves the robot from electrocution after it chomps on some live wires. That makes the Giant his friend forever, and now all Hogarth has to do is keep the robot a secret from his mom and the federal government.

The Iron Giant is still another example of the freedom that filmmakers find in animation: This would have been a $100 million live-action special-effects movie, but it was made for a fraction of that cost because the metal man is drawn, not constructed. And here is a family movie with a message: a Cold War parable in which the Iron Giant learns from a little boy that he is not doomed to be a weapon because "you are what you choose to be."

The movie is set in the 1950s because that's the decade when science fiction seemed most preoccupied with nuclear holocaust and invaders from outer space. It includes a hilarious cartoon version of the alarming *Duck and Cover* educational film in which kids were advised to seek shelter from H-bombs by hiding under their desks. And the villain is a Cold Warrior named Kent Mansley (voice by Christopher McDonald), a G-man who, of course, sees the Iron Giant as a subversive plot and wants to blast it to pieces.

That political parable is buried beneath a lot of surface charm; the film's appeal comes from its *E.T.*-type story about a boy trying to hide an alien from his mom. The Iron Giant is understandably too big to conceal in the closet, but there's a funny sequence where Hogarth brings the creature's hand into the house and it scampers around like a disobedient dog.

Like the new Japanese animated films, *The Iron Giant* is happy to be a "real movie" in everything but live action. There are no cute little animals and not a single musical number: It's a story, plain and simple. The director, Brad Bird, is a *Simpsons* veteran whose visual look here, much more complex than the *Simpsons,* resembles the "clear line" technique of Japan's Hayao Miyazaki *(My Neighbor Totoro).* It works as a lot of animation does, to make you forget from time to time that these are moving drawings, because the story and characters are so compelling.

As for the Iron Giant himself, he's surprisingly likable. He can't speak English at first, but is a quick study, and like E.T. combines great knowledge with the naïveté of a stranger in a puzzling land. His voice is by Vin Diesel, and sounds like it has been electronically lowered. He looks unsophisticated—something like a big Erector Set construction with a steamshovel mouth. But as we get to know him he turns into a personality before our very eyes— a big lunk we feel kind of sorry for. By the climax (which, also like *E.T.*, involves a threat from bureaucrats and technocrats), we're hoping Hogarth can help save his friend once again.

It must be tough to get a movie like this made. Disney has the traditional animation market locked up, but other studios seem willing to throw money at Disney musical lookalikes (like *The King and I*) even though they might have a better chance moving in the opposite direction—toward real stories told straight. *The Iron Giant*, based on a book by the late British poet laureate Ted Hughes, is not just a cute romp but an involving story that has something to say.

Isn't She Great? ★

R, 95 m., 2000

Bette Midler (Jacqueline Susann), Nathan Lane (Irving Mansfield), Stockard Channing (Florence Maybelle), David Hyde Pierce (Michael Hastings), John Cleese (Henry Marcus), John Larroquette (Maury Manning), Amanda Peet (Debbie). Directed by Andrew Bergman and produced by Mike Lobell. Screenplay by Paul Rudnick, based on an article by Michael Korda.

Perhaps it's appropriate that Jacqueline Susann's biopic has been written by Paul Rudnick, whose alter ego, "Libby Gelman-Waxner," waxes witty and bitchy in her *Premiere* magazine column every month. It was Truman Capote who said on a talk show that Jackie Susann "looks like a truck driver in drag," but whenever that image swims into view, it somehow seems to have the Gelman-Waxner byline attached.

Susann became famous writing potboilers about the sex and drug lives of the stars. Identifying the real-life models for her thinly veiled characters grew into a parlor game, and her *Valley of the Dolls* became the best-selling novel of all time. She also became famous for revolutionizing book retailing; Susann and her agent husband, Irving Mansfield, turned the book tour into a whistle-stop of America, and there was scarcely a bookseller, interviewer, or indeed shipping dockworker who didn't get the Susann treatment.

So tireless was her publicity that she even talked to me, at a time when I was twenty-three years old and had been on the *Sun-Times* for ten minutes. Jackie, Irving, and I had lunch at Eli's the Place for Steak, although all I can recall of the conversation is that she said, "I'm like Will Rogers. I never met a dog I didn't like." Full disclosure: Three years later I wrote the screenplay for the parody *Beyond the Valley of the Dolls*, and a few years after that, the Fox studio was sued by Mansfield on the grounds that the film diminished his wife's literary reputation. (Had I been called to testify, I would have expressed quiet pride in whatever small part I had played in that process.)

Susann's life would seem to be the perfect target for the Libby Gelman-Waxner sensibility; who better to write about the woman whose prose one reader described as "like overhearing a conversation in the ladies' room." My hopes soared when I learned that Andrew Bergman, who made the wacky comedies *Honeymoon in Vegas* and *Soapdish*, would be directing—and that John Cleese would play her publisher. I was hoping for satire, but they've made a flat and peculiar film that in its visual look and dramatic style might be described as the final movie of the 1950s.

Maybe that was the purpose. Maybe the whole look, feel, and sensibility of *Isn't She Great* is part of the joke. It's a movie that seems to possess the same color scheme and style sense as *Valley of the Dolls*, but, alas, without Jackie's dirty mind. So devout is this story that when Irving (Nathan Lane) walks out on Jackie (Bette Midler), we don't even find out why he really left. Jackie would have given us the scoopola.

And when they get back together again, is it with tearful recriminations and shocking accusations? Not at all. There is a tree in Central Park that they hold precious, because to them it represents God, and one day when Jackie visits the tree Irving is there already talking to God. To prove how much he loves her, on this and another occasion, he even wades into the Central Park lagoon. I think, although the movie isn't clear, that Irving left her not because of another person, but because the diamond brooch he bought for Jackie at the height of her success was upstaged by the diamond necklace given by her publisher. As her agent, shouldn't his gift be only 10 percent as expensive as her publisher's?

Money brings up another point: their lifestyle. Once Jackie makes it big time, they have a lot of money. But even before then, they live in Mansfield's lavishly expensive Manhattan apartment, reproduced on one of those spacious Hollywood sets where people make dramatic entrances and exits and the interior decorators have taste as vague as their budgets. Where did Mansfield get the money to live like this? When they first meet, he drops names like Perry Como and Frank Sinatra, but it turns out he represents their distant relatives.

Never mind. Factual accuracy is not what we're looking for anyway. What we want, I think, is the portrait of a funny trash-talker, not a secular saint who bravely bore the birth of an autistic son (visited on weekends in a luxury care center) and later battled cancer. Bette Midler would seem to be the right casting choice for Jackie, but not for this Jackie, who is not bright enough, vicious enough, ambitious enough, and complicated enough to be the woman who became world-famous through sheer exercise of will. Stockard Channing, who plays Jackie's boozy best friend, does a better job of suggesting the Susann spirit.

Jackie Susann deserved better than *Isn't She Great?* A woman who writes *Valley of the Dolls* shouldn't be punished with a biopic that makes her look only a little naughtier than Catherine Cookson. There's a scene here where Jackie and Irving visit with Jackie and Aristotle on the Onassis yacht. Consider for a moment what Susann could have done with that. Then look at the tepid moment where Ari sighs fondly, "Perhaps I married the wrong Jackie." Uh, huh. Here is a movie that needed great trash, great sex, and great gossip, and at all the crucial moments Susann is talking to a tree.

I Still Know What You Did Last Summer ★

R, 96 m., 1998

Jennifer Love Hewitt (Julie James), Freddie Prinze Jr. (Ray Bronson), Brandy (Karla Wilson), Mekhi Phifer (Tyrell), Muse Watson (Ben/Fisherman), Bill Cobbs (Estes), Matthew Settle (Will Benson), Jeffrey Combs (Mr. Brooks). Directed by Danny Cannon and produced by Neal H. Moritz, Erik Feig, Stokely Chaffin, and William S. Beasley. Screenplay by Trey Callaway.

I Still Know What You Did Last Summer assembles the building blocks of idiot-proof slasher movies: stings, Snicker-Snacks, false alarms, and POV bait-and-switches. We'll get back to those. The movie's R rating mentions "intense terror, violence, and gore," but only its publicist could consider it intense or terrifying. Gore it has.

The movie stars Jennifer Love Hewitt as Julie, survivor of the original *I Know What You Did Last Summer*, as a college student haunted by nightmares of what she did, in fact, the summer before last (last summer was actually the summer when the slasher knew what she did the previous summer, if you follow me). The pop star Brandy plays her roommate, Karla.

Together with their dates Will (Matthew Settle) and Tyrell (Mekhi Phifer), they go to the Bahamas after winning a radio contest by incorrectly naming Rio as the capital of Brazil. It wouldn't have helped to know that the correct answer is Brasilia, since they could have answered Schaumburg and still won: The contest is a hoax by the Fisherman, a spectral presence who dresses like the Groton's Fisherman and impales his victims with fishhooks. He wants to get them to the Bahamas for the obvious reason that the plot requires a seaside setting (the Fisherman would look oddly dressed anywhere else, and indeed one wonders how many victims he will have to claim before an APB is put out for a guy in a slicker with a fishhook).

Ominous signs have been portending even before they get to the Bahamas. After all those nightmares, Julie is so jumpy that the least little thing disturbs her. For example, the silly girl gets scared when her roommate creaks open the door, enters in the dark, makes assorted stealthy scary sounds, runs across a hallway in the background, and hides in the closet while allowing the clothing to rustle alarmingly. Julie grabs a knife from the kitchen, and that's when we get the first Snicker-Snack, which is the Movie Glossary term for the sound a blade makes in a movie whenever it is seen. (Blades can make this sound, which resembles a knife being drawn quickly across a steel surface, when they are touching absolutely nothing.)

Anyway, Julie darn near stabs Karla to death, when, hey, all Karla wanted to do was borrow a dress. This is the first of many false alarms, which are setups that look like danger but turn out to have an innocent explanation. They are usually followed by moments of real violence, in which we get a sting, which is the technical term for the loud, discordant, frightening chord that plays when the victim is confronted by sudden violence.

Now you'd think that Karla the roommate would figure out that since Julie has been living for two years with terrifying nightmares, and since most of her friends and neighbors have been filleted by the Fisherman, it would be unwise to sneak into her apartment in the dark, make suspicious noises, and hide in the closet. Roommates do not think like this in slasher movies.

The other standby is the POV bait-and-switch. This involves the manipulation of the camera to create a point of view that shows (a) what the character sees but we can't, (b) what we see but the character can't, or (c) what neither of us can see, since the camera is stalking the unwitting victim. It is an unwritten rule of slasher movies that killers are invisible until they actually leap into frame; if we can't see them, neither can the hero, even though the killer occupies space that should be visible from the hero's POV.

Now that we've analyzed the tawdry tricks the movie uses to pound the audience like a Playskool workbench, is there anything else to be said about *I Still Know What You Did Last Summer*? Not really. It contains no characters of any interest, no dialogue worth hearing, no originality of conception, no ambition other than to pocket the dollars of anyone unlucky enough to go to a movie named *I Still Know*

What You Did Last Summer. When a movie begins, I imagine an empty room in my mind that is about to be filled. This movie left the room furnished only with dust and a few dead flies.

I Went Down ★ ★ ★
R, 107 m., 1998

Brendan Gleeson (Bunny), Peter McDonald (Git), Tony Doyle (Tom French), Antoine Byrne (Sabrina), David Wilmot (Anto), Peter Caffrey (Frank Grogan), Rachel Brady (Young Woman). Directed by Paddy Breathnach and produced by Robert Walpole and Mark Shivas. Screenplay by Conor McPherson.

I was forbidden several years ago by a politically correct editor to write that the Irish "have the gift of gab." That was an unpermissable ethnic generalization, and probably racist, either by inclusion or exclusion, I forget which. I am reminded of that prohibition every time I review a new movie from Ireland, because so many of these movies are fueled with the music of speech, with the verbal poetry of a nation that until very recent times amused itself primarily by talking, singing, and reciting to one another. (Now that television has taken over I expect them to gradually subside like the rest of us into distracted mutterings the length of commercials.)

Paddy Breathnach's *I Went Down* is a crime movie in which the dialogue is a great deal more important than anything else. It takes the form of a road movie and the materials of gangster movies (do real gangsters learn how to act by watching movies?), but what happens is beside the point. It's what they say while it's happening that makes the movie so entertaining. Consider, for example, this observation of a kidnapped gangster: "Did you ever make love to a gangster's wife? It's like making love with the angel of (bleeping) death looking over your shoulder. Jeezsus, you just can't enjoy yourself."

The movie opens with Git (Peter McDonald) getting out of prison. He learns from his girlfriend that she has taken up with his friend Anto (David Wilmot), and when he goes to a pub looking for Anto, he ends up saving him from having his fingers smashed by the henchmen of Tom French, the local gang boss (Tony Doyle). Git pretty well smashes up French's men, and of course that is something he cannot hope to get away with. The usual punishment might be death or maiming, but French makes him an offer: He'll forgive him, and release Anto, if Git will go to Cork and collect some money for him. To keep an eye on him, French sends along the large and weathered Bunny (Brendan Gleeson).

Gleeson, who gave the best performance I saw at the 1998 Cannes Film Festival (in John Boormann's *The General*), is a rumpled giant, who as Bunny has problems with asthma and thinks he is getting too old for the workload of a gangster. He is a veteran without being an expert, as Git discovers early on when Bunny steals a car and then gets into a tricky situation at a gas station because he doesn't have the key to the gas cap.

The movie unfolds with a series of colorful characters, including Frank Grogan (Peter Caffrey), the villain in Cork. There is also an interlude with a young local girl Git meets on the way and spends a confessional night with. Ireland is small enough that you can drive across it in a day, but somehow it is such an intensely local place that such a journey seems almost epic, and every town and village is like a rich repository of densely packed local legends.

Despite the good supporting characters, the movie is basically a two-hander between McDonald and Gleeson (whose character likes to arrange everything in lists of threes). They talk, and as they talk they get to know one another, and as their personal colors emerge a friendship develops. The friendship is inconvenient, under the circumstances, but there you have it.

And when the inevitable violent showdown arrives, Breathnach makes an interesting decision: Instead of prolonging it with lots of clever shots and exploding body parts, he stylizes it—putting distance between the visuals and the action, so that *I Went Down* doesn't insult the audience it has carefully cultivated. I hate it when a movie treats the audience as if it's intelligent and alert to good dialogue, and then slaps on a bonehead ending. Much nicer this way. In Ireland, it's not so much what happens that matters, anyway, as what kind of a story you can turn it into.

J

Jack Frost ★
PG, 95 m., 1998

Michael Keaton (Jack Frost), Kelly Preston (Gabby Frost), Joseph Cross (Charlie Frost), Mark Addy (Mac MacArthur). Directed by Troy Miller and produced by Mark Canton and Irving Azoff. Screenplay by Mark Steven Johnson, Steve Bloom, Jonathan Roberts, and Jeff Cesario.

Jack Frost is the kind of movie that makes you want to take the temperature, if not feel for the pulse, of the filmmakers. What possessed *anyone* to think this was a plausible idea for a movie? It's a bad film, yes, but that's not the real problem. *Jack Frost* could have been co-directed by Orson Welles and Steven Spielberg and still be unwatchable because of that damned snowman.

The snowman gave me the creeps. Never have I disliked a movie character more. They say state-of-the-art special effects can create the illusion of anything on the screen, and now we have proof: It's possible for the Jim Henson folks *and* Industrial Light and Magic to put their heads together and come up with the most repulsive single creature in the history of special effects, and I am not forgetting the Chucky doll or the desert intestine from *Star Wars*.

To see the snowman is to dislike the snowman. It doesn't look like a snowman, anyway. It looks like a cheap snowman suit. When it moves, it doesn't exactly glide—it walks, but without feet, like it's creeping on its torso. It has anorexic tree limbs for arms, which spin through 360 degrees when it's throwing snowballs. It has a big, wide mouth that moves as if masticating Gummi Bears. And it's this kid's dad.

Yes, little Charlie (Joseph Cross) has been without a father for a year since his dad (Michael Keaton) was killed—on Christmas Day, of course. A year later, Charlie plays his father's magic harmonica ("If you ever need me . . .") and his father turns up as the snowman.

Think about that. It is an *astounding fact.* The snowman on Charlie's front lawn is a liv-ing, moving creature inhabited by the personality of his father. It is a reflection of the lame-brained screenplay that despite having a sentient snowman, the movie casts about for plot fillers, including a school bully, a chase scene, snowball fights, a hockey team, an old family friend to talk to mom—you know, stuff to keep up the interest between those boring scenes when *the snowman is TALKING.*

What do you ask a snowman inhabited by your father? After all, Dad's been dead a year. What's it like on the other side? Is there a heaven? Big Bang or steady state? When will the NBA strike end? Elvis—dead? What's it like standing out on the lawn in the cold all night? Ever meet any angels? Has anybody else ever come back as a snowman? Do you have to eat? If you do, then what? Any good reporter could talk to that snowman for five minutes and come back with some great quotes.

But Charlie, self-centered little movie child, is more concerned with how Jack Frost (his father's real name) can help *him*. His dad has been dead for a year and comes back as a snowman, and all he can think of is using the snowman to defeat the school bully in a snowball fight. Also, the kid tries to keep Dad from melting. (What kind of a half-track miracle is it if a snowman can talk, but it can't keep from melting?) Does the snowman have any advice for his son? Here is a typical conversation:

Jack Frost: *You da man!*
Charlie: *No, YOU da man!*
Jack: *No, I da SNOWMAN!*

Eventually the snowman has to leave again—a fairly abrupt development announced with the cursory line, "It's time for me to go . . . get on with your life." By this time the snowman's secret is known not only to his son but to his wife (Kelly Preston), who takes a phone call from her dead husband with what, under the circumstances, can only be described as extreme aplomb. At the end, the human Jack Frost materializes again, inside swirling fake snow, and tells his wife and son, "If you ever need me, I'm right here." And Charlie doesn't even ask, "What about on a hot day?"

Jakob the Liar ★ ★
PG-13, 114 m., 1999

Robin Williams (Jakob), Alan Arkin (Frankfurter), Bob Balaban (Kowalski), Mathieu Kassovitz (Herschel), Armin Mueller-Stahl (Kirschbaum), Liev Schreiber (Mischa), Hannah Taylor Gordon (Lina), Nina Siemaszko (Rosa), Michael Jeter (Avron). Directed by Peter Kassovitz and produced by Marsha Garces Williams and Steven Haft. Screenplay by Kassovitz and Didier Decoin, based on the book by Jurek Becker.

The last shot of *Jakob the Liar* (don't worry, it has nothing much to do with the rest of the film) shows an American jazz band playing in a field near the death camps of World War II. Three women who resemble the Andrews Sisters are singing. This shot is a fantasy, imagined by a character who wouldn't have the slightest notion what such a performance would look like. What is it doing in the movie? I fear it is there for one reason only, to provide an uplifting conclusion even if it has to be hauled in by the ears.

The first shots of the film show a man chasing a newspaper. Special effects give the paper a mind of its own. Every time the man is almost ready to pounce on it, a gust of wind comes along and blows it away. Hither and yon it blows, more versatile even than the feather at the beginning of *Forrest Gump* (which is, I suspect, its inspiration). Why is it so tantalizingly out of reach? It is a metaphor for the movie, which is about a man who pursues the illusive goal of news about the war.

These two contrived images bracket a movie that reflects their manipulative sensibility. *Jakob the Liar* takes place inside the ghetto of an unnamed Polish city where Nazis have walled off the streets and installed searchlights and guards with machine guns. Inside, Jewish captives live crowded into tiny apartments, waiting for news. The news they fear most is that they're going to be shipped to concentration camps, never to be heard of again.

Early in the film, a Jew named Jakob (Robin Williams) finds himself inside Nazi headquarters and accidentally overhears a news broadcast indicating that the war is going badly for Germany. He shares this news with his fellow captives, and it gives them hope. If the war is going to end soon, then perhaps it's worth holding on against despair and suicide.

Rumors spread that Jakob has a radio. Using the bigmouthed former boxer Mischa (Liev Schreiber) as a conduit, Jakob reluctantly leaks hints of more bad news for the Nazis. He's making it all up, of course, but in a situation like this every shred of hope could save lives. We meet various other members of the population: an old doctor (Armin Mueller-Stahl), an actor (Alan Arkin), a deeply depressed man (Bob Balaban), and a ten-year-old girl named Lina (Hannah Taylor Gordon), who was helped to escape from a death train by her parents and found by Jakob, who is hiding her.

That Jakob has room to hide both a girl and an imaginary radio is odd in a ghetto where most apartments house a dozen people. Also contrived is the way the Jews and the Nazis share a closed universe in which all important activities are limited to a few broadly drawn characters with stage accents and simple personality traits. There is little sense that a real war is lurking outside the frame.

Such a parable invites comparison with Roberto Benigni's *Life Is Beautiful,* the 1998 film about a clown who tries to use his gift of humor and imagination to save his little boy in a Nazi camp. *Jakob,* directed by Peter Kassovitz, was not inspired by Benigni's success; based on a 1975 East German movie, it was filmed before *Life Is Beautiful* was released, and (if you were wondering, and I'll bet you were) before Williams's schmaltzfest *Patch Adams.*

Both films are about extroverts using imagination as a weapon against the Holocaust. I prefer *Life Is Beautiful,* which is clearly a fantasy, to *Jakob the Liar,* which is just as contrived and manipulative but pretends it is not. You have to earn the dividends of realism. *Life Is Beautiful* is all of a piece, the opening hour showing us the limitations the hero will have to work with once he's inside the camp. *Jakob the Liar* wants the freedom of the Benigni film but doesn't want to pay the dues.

Williams is a talented performer who moves me in the right roles but has a weakness for the wrong ones. He needs a director like Billy Wilder, who once asked Jack Lemmon for "Less! Less! A little less!" so many times that Lemmon finally exploded: "Whaddaya want?

Nothing?" To which Wilder replied, "Please God!" If less is more, then Williams often demonstrates that more is less.

Movies as different as *The Dead Poets Society* and *Patch Adams* have been brought to a halt by interludes in which Williams darts in a frenzy from one character and accent to another. Here, in a scene that passes for restrained, he imitates Churchill, and uses a kitchen funnel and a flour can to create sound effects (only sneezing a little because of the flour). These scenes demonstrate that Williams cannot use shtick in a serious movie without damaging the fabric.

The other actors do their best (Schreiber is convincing, although hampered by a hat with funny ear flaps), but the screenplay and direction are lugubrious, as the characters march in their overwritten and often overacted roles toward a foregone conclusion. And then the Andrews Sisters. What a cheap shot. I wonder if it was forced on the director. It denies the truth of the film; is the audience supposed to be much relieved as it taps its feet to the tune?

I can imagine this material in black-and-white, grubbier, without stars, with subtitles to spare us the accents. It could work. Maybe I'm actually describing the 1975 East German film, which won the Silver Bear at the Berlin Film Festival. When this one opened at the Toronto festival, Williams got more applause for walking out on the stage before the screening than the whole movie got afterward.

Jawbreaker ★ ½

R, 91 m., 1999

Rose McGowan (Courtney), Rebecca Gayheart (Julie), Julie Benz (Marcie), Judy Evans Greer (Fern Mayo), Chad Christ (Zach), Charlotte Roldan (Liz Purr), Pam Grier (Detective Vera Cruz), Ethan Erickson (Dane Sanders). Directed by Darren Stein and produced by Stacy Kramer and Lisa Tornel. Screenplay by Stein.

I knew high school comedies were desperate for new ideas, but *Jawbreaker* is the first one I've seen where the bad girl is stoned with corsages. The movie is a slick production of a lame script, which kills time for most of its middle hour. If anyone in the plot had the slightest intelligence, the story would implode.

The film opens with an accidental death. The "Fearless Four" are the coolest girls in Reagan High School (and no wonder, since they look well into their twenties). One morning three of them surprise their friend Liz by sticking a jawbreaker into her mouth, taping it shut, and locking her in a car trunk for a ride to a restaurant where they plan a birthday breakfast. Liz chokes to death.

What to do? Cover it up, of course. The ringleader is Courtney (Rose McGowan), a rhymes-with-witch who fakes a phone call from Liz's mother, saying she'll be absent from school. Then she has her pals Julie (Rebecca Gayheart) and Marcie (Julie Benz) help her carry the corpse back to Liz's bed, where they fake a rape scene. Meanwhile, a school wallflower named Fern Mayo (Judy Evans Greer) delivers Liz's homework to her house, overhears the girls talking, and learns of their crime.

What to do? Part II. Make Fern one of them, of course, by giving her a beauty makeover, a new name (Vylette), and instructions on how to be a babe ("Never, ever, eat at lunch—period!"). Vylette, of course, turns out to be even more spiteful than the other girls, and indeed one of the original team, Julie (Rebecca Gayheart), drops out of the clique because she's disgusted with the whole deception.

Once poor Liz is dead and the cover-up begins, the film has to delay the obvious resolution of the situation in order to sketch in two tired subplots: Julie's romance with the star drama student (Chad Christ) and Fern/Vylette's transformation into a monster. Julie could end it all by speaking out, but she delays, because that would not be convenient for the plot.

Another problem. A local detective is investigating the death. She's played by Pam Grier, so cloaked in vast black garments and long hair that she seems to be peeking out from behind the wardrobe department. She has a scene where she's strong and angry, and then the movie forgets that personality trait and makes her into a stooge who listens to unbelievable stories. She arrests a man as a suspect in the case, disregarding a crucial clue: The school received that call from Liz's "mother," and since Liz's real mother didn't make it, it must have come from a female who knew what school Liz went to. Thus, probably not a random male rapist.

And on and on. The movie's fugitive pleasure is Rebecca Gayheart as the good girl; she is wonderfully photogenic, we reflect, as she and the rest of the cast founder in amateur-night dialogue and a plot that desperately stretches its thin material and still barely struggles to the ninety-one-minute mark—and that's counting end credits and various songs including, inexplicably, Frank Sinatra's "Young at Heart."

Joe Gould's Secret ★ ★ ★ ½
R, 108 m., 2000

Ian Holm (Joe Gould), Stanley Tucci (Joe Mitchell), Hope Davis (Therese Mitchell), Sarah Hyland (Elizabeth Mitchell), Hallee Hirsh (Nora Mitchell), Celia Weston (Sarah), Patrick Tovatt (Harold Ross), Susan Sarandon (Alice Neel). Directed by Stanley Tucci and produced by Elizabeth W. Alexander, Tucci, and Charles Weinstock. Screenplay by Howard A. Rodman, based on *Professor Seagull* and *Joe Gould's Secret* by Joseph Mitchell.

The secret of *Joe Gould's Secret* is that it is not Joe Gould's secret at all. It is Joe Mitchell's secret. Joe Gould is easy to understand, because like many madmen he is consistent from day to day—stuck in the rut of his delusions. But Joe Mitchell is a hard case, a man who hides his elusive nature behind a facade of shyness and courtly southern manners. Stanley Tucci's lovingly crafted film pretends to be about Joe Gould, and all the time its real subject is hidden right there before us in plain view.

Joseph Mitchell was a writer for the *New Yorker* in its glory days, in the 1930s and 1940s, when Harold Ross was the editor and the staff included Robert Benchley and E. B. White. He wrote stories about the people of the city, characters he encountered or heard about. One of them was Joe Gould, a bearded bohemian who marched through the streets of Greenwich Village clutching his tattered portfolio and demanding donations to the "Joe Gould Fund."

Gould claimed to be writing an oral history of New York, a million-word record of the daily conversations of the citizens, and had collected many patrons who believed him. "Gimme a bowl of soup—I don't have all day," he announces, marching into a restaurant the first time Mitchell sees him. He gets his soup. Max Gordon of the Village Vanguard donates to the "fund," and so does the poet e. e. cummings. In the film, the painter Alice Neel (Susan Sarandon) tells Mitchell: "I have always felt that the city's unconscious is trying to speak to you through Joe Gould."

Gould (Ian Holm) is a man of swiftly changing emotional weather. He can be sweet, perceptive, philosophical, and then burst out in sudden rage. The first time he has a conversation with Joe Mitchell (Stanley Tucci), he gets right to the heart of the matter. "Say 'I may marry Mary,'" he orders Mitchell, and then, after listening to the writer's accent, asks, "How did your father feel when you didn't want to go into the tobacco industry?" He has correctly clocked Mitchell as a refugee from a southern tobacco state, who became a writer against his father's wishes.

In another scene, Mitchell brings home watermelon for his wife and daughters, and cuts it on a piece of newspaper. "My father always said this was the only thing a newspaper was good for," he recalls. "And what did you say?" his wife asks the writer. He replies evenly, "I said not a thing."

There are clues to the film's real subject all through the movie. Mitchell's opening narration observes that Joe Gould felt at home among the city's outcasts and homeless, cranks and crazies. Mitchell says he did, too, and adds, "As time went on, I would find that this was not the only thing we had in common." What else they had in common is saved for the movie's end title, and suddenly illuminates the whole film.

Stanley Tucci is a director and actor with an openhearted generosity for his characters; he loves and forgives them. His first film, *Big Night,* codirected with Campbell Scott, was a perfect little masterpiece about an Italian restaurant run with too many ideals and not enough customers. Here he's made a chamber piece of quiet scenes, acutely heard dialogue, and subterranean emotional shifts. Ian Holm's role as Joe Gould is the flashy one, and some viewers will be fooled into thinking the film is about Gould. But he isn't the one who changes. He is himself from beginning to end, repeating the same notes, sometimes touchingly, sometimes maddeningly.

The movie is about Joe Mitchell, a man who avoids confrontation with such determination that he even hesitates to finish a sentence, lest it not be to his interrogator's liking. He pauses and backtracks, stammers and corrects himself, qualifies every word, and phrases everything with elusive southern courtesy. Joe Gould enters his life like a cautionary tale. Toward the end of the film, at a Greenwich Village party, Mitchell finds himself describing the book he plans to write, and we realize (if he does not) that he is describing a version of Joe Gould's oral history. Indeed, most of Mitchell's *New Yorker* articles did what Gould claimed to do; Mitchell wandered the city, stumbling bemusedly on people and their stories.

There is a dark, deep, and sad undercurrent in the movie. There is a whole story to be extracted from Mitchell's hints about himself. We sense it from the opening moments. It tantalizes us as the subtext of most of the scenes. Where is he headed? At the movie's very end we learn that one additional piece of information about Joseph Mitchell, and everything becomes clear. Tucci and Howard A. Rodman, who wrote the screenplay, based it on Mitchell's two articles about Gould, but they discovered something unwritten in those articles that gave them the clue to this movie. Some have said the film is too quiet and slow. There is anguish here that makes *American Beauty* pale by comparison.

Joe the King ★ ★
R, 100 m., 1999

Noah Fleiss (Joe), Karen Young (Theresa), Camryn Manheim (Mrs. Basil), Austin Pendleton (Winston), John Leguizamo (Jorge), Ethan Hawke (Len Coles), Val Kilmer (Bob), Max Ligosh (Mike). Directed by Frank Whaley and produced by Robin O'Hara, Scott Macaulay, Jennifer Dewis, and Lindsay Marx. Screenplay by Whaley.

Frank Whaley's *Joe the King* has been described as "semiautobiographical," and you can feel the pain behind this story of a boy from a gloomy home whose bad luck never seems to change. What you can also sense is too much self-pity: The film is so steeped in resentment that it's not able to pull back and let us see the boy behind the shield of his misery.

The film takes place in the mid-1970s, when Joe, played for most of the film by Noah Fleiss, is a dour loner who works after school in a diner and comes home to an alcoholic father (Val Kilmer), a bitter mother (Karen Young), and an older brother who tries his best but isn't much help (Max Ligosh). Joe is one of those kids whom other kids take a sadistic satisfaction in picking on. It doesn't help that his father is the school janitor; when Joe makes up stories about his dad on Careers Day, a fellow student blurts out the truth: "He cleans our toilets."

A sadistic teacher always seems to have Joe in her sights, and one day she calls him in front of the class, pulls down his pants, and smacks his bare bottom. This scene reveals a filmmaker so angered by his memories that he goes over the top: In the 1970s, in upstate New York, would a teacher really have gotten away with this? For Joe, every day is more or less the same: a round of humiliation at school, hard labor at the diner, fights between his parents at home.

The film has been compared to Truffaut's *The 400 Blows*, also about a boy whose parents' unhappy marriage sends him out into the streets, where crime beckons. Joe would also be at home in a novel by Dickens. He is hungry a lot of the time, steals food at the diner, and moves on to petty theft. After he gets in trouble with the law, there's a touching scene where he goes to the diner, orders platefuls of food, eats what he can, is overcome by grief, and throws up.

A movie like this needs some kind of arc to suggest a future for the boy. Truffaut's hero, who has an altar to Balzac in his room, at least had his dreams; no child, however unhappy, is completely without hope if he can get his hands on good books. Joe's prospects seem barren. His parents have surrendered, the system sees no good in him, and he's such a sad sack that when he's sent to a juvenile facility it plays less like an injustice than like an opportunity.

Frank Whaley, who wrote and directed, is an actor who works a lot and has a line on creepy connivers. He played the subversive assistant to studio executive Kevin Spacey in *Swimming With Sharks* (1994), studying his moves and then taking his revenge; in the underappreciated *Homage* (1996), he was a celebrity stalker who becomes indispensable to the mother of his favorite TV star; and in *Cafe Society* (1995) he was Mickey Jelke, the rich playboy who lived for headlines and made one too many.

In those roles you can sometimes see something in his eyes that can also be glimpsed in the eyes of Joe the King. However "semiautobiographical" this movie is, its author has become a successful and talented actor. I would be interested in seeing what Joe does with the rest of his life.

John Carpenter's Vampires ★ ★
R, 107 m., 1998

James Woods (Jack Crow), Daniel Baldwin (Montoya), Sheryl Lee (Katrina), Thomas Ian Griffith (Valek), Maximilian Schell (Cardinal Alba), Tim Guinee (Father Adam Guiteau), Mark Boone Jr. (Catlin), Gregory Sierra (Father Giovanni). Directed by John Carpenter and produced by Sandy King. Screenplay by Don Jakoby, based on the novel *Vampire$*, by John Steakley.

When it comes to fighting vampires and performing exorcisms, the Catholic Church has the heavy artillery. Your other religions are good for everyday theological tasks, like steering their members into heaven, but when the undead lunge up out of their graves, you want a priest on the case. As a product of Catholic schools, I take a certain pride in this preeminence.

Oh, I'm aware that Rome takes a dim view of sensationalist superstition. The pope wrote an encyclical about New Age tomfoolery just last week. But *John Carpenter's Vampires* gets its imprimatur from the Hollywood Catholic Church, a schism that broke off about the time the priest climbed the stairs to Linda

Blair's bedroom in *The Exorcist*. This is the kind of movie where the vampire killers hang rosaries from their rearview mirrors, and are blessed by a priest before they harpoon the vile creatures and drag them into the sunlight for spontaneous combustion.

The movie stars James Woods as Jack Crow, hard-bitten vampire hunter, whose family was destroyed by vampires. He's always fun to watch, with the dark glasses, the little cigar, and the sneer. He's informed by a cleric after the first raid: "I've notified Rome. They're wiring your payment to the Monterey account." Yes, the Church, which once relied on prayer, holy water, and crucifixes, now employs mercenaries to kill vampires. First the lay teachers in the parochial schools, now this.

Crow's partner is Montoya (Daniel Baldwin, jowliest of the Baldwin boys). They use a steel cable attached to a winch on a Jeep to drag the vampires into the sunlight, where they ignite in a way that looks uncannily as if they had roman candles in their pants pockets.

After the big raid in the opening sequence, they line up the skulls of their victims on the hood of their Jeep. One is missing: the Master. The vampire killers celebrate at a local motel with a wild party, but then Valek (Thomas Ian Griffith), the Master, attacks and wipes out all but Crow, Montoya, and a hooker named Katrina (Sheryl Lee). True, she's been bitten by Valek, but Crow explains that since masters communicate telepathically with their conquests, he can use her as a kind of ESP surveillance camera until she "turns."

There's a lot of Catholicism. We meet a cardinal (Maximilian Schell) who apparently supervises Rome's vampire squad. And an innocent priest in a Spanish mission that harbors the Black Cross that Valek covets. Why does he need it? It was used centuries ago in an attempted exorcism that used an "ancient forbidden form of ritual" that led to an "inverse exorcism," which means that instead of driving the evil spirit from the body and leaving the person behind, the person is cast out and the spirit retains rights of tenancy.

It is inevitable that Montoya and Katrina will be drawn to each other. She has wonderful qualities, including the ability to wear the same costume throughout the movie, survive a vampire massacre and a pickup truck crash in it, and still have it look perky the next day, with a neckline that displays the precise 2.2 inches of cleavage that Carpenter's heroines always display, as if just that much and no more or less comforts his libido.

One detail puzzled me. One of the characters is bitten by a vampire, takes out his butane lighter, and cauterizes the wound by holding his flesh above the flame. Yet later the film suggests that he may be infected after all. My thought: Either cauterizing a fresh vampire wound works or it doesn't. If it doesn't, it's not the sort of thing you do for fun.

The movie has a certain mordant humor and some macho dialogue that's funny. Woods manfully keeps a straight face through goofy situations where many another actor would have signaled us with a wink. But the movie is not scary, and the plot is just one gory showdown after another. I was disappointed to find that the traditional spiritual weapons against vampires no longer seem to work. But maybe it's just that Jack Crow's theology is rusty. At the end of the movie, bidding farewell to a couple of vampires he sort of likes, he tells them, *Vaya con dios!* Not a tactful thing to say to a vampire.

julien donkey-boy ★ ★ ★
R, 94 m., 1999

Ewen Bremner (Julien), Chloe Sevigny (Pearl), Werner Herzog (Father), Evan Neumann (Chris), Joyce Korine (Grandma), Chrissy Kobylak (Chrissy), Alvin Law (Neighbor), Victor Varnado (Albino Rapper). Directed by Harmony Korine and produced by Cary Woods, Scott Macaulay, and Robin O'Hara. Screenplay by Korine.

Is there an audience for movies like Harmony Korine's *julien donkey-boy*? The campus film freaks who used to support underground films have migrated to slick aboveground indie productions. There's no longer a fascination with films that are difficult and experimental. They can't fill a classroom these days, let alone a theater. Korine, who at twenty-five is one of the most untamed new directors, belongs on the list with Godard, Cassavetes, Herzog, Warhol, Tarkovsky, Brakhage, and others who smash conventional movies and reassemble the pieces.

Werner Herzog, the great German free spirit, is indeed one of the stars of *julien donkey-boy,* which is the story of a schizophrenic, told more or less through his own eyes. The film's style is inspired by Dogma 95, the Danish manifesto calling for movies to be made with handheld cameras, available light and sound, and props found on location. Korine shot his basic material using that approach, and then passed it through a lot of postproduction stages, so that at times it looks like abstract art seen through a glass, murkily. (The outtakes on the Website look like straightforward digital video; the movie rarely does.)

julien doesn't always work in its individual moments, but it works as a whole. It adds up to something, unlike a lot of movies where individual shots are sensational, but they add up to nothing. The characters emerge gradually from the kaleidoscopic style. We learn that Julien (Ewen Bremner, from *Trainspotting*) is a schizophrenic who lives at home with his bizarre father (Herzog), his fairly normal brother, Chris (Evan Neumann), and a sister, Pearl (Chloe Sevigny), who is carrying his child.

Life in this household consists of mind games, wrestling matches, and family fights. Herzog, as the father, is the ringleader. At various times he listens to bluegrass music while wearing a gas mask, lectures on the world championship for talking birds, praises *Dirty Harry* movies, and belittles his daughter's musical ambitions: "Why don't you tell your sister she is never going to learn to play this harp? She's a dilettante and a slut."

Sometimes this is funny. Sometimes it is sad. Some of it takes place so completely within Julien's mind that we can't be sure what really happens—the opening scene involving an attack on a boy and his pet turtle, for example. Other scenes take on a heartbreaking realism, as when Pearl has a miscarriage at an ice rink and Julien takes the stillborn infant in his arms, carries it home with him on the bus, and hides under his covers, cradling it and weeping.

The experience of seeing a movie like this is shocking for most moviegoers, and while some are stimulated by it, most resist and resent it. That's as it should be. No movie is made for everybody. *julien donkey-boy* is hardly made for anybody. It seems at first to be merely a jumble of discordant images (*Freaks* shot by the *Blair Witch* crew), but then, if you stay with it, the pattern emerges from the jumble.

You understand, first of all, that the point of view is that of a schizophrenic person. Second, that the family is dysfunctional to any outside observer but functions in its own way for its members. Third, that the story is filled with genuine emotion and even love (the movie is dedicated to Korine's schizophrenic uncle). An operatic aria plays in snatches throughout the film, and when it swells up at the end, it is a sad lament for the suffering of these characters.

Korine's background is well known. He was a skateboarder in New York when his screenplay about his friends was made into Larry Clark's *Kids* (1995), a harrowing portrait of street kids and their society. His second film, *Gummo*, unseen by me, won festival prizes at Venice and Rotterdam and was despised by a good majority of mainstream critics. Now comes *julien,* and it demonstrates that Korine is the real thing, an innovative and gifted filmmaker whose work forces us to see on his terms.

To be sure, Korine is sometimes too willing to shock for fun. A talent show at a school for the blind is excessive, especially the cigarette-eating act; and appearances by an armless drummer and a black albino rap artist are not persuasively integrated into the rest of the film. But a scene in an African-American gospel church service begins as tourism and then deepens into something very moving, as Julien's eyes brim with tears. The odds are good that most people will dislike this film and be offended by it. For others, it will provoke sympathy rather than scorn. You know who you are.

Note: In a "confession" published on the movie's Website, Korine kids Dogma 95 at the same time he genuflects to it. He admits that although Dogma requires all props to be found on location, he imported a can of cranberries from a supermarket. And he apologizes that Chloe Sevigny, his real-life girlfriend, was not really pregnant in the movie ("I did try, though"), but only had a pillow stuffed under her clothes. He proudly adds that the pillow was found on the location, in his grandmother's bedroom closet. All this and more at www.juliendonkeyboy.com.

Junk Mail ★ ★ ★
NO MPAA RATING, 83 m., 1998

Robert Skjaerstad (Roy), Andrine Saether (Line), Per Egil Aske (Georg), Eli Anne Linnestad (Betsy). Directed by Pal Sletaune and produced by Petter Boe and Dag Nordahl. Screenplay by Jonny Halberg and Pal Sletaune. In Norwegian with English subtitles.

Roy is not someone you would want to know. Or stand very close to. Or get your mail from. He brings new aromas to the concept of grunge. He is a mailman in Oslo who reads any letters that look interesting, and then delivers them smeared with cold spaghetti that he eats out of cans. He dumps junk mail into a cave by the railroad tracks. He's so low on the mailman evolutionary chain that even if you crossed him with Kevin Costner in *The Postman,* the result would frighten dogs.

Roy stumbles into the life of Line, a hearing-impaired woman who lives on his route. One day she forgets and leaves her house keys in the lock of her mailbox. He lets himself in, sniffs around, tastes some of her food, looks through her drawers and hears a message from "Georg" on her answering machine: "We did it together. You were as much a part of it as I was."

On another day he returns, falls asleep, and hides under the bed when she comes home early. Hearing nothing after a while, he finds her underwater in the bathtub. He saves her from suicide, calls an ambulance, and escapes. In a nightclub, he meets a blowzy, bosomy blonde in leopard-skin pants, who is long past her sell-by date. He takes her back to Line's apartment, knowing of course that it will be unoccupied. The blonde gets drunk, vomits, and throws things around.

I've been hearing about *Junk Mail* ever since the 1997 Sundance festival. People would mention it with that little smile that suggests a lot is being left unsaid. It's a film about a voyeur, and it appeals to the voyeur in us: We don't like Roy or approve of him, but we watch fascinated because he lives so casually outside the rules. He's the kind of guy who will steal candy from a patient in a coma.

Every once in a while I recommend a film and get an indignant postcard from someone informing me the characters were *disgusting*. I invariably agree. Roy, for example, is disgusting. So is Line (she and Georg mugged a security guard, who is the man in the coma). So is Georg. So is the leopard-skin blonde. In Norway, a land we think of as wholesome and enlightened, it is almost a relief to discover they still have room for a few token outcasts.

But why, oh why, the postcard always continues, should we pay our good money to see a film about *such disgusting people?* The postcards never have a return address, or I would write back arguing that my review described the film accurately, so why did they go? I might even cite Ebert's Law, which teaches us: "A film is not about what it is about. It is about how it is about it." Films about disgusting people can be amusing and interesting, or they can be worthless. But they are not bad simply because of their subject matter. Subjects are neutral. Style is all.

Consider, for example, that Roy does not kill anyone. What are his worst crimes? He is a bad mailman. He eats cold spaghetti out of a can. He needs a bath and a shave. He shouldn't sneak into that poor woman's apartment, although at least he saves her from suicide instead of simply sneaking out again. Compare Roy with—oh, I dunno, how about Art, the FBI guy played by Bruce Willis in *Mercury Rising*? Art also needs a bath and a shave. He kills countless people, speeds dangerously down the streets of Chicago, is associated with explosions and fires, and participates in a shootout at an old folks' home. He is a much more alarming specimen than Roy, even if he is the good guy—and yet no one sent me a postcard describing him as *disgusting*.

Why not? It is not because of the behavior or the values, but because of the hygiene. Roy is not attractive, muscular, and well coordinated. He is a scuzzy loser. If he were in a cartoon, flies would be buzzing around his head. And yet we are more likely to meet Roy than Art, because Roy exists in the world and Art exists only in a cinematic machine called a thriller. Roy wants love too. He asks Line out for a cup of coffee. He shares a few meager secrets about his existence with her. And at the end, when the bad guys come, he tries to protect her, just as Art tries to protect Stacy and the cute little autistic kid in *Mercury Rising*. What more can a hero do?

Junk Mail is a first film by Pal Sletaune, who has plunged headfirst into a world of rain, mud, desolate cityscapes, sickly greens, depressing blues, and sad struggling people. His mailman is not admirable, but he is understandable. And at least he doesn't have a hole in the back of his head, so that a director can stick in a key and wind him up.

K

Kadosh ★ ★ ★
NO MPAA RATING, 110 m., 2000

Yael Abecassis (Rivka), Yoram Hattab (Meir),
Meital Barda (Malka), Uri Ran Klausner
(Yossef), Yussef Abu Warda (Rav Shimon),
Sami Hori (Yaakov), Lea Koenig (Elisheva).
Directed by Amos Gitai and produced by
Laurent Truchot, Michel Propper, and Amos
Gitai. Screenplay by Amos Gitai, Eliette
Abecassis, and Jacky Cukier.

Kadosh is an Israeli film about the ultraorthodox Jewish sect of Hassidim, where men make the decisions and women are seen, narrowly, as vessels for the production of more sons. It is a very angry film, and has caused much discussion in Israel and within American Jewish circles, where most share its anger. Tolerance is not the strong point of the Hassidim, and a Jewish friend of mine was much saddened when his family was spat upon in Jerusalem for mistakenly entering a place where they were not welcome.

The film takes place in Mea Shearim, an area of Jerusalem where life is regulated according to ancient and unwavering laws. It tells the stories of two sisters, one married and one single but in love with an unacceptable man. Rivka and her husband, Meir, have been married for ten years and still have no children, a fact that preys on the mind of Meir's father, a rabbi. "The only task of a daughter of Israel is bringing children into the world," he believes, and eventually he orders his son to divorce his wife and marry a younger woman who might give him children. Meir protests—he loves his wife—but eventually he obeys. (Rivka has learned that her husband is sterile, but cannot share this information because such tests are forbidden.)

The other sister, Malka, has been in love for years with a man named Yaakov (Sami Hori), who was once a member of the sect but had to leave it when he joined the Israeli army; his religion did not permit him to serve. There is great family pressure on her to marry another man, a religious zealot who cruises the streets with a loudspeaker attached to his car, exhorting his listeners at deafening volume to see things his way.

The film, directed by a longtime Israeli documentarian named Amos Gitai, sees the story largely through the eyes of the women, who sometimes share rebellious thoughts like naughty schoolgirls: Their men spend their days in the study of the Torah, they observe, but women are not allowed to read it—perhaps because they might not agree that it prescribes such a limited life for women. Although some marriages, like Rivka's, are happy, women are actually told that their primary function in life is to bear as many children as possible, to "help vanquish the secular movement"—which includes Jews whose observance does not mirror the strict ways of the sect.

The women are restive, but obedient. Rivka leaves her house and goes to live alone, sinking into solitude and depression. Malka marries the zealot, and her wedding night brings into cruel focus the definition of husbandly duties. Their mother does not agree with what has happened to them but dares not oppose her husband. The men spend their days closed off together in ceaseless study and debate, even over the details for brewing (or not brewing) tea on the Sabbath. (This particular discussion seems more interested in finding theological loopholes than in honoring the underlying ideas.)

As I watched the film, I was reminded of *Two Women,* an Iranian film I saw recently, in which a woman was given a brief taste of freedom before being yanked out of college and married to her father's choice of a mate. Extreme forms of belief in both films seem designed to rationalize a fear of sex and distrust of women. My own notion is: I would be more persuaded by religious laws that are harder on the enforcers than on those under their authority, but it never seems to work out that way.

It occurred to me, during *Kadosh,* that while the Hassidim are a sect, the men within it have essentially formed a cult—excluding women, suspicious of others, dressing in such a way that they cannot mix unnoticed with outsiders, denying their own natures and instincts in order to follow their leaders. Although I am sure happy lives can be led and happy marriages created within such boundaries—and I realize the story of *Kadosh* may be an extreme example, not typical—I left the film with the thought that if God in his infinite love cannot gather both sexes into his arms equally, then I would like to sit down with him and ask him, respectfully, what his problem is.

Keeping the Faith ★ ★ ★
PG-13, 129 m., 2000

Ben Stiller (Jake), Edward Norton (Brian), Jenna Elfman (Anna), Anne Bancroft (Ruth), Eli Wallach (Rabbi Lewis), Ron Rifkin (Larry Friedman), Lisa Edelstein (Ali Decker), Milos Forman (Father Havel), Holland Taylor (Bonnie Rose), Rena Sofer (Rachel Rose). Directed by Edward Norton and produced by Hawk Koch, Norton, and Stuart Blumberg. Screenplay by Blumberg.

Edward Norton's *Keeping the Faith* is a profoundly secular movie about the love lives of a priest and a rabbi. It shares the universal Hollywood presumption that love should conquer all—that gratification of immediate emotional needs is more important than ancient values. Both the rabbi and the priest are in love with the same girl, and if only priests were allowed to marry, or if only Jews didn't mind a rabbi with a gentile wife, their problems would be over—except for the problem of which one the girl chooses.

We in the audience have been trained by a multitude of other movies to cheer for romance, especially when the girl is played by the sunny and lovable Jenna Elfman, and the boys are Rabbi Ben Stiller and Father Ed Norton. The movie does finally nod toward tradition at the end, with a loophole in the form of one brief dialogue exchange that is easily missed. But make no mistake: Both of these boys are ready to sleep with this girl no matter what their theology teaches.

The screenplay by Stuart Blumberg, of course, casts the story as a romantic comedy, not an ethical dilemma, and on that level I enjoyed it, especially since the dialogue makes the characters more thoughtful than we might expect. The story begins when all three characters are best friends as children. They go everywhere together, share everything, and then the parents of Anna (Elfman) move to California. Jake (Stiller) grows up to be a rabbi, Brian (Norton) grows up to be a priest, and they remain best friends whose church and synagogue even share development of a community center. Then Anna moves back to New York.

She's very successful. "I'm like a plumber except I fix leaky corporations," she explains. The three old friends go out together to dinner and the movies, and it's clear both guys are thunderstruck with love. But Jake is the one she likes, although she also has a conversation with Brian about the "sex thing" that, in his mind at least, contains faint echoes of invitation.

Written by a Jew and directed by a Catholic, the film has an evenhanded approach where possible. But there is one imbalance. The priest, with his vow of chastity, is not supposed to date or marry. The rabbi, who is not getting any younger and is still a bachelor, is under enormous pressure from his mother (Anne Bancroft) and his entire congregation to date and marry a Jewish woman. Indeed, his job depends on it. And since the mechanics of the screenplay require him to love only Anna, it follows that he is unable to find a Jewish woman he likes enough to marry.

This dilemma leads to a series of scenes in which romantic candidates are paraded before him like exhibits from a bachelor's nightmares. We meet Ali, the pushy physical fitness nut (Lisa Edelstein), and Rachel (Rena Sofer), the glamorous ABC correspondent, and lots of other available women, who all seem to crowd the lens and gush all over the film, with their mothers smiling and nodding behind them. We get the point, but we question it: Isn't it possible to write a movie in which Jake just plain loves Anna, period—without making every visible Jewish girl obnoxious? My guess is that if Anna had stayed in California, Jake would have been crawling through broken glass to date the ABC correspondent.

These are the kinds of thoughts that occur after the film. During the film, we're swept up in the story's need to find a happy ending. In conservative moral terms, the happiest ending, of course, would be: (1) priest remains celibate, offers up his sacrifice; (2) rabbi explains "two different worlds we come from," wishes Anna well, marries nice Jewish girl, and (3) Anna returns to California, where all things are possible. It is safe to say that no audience would accept this ending, however, as there is an emotional conservatism that runs much deeper in movie audiences than any other form of belief, and which teaches: If a movie shows us a boy and a girl who are really in love, there *must* be a happy ending.

What helps is that all of the major characters in the movie are good people — yes, even Jake's mother, who is played gently by Anne Bancroft as a woman willing to admit her mistakes and learn from them. And I like the way the filmmakers bring in older role models for the two young men. Jake turns to old Rabbi Lewis (Eli Wallach) and the wise Larry Friedman (Ron Rifkin), the head of his congregation. Brian turns to old Father Havel (Milos Forman), who confesses to having fallen in love, big time, at least every decade of his priesthood.

Why are love stories comedies and not tragedies? Because it is funny when we lose control of ourselves despite our best efforts to remain dignified. A man in love has stepped on an emotional banana peel. When a woman falls in love with an unavailable man, he *is* a banana peel.

Kikujiro ★ ★ ½
PG-13, 116 m., 2000

Beat Takeshi (Kikujiro), Yusuke Sekiguchi (Masao), Kayoko Kishimoto (Kikujiro's Wife), Yuko Daike (Masao's Mother), Kazuko Yoshiyuki (Masao's Grandmother), Beat Kiyoshi (Man at Bus Stop), Great Gidayu (Biker/Fatso), Rakkyo Ide (Biker/Baldy). Directed by Takeshi Kitano and produced by Masayuki Mori and Takio Yoshida. Screenplay by Kitano.

The little boy lives with his grandmother, who leaves food for him before she goes to work. The summer days stretch long, and the streets are empty. He is lonely, and finds the address of his mother, who works far away. He wants to visit her. The grandmother has a friend who has a husband who is a low-level gangster. The gangster is assigned to take the kid to find the mother, and that's the setup for *Kikujiro,* which

is a lot of things, although one of them is not a sweet comedy about a gangster and a kid.

The movie was made by Takeshi Kitano, currently Japan's most successful director, and he stars in it under the name he uses as an actor, Beat Takeshi. Kitano is a specialist in taut, spare crime dramas where periods of quiet and tension are punctuated by sharp bursts of violence. *Kikujiro* is the last sort of film you would expect him to make—even though he skews the material toward his hard-boiled style and away from the obvious opportunities for sentiment.

Kikujiro, known only as "Mister" to the little boy, is played by Kitano as a man who is willing to seem a clown, but keeps his thoughts to himself. His dialogue to the kid is not funny to the kid, but might be funny to a third party, and since there is none (except for the audience), it seems intended for self-amusement. Unlike *Gloria* or *Little Miss Marker,* this movie's kid doesn't have much of a personality; he pouts a lot, and looks at Mister as if wondering how long he will have to bear this cross.

The two of them are essentially broke for most of the movie, after Mister trusts the kid's ability to pick the winners at a bicycle race track. The kid guesses one race right and all the others wrong, and so the man and the boy are reduced to hitching to the remote city where the mother may live. This turns the movie into a road picture that develops slapstick notes, as when Mister tries to stop cars by lying down in the road or positioning nails to cause flat tires. (His efforts produce one puncture, which results in a great sight gag.)

Some of the adventures, like the kid's run-in with a child molester in a park, are fairly harrowing; the movie is rated only PG-13, but we can see why one paper mistakenly self-applied an R rating; scenes like this would be impossible in an American comedy, and it's all Kitano can do to defuse them enough to find comedy (very little, it is true) in them. Other scenes are funnier, including a road relationship with a couple of Hells Angels named "Baldy" and "Fatso," who despite their fearsome appearance are harmless. One extended sequence, when the man and boy are stranded at a remote bus stop, has a Chaplinesque quality.

If the movie finally doesn't work as well as it should, it may be because the material isn't a good fit for Kitano's hard-edged underlying style. Japanese audiences would know he is a movie tough guy (Clint Eastwood's Dirty Harry is our equivalent), and so they'd get the joke that he seems ineffectual and clueless. Western audiences, looking at the material with less of the context, are likely to find some scenes a little creepy, even though the cheerful music keeps trying to take the edge off. This same movie, remade shot-for-shot in America, wouldn't work at all, and only its foreign context blunts the bite of some scenes that are a little cruel or gratuitous.

Still, Takeshi Kitano is a fascinating filmmaker—a man with a distinctive style that's comfortable with long periods of inactivity. As an action director, he relishes the downtime, and keeps the action to a minimum; there is a relaxed rhythm, a willingness to let scenes grow at their own speed instead of being pumped out at top volume. I like the director and his style, but the material finally defeats him. You can't smile when you keep feeling sorry for the kid—who is not, after all, in on the joke.

The King of Masks ★ ★ ★
NO MPAA RATING, 101 m., 1999

Zhu Xu (Bian Lian Wang), Zhou Ren-Ying (Doggie), Zhang Riuyang (Tien Che), Zhao Zhigang (Liang Sao Lang). Directed and produced by Wu Tianming. Screenplay by Wei Minglung.

In a remote area of China, in the 1930s, we meet an old street performer. His profession is humble but his secrets are a great prize. One day a famous female impersonator from the Sichuan opera sees him performing, gives him a big coin, invites him to tea, and offers him a job in his troupe. But the old man, whose name is Wang, refuses this offer because it is a tradition in his family that the secrets are passed only from father to son.

Alas, Wang (played by Zhu Xu with touching appeal) has no son. And at his age, traveling the rivers in his little houseboat from one town to another, it is unlikely he will ever have one. The female impersonator begs him: "Do not die without an heir, or your magic will die too." Wang takes this advice to heart. It is a time of floods and homelessness, and in the next city there is a baby market where desperate parents look for homes for their hungry children—and cash. Wang is about to leave when an urchin cries out "Grandpa!" and captures his heart. He pays $10 for the eight-year-old, returns with him to his boat, and nicknames him Doggie. Together they will study the ancient art of silk masks, by which a man's face can take on a new and startling visage in the flash of a second.

That's the setup for *The King of Masks*, a new Chinese film of simplicity, beauty, and surprising emotional power. Like *Central Station*, it tells the story of a journey involving an old curmudgeon and a young child in search of a father. The difference is that the curmudgeon can become the father, if he chooses. And another one: Doggie is not a little boy, but a little girl.

Girls are not highly valued in China. When he discovers the deception, Wang feels cheated and wants to send Doggie away, but Doggie tearfully explains that she pretended to be a boy because she had been sold seven times already: The man who sold her was not her father, but a man who beat her. She promises to scrub the deck, do the cooking, and be a good doggie. The little girl, played with utter simplicity and solemnity by Zhou Ren-Ying, has already touched the old man's heart and he allows her to stay.

The King of Masks benefits by the survival of ancient ways into modern times. Today a street performer might be scorned, but in the 1930s he was seen as a member of an elite fraternity. Wang has a certain fame in the cities where he appears, and gains respect from his colleagues—even the female impersonator who is a great opera star, doted on by army generals. (The character, Liang, who dresses elegantly and travels in state, is played by the opera star Zhao Zhigang; we recall the tradition of female impersonators in Chinese opera from *Farewell, My Concubine*.)

Wang's life is happy, but he frets for a son and visits Buddhist temples (where Doggie plays happily among the toes of vast statues hewn from the hillside). One day Doggie comes upon a homeless little boy, and brings him home as a prize for old Wang, who is overjoyed. But the boy comes attached to great complications, and soon only Doggie can save Wang from imprisonment.

The King of Masks was directed by Wu Tianming, who as a studio head in the 1980s helped bring the Fifth Generation of Chinese filmmakers to prominence. After Tiananmen Square he moved to the United States, and returned only in 1995. This is his first film after his homecoming, and although it has no overt political message, perhaps it is no accident that its hero is a stubborn old artist who clings to his secrets.

Like so many recent Chinese films, it benefits enormously from the beauty of the setting, the costumes, and the customs. It's poignant to realize that a society of such unique beauty existed so recently. The river life of Wang and Doggie may be at the poverty level, but it has a quality that no modern rich man can afford. The story contains elements of fable (the changeling, ancient secrets), but gains weight because we know that to Wang it makes a great difference whether Doggie is a boy or a girl. And Doggie's heroics at the end seem like melodrama until we reflect that, trained by a street artist, she would have known what she was doing.

Note: The King of Masks *is being marketed as an art film for grown-ups. But as I watched it, I realized it would be an absorbing experience for bright children. Yes, there are subtitles, but no words a good reader wouldn't know. And the focus on the eight-year-old girl (not to mention Wang's beloved pet monkey) make this a magical film for third-graders and up. If you know the right child, this is the right film.*

Kissing a Fool ★
R, 105 m., 1998

David Schwimmer (Max Abbott), Jason Lee (Jay Murphy), Mili Avital (Samantha Andrews), Bonnie Hunt (Linda), Vanessa Angel (Natasha), Kari Wuhrer (Dara), Frank Medrano (Cliff Randal), Bitty Schram (Vicki Pelam). Directed by Doug Ellin and produced by Tag Mendillo, Andrew Form, and Rick Lashbrook. Screenplay by James Frey and Ellin.

One of the requirements of TV sitcoms is that the characters live in each other's pockets. They pop into their friends' apartments at any time of day or night, and every development becomes the subject of a group discussion. That works fine on *Seinfeld,* but on the big screen it looks contrived. Consider, for example, the new comedy *Kissing a Fool* in which none of the characters behave at any moment like any human being we have ever met.

The movie involves situations that wouldn't even exist if it were not for the tortuous contortions of the plot. Jay (Jason Lee) introduces his best friend, Max (David Schwimmer), to Sam (Mili Avital), the woman who is editing his book—even though Jay loves Sam himself. Why does he do this? Otherwise there wouldn't be a role for Max, who is such a hapless shmoe that the only reason Sam dates him is because the plot requires her to. It's crashingly obvious to everyone in the audience, but not to anyone in the movie, that Jay and Sam will eventually realize that they are really in love with one another. When we're that much smarter than the characters, you have to wonder why they aren't buying tickets to watch us.

The film begins at a wedding, with a kiss between two newlyweds. Because the shot is obviously and laboriously contrived to conceal the face of one of the newlyweds, we in the audience of course know immediately that there is a reason for this. Could it be that the two people who are getting married are not the two people the movie will spend the next ninety minutes pretending are going to get married?

At the wedding, we meet Linda (Bonnie Hunt), who runs the publishing company where Sam is editing Jay's book. Linda is the film's narrator. She tells two obnoxious guests at the wedding the whole story of how the newlyweds wound up at the altar. She tells this story without ever once using both of their names, and as she picks her way through a minefield of synonyms and vague adverbial evasions, we get downright restless. Obviously, she's concealing something. And we know what it is, so who's she kidding?

Why is this story, pea-brained to begin with, filtered through the annoying device of a narration? Maybe because the filmmakers thought we would be delighted at the wonderful surprise they are concealing for the last shot. I wonder: Do they know anyone that dumb in their own lives, or do they just think the rest of us are clueless?

Sitcoms like to supply their characters with physical props, and so poor Bonnie Hunt is required to hold a cigarette in every single scene she appears in. And not any cigarette. A freshly lit one, in her right hand, held in the air roughly parallel to her ear. I hope they had a masseuse to give her shoulder rubs between takes. Ms. Hunt, who I hope is suing her agent, does what she can with a character whose IQ is higher than those of the other three characters combined.

Max, the Schwimmer character, plays a WGN sportscaster who thinks Australia is in Europe. Sam and Jay immediately compare notes about charming little trattorias in Florence. Max is obviously not the right choice for this woman, but the movie explains their attraction as first love—a love so strong that Max is actually moved to take his toothpick (sitcom prop) out of his mouth when he sees her.

We are then made to endure a lame contrivance in which Max grows fearful that Sam will not remain faithful to him, and so enlists Jay to attempt to seduce her—as a test. Not since Restoration comedy has this plot device been original, but in *Kissing a Fool* it is taken so seriously that it leads to moments of heartfelt dismay, carefully cued by the sound track, and one of those "darkness before the dawn" sequences in which it appears, for a teeth-gnashing instant, that the right people will not end up together. One character, in dismay, goes into a bar and orders four vodkas at once; the movie doesn't even know how drinkers drink.

If James Frey and the director Doug Ellin, who wrote this screenplay, didn't have an outline from a script workshop tacked to the wall in front of them, then they deserve an Oscar for discovering, all by themselves, a basic story formula that was old, tired, and moronic long before they were born.

I like the title, though. *Kissing a Fool.* They got that right.

Krippendorf's Tribe ★ ★
PG-13, 94 m., 1998

Richard Dreyfuss (James Krippendorf), Jenna Elfman (Veronica), Natasha Lyonne (Shelly), Gregory Smith (Mickey), Carl Michael Lindner (Edmund), Lily Tomlin (Ruth Allen). Directed by Todd Holland and produced by Larry Brezner. Screenplay by Charlie Peters, based on the book by Frank Parkin.

Is it possible to recommend a whole comedy on the basis of one scene that made you laugh almost uncontrollably? I fear not. And yet *Krippendorf's Tribe* has such a scene, and many comedies have none. I was reminded of the dead parakeet that had its head taped back on in *Dumb and Dumber.* A scene like that can redeem a lot of downtime.

The scene in *Krippendorf's Tribe* involves the backyard fakery of a primitive circumcision ritual. But I am getting ahead of the story. The movie stars Richard Dreyfuss as James Krippendorf, an anthropologist who has gone to New Guinea, utterly failed to find a lost tribe, and returned to his campus, having spent all of his grant money. Now it is time to produce results, of which he has none.

Krippendorf has two small sons and a teenage daughter; his wife died in New Guinea, but she's handled so remotely in the film that I wonder why they bothered with her. No matter. Back home, Krippendorf has descended into sloth and despond, and pads about the house aimlessly. Then an enthusiastic colleague named Veronica, played with zest and wit by Jenna Elfman, pounds on his door with a reminder that he is to lecture on his findings that very night.

Krippendorf's lack of any findings takes on a whole new meaning when his department head informs him that another colleague will do prison time for misappropriating grant money. Terrified, Krippendorf improvises a lecture in which he claims to have found a lost tribe. He even produces one of its artifacts—a sexual aid, he claims, although sharp eyes might recognize it as a toy space shuttle, belonging to one of his sons who left it in the oven.

Krippendorf has promised home movies of the lost tribe, which, in desperation, he has named the Shelmikedmu, after his children Shelly, Mike, and Edmund. At home, he fakes the footage, dressing his children up like New Guinea tribesmen and intercutting their romps in the backyard with actual footage from his trip. It's at about this point that he hits on the inspiration of the circumcision ritual, which his two boys enter into with such zeal that the scene takes on a comic life of its own.

The movie as a whole isn't that funny. It introduces characters and doesn't really develop them. Lily Tomlin, for example, is Krippendorf's rival. She is given various props, including a pet monkey and an adoring female admirer, and then packed off to New Guinea, where the movie seems to forget her between brief remote appearances. David Ogden Stiers is likewise misused as a video producer who is brought onstage and then never really used. I did like Jenna Elfman's work as Veronica, who towers over Dreyfuss and eventually becomes an accomplice in the deception. Comic momentum threatens to build up during a late scene at a banquet, where the university's aged benefactor unexpectedly discovers the secret of the fraud. But the movie can't find that effortless zaniness that good screwball comedy requires. Dreyfuss and Elfman change into and out of a tribal disguise, and we can see how it's meant to be funny, but it isn't. *Krippendorf's Tribe* contains that one scene that reminds us of what great comedy can play like, and other scenes that don't benefit from the reminder.

Kundun ★ ★ ★
PG-13, 128 m., 1997

Tenzin Yeshi Paichang (Dalai Lama, age two), Tulku Jamyang Kunga Tenzin (Dalai Lama, age five), Gyurme Tethong (Dalai Lama, age twelve), Tenzin Thuthob Tsarong (Adult Dali Lama), Tencho Gyalpo (Dalai Lama's Mother), Tsewang Migyur Khangsar (Dalai Lama's Father), Lobsang Samten (Master of the Kitchen), Sonam Phuntsok (Reting Rinpoch). Directed by Martin Scorsese and produced by Barbara De Fina. Screenplay by Melissa Mathison.

At a midpoint in Martin Scorsese's *Kundun*, the fourteenth Dalai Lama reads a letter from the thirteenth, prophesying that religion in Tibet will be destroyed by China—that he and his followers may have to wander helplessly like beggars. He says, "What can I do? I'm only a boy." His adviser says, "You are the man who wrote this letter. You must know what to do."

This literal faith in reincarnation, in the belief that the child at the beginning of *Kundun* is the same man who died four years before the child was born, sets the film's underlying tone. *Kundun* is structured as the life of the fourteenth Dalai Lama, but he is simply a vessel for a larger life or spirit, continuing through centuries. That is the film's strength, and its curse. It provides a deep spirituality, but denies the Dalai Lama humanity; he is permitted certain little human touches, but is essentially an icon, not a man.

Kundun is like one of the popularized lives of the saints that Scorsese must have studied as a boy in Catholic grade school. I studied the same lives, which reduced the saints to a series of anecdotes. At the end of a typical episode, the saint says something wise, pointing out the lesson, and his listeners fall back in amazement and gratitude. The saint seems to stand above time, already knowing the answers and the outcome, consciously shaping his life as a series of parables.

In *Kundun,* there is rarely the sense that a living, breathing, and (dare I say?) fallible human inhabits the body of the Dalai Lama. Unlike Scorsese's portrait of Jesus in *The Last Temptation of Christ,* this is not a man striving for perfection, but perfection in the shape of a man. Although the film is wiser and more beautiful than Jean-Jacques Annaud's recent *Seven Years in Tibet,* it lacks that film's more practical grounding; Scorsese and his writer, Melissa Mathison, are bedazzled by the Dalai Lama.

Once we understand that *Kundun* will not be a drama involving a plausible human character, we are freed to see the film as it is: An act of devotion, an act even of spiritual desperation, flung into the eyes of twentieth-century materialism. The film's visuals and music are rich and inspiring, and like a Mass by Bach or a Renaissance church painting, it exists as an aid to worship: It wants to enhance, not question.

That this film should come from Scorsese, master of the mean streets, chronicler of wise guys and lowlifes, is not really surprising, since so many of his films have a spiritual component, and so many of his characters know they live in sin and feel guilty about it. There is a strong impulse toward the spiritual in Scorsese, who once studied to be a priest, and *Kundun* is his bid to be born again.

The film opens in Tibet in 1937, four years after the death of the thirteenth Dalai Lama, as monks find a young boy who they sense may be their reincarnated leader. In one of the film's most charming scenes, they place the child in front of an array of objects, some belonging to the thirteenth, some not, and he picks out the right ones, childishly saying, "Mine! Mine! Mine!"

Two years later, the monks come to take the child to live with them and take his place in history. Roger Deakins's photography sees this scene and others with the voluptuous colors of a religious painting; the child peers out at his visitors through the loose weave of a scarf, and sits under a monk's red cloak as the man tells him, "You have chosen to be born again."

At his summer palace, he sees dogs, peacocks, deer, and fish. He is given a movie projector, on which a few years later he sees the awful vision of Hiroshima. Soon the Chinese are invading Tibet, and he is faced with the challenge of defending his homeland while practicing the tenets of nonviolence. There is a meeting with Chairman Mao at which the Dalai Lama hears that religion is dead and can no longer look in the eyes of a man who says such a thing. He focuses instead on Mao's polished Western shoes, which seem to symbolize the loss of older ways and values.

The film is made of episodes, not a plot. It is like illustrations bound into the book of a life. Most of the actors, I understand, are real Tibetan Buddhists, and their serenity in many scenes casts a spell. The sets, the fabrics and floor and wall coverings, the richness of metals and colors, all place them within a tabernacle of their faith. But at the end I felt curiously unfulfilled; the thing about a faith built on reincarnation is that we are always looking only at a tiny part of it, and the destiny of an individual is froth on the wave of history. Those values are better for religion than for cinema, which hungers for story and character.

I admire *Kundun* for being so unreservedly committed to its vision, for being willing to cut loose from audience expectations and follow its heart. I admire it for its visual elegance. And yet this is the first Scorsese film that, to be honest, I would not want to see again and again. Scorsese seems to be searching here for something that is not in his nature and never will be. During *The Last Temptation of Christ*, I believe Scorsese knew exactly how his character felt at all moments. During *Kundun*, I sense him asking himself, "Who is this man?"

Kurt & Courtney ★ ★ ★
NO MPAA RATING, 99 m., 1998

A documentary directed by Nick Broomfield and produced by Tine Van Den Brande and Michael D'Acosta.

Nick Broomfield does not like Courtney Love. Neither do some of the other people in her life. In Broomfield's rambling, disorganized, fascinating new documentary named *Kurt & Courtney*, Love's father teases us with the possibility that she could have killed her rock star husband, Kurt Cobain. An old boyfriend screams his dislike into the camera. A nanny remembers there was "way too much talk about Kurt's will." A deranged punk musician says, "She offered me fifty grand to whack Kurt Cobain." A private eye thinks he was hired as part of a cover-up.

Broomfield is a one-man band, a BBC filmmaker who travels light and specializes in the American sex 'n' violence scene. After an exposé of the evil influences on Hollywood madam Heidi Fleiss, and an excursion into a Manhattan S&M parlor *(Fetishes)*, he takes his show to the Pacific Northwest to examine the unhappy life and mysterious death of Cobain—the lead singer of the grunge rock band Nirvana, apparently dead by his own hand.

Did Cobain really kill himself? No fingerprints were found on his shotgun, we're told, and the movie claims his body contained so many drugs it was unlikely he could have pulled the trigger. Broomfield's film opens with Love as a suspect, only to decide she was probably not involved, and the movie ends in murky speculation without drawing any conclusions. It's not so much about a murder investigation as about two people who won fame and fortune that only one was able to handle. Cobain probably did kill himself, but it was a defeat as much as a decision; he could no longer endure his success, his drug addiction, and his demanding wife.

When Courtney met Kurt, we learn, Cobain was already a star; she was lead singer in a second-tier local band. In 1992, in her words, "We bonded pharmaceutically over drugs." In the words of a friend, she came into his life and in a three-year period took over everything. Then, as Kurt descended, lost into drugs, she got her own act together, and after his death in 1994 she won a Golden Globe nomination for *The People vs. Larry Flynt* and, in the doc's closing scenes, is a presenter of a "freedom of information" banquet of the L.A. chapter of the ACLU. As she takes the stage, it is impossible not to think uneasily of *A Star Is Born.*

Broomfield is not objective. He's in the foreground, narrating everything. The real subject of his films is what he goes through to shoot them. We learn that Courtney refused permission to use her music or Kurt's (no kidding), and he tells us what songs he "would have used" over certain scenes. He hires paparazzi to stalk Love into a recording studio, and at the end, at the ACLU event, he barges onto the stage, grabs the microphone, and accuses her (accurately) of making implied death threats against journalists. One gathers that the ACLU, focusing on the message of *The People vs. Larry Flynt* and desiring a high-profile star for their benefit, invited Love a little prematurely.

In all of Broomfield's films, you meet people you can hardly believe exist. El Duce, for example, the punker who claims Love offered him money to kill Cobain, is a character out of Fellini, or hell. At the end of the movie, we are not surprised to learn he died after stumbling into the path of a train, but we are astonished to learn he was in his mid-thirties; he looks like a well-worn fifty-year-old bouncer. Love's father, a former manager for the Grateful Dead, has written two books about Kurt's death, both of them unflattering to his daughter, and speaks of buying pit bulls "to put peace into our house." Assorted old friends, flames, and hangers-on make appearances that seem inspired by the characters in Andy Warhol's *Chelsea Hotel.* Only Kurt's Aunt Mary, who plays tapes of him singing joyously as a child, seems normal.

Why did Kurt Cobain die? Because of his drug use, obviously, from which everything else descended, including his relationship with Courtney. He was filled with deep insecurities that made him unable to cope with the adulation of his fans; he was far too weak for Love's dominating personality; drugs and booze led to chronic stomach pain, and when he climbed over the wall of his last rehab center, he was fleeing to his death.

We learn from one of his old girlfriends that Cobain was acutely sensitive to how scrawny he was. We see a skeletal self-portrait. "He wore lots and lots of layers of clothing to make himself look heavier," she says. It is one of the film's many ironies that the grunge rock fashion statement, with its flannel shirts beloved by millions, may have come about because Kurt Cobain was a skinny kid.

L

La Ciudad (The City) ★ ★ ★
NO MPAA RATING, 88 m., 2000

Bricks—Ricardo Cuevas (Man), Anthony Rivera (Boy), Joe Rigano (Contractor). *Home*—Cipriano Garcia (Young Man), Leticia Herrera (Young Woman). *The Puppeteer*—Jose Rabelo (Father), Stephanie Viruet (Daughter). *Seamstress*—Silvia Goiz (Seamstress), Rosa Caguana (Friend), Guillermina de Jesus (Friend). Directed by David Riker and produced by Riker and Paul S. Mezey. Screenplay by Riker.

Those who leave their native land and immigrate to another are often, almost by definition, the boldest and most capable, able to imagine a new life for themselves. Arriving in a new land without language or connections, they are likely to be shuttled into low-paying jobs and scorned by the lucky citizens who are already onboard. They earn their living by seizing opportunities.

Consider the puppeteer (Jose Rabelo), who is the third subject of David Riker's *La Ciudad* (The City). He lives in a station wagon with his daughter (Stephanie Viruet). He supports them both by performing Punch and Judy shows for city kids, whose video games must make this entertainment look quaint. His daughter loves to read, is bright, wants to go to school. He tries everything to get her accepted. Every child is guaranteed a place in school, he has been told, but there is a hitch: He needs a receipt for rent or a telephone to show where he lives. And, of course, he lives in a car.

His story is one of four in *The City*, a direct, spare, touching film developed by Riker during six years of acting workshops with immigrants in New York City. His characters come from the Spanish-speaking lands to the south, have arrived in New York filled with hope, and now are exploited as cheap labor.

The first of his stories, *Bricks*, is about day laborers. They're hired a truckload at a time to be carted out to a work site, where they're promised $50 a day only to find out that is a theoretical sum and the job is piecework—fifteen cents for every brick they chip clean of mortar. A man (Ricardo Cuevas) wants to bring along his boy (Anthony Rivera). "This isn't a

day-care center," growls the foreman. But if the man is to work, is the boy to wait alone on the streets? There is an accident at the construction site, and we see how expendable these day workers are considered to be.

The second story, named *Home*, is the most bittersweet because it suggests the possibility of hope, even love. A young man (Cipriano Garcia) arrives in the city from Mexico. He crashes a party and finds himself dancing with a woman (Leticia Herrera) who, wonder of wonders, is from his hometown. He confesses to her: "My whole life is in this bag I am carrying." She responds with sweet formality, "I invite you to my home." They have the promise of happiness. And then, in an O. Henry ending, the man's hand closes on air.

Seamstress, the final story, is about a woman (Silvia Goiz) who has left her village and country to earn money to buy medicine for a sick child. Now she works in a sweatshop where no wages have been paid for weeks—and when she asks for her pay, she is fired. The other workers listen silently and glance out of the corners of their eyes. They have no job security, and they need this work desperately; will they express solidarity with her?

The Italian neorealists Rossellini and De Sica believed that everyone could play at least one role in a movie—himself. The movie camera is an effortless recorder of authenticity (it does just as well when exposing the false), and in *The City* we sense in the faces and voices of the performers an experience shared at firsthand. Their stories may be fictional, but their knowledge of them is true. The film is in black and white, as it must be; these spare outlines would lose so much power in color. Riker does an interesting thing with his writing: He never quite closes a story. The open endings are a way of showing that these lives continue from one trouble to another, without happy endings.

I saw this film at its first public screening at the 1998 Toronto Film Festival. Finally it is making its way around the country, at venues like the Film Center of the Art Institute of Chicago. It is a film that would have great power for Spanish-speaking working people, who, of course, are not likely to find it at the Art Institute. Eventually, on television, it may find broader audiences. It gives faces to the faceless, and is not easily forgotten.

La Cucaracha ★ ★ ★
R, 94 m., 1999

Eric Roberts (Walter), Tara Crespo (Lourdes), Alejandro Patino (Fruit Vendor), Joaquim de Almeida (Jose Guerras). Directed by Jack Perez and produced by Michael A. Candela and Richard Mann. Screenplay by James McManus.

One moment Walter is sleeping the sleep of the damned. The next moment his eyes snap open, he sits bolt upright, and runs in terror out of his shack, running through the sagebrush to the nearest cantina, where he gasps out an order for cerveza. Lots of cerveza. Eventually he is passed out at his table, sleeping now the sleep of a man who keeps terror at bay with drunkenness.

The title of La Cucaracha is possibly inspired by Walter, who like a cockroach hides in cracks and crannies and lives on the crumbs he picks up in bars. Once he was a would-be novelist, and sometimes he writes (or hallucinates that he writes) letters back home about how he cannot write his novel. He claims he is hiding out in Santiago, Mexico, because he killed a man. Unlikely. Like the consul who is the hero of Malcolm Lowry's great novel Under the Volcano, reality and fantasy both look the same to him.

Walter is played by Eric Roberts, often an intense and passionate actor, rarely more so than here, where with a bandage holding his broken glasses together, he peers out at a world that terrifies him. He is at the end of his rope, so strung out on booze that sobriety is only an invitation for the DTs. How does a man arrive at such a dead end, so far from home? By accident, bad habits, and rotten luck.

There is a beautiful woman in the town. He yearns for her. He stands in the night and watches her inside her house. He has nothing to offer her. A stranger approaches him in the bar with an offer of $100,000 if he will kill a man. A man, he is told, who is a child killer. He is not sure he can kill, but he is sure he needs $100,000. Soon he is holding a gun on the man he has been paid to kill. He does not pull the trigger.

"If you were worth the money they paid you, I would be dead five minutes ago," the man tells him. "Please—do what you came for." He hesitates. Now the man says: "The man who really killed the boy was the man who hired you. He could not stand the idea that his son was a homosexual."

Does he pull the trigger? The beauty of La Cucaracha is that it doesn't matter. This is a movie gloriously free of plot, and all the boring obligatory twists and turns that plot drags along with it. It is a character study about a man in peril. It was directed by Jack Perez and written by James McManus, who at one point includes dialogue mentioning Hemingway, Lowry, and Graham Greene—who wrote about men at the end of the line, drunken writers and whiskey priests. Walter is in that tradition.

The movie won the Austin Film Festival in 1998 and then disappeared until its current limited release. Perez's two earlier credits are The Big Empty (1997), which despite its promising title apparently never opened anywhere, and America's Deadliest Home Video, which went straight to same.

Now comes this intriguing, stylish little film. In superficial ways it's like El Mariachi, the film that made Robert Rodriguez's reputation, except that it lacks a strong marketing push, is not as cheaply made, and is more interested in character than action. It also has a wicked strain of humor, leading to such lines as, "If it's any consolation, this money will now be spent to build a pediatric ward in Santiago hospital."

It must have required a certain courage for Eric Roberts to take a role like this. It's not a prestigious job for a former Oscar nominee. But it's a juicy role for an actor whose career has meandered recently (what was he doing in Best of the Best 2?). His performance evokes some of the same desperation and determination as Warren Oates's work in Peckinpah's great Bring Me the Head of Alfredo Garcia. He's willing to go over the top with it—and yet his performance is not the manic hyperactivity we sometimes see from him; he finds a sadder, more controlled note.

The movie is not for everybody. Some people will no doubt find it silly, or yearn for the consolations of formula and genre. But the more you're into nuance and atmosphere, the more you appreciate a movie that evokes instead of explains, the more you might like it.

Lake Placid ★
R, 82 m., 1999

Bridget Fonda (Kelly Scott), Bill Pullman (Jack Wells), Oliver Platt (Hector Cyr), Brendan Gleeson (Sheriff Keough), Betty White (Mrs. Bickerman), Meredith Salenger (Deputy Sharon Gare). Directed by Steve Miner and produced by David E. Kelley and Michael Pressman. Screenplay by Kelley.

"What an animal does in the water is his own business—unless he does it to man." So says Sheriff Keough, one of the crocbusters of *Lake Placid*. I couldn't disagree with him more. The thirty-foot crocodile in this movie stays peacefully in the water, contentedly munching on bears and cows, until scuba-diving beaver-taggers invade his domain. It's their own fault that the beast gets mad and eats a scientist and half a game warden.

The croc inhabits Black Lake in Maine. (There is no Lake Placid in the movie, which may be its most intriguing mystery.) It is, we learn, an Asian crocodile. "How did he swim across the sea?" a lawman asks, not unreasonably. "They conceal information like that in books," one of the movie's croc lovers answers sarcastically. I dunno; I thought it was a pretty good question.

As the movie opens, two game wardens are tagging beavers to study their movements. Suddenly they're attacked by an underwater camera, which lunges at them in an unconvincing imitation of an offscreen threat. It becomes clear that Black Lake harbors more than beavers, although for my money the scenes involving beavers were the scariest in the movie. Can you imagine being underwater inside a beaver dam with angry animals the size of footstools whose teeth can chomp through logs?

When it becomes clear that Black Lake harbors a gigantic beast, an oddly assorted crew assembles to search for it. There's fish warden Jack Wells (Bill Pullman), museum paleontologist Kelly Scott (Bridget Fonda), Sheriff Keough (Brendan Gleeson), and millionaire croc-lover Hector Cyr (Oliver Platt), a mythology professor who believes "crocodiles are

divine conduits." Oh, and there's Mrs. Bickerman (Betty White), who lives in a cute little farm cottage on the shores of the lake and lost her husband a few years ago. That's her story, anyway.

Whether the movie was intended at any point to be a serious monster thriller, I cannot say. In its present form it's an uneasy compromise between a gorefest and a comedy—sort of a failed *Anaconda*. One peculiar aspect is the sight of an expensive cast in such a cheap production. We're looking at millions of dollars' worth of actors in the kind of aluminum boat you see on display outside Sam's Club. Given the size of the crocodile, this movie lends a new meaning to the classic *Jaws* line, "We're going to need a bigger boat."

There's tension between the locals and the visitors, between the croc lovers and the croc killers, between the sheriff and the state game officials, between the sexes, and between everybody else and Betty White, who uses language that would turn the Golden Girls green. Almost all of the disagreements involve incredibly stupid decisions (would you go scuba-diving in a lake with a hungry giant crocodile?). New meaning also is given to the disclaimer "no animals were harmed during the filming of this movie" by a scene where a cow is dangled from a helicopter as bait for the crocodile. I believe the cow wasn't harmed, but I'll bet she was really upset.

Occasional shots are so absurd they're just plain funny. Consider the way thousands of perch jump into the air because they're scared of the crocodile. What's their plan? Escape from the lake? I liked the way the croc's second victim kept talking after he'd lost half his body. And the way the Fonda character was concerned about toilet and tent facilities in their camp; doesn't she know she's an hour's drive from Freeport, Maine, where L.L. Bean can sell her a folding condo?

The movie is pretty bad, all right. But it has a certain charm. It's so completely wrongheaded from beginning to end that it develops a doomed fascination. We can watch it switching tones within a single scene—sometimes between lines of dialogue. It's gruesome, and then camp, and then satirical, and then sociological, and then it pauses for a little witty intellectual repartee. Occasionally the crocodile leaps out of the water and snatches victims from the shore, looking uncannily like a very big green product from the factory where they make Barney dolls. This is the kind of movie that actors discuss in long, sad talks with their agents.

The Land Girls ★ ★ ½
R, 112 m., 1998

Catherine McCormack (Stella), Rachel Weisz (Ag), Anna Friel (Prue), Steven Mackintosh (Joe Lawrence), Tom Georgeson (Mr. Lawrence), Maureen O'Brien (Mrs. Lawrence), Gerald Down (Ratty). Directed by David Leland and produced by Simon Relph. Screenplay by Keith Dewhurst and Leland, based on the novel *Land Girls* by Angela Huth.

The Land Girls tells the story of the Land Army, the volunteer force of civilians raised in England during World War II to take the place of farmworkers who enlisted in the armed forces. The movie takes place during a green, wet winter on a beautiful farm in Dorset, where three "land girls" from the city are sent to become farm laborers.

Their lessons begin, predictably, with the challenge of milking cows. Mr. Lawrence (Tom Georgeson), the farmer, is unimpressed: "It's not an army—it's just an excuse for a lark!" But the girls learn quickly and work hard, and in one way or another all three are attracted to Joe Lawrence (Steven Mackintosh), the farmer's son.

Prue (Anna Friel), who before the war was a hairdresser, is the boldest of the girls, and tells Agatha (Rachel Weisz), who is a Cambridge graduate but still a virgin at twenty-six, she should seize her opportunity with Joe. "Fornication? With him? He's unspeakable!" "So what?" Ag thinks it over and approaches Joe in all seriousness: "I'll come straight to the point. Would you mind giving me a go?"

Joe would not. He is more seriously attracted, however, to Stella (Catherine McCormack from *Dangerous Beauty*), who is engaged to a pilot. She tries to remain loyal to her man, but Joe has an appeal that's apparently irresistible to the women in the movie, although less compelling to the audience.

What happens to the characters is more or less predictable (we guess there will be some setbacks, some wartime tragedies, some angry partners, and weepy reunions). What I liked about the movie—what I preferred to the romances and relationships, indeed—was the look of the film, its sensual evocation of the British countryside in winter.

The cinematographer, Henry Braham, uses a saturated, high-contrast color style that makes the woods look dark and damp and the grass wet, cold, and green. The vast skies are that lonely and yet reassuring shade that watercolorists call Payne's gray. Farmer Lawrence loves his land, which he tramps morning and night in the company of his dog, Jack. His wife (Maureen O'Brien) loves it just as much, and acts as a quiet influence on his temper.

In one of the best sequences in the movie, Farmer Lawrence tells a government official he will not plow his east meadow, no matter how much the land is needed for wartime crops. "You should see this field in the spring," he tells Stella. "It's beautiful—just beautiful." He remembers courting his wife there. But Stella, stung in love and by what she perceives as the farmer's dislike, fires up the tractor one morning and plows it. This act of rebellion is what wins the farmer's respect.

I'll remember that scene, and another one where the land girls wait for the mailman to arrive, and one of them balances on a rail of the farm gate, like a figurehead in the mist. More than with most movies, I felt the reality of the rural setting, the earth beneath the grass, the closeness of the animals to their masters. But the story itself seemed thin in comparison: flirtations, broken hearts, bittersweet regret, all pretty routine.

The Last Days ★ ★ ★ ½
NO MPAA RATING, 88 m., 1999

A documentary directed by James Moll and produced by June Beallor and Ken Lipper for Steven Spielberg's Survivors of the Shoah Visual History Foundation. Featuring U.S. representative Tom Lantos, Alice Lok Cahana, Renee Firestone, Bill Basch, and Irene Zisblatt.

The Holocaust is so overwhelming that it threatens literally to become unthinkable—to become an abstraction of evil. *The Last Days* and other documentaries make it real by telling some of the countless small stories that make up the larger ones. To say that 6 million died is one thing. To listen to a woman's memories of her girlhood, when she hid from her father in a Nazi death camp because she wanted to spare them both the sight of each other—and how their eyes nevertheless met for a last time as he was marched to his death—is another thing altogether.

Steven Spielberg's Survivors of the Shoah Visual History Foundation is engaged in making a record of as many such memories as can be recorded from those who saw the tragedy with their own eyes. The eventual goal is 50,000 taped interviews. *The Last Days* features five of those survivors and others, telling their own stories. It focuses on the last year of the war, when Hitler, already defeated and with his resources running out, revealed the depth of his race hate by diverting men and supplies to the task of exterminating Hungary's Jews. At that late point, muses one of the witnesses in this film, couldn't the Nazis have just stopped? Used their resources where they were needed for the war effort? Even gotten some "brownie points" by ending the death camps?

No, because for the fanatic it is the fixed idea, not the daily reality, that obsesses the mind. Those apologists like the British historian David Irving, who argue that Hitler was not personally aware of many details of the Holocaust, are hard pressed to explain why his military mind could approve using the dwindling resources of a bankrupt army to kill still more innocent civilians.

In Spielberg's *Schindler's List* there are the famous shots of the little girl in the red coat (in a film otherwise shot in black and white). Her coat acts as a marker, allowing us to follow the fate of one among millions. *The Last Days*, directed by James Moll, is in a way all about red coats—about a handful of survivors, and what happened to them.

One describes the Nazis' brutality toward children, and says, "That's when I stopped talking to God." Another, Renee Firestone, confronts the evasive Dr. Hans Munch, who was acquitted in war crimes trials; his defense was that he spared the lives of some prisoners by conducting harmless medical experiments on them. But Firestone believes he was responsible for the death of her sister, Klara, and when he grows vague in his answers, she grows angry. Anyone who worked in a death camp has much to be vague about.

There is another passage where a woman, now around seventy, remembers instructions to Hungarian Jews to gather up their belongings for a trip by train. She took along a precious bathing suit, one she looked forward to wearing at the pool as any teenage girl might, and as she describes the fate of that suit, and of herself and her family, we hear a lifelong regret: In a moment, she was denied the kind of silly, carefree time a teenage girl deserves.

There is a final passage of joy that affected me with the same kind of emotional uplift as the closing scenes in *Schindler's List*. We have met during the film the only Holocaust survivor to be elected to the U.S. Congress—Representative Tom Lantos, whose wife is also a survivor. Both lost all of the members of their families. But they had two daughters, who came to them with the promise of a gift: They would have a lot of children. And then there is a shot of the Lantos family and its seventeen grandchildren.

That scene provides release after a harrowing journey. The movie contains footage of the survivors as they looked on the day their camps were liberated by the Allies—walking skeletons, whose eyes bear mute witness to horror. And the film has angry memories of an aftermath. One witness, an American soldier, describes shooting an unarmed German dead in cold blood, after being spat at. The film doesn't follow up on the implications of that, and because we can understand his rage, perhaps we let it go. But I feel the film should have either left out that memory or dealt with it. The soldier was wrong for the same reason the Holocaust was wrong.

The Holocaust is the most tragic and deadly outburst of the once useful, now dangerous, human trait of tribalism, in which we are right and you are wrong because we are we and you are not. In recent years in Serbia, in Africa, in Cambodia, in Northern Ireland, the epidemic is alive and well. Just the other day in Israel, Orthodox Jewish students booed and insulted visiting Reform rabbis who hoped to pray at the Western Wall, and the *New York Times* reported that some of the attackers "screamed that the rabbis should 'go back to Germany,' to be exterminated, one explained later." Any belief that does not allow others the right to believe something else is based more on fear than on faith. If that is not the lesson of the Holocaust, then what has been learned?

The Last Days of Disco ★ ★ ★ ½
R, 112 m., 1998

Chloe Sevigny (Alice), Kate Beckinsale (Charlotte), Chris Eigeman (Des), MacKenzie Astin (Jimmy), Matt Keeslar (Josh), Robert Sean Leonard (Tom), Jennifer Beals (Nina), Matthew Ross (Dan). Directed by Whit Stillman and produced by Edmon Roch and Cecilia Kate Roque. Screenplay by Stillman.

The Last Days of Disco is about people who *would* like to belong to the kinds of clubs that would accept them as members. It takes place in "the very early 1980s" in Manhattan, where a group of young, good-looking Ivy League graduates dance the night away in discos.

Unlike the characters in *Saturday Night Fever,* who were basically just looking for a good time, these upwardly mobile characters are alert to the markers of social status. *New York* magazine is their textbook, and being admitted to the right clubs is the passing grade.

The movie is the latest sociological romance by Whit Stillman *(Metropolitan, Barcelona),* who nails his characters with perfectly heard dialogue and laconic satire. His characters went to good schools, have good jobs, and think they're smarter than they are. "Alice, one of the things I've noticed is that people hate being criticized," says Charlotte, who seems quietly proud of this wisdom. They are capable of keeping a straight face while describing themselves as "adherents to the disco movement."

Alice (Chloe Sevigny, from *Kids*) is the smartest member of the crowd, and definitely the nicest. She has values. Her best friend, Charlotte (Kate Beckinsale), only has goals: to meet the right guys, to be popular, to do exactly what she imagines someone in her position should be doing. Both girls are regulars at a fashionable disco. Charlotte is forever giving poor Alice advice about what to say and how to behave; she says guys like it when a girl uses the word "sexy," and a few nights later, when a guy tells Alice he collects first editions of

Scrooge McDuck comic books, she faithfully observes that she has always found Uncle Scrooge sexy.

As the movie opens, a junior ad executive named Jimmy Steinway (MacKenzie Astin) has just failed to get his boss into the club (he was wearing a brown suit). Jimmy goes in anyway. Alice and Charlotte, working as a team (Charlotte is the coach), forcibly introduce themselves. During the opening scenes we meet other regulars, including Des (Christopher Eigeman), the floor manager, who gets rid of girls by claiming to be gay, and who has his doubts about the club's management ("To me, shipping cash to Switzerland in canvas bags doesn't sound legal"). Other regulars include Josh (Matthew Keeslar), who casually mentions that he's an assistant district attorney, and Tom (Robert Sean Leonard), who has a theory that "the environmental movement was spawned by the rerelease of *Bambi* in the late 1950s."

During the movie these people will date each other with various degrees of intensity. Charlotte's approach is to take no hostages; she invites the D.A. to dinner at a time when she doesn't even have an apartment, and then rents one. A real-estate agent explains the concept of a "railroad flat" to her (you have to walk through both bedrooms and the kitchen to get to the bathroom, but the flat has two hall doors, so the best way to get from the front to the back is to walk down the hall).

If Scott Fitzgerald were to return to life, he would feel at home in a Whit Stillman movie. Stillman listens to how people talk and knows what it reveals about them. His characters have been supplied by their Ivy League schools with the techniques but not the subjects of intelligent conversation, and so they discuss *Lady and the Tramp* with the kind of self-congratulatory earnestness that French students would reserve for Marx and Freud. (Their analysis of the movie is at least as funny as the Quentin Tarantino character's famous deconstruction of *Top Gun* in the movie *Sleep With Me.*)

Stillman has the patience to circle a punch line instead of leaping straight for it. He'll establish something in an early scene and then keep nibbling away until it delivers. The guy who dumps girls by claiming to be gay, for example, eventually explains that he always thought he was straight until, one day, he felt "something different" while watching Jim Fowler on *Wild Kingdom.*

The movie has barely enough plot to hold it together; it involves drugs and money laundering, but it's typical of Stillman that most of the suspense involves the young D.A. fretting about a romantic conflict of interest. The underlying tone of the film is sweet, fond, and a little sad: These characters believe the disco period was the most wonderful period of their lives, and we realize that it wasn't disco that was so special, but youth. They were young, they danced, they drank, they fell in love, they learned a few lessons, and the music of that time will always reawaken those emotions.

It's human nature to believe that if a club admits people like you, you will find the person you are looking for inside. The problem with that theory is that wherever you go, there you are. At the end of *The Last Days of Disco*, as the club scene fades, people are hired to stand outside and pretend they have been turned away. When they get off work, what clubs do they go to? So it goes.

Last Night ★ ★ ★
R, 93 m., 1999

Don McKellar (Patrick), Sandra Oh (Sandra), Callum Keith Rennie (Craig), Sarah Polley (Jennifer), David Cronenberg (Duncan), Tracy Wright (Donna), Genevieve Bujold (Mrs. Carlton), Roberta Maxwell (Patrick's Mother). Directed by Don McKellar and produced by Niv Fichman and Daniel Iron. Screenplay by McKellar.

I am writing in the closing days of December 1999. There are those who expect an apocalypse in a week or so, when Y2K shuts down the power grid and roving bands of carnivorous Americans stalk heavily armed into the streets to steal one another's Christmas presents. My own guess is that New Year's Eve will be more uneventful than usual, as most of us pause, awestruck, at the chiming of the millennium clock.

Don McKellar's *Last Night* is a Canadian film about the end of the world, and paints a picture more bittersweet than violent. While American fantasies run toward riot, rape, and pillage, life will end in Toronto, we learn, with

farewell dinners, favorite songs, and people deciding they have put off far too long their intention to sleep with one another.

The movie wisely offers no explanation for the coming apocalypse. All we know is that the world will end at midnight precisely, and that darkness never comes. As a soft, early evening twilight hangs late over the city, radio stations count down the 500 top songs of all time, revelers in a city square treat the event like New Year's Eve, and we meet a small group of people as they try to face the end with a certain grace and dignity.

One couple meets by accident. Sandra (Sandra Oh) is marooned in a distant part of the city with no way to get back for a planned final meal with her husband. She asks a stranger named Patrick (McKellar) for the use of his phone, but can't find her husband at home or his office. And she has lost her car. Now they sit there in his apartment, two strangers. He has planned to spend this evening alone. What is the etiquette for two people in a situation like this?

We meet other characters. One is Craig (Callum Keith Rennie), who has a rendezvous with his high school teacher (Genevieve Bujold). We sense they'd always been attracted to each other, but never acted on their impulses. Now years have passed and it is time to take care of unfinished business. Turns out Patrick knows Craig, and thinks perhaps he might loan Sandra a car. Craig protests that his cars are not just any cars, but valuable antiques. As if it makes a difference.

Downtown in an office building, an employee of the gas company (David Cronenberg) reassures customers their service will continue until the end. Elsewhere in town, a mother holds a Christmas dinner, since Christmas will not come, and gives her children the favorite toys she has saved for since they were children. Many of these characters turn out to be connected in one way or another.

Perhaps nothing tests our dignity more than how we behave when we know for certain the hour of our death. That knowledge must be the worst thing about being on death row—worse than the gallows itself. Better to die suddenly, or in oblivion. What makes life bearable is our personal conviction that we will never die—or at least, not yet.

As the final hour approaches for the characters in *Last Night*, there are moments of startling poignancy. Sandra and Patrick, for example, find themselves stranded together, their plans for the end interrupted. She suggests they tell each other the stories of their lives. He lists the usual biographical details. "You'd better hurry up," she tells him. "Tell me something to make me love you."

Note: On a talk show in Toronto, I was asked to define the difference between American and Canadian films, and said I could not. Another guest was Wayne Clarkson, the former director of the Toronto Film Festival. He said he could, and cited this film. "Sandra Oh goes into a grocery story to find a bottle of wine for dinner," he said. "The store has been looted, but she finds two bottles still on the shelf. She takes them down, evaluates them, chooses one, and puts the other one politely back on the shelf. That's how you know it's a Canadian film."

The Last September ★ ★
R, 104 m., 2000

Maggie Smith (Lady Myra), Michael Gambon (Sir Richard Naylor), Jane Birkin (Francie Montmorency), Fiona Shaw (Marda Norton), Lambert Wilson (Hugo Montmorency), David Tennant (Captain Gerald Colthurst), Richard Roxburgh (Daventry), Keeley Hawes (Lois Farquar), Gary Lydon (Peter Connolly). Directed by Deborah Warner and produced by Yvonne Thunder. Screenplay by John Banville, based on the novel by Elizabeth Bowen.

Years ago I visited one of the great country houses built by the Anglo-Irish in Ireland. It was Lissadell, the very one Yeats wrote about, its "great windows open to the south." The Gore-Booth family lived there; one of its daughters, Constance, Countess Markiewicz, was a leader in the Easter Rebellion of 1916, which marked the beginning of the Irish republic and the end for the Anglo-Irish. I went with an Irish friend whose family had grown up nearby. The tour was conducted by a distant relative of the family. As we left, my friend chortled all the way down the drive—that the gentry had so fallen that the son of a workingman could drop some coins in the collection pot near the door.

Deborah Warner's *The Last September* is set during the slow decline of the Anglo-Irish. It takes place in 1920 in county Cork, where Sir Richard Naylor and his wife, Lady Myra, preside over houseguests who uneasily try to enjoy themselves while the tide of Irish republicanism rises all around them. British Army troops patrol the roads and hedgerows, and Irish republicans raid police stations and pick off an occasional soldier. It is the time of the Troubles.

We meet the owners of the great house: pleasant and befuddled Sir Richard (Michael Gambon) and Lady Myra (Maggie Smith), a sharp and charming snob. She notices that her niece, Lois (Keeley Hawes), is sweet on Gerald Colthurst, a British captain (David Tennant), and warns her that, socially, the match won't do. It would be bad enough if the captain's parents were "in trade," but that at least would produce money; it is clear to Lady Myra that the suitor is too poor to afford thoughts of Lois.

Lois keeps her own thoughts to herself, and knows that Peter Connolly (Gary Lydon), a wanted Irish killer, is hiding in the ruined mill on their property. She brings him food, but he wants love, too, and she is not so sure about that—although she returns despite his roughness. Does she love either man? She is maddeningly vague about her feelings, and may simply be entertaining herself with their emotions.

Also visiting: Hugo and Francie Montmorency (Lambert Wilson and Jane Birkin), who have had to sell their place and become full-time guests, and Marda Norton (Fiona Shaw), a woman from London who is uncomfortably aware that she is approaching her sell-by date. She and Hugo were once lovers; she wouldn't marry him, Francie would, and now volumes go unspoken between them.

The weakness of the movie is that these characters are more important as types than as people. The two older women, Marda and Lady Myra, are the most vivid, the most sure of who they are. Hugo is an emasculated freeloader, and Captain Colthurst is a young man in love with infatuation. As for Connolly, the IRA man, he is a plot device.

The movie is based on a novel by Elizabeth Bowen, whose stories of London during the

Blitz capture the time and place exactly. She grew up at Bowen's Court, a country house in county Cork, was a member of an Anglo-Irish family, and would have been twenty-one in 1920—about the same age as Lois. But if Bowen modeled Lois on herself, she did herself no favor; Lois is bright and resourceful and likes attention, but is irresponsible and plays recklessly at a game that could lead to death.

The movie is elegantly mounted, and the house is represented in loving detail, although the opening scenes allow so much of the red-gold sunset to pour into the drawing room that we fear the conservatory is on fire. The tone is one of languid hedonism; life is pleasant for these people, who speak of themselves as Irish even though to the native Irish they are merely trespassers for the British empire. I'm not sure the movie should have pumped up the melodrama to get us more interested, but something might have helped.

Lawn Dogs ★ ½
R, 101 m., 1998

Mischa Barton (Devon), Sam Rockwell (Trent), Kathleen Quinlan (Clare), Christopher McDonald (Morton), Bruce McGill (Nash), Eric Mabius (Sean), David Barry Gray (Brett), Miles Meehan (Billy). Directed by John Duigan and produced by Duncan Kenworthy. Screenplay by Naomi Wallace.

John Duigan's *Lawn Dogs* is like a nasty accident at the symbol factory. Pieces are scattered all over the floor, as the wounded help each other to the exits. Some of the pieces look well made and could be recycled. We pick up a few of them, and put them together to see if they'll fit. But they all seem to come from different designs.

The movie isn't clear about what it's trying to say—what it wants us to believe when we leave. It has the form of a message picture, without the message. It takes place in an upscale Kentucky housing development named Camelot Gardens, where the $300,000 homes sit surrounded by big lawns and no trees. It's a gated community; the security guard warns one of the "lawn dogs"—or yard workers—to be out of town by 5:00 P.M.

In one of the new houses lives ten-year-old Devon (Mischa Barton), who has a scar running down her chest after heart surgery. Her insipid parents are Morton (Christopher McDonald) and Clare (Kathleen Quinlan). Morton plans to run for office. Clare has casual sex with local college kids. And Trent (Sam Rockwell) mows their lawn.

Devon is in revolt, although she doesn't articulate it as interestingly as the heroine of *Welcome to the Dollhouse.* She wanders beyond the gates, finds Trent's trailer home in the woods, and becomes his friend. There are unrealized undertones of sexuality in her behavior, which the movie never makes overt, except in the tricky scene where she asks Trent to touch her scar. He has a scar, too; here's a new version of you show me yours and I'll show you mine.

The people inside Camelot Gardens are all stupid pigs. That includes the security guard, the parents, and the college kids, who insult and bully Trent. Meanwhile, Trent and Devon spend idyllic afternoons in the woods, being friends, until there is a tragic misunderstanding that leads to the death of a dog and even more alarming consequences.

Nobody makes it into the movie just as an average person. Trent's dad is a Korean vet whose lungs were destroyed by microbes in the K rations, and who is trying to give away his American flag collection. Trent is the kind of guy who stops traffic on a one-lane bridge while he strips, dives into the river, and walks back to his pickup boldly nude. Devon is the kind of little girl who crawls out onto her roof, throws her nightgown into the sky, and utters wild dog cries at the Moon.

All of these events happen with the precision and vivid detail of a David Lynch movie, but I do not know why. It is easy to make a film about people who are pigs and people who are free spirits, but unless you show how or why they got that way, they're simply characters you've created. It's easy to have Devon say, "I don't like kids—they smell like TV." But what does this mean when a ten-year-old says it? It's easy to show good people living in trailers and awful people living in nice homes, but it can work out either way. It's easy to write about a father who wants his little girl to have plastic surgery so her scar won't turn off boys, and then a boy who thinks it's "cool." But where is it leading? What is it saying? Camelot Gardens is a hideous place to live. So? Get out as fast as you can.

The Leading Man ★ ★ ★
R, 96 m., 1998

Jon Bon Jovi (Robin Grange), Lambert Wilson (Felix Webb), Anna Galiena (Elena Webb), Thandie Newton (Hilary Rule), Barry Humphries (Humphrey Beal), David Warner (Tod), Patricia Hodge (Delvene), Diana Quick (Susan). Directed by John Duigan and produced by Bertil Ohlsson and Paul Raphael. Screenplay by Virginia Duigan.

The Leading Man begins as a backstage story about the London theater world, and then a little Hitchcockian intrigue edges into the frame. The movie's about "Britain's greatest living playwright," a bedeviled middle-aged man with a wife and a mistress, both angry with him. A Hollywood sex symbol, who is starring in his new play, offers to solve all his problems by seducing the wife.

This is a little like Hitchcock's setup in *Strangers on a Train,* where an outsider sees a need and volunteers to meet it—at a price. The neat trick in *The Leading Man* is that we never quite understand the movie star's complete plan. Why is he doing this (apart from getting the husband's license to seduce the wife?). What else does he have in mind?

The movie star, Robin Grange, is played by the rock musician Jon Bon Jovi, who is convincing as a man who is completely confident of his ability to seduce any woman, anywhere, anytime. Like Richard Gere, he has a way of looking at a woman as if they're both thinking the same thing. The playwright, Felix Webb (Lambert Wilson), is one of those men for whom romantic intrigue is hardly worth the trouble: His wife is bitter at his treatment of his family, and his mistress is tired of listening to his promises about how someday, very soon, he will leave his wife. He can't be happy anywhere.

Felix's problems come to a boil during rehearsals for his new play, which stars both Robin and Hilary (Thandie Newton), his mistress. It also stars two dependable British vet-

erans, played by David Warner and Patricia Hodge, who have seen backstage affairs before, and will see them again, and simply turn up to do their jobs. (While the younger actors are doing nervous deep-breathing exercises before the curtain goes up, Warner's character listens to cricket and plays solitaire.)

The playwright could be leading a very happy life. He has a big, old house on the banks of the Thames, down from Hammersmith Bridge, where his happy children play in the garden while his wife, Elena (Anna Galiena), steeps in resentment (one night as he sleeps she takes a scissors and chops off his famous forelock). Elena is younger than Felix, and Hilary is younger still, living with roommates who race out to dance clubs and are amused by the fogey she has taken into her bed. But here's a twist: The young girl is steadfast and sincere in her love for him, and not portrayed as a flirt or a siren.

Robin, the American, quickly sees what Felix thinks is a secret, his affair with his leading lady. Robin makes the great man an offer: He will seduce Elena, clearing the field. "It would be doing a favor for a friend," he explains. "Besides, I've seen her photographs. She's a beautiful woman."

So she is, and a faithful one, up to a point. But Robin studies his quarry carefully, making lists of the books she reads and the music she listens to (these details are not very convincing), and discovering her own secret—she is also a playwright, but her writing is hidden in the shadow of Felix's great reputation. He can help her, but is something sinister concealed in Robin's helpfulness? Robin is also growing closer to his costar, Hilary. Does he plan to take both women away from the playwright? And what about the gun he likes to play with?

The film, directed by John Duigan and written by his sister Virginia, is completely familiar with its showbiz world. Virginia is married to the director Bruce Beresford, and Duigan himself has long been linked romantically with Newton, whom he directed in the wonderful film *Flirting* (1992). Little biographical details—like Newton's degree from Oxford—are lifted from life.

But the climax does not, I'm afraid, do justice to the setup. Hitchcock, having brought the gun and the matching love triangles onstage, would have delivered. Still, Duigan keeps us interested right up to the overwrought final developments, and his portrait of the London theater world is wry and perceptive. The way he uses the actor Barry Humphries as the director of Felix's play, and Warner and Hodge as the seasoned pros, adds a certain ironic perspective to all the heavy breathing in the foreground.

The Legend of 1900 ★ ★ ½
R, 110 m., 1999

Tim Roth (1900), Pruitt Taylor Vince (Max), Bill Nunn (Danny Boodmann), Clarence Williams III (Jelly Roll Morton), Melanie Thierry (The Girl), Cory Buck (Younger 1900), Easton Gage (Youngest 1900). Directed by Giuseppe Tornatore and produced by Francesco Tornatore. Screenplay by Giuseppe Tornatore, based on a dramatic monologue by Alessandro Baricco.

Because life is at such hazard, we value those who lead their lives all in one place, doing one thing. Such continuity is reassuring. We are buffeted by the winds of fate, but the Trappist tills his field and the blacksmith stands beneath his tree. There is a certain charm in the notion of a man who is born on board an ocean liner and never gets off. He does not move, yet is never still.

The man's full name is Danny Boodmann T. D. Lemon 1900. That is because as a squawling infant he was discovered on the luxury liner *Virginian* by a man named Boodmann, in a lemon box, in the year 1900. He is raised in the engine room, his cradle swaying as the ship rolls, and as an adult plays piano in the ship's lounge. And what piano! So great is his fame that even the great Jelly Roll Morton comes on board for a duel.

1900 is played as an adult by Tim Roth, he of the sad eyes and rueful grin. Night after night he sits at his keyboard, as crews change and ports slip behind. His best friend is Max (Pruitt Taylor Vince), a trumpet player in the ship's orchestra, and his story is told through Max's eyes. It begins almost at the end, when Max finds an old wax recording in an antique shop and recognizes it as 1900's love melody to the only woman who almost got him to leave the ship.

The movie has been directed by Giuseppe Tornatore, whose *Cinema Paradiso* was much beloved in 1988. Like a lot of European directors, he despairs of ever finding large American audiences with subtitles, and shot this movie in English. (Europeans do not object to dubbing.) *The Legend of 1900* nevertheless seems mournfully, romantically Italian, and could be an opera. There is something heroic about a man whose whole life is ruled by the fixed idea that he must not step foot on dry land.

There is also something pigheaded and a little goofy. That side of 1900 seems to lurk just out of sight in scenes like the one where he and Jelly Roll pound out tunes in what seems more like a test of speed and volume than musicianship. We sense, as 1900 plays, that he loves music less than himself—that he is defending not his ability as a pianist but his decision to stay on the ship: See, he seems to be saying, I never went to New Orleans and yet look at my fingers fly.

Decades come and go. Fashions change. 1900 remains steadfast even during the war. Then one day something happens to stir him to his fundament. A woman comes on board. The Girl, for so she is called, is played by Melanie Thierry as an angelic vision who never pauses on the deck unless she is perfectly framed by a porthole directly in the sight line of the moody pianist. It is true love. It must be: It gets him halfway down the gangplank.

There is a mystery to an ocean liner. It is vast, yet self-contained. It has secrets, but they can be discovered. Somewhere even today, hidden on the *Norway*, which used to be the *France*, is a private first-class courtyard. You can find it. 1900 is the secret of the *Virginian*, whose shadows and secret passages he haunts like the hunchback of Notre Dame or the phantom of the opera.

His story was originally written not as a screenplay or a novel, but as a dramatic monologue by Alessandro Barrico. The film has inevitably been compared to *Titanic*, but has more in common with the little-known French film *A Chambermaid on the Titanic* (1997), about a man who wins a free ticket on the *Titanic*. The night before sailing, he is seduced by a woman who says she works on the ship. Does she? Or does she only want to steal his ticket? The monologue he makes of his experience grows in popularity until he has to perform it professionally. You see how ships can make us storytellers.

The Legend of 1900 has moments of great imagination: a scene, for example, where the piano rolls back and forth across the polished dance floor in a storm, and 1900 keeps on playing. But it never quite develops the conviction we expect. What does it think of this man? Is he crazy or heroic? Nice or narcissistic? At the end we are left with Max the trumpet player, treasuring the sound of an old recording and assuring the antique dealer that this was some kinduva guy. Yes, but what kinduva guy? And why?

Les Miserables ★ ★ ½

PG-13, 129 m., 1998

Liam Neeson (Valjean), Geoffrey Rush (Javert), Uma Thurman (Fantine), Claire Danes (Cosette), Hans Matheson (Marius). Directed by Bille August and produced by Sarah Radclyffe and James Gorman. Screenplay by Rafael Yglesias, based on the novel *Les Miserables* by Victor Hugo.

Les Miserables is like a perfectly respectable Classics Illustrated version of the Victor Hugo novel. It contains the moments of high drama, clearly outlines all the motivations, is easy to follow, and lacks only passion. A story filled with outrage and idealism becomes somehow merely picturesque.

Liam Neeson stars as Jean Valjean, and the movie makes its style clear in an early scene where he stands, homeless and hungry, at the door of a bishop, and says: "I am a convict. My name is Jean Valjean. I spent nineteen years at hard labor. On my passport I am identified as a thief." And so on. "I know who you are," replies the bishop, but not before the audience has been spoon-fed its briefing. Valjean is taken in, fed and sheltered, and tries to steal the bishop's silver. In one of the most famous episodes from Hugo's novel, the bishop tells the police he *gave* the tramp the silver, and later tells Valjean: "I've ransomed you from fear and hatred and now I give you back to God." There was a similar scene in Claude Lelouch's 1995 *Les Miserables,* which intercut passages from the novel with a story set during World War II; it was touching, but this version feels more like a morality play.

Valjean sells the silver, gets a job in a provincial factory, and uses the nest egg to buy the factory. As we rejoin him some years later, he is the local mayor, respectable and beloved, trying to teach himself to read and write. Then fate reenters his life in the person of Inspector Javert (Geoffrey Rush), a police official who recognizes him from his years at hard labor and wants to expose him: In this world, if you once do something wrong, you are banished forever from the sight of those lucky enough not to have been caught.

Consider, in the same light, poor Fantine (Uma Thurman), fired from the factory and forced into prostitution because it is discovered she has a child out of wedlock. Valjean discovers her plight (he was unaware of the firing), nurses her through a fatal illness, and promises to care for the child. Thurman's performance is the best element of the movie.

With the unyielding Javert forever at his back, Valjean takes his money and flees to Paris, taking refuge in a convent he had once (foresightedly) given money to. There he and the child, Cosette, spend ten years. Then Cosette, now a young woman played by Claire Danes, yearns for freedom; Valjean, against his better wisdom, takes a house for them. Cosette falls for the fiery radical Marius (Hans Matheson), who is being tailed by the police, which puts Javert once more onto the trail of poor Valjean.

Javert is the kind of man who can say with his dying breath, "I've tried to lead my life without breaking a single rule." He means it, and will never cease his pursuit of Valjean, even though the other man, as mayor, spared his job: "I order you to forgive yourself." As Javert pursues his vendetta against a man who has become kind and useful, Marius leads the mobs to the barricades, which look a lot here as they do in the stage musical.

That musical, by the way, is a long time coming. This is the second movie made of *Les Mis* during a decade when the "musical version" has been promised annually. There is, I think, an obvious person to direct it: Alan Parker, whose *Evita* and *Pink Floyd the Wall* show he is one of the few modern filmmakers who understands musicals. In the meantime, this dramatic version is by the Danish director

Bille August, whose work *(Pelle the Conqueror, The Best Intentions* from the Bergman screenplay, *The House of the Spirits)*, while uneven, has shown a juiciness and complexity.

Here we have a dutiful, even respectable, adaptation that lacks the rabble-rousing usually associated with *Les Miserables.* The sets and locations are handled well, the period looks convincing, but the story is lame. When Cosette pleads with her father to leave the convent, she sounds more like a bored modern teenager than a survivor of murderous times. ("Don't leave the cab!" he tells her on their first venture into the world, so of course she immediately does.)

Her father could, of course, settle all her objections with a few words of explanation, but in the great movie tradition of senselessly withholding crucial information, he refuses to; it must have been difficult for Neeson to maintain that expression of fearful regret in scene after scene. Rush, in his first major role since *Shine,* somehow doesn't project the fevered ethical madness that drives Javert; he comes across more as a very stubborn bore.

It's hard to make a period picture come alive, but when it happens *(Restoration, Dangerous Beauty, Amistad)* we feel transported back in time. *Les Miserables* only made me feel transported back to high school history class.

Lethal Weapon 4 ★ ★
R, 128 m., 1998

Mel Gibson (Martin Riggs), Danny Glover (Roger Murtaugh), Joe Pesci (Leo Getz), Rene Russo (Lorna Cole), Chris Rock (Lee Butters), Steve Kahan (Captain Travis). Directed by Richard Donner and produced by Donner and Joel Silver. Screenplay by Channing Gibson, Jonathan Lemkin, Alfred Gough, and Miles Millar.

Lethal Weapon 4 has all the technical skill of the first three movies in the series, but lacks the secret weapon, which was conviction. All four movies take two cop buddies and put them into spectacular and absurd action sequences, but the first three at least went through the motions of taking the plot seriously (and the first one did such a good job it made my "best 10" list). This time, we're watching an exercise.

Mel Gibson and Danny Glover star once again, as Riggs and Murtaugh, two cops who alternate between nonstop banter and dangerous action. Along the way, they've picked up a supporting cast: Leo Getz (Joe Pesci), the obnoxious but lovable accountant who joined them in the second film; Lorna Cole (Rene Russo), the Internal Affairs investigator and karate expert who came aboard in the third; Captain Travis (Steve Kahan), their long-suffering commanding officer; and, new this time, Lee Butters (Chris Rock), the cop who is secretly married to Murtaugh's pregnant daughter.

Most action movies don't stop for dialogue, but the *Lethal Weapon* pictures have always had a soft spot for human comedy, and there's a lot of repartee in this movie, some of it funny, as when Murtaugh and Riggs debate whether to take another deadly chance or not. There's a scene where they all wind up inhaling laughing gas in a dentist's office, and it works, too, but other dialogue scenes are just mechanical exercises: characters talking as if oblivious to danger.

The other trademark of the series is its spectacular special effects and stunt sequences. Here there's a brilliant freeway chase that involves a mobile home and a long sheet of plastic that drags Gibson behind it down the highway. Also one of those obligatory self-contained opening sequences (man in armor sprays city with flame-thrower and automatic rifle fire, is distracted by Murtaugh in underwear while Riggs shoots his fuel tank and he jets into a gas truck, etc.). And a climax in one of those factory spaces that seems to manufacture mostly water and steam.

The plot is so impenetrable that at one point the dialogue simply stops to explain it: A corrupt Chinese general has brought the Four Fathers of organized crime to the United States, and the Triads are trying to buy them back with counterfeit money. Yes. And that also involves a shipload of Chinese slave laborers, which is intercepted by Murtaugh, Riggs, and Getz, and Murtaugh ends up adopting one of the refugee families. Oh, and there's a sequence where all of the good guys are tied up on the floor of a burning house. And an underwater fight and rescue. And so on.

All done very well, you understand. Richard Donner is a master of what might be called elevated action. Martial arts fans will enjoy a newcomer named Jet Li, who has a lot of neat moves. And there are parallel pregnancies to create human interest, and a switch on the obligatory scene where the captain calls the rogue cops on the carpet: to control them, he tries promoting them.

But somehow it's all kind of hollow. By the numbers. I really did care for Murtaugh and Riggs in the first movie—and Leo, the Pesci character, was so much fun in the second one, he deserved an Oscar nomination. There was human interest in all the family scenes (especially involving Murtaugh's concern for his wife and kids), and poignancy in Riggs's lonely widower status. But all that has already happened by the beginning of this movie, and in a funny sense I felt like *Lethal Weapon 4* was outtakes—stuff they didn't use earlier, pieced together into a movie that doesn't really, in its heart, believe it is necessary.

Let's Talk About Sex ★
R, 82 m., 1998

Troy Beyer (Jazz), Paget Brewster (Michelle), Randi Ingerman (Lena), Joseph C. Phillips (Michael), Michaline Babich (Morgan), Tina Nguyen (Drew). Directed by Troy Beyer and produced by Deborah Ridpath. Screenplay by Beyer.

It's hard to feel much sympathy for the heroine of *Let's Talk About Sex*, as she regards the wreckage of her dreams. Jazz (Troy Beyer) is a newspaper advice columnist in Miami who wants her own TV show, and the movie is about a very long weekend during which she interviews lots of women about lots of sex, and then edits together a pilot of a show to be called "Girl Talk."

Alas, the pilot tape is mistakenly destroyed. When Jazz hears the news, she is as distraught as a heroine in Greek tragedy. She doubles up in pain. Her body is wracked by great, cataclysmic sobs. Her two friends weep in sympathy, the three of them wailing and gnashing. So great is their grief that mere words cannot encompass it, and they sink to the ultimate form of lamentation: They clean house. Bitter salt tears course down their cheeks as they Ajax the bathtub and Bab-O the pots and

pans, while the audience collapses in disbelieving laughter.

Jazz's reaction seems a tad extreme, especially in comparison with her other big tearful moment, when she confesses she cannot have children. That merely makes her sob. Losing the tape turns her into Lady Macbeth. She was so distraught I wanted to climb right up there on the screen, squeeze her hand, and comfort her. "Look," I would have said, "first of all, you still have all the raw footage, so you can easily re-create the film in no time. Second, almost everything you had on your pilot tape is too raunchy to be played on a commercial television station anyway, so maybe it's better this way."

Let's Talk About Sex, written and directed by Beyer, plays like two bad films trying to elbow each other out of the frame. Film One consists of the documentary footage gathered by Jazz and her friends as they ask Miami Beach women to talk about sex (a lot of this footage seems to involve real women who think they are in a real documentary). Film Two involves the romantic ordeals of Jazz and her two roommates, Michelle (Paget Brewster) and Lena (Randi Ingerman).

They all have problems. Jazz has just broken off a long-running engagement with her boyfriend. Michelle dates men for sex but not for intimacy. Lena attracts men who treat her the way Michelle treats men. All three women are drop-dead beautiful and live in a Miami Beach penthouse that illustrates the rule that characters in movies always live in more expensive housing than they could afford in real life.

Leaving aside the melodrama about the three friends (and the sub-melodramas of Michelle's lesbian sister and Lena's no-good musician boyfriend), we're left with a lot of footage of very strange women describing their very strange sex lives. The movie shows the women being recruited with fliers, but they talk more like they're involved in a slam at Penthouse Forum. It's enlightening to learn you can practice for deep throat by using antiseptic throat spray and a cucumber, but even in the post-Monica age, the audience for this information must be finite.

Few of the interviews will give male audience members even a shred of hope that they will ever succeed in truly pleasing a female. We learn that men are uncaring, unskilled, and underequipped; worse, we go to sleep after sex, when women know that's the perfect time for deep, meaningful conversation. Remember that old college boy joke about how, after sex, the ideal women turns into a pizza and a six-pack? In this movie, the ideal man turns into a vibrator and Ted Koppel.

L'Humanite ★ ★ ★ ½
NO MPAA RATING, 148 m., 2000

Emmanuel Schotte (Pharaon De Winter), Severine Caneele (Domino), Philippe Tullier (Joseph), Ghislain Ghesquiere (Commandant), Ginette Allegre (Eliane). Directed by Bruno Dumont and produced by Rachid Bouchareb and Jean Brehat. Screenplay by Dumont.

Bruno Dumont's *L'Humanite* has the outer form of a police movie, but much more inside. It is not about a murder, but about the policeman in charge of the investigation. It asks us to empathize with the man's deepest feelings. I saw the film a week after *Shaft*. Both films are about cops driven to the edge of madness by a brutal crime. *Shaft* is about the story; *L'Humanite* is about the character.

It is not an easy film and is for those few moviegoers who approach a serious movie almost in the attitude of prayer. A great film, like a real prayer, is about the relationship of a man to his hopes and fate.

The man this time is named Pharaon De Winter. He is played by Emmanuel Schotte as a man so seized up with sadness and dismay that his face is a mask, animated by two hopeless eyes. He lives on a dull street in a bleak French town. Nothing much happens. He once had a woman and a child, and lost them. We know nothing else about them. He lives with his mother, who treats him like a boy. Domino (Severine Caneele) lives next door. She has an intense physical relationship with her lover, Joseph, that gives her no soul satisfaction. It is impossible to guess if Joseph even knows what that is.

There is a scene where Pharaon walks in as they are making love, and regards them silently. Their lovemaking is not erotic or tender, but just a matter of plumbing arrangements. Domino sees him standing in the doorway.

Later she asks him, "Get an eyeful?" He mumbles a lame excuse. She says something hurtful and leaves. Then she returns, touches him lightly, and says, "I'm sorry." When she leaves again, he pumps his fists in the air with joy.

Why? Because he loves her or wants her? It isn't that simple. He is like those children or animals who go mad from lack of touching and affection. His sadness as he watched them was not because he wanted sex, but because they were getting nothing out of it. His joy was because she touched him and indicated that she knew how he felt, and that she had hurt him.

He is a policeman, but he has no confidence or authority. The opening shots show him running in horror from a brutal murder scene, and falling inarticulate on the cold mud. He tells his chief how upset he is by the crime. He doesn't have the chops to be a cop. He watches a giant truck race dangerously through the narrow lanes of the little town, and then exchanges a sad shrug with the old lady across the street. His police car is right there, but he doesn't give chase.

His relationship with Domino and Joseph is agonizing. He goes along with them on their dates for sad reasons: He has nothing else to do, they have nothing to talk about with each other, he's no trouble. Because Joseph is the dominant personality, he enjoys flaunting the law in front of Pharaon, who is so cowed he can't or won't stop him. There's a scene with the three of them in a car, Joseph speeding and running stop signs and Pharaon impotently saying he shouldn't. Domino listens, neutral. And a scene where Joseph behaves piggishly to bystanders, and Pharaon is passive. The dynamic is: Joseph struts so that Domino can observe that he is more of a man than Pharaon the cop. Pharaon implodes with self-loathing.

The murder investigation continues, sending Pharaon to England and to an insane asylum. His efforts are not really crucial to the solution of the case. In a way, the rape and death of the girl at the beginning is connected with his feelings for Domino—because she offers him sex (in a friendly way) and he cannot separate her body from the memory of the victim in the field. The rapist has taken away Pharaon's ability to see women in a holy light.

The movie is long and seemingly slow. The

actors' faces can be maddening. We wait for something to happen, and then realize, something *is* happening—*this* is happening. In the spiritual desert of a dead small town, murder causes this cop to question the purpose of his life. Eventually he goes a little mad (notice the way he sniffs at the possible drug dealer).

The film won the Grand Jury Prize at the 1999 Cannes Film Festival; Emmanuel Schotte won as Best Actor, and Severine Caneele shared the Best Actress Award. On stage, Schotte seemed as closed-off as in the film. Perhaps Bruno Dumont cast him the way Robert Bresson sometimes cast actors—as figures who did not need to "act" because they embodied what he wanted to communicate.

The Cannes awards were not popular. Well, the movie is not "popular." It is also not entirely successful, perhaps because Dumont tried for more than he could achieve, but I was moved to see how much he was trying. This is a film about a man whose life gives him no source of joy, and denies him the consolation of ignorance. He misses, and he knows he misses. He has the willingness of a saint, but not the gift. He would take the suffering of the world on his shoulders, but he is not man enough. The film is not perfect but the character outlives it, and you will not easily forget him.

Liberty Heights ★ ★ ★ ½
R, 122 m., 1999

Adrien Brody (Van), Ben Foster (Ben), Rebekah Johnson (Sylvia), Carolyn Murphy (Dubbie), Joe Mantegna (Nate), Orlando Jones (Little Melvin), Bebe Neuwirth (Ada), David Krumholtz (Yussel), Richard Kline (Charlie), Vincent Guastaferro (Pete). Directed by Barry Levinson and produced by Levinson and Paula Weinstein. Screenplay by Levinson.

Baltimore, 1955. Integration is the law of the land, and none too soon for Ben Kurtzman and his best pals, who are freshmen in high school. They regard the sign outside a municipal swimming pool: "No Jews, dogs, or colored." Dogs they understand. They ask themselves why Jews are listed first, and decide it's because "you never see any colored at the beach, so it must be directed mainly at Jews." Not

deep, analytical thinking, but they are distracted by the girls on the other side of the chain-link fence, their plump bits displayed in frilly bathing suits. This will be a year of discovery for Ben, and by the time it is over, he will understand more about Negroes, Jews, segregation, and himself.

Ben (Ben Foster) has been raised in a neighborhood so Jewish that when he is offered the gentile staff of life, Wonder Bread, he looks at it in amazement: "I've never seen raw bread before. We toast it." At school, he is interested in Sylvia (Rebekah Johnson), an African-American girl whose presence in their classroom is an aftershock from the earthquake of *Brown vs. the Board of Education.* The morning begins with the recitation of the Twenty-third Psalm, and Ben notices that Sylvia closes her eyes and really seems to be praying, and that touches him.

Liberty Heights understands in that scene an important element of adolescent romance: It can be based more on idealism than lust. Yes, in locker rooms teenage boys make crude remarks about girls. But in their hearts the girl they idealize is perfect, blessed, the embodiment of their most fervent desire (which is to be noticed and loved by the girl they have chosen for sainthood). Ben thinks Sylvia is "pretty attractive," he tells his mother, who is stopped in her tracks that her son would say this of a Negro girl: "Just kill me now!" Ben backtracks: "I said she was attractive. That doesn't mean that I'm necessarily attracted to her."

But he is. Yet *Liberty Heights* is not so much about romance, interracial or otherwise, as about coming of age and finding your own two feet in the world. Ben's older brother, Van (Adrien Brody), is also in love, with a gentile girl he has seen at a party. She is Dubbie (Carolyn Murphy), a blond Cinderella to his eyes, and he spends much energy trying to get an introduction through a WASP friend. Will either Van or Ben end up marrying a girl who is not Jewish? Not the point. The point is that the residential and social segregation that raised walls between all of Baltimore's communities is coming to an end.

Liberty Heights is the fourth of Barry Levinson's films set in his hometown of Baltimore (the others are *Diner, Tin Men,* and *Avalon*). He makes big Hollywood films *(Rain Man,*

Sphere, Good Morning, Vietnam) and then he makes these more personal Baltimore pieces, and you can feel the love and nostalgia in them.

I assume the character of Ben is based on Levinson himself, or someone he knew very well. The best thing about Ben is that he doesn't know then what we all know now. The movie doesn't give itself the benefit of hindsight: It remembers the racial divides of forty-five years ago, but it also remembers the innocence of a time when a high school freshman would probably not have smoked, would know nothing of drugs, would have little sexual experience, would be big-eyed with wonder at the unfolding world.

For me, the truest scene is the one where Ben goes over to Sylvia's house and they listen to Redd Foxx records (probably her father's). In the time just before rock 'n' roll broke loose, it was not so much music as comedy albums that spoke to young teenagers of freedom, risk, and daring. That scene ends with Sylvia's father, a doctor, coming home early, and Ben hiding in the closet. The doctor's conversation with the closed closet door is funny and terrifying at the same time.

We meet Ben's parents, Nate and Ada (Joe Mantegna and Bebe Neuwirth), and the rest of his family. We see family dinners interrupted by mysterious phone calls. "What does Dad *do?*" asks one of the kids. Mantegna runs a burlesque house and a numbers game, yet is a good provider and faithful family man, and scrupulously honest—so honest that he risks losing everything when a lowlife named Little Melvin (Orlando Jones) wins a $100,000 lottery that Nate unwisely tacked on top of the numbers payoff in the expectation that no one would ever get lucky.

One of the film's best sequences involves a sort of date that Sylvia and Ben go on, separately. A young singer named James Brown is playing at the Royal, and both kids want to see him. They dare not go as a couple. So they both go with their best friends, sitting a few rows apart, loving the music, happy to be in the same balcony together.

The film leads to a final scene that is one of those perfect public displays of poetic justice. I didn't quite believe it, but I'm glad it was there anyway, especially in the way it plays against the parents without making them the bad guys.

The film has some weaknesses. I thought the Little Melvin character was too broadly drawn, and I thought the whole subplot about how he tries to collect his winnings could not unfold as it does here. (The Mantegna character comes across not merely as a nice guy, but positively Gandhi-like.) But those flaws are not fatal, and the movie emerges as an accurate memory of that time when the American melting pot, splendid as a theory, became a reality.

Life ★ ★ ★
R, 100 m., 1999

Eddie Murphy (Ray Gibson), Martin Lawrence (Claude Banks), Obba Babatunde (Willie Long), Ned Beatty (Dexter Wilkins), Bernie Mac (Jangle Leg), Rick James (Spanky), Miguel A. Nunez Jr. (Biscuit), Clarence Williams III (Winston Hancock), Bokeem Woodbine (Can't Get Right). Directed by Ted Demme and produced by Brian Grazer and Eddie Murphy. Screenplay by Robert Ramsey and Matthew Stone.

Eddie Murphy and Martin Lawrence age more than fifty years in *Life,* the story of two New Yorkers who spend their adult lives on a Mississippi prison farm because of some very bad luck. It's an odd, strange film—a sentimental comedy with a backdrop of racism—and I kept thinking of *Life Is Beautiful,* another film that skirts the edge of despair. *Life Is Beautiful* avoids it through comic inspiration, and *Life* by never quite admitting how painful its characters' lives must really have been.

The movie is ribald, funny, and sometimes sweet, and very well acted by Murphy, Lawrence, and a strong supporting cast. And yet the more you think about it, the more peculiar it seems. Murphy created the original story line, and Ted Demme *(The Ref)* follows his lead; the result is a film that almost seems nostalgic about what must have been a brutal existence. When was the last time a movie made prison seem almost pleasant?

Life opens in 1932 in a Harlem nightclub, with a chance encounter between a bank teller named Claude (Lawrence) and a pickpocket named Ray (Murphy). They both find themselves in big trouble with Spanky, the club owner (Rick James), who is in the process of drowning Claude when Ray saves both their lives by talking them into a job: They'll drive a truck to Mississippi and pick up a load of moonshine.

The trip takes them into Jim Crow land, where Claude is outspoken and Ray more cautious in a segregated diner that serves "white-only pie." Then they find the moonshiner, load the truck, and allow themselves to get distracted by a local sin city, where Ray loses all his money to a cheat (Clarence Williams III) and Claude goes upstairs with a good-time girl. The cheat is found dead and Claude and Ray are framed by the sheriff who actually killed him, and given life in prison.

The early scenes move well (although why was it necessary to send all the way to Mississippi for moonshine, when New York was awash in bootleg booze during Prohibition?). The heart of the movie, however, takes place in prison, where after an early scene of hard physical labor, life settles down into baseball games, talent shows, and even, at one point, a barbecue. Bokeem Woodbine plays Can't Get Right, a retarded prisoner who hits a homer every time at the plate, and Ray and Claude become his managers, hoping to get a free ride out of prison when he's recruited by the Negro Leagues.

But it doesn't work that way, and life goes on, decade after decade, while the real world is only hearsay. Demme has two nice touches for showing the passage of time: Prison inmates are shown simply fading from the screen, and in the early 1970s Claude gets to drive the warden (Ned Beatty) into nearby Greenville, where he sees hippie fashions and his first Afro. Meanwhile, Rick Baker's makeup gradually and convincingly ages the two men, who do a skillful job of aging their voices and manners.

All of this time, of course, they dream of escaping. And they maintain the fiction that they don't get along, although in fact they've grown close over the years (comparisons with *The Shawshank Redemption* are inevitable). Ray remains the realist and compromiser, and Claude remains more hotheaded; the warden

likes them both, and eventually assigns them to his house staff.

But what are we to make of their long decades together? That without the unjust prison term, they would never have had the opportunity to enjoy such a friendship? That prison life has its consolations? That apart from that unfortunate lifetime sentence, the white South was actually pretty decent to the two friends? *Life* simply declines to deal with questions like that, and the story makes it impossible for them to be answered. It's about friendship, I guess, and not social issues.

Murphy and Lawrence are so persuasive in the movie that maybe audiences will be carried along. Their characters are likable, their performances are touching, they age well, they survive. And their lives consist of episodes and anecdotes that make good stories—as when the white superintendent's daughter has a black baby, and the super holds the kid up next to every convict's face, looking for the father. That's a comic scene in the movie; real life might have been different. But life flows along and we get in the mood, and by the end we're happy to see the two old-timers enjoying their retirement. After all, they've earned it.

Life Is Beautiful ★ ★ ★ ½
PG-13, 114 m., 1998

Roberto Benigni (Guido), Nicoletta Braschi (Dora), Giorgio Cantarini (Giosue), Giustino Durano (Zio), Sergio Bustric (Ferruccio), Marisa Paredes (Dora's Mother), Horst Buchholz (Doctor Lessing), Lydia Alfonsi (Guicciardini). Directed by Roberto Benigni and produced by Elda Ferri and Gianluigi Braschi. Screenplay by Vincenzo Cerami and Benigni.

Some people become clowns; others have clownhood thrust upon them. It is impossible to regard Roberto Benigni without imagining him as a boy in school, already a cut-up, using humor to deflect criticism and confuse his enemies. He looks goofy, and knows how he looks. I saw him once in a line at airport customs, subtly turning a roomful of tired and impatient travelers into an audience for a subtle pantomime in which he was the weariest and most put-upon. We had to smile.

Life Is Beautiful is the role he was born to play. The film falls into two parts. One is pure comedy. The other smiles through tears. Benigni, who also directed and cowrote the movie, stars as Guido, a hotel waiter in Italy in the 1930s. Watching his adventures, we are reminded of Chaplin.

He arrives in town in a runaway car whose brakes have failed, and is mistaken for a visiting dignitary. He falls in love instantly with the beautiful Dora (Nicoletta Braschi, Benigni's wife). He becomes the undeclared rival of her fiancé, the fascist town clerk. He makes friends with the German doctor (Horst Buchholz), who is a regular guest at the hotel and shares his love of riddles. And by the fantastic manipulation of carefully planned coincidences, he makes it appear that he is fated to replace the dour fascist in Dora's life.

All of this early material, the first long act of the movie, is comedy—much of it silent comedy involving the fate of a much-traveled hat. Only well into the movie do we even learn the crucial information that Guido is Jewish. Dora, a gentile, quickly comes to love him, and in one scene even conspires to meet him on the floor under a banquet table; they kiss, and she whispers, "Take me away!" In the town, Guido survives by quick improvisation. Mistaken for a school inspector, he invents a quick lecture on Italian racial superiority, demonstrating the excellence of his big ears and superb navel.

Several years pass, offscreen. Guido and Dora are married, and dote on their five-year-old son, Giosue (Giorgio Cantarini). In 1945, near the end of the war, the Jews in the town are rounded up by the fascists and shipped by rail to a death camp. Guido and Giosue are loaded into a train, and Guido instinctively tries to turn it into a game, to comfort his son; he makes a big show of being terrified that somehow they will miss the train and be left behind. Dora, not Jewish, would be spared by the fascists, but insists on coming along to be with her husband and family.

In the camp, Guido constructs an elaborate fiction to comfort his son and protect his life. It is all an elaborate game, he explains. The first one to get 1,000 points will win a tank—not a toy tank but a real one, which Giosue can drive all over town. Guido acts as the translator for a German who is barking orders

at the inmates, freely translating them into Italian designed to quiet his son's fears. And he literally hides the child from the camp guards, with rules of the game that have the boy crouching on a high sleeping platform and remaining absolutely still.

Benigni told me at the Toronto festival that the movie has stirred up venomous opposition from the right wing in Italy. At Cannes, it offended some left-wing critics with its use of humor in connection with the Holocaust. What may be most offensive to both wings is its sidestepping of politics in favor of simple human ingenuity. The film finds the right notes to negotiate its delicate subject matter. And Benigni isn't really making comedy out of the Holocaust, anyway. He is showing how Guido uses the only gift at his command to protect his son. If he had a gun, he would shoot at the fascists. If he had an army, he would destroy them. He is a clown, and comedy is his weapon.

The movie actually softens the Holocaust slightly, to make the humor possible at all. In the real death camps there would be no role for Guido. But *Life Is Beautiful* is not about Nazis and fascists, but about the human spirit. It is about rescuing whatever is good and hopeful from the wreckage of dreams. About hope for the future. About the necessary human conviction, or delusion, that things will be better for our children than they are right now.

Light It Up ★ ★ ½
R, 103 m., 1999

Usher Raymond (Lester Dewitt), Forest Whitaker (Officer Dante Jackson), Rosario Dawson (Stephanie Williams), Robert Ri'chard ("Ziggy" Malone), Judd Nelson (Ken Knowles), Vanessa L. Williams (Audrey McDonald), Fredro Starr (Rodney J. Templeton), Sara Gilbert (Lynn Sabatini), Clifton Collins Jr. (Robert "Rivers" Tremont). Directed by Craig Bolotin and produced by Tracey E. Edmonds and Kenneth Edmonds. Screenplay by Bolotin.

As recently as 1985, our view of high school was so innocent that a movie like *The Breakfast Club* could involve five teenage troublemakers working things out in unsupervised detention. Now look at *Light It Up*. The same kinds of kids take hostages and get involved in an armed standoff with the police.

The movie takes place at an inner-city high school where the heat doesn't work, the winter wind blows in through broken windows, and most students don't have copies of the textbook. But the students are basically good kids—not the crazed dopers and gang bangers depicted in so many movies about high schools in trouble.

The ingredients for a tragedy are assembled early. A new security guard with the ominous name of Dante Jackson (Forest Whitaker) has come to work. He's got problems. One student pegs him: "A $5 cop with a $50 attitude." Meanwhile, a teacher named Knowles (Judd Nelson, from the original *Breakfast Club*) is wandering the halls with his students, looking for a heated classroom. He eventually takes them to a fast-food restaurant. Misunderstandings multiply when they return to the school. The guard gets into a shoving match with some of the students, his gun goes off and wounds him, and a routine day turns into a hostage crisis.

The ringleader is a good student and star athlete named Lester, played by R&B singer Usher Raymond, who shows real screen presence. Other students include Rosario Dawson, as a girl who counsels moderation; Sara Gilbert, as a girl so steeped in misery she's basically just along for the ride; Robert Ri'chard as a goofy kid who unwittingly starts the trouble; Fredro Starr as a hothead with a police record; and Clifton Collins Jr. as Lester's lieutenant.

As these six students barricade themselves in the library with the wounded guard, we're reminded of the young actors in *The Breakfast Club*'s library: Emilio Estevez, Anthony Michael Hall, Judd Nelson, Molly Ringwald, and Ally Sheedy. Although their careers have had ups and downs, they all became stars, and the *Light It Up* cast is similarly promising.

The arc in the movie is predictable—so predictable that it keeps it from truly generating suspense (*The Breakfast Club* wisely went for discovery and revelation instead). Cops surround the school, which is in New York (although the movie was filmed in Chicago). Searchlights bathe it, Vanessa L. Williams plays the hostage negotiator who gets Lester on the

telephone. Of course, the library is equipped with computers, and soon the students are e-mailing their defense to CNN.

I am not sure I buy the way the movie thinks the crisis would play out. With the hostage-takers portrayed on TV as good kids, with their friends demonstrating their support, with even their teacher (Nelson) backing them, is it possible a hothead cop would seize control from the negotiator "because we want this wrapped up before the morning news"? Maybe that's necessary because in these souped-up times, a more rational conclusion is unthinkable. *The Breakfast Club* ended with the students, slightly older and wiser, driving off with their parents. This one has a SWAT team poised in a stairwell while the gang members prepare Molotov cocktails. Connect the dots.

The movie was directed by Craig Bolotin and produced by musician Kenneth (Babyface) Edmonds and his wife, Tracey. It has a refreshing lack of heated racial attitudes. Twenty years ago, there would have been some kind of obligatory shouting match in the library between the white girl and the black one. The teacher might not have been white. The principal would have been. The negotiator might not have been black. Bolotin's screenplay considers the characters as individuals, and they're not color-coded. Obligatory racial side-taking and name-calling is gradually (too gradually) being phased out of situations like this, in fiction and life, at the end of the century.

If I can't quite recommend the movie, it's because so much of the plot is on autopilot. The dialogue spells out too much that doesn't need to be said. The dynamic of the Internet-media angle is not really exploited. The final scenes seem contrived to supply action where it is not needed or convincing. But there's a lot in the movie that's good, including its introduction of a cast of gifted newcomers.

Limbo ★ ★ ★ ½
R, 126 m., 1999

Mary Elizabeth Mastrantonio (Donna De Angelo), David Strathairn (Joe Gastineau), Vanessa Martinez (Noelle De Angelo), Casey Siemaszko (Bobby Gastineau), Kris Kristofferson (Smilin' Jack), Kathryn Grody (Frankie), Rita Taggart (Lou). Directed and edited by

John Sayles and produced by Maggie Renzi. Screenplay by Sayles.

Limbo sure isn't heaven and it's too cold to be hell.
—From the diary read by Noelle

Juneau is the only state capital with roads that lead nowhere. Every highway out of town ends in the wilderness. That serves as a metaphor for the characters in John Sayles's *Limbo*, a movie about people whose lives are neither here nor there, but stuck in between. It also helps explain the movie's surprising story structure, which doesn't obediently follow our expectations, but reflects the way a wilderness like Alaska can impose its own abrupt reality.

We meet a local handyman named Joe (David Strathairn), who was a high school All-American until he wrecked his knee, and a fishing boat skipper until he lost two lives and quit the trade. And we meet a singer named Donna (Mary Elizabeth Mastrantonio), whose career on the club circuit has ended her up at the Golden Nugget Lounge, pretty much the end of the line. She's had bad luck with men, and we see her breaking up with her latest guy at a wedding reception. Joe gives her a lift back to town.

The movie seems to be announcing it is about a relationship. We meet Donna's daughter, Noelle (Vanessa Martinez), who is exasperated by her mom's taste in men but begins to like Joe. The backdrop also seems to fall into place. We learn about local campaigns to save the environment, and about ways to get around them ("Quit with the chain saws when you get to where people can see"). We meet some of the local fauna, including the high-spirited lesbian couple, Lou (Rita Taggart) and Frankie (Kathryn Grody), who have taken over a valued commercial fishing license.

Mastrantonio is a splendid presence in her role. She can sing well and talks about how sometimes in a song she'll find a moment of grace. She doesn't know what she's doing in Alaska: "Anything where you need equipment instead of clothing, I don't do." Strathairn's character has lived in Alaska most of his life, and it has taught him not to hope for much, and to expect anything. But just now it's summer, and the living looks easy. A romance seems to be forming.

We assume we're in familiar John Sayles territory; he likes to populate his stories with large, interlocking casts, and then show how the local politics and economy work. That's what he did in *City of Hope* (1991), set in New Jersey, and the great *Lone Star* (1996), set on the Tex-Mex border. But he has a surprise ready for us. (Although the ads and review clips reveal it, you might not want to read beyond this point before seeing the movie.)

The surprise is a complete overthrow of all of our expectations for the story, a sharp turn in the narrative that illustrates how Alaska is domesticated only up to a point—that the wilderness is only a step away, and death only a misstep. I was reminded of the chilling book *Into the Wild*, about the young dropout who went on an Alaskan camping trip where everything went wrong.

Joe has a half-brother named Bobby (Casey Siemaszko), who talks him into crewing his boat on a "business trip." Joe innocently invites Donna and Noelle along. The purpose of the trip is far from innocent. After narrowly surviving a storm, Joe guides the boat into an inlet where few boats ever come. And then there are more unexpected developments, and three of them (Joe, Donna, and Noelle) find themselves castaways on an island far from anyone else.

What I liked so much about this story structure is that it confounded my expectations at every step. I expected the story to stay in Juneau, but it didn't. When it took a turn toward adventure, I thought the threat would come from nature—but it comes from men. After the three characters are stranded, I expected—I don't know what, maybe Swiss Family Robinson-style improvisation.

But Sayles gradually reveals his buried theme, which is that in a place like the Alaskan wilderness you can never be sure what will happen next. And that optimism, bravery, and ingenuity may not be enough. Some of the best dialogue passages in the film involve Joe's quiet realism. He refuses to raise false hopes. And of course even the hope of rescue comes with a hidden barb: Will they be found by friends, or death?

The movie leaves conventional plot structure behind and treks off into the wilderness itself. There's even a story within the story, based on a journal Noelle finds—and it contains a surprise too. Then comes the film's ending. Watching the screen, I felt confident that I knew exactly what would have to happen. What, and how, and why. And I was wrong. The more you think about the way *Limbo* ends, the more you realize that any other ending would betray the purpose of the story. Sayles has started with a domestic comedy, and led us unswervingly into the heart of darkness.

The Limey ★ ★ ★
R, 89 m., 1999

Terence Stamp (Wilson), Lesley Ann Warren (Elaine), Luis Guzman (Ed), Peter Fonda (Valentine), Barry Newman (Avery), Joe Dallesandro (Uncle John), Nicky Katt (Stacy), Amelia Heinle (Adhara). Directed by Steven Soderbergh and produced by John Hardy and Scott Kramer. Screenplay by Lem Dobbs.

If you live like a villain all your life, sooner or later you will be sixty and still being shot at. Although violence may be a way of life for the poor, it is a nuisance to the rich, and they try to hire out the work wherever possible. Steven Soderbergh's *The Limey* is the story of two older guys who hire their killers, and another who is a do-it-yourselfer. In its quiet and murderous way, it is like the delayed final act of an old movie about drugs, guns, and revenge.

The movie opens with close-ups of Terence Stamp's tight, closed, angry face. His features were chiseled in those Westerns he made thirty years ago, and you can still see the skull beneath the skin. He has been released from a British prison, and is flying to Los Angeles to seek revenge for the murder of his daughter. He is not a sophisticate, but a smart, working criminal who amuses himself with Cockney slang.

He believes a man named Valentine has killed the girl. Valentine, played by Peter Fonda, is a legendary record producer who lives in an architectural showcase in the hills above L.A.—one of those places with a swimming pool cantilevered out over the valley. It is a nice irony that both Valentine and Wilson (the Stamp character) made their money from rock music: Valentine by selling the tickets, Wilson by stealing the receipts of a Pink Floyd concert.

Valentine's security problems are dealt with, we learn, by Avery (Barry Newman), also around sixty, with the expensive suit and the tinted glasses. The men have recently been involved in a drug deal. Valentine is nervous; he doesn't want anything to "touch" him. Avery is paid well to reassure him: "The goods have been turned around, the money's been laundered, the guys are dead. This is a *good* thing." The two men have the kind of relationship you sometimes see between two business partners who have long since lost interest in their business or each other, but stay together because they need to drive a Mercedes.

Soderbergh's direction of the film takes the underlying story, which is basic Ross Macdonald, and uses the visuals to add an ironic amusement. Notice, for example, the scene where Wilson and *his* acting security guy (a big, tough Mexican-American played by Luis Guzman) arrive for a party at Valentine's house. We get a POV shot through binoculars, which is standard, and shows guests arriving at the hilltop house. But now listen to Wilson, who has never seen valet parkers before, and thinks all those guys in uniforms are minders and bodyguards.

And watch a later scene, where Wilson has a run-in with one of Valentine's actual bodyguards, a tough guy dispatched by Avery to bounce him out of the party. Wilson throws him over the edge of the swimming deck and to his death on the hillside below. Standard. But the cinematographer, Ed Lachman, keeps it in a long shot, in the background; the foreground is filled with Valentine relaxing in what he thinks is safety. Neat.

Avery realizes he needs to have Wilson killed, and goes to a pool hall to hire a hit man. The hired hand is one of those wise guys who always has the verbal commentary going. "I embrace my lifestyle," he says. We realize he isn't a kid, either. Forty, maybe. In Southern California youth is eternal, and these guys, with their tans and haircuts and clothes and cars and young girlfriends, believe their own images and think they're still nimble and tough.

Soderbergh makes full use of the screen history of both Terence Stamp and Peter Fonda. We get flashbacks of Wilson as a young man—actually Stamp in the movie *Poor Cow* (1968). If the Fonda character in *Easy Rider* had lived, he might have turned out like this. We learn the Valentine character "took the whole sixties Southern California zeitgeist and ran with it."

What is *The Limey* about? Drugs, girls, guns, and revenge? Not at all. It's about retirement. It's about tough guys who talk big but are past their sell-by dates. They're not fast enough for the ageless limey, who was cured in prison like beef jerky, and comes in low and fast. Soderbergh's visuals place them in the eternal world of California wealth and sun, heaven's waiting room, where the old look young until they look dead. When Wilson gets off the plane from London, they might as well take their zeitgeist and stick it where the zeit don't geist.

Little Dieter Needs to Fly ★ ★ ★ ½
NO MPAA RATING, 80 m., 1998

Dieter Dengler (Himself). A documentary directed and produced by Werner Herzog.

"Men are often haunted," Werner Herzog tells us at the beginning of *Little Dieter Needs to Fly*. "They seem to be normal, but they are not." His documentary tells the story of such a haunted man, whose memories include being hung upside down with an ant nest over his head, and fighting a snake for a dead rat they both wanted to eat.

The man's name is Dieter Dengler. He was born in the Black Forest of Germany. As a child, he watched his village destroyed by American warplanes, and one flew so close to his attic window that for a split second he made eye contact with the pilot flashing past. At that moment, Dieter Dengler knew that he needed to fly.

Dengler is now in his fifties, a businessman living in northern California. He invites us into his home, carefully opening and closing every door over and over again, to be sure he is not locked in. He shows us the stores of rice, flour, and honey under his floor. He obsesses about being locked in, about having nothing to eat. He tells us his story.

As an eighteen-year-old, he came penniless to America. He enlisted in the navy to learn to fly. He flew missions over Vietnam, but "that there were people down there who suffered, who died—only became clear to me after I was their prisoner." He was shot down, made

a prisoner, became one of only seven men to escape from prison camps and survive. He endured tortures by his captors and from nature: dysentery, insect bites, starvation, hallucinations.

Werner Herzog's *Little Dieter Needs to Fly* lets Dieter tell his own story, which he does in rushed but vivid English, as if fearful there will not be time enough if he doesn't speak fast. As he talks, Herzog puts him in locations: his American home, his German village of Wildberg, and then the same Laotian jungles where he was shot down. Here certain memories are reenacted: He is handcuffed by villagers, made to march through the forest, and demonstrates how he was staked down at night. "You can't imagine what I'm thinking," he says.

The thing about storytelling is that it creates pictures in our heads. I can "see" what happened to Dieter Dengler as clearly as if it has all been dramatized, and his poetry adds to the images. "As I followed the river, there was this beautiful bear following me," he remembers. "This bear meant death to me. It's really ironic—the only friend I had at the end was death." At another point, standing in front of a giant tank of jellyfish, he says, "This is basically what Death looks like to me," and Herzog's camera moves in on the dreamy floating shapes as we hear the sad theme from *Tristan and Isolde*.

Now here is an interesting aspect. Dieter Dengler is a real man who really underwent all of those experiences (and won the Medal of Honor, the Distinguished Flying Cross, and the Navy Cross because of them). His story is true. But not all of his words are his own. Herzog freely reveals in conversation that he suggested certain images to Dengler. The image of the jellyfish, for example—"That was my idea," Herzog told me. Likewise the opening and shutting of the doors, although not the image of the bear.

Herzog has had two careers, as the director of some of the strangest and most fascinating features of the last thirty years, and some of the best documentaries. Many of his docs are about obsessed men: the ski-jumper Steiner, for example, who flew so high he overjumped his landing areas. Or Herzog himself, venturing onto a volcanic island to interview the one man who would not leave when he was told the volcano would explode.

Herzog sees his mission as a filmmaker not to turn himself into a recording machine, but to be a collaborator. He does not simply stand and watch, but arranges and adjusts and subtly enhances, so that the film takes the materials of Dengler's adventure and fashions it into a new thing.

You meet a person who has an amazing story to tell, and you rarely have the time to hear it, or the attention to appreciate it. The attendants in nursing homes sit glued to their Stephen King paperbacks; the old people around them have stories a thousand times scarier to tell. A colorful character dies and the obituaries say countless great stories were told about him—but at the end, did anybody still care to listen?

Herzog starts with a balding, middle-aged man driving down a country lane in a convertible, and listens, questions, and shapes until the life experience of Dieter Dengler becomes unforgettable. What an astonishing man! we think. But if we were to sit next to him on a plane, we might tell him we had seen his movie, and make a polite comment about it, and go back to our magazine. It takes art to transform someone else's experience into our own.

Little Men ★ ½
PG, 98 m., 1998

Michael Caloz (Nat Blake), Mariel Hemingway (Jo Bhaer), Ben Cook (Dan), Ricky Mabe (Tommy Bangs), Chris Sarandon (Fritz Bhaer), Kathleen Fee (Narrator). Directed by Rodney Gibbons and produced by Pierre David and Franco Battista. Screenplay by Mark Evan Schwartz, based on the novel by Louisa May Alcott.

In my review of *Little Women* (1994), I wrote, "the very title summons up preconceptions of treacly do-gooders in a smarmy children's story." I was relieved to report, however, that the movie itself was nothing of the sort; it was a spirited and intelligent retelling of the Louisa May Alcott classic. Now, alas, comes *Little Men*, which is indeed about treacly do-gooders in a smarmy children's story.

Although younger children may enjoy the movie on a simple and direct level, there's little depth or texture to make it interesting for viewers over the age of, say, about ten. It's all on one note. The adults are all noble and enlightened, the boys are all basically good, and the story is all basically a sunny, innocent fable.

The year is 1871. The "little women" have all grown up, according to a narrator who tells us far more than she should have to. Jo (Mariel Hemingway) has married Fritz Bhaer (Chris Sarandon), and together they run Plumfield School, a country home for wayward or orphaned boys.

To Plumfield comes the Boston street urchin Nat (Michael Caloz) and, not long after, his best friend Dan (Ben Cook). There they find love, acceptance, and such lessons as, "If a pie has twelve pieces and three-quarters of them are served at dinner, how many pieces are left?" All of the boys scribble industriously on their chalkboards to solve the puzzle, although since several of them are later involved in a game of poker, they would seem to have the necessary skills for mental calculation.

Plumfield has limited funds, and perhaps cannot afford to keep Dan. And then Dan causes some problems, as when he sponsors the secret poker game (complete with beer and cigars) and it almost results in Plumfield being burned down. Apart from such hitches, Plumfield is an ideal haven, with pillow fights scheduled every Saturday night, and the narrator informs us that "the feeling that someone cared for him made that playroom seem like heaven for the homeless child."

There is a certain complexity in Fritz, Jo's husband, who recalls that his grandmother taught him to think before he spoke by cutting the end of his tongue with her scissors. His idea of punishment is to have the boys cane him, a practice that will not withstand a single moment's more thought than the movie gives it. He rumbles suspiciously about Dan, but Dan "has the makings of a fine man," Jo declares, and although another boy is sent away for stealing, Dan survives the poker, beer, and cigar scandal.

There is a horse at Plumfield. Only one, untamed and unruly. In an early scene, we see the hired man trying to tame it. We know with complete certainty that Dan was born to tame that horse, which indeed is waiting (all saddled up) when the lad's rebellious spirit requires such a test.

I have no doubt that Louisa May Alcott wrote something resembling this plot, although nothing in it sends me hurrying to the bookshelf. *Little Men* is an example of the kind of movie that wins approval because of what it doesn't have, not for what it has. It is wholesome, blameless, positive, cheerful, well photographed, and nicely acted (especially by Ben Cook), and it has a PG rating. But, man, is it smarmy.

Little Voice ★ ★ ★
R, 99 m., 1998

Jane Horrocks (Laura [Little Voice]), Brenda Blethyn (Mari), Michael Caine (Ray Say), Jim Broadbent (Mr. Boo), Ewan McGregor (Billy), Philip Jackson (George), Annette Badland (Sadie). Directed by Mark Herman and produced by Elizabeth Karlsen. Screenplay by Herman, based on the stage play by Jim Cartwright.

Little Voice is unthinkable without the special and unexpected talent of its star. She is Jane Horrocks, from TV's *Absolutely Fabulous* and the Mike Leigh movie *Life Is Sweet,* and nothing I've seen her do prepared me in any way for the revelation that she is a singer. And not just a singer, but an impressionist who can perform in the voices of Judy Garland, Shirley Bassey, Marilyn Monroe, and Billie Holiday, among others. And not just an impressionist, but a mimic so skillful that the end credits make it a point to inform us that Horrocks sang all her own songs in the movie. We need to know that, because her mimicry is so exact that we assume it must be lip-synching.

Horrocks first appeared in this story on the stage (it was written for her by Jim Cartwright), and now in the movie she repeats an astonishing performance, which is plopped down into an amusing but uneven story about colorful characters in a northern England seaside resort town. She plays a young woman named Laura, who mopes in her bedroom above the record store that her late, beloved dad used to run. She shares his taste for classic pop records, and plays them again and again, memorizing the great performances.

The rest of the house is ruled by her mother, Mari (Brenda Blethyn, the Oscar nominee from *Secrets and Lies*). She's a loud, blowzy tart who picks up lads at pubs and brings them home. Her new squeeze is Ray Say (Michael Caine), a onetime London club promoter now reduced to managing strippers in this northern backwater. Mari's approach to Ray is direct. She brings him home from a pub and suggests, "Let's roll about."

One night a duel develops between Mari playing "It's Not Unusual" downstairs while Laura does "That's Entertainment" upstairs. Ray hears the singing, and realizes at once that he's in the presence of an extraordinary talent. But Laura's voice is not reflected in a big personality; she's a shy recluse who speaks in such a small voice that it has supplied her nickname.

Ray brings home his friend Mr. Boo (Jim Broadbent), owner of a local club, to audition Little Voice. They can't get her to sing, but afterward, while they're standing on the sidewalk, they hear her doing "Over the Rainbow" and Mr. Boo knows a big draw when he hears one. (His club books acts more along the lines of an elderly knife-thrower who aims blades at his wife to the strains of "Rawhide.")

The plot involves Ray's struggle to lure Little Voice onto the stage (he tells her a touching parable about a little bluebird) and his struggle to discourage Mari's amorous intensity. There is also a struggle going on for Little Voice's heart. A telephone lineman (Ewan McGregor) is in love with her, and uses his cherry-picker to levitate himself to her bedroom window. Will he win her love? Will she agree to sing?

Little Voice, written and directed by Mark Herman *(Brassed Off),* seems to have all the pieces in place for another one of those whimsical, comic British slices of life. But the movie doesn't quite deliver the way we think it will. One problem is that the Michael Caine character, sympathetic and funny in the opening and middle scenes, turns mean at the end for no good reason. Another is that the romance, and a manufactured crisis, distract from the true climax of the movie.

That would be Jane Horrocks's vocal performance. Watching her belt out one great standard after another, I was reminded of old musicals that were handmade as showcases for big stars. The plot was just a clothesline for Astaire's big dance number or Mario Lanza's solo. Here everything leads up to (and wilts after) Horrocks's show-stopper. But she is amazing. Absolutely fabulous.

Live Flesh ★ ★ ★ ½
R, 101 m., 1998

Liberto Rabal (Victor Plaza), Francesca Neri (Elena), Javier Bardem (David), Angela Molina (Clara), Jose Sancho (Sancho). Directed by Pedro Almodovar and produced by Agustin Almodovar. Screenplay by Pedro Almodovar, based on the novel by Ruth Rendell.

Pedro Almodovar's *Live Flesh* is the kind of overwrought melodrama, lurid and passionate, that I have a weakness for. It dives in headfirst, going for broke, using the entire arsenal of coincidence, irony, fire, and surprise. It's about cops, lovers, paralysis, prostitution, adultery, deception, and revenge, and it is also surprisingly tender in its portrait of a man who gets into a lifetime of trouble just because he wants to make a woman happy.

Because it is by Almodovar, that Spanish poet of the perverse, none of these elements are come by easily. Victor, the hero, is born on a bus, the child of a prostitute, with a madam as midwife (the Madrid bus company gives him a lifetime pass). Twenty years pass and we find him ringing the doorbell of Elena, a woman he has met only briefly. He recalls their brief encounter at a disco: "The guy you had sex with in the toilet—remember?" She does, but wants nothing to do with him. She's waiting for her drug dealer and all Victor has brought her is a pizza.

But Victor is stubborn. His encounter with Elena was his first sexual experience, and he is doe-eyed with desire to know her better. She's in no condition to be known. They argue, the cops are called, and a gun discharges, striking a young cop and paralyzing him. Flash forward: Victor, in prison, is surprised to see that the cop is now a wheelchair basketball star,

and Elena, cheering from the sidelines, has cleaned up her act and is now his devoted wife. Meanwhile, Victor rots behind bars, an innocent man.

Innocent, yes, because he did not fire the gun. In the struggle, it was the other cop—the alcoholic Sancho (Jose Sancho)—who pulled the trigger and hit his young partner, David (Javier Bardem). Why? Because he suspected David of having an affair with his wife, Clara. Of course, it is only a matter of time until Victor, released from prison, is having an affair with Clara himself.

Don't be concerned if you have not quite followed every twist and turn of this convoluted story. Almodovar makes it clear as it unfolds; his screenplay is based on a novel by Ruth Rendell, the British mistress of plots that fold back upon themselves. Another source for the film's style is Douglas Sirk, the master of 1950s Hollywood melodrama, whose films Almodovar claims to have seen hundreds of times, and who manufactured melodramatic plots with the ingenuity of chess puzzles.

Almodovar's films are often intended as put-ons. This one may be, too, but it's played more or less straight (for him, anyway). The actors understand that in melodrama of this sort, the slightest suggestion of irony is fatal, and they play everything with desperate intensity, while inhabiting screens so filled with bright colors it's a wonder they don't wince.

For Victor (Liberto Rabal), life has not been fair. But his luck changes when, after being released from prison, he goes to visit the grave of his mother. There he meets Clara (Angela Molina), an older woman, and after a strictly routine night of love he pleads inexperience and begs her to teach him everything she knows. She proves to be a gifted teacher. His long-term plan is to spend one night with the cruel Elena, proving himself the world's greatest lover and leaving her sobbing for more. Many men dream of such scenarios, but few have Victor's dedication to the necessary training regimen.

There are many other coincidences in the film, which I will not reveal. Some we can anticipate; others are complete surprises. It's interesting how Almodovar anchors the story so concretely in a real world, with everyday jobs and concerns; in the midst of jealousy and lust, the characters somehow retain a certain depth and plausibility. I especially liked the work of Molina, a frequent actress in Almodovar's films, as an older woman whose experience and wisdom have not been enough to protect her from a brutish husband.

And Javier Bardem takes a refreshing approach to the role of the paralyzed ex-cop: Of all the men in the movie, he has the strongest physical presence and the greatest menace. There's a scene where he goes in his chair to call on the young ex-convict, and the way he enters the room and establishes himself makes him the aggressor, not the handicapped one.

Movies like *Live Flesh* exist for the joy of telling their stories. They recall a time before high romance was smothered by taste. They don't apologize for breathless energy and cheerful implausibility, and every time a character walks into a room we feel like bracing ourselves for a new shock. Almodovar cannot be called "sincere" on the basis of this film— there's still a satirical glint in his eye—but by choosing to stick with the story and downplay his usual asides, nudges, and in-jokes, he's made a *film noir* of great energy.

Living Out Loud ★ ★ ★ ½
R, 102 m., 1998

Holly Hunter (Judith), Danny DeVito (Pat), Queen Latifah (Liz Bailey), Martin Donovan (Dr. Nelson), Elias Koteas (Stranger). Directed by Richard LaGravenese and produced by Danny DeVito, Michael Schamberg, and Stacey Sher. Screenplay by LaGravenese.

He is a short, pudgy elevator operator. She is the newly dumped wife of a doctor. They meet in his elevator, in her co-op building on Fifth Avenue. They seem to have little in common, until they start talking. This is a setup for a love story involving all the usual clichés, but *Living Out Loud* isn't a love story and is not made from standard parts. It's the film you need to see in order to understand why the ending of *As Good As It Gets* was phony.

The movie stars two of the most intensely interesting actors in the movies today, Danny DeVito and Holly Hunter. Not many actors can hold the screen against them. There's a dialogue scene where they talk about whether he should ask her out for dinner, and we're seeing a master class on the craft of acting in the movies. We don't *want* them to live happily ever after, because that would drain all of the interest out of their situation.

The movie has been written and directed by Richard LaGravenese, the gifted screenwriter of *The Horse Whisperer, The Bridges of Madison County,* and *Beloved.* He's more interested in characters and dialogue than in shaping everything into a conventional story. He aims for the kind of bittersweet open ends that life itself so often supplies; he doesn't hammer his square pegs into round holes, as James L. Brooks did by insisting in *As Good As It Gets* that the Jack Nicholson character could, should, or would ever be able to live happily with anyone else.

The movie opens with Judith (Hunter) breaking up with her husband of fifteen years (Martin Donovan). He's been cheating on her— and, worse, insulting her intelligence by thinking he could get away with it. Later we meet Pat (DeVito), an elevator operator whose wife has thrown him out because of his gambling debts and a whole lot more, and whose daughter is dying. Pat's brother, a saloon keeper, offers him a job, but Pat clings to his independence. The elevator job is temporary. He has plans.

To be cut adrift in uncertainty and grief is something to share, and soon they are sharing it. Feeling sorry for him and having drunk too much, which she often does, she hugs him, causing unruly feelings to stir within Pat. He subtly borrows $200 (the loan sharks are after him), and when he repays her he brings along a bottle of wine, and she confesses she saw through his story about why he needed the money, but gave it to him anyway, because . . . because . . .

Well, because it was a point of contact in a life that has become empty. (She has a day job as a caregiver for a singularly uncareworthy old lady.) Will they go on to share their innermost feelings and fall in love, as in a standard plot? Not necessarily. He thinks she's the perfect woman. But when she drinks she fantasizes about hunks, which is maybe how she wound up with a creep for a husband.

Need draws them together. Fantasies keep

them apart. And then an extraordinary third character enters their lives. This is Liz Bailey (Queen Latifah), a torch singer in a nightclub where Judith likes to drink too many martinis, smoke too many cigarettes, and display too much grief. Liz is tall, striking, carries herself with placid self-confidence, and wears dresses that display her magnificent bosom—not as an advertisement, but more in a spirit of generosity toward the world.

Liz and Judith become unlikely confidantes one boozy night, after Judith blurts out that she's sure Liz's boyfriend is gay. Well, he is: "I've always had this thing for beautiful, sensitive men." She takes Judith to a lesbian nightclub that looks recycled from German expressionist wet dreams; the scene doesn't seem out of place, but falls into the flow of a long, confusing, drunken night.

Judith and Pat both become friends of Liz, who is a confidante and counselor. But LaGravenese is too smart to involve Liz in an affair with Pat (or Judith). He's intrigued by how people can bounce around town when they're cut loose from their routines and marriages. How they find relief in a flood of confession and autobiography. ("His father was one of the first neurosurgeons in the city," Judith tells Pat about her first husband, and he nods and notes that his wife was an Oldsmobile saleswoman on Staten Island.)

Another man turns up in Judith's life, unexpectedly and accidentally, but I will leave it to you to find out how and why. And there's an appointment with an agreeable masseuse (an encounter that's just about perfectly written and acted). It's always confusing to meet your sexual fantasies in the flesh, because you have to deal with them—they won't obligingly evaporate when you're finished.

Living Out Loud is based on two short stories by Chekhov. It plays like a short story. A novel has beginning, middle, end, theme, conflict, resolution. A short story looks intensely at a shorter period of time during which closely observed characters go through experiences that change them. No doubt Judith, Pat, and Liz will drift apart again. There are more happy endings (and endings of any kind) in the movies than in life, which more closely resembles the beginnings of one unfinished story after another.

What I enjoyed in *Living Out Loud* was the comfort of these lives flowing briefly in the same stream. The sense that the unexpected was free to enter the story, and would not be shouldered aside by the demands of conventional plotting. And delight at the voluptuous complications of Liz Bailey. Queen Latifah shows here (as she did in *Set It Off*) that her screen presence makes a scene stand up and hum. Anyone who can steal a scene from Danny DeVito and Holly Hunter can do just about anything in a movie.

Lock, Stock and Two Smoking Barrels
★ ★ ★
R, 106 m., 1999

Jason Flemyng (Tom), Dexter Fletcher (Soap), Nick Moran (Eddy), Jason Statham (Bacon), P. H. Moriarty (Hatchet Harry), Lenny McLean (Barry the Baptist), Steven Mackintosh (Winston), Sting (JD), Nicholas Rowe (J), Vinnie Jones (Big Chris). Directed by Guy Ritchie and produced by Matthew Vaughn. Screenplay by Ritchie.

Lock, Stock and Two Smoking Barrels is like Tarantino crossed with the Marx Brothers, if Groucho had been into chopping off fingers. It's a bewilderingly complex caper film, set among the lowlifes of London's East End, and we don't need to be told that the director used to make TV commercials; we figure that out when a cook throws some veggies into water, and the camera shoots up from the bottom of the pot.

The movie is about a poker player named Eddy (Nick Moran), who is bankrolled by three friends for a high-stakes game with Hatchet Harry (P. H. Moriarty), a gambling and porn kingpin. Harry cheats, Eddy runs up an enormous debt, and Harry's giant enforcer, Barry the Baptist (Lenny McLean), explains that he will start chopping fingers if the friends don't pay up—or hand over a pub belonging to Eddy's father (Sting).

What to do? Eddy and his mates eavesdrop on neighbors in the next flat—criminals who are planning to rob a rich drug dealer. Meanwhile, Barry assigns two dimwits to steal a couple of priceless antique shotguns for Harry. The shotguns end up in the hands of Eddy and friends, who steal the drug money from the other thieves, and then—but you get the idea.

Or maybe you don't. The movie, which is an enormous hit in Britain, had its American premiere at the Sundance Film Festival, where I lost track of the plot and some of the dialogue. Seeing it again recently, I found the dialogue easier to understand, and the labyrinthine plot became a little clearer—although it's designed to fold back upon itself with unexpected connections.

The actors seem a little young for this milieu; they seem to be playing grown-up. Tarantino's *Reservoir Dogs* had characters with mileage on them, played by veterans like Harvey Keitel, Lawrence Tierney, and Michael Madsen.

But the heroes of *Lock* (Jason Flemyng, Dexter Fletcher, Jason Statham, and Moran) seem a little downy-cheeked to be moving in such weathered circles. And as the cast expands to include the next-door neighbors and the drug dealers, there are times when, frankly, we wish everybody would wear name tags ("Hi! I'm the effete ganja grower!").

I was convinced, however, by Harry and Barry—and also by Harry's collector, Big Chris, who is played by a soccer star named Vinnie Jones who became famous for squeezing in his vicelike grip that part of an opponent's anatomy that most quickly gains his full attention. They seemed plausible as East End vice retailers—seamy, cynical, middle-aged professionals in a heartless business.

I also liked the movie's sense of fun. The sound track uses a lot of rock music and narration to flaunt its attitude, it keeps most of the violence offscreen, and it's not above throwaway gags. While Eddy plays poker, for example, his three friends go next door to a pub. A man on fire comes staggering out of the door. They look at him curiously, shrug, and go in. The pub is named Samoa Joe's, which seems like a sideways nod to *Pulp Fiction* (Big Kahuna burgers crossed with Jack Rabbit Slim's restaurant). The guys sip drinks with umbrellas in them.

I sometimes feel, I confess, as if there's a Tarantino reference in every third movie made these days. *Lock, Stock and Two Smoking Barrels* is the kind of movie where you naturally play Spot the Influence: Tarantino, of course,

and a dash of Hong Kong action pictures, and the old British crime comedies like *The Lavender Hill Mob*. The director, Guy Ritchie, says his greatest inspiration was *The Long Good Friday* (1980), the Cockney crime movie that made a star out of Bob Hoskins. Lurking beneath all the other sources, I suspect, is *Night and the City* (1950), Jules Dassin's masterful *noir*, also about crime in the East End, also with a crime kingpin who employs a giant bruiser.

By the end of it all, as you're reeling out trying to make sense of the plot, *Lock, Stock, etc.* seems more like an exercise in style than anything else. And so it is. We don't care much about the characters (I felt more actual affection for the phlegmatic bouncer, Barry the Baptist, than for any of the heroes). We realize that the film's style stands outside the material and is lathered on top (there are freeze-frames, jokey subtitles, speed-up, and slo-mo). And that the characters are controlled by the demands of the clockwork plot. But it's fun, in a slapdash way; it has an exuberance, and in a time when movies follow formulas like zombies, it's alive.

The Loss of Sexual Innocence ★ ★ ★ ½
R, 101 m., 1999

Julian Sands (Adult Nic), Johanna Torrel (His Wife), Saffron Burrows (Twins), Stefano Dionisi (Lucca), Kelly MacDonald (Susan), Jonathan Rhys-Meyers (Nic, Age Sixteen), Hanne Klintoe (Eve), Femi Ogumbanjo (Adam). Directed by Mike Figgis and produced by Figgis and Annie Stewart. Screenplay by Figgis.

Mike Figgis, who pays so much attention to the music in his films, has made one that plays like a musical composition, with themes drifting in and out, and dialogue used more for tone than speech. *The Loss of Sexual Innocence* is built of memory and dreams, following a boy named Nic as he grows from a child into a man, and intercutting his story with the story of Adam and Eve. Not all of it works, but you play along, because it's rare to find a film this ambitious.

Figgis knows how to tell a story with dialogue and characters (*Leaving Las Vegas* is his masterpiece), but here he deals with impressions, secrets, desires. His story is about the way the world breaks our own Gardens of Eden, chopping down the trees and divesting us of our illusions. The process begins early for Nic, a British boy being raised in Kenya in 1953, when through a slit in a window he observes an old white man watching while a young African girl, dressed only in lingerie, reads to him from the Bible.

We move forward ten years or so to England, where Nic, now sixteen or so, is ignored by his girlfriend, Susan, at a family function. Susan gets drunk, and Nic discovers her upstairs, necking with an older man on the bed. Later there is an earlier scene from their courtship, when Nic and Susan are younger and steal into her house at night. She makes him coffee, they kiss by the fire, and then her father enters. He doesn't "catch" them and hardly notices them; he is in pain, and takes pills. Their young love is contrasted with the end that awaits us all.

These episodes are intercut with "Scenes from Nature," as Adam and Eve (Femi Ogumbanjo and Hanne Klintoe) emerge from a pond and explore the world, and their own bodies, with amazement. The nudity here, while explicit, is theologically correct; we didn't need clothing until we sinned. The whole Eden sequence could have been dispatched with, I think (its surprise payoff tries too hard to make a point that the ending of *Walkabout* made years ago). Yet the Eden scenes are so beautifully photographed that you enjoy them even as you question them. (The first shot of Eden is a breathtaking optical illusion.)

Nic's story, as it unfolds, reveals unhappiness. As he becomes an adult, now played by Julian Sands, we see glimpses of a marriage underlined with tension. He is a film director, and there is a trip to Tunisia that ends with a surprise development that is a sudden, crushing loss of innocence. And Figgis also weaves in a strand involving twins (played by Saffron Burrows) who are separated shortly after birth, and come face-to-face with one another in an airport years later. To look at your own face on another person is a fundamental loss of innocence, because it deprives you of the assumption that you are unique.

The film has no particular statement to make about its material (apart from the symbolism of the Eden sequence). It wants to share feel-ings, not thoughts. A lot of the dialogue sounds remembered, or overheard from a distance. (I was reminded of the dialogue treatment in *Bonnie and Clyde* when Bonnie goes to a family picnic and talks with her mother). We get the points that are being made, but this movie isn't about people talking to one another.

The film itself moves forward, but there are flashbacks of memory, as Nic, driving, recalls scenes from earlier life. There are two dream sequences—one for him, one for his wife, played by Johanna Torrel. Hers is about his indifference as he plays the piano while she makes love with another man. His is about his own death. We don't know if this material comes from Mike Figgis's life, but we're sure it comes from his feelings.

The Loss of Sexual Innocence is an "art film," which means it tries to do something more advanced than most commercial films (which tell stories simple enough for children, in images shocking enough for adults). It wants us to share in the process of memory, especially sexual memory. It assumes that the moments we remember most clearly are those when we lost our illusions—when we discovered the unforgiving and indifferent nature of the world. It's like drifting for a time in the film's musings, and then being invited to take another look at our own.

Lost & Found ★

PG-13, 98 m., 1999

David Spade (Dylan), Sophie Marceau (Lila), Artie Lange (Wally), Patrick Bruel (Rene), Mitchell Whitfield (Mark), Martin Sheen (Millstone), Jon Lovitz (Uncle Harry). Directed by Jeff Pollack and produced by Wayne Rice, Morrie Eisenman, Andrew A. Kosove, and Broderick Johnson. Screenplay by J. B. Cook, Marc Meeks, and David Spade.

Lost & Found is a movie about characters of limited intelligence who wander through the lonely wastes of ancient and boring formulas. No one involved seems to have had any conviction it could be great. It's the kind of movie where the hero imitates Neil Diamond—and he's not making fun of him, he's serious.

In asking us to believe David Spade as a romantic lead, it miscalculates beyond all reason.

Spade is wrong by definition for romantic leads, because his persona is based on ironic narcissism and cool detachment. A girl has to be able to believe it when a guy says he loves her more than anything else in the world. When Spade says it, it means he doesn't love anything else in the world, either.

Spade plays the owner of an Italian restaurant in Los Angeles. Like not very many owners of Italian restaurants, his name is Dylan. I have three hints for Dylan: (1) Unless you know them very well, customers do not like to be caressed on their arms as you pass their tables. (2) Although waiters must touch plates while serving them, it is bad form for the owner to put his thumb on a plate while it is being eaten from. (3) During renovations, do not seat customers directly below drywall with holes ripped in it.

Most L.A. restaurant owners do not live in colorful apartment buildings where all the neighbors know each other and little old ladies play strip poker. But the screenplay throws in the colorful rental units as a way of supplying recycled sitcom characters, and to place Dylan near the apartment of Lila (Sophie Marceau), a French cellist. She has a former boyfriend named Rene (Patrick Bruel), whose function is to look pained and supply straight lines to Dylan. And she has a dog named Jack, who is treated as much like the dog in *There's Something About Mary* as is possible without actually including clips from the other movie.

Dylan and Lila have a Meet Cute. She runs into him and knocks him flat, with her landing on top, which is about the cheapest Meet Cute you can buy at the Movie Cliché Store. He falls in love with Lila, gets nowhere, and steals her dog so that he can claim to have found it and thus win her love. Lila is so unobservant that Dylan often carries the dog past her windows, and even walks it in a nearby park, without Lila ever seeing them together. When the dog needs to poop, Dylan wears one of those tool belts you see on power company linemen, with eight or nine bright plastic pooper-scoopers dangling from it. Supplying a character with too much equipment is a creaky comedy wheeze; in a good movie, they'd give him one pooper-scooper and think of something funny to do with it.

Anyway. Dylan has an employee at the restaurant named Wally (Artie Lange), who is tall, fat, and dumb, sleeps over one night, and ends up in Dylan's bed because he gets scared. As they leap to attention in the morning, they can't even think of a funny payoff (such as Steve Martin in *Planes, Trains & Automobiles*, shouting at John Candy, "That wasn't a pillow!"). Instead, when Lila rings the doorbell, they both answer the door in their underpants and she assumes they're gay. Ho, ho.

Meanwhile, Jack the dog eats junk food and throws up. When Dylan comes home, we get a nauseated-dog's-eye-view of an optically distorted Dylan dressed in 1970s disco gear while dancing to a record on the sound track. Don't ask how a dog could have this hallucination; be thankful instead that the dog's fantasies are more interesting than any other visual in the movie.

Lost & Found ends at a big lawn party for rich people, which in movies about people over twenty-one is the equivalent of the Senior Prom scene in all other movies. There is a role for Martin Sheen, as Mr. Millstone, the tight-fisted banker who wants to fly in Neil Diamond as a surprise for his wife. In 1979, Martin Sheen starred in *Apocalypse Now*. In 1999, he plays Mr. Millstone. I wish he had taken my advice and gone into the priesthood.

As for the Neil Diamond imitation, my best guess is that David Spade secretly thinks he could have a parallel career as a Las Vegas idol, and is showing us how he can do Neil Diamond better than Diamond himself. All that's lacking is for Spade to take that hank of hair that hangs in front of his eyes and part it, so that it hangs over his ears.

Truth in Criticism: The movie has one funny scene, starring Jon Lovitz, as a dog whisperer.

Lost in Space ★ ½
PG-13, 130 m., 1998

Matt LeBlanc (Major Don West), Gary Oldman (Dr. Zachary Smith), William Hurt (Professor John Robinson), Mimi Rogers (Maureen Robinson), Heather Graham (Judy Robinson), Lacey Chabert (Penny Robinson), Jack Johnson (Will Robinson). Directed by Stephen Hopkins and produced by Mark W. Koch, Hopkins, and Akiva Goldsman. Screenplay by Goldsman.

Lost in Space is a dim-witted shoot-'em-up based on the old (I hesitate to say "classic") TV series. It's got cheesy special effects, a muddy visual look, and characters who say obvious things in obvious ways.

If it outgrosses the brilliant *Dark City*, the previous science-fiction film from the same studio, then audiences must have lost their will to be entertained.

The TV series was loosely modeled on the novel *The Swiss Family Robinson*, about a family shipwrecked far from home and using wit and ingenuity to live off the land. I loved that book, especially its detailed description of how the family made tools, machines, and a home for themselves, and trained the local animals.

The movie doesn't bother with such details. After a space battle that is the predictable curtain-raiser, and a quick explanation of why and how the Robinson family is setting off for a planet called Alpha Prime, the film takes place mostly on board their saucer-shaped ship, and involves many more space battles, showdowns, struggles, attacks, hyperspace journeys, and exploding planets. In between, the characters plow through creaky dialogue and exhausted relationship problems.

Imagine the film that could be made about a family marooned on a distant planet, using what they could salvage from their ship or forage from the environment. That screenplay would take originality, intelligence, and thought. *Lost in Space* is one of those typing-speed jobs where the screenwriter is like a stenographer, rewriting what he's seen at the movies.

The story: Earth will not survive another two decades. Alpha Prime is the only other habitable planet mankind has discovered. Professor John Robinson (William Hurt) and his family have been chosen to go there and construct a hypergate, to match the gate at the Earth end. Their journey will involve years of suspended animation, but once the other gate is functioning, humans can zip instantaneously to Alpha Prime.

There needs to be a hypergate at both ends, of course, because otherwise there's no telling where a hyperdrive will land you—as the Robinsons soon find out. Also on board are the professor's wife, Maureen (Mimi Rogers), their scientist daughter, Judy (Heather Graham), their younger daughter, Penny (Lacey Chabert),

and their son, Will (Jack Johnson), who is the brains of the outfit. The ship is piloted by ace space cadet Don West (Matt LeBlanc), and includes an intelligent robot who will help with the tasks at the other end.

Oh, and lurking below deck is the evil Dr. Zachary Smith (Gary Oldman), who wants to sabotage the mission, but is trapped on board when the ship lifts off. So he awakens the Robinsons, after which the ship is thrown off course and seems doomed to fall into the Sun.

Don West has a brainstorm: They'll use the hyperdrive to zap right *through* the Sun! This strategy of course lands them in a galaxy far, far away, with a sky filled with unfamiliar stars. And then the movie ticks off a series of crises, of which I can enumerate a rebellious robot, an exploding planet, mechanical space spiders, a distracting romance, and family issues of trust and authority.

The movie might at least have been more fun to look at if it had been filmed in brighter colors. Director Stephen Hopkins and his cinematographer, Peter Levy, for some reason choose a murky, muted palate. Everything looks like a drab brown suit or a cheap rotogravure. You want to use some Windex on the screen. And Bruce Broughton's musical score saws away tirelessly with counterfeit excitement. When nothing of interest is happening on the screen, it just makes it worse when the music pretends it cares.

Of the performances, what can be said except that William Hurt, Gary Oldman, and Mimi Rogers deserve medals for remaining standing? The kids are standard-issue juveniles with straight teeth and good postures. And there is a monkeylike little alien pet who looks like he comes from a world where all living beings are clones of Felix the Cat. This is the kind of movie that, if it fell into a black hole, you wouldn't be able to tell the difference.

Love & Basketball ★ ★ ★
PG-13, 118 m., 2000

Sanaa Lathan (Monica Wright), Omar Epps (Quincy McCall), Alfre Woodard (Camille Wright), Dennis Haysbert (Zeke McCall), Debbi Morgan (Mona McCall), Harry J. Lennix (Nathan Wright), Kyla Pratt (Young Monica), Glenndon Chatman (Young Quincy), Jess

Willard (Jamal), Chris Warren Jr. (Kelvin), Naykia Harris (Young Lena). Directed by Gina Prince-Bythewood and produced by Spike Lee and Sam Kitt. Screenplay by Prince-Bythewood.

Love & Basketball is about how you can either be in love or play basketball, but it's tricky to do both at the same time. It may be unique among sports movies in that it does *not* end with the Big Game. Instead, it's a thoughtful and touching story about two affluent black kids, a boy and a girl, who grow up loving each other, and the game.

Monica is a tomboy. Her parents and older sister despair of getting her to act like a girl. She'd rather shoot baskets. In 1981, when she's about twelve, her family moves into a new house in Baldwin Hills, a good Los Angeles neighborhood. Next door lives a star for the L.A. Clippers and his son, Quincy. The first time the kids meet, they play a pickup game. Monica goes for a score, Quincy pushes her, and she gets a little scar that will be on her right cheek for the rest of her life.

He likes her. "You wanna be my girl?" he asks. She wants to know what that means. "We can play ball and ride to school together and when you get mad I gotta buy you flowers." She doesn't like flowers, she says. But she kisses him (they count to five), and the next day he wants her to ride to school on the handlebars of his bike. She wants to ride her own bike. This will be the pattern of a lifetime.

Flash forward to 1988. Monica, now played by Sanaa Lathan, and Quincy (Omar Epps) are high school stars. They're not dating but they're friends, and when Quincy's parents (Dennis Haysbert and Debbi Morgan) start fighting, he slips out his bedroom window and sleeps on the floor of her room. In a sequence of surprising effectiveness, she takes the advice of her mom and sister to "do something" with her hair, and goes to a school dance with a blind date. Quincy is there too. They dance with their dates but they keep looking at each other. You know how it is.

They're both recruited by USC, and both turn into college basketball stars, although Monica, on the women's team, feels she's penalized for an aggression that would be rewarded on the men's team. Their romance has its ups and downs, and eventually they're both

playing in the pros—he in America, she in Spain. The ending reunites them a little too neatly.

But these bare bones of the plot don't convey the movie's special appeal. Written and directed by first-timer Gina Prince-Bythewood (and produced by Spike Lee), it is a sports film seen mostly from the woman's point of view. It's honest and perceptive about love and sex, with no phony drama and a certain quiet maturity. And here's the most amazing thing: It considers sports in terms of career, training, motivation, and strategy. The Big Game scenes involve behavior and attitude, not scoring. The movie sees basketball as something the characters do as a skill and a living, not as an excuse for audience-pleasing jump shots at the buzzer.

Omar Epps is an accomplished actor, effective here if a little too old (twenty-seven) to be playing a high schooler. Sanaa Lathan is the discovery. This is her sixth movie (she was in the look-alike films *The Wood* and *The Best Man*) and her chance to flower, and she does, with a combination of tomboy stubbornness and womanly pride. She has some wonderful scenes with her mother (Alfre Woodard), a housewife who defends her choices in life against her daughter's half-formed feminist notions.

Epps has effective scenes, too, with his parents. His dad retires from pro ball and is socked with a paternity suit, and Quincy has to reevaluate how he feels about both parents in a couple of strong truth-telling scenes.

The movie is not as taut as it could have been, but I prefer its emotional perception to the pumped-up sports clichés I was sort of expecting. Like Robert Towne's *Personal Best*, it's about the pressures of being a star athlete—the whole life, not the game highlights. I'm not sure I quite believe the final shot, though. I think the girl suits up for the sequel.

Love and Death on Long Island
★ ★ ★ ½
PG-13, 93 m., 1998

John Hurt (Giles De'Ath), Jason Priestley (Ronnie Bostock), Fiona Loewi (Audrey), Sheila Hancock (Mrs. Barker), Maury Chaykin (Irving), Gawn Grainger (Henry), Elizabeth Quinn (Mrs.

Reed), Linda Busby (Mrs. Abbott). Directed by Richard Kwietniowski and produced by Steve Clark-Hall and Christopher Zimmer. Screenplay by Kwientniowski, based on the novel by Gilbert Adair.

A creaky British writer, who has lived for decades in a cocoon of his books and his musings, locks himself out of the house one day in the rain. He takes refuge in a nearby movie theater, choosing a film based on a novel by Forster. After a time he murmurs, "This isn't E. M. Forster!" And he begins to collect his coat and hat so that he can leave.

Indeed it is not Forster. The film is *Hotpants College II,* about the hijinks of a crowd of randy undergraduates. But as the writer, named Giles De'Ath, rises to his feet, he sees an image that causes him to pause. The camera slowly zooms in on his face, illuminated by the flickering light reflected from the screen, as he stands transfixed by the sight of a young actor named Ronnie Bostock.

It is this moment of rapture that gives *Love and Death on Long Island* its sly comic enchantment. Giles De'Ath, played by John Hurt as a man long settled in his dry and dusty ways, has fallen in love with a Hollywood teen idol, and his pursuit of this ideal leads him stumbling into the twentieth century. He finds that films can be rented, and goes to a video store to obtain two other Ronnie Bostock titles, *Tex Mex* and *Skidmarks.*

Dressed like an actor playing T. S. Eliot, discussing the titles with the clerk as if he were speaking to a librarian in the British Museum, he rents the tapes and brings them home, only to find that he needs a VCR. He purchases the VCR, and has it delivered to his book-lined study, where the delivery man gently explains why he will also require a television set.

At last, banishing his housekeeper from his study, Giles settles down into a long contemplation of the life and work of Ronnie Bostock. He even obtains teenage fan magazines (the cover of one calls Bostock "snoggable!"), and cuts out Ronnie's photos to paste them in a scrapbook, which in his elaborate cursive script he labels "Bostockiana." He sneaks out to dispose of the magazines as if they were pornography, and daydreams of a TV quiz show on which he would know all the answers to trivia questions about Ronnie (Favorite author: Stephen King. Favorite musician: Axel Rose).

These opening scenes of *Love and Death on Long Island* are funny and touching, and Hurt brings a dignity to Giles De'Ath that transcends any snickering amusement at his infatuation. It's not even perfectly clear that Giles's feelings are homosexual; he has been married, now lives as a widower, and there is no indication that he has (or for that matter had) any sex life at all. At lunch with his bewildered agent, he speaks of "the discovery of beauty where no one ever thought of looking for it." And in a lecture on "The Death of the Future," he spins off into rhapsodies about smiles (he is thinking only about Ronnie's).

There is something here like the obsession of the little man in *Monsieur Hire,* who spies adoringly on the young woman whose window is opposite his own. No physical action is contemplated: Sexual energy has been focused into the eyes and the imagination. The cinema of Ronnie Bostock, Giles believes, "has brought me into contact with all I never have been."

It is always a disappointment when fantasies become real; no mere person can equal our imaginings. Giles actually flies to Long Island, where he knows Bostock has a home, and sets out to find his idol. This journey into the new land is not without hazards for the reclusive London writer, who checks into a hot-sheets motel and soon finds himself hanging out at Chez D'Irv, a diner where the owner (Maury Chaykin) refers to almost everything as "very attractive."

But eventually Giles does find his quarry. First he meets Audrey (Fiona Loewi), Ronnie's girlfriend, and then Ronnie himself, played by Jason Priestley with a sort of distant friendliness that melts a little when Giles starts comparing his films with Shakespeare's bawdy passages. The film doesn't commit the mistake of making Ronnie stupid and shallow, and Audrey is very smart; there's a scene where she looks at Giles long and hard, as his cover story evaporates in her mind.

I almost wish Giles had never gotten to Long Island—had never met the object of his dreams. The film, directed by Richard Kwietniowski and based on a novel by the British film critic Gilbert Adair, steps carefully in the American scenes, and finds a way to end without cheap melodrama or easy emotion. But the heart of the film is in Giles's fascination, his reveries about Ronnie's perfection.

There is a scene in *Hotpants College II* in which Ronnie reclines on the counter of a hamburger joint, and his pose immediately reminds Giles of Henry Wallis's famous painting *The Death of Chatterton,* in which the young poet is found dead on his bed in a garret. Thomas Chatterton was to the eighteenth century as Bostock is to ours, I suppose: sex symbol, star, popular entertainer, golden youth. It's all in how you look at it.

Love Is the Devil ★ ★ ★ ½
NO MPAA RATING, 91 m., 1998

Derek Jacobi (Francis Bacon), Daniel Craig (George Dyer), Tilda Swinton (Muriel Belcher), Anne Lambton (Isabel Rawsthorne), Adrian Scarborough (Daniel Farson), Karl Johnson (John Deakin), Annabel Brooks (Henrietta Moraes). Directed by John Maybury and produced by Chiara Menage. Screenplay by Maybury.

I almost climbed the stairs to the Colony Room once. I wanted to see what it looked like inside. I'd read Daniel Farson's *Soho in the 1950s,* and knew that in a shabby room over Trattoria Otello on Dean Street a woman named Muriel Belcher had long presided over the maintenance and upkeep of a generation of Soho alcoholics. After her death, Ian Board continued the tradition, but did not insult the inmates as much.

I knew that the painters Francis Bacon and Lucian Freud, the writer Jeffrey Bernard, the disgraced *Vogue* photographer John Deakin, and Farson himself had frequented the club, along with such celebrity visitors as Peter O'Toole and Richard Harris. In a time when the London pubs closed in the afternoons and again at 11 P.M., it was a place where you could get a drink pretty much whenever you wanted one.

I didn't climb the stairs. I felt too acutely that I didn't belong. I was not and never would be a member. No matter all the books I'd read, all the things I thought I knew about the Colony Room, I would be seen as a tourist, a foolish grin on my face. That was something I could not abide. I stood on the street and looked upstairs and walked on.

Love Is the Devil, the new film by John Maybury, takes me at last up those stairs and back in time to the decades when Francis Bacon presided over a scruffy roomful of bohemians—some rich, some poor, some gay, some straight, all drunks. The movie is loosely inspired by Farson's *The Gilded Gutter Life of Francis Bacon,* which documents the life of the greatest modern English painter as a dour and bitter ordeal, the bitchiness relieved intermittently by a good vintage and the Dover sole at Wheeler's. (Bacon liked a crowd at lunch, and didn't mind picking up the check.)

To look at a Francis Bacon painting is to get a good idea of the man who painted it. In an era of abstract expressionism, he defiantly painted the figure, because he wanted there to be no mistake: His subject was the human body seen in anguish and ugliness. Flesh clung to the bones of his models like dough slapped on by a careless god. His faces were often distorted into grimaces of pain or despair. His subjects looked like mutations, their flesh melting from radiation or self-loathing. His color sense was uncanny, his draftsmanship was powerful and unmistakable, his art gave an overwhelming sense of the artist.

There are no paintings by Francis Bacon in *Love Is the Devil.* Permission was refused by the estate. What are they waiting for, a film that shows him as a nice guy? It is an advantage to the movie, actually, to do without the actual work: Maybury doesn't have to photograph it devoutly, and the flow of the film is not interrupted by our awareness that we are looking at the real thing. Instead, Maybury and his cinematographer, John Mathieson, make the film itself look like a Bacon. They use filters and lenses to distort faces. They shoot reflections in beer mugs and ashtrays to elongate and stretch images. They use reflections to suggest his diptychs and triptychs. A viewer who has never seen a Bacon would be able to leave this film and identify one instantly in a gallery.

Bacon is played by Derek Jacobi (the king in Branagh's *Hamlet*) as a cold and emotionally careless man, a ginger-haired chipmunk who occupies a studio filled with the debris of his art. (He worked from photographs that fell to the floor and built up into a mulch beneath his feet.) One night while he is sleeping, a burglar breaks in through the skylight. The paintings inside are worth millions, but this burglar, named George Dyer (Daniel Craig), knows nothing of Bacon or his paintings. He's looking for pawnable loot. Bacon awakens and makes him a deal: "Take your clothes off and come to bed. Then you can have whatever you want."

George stays on as Bacon's lover. Bacon is a masochist in private, a sadist in public; at first he is touched by George's naïveté ("You actually make money out of painting?"), but eventually he tires of him. George is neurotic, always obsessively scrubbing his nails, and when he threatens suicide Bacon leaps to the attack, referring to "the beam in the studio screaming to have a rope thrown over it."

Whether *Love Is the Devil* is an accurate portrait of Bacon I have no idea. It faithfully reflects the painter as he is described in Farson's book, which is cited as a source for the movie. No one who has seen a Bacon painting expects a portrait much different than this one. From glimpses of the same Soho haunts in books by the late, celebrated drunk Jeffrey Bernard (whose weekly column in the *Spectator* was described as the world's longest-running suicide note), I recognized Belcher and Board and all the others who used the Colony Room as a refuge from an outer world in which they were always two or three drinks behind.

Lovers of the Arctic Circle ★ ★ ★
R, 112 m., 1999

Fele Martinez (Otto), Najwa Nimi (Ana), Nancho Novo (Alvaro), Maru Valdivielso (Olga), Peru Medem (Otto [Child]), Sara Valiente (Ana [Child]), Victor Hugo Oliveira (Otto [Teenager]), Kristel Diaz (Ana [Teenager]). Directed by Julio Medem and produced by Fernando Bovaira and Enrique Lopez Lavigne. Screenplay by Medem.

palindrome, n. Word, verse, sentence, etc., that reads the same backward as forward (e.g., madam, radar).

There is a certain kind of mind that enjoys difficulties. It is not enough to reach the objective; one must do it in a certain way. We begin by not stepping on the cracks in the sidewalk. Some never stop. Ernest Wright wrote an entire novel without using the letter "e." Hitchcock made a film without a single visible edit. There are paintings made of dots, piano compositions for one hand, and now here is a strange and haunting movie that wants to be a palindrome.

Lovers of the Arctic Circle tells the story of Ana and Otto, whose names are palindromes, and whose lives seem governed by circular patterns. Events at the beginning are related to events at the end. The movie is about love—or, rather, about their grand ideas of romance. It is comforting to think that we can love so powerfully that fate itself wheels and turns at the command of our souls.

Ana and Otto are seen at three periods of their lives. When they are small, they have a chance meeting in the woods, and Otto falls in love with Ana. A message he writes on a paper airplane leads to a meeting between their parents, who fall in love, and there is a marvelous shot of Otto's face when he realizes that the girl he loves is going to become his stepsister. As teenagers, they are lovers. As adults, they are separated—although for one heart-stopping moment they sit back to back in a Spanish café, each unaware of the other. And then fate takes them both to Finland, where the great circles of their lives meet again.

Julio Medem, who wrote and directed *Lovers of the Arctic Circle,* suggests that plot alone is not enough to explain a great love; faith is necessary, and an almost mystical belief that one is destined to share life with a single chosen person. His film more or less begins when Ana and Otto are young, and ends when they are older, but the story line is intercut with scenes and images that move back and forth in time and only gradually reveal their meanings. The shot at the beginning, for example, when one character is reflected in the eyes of another— we find out what that means at the end. And there are moments when a car either does, or does not, crash into a red bus. All becomes clear.

When you have a metaphysical system tiptoeing through a film, it's important that the actors provide a grounding of reality; otherwise, we're down the rabbit hole. There are many stretches in *Lovers of the Arctic Circle* that play just like ordinary drama, as we see the children growing up, we see their parents falling in love, we share the anger of Otto's mother when his father chooses the other woman, and we sense her hurt when Otto announces he wants to move in with the other family (it's not that he doesn't love his mother—but that he loves Ana more). There's even room for Ana's discovery that her mother may not be entirely faithful.

The romance between Ana and Otto (played by three sets of actors) is seen growing over many years, from a moment when young Otto wants to tell Ana he loves her, to a moment when he touches her leg, to a moment in their adolescence when she sends him a note: "Come to me tonight! Jump through the window. Be brave!" The movie doesn't linger on sexual details, but is interested instead in the whole arc of a life. It reminded me of the Kieslowski films in which characters are buffeted by chance, fate, and coincidence. And of Vincent Ward's *A Map of the Human Heart.* Yes, we have free will, such films are saying, and can choose as we want—but what ungoverned forces produce the choices we choose from?

Everything in the film is connected. A German pilot in World War II is linked to another pilot, years later. A story in a newspaper changes its meaning the more we learn. Who steps into the street at the wrong moment, and what happens then? It would be unfair to the film to tell. This is not the sort of movie where you can give away the ending. It is all ending. "In my end is my beginning," T. S. Eliot wrote. By now you are either confused by my description of the film, or intrigued by it. There is a certain kind of mind that enjoys difficulties. Are we not drawn onward to a new era? Give or take an "a"?

The Lovers on the Bridge ★ ★ ★
R, 125 m., 1999

Juliette Binoche (Michele Stalens), Denis Lavant (Alex), Klaus-Michael Gruber (Hans). Directed by Leos Carax and produced by Alain Dahan. Screenplay by Carax.

Leos Carax's *The Lovers on the Bridge* arrives trailing clouds of faded glory. It was already one of the most infamous productions in French history when it premiered at the Cannes festival in 1992, where some were stunned by its greatness and more were simply stunned. Its American release was delayed, according to Carax, because its distributor vindictively jacked up the asking price. Now it has arrived at last, a film both glorious and goofy, inspiring affection and exasperation in about equal measure.

The story could have been told in a silent melodrama, or on the other half of a double bill with Jean Vigo's great *L'Atalante* (1934), which was Carax's inspiration. On the ancient Pont-Neuf, the oldest bridge in Paris, two vagrants discover one another. One is Michele (Juliette Binoche), an artist who is going blind. The other is Alex (Denis Lavant), a drunk and druggie who supports himself by fire-breathing. The bridge has been closed for a year for repairs, bags of cement and paving blocks are tossed about, and they make it their home for the summer; their landlord, so to speak, is a crusty old bum named Hans (Klaus-Michael Gruber).

This three-hander could have made a nice little film in other hands, but Carax's production costs became legendary. His permission to shoot on the Pont-Neuf ran out while delays stalled his production; Lavant broke his leg, which held up the film a year, according to some sources, although since he uses a crutch and wears a cast in the film, one wonders why. (The broken leg is simply explained: Alex passes out in the middle of a boulevard late one night.) Thrown off the real bridge, Carax moved his entire production to the South of France and built a giant set of the Pont-Neuf, including the facades of three buildings of the famous Samaritaine department store. This was not cheap.

The lovers are both reckless and secretive. Michele, who wears a dressing over one eye, doesn't reveal for a long time that she is going blind. Alex loves her and yet would rather read her mail and break into her former home than ask her flat-out about herself. The bum keeps trying to throw her off the bridge ("It's all right for Alex, but not for a young girl like you"), but when he finally shares his own story, it opens the floodgates for all three.

There is much here that is cheerfully reckless, as when Alex does cartwheels on the bridge parapet above the Seine (did no authorities see him?). Or when the two of them steal a police speedboat so she can water-ski past the fireworks display on the night of the French bicentennial. Alex raises money by his fire-eating, his sweaty torso dancing in the middle of smoke and flames, and she pours drugs into the drinks of tourists to steal their money.

All well and good in a different kind of film. But other scenes break with the gritty reality and go for Chaplinesque bathos. Posters go up all over Paris—*all* over, on every Metro wall and construction site—and Alex sets them afire (why is there no one else in the Metro?). Then he torches the van of the man who is hanging the posters, and the man burns alive. This melodramatic excess leads, after a time, to a romantic conclusion that seems to dare us to laugh; Carax piles one development on top of another until it's not a story; it's an exercise in absurdity.

All of this is not without charm. Juliette Binoche, from *The English Patient*, the Kieslowski Red-White-Blue trilogy, and Louis Malle's *Damage*, dares to play her character with the kind of broad strokes you'd find in a silent film, and old Klaus-Michael Gruber has a touching moment of confession as Hans. Denis Lavant is not a likable Alex, but then how could he be? His approach to romance is simple: He makes his most dramatic demonstration of love in her absence, by burning the posters so she will not leave him; when she's there, he's likely to be sullen, petulant, or drunk. For two strong young people to embrace their lifestyle is itself an exercise in stylish defeatism; they have to choose to be miserable, and they do, wearing it well.

I felt a certain affection for *The Lovers on the Bridge*. It is not the masterpiece its defenders claim, nor is it the completely self-indulgent folly described by its critics. It has grand gestures and touching moments of truth, perched precariously on a foundation of horsefeathers.

So troubled was its distribution history that Carax waited seven years to make another film, which confirmed his unshakably goofy worldview. That was *Pola X*, which opened the 1999 Cannes festival, and was a modern telling of Melville's nineteenth-century novel *Pierre*, about a young man's idyllic relationship with his mother and his happy plans for marriage,

all destroyed by the appearance of a strange, dark woman who claims to be his father's secret daughter. The movie "exists outside the categories of good and bad," I wrote from Cannes; "it is a magnificent folly."

The Lovers on the Bridge, on the other hand, exists just inside the category of good. I am not sure, thinking about the two films, that I don't prefer *Pola X*. If you have little taste or discipline as a filmmaker but great style and heedlessness, it may be more entertaining to go for broke than to fake a control you don't possess.

Love's Labour's Lost ★ ★ ½
PG, 95 m., 2000

Kenneth Branagh (Berowne), Alessandro Nivola (King), Nathan Lane (Costard), Adrian Lester (Dumaine), Matthew Lillard (Longaville), Natascha McElhone (Rosaline), Alicia Silverstone (Princess), Timothy Spall (Don Armado), Carmen Ejogo (Maria), Emily Mortimer (Katherine). Directed by Kenneth Branagh and produced by David Barron and Branagh. Screenplay by Branagh, based on the play by William Shakespeare.

Shakespeare supplies not so much the source of Kenneth Branagh's *Love's Labour's Lost* as the clothesline. Using the flimsy support of one of the least of the master's plots, Branagh strings together ten song-and-dance numbers in a musical that's more like a revue than an adaptation. After daring to film his great version of *Hamlet* using the entire, uncut original play (the first time that had been done), Branagh here cuts and slashes through Shakespeare's text with an editorial machete.

What is left is winsome, charming, sweet, and slight. It's so escapist it escapes even from itself. The story pairs off four sets of lovers, supplies them with delightful songs and settings, and calls it a day. The cast is not especially known for being able to sing and dance (only the British Adrian Lester and the Broadway veteran Nathan Lane are pros in those departments), but that's part of the charm. Like Woody Allen's *Everyone Says I Love You*, this is one of those movies were real people are so seized with the need to break into song that a lack of talent can't stop them.

Not, in fact, that they are untalented. The songs here are well within the abilities of the cast to sing them, and indeed several of them were originally sung on the screen by Fred Astaire, whose vocal range was as modest as his footwork was unlimited. (Most of the songs have been recorded on albums by the British singer Peter Skellern, who can hit a note and the one below it and the one above it, and that's about it—and he makes them entertaining too.)

The plot: The king of Navarre (Alessandro Nivola) has declared that he and three of his comrades (Kenneth Branagh, Adrian Lester, Matthew Lillard) will withdraw from the world for three years of thought and study. During this time, they will reject all worldly pleasures, most particularly the company of women. No sooner do they make their vow and retire to their cloister than the princess of France (Alicia Silverstone) arrives for a visit, accompanied by three friends (Natascha McElhone, Carmen Ejogo, Emily Mortimer).

The men find it acutely poignant that they have sworn off the company of women (with a severe penalty for the first who succumbs). They search for loopholes. Perhaps if the ladies camp *outside* the palace walls, that won't count as a visit. Perhaps if the visit is a state occasion, it is not a social one . . .

All of these rationalizations collapse before the beauty of the women, and the eight men and women pair off into four couples so quickly it's like choosing sides for a softball game. Then we get the songs, some of them wonderfully well staged, as when "Cheek to Cheek" (with its line "Heaven . . . I'm in heaven . . .") has them floating in midair beneath the stars painted on the underside of the dome of the king's library.

The eight starters are joined by low-comedy relief pitchers, in the tradition of all Shakespeare comedies. They include Timothy Spall as a Spaniard whose "I Get a Kick Out of You" is a charmer, and Nathan Lane (who does a nice slow-tempo "There's No Business Like Show Business"). Alicia Silverstone is the lead among the women, who playfully do a synchroswimming version of "Fancy Free," and Branagh gives himself the best male role, although not tilting the scales to an unseemly degree.

All is light and winning, and yet somehow empty. It's no excuse that the starting point was one of the weaker of Shakespeare's plays. *Love's Labour's Lost* is hardly ever performed on the stage and has never been previously filmed, and there is a reason for that: It's not about anything. In its original form, instead of the songs and dances we have dialogue that's like an idle exercise in brainy banter for Shakespeare.

It's like a warm-up for the real thing. It makes not the slightest difference which boy gets which girl, or why, and by starting the action in 1939 and providing World War II as a backdrop, Branagh has not enriched either the play or the war, but fit them together with an awkward join. There's not a song I wouldn't hear again with pleasure, or a clip that might not make me smile, but as a whole, it's not much. Like cotton candy, it's better as a concept than as an experience.

Love Walked In ★ ★

R, 90 m., 1998

Denis Leary (Jack Hanaway), Terence Stamp (Fred Moore), Aitana Sanchez-Gijon (Vicki Rivas), Danny Nucci (Cousin Matt), Moira Kelly (Vera), Michael Badalucco (Eddie Bianco), Gene Canfield (Joey), Marj Dusay (Judith Moore). Directed by Juan J. Campanella and produced by Ricardo Freixa. Screenplay by Campanella, Lynn Geller, and Larry Golin, based on a novel by Jose Pablo Feinmann.

Love Walked In proves something that nobody ever thought to demonstrate before: You can't make a convincing *film noir* about good people. *Noir* is about weakness and temptation, and if the characters are going to get soppy and let their better natures prevail, what's left? Has there ever been a thriller about resisting temptation?

The movie has two other problems: It requires the female lead to behave in a way that's contrary to everything we know about her. And it intercuts the action with an absurd parallel story, a fantasy the hero is writing. He hopes to become a novelist, but on the basis of this sample he should stick to playing the piano. Oh, and the filmmakers should have guessed that the big ending, where the hero falls out of a tree, would inspire laughs just when the movie doesn't need any.

Yet the elements are here for a decent *film noir*. There is, first of all, good casting. Denis Leary plays Jack, a world-weary pianist in a fleapit lounge named the Blue Cat. Aitana Sanchez-Gijon is Vicki, his wife, a songstress who has a way with the pseudo-Gershwin tunes Jack writes. And Terence Stamp, he of the penetrating blue eyes and saturnine features, is a rich man named Moore who frequents the lounge and whose desire stirs for Vicki. Leary has been in a lot of movies lately (*The Real Blonde, Wag the Dog*), but this is the one where he really emerges: He began as a comedian learning to act, but now you can see that he has the stuff, that given a good script he could handle an important role.

Aitana Sanchez-Gijon (Keanu Reeves's love in *A Walk in the Clouds*) is also just right; you can see how this situation could have been rewritten into a workable *noir*. But neither she nor any other actress could convincingly handle the scenes where she is required to mislead Moore. Women don't work that way. Oh, a femme fatale might, but the whole point is that Vicki's heart is in the right place.

The setup: Jack and Vicki are desperately poor after ten years of touring crummy clubs. (Strange, since they're talented.) Jack's old buddy Eddie (Michael Badalucco), now a private eye, turns up and reveals he's been hired by Moore's jealous wife to get the dirt on him. Since Moore has the hots for Vicki, Eddie says, why not blackmail him—which would rescue Vicki and Jack from poverty row: "You guys have the real thing. All you need is a little dough to complete the picture."

This is a classic *noir* suggestion. And in a different kind of film we'd believe it when Jack suggests this plan to Vicki. But we never sense that Vicki is that kind of girl. She's wounded when she first hears the plan; Jack says she'd only have to "make out" with Moore long enough for Eddie to take photos, and Vicki shoots back, "Make out? How much? Second base? Third? Home run?" But she goes along with the scheme, even though the movie lacks any scene or motivation to explain her change of heart—or indeed, any way of telling what

she's really thinking most of the time. Her character is seen entirely from the outside, as an enigma, and maybe that's exactly what she was to the writer-director, Juan J. Campanella.

As for Jack, his character is confusingly written, and it doesn't help that he constantly interrupts the action with cutaways to a parallel story, which he narrates with Rod Serlingesque solemnity. The plot whips itself into a frenzied payoff, with thunder and lightning on cue, as Jack finds himself out on a limb in a scene that would be plausible, unfortunately, only if played by John Belushi in *Animal House*.

Love Walked In has the right moves for *noir*: the melancholy, the sexiness, the cigarettes, the shadows. But you have to believe in the characters and their capacity for evildoing. These characters act like they saw *Double Indemnity* on TV once and thought they could do that stuff themselves, and were wrong.

Lucie Aubrac ★ ★ ½
R, 116 m., 1999

Carole Bouquet (Lucie), Daniel Auteuil (Raymond), Patrice Chereau (Max), Jean-Roger Milo (Maurice), Eric Boucher (Serge), Heino Ferch (Barbie), Bernard Verley (Charles-Henri), Jean Martin (Paul Lardanchet), Marie Piller (Marie). Directed and produced by Claude Berri. Screenplay by Berri, based on the novel *Ils partiront dans l'ivresse* by Lucie Aubrac.

Lucie Aubrac is set in Lyon in 1943, and tells the story of a brave, pregnant woman who leads a daring raid to free her husband, a Resistance leader who has been condemned to death by the Gestapo. It is based on a novel by the real Lucie Aubrac, who says in a final screen note that she chose Claude Berri to direct the film because of his support for a foundation that commemorates the Resistance. It is a quiet and bitter joke in France, of course, that once the war was over everyone turned out to have been in the Resistance; the Nazis ran things with no help at all.

The opening titles tell us that *Lucie Aubrac* is based on fact, although "certain liberties" have been taken for the purposes of drama. On a whim, I searched for Raymond and Lucie Aubrac on the Web, and turned up many pages from *Liberation,* the Paris daily, involving a controversy over the most basic facts of all. Were the Aubracs indeed Resistance heroes, as her novel presents them, or did Raymond crack under Gestapo torture and identify the Resistance leader Jean Moulin? Detractors point to the coincidence that soon after Raymond's escape, Moulin was betrayed.

I don't have a clue about these facts, any of them. I doubt Lucie Aubrac would draw the attention of a novel and film to her story if she felt it could be disproved. At this point the Gestapo witnesses involved are certainly dead (among them Klaus Barbie, the "Butcher of Lyon," who makes a brief appearance here). What we are left with is a story which, if true, is certainly heroic. But since we are attending a movie and not a benefit, we must ask if we are moved and entertained.

I must say, not enough. There are some moments of true tension, as when Lucie (Carole Bouquet) confronts local Nazi officials and claims she is pregnant by the man they are holding prisoner, and wants to be married so her child can have a name. And more tension when she is permitted to meet with her husband in front of the Nazis. He has claimed to be somebody else, has denied he knows her, and now must somehow intuit that the time is right to admit his real identity—since her plan involves hijacking the truck that would carry him from prison to the wedding ceremony.

Those scenes work. Other scenes, including the planning and execution of the snatch, would not be remarkable if we saw them in a fiction film. They take on a certain interest because they are based on fact, yes, but the bones of the action are not very meaty. A map is drawn, showing an intersection of two streets. A plan is devised: Partisans will drive their cars in front of the truck, blocking it. Others will shoot the driver and guards. Raymond Aubrac and his fellow prisoners will escape. This is not the stuff of a caper movie.

Raymond is played by Daniel Auteuil, who has the best nose among French actors, ahead even of Depardieu (whose nose has been broken more often than Auteuil's but with less dramatic effect). He is a wonderful actor *(A Heart in Winter, My Favorite Season, Les Voleurs).* Here he seems constrained by the tradition of brave understatement that inflicts so many movie Resistance heroes. He is tender in quiet, private moments with his wife, but otherwise is essentially a pawn in her scheme.

Bouquet is an enigma. A beautiful woman, she somehow lacks juice in this role. She is too perfectly coiffed, dressed, made up; there should be more smudges on a girl who has been seduced and abandoned. Opportunities are lost in her meetings with Nazi officials, including one beefy general who in civilian life could have been typecast as a real butcher, in Lyon or anywhere. The confrontations are too dry, too restrained by unexpressed hostility. The movie has too much docudrama and not enough soul.

As a heroine, Lucie Aubrac has much to recommend her. After the screening I informed my wife that in the event of my being taken prisoner by villains, I would expect her, like Lucie, to lead a raid to free me. She agreed. I hope she springs me before I crack under torture.

M

Madadayo ★ ★ ★
NO MPAA RATING, 134 m., 1998

Tatsuo Matsumura (Hyakken Uchida), Kyoko Kagawa (Uchida's wife), Hisashi Igawa (Takayama), George Tokoro (Amaki). Directed by Akira Kurosawa and produced by Hisao Kurosawa. Screenplay by Akira Kurosawa.

Made in 1993 when he was eighty-three, *Madadayo* is possibly the last film by the Japanese master Akira Kurosawa, who is the greatest living filmmaker. And yet the very title of the film argues otherwise; it means "not yet!" That is the ritual cry that the film's old professor shouts out at the end of every one of his birthday parties, and it means that although death will come and may be near, life still goes on.

This is the kind of film we would all like to make, if we were very old and very serene. There were times when I felt uncannily as if Kurosawa were filming his own graceful decline into the night. It tells the story of the last two decades in the life of Hyakken Uchida, a writer and teacher who retires in the war years of the early 1940s. He was the kind of teacher who could inspire great respect and affection from his students, who venerate him and, as a group, help support him in his old age.

In Japan they have a tradition of "living national treasures"—people who because of their gifts and knowledge are treated like national monuments. Uchida is such a man, who has taught all his life and now finds that his books are selling well enough that he can move with his wife to a pretty little house, and sit in the entranceway: "That will be my study, and at the same time I will be the gatekeeper."

Kurosawa's career has itself spanned some sixty years, and the titles of his films are spoken with awe by those who love them. Consider that the same man made *Rashomon, Yojimbo, Ikiru, The Seven Samurai, The Hidden Fortress, Red Beard, Throne of Blood, Kagemusha, Ran,* and twenty-five more. His movies have been filled with life and spectacle, but here, in *Madadayo,* he has made a film in the spirit of his near-contemporary Yasujiro Ozu, whose domestic dramas are among the most quietly observant and contemplative of all films.

Very little happens in *Madadayo.* The old man (Tatsuo Matsumura) and his wife (Kyoko Kagawa) are feted by his students on his sixtieth birthday, and go to live in the fine little house. The house is destroyed in an air raid. They move to a little hut, hardly more than a room and a half, and there the professor also sits in the doorway and writes. His students come to see him, and every year on his birthday they have the ritual party at which he downs a big glass of beer and cries out "not yet!"

The students conspire to find the professor a larger house. Then something very important happens. A cat named Nora wanders into their house, and the professor and his wife come to love it. Nora disappears. The professor is grief-stricken. Leaflets are circulated, and his students, now middle-aged businessmen, scour the neighborhood for Nora, without success. Then another cat walks into their house, and the wound is healed.

At the professor's seventy-seventh birthday dinner, we see that things have changed. The early events were held Japanese-style, with men only. Now women are present, too: wives, daughters, even grandchildren, in a Western-style banquet room. And still the cry is "not yet!"

Like Ozu, Kurosawa is content to let his camera rest and observe. We never quite learn what sorts of things the professor writes (the real Uchida was in fact a beloved essayist), but we know he must be a great man because his students love him so. We learn few intimate details about his life (not even, if I recall, his wife's first name). We see him mostly seated in his front door, as a stranger might.

Like his students, we are amused by his signs forbidding visitors and warning away those who would urinate on his wall. We learn about the burglar-proofing strategies in his first, larger, house: He leaves a door open, with a sign saying "Burglar's Entrance." Inside, signs indicate "Burglar's Passage," "Burglar's Recess Area" and "Burglar's Exit." He guesses right that burglars would prefer to operate in a house that grants them more anonymity.

The movie is as much about the students as the professor, as much about gratitude and love as about aging. In an interview at the time of the film's release, Kurosawa said his movie is about "something very precious, which has been all but forgotten: the enviable world of warm hearts." He added, "I hope that all the people who have seen this picture will leave the theater feeling refreshed, with broad smiles on their faces."

Madeline ★ ★ ★
PG, 89 m., 1998

Frances McDormand (Miss Clavel), Nigel Hawthorne (Lord Covington), Hatty Jones (Madeline), Ben Daniels (Leopold the Tutor), Stephane Audran (Lady Covington), Arturo Venegas (Mr. Spanish Ambassador), Katia Caballero (Mrs. Spanish Ambassador), Chantal Neuwirth (Helene the Cook). Directed by Daisy von Scherler Mayer and produced by Saul Cooper, Pancho Kohner, and Allyn Stewart. Screenplay by Mark Levin and Jennifer Flackett, based on the book *Madeline* by Ludwig Bemelmans.

It is a great sadness that a witty and graceful prose stylist like Ludwig Bemelmans should today be remembered primarily for his children's books about Madeline. His works should be in every bookstore, somewhere near Waugh and Thurber, and studied by anyone who wants to learn how to put a sentence together without any nails.

Still, to have a degree of immortality is a blessing, and today there are little girls (and some boys) all over the world who can recite for you the opening lines of Bemelmans's first book about Madeline:

In an old house in Paris that was covered with vines,
Lived 12 little girls in two straight lines.

Bemelmans illustrated the books himself—made the drawings, indeed, for many of his books, which involved sophisticated but penniless European exiles who found themselves in such unfamiliar places as South American palaces and Manhattan hotels. There is a prejudice against adult books with illustrations; readers generally put them down with a sniff. In the case of Bemelmans, they are missing

some of the slyest and most seductive writing of the century. And enchanting drawings.

But the riches of Bemelmans are years in the future for the intended audience for *Madeline*, a family movie that does a surprisingly good job of using real actors and locations and making them look and feel like the books it is based on.

Some of the episodes are by Bemelmans, such as Madeline's appendectomy, or her fall into the Seine and rescue by the brave dog Genevieve. Others are invented. Even though the inventions involve an attempted kidnapping, this is not one of those children's movies that depends on noise and action to keep the attention of the audience. The movie has some of the same decorum and understated humor as the books.

Madeline is, of course, one of the twelve little girls who attends a boarding school in Paris run by Miss Clavel (Frances McDormand). An orphan, she is the smallest of the girls, who line up according to height before marching out in their straw hats for processions past Paris landmarks. Both her school and the house next door, which is purchased for the Spanish embassy, look gratifyingly like the Bemelmans drawings (there's a perfect match in the opening fade from drawing to real life).

The plot also involves Pepito, the show-off son of the Spanish ambassador, who roars around the courtyard on his motor scooter and dresses as a matador for his birthday. The girls peer at him from their windows, endure his bragging, and survive his willingness to demonstrate how to decapitate a white mouse before feeding it to his pet snake. Little does Pepito suspect that he figures in the plans of his tutor and a circus clown, who plot to abduct him.

Meanwhile, kind Lady Covington (Stephane Audran), who provides for the school, dies in the hospital, and her glint-eyed husband, Lord Covington (Nigel Hawthorne, from *The Madness of George V*), starts leading potential purchasers through the house. He wants to sell it for an embassy, and his ruthlessness is such that he even paints over the marks on the wall showing how the girls have grown during the year.

Hatty Jones makes an admirable Madeline, small and intent, and I liked her determination. When it appears the school will be sold, she decides to run away to join the circus, and that's how she discovers the plot against Pepito. Amazing that Miss Clavel didn't sniff it out first; she has a way of stopping stock-still, listening to unheard sounds, and announcing, "Something . . . is not right!"

Madeline is a quietly charming movie for kids not too hyped on action and candy. It's assisted mightily by the presence of McDormand and Hawthorne, who play their roles precisely, not broadly, and come across as people, not caricatures. It's not the noisy kind of movie that steamrollers kids into acceptance, like *Mortal Kombat*—but one, like *Mulan* or *Doctor Dolittle*, that actually expects them to listen, and pick up on some of the character humor. Observe, for example, how the movie handles the impending death of the chicken Fred, and Madeline's conversion to vegetarianism.

Mafia! ★ ★
PG-13, 86 m., 1998

Jay Mohr (Anthony Cortino), Billy Burke (Joey Cortino), Christina Applegate (Diane), Pamela Gidley (Pepper Gianini), Olympia Dukakis (Sophia), Lloyd Bridges (Vincenzo Cortino), Jason Fuchs (Young Vincenzo), Joe Viterelli (Clamato). Directed by Jim Abrahams and produced by Bill Badalato. Screenplay by Abrahams, Greg Norberg, and Michael McManus.

Yes, I laughed during Jim Abrahams's *Mafia!*, but even in midchortle I was reminded of the gut-busting experience of seeing *There's Something About Mary*. It is the new movie's misfortune to arrive after, instead of before, the funniest comedy of the year. I suppose it's not fair to penalize *Mafia!* for its timing, but on the other hand, how can I ignore it?

The movie, titled *Jane Austen's Mafia!* on the screen but not in the ads, is another in the series of gag-a-minit parodies worked on by Abrahams, like *Airplane!*, *Top Secret*, and the *Naked Gun* movies. It's a takeoff on Coppola's *The Godfather* and *Godfather, Part II* and Scorsese's *Casino*, with a few touches of *Il Postino*.

The opening shot is the best one, as Anthony Cortino (Jay Mohr), the mob's man in a

Las Vegas casino, turns the ignition on his Cadillac and is blown sky-high. In the Scorsese picture Robert De Niro rotated dreamily against a backdrop of flames; here the actor catches a Frisbee in his mouth, scores a basket, and watches the *Twister* cow drift by.

The movie, narrated by this character, tells the story of his father's youth in Sicily *(Godfather II)* and his own rise through the mob. Young Vincenzo Cortino, who is raised in the town of Salmonella ("Home of Warm Mayonnaise"), is played by Jason Fuchs. He immigrates to America (where the Ellis Island guards try to name him "Armani Windbreaker" after his jacket), and by the time he reaches Godfather status he's played by the late Lloyd Bridges, who has fun kidding Brando's famous tomatoes-and-death scene.

The don's older son, Joey (Bully Burke), is a short-tempered hothead, and power in the family devolves to Anthony (Mohr), based on the Al Pacino character. Familiarity with the earlier films is helpful, but then who isn't familiar with the *Godfather* movies—and who won't appreciate it when the Diane Keaton character (played by Christina Applegate) complains, "I'm always gonna just be that Protestant chick who never killed anyone."

In Vegas, Cortino runs a casino that includes such games as Go Fish and Snakes and Ladders. My favorite: Guess the Number. "Two?" says a gambler. "Sorry," says the dealer. "I was thinking of three." When cheats are discovered signaling to one another, a tough enforcer with a cattle prod sidles up to the wrong man, zaps him, and then zaps everyone else in the area. Anthony's life in Vegas gets complicated when he falls for a dancer named Pepper Gianini (Pamela Gidley), based on the Sharon Stone character in *Casino*.

I smiled through a lot of this, including Cortino's tip for the casino doorman ("Keep the car"), but by the time the projectile vomiting came around I was wondering if that was a homage to *Animal House* or only a lift. *Mafia!* is the kind of movie that can never entirely fail, but can succeed to various degrees. It doesn't rank with Abrahams's earlier efforts. And in a town where *There's Something About Mary* is playing, it's not the one to choose.

Magnolia ★ ★ ★ ★
R, 179 m., 2000

Jason Robards (Earl Partridge), Julianne Moore (Linda Partridge), Tom Cruise (Frank Mackey), Philip Seymour Hoffman (Phil Parma), John C. Reilly (Officer Kurring), Melora Walters (Claudia Gator), Jeremy Blackman (Stanley Spector), Michael Bowen (Rick Spector), William H. Macy (Donnie Smith), Philip Baker Hall (Jimmy Gator), Melinda Dillon (Rose Gator), April Grace (Reporter). Directed by Paul Thomas Anderson and produced by Joanne Sellar. Screenplay by Anderson.

Magnolia is operatic in its ambition, a great joyous leap into melodrama and coincidence, with ragged emotions, crimes and punishments, deathbed scenes, romantic dreams, generational turmoil, and celestial intervention, all scored to insistent music. It is not a timid film. Paul Thomas Anderson here joins Spike Jonze *(Being John Malkovich),* David O. Russell *(Three Kings),* and their master, Martin Scorsese *(Bringing Out the Dead),* in beginning the new decade with an extroverted self-confidence that rejects the timid postmodernism of the 1990s. These are not movies that apologize for their exuberance or shield themselves with irony against suspicions of sincerity.

The movie is an interlocking series of episodes that take place during one day in Los Angeles, sometimes even at the same moment. Its characters are linked by blood, coincidence, and by the way their lives seem parallel. Themes emerge: the deaths of fathers, the resentments of children, the failure of early promise, the way all plans and ambitions can be undermined by sudden and astonishing events. Robert Altman's *Short Cuts* was also a group of interlinked Los Angeles stories, and both films illustrate former district attorney Vincent Bugliosi's observation in *Till Death Do Us Part* that personal connections in L.A. have a way of snaking around barriers of class, wealth, and geography.

The actors here are all swinging for the fences, heedless of image or self-protective restraint. Here are Tom Cruise as a loathsome stud, Jason Robards looking barely alive, William H. Macy as a pathetic loser, Melora Wal-

ters as a despairing daughter, Julianne Moore as an unloving wife, Michael Bowen as a browbeating father. Some of these people are melting down because of drugs or other reasons; a few, like a cop played by John C. Reilly and a nurse played by Philip Seymour Hoffman, are caregivers.

The film's opening sequence, narrated by an uncredited Ricky Jay, tells stories of incredible coincidences. One has become a legend of forensic lore; it's about the man who leaps off a roof and is struck by a fatal shotgun blast as he falls past a window before landing in a net that would have saved his life. The gun was fired by his mother, aiming at his father and missing. She didn't know the shotgun was loaded; the son had loaded it some weeks earlier, hoping that eventually one of his parents would shoot the other. All (allegedly) true.

This sequence suggests a Ricky Jay TV special, illustrating weird coincidences. But it is more than simply amusing. It sets up the theme of the film, which shows people earnestly and single-mindedly immersed in their lives, hopes, and values, as if their best-laid plans were not vulnerable to the chaotic interruptions of the universe. It's humbling to learn that existence doesn't revolve around us; worse to learn it revolves around nothing.

Many of the characters are involved in television, and their lives reflect on one another. Robards plays a dying tycoon who produces many shows. Philip Baker Hall, also dying, is a game show host. Cruise is Robards's son, the star of infomercials about how to seduce women; his macho hotel ballroom seminars could have been scripted by Andrew Dice Clay. Walters is Hall's daughter, who doesn't believe anything he says. Melinda Dillon is Hall's wife, who might have been happier without his compulsion for confession. Macy plays "former quiz kid Donnie Smith," now a drunk with a bad job in sales, who dreams that orthodontics could make him attractive to a burly bartender. Jeremy Blackman plays a bright young quiz kid on Hall's program. Bowen plays his father, a tyrant who drives him to excel.

The connections are like a game of psychological pickup sticks. Robards alienated Cruise, Hall alienated Dillon, Bowen is alienating Blackman. The power of TV has not spared Robards or Hall from death. Childhood success left Macy unprepared for life, and may be doing the same thing for Blackman. Both Hall and Robards have employees (a producer, a nurse) who love them more than their families do. Both Robards and Hall cheated on their wives. And around and around.

And there are other stories with their own connections. The cop, played by Reilly, is like a fireman rushing to scenes of emotional turmoil. His need to help is so great that he falls instantly in love with the pathetic drug user played by Walters; her need is more visible to him than her crime. Later, he encounters Macy in the middle of a ridiculous criminal situation brought about to finance braces for his teeth.

There are big scenes here for the actors. One comes as Cruise's cocky TV stud disintegrates in the face of cross-examination from a TV reporter (April Grace). He has another big scene at Robards's deathbed. Philip Baker Hall (a favorite actor of Anderson's since *Hard Eight*) also disintegrates on TV; he's unable to ask, instead of answer, questions. Julianne Moore's breakdown in a pharmacy is parallel to Walters's nervousness with the cop: Both women are trying to appear functional while their systems scream because of drugs.

All of these threads converge, in one way or another, upon an event there is no way for the audience to anticipate. This event is not "cheating," as some critics have argued, because the prologue fully prepares the way for it, as do some subtle references to Exodus. It works like the hand of God, reminding us of the absurdity of daring to plan. And yet plan we must, because we are human, and because sometimes our plans work out.

Magnolia is the kind of film I instinctively respond to. Leave logic at the door. Do not expect subdued taste and restraint but instead a kind of operatic ecstasy. At three hours it is even operatic in length, as its themes unfold, its characters strive against the dying of the light, and the great wheel of chance rolls on toward them.

The Man in the Iron Mask ★ ★ ½
PG-13, 117 m., 1998

Leonardo DiCaprio (King Louis/Phillippe), Jeremy Irons (Aramis), John Malkovich (Athos), Gérard Depardieu (Porthos), Gabriel Byrne (D'Artagnan), Anne Parillaud (Queen Anne), Judith Godreche (Christine), Peter Sarsgaard (Raoul). Directed by Randall Wallace and produced by Wallace and Russell Smith. Screenplay by Wallace, based on the novel by Alexandre Dumas.

On the island of St. Marguerite, offshore from Cannes of all places, still stands the rude stone fortress where the Man in the Iron Mask spent his lonely days. I have sat below his window while the owner of the little Italian trattoria assured me that the man in the mask was no less than the twin brother of Louis XIV, held there because the state could not tolerate another claimant to the throne.

No one knows who the man in the mask was, but his dangerous identity must have been the whole point of the mask, so the twin brother theory is as good as any. *The Man in the Iron Mask* is "loosely based" on the Dumas novel, and includes a return appearance by the Three Musketeers. They come out of retirement in a scheme to rescue France from the cruel fist of the young, spoiled king.

Louis XIV and his brother are played by Leonardo DiCaprio in a dual role, his first film since *Titanic*. He looks well fed as the despotic ruler and not particularly gaunt, for that matter, as the man in the mask. As the film opens, he presides over a court that lives in decadent luxury, while mobs riot for bread in the streets. The beautiful Christine (Judith Godreche) catches his eye, and since she's engaged to the young Raoul (Peter Sarsgaard), the king sends Raoul off to war and makes sure he gets killed there.

The death of Raoul enrages his father, Athos (John Malkovich), one of the original musketeers, who enlists his comrades Aramis (Jeremy Irons) and Porthos (Gérard Depardieu) in a plan for revenge. Also involved, on the other side, is the original fourth musketeer, D'Artagnan (Gabriel Byrne), who remains loyal to Louis XIV and the twins' mother, Queen Anne (Anne Parillaud).

This setup, easy enough to explain, takes director Randall Wallace too long to establish, and there are side plots, such as the king's war against the Jesuits, that will confuse audiences. There was once a time when everyone had heard of the musketeers and the Man in the Iron Mask, but history these days seems to start with the invention of MTV, and those not familiar with the characters will take some time to get oriented.

The screenplay by Wallace (who wrote *Braveheart*) is not well focused, and there are gratuitous scenes, but finally we understand the central thread: The musketeers will spring the Man in the Iron Mask from captivity, and secretly substitute him for his brother. The actual mechanics of their plan left me shaking my head with incredulity. Does anyone think Jeremy Irons is large enough to smuggle Leonardo DiCaprio past suspicious guards under his cloak? Wallace should have dreamed up a better plan.

The substitution of the king and his twin is accomplished at a fancy dress ball, where the conspirators drive Louis XIV wild with fear by convincing him he sees iron masks everywhere. But the movie, alas, limits itself to the action in the plot—escapes, sword fights, the frequent incantation "all for one and one for all"—and ignores the opportunity to have more fun with the notion of a prisoner suddenly finding himself king.

Leonardo DiCaprio is the star of the story without being its hero, although his first emergence from the mask is an effective shot. The three musketeers are cast with big names (Irons, Malkovich, Depardieu), but to my surprise the picture is stolen by Gabriel Byrne, who has the most charisma and is the most convincing. His scenes with Parillaud (from *La Femme Nikita*) are some of the best in the movie. Once all the pieces of the plot were in place, I was at least interested, if not overwhelmed; I could see how, with a rewrite and a better focus, this could have been a film of *Braveheart* quality instead of basically just a costume swashbuckler.

Man of the Century ★ ★ ★
R, 78 m., 1999

Gibson Frazier (Johnny Twennies), Susan Egan (Samantha Winter), Anthony Rapp (Timothy Burns), Cara Buono (Virginia Clemens), Brian Davies (Victor Young), Dwight Ewell (Richard Lancaster), Frank Gorshin (Roman Navarro), David Margulies (Mr. Meyerscholtz), Bobby Short (Chester), Marisa Ryan (Gertrude). Directed by Adam Abraham and produced by Gibson Frazier and Abraham. Screenplay by Frazier and Abraham.

I have a friend named Jay Robert Nash who seems to be a character written by Ben Hecht. He embodies a personal style of speech and dress that would be at home in a classic old crime film or screwball comedy, and indeed he is an expert on both; he has penned encyclopedias on both film and crime. Nash talks with a cigarette bobbing in his mouth, likes to wear fedoras, and calls you "mug." Not only did he write a book proving that the FBI didn't kill John Dillinger outside the Biograph Theater, he actually met Dillinger in the 1960s ("I could see him through the screen door—an old man now, a hand on the heavy gat in his bathrobe pocket . . .").

Nash is a work of art, and the only person I know who does not need to see *Man of the Century*. This film is about a man with the style of a character in a 1920s wisecracking movie, who lives in the 1990s. Johnny Twennies (Gibson Frazier) walks, talks, dresses, behaves, and thinks like a character that might have been played by Jimmy Cagney or Pat O'Brien.

He writes a column for a modern New York newspaper, but on his desk there's a battered old Smith-Corona typewriter. There's no smoking in the office, of course, but Johnny always has one lit. When he grabs the phone, it's to say things like, "Hello, sweetheart! Give me rewrite!" And when he takes a date to a nightclub, a song and dance number breaks out and the movie stops to savor it.

Johnny lives in a world of street crime and casual four-letter vulgarity, but he doesn't seem to notice the shocking language that surrounds him. When he wants to ask his "best girl" out on a date, he sends her a telegram. His girl, Samantha (Susan Egan), runs an art gallery in SoHo and is a liberated woman, who finds it peculiar that Johnny hasn't made a move. One night she pins him to the sofa and tries to get a kiss, but—hey, what kindofa guy does she think he is?

Johnny writes his column about no-news stories like a ribbon-cutting at a library. But readers love it because of its innocence. The paper assigns him a photographer named Tim

(Anthony Rapp) who is gay, but Johnny doesn't comprehend homosexuality, or indeed much of anything else in the modern world. When he sees a mugging under way, he breaks it up instead of Not Getting Involved.

Gibson Frazier, who not only stars but cowrote the screenplay with director Adam Abraham, has a natural affinity for this material. You can't fake rapid-fire screwball dialogue. It has to be in your blood. *Man of the Century* is a peculiar delight, a one-of-a-kind movie that was obviously inspired by his love of old movies.

Watching those old films, I wonder if anybody ever really talked that way. And then I remember a story about Ben Hecht, who wrote dozens of crime movies, and realized that gangsters were learning how to talk by studying his movies. Stylized speech and behavior in the movies took a body blow from the Method, which prized realism above mannerism. *Man of the Century* is like a prizefight between the two acting styles, as if a character from *The Front Page* has been teleported into a movie from 1999. You review a movie like this, and you don't want to e-mail it to the office. You want to get on the horn and ask for rewrite, sister—on the double, see?

Man on the Moon ★ ★ ★ ½
R, 118 m., 1999

Jim Carrey (Andy Kaufman), Courtney Love (Lynne Margulies), Paul Giamatti (Bob Zmuda), Danny DeVito (George Shapiro), Jerry Lawler (Himself). Directed by Milos Forman and produced by Danny DeVito, Michael Shamberg, and Stacey Sher. Screenplay by Scott Alexander and Larry Karaszewski.

Our inner child embraces Andy Kaufman. We've been just like that. Who cannot remember boring our friends for hour after hour after *hour* with the same dumb comic idea, endlessly insisted on? Who hasn't refused to admit being wrong? "I won't give up on this," we're saying, "until you give up first. Until you laugh, or agree, or cry 'uncle.' I can keep this up all night if necessary."

That was Andy Kaufman's approach to the world. The difference was, he tried to make a living out of it, as a stand-up comedian. Audiences have a way of demanding to be entertained. Kaufman's act was essentially a meditation on the idea of entertainment. He would entertain you, but you had to cave in first. You had to laugh at something really dumb, or let him get away with something boring or outrageous. If you passed the test, he was like a little kid, delighted to be allowed into the living room at last. He'd entertain, all right. But you had to pass the entry exam.

He was not the most successful comedian of his time. The last years of his life, his biographer Bill Zehme tells me, were spent in mostly unemployed showbiz free-fall. But Kaufman enjoyed that, too: He was fascinated by the relationship between entertainer and audience, which is never more sincere than when the entertainer is hated. It is poetic justice that Andy Kaufman now has his own biopic, directed by Milos Forman and starring Jim Carrey. He wins. Uncle.

What is most wonderful about *Man on the Moon*, a very good film, is that it remains true to Kaufman's stubborn vision. Oh, it brightens things up a little (the cookie-and-milk evening at Carnegie Hall wasn't his farewell concert, because by then he was far too unemployable for a Carnegie booking). But essentially it stays true to his persona: a guy who would test you, fool you, lie to you, deceive you, and stage elaborate deceptions, put-ons, and hoaxes. The movie doesn't turn him into a sweet, misunderstood guy. And it doesn't pander for laughs. When something is not working in Kaufman's act, it's not working in the movie either, and it's not funny; it's painful.

The film has a heroic performance from Jim Carrey, who successfully disappears inside the character of Andy Kaufman. Carrey is as big a star as Hollywood has right now, and yet fairly early in *Man on the Moon*, we forget who is playing Kaufman and get involved in what is happening to him. Carrey is himself a compulsive entertainer who will do anything to get a laugh, who wants to please, whose public image is wacky and ingratiating. That he can evoke the complexities of Kaufman's comic agonies is a little astonishing. That he can suppress his own desire to please takes a kind of courage. Not only is he working without his own net, but he's playing a guy who didn't use a net.

The film, directed by Forman and written by Scott Alexander and Larry Karaszewski, begins with Kaufman as a troublesome kid in his room, refusing to go out and play, preferring to host his own TV variety program for the cameras he believed were hidden in his bedroom walls. His material was inspired by shabby nightclub and lounge acts. He understood that a live performance is rarely more fascinating than when it is going wrong.

I myself, for example, have seldom been more involved than I was one night at a thirty-six-seat theater in London during a performance of a one-man show called "Is It Magic—or Is It Manilow?" The star was a bad magician who did a bad imitation of Barry Manilow, alternating the two elements of his act. There were twelve people in the audience, and we were desperately important to him. The program notes said he had once been voted most popular entertainer on a cruise ship out of Goa. Andy Kaufman would have been in ecstasy.

The movie follows Kaufman into the L.A. stand-up circuit, where a talent manager (Danny DeVito) sees something in his act and signs him. Kaufman is soon a sitcom star, a regular on *Taxi* (we see cast veterans Marilu Henner, Carol Kane, Christopher Lloyd, and Judd Hirsch playing themselves—DeVito, of course, is otherwise engaged). He insists on "guest bookings" for his "protégé," an obnoxious lounge act named Tony Clifton, who is played behind impenetrable makeup by Kaufman and sometimes by his accomplice Bob Zmuda. Kaufman steadfastly refuses to admit he "is" Clifton, and in a way, he isn't.

The parabolas of Kaufman's career intersect as *Taxi* goes off the air. He has never been more famous, or had bleaker prospects. He's crying wolf more than the public is crying uncle. He starts wrestling women in his nightclub act, not a popular decision, and gets involved in a feud with Memphis wrestling star Jerry Lawler. They fight on the Letterman show. It looks real. The movie says it was staged (Lawler plays himself). Okay, so it was staged—but Lawler's blow to Kaufman's head was real enough to tumble him out of his chair. And no doubt Kaufman made Lawler vow to hit him that hard. He always wanted to leave you in doubt.

Courtney Love is back in her second Milos Forman movie in a row, playing the lover of an impossible man (she was the *Hustler* publisher's lover in Forman's *The People vs. Larry Flynt*). She comes to wrestle Kaufman and stays to puzzle at him. She likes him, even loves him, but never quite knows who he is. When he tells her he's dying of cancer, her first reaction is anger that he would toy with her feelings in yet another performance piece. Love shows again here that she is a real actress and can, if she wants to, give up the other job.

What was it with Kaufman? The movie leaves us with a mystery, and it should. In traditional Hollywood biopics, there would be Freudian shorthand to explain everything. Nothing explains Andy Kaufman. If he had been explicable, no one would have wanted to make a movie about him.

The Chicago talk jock Steve Dahl told me the other day that Kaufman once recruited him for a performance. "He told me I would be inside a box on the stage, and people would try to guess what was in the box," Dahl recalled. "He gave me a six-pack of Heinekens to keep me company. What he didn't tell me was that I would be in the box for three hours. There I was in the dark, trying to pee back into the can." Dahl thought he was in the show, but from Kaufman's point of view, he was the ideal member of the audience.   ☞

Mansfield Park ★ ★ ★
PG-13, 110 m., 1999

Embeth Davidtz (Mary Crawford), Jonny Lee Miller (Edmund Bertram), Alessandro Nivola (Henry Crawford), Frances O'Connor (Fanny Price), Harold Pinter (Sir Thomas Bertram), Lindsay Duncan (Lady Bertram/Mrs. Price), Sheila Gish (Mrs. Norris), James Purefoy (Tom Bertram), Hugh Bonneville (Mr. Rushworth), Justine Waddell (Julia Bertram), Victoria Hamilton (Maria Bertram), Sophia Myles (Susan), Hilton McRae (Mr. Price), Hannah Taylor Gordon (Young Fanny), Charles Edwards (Yates). Directed by Patricia Rozema and produced by Sarah Curtis. Screenplay by Rozema, based on the novel by Jane Austen, her letters, and early journals.

Patricia Rozema's *Mansfield Park* makes no claim to be a faithful telling of Jane Austen's novel, and achieves something more interesting instead. Rozema has chosen passages from Austen's journals and letters and adapted them to Fanny Price, the heroine of *Mansfield Park*, and the result is a film in which Austen's values (and Fanny's) are more important than the romance and melodrama.

The film begins with a young girl whispering a lurid story into the ear of her wide-eyed little sister. This is Fanny (Hannah Taylor Gordon), whose family lives in poverty in a dockside cottage in Portsmouth. Fanny's mother married unwisely for love. Her sister Lady Bertram married for position, and now lives in the great country estate Mansfield Park. Lady Bertram spends her days nodding in a haze of laudanum, but rouses herself sufficiently to send for one of her nieces, and so with no warning Fanny is bundled into a carriage and taken away from her family. "It seems that mother has given me away," she writes her sister. "I can augur nothing but misery with what I have seen at Mansfield Park."

The narrative springs forward, and we meet a twentyish Fanny, now played by Frances O'Connor. Great English country houses in those days were truly family seats, giving shelter and employment to relatives, dependents, and servants, and we meet Lord Bertram (the playwright Harold Pinter, magisterial and firm), his drug-addled wife (Lindsay Duncan), his drunken older son, Tom (James Purefoy), his likable younger son, Edmund (Jonny Lee Miller), his two inconsequential daughters, and the attractive Crawfords, Henry and his sister, Mary (Alessandro Nivola and Embeth Davidtz). The Crawfords have rented the estate's parsonage with the aim of marrying into the Bertram family.

This may seem like a large cast (I have left out three or four characters), but it is important to understand that in that time and place, it would have seemed a small enough one, because these were literally the only people Fanny Price could expect to see on a regular basis. If she is to marry, her husband will probably come from among them, and nobody has to tell her that the candidates are Tom, Edmund, and Henry. All of Austen's novels, in one way or another, are about capable young women trapped in a strata of country society that assigns them to sit in drawing rooms looking pretty while they speculate on their matrimonial chances and risks.

In crossing this theme with the idea that Fanny is a writer, Rozema cuts right to the heart of the matter. We assume that women have always written, but actually until 200 years ago women authors were rare; Austen found her own way into the profession. Most women did not have the education, the freedom, or the privacy to write. Virginia Woolf is eloquent about this in *A Room of One's Own*, speculating that someone like Austen might literally have never been alone in a room to write, but should be pictured in the corner of a drawing room containing all the other members of her household—writing her novels while conversation and life carried on regardless, dogs barked and children urged.

In *Mansfield Park*, we see Fanny thrilled to receive a quire of writing paper, and sending letters to her sister Susie that contain a great deal more observation and speculation than family correspondence really requires. This young woman could grow up to write—well, *Pride and Prejudice*. We are so accustomed to the notion of Austen's wit and perception that we lose sight of the fact that for her to write at all was a radical break with the role society assigned her.

Women in the early years of the nineteenth century were essentially commodities until they were married, and puppeteers afterward, exerting power through their husbands and children and in the management of their households. Thus all of Austen's novels (and those of George Eliot, Mrs. Gaskell, and the Brontës) can be seen as stories about business and finance—for a woman's occupation and fortune came through marriage.

The key thing about Fanny Price, and about many of Austen's heroines, is that she is ready to say no. Her uncle, Lord Bertram, informs her that Henry Crawford has asked for her hand, and "I have agreed." Fanny does not love Henry. She loves her cousin Edmund, who is engaged to the worthless Mary Crawford. When she says she does not trust Henry, there is a ruthless exchange with her uncle. "Do you trust me?" he asks. "Yes, sir." "Well, I trust him, and you will marry him."

Later in the film there is a bloodcurdling scene in the drawing room after a scandal has threatened the family's reputation. Without revealing too much, let me ask you to listen for Mary Crawford's chilling analysis of the emergency and her plan for what must be done. To modern ears it sounds crass and heartless. In 1806, just such conversations would have sounded reasonable to people schooled to think of the family fortune above any consideration of love or morality.

Mansfield Park is a witty, entertaining film, and I hope I haven't made it sound too serious. Frances O'Connor makes a dark-haired heroine with flashing eyes and high spirits. Harold Pinter is all the country Tory one could possibly hope for. Alessandro Nivola makes a rakish cad who probably really does love Fanny, after his fashion. And Embeth Davidtz's cold-blooded performance as Mary strips bare the pretense and exposes the family for what it is—a business, its fortune based on slave plantations in the Caribbean. This is an uncommonly intelligent film, smart and amusing, too, and anyone who thinks it is not faithful to Austen doesn't know the author but only her plots.

A Map of the World ★ ★ ★ ½
R, 127 m., 2000

Sigourney Weaver (Alice Goodwin), Julianne Moore (Theresa Collins), David Strathairn (Howard Goodwin), Ron Lea (Dan Collins), Arliss Howard (Paul Reverdy), Chloe Sevigny (Carole Mackessy), Louise Fletcher (Nellie), Sara Rue (Debbie), Aunjanue Ellis (Dyshett). Directed by Scott Elliott and produced by Kathleen Kennedy and Frank Marshall. Screenplay by Peter Hedges and Polly Platt, based on the novel by Jane Hamilton.

There is a pounding that starts inside the heads of certain kinds of people when they're convinced they're right. They know in theory all about being cool and diplomatic, but in practice a great righteous anger takes hold, and they say exactly what they think in short and cutting words. Later they cool off, dial down, and vow to think before they speak, but then the red demon rises again in fury against those who are wrong or stupid—or seem at the moment to be.

Alice Goodwin, the Wisconsin farm woman played by Sigourney Weaver in *A Map of the World,* is a woman like that. She has never settled comfortably inside her own body. She is not entirely reconciled to being the wife of her husband, the mother of her children, the teacher of her students. She is not even sure she belongs on a farm. You sense she has inner reservations about everything, they make her mad at herself, and sometimes she blurts out exactly what she's thinking, even when she shouldn't be thinking of it.

This trait leads to a courtroom scene of rare fascination. We've seen a lot of courtrooms in the movies, and almost always we know what to expect. The witnesses will tell the truth or lie, they will be effective or not, and suspense will build if the film is skillful. *A Map of the World* puts Alice Goodwin in the witness box, and she says the wrong thing in the wrong way for reasons that seem right to her but nobody else. She'd rather be self-righteous than acquitted.

This quality makes her a fascinating person, in one of the best performances Weaver has given. We can't take our eyes off her. She is not the plaything or the instrument of the plot. She fights off the plot, indeed: The movement of the film is toward truth and resolution, but she hasn't read the script and is driven by anger and a deep wronged stubbornness. She begins to speak and we feel enormous suspense. We care for her. We don't want her to damage her own case.

The plot involves her in a situation that depends on two unexpected developments, and I don't feel like revealing either one. Neither one is her fault, morally, but bad things happen all the same. She's smart enough to see why she's not to blame for the first event, but human enough to feel terrible about it anyway. And the second development is sort of a combination of the first, plus her own big mouth. Her family is terrified. Her husband doesn't know what to make of her, and her kids don't have the comfort of thinking of their mom as an innocent in an unfair world, because she doesn't act like a victim—she acts like a woman who plans to win the game in the last quarter.

There are good performances all through the movie, which was directed by Scott Elliott and written by Peter Hedges and Polly Platt. David Strathairn plays Howard, Alice Goodwin's husband, and Julianne Moore and Ron Lea play their farm neighbors—just about their only friends. When Alice spends time in prison, she gets a hard time from an inmate (Aunjanue Ellis), who senses (correctly) that this woman may have dug her own grave. And there is a small but crucial role for Chloe Sevigny, who in several recent movies *(Boys Don't Cry, julien donkey-boy, American Psycho)* shows an intriguing range. As for Julianne Moore, see Stanley Kauffmann's praise in his *New Republic* review, where he finds her grief "a small gem of truthful heartbreak."

The movie is not tidy. Like its heroine, it doesn't follow the rules. It breaks into parts. It seems to be a family story, and then turns into a courtroom drama, and then into a prison story, and there is intercutting with romantic intrigue, and there aren't any of the comforting payoffs we get in genre fiction. I'm grateful for movies like this; *Being John Malkovich* and *Three Kings,* so different in every other way, resemble *A Map of the World* in being free—in being capable of taking any turn at any moment, without the need to follow tired conventions. And in Sigourney Weaver, the movie has a heroine who would be a lot happier if she weren't so smart. Now there's a switch.

Marie Baie des Anges ★
R, 90 m., 1998

Vahina Giocante (Marie), Frederic Malgras (Orso), Amira Casar (Young Woman), David Kilner (Larry), Jamie Harris (Jim), Frederic Westerman (Ardito), Nicolas Welbers (Goran), Swan Carpio (Jurec). Directed by Manuel Pradal and produced by Philippe Rousselet. Screenplay by Pradal.

At the height of the storm over *Last Tango in Paris,* Art Buchwald, who had lived in Paris for years, weighed in with some common sense: The movie, he explained, is really about real estate. Both characters want the same apartment and are willing to do anything to get it.

Marie Baie des Anges is not really about real estate. It is about sex. But I thought a lot about real estate while I was watching it. It takes place on the French Riviera, which is pictured here as an unspoilt Eden in which the film's adolescent lovers gambol and pose, nude much

of the time, surfacing only occasionally for the dangers of the town.

Anyone who has visited the French Riviera knows that it has more in common with Miami than with Eden. It is a crowded, expensive perch for ugly condos and desperate beachgoers, and the only place where teenage lovers can safely gambol is in their bathtubs. *Marie Baie des Anges* is as realistic as *Blue Lagoon,* although without any copulating turtles.

The movie stars Vahina Giocante as Marie, a fifteen-year-old who spends her vacations on the Riviera picking up American sailors and sleeping under the stars. No mention of her parents, home, income, past, experience, etc. She is the pornographer's dream: an uncomplicated, nubile teenager who exists only as she is. Giocante has been billed as "the new Bardot," and she's off to a good start: Bardot didn't make many good films either.

On the beach, she meets Orso (Frederic Malgras), a sullen lout who lurks about looking like a charade, with the answer "Leonardo DiCaprio." Together they run, play, boat, swim, eat strawberries, and flirt with danger, and inevitably a handgun surfaces, so we will not be in suspense about the method used to bring the film to its unsatisfactory conclusion. "Get me the best-looking gun you can find," Orso tells Marie, who steals it from a one-night stand.

The movie is yet one more evocation of doomed youth, destined for a brief flash of happiness and a taste of eroticism before they collide with the preordained ending. All of these movies end the same way, with one form of death or another, which casts a cold light on the events that went before, showing you how unlucky these young people were to be in a story written by a director who lacked the wit to think of anything else that might happen.

The filmmaker is Manuel Pradal, who in addition to recycling exhausted clichés also fancies himself at the cutting edge of narrative. He tells his story out of sequence, leaving us to collect explanations and context along the way; one advantage of this style is that only at the end is it revealed that the story was not about anything. We get glimpses and fragments of actions; flashforwards and flashbacks; exhausting, self-conscious artiness.

Yes, there is beautiful scenery. And nice compositions. Lots of pretty pictures. Giocante and Malgras are superficially attractive, although because their characters are empty vessels there's no reason to like them much or care about them. The movie is cast as a tragedy, and it's tragic, all right: Tragic that these kids never developed intelligence and personalities.

Marius and Jeannette ★ ★
NO MPAA RATING, 1998

Ariane Ascaride (Jeannette), Gerard Meylan (Marius), Pascale Roberts (Caroline), Jacques Boudet (Justin), Frederique Bonnal (Monique), Jean-Pierre Darroussin (Dede), Laetitia Pesenti (Magali), Miloud Nacer (Malek). Directed by Robert Guediguian and produced by Gilles Sandoz. Screenplay by Guediguian and Jean-Louis Milesi. In French with English subtitles.

Marius and Jeannette is a sentimental fantasy of French left-wing working-class life, so cheerful and idealized that I expected the characters to break into song; they do all dance together, in the forecourt of a shuttered cement factory. Set in a blue-collar district of Marseilles, it plays like a sitcom spin-off of *Carmen*, with everyone popping in and out of each other's houses and lives, while all personal emergencies are handled in public, collectively.

The director, Robert Guediguian, has visited this territory before; his 1980 film *Last Summer* dealt with workers in the same factory when it was still in operation. Now the jobs have fled to Malaysia, the workers tell each other, although they are none too sure where that is, and they sit outside their doors in beach chairs, unemployed but unbowed.

The movie's heroine is Jeannette (Ariane Ascaride, the director's wife). She's raised two kids by different fathers, and as the movie opens she tries to steal cans of paint from the factory. She's stopped by a security guard, Marius (Gerard Meylan), who limps around in an orange one-piece suit, patrolling the ruins. "My house will collapse without a paint job!" Jeannette shouts, calling him a fascist. The next day, he delivers the cans to her door, and that's the beginning of a romance.

Well, we like these two people, and that's the argument for liking the movie. Jeannette is irredeemably cheerful and upbeat, a pal to her children, a no-nonsense figure in jeans and a Levi's jacket. Sample dialogue: "You're beautiful," she tells her teenage daughter Magali, who tries on a lacy minidress. "But I look cheap," the daughter says. "Yes, but it suits you." "If I wear this I'll be pregnant before I get to the end of the street," Magali says. Jeannette smiles: "I'd like to be a grandma."

Not your typical mother, eh? Jeannette combines elements of old-time leftist idealism with the hippie commune spirit. She and her neighbors live in each other's pockets; they occupy a little courtyard with windows that open onto a common space, and even the most intimate matters are freely discussed. They also laugh a lot—too much, I thought. At one point the neighbor's husband lands in the hospital after getting drunk and throwing rocks at right-wing political posters. The rocks bounce back and hit him in the head. At this news everyone laughs so uproariously that they have to wipe away the tears. I didn't believe I was looking at laughter: It looked more like overacting in response to the screenplay instruction, "They laugh uncontrollably."

There must be an arc in all romances, a darkness before the dawn. Marius and Jeannette fall in love, but then he unexpectedly disappears, and the movie falls back on that most ancient of clichés, that in wine there is truth. The neighborhood guys get him drunk, and he confesses his innermost fears and insecurities. There is also an unnecessary and unmotivated bar brawl. Then, in a tactic that takes communal living too far, they haul him unconscious back to Jeannette's bed.

Meanwhile, Jeannette conducts her private war against the bosses. She's a checkout clerk at a supermarket, where the chair hurts her back (she should try standing up like an American grocery clerk). She shouts at the manager, "The Gestapo could have used these chairs for torture!" Since the movie is set much too late for Jeannette to have had any experience of World War II, this seems more like a dated, ritualized left-wing attribution of fascism to all the enemies of the workers.

By the end of the film, I was fed up. Yes, I liked Jeannette and Marius as individuals; they're a warm, attractive, funky couple on the shores of middle age who find happiness. But the movie forces its politics until it feels like a

Pete Seeger benefit. And, hey, I like Pete Seeger. It's just that the love story of *Marius and Jeannette* is at an awkward angle to the politics, and the lives and dialogue of these characters seem impossibly contorted to reflect the director's politics.

The Mask of Zorro ★ ★ ★
PG-13, 136 m., 1998

Antonio Banderas (Alejandro/Zorro), Anthony Hopkins (Don Diego/Zorro), Catherine Zeta-Jones (Elena Montero), Stuart Wilson (Don Rafael Montero). Directed by Martin Campbell and produced by Doug Claybourne and David Foster. Screenplay by John Eskow, Ted Elliott, and Terry Rossio.

The Mask of Zorro has something you don't often see in modern action pictures, a sense of honor. The character takes sides, good versus evil, and blood debts are nursed down through the generations. It also has a lot of zest, humor, energy, and swordplay; it's fun, and not an insult to the intelligence.

The movie resurrects a character first played in silent films by Douglas Fairbanks Sr., and again on TV in the 1950s by Guy Williams, and launches him in what the producers no doubt hope will be a series. The director, Martin Campbell, did the Bond picture *GoldenEye,* and in a sense, *The Mask of Zorro* is a Bond picture on horseback: There's the megalomaniac villain, the plan to take over the world (or, in this case, California), the training of the hero, the bold entry into the enemy's social world, the romance with the bad guy's stepdaughter, and the sensational stunts. There's even the always-popular situation where the hero and the girl start out in a deadly struggle and end up in each other's arms.

All of this action is set in Mexico and California as they were in the first half of the nineteenth century, when the evil Don Rafael Montero (Stuart Wilson) rules the land, chooses peasants at random to be shot by a firing squad, and earns the enmity of the mysterious masked man Zorro.

In an opening setup, Zorro interrupts a public killing, inspires the population, and escapes back into domestic bliss. He's played by Anthony Hopkins, who in his daytime identity as Don Diego de la Vega has a beautiful wife and child. But Don Rafael invades his home, his men shoot the wife, Don Diego is imprisoned, and Don Rafael raises the daughter as his own.

Twenty years pass, and the movie's central story begins. It involves a street urchin named Alejandro, once befriended by Zorro, now grown into a bandit played by Antonio Banderas. Alejandro and Don Diego, now older and gray, meet and join forces, and Don Diego trains the youth to inherit the legend of Zorro. "You know how to use that?" the old man asks, pointing to the younger one's sword. "Yes," he says, "the point goes into the other man." Ah, but it's not as simple as that, and after lessons in fencing, horsemanship, hand-to-hand combat, and the arts of swinging from ropes and somersaulting out of danger, the older man thinks the younger one might be ready to foil old Don Rafael's plans. There's just one final lesson: "I must teach you something that is completely beyond your reach—charm."

Don Rafael's plans have now matured: He's amassed a fortune in gold from secret mines on Mexican land, and now wants to use the gold to buy California from General Santa Anna, who needs cash to fund his war against the United States. Since it's Santa Anna's gold, this is a brilliant plan—if Don Rafael can pull it off. As the rich plot unfolds, the new young Zorro, disguised as a Spanish nobleman, infiltrates Don Rafael's social circle, and romance blossoms between the newcomer and the beautiful daughter, Elena (Catherine Zeta-Jones).

The best scenes in the movie are between Banderas and Zeta-Jones, who share chemistry and, it turns out, a sense of justice. There is a dance at Don Rafael's house at which the daughter and the visitor take over the dance floor in a passionate pas de deux, and another scene where the outlaw hides in a confessional and listens with great interest as the young woman confesses her feelings of lust for a mysterious masked man. All of these threads come together in what starts as a duel to the death between the man and the woman, and ends in a surprised embrace.

The movie celebrates the kind of Western location shooting that's rarely seen these days: horses and haciendas, gold mines and dungeons, and a virtuoso display of horsemanship. The back story, involving the first Zorro's abiding love for the daughter who was stolen from him, is pure melodrama, but Anthony Hopkins brings it as much dignity and pathos as possible, and Zeta-Jones does a good job of handling the wide-eyed, heaving bosom, tears-in-eyes kind of stuff.

The movie is a display of traditional movie craftsmanship, especially at the level of the screenplay, which respects the characters and story and doesn't simply use them for dialogue breaks between action sequences. It's a reminder of the time when stunts and special effects were integrated into stories, rather than the other way around. And in giving full weight to the supporting characters and casting them with strong actors, *The Mask of Zorro* is involving as well as entertaining. I was surprised how much I enjoyed it.

The Matrix ★ ★ ★
R, 135 m., 1999

Keanu Reeves (Neo), Laurence Fishburne (Morpheus), Carrie-Anne Moss (Trinity), Hugo Weaving (Agent Smith), Joe Pantoliano (Cypher), Gloria Foster (Oracle). Directed by Larry and Andy Wachowski and produced by Joel Silver and Dan Cracchiolo. Screenplay by Larry and Andy Wachowski.

The Matrix is a visually dazzling cyberadventure, full of kinetic excitement, but it retreats to formula just when it's getting interesting. It's kind of a letdown when a movie begins by redefining the nature of reality and ends with a shoot-out. We want a leap of the imagination, not one of those obligatory climaxes with automatic weapons fire.

I've seen dozens if not hundreds of these exercises in violence, which recycle the same tired ideas: Bad guys fire thousands of rounds, but are unable to hit the good guy. Then it's down to the final showdown between good and evil—a martial arts battle in which the good guy gets pounded until he's almost dead, before he finds the inner will to fight back. Been there, seen that (although rarely done this well).

Too bad, because the setup is intriguing.

The Matrix recycles the premises of *Dark City* and *Strange Days,* turns up the heat and the volume, and borrows the gravity-defying choreography of Hong Kong action movies. It's fun, but it could have been more. The directors are Larry and Andy Wachowski, who know how to make movies (their first film, *Bound,* made my ten best list in 1996). Here, with a big budget and veteran action producer Joel Silver, they've played it safer; there's nothing wrong with going for the Friday night action market, but you can aim higher and still do business.

Warning; spoilers ahead. The plot involves Neo (Keanu Reeves), a mild-mannered software author by day, a feared hacker by night. He's recruited by a cell of cyber-rebels, led by the profound Morpheus (Laurence Fishburne) and the leather-clad warrior Trinity (Carrie-Anne Moss). They've made a fundamental discovery about the world: It doesn't exist. It's actually a form of Virtual Reality, designed to lull us into lives of blind obedience to the "system." We obediently go to our crummy jobs every day, little realizing, as Morpheus tells Neo, that "Matrix is the wool that has been pulled over your eyes—that you are a slave."

The rebels want to crack the framework that holds the Matrix in place and free mankind. Morpheus believes Neo is the Messianic "One" who can lead this rebellion, which requires mind power as much as physical strength. Arrayed against them are the Agents, who look like Blues Brothers. The movie's battles take place in Virtual Reality; the heroes' minds are plugged into the combat. (You can still get killed, though: "The body cannot live without the mind.")

"Jacking in" like this was a concept in *Strange Days* and has also been suggested in novels by William Gibson *(Idoru)* and others. The notion that the world is an artificial construction, designed by outsiders to deceive and use humans, is straight out of *Dark City.* Both of those movies, however, explored their implications as the best science fiction often does. *Dark City* was fascinated by the Strangers who had a poignant dilemma: They were dying aliens who hoped to learn from human methods of adaptation and survival.

In *Matrix,* on the other hand, there aren't flesh-and-blood creatures behind the illusion—only a computer program that can think and learn. The Agents function primarily as opponents in a high-stakes computer game. The movie offers no clear explanation of why the Matrix-making program went to all that trouble. Of course, for a program, running is its own reward—but an intelligent program might bring terrifying logic to its decisions.

Both *Dark City* and *Strange Days* offered intriguing motivations for villainy. *Matrix* is more like a superhero comic book in which the fate of the world comes down to a titanic fistfight between the designated representatives of good and evil. It's cruel, really, to put tantalizing ideas on the table and then ask the audience to be satisfied with a shoot-out and a martial arts duel.

Let's assume Neo wins. What happens then to the billions who have just been "unplugged" from the Matrix? Do they still have jobs? Homes? Identities? All we get is an enigmatic voice-over exhortation at the movie's end. The paradox is that the Matrix world apparently resembles in every respect the pre-Matrix world. (I am reminded of the animated kid's film *Doug's 1st Movie*, which has a VR experience in which everything is exactly like in real life, except more expensive.)

Still, I must not ignore the movie's virtues. It's great-looking, both in its design and in the kinetic energy that powers it. It uses flawlessly integrated special effects and animation to visualize regions of cyberspace. It creates fearsome creatures, including mechanical octopi. It morphs bodies with the abandon of *Terminator II*. It uses f/x to allow Neo and Trinity to run horizontally on walls, and hang in the air long enough to deliver karate kicks. It has leaps through space, thrilling sequences involving fights on rooftops, helicopter rescues, and battles over mind control.

And it has performances that find the right notes. Keanu Reeves goes for the impassive Harrison Ford approach, "acting" as little as possible. I suppose that's the right idea. Laurence Fishburne finds a balance between action hero and Zen master. Carrie-Anne Moss, as Trinity, has a sensational title sequence, before the movie recalls that she's a woman and shuttles her into support mode. Hugo Weaving, as the chief Agent, uses a flat, menacing

tone that reminded me of Tommy Lee Jones in passive-aggressive overdrive. There's a well-acted scene involving Gloria Foster as the Oracle, who like all oracles is maddeningly enigmatic.

The Matrix did not bore me. It interested me so much, indeed, that I wanted to be challenged even more. I wanted it to follow its material to audacious conclusions, to arrive not simply at victory, but at revelation. I wanted an ending that was transformational, like *Dark City*'s, and not one that simply throws us a sensational action sequence. I wanted, in short, a third act. ☞

Ma Vie en Rose ★ ★ ★
R, 88 m., 1998

Georges Du Fresne (Ludovic), Michele Laroque (Hanna), Jean-Philippe Ecoffey (Pierre), Helene Vincent (Elisabeth), Julien Riviere (Jerome), Cristina Barget (Zoe), Gregory Diallo (Thom), Erik Cazals De Fabel (Jean). Directed by Alain Berliner and produced by Carole Scotta. Screenplay by Chris vander Stappen and Berliner.

Ludovic is a seven-year-old boy who likes to dress in girl's clothes, not so much because he likes the clothes as because he is convinced he is a girl. It all seems very clear. After he learns about chromosomes, he explains to his parents that instead of the female XX chromosomes he was intended to get, he received the male XY after "my other X fell in the garbage."

Ludovic's parents have just moved to a suburb of Paris that looks for all the world like a set for *Ozzie and Harriet*. Ominously, they live next door to his father's boss. A barbecue is planned to welcome the newcomers, and it's at this party that Ludovic makes his dramatic entrance, dressed in pink. The adults, who would not have looked twice at a little girl wearing jeans and sneakers, are stunned. "It's normal until seven," Ludovic's mother explains bravely. "I read it in *Marie-Claire*."

Ma Vie en Rose offers gentle fantasy, and a little hard reality, about Ludovic's predicament. He is convinced he is a girl, knows some sort of mistake was made, and is serenely intent on correcting it. Soon he's making the arrangements for a play "marriage" with Jerome, his best friend, who lives next door and is therefore, unluckily, the boss's son. Since the boss is a blustering bigot, this is not a good idea. Indeed, most of the adults in the movie seem like members of the Gender Role Enforcement Police.

The film is careful to keep its focus within childhood. It's not a story about homosexuality or transvestism, but about a little boy who thinks he's a little girl. Maybe Ludovic, played by a calmly self-possessed eleven-year-old named Georges Du Fresne, will grow up to be gay. Maybe not. That's not what the movie is about. And the performance reflects Ludovic's innocence and naïveté; there is no sexual awareness in his dressing up, but simply a determination to set things right.

The movie is about two ways of seeing things: the child's and the adult's. It shows how children construct elaborate play worlds out of dreams and fantasies, and then plug their real worlds right into them. Ludovic's alternate universe is ruled by his favorite TV personality, named Pam, who dresses like a princess and has a boyfriend named Ken and flies about the house with her sparkling magic wand. It also contains his beloved grandmother. In this world Ludovic is sort of an assistant princess, and we can see how his worship of Pam has made him want to be just like her.

Adults, on the other hand, see things in more literal terms and are less open to fantasy. No one is threatened by a girl who dresses like a boy, but the father's boss is just one of the people who sees red whenever Ludovic turns up in drag. This innocent little boy is made to pay for all the gay phobias, fears, and prejudices of the adult world.

Because *Ma Vie en Rose (My Life in Pink)* is a comedy, however, the going never gets too heavy. Ludovic is taken to a psychiatrist, he is shouted at by his (mostly sympathetic) parents, he is a figure of mystery to his three well-adjusted siblings, and he is a threat to the stability of his neighborhood. Since it's one of those sitcom neighborhoods where everyone spends a lot of time out on the lawn or gossiping over the driveways, what happens to one family is the concern of all.

Ma Vie en Rose is the first film by Alain Berliner, a Belgian, who worked from the orig-

inal screenplay of Chris vander Stappen, herself a tomboy who got a lot of heat as a child. There are clearly important personal issues at work beneath the surface, especially for Ms. vander Stappen, who identifies herself as a lesbian, but they skate above them. And there is a certain suspense: Surely Ludovic cannot simply be humored? Simply allowed to dress as a girl? Or can he?

Meet Joe Black ★ ★ ★
PG-13, 174 m., 1998

Brad Pitt (Joe Black), Anthony Hopkins (William Parrish), Claire Forlani (Susan Parrish), Jake Weber (Drew), Marcia Gay Harden (Allison), Jeffrey Tambor (Quince), David S. Howard (Eddie Sloane), Lois Kelly-Miller (Jamaican Woman). Directed and produced by Martin Brest. Screenplay by Ron Osborn, Jeff Reno, Kevin Wade, and Bo Goldman.

Meet Joe Black is a movie about a rich man trying to negotiate the terms of his own death. It is a movie about a woman who falls in love with a concept. And it is a meditation on the screen presence of Brad Pitt. That there is also time for scenes about sibling rivalry and a corporate takeover is not necessarily a good thing. The movie contains elements that make it very good, and then a lot of other elements besides. Less is more.

As the movie opens, a millionaire named William Parrish (Anthony Hopkins) is pounded by a heart attack, the sound track using low bass chords to assault the audience. He hears a voice—his own—in his head. On the brink of his sixty-fifth birthday, he senses that death is near. He tells his beloved younger daughter, Susan (Claire Forlani), that he likes her fiancé, but doesn't sense that she truly loves him: "Stay open. Lightning could strike."

It does. A few hours later in a coffee shop, she meets a stranger (Brad Pitt). They talk and flirt. He says all the right things. Lightning makes, at the very least, a near miss. They confess they really like one another. They part. He is killed. That night at dinner, she is startled to find him among her father's guests. The body of the young man is now occupied by Death, who has come to inform Parrish that his end is near.

He does not recognize Susan. That's odd. Isn't Death an emissary from God? Shouldn't he know these things? He's been around a long time (one imagines him breaking the bad news to amoebas). This Death doesn't even know what peanut butter tastes like, or how to kiss. A job like that, you want a more experienced man.

No matter. We accept the premise. We're distracted, anyway, by the way Brad Pitt plays the role. As both the young man in the coffee shop and as "Joe Black" (the name given him by Parrish), he is intensely aware of himself—too aware. Pitt is a fine actor, but this performance is a miscalculation. Meryl Streep once said that an experienced actor knows that the words "I love you" are really a question. Pitt plays them as a compliment to himself. There is no chemistry between Joe Black and Susan because both parties are focused on him.

That at least leads to the novelty of a rare movie love scene where the camera is focused on the man's face, not the woman's. Actresses have become skilled over the years at faking orgasms on camera, usually with copious cries of delight and sobs of passion. (As they're buffeted by their competent male lovers, I am sometimes reminded of a teenager making the cheerleader team, crossed with a new war widow.) A male actor would have to be very brave to reveal such loss of control, and Pitt's does not cry out. His orgasm plays in slow motion across his face like a person who is thinking, "This is way better than peanut butter."

I was not, in short, sold on the relationship between Susan and Joe. She spends most of the movie puzzling about a very odd man who briefly made her heart feel gooey. There is no person there for her, just the idea of perfect love. Joe Black is presented as a being who is not familiar with occupying a human body or doing human things. One wonders—is this the first time Death has tried this approach? Parrish strikes a deal with him (he won't die as long as he can keep Joe interested and teach him new things) and he takes him everywhere with him, including board meetings, where Joe's response to most situations is total silence, while looking like the cat that ate the mouse.

The Parrish character, and Anthony Hopkins's performance, are entirely different matters. Hopkins invests the dying millionaire with intelligence and acceptance, and he talks wonderfully well. Meet Joe Black consists largely of conversations, which are well written and do not seem false or forced as long as Parrish is involved in them. His key business relationships are with the snaky Drew (Jake Weber), whom Susan dumps for Joe, and with the avuncular Quince (Jeffrey Tambor), his loyal but bumbling son-in-law. Quince is married to Allison (Marcia Gay Harden), who knows Susan is her father's favorite but can live with that because Parrish is such a swell guy. (He's ethical, sensitive, and beloved—the first movie rich man who could at least squeeze his head and shoulders through the eye of the needle.)

What's fascinating about Parrish is that he handles death as he has handled everything else. He makes a realistic assessment of his chances, sees what advantages he can extract, negotiates for the best possible terms, and gracefully accepts the inevitable. There are times when he handles his talks with Death so surely that you wish heaven had sent a more articulate negotiator.

The movie's ending takes too long. There are farewells, reflections, confessions, reassurances, reconciliations, partings, and surprises. Joe Black begins to get on our nerves with his knack of saying things that are technically true, but incomplete and misleading. The film would play better if he didn't always have to talk in epigrams. Even at the very end, when a line or two of direct dialogue would have cleared the air, he's still talking in acrostic clues.

Still, there's so much that's fine in this movie, directed by Martin Brest (Scent of a Woman). Claire Forlani has a touching vulnerability as she negotiates the strange terms of her love. Marcia Gay Harden plays a wise, grown-up scene with Hopkins, as a loving daughter who knows she isn't the favorite. Jeffrey Tambor's performance is crucial; through his eyes, we understand what a good man Parrish is. And Anthony Hopkins inhabits a story that tends toward quicksand and finds dry land. You sense a little of his Nixon here: A man who can use anger like a scalpel, while still standing back to monitor the result.

Meet the Deedles ★ ½
PG, 90 m., 1998

Steve Van Wormer (Stew Deedle), Paul Walker (Phil Deedle), A. J. Langer (Jesse Ryan), John Ashton (Captain Douglas Pine), Dennis Hopper (Frank Slater), Eric Braeden (Elton Deedle), Richard Lineback (Crabbe), Robert Englund (Nemo). Directed by Steve Boyum and produced by Dale Pollock and Aaron Meyerson. Screenplay by Jim Herzfeld.

The cult of stupidity is irresistible to teenagers in a certain mood. It's a form of rebellion, maybe: If the real world is going to reject them, then they'll simply refuse to get it. Using jargon and incomprehension as weapons, they'll create their own alternate universe.

All of which is a tortuous way to explain *Meet the Deedles*, a movie with no other ambition than to create mindless slapstick and generate a series in the tradition of the *Bill and Ted* movies. The story involves twin brothers Stew and Phil Deedle (Steve Van Wormer and Paul Walker), slackers from Hawaii who find themselves in the middle of a fiendish plot to sabotage Old Faithful in Yellowstone National Park.

As the movie opens, Stew and Phil are hanging beneath a balloon being towed above the Hawaiian surf, while being pursued by a truant officer on a Jet Ski. Soon they're called on the carpet before their millionaire father (Eric Braeden), who snorts, "You will one day take over the entire Deedles empire—and you are surf bums!" His plan: Send them to Camp Broken Spirit, a monthlong experience in outdoor living that will turn them into men.

Through plot developments unnecessary to relate, the Deedles escape the camp experience, are mistaken for Park Ranger recruits, come under the command of Ranger Pine (John Ashton), and stumble onto the solution to a mysterious infestation of prairie dogs.

Now prairie dogs can be cute, as anyone who has seen Disney's *The Living Prairie* nature documentary can testify. But in large numbers they look alarmingly like herds of rats, and the earth trembles (slightly) as they scurry across the park. Why so many prairie dogs? Because an evil ex-ranger named Slater (Dennis Hopper) has trained them to burrow

out a cavern around Old Faithful, allowing him to redirect the geyser's boiling waters in the direction of New Faithful, to which he plans to sell tickets.

Hopper lives in the cavern, relaxing in his E-Z-Boy recliner and watching the surface on TV monitors. His sidekicks include Nemo, played by Robert Englund, Freddy of the *Nightmare on Elm Street* pictures. At one point he explains how he trained the prairie dogs, and I will add to my permanent memory bank the sound of Dennis Hopper saying, "Inject kibble into the dirt, and a-tunneling they would go." Study his chagrin when the Deedles employ Mentholatum Deep Heat Rub as a weapon in this war.

While he schemes, the Deedles fumble and blunder their way through ranger training, and Phil falls for Jesse (A. J. Langer), the pretty stepdaughter of Ranger Pine. There are a lot of stunts, involving mountains, truck crashes, and river rapids, and then the big showdown over Old Faithful. The Deedles relate to everything in surfer terms (plowing into a snowbank, they cry, "We've landed in a Slurpy!").

I am prepared to imagine a theater full of eleven-year-old boys who might enjoy this movie, but I can't recommend it for anyone who might have climbed a little higher on the evolutionary ladder. The *Bill and Ted* movies had a certain sly self-awareness that this one lacks. Maybe that's a virtue. Maybe it isn't.

Me, Myself & Irene ★ ½
R, 116 m., 2000

Jim Carrey (Charlie/Hank), Renee Zellweger (Irene), Robert Forster (Colonel Partington), Chris Cooper (Lieutenant Gerke), Richard Jenkins (Agent Boshane), Daniel Green (Dickie Thurman), Anthony Anderson (Jamaal), Mongo Brownlee (Lee Harvey). Directed by Peter Farrelly and Bobby Farrelly and produced by the Farrellys and Bradley Thomas. Screenplay by the Farrellys and Mike Cerrone.

Me, Myself & Irene is a labored and sour comedy that rouses itself to create real humor, and then settles back glumly into an impenetrable plot and characters who keep repeating the same schtick, hoping maybe this time it will work. It stars Jim Carrey in a role that mires him in versions of the same gags, over and over. Renee Zellweger costars as a woman who stays at his side for no apparent reason except that the script requires her to.

The movie is by the Farrelly brothers, Peter and Bobby, whose *There's Something About Mary* still causes me to smile whenever I think about it, and whose *Kingpin* is a buried treasure. They worked with Carrey in *Dumb and Dumber*, which has some very big laughs in it, but this time their formula of scatology, sexuality, political incorrectness, and cheerful obscenity seems written by the numbers. The movie is as offensive as most of their work, which would be fine if it redeemed itself with humor. It doesn't. There is, for example, an extended passage making fun of an albino that is not funny at all, ever, in any part, but painfully drones on and on until the filmmakers cop out and make him the pal of the heroes.

Carrey plays a Rhode Island state trooper who puts up with shocking insults to his manhood and uniform and manages somehow to be a sunny Dr. Jeckyl, until he finally snaps and allows his Mr. Hyde to roam free. As the nice guy (named Charlie), he keeps smiling after his wife presents him with three black babies, fathered by a dwarf limo driver and Mensa member. He even keeps smiling when his neighbor allows his dog to defecate on his lawn, while the neighbor's wife steals his newspaper, and when the guys in the barbershop laugh at his attempts to enforce the law.

Years pass in this fashion. His wife runs off with the little genius. His sons stay with him, growing into enormous lads who are brilliant at school but use the MF-word as if it were punctuation (they learned it by watching Richard Pryor and Chris Rock videos). The movie must think all African-Americans are required by statute or genetics to repeat the word ceaselessly (it might have been funnier to have all three boys talk like Sam Donaldson).

After the evil side of his personality ("Hank") breaks free, Carrey starts kicking butt and taking no prisoners. Through twists unnecessary to describe, he hooks up with the perky, pretty Irene (Renee Zellweger), and they become fugitives from the law, pursued by the evil Lt. Gerke (Chris Cooper) for reasons that have something to do with environmental scandals, country clubs, bribery, and cover-ups;

the plot is so murky we abandon curiosity and simply accept that Carrey and Zellweger are on the run, and the bad guys are chasing them.

The movie has defecation jokes, urination jokes, dildo jokes, flasher jokes, and a chicken that must be thoroughly annoyed by the dilemma it finds itself in. Not many of the jokes are very funny, and some seem plain desperate. I did laugh a lot during a sequence when Carrey tries to put a wounded cow out of its misery, but most of the time I sat quietly reflecting that the Farrelly brand of humor is a high-wire act; it involves great risks and is a triumph if they get to the other side, but ugly when they fail.

Carrey has a plastic face and body, and does remarkable things with his expressions. As Charlie he's all toothy grins and friendliness. As Hank, his face twists into an evil scowl, and his voice is electronically lowered into a more menacing register. Problem is, although it's sort of funny to see Charlie reacting to the insulting ways people treat him, it is rarely funny to see him transform himself into Hank, who then takes revenge. Hank is not really a comic character, and it's a miscalculation to allow him to dominate most of the movie.

Irene, the Zellweger character, has not been invented fresh with a specific comic purpose, but is simply a recycled version of the character she usually plays. Her job is to be loyal and sensible, lay down the law, pout, smile, and be shocked. It is a thankless task; she's like the on-screen representative of the audience.

The Farrellys are gifted and have made me laugh as loudly as anyone since the golden age of Mel Brooks. They have scored before and will no doubt score again. This time they go for broke, and get there.   ☞

Note: The film is dedicated to the late Gene Siskel, whose enthusiasm for Kingpin *came at a crucial time for the Farrellys, encouraging them to push ahead with* There's Something About Mary.

Me Myself I ★ ★ ★
R, 104 m., 2000

Rachel Griffiths (Pamela), David Roberts (Robert), Sandy Winton (Ben), Yael Stone (Stacey), Shaun Loseby (Douglas), Trent Sullivan

(Rupert), Rebecca Frith (Terri), Felix Williamson (Geoff). Directed by Pip Karmel and produced by Fabien Liron. Screenplay by Karmel.

Consider now Rachel Griffiths. I first noticed her as the best friend with the infectious grin in *Muriel's Wedding*, the quirky Australian comedy. She was the lusty pig farmer's daughter who married the earnest student in *Jude*. In *Hilary and Jackie*, she played the sister of the doomed musician, and won an Oscar nomination. She was wonderful in two films that didn't find wide distribution: *My Son, the Fanatic*, where she played a hooker who forms a sincere friendship with a middle-aged Pakistani taxi driver in the British Midlands, and *Among Giants*, where she was a backpacking rock climber who signs up for the summer with a crew of British power pylon painters. That was the movie where, on a bet, she traversed all four walls of a pub with her toes on the wainscoting, finding fingerholds where she could.

It is quite possible that Griffiths made all of these movies without coming to your attention, since none of them were big box-office winners, and a depressing number of movie-goers march off like sheep to the weekend's top-grossing hot-air balloon. She's been in one hit, *My Best Friend's Wedding*, but not so's you'd notice. I think she is one of the most intensely interesting actresses at work today, and in *Me Myself I* she does something that is almost impossible: She communicates her feelings to us through reaction shots while keeping them a secret from the other characters. That makes us conspirators.

Griffiths is not a surface beauty but a sexy tomboy with classically formed features, whose appeal shines out through the intelligence in her eyes and her wry mouth. You cannot imagine her as a passive object of affection. If Hollywood romances were about who women were rather than how they looked, she'd be one of the most desirable women in the movies. To the discerning, she is anyway.

Me Myself I is a fantasy as contrived and satisfactory as a soap opera. Griffiths plays Pamela, a professional magazine writer in her thirties who smokes too much and keeps up her spirits with self-help mantras ("I deserve the best and I accept the best"). Her idea of a date is to open a bottle of wine and look at photos of guys she dated fifteen years ago. "Why did I let you go?" she asks the photo of Robert (David Roberts). She's attracted to a crisis counselor named Ben (Sandy Winton), but finds out he is happily married, with children.

Should she have married Robert all those years ago? An unexplained supernatural transfer takes place, and she gets a chance to find out. She's hit by a car, and the other driver is—herself. After a switch, she finds herself living in an alternate universe in which she did marry Robert, and they have three children. This, of course, is all perfectly consistent with the latest theories in movie metaphysics; only the mechanism of the transfer remains cloudy.

Here is the key to the transformation scenes: Pamela knows she is a replacement for the "real" Pamela in this parallel world, and so do we, but everyone else fails to notice the substitution (except for Rupert, the youngest, who asks her bluntly, "When's Mommy gonna be home?"). There are scenes involving cooking dinner, managing the house, and copiloting for Rupert during his toilet duties. And a sex life with Robert that he finds surprising and delightful, since he and his original Pamela had cooled off considerably.

In this parallel universe, Ben is single, not married, and she takes the chance to have an affair with him, despite the complication that now she is married, not single. When she thinks Robert has been unfaithful, she is outraged, as much on behalf of the other Pamela as for herself, although in the new geometries of the universe-switch they are equally guilty, or innocent. This new Robert also has to be trained to accept an independent woman. When she announces that she needs a new computer and he says, "We'll see," she jolts him with: "I'm not asking your permission."

There are sweet scenes in the film, and touching ones. My favorite moments come when Pamela does subtle double takes when she realizes how her life is different now, and why. The plot is not remarkably intelligent, but Pamela (or Griffiths) is, and her reaction shots, her conspiratorial sharing of her thoughts with us, is where the movie has its life.

Rachel Griffiths's career is humming right along, if the criteria is that she stars in good roles in interesting movies, and is able to use her gifts and her intriguing personality. It could stand some improvement if the criteria is that she appears in big hits and makes $20 million a picture. The odds are she is too unique to ever make that much money; she isn't generic enough. And remember that the weekend box-office derby is usually won by the movie appealing to teenage boys. She doesn't play the kinds of women who are visible to them yet. All of this is beside the point for evolved moviegoers such as ourselves, who know a star when we see one.

Men With Guns ★ ★ ★ ★
R, 128 m., 1998

Federico Luppi (Dr. Fuentes), Damian Delgado (Domingo, the Soldier), Dan Rivera Gonzalez (Conejo, the Boy), Tania Cruz (Graciela, the Mute Girl), Damian Alcazar (Padre Portillo, the Priest), Mandy Patinkin (Andrew), Kathryn Grody (Harriet). Directed by John Sayles and produced by R. Paul Miller and Maggie Renzi. Screenplay by Sayles.

Men With Guns tells the story of a doctor in an unnamed Central American country who makes a trip into the rain forest to visit the young medical students he trained some years earlier. They were supposed to fan out among the Indian villages, fighting tapeworm and other scourges. The doctor has reason to believe many of them have been killed.

The doctor's journey is enlarged by John Sayles into an allegory about all countries where men with guns control the daily lives of the people. Some of the men are with the government, some are guerrillas, some are thieves, some are armed to protect themselves, and to the ordinary people it hardly matters: The man with the gun does what he wants, and his reasons are irrelevant—unknown perhaps even to himself.

The film takes the form of a journey, sometimes harrowing, sometimes poetic. It has a backbone of symbolism, as many great stories do. As the doctor moves from the city to the country, from the shore to the mountains, he also moves through history. We see the ruins of older civilizations that lived in this land, and we see powerless villagers moved here and there according to arbitrary whims. They are

killed by the military for helping the guerrillas, and killed by the guerrillas for helping the military, and their men are killed simply because they are men without guns. There is no suggestion that either military or guerrillas have any larger program than to live well off the spoils of power.

The doctor (Federico Luppi), tall and white-haired, has a grave dignity. He is not an action hero, but a man who has been given a pass in life; while he has lived comfortably in the capital with a nice practice, his country's reality has passed him by. As he ventures into the countryside, he gathers four traveling companions. There is an army deserter, now a thief, who first steals from him, then joins him. A former priest ("his church calls it liberation theology, but he preferred to liberate himself"). A young boy who knows the area better than any of them and has an uncanny ability to judge the essence of a situation. And a woman who has not spoken since she was raped.

The critic Tom Keogh suggests that there is an element of *The Wizard of Oz* in the doctor and his companions, who need a heart, a voice, and courage. There are also suggestions of *Treasure of the Sierra Madre* and other stories in which a legendary goal—Oz, gold, El Dorado—is said to be hidden further on. In this case the travelers begin to hear about a village named "The Circle of Heaven," which is so high on a mountain and so deep in the trees that the helicopters cannot find it, and people live free. Sayles tells his story in a series of vignettes—encounters on the road, stories told, flashbacks of earlier experiences, a touch of magic realism.

From time to time, the travelers and their journey are interrupted by two other characters, chatty American tourists (Mandy Patinkin and Kathryn Grody) who are looking for "antiques" and haven't a clue about the reality of the land and people behind them.

The tourists serve a satirical purpose, but I found myself seeing them in a different light. From time to time, reviewing a movie, I'll say the leading characters were shallow but the people in the background seemed interesting. In that sense, *Men With Guns* is about the background. Sayles finances his own films. If he had taken this script to a studio executive, he no doubt would have been told to beef up the American tourist roles and cast the roles with stars. The film would have become an action sitcom with Indians, doctors, priests, and orphans in the background as local color.

If you doubt me, look again at *Medicine Man* (1992), with Sean Connery in the rain forest, or *Anaconda* (1997), with snake-hunters up the Amazon. In my bemusement, every time the American tourists turned up, I thought of them as visitors from the phantom Hollywood revision of this material: magic realism of a different sort. It's as if Sayles is saying, "Here's what the studios would have made this movie into."

When the history of the century's films is written, John Sayles will stand tall as a director who went his own way, made his own films, directed and edited them himself, and operated completely outside the traditional channels of distribution and finance. When we hear Francis Coppola's lament that he has to make a John Grisham film in order to make one of his "own" films, we can only reflect that Sayles has demonstrated that a director can be completely independent if he chooses.

Men With Guns is immensely moving and sad, and yet because it dares so much, it is an exhilarating film. It frees itself from specific stories about *this* villain or *that* strategy to stand back and look at the big picture: at societies in collapse because power has been concentrated in the hands of small men made big with guns. I understand guns in war, in hunting, in sport. But when a man feels he needs a gun to leave his house in the morning, I fear that man. I fear his fear. He believes that the only man more powerless than himself is a dead man.

Mercury Rising ★ ★

R, 108 m., 1998

Bruce Willis (Art Jeffries), Alec Baldwin (Kudrow), Miko Hughes (Simon), Chi McBride (Bizzi Jordan), Kim Dickens (Stacey), Robert Stanton (Dean), Bodhi Pine Elfman (Leo). Directed by Harold Becker and produced by Brian Grazer and Karen Kehela. Screenplay by Lawrence Konner, Ryne Douglas Pearson, and Mark Rosenthal, based on the novel by Pearson.

Mercury Rising is about the most sophisticated cryptographic system known to man, and about characters considerably denser than anyone in the audience. Sitting in the dark, our minds idly playing with the plot, we figure out what they should do, how they should do it, and why they should do it, while the characters on the screen strain helplessly against the requirements of the formula.

The movie begins with the two obligatory scenes of most rogue lawman scenarios: (1) Opening hostage situation, in which the hero (Bruce Willis) could have saved the situation if not for his trigger-happy superiors; (2) The calling on the carpet, in which his boss tells the lawman he's being pulled off the job and assigned to grunt duty. "You had it—but the magic's gone," the boss recites. Willis's only friend is a sidekick named Bizzi Jordan (Chi McBride), who has, as is the nature of sidekicks, a wife and child, so that the hero can gaze upon them and ponder his solitude.

Experienced moviegoers will know that in the course of his diminished duties, Willis (playing an FBI man named Jeffries) will stumble across a bigger case. And will try to solve it single-handedly, while he is the object of a police manhunt. And will eventually engage in a hand-to-hand struggle with the sinister man behind the scheme. This struggle will preferably occur in a high place (see "Climbing Killer," from *Ebert's Little Movie Glossary*). Plus, there's a good bet the hero will enlist a good-looking woman who will drop everything for a chance to get shot at while by his side.

The new twist this time is explained by the evil bureaucrat (Alec Baldwin) in one of several lines of dialogue he should have insisted on rewriting: "A nine-year-old has deciphered the most sophisticated cipher system ever known—and he's autistic!?!" Yes, little Simon (Miko Hughes) looks at a word game in a puzzle magazine, and while the sound track emits quasi-computeristic beeping noises, he figures out the code concealed there, and calls the secret phone number, causing two geeks in a safe room to leap about in dismay.

Agents are dispatched to try to kill the kid and his parents, who live in Chicago. FBI agent Jeffries comes late to the scene, eyeballs the dead parents, immediately intuits it wasn't really a murder-suicide ("How's a guy that's so broke afford a $1,500 handgun?"), and then finds Simon hiding in a crawl space. Putting two and two together (without beeping noises), he deduces that Simon knows a secret, and powerful people want to destroy him.

The movie then descends into formula again, with obligatory scenes in which the police guard is mysteriously pulled off duty in a hospital corridor (see *The Godfather*), and Jeffries runs down corridors with the kid under his arm while evil agents demonstrate that no marksman, however well trained, can hit anyone important while there's still an hour to go. (The David Mamet movie *The Spanish Prisoner*, which is as smart as *Mercury Rising* is dumb, has the hero ask a markswoman: "What if you had missed?" and supplies her with the perfect answer: "It would be back to the range for me!")

The movie's greatest test of credibility comes when Jeffries, object of a citywide manhunt, walks into a restaurant in the Wrigley Building, meets a complete stranger named Stacey (Kim Dickens), and asks her to watch the kid for him while he goes on a quick mission. Of course Stacey agrees, and cooperates again when the agent and the kid turn up at her house in the middle of the night and ask for a safe place to stay. Before long, indeed, she's blowing off a business trip to Des Moines because, well, what woman wouldn't instinctively trust an unshaven man in a sweaty T-shirt, with an autistic kid under his arm and a gun in his belt—especially if the cops were after him?

What is sad is that the performances by Willis, Dickens, and young Miko Hughes are really pretty good—better than the material deserves. Willis doesn't overplay or overspeak, which redeems some of the silly material, and Dickens somehow finds a way through the requirements of her role that allows her to sidestep her character's wildly implausible decisions.

But what happened to Alec Baldwin's BS detector? Better replace those batteries! His character utters speeches that are laughable in any context, especially this one: "You know," he says, "my wife says my people skills are like my cooking skills—quick and tasteless." And

listen to his silky speech in the rain as he defends his actions.

Here are the two most obvious problems that sentient audiences will have with the plot. (1) Modern encryption cannot be intuitively deciphered, by rainmen or anyone else, without a key. And (2) if a nine-year-old kid can break your code, don't kill the kid; kill the programmers.

A Merry War ★ ★ ★
NO MPAA RATING, 100 m., 1998

Richard E. Grant (Gordon Comstock), Helena Bonham Carter (Rosemary), Julian Wadham (Ravelston), Jim Carter (Erskine), Harriet Walter (Julia Comstock), Lesley Vickerage (Hermione), Liz Smith (Mrs. Meakin), Barbara Leigh Hunt (Mrs. Wisbeach). Directed by Robert Bierman and produced by Peter Shaw. Screenplay by Alan Plater, based on the novel by George Orwell.

A Merry War is the insipid and enigmatic new title for a film released in England as *Keep the Aspidistra Flying*. That may not be an inspired title either, but at least it is the title of the famous 1936 novel by George Orwell, and a play on the communist slogan "Keep the Red Flag Flying." In Orwell's England, the aspidistra, a house plant almost impossible to kill through neglect, was a symbol of suburban living rooms. And his hero, Gordon Comstock, seems determined to find out how much neglect he can endure.

Comstock is a version of Orwell with many autobiographical parallels, I suspect, and as played by Richard E. Grant, has the same long face, deep eyes, towering brow, and morose demeanor. The film begins with Comstock quitting his job at an advertising agency in order to write poetry, only to find that poets, like everyone else, need money.

He gets a job in a ratty used bookstore in the slums of Lambeth but is reminded by the dusty shelves and sparse business that his boss at the ad agency was probably right when he asked, "Isn't there enough poetry in the world already?" The final straw comes when Gordon finds his own slim volume of verse marked down to three pence.

In Gordon's life there is one sparkle of sunshine, and it is provided by Rosemary (Helena Bonham Carter), an artist at the agency, who rather improbably loves him and even believes in him. But Gordon has no money to take her out, no money for a clean shirt or laundry, no money for smokes or even for tea (he cadges off his sister, who works in a tea shop). The movie, and the novel, capture the desperation of the Great Depression, when people like Gordon, whose family had just barely slipped into the middle class, were in danger of slipping out again.

Orwell himself was a connoisseur of poverty. His book *Down and Out in Paris and London* chronicles time spent living among the poor; he supported himself as a dishwasher in Paris, inhabiting another universe from the diners who dirtied the dishes. And he worked for a time in a London used bookstore; you can see his face gazing down from the wall of a pizza parlor at 1 South End Street in Hampstead, where the bookstore once operated.

The novel is billed as "Orwell's only comedy," although a better case can be made for *Animal Farm,* and the humor in *Keep the Aspidistra Flying* is of a sardonic turn: "The public are swine; advertising is the rattling of a stick inside a swill-bucket." The movie plays more as a morality tale, in which Gordon thinks he can escape advertising and is proven wrong. "I was called 'promising' by the *Times Literary Supplement,*" he tells his long-suffering publisher. "I know," says the publisher. "I wrote it."

Gordon hardly deserves Rosemary's sweetness and trust, but she is his savior. As played by Helena Bonham Carter, she is a small, intense, focused, and serious young woman who has her standards. They are in love but have never made love, mostly because Gordon has a sharp-eyed landlady and no money to rent a room, and Rosemary sharply lays down the law: "I will not make love where dogs have peed." When they do finally achieve union, of course she gets pregnant, but even then offers him his freedom: "Remember—you're a poet. And a free man."

Babies. What does Gordon know of them? He goes to the public library and has a classic exchange with the librarian (Alan Plater's screenplay concisely punches up Orwell's dialogue). "Do you have any books on pregnancy?" he

asks. "Not for the general public!" she snaps. "I'm not the general public," he corrects her condescendingly. "I'm the father of an unborn child." And as he regards the engraving of a fetus, he knows what his duty is. After all, as his boss also observed, "Poetry and advertising all use the same words—just in a different order."

A Merry War is the kind of movie that doesn't reach large audiences, but some will find it appealing. For me it works not only as a reasonable adaptation of an Orwell novel I like, but also as a form of escapism since, if the truth be known, I would be happy as a clerk in a London used bookstore. For a time.

Message in a Bottle ★ ★
PG-13, 126 m., 1999

Kevin Costner (Garret Blake), Robin Wright Penn (Theresa Osborne), John Savage (Johnny Land), Illeana Douglas (Lina Paul), Robbie Coltrane (Charlie Toschi), Jesse James (Jason Osborne), Paul Newman (Dodge Blake). Directed by Luis Mandoki and produced by Denise Di Novi, Jim Wilson, and Kevin Costner. Screenplay by Gerald DiPego, based on the novel *The Notebook* by Nicholas Sparks.

Message in a Bottle is a tearjerker that strolls from crisis to crisis. It's curiously muted, as if it fears that passion would tear its delicate fabric; even the fights are more in sorrow than in anger, and when there's a fistfight, it doesn't feel like a real fistfight—it feels more like someone thought the movie needed a fistfight 'round about then.

The film is about a man and a woman who believe in great true love. The man believes it's behind him; the woman hopes it's ahead of her. One of their ideals in life is "to be somebody's true north." Right away we know they're in trouble. You don't just find true love. You team up with somebody, and build it from the ground up. But *Message in a Bottle* believes in the kind of love where the romantic music comes first, trembling and sweeping under every scene, and the dialogue is treated like the lyrics.

Yet it is about two likable characters—three, really, since Paul Newman not only steals every scene he's in, but puts it in the bank and draws interest on it. Robin Wright Penn plays Theresa, a researcher for the *Chicago Tribune*, who finds a letter in a bottle. It is a heartbreaking love note to "Catherine," by a man who wants to make amends to his true north.

Theresa, a divorced mother of one, is deeply touched by the message, and shares it with a columnist named Charlie (Robbie Coltrane), who of course lifts it for a column. Theresa feels betrayed. (If she thinks she can show a letter like that to a guy with a deadline and not read about it in tomorrow's paper, no wonder she's still a researcher.) The column leads to the discovery of two other letters on the same stationery. Charlie has the bottle, the cork, the stationery, and the handwriting analyzed, and figures the messages came from the Carolinas. A few calls to gift shops, and they know who bought the stationery.

It's Garret Blake (Kevin Costner). Theresa is sent out on a mission to do research about him. She meets his father (Newman), and then the man himself, a shipwright who handcrafts beautiful vessels. He takes her for a test sail. The wind is bracing and the chemistry is right. "You eat meat?" he asks her. "Red meat? I make a perfect steak. It's the best thing I do." With this kind of buildup, Linda McCartney would have tucked into a T-bone.

Soon it's time for Theresa to return home (where after she writes one column, the paper promotes her and gives her an office with a window view; at that rate, in six weeks she'll be using Colonel McCormick's ancestral commode). Of course she wants him to come and see her—to see how she lives. "Will you come and visit me?" she asks. His reply does not represent the proudest moment of the screenwriter: "You mean, inland?"

Sooner or later he's going to find out that she found his letter in a bottle and is not simply a beautiful woman who wandered onto his boat. That his secrets are known in those few places where the *Tribune* is still read. Yes, but it takes a long time, and when his discovery finally comes, the film handles it with a certain tact. It's not just an explosion about betrayal, but more complicated—partly because of the nature of the third letter.

As morose and contrived as the movie is, it has a certain winsome charm because of the personal warmth of the actors. This is Robin Wright Penn's breakthrough to a different kind of acting, and she has a personal triumph; she's been identified with desperate, hard-as-nails characters, but no more. Costner finds the right note of inarticulate pain; he loves, but doesn't feel he has the right to. Paul Newman handles his role, as Costner's ex-drunk father, with the relaxed confidence of Michael Jordan shooting free throws in your driveway. It is good to see all three of them on the screen, in whatever combination, and the movie is right to play down the sex scenes and underline the cuddling and the whispers.

But where, oh where, did they get the movie's ending? Is it in the original novel by Nicholas Sparks? Don't know. Haven't read it. The climactic events are shameless, contrived, and wildly out of tune with the rest of the story. To saddle Costner, Penn, and Newman with such goofy melodrama is like hiring Fred Astaire and strapping a tractor on his back.

The Messenger: The Story of Joan of Arc ★ ★
R, 141 m., 1999

Milla Jovovich (Joan), John Malkovich (Charles VII), Faye Dunaway (Yolande D'Aragon), Dustin Hoffman (Joan's Conscience), Pascal Greggory (Alencon), Vincent Cassel (Gilles de Rais), Tcheky Kary (Dunois), Richard Ridings (La Hire), Desmond Harrington (Aulon). Directed by Luc Besson and produced by Patrice Ledoux. Screenplay by Besson and Andrew Birkin.

Luc Besson's *The Messenger: The Story of Joan of Arc* labors under the misapprehension that Joan's life is a war story, and takes place largely on battlefields. In fact, it takes place almost entirely within the consciences of everyone involved. The movie does at least concede that a good part of Joan's legend involves her trial for heresy and her burning at the stake, and these scenes may prove educational for the test audience members who wrote on their sneak-preview cards, "Why does she have to die at the end?"

Two of the best films ever made are about Joan of Arc: *The Passion of Joan of Arc*, by Carl Dreyer (1928), and *The Trial of Joan of Arc*, by Robert Bresson (1962). Also one of the worst, *Saint Joan* (1957), by Otto Preminger, who had in common with Luc Besson the theory that Joan must look like a babe. Dreyer's Joan was Falconetti, a French actress whose haunted face mirrored one of the greatest performances in cinema—the only one she ever gave. Preminger's was Jean Seberg, found in Iowa after an international talent search. (The search for her talent continued after the film was completed, and it was finally found in Godard's *Breathless* two years later.)

Besson has cast Milla Jovovich as his Joan. She was his wife at the time they started shooting. They have since split, although he says they would still be together if they could only have made movies 365 days a year, a statement that may provide more insight than he intended. Jovovich, who also starred in Besson's *The Fifth Element,* is a healthy, cheerful, open-faced twenty-four-year-old actress who seems much too robust and uncomplicated to play Joan.

The movie is a mess: a gassy costume epic with nobody at the center. So deficient is Besson at suggesting the conscience that rules Joan's actions that the movie even uses another character, the Grand Inquisitor, as a surrogate conscience, and brings in Dustin Hoffman to play it; he is a creation of Joan's imagination. That Hoffman's performance is the best in the film should have been a nudge to the filmmaker that he could cut back on the extras and the battle scenes and make the movie about—well, about Joan.

Joan of Arc was a naive young French peasant woman, illiterate, who was told by voices that she must go to the aid of her king. France at that time was ill-supplied with kings; the best it could offer was the reluctant Dauphin (John Malkovich), later Charles VII. She informed him her destiny was to lead French troops on the battlefield against the English, who were godless (or foreign, which to the French was a negligible distinction). Legend has it she ended the siege of Orleans.

Legend may be wrong. A book published in France by the historian Roger Caratini claims "precious little of what we French have been taught in school about Joan of Arc is true." He finds scant evidence that Joan did much more than go along for the ride, and adds cruelly that she could not have raised the siege of

Orleans because the city was never besieged in the first place. Her trial for heresy was not at the hands of the British but under the French Inquisition at the University of Paris, and her greatest crime may have been dressing like a boy and offending the ecclesiastical gender police. Her legend was "more or less invented" in the nineteenth century, we learn, as a tonic for emerging French nationalism, which had a "desperate need for a patriotic mascot."

Of course we do not expect *The Messenger* to be a revisionist downgrading of the French national heroine, who was burned by a schismatic branch of the church and canonized by Rome five centuries later without having, perhaps, done much to deserve either. We expect a patriotic epic, in which the heroic young woman saves her country but is destroyed by an effete ruler and a lot of grim old clerics. Even if the film is not about a battle of opposing moralities, even if it is not about conscience (as the Dreyer and Bresson films are), it can at least be as much fun as, say, *Braveheart*, wouldn't you say?

No such luck. Besson's film is a thin, uninvolving historical romp in which the only juicy parts are played by supporting characters, such as the Dauphin, made by John Malkovich into a man whose interest in the crown essentially ends with whether it fits. Faye Dunaway has fun as his stepmother, Yolande D'Aragon, who schemes against Joan as any mother would when her son falls under the sway of a girl from the wrong side of the class divide. And Dustin Hoffman is really very good as Joan's surrogate conscience, the Inquisitor, even if his role seems inspired by the desperate need to somehow shoehorn philosophy into the film. I was reminded of the Roger Corman horror picture where holes in the plot were plugged by hiring two bit players and having one ask the other, "Now explain what all this means."

Metroland ★ ★ ★

NO MPAA RATING, 101 m., 1999

Christian Bale (Chris), Emily Watson (Marion), Lee Ross (Toni), Elsa Zylberstein (Annick), Rufus (Henri), Jonathan Aris (Dave), Ifan Meredith (Mickey), Amanda Ryan (Joanna). Directed by Philip Saville and produced by

Andrew Bendel. Screenplay by Adrian Hodges, based on the novel by Julian Barnes.

There are a lot of movies about escaping from the middle class, but *Metroland* is one of the few about escaping into it. In 1968, Chris is a footloose British photographer in Paris, who has an affair with a French woman and drifts through streets alive with drugs and revolution. In 1977, Chris has become a married man with a child, living in a London suburb at the end of the Metropolitan line of the Underground. Is he happier now?

Not according to his friend Toni, who joined Chris in sixties hedonism and never looked back. Toni (Lee Ross) has just returned from America, after dropping out in Africa and Asia. He's returned to the United Kingdom for one reason only: to convince Chris (Christian Bale) to leave his family behind and join him on the road. *Metroland,* based on a 1980 novel by Julian Barnes, who became famous after *Flaubert's Parrot,* watches Chris as he is enticed by temptation and memory.

The memories are often about the two women he met in Paris that year—the one he married and the one he didn't. Annick (Elsa Zylberstein) is one of those young Parisians who live on air and use the cafés as living rooms. They meet, they flirt, they become a couple. The sound track of their romance is sixties rock, mixed with Django Reinhardt, and with Annick he learns about sex ("Is it the first time?" she asks, with reason). Then into his world drifts a visiting English girl, Marion (Emily Watson), who is sensible, cheerful, supportive, reassuring, and wholesome. She sizes him up and informs him that he will get married, probably to her, because "you're not original enough not to."

He does, and life in Metroland continues happily until Toni calls at 6 A.M. one morning. Toni tempts Chris with tastes of the life he left behind, and at a party they attend, an available girl makes him an offer so frank and inviting he very nearly cannot refuse. Yet the movie is not about whether Chris will remain faithful to Marion; it's about whether he chose the right life in the first place.

Philip Saville, who directs from a screenplay by Adrian Hodges, starts with a straight-forward story of life choices (the plot could as easily be from Joanna Trollope as Julian Barnes), and slips in teasing asides, as in a scene where Toni almost has Chris and Marion believing he has "always been in love with Chris." Or when Chris daydreams about Marion telling him, "of course, I expect you to have affairs." What Saville doesn't do, mercifully, is depend on sentiment: Chris is not asked to make his decision based on loyalty to wife and daughter, but on the actual issue of his choice to live in the London outskirts and raise a family. There is a cold-blooded sense in which he could decide, objectively, dispassionately, that he took the wrong turn—that it is his right to join Toni in a life of wandering, sex, and mind-altering.

What's curious, given how everything depends on Chris, is the way the movie is really centered on the two women. Annick almost deliberately plays the role of a cliché—the brainy, liberated French woman showing the Englishman the sensual ropes. Elsa Zylberstein finds the right note: The woman proud to have "a beautiful British boyfriend," and hurt when she's dumped, but not blinded by dreams of eternal love. And then there's Marion, played by Emily Watson in a radical departure from her tormented characters in *Breaking the Waves* and *Hilary and Jackie.* Here she is cheerfully normal—an ideal wife, if that's what Chris is looking for. "No wonder you're bored," says Toni. But why did Toni come back, if he wasn't bored too?

Michael Jordan at the Max ★ ★
NO MPAA RATING, 45 m., 2000

A documentary directed by Jim Stern and John Kempf and produced by John Kempf, Steve Kempf, and Stern.

It is awesome to see Michael Jordan on the five-story IMAX screen, and to hear the roar of the crowd in surround stereo. Any Jordan fan will enjoy *Michael Jordan at the Max* on that level. Unfortunately, that's the only level there is. As a documentary, the film plays like one of those packages NBC cobbles together before a semifinals round: game footage, talking heads, and a narrator who intones the usual mantras about His Airness.

We might as well get used to the idea that there will never be a real documentary about Michael Jordan—one made with the full tools of the filmmaker's art, with its own point of view and insights beneath the surface. *Michael Jordan at the Max,* like almost everything that has been filmed or written about Jordan, is essentially just a promotional film for Jordan as a product. It plays like a commercial for itself.

Jordan is a private man—so private, that although he talks about his dead father in this film, there is no mention of his mother, his wife, or his children. His mother is seen and heard once; his wife is (I think) glimpsed briefly. I didn't expect an intimate display of private matters, but in this film Jordan is a man who lives on the basketball court and evaporates otherwise, except when starring in commercials. The only time we see him not wearing a basketball uniform is when he's wearing a suit while walking into the dressing room.

Michael Jordan at the Max takes as its framework that remarkable final championship season, and there are moments from games we remember so well, against Indiana, Seattle, and Utah. But they aren't analytical or even very informative—just colorful shots of Michael scoring again and again (he misses two shots in the entire film). Sometimes you have to know the story to realize what you're seeing, as when we overhear Steve Kerr, during a time out, tell Michael that if he gets the ball he will not miss the shot—and then sinking his famous game-winning two-pointer. The movie shows this, but doesn't underline it or explain it.

Jordan's career is commented on in interviews with Bob Greene, Phil Jackson, Bob Costas, Johnny "Red" Kerr, and others. The professional sportswriters who covered the games are not consulted. Not a word by the others seems spontaneous; the photography is flawless, like a studio portrait, and so are their comments, which sound (even if they aren't) scripted and rehearsed. I don't think we're seeing take one. Nobody ever fumbles, or pauses, or searches for a thought. They're all so sure what they want to say—and so is Jordan, interviewed in the United Center, his words so familiar they are like a politician's basic stump speech, perfected after many deliveries.

Season after season, Gene Siskel explained the Bulls to me (and anyone else who would listen). He was smarter on basketball than anyone else I've ever encountered. He noticed small things and drew lessons from them (why Dennis Rodman missed the first free throw, why Toni Kukoc was more willing to take a bad shot than a good one). He watched the games not only as a fan, but as an analyst. He was to fans as Jackson is to coaches.

That taste of real insight left me feeling empty after *Michael Jordan at the Max,* with its platitudes and the same familiar sentences of praise we've heard so many times before, about how hard Jordan practiced, and how fierce was his desire to win, and what a leader he was. Yes, yes, yes, but there was *strategy* at work too. Jordan outplayed his opponents on some nights. He outthought them on every night. By treating him like a god the movie diminishes the achievement of the man.

This movie has no curiosity about the way Jordan read the game and its players. It has the spirit of a promotional film. It's bright and colorful, and it makes it fun for us to revisit those cherished Bulls triumphs, but there is no bite. It's the official, authorized version. On the giant IMAX screen it has an undeniable impact, and as a Bulls fan I enjoyed it. But as a film critic I was disappointed: Shrink this to a videocassette, pop it into your VCR machine, and you might as well be looking at an NBA highlight reel.

Mickey Blue Eyes ★ ★
PG-13, 103 m., 1999

Hugh Grant (Michael Felgate), James Caan (Frank Vitale), Jeanne Tripplehorn (Gina Vitale), Burt Young (Vito Graziosi), James Fox (Philip Cromwell), Joe Viterelli (Vinnie), Scott Thompson (Agent Lewis), Paul Lazar (Ritchie Vitale). Directed by Kelly Makin and produced by Elizabeth Hurley and Charles Mulvehill. Screenplay by Adam Scheinman and Robert Kuhn.

Mickey Blue Eyes has most of the ingredients in place for another one of those married-to-the-mob comedies, but the central character has to hold it together, and Hugh Grant is wrong for the role. More than some actors, perhaps, he depends on correct casting for his appeal—and here, as an art auctioneer who gets into danger after falling in love with a mobster's daughter, he strikes one wrong note and then another.

The setup is ingenious. He's Michael Felgate, an art expert, proper, reserved, with a mid-Atlantic accent, and he falls in love with a dazzling young woman named Gina Vitale, who loves him too—but explains they can never marry. Why not? She's reluctant to tell him, but she fears for his life if he gets too close to her dad's mob connections.

Michael blunders ahead anyway. He meets her dad (James Caan), who runs a restaurant where the customers all seem supplied by Central Casting, Gangster Division. The inimitable Joe Viterelli, who was so funny as the bodyguard in *Analyze This*, is even on hand. Michael's slow to catch on: "Your dad is some kind of mob caterer?" And he asks the wrong questions for the right reasons ("Are you mostly family?"). But before she realizes what's happening, her dad has taken a liking to Michael and the wedding is on.

Complications. The big boss (nicely played by Burt Young) doesn't know the real story. There are misunderstandings. Michael has to pose as a mobster to save his life. He gets lessons in pronunciation to learn to talk like a gangster, and these scenes are so badly handled by Grant that the movie derails and never recovers. Either he can't do a plausible mob accent, or he thought it wasn't called for. The squawks and gurgles he produces, both during the lessons and later, are so strangled and peculiar that we wonder why the other actors don't just break off and wait for the next take.

Grant is wrong for the role anyway. He has a good line in charm and wit, he can play intelligent and vulnerable, and he's likable. But there's never a moment here where he convinces us he's truly desperate or in danger. He drops into the movie like a dinner guest; we're reminded of somebody unflappable like David Niven, although Niven could play desperate when he had to.

Jeanne Tripplehorn is sufficiently convincing as the woman who loves him, although it must have seemed odd to her, being so intense in the face of his cool. James Caan and Burt Young are right at home (Young's thin lips releasing each word grudgingly), and Viterelli is a mountain of plausibility. But without a strong

center, there's not enough for them to play against.

A side plot, involving James Fox as a major player in the art world, seems like an afterthought, but there is funny stuff about art in the movie. I liked the plot device of a mobster's son who paints unspeakably awful pictures (Jesus with a machine gun, etc.). They end up at auction, where they turn out to be a handy way to launder money (mob pays big for painting, son therefore has legitimate income from art). There are interesting consequences when the paintings become sought-after, especially by a sweet little old lady who is tempted by dangerous investments.

All good stuff, but it doesn't add up. Is this movie Hugh Grant's fault? I don't know. Not many actors can save themselves from wrong casting. On paper perhaps Grant looked right. But consider his success in *Notting Hill*. Even there, faced with the loss of the woman he loved, his instincts were not to scream but to apologize. Some actors can convey charm and desperation in a romantic farce (Matt Dillon comes to mind) and some need to be a little more grounded in reality. After the bite and freshness of *Analyze This*, *Mickey Blue Eyes* plays like an afterthought.

Mifune ★ ★ ★
R, 99 m., 2000

Anders W. Berthelsen (Kresten), Iben Hjejle (Liva), Jesper Asholt (Rud, Kresten's Brother), Sofie Grabol (Claire, Kresten's Wife), Emil Tarding (Bjarke, Liva's Brother), Anders Hove (Gerner), Paprika Steen (Pernille), Mette Bratlann (Nina). Directed by Soren Kragh-Jacobsen and produced by Birgitte Hlad. Screenplay by Kragh-Jacobsen and Anders Thomas Jensen.

Mifune is the latest work with the imprimatur of Dogma '95, a group of Danish filmmakers who signed a cinematic "vow of chastity"—reserving poverty and obedience, apparently, for TV directors. Dogma films are encouraged to use natural light and sound, real locations, no props or music brought in from outside, handheld cameras and "no directorial touches," as if the auteur theory was shamelessly immodest. Of the Dogma films I have seen (*The*

Idiots, Celebration) and the Dogma wanna-be *julien donkey-boy, Mifune* is the most fun and the least dogmatic. With just a few more advances, like props, sets, lighting, music, and style, the Dogma crowd will be making real movies.

Only kidding. But in truth, Dogma '95 is as much publicity as conviction, and its films contain more, not less, directorial style. Like the American indie movement, they use small budgets and unsprung plots, but that's not a creed; it's a strategy for making a virtue of necessity. That the Dogma films have been good and interesting is encouraging, but a coincidence.

The story of *Mifune* breaks down no barriers but is in the tradition of offbeat romantic comedy, and one can imagine it being remade by Hollywood with Jeff Daniels as the hero, Martin Short as the retarded brother, and Angelina Jolie as the hooker. It is a "commercial" story, and all the more entertaining for being so, but Soren Kragh-Jacobsen's low-rent version has a freshness and spontaneity that the Hollywood version would probably lose. There's something about ground-level filmmaking that makes an audience feel a movie is getting away with something.

The story begins with the wedding of Kresten (Anders W. Berthelsen) and Claire (Sofie Grabol). If the eye contact between Kresten and Claire's sexy mother is any indication, this marriage might have soon grown very complicated, but Kresten's past catches up with him and dooms the marriage (not, luckily for Claire, before a wedding night that seems to set Guinness records). Kresten learns that his father has died, and he has avoided telling his wife and snotty in-laws about his family's ramshackle farm, his retarded brother, or his mother who hung herself on "one of the oldest trees in Denmark." ("He grew up," observes A. O. Scott, "in the Danish translation of a Tennessee Williams play.")

Kresten returns to the farm, which is a run-down shambles with water damage and animals making free use of the house, and finds his brother, Rud (Jesper Asholt), drinking under the table that bears the father's corpse. What to do? Rud cannot take care of himself, the farm is falling to pieces, and this is not the kind of situation he can bring Claire into. Desperate, Kresten hires a housekeeper named

Liva, played by Iben Hjejle (she plays Laura, the lost love, in *High Fidelity*). Liva is desperate, too; we learn she was a hooker, is being pursued by an angry pimp, and receives alarming phone calls.

At this point in the story not even the most stringent application of Dogma vows can prevent the director and his audience from hurtling confidently toward the inevitable development in which Kresten and Liva fall in love and form a sort of instant family with Rud as honorary child. Dogma forbids genre conventions, but this story is made from the ground up of nothing else—and more power to it.

If the story is immensely satisfying in a traditional way, the style has its own delights. Kragh-Jacobsen feels free to meander. Every single scene doesn't have to pull its weight and move the plot marker to the next square. Asides and irrelevant excursions are allowed. Characters arrive at conclusions by a process we can follow on the screen, instead of signaling us that they are only following the script. And there is an earthiness to the unknown actors, especially Asholt as Rud, that grounds the story in the infinite mystery of real personalities.

Watching *Mifune* and the other Dogma films (except for *julien,* which is more of an exercise in video art), we're taught a lesson. It's not a new lesson; John Cassavetes taught it years ago and directors as various as Mike Leigh and Henry Jaglom demonstrate it. It has to do with the feel of a film, regardless of its budget or the faces in the cast. Some films feel free, and others seem caged. Some seem to happen while we watch, and others seem to know their own fates. Some satisfy by marching toward foregone conclusions, and others (while they may arrive at the same place) seem surprised and delighted by how they turn out.

Mifune is like a lesson in film watching. If you see enough films like this, you learn to be suspicious of high-gloss films that purr along mile after mile without any bumps. If a film like this were a car and it stalled, you could go under the hood with a wrench. When fancy films stall, you need a computer expert.

The Mighty ★ ★ ★
PG-13, 100 m., 1998

Elden Henson (Max), Kieran Culkin (Kevin), Sharon Stone (Kevin's Mother), Gena Rowlands (Max's Grandmother), Harry Dean Stanton (Max's Grandfather), Gillian Anderson (Loretta Lee), James Gandolfini (Max's Father), Meat Loaf (Iggy). Directed by Peter Chelsom and produced by Jane Startz and Simon Fields. Screenplay by Charles Leavitt, based on the novel *Freak, the Mighty* by Rodman Philbrick.

"You need a brain, I need legs—and the Wizard of Oz doesn't live in South Cincinnati."

So speaks a twisted little boy named Kevin to a hulking giant named Max, in the new movie *The Mighty*. They're both in the seventh grade in Cincinnati—Max for the third time—and they're both misfits.

Max, known to his cruel classmates as the Missing Link, feels like Godzilla as he lumbers down the school corridors, and says, "... sometimes seems like the whole world has just seen me on *America's Most Wanted*." Kevin has Morquio's Syndrome, which causes his bones to stop growing even though his organs continue to expand, until finally, in the movie's words "his heart will get too big for his body."

Kevin and Max are the heroes of *Freak, the Mighty*, a best-selling children's book by Rodman Philbrick that has been embraced by kids who feel they stand out like sore thumbs (and what kid doesn't?). It's a fable about how two friends can work together to take on the world, and it's about how Kevin's example helps Max repair a life that began with his father killing his mother.

At first, it's not a friendship made in heaven. Kevin moves in next door to Max, who spies across the back fence as the little kid, who wears braces and glasses, test-flies a birdlike model flying machine he calls an "Ornothopter." ("I gave birth to a seven-and-a-half-pound dictionary," sighs his mother.) In gym class, a cruel kid throws a basketball to knock Kevin off his crutches, and Max is blamed for the stunt. It's ironic when Max goes for remedial reading lessons and finds out that Kevin is his tutor. "I didn't throw the basketball," he tells the little kid, who says he was a chump to take the rap for someone else.

The book they read is *King Arthur and the Knights of the Round Table*, and it is Arthurian chivalry that Kevin believes should guide their lives. Soon they arrive at a working arrangement that takes advantage of both their needs: Kevin rides around on Max's shoulders, and they even play basketball that way. The extra height is great for layups. (Did the book's author see *Mad Max Beyond Thunderdome*, where another giant and another dwarf teamed up to create the character Master-Blaster?)

We meet the people in their lives. Kevin's mother (Sharon Stone) struggles to keep him out of "special schools" and help him lead the fullest possible life. Max's grandparents, Gram and Grim (Gena Rowlands and Harry Dean Stanton), are raising him, not without love, after the death of his mother and the imprisonment of his father (James Gandolfini).

The last third of the movie involves derring-do that's highly improbable, especially a make-shift toboggan ride. But for the younger audiences the movie is aimed at, these adventures will be thrilling and not too violent, and they do give both boys a chance to put the code of the Round Table into practice.

The Mighty is an emotionally affecting movie (much like the somewhat similar *Simon Birch*, which is about a friendship between a fatherless boy and a dwarf). It is a little stronger in its central theme, which is that we all have weaknesses, we are not perfect, but together we can be more than the sum of our parts.

Much of the film's appeal comes from the performances. Elden Henson, with his big, round, Scandinavian face and football lineman's body, brings a shyness and vulnerability to Max. He's stronger than the bullies who pick on him, but he has retreated into himself. Kieran Culkin, as Max, looks like his older brother Macaulay, but doesn't play the cute card as much, and has a nice unsentimental streak when he levels with Max. And the adults tactfully do what their roles require without trying to steal the movie from its heroes. (There's also a nice supporting role for Gillian Anderson as a woman whose stolen purse sets up the movie's climax.)

What I liked most about the movie is the way it shows that imagination can be a weapon in life. At their first reading lesson, Kevin tells Max that every word is part of a picture, and every sentence is a picture, and you put them all together in your head. That has never occurred to Max, who in reading about the Round Table is taken to a place outside his lonely bedroom and solitary school existence, and learns of nobility and romance. No child is completely a captive of a sad childhood if he can read and has books; they are the window to what can be, and that is the underlying message of *The Mighty*.

Mighty Joe Young ★ ★ ★
PG, 114 m., 1998

Charlize Theron (Jill Young), Bill Paxton (Gregg O'Hara), Rade Serbedzija (Strasser), Peter Firth (Garth), David Paymer (Harry Ruben), Regina King (Cecily Banks), Robert Wisdom (Kweli), Naveen Andrews (Pindi). Directed by Ron Underwood and produced by Ted Hartley and Tom Jacobson. Screenplay by Mark Rosenthal and Lawrence Konner, based on a screenplay by Ruth Rose.

Mighty Joe Young is an energetic, robust adventure tale: not too cynical, violent, or fragmented for kids, not too tame for adults. After all the calculation behind *Godzilla* or *Armageddon*, it has a kind of innocence to it. It's not about a monster but about a very big, well-meaning gorilla that just wants to be left in peace. And about a woman who treasures the gorilla. And about a zoologist who loves the woman. All that stuff.

Charlize Theron stars as Jill Young, a woman whose mother is a famed gorilla expert of the *Gorillas in the Mist* variety. Jill is raised with Joe, who even as a baby is big for his size. They grow up together, and Joe just keeps on growing, until you can tell he's approaching because the treetops shake.

Bill Paxton, from *Twister*, stars as Gregg O'Hara, a zoologist who wants samples of Joe's blood. Alas, the snaky types he hires as assistants are crooked, and try to sell information about the gorilla to a sleazy Los Angeles promoter named Strasser (Rade Serbedzija). This same Strasser is a poacher with a history with Joe, who once bit off his thumb and forefinger.

The African scenes are remarkable in the way they create a convincing giant gorilla and place him in the wild. The majority of the shots of Joe in this movie are special effects; we are rarely looking at a real gorilla. You can't tell that by anything on the screen—apart from Joe's size, of course. Joe isn't simply seen as he lumbers past. The camera is free to circle and approach him. In a sequence where he's being pursued by men in Land Rovers, the camera parallels him, then swings in front of him, then moves in for a close-up. It's a remarkable demonstration of technical skill.

Close-ups of Joe's face and upper body use superb animatronics. The only thing dubious about Joe is his attitude; when Jill cuddles and comforts him, he's more like a gentle little chimp than a fearsome beast. His eyes, lips, and facial movements are expressive even in the close shots. Theron treats him like a pet, whistling to make him approach her, sure of her authority.

The romance between Theron and Paxton is inevitable, but not intrusive. It's more of an obligatory subplot than a big deal. More interesting is the devious scheming of Strasser and his henchmen after Joe is brought to California. There's a scene where Mighty Joe freaks out at a charity benefit, and then the payoff as he scales Graumann's Chinese Theater, visits the Hollywood sign, and ends up in that dependable refuge of all thrillers, a carnival midway, where a child is in danger on top of a Ferris wheel.

The payoff of that scene owes more than a little to a certain scene in *E.T.*, and indeed the director, Ron Underwood, shows he's studied *E.T.* carefully. An early scene of poachers in the jungle is framed much like the early hunt for *E.T.* The camera is at boot level, there are loud jangles of keys and weapons on the sound track, and powerful flashlight beams cut Spielbergian laser-tracks through the mist.

One positive aspect is the film's relative civility. So many special-effects movies seem angry and aggressive; smaller kids are blown out of the theater by the force of the noise and special effects. *Mighty Joe Young* is not meek and harmless; it's a full-blooded action picture, all right, but with a certain warmth and humor instead of a scorched-earth approach. You feel good at the end, instead of merely relieved.

Mighty Peking Man ★ ★ ★
NO MPAA RATING, 100 m., 1977 (rereleased 1999)

Danny Lee (Li Hsiu-Hsien) (Johnny Feng),
Evelyne Kraft (Samantha [Ah Wei]), Hsiao Yao
(Huang Tsui-Hua), Ku Feng (Lu Tien), Lin Wei-
Tu (Chen Shi-Yu), Hsu Shao-Chiang (Ah Lung),
Wu Hang-Sheng (Ah Pi), Cheng Ping (Lucy).
Directed by Ho Meng-Hua and produced by
Runme Shaw. Screenplay by I. Kuang.

There is an earthquake near the beginning of
Mighty Peking Man, but unlike the earthquake
in the fondly remembered *Infra-Man,* it does
not unleash the Slinky-necked robots and hairy
mutant footstools controlled by Princess Dragon
Mom. Still, it offers attractions of its own. It
disturbs a giant ape, for example, which lumbers down from its mountain home and heads
for the jungles of India. And it is no ordinary
tremor; it unfolds progressively.

First, a character shouts that there's an earthquake. Then we hear it, although we do not see
anything alarming. Then the back-projected
landscape begins to shake violently, although
the foreground does not shake. Then the camera begins to shake, while the foreground still
holds steady. Later, finally, Earth moves. This
may be the first special effects–generated
earthquake in which the back projection shakes
so hard it moves Earth.

The earthquake doesn't really have an impact on the plot. It's simply an earthquake
scene, just as later there is a quicksand scene, a
scene where a python fights a tiger, etc. *Mighty
Peking Man,* made in 1977, is being rereleased
by Quentin Tarantino's Rolling Thunder Pictures, and we can only imagine young QT behind the counter of that legendary video store
of his youth, watching this on the monitor
and realizing he'd struck gold.

The plot involves an expedition to discover
the giant apelike Peking Man, who is said at
one point to be ten feet tall—although a grown
man is able to stand inside one of its foot-
prints. Later in the film, however, the creature
has grown enough to knock down tall buildings, although later still it has shrunk enough
to climb one.

The dialogue is to the point. After the expedition is suggested, a character says: "I know
an explorer here in Hong Kong! He just lost

his girl! He wants to get away!" The explorer,
whose name is Johnny Feng (Danny Lee), is
drunk when we first meet him; a flashback reveals that his girlfriend is having an affair with
his brother. That doesn't dissuade Lu Tien, the
hunt financer: "You're going to lead our expedition into the Himalyan jungle! You're the
only one I trust!"

Soon the expedition sets off, not in Land
Rovers as we might expect, but in tall two-
wheeled ox carts. There are hazards along the
way. My favorite is when a Sherpa gets his leg
bitten off above the knee. Johnny wants to
summon medical help, but Lu Tien simply
shoots the man in the head. The expedition
soon encounters a blond woman named Samantha (Evelyne Kraft) who has lived in the
jungle since the crash long ago of a plane carrying her family (in a flashback, we see the tot
crying out, "Mama! Papa!"). Mighty Peking
Man and Samantha hang out together, but are
just friends.

Samantha doesn't speak English at first, but
quickly learns, no doubt in the same way the
other actors have learned: by speaking their
usual language and having it dubbed. What is
amazing is that Mighty Peking Man, when encountered, also speaks English. Samantha's
savage existence has given her time to design
an off-the-shoulder leopard-skin brassiere,
and to find a supply of lip gloss and eyeliner.
Soon Samantha and Johnny are an item.

Lu Tien sees a fortune in Mighty Peking
Man, and brings him to Hong Kong, where he
is displayed in a stadium before thousands of
people, while chained to big trucks. Samantha
meanwhile has found Johnny in bed with his
original girlfriend, and races distraught to the
stadium when she sees Mighty Peking Man on
TV, tossing the trucks around like large toys
(which they are). She desperately pleads with
the implacable security forces to spare the
beast because he has been misunderstood. But
too late: MPM goes on a rampage through
downtown Hong Kong, knocking over buildings and batting helicopters out of the sky in a
sequence that was surely not an attempt to rip
off Dino De Laurentiis's *King Kong,* made a
year earlier.

Mighty Peking Man is very funny, although
a shade off the high mark of *Infra-Man,* which
was made a year earlier and is my favorite

Hong Kong monster film. Both were produced by the legendary Runme Shaw, who, having tasted greatness, obviously hoped to repeat. I find to my astonishment that I gave *Infra-Man* only two and a half stars when I reviewed it. That was twenty-two years ago, but a fellow will remember a lot of things you wouldn't think he'd remember. I'll bet a month hasn't gone by since that I haven't thought of that film. I am awarding *Mighty Peking Man* three stars, for general goofiness and a certain level of insane genius, but I cannot in good conscience rate it higher than *Infra-Man*. So, in answer to those correspondents who ask if I have ever changed a rating on a movie: Yes, *Infra-Man* moves up to three stars.

The Minus Man ★ ★ ★
R, 115 m., 1999

Owen Wilson (Van), Janeane Garofalo (Ferrin), Brian Cox (Doug), Mercedes Ruehl (Jane), Dwight Yoakam (Blair), Dennis Haysbert (Graves), Sheryl Crow (Caspar). Directed by Hampton Fancher and produced by David Bushell and Fida Attieh. Screenplay by Fancher, based on the novel by Lew McCreary.

"I take the natural momentum of a person and draw it toward me," Van tells us during *The Minus Man*. He is like the narrator of a how-to tape for serial killers. In musings on the sound track, he talks about his methods, as he drifts from place to place, poisoning people. His approach is not violent, "just the minimum necessary." He is an enigma. People seem to like him, and we wonder why.

We are curious about such killers, because they fit in so easily. A mad-dog psychopath, shooting up a church or school, is clearly nuts and evil. But what about mild-mannered Van (Owen Wilson), polite and quiet, able to win the confidence of girls in bars, landlords, strangers? It is one thing to be the victim of random violence, another to welcome your killer into your life.

Van's act is that he just wants to help out and not make waves. In an opening sequence, he meets a sad addict (Sheryl Crow) in a bar, and offers her a lift. He's like a good Samaritan. He says what people want to hear, or need to hear. He's quiet; he doesn't frighten them

away with loud noises or sudden moves. Even his killing method is subdued. Retracing the movements of serial killers, we often find they had contact with the law, without the law knowing who they were. Maybe part of the thrill is in edging close to capture and then dancing away. There's a dicey scene in *The Minus Man* where Van is awakened by a cop as he sleeps in his car. A search would turn up incriminating evidence, but he's so respectful that he gets off with a warning.

Soon he's a boarder in the home of Doug and Jane (Brian Cox and Mercedes Ruehl). Doug is a postal worker. Jane is suspicious. They need the income from renting the extra room, but she warns Doug, "Don't make a boarder your guest." But Doug is lonely, and Jane is always picking on him. He needs a friend. Soon he's found Van a job he loves, at the post office. And there he meets Ferrin (Janeane Garofalo), who likes him.

All of these developments are done in low-key, understated style. The suspense beats away underneath because we know what Van is capable of. Will Doug get a pass because he provided a job? What about Ferrin? Does he like her, or is he leading her on? What is Van thinking about, in his rented room? I was reminded of the Joseph Cotten character in Hitchcock's *Shadow of a Doubt*—the man of unspeakable evil, moving blandly through small-town society. And of Joyce Carol Oates's chilling novel *Zombie,* about a character not unlike Van.

Both Van and the Oates character narrate their own stories, dwelling on methods, giving helpful advice to anyone hoping to follow in their footsteps. There's never a second's introspection. They don't ask why they kill because the question doesn't occur to them; they act according to their natures. It is for us to wonder that our species could produce a creature that will not sign the truce that makes civilization possible.

The Minus Man, based on a novel by Lew McCreary, was written and directed by Hampton Fancher, who wrote *Blade Runner*. This is his directing debut; a curious choice, but since he pulls it off he must feel a connection with it. Owen Wilson, who can look reassuring or not, depending on how much tension he allows into his face, finds the right insidious, ingratiating tone for Van. And the three closest people in his life (Garofalo's postal worker and Ruehl and Cox as the landlords) are able to meet one of an actor's trickiest challenges: to stand in harm's way and be oblivious to it.

Karl Malden told me that the most difficult scene he ever had as an actor was in *On the Waterfront,* where he played a priest who had to make a speech while unaware that a beer can was about to be thrown at his head. The priest didn't know about the can, but the actor did. You see the problem. In *The Minus Man,* Garofolo, Ruehl, and Cox successfully spend the whole movie acting as if the can hasn't been thrown.

Mission: Impossible 2 ★ ★ ★
PG-13, 120 m., 2000

Tom Cruise (Ethan Hunt), Dougray Scott (Sean Ambrose), Thandie Newton (Nyah Hall), Richard Roxburgh (Hugh Stamp), John Polson (Billy Baird), Brendan Gleeson (McCloy), Rade Sherbedgia (Dr. Nekhorvich), Ving Rhames (Luther Stickell). Directed by John Woo and produced by Tom Cruise and Paula Wagner. Screenplay by Robert Towne, based on a story by Ronald D. Moore and Brannon Braga and the television series created by Bruce Geller.

If James Bond is still around at the end of the twenty-first century, he will look a lot like Ethan Hunt. The hero of the *Mission: Impossible* series is a 007 for our time.

That means: Sex is more of a surprise and a distraction than a lifestyle. Stunts and special effects don't interrupt the plot, but *are* the plot. The hero's interest in new consumer items runs more toward cybergadgets than sports cars. He isn't a patriot working for his government, but a hired gun working for a shadowy international agency. And he doesn't smoke, hardly drinks, and is in the physical condition of a triathlete.

The new Bond, in short, is a driven, over-achieving professional—not the sort of gentleman sophisticate the British spy family used to cultivate. His small talk consists not of lascivious puns, but geekspeak. When he raises an eyebrow, it's probably not his, because he's a master of disguise and can hide behind plastic masks so realistic even his cinematographer doesn't know for sure.

The first *Mission: Impossible* (1996) had a plot no one understood. *Mission: Impossible 2* has a plot you don't need to understand. It's been cobbled together by the expert Hollywood script doctor Robert Towne out of elements of other movies, notably Hitchcock's *Notorious,* from which he takes the idea that the hero first falls in love with the heroine, then heartlessly assigns her to resume an old affair with an ex-lover in order to spy on his devious plans. In both films, the woman agrees to do this because she loves the hero. In *Notorious,* the hero loses respect for the woman after she does what he asks. The modern hero is too amoral to think of this.

Towne's contribution is quite skillful, especially if it's true, as I've heard, that he had to write around major f/x sequences that director John Woo had already written and fine-tuned. His strategy is to make Ethan Hunt (Tom Cruise) into a sympathetic yet one-dimensional character, so that motivation and emotion will not be a problem. He's a cousin of Clint Eastwood's Man With No Name—a hero defined not by his values but by his actions.

The villain remains in the Bond tradition: A megalomaniac who seeks power or wealth by holding the world ransom. In this case, he seeks control of a deadly virus, but the virus is what Hitchcock called a MacGuffin; it doesn't matter what it is, just so it's something everyone desires or fears. The movie wisely spends little time on the details, but is clever in the way it uses the virus to create time pressure: Twenty-four hours after you're exposed, you die, and that leads to a nicely timed showdown involving the hero, the woman he loves, the villain, the virus, and a ticking clock.

Thandie Newton plays the woman, and the most significant thing about her character is that she's still alive at the end, and apparently available for the sequel. The Bond girls have had a depressing mortality rate over the years, but remember that 007 was formed in the promiscuous 1960s, while Ethan Hunt lives in a time when even spies tend to stay with old relationships, maybe because it's so tiresome to start new ones.

Newton's character is unique in the way she plays a key role in the plot, taking her own initiative. Bond girls, even those with formidable fighting skills, were instruments of the plot;

Newton's Nyah Hall not only lacks a name that is a pun, but shockingly makes a unilateral decision that influences the outcome of the movie. The playing field will be more level in the *M:I* battle of the sexes.

For Tom Cruise, the series is a franchise, like Mel Gibson's *Lethal Weapon* movies. *M:I3* is already on the drawing board, again with John Woo as director, and there's no reason the sequels can't continue as long as Cruise can still star in action scenes (or their computer-generated manifestations). This is good for Cruise. By more or less underwriting his box-office clout, it gives him the freedom to experiment with more offbeat choices like *Eyes Wide Shut* and *Magnolia*.

As for the movie itself: If the first movie was entertaining as sound, fury, and movement, this one is more evolved, more confident, more surefooted in the way it marries minimal character development to seamless action. It is a global movie, flying no flag, requiring little dialogue, featuring characters who are Pavlovian in their motivation. It's more efficient than the Bond pictures, but not as much pure fun. In this new century, I have a premonition we'll be seeing more efficiency and less fun in a lot of different areas. The trend started about the time college students decided management was sexier than literature. ☞

Mission to Mars ★ ★ ½
PG, 113 m., 2000

Gary Sinise (Jim McConnell), Tim Robbins (Woody Blake), Don Cheadle (Luke Graham), Connie Nielsen (Terri Fisher), Jerry O'Connell (Phil Ohlmyer), Peter Outerbridge (Sergei Kirov), Kavan Smith (Nicholas Willis), Jill Teed (Renee Cote). Directed by Brian De Palma and produced by Tom Jacobson. Screenplay by Jim Thomas, John Thomas, Graham Yost, and Lowell Cannon.

Well, here it is, I guess, a science-fiction movie like the one I was wishing for in my review of *Pitch Black*. That film transported its characters to an alien planet in a three-star system and then had them chase each other around in the desert and be threatened by wicked bat-creatures. Why go to all the trouble of trans-porting humans millions of miles from Earth, only to mire them in tired generic conventions?

Mission to Mars is smarter and more original. It contains some ideas. It also has its flaws. It begins with an astronaut's backyard picnic so chirpy it could easily accommodate Chevy Chase. It contains conversations that drag on beyond all reason. It is quiet when quiet is not called for. It contains actions that deny common sense. And for long stretches the characters speak nothing but boilerplate.

And yet those stretches on autopilot surround three sequences of real vision, awakening the sense of wonder that is the goal of popular science fiction. The film involves a manned mission to Mars, which lands successfully and then encounters . . . something . . . that results in the death of three of the crew members, and loss of radio contact with the fourth (Don Cheadle).

A rescue mission is dispatched, led by co-pilots Tim Robbins and Gary Sinise, with Connie Nielsen as Robbins's wife and Jerry O'Connell as the fourth member. They run into a clump of tiny meteorites that puncture the hull and lead to a loss of air pressure. (It's here that the Sinise character defies logic by refusing, for no good reason, to put on his helmet and draw oxygen from his suit.) Then there's another crisis, which leads to a surprisingly taut and moving sequence in which the four characters attempt a tricky maneuver outside their ship and are faced with a life-or-death choice.

Arriving on the red planet, they find the survivor, hear his story, and then are led into a virtual reality version of a close encounter of the third kind. They learn the history of Mars, and the secret of life on Earth, and Sinise continues his journey in an unexpected way.

I am being deliberately vague here because one of the pleasures of a film like this is its visual and plot surprises. I like a little science in science fiction, and this film has a little. (The emphasis is on "little," however, and its animated re-creation of the evolution of species lost me when the dinosaurs evolved into bison—and besides, how would the makers of that animation know the outcome of the process?) The movie also has some intriguing ideas, and some of the spirit of *2001: A Space Odyssey*. Not a lot, but some. (It pays homage to Kubrick's film by giving us space suits and spaceship interiors that seem like a logical evolution of his designs.)

I watched the movie with pleasure that was frequently interrupted by frustration. The three key sequences are very well done. They are surrounded by sequences that are not—left adrift in lackluster dialogue and broad, easy character strokes. Why does the film amble so casually between its high points? Why is a meditative tone evoked when we have been given only perfunctory inspiration for it? Why is a crisis like the breached hull treated so deliberately, as if the characters are trying to slow down their actions to use up all the available time? And why, oh why, in a film where the special effects are sometimes awesome, are we given an alien being who looks like a refugee from a video game?

I can't recommend *Mission to Mars*. It misses too many of its marks. But it has extraordinary things in it. It's as if the director, the gifted Brian De Palma, rises to the occasions but the screenplay gives him nothing much to do in between them. It was old Howard Hawks who supplied this definition of a good movie: "Three great scenes. No bad scenes." *Mission to Mars* gets only the first part right.   ☞

Miss Julie ★ ★ ★
R, 100 m., 2000

Saffron Burrows (Miss Julie), Peter Mullan (Jean), Maria Doyle Kennedy (Christine), Tam Dean Burn (Servant), Heathcote Williams (Servant), Eileen Walsh (Servant). Directed by Mike Figgis and produced by Figgis and Harriet Cruickshank. Screenplay by Helen Cooper, based on the play by August Strindberg.

Mike Figgis's *Leaving Las Vegas* was about a self-destructive man who pauses briefly for sex and kindness from a Vegas call girl on his way to the grave. Now Figgis has made *Miss Julie*, a film based on the Strindberg play about the daughter of a count and her footman—two people who use sex as their instrument of self-destruction. Both films are intense, erotic, and willful; the difference is that we pity and love the characters in the first, while Strindberg and Figgis allow only pity in the second.

It is Midsummer's Eve in the house of a wealthy Swedish count. In the kitchen, there's much cheerful toing-and-froing from the downstairs staff, while upstairs a party is under way. We meet Jean, the footman, played by Peter Mullan as a compact, self-assured man who polishes boots as if they were his enemies. His fiancée, Christine (Maria Doyle Kennedy), is a plump, jolly woman who not only knows her place, but approves of it.

Miss Julie walks down the stairs. Played by Saffron Burrows, she is several inches taller than Jean, and bold, the kind of woman who learned to handle men by first mastering horses. She's come for a little sport with the servants, or because she's bored with the aristocrats upstairs, or because she has noticed how Jean looks at her, or perhaps because her fiancé has left her. He left, we learn, because she was too headstrong. On the rebound, she is angry and reckless.

For the next hour and a half, Jean and Miss Julie will engage in a duel of wills. The movie is almost exactly as long as Strindberg's one-act play, which traps them in the same time and space, and calls their mutual bluff: Each wants to prove the other doesn't have the nerve to have sex. Intimacy between them, of course, is forbidden by all the codes that apply in this kitchen: the class system, religious beliefs, the separation of servant and master, Jean's engagement to Christine, and not least the fact that they do not like each other.

Their dislike is, however, an aphrodisiac, and so is the danger they place themselves in, because a servant and a mistress who have sex can never be accepted again by the society that contains them. They must leave—flee to Paris, perhaps—or find some other kind of escape. Ah, you say, but what if no one finds out? The whole point is that they themselves will know. They've been instructed by the class system to see themselves in a certain way, and sex would destroy that way of seeing.

Of course, their danger makes it all the more enticing, and the drama is a verbal duel in which words are foreplay. There is a lot of sadomasochism in their fencing. She at first wants him to grovel, and towers over him. Then he takes the upper hand and lashes her with harsh truths about herself. When they

381

finally do have sex, it is not pleasurable but more like a mutual wounding: As you destroy me, I destroy you.

The actors are compelling. Mullan *(My Name Is Joe)* can be a hard man, roughened by his servant's life. Burrows *(The Loss of Sexual Innocence)* is a great beauty but, like Sigourney Weaver, another tall woman, possessed of angularity: She can be soft, and then all sharp corners. They talk, they fence, they dream, they are tender, they tease, they taunt, they dance closer and closer to the film's outcome, which, once you experience it, you know you saw coming right from the first.

The Mod Squad ★ ★
R, 94 m., 1999

Claire Danes (Julie), Giovanni Ribisi (Pete), Omar Epps (Linc), Dennis Farina (Greer), Josh Brolin (Billy), Michael Lerner (Wiseman), Steve Harris (Briggs), Richard Jenkins (Mothershed), Larry Brandenburg (Eckford). Directed by Scott Silver and produced by Ben Myron, Alan Riche, and Tony Ludwig. Screenplay by Stephen Kay, Silver, and Kate Lanier.

The Mod Squad has an intriguing cast, a director who knows how to use his camera, and a lot of sly humor. Shame about the story. When you see this many of the right elements in a lame movie, you wonder how close they came to making a better one. The director, Scott Silver, cowrote the script himself, and has to take some of the blame: This is a classy production and deserves better.

The premise is from the old TV series. Three young screw-ups are interrupted at the beginning of criminal careers and recruited by a police captain to form an undercover squad. Their assignment: Infiltrate a club where prostitution and drug dealing seem to be happening. The mod squad doesn't carry guns (officially, anyway), doesn't have badges, and I'm not sure if they can make arrests; maybe they're more like high-level snitches.

The members are described by a Rod Serling–type voice over the opening credits. Julie (Claire Danes) was "a runaway—an addict at eighteen." Pete (Giovanni Ribisi) "went straight from Beverly Hills to county jail." Linc (Omar Epps) "doesn't blame his crimes on anything." (He's black, and so the implication, I guess, is that this is worthy of comment.) In the good-looking opening sequence, filmed by Ellen Kuras, they're intercut with dancers at a club, get into a fight, and then find themselves being debriefed and lectured by Captain Greer (Dennis Farina), who orders them to stand up when they talk to him, quit sitting on his desk, etc. Of course, their bad manners are a curtain-raiser to bravery, heroism, and astonishing crime-fighting skills.

The skills, alas, are astonishing because they're so bush-league. The main investigative technique in this movie consists of sneaking up on people and eavesdropping while they explain the entire plot and give away all the secrets. Julie falls for a former lover, follows him to a rendezvous with a drug kingpin (Michael Lerner), and overhears choice nuggets of conversation ("None of them have any idea I know they're cops!"). Then she follows him home and hides in his closet while the faithless louse does the rumpy-pumpy with another woman.

Petey, meanwhile, is even more clever. He creeps up on a hideout and hides behind a wall while tape-recording a full confession. It goes without saying his tape will later be played over a loudspeaker in order to incriminate the bad guys. He uses one of those little $29 microcassette recorders—you know, the kind that can record with perfect fidelity at twenty yards outdoors on a windy day.

As the mod squaders were creeping around, eavesdropping and peeping through windows, I grew restless: This is the kind of stuff they rewrote the Nancy Drew books to get rid of. Too bad, because I liked the pure acting touches that the cast brought to their roles. Ribisi (from *Friends, Saving Private Ryan,* and *The Other Sister)* has a kind of poker-faced put-upon look that's appealing, especially when he gets beat up and goes back to Beverly Hills and his dad chortles heartily at the claim that his kid is now a cop. Danes *(Romeo and Juliet)* has a quick intelligence that almost but not quite sells the dumb stuff they make her do. Epps *(Scream 2, Higher Learning)* is the dominant member of the squad, who tries to protect the others from their insane risk-taking.

And there's a small but indispensable supporting role by Michael Lerner as the crewcut evil kingpin, who intimidates his enemies by dancing with them ("I'm not a fairy—I just like to dance"). He delivers his dialogue indirectly, as an ironic commentary on the horrible things he always seems about to do.

So all of this is a good start, but the screenplay just doesn't provide the foundation. Consider Billy, the Josh Brolin character, who is Julie's once and future boyfriend. We know from the first moment we see him that he's no good. We're tipped off by how suddenly Julie goes for him; if the point were romance, the movie would let them take longer, but since the point is for her to be deceived, she has to rush in heedlessly. No girl meets a guy who dumped her and broke her heart, and immediately drags him into a toilet stall for sex. Especially not now that she's clean and sober, as Julie is (although the movie repeats the tiresome cliché that all recovering alcoholics immediately turn to drink after a setback—preferably swigging from a fifth).

What I'd love to know is how the screenplay got green-lighted. This is a top-drawer film with a decent budget and lots of care about the production values. The cast is talented and well chosen. The movie is even aware of potential clichés (before the last shoot-out, Julie says, "At least it's not going down in an abandoned warehouse"). And then what do they end up with? The most expensive Nancy Drew mystery ever filmed.

Mon Homme ★ ★
NO MPAA RATING, 95 m., 1998

Anouk Grinberg (Marie), Gérard Lanvin (Jeannot), Valeria Bruni-Tedeschi (Sanguine), Olivier Martinez (Jean-Francois), Sabine Azema (Berangere), Dominique Valadie (Gilberte), Mathieu Kassovitz (First Client), Jacques Francois (Second Client). Directed by Bertrand Blier and produced by Alain Sarde. Screenplay by Blier. In French with English subtitles.

"What I sell is true love," says the heroine of Bertrand Blier's *Mon Homme.* "With me they hear the music." She says her name is Marie (Anouk Grinberg) and she is the hooker of a john's dreams: "I should pay you," she tells one client. As the film opens, we find her sitting outside a hotel ("This is where I spin my web"), explaining how much she enjoys prostitution.

"Ever thought of being paid for it?" she asks a matron who is passing by. The matron has. In no time at all, Marie has talked her into turning her first trick.

Blier's films are often about men in the service of their sexual needs. *Too Beautiful for You* (1988) starred Gérard Depardieu as a man who leaves his elegant wife for the dowdy secretary who obsesses him. The Oscar winner *Get Out Your Handkerchief* (1977) starred Depardieu as a man who despairs of satisfying his wife. In *Mon Homme,* Blier in a sense has cast the male role with a woman: Marie calls the shots, satisfies herself, sleeps with whom she wants, and gets paid for it.

But her life is not perfect until one day she discovers a derelict sleeping near a garbage heap. She brings him home, feeds him (leftover veal stew; French refrigerators never contain old pizzas and doggie bags from the Chinese restaurant). Then they make love. Grinberg is awesome in suggesting her passion; the earth shakes because she's shaking it. There is a small detail that's just right: the way she bites his chin through his beard. Jeannot (Gérard Lanvin) is expert and enduring. She bathes him, shaves him, and asks him to be her pimp and take all her money.

He: What if you want money?
She: I'll ask you for it.
He: And if I refuse?
She: Then you'll be a real pimp.

I wouldn't go so far as to say there are *no* hookers like this in Paris, but Blier may have found the only one.

I was distracted, during their lovemaking, by the thought that a homeless man, found on a garbage heap, would be aromatic. Shouldn't she have bathed him before sex? But a moment's thought reveals that Marie is not being entirely truthful about her needs: It is not so much that she loves sex and prostitution as that she's a masochist, as Jeannot intuits when he slaps her after she has given him stew, sex, and what he concedes is a rather nice red wine. ("Like the smack?" She nods. Later, good fellow that he is, he instructs her on how to duck when she senses a slap on its way.)

If Blier had been true to the logic of the story, he would have followed Marie's compulsions to their bitter end. Instead, he spins off into Jeannot's story, as the new pimp (who cleans up nicely) who seduces a manicurist, names her Tangerine, and tries to set her up in business. Tangerine, who thinks with her mouth open, does not have enough wit for the game, and soon Jeannot is being slapped around by the cops; in France, it is legal to be a prostitute but not to be a pimp.

The film drifts away into developments, fantasies, whimsy, and conceit. Its energy is lost. Blier has a strong central character and abandons her rather than accept the inescapable implications of her behavior. I do not argue that prostitutes cannot be happy (indeed, I have here a letter from a prostitute taking me to task for calling all the characters in *Boogie Nights* sad). But I argue that Marie is not happy, and that Blier's view of women and their sexuality is so narrow that he simply cannot accommodate that inconvenience.

Monument Ave. ★ ★ ★
NO MPAA RATING, 90 m., 1998

Denis Leary (Bobby), Colm Meaney (Jackie), Billy Crudup (Teddy), Jason Barry (Seamus), Ian Hart (Mouse), Famke Janssen (Katy), Martin Sheen (Hanlon), John Diehl (Digger), Greg Dulli (Shang), Jeanne Tripplehorn (Annie). Directed Ted Demme and produced by Joel Stillerman, Demme, Jim Serpico, Nicolas Clermont, and Elie Samaha. Screenplay by Mike Armstrong.

Watching *Monument Ave.*, I was reminded of the recent tragedy in Chicago when a young black man, bicycling through Bridgeport, was beaten almost to death. There is a chillingly similar scene in this movie, with a revealing twist on the sickness of racism.

The film takes place in an Irish-American section of Boston, where a gang of childhood friends, now in their thirties, support their booze and coke habits with a loosely organized car theft ring. Their leader is Jackie (Colm Meaney), who is capable of ordering an informer to be shot dead in a saloon, and then attending the wake to pass out $100 bills to the dead boy's relatives. Second in command is Bobby (Denis Leary), who is drifting out of control, and is usually in debt to Jackie because of gambling bets made during blackouts.

One night Bobby and his friends are cruising their neighborhood in a friend's cab, when they see a young black man walking alone on the street. One of the gang says they ought to beat him up "to teach him a lesson." The others are not so enthusiastic, but the guy keeps talking, until finally Bobby, fueled by cocaine and booze, orders the driver to turn the cab around. "Give me the gun," Bobby says.

With Bobby as the instigator, they pile out of the taxi and force the black man inside. They drive around, as Bobby makes violent threats. There is a fake execution before Bobby sets his victim free. "There's a subway stop a block from here," he says. "Ask around at school to see where it's safe to go."

Then he turns on his racist friend and berates him for talking big but being gutless. And we get the point: Bobby never intended to harm the black man, but staged the whole charade to teach his friend a lesson—to show him up as a phony. Bobby is the good guy here. And as that sinks in, we realize the depth of the sickness in Bobby's society. He was concerned only with making a point to his friend. He felt not a shred of empathy for the victim. He was incapable of sharing or perhaps even seeing the man's terror. Bobby, like the others, is trapped inside a watertight, airtight, thoughtproof cocoon of blind tribalism.

Gangs of every color are like that. Their values are entirely within the gang structure; outsiders are irrelevant. In *Monument Ave.*, the characters drink together, snort together, play stick hockey together. The movie, directed by Ted Demme and written by Mike Armstrong, has a good ear for their dialogue, and it's not the funny, colorful dialogue of other lowlife movies; a kind of exhausted desperation creeps even into their humor.

There's a minimal plot; the movie is mostly concerned with showing the lifestyle. In a key early scene, Bobby goes to the local bar and sees that his friend Teddy (Billy Crudup) is home from prison. Teddy is obviously high in a dangerous way. Bobby tries to give him money and send him home. No luck. Teddy settles in, and when Jackie the ringleader turns up, he unwisely goes into a disorganized ramble about what he did, and didn't, tell the cops who quizzed him. Everybody at the table knows that Teddy has made a big mistake. Bobby tells a funny story. Jackie's men shoot Teddy dead.

The beat detective (Martin Sheen) arrives and makes cynical noises about how he supposes all the witnesses were in the men's room at the time.

As the central character, Denis Leary gives a thoughtful and effective performance. He is tired of his life of crime, tired of drugs and drinking, tired of always playing catch-up. Teddy's friends huddle in a corner at the funeral home and watch disbelievingly as Jackie, the big man, hands out the bills and sympathy. His mother, after still another wake, tells him, "Somebody ought to say something this time." But nobody ever does.

The characters talk about family, neighborhood, loyalty, tradition, as if their gang represents the neighborhood (which is terrified of them). Certainly there are a lot of good people in the neighborhood, and we glimpse them in the background, but in Bobby's crowd, all of the good has been drained out, and they are demoralized by the half-realized fact that they are bad and worthless, their code a hollow shell.

The film is populated with many other sharply seen characters. Katy (Famke Janssen) is officially Jackie's girlfriend, but gets drunk and comes over to Bobby's house. All life centers in the tavern, which is a stage for nightly dramas, as when Bobby sees Katy with Jackie, and deliberately picks up a yuppie girl (Jeanne Tripplehorn) just to make her mad at him. It's the kind of bar where two men put their bare arms side by side, and the bartender puts a lighted cigarette on them, and they bet on who'll be the first to pull his arm away. You see somebody playing that game, you know all you need to know about them.

There is a whole genre of films about childhood friends still living in the old neighborhood, and going down the drain of crime and drugs. Few of them capture the fatigue and depression, the futility, as well as this one, in which the characters hold on to their self-respect by obeying the very rules that are grinding them down.

The Mother and the Whore ★ ★ ★ ★
NO MPAA RATING, 215 m., 1973 (rereleased 1999)

Jean-Pierre Leaud (Alexandre), Bernadette Lafont (Marie), Francoise Lebrun (Veronika), Isabelle Weingarten (Gilberte), Jean Douchet (Man at Café Flore), Jean-Noel Picq (Offenbach Lover). Directed by Jean Eustache and produced by Pierre Cottrell. Screenplay by Eustache.

When Jean Eustache's *The Mother and the Whore* was released in 1973, young audiences all over the world embraced its layabout hero and his endless conversations with the woman he lived with, the woman he was dating, the woman who rejected him, and various other women encountered in the cafés of Paris. The character was played by Jean-Pierre Leaud, star of *The 400 Blows* and two other autobiographical films by François Truffaut. In 1977, Truffaut made *The Man Who Loved Women.* This one could have been titled *The Man Who Loved to Hear Himself Talk.*

At three and a half hours, the film is long, but its essence is to be long: Make it any shorter, and it would have a plot and an outcome, when in fact Eustache simply wants to record an existence. Alexandre (Leaud), his hero, lives with Marie (Bernadette Lafont), a boutique owner who apparently supports him; one would say he was between jobs if there were any sense that he'd ever had one. He meets a blind date named Veronika (Francoise Lebrun) in a café, and subjects her to a great many of his thoughts and would-be thoughts. (Much of Lebrun's screen time consists of close-ups of her listening.) In the middle of his monologues, Alexandre has a way of letting his eyes follow the progress of other women through his field of view.

Alexandre is smart enough, but not a great intellect. His favorite area of study is himself, but there he hasn't made much headway. He chatters about the cinema and about life, sometimes confusing them ("films tell you how to live, how to make a kid"). He wears a dark coat and a very long scarf, knotted around his neck and sweeping to his knees; his best friend dresses the same way. He spends his days in cafés, holding (but not reading) Proust. "Look there's Sartre—the drunk," he says one day in Café Flore, and Eustache supplies a quick shot of several people at a table, one of whom may or may not be Sartre. Alexandre talks about Sartre staggering out after his long intellectual chats in the café, and speculates that the great man's philosophy may be alcoholic musings.

The first time I saw *The Mother and the Whore,* I thought it was about Alexandre. After a viewing of the newly restored 35mm print being released for the movie's twenty-fifth anniversary, I think it is just as much about the women, and about the way that women can let a man talk endlessly about himself while they regard him like a specimen of aberrant behavior. Women keep a man like Alexandre around, I suspect, out of curiosity about what new idiocy he will next exhibit.

Of course, Alexandre is cheating—on Marie, whom he lives with, and on Veronika, whom he says he loves. Part of his style is to play with relationships, just to see what happens. The two women find out about each other, and eventually meet. There are some fireworks, but not as many as you might expect, maybe because neither one would be that devastated at losing Alexandre. Veronika, a nurse from Poland, is at least frank about herself: She sleeps around because she likes sex. She has a passionate monologue about her sexual needs and her resentment that women aren't supposed to admit their feelings. Whether Alexandre has sex with Marie is a good question; I suppose the answer is yes, but you can't be sure. She represents, of course, the mother, and Veronika thinks of herself as a whore; Alexandre has positioned himself in the cross-hairs of the classic Freudian dilemma.

Jean-Pierre Leaud's best performance was his first, as the fierce young thirteen-year-old who roamed Paris in *The 400 Blows,* idolizing Balzac and escaping into books and trouble as a way of dealing with his parents' unhappy marriage. In a way, most of his adult performances are simply that boy, grown up. Here he smokes and talks incessantly, and wanders Paris like a puppet controlled by his libido. It's amusing the way he performs for the women; there's one shot in particular, where he takes a drink so theatrically it could be posing for a photo titled, "I Take a Drink."

The genuine drama in the movie centers on Veronika, who more or less knows they are only playing at love while out of the sight of Marie. We learn a lot about her life—her room in the hospital, her schedule, her low self-esteem. When she does talk, it is from brave, unadulterated self-knowledge.

The Mother and the Whore made an enormous impact when it was released. It still works a quarter-century later, because it was so focused on its subjects and lacking in pretension. It is rigorously observant, the portrait of an immature man and two women who humor him for a while, paying the price that entails. Eustache committed suicide at forty-three, in 1981, after making about a dozen films, of which this is by far the best-known. He said his film was intended as "the description of a normal course of events without the shortcuts of dramatization," and described Alexandre as a collector of "rare moments" that occupy his otherwise idle time. As a record of a kind of everyday Parisian life, the film is superb. We think of the cafés of Paris as hotbeds of fiery philosophical debate, but more often, I imagine, they are just like this: people talking, flirting, posing, drinking, smoking, telling the truth, and lying, while waiting to see if real life will ever begin.

Mr. Death: The Rise and Fall of Fred A. Leuchter Jr. ★ ★ ★ ★
PG-13, 96 m., 2000

A documentary directed by Errol Morris and produced by Michael Williams, David Collins, and Dorothy Aufiero.

The hangman has no friends. That truth, I think, is the key to understanding Fred A. Leuchter Jr., a man who built up a nice little business designing death-row machines, and then lost it when he became a star on the Holocaust denial circuit. Leuchter, the subject of Errol Morris's documentary *Mr. Death: The Rise and Fall of Fred A. Leuchter Jr.,* is a lonely man of limited insight who is grateful to be liked—even by Nazi apologists.

This is the seventh documentary by Morris, who combines dreamlike visual montages with music by Caleb Sampson to create a movie that is more reverie and meditation than reportage. Morris is drawn to subjects who try to control that which cannot be controlled—life and death. His heroes have included lion tamers, topiary gardeners, robot designers, wild turkey callers, autistics, death row inmates, pet cemetery owners, and Stephen Hawking, whose mind leaps through space and time while his body slumps in a chair.

Fred Leuchter, the son of a prison warden, stumbled into the death row business more or less by accident. An engineer by training, he found himself inspired by the need for more efficient and "humane" execution devices. He'd seen electric chairs that cooked their occupants without killing them, poison gas chambers that were a threat to the witnesses, gallows not correctly adjusted to break a neck. He went to work designing better chairs, trapdoors, and lethal injection machines, and soon (his trade not being commonplace) was being consulted by prisons all over America.

Despite his success in business, he was not, we gather, terrifically popular. How many women want to date a guy who can chat about the dangers of being accidentally electrocuted while standing in the pool of urine around a recently used electric chair? He does eventually marry a waitress he meets in a doughnut shop; indeed, given his habit of forty to sixty cups of coffee a day, he must have met a lot of waitresses. We hear her offscreen voice as she describes their brief marriage, and demurs at Fred's notion that their visit to Auschwitz was a honeymoon (she had to wait in a cold car, serving as a lookout for guards).

Leuchter's trip to Auschwitz was the turning point in his career. He was asked by Ernst Zundel, a neo-Nazi and Holocaust denier, to be an expert witness at his trial in Canada. Zundel financed Leuchter's 1988 trip to Auschwitz, during which he chopped off bits of brick and mortar in areas said to be gas chambers, and had them analyzed for cyanide residue. His conclusion: The chambers never contained gas. The "Leuchter Report" has since been widely quoted by those who deny the Holocaust took place.

There is a flaw in his science, however. The laboratory technician who tested the samples for Leuchter was later startled to discover the use being made of his findings. Cyanide would penetrate bricks only to the depth of a tenth of a human hair, he says. By breaking off large chunks and pulverizing them, Leuchter had diluted his sample by 100,000 times, not even taking into account the fifty years of weathering that had passed. To find cyanide would have been a miracle.

No matter; Leuchter became a favorite after-dinner speaker on the neo-Nazi circuit, and

the camera observes how his face lights up and his whole body seems to lean into applause, how happy he is to shake hands with his new friends. Other people might shy away from the pariah status of a Holocaust denier. The hangman is already a pariah, and finds his friends where he can.

Just before *Mr. Death* was shown in a slightly different form at the 1999 Sundance Film Festival, a *New Yorker* article by Mark Singer wondered whether the film would create sympathy for Leuchter and his fellow deniers. After all, here was a man who lost his wife and his livelihood in the name of a scientific quest. My feeling is that no filmmaker can be responsible for those unwilling or unable to view his film intelligently; anyone who leaves *Mr. Death* in agreement with Leuchter deserves to join him on the loony fringe.

What's scary about the film is the way Leuchter is perfectly respectable up until the time the neo-Nazis get their hooks into him. Those who are appalled by the mass execution of human beings sometimes have no problem when the state executes them one at a time. You can even run for president after presiding over the busiest death row in U.S. history.

Early sequences in *Mr. Death* portray Leuchter as a humanitarian who protests that some electric chairs "cook the meat too much." He dreams of a "lethal injection machine" designed like a dentist's chair. The condemned could watch TV or listen to music while the poison works. What a lark. There is irony in the notion that many American states could lavish tax dollars on this man's inventions, only to put him out of work because of his unsavory connections. The ability of so many people to live comfortably with the idea of capital punishment is perhaps a clue to how so many Europeans were able to live with the idea of the Holocaust: Once you accept the notion that the state has the right to kill someone, and the right to define what is a capital crime, aren't you halfway there?

Like all of Errol Morris's films, *Mr. Death* provides us with no comfortable place to stand. We often leave his documentaries not sure if he liked his subjects or was ridiculing them. He doesn't make it easy for us with simple moral labels. Human beings, he argues, are fearsomely complex, and can get their minds around very strange ideas indeed. Sometimes it is possible to hate the sin and love the sinner. Poor Fred. What a dope, what a dupe, what a lonely, silly man.

Mr. Jealousy ★ ★ ½
R, 103 m., 1998

Eric Stoltz (Lester Grimm), Annabella Sciorra (Ramona Ray), Chris Eigeman (Dashiell Frank), Carlos Jacott (Vince), Marianne Jean-Baptiste (Lucretia), Brian Kerwin (Stephen), Peter Bogdanovich (Dr. Poke), Bridget Fonda (Irene). Directed by Noah Baumbach and produced by Joel Castleberg. Screenplay by Baumbach.

Lester Grimm, the hero of *Mr. Jealousy,* is the kind of guy who can grow so obsessed with a girl that he shadows her all the time, hiding in shrubbery to see where she goes and what she does—until she drops him because he never seems to be around. His insecurity started early. At fifteen, he took a girl to a movie and an Italian restaurant on what he thought was a perfectly acceptable date, only to spot her later at a party, making out with a twenty-four-year-old club promoter.

Ever since, Lester (Eric Stoltz) has been tormented by images of his dates in the arms of other guys. Who did they date before they met him? How did they feel about their former lovers? How do they still feel? At thirty-one, Lester is still single, and working as a substitute teacher of Spanish, a language he does not speak. He is dating Ramona (Annabella Sciorra), who conducts museum tours and is getting her doctoriate in abstract expressionism. Can he trust her? Did she have a life before he met her?

She sure did. She used to date Dashiell Frank (Chris Eigeman), "the generation-defining writer" whose novels speak powerfully to Generation Xers. When Ramona and Dashiell accidentally encounter one another, Lester's jealousy is inflamed by their air of easy affection, and he starts following Dashiell. Discovering that the writer is a member of a therapy group, Lester signs up for the same group—not under his own name, but as "Vince," the name of his best friend (Carlos Jacott).

That's the setup for Noah Baumbach's film, which, like his observant *Kicking and Scream-*

ing (1995), is about characters who are too old for college but unready for real life. Baumbach has a good ear for how these characters talk, but the unforced originality of his earlier film is joined here by homages to other directors; he gets the iris shots and narration from Francois Truffaut, the nebbishy insecurity from Woody Allen and Henry Jaglom, and the self-analytical dialogue from Whit Stillman. I'm not bothered by his homage to them so much as I miss his confidence in himself.

That earlier film nailed the characters and the dialogue so accurately that you remembered people exactly like that; indeed, you recalled *being* like that. *Mr. Jealousy* pumps in more plot, and I'm not sure that's the right decision. Mistaken identities and mutual misunderstandings can only be taken so far before the plot seems to be leading the characters. That's okay in farce, but in more thoughtful comedies the characters should appear to be making their decisions entirely unprompted by the requirements of the genre.

Baumbach is a gifted filmmaker, however, and many of his scenes are just right, including a sequence where Dashiell, the writer, reads a story to the group and Lester thinks it must be based on Dashiell's relationship with Ramona. He challenges the writer to "reveal more about his characters," and learns what he didn't want to know, that the original of the woman in the story "was a bit of a tart."

Well, was she? Ramona strikes us as sensible and restrained, and discriminating enough in her relationships that she probably shouldn't even be dating Lester. But we begin to sense uneasily that a story arc is being shaped here, and that the movie will require Lester to almost lose Ramona, and for secrets to be revealed and emotional showdowns to be arrived at, and for events to replace insights.

Eric Stoltz, who also starred in *Kicking and Screaming,* is well cast as Lester; he has a quiet intelligence matched with a kind of laconic earnestness about himself. Chris Eigeman, a veteran of Stillman's films, finds and holds a difficult note as a writer who is young and famous without being any more insufferable as a result than is absolutely necessary. Annabella Sciorra does a good job of creating the kind of woman who puts up with a lot from a guy if she likes him; she has her own life, doesn't need to live through his, and only gradually realizes that in a quiet, elusive way he is stark staring mad.

Mr. Jealousy isn't quite successful, but it does provide more evidence of Baumbach's talent. So many young filmmakers aim merely for success, and throw anything at us that they think we'll buy. Only a few are trying to chronicle their generation, listening to how it talks and watching how it behaves. That number includes the Whit Stillman of *The Last Days of Disco*, the Richard Linklater of *subUrbia*, the Kevin Smith of *Chasing Amy*, and the Nicole Holofcener of *Walking and Talking*. *Mr. Jealousy* shows that Baumbach is the real thing, but he needs to focus.

Mr. Nice Guy ★ ★ ★
PG-13, 90 m., 1998

Jackie Chan (Jackie), Richard Norton (Giancarlo), Gabrielle Fitzpatrick (Diana), Miki Lee (Miki), Karen McLymont (Lakeisha), Vince Poletto (Romeo), Barry Otto (Baggio), Sammo Hung (Cyclist). Directed by Sammo Hung and produced by Chua Lam. Screenplay by Edward Tang and Fibe Ma.

Jackie Chan's *Mr. Nice Guy* was originally titled *No More Mr. Nice Guy*, which would also have worked; as the film opens he's a smiling chef on a TV show, and as it closes he's single-handedly destroying a house with a giant piece of earthmoving equipment. Still, I like the new title, because Chan *is* a nice guy, with his infectious grin, potato nose, and astonishing physical comedy.

In a seminar last year at the Hawaii Film Festival, I compared some of Chan's action sequences to work by Buster Keaton. That may seem like a stretch, but look at his films and it's obvious Chan is more in the tradition of silent comedy than of the chop-socky genre. He kids himself, he pretends to be in over his head, and he survives by luck and skill instead of brute force.

In *Mr. Nice Guy*, he's the innocuous bystander who gets involved only to save a pretty girl, and wanders into a drug war by accident. The plot is a clothesline for the action sequences. A TV reporter (Gabrielle Fitzpatrick) has a videotape incriminating some drug lords.

The bad guys want it back. They chase her. Jackie helps her. The bad guys become convinced Jackie has the tape. They chase both of them. Jackie's TV show assistant (Karen McLymont) turns up and gets chased too. Jackie's girlfriend from Hong Kong (Miki Lee) flies into town. Then the bad guys chase Jackie and all three women.

Sample dialogue. Goon tells boss: "I'm sorry, boss. We didn't get the tape, and four of our guys got blown up!" Boss tells goon: "Get the tape or you'll never be seen again." So far, so good, but then the boss grabs the goon's tie and starts slapping him on his face with the end of it, and this is so unexpected and weirdly goofy that it gets a laugh.

The plot is an excuse for sight gags, physical humor, stunts, and exquisite timing. There are big action ballets, but one of my favorite moments is a quieter one that happens so fast you'll miss it if you blink. Jackie is holding a gun he knows is not loaded. He comes around a corner and is face-to-face with a bad guy, also with a gun. The guy points the gun at Jackie. Jackie hands his own gun to the guy. The guy looks at the gun he's been given, and Jackie simply takes the other gun, as if in trade. Then the guy shoots Jackie—but with the unloaded gun. It's like a three-card monte trick. I think I've left out a couple of steps, but you get the idea: The logic of the physical movements drives the drama.

Another neat sequence: Jackie is demonstrating cooking skills in a shopping center by flipping bite-sized pieces of crepes twenty yards into the mouths of his fans. A bad guy steps in front of a fan, and intercepts one of the bites. Jackie grins and flips him another bite. This time it's a fiery pepper. Okay, so this isn't Antonioni.

The big action sequences involve runaway horses, a chase through a shopping center, the use of a crane, and an escape across a steel beam high in the air. Some of the stunts are amazing. That giant earthmoving vehicle, for example, has wheels that look twelve feet high. In one shot, as a wheel approaches Jackie to crush him, he keeps himself away from it—by pushing off with his feet against the moving wheel to scoot himself along on his back. Get that one wrong, and you have tire treads where your face used to be.

There's a stunt, too, where Jackie is hanging

389

out the side of a moving carriage, about to fall, and braces himself by running sideways, as it were, down the side of a passing trolley car. Hard to describe, and almost impossible to do, but for Chan it's a throwaway, a few seconds in length.

The movie ends, as always, with credit cookies showing outtakes of Jackie landing wrong and nearly getting creamed. They prove what we know, that he does his own stunts. You watch how good he is and how hard he works, and you're glad his plots are an afterthought, because you don't want anything distracting from his sheer physical exuberance.

Mrs. Dalloway ★ ★ ★ ½
PG-13, 97 m., 1998

Vanessa Redgrave (Mrs. Dalloway), Natascha McElhone (Young Clarissa), Rupert Graves (Septimus Smith), Michael Kitchen (Peter Walsh), Alan Cox (Young Peter), Sarah Badel (Lady Rosseter [Sally]), Lena Headey (Young Sally), John Standing (Richard Dalloway), Robert Portal (Young Richard), Amelia Bullmore (Rezia Smith). Directed by Marleen Gorris and produced by Stephen Bayly and Lisa Katselas Pare. Screenplay by Eileen Atkins, based on a novel by Virginia Woolf.

In many lives there is a crossroads. We make our choice and follow it down to the present moment. Still inside of us is that other person, who stands forever poised at the head of the path not chosen. *Mrs. Dalloway* is about a day's communion between the woman who exists and the other woman who might have existed instead.

The film's heroine muses that she is thought of as "Mrs. Dalloway" by almost everybody: "You're not even Clarissa any more." Once she was young and fair, and tempted by two daring choices. Young Peter would have been a risk, but he was dangerous and alive. Even more dangerous was Sally, with whom flirtation threatened to develop into something she was unwilling to name. Clarissa took neither choice, deciding instead to marry the safe and sound Richard Dalloway, of whom young Peter sniffed, "He's a fool, an unimaginative, dull fool."

Now many years have passed. Mrs. Dalloway is giving a party. The caterer has been busy since dawn, the day is beautiful, and she walks through Hyde Park to buy the flowers herself. So opens Virginia Woolf's famous 1923 novel, which follows Clarissa Dalloway for a day, using the new stream-of-consciousness technique James Joyce was experimenting with. We will follow her through until the end of her party, during a day in which no one she meets will know what she's really thinking: All they will see is her reserved, charming exterior.

The novel stays mostly within the mind of Clarissa, with darts into other minds. Film cannot do that, but *Mrs. Dalloway* uses a voiceover narration to let us hear Clarissa's thoughts, which she never, ever, shares with anybody else. To the world she is a respectable, sixtyish London woman, the wife of a Cabinet official. To us, she is a woman who will always wonder what might have been.

Vanessa Redgrave so loved the novel that she commissioned this screenplay by Eileen Atkins, an actress who has been involved in a lot of Woolf-oriented stage work. Redgrave, of course, seems the opposite of a woman like Clarissa Dalloway, and we assume she has few regrets. But we all wonder about choices not made, because in our memories they still glow with their original promise, while reality is tied to the mundane.

As the film makes its way through Clarissa's day, there are flashbacks to long-ago summers when young Peter (Alan Cox) was courting young Clarissa (Natascha McElhone), and young Sally (Lena Headey) was perhaps courting her, too, although the movie is cagier about that than the novel. But Woolf is too wise to let Peter and Sally remain in the sunny past of memory. They both turn up on this day.

In middle age, Peter (Michael Kitchen) is rather pathetic, just returned from what seems to have been an unsuccessful romance and career in India. And Sally (Sarah Badel) is now the distinguished Lady Rosseter. There is a wonderful scene where Peter and Sally find a quiet corner of the party, and he tells her of Clarissa, "I loved her once, and it stayed with me all my life, and colored every day." Sally nods, keeping her own thoughts to herself. We gather that Sally, in middle age, may be practicing the same sort of two-track thinking that

Clarissa uses: Both women see more sharply, and critically, than anyone imagines, although with Sally we must guess this from the outside.

There is another crucial character in the film. Unless you've read the novel you may have trouble understanding his function. This is Septimus Warren Smith (Rupert Graves), who in an early scene watches as a friend is blown up in the no-man's-land of the trenches in France. Now five years or more have passed, but he suffers from shell shock, and has a panic attack outside a shop where Clarissa pauses. She sees him, and although they never meet, there is a link between them: Both have seen beneath the surface of life's reassurance, to the possibility that nothing, or worse than nothing, lurks below. Woolf is suggesting that World War I unleashed horrors that poisoned every level of society.

The subtext of the story is suicide. Woolf is asking what purpose is served by the decisions of Clarissa and Septimus to go on living lives that they have seen through. A subtle motif throughout the film is the omnipresence of sharp fence railings—spikes, like life, upon which one could be impaled.

The director, Marleen Gorris, previously made the Oscar-winning Dutch film *Antonia's Line,* about a woman who makes free choices, survives, and prevails. Here is the other side. It's surprising that Gorris, who was so open about Antonia's sexuality, is so subtle about the unspoken lesbianism in Woolf's story, but it's there for those who can see it.

More important is the way she struggles with form, to try to get an almost unfilmable novel on the screen. She isn't always successful; the first act will be perplexing for those unfamiliar with the novel, but Redgrave's performance steers us through, and by the end we understand with complete, final clarity what the story was about. Stream-of-consciousness stays entirely within the mind. Movies photograph only the outsides of things. The narration is a useful device, but so are Redgrave's eyes, as she looks at the guests at her party. Once we have the clue, she doesn't really look at all like a safe, respectable, middle-aged hostess. More like a caged animal—trained, but not tamed.

Mulan ★ ★ ★ ½
G, 98 m., 1998

With the voices of: Ming-Na Wen (Mulan), Lea Salonga (Mulan, Singing), Eddie Murphy (Mushu), B. D. Wong (Shang), Donny Osmond (Shang, Singing), Harvey Fierstein (Yao), Jerry Tondo (Chien-Po), Gedde Watanabe (Ling). Directed by Barry Cook and Tony Bancroft and produced by Pam Coats. Screenplay by Rita Hsiao, Christopher Sanders, Philip LaZebnik, Raymond Singer, and Eugenia Bostwick-Singer, based on a story by Robert D. San Souci.

Mulan charts a new direction for Disney's animation studio, combining the traditional elements (brave heroine, cute animal sidekicks) with material that seems more adventuresome and grown-up. Like Fox's *Anastasia,* this is a film that adults can enjoy on their own, without feeling an obligation to take along kids as a cover.

The story this time isn't a retread of a familiar children's classic, but original material, about a plucky Chinese teenage girl who disguises herself as a boy to fight the invading Huns. When the invaders and their implacable leader Shan-Yu (who looks alarmingly like Karl Malone) sweep down on the Great Wall, the emperor calls up all able men to defend the kingdom. Mulan's father is old and feeble, but throws away his crutch to volunteer. To spare him, Mulan steals the family sword, summons the family ancestors for aid, and secretly goes in his place.

Ah, but it isn't as simple as that. Mulan is defying not simply convention, but her family's desire that she abide by the plans of a matchmaker and marry whomever she selects for her. Opening scenes in the film show her botching the interview with the matchmaker (she sets her pants on fire, a nice Freudian touch), and asking, "When will my reflection show who I am inside?"

The message here is standard feminist empowerment: Defy the matchmaker, dress as a boy, and choose your own career. But *Mulan* has it both ways, since inevitably Mulan's heart goes pitty-pat over Shang, the handsome young captain she's assigned to serve under. The movie breaks with the tradition in which the male hero rescues the heroine, but is still totally sold on the Western idea of romantic love. (In an Eastern culture, the ending might have involved an arranged match between Mulan and Shang, which she has earned by her exploits.)

Disney movies since time immemorial have provided their leads with low-comedy sidekicks, usually in the form of animals, although teacups and chandeliers are not unheard-of. Mulan is accompanied on her journey by a scrawny dragon named Mushu, whose voice is performed by Eddie Murphy. It's a little disconcerting the first time we hear his streetsmart lingo (a black dude in medieval China?), but Mushu quickly grows on us. Murphy, working in the tradition of Robin Williams's genie in *Aladdin*, is quick, glib, and funny. He is also offended when people doubt he is a real dragon and refer to him as a lizard.

The action plot involves Mulan training for battle (the song promises, "I'll make a man out of you"), and using quick thinking to save Shang's troops from certain defeat. There are a couple of scenes where she narrowly escapes detection, including one at a swimming hole, and then, when she's unmasked, Shang's snaky adviser whispers that to impersonate a man is "treason." The outcome manages somehow to be true simultaneously to feminist dogma and romantic convention.

The visual style breaks slightly with the look of modern Disney animation to draw from Chinese and Japanese classical cartoon art; in the depiction of nature, there's an echo of the master artist Hiroshige. In a scene where the Hun troops sweep down the side of a snowy mountain, I was reminded of the great battle sequence in Eisenstein's *Alexander Nevsky*. There are scenes here, indeed, where the Disney artists seem aware of the important new work being done in Japanese anime; if American animation is ever going to win an audience beyond the family market, it will have to move in this direction, becoming more experimental in both stories and visual style.

Animation often finds a direct line to my imagination: It's pure story, character, movement, and form, without the distractions of reality or the biographical baggage of the actors. I found myself really enjoying *Mulan,* as a story and as animated art. If the songs were only more memorable, I'd give it four stars,

but they seemed pleasant rather than rousing, and I wasn't humming anything on the way out. Still, *Mulan* is an impressive achievement, with a story and treatment ranking with *Beauty and the Beast* and *The Lion King*.

Mumford ★ ★ ★ ½
R, 111 m., 1999

Loren Dean (Mumford), Hope Davis (Sofie Crisp), Jason Lee (Skip Skipperton), Alfre Woodard (Lily), Mary McDonnell (Althea Brockett), Ted Danson (Jeremy Brockett), Pruitt Taylor Vince (Henry Follett), Zooey Deschanel (Nessa Watkins), Martin Short (Lionel Dillard), David Paymer (Ernest Belbanco), Jane Adams (Phyllis Sheeler). Directed by Lawrence Kasdan and produced by Charles Okun and Kasdan. Screenplay by Kasdan.

In a little town right down the imaginary road from Pleasantville and Seaside (where Truman lives), a psychologist sets up shop. His name is Mumford. The town's name is Mumford. Mumford is also the name of a great writer on towns and cities, but any connections among these Mumfords are left unexplored. Folks are too busy living their lives to spare the time.

Mumford is so carefully visualized in Lawrence Kasdan's new film that you'd sort of like to live there. Yes, it has its problems, its troubled people, and lonely lives. But the arrival of Mumford (Loren Dean) seems to help. He rents a room from Lily (Alfre Woodard), who owns the coffee shop, and begins to listen to people's problems. Soon he is the most popular psychologist in town, and it's hard to say exactly why.

His dialogue, as written by Kasdan, is so circular and comforting that at times we almost feel we're on the couch ourselves. He rarely responds directly to anything, but on the other hand he doesn't use the old professional formulas, either; you won't hear him asking, "What do *you* think about that?" Instead, he has a kind of oblique conversational style. He angles off in new directions. He encourages lateral thinking. People provide a lot of their own answers.

Kasdan has been attracted over the years to movies with large casts; like Robert Altman, he wants to know everybody in town. His credits include *The Big Chill* and *Grand Canyon*, and *Mumford* is another ensemble piece. Sooner or later most everyone wanders across Doc Mumford's path.

We meet: Sofie Crisp (Hope Davis), so chronically fatigued she's afraid to lie down on the couch for fear she may never rise again; Skip Skipperton (Jason Lee), the local Bill Gates type, a zillionaire so lonely he has a secret lab trying to develop a bionic woman; Althea Brockett (Mary McDonnell), who shops till she drops, and her husband, Jeremy (Ted Danson), who treats her badly and himself very, very well; the local druggist Henry Follett (Pruitt Taylor Vince), his fantasies inflamed by pulp magazines; Nessa Watkins (Zooey Deschanel), a troubled teenager; and Lionel Dillard (Martin Short), an attorney who is fired as a patient by Mumford and wants to get even. There are also two other local shrinks, Ernest Belbanco (David Paymer) and Phyllis Sheeler (Jane Adams), who don't violently resent Mumford's success, but would be interested to learn any scandal about him.

During the course of this movie some of these people find they are made for one another, and others find they are made for better things than they have permitted themselves to try. The film makes us feel good, and we bathe in it. There's no big climax or crisis, and we can see the secrets coming a mile away, but this isn't a plot movie anyway. It's a feeling movie, a mood movie, an evocation of the kind of interaction we sometimes hunger for. In an age when nobody has time for anybody else, when people's pockets are buzzing with urgent electronic input, when the way to get someone's attention is to walk away and call them on a cell phone, *Mumford* is about a man who listens, and whose questions are nudges in the direction of healing.

This must read like a peculiar review. Does it make you want to see the movie? There are no earthshaking payoffs here. No dramatic astonishments, vile betrayals, or sexual surprises. Just the careful and loving creation of some characters it is mostly a pleasure to meet. And at its deepest level, profoundly down there below the surface, it is something more, I think: an expression of Kasdan's humanist longings, his wish that people would listen better and

value each other more. It is the strangest thing, how this movie sneaks up and makes you feel a little better about yourself.

The Mummy ★ ★ ★
PG-13, 124 m., 1999

Brendan Fraser (Rick O'Connell), Rachel Weisz (Evelyn), John Hannah (Jonathan), Kevin J. O'Connor (Beni), Arnold Vosloo (Imhotep), Jonathan Hyde (Egyptologist), Oded Fehr (Ardeth Bay), Omid Djalili (Warden). Directed by Stephen Sommers and produced by James Jacks and Sean Daniel. Screenplay by Sommers.

There is within me an unslaked hunger for preposterous adventure movies. I resist the bad ones, but when a *Congo* or an *Anaconda* comes along, my heart leaps up and I cave in. *The Mummy* is a movie like that. There is hardly a thing I can say in its favor, except that I was cheered by nearly every minute of it. I cannot argue for the script, the direction, the acting, or even the mummy, but I can say that I was not bored and sometimes I was unreasonably pleased. There is a little immaturity stuck away in the crannies of even the most judicious of us, and we should treasure it.

This is a movie about a man who fooled around with the pharaoh's mistress and lived (and died, and lived again) to regret it. As his punishment he is "mummified alive," sealed inside a sarcophagus with thousands of flesh-eating beetles (which eat flesh "very slowly," we learn). Millennia pass. In the 1920s, a French foreign legionnaire named Rick meets a librarian named Evelyn, and joins with her and her brother in an unwise quest to find Hamunaptra, the City of the Dead. (Sample dialogue: "Are we talking about *the* Hamunaptra?") They get into a race with other fortune-hunters, who have heard of untold treasure buried beneath the sands, and meanwhile the descendants of the high priests, who have guarded the city for 3,000 years, move against them.

There is good reason not to disturb the mummy, named Imhotep. If he is brought back to life, he will "arise a walking disease," we learn, and unleash the ten proverbial plagues upon Egypt, of which in the course of the movie I counted locusts, fireballs from the sky, rivers running with blood, earthquakes, and flies. Also, of course, the flesh-eating beetles, although I was not certain whether they were a plague or came with the territory.

Brendan Fraser plays Rick, a low-rent Indiana Jones who single-handedly fights his way through a bewildering series of battles. Evie (Rachel Weisz) is too clumsy to be much help (in a delightful early scene, she knocks over one bookcase and the domino effect knocks over every single bookcase in the Museum of Antiquities). Her brother Jonathan (John Hannah) is a spoiled rich kid who specializes in the sorts of asides that butlers used to make. Arnold Vosloo plays Imhotep the mummy in the later scenes, after Imhotep has absorbed the inner organs of enough victims to reconstitute himself. In the earlier scenes, Imhotep is a ghastly special-effects creature who seems made of decomposed cardboard, and lets out a cloud of dust every time Rick slices him.

None of this has anything to do with the great horror classic *The Mummy* (1932), which starred Boris Karloff in a strangely poignant performance as a long-dead priest who returns to life and falls in love with the modern reincarnation of the woman he died for. The 1932 movie contains no violence to speak of; there's hardly any action, indeed, and the chills come through slow realizations (hey, did that mummy move?). This 1999 mummy does indeed mumble something about his feelings for Evie, who may be descended from the pharaoh's mistress on her mother's side. But the bass on his voice synthesizer was set to Rumble, and so I was not quite sure what he said. It sounded vaguely affectionate, in the way that a pit bull growling over a T-bone sounds affectionate, but how can Imhotep focus on rekindling a 3,000-year-old romance when he has ten plagues to unleash?

There's a lot of funny dialogue in the movie, of which my favorite is a line of Evie's after she hears a suspicious noise in the museum library: "Abdul? Mohammed? Bob?" I liked the Goldfinger paint job on the priests in ancient Thebes. And the way a beetle burrowed in through a guy's shoe and traveled through his body, a lump under his flesh, until it could dine on his brain. And the way characters were always reading the wrong pages of ancient books, and raising the dead by accident.

Look, art this isn't. Great trash, it isn't. Good trash, it is. It's not quite up there with *Anaconda*, but it's as much fun as *Congo* and *The Relic*, and it's better than *Species*. If those four titles are not intimately familiar to you, *The Mummy* might not be the place to start.

Muppets from Space ★ ★
G, 82 m., 1999

Dave Goelz (Gonzo), Jeffrey Tambor (K. Edgar Singer), Steve Whitmire (Kermit the Frog), Bill Barretta (Pepe the Prawn), Ray Liotta (Security Guard), Hulk Hogan (Man in Black), Jerry Nelson (Robin), Brian Henson (Dr. Phil Van Neuter), Kevin Clash (Clifford), Frank Oz (Miss Piggy). Directed by Tim Hill and produced by Brian Henson and Martin G. Baker. Screenplay by Jerry Juhl, Joseph Mazzarino, and Ken Kaufman.

The funniest scene in *Muppets from Space* is the first one, where Gonzo is refused a place on Noah's Ark because he is one of a kind. Then he wakes up and realizes it was all only a nightmare. But when it's later revealed that Gonzo is, in fact, an alien from outer space, stranded on our planet, we can sympathize with his feelings: Ever since the crash landing near Roswell, New Mexico, he's been alone and lonely, the odd man out, living in a Muppet boardinghouse. Poor guy (or whatever he is).

The new Muppets movie lacks the kind of excitement the first ones generated, maybe because Muppets have become a little dated except for younger viewers, maybe because the kinds of animals in the two *Babe* movies show such an advance in special effects that we almost wonder why the Muppeteers go to all that trouble to physically manipulate their creatures.

I know that's heresy. I know we're supposed to embrace and defend Muppets because they are real, or at least more real than digital creatures, and because their personalities are more important than their special effects. But somehow *Muppets from Space* seemed a little disconsolate, a little low in energy, as if the ship (or the ark) had sailed.

Maybe that's because the best of the Muppets don't star this time. Kermit is reduced to a hop-through, Miss Piggy is a TV journalist, and most of the big moments belong to Gonzo, the weird-nosed one, who moons about looking alienated and lonely and eats alphabet cereal that spells out messages for him, like "Watch the Sky."

His space people are returning for him, forcing him to choose between Muppets and his alien relatives. This alien visit to Earth excites the attention of a government agent (Jeffrey Tambor, who plays the announcer on *The Larry Sanders Show*), and there are nudges of satire in the direction of *Men in Black* (Hulk Hogan is a man in black), but after the excitement of the human/animal interaction in *Babe* and *Babe, Pig in the City,* I dunno: It's like we've been there, done that.

I feel guilty even writing those words. I recall the charm of the original *Muppet Movie,* when Kermit actually rode a bicycle and we all gasped. I suppose it seemed then that the Muppets could continue indefinitely, with their outsize personalities and effortless interaction with human characters. But now . . . well, maybe it's just this movie. Maybe *Muppets from Space* is just not very good, and they'll make a comeback. I hope so. Because I just don't seem to care much anymore. Sorry, Miss Piggy. Really sorry.

The Muse ★ ★ ★
PG-13, 97 m., 1999

Albert Brooks (Steven Phillips), Sharon Stone (Sarah), Andie MacDowell (Laura Phillips), Jeff Bridges (Jack Warrick), Wolfgang Puck (Himself), Jennifer Tilly (Herself), Lorenzo Lamas (Himself), Cybill Shepherd (Herself), Martin Scorsese (Himself), James Cameron (Himself). Directed by Albert Brooks and produced by Herb Nanas. Screenplay by Brooks and Monica Johnson.

The Muse opens with its hero winning a humanitarian award. "Daddy," his daughter asks at bedtime, "what exactly is a humanitarian?" "It's someone who's never won the Oscar," he tells her. That ability to snatch failure from the ashes of success is common to many of Albert Brooks's characters, and in *The Muse* he plays Steven Phillips, writer of "over seventeen mov-

ies," who is fired by his studio for having lost his "edge." This is a man who is all edge, but never mind: The Hollywood executive credo is, "I fire people, therefore I am."

Steven Phillips is a man with expenses. He needs income. In desperation he visits his friend Jack (Jeff Bridges), a writer who moves from one success to another. Just as he's arriving at Jack's house, he sees a good-looking blonde on her way out. Who can this be? Is Jack having an affair? Steven presses him until Jack finally confesses that the woman is his muse: "I met her at a party a couple of years ago. Rob Reiner introduced us."

Steven begs to be introduced to the muse. Jack relents. Her name is Sarah (Sharon Stone), and she doesn't come cheap. "Bring her a gift," Jack suggests. She likes things that come in those little blue Tiffany's boxes. Soon Steven has moved her into a $1,700 suite at the Four Seasons and is fielding her midnight phone calls complaining that room service won't bring her a Waldorf salad. When Steven's wife, Laura (Andie MacDowell), finds him at the supermarket buying for Sarah that product which no man needs for himself, he confesses everything. At first Laura suspects he's having an affair. Then she realizes he's telling the truth. She knows him too well: There's no way he would bring someone a Waldorf salad just to get sex. Soon Sarah is living in Jack's guest house and receiving visitors like James Cameron ("I don't see you going back in the water," she tells him).

There is desperation in all the best Albert Brooks characters; the precision in his speech barely masks anger and melancholy. As Steven Phillips, he is a man like many others in Hollywood who has stumbled into success and now is stumbling out of it, clueless in both directions. For him, perhaps, the muse is therapeutic: If he believes she's helping him, then she is. Sarah explains early on that she doesn't do any actual writing; she just hangs around, and interesting ideas occur to her clients. This is consistent with my own belief that the muse visits during the act of creation, not before.

There is, of course, the possibility that Sarah is not a Muse, not one of the nine daughters of Zeus, but simply another Hollywood female who likes the little blue boxes and has found a sweatless way to get them. She may work as a placebo. If you believe something will help you write, it will. Ask anyone who has signed up for a screenwriting seminar. Or ask Sarah's clients; in addition to Cameron, we get a series of funny cameos starring Martin Scorsese ("I'm thinking of a remake of *Raging Bull* with a thin and angry guy"), Rob Reiner ("Thanks for *The American President!*"), and Spago chef Wolfgang Puck (after Sarah inspires a new cookie recipe for Steven's wife, Laura and Wolfgang form a partnership).

The Muse was released two weeks after *Bowfinger*, Steve Martin's comedy about desperation in Hollywood. The two movies exist in Hollywoods that never meet. Bowfinger is a mongrel stealing scraps from the feast; Phillips is a man unwilling to push back from the table. *Bowfinger* uses physical comedy; *The Muse* depends on Brooks's sharp ear for dialogue. When the studio executive rejects his screenplay using what he describes as "a form that's not insulting: It's no good," Phillips asks, "What would the insulting form be?"

The movie is good but not great Brooks; not the equal of *Lost in America* or *Mother*, but smart, funny, and—edgy. And there's something fascinating about the way Brooks, as an actor, is ingratiating and hostile at the same time. He projects the feeling of a man trying to conceal his awareness that everyone around him is stupid, or mad. Like a grade school teacher he patiently tries to lead his enemies through their lessons, while they cheerfully frustrate him. There are days and even weeks when we all feel like Steven Phillips. The sneaky thing about this movie is its insinuation that the answer is not to find a muse, but to be one.

Music of the Heart ★ ★ ★
PG, 123 m., 1999

Meryl Streep (Roberta Guaspari), Angela Bassett (Janet Williams), Aidan Quinn (Brian Sinclair), Cloris Leachman (Assunta Guaspari), Jane Leeves (Dorothea von Haeften), Kieran Culkin (Lexi "Teen"), Michael Angarano (Nick "Young"), Gloria Estefan (Isabel Vasquez), Jay O. Sanders (Dan). Directed by Wes Craven and produced by Marianne Maddalena, Walter Scheuer, Allan Miller, and Susan Kaplan. Screenplay by Pamela Gray, based on the life story of Roberta Guaspari and inspired by the documentary *Small Wonders*.

Music of the Heart is based on the true story of a violin teacher named Roberta Guaspari, who created a high school music program more or less out of thin air in East Harlem, and eventually found herself and her students on the stage of Carnegie Hall. Most movies claiming to be based on fact pour on the melodrama, but this one basically just sticks to the real story, which has all the emotional wallop that's needed.

Meryl Streep stars as Guaspari, a mother of two whose husband leaves her. On her own, she has hard times in the job market; she's gift-wrapping presents in a department store one day when she's spotted by an old friend (Aidan Quinn) who knew her in her days as a gifted music student. He tells her about a high school that might have an opening, and soon Guaspari is trying to sell a reluctant principal (Angela Bassett) on what could be accomplished with fifty violins she just happens to have purchased cheap in Greece.

The principal doesn't think so. And, of course, the school has no funds anyway (think what our society might be like if the funds spent on high school sports were used to help kids access the humanities). But Guaspari is persistent, and establishes a music program despite predictable difficulties, including the obligatory mother who complains her children are being taught the music of "dead white men." (The mother is correct, but man, could those guys compose!)

The screenplay has the courage to go easy on the scenes involving movie romance. The Quinn character is disqualified as a candidate, and although another guy (Jay O. Sanders) comes along, this movie is not so much about romance as about practice, practice, practice. Ten years pass. The program has expanded to three schools, and is so popular kids enter a lottery to get into it. Then funds are cut, and the program is threatened. "Do you know anybody who works for the *New York Times?*" Guaspari thoughtfully asks a friend, and soon an article in the *Times* leads to a benefit concert at Carnegie Hall, with violinists Isaac Stern, Itzhak Perlman, and Arnold Steinhardt playing themselves.

This second half of the film feels almost like a documentary, and no wonder; there *was* a documentary about this same material (*Small Wonders*, 1996), unseen by me, and you can guess how Guaspari must have seemed like a natural for someone like Streep to play. The movie doesn't punch up the drama, but simply shows good people trying to work together and get something done. That's why it's so effective.

Meryl Streep is known for her mastery of accents; she may be the most versatile speaker in the movies. Here you might think she has no accent, unless you've heard her real speaking voice; then you realize that Guaspari's speaking style is no less a particular achievement than Streep's other accents. This is not Streep's voice, but someone else's—with a certain flat quality, as if later education and refinement came after a somewhat unsophisticated childhood.

The movie was directed by Wes Craven, known for his horror films (*Scream, A Nightmare on Elm Street*) and he may seem like a strange choice for this material. Not at all. He is in fact a cultured man who broke into movies doing horror and got stuck in the genre; he's been trying to fight his way free from studio typecasting for twenty years, and this movie shows that he can get Meryl Streep to Carnegie Hall just as easily as a phantom to the opera. ☞

My Best Fiend ★ ★ ★
NO MPAA RATING, 95 m., 2000

A documentary directed by Werner Herzog and produced by Lucki Stipetic.

Werner Herzog made five films starring Klaus Kinski. Few other directors wanted to work with him more than once. Midway in their first film, *Aguirre, the Wrath of God* (1972), Kinski threatened to walk off the set, deep in the Amazon rain forest, and Herzog said he would shoot him dead if he did. Kinski claims in his autobiography that he had the gun, not Herzog. Herzog says that's a lie. Kinski describes Herzog in the book as a "nasty, sadistic, treacherous, cowardly creep." Herzog says in the film that Kinski knew his autobiography would not sell unless he said shocking things—so Herzog helped him look up vile words he could use in describing the director.

And so it goes on, almost a decade after Kinski's death, the unending love-hate relationship between the visionary German filmmaker and his muse and nemesis in five films. Herzog's new documentary, *My Best Fiend*, traces their history together. They had one of the most fruitful and troubled relationships of any director-actor team.

Together they made *Aguirre*, about a mad conquistador in the Peruvian jungle; *Fitzcarraldo* (1982), about a man who used block-and-tackle to pull a steamship from one Amazonian river system to another; *Nosferatu* (1979), inspired by Murnau's silent vampire classic; *Woyzeck* (1979), about a nineteenth-century army private who seems mad to others because he sees the world in his own alternative way; and *Cobra Verde* (1988), about a slave trader in Africa. All of their collaborations contain extraordinary images, but the sight in that one of Kinski running wild inside an army of naked, spear-carrying amazons may be the strangest.

Reviewing *Woyzeck*, I wrote: "It is almost impossible to imagine Kinski without Herzog; reflect that this 'unforgettable' actor made more than 170 films for other directors—and we can hardly remember a one." Consider, too, that their strange bond began long before Herzog stood behind a camera.

Herzog told me how they met. When he was twelve, he said, "I was playing in the courtyard of the building where we lived in Munich, and I looked up and saw this man striding past, and I knew at that moment that my destiny was to direct films and that he would be the actor." Kinski was known for his scorn of both films and acting, and claimed to choose projects entirely on the basis of how comfortable he would be on the location. Yet when Herzog summoned him to the rain forest for *Aguirre*, where he would have to march through the jungle wearing Spanish armor and end up on a sinking raft with gibbering monkeys, he accepted. Why? I asked him once, and he replied grimly: "It was my fate."

Herzog believes in shooting on location, arguing that specific places have a voodoo that penetrates the film. *Fitzcarraldo* could have been shot in comfort, not 900 miles up the Amazon, and with special effects and a model boat—but Herzog insisted on isolating his crew, and in hauling a real boat up a real hill. When engineers warned him the ropes would snap and cut everyone in two, he dismissed the engineers. That's all the more intriguing when you learn that Kinski was even more hated than Herzog on the location. In *My Best Fiend,* Herzog recalls that local Indians came to him with an offer to kill Kinski. "I needed Kinski for a few more shots, so I turned them down," he says. "I have always regretted that I lost that opportunity."

He learned early about Kinski's towering rages. The actor actually lived for several months in the same flat with Herzog's family, and once locked himself in the bathroom for two days, screaming all the while, and reducing the porcelain fixtures "to grains the size of sand." Only once, on *Aguirre,* was he able to fully contain his anger in his character—perhaps because Aguirre was as mad as Kinski—and there he gave one of the great performances in the cinema. Herzog revisits the original locations, recalling fights they had and showing the specific scenes that were shot just afterward.

There must have been good times, too, although Herzog shows only one of them—a happy day at the Telluride Film Festival. *My Best Fiend* suffers a little by not having footage to cover more of Herzog's sharpest memories (Les Blank's legendary documentary *Burden of Dreams,* shot on location during *Fitzcarraldo,* shows the two men at each other's throats). But as a meditation by a director on an actor, it is unique; most show biz docs involve the ritual exchange of compliments. *My Best Fiend* is about two men who both wanted to be dominant, who both had all the answers, who were inseparably bound together in love and hate, and who created extraordinary work— while all the time each resented the other's contribution.

My Dog Skip ★ ★ ★
PG, 95 m., 2000

Frankie Muniz (Willie Morris), Diane Lane (Ellen Morris), Luke Wilson (Dink), Kevin Bacon (Jack Morris), Mark Beech (Army Buddy), Harry Connick Jr. (Narrator). Directed by Jay Russell and produced by Broderick Johnson and Andrew Kosove. Screenplay by Gail Gilchriest, based on the book by Willie Morris.

Don't trust any critic who writes about *My Dog Skip* without remembering his childhood dog. My dog was named Blackie. He was part cocker, part beagle, and he was my friend. The sweet thing about *My Dog Skip* is the way it understands the friendship between a kid and a dog. Dogs accomplish amazing things in the movies, but the best thing Skip does is look up at his master, eager to find out what they're gonna do next.

The movie is much elaborated from a memoir by Willie Morris, who grew up in Yazoo, on the Mississippi Delta, and went on to become the editor of *Harper's* magazine. Not everything in the movie actually happened. Its embroideries remind me of Huck Finn's comment about Tom Sawyer: "He told the truth, mainly. There was things which he stretched, but mainly he told the truth."

It is probably not true, for example, that young Willie (Frankie Muniz) volunteered Skip to become an army para-puppy. Oh, I believe Willie (and Skip) saw a newsreel about the brave dogs in our fighting forces. And I believe that Willie trained Skip to become what the newsreel calls a "Yankee Doodle doggy." What I don't believe is that any kid would send his dog away to war. Let him serve on the home front.

The movie is set in the summer of 1942. Willie is a lonely child. He's no good at sports, he doesn't make friends easily, and he has a standoffish relationship with his dad (Kevin Bacon), who lost a leg in the Spanish Civil War, "and a piece of his heart." Will's mom (Diane Lane) tries to make her child happy, but look at that birthday party she throws, where all the guests are old folks, and one of them gives him a bow tie. Will's "older and only friend" is Dink (Luke Wilson), a high school sports star, who lives next door and goes off to war before he can teach Will the secrets of the curveball.

Mom decides Will needs a dog. Dad is against it. "He needs a friend," Mom says, snatching the cigar out of Dad's mouth and puffing on it herself, as a Freudian signal of her takeover. She gives the dog to Will, and Will's life is changed forever. With Skippy, he runs all over town, and the fields outside of town, and other kids want to be his friend because he has a dog.

This is some dog. It knows everybody in town, and makes a daily stop at the butcher shop for a slice of bologna. When Will makes several errors in a baseball game, Skip runs onto the field to help Will. When Will, distraught, slaps his dog, I found to my amazement that I recoiled with dismay. That's when I discovered how the movie had gotten to me. How I had shelved a movie critic's usual reserve and just started identifying with Will and Skip. I wasn't good at sports, either, and Blackie helped me make friends.

There's a subplot about moonshiners that isn't too convincing. I don't know why they'd need to hide their booze in a cemetery crypt, and I wasn't convinced when that led to a crisis for Skip at the end. But I did remember riding my bike all over the neighborhood once when Blackie ran away, calling out his name again and again as dusk fell, and the movie has that right.

Another subplot has to do with Dink, who comes back from the war in a different mood than when he left, and tells Will, "It isn't the dying that's scary—it's the killing." And there's a scene where Will sees a deer die before his eyes. We understand that in every childhood there are lessons burned into your memory. They shape you. In Willie Morris's case, they guided him out of Yazoo and to Oxford on a Rhodes scholarship, and then to New York and a literary career. But he never forgot Skip.

A movie like this falls outside ordinary critical language. Is it good or bad? Is there too much melodrama? I don't have any idea. It triggered too many thoughts of my own for me to have much attention left over for footnotes. I realize, for example, that the movie doesn't deal in any substantial way with the racial situation in Mississippi in 1942, and I know that Will's dad undergoes a rather miraculous transformation, and that Dink seems less like a neighbor than like a symbol of lost innocence. I know those things, but they don't seem relevant to the actual experience of this movie. If there was ever a day or even a minute when your dog was not your best but your only friend, you'll see what I mean.

My Favorite Martian ★ ★
PG, 93 m., 1999

Christopher Lloyd (Uncle Martin), Jeff Daniels (Tim O'Hara), Elizabeth Hurley (Brace Channing), Daryl Hannah (Lizzie), Wallace Shawn (Coleye), Christine Ebersole (Mrs. Brown), Michael Lerner (Mr. Channing), Ray Walston (Armitan). Directed by Donald Petrie and produced by Robert Shapiro, Jerry Leider, and Mark Toberoff. Screenplay by Sherri Stoner and Deanna Oliver.

My Favorite Martian is slapstick and silliness, wild sight gags and a hyped-up acting style. The Marx Brothers would have been at home here. The movie is clever in its visuals, labored in its audios, and noisy enough to entertain kids up to a certain age. What age? Low double digits, I'd say.

It stars Jeff Daniels, a seasoned straight man *(Dumb and Dumber)*, as a TV producer named Tim. He sees a flying saucer crash and is soon adopted by its occupant, a Martian named, for purposes of the human appearance he assumes, Uncle Martin. The Martian is played by Christopher Lloyd with zestful looniness, and the Martian's space suit, named Zoot, becomes a character in its own right. Both Uncle Martin and Zoot are capable of instant shapeshifting, and depending on what color of extraterrestrial gumball they're chewing, Martin (and the humans) can turn into a variety of monsters.

There's a love story in the frenzy. As the film opens, Tim is in love with his on-air talent, a reporter named Brace (Elizabeth Hurley). By the end, he has come to realize that Lizzie (Daryl Hannah), his technician, is a better choice in every way. All of this is decided at breakneck speed, and at one point Lizzie even turns into a bug-eyed monster and entirely devours a bad guy. (Soon after, defying one of Newton's laws, I'm not sure which one, she turns back into a lithesome young woman who has not put on any weight.)

The villains are all government scientists, led by Coleye (pronounced "coli," as in "e coli"), a bureaucrat obsessed with aliens. Played by Wallace Shawn, who often looks as if he is about to do something immoral with a clipboard, he desperately chases Tim and Uncle Martin because he wants to prove there is intelligent life on other planets. Uncle Martin, on the other hand, only wants to lie low, be friends with Tim and Lizzie, repair his spaceship, and go home. Then he discovers ice cream, and all he wants to do is eat ice cream.

There are some good moments in *My Favorite Martian,* and the best comes right at the top, where we see one of NASA's Martian exploratory vehicles roll up to a rock, stop, and run out of juice just before it would have stumbled upon an amazing sight. I also liked the gyrations of Zoot the suit, which develops an addiction to washing machines. And the scene where Martin chug-a-lugs a lava lamp. I also appreciated the information that a space probe contained the ashes of Jerry Garcia.

It looks as if everyone who made this film had a lot of fun. Spirits and energy are high, mugging is permitted, dialogue is rapid-fire, nobody walks if they can run. As kids' entertainment, it's like a live-action cartoon, and I can recommend it on that level, although not on a more ambitious plane. I came upon the movie just a few days after seeing *Children of Heaven,* a children's film from Iran that has the power to absorb and teach any child, and I found *My Favorite Martian* noisy and superficial by comparison. (But of *course* it's noisy and superficial. That's its mission. I keep forgetting.)

My Giant ★ ★
PG, 107 m., 1998

Billy Crystal (Sammy), Kathleen Quinlan (Serena), Gheorghe Muresan (Max), Joanna Pacula (Lilianna), Zane Carney (Nick), Jere Burns (Weller), Steven Seagal (Himself). Directed by Michael Lehmann and produced by Billy Crystal. Screenplay by David Seltzer, based on a story by Crystal and Seltzer.

The posters for *My Giant* show the seven-foot, seven-inch basketball star Gheorghe Muresan holding Billy Crystal (who is at least two feet shorter) under his arm. That looks funny. Who could guess it's a heartfelt friendship?

We go into the movie and meet Crystal, who plays Sammy, a Hollywood agent visiting the set of his single remaining client, in Romania. He's not having a good day. His wife announces she's leaving him, his client fires him, and then his car swerves into a creek. It looks like he'll drown, until he is saved by two enormous hands.

Regaining consciousness later in a monastery, he discovers that the hands belong to Max (Muresan), a local giant who is the ward of the monks. In the monastery he reads Shakespeare and pines for his lost love, who jilted him and moved to New Mexico. He is a big, sweet guy. Very big. Muresan may not have heard of Rossellini's belief that everyone has at least one movie performance in him (playing himself), but he illustrates that principle nicely.

Sammy, a desperate hustler, sees Max as his meal ticket out of Romania and back into the business. Promising him an eventual reunion with his lost beloved, he flies the two of them back to America, where the plot grows mired in sentimentality and we gradually realize this is not a comedy after all, but a greeting card crossed with a guide to improved self-esteem. The movie, which could have been a funny send-up of Hollywood talent requirements, gets distracted by subplots: Can Sammy's marriage be saved? Will his son learn to trust him again? Will that heartless girl in New Mexico give a break to the big lug whose heart she shattered?

Why is it that comics are always the biggest pushovers when it comes to sentiment? Do people who are funny have a greater than ordinary need to be loved? Is that why they want to make us laugh in the first place? After its promising start, *My Giant* isn't a comedy about an agent and a giant, so much as the heartwarming tale of a guy who learns to be a better family man.

It's interesting, the way Muresan establishes himself on screen as a stable area of calm, while the plot scurries around him. His English is not the best, but we believe he is who he's playing, and that's a test not every actor can pass. There are a few attempts to insert him into the world of showbiz, and they provide the movie's biggest laughs. There's a talk show sequence, a wrestling gig, and a funny send-up of Steven Seagal, in which Seagal does a good job of cheerfully skewering himself. That comes as Sammy tries to get Max a job on the new Seagal thriller, being shot in Las Vegas, and suggests how the whole movie could have worked, if it hadn't headed straight for the heart-tug department.

But most of the movie is lugubrious. Way too much dialogue is about whether Sammy forgot his son's birthday, and whether his wife (Kathleen Quinlan) can trust him to ever remember it again, and whether Max's lifelong happiness really does depend on the cold-hearted woman in New Mexico. Do you know anyone who wanted to see a heartwarming story about Gheorghe Muresan helping Billy Crystal get in touch with his better nature? I don't think I do.

My Life So Far ★ ★ ★
PG-13, 92 m., 1999

Colin Firth (Edward), Rosemary Harris (Gamma), Irene Jacob (Heloise), Mary Elizabeth Mastrantonio (Moira), Malcolm McDowell (Uncle Morris), Robert Norman (Fraser), Tcheky Karyo (Gabriel Chenoux), Kelly MacDonald (Elspeth). Directed by Hugh Hudson and produced by David Puttnam and Steve Norris. Screenplay by Simon Donald, based on the book *Son of Adam* by Sir Denis Forman.

It's been said that the most pleasant of all lives were lived in the great British country houses in the years between the wars—for those who lived there, of course. The rest of us can only enviously imagine those days as idealized in the works of P. G. Wodehouse, whose characters occupy an endless summer of dotty earls, alcoholic younger brothers, eccentric inventors, ferocious aunts, hopeful suitors, and prize-winning pigs. Their household staff functions not as servants but as keepers.

My Life So Far, set in the late 1920s on an estate near Argyle, Scotland, is based on the memoirs of a real person—Sir Denis Forman, director of the Royal Opera House. I've always thought of the Wodehouse universe as essentially a fantasy, but perhaps not. Sir Denis's childhood at times seems to be taking place at Plum's Blandings Castle, where Lord Emsworth doted on his blue-ribbon pig, the Empress of Blandings.

The hero of this film, a ten-year-old named Fraser Pettigrew (Robert Norman), grows up in Kiloran House, where his father, Edward (Colin Firth), invents airships and paddleboats, and commits a large part of the family fortune to the cultivation of sphagnum moss (which is, he boasts, "better than cotton wool for wounds"). Fraser's mother, Moira (Mary Elizabeth Mastrantonio), smiles indulgently and a little wearily upon her husband the enthusiast.

Her own mother (Rosemary Harris), called "Gamma" by the kids, owns the estate, which Edward hopes she will leave to him. But there is another claimant—Uncle Morris (Malcolm McDowell), Moira's brother, a hard-boiled businessman who arrives one day with his new French wife, Heloise (Irene Jacob). Soon both Fraser and (alas) his father are in love with the young woman, causing complications in Eden.

My Life So Far, directed by Hugh Hudson *(Chariots of Fire),* is not plot-driven, and even a crisis (like the opening scene where the infant Fraser is happily climbing on the roof) is handled with a certain detachment. These are characters for whom tone is more important than content; they live their lives according to the teaching of Billy Crystal's Hernando: "It is better to look good than to feel good."

The household contains a large family, many servants, and a ceaseless stream of visitors (including Tcheky Karyo as a legendary pilot named "The Emperor of the Air"). The big scenes play out at dinner or in the drawing room before an audience of most of the other characters; these lives are so public they almost take place onstage. The reason modern American conversation has declined so sadly is because most of us no longer have fireplaces to stand before while declaiming epigrams, or dinner parties for eighteen at which precocious youngsters can suggest that the family finances could be improved if the women sold themselves into prostitution.

That is indeed a suggestion brightly made

by young Fraser, who has found his father's secret library and devoured books he does not quite understand. Meanwhile, darker currents gather as his father and his uncle jostle for position. And his father, who has seemed so carefree and steadfast for the first half of the movie, actually seems prepared to sacrifice everything—family, children, estate—for the love of Heloise, who is not even a femme fatale but only a pleasant sweetheart.

Did worlds like this exist? Yes, until death duties and taxes forced the old families to earn their own livings, while the great houses were opened to tourists and the servant quarters became tea shops. Today there are people with as much money or more, but they have had to be smart enough to earn it; they may occupy houses like this, but they lack the dreamy naïveté to enchant them. It has been a melancholy progression from the Empress of Blandings to pork bellies. Sir Denis Forman may have his knighthood and the Royal Opera House to run, but there is a poignancy that colors every scene of *My Life So Far*. He is homesick for Kiloran. So am I, and I never even lived there.

My Name Is Joe ★ ★ ★ ½
R, 108 m., 1999

Peter Mullan (Joe), Louise Goodall (Sarah), Gary Lewis (Shanks), Lorraine McIntosh (Maggie), David McKay (Liam), Anne-Marie Kennedy (Sabine), David Hayman (McGowan), Scott Hannah (Scott), David Peacock (Hooligan). Directed by Ken Loach and produced by Rebecca O'Brien. Screenplay by Paul Laverty.

His name is Joe, and he's an alcoholic. He's been sober for only ten months, and although AA advises against romance in the first year of recovery, Joe falls in love with a nurse named Sarah. She's a social worker who has seen a lot of guys like Joe, but there's something about him—a tenderness, a caring—that touches her.

They're both wounded and cautious, but a romance slowly grows at moments like the one where he invites her in for tea and plays some classical music. He explains: In his drinking days he stole some cassettes and sold them,

but the classical tape didn't sell. One night he got drunk and played it, and "it was just lovely."

Joe is played by Peter Mullan, who won the 1998 Best Actor Award at Cannes. He's a compact, ginger-haired man around forty, who moves with a physical efficiency that suggests he's focused and impatient. He looks a little like Paul Newman, with the same slender energy. He keeps busy. He doesn't have work, but he manages a soccer team and picks up the members in a city van, fussing over them like a brood hen. He wears a windbreaker and sneakers, and is always in a hurry. And he takes his newfound sobriety seriously (the opening scene shows him telling his story at an AA meeting).

Joe lives in a rough neighborhood of Glasgow, where drugs and crime are a way of life. One of his friends is Liam (David McKay), a kid who did time for drugs. Liam's wife, Sabine (Anne-Marie Kennedy), dealt while Liam was inside, but now he's out and, Joe thinks, clean and sober. But it's not that simple. Sabine is using, and they're into the local druglord, McGowan, for a total of 2,000 pounds. McGowan's thugs have offered to break Liam's legs, and nobody thinks they're kidding.

My Name Is Joe takes these elements and puts them together into a story that forces Joe to choose between the twelve steps of AA and the harder, more painful steps he learned on the street. In theory, a recovering alcoholic doesn't allow himself anywhere near drink or drugs. But McGowan offers Joe a deal: If he makes two trips up north and drives back cars containing drugs, Liam's debt will be forgotten. Why doesn't McGowan simply have Liam do this? Because McGowan isn't dumb. He knows Liam can't be trusted—and he also enjoys, perhaps, compromising a community leader who no longer adorns McGowan's pub.

The film is another one of Ken Loach's tales of working-class life; like *Riff-Raff*, it is told in a regional British accent that's so thick it has been subtitled. (I understood most of it when I saw it without subtitles in Cannes, but I have to say they help.) His screenplay is ingenious in bringing together the romance, the crime elements, and the challenge of being sober in a community where drink and drugs provide the primary pastime (and employment).

The romance is all the more absorbing because it's between two streetwise people in early middle age who have no illusions. The nurse, Sarah, is played by Louise Goodall with a careworn face but a quick smile; she's had to harden herself against the sad cases she encounters as a community health worker, but she's able to be moved by Joe's spirit and sincerity.

I have made the film sound too depressing, perhaps. It is about depressing events, but its spirit is lively, and there's a lot of humor wedged here and there, including a walk-on for a bagpiper who knows three songs, plays them, and then peddles shortbread to tourists. And there's humor involving the soccer team, their bad luck and their uniforms.

Often with a film like this you think you know how it has to end. The ending of *My Name Is Joe* left me stunned. I've rarely seen a film where the conclusion is so unexpected, and yet, in its own way, so logical, and so inevitable.

My Son the Fanatic ★ ★ ★ ½
R, 86 m., 1999

Om Puri (Parvez), Rachel Griffiths (Bettina), Akbar Kurtha (Farid), Stellan Skarsgard (Schitz), Gopi Desai (Minoo), Bhasker Patel (The Maulvi), Harish Patel (Fizzy), Sarah Jane Potts (Madeleine), Judi Jones (Mrs. Fingerhut), Geoffrey Bateman (Inspector Fingerhut). Directed by Udayan Prasad and produced by Chris Curling. Screenplay by Hanif Kureishi.

My Son the Fanatic tells the story of a taxi driver of Pakistani origins, who for many years has lived in the British midlands. He works at night to make better money, and finds himself giving rides to hookers and their clients—and sometimes helping them to meet one another. There is one hooker he rather likes, because she sees him as an individual, something few other people in his life seem able to do.

The driver, whose name is Parvez, is played by Om Puri, an actor of great humor and wisdom, whose weathered face can be tough and sad. He shares an uneventful marriage with his wife, Minoo (Gopi Desai), who regards him with mute but unending disapproval. Their lives are briefly brightened when their son, Farid (Akbar Kurtha), is engaged to the daugh-

ter of the local police inspector, but then Farid breaks it off ("Couldn't you see how they looked at you?" he asks his father, after a visit to the girl's parents). The son turns to fundamentalism, and is soon listening to religious tapes, wearing a costume to set himself apart from others, and asking to move a visiting guru into Parvez's home.

Real life for Parvez takes place in his cab, and we meet Bettina (Rachel Griffiths), the tough, realistic hooker he has a soft spot for. He recommends her to a visiting German businessman (Stellan Skarsgard), who has low tastes and a lot of money and treats Bettina in ways that make Parvez wince. Parvez spends long hours at work, and at home has carved out a little space in the basement that he can call his own—playing jazz records, drinking Scotch, listening to the voices upstairs of the guru and his followers, discussing their "mad ideas."

There is, of course, racial discrimination in England (I sometimes wonder if North America, for all our faults, is not the most successful multiracial society on Earth). There's an ugly scene in a nightclub, where Parvez has taken Bettina and the German, and is singled out after a comic shines a spotlight on him. And another scene, ugly in a quieter way, when Parvez takes Bettina to the big restaurant operated by his old friend Fizzy, who immigrated from Pakistan with him. Fizzy does not approve of Parvez bringing any woman not his wife (and especially not this woman) into the restaurant, and officiously sets a table for them in an empty storeroom.

The film was written by Hanif Kureishi, the novelist whose screen credits include *My Beautiful Launderette*. His stories often involve children in rebellion against the values of their parents, but here he turns the tables: It is Parvez who lives like a teenager, staying out late and cherishing his favorite albums in the basement, and his son who occupies the upstairs and preaches conservatism and religion. Parvez is not a rebel, just a realist who asks himself, "Is this it for me? To sit behind the wheel of a cab for the rest of my life and never a sexual touch?" When Bettina kisses him, says she can't remember the last time she kissed a man, and quietly reveals that her real name is Sandra, we believe them as a couple, however unlikely:

403

In a lonely and cold world, they see each other's need.

Om Puri's performance is based on the substantial strength of his physical presence, and on his clear-sighted view of his world as an exile. When the guru comes to Parvez with requests that the son would be shocked to hear, he is not surprised: "You are so patriotic about Pakistan," he tells the guru. "That is always a sign of imminent departure." He instinctively suspects any religion, even his own, when it operates as a tribe: He is tolerant in his very bones, and dislikes religions that use costumes, fear, and peer pressure to set their members aside from the mainstream. In accepting the hooker, he accepts all outcasts and pariahs, judging them on their characters rather than their affiliations.

The movie contains a lot of humor, much of it generated by the creative differences between standard English and its variations in India and Pakistan. Parvez has a knack for putting a slight satirical spin on a phrase by not quite getting it right. When the police inspector is late to their meeting, he observes, "The law never sleeps at night!" When a man smokes in his taxi: "Please, sir! No smoking indoor! Smell is deafening."

There is humor, too, in his concern about his son's strange behavior. At first he suspects drugs rather than religion, and asks Bettina to write him out a list of the danger signals of addiction. When he tries the questions out on his son, the boy groans, "I can always tell when you have been reading *Daily Express*."

The film's director, Udayan Prasad, knows, as Kureishi does, that there are no simple solutions to the dilemmas of their story. For that reason, it is more than usually important to sit through the closing credits. The credits roll over a long shot that is not just a closing decoration, but really the resolution of the whole story, such as it is. In a way we are all exiles. In a way there is never going to be any home.

Mystery, Alaska ★ ★ ½
R, 118 m., 1999

Russell Crowe (John Biebe), Hank Azaria (Charles Danner), Mary McCormack (Donna Biebe), Burt Reynolds (Judge Walter Burns), Colm Meaney (Mayor Scott Pitcher), Lolita Davidovich (Mary Jane Pitcher), Maury Chaykin (Bailey Pruitt), Ron Eldard ("Skank" Marden). Directed by Jay Roach and produced by David E. Kelley and Howard Baldwin. Screenplay by Kelley and Sean O'Byrne.

Mystery, Alaska is sweet, pleasant, low-key, inoffensive, and unnecessary. It sticks up for underdogs, nice people, and small towns, and doesn't like big corporations, adulterers, TV producers, and New Yorkers in general. It contains not only a big game with a thrilling finish, but also a courtroom scene, a funeral scene, an innocent teenage sex scene, a change-of-heart scene, and a lot of scenery. No one falls through the ice and almost drowns, but we can't have everything.

The movie assembles a large cast in Mystery, Alaska, a fictional town where since time immemorial life has revolved around the Saturday Game, a hockey match played on black pond ice by local boys and men, who take it very seriously indeed. A former town resident (Hank Azaria) writes an article for *Sports Illustrated* about what fierce and brilliant hockey players they all are, and soon a sports network is promoting an exhibition game between the local team and the New York Rangers.

But this is not merely a hockey movie, leading up to the big game. It has many things on its mind. A foulmouthed representative for a big retail chain comes to town and gets shot in the foot by a general-store owner. The mayor's wife fools around with one of the hockey players. A veteran team member gets kicked upstairs to the coaching job to make room for a teenage phenom. There are scenes of young and middle-aged love, visits from high-powered media stars, and a drunken driving scene involving a Zamboni.

So cluttered is the plot that Burt Reynolds, sporting a Mephistophelian beard and a black overcoat he didn't get from Eddie Bauer, plays not only the local judge but also a strict and troubled husband and father, a former hockey coach who returns to the job, and a spoilsport who turns into a good guy. Since he gets only one big scene for some of these manifestations, the screenplay is like a test of versatility.

The film was written by David E. Kelley, one of the most successful writer-producers in TV today *(Ally McBeal)*, and Sean O'Byrne. They like lots of characters. Russell Crowe is the town sheriff and aging hockey star; Mary McCormack is his sweet wife; Maury Chaykin is the local attorney; Lolita Davidovich is married to the mayor (Colm Meaney); Ron Eldard is "Skank," the local ladies' man; Judith Ivey is the judge's wife and Rachel Wilson is his daughter; Ryan Northcutt is Stevie, her boyfriend, the speed demon on ice. Mike Myers has fun with a Canadian accent and word choices as a TV color commentator; no doubt he was recruited by the director, Jay Roach, who made the *Austin Powers* movies. Hockey legends Doug McLeod, Phil Esposito, and Jim Fox are also TV announcers. I will not reveal what celebrity they recruit to sing the "Star-Spangled Banner," or what he does for an encore, because that sequence is just about perfect.

All of these people are awfully nice. I don't know how they got an R rating for their movie, which seems pretty PG-13 to me. They have a fine little village there, and darned if I wasn't rooting for the home team in the big game. This is not a bad movie so much as a meandering one, lacking in dramatic tension because no one really turns out to be a villain.

I don't require that a sports movie end when the outcome of the big game is decided, but neither do I recommend that it linger while the locals and visitors say good-bye to one another, tidy up every plot strand, and demonstrate that their hearts are in the right place. I do, however, think this same cast, in this same town, could metamorphose into an entertaining sitcom. It almost feels as if they metamorphosed out of one.

Mystery Men ★ ★
PG-13, 111 m., 1999

Geoffrey Rush (Casanova Frankenstein), Greg Kinnear (Captain Amazing), Hank Azaria (Blue Raja), Janeane Garofalo (Bowler), William H. Macy (Shoveler), Kel Mitchell (Invisible Boy), Paul Reubens (Spleen), Ben Stiller (Furious), Lena Olin (Dr. Annabel Leek), Wes Studi (Sphinx), Ricky Jay (Publicist). Directed by Kinka Usher and produced by Lawrence Gordon, Mike Richardson, and Lloyd Levin. Screenplay by Neil Cuthbert, based on the Dark Horse Comic Book Series created by Bob Burden.

Mystery Men has moments of brilliance waving their arms to attract attention in a sea of dreck. It's a long, shapeless, undisciplined mess, and every once in a while it generates a big laugh. Since many of the laughs seem totally in the character of the actors who get them, they play like ad libs—as if we're hearing asides to the audience.

The premise: Captain Amazing (Greg Kinnear) is the top-rated superhero in Champion City, a special-effects metropolis made of skyscrapers, air buses, and dirigibles. He wears sponsor badges on his leather suit (Ray-O-Vac, Pennzoil) like Indy 500 drivers, but the sponsors are growing restless because his recent exploits are tired and dumb. Consulting with his publicist (Ricky Jay), he decides to spring his archenemy from jail. Maybe Casanova Frankenstein (Geoffrey Rush) can improve his Q rating by inspiring more colorful adventures.

The problem with this strategy is that Casanova is smart and the Captain is dumb, and soon Amazing is the villain's captive. That makes an opening for second-string superheroes to try to rescue Amazing and enhance their own reputations. The B team includes the Blue Raja (Hank Azaria), who hurls forks and spoons with amazing strength; Mr. Furious (Ben Stiller), who gets bad when he gets mad; and the Shoveler (William H. Macy), who whacks people with a spade. They're joined by new hopefuls, including the Spleen (Paul Reubens), whose weapon is voluminous flatulence; the Bowler (Janeane Garofalo), whose father's skull is inside her transparent bowling ball; Invisible Boy (Kel Mitchell), whose invisibility has to be taken mostly on trust, since you can't see if he's really there; and the Sphinx (Wes Studi), whose sayings make the Psychic Friends Network look deep.

All of these characters are hurled into elaborate special-effects scenes, where they get into frenetic human traffic jams. Comedy depends on timing, and chaos is its enemy. We see noisy comic book battles of little consequence, and finally we weary: This isn't entertainment; it's an f/x demo reel.

And yet the movie has its moments. I liked William H. Macy's version of Henry V's speech on the eve of battle ("We few . . .") and his portentous line, "We've got a blind date with Destiny, and it looks like she ordered the lobster." And a lot of Janeane Garofalo's lines, as when she says: "I would like to dedicate my victory to supporters of local music and those who seek out independent films." When the smoke clears, her character is ready to retire: "Okay, now I'm going back to graduate school; that was the agreement." We share her relief.

N

The Negotiator ★ ★ ★ ½
R, 141 m., 1998

Samuel L. Jackson (Danny Roman), Kevin Spacey (Chris Sabian), David Morse (Commander Adam Beck), Ron Rifkin (Commander Frost), John Spencer (Chief Al Travis), J. T. Walsh (Inspector Niebaum), Regina Taylor (Karen Roman). Directed by F. Gary Gray and produced by Arnon Milchan and David Hoberman. Screenplay by James DeMonaco and Kevin Fox.

The Negotiator is a triumph of style over story, and of acting over characters. The movie's a thriller that really hums along, and I was intensely involved almost all the way. Only now, typing up my notes, do I fully realize how many formula elements it contains.

Consider. In the opening scene, a Chicago police negotiator named Danny Roman (Samuel L. Jackson) calmly talks with a madman who has taken his own daughter hostage. The siege ends in victory, just as it does in every other cop movie. Next scene, of course, is the cops celebrating in a bar and watching coverage of themselves on TV. There's always one sorehead who makes a point of *not* celebrating the hero's triumph. Pay close attention to this character, who is the False Villain and is there to throw you off the track.

Next major sequence: Hero cop faces sudden disgrace. Is accused of embezzling funds from police pension fund. Is framed to look like bad guy. Has no friends anymore. I don't have to tell you this always leads to the Gun and Badge scene, in which the hero drops the tools of his trade on the chief's desk.

The film now moves quickly toward its central notion, which is that one trained negotiator faces another one—meaning that these men understand each other's strategies. Roman, facing jail as the victim of a frame-up, takes hostages, including Niebaum (J. T. Walsh), an investigator looking into the missing pension funds. Roman says there is only one negotiator he will deal with—Chris Sabian (Kevin Spacey), a man who is not part of the department and unlikely to be in on the frame-up.

Until Sabian's arrival on the scene, *The Negotiator* has been assembled from off-the-shelf parts. But then the movie comes alive. There's a chemistry between the negotiators played by Jackson and Spacey; sometimes they seem to be communicating in code, or by the looks in their eyes. The screenplay, by James DeMonaco and Kevin Fox, shows evidence of much research into the methods of negotiators, but it uses its knowledge only when it's needed. (I liked the little lecture on eye language.) And the direction by F. Gary Gray is disciplined, taut, and smart: When he touches a base, he's confident enough to keep on running, instead of jumping up and down on it like a lot of directors would.

I don't know a lot about Gray, but I know he has a greater curiosity about the human element than a lot of men who make thrillers. His first film was *Friday* (1995), written by and starring Ice Cube in a character study of two homeboys hanging out in the neighborhood, engaged in intense people-watching and dope-smoking. His second film, *Set It Off* (1996), was about four black women who get involved in a bank robbery, and who emerge as touching and convincing characters, vividly seen.

Now comes *The Negotiator,* which essentially consists of two men talking to one another, intercut with action. It could have dragged. It could have locked into sets. It doesn't. Gray makes us care about the characters, to share some of Roman's frustration and rage, to get involved in the delicate process of negotiations. The plot makes good use of the fact that the Chicago policemen surrounding Danny Roman (who has taken his hostages in a West Wacker Drive high-rise) may also be in on the embezzlement. They want him dead. Spacey, as Sabian, is fighting for time before the hotheads send in the SWAT teams.

There are also quiet passages, in which some of the hostages begin to feel sympathy for Danny Roman. J. T. Walsh, in one of his last performances before his untimely death, is effective at concealing how much he might really know, and what his involvement is. But Roman is right in suspecting that his loyal secretary might know where all the secrets are hidden and want to go home to her family in one piece.

Yes, there are clichés all through the movie, including the obligatory role of Roman's new wife (Regina Taylor), who wants him to stop taking the dangerous assignments. Yes, the TV news crews supply the usual breathless bulletins and obnoxious questions. Yes, the action scenes are unlikely (Roman uses the SWAT teams' own percussion bombs against them—but in a confined space wouldn't the percussion affect him as much as them?).

But *The Negotiator* works because it takes its conventional story and jacks it up several levels with Gray's craft and style. And because Jackson and Spacey are very good. Much of the movie simply consists of close-ups of the two of them talking, but it's not simply dialogue because the actors make it more than dialogue—investing it with conviction and urgency. Here is one of the year's most skillful thrillers.

Never Been Kissed ★ ★ ★

PG-13, 107 m., 1999

Drew Barrymore (Josie Geller), David Arquette (Rob Geller), Michael Vartan (Sam Coulson), Molly Shannon (Anita), Leelee Sobieski (Aldys), John C. Reilly (Gus), Garry Marshall (Rigfort), Sean Whalen (Merkin). Directed by Raja Gosnell and produced by Sandy Isaac and Nancy Juvonen. Screenplay by Abby Kohn and Marc Silverstein.

Never Been Kissed stars Drew Barrymore as a copy editor for that excellent newspaper the *Chicago Sun-Times*. I recommend its use as a recruiting film—not because it offers a realistic view of journalistic life, but because who wouldn't want to meet a copy editor like Barrymore? Even when she's explaining the difference between "interoffice" and "intraoffice," she's a charmer. The movie's screenplay is contrived and not blindingly original, but Barrymore illuminates it with sunniness and creates a lovable character. I think this is what's known as star power.

She plays a twenty-five-year-old named Josie Geller who, despite a few unhappy early experiences with spit-swapping, has indeed never *really* been kissed. At the paper, she issues copyediting edicts while hiding behind a mousy brown hairdo and a wardrobe inspired by mudslides. Her editor, played as subtly as one of the Three Stooges by Garry Marshall, likes to pound the conference table with a bat while conducting editorial meetings; he wants an undercover series on life in high school and assigns Josie because she looks young enough.

That sets up Josie's chance to return to high school and get it right. The first time around, she was known as "Josie Grossie," an ugly duckling with braces on her teeth, hair in her eyes, baby fat, and pimples. Barrymore does a surprisingly convincing job of conveying this insecure lump of unpopularity; it's one of the reasons we develop such sympathy for Josie.

Josie borrows a car from her brother Rob (David Arquette), a once-promising baseball player who now works in a store that's a cross between Kinko's and Trader Vic's. She adopts a new blond hairstyle and gets rid of the glasses. But her first day on her secret assignment gets off to the wrong start, thanks to a wardrobe (white jeans and a gigantic feather boa) that might have been Cruella DeVil's teenage costume. The popular girls mock her, but she's befriended by Aldys (Leelee Sobieski), leader of the smart kids: "How are you at calculus? How would you like to join the Denominators?" That's the math club, with matching sweatshirts.

Josie's unpopularity reaches such a height that her car is deposited by pranksters in the middle of the football field. Rob analyzes the situation and says she needs to be certified as acceptable by a popular kid. What kid? Rob himself. He enrolls in high school and is popular by lunchtime, after winning a coleslaw-eating contest. Following his example, the students accept Josie, while Rob reawakens his fantasy of playing for a state championship baseball team.

The title *Never Been Kissed* gives us reason to hope that Josie will, sooner or later, be kissed. Soon we have reason to believe that the kisser may be Mr. Coulson (Michael Vartan), the English teacher, and of course the taboo against student-teacher relationships adds spice to this possibility. Meanwhile, Josie's adventures in high school are monitored at the *Sun-Times* through a remarkable invention, a brooch pin that contains a miniature TV camera and transmits everything she sees back to the office. We do not actually have such technology at the *Sun-Times*, and thank heavens, or my editors would have had to suffer through *Baby Geniuses.*

The story develops along a familiar arc. Josie has flashbacks to her horrible high school memories, but this time around, she flowers. Unspoken romance blooms with Mr. Coulson. Comic relief comes from Josie's friend Anita (Molly Shannon), who is mistaken for a high school sex counselor and offers advice startling in its fervor. Alas, Josie gets scooped on a story about the local teenage hangout, and her editor bangs the conference table some more. We are left to marvel at the portrait of Chicago journalism in both this movie and *Message in a Bottle*, which had Robin Wright Penn as a researcher at the *Tribune.* Apparently at both papers the way to get a big salary and your own office is to devote thousands of dollars and weeks of time to an assignment where you hardly ever write anything.

Never Been Kissed is not deep or sophisticated, but it's funny and bighearted and it wins us over. The credit goes to Barrymore. In this movie and *Ever After* (and in *The Wedding Singer*, where I liked her a lot more than the movie), she emerges as a real star—an actor whose personality and charisma are the real subject of the story. *Never Been Kissed* ends in a scene that, in any other movie, I would have hooted at. Without revealing it, I'll identify it as the five-minute wait. This scene is so contrived and artificial it could be subtitled "Shameless Audience Manipulation." But you know what? Because the wait involved Barrymore, I actually cared. Yes, I did.

The Newton Boys ★ ★
PG-13, 122 m., 1998

Matthew McConaughey (Willis Newton), Skeet Ulrich (Joe Newton), Ethan Hawke (Jess Newton), Julianna Margulies (Louise Brown), Dwight Yoakam (Brentwood Glasscock), Vincent D'Onofrio (Dock Newton), Gail Cronauer (Jess Newton), Chloe Webb (Avis Glasscock). Directed by Richard Linklater and produced by Anne Walker-McBay. Screenplay by Linklater, Claude Stanush, and Clark Lee Walker, based on the book by Stanush.

The Newton boys were the most successful bank robbers in American history, up until the savings and loan bandits of the 1980s. Operating in the Roaring Twenties, they hit as many as two hundred banks, and then pulled off the nation's biggest train robbery, a mail train heist in northern Illinois. Despite their remarkable record, they never became as famous as John Dillinger or Bonnie and Clyde. On the basis of this movie I suspect it was because they were too respectable.

The Newton Boys tells the story of the four brothers and a friend who knew how to handle nitroglycerine. Operating mostly at night, blowing up safes that were no match for their skill, they worked under a simple code: no killing, no stealing from women and children, and no snitching. According to the film, they actually managed to complete their criminal careers without shooting anybody except for one of their own brothers, by accident.

The brothers are played by a roll call of gifted young actors: Matthew McConaughey (Willis, the oldest), Skeet Ulrich (Joe), Ethan Hawke (Jess), and Vincent D'Onofrio (Dock). Dwight Yoakam is Brentwood Glasscock, their explosives expert, who pours nitro as if intensely curious about what it would feel like to be vaporized in the next nanosecond. Julianna Margulies plays Louise, the cigar-store girl who hitches up with Willis without knowing his real name or occupation, and Chloe Webb is Glasscock's approving wife. It's not an enormous cast, and yet somehow the Newtons are hard to tell apart—not in appearance, but in personality. Their dialogue mostly strikes the same musing, loquacious note.

The film chronicles their criminal career in a low-key, meandering way; we're hanging out with them more than we're being told a story. There are a lot of conversations about the profession of bank robbery—which, as a topic for conversation, is not a whole lot more interesting than double-entry bookkeeping. And when there is action (as in a scene where they're unexpectedly chased by bank guards), it plays like a pale shadow of this film's master, *Bonnie and Clyde.*

The *B&C* influences are everywhere: in the period, the clothes, the cars, the banjo music on the sound track, the reunions between brothers, the suspicions of girlfriends, and even in the character of Texas Ranger Frank Hamer, who arrests the Newtons. Hamer was the ranger forced to pose for photos with Bonnie and Clyde; to be fair, his inclusion is probably a deliberate in-joke by Richard Linklater, the director and cowriter, but the film as a whole seems drained of thrust and energy—especially compared to his earlier films.

Linklater is the talented maker of *Slacker, Dazed and Confused, Before Sunrise,* and the underrated *subUrbia.* Those have all been pigeonholed as Gen-X movies, although there's a wide range of material. What none of them lack is energy: He's intensely involved in the lives of his characters, whether the preppies of *Before Sunrise* or the losers hanging out in a strip-mall parking lot in *subUrbia.*

He just doesn't seem as interested in the Newton Boys. Sure, they were great bank robbers—but their very success may help explain why their legend hasn't placed as high in the charts as Dillinger, Baby Face Nelson, or Pretty Boy Floyd. They were efficient professionals. And the movie sits there on the screen like a biopic of traveling salesmen who crack safes instead of prospects.

The most entertaining footage in the film comes at the end, during the credits, when we see the real Willis Newton, in his eighties, being interviewed by Johnny Carson, and see scenes from a home movie interview with the real Joe Newton. Willis makes a spirited defense of their trade to Carson. Since the insurance companies were crooks, too, and since the banks always exaggerated the amount of their losses, he says, it was "just one thief a-stealing from another."

The Next Best Thing ★
PG-13, 110 m., 2000

Rupert Everett (Robert), Madonna (Abbie), Benjamin Bratt (Ben), Michael Vartan (Kevin), Malcolm Stumpf (Sam), Neil Patrick Harris (David), Illeana Douglas (Elizabeth Ryder), Josef Sommer (Richard Whittaker), Lynn Redgrave (Helen Whittaker). Directed by John Schlesinger and produced by Tom Rosenberg, Leslie Dixon, and Linne Radmin. Screenplay by Thomas Ropelewski.

The Next Best Thing is a garage sale of gay issues, harnessed to a plot as exhausted as a junk man's horse. There are times when the characters don't know if they're living their lives or enacting edifying little dramas for an educational film. The screenplay's so evenhanded it has *no* likable characters, either gay or straight; after seeing this film, I wanted to move to Garry Shandling's world in *What Planet Are You From?* where nobody has sex.

Not that anybody has a lot of sex in this PG-13 film. The story hinges on a murky alcoholic night spent by Abbie (Madonna) and her gay best friend Robert (Rupert Everett). They were both in drunken blackouts, although of course by the next morning they're able to discuss their blackouts with wit and style, unlike your average person, who would be puking. Abbie gets pregnant and decides to have the baby, and Robert announces he will be a live-in father to the child, although he doesn't go so far as to become a husband to its mother.

Both Abbie and Robert are right up-to-date when it comes to sexual open-mindedness. Robert still dates, and Abbie's okay with that, although when Abbie meets a guy named Ben (Benjamin Bratt), Robert turns into a green-eyed monster. That's because Ben wants to marry Abbie and move to New York, and where would that leave Robert? If you think this movie, which begins as a sexual comedy, is going to end up as a stultifying docudrama about child custody, with big courtroom scenes before the obligatory stern black female judge, you are no more than ordinarily prescient.

The movie's problem is that it sees every side of all issues. It sides with Robert's need to be a father, and Benjamin's need to be a husband and lover, and Abbie's need to have a best friend, a husband, a lover, a son, and a lawyer. Luckily there is plenty of money for all of this, because Abbie is a yoga instructor and Robert is a gardener, and we know what piles of money you can make in those jobs, especially in the movies. I wish the film had scaled its lifestyles to the realities of service industry workers, instead of having the characters live in the kinds of places where they can dance around the living room to (I am not kidding) Fred Astaire's "Steppin' Out With My Baby" and have catered backyard birthday parties that I clock at $10,000, easy.

In describing the plot, I've deliberately left out two or three twists that had me stifling groans of disbelief. It's not that they're implausible; it's that they're not necessary. Any movie is bankrupt anyway when it depends on Perry Mason–style, last-minute, unexpected courtroom appearances to solve what should be an emotional choice.

Rupert Everett, "openly gay," as they say, must have had to grit his teeth to get through some of his scenes. Consider a sequence where, as Abbie's best friend, he is delegated to pick up her house keys after she breaks up with her early boyfriend, Kevin ("I want to date less complicated women," Kevin tells her). Kevin is a record producer, and we see him mixing the tracks for a rap group when Robert swishes in and pretends to be his ex-lover, while there are lots of yuks from the homophobic black rappers. Give the scene credit: At least it's not politically correct.

Madonna never emerges as a plausible human being in the movie; she's more like a spokesperson for a video on alternative parenting lifestyles. She begins the movie with a quasi-British accent, but by the halfway mark we get line readings like "we can be in each other's lifes" (a Brit, and indeed many an American, would say "lives").

This and other details should have been noticed by the director, John Schlesinger, whose career has included *Midnight Cowboy, Sunday Bloody Sunday, The Falcon and the Snowman, Madame Sousatzka,* and now . . . this?

Watching the movie, I asked myself why so many movies with homosexuals feel they need to be about homosexuality. Why can't a movie just get over it? I submit as evidence the magical film *Wonder Boys,* in which the homosexuality of the character played by Robert Downey Jr. is completely absorbed into the much larger notion of who he is as a person. Nobody staggers backward and gasps out that his character is gay, because of course he's gay and everybody has known that for a long time and, hey, some people *are* gay, y'know? Watching *The Next Best Thing,* we suspect that if sexuality were banned as a topic of conversation,

Abbie and Robert would be reduced to trading yoga and gardening tips. ☞

Niagara, Niagara ★ ★ ★
R, 93 m., 1998

Robin Tunney (Marcy), Henry Thomas (Seth), Michael Parks (Walter), Stephen Lang (Claude), John MacKay (Seth's Father), Alan Pottinger (Lot Cop), Sol Frieder (Pawn Broker), Candy Clark (Sally). Directed by Bob Gosse and produced by David L. Bushell. Screenplay by Matthew Weiss.

Niagara, Niagara is about two misfits who become lovers and hit the road, where the cruel world boots them toward a tragic conclusion. This is not a new idea, as the current revival of *Badlands* (1973) reminds us. But the movie contains three strong performances and a subject I haven't seen before: the affliction of Tourette's syndrome.

Marcy (Robin Tunney) and Seth (Henry Thomas) meet while shoplifting. In the parking lot outside the store, they share a broken conversation, until Marcy finally admits that she can't look at people while talking to them and notices that Seth can't either: "I like that." Outsiders and loners, they fall into one another's arms by default, and Seth is too shy or uncertain to show that he notices her sometimes strange behavior.

She levels with him: She has Tourette's syndrome, which in her case takes the form of sudden tics, contortions, arm-flailing, bursts of aggressive behavior, and acting out. There's medication to control it. And she constantly takes little drinks out of a flask because booze seems to help. "And sex helps. For some reason, sex helps."

We get a glimpse of their home lives. Seth lives with a violent, abusive father. Marcy lives in a cluttered school bus behind a mansion that I assume belongs to her parents. She has always wanted a "black Barbie head," but cannot find one on local shelves, so they decide to run away together. Maybe she can find one in Toronto.

The parabola of a road movie is as reassuring as a nursery rhyme. It is required that the heroes drive a full-sized American car, preferably an older model. That there be long shots showing them on the open road. That there be a montage of the roadside sights and signs. And eventually that there be a collision with the unbending requirements of society.

Marcy needs pills. They try to get them from a drugstore. They don't have a prescription. Since the medication she needs isn't a controlled substance, it's likely she could find someone to prescribe it for her, maybe in a free clinic, but no: They stick up the store that night, Seth is wounded, their car overturns in the getaway, and then the movie's strange, enchanted centerpiece begins.

They're found by an old geezer named Walter (Michael Parks) in a tow truck. He takes them to his ramshackle spread, tends the wound, and tells them of his late wife, whom he loved, and his favorite chicken, which he still loves. Seth is afraid of fish, but somehow finds the courage to go fishing with Walter. The writing and acting here blossom, and we get a glimpse of how the movie might have developed without the road formula to contain it.

What happens later in their journey I shall not reveal. We do indeed see Niagara Falls, which inspires some easy symbolism, and we do eventually see the rare Barbie head. But what disappointed me was the film's need to hold itself within the narrow requirements of the genre.

How many times have we seen Tourette's syndrome on the screen? Hardly ever. So why not devise a story that would be about these two characters and their problems, rather than plugging them into a road movie? They're packaged much as Barbie comes boxed in different roles. The movie is good, but could have been better if it has been set free to explore.

Robin Tunney is sometimes scary, she's so good at conveying her character's torment (she won the Best Actress Award at Venice). And Henry Thomas, who fifteen years ago was the little boy in *E.T.*, has developed into a fine actor, able to be quiet and absorbed. The materials were here for a different kind of film, in which the souls of the characters had an effect on the outcome. In *Niagara, Niagara*, we want to warn them there's no hope. They're in the wrong genre for that.

A Night at the Roxbury ★
PG-13, 84 m., 1998

Will Ferrell (Steve Butabi), Chris Kattan (Doug Butabi), Molly Shannon (Emily Sanderson), Richard Grieco (Himself), Loni Anderson (Barbara Butabi), Dan Hedaya (Kamehl Butabi), Chazz Palminteri (Club Owner), Elisa Donovan (Cambi), Gigi Rice (Vivica), Lochlyn Munro (Craig). Directed by John Fortenberry and produced by Lorne Michaels and Amy Heckerling. Screenplay by Steve Koren, Will Ferrell, and Chris Kattan.

D. Kepesh of Chicago writes: "Do you ever find yourself distracted during a screening by thoughts of the review you will later write? Distracted to the point of missing part of the film?" Sometimes it gets much worse than that, D. Sometimes a movie is so witless that I abandon any attempt to think up clever lines for my review, and return in defeat to actually watching the film itself. I approach it as an opportunity for meditation. My mantra is "aargh . . . aargh. . . ."

A Night at the Roxbury is such a movie. It's based on the *Saturday Night Live* skits about the Butabi brothers, Steve and Doug (Will Ferrell and Chris Kattan), who snap their heads in unison with the music and each other, while trying out pickup lines in spectacularly unlikely situations. I liked the first sixty seconds of the first Butabi brothers sketch I saw because I found the head-snapping funny. Apart from that, I relate to the sketches basically as a waste of the talent of Kattan, who as Mr. Peepers, the Missing Link, is very funny.

No doubt we will get a Mr. Peepers movie one of these days. Lorne Michaels seems determined to spin out every one of the *SNL* characters into a feature-length movie—even if this one barely makes it to that length (the studio pegs it at eighty-four minutes but I didn't stay for the closing credits and was out in closer to seventy-five).

The sad thing about *A Night at the Roxbury* is that the characters are in a one-joke movie, and they're the joke. The premise: The Butabi brothers work for their dad (Dan Hedaya) in his artificial flower store. They still live at home with Dad and Mom (Loni Anderson), but dream of meeting great chicks in Los Angeles night clubs, where the bouncers treat them like target practice. Finally they get inside on the coattails of TV star Richard Grieco (playing himself, none too well), find a wonderland of improbably buxom babes (Elisa Donovan and Gigi Rice), and get picked up under the mistaken impression that they're part of Grieco's entourage. One suspects that the movie is poking fun at Grieco, but the cues are so muddled that on the other hand, maybe not. The whole party moves on to the home of the club's owner (Chazz Palminteri in an unbilled role), where the brothers demonstrate that, for them, getting lucky and falling in love are synonymous.

Meanwhile, Emily (Molly Shannon), daughter of the man who owns the store next door, dreams of marrying Steve so her dad can merge their retail empires. She's up-front about sex (especially as a means of fulfilling her business ambitions), and although the boys would rather throw themselves away on mindless bimbos, they're no match for her strategy, perhaps because the boys *are* mindless bimbos.

Steve and Doug, who took seven years to graduate from high school, still share the same bedroom, which seems to have been decorated when they were in junior high. They have a falling out and Doug moves into the pool house. And then there's an engagement, and a wedding, and . . . the script fairly wheezes with exhaustion. *A Night at the Roxbury* probably never had a shot at being funny anyway, but I don't think it planned to be pathetic. It's the first comedy I've attended where you feel that to laugh would be cruel to the characters.

Nightwatch ★ ★
R, 105 m., 1998

Ewan McGregor (Martin Bells), Nick Nolte (Inspector Gray), Josh Brolin (James), Patricia Arquette (Katherine), Alix Koromzay (Joyce), Lauren Graham (Marie), Erich Anderson (Newscaster), Lonny Chapman (Old Watchman), Scott Burkholder (College Professor), Brad Dourif (Duty Doctor). Directed by Ole Bornedal and produced by Michael Obel. Screenplay by Bornedal and Steven Soderbergh, based on the film *Nattevagten* by Bornedal.

Horror films often bring out the best in a director's style but not in his intelligence. *Nightwatch* is an example. It's a visually effective and often scary film to watch, but the story is so leaky that we finally just give up: Scene after scene exists only to toy with us and prop up the impossible plot.

Ewan McGregor, from *Trainspotting,* stars as Martin Bells, a law student who takes a night watchman's job in the local morgue. It's a creepy building, not improved by two giant pine trees that flank the doors and have been wrapped in plastic, so that they look like swaying bodies in huge garbage bags.

Inside, we find the usual lighting problem: Corridors have small bulbs and are spooky, but the cold room for the corpses is brightly lit so we can see what we don't much want to see. The building itself has a certain eerie charm, with its large empty spaces and its institutional chill.

There's a nice sequence with Lonny Chapman as the retiring watchman, who shows the kid the ropes, filling him in on creepy old stories, and entreating, "Get a radio!" Much is made of the alarm that will go off if one of the corpses should suddenly come to life ("It's not going to happen," the old man assures Martin). The story is repeated about a watchman from "several years ago," who was dismissed in a messy scandal. There are murky shots of vats of chemicals, one of which, Martin is disturbed to discover, contains "feet—nothing but feet!"

Of course, the watchman's rounds include a time clock on the far wall of the cold room, which must be punched once an hour. (The morgue door has no handle on the inside, which if you really think about it makes sense, from the point of view of the corpses.) Each marble palette has a cord above it, within reach of a body that returns to life, although in the absolute dark of the storage room it would be a clever resurrectionist who thought to wave his hand in search of it.

The other characters: Martin's best friend, James (Josh Brolin), who gets in bar fights because he likes the rush ("my tolerance level has increased"). Martin's girlfriend, Katherine (Patricia Arquette), who puts up with his bad breath, a by-product of working around formaldehyde. The creepy doctor (Brad Dourif) who works in the morgue. The frightened hooker (Alix Koromzay), who has a client who wants her to play dead. And the cop, Inspector Gray (Nick Nolte), who is sad, rumpled, and wise, and warns Martin that he is being framed for murder: "There's someone really dangerous standing right behind you."

One of these people is responsible for a series of murders of local prostitutes. I was able to guess which one in the opening credits, although I wasn't sure I was right for a while—and the movie gives him (or her) away in such a sneaky way that for a moment there even seems to be another explanation for his (or her) presence at the murder scene.

The movie is a remake of *Nattevagten,* a Danish film by Ole Bornedal, who also directed this English-language version. Dimension Films bought the original film, a hit in Europe, and kept it off the market here while producing the retread, no doubt to forestall the kinds of unfavorable comparisons that came up when the Dutch director George Sluizer remade his brilliant *The Vanishing* (1988) into a sloppy, spineless 1993 American film.

I haven't seen *Nattevagten,* and don't know how it compares with *Nightwatch,* but this film depends so heavily on horror effects, blind alleys, false leads, and red herrings that eventually watching it stops being an experience and becomes an exercise.

Nil by Mouth ★ ★ ★ ½
R, 128 m., 1998

Ray Winstone (Raymond), Kathy Burke (Valerie), Charlie Creed-Miles (Billy), Laila Morse (Janet), Edna Dore (Kath), Chrissie Coterill (Paula), Jon Morrison (Angus), Jamie Forman (Mark), Steve Sweeney (Danny). Directed by Gary Oldman and produced by Luc Besson, Douglas Urbanski, and Oldman. Screenplay by Oldman.

Gary Oldman's *Nil by Mouth* descends into a domestic hell of violence, drugs, and booze, where a man can kick his pregnant wife and then, drunk, scrape out the words "My Baby" on the wallpaper with his bloody fingernails. It takes place in the pubs and streets of South London, where the actor grew up, and is dedicated enigmatically, "In memory of my fa-

ther." We want to stand back out of the way; something primal, needful, and anguished is going on here.

Using a handheld camera and close-up style, Oldman plunges into the middle of this family as they spend a night at their local pub. At first we don't understand all the relationships, but Oldman uses the right approach: These people know each other so intimately and in such fearsome ways that any "establishing" scenes would dilute the impact.

The center of authority in the film is Janet (Laila Morse), the worn blond mother whose factory job is one of the family's few steady sources of income. Her own aged, feisty mother, Kath (Edna Dore), is still around. Janet's daughter is Valerie (Kathy Burke, who won the Best Actress award at Cannes). Val's husband, Ray (Ray Winstone), is a violent drunk whose rage alternates with self-pity. Val's brother, Janet's son, is Billy (Charlie Creed-Miles). He has a drug habit. Ray's best friend Mark (Jamie Forman) is emotionally dependent on him— maybe he's an excitement junkie, who feeds on the moments when Ray explodes.

This family weeps, bleeds, and endures. Billy, who lives with Val and Ray, is thrown out of the house after some money is missing; Ray beats him and bites his nose, and Billy staggers into a bleak dawn—homeless, although he still lives on the outskirts of the family, like a wounded wolf following the pack.

A day or so later, Ray walks into a pub and finds his wife, Val, playing pool with a casual friend. Ray seems cheerful at first, but he has the personality changes of the alcoholic, and orders her home, where he weeps and explodes in a jealous rage, sure Val (who is large with child) was having an affair with the man. She miscarries after his beating.

One of the film's key scenes comes after Val returns home and is seen, black, blue, and bandaged, by her mother. She tells Janet she was struck by a hit-and-run driver. Janet clearly knows Ray beat her daughter, but accepts the story. The dialogue here is precise in its observation; Val's details all have to do with the location ("You know, down by the shops"), as if the story is proven by the fact that the shops exist. Her mother vows revenge on the bastard driver who committed the hit and run; both women understand this is code for Ray. ("You know what it's like going to hospitals late at night," Janet says at one point. In most healthy families this is not something everyone knows.)

The film's portrait of street life in South London is unflinching and observant. Billy, drifting, looking for a fix, gets involved in a strange fight over a tattooed street person and his little pet dog. He goes to his mother's factory to borrow money for a fix, and then asks her to drive him to a dealer. Back in her van, he starts to shoot up, and she snaps, "Get in the back of the van where no one can see you." Just like a mother. The cost of Billy's habit is something Janet knows, just as in another family the mother would know the size of her son's paycheck.

Gary Oldman is clearly dealing here with autobiographical wounds. I saw him after the film played at Cannes, and he volunteered the information that a chair in the film is the same one his father sat in while drinking at home. He spoke in a flat voice, giving information, but I sensed that the chair was still occupied by the stabbing ghosts of days and words.

Yet *Nil by Mouth* is not an unrelieved shriek of pain. There is humor in it, and tender insight. After he almost kills himself on a bender, Ray is hospitalized, and Mark visits him. In a monologue brilliantly delivered by Winstone, Ray complains about the lack of love from his own father: "Not one kiss. Not one cuddle." In Ray's mind, he is the abused child. We sense Oldman's ability to understand, if not forgive.

At the beginning of *Nil by Mouth* we cannot understand the South London dialect very easily, and aren't sure who all the characters are. By the end, we know this family and we understand everything they say, and many things they do not say. And we remember another very minor character in the film, the small child of Ray and Val, who sits at the top of the stairs during a bloody fight and sees everything.

Footnote: Dedicated to Oldman's father, the film is filled with personal touches. The actress who plays Janet, billed as "Laila Morse," is the author's sister; her stage name is an anagram of "my sister" in Italian. When Kath sings "Can't Help Lovin' That Man" over the closing credits, the voice dubbed onto the track belongs to Oldman's seventy-five-year-old mother. And that is his father's chair.

The Ninth Gate ★ ★
R, 132 m., 2000

Johnny Depp (Dean Corso), Frank Langella (Boris Balkan), Lena Olin (Liana Telfer), Emmanuelle Seigner (The Girl), Barbara Jefford (Baroness Kessler), Jack Taylor (Victor Fargas), Jose Lopez Rodero (Ceniza Brothers), Toni Amoni (Liana's Bodyguard). Directed and produced by Roman Polanski. Screenplay by Enrique Urbizu, Polanski, and John Brownjohn, based on the novel *El Club Dumas* by Arturo Perez Reverte.

Roman Polanski's *The Ninth Gate,* a satanic thriller, opens with a spectacularly good title sequence and goes downhill from there—but slowly, so that all through the first hour there is reason for hope, and only gradually do we realize the movie isn't going to pay off. It has good things in it, and I kept hoping Polanski would take the plot by the neck and shake life into it, but no. After the last scene, I underlined on my notepad: "What?"

The film stars Johnny Depp in a strong if ultimately unaimed performance, as Dean Corso, a rare-book dealer whose ethics are optional. He's hired by Boris Balkan (Frank Langella), a millionaire collector who owns a copy of *The Nine Gates of the Kingdom of the Shadows,* published in Venice in 1666 by one Aristide Torchia—who, legend has it, adapted the engravings from the work of Satan himself. Two other copies of the book survive, and Balkan wants Depp to track them down and compare the engravings.

Torchia was burned to death by the Inquisition, and indeed Andrew Telfer, one of the recent owners of the book, hangs himself in an early scene, after selling his copy to Balkan. Liana (Lena Olin), his widow, tries to appear indifferent, but has an unwholesome interest in getting the book back. Corso flies to Europe and meets the other two owners, a stately aristocrat (Jack Taylor) in Portugal and an elderly Parisian baroness (Barbara Jefford) in a wheelchair.

What's best about Corso's quest is the way he conducts it. Depp and Polanski bring a *film noir* feel to the film; we're reminded of Bogart pretending to be a rare-book buyer in *The Big Sleep.* As Corso moves from one bizarre millionaire collector to another, he narrowly avoids several threats on his life and realizes he's being followed by a young woman (Emmanuelle Seigner), whose purpose and identity remain obscure, although at one point she uses martial arts to save his life, and at another point we (but not he) see her fly.

The secret of the engravings in the three editions of the book will not be revealed here. Nor will various additional motives of Balkan, the Telfer widow, and the inexplicable young woman. Their stories are told with a meticulous attention to details, which are persuasive until we realize they are accumulating instead of adding up. If some of the engravings were indeed drawn by Satan, and if assembling them can evoke the Prince of Darkness, then that would be a threat, right? Or would it be a promise? And what happens at the end—that would be an unspeakably evil outcome, right? But why does it look somehow like a victory? And as for the woman—good or bad? Friend or foe? You tell me.

What's intriguing about the material is the way Polanski trusts its essential fascination, and doesn't go for cheesy special effects, as in the Schwarzenegger thriller *End of Days*. Satan need not show himself with external signs, but can work entirely within human nature, which is, after all, his drafting board. When Corso goes to visit the baroness in her wheelchair, I was reminded of Bogart's similar call on an elderly eccentric in *The Big Sleep*, and I relished a sequence where Corso calls on two booksellers, the twin Ceniza brothers, who in a neat f/x touch are played by one actor, Jose Lopez Rodero.

The movie does a good job of mirroring its deaths with situations from the Tarot deck, and making the Telfer widow (Olin) more sinister by (I think) inserting electronic undertones beneath her speech. I also liked the atmosphere evoked by the dialogue, which isn't too dumbed down, uses some of the jargon of the book trade, and allows us to follow Corso's process of deduction as he figures out what the engravings mean and what Balkan's true motives are. It's just that a film of such big themes should be about more than the fate of a few people; while at the end I didn't yearn for spectacular special effects, I did wish for spectacular information—something awesome, not just a fade to white. ☞

No Looking Back ★ ★
R, 96 m., 1998

Jon Bon Jovi (Michael), Edward Burns (Charlie), Lauren Holly (Claudia), Connie Britton (Kelly), Blythe Danner (Claudia's Mom), Jennifer Esposito (Teresa), Shari Albert (Shari), Kathleen Doyle (Mrs. Ryan). Directed by Edward Burns and produced by Ted Hope, Michael Nozik, and Burns. Screenplay by Burns.

Hobbies. That's what the characters in *No Looking Back* need. Bowling or yard sales or watching the Knicks on television. Anything. Although the movie wants us to feel sympathy for them, trapped in meager lives and empty dreams, I saw them as boring slugs. There is more to existence than moping about at bars and kitchen tables, whining about unhappiness while endlessly sipping from long-neck Budweiser bottles. Get a life.

The movie is the latest from Ed Burns, who won the Sundance Film Festival in 1995 with his rich and moving *The Brothers McMullen*, but has since made two thin and unconvincing films: *She's the One* (1996) and now this one, in which self-absorbed characters fret over their lives. I have no brief against that subject matter; I simply wish the characters and their fretting were more interesting, or their unhappiness less avoidable.

The film is set in the bleak, wintry landscape of Rockaway Beach, New York, where Claudia (Lauren Holly) works in a diner and lives with Michael (Jon Bon Jovi), a mechanic. They are engaged, in a sense, but with no plans for marriage; Michael wants to marry her, but she's "afraid to wake up ten years from now" still working in the diner.

As the film opens, Charlie (Edward Burns) returns to town on the bus after an absence of three years. He was once Claudia's lover, but ditched her without a farewell. Now he apparently hopes to pick up where they left off. He moves into his mother's house; she has his number and tells him to get a job. And then Michael, who was his best friend, comes over for more beer and conversation, and explains that he and Claudia are "together" now.

Will Claudia accept the dependable Michael? Or will she be swept off her feet once again by the flashier, more charismatic Charlie? "It's different this time," he tells her. "This time I need you. I love you." He's not the soul of eloquence, but she is willing to be persuaded.

The problem is, Charlie is an enigma. Where was he for three years? Why is he back? What are his skills, his plans, his strategies? His vision for the two of them is not inspiring: They'll leave town and go to Florida, where he has no prospects, and "start over." Still, Charlie paints a seductive picture.

Or does he? The film wants us to see Michael, the Bon Jovi character, as a boring, safe, faithful, but unexciting choice. But I sort of liked him; Bon Jovi plays the role for its strengths, which involve sincerity and a certain bottom line of integrity. Charlie, on the other hand, is one of those men who believe that true happiness, for a woman, consists of doing what he wants. He offers Claudia not freedom, but the choice of living in his shadow instead of her own.

The story plays out during overcast days and chilly nights, in lonely barrooms and rented houses. Some small life is provided by Claudia's family, which includes her mother (Blythe Danner) and her sister. The mother is convinced her husband, who has deserted her, will return someday. The sister is dating the local fishmonger. As the three women discuss the comings and goings of the men in their lives, they scheme like some of Jane Austen's dimmer characters, for whom the advent of the right man is about the most a girl can hope for.

It is extremely important to some men that the woman of their choice sleep with them. This is a topic not of much interest to outside observers, and often not even to the woman of their choice. *No Looking Back* is really only about whether Claudia will sleep with Charlie, stay with Michael, or leave town. As the characters unhappily circled those possibilities, I felt like asking Claudia to call me back when she made up her mind.

Not One Less ★ ★ ★
G, 100 m., 2000

Wei Minzhi (Herself [Young Student]), Zhang Huike (Himself [Young Student]), Tian Zhenda (Mayor Tian), Gao Enman (Teacher Gao), Feng Yuying (TV Receptionist), Li Fanfan (TV Host).

Directed by Zhang Yimou and produced by Zhao Yu. Screenplay by Shi Xiangsheng.

Not One Less is not only about the poor in China's remote rural areas, but could be dedicated to them; we sense that Zhang Yimou, the director of such sophisticated films as *Raise the Red Lantern* and *Shanghai Triad*, is returning here to memories of the years from 1968 to 1978, when he worked as a rural laborer under the Cultural Revolution. His story is simple, unadorned, direct. Only the margins are complicated.

The actors are not professionals, but local people, playing characters with their own names. Wei Minzhi, a red-cheeked thirteen-year-old who usually looks very intent, stars as Wei, a substitute teacher, also very intent. The village's schoolmaster has been called away to his mother's deathbed, and Wei's assignment is to teach his grade school class.

To assist her in this task, she is supplied with one piece of chalk for every day the teacher will be away. And she gets strict instructions: Since the school's subsidy depends on its head count, she is to return the full class to the teacher—"not one less." Keeping all the students in class is more important than anything she teaches them, and indeed she isn't a lot more advanced than her students. This isn't one of those movies where the inspired teacher awakens the minds and spirits of her class; Wei copies lessons on the board and blocks the door.

These early scenes are interesting in the way they don't exploit the obvious angles of the story. This isn't a pumped-up melodrama or an inspirational tearjerker, but a matter-of-fact look at a poor, rural area where necessity is the mother of invention and everything else.

When one of her students, Zhang (Zhang Huike), runs away to look for work in the big city, Wei determines to follow him and bring him back. This is not an easy task. It involves buying a bus ticket, and that means raising the money for the ticket. Wei puts the whole class to work shifting bricks for a local factory to earn the funds. She eventually does get to the city, Jiangjiakou, and her encounters with bureaucracy there are a child's shadow of the heroine's problems in Zhang Yimou's famous film *The Story of Qui Ju* (1992).

417

The city scenes were not as compelling for me as the earlier ones, maybe because Wei's patience tried my own. She waits what seems like forever outside the gates of a TV studio, hoping to talk to the man in charge, and although her determination is admirable, it could have been suggested in less screen time. Once she does get on TV, there's a moment of absolute authenticity when the anchorwoman asks her a question, and Wei just stares dumbfounded at the camera.

For Chinese viewers, this film will play as a human drama (end titles mention how many children drop out of school in China every year). For Western viewers, there's almost equal interest at the edges of the screen, in the background, in the locations and incidental details that show daily life in today's China. One of the buried messages is the class divide that exists even today in the People's Republic, where TV bureaucrats live in a different world than thirteen-year-old rural schoolgirls. Zhang Yimou, whose films have sometimes landed him in trouble with the authorities, seems to have made a safe one this time. But in the margins he may be making comments of his own.

Note: Parents looking for intelligent films for children might consider Not One Less. *Like the Chinese film* King of Masks *and the Iranian film* Children of Heaven *(both available on video), it has subtitles, but none too difficult for a good young reader.*

Notting Hill ★ ★ ★
PG-13, 125 m., 1999

Julia Roberts (Anna Scott), Hugh Grant (William Thacker), Richard McCabe (Tony), Rhys Ifans (Spike), Emma Chambers (Honey), Tim McInnerny (Max), Gina McKee (Bella), Hugh Bonneville (Bernie), James Dreyfus (Martin). Directed by Roger Michell and produced by Duncan Kenworthy. Screenplay by Richard Curtis.

Well of course the moment we see Julia Roberts and Hugh Grant together on the screen, we want to see them snoggling, but a romantic comedy like *Notting Hill* is about delaying the inevitable. After all, two different worlds they live in. Her character, Anna, is one of the most famous movie stars in the world. His character, William, runs a modest little travel bookshop in London. We know they're destined for one another, but we're always quicker to see these things than the characters are.

Notting Hill reassembles three of the key players from *Four Weddings and a Funeral* (1994), which made Hugh Grant a star: Grant, screenwriter Richard Curtis, and producer Duncan Kenworthy. In the earlier film Grant fell for a beautiful American (Andie MacDowell), and that's what happens this time too. And both films surround the romantic couple with a large, cheerful assortment of weird but lovable friends.

The film, of course, begins with a Meet Cute; she wanders into his bookstore, enjoys the way he handles a would-be shoplifter, and their eyes, as they say, meet. He tries to keep his cool, although he's as agog as if she were, well, Julia Roberts. She acknowledges his unspoken adoration, and is grateful that it remains unspoken, and although there's enough electricity between them to make their hair stand on end, she leaves. They will have to meet again. If there's one thing this movie has, luckily, it's an endless supply of Meet Cutes. The next time they meet, it's by accident, and he spills orange juice all over her. That leads to an invitation to clean up at his nearby flat, which leads to some flirtatious dialogue and a kiss, but then they separate again.

Will Anna and William never find the happiness they deserve? We slap our foreheads in frustration for them. Eventually they meet again during her press junket at the Ritz Hotel, where he is mistaken for a journalist, identifies himself as the film critic for *Horse & Hound* magazine, and quizzes her about her horses—and hounds, I think. The absurdities of a press junket are actually pretty clearly seen, allowing for some comic exaggeration, and the movie is more realistic about the world of a movie star than I expected it to be.

Anna Scott, the Julia Roberts character, is seen not simply as a desirable woman, but as a complicated one, whose life doesn't make it easy for her to be happy. There are moments of insight in the middle of this comedy that bring the audience to that kind of hushed silence you get when truths are told. One comes when Roberts looks into the camera and predicts Anna's future: "One day my looks will go, and I'll be a sad middle-aged woman who looks like someone who was famous for a while." Another comes when she kids with the bookseller that the price of her beauty was two painful operations. She points silently to her nose and her chin. Is Roberts talking about herself? Doesn't matter. The scene is based on a fact of life: Anyone who gets paid $15 million a picture is going to perform the necessary maintenance and upkeep.

To be beautiful and famous is, the movie argues, to risk losing ordinary human happiness. The first "date" between Anna and William is at his sister's birthday party, where a mixed bag of friends take her more or less at face value, and allow her to enjoy what is arguably the first normal evening she's had in years. There are other moments when they are basically just a boy and a girl, hand in hand, wandering at night through London. And then her "real life" kicks in, complete with a movie star boyfriend (Alec Baldwin) who thinks William is from room service.

From *Four Weddings,* we remember the extended family and friends such as Simon Callow, so good as the gay friend who has the heart attack. In *Notting Hill* William's circle includes his airhead sister Honey (Emma Chambers); his best friend Max (Tim McInnerny); Max's beloved wife, Bella (Gina McKee), who is in a wheelchair; and his stockbroker pal Bernie

(Hugh Bonneville), who is like one of those friends we all accumulate—boring, but reassuring to have around. William also has a Welsh roommate named Spike (Rhys Ifans), who seems to regard his bodily functions as performance art. These friends and others, like a restaurant owner, represent a salt-of-the-earth alternative to Anna's showbiz satellites.

The movie is bright, the dialogue has wit and intelligence, and Roberts and Grant are very easy to like. By the end, as much as we're aware of the ancient story machinery groaning away below deck, we're smiling. I have, however, two quibbles. The first involves the personality of Grant's character. Nobody is better at being diffident, abashed, and self-effacing than Hugh Grant, but there comes a point here where the diffidence becomes less a manner, more of a mannerism. Hint: Once a woman spends the night with you, you can stop apologizing for breathing in her presence.

My other problem is with the sound track, which insists on providing a running commentary in the form of song lyrics that explain everything. There is a moment, for example, when Anna disappears from William's life, and he is sad and lonely and mopes about the city. A few violins and maybe some wind in the trees would have been fine. Instead, the sound track assaults us with "Ain't No Sunshine When She's Gone," which is absolutely the last thing we need to be told.

O

The Object of My Affection ★ ★
R, 111 m., 1998

Jennifer Aniston (Nina Borowski), Paul Rudd (George Hanson), John Pankow (Vince McBride), Alan Alda (Sidney Miller), Tim Daly (Dr. Robert Joley), Nigel Hawthorne (Rodney Fraser), Allison Janney (Constance Miller), Amo Gulinello (Paul James). Directed by Nicholas Hytner and produced by Laurence Mark. Screenplay by Wendy Wasserstein, based on the novel by Stephen McCauley.

There is a movie fighting to get out of *The Object of My Affection*, and I like it better than the movie it's trapped in. It involves a wise old man who has arrived at some useful insights about life. If they did spin-offs of movie characters the way they do on TV, he'd be in a movie of his own.

Alas, this touching and fascinating character is mired in the worst kind of sitcom—a serious one (seriocom?). *The Object of My Affection* deals with some real issues and has scenes that work, but you can see the wheels of the plot turning so clearly that you doubt the characters have much freedom to act on their own.

The story involves a social worker named Nina (Jennifer Aniston) and a first-grade teacher named George (Paul Rudd). Nina is engaged to a creep named Vince (John Pankow), and George is living with a literary critic named Robert (Tim Daly), who, like all Bernard Shaw experts, can afford a BMW convertible and a luxurious apartment in Manhattan. At a dinner party, Nina finds out that Robert is leaving George, and tells George—alas, before Robert has. George is crushed, but soon has moved into Nina's Brooklyn apartment, where they will live as good friends.

Then Nina gets pregnant. Vince, the father, keeps talking about "our" baby until Nina announces it is her baby and she has no plans to marry Vince, and Vince stalks out after declaring, "I never want to see you again," a line that sounds for all the world like a screenwriter's convenience to get him out of the cluttered plot for a scene or two. Nina, who really likes George, asks him to share the fathering: They could be a couple in everything but sex. George agrees, but then he falls for Paul (Amo Gulinello), and Nina feels hurt and jealous.

All of this material, which is promising, is dealt with on that level where characters are not quite allowed to be as perceptive and intelligent as real people might be in the same circumstances. That's because they're shuttled hither and yon by the plot structure, which requires, of course, a false crisis and false dawn (Nina and George dance to "You Were Meant for Me") before the real crisis and real dawn. At least we're spared a live childbirth scene, although to be sure, we do get the listening-to-the-embryo's-heartbeat scene.

Aniston and Rudd are appealing together; however, Pankow's crudely written role puts him through bewildering personality shifts. But then, suddenly, a character walks in from nowhere and becomes the movie's center of interest. This is the aging drama critic Rodney, played by Oscar nominee Nigel Hawthorne of *The Madness of King George.* He is gay, and Paul is his young protégé. They do not have sex, Paul makes clear to George. But Rodney clearly loves the young man, and there are a couple of scenes in which he says and does nothing, and achieves a greater emotional effect than is reached by any dialogue in the movie.

He also offers Nina hard-won advice: In the long run, her arrangement with George will not work. "Don't fix your life so that you're left alone just at the middle of it," he says, and we sense that the movie has quieted down and found its focus and purpose. You ask yourself, what would the whole film have been like if it had been written and acted at this level? The answer, sadly, is—not much like *The Object of My Affection.*

October Sky ★ ★ ★ ½
PG, 108 m., 1999

Jake Gyllenhaal (Homer Hickam), Chris Cooper (John Hickam), Laura Dern (Miss Riley), Chris Owen (Quentin), William Lee Scott (Roy Lee), Chad Lindberg (Odell), Natalie Canerday (Elsie Hickam), Scott Thomas (Jim Hickam), Chris Ellis

(Principal). Directed by Joe Johnston and produced by Charles Gordon and Larry Franco. Screenplay by Lewis Colick, based on the book *Rocket Boys* by Homer H. Hickam Jr.

Like the hero of *October Sky,* I remember the shock that ran through America when the Russians launched *Sputnik* on October 4, 1957. Like the residents of Coalwood, West Virgina, in the movie, I joined the neighbors out on the lawn, peering into the sky with binoculars at a speck of moving light that was fairly easy to see. Unlike Homer Hickam, I didn't go on to become a NASA scientist or train astronauts. But I did read Willy Ley's *Rockets, Missiles and Space Travel* three or four times, and Arthur Clarke's *The Making of a Moon.* I got their autographs, too, just as Homer sends away for a signed photo of Werner von Braun.

That first shabby piece of orbiting hardware now seems like a toy compared to the space station, the shuttle, and the missions to the moon and beyond. But it had an impact that's hard to describe to anyone who takes satellite TV for granted. For the first time in history, man had built something that went up, but did not come down—not for a long time, anyway. *Sputnik* was a tiny but audacious defiance of the universe.

October Sky tells the story of four boys in a poverty-stricken corner of Appalachia who determine to build their own rocket and help get America back in the "space race." It's seen through the eyes of their leader, young Homer Hickham (Jake Gyllenhaal), who sees the speck of light in the sky and starts reading the science fiction of Jules Verne. Homer is a good student, but math and science are his weak points. He knows he needs help, and breaks all of the rules in the school lunchroom by approaching the class brain, an outcast named Quentin (Chris Owen).

They talk about rocket fuel, nozzles, velocity. Two other boys get involved: Roy Lee (William Lee Scott) and Odell (Chad Lindberg). Their first rocket blows a hole in the picket fence in front of Homer's house. The second one narrowly misses some miners at the coal mine, and Homer's dad, John (Chris Cooper), the mine supervisor, forbids further experimentation and confiscates all of the "rocket stuff"

from the basement. But the kids labor on in an isolated patch of woods, building a shelter to protect themselves from exploding rockets. They talk a machinist at the mine into building them a rocket casing of stronger steel, and they use alcohol from a moonshiner as an ingredient in the fuel.

The tension in the movie is not between the boys and their rockets, but between the boys and those who think that miners' sons belong down in the mines and not up in the sky. Homer's father is not a bad man; he fights for the jobs of his men, he rescues several in a near-disaster, he injures his eye in another emergency. He wants Homer to follow in his footsteps. The mine may seem an unhealthy and hateful place to some, but when John takes Homer down for his son's first day on the job, his voice glows with poetry: "I know the mine like I know a man. I was born for this."

The high school principal (Chris Ellis) believes the job of the school to is send miners' sons down to the coal face. But a young teacher (Laura Dern) tells Homer she feels her life will have failed if some of the kids don't get out and realize their dreams. Then there's a crisis (did a rocket set a forest fire?), and a scene in which Homer and his friends use trigonometry to argue their innocence.

There have been a lot of recent movies set in high school: *She's All That, Varsity Blues, Jawbreaker.* In those movies, even the better ones, "teenagers" who look like soap stars in their twenties have lives that revolve around sex and popularity. The kids in *October Sky* look like they're in their mid-teens, and act that way too. Watching Homer get out the trig book, I was reminded how rarely high school movies have anything to do with school—with how an education is a ticket to freedom.

Perhaps because *October Sky* is based on a real memoir, Homer Hickam's *Rocket Boys,* it doesn't simplify the father into a bad guy or a tyrant. He understandably wants his son to follow in his footsteps, and one of the best elements of the movie is when the son tries to explain that in breaking free, he is respecting his father. This movie has deep values.

The Odd Couple II ★ ½
PG-13, 107 m., 1998

Jack Lemmon (Felix Ungar), Walter Matthau (Oscar Madison), Christine Baranski (Thelma), Barnard Hughes (Beaumont), Jonathan Silverman (Brucey Madison), Jean Smart (Holly), Lisa Waltz (Hannah Ungar), Mary Beth Peil (Felice). Directed by Howard Deutch and produced by Neil Simon, Robert W. Cort, and David Madden. Screenplay by Simon.

Watching Walter Matthau and Jack Lemmon make the talk show circuit, trading one-liners and barbs like a vaudeville team, I imagined a documentary simply showing them promoting this film. They're funny, familiar, edgy, and smart. *The Odd Couple II* is none of those things, and a much longer list could be made of other things it is not.

Lemmon and Matthau are perfectly suited for working together. In life as in fiction, they *are* a little like the original odd couple, Felix and Oscar: Lemmon concise and tidy, Matthau rambling, shambling, and gambling. When they're given a decent screenplay, as in the original *Odd Couple* (1968) or last year's engaging *Out to Sea*, they're fun to watch; their timing is impeccable, and you can sense their joy of work.

Odd Couple II is not, alas, such a screenplay. It has been written by the master, Neil Simon, who in this case is an emperor without any clothes. Did no one have the nerve to suggest a rewrite? To tell him that his story was slight, contrived and flat? Perhaps it seemed to the film's producers that the combination of Simon, Lemmon, Matthau, and the words "odd couple" were a sufficient guarantee of success. The difference between a creative executive and a contract signer lies precisely in the ability to see, in a case like this, that they were not. (Of course, Simon himself is one of the producers on this film, so in a way he was working without a net.)

The story opens seventeen years after Oscar and Felix last saw one another. (It's thirty years since the movie, but that would make their children middle-aged, so never mind.) Both now live in Florida, where Felix plays cards with old cronies and fusses over the snacks, while Oscar practices trying to hit his garbage can with a Hefty bag from an upper floor. They get calls: Oscar's son is engaged to marry Felix's daughter.

This inevitably requires them to fly to Los Angeles, where they plan to rent a car and drive to the town where the wedding is being held (it's "San something," but they can't remember what). Felix injures his foot while crashing into Oscar at the airport, they rent a car, the car rolls over a cliff and explodes, etc., and they find themselves in a road movie, complete with seamy motels and colorful characters along the way.

Simon's borscht-belt humor still prevails in the dialogue. ("My sister lost three pairs of dentures in the earthquake." "What did she do to eat?" "She sent out.") There are jokes about age, sex, and death, and a nice sight gag after they get a lift in a Rolls-Royce driven so slowly by a millionaire that they are passed up first by runners, and then by walkers.

But the movie has no purpose for being. That's revealed by the road movie premise: The genre is ideal for throwing characters and dialogue at situations without the bother of contriving any kind of a dramatic or comedic reason for them to be together. More honest, and maybe even funnier, would have been the story of the two old adversaries forced to be roommates in a retirement village. The movie slogs on and on, Matthau and Lemmon gamely delivering lines that may contain mechanical wit, but no impulse or dramatic purpose.

Office Space ★ ★ ★
R, 90 m., 1999

Ron Livingston (Peter), Jennifer Aniston (Joanna), Stephen Root (Milton), Gary Cole (Bill Lumbergh), David Herman (Michael Bolton), Ajay Naidu (Samir), Richard Riehle (Tom Smykowski), Diedrich Bader (Lawrence), Alexandra Wentworth (Anne). Directed by Mike Judge and produced by Michael Rotenberg and Daniel Rappaport. Screenplay by Judge, based on his *Milton* animated shorts.

Mike Judge's *Office Space* is a comic cry of rage against the nightmare of modern office life. It has many of the same complaints as *Dilbert* and the movie *Clockwatchers*—and, for that matter, the works of Kafka and the Book of Job. It is about work that crushes the spirit. Office cubicles are cells, supervisors are the wardens, and modern management theory is skewed to employ as many managers and as few workers as possible.

As the movie opens, a cubicle slave named Peter (Ron Livingston) is being reminded by his smarmy supervisor (Gary Cole) that all reports now carry a cover sheet. "Yes, I know," he says. "I forgot. It was a silly mistake. It won't happen again." Before long another manager reminds him about the cover sheets. "Yes, I know," he says. Then another manager. And another. Logic suggests that when more than one supervisor conveys the same trivial information, their jobs overlap, and all supervisors after the first one should be shredded.

Peter hates his job. So do all of his coworkers, although one of them, Milton (Stephen Root), has found refuge through an obsessive defense of his cubicle, his radio, and his stapler. Milton's cubicle is relocated so many times that eventually it appears to have no entrance or exit; he's walled in on every side. You may recognize him as the hero of cartoons that played on *Saturday Night Live,* where strangers were always arriving to use his cubicle as storage space for cardboard boxes.

Mike Judge, who gained fame through TV's *Beavis and Butt-head,* and made the droll animated film *Beavis and Butt-head Do America* (1996), has taken his *SNL Milton* cartoons as an inspiration for this live-action comedy, which uses Orwellian satirical techniques to fight the cubicle police: No individual detail of office routine is too absurd to be believed, but together they add up into stark, staring insanity.

Peter has two friends at work: Michael Bolton (David Herman) and Samir (Ajay Naidu). No, not that Michael Bolton, Michael patiently explains. They flee the office for coffee breaks (demonstrating that Starbucks doesn't really sell coffee—it sells escape from the office). Peter is in love with the waitress at the chain restaurant across the parking lot. Her name is Joanna (Jennifer Aniston), and she has problems with management too. She's required to wear a minimum of fifteen funny buttons on the suspenders of her uniform; the buttons are called "flair" in company lingo, and her manager suggests that wearing only the minimum flair suggests the wrong spirit (another waiter has "forty-five flairs" and looks like an exhibit at a trivia convention).

The movie's dialogue is smart. It doesn't just chug along making plot points. Consider, for example, Michael Bolton's plan for revenge against the company. He has a software program that would round off payments to the next-lowest penny and deposit the proceeds in his checking account. Hey, you're thinking—that's not original! A dumb movie would pretend it was. Not *Office Space,* where Peter says he thinks he's heard of that before, and Michael says, "Yeah, they did it in *Superman 3*. Also, a bunch of hackers tried it in the seventies. One got arrested."

The movie's turning point comes when Peter seeks help from an "occupational hypnotherapist." He's put in a trance with long-lasting results; he cuts work, goes fishing, guts fish at his desk, and tells efficiency experts he actually works only fifteen minutes a week. The experts like his attitude and suggest he be promoted. Meanwhile, the Milton problem is ticking like a time bomb, especially after Milton's cubicle is relocated into a basement storage area.

Office Space is like the evil twin of *Clockwatchers.* Both movies are about the ways corporations standardize office routines so that workers are interchangeable and can be paid as little as possible. *Clockwatchers* was about the lowest rung on the employment ladder—daily temps—but *Office Space* suggests that regular employment is even worse, because it's a life sentence. Asked to describe his state of mind to the therapist, Peter says, "Since I started working, every single day has been worse than the day before, so that every day you see me is the worst day of my life."

Judge, an animator until now, treats his characters a little like cartoon creatures. That works. Nuances of behavior are not necessary, because in the cubicle world every personality trait is magnified, and the captives stagger forth like grotesques. There is a moment in the movie when the heroes take a baseball bat to a malfunctioning copier. Reader, who has not felt the same?

Onegin ★ ★ ½

NO MPAA RATING, 106 m., 2000

Ralph Fiennes (Evgeny Onegin), Liv Tyler (Tatyana Larin), Toby Stephens (Vladimir Lensky), Lena Headey (Olga Larin), Martin Donovan (Prince Nikitin), Irene Worth (Princess Alina). Directed by Martha Fiennes and produced by Simon Bosanquet and Ileen Maisel. Screenplay by Michael Ignatieff and Peter Ettedgui, based on the novel by Alexander Pushkin.

Onegin is a man bemused by his own worthlessness. He has been carefully prepared by his aristocratic nineteenth-century upbringing to be unnecessary—an outside man, hanging on, looking into the lives of others. Even when he's given the opportunity to play a role, after he inherits his uncle's estate, his response is to rent the land to his serfs. In another man, this would be seen as liberalism. In Evgeny Onegin, it is more like indifference.

Onegin is a leisurely, elegant, detached retelling of Pushkin's epic verse novel, with Ralph Fiennes as the hero. It is the kind of role once automatically assigned to Jeremy Irons. Both men look as if they have stayed up too late and not eaten their greens, but Irons in the grip of passion is able to seem lost and heedless, while Fiennes suggests it is heavy lifting, with few rewards. "I am not one who is made for love and marriage," his Onegin says soulfully.

As the film opens, Onegin is returning to inherit his uncle's estate outside St. Petersburg, after having lost his own fortune at the gambling tables. He is welcomed by receptions, teas, and balls, and embraced by his neighbor, Lensky (Toby Stephens). Lensky has a young bride named Olga (Lena Headey), and she has an older sister named Tatyana (Liv Tyler), who is a lone spirit and visits Onegin's estate to borrow books from his library.

Tyler has the assignment of suggesting passionate depths beneath a cool exterior, and succeeds: She is grave and silent, with an ethereal quality that is belied by her bold use of eye contact. Onegin probably falls in love with her the first time he sees her, but is not, of course, made for love, and shrugs off his real feelings in order to enter into a flirtation with Olga, who is safely married.

Tatyana's waters run deep. She declares herself in a passionate love letter to Onegin (the moment she saw his face, she knew her heart was his, etc.), but such passion only alarms him. "Any stranger might have stumbled into your life and aroused your romantic imagination," he tells her tactlessly. "I have no secret longing to be saved from myself." "You curse yourself!" she cries, rejected. The heartless Onegin continues his dalliance with Olga. This leads to a duel with Lensky. His heart is broken when he kills his friend; that will teach him to call a nineteenth-century Russian nobleman's wife "easy."

Onegin flees to exile (or Paris, which are synonymous). Six years pass. He returns to St. Petersburg and sees Tatyana again, at a ball. But now the tables are turned, in ironic revelations and belated discoveries, and Onegin pays the price for his heartlessness.

There is a cool, mannered elegance to the picture that I like, but it's dead at its center. There is no feeling that real feelings are at risk here. Liv Tyler seems sincere enough, but Fiennes withholds too well. And the direction, by his sister Martha Fiennes, is deliberate and detached when it should perhaps plunge into the story. The visuals are wonderful, but the drama is muted.

There is a tendency to embalm classics, but never was literature more tempestuous and heartfelt than in nineteenth-century Russia. Characters joyously leap from the pages of Pushkin, Dostoyevsky, and Tolstoy, wearing their hearts on their sleeves, torn between the French schoolmasters who taught them manners, and the land where they learned passion—inhaled it, absorbed it in the womb. I know *Eugene Onegin* is a masterpiece, but the story it tells is romantic melodrama, and requires some of the same soap-opera zest as David Lean's *Dr. Zhivago*. This film has the same problem as its hero: Its manners are so good it doesn't know what it really feels.

One Tough Cop ★
R, 92 m., 1998

Stephen Baldwin (Bo Dietl), Chris Penn (Duke), Mike McGlone (Richie La Cassa), Gina Gershon (Josephine "Joey" O'Hara), Paul Guilfoyle (Frankie "Hot" Salvano), Amy Irving (Jane Devlin), Victor Slezak (Bruce Payne). Directed by Bruno Barreto and produced by Michael Bregman and Martin Bregman. Screenplay by Jeremy Iacone, inspired by the novel by Bo Dietl.

As the opening credits on *One Tough Cop* rolled, I made a bet with myself that the opening sequence would involve a hostage crisis. I lost. There was another short scene first, and *then* the hostage crisis. A tough cop named Bo Dietl (Stephen Baldwin) walks past the uniformed officers and confronts the madman who has taken his daughter hostage. Just like in dozens of other cop movies. Of course, the hostage sequence must stand alone, and not have any attachment to the rest of the movie.

Okay, I'm thinking. What scene *always* follows a hostage scene in a cop movie? A bar scene. Cops drinking. I am correct. Dietl and his partner Duke (Chris Penn) are in a bar, while the movie establishes that Duke has drinking and gambling problems. (It's always a danger signal when your partner advises you to "put something on your stomach.") Then Dietl ends up at a birthday party for Richie La Cassa (Mike McGlone), his friend since kindergarten. Is Richie in the mob? (It's always a danger signal when your best friend has an uncle named Sal who travels with bodyguards.)

I'm checking my Timex Indiglo, waiting to see how long it will take for the rogue cop to be called on the carpet by his superior. Answer: Four minutes. "Bo," says the chief, "you're the best cop I have working for me, but, swear to God, you're your own worst enemy!"

Bo is confronted by two feds (Amy Irving and Victor Slezak), who show him photos of himself hugging his childhood buddy Richie at last night's party. In a dialogue scene so talky it brings the movie to a halt, they want him to turn rat and plant a bug on Richie. But Bo won't. The movie is filled with speeches in which he explains that these Mafia guys are his childhood friends from the old neighborhood, who he saw on Sundays at church and never asked what they did for a living.

Meanwhile, Duke continues to drink and gamble, and then the two cops happen upon a crime scene in which a nun has been raped and tortured. I'm counting down, five, four, three . . . and sure enough, on two we hear the obligatory line, "What kind of an animal would do this?"

This Bo Dietl is apparently a real person, an ex-cop who reviews movies on the Don Imus radio program. *One Tough Cop* is based on a book that is somewhere between memoir and fiction. The movie ends with its only laugh, a title card which informs us: "Except for the character of Bo Dietl, all characters and events in this movie are fictional." How real can a character be, you ask, in a totally fictional story? Think Michael Jordan in *Space Jam*.

To the degree that Dietl's book does reflect events in his life, his life has been remarkable in incorporating all the clichés of cop movies. There's even a *noir* heroine, Joey (Gina Gershon), whose purpose is to be backlit in slinky poses while making me wonder why this movie got released when her infinitely better work in the incomparably better murder-'n'-incest film *This World, Then the Fireworks* (1997) never got a theatrical run.

The movie misses sure bets in scene after scene. Consider a confrontation in a bawdy house between Duke and Frankie "Hot" Salvano (Paul Guilfoyle), a mob gambling collector. "Hot" insultingly throws crumpled $100 bills at Duke, who boils over, smashes "Hot" against a table, and stalks out. My best guess is that the hookers would immediately dive for the floor, butting heads in the scramble for the C-notes, but no. They just sit there, forgotten by the screenplay.

The movie forgets lots of things. If you were Bo Dietl, for example, and had already been shown eight-by-ten glossies of yourself at a private birthday party with your mob friend Richie, would you select a table in the front window of a coffee shop as the ideal place to openly hand $5,000 in gambling debts to "Hot"? That's professional suicide. Maybe Dietl is thinking, one tough cop is one tough cop too many.

One True Thing ★ ★ ★
R, 121 m., 1998

Meryl Streep (Kate Gulden), Renee Zellweger (Ellen Gulden), William Hurt (George Gulden), Tom Everett Scott (Brian Gulden), Lauren Graham (Jules), Nicky Katt (Jordan Belzer), James Eckhouse (District Attorney), Patrick Breen (Mr. Tweedy). Directed by Carl Franklin and produced by Harry Ufland and Jesse Beaton. Screenplay by Karen Croner, based on the novel by Anna Quindlen.

No matter how well we eventually come to understand our parents, our deepest feelings about them are formed at a time when we are young and have incomplete information. *One True Thing* is about a daughter who grows up admiring her father and harboring doubts about her mother, and finds out she doesn't know as much about either one as she thinks she does.

The movie is based on the 1995 novel by Anna Quindlen, about a New York magazine writer whose father is "Mr. American Literature" and whose mother seems to have been shaped by the same forces that generated Martha Stewart's hallucinations. Ellen (Renee Zellweger) is bright and pretty, but with a subtle wounded look: She has that way of signaling that she's been hurt and expects to be hurt again.

She comes home to upstate New York for a surprise birthday party for her father, a professor named George (William Hurt), and is not surprised to see her mother, Kate (Meryl Streep), prancing around the house dressed like Dorothy in *The Wizard of Oz*. Yes, it's a costume party, but Kate is the kind of woman who can find costumes like that right in her own closet. Eventually Ellen gets a chance to ask her dad about her latest magazine article, which he has read, and, "writer to writer," thinks should be "more muscular."

Later he muses, "When I was twenty and working at *The New Yorker* I would spend a whole day working on a single sentence." That's the kind of statement that deserves pity rather than respect; if it is true, then to meet his deadlines he must have had to dash off his other sentences in heedless haste. Ellen should be able to feel a certain contempt for her father for even using such a ploy, but she is blinded by his tweeds, his National Book Award, his seminars, his whole edifice of importance. He thinks he's a big shot, and she buys it.

Ellen's hurt, we see, comes because her father, who she admires, does not sufficiently show his love for her—while her mother, of whom she disapproves, has a love that is therefore unwelcome. All of this begins to matter in the next months, as it develops that Kate has cancer, and George wants his daughter to move back home and take care of her.

But, I have a career, Ellen argues. "You can work as a freelancer from home," the professor says, clearly not convinced that whatever his daughter has can be described as a career. He, of course, is too busy with midterms to take care of Kate. The family's younger brother, Brian (Tom Everett Scott), must stay in school. Yes, a nurse could be hired, but the professor doesn't want a nurse poking around the house and disturbing his routine. Kate herself doesn't want Ellen to stay but wasn't consulted (by her husband or her daughter) about the decision.

As autumn winds down into winter, Ellen coexists in the house with a mother who is clearly demented in the area of domestic activities. She belongs to a local group named the Minnies, who decorate Christmas trees with the fury of beavers rebuilding a dam. The luncheon meetings of the Minnies could be photographed for layouts in food magazines, and of course the Minnies cook everything themselves. When Ellen breaks a piece of Kate's china, Kate asks her to save the pieces because she can use them in her mosaic table. Ellen finally tells Kate she thinks the Minnies are like a cult group.

George, on the other hand, throws his daughter a bone; he asks her to write an introduction to his collected essays. She is flattered, although a little wounded that he immediately afterward asks her, in more or less the same spirit, to launder some shirts. As winter unfolds and Kate's illness grows more severe, Ellen begins to suspect things about her father, and her mother observes this and finally tells her: "There's nothing that you know about your father that I don't know—and better." And we see that the buried story of the movie is the hurt that Kate has borne, all these years, over the way her daughter's love was quietly directed away from her.

It is the craftsmanship that elevates *One True Thing* above the level of a soaper. The director, Carl Franklin *(One False Move)*, goes not for big melodramatic revelations but for the accumulation of emotional investments. Hurt and Streep are so well cast they're able to overcome the generic natures of their roles and make them particular people. And Renee Zellweger, as Streep observed at the Telluride Film Festival, is able to create a place for herself and work inside of it, not acting so much as fiercely possessing her character. The movie's lesson is that we go through life telling ourselves a story about our childhood and our parents, but we are the authors of that story, and it is less fact than fiction.

On the Ropes ★ ★ ★ ★
NO MPAA RATING, 90 m., 1999

A documentary featuring boxers Tyrene Manson, George Walton, Noel Santiago, trainer Harry Keitt, manager Mickey Marcello, and Randy Little. Directed and produced by Nanette Burstein and Brett Morgen.

On the Ropes tells the true stories of three young boxers. One of them is sent to prison although she is apparently innocent. We watch as she is represented by an incompetent lawyer, crucified by uncaring prosecutors, and sentenced by a judge who exhibits the worst kind of barbarism: indifference to those whose lives he has power over.

The most amazing thing about the trial and conviction of Tyrene Manson is not that it happened. Justice miscarries all the time in America, frequently when poor black defendants are involved. The new movie *Hurricane* tells the true story of a boxer much more famous than Manson, who was railroaded for life on three fabricated murder convictions.

No, what is amazing is that the lawyer, the prosecutors, and the judge allowed themselves to be filmed as they toyed recklessly with Tyrene Manson's life. You'd think that even the most indifferent of jurists would be on good behavior before the camera. Perhaps the camera itself explains their lack of prudence. *On the Ropes* was filmed by Nanette Burstein and Brett Morgen with a low-tech Sony Handycam; its subjects might not have expected a real movie

to result. But it did, and it won the Special Jury Award at Sundance. Now they know.

On the Ropes is a sports documentary as gripping, in a different way, as *Hoop Dreams*. Both films are about ambitious young people from the ghetto who see sports as a road out of poverty. *On the Ropes* centers on the New Bed-Stuy Gym in New York, where a wise trainer, himself a survivor of hard times, guides the careers of three boxers.

The trainer's name is Harry Keitt, and his story will also figure here. The boxers are Tyrene Manson, a young Golden Gloves contender who has already knocked out the defending champion; George Walton, who seems to have genuine professional potential; and Noel Santiago, who is quick and promising, but easily discouraged. As they prepare for upcoming fights, we learn something of their stories.

Tyrene Manson's is the most inspiring— and therefore most heartbreaking. She is determined to be "the first member of my family to make something of myself." Trapped in poverty, she lives in a house with assorted other family members, and is raising two nieces who belong to her Uncle Randy, described in the movie as a crackhead. During her training for the Golden Gloves, disaster strikes when Randy is arrested for selling drugs to undercover police. They search the house, find cocaine in a bedroom, and charge Tyrene with possession with intent to sell.

Now pause a moment for Tyrene's story, which is more than the court did. She is a woman with no previous history of drug crimes. She does not use drugs. Five people shared that bedroom as their sleeping quarters. There was no lock on the door. She had been trying desperately to find other houses for herself and her nieces, to get them away from the crackhead and his life. Why was she the one charged? Because she was there.

Now follow the progress of the court case. Because her court-appointed attorney forgets a key appointment, her trial is postponed until four days before the Golden Gloves. She asks for a postponement so she can fight. Request denied. On the very day of her cancelled fight, she is sentenced to four and a half to nine years, after a "trial" that is an incompetent assembly-line procedure. One wonders if the judge even really saw her. Certainly he took no notice of her story. Her lawyer is so inept we want to shout obvious suggestions from the audience. Her own tearful speech in her own defense does her no good.

The message is clear: The drug epidemic is so widespread and the courts so overburdened and cynical that a defendant without a competent lawyer is more or less routinely doomed to be locked up. In this case, the evidence suggests that Tyrene Manson was innocent. But to be cynical, even if she were guilty, if she had been white, rich, or well represented, she would never have done a day because of the tainted evidence trail.

There is more heartbreak in the film. We watch as George Walton shows such promise that he gets a shot at the big time, and promptly allows himself to be fast-talked by Vegas types, while hardworking Harry Keitt gets left behind. We see how hard Harry works to help Noel Santiago find direction in his life. We learn something about Harry himself, his own past history of drug problems, his homelessness, and how the gym represents his own comeback. And we see the almost unimaginable disappointments he has to bear.   ☞

Note: In one of those notes of irony that life produces so freely, Tyrene Manson was given a brief pass out of prison to attend the Oscars when On the Ropes *was nominated for an Academy Award.*

The Opposite of Sex ★ ★ ★
R, 105 m., 1998

Christina Ricci (Dedee Truitt), Martin Donovan (Bill Truitt), Lisa Kudrow (Lucia), Lyle Lovett (Carl Tippett), Johnny Galecki (Jason), Ivan Sergei (Matt Mateo), William Lee Scott (Randy). Directed by Don Roos and produced by David Kirkpatrick and Michael Besman. Screenplay by Roos.

The Opposite of Sex is like a movie with the *Mystery Science Theater 3000* commentary built right in. It comments on itself, with the heroine as narrator. Dedee Truitt, a trash-talking teenager from Louisiana, chats on the sound track during and between many of the scenes, pointing out the clichés, warning us about approaching plot conventions, and debunking

our desire to see the story unfold in traditional ways.

Watching the movie is like sitting through a film in front of a row of wisecracking cult movie fans. It's also sometimes very funny. Dedee (the name may relate to her bra size) is played by Christina Ricci, who is having a very good year, and has left all memories of *The Addams Family* far behind with roles in movies such as *The Ice Storm* and *Fear and Loathing in Las Vegas*. Here she shows a cocky, smart-aleck side. She's the kind of actress who makes an audience sit up and take notice, because she lets us know she's capable of breaking a movie wide open.

In *The Opposite of Sex,* her sixteen-year-old character Dedee bails out from an unhappy home life in Louisiana and makes her way to Indiana, where an older half-brother named Bill (Martin Donovan) teaches high school. Bill is gay, and until recently lived with a stockbroker named Tom, who died of AIDS and left him all his money. Now he lives with a younger man named Matt (Ivan Sergei) and gets frequent visits from Lucia (Lisa Kudrow), who was Tom's sister.

It's a good thing we have Dedee to explain all of this to us, usually in cynical terms. Dedee is advanced sexually, if not intellectually, and soon sets about trying to convince Matt that he is not really gay at all, but has just been killing time while waiting for Dedee to come along. She has a good reason for snaring Matt: She got pregnant in Louisiana and is recruiting a partner.

Dedee and her brother Bill have obviously had quite different childhoods. Bill is quiet, civilized, accepting. When he finds a student writing a crude graffiti about him on the wall of the high school men's room, he suggests grammatical improvements. Dedee is loud, brash, and in your face—a hellion whose master plan includes seducing Matt and stealing $10,000 from Bill so she and Matt can flee to Los Angeles for the good of "their" baby.

Meanwhile, an obnoxious dropout named Jason (Johnny Galecki from *Roseanne*) claims Bill has molested him. It's a blackmail scheme, but the sheriff (Lyle Lovett) has to investigate anyway, even though he more or less sees through Jason. Working behind the scenes,

Lucia, the Kudrow character, wonders if maybe Bill would like to live with her in whatever arrangement might seem to work. The sheriff likes Lucia in his earnest and plodding way, but she can't really focus on him.

In its plot outlines, *The Opposite of Sex* is an R-rated sitcom. But first-time director Don Roos (who wrote *Single White Female* and *Boys on the Side*) redeems it with Dedee's narration. When a gun turns up on the screen, Dedee tells us: "This is foreshadowing. Duh!" She likes to tell us she knows what we're thinking, and we're wrong.

The approach is refreshing. Most movies are profoundly conservative at the level of plot construction, no matter how offbeat their material may be. They believe that all audiences demand happy endings, and want to be led lockstep through traditional plot construction. When you've seen enough movies, alas, you can sense the gears laboriously turning, and you know with a sinking heart that there will be no surprises. The Dedee character subverts those expectations; she shoots the legs out from under the movie with perfectly timed zingers. I hate people who talk during movies, but if she were sitting behind me in the theater, saying all of this stuff, I'd want her to keep right on talking.

Orgazmo ½★
NC-17, 94 m., 1998

Trey Parker (Elder Joe Young), Matt Stone (His Friend), Dian Bachar (Ben [Choda-Boy]), Michael Dean Jacobs (Maxxx Orbison), Robyn Lynne (Joe's Fiancée), Masad "Maki" San (G-Fresh), Ron Jeremy (Clark), Chasey Lain (Candi). Directed by Trey Parker and produced by Fran Rubel Kuzui, Jason McHugh, and Matt Stone. Screenplay by Parker.

When a critic uses the word "sophomoric," it's a good sign you're dealing with an amateur. Once you get to be a junior, you should more or less retire "sophomoric" from your vocabulary, unless no other word will do.

A database search through my old reviews reveals that I have used it only twice in the 1990s (once to refer to the plot of *Wild at Heart*, and again to describe Jim Morrison's lyrics) and in only eleven reviews in total. (They included *National Lampoon's Animal House, Airplane!* and the surfing documentary *Endless Summer;* in all three cases I'm sure the directors themselves would agree it was appropriate.)

Now I must use the word again. *Orgazmo,* a comedy by *South Park* cocreator Trey Parker, is the very soul of sophomorism. It is callow, gauche, obvious, and awkward, and designed to appeal to those with similar qualities. It stars Parker himself as Elder Joe Young, a Mormon missionary who agrees to appear in a porn film in order to raise $20,000 so that he can be married in the temple in Salt Lake City. True to the film's sophomorism, it is not a satire of Mormonism, but simply uses Mormons in the conviction that their seriousness will be funny to gapejaws in the audience—to whom all sincerity is threatening, and therefore funny.

Sophomorism uses a sledgehammer; wit uses a scalpel. Sophomorism cries out for your attention; wit assumes it has it. Sophomorism shocks by presenting sexuality; wit shocks by using it. A sophomoric film will think it is funny when hairy buttocks block the camera's view. A witty film will ask, whose buttocks? Why now? What next?

I will provide an example. Early in the film, Elder Young (whose name would have been funnier if it had been Elder Younger) and another missionary are knocking on doors in Los Angeles, seeking converts. One door is opened by a sweet little old lady. The instant I saw her, I knew, with the same certainty that a Mormon missionary knows he will go to heaven, that the sweet little old lady would shout a stream of vile obscenities. She did.

That is sophomorism. What would wit have done? The missionaries would have knocked on the door, the sweet little old lady would have opened it, and wit would have known that the audience anticipated obscenities, so wit would have had the little old lady say: "I know that in the movies we sweet little old ladies are always getting a cheap laugh by using the f-word to missionaries, but that lacks imagination, don't you think? That's what my son, Quentin Tarantino, always says. Here, have some cookies."

The plot thickens when Elder Young knocks on the door of Maxxx Orbison (Michael Dean Jacobs), a porno filmmaker. After Young beats up the pornographer's bodyguards, the director offers him $20,000 for two days' work, and even agrees that a body-part double will be used. That he will pay extra for star quality is proven by the presence of Ron Jeremy as the costar of the movie he is making. Ron Jeremy, for those not willing to admit they know who he is, has been in more porn films than anyone else. His popularity is easily explained: Every man alive believes that any woman would prefer him to Ron Jeremy.

Elder Young is given the role of Orgazmo, a porno superhero with a sidekick named Choda-Boy (Dian Bachar). They crash through cardboard walls to rescue damsels in distress (or damsels being ravished by Ron Jeremy, which amounts to the same thing). His weapon (Orgazmo's) is an Orgazmorator, which immobilizes his enemies with multiple orgasms. In a movie with wit, people would be lining up to become Orgazmo's enemies.

Elder Young calls his fiancée, Lisa (Robyn Lynne), in Utah and explains that he has been cast in a movie. She wants to know the title. *Death of a Salesman,* he says, and Lisa intuits that he has bagged the plum role of Biff. She flies to L.A. and is soon tied to the bed in Maxxx Orbison's house. I was by now so desperately longing for a reason to laugh that, yes, I did laugh at a scene where all of the characters leave the frame and fight offscreen, and debris is thrown on-screen from beyond the edges to indicate what a battle it is.

Orgazmo was made before Trey Parker and Matt Stone became famous for the *South Park* cable cartoon program. (There is an even earlier film, *Cannibal: The Musical,* which is unseen by me and has an excellent chance of remaining so.) *South Park* is elegant, in its way: a self-contained animated universe that functions as a laboratory to conduct experiments in affronting the values of viewers, who, if they held them, would not be watching. I like *South Park.* It has wit. I guess *Orgazmo* was a stage the boys had to go through. They're juniors now.

Orphans ★ ★ ½
NO MPAA RATING, 102 m., 2000

Gary Lewis (Thomas), Douglas Henshall (Michael), Rosemarie Stevenson (Sheila), Stephen McCole (John), Frank Gallagher (Tanga), Alex Norton (Hanson). Directed by Peter Mullan and produced by Frances Higson. Screenplay by Mullan.

How seriously does *Orphans* intend to be taken? On one hand it tells the gritty story of three Glasgow brothers and their handicapped sister in the twenty-four hours after their mother dies. On the other hand, it involves events that would be at home in a comedy of the absurd. When the sister's wheelchair topples a statue of the Virgin Mary and the damage is blamed on high winds that lifted the roof off a church, we have left the land of realism.

We have not, however, entered the land of boredom. *Orphans* is a film of great intensity and weird events, in which four suddenly parentless adults come unhinged in different ways. For Thomas, the oldest, the mother's death is an occasion for piety, and he spends the night with her coffin in the church and later tries to carry it on his back to the grave. For Michael, it's an occasion for boozing, a pub fight, and a spiral of confusion after he gets knifed. For John, the youngest, it provides a mission: to find and kill the man who stabbed Michael. And for Sheila, in the wheelchair, it leads to an act of defiance as she ventures out into the night alone.

The movie was written and directed by Peter Mullan. You may remember him as the title character in *My Name Is Joe,* Ken Loach's heartrending film about a recovering alcoholic in Glasgow. He won the Best Actor prize at Cannes for that role, and with *Orphans* focuses on at least two characters in urgent need of AA.

It's one of those sub–Eugene O'Neill family dramas in which a lifetime of confusion and anguish comes to a head during a family crisis. We see how each brother has hewn out his space in the family in reaction to the others, while the sister basically just wants out. The brothers Michael and John inhabit a world of hard characters and pub desperadoes (sample dialogue: "We'd cut your legs off for twenty

Silk Cut [cigarettes] and a rubber bone for his dog"). Thomas likes to see himself as older, wiser, saner, more religious, and yet he's the maddest of them all. And the movie staggers like its drunken characters from melodrama to revelation, from truth-telling to incredible situations, as when Michael finds himself used as a dart board by a pub owner.

How are we to take this? There are times when we want to laugh, as when Thomas tries to glue the shattered Virgin back together with hot wax candle drippings ("She's a total write-off," he observes morosely). We see the roof lifting off the church in a nice effects shot, but why? To show God's wrath, or simply bad weather conditions? It's a nice point when the funeral goes ahead inside the ruined church—but wouldn't the insurance company and public safety inspectors have something to say about that?

Maybe we're not supposed to ask such realistic questions, but we can't resist. Yet other moments seem as slice-of-life as anything in *My Name Is Joe.* My guess is that Mullan never decided what tone his film should aim for; he fell in love with individual sequences without asking how they fit together.

Note: Because of its Glasgow accents, the film has been subtitled. But we can understand most of what the characters say, and that leads to disconnections, since the subtitles are reluctant to use certain four-letter Anglo-Saxonisms we can clearly hear being uttered by the characters.

Oscar and Lucinda ★ ★ ★ ★
R, 133 m., 1998

Ralph Fiennes (Oscar Hopkins), Cate Blanchett (Lucinda Leplastrier), Ciaran Hinds (Reverend Dennis Hasset), Tom Wilkinson (Hugh Stratton), Richard Roxburgh (Mr. Jeffris), Clive Russell (Theophilus), Bille Brown (Percy Smith), Josephine Byrnes (Miriam Chadwick), Geoffrey Rush (Narrator). Directed by Gillian Armstrong and produced by Robin Dalton and Timothy White. Screenplay by Laura Jones from the original novel by Peter Carey.

"In order that I exist," the narrator of *Oscar and Lucinda* tells us, "two gamblers, one obsessive, one compulsive, must declare themselves." The gamblers are his grandparents, two oddball nineteenth-century eccentrics, driven by faith and temptation, who find they are freed to practice the first by indulging in the second. Their lives form a love story of enchantment and wicked wit.

When we say two people were born for each other, that sometimes means their lives would have been impossible with anyone else. That appears to be the case with Oscar and Lucinda. Their story, told as a long flashback, begins with Oscar as the shy son of a stern English minister, and Lucinda as the strong-willed girl raised on a ranch in the Australian outback. We see them formed by their early lives; he studies for the ministry, she inherits a glassworks and becomes obsessed with glass, and they meet during an ocean voyage from England to Australia.

They meet, indeed, because they gamble. Oscar (Ralph Fiennes) has been introduced to horse racing while studying to be a clergyman, and is transformed by the notion that someone will actually pay him money for predicting which horse will cross the line first. Lucinda (Cate Blanchett) loves cards. Soon they're playing clandestine card games on board ship, and Oscar is as thrilled by her descriptions of gambling as another man might be by tales of sexual adventures.

Oscar and Lucinda is based on a novel by Peter Carey, a chronicler of Australian eccentricity; it won the 1988 Booker Prize, Britain's highest literary award. Reading it, I was swept up by the humor of the situation and by the passion of the two gamblers. For Oscar, gambling is not a sin but an embrace of the rules of chance that govern the entire universe: "We bet that there is a God—we bet our life on it!"

There is also the thrill of the forbidden. Once ashore in Sydney, where Oscar finds rooms with a pious church couple, they continue to meet to play cards, and when they are discovered, they're defiant. Oscar decides he doesn't fit into ordinary society. Lucinda says it is no matter. Even now they are not in love; it is gambling that holds them together, and Oscar believes Lucinda fancies another minister who has gone off to convert the outback. That gives him his great idea: Lucinda's glassworks will fabricate a glass cathedral, and Oscar will superintend the process of floating it upriver to the remote settlement.

For madness, this matches the obsession in Herzog's *Fitzcarraldo* to move a steamship across a strip of dry land. For inspiration, it seems divine—especially since they make a bet on it. Reading the novel, I pictured the glass cathedral as tall and vast, but of course it is a smaller church, one suitable for a growing congregation, and the photography showing its stately river progress is somehow funny and touching at the same time.

Oscar and Lucinda has been directed by Gillian Armstrong, whose films often deal with people who are right for each other and wrong for everyone else (see her neglected 1993 film *The Last Days of Chez Nous*, about a troubled marriage between an Australian and a Frenchman, or recall her 1979 film *My Brilliant Career*, in which Judy Davis played a character not unlike Lucinda in spirit). Here there is a dry wit, generated between the well-balanced performances of Fiennes and Blanchett, who seem quietly delighted to be playing two such rich characters.

The film's photography, by Geoffrey Simpson, begins with standard, lush nineteenth-century period evocations of landscape and sky, but then subtly grows more insistent on the quirky character of early Sydney, and then cuts loose altogether from the everyday in the final sequences involving the glass church. In many period films, we are always aware that we're watching the past: Here Oscar and Lucinda seem ahead of us, filled with freshness and invention, and only the narration (by Geoffrey Rush of *Shine*) reminds us that they were, incredibly, someone's grandparents.

Oscar and Lucinda begins with the look of a period literary adaptation, but this is not Dickens, Austen, Forster, or James; Carey's novel is playful and manipulative, and so is the film. Oscar is shy and painfully sincere, Lucinda has evaded her century's strictures on women by finding a private passion, and they would both agree, I believe, that people who worship in glass churches should not throw stones.

The Other Sister ★

PG-13, 130 m., 1999

Juliette Lewis (Carla), Diane Keaton (Elizabeth), Tom Skerritt (Radley), Giovanni Ribisi (Danny), Poppy Montgomery (Caroline), Sarah Paulson (Heather), Linda Thorson (Drew), Joe Flanigan (Jeff). Directed by Garry Marshall and produced by Mario Iscovich and Alexandra Rose. Screenplay by Marshall and Bob Brunner.

The Other Sister is shameless in its use of mental retardation as a gimmick, a prop, and a plot device. Anyone with any knowledge of retardation is likely to find the film offensive. It treats the characters like cute little performing seals—who always deliver their "retarded" dialogue with perfect timing and an edge of irony and drama. Their zingers slide out with the precision of sitcom punch lines.

The film stars Juliette Lewis as Carla, a rich San Francisco girl of seventeen or eighteen who has just returned home after several years in an institution. Her ambition is to train as a veterinarian's assistant. Her father (Tom Skerritt) thinks she should go for it, but her mother (Diane Keaton) is opposed. If there is a convincingly retarded character in the movie, it's the mother. She's borderline hysterical in insisting her daughter is not ready for junior college, dating, dancing, sex, living in her own apartment, or anything else.

In flashbacks to the girl's childhood, we see the mother crying out, "I don't want her to be retarded!" Now she doesn't want her to be anything else. Her opposition to any sign of Carla's independence is handled oddly, however. Every once in a while, she has a brief moment of humanity, in which she softens and says sensible things like, "I'll try to see it your way." These interludes play suspiciously as if they were inserted into the script to lighten the character and make her less of a harridan. Then it's back to bullheaded denial again.

Carla does eventually get into the local polytechnic, where she makes a friend of Danny (Giovanni Ribisi). The two of them are the butts of some cruel treatment, but Danny has found a haven in the music department, where, he proudly tells Carla, he has a real job: "cleaning the marshmallows out of the tubas."

That's because at football games students throw marshmallows at the tubas in the marching bands. I am prepared to believe they do that, but not so prepared to believe that something equally cute comes up at every juncture, as when Carla and her mother attend a benefit at a dog shelter and Carla starts barking at the strays and releases them, disrupting a reception. Or when she gets a free beauty makeover at the mall and is surprised to find it covers only half her face. Or when she's garbed in an absurd swan costume for a social event. Or when she and Daniel, alone at last, study positions in *The Joy of Sex*.

The movie's dialogue knows it's funny—a fatal error. "I wonder who thought up sex in the first place?" one of them muses, studying the sex books. The answer: "I think it was Madonna." Sure, that's exactly what would be said. And how about when Daniel tells Carla, "I love you more than band music and cookie making." All of their words are pronounced as if the characters have marbles in their mouths, and when they walk, it's a funny little modified duck walk. It's like they learned how to act retarded by studying under Jerry Lewis.

Moment after moment is utterly false. Take the climax at the country club, where a bartender keeps pouring triple shots of green Chartreuse for Danny. Not likely, because: (1) Danny is obviously a novice drinker. (2) He is obviously underage. (3) Green Chartreuse is one of the strongest liquors in the world, so that several full snifters would paralyze an inexperienced drinker. And (4) country club bartenders like their jobs and know they can get fired for getting underage drinkers blind drunk.

Of course, Danny doesn't get *really* drunk— only drunk enough to make a speech that is cunningly calculated to offend those who need to be offended, please those who need to be pleased, and move the wheels of the plot. All in "retarded" language that is perfectly chosen and timed, of course.

Am I getting too technical here? I don't think so. The truth is in the details. The details of *The Other Sister* show a movie with no serious knowledge of retardation and no interest in learning or teaching. I never tire of quoting Godard, who tells us that the way to criticize a movie is to make another movie. The movie that shames *The Other Sister* was made in 1988 by Robert M. Young. It is called *Dominick and Eugene*, and it stars Tom Hulce and Ray Liotta in the story of a retarded man and his brother. See that, and you will cringe when you compare it to *The Other Sister*.

Out of Sight ★ ★ ★ ½
R, 123 m., 1998

George Clooney (Jack Foley), Jennifer Lopez (Karen Sisco), Ving Rhames (Buddy Bragg), Isaiah Washington (Kenneth), Don Cheadle (Maurice Miller), Steve Zahn (Glenn Michaels), Keith Loneker (White Boy Bob), Dennis Farina (Marshall Sisco), Albert Brooks (Ripley). Directed by Steven Soderbergh and produced by Danny DeVito, Michael Shamberg, and Stacey Sher. Screenplay by Scott Frank, based on the novel by Elmore Leonard.

Steven Soderbergh's *Out of Sight* is a crime movie less interested in crime than in how people talk, flirt, lie, and get themselves into trouble. Based on an Elmore Leonard novel, it relishes Leonard's deep comic ease; the characters mosey through scenes, existing primarily to savor the dialogue.

The story involves a bank robber named Foley (George Clooney) and a federal marshal named Sisco (Jennifer Lopez), who grow attracted to one another while they're locked in a car trunk. Life goes on, and in the nature of things, it's her job to arrest him. But several things might happen first.

This is the fourth recent adaptation of a Leonard novel, after *Get Shorty, Touch,* and *Jackie Brown,* and the most faithful to Leonard's style. What all four movies demonstrate is how useful crime is as a setting for human comedy. For example: All caper movies begin with a self-contained introductory caper that has nothing at all to do with the rest of the plot. A cop will disarm a hostage, or a terrorist will plant a preliminary bomb. *Out of Sight* begins with as laid-back a bank robbery as you'd want to see, as Clooney saunters up to a teller's window and politely asks, "This your first time being held up?" How he cons the teller is one of the movie's first pleasures. The point of the scene is behavior, not robbery.

It turns out that this robbery is not, in fact, self-contained—it leads out of and into something—and it's not even really the first scene in the story. *Out of Sight* has a time line as complex as *Pulp Fiction*, even though at first we don't realize that. The movie's constructed like hypertext, so that, in a way, we can start watching at any point. It's like the old days when you walked in to the middle of a film and sat there until somebody said, "This is where we came in."

Elmore Leonard is above all the creator of colorful characters. Here we get the charming, intelligent Foley, who is constitutionally incapable of doing anything but robbing banks, and Sisco, the marshal, who has already had a previous liaison with a bank robber (admittedly, she eventually shot him). They are surrounded by a rich gallery of other characters, and this movie, like *Jackie Brown*, takes the time to give every character at least one well-written scene showing them as peculiar and unique.

Among Foley's criminal accomplices is his criminal partner, Buddy Bragg (Ving Rhames, who played Marcellus Wallace in *Pulp Fiction*). He's waiting on the outside after the prison break. In prison, Foley met a small-time hood named Glenn (Steve Zahn), who "has a vacant lot for a head." They're highly motivated by one of their fellow prisoners, a former Wall Street leverage expert named Ripley, who unwisely spoke of a fortune in uncut diamonds that he keeps in his house. (Ripley is played by Albert Brooks with a Michael Milkin hairstyle that is not a coincidence.)

Then there's the threesome that join Foley and his friends in a raid on Ripley's house. Snoopy Miller (Don Cheadle) is a nasty piece of work, a hard-nosed and violent former boxer; Isaiah Washington plays his partner; and Keith Loneker is White Boy Bob, his clumsy but very earnest bodyguard. It's ingenious how the raid involves shifting loyalties, with Foley and Sisco simultaneously dueling and cooperating.

All of these characters have lives of their own and don't exist simply at the convenience of the plot. Consider a tender father-daughter birthday luncheon between Karen Sisco and her father (Dennis Farina), a former lawman who tenderly gives her a gun.

At the center of the film is the repartee between Jennifer Lopez and George Clooney, and these two have the kind of unforced fun in their scenes together that reminds you of Bogart and Bacall. There's a seduction scene in which the dialogue is intercut with the very gradual progress of the physical action, and it's the dialogue that we want to linger on.

Soderbergh edits this scene with quiet little freeze-frames; nothing quite matches up, and yet everything fits, so that the scene is like a demonstration of the whole movie's visual and time style.

Lopez had star quality in her first role in *My Family,* and in *Anaconda, Selena,* and the underrated *Blood and Wine* she has only grown; here she plays a role that could be complex or maybe just plain dumb, and brings a rich comic understanding to it. She wants to arrest the guy, but she'd like to have an affair with him first, and that leads to a delicate, well-written scene in a hotel bar where the cat and mouse hold negotiations. (It parallels, in a way, the "time out" between De Niro and Pacino in *Heat.*)

Clooney has never been better. A lot of actors who are handsome when young need to put on some miles before the full flavor emerges; observe how Nick Nolte, Mickey Rourke, Harrison Ford, and Clint Eastwood moved from stereotypes to individuals. Here Clooney at last looks like a big-screen star; the good-looking leading man from television is over with.

For Steven Soderbergh, *Out of Sight* is a paradox. It's his best film since *sex, lies, and videotape* a decade ago, and yet at the same time it's not what we think of as a Soderbergh film—detached, cold, analytical. It is instead the first film to build on the enormously influential *Pulp Fiction* instead of simply mimicking it. It has the games with time, the low-life dialogue, the absurd violent situations, but it also has its own texture. It plays like a string quartet written with words instead of music, performed by sleazeballs instead of musicians.

The Out-of-Towners ★ ½
PG-13, 91 m., 1999

Steve Martin (Henry Clark), Goldie Hawn (Nancy Clark), John Cleese (Hotel Manager), Tom Riis Farrell (Mugger). Directed by Sam Weisman and produced by Robert W. Cort, Robert Evans, and Christine Forsyth-Peters. Screenplay by Marc Lawrence, based on the screenplay by Neil Simon.

The Out-of-Towners jogs doggedly on the treadmill of comedy, working up a sweat but not getting much of anywhere. It's a remake of the

1970 Neil Simon screenplay, with Steve Martin and Goldie Hawn now taking the roles played by Jack Lemmon and Sandy Dennis. The most valuable addition to the cast is John Cleese, as the hotel manager; he's doing his character from *Fawlty Towers,* but at least it's a role worth repeating.

Martin and Hawn play the Clarks, Henry and Nancy, who are empty nesters in Ohio now that their daughter has moved to New York and their son is studying abroad. Henry has a secret: He's been fired at his ad agency. He flies to New York for a job interview, Nancy tags along, and we sense the movie's desperation in a scene on the plane. She's seated several rows behind him, and asks the passengers in between to pass up his Foot Chums and rash ointment. A woman like that deserves to be in an empty nest all by herself.

But the thing is, Nancy isn't really that lame-brained. She can be smart, or tender, or goofy, or stubborn—or whatever the screenplay requires from moment to moment. That's because she isn't really anybody at all, and neither is Henry. They're devices to be manipulated by the film—figures on a chessboard.

Lots of things go wrong on the trip, which is taken by plane, train, and automobile, providing a melancholy reminder of Martin's much better 1987 movie—and also of *Forces of Nature,* in which Ben Affleck and Sandra Bullock go through a similar ordeal. The trick in a film like this is to keep the characters consistent as the situations change. If both the characters and the situations are slippery, there's no place to stand. And if you're determined to have a sweet, uplifting ending, all is lost.

It helps to observe situations closely, to find humor in the details rather than trusting the general scene. Consider, for example, a sequence where Henry and Nancy blunder into a meeting of Sex Addicts Anonymous because they're starving and spot the free sweet rolls. They don't realize what kind of a meeting it is, and the movie thinks that's joke enough, so it doesn't really "see" the other people at the meeting. I'm reminded of a scene in John Waters's *Polyester,* where Tab Hunter blunders into an AA meeting and is asked to introduce himself. He gives his name. "And?" ask the assembled members. "AND? AAANNNDDD???" They're shot with a fish-eye lens as they peer at

him, waiting for the magic words, "and I'm an alcoholic."

In *The Out-of-Towners,* the filmmakers think it's funny enough that the sex addicts are creepy, and Henry and Nancy are grossed out by their stories. That misses the point. In comedy, you figure out what the objective is, and go for it single-mindedly. Why are Henry and Nancy at the meeting? Because they want those sweet rolls! So what should they do? Win the sweet rolls by any means necessary, telling the members whatever they want to hear. I can imagine Martin and Hawn improvising sexual addictions all night long. But not in this movie, which skims the surface.

There are a couple of sequences that work. I liked the absurdity of the scene where they're approached on the street by a well-dressed, well-spoken man (Tom Riis Farrell) who asks for $5 to get to a business meeting. He doesn't look like a panhandler, and his British accent is curious. Nancy finally asks, "Aren't you . . . Andrew Lloyd Webber?" Well, yes, he confesses, it's embarrassing to be caught short of funds, but yes, he is. The scene develops nicely.

And then there is John Cleese, who perhaps had a hand in the precise wording of some of his own dialogue, which spins easily between ingratiating toadiness and loathsome sneering. There are few things funnier than Cleese playing a snob who is pretending to be a democrat.

But even some of the movie's surefire ideas don't seem to work. There's a moment, for example, when the Clarks are embracing on the grass in Central Park, and are suddenly hit with spotlights and seen by dozens of people inside the Tavern on the Green, including Mayor Rudy Giuliani, playing himself. Incredible as it may seem, this is not funny.

We observe that, yes, it's the mayor. We understand that the Clarks are embarrassed. But the movie stands flat-footed and smugly regards the situation, instead of doing something with it. If you're going to have a celebrity in your movie, make him work for his cameo. Why not have Giuliani personally take charge of the police investigation? Or claim the spectacle as an example of how people-friendly the park is? Or get turned on?

As it became increasingly clear that *The Out-of-Towners* was not a proud moment in the often inspired careers of Martin and Hawn,

I started looking for evidence of little moments of genius that the stars may have slipped into the crevices of the movie on their own. Surely it was Martin's idea to suggest renting advertising space on the tongues of dogs to tattoo the word "Alpo."

Outside Ozona ★ ★
R, 98 m., 1998

Robert Forster (Odell Parks), Kevin Pollak (Wit Roy), Sherilyn Fenn (Marcy Duggan), David Paymer (Alan Defaux), Penelope Ann Miller (Earlene Demers), Swoosie Kurtz (Rosalee), Taj Mahal (DJ), Meat Loaf (Floyd Bibbs), Lois Red Elk (Effie Twosalt), Kateri Walker (Reba Twosalt), Lucy Webb (Agent Deene). Directed by J. S. Cardone and produced by Avi Lerner. Screenplay by Cardone.

When I say that all the plot threads in *Outside Ozona* come together in one closing scene, you can't imagine how literally I mean that. The movie builds up an incredible series of coincidences, in which the good are rewarded, the evil are punished, the lovelorn are thrown into one another's arms, all mysteries are solved, and a homeless dog named Girl lives to bark another day. There was feverish scribbling in the dark as my colleagues and I tried to keep up with the cascade of developments.

An ending like this is either naive or deeply profound. After all the slick formula movies, it's refreshing sometimes to see a film that isn't working from the rule book. J. S. Cardone, who wrote and directed, provides clumsy parallels and too many speeches that sound written, but his heart is sound: He's going for something touching and sincere, and some of his scenes get there.

The movie takes place during a long night on the lonely highways outside Ozona, Oklahoma. The local radio DJ (Taj Mahal) calls this area the "badlands," and indeed it's so far from anywhere else that everyone has to listen to the same radio station. In movie theory, much is made of "offscreen space," which is the implied environment outside the frame. Cardone creates an almost palpable sense that the offscreen space is dark, hostile, and abandoned to the wolves.

We meet a lot of characters. The movie will cut between their stories. Many of the scenes are conversations in the front seats of cars that are allegedly traversing the lonely badlands highways, but are obviously on darkened sound stages. This is a stylistic decision, not a weakness; it increases focus as the film breaks out into dialogues between the people whose lives we glimpse.

Among them are a circus clown (Kevin Pollak) who has just been fired and his girlfriend, an ex–lap dancer (Penelope Ann Miller). They have a clever scene in which she interrupts his robbery attempt and makes him apologize, but we could have been spared his monologue about the fate of Jumbo the famous elephant.

Then there's a lonely trucker (Robert Forster, who stepped into the role after J. T. Walsh died) and a Navaho woman (Lois Red Elk). He gives her a ride, and there is mutual attraction. Later, in a car with her grandmother (Kateri Walker), she learns the old woman's lessons about love.

Sherilyn Fenn plays one of two sisters who pick up a hitchhiker (David Paymer) who may or may not be the serial killer haunting these highways. And we meet a truck stop waitress (Swoosie Kurtz), a radio station manager (Meat Loaf), and the FBI. For lost highways in the badlands, these are well-traveled roads.

The dialogue exchanged by these people doesn't further the plot, because there is no central plot; the strategy of the movie is simply to watch and listen as its characters speed toward their rendezvous with destiny. There are some grisly interludes (the killer's victims are left holding their own hearts), some heavy-handed preaching (the DJ uses the killer's calls as his cue for a political rant), and some oddly low-key FBI work.

I'm not sure what the movie thinks its purpose is; at the end, we are pleased with the outcome but not enlightened. But there are moments I will remember, and Cardone evokes a real sense for the deserted night highways.

Outside Providence ★ ½
R, 102 m., 1999

Shawn Hatosy (Tim Dunphy), Alec Baldwin (Old Man Dunphy), Amy Smart (Jane Weston), Jon Abrahams (Drugs Delaney), Tommy Bone (Jackie Dunphy), Jonathan Brandis (Mousy),

Jack Ferver (Irving Waltham), Gabriel Mann (Jack Wheeler). Directed by Michael Corrente and produced by Corrente, Peter Farrelly, Bobby Farrelly, and Randy Finch. Screenplay by Peter Farrelly, Corrente, and Bobby Farrelly, based on the novel by Peter Farrelly.

The brothers Farrelly, Peter and Bobby, have had stupendous success with their comedies *Dumb and Dumber* and *There's Something About Mary*. So much success they have the clout to get a project made just because they want to make it. Their wish is Miramax's command—which suggests a valuable exhortation: Be careful what you wish for, because you might get it.

This is a coming-of-age movie, set in the 1970s, about a working-class kid from Pawtucket, Rhode Island, who gets in trouble and then, because his dad's mob friend knows a judge, gets sent to a private academy for his last year of high school. Here he's a fish out of water (instead of luggage, he arrives with his clothing in a plastic garbage bag). But soon he's dating the most popular girl in school, getting into and out of trouble, learning life's lessons, and having the kinds of experiences people must really actually have, since so many movies have been made about them.

If it had been well made, *Outside Providence* might have overcome its genre and amounted to something. Alas, it is badly written and severely miscast; Alec Baldwin, as a working-class stiff with a Rhode Island accent, sweats over every syllable. Its construction is so amateurish that a basic character change (the hero stops screwing around and starts studying) is blown off with a film-school montage (reads books, gets approving nod from teacher, etc.). And the school faculty contains nothing but archetypes (a befuddled Mr. Chips, a vindictive martinet).

The movie was directed by Michael Corrente and written by Corrente and the Farrellys, based on a novel by Peter Farrelly. Corrente can direct (I liked his 1995 film *Federal Hill*, set in Providence), but this time he has an underdone screenplay and compensates by pushing too hard. What are we to make of a scene where the characters are smoking dope in a car, and an exterior shot shows the car trailing so much smoke it looks on fire? In Cheech and Chong, yes. In the real world, no. I could also

have done without the little brother in the wheelchair and the three-legged family dog with an eye patch. The kid brother would have been okay if he'd been better developed as a character, not just window dressing and a setup for one-liners ("We were playing touch football and he fell off the roof").

The hero is a Pawtucket teenager named Tim Dunphy (Shawn Hatosy), whose father (Baldwin) calls him "Dildo"—the kind of detail that could be true in life but never feels true in the movies. "Dunph" (as he understandably prefers to be called) hangs out with his dopehead friends, smoking reefer atop the local water tower (surely the police would never notice them there). Sent away to an exclusive Connecticut boarding school, he finds richer versions of the same kinds of friends; now they smoke dope on the roof outside their dorm windows.

The screenplay lumbers from one obligatory scene to the next, pausing most painfully at a big dramatic climax where Dunph and his dad have a heart-to-heart about his dead mother. What happened, and why, and should Dunph blame his father? We hardly care, because the dialogue is so ham-handed that the illusion of reality is broken and we can see the acting itself; we're aware of Baldwin and Hatosy struggling with lines that contain information but don't put it in context—it's payoff without setup, bathos when it should be pathos.

There's an uneasy truce between the heartfelt family stuff and the standard prep school high jinks. When Dunph gets in big trouble for having Jane in his room, it's handled as a life-changing experience on the one hand, and as a sitcom opportunity on the other. Which is it? Moment of decision, or setup for a silly scene where he hops up and down outside a dean's window to get his attention?

Outside Providence is so unsuccessful in so many different ways that maybe the whole project was doomed. At the least, the screenplay should have been rewritten in a consistent tone, and Old Man Dunphy should have been recast with a grittier actor and rewritten into a real father and not just a collection of blue-collar clichés. *Outside Providence* no doubt embodies many memories that are sacred to the Farrelly brothers, but in this form it might prudently have been left unmade.

P

Palmetto ★ ★
R, 113 m., 1998

Woody Harrelson (Harry Barber), Elisabeth Shue (Rhea), Gina Gershon (Nina), Rolf Hoppe (Felix Malroux), Michael Rapaport (Donnelly), Chloe Sevigny (Odette), Tom Wright (John Renick), Marc Macaulay (Miles Meadows). Directed by Volker Schlondorff and produced by Matthias Wendlandt. Screenplay by E. Max Frye, based on the novel *Just Another Sucker* by James Hadley Chase.

Florida is the ideal state for *film noir*. Not the Florida of retirement villas and golf condos, but the Florida of the movies, filled with Spanish moss and decaying mansions, sweaty trophy wives and dog-race gamblers, chain-smoking assistant DAs and alcoholic newspaper reporters. John D. Macdonald is its Raymond Chandler and Carl Hiaasen would be its Elmore Leonard, if Leonard hadn't gotten there first.

Noir is founded on atmosphere, and Florida has it: tacky theme bars on the beach, humid nights, ceiling fans, losers dazed by greed, the sense of dead bodies rotting out back in the Everglades. (Louisiana has even more atmosphere, but in *noir* you need a society where people are surprised by depravity, and Louisiana takes it for granted.)

Palmetto is the latest exercise in Florida *noir*, joining *Key Largo, Body Heat, A Flash of Green, Cape Fear, Striptease*, and *Blood & Wine*. The movie has all the elements of the genre, and lacks only pacing and plausibility. You wait through scenes that unfold with maddening deliberation, hoping for a payoff—and when it comes, you feel cheated. Watching it, I was more than ever convinced that Bob Rafelson's *Blood & Wine* was the movie that got away in 1997—a vastly superior Florida *noir* (with a Jack Nicholson performance that humbles his work in *As Good As It Gets*).

Both films depend on our sense of rich, eccentric people living in big houses that draw the attention of poor people. Both involve deception and hidden identities. Both heroes are once-respectable outsiders, driven to amateurish crime by desperation. Both involve older men blinded to danger by younger women with beckoning cleavage. *Blood & Wine* is the film that works. *Palmetto* is more like a first draft.

Woody Harrelson stars as Harry Barber, a newspaper reporter who tried to expose corruption in the town of Palmetto and was framed and sent to prison. After two years his conviction is overturned and he's released—by a judge who renders the verdict over closed-circuit TV. When Harry starts screaming that he wants his two years back, the judge dismisses him by clicking the channel-changer.

Harry wants to start over, anywhere but in Palmetto. But he's drawn back by his ex-girlfriend, Nina, an artist played by Gina Gershon. He looks for work, can't find it, and amuses himself by hanging around daytimes in bars, ordering bourbon and not drinking it (this is not recommended for ex-drinkers). One day a blonde named Rhea (Elisabeth Shue) undulates into the bar, makes a call, and out-dulates without her handbag. Harry finds it in the phone booth, she reundulates for it, and they fall into a conversation during which Harry does not drink bourbon and Rhea holds, but does not light, a cigarette ("I don't smoke").

The sense that Harry and Rhea are holding their addictions at bay does not extend to sex, which Rhea uses to enlist Harry in a mad scheme. She's married to a rich old coot named Felix who is dying of cancer but may linger inconveniently; meanwhile, her stepdaughter, Odette (Chloe Sevigny, from *Kids*), is threatening to run away rather than be parked in a Swiss boarding school. Rhea's proposal: Harry fakes Odette's kidnapping, Felix pays $500,000 in ransom, Harry keeps 10 percent for his troubles, Odette has her freedom with the rest. Lurking in the background: Michael Rapaport, as Felix's stern houseboy.

Well, what mother wouldn't do as much for a child? Harry's misgivings about this plot are silenced by Rhea's seductive charms, while Nina observes in concern (her role here reminded me of Barbara Bel Geddes in *Vertigo*—the good girl with the paint brush, looking up from her easel each time the bad boy slinks in after indulging his twisted libido).

Harry is, of course, spectacularly bad as a kidnapper (I liked the scene where he types a ransom note on his typewriter and flings the machine from a bridge, only to see that he has misjudged the water depth and it has landed in plain sight on the mud). While he busies himself leaving about fingerprints and cigarette butts ("DNA? They can test for that?"), there's a neat twist: The assistant DA in charge of the kidnapping case (Tom Wright) hires Harry as a press liaison. So the kidnapper becomes the official police spokesman.

All of the pieces are here for a twisty *film noir,* and Harry's dual role—as criminal and police mouthpiece—is Hitchcockian in the way it hides the perp in plain sight. But it doesn't crackle. The director, Volker Schlondorff *(The Tin Drum),* doesn't dance stylishly through the genre, but plods in almost docudrama style. And screenwriter E. Max Frye, working from James Hadley Chase's novel *Just Another Sucker,* hasn't found the right tone for an ending where victims dangle above acid baths. The ending could be handled in many ways, from the satirical to the gruesome, but the movie adopts a curiously flat tone. Sure, we have questions about the plot twists, but a better movie would sweep them aside with its energy; this one has us squinting at the screen in disbelief and resentment.

The casting is another problem. Gina Gershon and Elisabeth Shue are the wrong way around. Gershon is superb as a lustful, calculating femme fatale (she shimmers with temptation in *Bound* and *This World, Then the Fireworks).* Shue is best at heartfelt roles. Imagine Barbara Stanwyck waiting faithfully behind the easel while Doris Day seduces the hero and you'll see the problem. Woody Harrelson does his best, but the role serves the plot, not his character, and so he sometimes does things only because the screenwriter needs for him to. *Palmetto* knows the words, but not the music.

Paradise Lost 2: Revelations ★ ★ ★
NO MPAA RATING, 2000

A documentary directed by Joe Berlinger and Bruce Sinofsky.

Three second-graders were brutally murdered on May 5, 1993, in West Memphis, Arkansas, and three young men are still in prison for the crimes, convicted in a climate that stereotyped them as members of a satanic cult.

The possibility that they are innocent gnaws at anyone who has seen *Paradise Lost: The Child Murders at Robin Hood Hills.* That 1996 documentary argued they were innocent, and implied that the father of one of the victims might have been involved. He even supplied a knife to the filmmakers that seemed to match the profile of the murder weapon, but DNA tests on bloodstains were botched.

When *Paradise Lost* played on HBO, it inspired a national movement to free the three prisoners—Damien Echols, now twenty-four, under sentence of death, and Jessie Misskelley, twenty-three, and Jason Baldwin, twenty-one, with life sentences. Now comes *Paradise Lost 2: Revelations,* a sequel that involves their appeals, and also features extraordinarily creepy footage of Mark Byers, the father under suspicion, whose wife has died in mysterious circumstances in the meantime.

The new documentary is directed like the first by Joe Berlinger and Bruce Sinofsky. There is unlikely to be anything else on TV more disturbing than this film. Watching it, you feel like an eyewitness to injustice.

Among new evidence introduced on appeal is the finding that human bite marks, found on one of the child's bodies, do not match the bites of the three defendants. The film points out that Mark Byers had his teeth extracted in 1997, four years after the murders, although on camera he places the extraction much earlier, and gives several contradictory reasons for it.

What does this prove? Not much to prosecution forensic experts, who testify the bite marks were caused by a belt.

Byers spends a lot of time on-camera (he accepted a payment for appearing in this film). He is described by Echols as "the fakest creature to ever walk on two legs," and that seems the simple truth: He has an odd way of speaking in rehearsed sound bites, avoiding eye contact while using lurid prose that sounds strikingly insincere. Visiting the murder scene, he stages a mock burial and cremation of the three defendants, saying, "There's your head-marker, you animal," and then pouring on charcoal lighter, chortling, "Now we're gonna have some fun," and lighting his cigar before dropping the match.

Did he do it? We hear a litany of his problems: a brain tumor, manic depression, bad checks, drug abuse, DUIs, hallucinations, black-outs, neighbors who got a restraining order after he spanked their child, and the death of his wife. Byers rants about those who accused him of her death and says she died in her sleep of natural causes. Later, possibly in a Freudian slip, he says, "after my wife was murdered."

The legal establishment in West Memphis seems wedded to their shaky case—dug in too deep to reconsider. Echols's new attorney claims the original defense was underfunded and incompetent, and indeed we find that one attorney was paid only $19 an hour, and the defense was limited to $1,000 for tests and research in a case dripping with forensic evidence.

Questions remain. If the victims were killed in the wooded area where they were found, why was there no blood at the scene? Can a confession by Misskelley be trusted? He has an IQ of 72, was questioned by police for twelve hours without a parent or attorney present, and then was tape-recorded only long enough to recite a statement, which he later retracted.

On June 17, 2000, the appeal was turned down by the same judge who officiated at the original trial. A federal habeus corpus motion is the defendants' last chance.

Near the end of the film, Byers takes a lie detector test and passes. The film notes that at the time he was on five mood-altering medications. The last shots show him singing "Amazing Grace," very badly.

The Parent Trap ★ ★ ★
PG, 123 m., 1998

Lindsay Lohan (Hallie Parker/Annie James), Dennis Quaid (Nick Parker), Natasha Richardson (Elizabeth James), Elaine Hendrix (Meredith Blake), Lisa Ann Walter (Chessy), Simon Kunz (Martin). Directed by Nancy Meyers and produced by Charles Shyer. Screenplay by David Swift, Meyers, and Shyer.

The Parent Trap is based on story elements so ancient and foolproof they must have their roots in Shakespeare's day: The twins changing places, their divorced parents falling in love again, and, for low comedy, their servants falling in love too. And of course there's a wicked would-be stepmother lurking about. It's the stuff of Elizabethan comedy, resurrected in modern times as the British film *Twice Upon a Time* in 1953, and in the classic 1961 film *The Parent Trap.*

The story is ageless and so is the gimmick: The twins are played by the same actress, using trick photography. Hayley Mills did it in 1961 and Lindsay Lohan does it this time, seamlessly. Although I was aware that special effects and over-the-shoulder doubles were being used, I simply stopped thinking about it, because the illusion was so convincing. One twin is American, one is British, but even their accents don't help us tell them apart, since half of the time they're pretending to be each other.

"I'll teach you to be me, and you teach me to be you," one twin says after they meet by chance at summer camp and realize that they've been raised separately by divorced parents. It's a splendid story premise, but in a way the switch is just the setup, and the real story involves the parents. They're played by Dennis Quaid and Natasha Richardson, who bring such humor and warmth to the movie that I was amazed to find myself actually caring about their romance.

The three important supporting roles are also well filled. Plump, spunky Lisa Ann Walter plays the nanny and housekeeper on Quaid's spread (he runs a vineyard in Napa Valley), and bald, droll Simon Kunz is Richardson's butler (she's a trendy London fashion designer). Elaine Hendrix, coming across a little like Sharon Stone, is the snotty publicist who plans to marry Quaid—until the parent trap springs. She has a thankless role—the only person in the movie we're not supposed to like—but at least they don't make her just stand there and be obnoxious. She gets to earn her stripes in a camping trip during which she demonstrates, for once and all, that she is not the ideal wife for Quaid.

A movie like this has to cover a lot of ground in several different locations. That's why good casting is so important. There's not time to establish the characters carefully, so they have to bring their personalities along with them almost from the first shot. Quaid is instantly likable, with that goofy smile. Richardson, who almost always plays tougher roles and harder women, this time is astonishing, she's so warm and attractive. The two of them have a conversation over an old bottle of wine, and, yes, it's cornball—but quality cornball, earning its sentiment.

Movies like this remember how much fun escapism can be. The film opens with Quaid and Richardson falling in love on the *QE2* and being married in mid-Atlantic. It includes the kind of summer camp where when the kids play pranks, it looks like they had the help of a platoon of art directors and special-effects coordinators. And, of course, both parents live in great houses: Richardson in a London town house with sweeping staircases and *Architectural Digest* interiors, Quaid in a Napa ranch home with a shaded veranda.

The key task in the movie is to make the double photography of the "twins" work. All kinds of tricks are used, and of course the techniques are more advanced than they were in 1961, but since you can't see them anyway, you forget about them. Lindsay Lohan has command of flawless British and American accents, and also uses slightly flawed ones for when the girls are playing each other. What she has all the time is the same kind of sunny charm Hayley Mills projected, and a sense of mischief that makes us halfway believe in the twins' scheme.

The movie was directed by Nancy Meyers and produced by Charles Shyer; they wrote the script with David Swift. Meyers and Shyer have specialized in light domestic comedies *(Baby Boom, Father of the Bride)* and they make this into a good one—a family picture that's not too soppy for adults. My only reservation involves the ear-piercing scene, which I suspect will lead to an epidemic of do-it-yourself home surgery.

Pariah ★ ★ ★
NO MPAA RATING, 105 m., 1999

Damon Jones (Steve), Dave Oren Ward (Crew), David Lee Wilson (David Lee), Aimee Chaffin (Sissy), Angela Jones (Angela), Anna Padgett (Lex), Dan Weene (Joey), Ann Zupa (Babe), Brandon Slater (Doughboy), Jason Posey (Kewvin), Elexa Williams (Sam). Directed by Randolph Kret and produced by Scott Grusin, David J. Hill, Shaun Hill, and Vince Rotonda. Screenplay by Kret.

Godard said that one way to criticize a movie is to make another movie. *Pariah,* a raw and unblinking look at the skinhead subculture, is a movie I'd like to show to those admirers of *Fight Club* who have assured me of their movie's greatness. This is the real thing, with *Fight Club*'s implicit skinhead doom-worship made visible. Its characters don't take the high road in rejecting straw targets like "consumerism," but the low road, in rejecting everything outside their small, infected circle of hate. The movie understands that it's not what you reject that defines you, but the act of rejection—the very decision to scorn and offend. *Fight Club* is *Pariah* made palatable.

To be sure, the demented subjects of *Pariah* are racists, and the heroes of *Fight Club* are not. But there are scenes in *Pariah* that look uncannily like scenes in *Fight Club,* except that they are uglier, more violent, and more brutal. And the group dynamic is similar: Society is corrupt, so we will set ourselves against society, behaving in such a way that citizens will fear and hate us.

Pariah takes place within a Los Angeles neighborhood mostly devoid of ordinary people. Everyone seems to live by violence and fear. If the skinheads attack gays and attempt the murder of a transvestite in a park—well, there is a gay gang, too, to pound the skinheads with baseball bats. And if white gangs attack interracial couples because the woman is black, black gangs attack them because the man is white. When not enforcing their dating theories, the gangs fight with each other.

As the film opens, we meet Steve (Damon Jones), a peaceable white guy who dates a black woman (Elexa Williams). They are attacked by skinheads in a parking garage, and he is beaten and then made to watch while she is raped. He attempts to comfort her, in an observant if somewhat awkward scene, but she is beyond comfort. Rage then transforms Steve into an instrument of vengeance, and he becomes a skinhead, tattooed, belted, and booted, and joins the gang that attacked them. He wants revenge, especially against David Lee (David Lee Wilson), who led the attack, and Crew (Dave Oren Ward), the pack's top dog.

Only the reasonable would point out that once Steve identifies the gang, it would be fairly easy for him to kill David without going through the painful and dangerous ordeal of trying to ingratiate himself. But then there would be no movie—and also no opportunity for Randolph Kret, the writer-director, to show us Steve gradually becoming brutalized by the skinhead culture. He doesn't change his ideas, but he becomes comfortable within a world of hate-talk, rough sex, and fights that lead to bonding and friendship (ahem).

Pariah is sometimes an ungainly movie, carelessly constructed and too long, but it contains the seed of truth, and that redeems it. It shows us a male-dominated group in which sex is uninteresting unless forced, in which women are treated as slaves and receptacles, in which the rhetoric of white supremacy begs the question: How do these people not see that their values reflect pathology and zero self-esteem?

The dynamic of the skinheads and *Fight Club* is similar. Society is corrupt and unworthy, and its values are boring and materialistic. Only by a descent to the animal level can men regain self-respect. (Yes, *Fight Club* rejects this message, but its imagery makes it fleetingly attractive; *Pariah* does a better job of not making seductive what it is against.) To spend time in this movie is to reap the harvest of cruel childhoods, broken parents, poverty, ignorance, and despair. You would need to think yourself desperately without resources to turn to skinheads for improvement.

Will the film cause the kind of behavior it opposes? (It opened in Los Angeles in spring 1999, then was withdrawn after Columbine.) I doubt that any film can persuade anybody to do what he is not already fully prepared to do. Films may suggest methods, but do not force decisions. What it does do is show *Fight Club* fans what their movie is really about. I received an actual e-mail, which I believe to be genuine, from a *Fight Club* admirer who complained: "My generation was denied a war in which to test itself. We need movies like this."

Passion in the Desert ★ ★
PG-13, 93 m., 1998

Ben Daniels (Augustin), Michel Piccoli (Venture), Paul Meston (Grognard), Kenneth Collard (Officer), Nadi Odeh (Bedouin Bride), Auda Mohammed Badoul (Shepherd Boy), Mohammed Ali (Medicine Man). Directed and produced by Lavinia Currier. Screenplay by Currier, adapted from the novella *A Passion in the Desert* by Honoré de Balzac.

Passion in the Desert is a brave folly of a film, easy to laugh at but deserving a certain respect, if only because it involves such a foolish and difficult story. For most of its length, it is about a man and a leopard who seem to fall in love with one another (if leopards can be said to fall in love). As they gaze happily into each other's eyes, we agree they make a handsome couple, but what exactly is the filmmaker trying to say?

The film, acted in English despite its French origins, opens in 1798, during Napoleon's North African campaign. The soldier Augustin (Ben Daniels) has been attached as a guide to an artist named Venture (Michel Piccoli), assigned to the campaign. After a bloody attack, Augustin observes, "We seem to have misplaced the French army." No matter: "How can you get lost in Egypt? You have the Nile and the sea."

Yes, but that isn't much help if neither is in walking distance. The two men struggle under the blazing sun until death seems near. Venture drinks his paints and dies. Augustin stumbles across a tent, water, a woman in jewels, but after his depredations are discovered he is chased toward an ancient gathering of monuments, which is guarded by a female leopard.

The beast has already killed a man, but now soldier and leopard make a wary peace, which gradually grows into acceptance and fondness; the soldier even grooms the leopard's coat by licking it. When a male leopard appears and a courtship seems on the horizon, the jealous soldier uses mud to cover himself with spots, so he can seem to be a male leopard too.

The actor worked with three trained leopards in filming these scenes, which win our admiration for their beauty and difficulty even as we're trying to puzzle them out on some plane above the *Wild Kingdom* level. And the film is beautifully photographed. But the longer the courtship continues, the more it seemed like a weird exercise in surrealism; I didn't believe it on a literal level and couldn't get it to work on any other.

Where did the writer-director, Lavinia Currier, get the idea for this story? Not in a million years would I have guessed the answer: from Balzac. Yes, from Honoré de Balzac, the nineteenth-century French saint of social realism. The critic Michael Atkinson has pointed out that Balzac's story, however, is titled *A Passion in the Desert,* and that little "A" makes all the difference—suggesting the suffering of Christ rather than, as Atkinson puts it, "a soft porn Bo Derek film from the '80s."

I am informed by a reader that the Vancouver movie ratings board has, in addition to everything our own MPAA warns us about, a warning about "animal husbandry" scenes in which animals engage in reproductive frolic. Mercifully, Augustin and the leopard hold the line at goo-goo eyes.

Passion of Mind ★ ★
PG-13, 105 m., 2000

Demi Moore (Marie/Marty), Stellan Skarsgard (William), William Fichtner (Aaron), Sinead Cusack (Jessie), Peter Riegert (Dr. Peters), Joss Ackland (Dr. Langer), Gerry Bamman (Edward Youngerman), Julianne Nicholson (Kim). Directed by Alain Berliner and produced by Carole Scotta, Tom Rosenberg, and Ron Bass. Screenplay by Bass and David Field.

When Marie is asleep in France, Marty is awake in New York. When Marty is asleep in New York, Marie is awake in France. Both women are played by Demi Moore in Alain Berliner's *Passion of Mind,* a film that crosses the supernatural with "an interesting case of multiple personality," as one of her shrinks puts it. She has two shrinks. She needs them. She doesn't know which of her lives is real and which is the dream. Whenever she goes to sleep in one country, she wakes up in the other. Multiple personalities are bad enough, but at least she doesn't have eager kidneys; getting up in the middle of the night to go to the bathroom could lead to whiplash.

The movie uses its supernatural device to show Moore's characters living two contrasting lifestyles. In France, she leads a quiet life as a book reviewer and raises her two daughters. In New York, she's a powerful literary agent who dedicates her life to her career. In France, she meets William (Stellan Skarsgard). In New York, she meets Aaron (William Fichtner). They both love her. Each of her personalities, Marty and Marie, is aware of the other and remembers what happens in the other's life.

Like *Me Myself I,* the recent movie starring Rachel Griffiths, this movie is about a woman's choice between family and career. In the Griffiths film, a busy single writer is magically transported into a marriage with a husband and three kids. If she could have led both lives at once, as Marie/Marty does, I think she would have been okay with that. And as Marty and Marie trudge off to complain to their shrinks, I was wondering why it was so necessary to solve their dilemma. If you can live half of your life quietly in France and the other half in the fast lane of Manhattan, enjoy parenthood and yet escape the kids, and be in love with two great guys without (technically) cheating on either one—what's the problem? When you're not with the one you love, you love the one you're with. If it works, don't fix it.

Of course it doesn't work. If one of the worlds is real and the other is a dream, and if you cannot be in love with two men at once, then what happens if you commit to the dream man and lose the real one? This preys on the mind of Marie/Marty, who also dreads what could happen if the two worlds mix in some way. She won't let one guy spend the night, because "if someone were to be with me and wake me up, something bad might happen."

It is that very problem that the movie never quite solves logically. Forgive me for being literal. The time difference between New York and France is six hours. How does that fit into your sleep schedule? If she is awake until midnight in France, does that mean she's asleep all day in New York, and wakes up at six P.M.? Are there twenty-four hours in a day for both characters?

These questions are cheating. Forgive me for thinking of them. They obviously occurred to the screenwriters, Ron Bass and David Field, who just as obviously decided to ignore them. The movie is not about timetables but life choices, and to a degree it works. We see Marty/ Marie pulled between two worlds, in love with her children, attracted to the two guys. The problem is, that's it. We master the situation in the first forty minutes, and then the wheels start spinning. What's needed is a way to take the story through some kind of U-turn.

Why not have the woman accept her situation, work with it, willfully experiment with her two lives, self-consciously engage with it? Don't make her a victim but a psychic explorer. Why, if we are dealing with a woman who is liberated half of the time from each lifestyle, does the movie fall back on the tired formula that there is something wrong with her, and she must seek psychiatric help to cure it? The joy in *Me Myself I* is that the woman self-reliantly deals with the vast change in her life, instead of diagnosing herself as a case study.

Another difficulty in *Passion of Mind* is with the men. Stellan Skarsgard and William Fichtner bring more to the movie than is needed. These are complex actors with subtly disturbing undertones. They both play nice guys, but we can't quite believe them. We suspect secrets or hidden agendas. They smile, they're warm and pleasant and supportive, and we're wondering, what's their angle? For this particular story, it might have been better to cast actors who were more bland and one-dimensional, so that they could represent only what is needed (two nice guys) rather than veiled complications.

Demi Moore does what she can with a screenplay that doesn't seem confident about what to do with her. She is convincing as either woman, but not as both, if you see what I mean. She makes a wonderful mother in France and a convincing businessman in Manhattan, but when she is either one, we wonder where she puts the other one. The screenplay doesn't help her.

By the end of the film, which is unconvincingly neat, I was distracted by too many questions to care about the answers. The structure had upstaged the content. It wasn't about the heroine; it was about the screenplay. In *Me Myself I*, which has a much simpler premise (the woman goes from one life to another with an unexplained magical zap), there was room for a deeper and more human (and humorous) experience. First the heroine was one, then the other. In *Passion of Mind*, by being

both, she is neither. Is her problem a split personality, or psychic jet lag?

Patch Adams ★ ½
PG-13, 110 m., 1998

Robin Williams (Patch Adams), Daniel London (Truman), Monica Potter (Carin), Philip Seymour Hoffman (Mitch), Bob Gunton (Dean Walcott), Josef Sommer (Dr. Eaton), Irma P. Hall (Joletta), Frances Lee McCain (Judy). Directed by Tom Shadyac and produced by Barry Kemp, Mike Farrell, Marvin Minoff, and Charles Newirth. Screenplay by Steve Oedekerk, based on the book *Gesundheit: Good Health Is a Laughing Matter* by Hunter Doherty Adams with Maureen Mylander.

Patch Adams made me want to spray the screen with Lysol. This movie is shameless. It's not merely a tearjerker. It extracts tears individually by liposuction, without anesthesia. It is allegedly based on the life of a real man named Patch Adams, whom I have seen on television, where he looks like Salvador Dali's seedy kid brother. If all of these things really happened to him, they should have abandoned Robin Williams and brought in Jerry Lewis for the telethon.

As the movie opens, a suicidal Patch has checked into a mental hospital. There he finds that the doctors don't help him, but the patients do. On the outside, he determines to become a doctor in order to help people, and enrolls in a medical school. Soon he finds, not to our amazement, that medicine is an impersonal business. When a patient is referred to by bed number or disease, Patch reasonably asks, "What's her name?"

Patch is a character. To himself, he's an irrepressible bundle of joy, a zany live wire who brings laughter into the lives of the sick and dying. To me, he's a pain in the wazoo. If this guy broke into my hospital room and started tap-dancing with bedpans on his feet, I'd call the cops.

The lesson of *Patch Adams* is that laughter is the best medicine. I know Norman Cousins cured himself by watching Marx Brothers movies, but to paraphrase Groucho, I enjoy a good cigar, but not when it explodes. I've been lucky enough to discover doctors who never once found it necessary to treat me while wearing a red rubber nose.

In the movie, Patch plays the clown to cheer up little tykes whose hair has fallen out from chemotherapy. Put in charge of the school welcoming committee for a gynecologist's convention, he builds a papier-mâché prop: enormous spread legs reaching an apex at the entrance to the lecture hall. What a card. He's the nonconformist, humanist, warmhearted rebel who defies the cold and materialist establishment and stands up for clowns and free spirits everywhere. This is a role Robin Williams was born to play. In fact, he was born playing it.

We can see at the beginning where the movie is headed, but we think maybe we can jump free before the crash. No luck. (Spoiler warning!) Consider, for example, the character named Carin (Monica Potter), who is one of Patch's fellow students. She appears too late in the movie to be a major love interest. Yet Patch does love her. Therefore, she's obviously in the movie for one purpose only: to die. The only suspense involves her function in the movie's structure, which is inspired by those outlines that Hollywood writing coaches flog to their students: Will her death provide the False Crisis, or the Real Crisis?

She's only good for the False Crisis, which I will not reveal, except to say that it is cruel and arbitrary, stuck in merely to get a cheap effect. It inspires broodings of worthlessness in Patch, who ponders suicide, but sees a butterfly and pulls himself together for the False Dawn. Life must go on, and he must continue his mission to save sad patients from their depression. They may die, but they'll die laughing.

The False Dawn (the upbeat before the final downbeat) is a lulu. A dying woman refuses to eat. Patch convinces her to take nourishment by filling a plastic wading pool with spaghetti and jumping around in it. This is the perfect approach, and soon the wretched woman is gobbling her pasta. I would have asked for some from the part he hadn't stepped in.

Next comes the Real Crisis. Patch is threatened with expulsion from medical school. I rubbed my eyes with incredulity: *There is a courtroom scene!* Courtrooms are expected in legal movies. But in medical tearjerkers, they're the treatment of last resort. Any screenwriter who uses a courtroom scene in a nonlegal movie is not only desperate for a third act, but didn't have a second act that led anywhere.

What a courtroom. It's like a John Grisham wet dream. This could be the set for *Inherit the Wind.* The main floor and balcony are jammed with Patch's supporters, with a few seats up front for the villains. There's no legalistic mumbo-jumbo; these people function simply as an audience for Patch's narcissistic grandstanding. (Spoiler warning No. 2.) After his big speech, the courtroom doors open up and who walks in? All those bald little chemotherapy kids that Patch cheered up earlier. And yes, dear reader, each and every one is wearing a red rubber nose. Should these kids be out of bed? Their immune systems are shot to hell. If one catches cold and dies, there won't be any laughing during the malpractice suit.

I have nothing against sentiment, but it must be earned. Cynics scoffed at Robin Williams's previous film, *What Dreams May Come,* in which he went to heaven and then descended into hell to save the woman he loved. Corny? You bet—but with the courage of its convictions. It made no apologies and exploited no formulas. It was the real thing. *Patch Adams* is quackery.

The Patriot ★ ★ ★
R, 157 m., 2000

Mel Gibson (Benjamin Martin), Heath Ledger (Gabriel Martin), Joely Richardson (Charlotte Selton), Jason Isaacs (Colonel William Tavington), Chris Cooper (Colonel Harry Burwell), Tcheky Karyo (Jean Villeneuve), Rene Auberjonois (Reverend Oliver), Lisa Brenner (Anne Howard), Tom Wilkinson (General Cornwallis). Directed by Roland Emmerich and produced by Mark Gordon and Gary Levinsohn. Screenplay by Robert Rodat.

The Patriot is a fable arguing the futility of pacifism, set against the backdrop of the Revolutionary War. It is rousing and entertaining and you get your money's worth, but there isn't an idea in it that will stand up to thoughtful scrutiny. The British are seen as gentlemanly fops or sadistic monsters, and the Americans come in two categories: brave or braver. Those who have a serious interest in the period will find it a cartoon; those raised on summer action pictures will find it more stimulating than most.

Mel Gibson stars, in a powerful and effective performance, as a widower named Benjamin Martin with seven children. He saw enough of battle in the French and Indian War, and was frightened by what he learned about himself. He counsels a treaty with King George. Asked about his principles by an old comrade in arms (Chris Cooper), he replies, "I'm a parent. I haven't got the luxury of principles." But he gets some in a hurry after the monstrous British Colonel Tavington (Jason Isaacs) arrests Martin's eldest son, Gabriel (Heath Ledger), and takes him away to be hanged, after first shooting another of Martin's sons just for the hell of it, and then burning down his house.

Since Martin had just been treating the wounded of both sides in his home, this seems excessive, and in the long run turns out to be extremely unwise for the British, since Martin goes on to more or less single-handedly mastermind their defeat. There must have been many British officers less cruel—but none would have served the screenplay's purpose, which is to show Martin driven berserk by grief, rage, and the need for revenge.

The following sequence is the film's most disturbing. Martin and his sons hide in the woods and ambush Tavington and his soldiers; eventually the battle comes down to hand-to-hand fighting (Martin wielding a tomahawk). Gabriel is freed, and the younger adolescent boys get a taste for blood ("I'm glad I killed them!" one of the tykes cries. "I'm glad!"). The movie's scenes of carnage have more impact than the multiple killings in a film like *Shaft*, because they are personal, not technical; individual soldiers, frightened and ill-prepared, are fighting for their lives, while in the modern action pictures most of the victims are pop-up arcade targets.

The big players in the war (George Washington, King George) are far offscreen, although we do meet General Cornwallis (Tom Wilkinson), a British leader who counsels a "gentlemanly" conduct of the war and rebukes Tavington for his brutality. Still, when the Americans refuse to "fight fair" and adopt hit-and-run guerrilla tactics against the British (who march in orderly ranks into gunfire), he bends enough to authorize the evil colonel to take what steps are necessary to bring down Martin (by now legendary as "the Ghost").

The movie's battle scenes come in two flavors—harrowing and unlikely. Two battles near the beginning of the film are conveniently fought in open fields overlooked by the upper windows of houses, so onlookers have excellent seats for the show and can supply a running narration. No doubt revolutionary battles were fought right there in the pasture, but would Benjamin Martin allow his kids to stand in the windows, or tell them to hide in the barn?

The "real" battles are grueling tests of men and horses, as soldiers march into withering fire and the survivors draw their swords or fix their bayonets for blood-soaked combat in close quarters. These battles seem anarchic and pitiless, and respect the movie convention that bitter rivals will sooner or later find themselves face-to-face. The scenes are well staged by the director, Roland Emmerich, working from a screenplay by Robert Rodat, the same man who wrote *Saving Private Ryan,* with its equally appalling battle scenes.

Hollywood movies are at pains these days to provide a role for a heroic African-American or two. A role for a black sailor was found in the segregated U.S. Navy submarine corps in *U-571* (he was a mess orderly). Now we have a black slave who fights beside white men (even those who hate him) because General Washington has decreed freedom for all slaves who fight for a year. Good enough, but why not go all the way and give this character dialogue and a real role to play, instead of demeaningly using him only to count down the months and days until his freedom? When the former slave finally gets two whole sentences in a row, at the end, he quotes Martin's son: "Gabriel said if we won the war, we could build a whole new world. We could get started right here with your home." Uh-huh. Why not get started with your own home?

The movie has light comic relief to ease the tension (Martin's handmade chairs keep collapsing beneath him), and a love story (Gabriel loves Anne, a plucky colonial girl who catches his eye with a patriotic speech). Anne's father is a deaf man who misunderstands things. When Gabriel asks permission to write Anne, the old man at first takes offense. Then he says,

"Oh . . . *write* her! Of course you may." What did he think Gabriel had asked? Meanwhile, there's even female company for hard-bitten Benjamin Martin, who asks the sister of his dead wife, "May I sit here?" Her answer got laughs in the screening I attended: "It's a free country—or at least, it will be."

These passages and others (including The Dead Man Who Is Not Really Dead) have been trucked directly into *The Patriot* from the warehouse of timeless clichés. They betray the movie's lack of serious intentions. It basically wants to be a summer action movie with a historical gloss. At that, it succeeds. I enjoyed the strength and conviction of Gibson's performance, the sweep of the battle scenes, and the absurdity of the British caricatures. None of it has much to do with the historical reality of the Revolutionary War, but with such an enormous budget at risk, how could it? ☞

Paulie ★ ★
PG, 92 m., 1998

Gena Rowlands (Ivy), Tony Shalhoub (Misha), Cheech Marin (Ignacio), Bruce Davison (Dr. Reingold), Jay Mohr (Paulie/Benny), Trini Alvarado (Adult Marie), Buddy Hackett (Artie), Hallie Kate Eisenberg (Marie). Directed by John Roberts and produced by Mark Gordon, Gary Levinsohn, and Allison Lyon Segan. Screenplay by Laurie Craig.

Paulie tells the story of a parrot who can think like a human and talk like a stand-up comic, but a parrot who really had those gifts wouldn't have the problems this one does. He doesn't come across as a bird at all, but as a small, wisecracking person wearing feathers. He's just a little more interesting than the other guy with the same first name who also stars in—but no, that sentence was headed in an unkind direction.

The film is aimed at children, I suppose, although I don't think they'll like Paulie all that much. I didn't. I know there are people who love parrots, but they love them for being parrots. Would you want to live with a parrot who talked and thought like Buddy Hackett? You would? As long as he cleaned his own cage?

As the movie opens, Paulie is in "purgatory" in the basement of a research lab, where he's been banished for refusing to cooperate with an ambitious scientist (Bruce Davison). How did Paulie get there? After he's befriended by a Russian-American janitor (Tony Shalhoub), he offers to tell his story, and we see it in flashback as an odyssey across the country.

Paulie started, we learn, as the friend of a little girl named Marie. After he's blamed for her fall from a roof, he's dispatched to Buddy Hackett's pawnshop, where he picks up some of his vocal style before he's purchased by a lovable woman named Ivy (Gena Rowlands) who (kids! hide your eyes!) goes blind and dies. Then he travels cross-country to Los Angeles, where he has an unconsummated romance with a girl parrot, and no wonder: If you were as smart as Buddy Hackett, how long would you be able to sustain a relationship with a parrot? Cheech Marin makes a brief appearance as another of Paulie's owners, and the bird even becomes expert at stealing from ATM machines before he ends up in the hands of the scientist.

The movie's slant is that it's wrong to keep animals in cages and do experiments on them, and Paulie makes some dramatic gestures toward this end, but by then my attention was drifting. Dogs and cats, horses and monkeys, and even bears make charismatic movie stars, but *Paulie,* I think, suggests that birds are more decorative than dramatic.

On the other hand, just to be fair, I should mention that parrots make great subjects for jokes. I know about a dozen, including the ones about the parrot in the deep freeze, the insulting parrot, the 300-pound parakeet, and the parrot whose last words were, "Who moved the ladder?"

I even made up a brand-new parrot joke while watching this movie. A parrot has a memory that will hold only the last two things it has heard. A guy buys him, puts him by the front door and tests him. "One, two," the man says. "One, two," the parrot says. "Three," says the man. "Two, three," says the parrot. "Four," says the man. "Three, four," says the parrot. Then the guy shouts to his wife: "So long, honey, I'm going to the office!" When the guy comes home, what does the parrot say?

I'd tell you, but this is a family movie.

Payback ★ ★ ★
R, 102 m., 1999

Mel Gibson (Porter), Gregg Henry (Val), Maria Bello (Rosie), David Paymer (Stegman), Deborah Kara Unger (Lynn), William Devane (Carter), Bill Duke (Detective Hicks), Kris Kristofferson (Bronson), James Coburn (Mr. Fairfax), Lucy Liu (Pearl). Directed by Brian Helgeland and produced by Bruce Davey. Screenplay by Helgeland and Terry Hayes, based on the novel *The Hunter* by Richard Stark.

"Not many people know what their life's worth," the hero of *Payback* tells us right at the beginning. "I do. Seventy grand. That's what they took from me. And that's what I'm gonna get back." If you absorb that statement and take a close look at the title, you'll have a good idea of what the movie's about. The only remaining question: Is it about it entertainingly? Yes.

The movie's publicity makes much of the fact that the hero, named Porter, is a bad guy. It quotes the director, Brian Helgeland: "I wanted to see a bad guy as the hero, but I didn't want to make excuses for him." Of course, if the bad guy is played by Mel Gibson, you don't have to make the same kinds of excuses as if he's played by, say, James Woods. Gibson has a whimsical charm, a way of standing outside material like this and grinning at it. Oh, he's earnest and angry, blood-soaked and beaten nearly to death. But inside, there's a grin. His fundamental personality is comic—he's a joker and a satirist—and he only rarely makes an effort to hide that side (as he did, say, in *The Year of Living Dangerously*).

Brian Helgeland has a sense of style, too (he wrote *L.A. Confidential*), and we get the sense that *Payback* is more interested in style than story; it wants to take a criminal's revenge and make it the story of a guy whose mission edges into monomania. He wants exactly $70,000, no more, no less. More than once in the movie, Porter's enemies try to pay him more than $70,000. They're missing the point. (Porter could save himself a lot of wear and tear by taking $130,000 and mailing the rest back, but you know how it is.)

The setup contains a fundamental double-cross that I dare not reveal, and that will make it a little hard to discuss certain other aspects of the story. Perhaps selected details will give you the flavor. As when Porter's friend Val (Gregg Henry) shows him the weekly routine of some Chinese mobsters picking up cash. "They're not wearing their seat belts," Porter observes, and of course that leads to the logical conclusion that the way to get their money is to crash head-on into their car.

There are also action gags involving severed gas lines on a car, a trick telephone, blackmail by cell phone, kidnapping, and a scene in which Porter comes closer than anyone since James Bond to being killed crotch-first. The film also contains a hooker with a heart of gold (Maria Bello), a two-timing dame (Deborah Kara Unger), a laconic cop (Bill Duke), a big mobster (Kris Kristofferson), and an even bigger one (James Coburn).

Writing a screenplay like this essentially involves finding new bottles for old wine. Tricking the enemy is routine, but doing it in a new way is fun. Turning the tables is standard, but not when you don't expect when, and how, they'll be turned. And cinematographer Ericson Core finds a nice blue-green grittiness in the streets of Chicago, where the exterior scenes are punctuated by elevated trains rumbling past on such a frequent schedule that actual el riders will be chuckling to themselves.

There is much cleverness and ingenuity in *Payback,* but Mel Gibson is the key. The movie wouldn't work with an actor who was heavy on his feet, or was too sincere about the material. Gibson is essentially an action comedian, who enters into violence with a bemused detachment *(Mad Max Beyond Thunderdome).* Here he has fun as the movie goes over the top, as when a doctor operates on him for gunshot wounds, using whiskey as a painkiller (for the doctor, not Gibson). Or when he helps himself to the dollars from a beggar's hat. Or when, and how, he recites "This little piggy."

Pecker ★ ★
R, 87 m., 1998

Edward Furlong (Pecker), Christina Ricci (Shelley), Mark Joy (Jimmy), Mary Kay Place

(Joyce), Martha Plimpton (Tina), Brendan Sexton III (Matt), Lili Taylor (Rorey Wheeler), Jean Schertler (Memama), Lauren Hulsey (Little Crissy). Directed by John Waters and produced by John Fiedler and Mark Tarlov. Screenplay by Waters.

The hero of John Waters's *Pecker* got his nickname as a kid, we are told, by pecking at his food. Uh, huh. And guys named Studs had fathers in the tuxedo business. Pecker (Edward Furlong) works in a Baltimore sandwich shop and takes photos of the seamy side of life. He has an exhibit in the restaurant, a famous New York art dealer (Lili Taylor) happens to see it, and she mounts a show of his work in her gallery.

Of course all Manhattan is soon agog at the young genius, providing Waters with easy targets in the world of modern art. "Pecker's like a humane Diane Arbus," one critic gushes, when in fact he's more like just plain Diane Arbus. But *Pecker* isn't really about art so much as about the way that fame and fortune upset Pecker's little world.

There is a strong streak of domesticity in Waters's plots (even the characters in *Pink Flamingos* have home lives, although you might need to leave the room if I described them). Pecker's dad (Mark Joy) operates a failing bar. His mom (Mary Kay Place) runs a thrift shop and sells the homeless "a complete Easter outfit" for twenty-five cents. (Pecker assures one of her potential customers that a winter coat is "flameproof—in case someone tries to set you on fire.")

His sister Tina (Martha Plimpton) is the emcee in a male go-go bar, issuing dire warnings against such misbehavior as "tea-bagging." His grandmother (Jean Schertler) has a stand in front of the house to sell something called "pit beef," and has a Virgin Mary statue that talks uncannily like one of Conan O'Brien's speaking TV pictures. And there is a kid sister named Little Crissy (Lauren Hulsey) who stuffs candy into her mouth as if she only feeds on payday; she continues the Waters tradition of at least one addictive character in every movie.

Pecker is the most normal member of the family, I'd say. His girlfriend Shelley (Christina Ricci) runs a Laundromat, is an expert on stains, and sometimes slightly unzips the top of her jumper so Pecker can snap off a few quick shots. His best friend, Matt (Brendan Sexton III), is a compulsive shoplifter who poses while committing crimes and suffers the most from Pecker's fame; he complains, "If I can't shoplift, I don't want to be an artist!"

Waters follows these characters through their fifteen minutes of fame without ever churning up very much interest in them. One problem is that Furlong's performance doesn't project much heat or charisma, while the girlfriend played by Ricci seems constantly to be dampening her own. A simple casting switch, making Ricci the photographer and Furlong the boyfriend, might have improved the movie considerably.

There's also a certain tension between the gentler new Waters and his anarchic past. In the scenes in the male strip bar, for example, we keep waiting for Waters to break loose and shock us, and he never does, except with a few awkward language choices. The miraculous statue of Mary could have provided comic possibilities, but doesn't. In the early scenes it's clear that the grandmother is a ventriloquist, but in the later scenes, when the statue actually does talk, the best it can come up with are some disconnected phrases; one is reminded of HAL 9000 as the memory is being disconnected. Better if Mary had become an art critic.

Some scenes are so flat we squint a little at the screen, trying to see why anyone thought they might be funny. After Shelley the girlfriend thinks she sees Pecker kissing the art dealer, for example, she flees brokenhearted into a voting booth, and Pecker follows her into the booth, where they have loud and active sex. This is supposed to shock the bourgeoisie, but it plays like a bad idea.

The movie is filled with cameos, of which the most suggestive is the artist/photographer Cindy Sherman. She eyes the pit-beef grandma as a possible subject, and started me thinking maybe *that* would have been a better approach: Every member of the family is taken up by a different artist, and the Virgin Mary examines the results and says she doesn't know much about art, but she knows what she likes. After all, she's been in a lot of good paintings herself.

A Perfect Murder ★ ★ ★

R, 107 m., 1998

Michael Douglas (Steven Taylor), Gwyneth Paltrow (Emily Bradford Taylor), Viggo Mortensen (David Shaw), David Suchet (Detective Karaman), Constance Towers (Sandra Bradford), Sarita Choudhury (Raquel Martinez). Directed by Andrew Davis and produced by Arnold Kopelson, Anne Kopelson, Christopher Mankiewicz, and Peter MacGregor-Scott. Screenplay by Patrick Smith Kelly, based on the play *Dial M for Murder* by Frederick Knott.

Michael Douglas is about as good as anyone can be at playing greedy, coldhearted SOBs. He's also good at playing nice guys and victims—he's a versatile pro—but when he goes into his Gordon Gekko mode there's an extra charge on the screen, because we know everything his character says and does will be deceitful and self-interested.

Consider an early scene in Andrew Davis's *A Perfect Murder*. Douglas plays Steven Taylor, a wealthy currency trader. Gwyneth Paltrow plays Emily, his wife. She comes home to their designer apartment to find him dressed for a museum opening. They kiss. She says how nice he looks: "I'll hurry and get dressed so I can catch up." Throughout this entire scene, dislike hangs in the air. There's nothing overt. It's simply a way Douglas has of pronouncing his words, as if he wants to say all the proper things even though he doesn't mean them.

The Paltrow character is an heiress who is having an affair with an artist named David Shaw (Viggo Mortensen). We learn that in the first scene. *A Perfect Murder* doesn't fool around with a misleading opening charade to deceive us. This is not a happy marriage and the movie never pretends otherwise, and when the husband confronts the artist in his studio, there is a kind of blunt savagery to the way he cuts to the bottom line. ("You steal the crown jewel of a man's life, and all you can come up with is some candy-ass Hallmark sentiment?")

A murder is arranged in the movie, but for once the TV ads leave you with a certain doubt about who is doing what and with which and to whom, so I won't reveal the secret. I will say that Paltrow does a convincing job of playing a chic wife who considers love to be a choice more than a destiny. Viggo Mortensen undergoes an interesting transformation in his key scene with Douglas; we believe him when he's a nice guy, and we believe him even more when he's not; he doesn't do a big style shift, he simply turns off his people-pleasing face.

The screenplay, by Patrick Smith Kelly, is based on the play *Dial M for Murder* and the Hitchcock film of the same title. It has little in common with its predecessors. It's about negotiation more than deception, money more than love. Everybody's motives are pretty much clear from the beginning, and when the body is found on the kitchen floor the only mystery is how long it will take the survivor to find the key to the scheme.

Surprisingly, the movie got some negative early reviews. I think it works like a nasty little machine to keep us involved and disturbed; my attention never strayed, and one of the elements I liked was the way Paltrow's character isn't sentimentalized. She says she's in love with the artist, yes, but she gets over it in a hurry; it takes her about one line of dialogue. And there is a moment when it appears that husband and wife will put adultery and violence behind them, and continue their pragmatic liaison as a rich guy and his multilingual trophy wife. Who wouldn't want to keep living in that great apartment?

But there's another problem: Steven is having a portfolio meltdown (his adviser tells him, "Think Chernobyl"). Steven is driven not only by jealousy but by need and greed. Emily has a $100 million trust fund that would help Steven cover those margins (although the markets move a lot faster than probate, and the inheritance is unlikely to arrive in time to do much good).

The movie is a skilled example of what I call the Fatal Basic Genre. Like *Fatal Attraction*, *Basic Instinct*, and all of their lesser imitators, it's about sex between bad people who live in good houses. Nobody is better at Fatal Basic than Michael Douglas, who doesn't need to read *GQ* because he instinctively knows what clothes to wear and which cigars to smoke.

My only real disappointment with the movie comes at the end, when various differences are resolved with gunshots. This is such a tired story solution. I realize that the Hollywood bylaws require all action movies to end in shoot-outs, but is a gun really necessary in a Fatal Basic movie? I'd prefer the chessmaster approach to the problem, in which a single line of logical dialogue seals a character's fate, and then we get a big close-up of him realizing he's screwed. Gunshots release tension, but they don't provide audience pleasure, because the victim is dead and therefore cannot feel as bad as he deserves to.

The Perfect Storm ★ ★ ★ ½
PG-13, 129 m., 2000

George Clooney (Captain Billy Tyne), Mark Wahlberg (Bobby Shatford), Mary Elizabeth Mastrantonio (Linda Greenlaw), John C. Reilly (Murph), William Fichtner (Sully), Karen Allen (Melissa Brown), Allen Payne (Alfred Pierre), Diane Lane (Christina Cotter), John Hawkes (Bugsy), Cherry Jones (Edie Bailey). Directed by Wolfgang Petersen and produced by Paula Weinstein, Petersen, and Gail Katz. Screenplay by Bill Wittliff, based on the book by Sebastian Junger.

The Perfect Storm is a well-crafted example of the film of pure sensation. It is about ships tossed by a violent storm. The film doesn't have complex and involving characters, but they are not needed. It doesn't tell a sophisticated story, and doesn't need to; the main events are known to most of the audience before the movie begins. All depends on the storm. I do not mind admitting I was enthralled.

The movie, based on the best-seller by Sebastian Junger, is mostly about a fishing ship named the *Andrea Gail,* out of Gloucester, Massachusetts, which had the misfortune in 1991 of running into "the middle of the monster" when three great storm systems collided in the Atlantic. We learn about the economic pressures of the swordfishing industry, we meet the crew members and their women, we learn a little of their stories, and then the film is about the ship, the storm, and the people waiting in port for news. A parallel story, about a luxury sailboat in distress, cranks up the suspense even further.

The crew members of the *Andrea Gail* are a job lot of basic movie types. We count Captain Billy Tyne (George Clooney), whose pride has been stung because his catch has fallen behind this season. His crew includes Bobby Shatford (Mark Wahlberg), who is in love with divorced mom Diane Lane; Murph (John C. Reilly), whose seafaring life has led to a friendly but sad separation from his wife and son; Bugsy (John Hawkes), the sort of character who gets overlooked in crowds; Alfred Pierre (Allen Payne), a Jamaican who has ventured into northern waters for the paycheck; and a last-minute addition, Sully (William Fichtner). He and Murph don't like each other. Why not? Jealousy over Murph's wife, the movie says. To provide the plot with some onboard conflict, is my guess.

These characters are not developed in the way that similar seafarers might be developed in a novel by Joseph Conrad or Herman Melville. We learn only their external signs and characteristics; we don't know or much care what makes them tick. That's not a fatal flaw to the film because *The Perfect Storm* is not about the people, but about the storm. When Conrad writes *Lord Jim* or Melville writes *Moby-Dick,* the stories are about the way men's characters interact with the sea and with their shipmates. They are novels about people.

If *The Perfect Storm* had taken that approach, there would be fewer characters and a lot more dialogue; it might be a better film and would certainly be a different one. Its director, Wolfgang Petersen, also made *Das Boot,* the submarine drama, that does develop the deeper human complexities of its characters—but that took so long that the original 210-minute cut was trimmed back to 145 more action-packed minutes for the first U.S. release. At 129 minutes, *The Perfect Storm* delivers the goods but little human insight.

The film's best scenes are more or less without dialogue, except for desperately shouted words. They are about men trapped in a maelstrom of overpowering forces. They respond heroically, because they must, but they are not heroes; their motivation is need. They have had a bad season, have made one risky last trip, have ventured beyond the familiar Grand Banks fishing grounds to the problematical Flemish Cap. Quentin, the salty old dog who sits at the bar and provides color commentary, gives us the background: "I was last there in '62. Lots of fish. Lots of weather."

They have good luck: a catch of 60,000 pounds of swordfish. Then bad luck: The ice machine breaks down. The catch will spoil unless they get it quickly back to port. There are reports of a gathering storm. Billy lists their choices: "Either we hang out here, or say the hell with it and drive right through." The crew votes to plow right through the storm and collect those paychecks. Of course, they don't understand how big the storm really is, and when another fishing boat skipper (Mary Elizabeth Mastrantonio) tries to tell them, their antenna has blown overboard.

The scenes at sea are intercut with scenes in the bar where most of the Gloucester fishing industry seems to drink; it is conveniently located right at the end of the dock (and Diane Lane conveniently lives right upstairs). This is about right; I do not doubt that the owners, retired sailors, wives, girlfriends, and drinking buddies all stand watch in a saloon during a storm, ordering rounds and eyeing the Weather Channel.

Even before the storm, there are terrific set pieces, as when Murph is yanked overboard by a fishing line, and two men dive in to save him (Sully, his enemy, is the first in the water). But the heart of the film is in the ordeal of two ships caught in the tempest. As the men of the *Andrea Gail* battle wearily against their fate, the skipper attempts to cut loose an anchor. He clings to a swaying beam while holding an acetylene torch; the wonder is that he doesn't burn a hole in himself in the attempt.

Even more exciting is the parallel plot involving a Coast Guard rescue of the sailboat. A passenger (Cherry Jones) pleads with its owner to seek safer waters, but he is a pig-headed millionaire yachtsman with no respect for nature ("This is *my* boat!"). A helicopter rescue is attempted, shown in amazing action footage, and then the tension escalates as the chopper tries to go on to the *Andrea Gail*, a midair refueling is attempted, and eventually men are risking their lives in what seems like a doomed struggle (at one point, a Guardsman who is safe goes back into the sea after a crew mate).

We know intellectually that we're viewing special effects. Tanks and wind machines are involved, and computer graphics and models. This is not important. The impetus of the story drives us forward, and by the end of the film I was wrung out. It's possible to criticize the sketchy characters, but pointless. The movie is about the appalling experience of fighting for your life in a small boat in a big storm. If that is what you want to see, you will see it done here about as well as it can be done. ☞

Permanent Midnight ★ ★ ★
R, 95 m., 1998

Ben Stiller (Jerry Stahl), Elizabeth Hurley (Sandra), Janeane Garofalo (Jana), Maria Bello (Kitty), Owen C. Wilson (Nicky), Lourdes Benedicto (Volo), Fred Willard (Craig Ziffer), Cheryl Ladd (Pamel Verlaine), Peter Greene (Dealer). Directed by David Veloz and produced by Jane Hamsher and Don Murphy. Screenplay by Veloz, based on the book by Jerry Stahl.

"You're too darn sad-looking to just be another retard in a pink visor," the customer tells the fast-food clerk. That leads into a conversation, and in no time at all they're in bed together, and he's telling her the story of his life—which, in recent years, played more like his slow and agonizing death.

The guy with the drive-thru job is Jerry Stahl (Ben Stiller), who at one point was making $5,000 a week as a TV writer in Hollywood. Nice work, unless your drug habit is running you $6,000 a week. It's a true story. The movie *Permanent Midnight,* based on the autobiography of Stahl, tells how his life spiraled into increasing desperation, even while his TV bosses let him get away with almost everything—as long as he produced.

Stahl, a smart guy with good ideas, gets his TV job through Sandra (Elizabeth Hurley), a British woman he marries for money, so she can get a green card. His first job interview goes strangely. "I'm wondering if your mind can function down at our level," muses his prospective boss (Fred Willard). Asked what he thinks about the show (a puppetcast named Mr. Chompers), he insults the show and is hired. Soon he's turning his own life into fodder for comedy; his father's suicide is recycled into an episode.

The story of every drunk or addict is different in the details but similar in the outlines:

Their days center around locating and using a sufficient supply of their substance of choice to avoid acute mental and physical discomfort. Eventually it gets to the point where everything else—job, family, self-image—is secondary. Stahl steals drugs from the medicine cabinet of his friends ("If I was Percodan, where would I be?") and buys drugs from very dangerous people (he's safe only because there's more money in customers who are not dead). He shoots up in risky places, is sometimes caught or almost caught, and finds his anger mounting because it is so very hard and exhausting to get high all the time.

There are bizarre episodes at work and in his private life, where the green-card girl inexplicably begins to take a liking to him, gets pregnant, and finds out too late that he is the wrong pony to bet on. One day, in desperation, she begs him to baby-sit. He sticks the kid in the car and goes looking for drugs; he's eventually stopped by the cops, who arrest him and call family services for the child. Does he learn his lesson? Does it help that when he gets out of rehab a friendly dealer (Peter Greene) is waiting to sell him drugs in the parking lot?

The story in *Permanent Midnight* has been told many times in many forms. Someday I'd like to see a movie based on Julia Phillips's harrowing memoir, *You'll Never Have Lunch in This Town Again.* What Ben Stiller brings to the role is a kind of savage impatience; his character stabs his body anywhere with the needle—even in the neck—because the niceties are no longer of interest to a man who simply needs to get the stuff into his veins, right away.

The movie gets credit for not making the highlife seem colorful or funny. It is not. It is boring, really, because when the drugs are there they simply clear the pain and allow the mind to focus on getting more drugs. Stahl doesn't seek drugs because he wants to feel good but because he wants to stop feeling bad. It isn't the high that makes people into addicts; it's the withdrawal.

Last month I saw a revival of Otto Preminger's *The Man With the Golden Arm,* the first of the Hollywood drug movies, with Frank Sinatra in the title role. Sinatra got an Oscar nomination for the role, in which he portrayed the pain of withdrawal. Stiller, playing Stahl,

makes it look incomparably worse. Either the drugs are getting stronger, or the actors are.

Phantoms ★
R, 91 m., 1998

Peter O'Toole (Timothy Flyte), Rose McGowan (Lisa Pailey), Joanna Going (Jenny Pailey), Liev Schreiber (Deputy Stu Wargle), Ben Affleck (Sheriff Bryce Hammond), Nicky Katt (Deputy Steve Shanning). Directed by Joe Chappelle and produced by Joel Soisson, Michael Leahy, Robert Pringle, and Steve Lane. Screenplay by Dean Koontz, based on his book.

Did you know that if a certain kind of worm learns how to solve a maze, and then you grind it up and feed it to other worms, the other worms will then be able to negotiate the maze on their first try? That's one of the scientific nuggets supplied in *Phantoms,* a movie that seems to have been made by grinding up other films and feeding them to this one.

As the movie opens, two sisters arrive by Jeep in a quaint mountain town that seems suspiciously quiet, and no wonder: Everybody in town seems to be dead. Some of them have died rather suddenly. The baker's wife, for example. Her hands still grip the rolling pin. Just her hands. The rest of her is elsewhere.

The sisters (Rose McGowan and Joanna Going) find more ominous signs. A dead deputy sheriff, for example. And phones that don't work—but then one does. The older sister picks it up. "Who are you? What do you want?" she asks. It is a test of great acting to be able to say those ancient lines as if you mean them. A test like many others that this movie fails.

The sheriff turns up. He is played by Ben Affleck, wearing an absurd cowboy hat that looks like the kind of unsold stock they unload on city slickers at the end of the season. He is accompanied by another deputy (Nicky Katt), who wears an identical hat. Don't they know it's a rule in the movies: Hero wears neat hat, sidekick wears funny hat?

Joining the two young women, they search the town and find a desperate message written in lipstick on a mirror, which (I'm jumping ahead now) leads them to Dr. Timothy Flyte (Peter O'Toole), an editor of the kind of supermarket rag that features babies with nine-pound ears. Dr. Flyte and U.S. Army troops soon arrive in the small town, dressed like ghostbusters, to get to the bottom of the mystery. "What kind of threat are we dealing with here—biological, chemical, or other?" he's asked. "I'm leaning toward 'other,'" he replies, with all the wisdom and poignancy of a man who once played Lawrence of Arabia and is now playing Dr. Timothy Flyte.

The movie quickly degenerates into another one of those Gotcha! thrillers in which loathsome, slimy creatures leap out of drain pipes and sewers and ingest supporting actors, while the stars pump bullets into it. There are a few neat touches. In front of an altar at the local church, the heroes discover a curious pile of stuff: watches, glasses, ballpoints, pacemakers. At first they think it's an offering to the Virgin Mary. But no: "That's not an offering. Those are undigested remains."

How common are these films getting to be? Two out of the three films I saw today used the formula. With a deep bow (almost a salaam) to *Tremors,* they locate their creatures beneath the surface of the land or sea, so that most of the time, although not enough of the time, you can't see them.

Peter O'Toole is a professional and plays his character well. It takes years of training and practice to be able to utter lines like, "It comes from the deep and secret realms of our Earth" without giggling. It is O'Toole who gets to float the educated tapeworm theory. When these creatures eat a human, they learn everything it knows—and even everything it thinks it knows, so that since many humans think they are being eaten by the devil, the creatures think they are the devil too. If only we could learn to think more kindly of those who digest us, this movie could have ended happily.

π ★ ★ ★ ½
R, 85 m., 1998

Sean Gullette (Maximillian Cohen), Mark Margolis (Sol Robeson), Ben Shenkman (Lenny Meyer), Pamela Hart (Marcy Dawson), Stephen Pearlman (Rabbi Cohen), Samia Shoaib (Devi), Ajay Naidu (Farrouhk). Directed by Darren Aronofsky and produced by Eric Watson. Screenplay by Aronofsky.

π is a study in madness and its partner, genius. A tortured, driven man believes (1) that mathematics is the language of the universe, (2) nature can be expressed in numbers, and (3) there are patterns everywhere in nature. If he can find the patterns, if he can find the key to the chaos, then he can predict anything—the stock market, for example. If the man is right, the mystery of existence is unlocked. If he is wrong, the inside of his brain begins to resemble a jammed stock ticker.

The movie, written and directed by Darren Aronofsky, is a study in mental obsession. His hero, named Maximillian Cohen, lives barricaded behind a triple-locked door, in a room filled with high-powered, customized computer equipment. He wants nothing to do with anybody. He writes programs, tests them, looks for the pattern, gets a 216-digit bug, stomps on his chips in a rage, and then begins to wonder about that bug. Exactly 216 digits. There is a theory among some Jewish scholars, he learns, that the name of God has 216 letters.

The movie is shot in rough, high-contrast black and white. Max, played by Sean Gullette, is balding, restless, paranoid, and brilliant. He has debilitating headaches and nosebleeds, symptoms of high blood pressure—or of the mental torment he's putting himself through. He's suspicious of everyone. The friendly Indian woman next door puts food by his door. He avoids her. He trusts only his old teacher, Sol (Mark Margolis). They play Go, a game deeper than chess, and Sol tells him to stop with the key-to-the-universe business already. He warns that Max's spinning away from science and toward numerology.

Not everybody thinks so. Max's phone rings with the entreaties of Marcy (Pamela Hart), who works for a high-powered Wall Street analysis firm. They want to hire him as a consultant. They think he's onto something. He has predicted some prices correctly. At the deli, he runs into a Hasidic Jew named Lenny (Ben Shenkman), who seems casual and friendly but has a hidden mission: His group believes the Torah may be a code sent from God, and may contain God's name.

Of course, if one finds the mathematical key to everything, that would include God, stock prices, the weather, past and future history, baseball scores, and the response to all moves in Go. That assumes there is a key. When you're looking for something that doesn't exist, it makes you crazier the closer you get to it.

The seductive thing about Aronofsky's film is that it is halfway plausible in terms of modern physics and math. What was numerology a century ago has now been simplified into a very, very vast problem. Chaos theory looks for patterns where common sense says there are none. A computer might be able to give you the answer to anything, if (1) it is powerful enough, and (2) it has all the data. Of course, you might need a computer the size of the universe and containing everything in it, but we're talking theory here.

π is a thriller. I am not very thrilled these days by whether the bad guys will get shot or the chase scene will end one way instead of another. You have to make a movie like that pretty skillfully before I care. But I am thrilled when a man risks his mind in the pursuit of a dangerous obsession. Max is out on a limb. There are hungry people circling him. He may be onto something. They want it too. For both the stock market people and the Hasidic cabal, Max's formula represents all they believe in and everything they care about.

And then there is a level, of course, at which Max may simply be insane or physically ill. There are people who work out complicated theories involving long, impenetrable columns of numbers. Newspapers get envelopes filled with their proofs every day. And other people who sit in their rooms, wrapping themselves in the webs of chess or numbers theory, addicted to their fixes. And game players, gamblers, horse players—people bewitched by the mirage of a system.

The beautiful thing about mathematics is that you can't prove it except by its own terms. There's no way to put some math in a test tube and see if it turns purple or heats up. It sits there smugly in its own perfect cocoon, letting people like Max find anything he wants in it— or to think that he has.

Note: Sean Gullette, the star of π, has authored the movie's fascinating Web page at www. pithemovie.com/.

A Piece of Eden ★ ½
NO MPAA RATING, 112 m., 2000

Marc Grapey (Bob Tredici), Rebecca Harrell (Happy), Robert Breuler (Franco Tredici), Tyne Daly (Aunt Aurelia), Marshall Efron (Andres), Frederic Forrest (Paulo Tredici), Andreas Katsulas (Giuseppe Tredici), Jeff Puckett (Greg Tredici), Tristan Rogers (Victor Hardwick). Directed by John Hancock and produced by Hancock and Ken Kitsch. Screenplay by Dorothy Tristan.

A Piece of Eden is a good-hearted film with many virtues, although riveting entertainment value is not one of them. It's a family comedy that ambles down well-trodden paths toward a foregone conclusion, neither disturbing nor challenging the audience. It was filmed in and around LaPorte, Indiana; the only review I have seen so far comes from a Utah critic, Fawna Jones, who finds it predictable, and describes it quite accurately: "This a movie for those who generally stay away from the theater for fear of being offended and who like their movies to have happy endings."

Going to a movie so you won't be offended is like eating potato chips made with Olestra; you avoid the dangers of the real thing, but your insides fill up with synthetic runny stuff. Watching *A Piece of Eden,* I found myself wanting to be shocked, amazed, or even surprised. The most unexpected thing in the movie is a machine that shakes apple trees to make the apples fall off. That could have prevented a lot of heartbreak in *The Cider House Rules.*

The film opens in New York, where Bob Tredici (Marc Grapey) runs the struggling Television Publicity Bureau with his secretary, Happy (Rebecca Harrell). She's been late four out of the last five days, and even more ominously, has a psychological block that prevents her from pronouncing the word "publicity" correctly when she answers the phone. (She comes from a family of high-powered analysts, and thinks her block may be approach avoidance.)

Bob gets a call from northeast Indiana, where his family has run a fruit farm since time immemorial. His father, Franco (Robert Breuler), is dying. Bob has an unhappy relationship with the old man but returns home anyway, to learn that the patriarch has rallied enough to spend endless hours in a hospital bed in the living room, making life miserable for everyone with his salt-of-the-earth routine. Franco plans to leave the farm not to Bob but to a relative who has stayed behind in Indiana.

Bob has bright ideas for the farm, including using computers for cost control and starting a petting zoo. But he needs to appear more stable, less like a decadent Manhattanite, and so in desperation he imports Happy to pose as his wife. This leads to scenes that could exist only in a movie, as when they are assigned to bunk down in the barn, and he gets a glimpse of her silhouette through the sheet that hangs from the ceiling just as it did in *It Happened One Night* (1934).

The choices available to the story are limited and obvious. Either Bob will get the farm, or another happy solution will be found, since Fawna Jones is quite correct that this is not a film destined for an unhappy ending. There must also be a near disaster, and there is, when Bob holds an open house for the petting zoo concept and imports a friendly soap opera star (Tristan Rogers) as his celebrity guest. First no members of the public show up. Then they're swamped.

It must be said that the character of the father is a major pain in the netherlands. He is one of those blowhard bearded patriarchs so full of himself and so colorful in unconvincing ways that to have such a person as a parent would be enough to—well, inspire you to flee to New York and open a Television Publicity Bureau. His personality is so insufferable that when he has a change of heart, you don't believe it—you just figure, there goes Dad again, faking it for the evening news.

John Hancock, whose credits include the powerful *Bang the Drum Slowly* and the sweet *Prancer* (a much better family film also set in the same area), does indeed own a fruit farm near LaPorte, and no doubt *A Piece of Eden* flows from his experiences and memories, and those of his wife, the actress Dorothy Tristan, who wrote the screenplay. But the story line runs out of steam about four-fifths of the way through, and the closing scenes lack dramatic interest, dissolving in a haze of landscapes and blue skies and happily-ever-after music.

Pitch Black ★ ★
R, 107 m., 2000

Vin Diesel (Riddick), Radha Mitchell (Fry), Cole Hauser (Johns), Keith David (Imam), Lewis Fitz-Gerald (Paris), Claudia Black (Shazza), Rhiana Griffith (Jack). Directed by David Twohy and produced by Tom Engelman. Screenplay by Twohy and Jim and Ken Wheat.

No other movie opening thrills me more than a vast ship in interstellar space. The modern visual rules for these shots were set by Stanley Kubrick's *2001*, which used a detailed model moving slowly instead of a cheesy model moving fast. Kubrick had the good sense to know that sound does not travel in space, but *Star Wars*, with its deep bass rumbles, demonstrated that it certainly should. And then in the *Alien* and *Star Trek* pictures and in countless others, gigantic space cruisers aimed majestically at the stars, and I felt an inner delight that has its origins in those long-ago days when I devoured pulp space opera by Robert Heinlein and such forgotten masters as Murray Leinster and Eric Frank Russell.

My state of mind is best captured by a pulp mag that was defunct even before I started reading science fiction: *Thrilling Wonder Stories*, without doubt the best title in the history of magazines. I hope for strange and amazing adventures. Sometimes I am gratified. More often I am disappointed. *Pitch Black*, which begins in deep space and ends with a manhunt on a desert planet, falls somewhere in between: clever, done with skill, yet lacking in the cerebral imagination of the best science fiction. How sad it is that humans travel countless light years away from Earth, only to find themselves inhabiting the same tired generic conventions.

The movie begins during an interstellar mission, with the crew and a dangerous prisoner all in cryo-sleep. The ship collides with a cluster of tiny rock fragments, which penetrate the hull like BBs through cellophane. The captain and several other sleepers are terminally perforated, and Fry (Radha Mitchell) assumes command. The ship crash-lands on a planet that circles somehow within a three-star system, where at least one sun never seems to set, and the surviving crew members have to fight it out with the vicious and cunning prisoner, Riddick (Vin Diesel).

You may remember Diesel from *Saving Private Ryan,* where he was the hard-bitten Private Caparzo. He looks like a mean customer, and he is; he shares no fellow feeling with the other survivors, expresses no responsibility to them, does not consider himself in the same boat, and thinks only of escaping. Oh, and his eyes have a remarkable quality: He can see in the dark. Not a very useful ability on a planet with three suns and no night, right? (Hollow laugh.)

What disappointed me about *Pitch Black,* directed by David Twohy, is that it didn't do more with its alien world and less with its recycled human conflicts. I feel underwhelmed when humans land on another world and are so quickly reduced to jumping out from behind rocks at one another and playing hostage games. *Pitch Black* does have a nice look, all bleached blues and desert sands. And there are some promising story elements, one of which I am about to discuss, so you might want to set this review aside if you plan to see the movie.

The spoiler commences: Yes, night does fall on the planet, every once in a long while when all three suns are in eclipse. I am not sure what complex geometries of space and trajectory are necessary for a planet to exist in a three-star system and somehow manage to maintain any continuity of climate and temperature, but never mind: What is maybe more difficult to accept is that it would develop a life form that appears only in the dark. Since sunlight is the source of heat and energy, Darwinian principles would seem severely challenged by the task of evolving living things that hibernate for twenty-two years between eclipses. How does a thing that lives in the dark evolve in a planet where it is almost always daytime? This is not the kind of question you're supposed to ask about *Pitch Black,* but I'd rather have the answer than any forty-five minutes of this movie.

The story also poses the problem (less challenging from a Darwinian view, to be sure) of whether the Diesel character will cooperate with his species-mates or behave entirely like a selfish gene. Whether this happens or not I

leave it to you to discover. By the end of the movie, however, I was wondering if the trip had been necessary; most of this movie's plot could be ported into a Western or a swashbuckler with little alteration. For Twohy, it's a step backward from *The Arrival* (1996), one of the smartest recent science-fiction films—one that really does develop suspense out of challenging ideas of alien conduct (space visitors are secretly warming the Earth to their comfort zone).

My suggestion for his next film: an expedition to the seas beneath the ice of Europe, where volcanic warmth may have allowed life to occur. Consider the physical properties of a life form that evolves under the tiny gravity of such a moon. It could be amorphous, tenuous, and enormous. In sailing a stellar sub through the seas of Io, you might be navigating not toward life, but . . . through it. What would a human crew do in such a situation? Not get into fights and start chasing each other through the sub, I hope.

Player's Club ★ ★ ★
R, 103 m., 1998

Lisa Raye (Diana Armstrong), Bernie Mac (Dollar Bill), Chrystale Wilson (Ronnie), Adele Givens (Tricks), A. J. Johnson (Li'l Man), Larry McCoy (St. Louis), Jamie Foxx (Blue [DJ]), Monica Calhoun (Ebony). Directed by Ice Cube and produced by Patricia Charbonnet and Carl Craig. Screenplay by Ice Cube.

Player's Club, written and directed by the rapper Ice Cube, is a gritty black version of *Showgirls,* set in a "gentlemen's club" where a young college student hopes to earn her tuition. Rich with colorful dialogue and characters, it's sometimes ungainly but never boring, and there's a core of truth in its portrait of sex workers.

Thirty years ago this material would have been forced into the blaxploitation genre— dumbed down and predictable. But *Player's Club* is observant and insightful, and beneath its melodrama lurks unsentimental information about why young women do lap dances for a living, and what they think about themselves and their customers.

The movie stars a convincing newcomer named Lisa Raye as Diana, who has a fight with her father over what college to attend. Pregnant and jobless, she moves away from home, gets a job in a shoe store, and is fairly happy until her child's father wants "more space" and abandons her.

That's when she meets Tricks and Ronnie, two dancers at the Player's Club, who tell her there are ways to make a lot more money. They are correct, but the money comes at a price. The film is knowledgeable about details of the clubs: the camaraderie of the dancers, the flamboyance of the owner and grandiloquence of the doorman, the way the bartenders and the disk jockey keep an eye on the action, and the needy absorption of the customers. "The first dance is degrading," Ronnie (Chrystale Wilson) tells her, "but you get used to it." Her advice to the newcomer: Don't look at the customers, look at yourself in the mirror.

Onto this semidocumentary material, Ice Cube grafts a crime story involving the mysterious St. Louis, a gangster who is owed a lot of money by Dollar Bill (Bernie Mac), the club's fast-talking owner. St. Louis wants his money, Dollar Bill doesn't have it, and at one point Bill is actually inside a car trunk and we think we know what has to happen next, but the action tilts toward farce rather than tragedy. (A lot of people get shot at in the movie, but I don't think anyone ever quite gets killed.)

Problems for Diana begin when Ebony (Monica Calhoun), her eighteen-year-old cousin, comes to stay with her. She wants to keep Ebony away from the club, but "Ebony jumped headfirst into the lifestyle," and soon Diana, who has drawn the line at prostitution, finds that Ebony treats it more like a career goal. Ice Cube uses strong dramatic intercutting to build suspense in a scene where Ebony, hired as a dancer at a bachelor party, is uneasy to find there aren't any other girls there.

What's interesting about *Player's Club* is the way it moves through various tones and kinds of material. There's the documentary stuff, the crime story, Diana's shaky romance with a new boyfriend, Ebony's problems, and comic relief from the stylized dialogue of Dollar Bill and his doorman, L'il Man (A. J. Johnson). And then a strong underpinning of economic reality, as Diana works hard to pay her bills,

and is encouraged by a professor after she finds herself falling asleep in class.

The movie has strong scenes for all its major characters, including a boozy after-hours party being held by some ATF agents who hire Ronnie and some of the other girls as strippers. Ronnie knows these guys from earlier parties and plays the role of dominatrix. (Slapping one officer on the behind with a paddle, she says, "That's one more for Rodney King.") The scene develops interestingly: At first we think Ronnie may be in danger, and when we see she knows what she's doing, Ice Cube resists the temptation to go for a comic putdown of the agents, and stays instead with the real tension of the tables being turned. The scene's effect depends on the way Wilson plays it; a less convincing performance, and we wouldn't buy it.

The movie doesn't preach, but it has values. It sees the Player's Club as a job, and the women there as workers, not sex objects. It's work that pays well, but at a price, and although Diana has rules about drugs and sex, Ebony seems like an excellent candidate to crash and burn. I liked Ice Cube's ambition in writing so many colorful characters and juggling them all at the same time. The movie isn't deep, but it's sophisticated about its people and places, and Diana and Ebony have the clarity of characters who seem drawn from life. It would be easy to dismiss *Player's Club* by looking only at its subject matter, but look a little harder and you see an ambitious filmmaker at work.

Playing by Heart ★ ★ ½
R, 120 m., 1999

Gillian Anderson (Meredith), Ellen Burstyn (Mildred), Sean Connery (Paul), Gena Rowlands (Hannah), Anthony Edwards (Roger), Angelina Jolie (Joan), Jay Mohr (Mark), Ryan Philippe (Keenan), Dennis Quaid (Hugh), Madeleine Stowe (Gracie), Jon Stewart (Trent), Patricia Clarkson (Allison), Nastassja Kinski (Melanie), Alec Mapa (Lana). Directed by Willard Carroll and produced by Meg Liberman, Carroll, and Tom Wilhite. Screenplay by Carroll.

Playing by Heart interweaves the stories of maybe a dozen characters, couples of one sort or another, who try to express how they feel and sometimes succeed. It's like one of those Alan Rudolph films (*Choose Me* or *Welcome to L.A.*) where lonely seekers cruise the city seeking solace. The difference is that Rudolph's characters have tough, wounded personalities, and the characters created here by Willard Carroll are mostly softies—they're in tune with the current trend toward movies that coddle the audience with reassuring sentiments.

Of course, there is some pain along the way. One of the most touching couples consists of a mother (Ellen Burstyn) whose son (Jay Mohr) is dying of AIDS. Their long sickroom conversations contain the stuff of truth. And there is a different kind of truth in the peppy wisecracks of Joan (Angelina Jolie), a club-crawler who meets Keenan (Ryan Philippe), a guy she likes, and can't understand why he goes hot and cold with her. Jolie steals the movie as a woman whose personal style has become so entertaining she can hide behind it.

Other couples include Paul and Hannah (Sean Connery and Gena Rowlands), who are approaching their fortieth wedding anniversary under an unexpected cloud. And Meredith (Gillian Anderson), a theater director who tries dating Trent (Jon Stewart), an architect. And Gracie (Madeleine Stowe), who meets her lover (Anthony Edwards) in hotel rooms, and then comes home to her cold husband, Hugh (Dennis Quaid). And we see Hugh in a different light in a series of deep and deceptive barroom conversations with Patricia Clarkson, Nastassja Kinski, and a drag queen played by Alec Mapa.

All of these people are articulate, and some of them are glib, and although the dialogue sometimes sounds exactly like dialogue, it's often entertaining. I liked the way the drag queen says he's twenty-nine, "and those are real years, not Heather Locklear years." And the way Keenan tells Joan, "What did I do to deserve this?" and means it gratefully, and she observes that's the kind of line that's usually hurled at her by someone on his way out the door.

In a movie with so many characters, there's no time to deeply develop any of them. Some don't really register. Others we enjoy because of their star power. It's a little unlikely that the couple played by Connery and Rowlands would have quite the conversation they have about an affair Connery almost had twenty-five years ago. That's especially true given more urgent circumstances facing them now. But the affection between the two feels real, and there is an invaluable moment when Connery imitates a puppy dog.

As the movie circled from one story to another, I found myself waiting for Angelina Jolie to come round again. With her pouty lips and punk chic look, she's an original; I like the way she's talking to her sister on the phone and when Keenan turns up unexpectedly, she says, "Let me take care of this call" and takes care of it by hanging up. Their relationship is the one that develops the most during the film—the one we care about.

Where it all ends up, the filmmakers have entreated critics not to say. I will obey. There is not a ban on deciding what it all adds up to, however, and I think it amounts to a near miss. It's easy to like the movie because we like the actors in it, and because the movie makes it easy on us and has charming moments. But it feels too much like an exercise. It's yuppie lite—affluent, articulate people who, except for those who are ill, have problems that are almost pleasant. It has been observed that a lot of recent movies about death have gone all soft and gooey at the center. Here's a movie about life that does the same thing.

Play It to the Bone ★ ½
R, 125 m., 2000

Antonio Banderas (Cesar Dominguez), Woody Harrelson (Vince Boudreau), Lolita Davidovich (Grace Pasi), Tom Sizemore (Joe Domino), Lucy Liu (Lia), Robert Wagner (Hank Goody), Richard Masur (Artie), Willie Garson (Cappie Caplan). Directed by Ron Shelton and produced by Stephen Chin. Screenplay by Shelton.

Play It to the Bone ends with a long, gruesome, brutal, bloody prizefight scene, which would be right at home in another movie but is a big miscalculation here, because it is between the two heroes of the story. We like them both. Therefore, we don't want either one to win, and we don't want either one to lose. What we basically want is for them to stop pounding one another. That isn't the way you want your audience to feel during a boxing movie.

The movie stars Antonio Banderas and Woody Harrelson as Cesar and Vince, a couple of has-been welterweights who get an emergency call from Las Vegas: Will they fight on the undercard before tonight's main event with Mike Tyson? Both slots have opened up after one of the scheduled fighters wiped himself out in a car crash and the other overdosed ("drugs are coming out of his ears"). Banderas and Harrelson are buddies and sparring partners who need a fresh start. The deal: They'll split $100,000, and the winner gets a shot at the title.

The movie was written and directed by Ron Shelton, an expert on sports movies; he wrote and directed *Bull Durham, White Men Can't Jump* and *Cobb*, and wrote *Blue Chips*. One of his trademarks is expertise, and yet *Play It to the Bone* isn't an inside job on boxing but an assembly of ancient and familiar prizefight clichés (the corrupt promoter, the dubious contract, the ringside celebrities, the cut that may not stop bleeding, the "I coulda been a contender" scene). Even at that level it doesn't have enough of a boxing story to occupy the running time, and warms up with a prolonged and unnecessary road movie.

The setup: Neither fighter can afford air fare to Vegas. It doesn't occur to them to have the casino prepay their tickets. Instead, they convince Grace (Lolita Davidovich), who is Cesar's girlfriend, to drive them there in her vintage Oldsmobile convertible (all road movies involve classic cars, which drive down back roads with gas stations recycled from *The Grapes of Wrath*). When their credit card is rejected at a pit stop, they pick up Lia (Lucy Liu), a hitchhiker with funds.

The road trip involves many scenes intended to be colorful, including an obligatory fight between the two women. Shelton is good at comic conversation, but here the dialogue doesn't flow and sounds contrived, as when Cesar explains that he was once gay for a year, "but only exactly a year," because he was "trying all sorts of things." Vince, a Jesus freak, is shocked—but only, we sense, because the screenplay tells him he is. Both Cesar's sex life and Vince's spiritual visions are like first-draft

ideas that don't flow convincingly from the characters. And what about Grace's motivation for the trip: Her hope of selling the rights to her gizmo inventions to high rollers? Uh, huh.

All leads up to the big fight, during which, as I've said, we want to hide our eyes. Shelton's approach is certainly novel: A match you want to stop before the fighters hit each other any more. It's bad enough that they're fighting, but why, in a silly comedy, did Shelton think he had to outdo *Raging Bull* in brutality? Vince and Cesar hammer each other until it is unlikely either fighter, in the real world, would still be conscious—or alive. It's a hideous spectacle, and we cringe because the movie doesn't know how odd it seems to cut from the bloodshed in the ring to the dialogue of the supporting players, who still think they're in a comedy.

Pleasantville ★ ★ ★ ★
PG-13, 116 m., 1998

Tobey Maguire (David/Bud), Reese Witherspoon (Jennifer/Mary Sue), Jeff Daniels (Mr. Johnson), Joan Allen (Betty Parker), William H. Macy (George Parker), J. T. Walsh (Big Bob), Don Knotts (TV Repairman), Paul Walker (Skip), Marley Shelton (Margaret), Jane Kaczmarek (David and Jennifer's Mom). Directed by Gary Ross and produced by Steven Soderbergh, Jon Kilik, and Bob Degus. Screenplay by Ross.

In the twilight of the twentieth century, here is a comedy to reassure us that there is hope—that the world we see around us represents progress, not decay. *Pleasantville*, which is one of the year's best and most original films, sneaks up on us. It begins by kidding those old black-and-white sitcoms like *Father Knows Best*, it continues by pretending to be a sitcom itself, and it ends as a social commentary of surprising power.

The movie opens in today's America, which we have been taught to think of as rude, decadent, and dangerous. A teenager named David languishes in front of the tube, watching a rerun of a 1950s sitcom named *Pleasantville*, in which everybody is always wholesome and happy. Meanwhile, his mother squabbles with her ex-husband and his sister Jennifer prepares for a hot date.

Having heard a whisper or two about the plot, we know that the brother and sister will be magically transported into that 1950s sitcom world. And we're expecting maybe something like *The Brady Bunch Movie*, in reverse. We are correct: While David and Jennifer are fighting over the remote control, there's a knock at the door, and a friendly TV repairman (Don Knotts) offers them a device "with more oomphs." They click it, and they're both in Pleasantville.

The movie has been written and directed by Gary Ross, who wrote *Big*, the 1988 movie where Tom Hanks was a kid trapped in an adult body. Here the characters are trapped in a whole world. He evokes the black-and-white 1950s sitcom world of picket fences and bobby sox, where everybody is white and middle class, has a job, sleeps in twin beds, never uses the toilet, and follows the same cheerful script.

Luckily, this is a world that David (Tobey Maguire) knows well; he's a TV trivia expert. It's a mystery to his sister Jennifer (Reese Witherspoon), so he briefs her: Their names are now Bud and Mary Sue, and their parents are Betty and George Parker (Joan Allen and William H. Macy). "We're, like, stuck in Nerdville!" Jennifer complains.

They are. Geography lessons at the local high school are limited to subjects like "Main Street" and "Elm Street" because the world literally ends at the city limits. Space twists back upon itself in Pleasantville, and "the end of Main Street is just the beginning again." Life always goes according to plan, and during basketball practice every shot goes in. (But things change. After one player experiences sex, he is capable of actually missing a shot; a dead silence falls as it rolls away. "Stand back, boys!" warns the coach. "Don't touch it!")

Pleasantville has fun during these middle sequences, as "Bud and Mary Sue" hang out at the malt shop run by Mr. Johnson (Jeff Daniels) and park on Lover's Lane (just to hold hands). Then sparks from the emerging future begin to land here and there in the blandness. Mary Sue shares information about masturbation with her mother, who of course has never dreamed of such a pastime (as a perfect housewife, she has never done anything just for herself). As her mother relaxes in her bath, a tree outside their house breaks into flames—in full color!

Ross and his cinematographer, John Lindley, work with special effects to show a black-and-white world in which some things and a few people begin switching to color. Is there a system? "Why aren't I in color?" Mary Sue asks Bud. "I dunno," he says. "Maybe it's not just the sex." It isn't. It's the change.

The kids at school are the first to start appearing in colors. They're curious and ready to change. They pepper Bud with questions. "What's outside of Pleasantville?" they ask. "There are places," he says, "where the roads don't go in a circle. They just keep going." Dave Brubeck's "Take Five" subtly appears on the sound track.

Bud shows Mr. Johnson a book of color art reproductions, and the soda jerk is thunderstruck by the beauty of Turner and van Gogh. He starts painting. Soon he and Betty Parker have discovered they're kindred spirits. (After Betty turns up in color, she's afraid to show herself, and in a scene of surprising tenderness her son helps her put on gray makeup.) George Parker, meanwhile, waits disconsolately at home for his routine to continue, and the chairman of the chamber of commerce (J. T. Walsh, in his last performance) notes ominously, "Something is happening in our town."

Yes, something, in a town where nothing ever did. The film observes that sometimes pleasant people are pleasant simply because they have never, ever been challenged. That it's scary and dangerous to learn new ways. The movie is like the defeat of the body snatchers: The people in color are like former pod people now freed to move on into the future. We observe that nothing creates fascists like the threat of freedom.

Pleasantville is the kind of parable that encourages us to reevaluate the good old days, and take a fresh look at the new world we so easily dismiss as decadent. Yes, we have more problems. But also more solutions, more opportunities, and more freedom. I grew up in the 1950s. It was a lot more like the world of *Pleasantville* than you might imagine. Yes, my house had a picket fence, and dinner was always on the table at a quarter to six, but things were wrong that I didn't even know the words for. There is a scene in this movie where it rains for the first time. Of course it never rained in 1950s sitcoms. Pleasantville's people in color go outside and just stand in it.

* * *

Note: *Pleasantville* contains the last major role by the much-admired character actor J. T. Walsh. He plays the head of the 1950s sitcom chamber of commerce, a man much threatened by change, who warns, "There is something happening in our town"—a town, we know, where nothing has ever happened.

Walsh, who played roles in nearly sixty movies in a busy acting career that began only in 1983, was also seen recently as an internal affairs investigator in *The Negotiator* and a murdering truck driver in *Breakdown*. He died unexpectedly on February 27, 1998, of a heart attack, at age fifty-three.

"He was so hard on himself," remembers Gary Ross, who directed him in *Pleasantville*.

"I met J. T. at seven in the morning and he was having a big whipped cream cheese, smoking a cigarette while he was eating. He smoked all the time. Tough on himself. And he was so hard on himself as an actor.

"As a director, you try to sort of find what it is they need, a little bit of reassurance, and with J. T. it was—boy, how do I get him to forgive himself and relax a little bit here? He was so brilliant, and I would go, 'This is great, this is great.' But he never believed it."

Walsh came late to acting, Ross said. "He was an encyclopedia salesman. He was so good right from the start. Remember him in *Good Morning, Vietnam*?"

He was also in *Sling Blade, Nixon* (as John Erlichman), *Contact, Red Rock West, Backdraft, Hoffa* (as union leader Frank Fitzsimmons), and many TV programs (he had a continuing role on *L.A. Law* in 1986).

In *Pleasantville*, he leads the forces of the status quo against the threat of change. "J. T. had the best way of describing the movie," Ross remembered. "He said the kids from the future (who stir up the 1950s sitcom universe) are like the sand that gets in the oyster. It was such a perfect metaphor—the irritation that produces something beautiful."

As for Walsh's death so soon after filming was completed: "It's just an insane loss."

Plunkett and Macleane ★ ½
R, 102 m., 1999

Robert Carlyle (Will Plunkett), Jonny Lee Miller (James Macleane), Alan Cumming (Lord Rochester), Michael Gambon (Lord Chief Justice Gibson), Liv Tyler (Lady Rebecca Gibson), Ken Stott (Chance). Directed by Jake Scott and produced by Tim Bevan, Eric Fellner, and Rupert Harvey. Screenplay by Robert Wade, Neal Purvis, and Charles McKeown, based on an original screenplay by Selwyn Roberts.

Plunkett and Macleane conducts an experiment: Can a movie be constructed entirely out of stylistic excess, without the aid of a story or characters we'd give two farthings for? Answer: Perhaps, but not this time. Here is a film overgrown with so many directorial flourishes that the heroes need machetes to hack their way to within view of the audience. It's not enough to want to make a movie. You have to know why, and let the audience in on your thinking.

The film, set in eighteenth-century London, tells the story of a gentleman named Macleane (Jonny Lee Miller) and an unwashed rogue named Plunkett (Robert Carlyle). Macleane is not entirely a gentleman (the movie opens with him being sentenced for public drunkenness), but at least he knows how to play one, and the accent is right. Plunkett has the better natural manners and charm. When they meet after an unlikely jailbreak, Plunkett suggests that with Macleane's accent and his own criminal expertise, they could make a living stealing from the rich.

When you extract this story from the morass of style through which it wades, it's as simpleminded as an old B Western. The two men lurk in the woods, spring upon the passing carriages of the rich, and relieve them of their wealth. Trouble looms when Macleane is smitten by the beautiful Lady Rebecca Gibson (Liv Tyler), who, wouldn't you know, is the niece of the Lord Chief Justice (Michael Gambon). The pair become known as the Gentlemen Highwaymen, the chief justice is enraged that they have not been captured, and the oily Chance (Ken Stott) is in charge of the chase.

Just as a random hypothesis, let us suppose that one of the pair is captured and sentenced to hang. Take the following multiple-choice quiz. Will he:

a. Hang by the neck until dead.

b. Escape in a daring jailbreak.

c. Receive a pardon on the tearful entreaties of Lady Rebecca.

d. Mount the gallows tree, have the noose slipped around his neck, have the trap door opened, fall to the end of the rope, and hang there for long seconds, before being cut down in a tardy last-moment rescue plan, leaving us in suspense about whether he is dead or alive (unless we have studied the immutable movie genre laws governing such matters).

I will publish the answer at the end of the next millennium or when the sequel to this movie is released, whichever comes first.

Plunkett and Macleane was directed by Jake Scott, son of Ridley Scott, whose own films *(Alien, Blade Runner)* are themselves dripping with dark, gloomy atmosphere, but who knows how to tell a story about interesting characters *(Thelma and Louise)*. The problem with Jake Scott is that he uses background as foreground. There are times early in *Plunkett and Macleane* when there are so many mysterious and opaque objects cluttering the screen that, as we try to peer around them, we wonder if the MPAA warmed up on this movie before obscuring the naughty bits in *Eyes Wide Shut.*

Dialogue and character are always secondary to atmosphere. The highwaymen and their prey are seen through a murk of fog, mist, overgrowth, lantern shadows, bric-a-brac, triglyphs, and metopes; their dialogue has to be barked out between the sudden arrival of more visual astonishments. The sound track is cluttered with a lot of anachronistic music, as if the movie began life as an MTV music video and then had its period violently wrenched back into the past before the contemporary music could be removed. How displaced is the music? The movie is set in 1748, but the song under the credits, if I heard correctly, mentions the Jedi.

If there's one thing that annoys me in a movie

(and there are many in this one), it's when the characters escape through a loophole in the cinematic technique. There's a scene where Plunkett and Macleane are trapped inside a carriage, which is riddled with countless bullets, just like a car in a gangster movie. The carriage is surrounded. When it is approached after the fusillade, Plunkett and Macleane have disappeared, and been replaced by a bomb with a burning fuse! How? Is this not physically impossible? We're not even supposed to ask, because we are so very, very entertained by such a clever, clever surprise. My movie history may be shaky, but I believe this sequence was inspired by a Loony Tune.

Note: Readers assure me that a sewer opening beneath the carriage was the means of escape.

Pokémon the First Movie: Mewtwo Strikes Back ★ ★
G, 69 m., 1999

With the voices of: Veronica Taylor, Philip Bartlett, Rachael Lillis, Eric Stuart, Addie Blaustein, and Ikue Otani. Directed by Kunihiko Yuyama and produced by Norman J. Grossfeld, Choji Yoshikawa, Tomoyuki Igarashi, and Takemoto Mori. Screenplay by Takeshi Shudo; adaptation written by Norman J. Grossfeld, Michael Haigney, and John Touhey.

There are times here on the movie beat when I feel like I'm plain in over my head. This is one of those times. My assignment is to review *Pokémon the First Movie: Mewtwo Strikes Back.* I have done research. I have even played a Pokémon card game with a six-year-old Pokémon trainer named Emil. The rules of the game seemed to bear a suspicious resemblance to War. At the end of the game, Emil had all fifty-two cards. I do not know if this is because of his mastery as a trainer, or because he stacked the deck.

The easiest way to understand Pokémon is as a major factor in the U.S.-Japanese balance of trade. It began as a Nintendo Game Boy game, and has since proliferated into spin-offs, clones, ancillary rights, books, videos, TV shows, toys, trading cards, and now this movie. All of this despite the fact that nobody over twelve seems able to explain the Pokémon universe coherently. In the on-line magazine Salon, for example, Cynthia Joyce did an interview with a ten-year-old named Sean Levine, who loves Pokémon. Please study the following exchange:

Cynthia: "Can you explain to me—in simple terms—what the game is about?"

Sean: "Well it's not just a game! It's a whole world. There's TV shows, comic books, little figures, and card game. . . . But my favorite is probably the Game Boy game. And the card game. The goal is to get all 151 types of Pokémon—that's the red and blue version. In the new versions there's 250 types of little creatures. I like collecting the cards—I have the red version and the blue version, so I can get all the Pokémon I need. Some Pokémon cards are actually worth a lot—for example, if you have a first edition Charizard, you can sell it for over 99 bucks."

The interview is longer, but no more helpful. Is there even a game at all, in the sense of Monopoly? Sean cleverly deflects the question into a description of the Pokémon empire, and how much money you can make as a Pokémon tycoon. I used to collect baseball cards, but at least there was a game called baseball, which existed separately from the cards. You don't "play" Pokémon in any sense that involves running around or catching anything or scoring runs or getting dirty. It sounds more like early training for commodities brokers.

Here is the movie. The plot: A villain has found a way to genetically clone one of the Pokémon (Pokemen?), named Mew. His invention is named Mewtwo. He also clones other Pokémon. Each Pokémon has a different kind of power. The hero, Ash Ketcham (so called because he wants to "catch 'em all" and have a complete set of Pokémon), ventures with his friends to the villain's island, where battles take place between lots of different kinds of Pokémon (Pokémi?) and their clones. After an hour of struggle that shakes the very firmament, the Pokémon collapse (they run down instead of dying). There are a lot of speeches about how we now see that fighting is wrong. There will be a sequel, in which no doubt there will be another hour of fighting before the same lesson is learned again.

The animation is bright, colorful, and vi-brant. It's eye candy. The story seems very thin, especially compared to such other Japanese anime titles as *My Neighbor Totoro*. The story is idiotic. The individual Pokémon have personalities that make the Teenage Mutant Ninja Turtles look like Billy Crystal. Kids will no doubt love this movie because they can see action involving figures they have collected themselves.

I can't recommend the film or work up much enthusiasm for it because there is no level at which it enriches a young viewer by encouraging thinking or observation. It's just a sound-and-light show linked to the marketing push for Pokémon in general. On the other hand, I may have completely bypassed the point and misinterpreted crucial Pokémon lore. This may disqualify me from ever becoming a Pokémon trainer. I can live with that.

Polish Wedding ★ ★
PG-13, 101 m., 1998

Lena Olin (Jadzia Pzoniak), Gabriel Byrne (Bolek Pzoniak), Claire Danes (Hala Pzoniak), Adam Trese (Russell Schuster), Mili Avital (Sofie Pzoniak), Daniel LaPaine (Ziggy Pzoniak), Rade Serbedzija (Roman Kroll). Directed by Theresa Connelly and produced by Tom Rosenberg, Julia Chasman, and Geoff Stier. Screenplay by Connelly.

A movie can get away with anything if it can convince you it believes in itself. Theresa Connelly's *Polish Wedding* doesn't succeed. Too many scenes float above reality, going for cuteness and colorful dialogue and zany quirks, until we begin to question the very possibility that these wonderful, full-hearted characters could actually exist in a suburb of Detroit—or anywhere.

The movie tells the story of a Polish-American family awash with secret romance, buried passion, and fierce pride. Jadzia Pzoniak (Lena Olin), the mother, is a cleaning woman. Bolek (Gabriel Byrne), the father, works nights as a baker. The family lives in one of those houses you see only in the movies—where everyone's always looking out the window and lots of things happen in the yard. There are four sons and a daughter, and the boys all seem to sleep in one bedroom, which is strictly speaking not impossible—but a thrifty Polish-American family that has had two working parents for more than twenty years is more likely, I think, to be living in a larger house by now, instead of one that seems artificially cramped for movie purposes.

Jadzia and Bolek are not happily married. Jadzia says she married her husband for a good reason, but just at the moment she can't remember what it was. She dresses in some kind of women's auxiliary outfit once a week and goes out to her "meeting," which consists of a liaison with her lover, Roman (Rade Serbedzija). He's her boss at work. You might therefore wonder why she's still a cleaning lady, instead of being promoted to receptionist or something, but there's a scene where he enters the restroom she's cleaning and she hurls him to the floor and pounces on him for some inappropriate behavior in the workplace; maybe he'd miss that.

Jadzia's daughter, Hala (Claire Danes), a teenager young enough to be cast as the virgin in the church procession, is sneaking out nights, too, to see a young cop named Russell (Adam Trese). She gets pregnant and tells her dad, "My clock stopped." What clock? "Every woman has that kind of clock that she tells her time by." That leads to the double climax, in which the serenity of the procession is much tested, and the entire Pzoniak family marches on Russell's house for a singularly unconvincing confrontation.

Polish Wedding is the kind of movie that cries out to be set in a country I know little or nothing about. Maybe I would believe this colorful behavior in Albania, or in one of those Italian comedies where Sophia Loren knew everybody in town, biblically and otherwise. In a Detroit suburb, I don't imagine carefree people gambol in the fields and gather around the breakfast table for family conversations apparently inspired by sitcom dialogue. Oh, I believe all the things happen in Detroit that happen in this movie; I simply don't believe people rant and rave and posture and emote so wildly while they're happening. A lot of the time I'll bet they're monosyllabic, and even during their emotional peaks still spend a lot of time watching TV.

Lena Olin is an actress who could have gotten away with this role, in another movie in another country. She brings it great life and conviction, but since the movie never connects with the world around it she seems, alas, more crazy than colorful. Gabriel Byrne's character is written as an enigma and he plays it as if it's certainly an enigma to him. Claire Danes seems too old for some scenes and too young for others; her character is a utility infielder, playing all positions and trying to field whatever the screenplay hits at her.

The movie's mixture of sex, religion, and family craziness reminded me of *Household Saints*, the Nancy Savocca film in which Lili Taylor's grandmother believes in saints, her parents believe in the American dream, and Lily, by seriously desiring to become a saint, does what would make her grandmother happy and her parents miserable. All the generational values are squished together in *Polish Wedding*. We're not looking at behavior, but at a lot of dubious anecdotes.

Post Coitum, Animal Triste ★ ★ ★
NO MPAA RATING, 95 m., 1998

Brigitte Rouan (Diane), Boris Terral (Emilio), Patrick Chesnais (Philippe), Nils Tavernier (Francois), Jean-Louis Richard (Weyman-Lebeau). Directed by Brigitte Rouan and produced by Humbert Balsan. Screenplay by Santiago Amigorena, Jean-Louis Richard, Rouan, and Guy Zylberstein.

The first shot is of a cat writhing in lust. The second shot is of a woman writhing in emotional agony. Both feel the same animal need, according to Brigitte Rouan, who directed, stars in, and cowrote the astonishing psychodrama *Post Coitum, Animal Triste*, which is about a woman's transition from wild sexual excitement to love to fury at rejection.

Rouan plays Diane, a Parisian book editor in her forties, who is trying to guide a young author named Francois (Nils Tavernier) through the ordeal of his second novel. At his apartment, she meets Emilio (Boris Terral), Francois's roommate. Their eyes lock. They seem almost immediately to fall into a mutual sexual trance and are making love before they know each other. He is young, wild, reckless. She is a bourgeoisie intellectual with a husband and two children. "I'm a lifetime ahead of you," she complains. "Want to help me buy some socks?" he asks.

The first stage of their relationship is one of urgent risk taking, as they meet whenever and wherever they can. She races across streets, crying out his name. Kissing, they fall onto the hood of a car in the middle of traffic, oblivious. Once they become so reckless that they are requested to leave a restaurant. Diane is amazed to feel so strongly and deeply; at one point, she is literally seen floating on air. The bewitched Emilio seems in a tumescent daze.

Her husband, Philippe (Patrick Chesnais), of course, soon suspects an affair. He is a lawyer, not stupid, whose current client plunged a carving fork into the jugular of her husband; the older woman had put up with years of infidelity and abuse, but could not deal with her husband's threat to leave her. As Philippe quizzes his client about her crime, he senses a certain serenity in her manner; by murdering her husband, she has at last ended her lifetime of suffering. The film teases us with the possibility that Philippe may take the hint.

Then, gradually, in steps as small as a few words murmured to his grandfather, Emilio begins to lose his passion. He is a "hydraulic engineer in the Third World," on leave after mending dikes in Bangladesh, and now he informs Diane he is going to Africa for six months. She interprets this, correctly, as an attempt to get away, and has a breakdown that escalates for most of the rest of the movie.

It is not a pretty sight, seeing a dignified and attractive woman of a certain age as she goes completely to pieces. "I hurt all over and you feel nothing," she tells Emilio. He might have been willing to extend their relationship in a reasonable way, but is frightened by her frenzy. She drinks to oblivion. She starts a fire in her office. She loses her job. She lives on the sofa. She forgets to eat. She cries for hours. Her family moves out. She doesn't kill herself only because, perhaps, she masochistically enjoys her agony.

This breakdown went on too long, I thought; a little forlorn hysteria goes a long way. But by the end of the film, we have come to admire Rouan's courage as a performer and a filmmaker in following Diane's mania as far as it will go. And I liked the way the central drama is surrounded by small, observant moments involving the husband, the children, and even the accused murderer (at one point, Philippe plays tapes of his wife's secret phone calls to his client—to get the benefit of her more direct experience with adultery).

The title translates loosely as "After sex, animal grief." Is it autobiographical? I don't know. My guess is, either these events are inspired by an affair that Rouan once had, or they are a memorandum to herself: Never have one.

Practical Magic ★ ★
PG-13, 105 m., 1998

Sandra Bullock (Sally Owens), Nicole Kidman (Gillian Owens), Aidan Quinn (Gary Hallett), Dianne Wiest (Aunt Jet), Stockard Channing (Aunt Frances), Goran Visnjic (Jimmy), Evan Rachel Wood (Kylie), Alexandra Artrip (Antonia). Directed by Griffin Dunne and produced by Denise Di Novi. Screenplay by Robin Swicord, Akiva Goldsman, and Adam Brooks, based on the novel by Alice Hoffman.

Practical Magic is too scary for children and too childish for adults. Who was it made for? On the one hand, you have cute witches making jokes about magic potions and herbal shampoos, and on the other hand you have a kidnapping by an abusive boyfriend who dies of an overdose—but not for long. Moldy evil spirits rise up out of other people's bodies, and teaspoons stir on their own.

The movie doesn't seem sure what tone to adopt, veering uncertainly from horror to laughs to romance. To cue us, it puts lots of songs on the sound track. A movie lacks confidence when it uses music to tell us how to feel; here the music intrudes, insists, explains, and tries to force segues between events that are not segueable. Example: Early in the film, an impending kiss is accompanied by "This Kiss," by Faith Hill.

The story involves a family that has had witches for 300 years. Because of an ancient curse, all of their husbands die. The chirp of a deathwatch beetle provides advance warning. So it is best for the womenfolk (and in the long run this family has nothing but womenfolk) to avoid heartbreak by not falling in love. Two sisters named Sally and Gillian (Sandra Bullock and Nicole Kidman) grow up with the curse, and Sally protects against it by casting a spell for a man she trusts will be impossible to find. He has to have one blue eye and one green eye, be able to flip pancakes in the air, and have other attributes that are not nearly as rare as Sally thinks.

Flash-forward. Sally marries. She is happy. She and her husband have two lovely daughters. One day she hears the deathwatch beetle beneath the floorboards. Desperate, she tears up one floorboard, then another. How does this work? Your husband lives if you squish the beetle in time? Soon she has torn up the entire floor—a job that would take union carpenters hours if not days, and is not necessary because anguish can actually be demonstrated by the manner in which you tear up floorboards, not by how many you are able to get through. The extra floorboards, like the extra songs, are overkill.

Later, Gillian sends Sally a psychic distress call, and Sally speeds to the rescue, finding Gillian shacked up in a motel with Jimmy (Goran Visnjic), a "Transylvanian cowboy" who beats her up. (She can't marry him and trigger the beetle scenario because she doesn't love him.) He kidnaps the two women, and eventually supplies the evil spirit that fuels the rest of the plot. Aidan Quinn plays Gary Hallett, a cop who comes to investigate the missing Transylvanian. "Is he cute?" asks Gillian about the cop. "Yeah," says Sally, "in a penal code sort of way." No prizes for guessing his eye color.

Comic relief is provided by the sisters' two maiden aunts, Jet (Dianne Wiest) and Frances (Stockard Channing). The whole movie would have been funnier if they, and not the younger women, had been involved with the Transylvanian cowboy and the cop, but that would have required wit and imagination beyond the compass of this material. Still pending at the outcome is whether pancake flipping somehow immunizes Gary from the knell of the deathwatch beetle.

A Price Above Rubies ★ ★ ★
R, 116 m., 1998

Renee Zellweger (Sonia), Christopher Eccleston (Sender), Julianna Margulies (Rachel), Allen Payne (Ramon), Glenn Fitzgerald (Mendel), Kim Hunter (Rebbitzn), John Randolph (Rebbe), Phyllis Newman (Mrs. Gelbart). Directed by Boaz Yakin and produced by Lawrence Bender and John Penotti. Screenplay by Yakin.

A Price Above Rubies tells the story of a woman who burns for release from the strictures of a closed society. We learn much about her during the film, but not much about her society—a community of Orthodox Hasidic Jews, living in Brooklyn. Perhaps that's in the nature of commercial filmmaking; there is a larger audience for a story about the liberation of proud, stubborn Renee Zellweger (from *Jerry Maguire*) than there is for a story about why a woman's place is in the home.

During the film, however, questions about the message were not foremost in my mind. I was won over by Zellweger's ferociously strong performance, and by characters and scenes I hadn't seen before: the world, for example, of Manhattan diamond merchants, and the parallel world of secret (untaxed) jewel shops in Brooklyn apartments, and the life of a young Puerto Rican who is a talented jewelry designer. The film also adds a level of magic realism in the character of an old homeless woman who may be "as old as God himself."

Zellweger plays Sonia, the daughter of gemologists who steer her away from the family business and into marriage with a young scholar named Mendel (Glenn Fitzgerald), who prefers prayer and study to the company of his wife. (During sex, he turns off the light and thinks of Abraham and Isaac.) Sonia's unhappiness makes her an emotional time bomb, and it is Mendel's older brother Sender (Christopher Eccleston) who sets her off. First he tests her knowledge of jewelry. Then he offers her a job in his business. Then he has sex with her. It's rape, but she seems to accept it as the price of freedom.

A Price Above Rubies is the second film by writer-director Boaz Yakin, whose *Fresh* (1994) was able to see clearly inside a black community; here, although he is Jewish, he is not able to bring the Hasidim into the same focus. All I learned for sure about them is that the men wear beards and black hats and suits, and govern every detail of daily life according to the teachings of rabbis and scholars. The women obey their fathers and husbands, and the group as a whole shuns the customs of the greater world and lives within walls of rules and traditions. There is not a lot of room for compromise or accommodation in their teachings, which is a point of tension in modern Israel between Orthodox and other Jews.

Sonia does not find this a world she can live in. She is rebellious when her husband insists their newborn son be named after the rabbi rather than after Sonia's beloved brother, who drowned when he was young. She is opposed to the boy's circumcision ("He's like a sacrifice!")— but, to be sure, her husband also faints at the sight of blood. She is as resentful at Mendel's long hours at study and prayer as another wife might be at a husband who spent all of his time in a bar or at the track. And there is that unquenched passion burning inside of her. (In equating her sexual feelings with heat, Yakin unwittingly mirrors the convention in porno films, where women complain of feeling "hot . . . so hot" and sex works like air-conditioning.)

After her brother-in-law sets her up in the jewelry business, she glories in her freedom. She wheels and deals with the jewelry merchants of the city, and runs his illicit store from a garden apartment. On a park bench one day, she sees a black woman with beautiful earrings, and this sends her on a search for their maker, Ramon (Allen Payne), a Puerto Rican who sells schlock in Manhattan to make money, and then does his own work for love.

This man is unlike any Sonia has ever met, but at first her love is confined to his jewelry. She encourages him, commissions him, reassures him that his work is special. But then Sender discovers their connection and tells Sonia's husband and family, and Sonia is locked out of her house, cut off from her child, and divorced.

It is hard to see why Sender would take that risk, considering what a powerful weapon Sonia has: She could accuse him of rape. But perhaps he knows she wouldn't be believed. His values are hardly those of his prayerful brother's; he believes we sin in order to gain God's forgiveness (or perhaps even his attention), and that "the quality of our sins sets us apart."

I was always completely absorbed in Sonia's quest. Zellweger avoids all the cute mannerisms that made her so lovable in *Jerry Maguire*,

and plays this young woman as quiet, inward, even a little stooped. She knows she must find a different kind of life for herself, and does.

The film has been protested by some Hasidic Jews, who especially disliked the circumcision scene. Yakin did little for his defense by claiming it was "comedic"—which it is not remotely. Like the Amish of *Kingpin* and the Catholics of the early scenes in *Household Saints*, these Jews come across as exotic outsiders and holdouts in the great secularized American melting pot. What may offend them as much as anything is that their community is reduced to a backdrop and props for Sonia's story. It would be an interesting challenge for a filmmaker to tell a story from inside such a community. *Witness* came close to suggesting the values of the Amish, I think, but then how would I really know?

Price of Glory ★ ★
PG-13, 118 m., 2000

Jimmy Smits (Arturo Ortega), Maria Del Mar (Rita Ortega), Jon Seda (Sonny Ortega), Clifton Collins Jr. (Jimmy Ortega), Ernesto Hernandez (Johnny Ortega), Ron Perlman (Nick Everson), Louis Mandylor (Davey Lane), Sal Lopez (Hector Salmon). Directed Carlos Avila and produced by Moctesuma Esparza, Robert Katz, and Arthur E. Friedman. Screenplay by Phil Berger.

Price of Glory made me feel like I was sitting in McDonald's watching some guy shout at his kids. You read the situation: Here's a man with problems of his own, who is projecting his troubles onto his children—because he thinks he can control them, and he knows he can't control himself. The world has him licked. The situation makes you feel sad and uncomfortable, but it's none of your business. You look away.

Price of Glory gives us two hours of that behavior, and it's a miscalculation so basic that it makes the movie painful when it wants, I guess, to be touching. Jimmy Smits plays Arturo Ortega, a Mexican-American father who was a boxer when he was young, was "brought along too fast" and beaten badly in a fight, and now leads a life obsessed with getting revenge through the lives of his three sons. He brings them up as boxers ("the Fighting Ortegas"), and tries to dominate their lives. But he does such a bad job of masterminding their careers that finally the sons and long-suffering wife see him less as a father than as their cross to bear. Even his rival, a boxing promoter who wants to handle the most promising son, comes across less as an enemy than as a man with more common sense than Arturo.

Smits is good in this performance—all too good. The movie is earnest and sincere, and an ordeal to watch, because there's no arc to his character, and learning and redemption are too little, too late. He's stuck. He keeps making the same mistakes over and over; he starts as tragic, and ends as a slow study. And he inflicts on his kids (and us) that tiresome strategy of the domineering parent who puts on an act of being reasonable, of "only wanting what's best" for his kids, when clearly his own issues are in charge. He even believes himself when he delivers his sanctimonious and self-serving speeches; the kids turn away, and we pity them.

The other arc in the film is that of a typical boxing movie. It opens with Arturo losing big in an early fight, and then we see him living in New Mexico with his wife, Rita (Maria Del Mar), who sees him clearly, loves him, but puts up with way too much. They have three kids, who are put in the ring at such young ages that we didn't know they made boxing gloves that tiny. (I don't even want to think about kids in the "Peewee Division.") He pushes them, browbeats them; even one kid's victory gets criticized because his style was wrong. We sense here a portrait of all parents who live through young children, pushing them onto the stage, forcing them into competitions they have no taste for, treating them not like kids but like puppets acting out the parents' fantasies.

Flash forward ten years and the kids are young men, but their father has learned nothing. They are Sonny (Jon Seda), Jimmy (Clifton Collins Jr.), and Johnny (Ernesto Hernandez). Sonny is the best boxer, but as the oldest he's the most driven to squirm from under his father's thumb. Jimmy is resentful and rebellious. Johnny has real promise, and as the youngest is most concerned with pleasing his dad. But the family by this point is twisted and distorted by years of Arturo's bullying, as Rita Ortega looks on helplessly.

Like many bullies, Arturo is filled with self-pity, and has a way of creating a family dynamic where guilt suppresses rage. Consider a scene where one of the boys proudly brings home the girlfriend he wants to marry and her parents, for dinner. Arturo behaves like such a jerk that we cringe. A family dinner quite like this could not exist anywhere outside a movie more concerned with making a point than drawing a convincing character.

The story's villain is a professional fight promoter named Nick Everson (Ron Perlman). With his deep-set eyes and burly physique, he's intimidating, and controls the bookings for big fights. I am sure there are people like him all through professional boxing, but what's amazing is that he comes as a surprise to Arturo, who wants to manage his sons himself. Everson has thugs working for him, but he and his men are not vicious, simply hard-boiled. By the end of the film, Everson is looking reasonable compared to Arturo Ortega—even to Arturo himself.

The character scenes are intercut with standard scenes from boxing movies: training, strategy, talking about moves, early fights. None of this stuff is remarkable. What's peculiar is that the film doesn't build toward anything because even as the boxing careers flourish, the character of Arturo drags everything down. At the end there is a victory, and it means nothing—it's ashes, because Arturo has taken out the fun. He just never learns.

Primary Colors ★ ★ ★
R, 135 m., 1998

John Travolta (Governor Jack Stanton), Emma Thompson (Susan Stanton), Billy Bob Thornton (Richard Jemmons), Kathy Bates (Libby Holden), Adrian Lester (Henry Burton), Maura Tierney (Daisy), Larry Hagman (Governor Fred Picker), Diane Ladd (Mamma Stanton). Directed and produced by Mike Nichols. Screenplay by Elaine May, based on the novel by "Anonymous."

Here's the surprising thing: *Primary Colors* would seem just about as good, as tough, and as smart if there had never been a president named Bill Clinton. Of course the movie resonates with its parallels to the lives of Bill and

Hillary Clinton, but it's a lot more than a disguised exposé. It's a superb film—funny, insightful, and very wise about the realities of political life.

The director, Mike Nichols, and the writer, his longtime collaborator Elaine May, have put an astonishing amount of information on the screen, yes, but that wasn't the hard part. Their real accomplishment is to blend so many stories and details into an observant picture that holds together. We see that Jack Stanton, the presidential candidate in the film, is a flawed charmer with a weakness for bimbos, but we also see what makes him attractive even to those who know the worst: He listens and cares, and knows how to be an effective politician.

John Travolta and Emma Thompson play Stanton and his wife, Susan, as a couple who, we feel, have spent many long hours and nights in mind-to-mind combat. Her true feelings about his infidelity remain unexpressed, but she is loyal to a larger idea of the man, and not as hurt that he fools around as that she's lied to about it. Much will be written about how much Travolta and Thompson do or do not resemble the Clintons, but their wisest choice as actors is to preserve their mystery.

By *not* going behind their bedroom door, by not eavesdropping on their private moments, the movie avoids having to explain what perhaps can never be understood: why a man is driven to self-destructive behavior, and how his wife might somehow remain at his side anyway. The movie wisely stays a certain distance from the Stantons. There are no important scenes in which they are alone together in a room.

Instead, *Primary Colors* centers its point of view in a character named Henry Burton (Adrian Lester), grandson of a civil rights leader, who doesn't join the campaign so much as get sucked into its wake. Before he has even agreed to join Stanton's team, he finds himself on a chartered plane to New Hampshire with the candidate asleep on his shoulder. Earlier, he saw Stanton at work. At an illiteracy class, a black man (Mykelti Williamson in a powerful cameo) tells of the pain of not being able to read. Stanton empathizes with him, telling the story of his Uncle Charlie, who was a Medal of Honor winner but passed up college scholarships because he was ashamed to admit his illiteracy, and instead "just laid down on his couch and smoked his Luckies."

Of course, the Uncle Charlie story may not be entirely true, and later that day Henry sees Stanton emerging from a hotel bedroom with the flustered woman who runs the illiteracy program, but for Henry and the other campaign workers it eventually comes down to this: All the candidates are flawed in one way or another, but some have good ideas, and of those only a few might be able to win.

John Travolta dominates the movie, in part, by his absence. Nichols and May must have decided it would be a mistake to put him into every scene: A man like Jack Stanton is important because of the way people talk, speculate, and obsess about him in his absence.

Through Henry, we meet the campaign's inner circle. Richard Jemmons (Billy Bob Thornton), obviously based on Clinton's strategist James Carville, is a cynical realist who provides running commentary on the stages of the campaign. Libby Holden (Kathy Bates), the "dust-buster," is a longtime Stanton confidant and recent mental patient who comes out of retirement, foul-mouthed and lusty, to dig up the dirt before the other side can. And Daisy (Maura Tierney), quiet and observant, is a scheduler who eventually finds herself in Henry's bed, not so much out of choice as default. Of the crowd, Bates is the dynamo, playing a hard-living lesbian with a secret center of idealism; it's an Oscar-caliber performance.

The movie ticks off episodes based on real life. There's a woman from the candidate's home state who claims to have had an affair with him and to have tapes to prove it. And a dramatic appearance on national TV, where Susan Stanton holds her husband's hand and defends him (her hand snaps away from his as the show goes off the air). It intercuts these with fiction, created in the novel by "Anonymous," now revealed as ex-*Newsweek* writer Joe Klein. There's the pregnancy of the teenage daughter of Stanton's favorite barbecue chef. And the populist Florida governor (Larry Hagman), who looks good against Stanton until his past returns to haunt him.

Much of the movie's ethical content revolves not around sex, but around how a primary campaign should handle damaging information it turns up about its opponent. Libby argues that they shouldn't use it. Jack says that if they don't, the other side will. Better to get it out before it does more harm.

In the way *Primary Colors* handles this issue, it shows more insight and maturity than all but a handful of recent mainstream movies: This is a grown-up film about real issues in the real world. Among its pleasures is the way it lets us examine the full frame, and observe how characters at the side or in the background react; whole characters are developed in asides.

It is also very funny at times, as when Stanton, Jemmons, and others get in a "mommathon," praising their mothers into the night. Or when Susan snatches Jack's ever-present chicken drumstick out of his hand. Or when the candidate, his wife, and his aides search a roadside for a cell phone thrown from a car in anger. The movie is endlessly inventive and involving: You get swept up in the political and personal suspense, and begin to understand why people are engulfed in political campaigns.

Will *Primary Colors* hurt or help the Clinton presidency? To some degree, neither; it's a treatment of matters the electorate has already made up its mind about. The film has certainly not in any sense "softened" its portrayal of its Clintonesque hero—those rumors are exposed by its almost brutal candor. But in a strange way *Primary Colors* may actually work to help Clinton. While a lesser film would have felt compelled to supply an "answer," this one knows that the fascination is in the complexity, in the strong and weak qualities at war with one another. The secret of what makes Jack Stanton tick is as unanswerable as the meaning of Citizen Kane's "Rosebud." And the resemblance doesn't stop there.

The Prince of Egypt ★ ★ ★ ½
PG, 99 m., 1998

With the voices of: Val Kilmer (Moses), Sandra Bullock (Miriam), Ralph Fiennes (Rameses), Danny Glover (Jethro), Jeff Goldblum (Aaron), Steve Martin (Hotep), Helen Mirren (Queen), Michelle Pfeiffer (Tzipporah), Patrick Stewart (Seti). Directed by Brenda Chapman, Steve Hickner, and Simon Wells and produced by Penney Finkelman Cox and Sandra Rabins. Screenplay by Philip LaZebnik.

Not long ago I saw the first of the great screen epics about Moses and his people, the 1923 silent version of Cecil B. DeMille's *The Ten Commandments.* Everyone must be familiar with DeMille's 1956 sound version, which plays regularly on television. Now here is *The Prince of Egypt,* an animated version based on the same legends. What it proves above all is that animation frees the imagination from the shackles of gravity and reality, and allows a story to soar as it will. If DeMille had seen this film, he would have gone back to the drawing board.

The story of Exodus has its parallels in many religions, always with the same result: God chooses one of his peoples over the others. We like these stories because in the one we subscribe to, we are the chosen people. I have always rather thought God could have spared Man a lot of trouble by casting his net more widely, emphasizing universality rather than tribalism, but there you have it. Moses gives Ramses his chance (free our people and accept our god) and Ramses blows it, with dire results for the Egyptian side.

Prince of Egypt is one of the best-looking animated films ever made. It employs computer-generated animation as an aid to traditional techniques, rather than as a substitute for them, and we sense the touch of human artists in the vision behind the Egyptian monuments, the lonely desert vistas, the thrill of the chariot race, the personalities of the characters. This is a film that shows animation growing up and embracing more complex themes instead of chaining itself in the category of children's entertainment.

That's established dramatically in the wonderful prologue scenes, which show the kingdom and Hebrew slaves building pyramids under the whips of the pharaoh's taskmasters. The "sets" here are inspired by some of the great movie sets of the past, including those in DeMille's original film and Griffith's *Intolerance.* A vast sphinx gazes out over the desert, and slaves bend to the weight of mighty blocks of stone. In crowd scenes, both here and when the Hebrews pass through the Red Sea, the movie uses new computer techniques to give the illusion that each of the countless tiny figures is moving separately; that makes the "extras" uncannily convincing.

The film follows Moses (voice by Val Kilmer) from the day when he is plucked from the Nile by the queen (Helen Mirren) to the day when he returns from the mountain with the Ten Commandments. What it emphasizes more than earlier versions is how completely the orphan child is taken into the family of the pharaoh (Patrick Stewart); he is a well-loved adopted son who becomes the playmate and best friend of Ramses (Ralph Fiennes), the pharaoh's son. As boys, they get in trouble together (one drag race in chariots, which speed excitingly down collapsing scaffolds, results in the destruction of a temple). And when Ramses is named regent, his first act is to name Moses as royal chief architect.

But something in Moses knows that the Egyptians are not his people. After he happens to meet his real brother and sister, Aaron (Jeff Goldblum) and Miriam (Sandra Bullock), and learns the truth about his heritage, he runs away into the desert. At an oasis, he encounters the former slave girl Tzipporah (Michelle Pfeiffer), whom he earlier helped escape from the pharoah's kingdom, and her father, Jethro (Danny Glover), the Hebrew high priest. While staying with them, Moses hears the voice from the burning bush: "I am that I am, the god of your fathers."

For Moses, accepting this god means renouncing untold power and riches, and Ramses (now the pharaoh) is first incredulous, then angered. "I am a Hebrew," Moses sternly informs him, "and the god of the Hebrews came to me and commands that you let my people go." When Ramses disagrees (and doubles the slaves' workload), God unleashes a series of punishments. Fire rains from the sky, locusts descend in clouds, and all the firstborn are killed. All leads up to the spectacular parting of the Red Sea, an event made for animation; unlike DeMille's oddly unconvincing vertical walls of water, the parting here has an almost physical plausibility; we can see how the water parts and where it goes.

The movie is not shy about being entertaining, but it maintains a certain seriousness. In place of the usual twosomes and threesomes of little characters doing comic relief, we get two temple magicians (voices by Steve Martin and Martin Short), and a duet ("You're Playing With the Big Boys Now") after Moses turns his staff into a snake to impress Ramses, and magicians show how the trick has been done. It's not that easy to explain the fire and the locusts.

The more movies I see, the more grateful I am for new films that go to the trouble of creating astonishing new images. One of the reasons I was so enthusiastic about *Dark City*, *What Dreams May Come*, and *Babe: Pig in the City* is that they showed me sights I had never imagined before, while most movies were showing me actors talking to one another. (Those who found *Dreams* cornball were correct, but they missed the point.)

Prince of Egypt is the same kind of film (as were, on quite a different scale, *A Bug's Life*, *Antz*, and *Kiki's Delivery Service*). It addresses a different place in the moviegoer's mind, one where vision, imagination, and dream are just barely held in rein by the story. One imagines that DeMille had a film like this in his mind before he had to plod out and translate it to reality.

Princess Mononoke ★ ★ ★ ★
PG-13, 133 m., 1999

With the voices of: Claire Danes (San [Princess]), Minnie Driver (Eboshi), Gillian Anderson (Moro the Wolf), Billy Crudup (Ashitaka), Jada Pinkett-Smith (Toki), Billy Bob Thornton (Jigo), John De Mita (Kohroku), John Di Maggio (Gonza). Directed by Hayao Miyazaki and produced by Toshio Suzuki. Screenplay by Miyazaki, English adaptation by Neil Gaiman.

I go to the movies for many reasons. Here is one of them: I want to see wondrous sights not available in the real world, in stories where myth and dreams are set free to play. Animation opens that possibility because it is freed from gravity and the chains of the possible. Realistic films show the physical world; animation shows its essence. Animated films are not copies of "real movies," are not shadows of reality, but create a new existence in their own right. True, a lot of animation is insipid and insulting, even to the children it is made for. But great animation can make the mind sing.

Hayao Miyazaki is a great animator, and his *Princess Mononoke* is a great film. Do not allow conventional thoughts about animation to prevent you from seeing it. It tells an epic story set in medieval Japan at the dawn of the Iron Age, when some men still lived in harmony with nature and others were trying to tame and defeat it. It is not a simplistic tale of good and evil, but the story of how humans, forest animals, and nature gods all fight for their share of the new emerging order. It is one of the most visually inventive films I have ever seen.

The movie opens with a watchtower guard spotting "something wrong in the forest." There is a disturbance of nature, and out of it leaps a remarkable creature, a kind of boar-monster with flesh made of writhing snakes. It attacks villagers, and to the defense comes Ashitaka, the young prince of his isolated people. He is finally able to slay the beast, but his own arm has been wrapped by the snakes and is horribly scarred.

A wise woman is able to explain what has happened. The monster was a boar god, until a bullet buried itself in its flesh and drove it mad. And where did the bullet come from? "It is time," says the woman, "for our last prince to cut his hair and leave us." And so Ashitaka sets off on a long journey to the lands of the west, to find out why nature is out of joint, and whether the curse on his arm can be lifted. He rides Yakkuru, a beast that seems part horse, part antelope, part mountain goat.

There are strange sights and adventures along the way, and we are able to appreciate the quality of Miyazaki's artistry. The drawing in this film is not simplistic, but has some of the same "clear line" complexity used by the Japanese graphic artists of two centuries ago, who inspired such modern work as Hergé's Tintin books. Nature is rendered majestically (Miyazaki's art directors journeyed to ancient forests to make their master drawings) and fancifully (as with the round little forest sprites). There are also brief, mysterious appearances of the spirit of the forest, who by day seems to be a noble beast and at night a glowing light.

Ashitaka eventually arrives in an area prowled by Moro, a wolf god, and sees for the first time the young woman named San. She is also known as Princess Mononoke, but that's more a description than a name; a "mononoke" is the spirit of a beast. San was a human child, raised as a wolf by Moro; she rides bareback on the swift white spirit-wolves, and helps the pack in their battle against the encroachments of Lady Eboshi, a strong ruler whose village is developing ironworking skills and manufactures weapons using gunpowder.

As Lady Eboshi's people gain one kind of knowledge, they lose another, and the day is fading when men, animals, and the forest gods all speak the same language. The lush green forests through which Ashitaka traveled west have been replaced here by a wasteland; trees have been stripped to feed the smelting furnaces, and on their skeletons, yellow-eyed beasts squat ominously. Slaves work the bellows of the forges, and lepers make the weapons.

But all is not black-and-white. The lepers are grateful that Eboshi accepts them. Her people enjoy her protection. Even Jigo, a scheming agent of the emperor, has motives that sometimes make a certain amount of sense. When a nearby samurai enclave wants to take over the village and its technology, there is a battle with more than one side and more than one motive. This is more like mythical history than action melodrama.

The artistry in *Princess Mononoke* is masterful. The writhing skin of the boar-monster is an extraordinary sight, one that would be impossible to create in any live-action film. The great white wolves are drawn with grace, and not sentimentalized; when they bare their fangs, you can see that they are not friendly comic pals, but animals who can and will kill. The movie does not dwell on violence, which makes some of its moments even more shocking, as when Ashitaka finds that his scarred arm has developed such strength that his arrow decapitates an enemy.

Miyazaki and his collaborators work at Studio Ghibli, and a few years ago Disney bought the studio's entire output for worldwide distribution. (Disney artists consider Miyazaki a source of inspiration.) The contract said Disney could not change a frame—but there was no objection to dubbing into English, because of course all animation is dubbed, into even its source language, and as Miyazaki cheerfully observes, "English has been dubbed into Japanese for years."

This version of *Princess Mononoke* has been well and carefully dubbed with gifted vocal talents, including Billy Crudup as Ashitaka, Claire Danes as San, Minnie Driver as Eboshi, Gillian Anderson as Moro, Billy Bob Thornton as Jigo, and Jada Pinkett-Smith as Toki, a commonsensical working woman in the village.

The drama is underlaid with Miyazaki's deep humanism, which avoids easy moral simplifications. There is a remarkable scene where San and Ashitaka, who have fallen in love, agree that neither can really lead the life of the other, and so they must grant each other freedom and only meet occasionally. You won't find many Hollywood love stories (animated or otherwise) so philosophical. *Princess Monokone* is a great achievement and a wonderful experience, and one of the best films of 1999. ☞

Note: Some of my information comes from an invaluable book, Hayao Miyazaki: Master of Japanese Animation, *by Helen McCarthy, Stone Bridge Press, $18.95.*

Private Confessions ★ ★ ★ ½
NO MPAA RATING, 127 m., 1999

Pernilla August (Anna), Samuel Froler (Henrik), Max von Sydow (Jacob), Thomas Hanzon (Tomas Egerman), Kristina Adolphson (Maria), Anita Bjork (Karin Akerblom), Gunnel Fred (Marta Gardsjo), Sven Lindberg (Bishop Agrell). Directed by Liv Ullmann and produced by Ingrid Dahlberg. Screenplay by Ingmar Bergman.

It is hard to imagine your parents as young people when you are older than they were when they raised you. We understand other adults, but it is so hard to see them clearly; we still regard them through the screens of childhood mystery. In his old age, the thoughts of the Swedish director Ingmar Bergman have turned toward his childhood, and particularly toward the secrets of his parents' marriage.

His father was a Lutheran minister. His films paint his mother as a high-spirited woman who often found her husband distant or tiresome. Both his parents were steeped in religion and theology, which did not prevent them from doing wrong, but equipped them to agonize over it. In four films, one as a director and three where others directed his screen-

plays, Bergman has returned to the years when he was a child and his parents were in turmoil. *Fanny and Alexander* (1983) was a memory of childhood. Bille August's *The Best Intentions* (1992) was the story of the parents' courtship. *Sunday's Children* (1994), directed by Bergman's son Daniel, was about the boy's uneasy relationship with his father. Now comes *Private Confessions,* the story of his mother's moral struggles. He calls these films fictions, because he imagines things he could not have seen, but there is no doubt they are true to his feelings about his parents. One would not live to eighty-one and tell these stories only to falsify them.

Private Confessions, based on Bergman's 1966 book, has been directed by Liv Ullmann, an actress in many of his best films. The cinematographer is wise old Sven Nykvist, his collaborator for thirty years. The actress playing Anna, his mother, is Pernilla August, who also played Anna in *The Best Intentions.* Uncle Jacob, Anna's spiritual adviser, is Max von Sydow, the tall, spare presence in so many Bergman films from *The Seventh Seal* onward.

The film is divided into five "conversations." An explanation is offered early, by Uncle Jacob. It is often wrongly thought, he tells Anna, that Luther abolished the Catholic sacrament of confession. Not exactly. He replaced it with "private conversations" in which sins and moral questions could be discussed with an adviser. Jacob led young Anna through her confirmation, and they meet again as the film opens in the summer of 1925. She confesses to him that she has been an unfaithful wife. She has cheated on her husband, Henrik, with a younger man, Tomas. Both men are theologians.

Jacob tells her she must break off the relationship, and tell everything to her husband. In the second conversation, set a few weeks later, she follows his advice, and we see that Henrik (Samuel Froler) is a cold man who views adultery less as a matter of passion than as a breach of contract. No wonder, he shouts, that the house contains "chipped glasses, stained cloths, dead plants."

The third conversation takes place before the other two, and involves a rendezvous between Anna and Tomas, which she has arranged in the home of a friend. Here we get insights into the nature of their relationship, and there is the possibility that for a lover, Anna may have selected a man similar to her husband. He feels "gray and inadequate," Tomas tells her the morning after, and keeps repeating, "One must be true." Is it Anna's fate to forever dash her passion against the stony shores of men who think before they feel?

The fourth conversation, which contains the heart of the film, takes place ten years later, when Jacob is dying and wants to know the truth about what happened—about whether Anna followed his advice. She lies to him to spare his feelings. They take communion together, and that sets up the fifth conversation, which takes place before all the others, the day before young Anna's confirmation. In it she confesses to Jacob that she does not feel ready to take communion the next day. One must, of course, be in a state of grace and readiness to take the sacrament, and she does not feel she is. His advice to her at this time is the best he ever gives her.

The film is not about sex or adultery. It is about loneliness and the attempt to defeat it while living within rigid moral guidelines. To understand it completely, we have to remember *The Best Intentions*, which tells the story of Anna and Henrik's courtship, and shows her as warm and generous, he as already crippled by a cold childhood and an inferiority complex. There is just the hint—the barest hint, a whisper only—that the one man in Anna's life who might have given her what she craved was Uncle Jacob.

A film like *Private Confessions* makes most films about romance look like films about plumbing. It is about Bergman's eternal theme, which is that we are all locked in our own boxes of time and space, and most of us never escape them. They have windows but not doors. Anna's problem is not morality but consciousness. To know herself is to accept that no one else will ever truly know her. Her final lie to Jacob accepts this truth, but at least as he dies she can make his own cell a little more peaceful.

Psycho ★ ½
R, 106 m., 1998

Vince Vaughn (Norman Bates), Anne Heche (Marion Crane), Julianne Moore (Lila Crane), Viggo Mortensen (Sam Loomis), William H. Macy (Milton Arbogast), Robert Forster (Dr. Simon), Philip Baker Hall (Sheriff Chambers), Anne Haney (Mrs. Chambers). Directed by Gus Van Sant, and produced by Brian Grazer and Van Sant. Screenplay by Joseph Stefano, based on the novel by Robert Bloch.

The most dramatic difference between Alfred Hitchcock's *Psycho* (1960) and Gus Van Sant's "shot-by-shot" remake is the addition of a masturbation scene. That's appropriate, since this new *Psycho* evokes the real thing in an attempt to re-create remembered passion.

Curious, how similar the new version is, and how different. If you have seen Hitchcock's version, you already know the characters, the dialogue, the camera angles, the surprises. All that is missing is the tension—the conviction that something urgent is happening on the screen at this very moment. The movie is an invaluable experiment in the theory of cinema, because it demonstrates that a shot-by-shot remake is pointless; genius apparently resides between or beneath the shots, or in chemistry that cannot be timed or counted.

Students of trivia will note the differences. The opening shot is now an unbroken camera move from the Phoenix skyline into the hotel room where Marion Crane (Anne Heche) is meeting with her lover, Sam Loomis (Viggo Mortensen). There is a shot of Loomis's buttocks, and when he turns toward her, a quick downward glance of appreciation by Marion. In the scene where Marion packs while deciding to steal the money, Heche does more facial acting than Janet Leigh did in the original—trying to signal what she's thinking with twitches and murmurs. Not necessary.

The highway patrolman who wakes her from her roadside nap looks much the same as in the original, but has a speaking voice which, I think, has been electronically tweaked to make it deeper—and distracting*. We never get the chilling closer shot of him waiting across the street from the car lot, arms folded on his chest. When Marion goes into the "parlor" of Norman Bates (Vince Vaughn), the stuffed birds above and behind them are in indistinct soft focus, so we miss the feeling that they're poised to swoop. There is a clearer shot of "Mrs. Bates" during the knife attack in the shower. And more blood.

As for the masturbation scene, as Norman

spies on Marion through the peephole between the parlor and Room No. 1: Even if Hitchcock was hinting at sexual voyeurism in his 1960 version, it is better not to represent it literally, since the jiggling of Norman's head and the damp offscreen sound effects inspire a laugh at the precise moment when one is not wanted.

All of these details would be insignificant if the film worked as a thriller, but it doesn't. One problem is the casting of Vaughn in the Norman Bates role. He isn't odd enough. Norman's early dialogue often ends in a nervous laugh. Anthony Perkins, in the original, made it seem compulsive, welling up out of some secret pool of madness. Vaughn's laugh doesn't seem involuntary. It sounds as if he intends to laugh. Possibly no actor could have matched the Perkins performance, which is one of the unique creations in the cinema, but Vaughn is not the actor to try. Among actors in the correct age range, my suggestion would be Jeremy Davies, who was the frightened Corporal Upham in *Saving Private Ryan*.

Anne Heche, as Marion Crane, lacks the carnal quality and the calculating detachment that Janet Leigh brought to the original film. She is less substantial. Van Sant's decision to shoot in color instead of black and white completes the process of de-eroticizing her; she wears an orange dress that looks like the upholstery from my grandmother's wingback chair. Viggo Mortensen is also wrong for Sam Loomis, the lover. Instead of suggesting a straight arrow like John Gavin in the original film, he brings an undertow of elusive weirdness. The only new cast members who more or less get the job done are William H. Macy, as the private eye Arbogast, and Philip Baker Hall, as Sheriff Chambers. By having a psychiatrist (Robert Forster) reproduce a five-minute speech of clinical diagnosis at the end of the film, Van Sant demonstrates that a completely unnecessary scene in the original, if reproduced, will be completely unnecessary in the remake as well.

I viewed Hitchcock's *Psycho* a week ago. Attending this new version, I felt oddly as if I were watching a provincial stock company doing the best it could without the Broadway cast. I was reminded of the child prodigy who was summoned to perform for a famous pianist. The child climbed into the piano stool and played something by Chopin with great speed and accuracy. When the child had finished, the great musician patted it on the head and said, "You can play the notes. Someday, you may be able to play the music."

I was wrong. That's the real voice of James Remar.

Pups ★ ★ ★
NO MPAA RATING, 103 m., 1999

Cameron Van Hoy (Stevie), Mischa Barton (Rocky), Burt Reynolds (Daniel Bender), Kurt Loder (Himself), Adam Ferrar (Wheelchair Man), David Allen Graf (Bank Manager), James Gordon (J.P.), Darling Narita (Joy). Directed by Ash and produced by Ash and Daniel M. Berger. Screenplay by Ash.

Pups looks ragged and slammed-together, but that's part of its appeal; the film has a wildness that more care would have killed. It's about a bank robbery and hostage crisis involving a thirteen-year-old and his girlfriend. Why this bank? "It was on the way to school."

The kids, named Stevie and Rocky, are played by Cameron Van Hoy and Mischa Barton in two of the most natural and freed performances I have seen by actors of any age. There is an unhinged quality about Van Hoy's acting; he waves his mother's loaded gun while ordering around the adults he's found in the bank, and although we know his character got his lines by watching TV, his energy level is awesome. He pumps out words and postures, flailing his arms, jazzed by the experience, implying a whole childhood in the way he seizes this power.

Van Hoy is a newcomer. Barton, who plays his girlfriend, has a lot of professional experience, but must never have found a role like this before. You can sense her exhilaration as she behaves the way a thirteen-year-old girl *would* behave—not dampened down by a conventional screenplay. Often they waltz through long takes, working without the net of editing.

The movie is persuasive in the way it shows the steps leading to their absurd decision to rob a bank. Stevie begins by videotaping a fake suicide message, shouting "final warnings" to a mother who, we learn, is out of town on business. Then he finds her loaded gun. His girlfriend, Rocky, comes over, he accidentally fires the gun, they are impressed, and then they head for school—at one point interrupting the trip to lie down in the street. The street scene isn't played for phony suspense; a guy in an SUV drives by and tells them they're jerks.

Stevie has brought along the gun. On an impulse, he walks into a bank and announces a stickup. Rocky tells him he's crazy, but eventually she joins him (what's a girlfriend for?). We meet some of the staff and customers, including an angry guy in a wheelchair (Adam Ferrar) who eggs them on, a bank manager (David Allen Graf) who can't believe this is happening to him, and a customer (Darling Narita) who sneaks puffs on a joint.

Burt Reynolds plays the FBI agent in charge of the force surrounding the bank. It is not a distinguished performance, and one of its peculiarities (the screenplay's fault?) is that instead of using psychological insights in negotiating with the kid, he simply shouts threats, profanities, and insults over the phone. Maybe Reynolds has been saving up those lines ever since he played the cop with the pint-size sidekick in *Cop and a Half*.

The details of the FBI siege are unconvincing, and an encounter between Rocky and her father rings false, but I think you have to buy the movie's flaws as the price of its anarchic freedom. The stories of the hostages are all loose ends—but then, they would be. *Pups* doesn't make everyone inside the bank into instant friends, but keeps them as strangers who puzzle one another. Orchestrating everything are the two kids, waving their gun and improvising their strategy as they go along.

At one point, having ordered pizzas, the kids think of another demand. "We could be on MTV," Rocky says, thinking of *Real Life*. "You know—like six strangers meet in a bank and are forced to live together." MTV personality Kurt Loder, playing himself, shows up, and his interview with the kids is the heart of the film. He asks them about sex. Stevie says, "I love her—we're gonna get married on the Internet." Loder is from MTV, all right: "You'll be divorced by fifteen and back on the market."

Pups is the second film by Ash, a British director whose *Bang* (1997) starred Darling Narita as an actress who is molested by a cop, hand-

cuffs him, steals his uniform, and spends the day on his motorcycle experiencing how this borrowed identity gives her power and unexpected responsibilities. That movie was shot guerrilla-style for $25,000 and has an eerie power; this one cost a little more, but it was shot in two weeks and has the same feeling that it's running free. Ash's films are unpolished but involving and untamed.

So much depends on the performances. If instead of Van Hoy and Barton the movie had starred safer or more circumspect actors, the energy would have flagged and the flaws of the quick production would have been more of a problem. As it is, *Pups* is a kind of headlong rush toward doom. "The only way to get us out of here is to carry us out in a box," Stevie boasts, using a line he learned from TV. But the FBI won't shoot thirteen-year-olds, will it?

Pushing Tin ★ ★ ★
R, 124 m., 1999

John Cusack (Nick Falzone), Billy Bob Thornton (Russell Bell), Angelina Jolie (Mary Bell), Cate Blanchett (Connie Falzone), Jake Weber (Barry Plotkin), Vicki Lewis (Tina). Directed by Mike Newell and produced by Art Linson. Screenplay by Glen and Les Charles, based on an article by Darcy Frey.

Like an overloaded airplane struggling to lift off, the characters in *Pushing Tin* leap free of the runway only to be pulled back down by the plot. John Cusack and Billy Bob Thornton play two air-traffic controllers who are prickly and complex, who take hold of a scene and shake it awake and make it live, only to be brought down by a simpering series of happy endings.

For at least an hour, there is hope that the movie will amount to something singular. It takes us into a world we haven't seen much of—an air-traffic control center. Controllers peer into their computer screens like kids playing a video game, barking instructions with such alarming quickness that we wonder how pilots can understand them. They use cynicism to protect themselves from the terrors of the job. One guy "has an aluminum shower in his future." The movie opens with the laconic observation, "You land a million planes safely, then you have one little midair, and you never hear the end of it." This movie is not going to be shown on airplanes.

Cusack plays Nick Falzone, hotshot controller, on top of his job, happily married to his sweet wife, Connie (Cate Blanchett, astonishingly transformed from Elizabeth I into a New Jersey housewife). He works a night shift, ingests a plateful of grease at the local diner, is tired but content. Then into his life comes Russell Bell (Billy Bob Thornton), a cowboy controller from out west, who gets under people's skins. He rides a hog, needs a shave, schedules planes so close together that the other controllers hold their breaths. He's married to a twenty-year-old sex bomb named Mary (Angelina Jolie), who dresses like a lap dancer.

These four characters are genuinely interesting. Russell is an enigma and likes it that way. He speaks seldom, has tunnel vision when concentrating on a task, and once stood on a runway to see what the backwash from a 747 felt like. (The controllers watch him doing this, in a video that shows him blown away like a rag doll; in real life, paralysis or death would probably result.) Thornton, who is emerging as the best specialist in scene-stealing supporting roles since Robert Duvall, is able to maintain the fascination as long as the screenplay maintains Russell's mystery.

Alas, Hollywood grows restless and unhappy with characters who don't talk much; that's why the typical American screenplay is said to be a third longer than most French screenplays. It's hard to be chatty and still maintain an air of mystery; the key to Bogart's appeal is in enigmatic understatement. When Russell does start speaking (or "sharing") with Nick, he turns out, alas, to have the mellow insights of a self-help tape, and at one point actually advises the younger man to learn to "let go." This is not what we want to hear from the same man who, earlier in the movie, when asked if he has any hobbies, growls, "I used to bowl, when I was an alcoholic."

The Cusack character is also given a rocky road by the screenwriters (Glen and Les Charles).

He's a happily married man, but when he sees the Angelina Jolie character, he melts. She's weeping in the supermarket over a cart full of vodka, and he helpfully invites her to a nearby restaurant. After predictable consequences, she has a line that would have made her husband proud ("Mr. Falzone, what's the fewest number of words you can use to get out that door?"), but instead of following the emotional and sexual consequences to some kind of bitter end, the movie goes all soft and sentimental.

Cusack does what he does best: incisive intelligence, combined with sincere but sensible emotion. Blanchett, eccentric in *Oscar and Lucinda* and regal in *Elizabeth,* is cheery and normal here, chatting about taking art classes. Jolie's sexuality is like a bronco that keeps throwing her; she's too young and vulnerable to control it. One can imagine a movie that linked these characters in unforgettable ways, and this one seems headed for a showdown before it veers off into platitudes.

At least it spares us an airplane crash. And it gives us a good scene where Nick, aboard a plane, becomes convinced that Russell is steering them through a thunderstorm. (His behavior here should get him handcuffed by the flight crew and arrested by the FBI, but never mind.) The movie also does an observant job of showing us the atmosphere inside an air-traffic control center, where the job description includes "depression, nervous breakdowns, heart attacks, and hypertension."

The movie is worth seeing for the good stuff. I'm recommending it because of the performances and the details in the air-traffic control center. The director is Mike Newell *(Donnie Brasco, Four Weddings and a Funeral).* His gift in making his characters come alive is so real that it actually underlines the weakness of the ending. We believe we know Russell and Nick—know them so well we can tell, in the last half-hour, when they stop being themselves and start being the puppets of a boring studio ending.

Q

Quest for Camelot ★ ★
G, 83 m., 1998

With the voices of: Jessalyn Gilsig (Kayley), Andrea Corr (Kayley Singing), Cary Elwes (Garrett), Bryan White (Garrett Singing), Gary Oldman (Ruber), Eric Idle (Devon), Don Rickles (Cornwall), Jane Seymour (Juliana), Celine Dion (Juliana Singing). Directed by Frederik Du Chau and produced by Dalisa Cooper Cohen. Screenplay by Kirk De Micco, William Schifrin, Jacqueline Feather, and David Seidler, based on the novel *The King's Damosel* by Vera Chapman.

Quest for Camelot is still another big-studio attempt to wrest the crown of family animation away from Disney. It's from Warner Bros., which scored with the bright and amusing *Space Jam*, but now seems to fall back into the pack of Disney wanna-bes. The animation isn't vivid, the characters aren't very interesting, and the songs are routine.

Space Jam and Fox's *Anastasia* are the only recent non-Disney features to steal some of the magic from Walt's heirs. Since *Quest for Camelot* cost a rumored $100 million and yet lacks the sparkle of a *Beauty and the Beast,* perhaps it's time for Warners to explore a different approach—perhaps animation aimed at the teenage and adult market, which does so well in Japan.

Quest for Camelot, like so many animated features, is a template into which superficially new characters are plugged. We need a young hero, and get one in Kayley, the brave teenage daughter of Lionel, one of Arthur's knights. Lionel, of course, is killed in an early scene while defending Arthur, because the heroes of animated films must always lack at least one parent (later, Kayley's mother is conveniently kidnapped).

We also need—let's see, a villain (Ruber, the evil and jealous knight), a villain's cruel sidekick (the wicked griffin), and a villain's good-hearted sidekick (Bladebeak the chicken). We need a young man to help the heroine on her quest (Garrett, the blind forest dweller), a hero's noble friend (a silver-winged falcon), and the hero's low comedy team (Devon and Cornwall, the two-headed dragon). Then have Ruber steal the magic sword Excalibur, and have Kayley and Garrett try to recapture it, throw in some songs and a lot of animated action, and you have your movie.

I'm not putting the formula down. Done well, it can work, and some version of these ingredients now seems to be required in all feature-length animated films. But *Quest for Camelot* does a fuzzy job of clearly introducing and establishing its characters, and makes them types, not individuals. Their personalities aren't helped by the awkward handling of dialogue; in some of the long shots, we can't tell who's supposed to be speaking, and the animated lip synch is unconvincing. Another problem is the way the songs begin and end abruptly; we miss the wind-up before a song and the segue back into spoken dialogue. The movie just doesn't seem sure of itself.

Will kids like it? I dunno. I saw it with a theater filled with kids, and didn't hear or sense the kind of enthusiasm that good animation can inspire. The two-headed dragon gets some laughs with an Elvis imitation. But there's a running joke in which one head is always trying to smooch the other one, and the kids didn't seem sure why they were supposed to laugh. There's also the problem that Ruber is simply a one-dimensional bad guy, with no intriguing personality quirks or weaknesses; he pales beside Rasputin in *Anastasia* or Scar in *The Lion King.*

Of the supporting animals, the falcon has no particular personality, and Bladebeak is a character in search of a purpose. Even the vast, monstrous dragon that ends up with Excalibur (as a toothpick) is a disappointment. When the heroes find him in a cave, he doesn't exude much menace or personality; he's just a big prop.

The most interesting character is Garrett, who (we learn) was rejected from Camelot because he was blind, and now lives in the forest with the falcon. "I stand alone," he sings, but his friendship with Kayley is the only meaningful one in the movie. It's also curious that the plants in his forest are more interesting than most of the animals. There are eyeball plants that snap at people, and helicopter plants that give free rides (more could have been

479

made of these), and plants that snap at ankles and elbows.

Really good animation can be exhilarating; I remember the "Under the Sea" sequence from *The Little Mermaid,* and "Be Our Guest" from *Beauty and the Beast.* In *Quest for Camelot* there are no sequences that take off and soar, and no rules to give shape to the action scenes (if Excalibur is really all-powerful, how is its power exercised, and why can its bearer be defeated?). The movie's underlying formula is so familiar that there's no use bothering with a retread unless you have compelling characters and good songs. Enormous resources went into the making of this film, but why wasn't there more stretching and creativity at the screenplay level? Why work so hard on the animation and run the plot on autopilot?

R

The Rage: Carrie 2 ★ ★
R, 104 m., 1999

Emily Bergl (Rachel Lang), Jason London (Jesse Ryan), Dylan Bruno (Mark), J. Smith-Cameron (Barbara Lang), Amy Irving (Sue Snell), Zachery Ty Bryan (Eric), John Doe (Boyd), Gordon Clapp (Mr. Stark). Directed by Katt Shea and produced by Paul Monash. Screenplay by Rafael Moreu.

The Rage: Carrie 2 opens with a woman painting a red stripe at eye-level completely around her living room, while screaming, "You can't have my daughter!" Soon the woman is being carried out of the house in restraints, and her daughter, little Rachel, is being reassured by a cop, who for some reason thinks they should stand outside in the pouring rain instead of inside where it's dry.

Why the rain? For the same reason the movie has all the other props of macabre thrillers, such as blinding flash-frames accompanied by loud whooshes on the sound track. And the snicker-snack noise of two blades clashing, even when there are no blades anywhere around. And, of course, a room filled with hundreds of burning candles. And flashbacks to blood-soaked horrors in the past.

After her mother is shipped off to the asylum, Rachel grows up to become an unpopular teenager (played pretty well, under the circumstances, by Emily Bergl). She's a loner, works at a Fotomat booth, lives with a cruel foster family (even its dog is always trying to run away). One day her best friend Lisa is distraught after a boy seduces and betrays her, and throws herself off the high school roof. Rachel is distraught, and all of the lockers in the high school spring open and start banging.

The wise teacher Mrs. Snell (Amy Irving) has seen this before. Twenty years earlier, she was the friend of Carrie, the jilted girl whose psychic meltdown at a prom killed seventy-three people and burned the high school to the ground. Mrs. Snell tries to counsel Rachel, who gets upset and causes the teacher's paperweight to explode. Soon Mrs. Snell tracks down the secret of Rachel's uncontrollable powers and offers her help.

Rachel is telekinetic, we learn. Well, we knew that. What we didn't know, what indeed has escaped the attention of the ESP industry, is that telekinesis is a genetic trait. Yes, Mrs. Snell tells Rachel: "There's a lab at Princeton working on this. The male is the carrier. It's an inherited recessive trait." Why recessive? If Darwin was right, since telekinesis is so useful, it should be a dominant trait, so that Mayflower guys could move the piano upstairs while relaxing in lawn chairs.

The Rage: Carrie 2 faithfully follows the story arc of Brian De Palma's 1976 thriller. Rachel, like Carrie, is a plain and unpopular girl who is unexpectedly asked out by a popular guy (Jason London). Instead of a prom, the movie leads up to a party after the opening game of the football season. The guy, named Jesse, really does like Rachel, but nevertheless she's set up for heartbreak by cruel girls and heartless football jocks, and responds in a terrifically unrecessive way.

All of this happens like dreamwalking, as if the characters in this movie knew they were doomed to follow the scenario laid down in the first one. Some scenes exist only for contrived distraction, like the utterly pointless one where Rachel's family dog runs into traffic. (Okay, to be fair, it doubles as a Meet Cute, when Jesse takes them to the all-night animal clinic.) There is a scene where Mrs. Snell takes Rachel on a tour of the ruins of the high school that Carrie burnt down, and even she thinks it's curious that the ruins (which are practically still smoldering) haven't been cleared after two decades. Amy Irving intones her dialogue in this scene as if evoking ancient disappointments.

The original *Carrie* worked because it was a skillful teenage drama grafted onto a horror ending. Also, of course, because De Palma and his star, Sissy Spacek, made the story convincing. *The Rage: Carrie 2* is more like a shadow. I can imagine the story conference: "Let's think up some reason why the heroine has exactly the same ability Carrie had, and then let's put her in a story where exactly the same things happen to her, with the same result." People actually get paid for thinking up things like that. Too much, if you ask me.

Random Hearts ★ ★ ½

R, 131 m., 1999

Harrison Ford (Dutch Van Den Broeck), Kristin Scott Thomas (Kay Chandler), Charles S. Dutton (Alcee), Bonnie Hunt (Wendy Judd), Dennis Haysbert (Detective George Beaufort), Sydney Pollack (Carl Broman), Richard Jenkins (Truman Trainor), Paul Guilfoyle (Dick Montoya). Directed by Sydney Pollack and produced by Pollack and Marykay Powell. Screenplay by Kurt Luedtke, based on the novel by Warren Adler.

There are so many good things in *Random Hearts*, but they're side by side instead of one after the other. They exist in the same film, but they don't add up to the result of the film. The film has no result—just an ending, leaving us with all of those fine pieces still waiting to come together. If this were a screenplay and not the final product, you'd see how with one more rewrite, it might all fall into place.

The movie is about two somber, private adults who find out their spouses were having an affair with one another. They find out in an abrupt and final way, when the two cheaters are killed in the crash of a plane they weren't supposed to be on. Curious, how neither of the survivors ever cries at first—not until late in the film, when there are more things to cry about. If you think you're happily married and your spouse dies and is exposed as a cheater, don't you cry anyway? Cry, because you loved them all the same, and now have lost not only your spouse but trust in your memories?

Sydney Pollack's *Random Hearts* is too intent on its agenda to stop and observe that; it is about the living, not the dead. Harrison Ford plays a District of Columbia police sergeant, and Kristin Scott Thomas is a Republican congresswoman from New Hampshire. They meet about forty-five minutes into the film, in a well-written scene in which he wants to find some kind of closure and she doesn't. "What's the last thing you remember about your husband that you *know* was true?" he asks her.

Although the movie is primarily about the relationship between the two survivors, the early scenes have their own fascination. The movie makes it clear to us that the two cheaters are crash victims, but Ford and Thomas walk through a minefield of available information without making a connection. When Ford finally understands that his wife was not taking the flight for business reasons, he asks, "Are you saying she lied to me?" and we understand how hard this is for him to understand.

How does he feel? Angry? Betrayed? In denial? Ford is an actor able to keep his hand hidden, and he creates interest by not letting us know. He feels *something* strongly, and he wants answers. The congresswoman absorbs the new facts quickly and efficiently: They cheated, they're dead, they're in the past, it's time to move on. Both of these acts are facades, broken by the survivors in a shocking moment when they fall upon each other in unseemly, and therefore convincing, passion.

There are subplots in the movie, but the emotional themes are more intriguing. The subplot involves Ford as an internal affairs investigator who is on the trail of a crooked cop who may have murdered a witness. All good stuff for another movie, but frankly it's just a distraction here. More interesting is her subplot, about the details of a congressional campaign, with Pollack convincing as an adviser who applies spin control to the story of the brave widow. We realize with a certain surprise that she is that rarity in a Hollywood movie, a good-hearted Republican, and later in the film there's amusing pillow talk. "Are you a Democrat?" she asks. "What if I am?" he says. "We talk," she says, "and I give you books to read."

The real interest in the movie involves her emotional discoveries about herself. Ford seems stuck in the fact of betrayal. Thomas seems freed. She reevaluates everything. Does she really want to run for office? What are her values? Startled to be plunged so quickly into a physical affair, she sees herself, the proper congresswoman, eagerly embracing physical abandon with this cop. "Nobody knows who I am anymore," she says. "Nobody knows how easily I can do this."

You hear dialogue like that, and you want more. You don't want the resolution of the cop subplot, even if it is handled with a minimum of cheap violence. You like the fact that the movie doesn't make one of these people good and the other bad, but makes both of them shell-shocked survivors with unexplored potential. You wish you could figure out what Harrison Ford is thinking, but then Ford has made a career out of hiding his thoughts.

Maybe the fundamental problem is the point of view. The interesting character here is the woman, but the movie's star is Harrison Ford, and so the film is told from his point of view, and saddled with the unnecessary crime plot he drags in (a plot with no thematic connection to the rest of the story). How about a movie about a Republican congresswoman who loses her husband and gains a cop who looks just like Harrison Ford? All seen through her eyes. Now there would be a movie.

Ravenous ★ ★ ★
R, 101 m., 1999

Guy Pearce (Boyd), Robert Carlyle (Colqhoun/Ives), David Arquette (Cleaves), Jeremy Davies (Toffler), Jeffrey Jones (Hart), John Spencer (General Slauson), Stephen Spinella (Knox), Neal McDonough (Reich). Directed by Antonia Bird and produced by Adam Fields and David Heyman. Screenplay by Ted Griffin.

I said no food. I didn't say nothing to eat.
—dialogue from *Ravenous*

Of course a vampire is simply a cannibal with good table manners, and *Ravenous* is a darkly atmospheric film about an epidemic of flesh-eating and the fearsome power that it brings. It takes place during the Mexican-American War in an isolated U.S. Army outpost in the Sierra Nevadas, when a half-dead man (Robert Carlyle) staggers into the fort with the story of snowbound travelers, starvation, and worse: "We ate the oxen, then the horses, then a dog, then our belts and shoes ..."

Eventually one of the party died of starvation, and they ate him. Then they ate others ... and by now the commander of the fort has heard enough, and determines to send out a party to investigate. All of this is shown in wet, dark colors, with a sound track of chimes and mournful cries, low, ominous, burbling percussion, and far-off female laments. *Ravenous* is the kind of movie where you savor the texture of the filmmaking, even when the story strays into shapeless gore.

The movie stars Guy Pearce, the honest cop

from *L.A. Confidential*, as a man named Boyd who becomes an accidental hero during a battle. Mistaken for dead, he's piled under corpses; blood trickles into his mouth and gives him the strength to capture an enemy outpost. He's decorated, but his commanding officer sees the cowardice beneath his luck, and sends him to a godforsaken outpost where the story takes place.

Fort Spencer is a caretaking operation in a vast wilderness, presided over by Hart (Jeffrey Jones), a genial commanding officer who acts more like a host. The soldiers are all cracking up in one way or another, except for Reich (Neal McDonough), a gung ho warrior. The others include the second in command, Knox (Stephen Spinella), the religious Toffler (Jeremy Davies), Cleaves the cook (David Arquette), and some Indians. From the Indians comes the legend that when you eat another man's flesh, you possess his past and assume his strength, and your hunger becomes insatiable.

The movie has established its cold, ominous tone long before the real story reveals itself. That happens when the characters return to the cave where the travelers are said to have taken shelter. There's a creepy sequence in which Reich and Toffler enter the cave, and then traverse into an inner cave where what they find is not a pretty sight. Then there are surprises and revelations, and unspeakable things happen to some of the characters, or at least we think they do.

The director is a British woman named Antonia Bird; I didn't admire her *Priest*, but she shows she's a real filmmaker. She is wisely more interested in atmosphere than plot, and has an instinct for scenes like the one where a visiting general savors the broth of a bubbling stew. Her shots of meat are all cheerfully off-putting; she revealed at the Sundance premiere that she is a vegetarian, which came as no surprise. She does what is very hard to do: She makes the weather feel genuinely cold, damp, and miserable. So much snow in the movies looks too pretty or too fake, but her locations (in Slovakia) are chilly and ominous.

The film's setup is more fun than its payoff because in a story of this nature we would rather dread what is going to happen than see it. The movie makes much of the strength to be gained by eating human flesh, and there is a final confrontation between two men, both much fortified by their fellows, that feels like one of those superhero battles in a comic book, where neither side can lose.

The screenplay, by Ted Griffin, provides nice small moments of color for the characters (I liked the way Jeffrey Jones's C.O. seemed reasonable in the most appalling ways), and short, spare lines of dialogue that do their work ("He was licking me!"). I also liked the way characters unexpectedly reappeared, and how the movie savors Boyd's inability to get anyone to believe him. And I admired the visceral music, by Michael Nyman and Damon Albarn, which calls attention to itself (common) but deserves to (rare). *Ravenous* is clever in the way it avoids most of the clichés of the vampire movie by using cannibalism, and most of the clichés of the cannibal movie by using vampirism. It serves both dishes with new sauces.

Reach the Rock ★
R, 100 m., 1998

Alessandro Nivola (Robin), William Sadler (Phil Quinn), Bruce Norris (Ernie), Brooke Langton (Lise), Karen Sillas (Donna). Directed by William Ryan and produced by John Hughes. Screenplay by Hughes.

Reach the Rock plays like an experiment to see how much a movie can be slowed down before it stops. It was produced and written by John Hughes, who should have donated his screenplay to a nearby day-care center for use by preschoolers in constructing paper chains. How can the man who made *Plains, Trains and Automobiles* have thought this material was filmable?

The story involves an unhappy young man named Robin (Alessandro Nivola), who in the opening scene uses a flagpole to break the window of a hardware store. When Ernie the small-town cop (Bruce Norris) arrives, he finds Robin seated in a beach chair before the window, cooling himself with an electric fan. Robin is returned to the station, where the only other cop on the overnight shift is Sergeant Phil Quinn (William Sadler).

Robin is well known to the officers. His arrest sheet lists such offenses as loitering, disturbing the peace, vandalism, etc. The sergeant and the kid dislike each other, and the actors demonstrate this with various reliable techniques, including the always dependable flaring of the nostrils.

The cops lock Robin in a cell. He steals the keys to the cell, lets himself out, steals a squad car, drives downtown, fires a shotgun through a coffee shop window, returns, and locks himself back in. This is a pattern that will repeat itself many times during the long night. "How are you gettin' out of here?" asks Sergeant Quinn, convinced that Robin is the culprit. It never occurs to him to search the prisoner for the keys. I can't say much for his police work. (That line is borrowed from *Fargo*, a movie I thought of during this one as a drowning man will think of an inflatable whale.)

Robin's sneaky activities unfold with the velocity of sleepwalking. There are two cells in the jail, and at various times Robin is locked in both, Ernie is locked in one, Quinn is locked in the other, a bunk catches fire, Robin's old girlfriend is locked in with him, and Quinn is locked out of the building. Sounds like a maelstrom of activity with all those cell doors banging open and shut, but imagine the stateroom scene in *A Night at the Opera*, enacted in slow motion, and with sadness.

Yes, *Reach the Rock* is very sad. Halfway through the film we learn that Sergeant Quinn blames Robin for the drowning death of his nephew. Even later, we learn that Robin has been moping and pining for four years because a rich local girl (Brooke Langton) dated him in high school but dropped him when she went to college—except, of course, for summers, when she comes home and resumes their sexual relationship, which seems sporting of her. "Time stopped for you about four years ago," somebody tells Robin, or maybe it is everybody who tells Robin that.

There is a subplot. When we first see Ernie the dim-witted deputy, he is drinking in a parked squad car with a local woman named Donna (Karen Sillas). He's about to make a move when he gets the call to check out the alarm at the hardware store. Throughout the entire movie, Ernie and Donna try to get horizontal and are repeatedly interrupted. This is a running gag, or, in this movie, a walking gag.

Donna grows frustrated and wanders the deserted night streets in her nightgown—forlorn, neglected, and in heat. At one point, when Ernie arrives for yet another rendezvous, she warns him, "This is your last chance," but one senses that with Donna there are as many last chances as with Publishers Clearing House.

All of the elements of the plot at long last fall into place, including an old tattoo that explains an earlier parable. Comes the dawn, and we are left with questions only a policeman could answer. (Spoiler Warning—read no further if you intend to see the film.)

Attention, officers! If a perpetrator has a three-page arrest record and during one night, angry at being dumped by an old girlfriend, he breaks a store window, breaks out of a jail cell, steals a police car, uses a police shotgun to shoot out another window, locks an officer out of the police station, locks two officers into cells, starts a fire, and tries to frame an officer for the crimes, would you, in the morning, release the kid and tell him to go home because "her old man has insurance"? Just wondering.

Ready to Rumble ★ ★
PG-13, 100 m., 2000

David Arquette (Gordie Boggs), Oliver Platt (Jimmy King), Scott Caan (Sean Dawkins), Bill Goldberg (Himself), Rose McGowan (Sasha), Diamond Dallas Page (Himself), Joe Pantoliano (Titus Sinclair), Martin Landau (Sal Bandini). Directed by Brian Robbins and produced by Bobby Newmyer and Jeffrey Silver. Screenplay by Steven Brill.

It must be a mixed blessing to be Michael Buffer. He is the man in the tuxedo famous for intoning, "Let's get . . . ready to RUMBLE?" before sporting events and, for all I know, weddings and bingo games. He is rich and famous, yes. But how many times a day/week/month/lifetime do you suppose he has to listen to people shouting Michael Buffer imitations into his ear? And is it discouraging that the excitement is over for him just as it's beginning for everyone else?

These thoughts ran through my mind during *Ready to Rumble*. Buffer appears in the movie and duly performs "Let's get ready to rumble," and so earnestly was I *not* ready to rumble that I wanted the camera to follow him out of the arena instead of staying for a three-cage fight to the death between Jimmy ("The King") King and Diamond Dallas Page.

It's not that I have anything against professional wrestling. I have a newfound respect for it after seeing the documentary *Beyond the Mat*, which establishes without a shadow of a doubt that when you are thrown out of the ring in a scripted fight with a prearranged winner, it nevertheless hurts when you hit the floor. I am in awe of wrestlers—not as athletes, but as masochists. They take a lickin' and keep on kickin'.

The problem with *Ready to Rumble* is that its hero is not a wrestler but an actor, Oliver Platt. Platt is a good comic actor and I have liked him in a lot of movies, but here he is not well used, and occupies a role that would have been better filled by a real wrestler. That is demonstrated every time Diamond Dallas Page is on the screen, playing himself with such ferocity that Platt seems to be playing Jimmy the King in a key heard only by himself.

The plot is easily summarized: *Dumb and Dumber Meet Dumbbell*. David Arquette and Scott Caan are Gordie and Sean, best pals in a Wyoming hamlet where watching the Monday night fights on cable brings the only joy into their lives as sanitation servicemen. By day they suction the contents out of Porta-Potties, and by night they hang out in the parking lot of the convenience store, lecturing callow youths on the glories of wrestling as America's finest sport.

They get tickets to The King's latest title defense, little realizing that the real kingmaker is Titus Sinclair (Joe Pantoliano), this movie's version of Vince McMahon. Titus has declared that The King will go down to Diamond Dallas, and by the end of the fight the loser has been kicked insensible by everyone on the card and banished from wrestling as a hopeless drunk.

When Gordie and Sean's tank truck overturns on the way home, creating a really nasty spill for the fire department to clean up, they take this as a sign that they must leave their town, find The King, and mastermind his comeback. Their plan involves enlisting the once-great, now aging Sal Bandini (Martin Landau) as a trainer. The King is not thrilled: "I don't need a trainer; I need a safe house!" He's right. Landau's scenes demonstrate that as an elderly wrestler he looks no more convincing than he did as a dying millionaire disco dancer in *B.A.P.S.* He's good in serious stuff (hint).

The movie is best when it deals with professional wrestling, and worst (which is most of the time) when it prefers a wheezy prefab plot to the possibilities of its subject. The machinations of a sexpot (Rose McGowan) are tired and predictable, and Platt, who might have done something with decent dialogue, is left on the sidelines while Arquette and Caan shout at each other in a forlorn attempt to reproduce the chemistry of Jim Carrey and Jeff Daniels in *Dumb and Dumber*. I gave that movie only two stars despite the fact that its dead parakeet scene caused me to laugh uncontrollably; now, after sitting through *Ready to Rumble*, with only the occasional grudging "ha!" I know better what a two-star movie looks like.

The Real Blonde ★ ★ ★
R, 107 m., 1998

Matthew Modine (Joe), Catherine Keener (Mary), Daryl Hannah (Kelly), Maxwell Caulfield (Bob), Elizabeth Berkley (Tina), Marlo Thomas (Blair), Bridgette Wilson (Sahara), Buck Henry (Dr. Leuter), Christopher Lloyd (Ernst), Denis Leary (Doug), Kathleen Turner (Dee Dee). Directed by Tom DiCillo and produced by Marcus Viscidi and Tom Rosenberg. Screenplay by DiCillo.

Tom DiCillo's *The Real Blonde* is a meandering movie that usually meanders in entertaining directions. It has too many characters and not much of a plot, but that didn't bother me while I was watching it. It's a sketchbook in which the director observes certain types he seems familiar with. A lot of them are actors and models, who are understandably confused because they don't know if they're being paid to be someone else, or just because of who they are.

The central couple are Joe (Matthew Modine) and Mary (Catherine Keener), who have been together so long they feel they should either break up or get married. Not that it isn't working the way it is, but they feel embarrassed, somehow, by not having chosen one path or the other. Joe is an actor with such high standards that he never works. Mary is a makeup artist in the fashion industry, skilled at calming restless models before they go in front of the camera.

The movie proceeds as a sort of tag game, as each new character introduces other ones. Through Mary we meet a famous photographer (Marlo Thomas) and an insecure model named Sahara (Bridgette Wilson). Through Joe we meet the punctilious caterer (Christopher Lloyd) he works for, and Joe's best friend Bob (Maxwell Caulfield), a soap opera actor obsessed with dating a real blonde. And then through Bob we meet a real blonde named Kelly (Daryl Hannah) and, full circle, Bob also meets Sahara.

Meanwhile, Mary's therapist (Buck Henry) leads her to discover a self-defense instructor (Denis Leary), while Joe's agent (Kathleen Turner) gets him a job in a Madonna video directed by Steve Buscemi, where he meets Madonna's body double (Elizabeth Berkley) and almost has an affair with her, while Mary is almost having an affair with the karate teacher.

You see what I mean. There are so many characters that none of them is really developed, except to a certain degree Joe and Mary. But the film isn't about psychological insight. It has about the same depth as many real relationships in the same circles, where ego and job demands fit right into the lifestyle: People meet and feel like they know one another because they share the same jargon and reference points. They flirt, talk, and dart away like mayflies who must mate before the end of the day—or the current shoot, whichever comes first.

DiCillo is a quixotic director, who began as a cinematographer for directors like Jim Jarmusch, and whose take is always a little skewed. His credits include the ambitious, oddball but not compelling *Johnny Suede* (an early Brad Pitt film); the satirical *Living in Oblivion*, about a cheap horror movie production; and *Box of Moonlight*, about a man who goes in search of . . . well, in search of something to go in search of.

Here he devises brief, sharply observed scenes. He notices, for example, the way a makeup artist makes up not only a model's face but also her attitude. The way the karate instructor, playing an aggressor, takes a sly pleasure in using sexist insults. The way people talk knowledgeably about movies they haven't seen. The way a guy who's embarrassed to be in a porno store will brazen it out. All of the actors are right for their roles, because a degree of typecasting has been done, but Daryl Hannah brings a particularly focused energy to the role of a soap opera actress who is not impressed that a guy is impressed by her. And Catherine Keener brings a kind of wry wit to her character; she sees models in billboards on Times Square and knows what it took to get them there.

The film's opening titles are a visual tease: We see parts of two torsos, gradually revealed, like shards of a giant sculpture, until finally they resolve themselves into a blonde with a man who kneels to embrace her. Later in the film, we see the Marlo Thomas photographer taking that shot, and we learn the real story: The model, a European Fabio clone, is embarrassed because he "released the gas," as he puts it, and the model consoles him. Thus are legends born.

As for Joe and Mary, their threatened relationship and their temptations to stray: *The Real Blonde* is so much more adult in its attitudes than a shallow film like, say, *Kissing a Fool*. The characters are articulate enough to talk about what really moves them; they don't play sitcom games. DiCillo never puts two and two together, but somehow it all adds up.

The Red Violin ★ ★ ★ ½
NO MPAA RATING, 126 m., 1999

Carlo Cecchi (Nicolo Bussotti), Irene Grazioli (His Wife, Anna), Samuel L. Jackson (Charles Morritz), Sylvia Chang (Xiang Pei), Colm Feore (Auctioneer), Don McKellar (Evan Williams), Greta Scacchi (Victoria Byrd), Jason Flemyng (Frederick Pope), Jean-Luc Bideau (Georges Poussin), Christoph Koncz (Kasper Weiss). Directed by Francois Girard and produced by Niv Fichman. Screenplay by Don McKellar with Girard.

There is a kind of ideal beauty that reduces us all to yearning for perfection. *The Red Violin* is about that yearning. It traces the story of a violin ("the single most perfect acoustical machine I've ever seen," says a restorer) from its maker in seventeenth-century Italy to an auction room in modern Montreal. The violin passes from the rich to the poor, from Italy to Poland to England to China to Canada. It is shot, buried, almost burned, and stolen more than once. It produces music so beautiful that it makes you want to cry.

The film is heedlessly ambitious. In a time of timid projects and easy formulas, it has the kind of sweep and vision we identify with elegant features from decades ago—films that followed a story thread from one character to another, like *Tales of Manhattan* or *La Ronde*. There really is a little something here for everyone: music and culture, politics and passion, crime and intrigue, history and even the backstage intrigue of the auction business. Not many films can encompass a British aristocrat who likes to play the violin while he is having sex, and a Chinese woman who risks her life to protect a violin from the martinets of the Cultural Revolution.

The violin is crafted in Cremona, Italy, in 1681—made by the craftsman Nicolo Bussotti (Carlo Cecchi) for his unborn son. But his wife, Anna (Irene Grazioli), dies in childbirth after hearing a series of prophecies from a village crone who reads the Tarot deck. The cards provide a structure for flash-forwards to the future adventures of the violin, and at the same time there is a flashback structure, as bidders arrive at the auction house in Montreal and we learn why they desire the instrument.

The film is easy to follow, and yet reveals its secrets slyly. The tale of the violin is a series of stories involving the people who own it over a period of 300 years. Then there is another story, hinted at, slowly revealing itself, involving an expert evaluator of instruments (Samuel L. Jackson). He is the person who proves that this is indeed Bussotti's famous red violin, and solves the mystery of its color. He is also perhaps the person best equipped to appreciate how rare and wonderful the instrument is—but, like many passionate connoisseurs, he lacks the wealth to match his tastes. His plans for the instrument supply a suspenseful ending to a movie that has already given us just about everything else.

The film was directed by the Canadian Francois Girard, and written by him and the actor-director Don McKellar. They also cowrote Girard's brilliant first film, *Thirty-two Short Films About Glenn Gould* (1994), which considered the life and work of the great Canadian pianist in thirty-two separate episodes. *The Red Violin* uses a similar approach, spinning stories and tones out of the central thread.

After the opening sequence involving Bussotti, the violin drifts into the hands of an order of monks, and we rejoin it 100 years later at their orphanage. They dote on a young prodigy named Kasper (Christoph Koncz), who plays with the purity of an angel. The musician Poussin (Jean-Luc Bideau), expert but poor, hears the boy play and adopts him on the spot, despite the doubts of his wife. This sequence develops tenderly, as the old couple grow to love the boy—who sleeps with his violin.

Flash-forward. The violin is in the possession of gypsies (I am not revealing the details of the transfers). It is played by many hands and travels from Poland to England where, in the nineteenth century, it is heard by a rich virtuoso named Frederick Pope (Jason Flemyng), who incorporates it into his concerts and into his lovemaking with his mistress, Victoria (Greta Scacchi). It is she who fires a bullet at it. The violin next surfaces in a pawn shop in Shanghai where, during the Cultural Revolution, it stands as a symbol of Western decadence. It's defended by a brave musician who points out that Beethoven and Prokofiev were revolutionaries, but is saved only when a music lover (Sylvia Chang) risks her life. Eventually the now-capitalist Chinese government sends it off to Montreal, where it attracts the attention of the Samuel Jackson character.

A brief outline doesn't begin to suggest the intelligence and appeal of the film. The story hook has been used before. *Tales of Manhattan* followed an evening coat from person to person, and *The Yellow Rolls-Royce* followed a car. Max Ophuls's *La Ronde* (1950), Luis Buñuel's *The Phantom of Liberty,* (1974) and Richard Linklater's *Slacker* (1991) all follow chains of characters, entering a scene with one person and exiting it with another. Such structures take advantage of two contradictory qualities of film: It is literal, so that we tend to believe what we see; and it is fluid, not tied down to

times and places. All of those titles more or less observe time and place, however; *The Red Violin* follows not a person or a coat, but an idea: the idea that humans in all times and places are powerfully moved, or threatened, by the possibility that with our hands and minds we can create something that is perfect. ☞

Regret to Inform ★ ★ ★
NO MPAA RATING, 72 m., 1999

A documentary directed by Barbara Sonneborn and produced by Kathy Brew, Janet Cole, Megan Jones, Daniel Reeves, Sonneborn, and Todd Wagner. Screenplay by Sonneborn.

On the twentieth anniversary of her first husband's death in Vietnam, Barbara Sonneborn woke up "and I knew I had to go to Vietnam." She was remarried and happy, "and yet Jeff's death and my feelings about the war were still not resolved." Jeff Gurvitz, her high school sweetheart, had been killed in 1968, on her twenty-forth birthday, eight weeks after arriving in Vietnam. He died while trying to help his radio operator out of a tight spot.

"We had talked about the possibility of Jeff dying," Barbara remembers, in the narration of *Regret to Inform*. "We never talked about the possibility that he would have to kill." After his death, she received a tape recording he had made. It took her twenty years to work up the courage to listen to it. On it, she heard his voice saying he felt like a bystander to his own life—"watching myself do things I never expected or desired to do."

Sonneborn enlists as her translator a woman named Xuan Ngoc Evans, who has memories of her own. One of them is of the day when her five-year-old cousin darted out of a safe place to get a drink of water and was shot dead by a GI. "I remember how his eyes looked," she says. "He had a horrified look in his eye, as much as I did." This woman later worked as a prostitute, dating American soldiers. "I wouldn't have," she says, "if I'd had another choice."

The distinctive thing about Sonneborn's film, which won awards for Best Documentary and Best Cinematography at the 1999 Sundance Festival, is that it remembers the war from both sides, as seen by the women who were touched by it. We meet the widow of a Native American rodeo cowboy, who signed up over her protests because it was his duty. The widow of a man killed by Agent Orange, the defoliant the United States tried to deny was harmful.

And there is the woman who so desperately wanted to deflect her husband's desire to serve that she considered injuring his hand with a hammer. "I wanted to stop him and I thought of smashing his hand, doing it the right way, so it would take six months to heal, time for our baby to be born."

Sonneborn, and her translator and small crew, take the train from one end of Vietnam to another. They talk to Vietnamese war widows. One remembers hiding under a pile of corpses, because to be dead was to be safe. The film makes little distinction between the widows of soldiers who died fighting for the south or the north. All of the memories are painful.

The movie is at pains to remain at the personal level; for women whose husbands fought on opposing sides, the war today is not a political dispute but a huge force that swept away their men, the fathers of their children. Left unsaid is what we see in the background. Vietnam today is independent and communist, the two things we fought to prevent, yet it is not regarded as a dangerous enemy, but a popular tourist destination for Americans—many of them, like Sonneborn, going back looking for answers.

There is one moment in particular that will stay with me a long time. Sonneborn goes to visit the Vietnam War Memorial in Washington, D.C., and talks to a woman who weeps that her husband's name is not included. "My husband should be on the wall," she says. "He left his soul in Vietnam. It took his body seven years to catch up. He went out in the garage and shot himself. He left a note that said, 'I love you sweetheart, but I just can't take the flashbacks anymore.'"

Reindeer Games ★ ½
R, 98 m., 2000

Ben Affleck (Rudy), Charlize Theron (Ashley), Gary Sinise (Gabriel), Clarence Williams III (Merlin), James Frain (Nick), Dennis Farina (Jack Bangs), Isaac Hayes (Zook). Directed by John Frankenheimer and produced by Marty Katz, Bob Weinstein, and Chris Moore. Screenplay by Ehren Kruger.

Reindeer Games is the first all-Talking Killer picture. After the setup, it consists mostly of characters explaining their actions to one another. I wish I'd had a stopwatch to clock how many minutes are spent while one character holds a gun to another character's head and gabs. Charlize Theron and Gary Sinise between them explain so much they reminded me of Gertrude Stein's line about Ezra Pound: "He was a village explainer, excellent if you were a village, but if you were not, not."

Just a nudge, and the movie would fall over into self-parody, and maybe work better. But I fear it is essentially serious, or as serious as such goofiness can be. It opens in prison with cellmates Rudy (Ben Affleck) and Nick (James Frain). Both are about to be set free. Nick has engaged in a steamy correspondence with Ashley (Theron), one of those women who have long-distance romances with convicts. His cell wall is plastered with photos that make her look like a model for cosmetics ads.

But then (I am not giving away as much as it seems, or perhaps even what it seems) Nick is knifed in a prison brawl, and when Rudy walks out of prison and lays eyes on Ashley—well, what would you do? That's what he does. "I'm Nick," Rudy tells her. Soon they make wild and passionate love, which inevitably involves knocking things over and falling out of bed and continuing on the floor. You'd think if people were that much into sex, they'd pay more attention to what they were doing.

Then there's a major reality shift, and perhaps you'd better stop reading if you don't want to know that . . . Ashley's brother Gabriel (Gary Sinise) heads a gang of scummy gunrunners who think Rudy used to work in an Indian casino in upstate Michigan—because, of course, they think Rudy is Nick, and that's what Nick told Ashley about himself. Gabriel and his gang try to squeeze info about the casino's security setup out of Rudy, who says he isn't Nick, and then says he is Nick after all, and then says he isn't, and has so many reasons for each of his answers that Gabriel gets very confused, and keeps deciding to kill him, and deciding not to kill him, and deciding to kill him after all, until both characters seem stuck in a time loop.

There are other surprises, too, a lot of them, each with its explanation, usually accompanied by an explanation of the previous explanation, which now has to be re-explained in light of the new explanation. They all got a lot of 'splainin' to do.

The movie's weakness is mostly in its ludicrous screenplay by Ehren Kruger. The director, John Frankenheimer, is expert at moving the action along and doing what can be done with scenes that hardly anything can be done with. Ben Affleck and Charlize Theron soldier through changes of pace so absurd it takes superb control to keep straight faces. Theron's character looks soft and sweet sometimes, then hard and cruel other times, switching back and forth so often I commend her for not just passing a hand up and down in front of her face: smile, frown, smile, frown.

Perhaps the movie was originally intended to open at Christmas. That would explain the title and the sequence where the casino, which looks like a former Target store, is stuck up by five Santas. But nothing can explain the upbeat final scene, in which, after blood seeps into the Michigan snow, we get a fit of Robin Hood sentimentality. The moment to improve *Reindeer Games* was at the screenplay stage, by choosing another one.

The Replacement Killers ★ ★ ★
R, 88 m., 1998

Chow Yun-Fat (John Lee), Mira Sorvino (Meg Coburn), Michael Rooker (Stan "Zeedo" Zedkov), Kenneth Tsang (Terence Wei), Jurgen Prochnow (Michael Kogan), Til Schweiger (Ryker), Danny Trejo (Collins), Clifton Gonzalez Gonzalez (Loco). Directed by Antoine Fuqua and produced by Brad Grey and Bernie Brillstein. Screenplay by Ken Sanzel.

The Replacement Killers is all style. It's a high-gloss version of a Hong Kong action picture, made in America but observing the exuberance of a genre where surfaces are everything. The characters are as flat as figures on a billboard, but look at the way everything is filmed in saturated color, and anything that moves makes a metallic whooshing sound that ends in a musical chord, and how when the hero walks down a corridor at a car wash, it's done with a tilt and a zoom. In a movie like this, the story is simply a device to help us tell the beginning from the end.

The film is the American debut for Chow Yun-Fat, a popular star in Asia for twenty years and for the last ten a frequent collaborator with John Woo, the Hong Kong action wizard also now working in Hollywood (he produced this film). Chow is good-looking, open-faced, with a hint of sadness that reminded me of Charles Bronson in repose. Here he plays a Chinese immigrant to America, who owes a favor to the drug lord Terence Wei (Kenneth Tsang), whose son has been killed by a cop (Michael Rooker).

Chow's assignment: Kill someone important to the cop. But with the target framed in his telescopic sights, Chow just can't do it. "I went against Mr. Wei," he tells a wise Buddhist monk. "There will be consequences." He knows Wei will go after his mother and sister in Shanghai, and he needs a forged passport to fly home and protect them. That leads him to the lair of Meg Coburn (Mira Sorvino), a master forger whose first appearance is a good example of the movie's visual lushness: Leaning over her computer, she's in red lipstick and a low-cut dress in a hideaway that looks like a cross between Skid Row and a cosmetics ad.

Meg is a tough girl, played by Sorvino with a nice flat edge (while Chow's posing for his passport picture, she says "Smile, and say, 'Flight from prosecution.'"). She wants no part of his troubles, but soon they've teamed up as Wei throws squadrons of killers at them, including two "replacements" flown in to kill the cop's son.

In movies like this, everyone knows everyone. Chow and Sorvino go into an amusement arcade, and she's hit on by a gold-toothed creep. Her reaction: "I try to stick to my own species." The creep of course is in the hire of Wei, and soon a gun battle rages through the arcade. Other elaborately choreographed shootouts take place in a car wash, and in a theater where the cop has taken his son for a cartoon festival (the gunfire is intercut with Mr. Magoo).

There's a moment in the recent *Desperate*

Measures where violence erupts as a father tries to save the life of his son, and a cop asks, "How many people are gonna have to die here tonight so that kid of yours can live?" I had the same thought in *The Replacement Killers*. Because Chow spares Wei's target, approximately two dozen people die, or maybe more (in the dark it's hard to see what happens to all the Magoo fans).

What I liked about the film was its simplicity of form and its richness of visuals. There's a certain impersonality about the story; Chow and Sorvino don't have long chats between the gunfire. They're in a ballet of Hong Kong action imagery: bodies rolling out of gunshot range, faces frozen in fear, guys toppling off fire escapes, grim lips, the fetishism of firearms, cars shot to pieces, cops that make *Dragnet* sound talky. The first-time director, Antoine Fuqua, is a veteran of commercials and music videos; with cinematographer Peter Lyons Collister he gets a sensuous texture onto the screen that makes you feel the roughness of walls, the clamminess of skin, the coldness of guns. *The Replacement Killers* is as abstract as a jazz instrumental, and as cool and self-assured.

Return to Me ★ ★ ★
PG, 115 m., 2000

David Duchovny (Bob Rueland), Minnie Driver (Grace Briggs), Carroll O'Connor (Marty O'Reilly), Robert Loggia (Angelo Pardipillo), Bonnie Hunt (Megan Dayton), James Belushi (Joe Dayton), David Alan Grier (Charlie Johnson), Joely Richardson (Elizabeth Rueland), Eddie Jones (Emmett McFadden). Directed by Bonnie Hunt and produced by Jennie Lew Tugend. Screenplay by Hunt and Don Lake.

Here's an old-fashioned love story so innocent, so naive, so sweet and sincere that you must leave your cynicism at the door or choose another movie. Bonnie Hunt's *Return to Me* could have been made in 1955, starring Doris Day and James Stewart. It has been made in 2000, starring Minnie Driver and David Duchovny, and I am happy that it has.

Duchovny stars as Bob, a Chicago architect married to Elizabeth (Joely Richardson), who works at the Lincoln Park Zoo. Scenes estab-

lishing their happiness are intercut with hospital scenes involving Grace (Driver), who will die of heart disease unless she receives a transplant. To the surprise of nobody in the audience, Elizabeth dies in a tragic accident, and Grace is given her heart.

At the very moment when it starts beating in her chest, Bob, grieving at home, seems to sense it, as heartbeats on the sound track underline the segue. And a year later, Grace and Bob meet in the Old Town family-run restaurant where she works and lives. It is, for both of them, love at first sight, and their romance blossoms until she discovers something that Bob does not know—it is Elizabeth's heart beating in her chest.

Do not fear I have revealed too much of the story, because all of this is essentially setup, easily anticipated. What gives the movie its gentle charm is not the melodramatic story, but the warmth of the performances and the way the movie pokes merrily along, teasing us with rewards and disappointments.

The key element in the success, I think, is the illusion that Bob and Grace are truly in love. Duchovny and Driver (who has a gift for vulnerability) have an unforced chemistry that feels right. It is crucial in a story of this sort that we want the couple to be together—that we care about them. Otherwise we are simply looking at the puppet strings. I did like them, and felt protective toward them, and apprehensive as their inevitable problems approached.

The setting of the film is also old-fashioned, and a little too picturesque for my taste. Many of the scenes play in O'Reilly's Italian restaurant (actually the Twin Anchors), where the Irish and Italian branches of Grace's family offer such contradictory menu choices as chicken vesuvio and corned beef and cabbage. What is strangest about the restaurant is not the menu but the hours: O'Reilly's seems to close early every night so that the old cronies who run the place can sit around the back table, playing poker and holding desultory debates on the relative merits of Frank Sinatra, Dean Martin, and Vic Damone.

These stalwarts include Carroll O'Connor and Robert Loggia as, of course, the Irish and Italian patriarchs, O'Connor's accent a shade too thick. The guys are all busybodies, peering through a back window into the rear garden where many of the key scenes take place, and playing matchmakers for all they're worth. A little trimming of their scenes wouldn't have hurt.

There is, however, a nice unforced feel to the home life of Grace's best friends, Megan and Joe Dayton, played by Hunt and James Belushi with a relaxed domesticity that makes their characters feel real, and not just helpers designed to speed a scene or two. The emphasis on the film is on friends and family, on a much-loved neighborhood woman who moves in a circle of people who want her to be happy.

Watching the film, I became aware that it lacked the gimmicks of many recent romances. It believes in love and fate, stuff like that. Its innocence is crucial to the plot, because much depends on Bob not seeing the scar on Grace's chest while their courtship moves along. In today's sex-happy movies, the secret would have been revealed when they slept together on their second date, but *Return to Me* convincingly lets them move slowly toward intimacy, so that Grace's delayed nudity creates effective tension.

No doubt this film will be disemboweled by cynics among the reviewers. It offers an easy target. It is almost an act of courage, the way it refuses to hedge its bets or cater to irony. It is what it is, without apology or compromise. It made me smile a lot. I have tried to describe it accurately, for the benefit of those who will like it, and those who will not. You know who you are.

Return to Paradise ★ ★ ★ ½
R, 109 m., 1998

Vince Vaughn (Sheriff), Anne Heche (Beth), Joaquin Phoenix (Lewis), David Conrad (Tony), Vera Farmiga (Kerrie), Nick Sandow (Ravitch), Jada Pinkett Smith (M. J. Major). Directed by Joseph Ruben and produced by Alain Bernheim, Steve Golin, and Ezra Swerdlow. Screenplay by Bruce Robinson and Wesley Strick.

Joseph Ruben's *Return to Paradise* is a thriller that traps its characters in an exquisite dilemma involving life and death. Lewis, Sheriff, and Tony are three Americans who meet in Malay-

sia and fool around in cheap huts on the beach, "God's own bathtub," enjoying the rum, the girls, and the hashish. Sheriff and Tony return to New York. Lewis plans to go on to Borneo for a Greenpeace project to protect the orangutan. Instead, he's arrested with the left-over hash and sentenced to death.

Two years pass before Sheriff (Vince Vaughn) and Tony (David Conrad) are contacted in Manhattan and told all of this by Lewis's advocate, Beth (Anne Heche). The problem, she explains, is that Lewis (Joaquin Phoenix) was over the legal limit for possession by one person, making him a trafficker, not a user. However, she's cut a deal with the authorities. If Sheriff and Tony will return to Malaysia and testify that they all owned the hashish together, Lewis will be allowed to live, and Sheriff and Tony will each have to spend three years apiece in prison. If only one of them returns, it'll be six years.

Students of logic will recognize this choice immediately. It's a variation of the Prisoner's Dilemma, one of the oldest puzzles in mathematics and philosophy. Obviously, neither Tony nor Sheriff want Lewis to die. But they didn't know him *that* well, and they hardly want to spend three years of their lives in a Third World prison—let alone six years. The ideal solution for either Tony and Sheriff would be for the other guy to do six years while one gets off free. But if both guys try this tactic, Lewis dies.

Hemingway, defining morality, once said that something is good if you feel good after doing it, and evil if you feel bad after doing it. How would you feel if you let Lewis hang? Good, because you were not spending three or six years in prison in Malaysia? Or bad, because you know it was your hashish too? *Return to Paradise* watches Sheriff and Tony as they decide. And they do decide; this is not going to be one of those teasers that sets you up for a moral dilemma and then pulls a switcheroo and solves everything with an action climax.

All of the performances are convincing, but Anne Heche's is especially effective. She walks a fine line between inviting Tony and Sheriff to save Lewis's life, and pummeling them with moral blackmail. It is not an easy decision to walk out of freedom in Manhattan and into three years in a jail where disease, brutality, malnutrition, and dysentery have been reported. Heche looks very concentrated in her scenes: intense, focused, trying to read all of the signs.

Sheriff (Vince Vaughn) is now working as a limo driver. He doesn't have much of a life, but at least it's his. Tony is engaged to be married. As for Beth, we only gradually learn her full story, which catches Sheriff in a tricky emotional vise. Joaquin Phoenix, as the prisoner, is not stoic or philosophical, but feels the way most people would when a death sentence appears out of the blue.

The director, Joseph Ruben (*The Stepfather, Sleeping With the Enemy*), uses a kind of flat, logical storytelling that leads us inexorably toward his conclusions. The suspense is not so much over what happens as about how it will happen to us—how the movie will make us experience what clearly must happen. His screenplay, by Bruce Robinson and Wesley Strick, doesn't make things easy by portraying the Malaysians as particularly villainous; the judge, indeed, makes sense when he expresses puzzlement that America would permit its streets to be endangered by drugs: Better that the drug dealers should suffer instead of the general population.

The only real villain in the movie, indeed, is a journalist played by Jada Pinkett Smith, whose eagerness to get Lewis's story may endanger the efforts to free him. She's seen as a little too eager and careless, but there is an element of truth in her behavior: Many journalists would and do get stories at a human cost that the story cannot possibly justify.

Return to Paradise has been compared to *Midnight Express*, another film about a thoughtless American facing the forfeit of his life in prison far from home. That was more of a visceral film. This one is more cerebral. Like Sheriff and Tony, we're pulled both ways by the story: We want them to go back and save Lewis, but we're not exactly sure we'd do the same. That's the Prisoner's Dilemma in a nutshell.

Return With Honor ★ ★ ★

NO MPAA RATING, 102 m., 1999

A documentary featuring Lieutenant (jg) Everett Alvarez, Lieutenant Commander Bob Shumaker, Commander Jeremiah (Jerry) Denton, Commander James Stockdale, Lieutenant Colonel Robinson Risner, Lieutenant Commander John McCain, Captain Douglas Peterson, Major Fred Cherry, Lieutenant John McGrath, Seaman Douglas Hegdahl. Directed and produced by Freida Lee Mock and Terry Sanders. Screenplay by Mock, Sanders, and Christine Z. Wiser.

Return With Honor is a documentary about the ordeals of the American prisoners of war in the infamous Hanoi Hilton, a torture facility. We see the faces of these men today, and we even see them in footage shot at the time. We hear their voices, which are level and sane, as military pilots are trained to speak, but which betray depths of emotion.

The war essentially ended for these men when they were captured, and a new chapter began, of personal test. They were so cut off from the world that they learned of the Moon landing only by seeing a Neil Armstrong postage stamp. Their lives were bounded by stone walls and controlled by their captors, who devised methods of torture so refined that "you'd sell your mother down the river in a minute."

And yet the men endured more than it is possible to comprehend. It is interesting that we hear little hate or anger in their voices; as professional soldiers they value a certain stoicism. To be captured was a risk of war. To "return with honor" was their goal, and one defines it: "To be able to say you didn't do anything you'd be ashamed to tell your children." Of course, that did not include napalming civilians and poisoning crops—because in the rules of war mass violence is sanctioned by both sides, and only personal violence, such as torture, is condemned.

The Hanoi Hilton, we learn, has a symbolic history. It was built by the French during the colonial era to hold disobedient Vietnamese subjects, then used by the Viet Cong to hold Americans. Leg clamps were bolted to the beds, and one witness says, "You could look at this place and hear the screams of fifty years." The Viet Cong torturers had refined methods, including a "rope trick" in which prisoners were bound in positions of excruciating pain. Their minds were worked on by morale-crushing video programs showing U.S. antiwar rallies

493

and congressional speeches. "We will win this war on the streets of New York," their captors told them after one show. In a sense they did.

The ingenuity of the prisoners is astonishing. They devised a code of taps to communicate through cell walls, developing friendships with prisoners they had never seen. Put in a propaganda film, Commander Jeremiah Denton blinked out the word "torture" in Morse code with his eyelids. A fellow prisoner held out his middle fingers to send an even more universal code. Lieutenant John McGrath drew on his cell wall with his own blood and pus; after being freed, he drew everything he remembered. Seaman Douglas Hegdahl memorized the names of 268 fellow prisoners.

Return With Honor was directed by Freida Lee Mock and Terry Sanders. Mock's *Maya Lin: A Strong Clear Vision* is a 1994 Oscar-winning documentary about the Vietnam Veteran's Memorial in Washington and the young woman who designed it. After seeing it, two former prisoners told Mock they had a story to be told. This film tells it simply and directly, without spin or flash, with no narration—just the voices of the men themselves, as they talk against a plain background. There is footage of the Hanoi Hilton as it is today (the screams in a way still echoing) and footage of the men at the time, taken by the Viet Cong and showing, for example, Hanoi mobs cursing them during a march through the city.

A few of the faces are familiar. There are short glimpses of Senator John McCain. We see Pete Peterson, who returned to Vietnam in 1997 as our ambassador. And Vice Admiral James Stockdale, Ross Perot's 1992 running mate. No attempt is made to introduce politics into the film: These were brave men who behaved honorably and patriotically, and we are moved by the strength of their spirits. The scenes of their homecoming are enormously affecting.

I saw another Vietnam documentary, *Regret to Inform*, by Barbara Sonneborn, the widow of an American who died in Vietnam. Her film talks with women on both sides about the husbands they lost. It is not really political either, although no one in her film thinks the war was a good idea (it is not much praised in *Return With Honor*, either). The films would

make a useful double feature, suggesting that when war places people under unimaginable pain, it is not politics that motivates them— but self-respect, pride, even stubbornness. The message, I think, is that they hope to be able to return with honor to themselves.

Ride With the Devil ★ ★
R, 138 m., 1999

Skeet Ulrich (Jack Bull Chiles), Tobey Maguire (Jake Roedel), Simon Baker-Denny (George Clyde), Jeffrey Wright (Daniel Holt), Jewel (Sue Lee Shelley), Jonathan Rhys Meyers (Pitt Mackerson), James Caviezel (Black John), Thomas Guiry (Riley Crawford), Tom Wilkinson (Orton Brown). Directed by Ang Lee and produced by Ted Hope, Robert F. Colesberry, and James Schamus. Screenplay by Schamus, based on the novel *Woe to Live On* by Daniel Woodrell.

Ride With the Devil is the first Civil War film I can recall that is not told with the benefit of hindsight. It's about characters who don't know the North will win—and sometimes don't much seem to care. It's said that all politics are local; this movie argues that some wars are local too. In Missouri, the only slaveholding state that sided with the Union, it tells the story of a small group of guerrillas with such complex personal motives that it even includes a black man who fights for the South.

The film has been made by Ang Lee, the gifted Taiwan-born, Illinois-educated director *(Sense and Sensibility, The Ice Storm)* who is able to see the Civil War from the outside. Based on a historical novel by Daniel Woodrell, Lee centers his story on Southwest Missouri, where the Missouri Irregulars, known as Bushwhackers, waged a hit-and-run fight against the Union troops, called Jayhawkers. This is basically a local war among neighbors with personal animosities and little interest in the war's ideological underpinnings.

We follow four Bushwhackers in particular: Jake Roedel (Tobey Maguire), Jack Bull Chiles (Skeet Ulrich), George Clyde (Simon Baker-Denny), and the freed black slave Daniel Holt (Jeffrey Wright). The film opens with a farm wedding they attend; later they see the farm burned and its owners murdered by a Jay-hawker raid.

Roedel and Chiles want revenge. Clyde, a southerner, believes in Dixie values and traditions, but is complex enough to have freed Holt, once his slave. Holt's motives are the most impenetrable. Why would a former slave fight for the South? He indicates it is out of personal loyalty to Clyde, who freed him and says he "trusts him with my life every day." Also perhaps because of a bond with his comrades. But Holt says little and his eyes often make a silent commentary on what he sees and hears; we wait through the film for a revelation of his deepest feelings.

History, it is said, is written by the victors. The southern side has had its share of historians, too, but before this movie I had not seen a Civil War story about characters whose feelings are local and personal, whose motives were unclear even to themselves, who were essentially young men with guns, forced to fight by the time and place they lived in. To some degree, they are only practicing self-defense. The movie is more interested in their personalities than their adventures—but not so interested that it makes their motives very clear. There is nothing quite so baffling as a character who acts from psychological reasons but possesses little insight into those buried feelings.

The movie is slow and deliberate—too slow. It begins with the enigma of heroes whose cause we do not share, and then has them spend much of their time hunched inside a hideout they have built into a hillside (where it never occurs to them that if they'd fill the chinks between the logs it might be warmer inside). They have long conversations, delivered in language that seems more suited to sermons and editorials than to everyday speech.

Their hideout is on the land of a Missouri family that supports the Confederacy, and soon Chiles is falling in love with Sue Lee (Jewel), a war widow. To give the film credit, it doesn't degenerate into a conventional romance, but plays both Chiles and Sue Lee as desperate in their own ways for an escape from an intolerable situation. There are also grim passages involving wounds, amputations, and desperate armed raids.

The technical and acting credits are first-rate. Frederick Elmes, who also shot *The Ice Storm,* has an uncanny ability to evoke cold and damp. The actors do a good job of being contained by their characters—by not letting modern insights peek through. Jeffrey Wright, who starred in *Basquiat,* is especially intriguing as the freed slave, who keeps his own counsel throughout the movie without sending out signals about what he's doing. Jewel deserves praise for, quite simply, performing her character in a convincing and unmannered way. She is an actress here, not a pop star trying out a new hobby. Ulrich is good, too, although Tobey Maguire's tone—tight, inward, controlled—is beginning to wear on me after this and *The Cider House Rules.* It's time for him to make a dumb teenage comedy (not because I want to see it, but more to clear the cobwebs).

Watching the film, I could see that Ang Lee and his frequent collaborator, the screenwriter James Schamus, were in search of something serious. *Ride With the Devil* does not have conventional rewards or payoffs, does not simplify a complex situation, doesn't punch up the action or the romance simply to entertain. But it is, sad to say, not a very entertaining movie; it's a long slog unless you're fascinated by the undercurrents. It's a film that would inspire useful discussion in a history class, but for ordinary moviegoers, it's slow and forbidding.

Ringmaster ★ ★
R, 95 m., 1998

Jerry Springer (Jerry Farrelly), Jaime Pressly (Angel Zorzak), Molly Hagan (Connie Zorzak), Michael Dudikoff (Rusty), Ashley Holbrook (Willie), Michael Jai White (Demond), Wendy Raquel Robinson (Starletta), Tangie Ambrose (Vonda), Nicki Micheaux (Leshawnette). Directed by Neil Abramson and produced by Jerry Springer, Gina Rugolo-Judd, Brad Jenkel, Steve Stabler, and Gary W. Goldstein. Screenplay by Jon Bernstein.

Jerry Springer's *Ringmaster* creates an understandable anticipation in the audience that the film will be largely about Springer. But Springer appears more as a by-product. He stands to one side looking morose and regretful, while human flotsam occupies his stage. He's like a sorrowful deer caught in the headlights, except for a big speech where he lectures sternly that the poor have just as much right as the rich to be humiliated in public.

The difference, of course, is that the rich have public humiliation thrust upon them, while the poor have to angle for it. The movie's plot is mostly about two sets of would-be guests who apply to the show, hoping for free airline tickets. The movie wisely focuses on them, and that's the key to its occasional charm: It doesn't make the mistake of thinking we're much interested in Springer himself. What we want to know is, what kind of people would want to be guests on that show?

Was ever the word "guest" more cruelly misused than as a description of the victims of the Springer program? And yet that's how they see themselves. "This is the first family vacation we've ever had," says Connie Zorzak (Molly Hagan), the heroine of the film, who volunteers her daughter, Angel (Jaime Pressly), and husband (Angel's stepfather), Rusty (Michael Dudikoff), for the Springer show after catching them in bed with one another. As a fillip, she throws in Angel's boyfriend, Willie (Ashley Holbrook), who she (Connie) has been having sex with—as revenge against Angel, of course.

They all live in a trailer park near Miami. Connie and Angel are employed, Connie as the proprietor of a snack wagon that never seems to have any customers, Angel as a maid in a motel where the male customers all seem to know that, for a good time, they should see Angel. Rusty sits at home drinking beer and watching the dog races on TV. Occasionally he has to deal with Connie calling him up and telling him about openings for fork lift operators. All three actors are effective at finding the note that passes caricature but stops short of parody; I was reminded of scenes from *The Positively True Adventures of the Alleged Texas Cheerleader-Murdering Mom*.

They're accepted for the TV segment "You Did WHAT With Your Stepdaddy?" Meanwhile, we meet other guests. Starletta (Wendy Raquel Robinson) has a straying boyfriend named Demond (Michael Jai White), who has cheated on her with two other women: Vonda (Tangie Ambrose) and Leshawnette (Nicki

Micheaux). They all qualify for the Jerry show "My Traitor Girlfriends," where almost inevitably some of these cheerful cheaters find new possibilities backstage.

You'd expect this material to be dealt with in a careless and seamy way, but *Ringmaster* is a better movie than I expected. The guests come across as pathetic but spirited, and are acted with some sympathy. And the show tapings look like outtakes from TV, including tongue-kissing lesbians and black-shirted security guards to pull apart hair-pulling guests. (The preshow announcements have a charm of their own: "The No. 1 rule is: No weapons whatsoever. Can you be arrested for a crime you commit on the Jerry show? The answer is, yes.")

Molly Hagan brings poignancy to Connie, the trailer park mom. She was pregnant at fifteen, we learn, and blames herself for the shabby life she has created for her daughter. When she finds Angel in bed with her husband, she sees it less as a betrayal than as an opportunity for free airfare. Like Robert De Niro in *Taxi Driver*, she practices her lines in the mirror: "You did WHAT with my husband?" Jaime Pressly has a good scene as she tries to cash her paycheck and is told she has the wrong ID; her lifestyle includes weekly challenges to accepted banking practices.

Jon Bernstein's screenplay has some nice lines ("I like to think of us as the Judds without the talent"). Jerry Springer probably supplied most of his own dialogue ("This is a slice of American life, and if you don't like it, bite something else"). At times he looks like he's trying to send us a telepathic appeal for forgiveness. True story: One day Springer encountered a Chicago news anchor. Out of a blue sky, he volunteered, "I know I'm going to go to hell for doing this show." He should learn to forgive himself (a current Oprah topic). Somebody must be watching. I watch sometimes. And so do you.

The Road to El Dorado ★ ★ ★
PG, 83 m., 2000

With the voices of: Kevin Kline (Tulio), Kenneth Branagh (Miguel), Rosie Perez (Chel), Armand Assante (Tzekel-Kan), Edward James Olmos (The Chief), Jim Cummings (Cortez), Frank

Welker (Altivo), Elton John (Narrator). Directed by Eric "Bibo" Bergeron and Don Paul and produced by Bonne Radford and Brooke Breton. Screenplay by Ted Elliott and Terry Rossio.

There is a moment in *The Road to El Dorado* where the two heroes and their profoundly dubious horse are in a rowboat somewhere in the ocean off of Central America. It looks like the end. Then a sea bird appears, circles, and lands on their boat. This is a good omen. Land must be near. Then the bird drops dead. Bad sign. Then a shark leaps out of the sea and snaps up the bird in one gulp. Piling gag on top of gag is the strategy of the film, a bright and zesty animated comedy from DreamWorks.

In the studio's quest to compete with Disney in the feature-length animation sweepstakes, it's a worthy entry. It's not as quirky as *Antz* or as grown-up as *The Prince of Egypt*, but as silly fun it does nicely, and no wonder: Its directors are Disney veterans, and the sound track includes such effective cartoon voices as Kevin Kline, Kenneth Branagh, Armand Assante, Edward James Olmos, and the unsinkable Rosie Perez.

As the movie opens, the heroes, Tulio (Kline) and Miguel (Branagh), are gambling in a waterfront dive in Spain, 1519. They win a map to the treasures of El Dorado, before it's discovered that their dice are loaded and they beat a hasty retreat—pretending to duel with each other to confuse their pursuers. One thing leads to another, and they find themselves on board Cortez's ship as the explorer sails for South America. They're discovered, sentenced to flogging and enslavement, and escape with their horse in a rowboat, which brings us to the bird, the shark, and landfall at a point that corresponds exactly with the treasure map.

The Road to El Dorado doesn't have a hero; it's about supporting characters. In other hands, the story might have centered around Cortez, the explorer, whose ship catches up to Tulio and Miguel in the new land. But this is the story of two pals caught up in events beyond their comprehension, after the roly-poly local chief (voice by Edward James Olmos) mistakes them for gods. The plot then recycles Kipling's *The Man Who Would Be King:* One likes being a god, the other doesn't. Along the way, they get a sidekick of their own, Chel, a local woman. She's voiced by Perez, and looks like her too. She learns their secret—they aren't gods, only men, but likes them anyway, and decides she wants in on their team when the priest (Armand Assante) devises a monster to destroy them.

The movie has songs by Elton John, which may grow on me, but haven't yet, and some funny comedy sequences. The best may be the invention of the game of basketball, with a living ball—a round little creature who contributes his own moves to the game. More comedy comes as the friends realize the game is up, and try to sneak away with some gold of their own.

Freed of a towering central figure like Pocahontas or Tarzan, *The Road to El Dorado* is liberated for goofiness. There are no serious themes lurking about, or uplifting lessons to learn—just a couple of con men in over their heads, their gal pal, and a horse that some of the time is smarter than the other three put together. (Since the horse doesn't speak, it's able to exploit the miming gifts of the animators.) This is not a landmark in the history of feature animation, but it's bright and has good energy and the kinds of witty asides that entertain the adults in the margins of the stuff for the kids.

Road Trip ★ ★

R, 91 m., 2000

Breckin Meyer (Josh), Seann William Scott (E.L.), Amy Smart (Beth), Paulo Costanzo (Rubin), D. J. Qualls (Kyle), Rachel Blanchard (Tiffany), Anthony Rapp (Jacob), Fred Ward (Earl Edwards). Directed by Todd Phillips and produced by Daniel Goldberg and Joe Medjuck. Screenplay by Todd Phillips and Scot Armstrong.

Road Trip is mellow and dirty, which is the wrong combination. It's sweet when it should be raunchy, or vice versa, and the result is a movie that seems uneasy with itself. It wants to be evil, really it does, but every so often its better nature takes over, and it throws sweetness right there in the middle of the dirty stuff and the nudity. We feel unkind, watching it. We'd enjoy the nudity more if it were ribald and cheerful, but it feels obligatory, as if the actresses were instructed to disrobe every five minutes in a movie that's only really interested in sex for commercial reasons.

Nude scenes should be inspired by the libido, not the box office. That's why I object to the phrase "gratuitous nudity." In a movie like this, the only nudity worth having is gratuitous. If it's there for reasons that are clankingly commercial, you feel sorry for the actresses, which is not the point.

The plot is a lamebrained contrivance about a frat boy named Josh (Breckin Meyer), who has been dating Tiffany (Rachel Blanchard of TV's *Clueless*) ever since high school. Now he's a student at Ithaca College, and she has decided she needs room to grow, or concentrate on her major, or something, and she enrolls at the University of Austin, which is not as far from Ithaca as you can get, but might as well be.

Josh and Tiff keep in touch by telephone, but Josh senses her attention waning, and then there's a period when she doesn't answer the phone. Josh meanwhile has been flirting with a campus sexpot named Beth (Amy Smart), and one night she seduces him and they make a video of themselves having sex, perhaps because they have seen the same thing done in *American Pie*, or perhaps because the makers of *Road Trip* are ripping off *American Pie*, which is probably more likely.

Josh has made a sweet video to send to Tiffany, but we get no points for foreseeing the obvious, which is that the wrong video gets mailed to Tiff, and so Josh and his friends, who lack airfare, have to make an emergency road trip to Austin to try to retrieve the video before Tiffany can see it. All of this is complicated by the presence of Jacob (Anthony Rapp), an unpleasant undergraduate whose minor seems to be in stalking.

Josh borrows a car that belongs to his geeky friend Kyle (D. J. Qualls), and takes along his friends Rubin (Paulo Costanzo) and E.L. (Seann William Scott), who is from *American Pie* and thus functions as a cross-cultural trivia bookmark. They have versions of the usual adventures along the way, including an awkward scene where these white boys try to convince the members of an African-American fraternity that they are members. This scene is as uncomfortable as comedy can be, because the

humor in it is latently racist, and so the movie lets it remain latent, which means that all the characters, black and white, seem to be standing around self-consciously avoiding tasteless material. (The movie is bereft, unfortunately, of any alternative material.)

Whether Josh gets to the tape before Beth sees it, I will leave for you to determine. And yes, I said "determine" and not "decide," because to be honest with you I was confused. I thought she had seen it, and then it appeared that she had not, all because of a dream sequence that was either (a) incompetently presented, or (b) failed to engage what I fondly think of as my full intelligence.

On the way out of the movie, I met three teenage girls who asked me what I thought of it, and I requested their opinion: Didn't it seem like Beth had seen the video and then that she hadn't? The three girls agreed with me, and said they'd been confused, too, and together we figured out what had happened, which was useful, but not the sort of conversation you should be having. When a movie doesn't have a brain in its head, don't you agree it's kind of unfair to require thought on the part of the audience?

Full disclosure requires me to report that there were several moments in the movie when I did indeed laugh, and that the characters are likable when they are not being required to act dirty for the transient purposes of the screenplay. Those virtues are not enough to redeem the film, but they suggest that the cast should be regarded more as victims than perpetrators.

Romance ★ ★ ★
NO MPAA RATING, 103 m., 1999

Caroline Ducey (Marie), Sagamore Stevenin (Paul), Francois Berleand (Robert), Rocco Siffredi (Paolo). Directed by Catherine Breillat and produced by Jean-Francois Lepetit. Screenplay by Breillat.

There is a fantasy scene in *Romance* where a woman's body is divided by a wall. On one side, from the waist down, she is in a brothel. On the other side, from the waist up, in a delivery room. What is the message of the scene? Don't be too sure you know. I know I don't. It isn't some kind of simplistic message linking childbirth with misuse by men. The woman having the fantasy isn't really against the activities on either side of the wall. Maybe the scene is intended as an illustration of her own confusion about sex.

The woman's name is Marie (Caroline Ducey). She could be the woman Freud was thinking about when he confessed he could not answer the question, "What does a woman want?" Marie asks herself the same question. She wants something, all right. She is unhappy with her boyfriend, Paul, who refuses to sleep with her, and unhappy, too, with the sexual adventures she has. It's like there's a disconnect between her body and her identity. She does things that sometimes make her feel good, but she doesn't feel good because she has done them.

Romance, written and directed by Catherine Breillat, became notorious on the festival circuit because it is an intelligent, radical film by a woman, and at the same time it contains explicit nudity and, as nearly as we can tell, actual sex. It is not arousing or pornographic, because the sex isn't presented in an erotic way; it's more like a documentary of a dogged woman's forced march toward orgasm, a goal she is not sure she values. Marie narrates the film herself, and also seems to be reading pages from her journal; she is baffled by herself, baffled by men, baffled by sex. Even after climax, her hand closes on air.

Of course the film is French. It is said that for the French, wine takes the place of flirting, dining takes the place of seduction, smoking takes the place of foreplay, and talking takes the place of sex. *Romance* is so analytical that you sometimes get the feeling Marie is putting herself through her sexual encounters simply to get material for her journal. These poor guys aren't lovers; they're case studies.

And yet the film has an icy fascination. Perhaps it is a test of how men and women relate to eroticism on the screen. I know few men who like it much (sure proof it is not pornographic). Women defend it in feminist terms, but you have the strangest feeling they're not saying what they really think. At a screening at the Toronto Film Festival, there was some laughter, almost all female, but I couldn't tell if it was nervous, or knowing.

Perhaps the sex content gets in the way, causing our old tapes to play. When we see a stud on the screen (like Rocco Siffredi, in real life an Italian porno actor famous for one very good reason), we go into porno mode and expect to see—well, what we usually see. But *Romance* doesn't have that mode. Marie relates to Paolo (Siffredi's character) as if he is a laboratory specimen. So this is the famous white rat she has heard so much about. Can he bring her pleasure? Is it perhaps a matter of physical endowment?

And what about Robert (Francois Berleand), who offers to tie her up? He is an ordinary man, not handsome, not exciting, but he has all the necessary equipment and skills, and when he makes his offer she agrees, as if he is a guide at Disney World suggesting one more ride she should try before leaving the park. Does she like bondage? She goes back for more. Perhaps it is not the sexual side that pleases her, but the fact that when Robert is arranging his ropes and restraints, at least he is thinking about her.

There is a scene in the movie that looks like rape, but is it? She more or less invites the stranger who mistreats her. She wants—well, she wants to take a chance, and then she finds out she didn't like it. So she's defiant toward the guy, but it's not anger at how he treated her; it's triumph that she feels undefeated. Later, there is a gynecological examination—perhaps the creepiest scene in the movie, as interns line up for their turn.

I did not really enjoy this movie, and yet I recommend it. Why? Because I think it's onto something interesting. Movies buy the whole romantic package, lock, stock, and barrel. People look great, fall in love, and have wonderful sex. Even intelligent characters in smart movies all seem to think more or less the same way while they're in the sack. Erogenous autopilot takes over. Here is a movie about a woman who never stops thinking. That may not be as good for you as it is for her. ☞

Romeo Must Die ★ ½
R, 110 m., 2000

Jet Li (Han Sing), Aaliyah (Trish O'Day), Isaiah Washington (Mac), Delroy Lindo (Isaak O'Day), DMX (Silk), D. B. Woodside (Colin), Anthony Anderson (Maurice), Henry O. (Ch'u Sing).

Directed by Andrzej Bartkowiak and produced by Joel Silver and Jim Van Wyck. Screenplay by Mitchell Kapner, Eric Bernt, and John Jarrell.

Shakespeare has been manhandled in countless modern-dress retreads, and I was looking forward to *Romeo Must Die*, billed as a war between Chinese and African-American families, based on *Romeo and Juliet*. After *China Girl* (1987), which sets the story in New York's Little Italy and Chinatown, and *Romeo + Juliet* (1996), which has a war between modern gangsters in a kind of CalMex strip city, why not a martial arts version in Oakland?

Alas, the film borrows one premise from Shakespeare (the children of enemy families fall in love), and buries the rest of the story in a creaky plot and wheezy dialogue. Much is made of the presence of Jet Li, the Hong Kong martial arts star *(Lethal Weapon 4)*, but his scenes are so clearly computer-aided that his moves are about as impressive as Bugs Bunny doing the same things.

Li stars as Han Sing, once a cop, now taking the rap for a crime he didn't commit. He's in a Hong Kong prison as the movie opens. His brother is killed in Oakland after a fight at an African-American dance club, and Sing breaks out of prison to travel to America and avenge his brother. In Oakland, he meets Trish O'Day (Aaliyah, the singer) and they begin to fall in love while she helps him look into the death of his brother.

But what a coincidence! Her father, Isaak (Delroy Lindo), may know more about the death than he should, and soon the two lovers are in the middle of a war between Chinese and black organizations who are involved in a murky plot to buy up the waterfront for a new sports stadium. This real-estate project exists primarily as a clothesline on which to hang elaborate martial arts sequences, including one Jackie Chan–style football game where Jet Li hammers half a dozen black guys and scores a touchdown, all at once.

It is a failing of mine that I persist in bringing logic to movies where it is not wanted. During *Romeo Must Die*, I began to speculate about the methods used to buy up the waterfront. All of the property owners (of clubs, little shops, crab houses, etc.) are asked to sell, and when they refuse, they are variously murdered, torched, blown up, or have their faces stuck into vats of live crabs. Don't you think the press and the local authorities would notice this? Don't you imagine it would take the bloom off a stadium to know that dozens of victims were murdered to clear the land?

Never mind. The audience isn't in the theater for a film about property values, but to watch Jet Li and other martial arts warriors in action. *Romeo Must Die* has a lot of fight scenes, but key moments in them are so obviously special effects that they miss the point. When Jackie Chan does a stunt, it may look inelegant, but we know he's really doing it. Here Jet Li leaps six feet in the air and rotates clockwise while kicking three guys. It can't be done, we know it can't be done, we know he's not doing it, and so what's the point? In *The Matrix,* there's a reason the guy can fly.

There's a moment in Jackie Chan's *Rumble in the Bronx* when he uses grace and athletic ability to project his entire body through the swinging gate of a grocery cart, and we say, "Yes!" (pumping a fist into the air is optional). Here Jet Li tries the Chan practice of using whatever props come to hand, but the football game looks overrehearsed and a sequence with a fire hose is underwhelming (anybody can knock guys off their feet with a fire hose).

Closing Notes: Many windows are broken in the movie. Many people fall from great heights. There are a lot of rap songs on the sound track, which distract from the action because their lyrics occupy the foreground and replace dialogue. Killers on motorcycles once again forget it is dangerous for them to chase cars at high speed, because if they get thrown off their bikes, it will hurt. The reliable Motorcycle Opaque Helmet Rule is observed (when you can't see the face of a character because the visor is down, chances are—gasp!—it's a woman). No great romantic chemistry is generated between the young lovers, and there is something odd about a martial arts warrior hiding behind a girl's bedroom door so her daddy won't catch him. Delroy Lindo projects competence, calm, and strength in every scene. This movie needs a screenplay.

Ronin ★ ★ ★
R, 121 m., 1998

Robert De Niro (Sam), Jean Reno (Vincent), Stellan Skarsgard (Gregor), Skipp Sudduth (Larry), Jan Triska (Dapper Gent), Natascha McElhone (Deidre), Sean Bean (Spence), Michael Lonsdale (Jean-Pierre). Directed by John Frankenheimer and produced by Frank Mancuso Jr. Screenplay by J. D. Zeik and Richard Weisz.

The "ronin" of Japanese legend were samurai whose lords were killed. Left with no leader to dedicate their lives to, they roamed the countryside, freelancers for hire. The same definition would apply to the rough band of killers who assemble in a Paris bistro at the beginning of John Frankenheimer's *Ronin.*

They're an international crew. From America comes Sam (Robert De Niro), who the others think is ex-CIA. From France, Vincent (Jean Reno). From Russia, Gregor (Stellan Skarsgard), who may be ex-KGB and is a computer expert. From England, Spence (Sean Bean), a munitions and bomb man. And there's another American, Larry (Skipp Sudduth)—who is supposed to be a great driver but is too much of a showboat, choosing as he does to replicate the Diana death chase (actually, that's just the movie's in-joke, if it's a joke at all).

The movie is essentially bereft of a plot. There's an explanation at the end, but it's arbitrary and unnecessary. *Ronin* is really about characters, locations, and behavior. Consider the elaborate opening setup in which Sam, the De Niro character, reconnoiters the bistro before going in. We assume he's going to attack those inside, but actually he's only attending a meeting of all the men that has been called by an IRA paymistress named Deidre (Natascha McElhone). "Why did you go around to the back?" she asks him. "I never walk into a place I don't know how to walk out of," says De Niro, who spends most of the rest of the movie walking into places he doesn't know how to walk out of.

Frankenheimer milks that opening for ten minutes of pure cinema. Once De Niro gets inside, the opening is revealed as just an exercise, but in a film like this you stay in the pres-

ent and don't ask questions (like, why hold the meeting in a public place?).

The IRA has assembled these five men to get a briefcase. We never learn what is in the briefcase. It's the perfect McGuffin, as defined by Hitchcock (something everyone cares about, although it doesn't matter what it is). My guess: Inside this briefcase is the briefcase from *Pulp Fiction.* The briefcase is in the possession of "five to eight men," Deidre tells them, and the ronin set out to track them to Cannes, Nice, and other attractive locations (an obligatory encounter in an ancient Roman arena is not overlooked). Every encounter leads to a violent bloodbath and a high-speed chase, so that in the real world the headlines would be screaming about streets in flames and dozens dead—but in a thriller, of course, to be dead is to be forgotten.

I enjoyed the film on two levels: for its skill and its silliness. The actors are without exception convincing in their roles, and the action makes little sense. Consider the Stellan Skarsgard character, who is always popping out his laptop computer and following the progress of chase scenes with maps and what I guess are satellite photos. Why does he do this? To affirm to himself that elsewhere something is indeed happening, I think.

The best scene is one of the quieter ones, as De Niro's character gives instructions on how a bullet is to be removed from his side. "I once removed a guy's appendix with a grapefruit spoon," he explains, and more urgently: "Don't take it out unless you really got it." The scene ends with a line that De Niro, against all odds, is able to deliver so that it is funny and touching at the same time: "You think you can stitch me up on your own? If you don't mind, I'm gonna pass out."

John Frankenheimer is known as a master of intelligent thrillers *(Manchurian Candidate, 52 Pick-Up)*, and his films almost always have a great look: There is a quality in the visuals that's hard to put your finger on, but that brings a presence to the locations, making them feel like more than backdrops.

Here, with a fine cast, he does what is essentially an entertaining exercise. The movie is not really about anything; if it were, it might have really amounted to something, since it comes pretty close anyway. The screenplay credits conceal the presence of hired hand David Mamet, who reportedly wrote most of the final draft, and who gives the dialogue a deadpan, professional sound. For a little more maybe he would have thrown in a plot.

Rosetta ★ ★ ★ ½
R, 95 m., 2000

Emilie Dequenne (Rosetta), Fabrizio Rongione (Riquet), Anne Yernaux (Mother), Olivier Gourmet (Boss), Bernard Marbaix (Campgrounds Manager), Frederic Bodson (Head of Personnel), Florian Delain (Boss's Son), Christiane Dorval (First Saleswoman), Mireille Bailly (Second Saleswoman). Directed by Luc and Jean-Pierre Dardenne and produced by the Dardennes and Michele and Laurent Petin. Screenplay by the Dardennes.

At night before she goes to sleep, Rosetta has this conversation with herself: "Your name is Rosetta. My name is Rosetta. You found a job. I found a job. You've got a friend. I've got a friend. You have a normal life. I have a normal life. You won't fall in a rut. I won't fall in a rut. Good night. Good night."

This is a young woman determined to find a job at all costs. She is escaping from the world of her alcoholic mother, a tramp who lives in a ramshackle trailer and runs away near the beginning of the story, leaving her daughter to fend for herself. Rosetta sees an abyss yawning beneath her and will go to any length to avoid it.

Her story is told in a film that astonishingly won the Palme d'Or at the 1999 Cannes Film Festival, as well as the Best Actress prize for its star, Emilie Dequenne. The wins were surprising not because this is a bad film (in its uncompromising way it's a very good one), but because films like this—neorealist, without pedigree, downbeat, stylistically straightforward—do not often win at Cannes. *Variety*'s grudgingly positive review categorized it as "an extremely small European art movie from Belgium." Not just European but Belgian.

Rosetta opens with its heroine being fired, unjustly, we think, from a job. She smacks the boss, is chased by the police, returns home to her mother's trailer, and we get glimpses of her life as she sells old clothes for money, and sometimes buries things like a squirrel. She fishes in a filthy nearby stream—for food, not fun. She makes a friend of Riquet (Fabrizio Rongione), a kid about her age who has a job in a portable waffle stand (yes, Belgian waffles in a Belgian art movie). He likes her, is kind to her, and perhaps she likes him.

One vignette follows another. We discover that unlike almost every teenage girl in the world, she can't dance. That she has stomach pains, maybe from an ulcer. One day Riquet falls in the river while trying to retrieve her fishing line, and she waits a strangely long time before helping him to get out. Later she confesses she didn't want him out. If he had drowned, she could have gotten his job. After all, the local waffle king likes her, and she'd have a job already, had it not gone to his idiot son.

What happens next I will leave for you to discover. The film has an odd, subterranean power. It doesn't strive for our sympathy or make any effort to portray Rosetta as colorful, winning, or sympathetic. It's a film of economic determinism, the story of a young woman for whom employment equals happiness. Or so she thinks until she has employment, and is no happier, perhaps because that is something she has simply never learned to be.

Two other films prowled like ghosts in my memory as I watched *Rosetta*. One was Robert Bresson's *Mouchette* (1966), about a poor girl who is cruelly treated by a village. The other was Agnes Varda's *Vagabond* (1986), about a young woman alone on the road, gradually descending from backpacker to homeless person. These characters are Rosetta's spiritual sisters, sharing her proud disdain for society and her desperate need to be seen as part of it. She'll find a job. She'll get a friend. She'll have a normal life. She won't fall in a rut. Good night.

Rounders ★ ★ ★
R, 115 m., 1998

Matt Damon (Mike McDermott), Edward Norton (Worm), John Malkovich (Teddy KGB), Gretchen Mol (Jo), John Turturro (Joey Knish), Martin Landau (Petrovsky), Famke Janssen

(Petra). Directed by John Dahl and produced by Joel Stillerman and Ted Demme. Screenplay by David Levien and Brian Koppelman.

Rounders cheerfully buys into compulsive gambling. The hero gambles away his tuition money, his girlfriend, his law degree, and nearly his life, and at the end he's still a happy gambler. If this movie were about alcoholism, the hero would regain consciousness after the DTs and order another double. Most gambling movies are dire warnings; this one is a recruiting poster.

I think that's because the movie would rather recycle the *Rocky* genre than end on a sour note. It stars Matt Damon as a New York law student who is a truly gifted poker player, and since the movie ends with a big game you somehow kinda know he's not going to lose it. Since the genre insists on a victory at the end, the movie has to be in favor of poker; you don't see Rocky deciding to retire because of brain damage.

As a poker movie, it's knowledgeable and entertaining. And as a mediocre player who hits the poker room at the Mirage a couple of times a year and has read a fair share of books about the World Series of Poker, I enjoyed it. It takes place within the pro poker underground of New York and Atlantic City, where everybody knows the big games and the key players. And it shows brash, clean-cut, young Mike McDermott (Damon) venturing into the world of cutthroats like Teddy KGB (John Malkovich), the poker genius of the Russian-American Mafia.

Mike is a law student, living with fellow student Jo (Gretchen Mol). As the movie opens, he gathers his entire stake of $30,000 and loses it all to Teddy KGB. Jo has been trying to talk him into quitting poker, and he promises to reform. But the next day his best friend, Worm (Edward Norton), gets out of prison, and of course he has to meet him at the prison gates, and of course that leads to a poker game that night, and to an escalating and dangerous series of problems.

Worm owes a lot of money to bad people. Mike unwisely becomes his coguarantor. It becomes necessary for them to win a lot of money in a short period of time or be hurt very badly, and the movie is about the places they go and the weird people they encounter in the process. Although it's not necessary to play poker to understand the movie, the screenwriters (David Levien and Brian Koppelman) have done their homework, and approvingly quote such truisms as, "If you can't spot the sucker in your first half-hour at the table, you are the sucker."

The movie buys into the seedy glamour of poker, romanticizing a game that essentially consists of exhausted technicians living off brief bursts of adrenaline generated by risking everything they own or can borrow. All gambling comes down to that—the queasy combination of thrill and fear as you win or lose—and real gambling ideally involves more of your money than it reasonably should.

Mike is established as a brilliant poker player in a scene where he walks into a game between some judges and tells every player what's in his hand. The movie doesn't have him in the room long enough to be able to do that, but never mind: The point is made, and one of the players is his mentor, Professor Petrovsky (Martin Landau), who tells him, "Our destiny chooses us." Sounds like Mike's destiny is not the law but poker, although I am not sure I follow the professor's reasoning when he lends his student $10,000 and calls it a mitzvah. (The professor remembers someone who helped him when he decided to become a lawyer instead of a rabbi, but that's not quite the same thing as deciding to become a gambler instead of a lawyer.)

The movie's best scenes contrast the personalities of Mike and Worm. Mike wants to win by playing well. Worm wants to hustle. He's a card mechanic who takes outrageous chances, and his intoxication with danger leads them both into trouble—not least when they find themselves in a high-stakes game in a roomful of state troopers. Not for Worm is the cautious lifestyle of Joey Knish (John Turturro), who has ground out a living for fifteen years by folding, folding, folding, until he draws a good hand.

There's humor in the film, especially when a lot of professional players find themselves at the same table in Atlantic City, and Mike's droll voice-over narration describes the unsuspecting suckers who sit down at the table.

("We weren't working with one another, but we weren't working against one another, either. It's like the Nature Channel; you don't see piranhas eating each other.")

The movie was directed by John Dahl, whose *Red Rock West* and *The Last Seduction* are inspired neo-*noirs*. *Rounders* sometimes has a *noir* look but it never has a *noir* feel, because it's not about losers (or at least it doesn't admit it is). It's essentially a sports picture, in which the talented hero wins, loses, faces disaster, and then is paired off one last time against the champ. For a grimmer and more realistic look at this world, no modern movie has surpassed Karel Reisz's *The Gambler* (1974), starring James Caan in a screenplay by self-described degenerate gambler James Toback. Compared to that, *Rounders* sees compulsive gambling as a lark—as long as it's not your money.

Rugrats ★ ★

G, 84 m., 1998

Voices of: E. G. Daily (Tommy Pickles), Christine Cavanaugh (Chuckie Finster), Kath Soucie (Phil and Lil DeVille), Cheryl Chase (Angelica Pickles), Tara Charendoff (Dil Pickles), Melanie Chartoff (Didi Pickles), Jack Riley (Stu Pickles), Joe Alaskey (Grandpa Pickles). Directed by Norton Virgien and Igor Kovalyov and produced by Arlene Klasky and Gabor Csupo. Screenplay by David N. Weiss and J. David Stem.

Rugrats is kind of an animated *Kids Say the Darndest Things* for kids. They also do the darndest things, many of them involving poo and pee. I don't know if I can use those words in the paper, but they use them all the time in this G-rated movie, which is pitched at kids so young that poo and pee are substances over which they are still celebrating recent victories.

Consider an opening musical number set in a maternity ward, where Tommy Pickles and his friends Chuckie Finster and Phil and Lil DeVille are hoping for a look at Tommy's new kid brother, Dilbert. (Dil Pickles—get it? For *Rugrats* fans, this is humor of the highest order.) They wake up the babies, who do a musical number that seems inspired by Busby Berkeley, except that the Berkeley girls never had to supply their own dancing waters, if you get my drift. The song is "This World Is Some-

thing New to Me," and like most of the movie, it's scored by pop performers—Busta Rhymes, Lou Rawls, and the B-52s among them. The sound track would be fun.

The movie, based on the popular Nickelodeon series, doesn't have a plot so much as a series of cliff-hanging adventures, many of them containing satirical movie references (I noticed *Raiders of the Lost Ark, The Fugitive,* and *2001*). Led by Tommy, who has a gift for finding danger, the Rugrats commandeer the new Reptorwagon designed by his dad, Stu. This vehicle, which may have some connection to the SUVs in *Jurassic Park: The Lost World,* or then again may not, takes them on a harrowing ride that ends shuddering at the edge of a precipitous drop.

Adventures in the woods include a run-in with a wolf. ("He ate that Little Red Riding Girl!" "The wolf ate a girl?" "They got her out.") And adventures with monkeys from a circus train. And adventures inside a mattress truck. And mud, a lot of mud. Much of the humor comes from the way the Rugrats talk, in a kind of marble-mouthed free association that leads to lines like, "I want those fugitives back in custard-y!"

I saw *Rugrats* the same day I saw *A Bug's Life,* and not long after seeing *Antz.* Both of the insect pictures were more to my taste. But when Adam Sandler's *The Waterboy* grossed $76 million in its first two weeks in release, all sorts of articles appeared that said that although critics hated it, they were "out of touch with the target audience." (At today's press screening, we took a twenty-two-year-old colleague severely to task for disliking the movie, since he was a member of the target audience and thus guilty of betraying his age group by a display of advanced taste.)

The target audience for *Rugrats* is, I think, kids under ten. Unlike both insect cartoons, the movie makes little effort to appeal to anyone over that age. There is something admirable about that. Trying to liberate myself from my box of space and time, I traveled in my memory back to my tenth year to ask if I would have liked *Rugrats.* The answer was, no—but when I was eight I might have. Is it bright, cheerful, colorful, and fast-moving? Yes. Is it for me? No. Would I recommend it to kids? Yeah, my guess is they would like it. I would also recommend it to those who liked *The Waterboy,* because *Rugrats* is the next step up the ladder of cinematic evolution.

Rules of Engagement ★ ★ ½
R, 123 m., 2000

Tommy Lee Jones (Colonel Hays Hodges), Samuel L. Jackson (Colonel Terry Childers), Guy Pearce (Major Mark Biggs), Philip Baker Hall (General Hodges), Bruce Greenwood (William Sokal), Blair Underwood (Captain Lee), Anne Archer (Mrs. Mourain), Mark Feuerstein (Captain Tom Chandler), Ben Kingsley (Ambassador Mourain). Directed by William Friedkin and produced by Richard D. Zanuck and Scott Rudin. Screenplay by Stephen Gaghan.

Rules of Engagement works splendidly as a courtroom thriller about military values, as long as you don't expect it to seriously consider those values. It's convincing on the surface, evasive beneath. I found myself involved in the story, and was pleased that for once I couldn't guess how a movie trial was going to turn out. Still, I expected the closing scenes to answer questions and close loopholes, and they evaded the questions and slipped through the loopholes.

The film centers on a relationship forged throughout the adult lifetimes of two marine colonels, Hodges (Tommy Lee Jones) and Childers (Samuel L. Jackson). They fought side by side in Vietnam, where Childers saved Hodges's life by shooting an unarmed POW. That's against the rules of war, but understandable, in this story anyway, under the specific circumstances. Certainly Hodges is not complaining.

Years pass. Hodges, whose wounds make him unfit for action, gets a law degree and becomes a marine lawyer. He also gets a divorce and becomes a drunk. Childers, much decorated, is a textbook marine who is chosen to lead a rescue mission into Yemen when the U.S. embassy there comes under threat from angry demonstrators.

Exactly what happens at the embassy, and why, becomes the material of a court-martial, after Childers is accused of ordering his men to fire on a crowd of perhaps unarmed civil-

ians, killing eighty-three of them. He convinces his old friend Hodges to represent him in the courtroom drama that occupies the second half of the film. Although the story marches confidently toward a debate about the ethical conduct of war, it trips over a villain who sidetracks the moral focus of the trial.

Remarkable, though, how well Jones, Jackson, and director William Friedkin are able to sustain interest and suspense even while saddled with an infuriating screenplay. Little is done to provide the characters with any lives outside their jobs, and yet I believed in them and cared about the outcome of the trial. If their work had been supported by a more thoughtful screenplay, this film might have really amounted to something.

Some of the lapses can't be discussed without revealing plot secrets. Here's one that can. Hodges makes a fact-finding visit to Yemen, and sees children who were victims of Childers's order to fire (the scene echoes one in *The Third Man*). He returns, drunk and enraged, and accuses Childers of lying to him. Childers punches him. Hodges fights back. They have a bitter brawl—two middle-aged men, gasping for breath—while we try not to wonder how a lame attorney can hold his own with a combat warrior. Finally, with his last strength, Hodges throws a pillow at Childers, and the two bloodied men start laughing. This works fine as an illustration of an ancient movie cliché about a fight between friends, but what does it mean in the movie? That Hodges has forgotten the reason for his anger? That it was not valid?

Much depends, during the trial, on a missing tape that might show what really happened when the crowd was fired on. The tape is destroyed by the national security adviser (Bruce Greenwood), who tells an aide: "I don't want to watch this tape. I don't want to testify about it. I don't want it to exist." How do you get to be the national security adviser if you're dumb enough to say things like that out loud to a witness? And dumb enough, for that matter, to destroy this particular tape in the first place—when it might be more useful to the United States to show it?

Much is made in the movie of the marine esprit de corps, of protecting the lives of the men under your command, of following a warrior code. Yet one puzzling close-up of Childers's eyes during the Vietnam sequence supplies an undertow that influences our view of the character all through the movie: Is he acting as a good marine, or out of rage? This adds usefully to the suspense (movie stars are usually found innocent in courtroom dramas, but this time we can't be sure). But eventually we want more of an answer than we get.

One entire subplot is a missed opportunity. We see the U.S. ambassador (Ben Kingsley) and his wife and son as they're rescued by Childers. Later we hear his testimony in court, and then there's a scene between Hodges and the ambassador's wife (Anne Archer). Everything calls for a courtroom showdown involving either the ambassador or his wife, but there isn't one. Why set it up if you're not going to pay it off?

I ask these questions and yet admit that the movie involved me dramatically. Jones and Jackson work well together, bringing more conviction to many scenes than they really deserve. The fundamental problem with *Rules of Engagement,* I suspect, is that the filmmakers never clearly defined exactly what they believed about the issues they raised. Expert melodrama conceals their uncertainty up to a point, but at the end we have a film that attacks its central issue from all sides, and has a collision in the middle.

Runaway Bride ★ ★

PG, 116 m., 1999

Julia Roberts (Maggie Carpenter), Richard Gere (Ike Graham), Joan Cusack (Peggy), Hector Elizondo (Fisher), Rita Wilson (Ellie), Paul Dooley (Walter), Christopher Meloni (Coach Bob), Jane Morris (Mrs. Pressman), Laurie Metcalf (Mrs. Trout), Jean Schertler (Grandma Julia). Directed by Garry Marshall and produced by Ted Field, Tom Rosenberg, Scott Kroopf, and Robert Cort. Screenplay by Josann McGibbon and Sara Parriott.

Sometimes I embrace contrivance and sometimes it makes me squirm. Sometimes a movie manipulates me in dumb ways, and I grin and purr. Sometimes I get grumpy. It all has to do with tone. The material may be unlikely, manipulative, and contrived, but sometimes it works and sometimes all you want to do is bark at it.

Consider two films. Garry Marshall's *Pretty Woman* (1990) starred Richard Gere and Julia Roberts as an executive who was shy of emotional commitment and the hooker he finds true love with. Garry Marshall's *Runaway Bride* (1999) stars Julia Roberts and Richard Gere as a woman who gets skittish at the altar and a newspaper columnist who finds true love with her. Same director, same stars, similar Meet Cutes. A hooker and a newspaper columnist are not precisely in the same occupation, but close enough—both enter the lives of strangers, for hire, the difference being that the hooker is invited.

The virtues of *Pretty Woman* do not need repeating. Even its utterly unlikely ending, so contrived it was bizarre, actually worked by the time we steamed up to it. Now here we have the same two actors—actors we like, actors it is good to look at, actors who work easily together—and the same directorial hand at the helm, and they just seem to be going through the motions.

Gere plays Ike Graham, a columnist for *USA Today.* His specialty is banging out last-minute prose off the top of his head (at one point he actually seems to be sitting in a bar and writing in longhand). A drunk tells him about a woman in his hometown named Maggie Carpenter who has left seven or eight guys stranded at the altar. He writes a female-bashing column, prints the woman's name, and is astonished when she writes a snarly letter to the editor. She stranded only three guys, she says, and there are fifteen other inaccuracies; doesn't he check his facts?

How about *USA Today?* Does it check? This guy wouldn't last a day in the real world. But hey, this is a movie, and so we accept the premise that he would quickly journey down to the bucolic movie hamlet where Maggie lives—Hale, Maryland, a village that looks like a postcard, where everybody lives in each other's pockets. I kept waiting for the town to fade to black and white and turn into Pleasantville.

In Hale we meet Maggie's jovial but harddrinking dad (Paul Dooley), who is a good sport, assuming he has to pay for all the weddings; her best friend, Peggy (Joan Cusack), a hairstylist who reads omens in the flights of geese; and Maggie's Grandma Julia (Jean Schertler), whose theory is that it's not the wedding Maggie is afraid of, but the wedding night. There is also the matter of Maggie's current fiancé, Coach Bob (Christopher Meloni). He's *Runaway Bride*'s equivalent of the guy in a cop picture who has one day to go before retirement.

Back at *USA Today*, Rita Wilson plays Ike's ex-wife, who is now his editor. Hector Elizondo plays her current husband, for the excellent reason that he has appeared in all eleven of Marshall's films and is the director's good-luck charm, or at least that was the theory. Their scenes have no dramatic or comedic importance, leaving us free time to reflect that a movie starring them as the runaway bride and the newspaper columnist instead of Roberts and Gere might have had more zing, if less hair.

It is crashingly obvious to everyone in the theater that Maggie and Ike will eventually find themselves at the altar together, after obligatory preliminary fights, negotiations, and scuffles. We click off the screenplay stops along the way. They have to fight. Suddenly see the other person in a different light. Share confidences. Be involved in a silly misunderstanding. Go to the brink of tragedy. Tell truths. Be saved. And, of course, just as they stand at the brink of False Happiness there has to be a False Crisis, before the Real Crisis and the Real Happiness can be permitted on-screen.

The movie has one great line ("Always a bride, never a bridesmaid"), but even that is sort of inevitable. Movies like this should have an explanatory note at the outset, to help us understand them. Something like, "The following characters all look really great, but don't know anything they haven't learned by watching sitcoms." Having seen Gere and Roberts play much smarter people (even in romantic comedies), it is painful to see them dumbed-down here. The screenplay is so sluggish, they're like derby winners made to carry extra weight.

Run Lola Run ★ ★ ★

R, 81 m., 1999

Franka Potente (Lola), Moritz Bleibtreu (Manni), Herbert Knaup (Lola's Father), Armin Rohde (Mr. Schuster), Joachim Krol (Tramp), Nina Petri (Mrs. Hanson). Directed by Tom Tykwer and produced by Stefan Arndt. Screenplay by Tykwer.

Run Lola Run is the kind of movie that could play on the big screen in a sports bar. It's an exercise in kinetic energy, a film of nonstop motion and visual invention. A New York critic called it "post-human," and indeed its heroine is like the avatar in a video game—Lara Croft made flesh.

The setup: Lola gets a phone call from her boyfriend, Manni. He left a bag containing 100,000 Deutschmarks on the subway, and a bum made away with it. Manni is expected to deliver the money at noon to a gangster. If he fails, he will probably be killed. His desperate plan: Rob a bank. Lola's desperate plan: Find the 100,000 DMs somehow, somewhere, in twenty minutes. Run, Lola, run!

The director, a young German named Tom Tykwer, throws every trick in the book at us, and then the book, and then himself. The opening credits spring a digital surprise, as a shot of a crowd turns into an aerial point of view and the crowd spells out the name of the movie. Lola sometimes runs so frantically that mere action cannot convey her energy, and the movie switches to animation. There's speed-up, instant replay, black and white, whatever. And the story of Lola's twenty-minute run is told three times, each time with small differences that affect the outcome and the fate of the characters.

Film is ideal for showing alternate and parallel time lines. It's literal; we see Lola running, and so we accept her reality, even though the streets she runs through and the people she meets are altered in each story. The message is that the smallest events can have enormous consequences. A butterfly flaps its wings in Malaysia, causing a hurricane in Trinidad. You know the drill.

Franka Potente, who plays Lola, has a certain offhand appeal. I liked her, though I can't say I got to know her very well, and she was usually out of breath. She runs down sidewalks and the middles of streets, arms pumping, bright red hair flying, stomach tattoo wrinkling in time with her footsteps. She loves Manni and wants to save him from his own stupidity. Occasionally the movie pauses for moments of sharply seen detail, as when her rich father refuses to give her the money, tells her he plans to leave home and marry his mistress, and throws in for good measure: "I'd have never fathered a girl like you. You're a cuckoo's egg."

Manni does his share of running, too, and there are various alternate scenarios involving car crashes, gunshot wounds, and the sly use of that ancient movie situation where guys are carrying a huge sheet of plate glass across the street. Tykwer also adds segments titled "Now and Then," in which he singles out minor characters on the screen and uses just a few startling flash-frames to foresee their entire lifelines.

Run Lola Run is essentially a film about itself, a closed loop of style. Movies about characters on the run usually involve a linear story (*The Fugitive* comes to mind), but this one is basically about running—and about the way that movie action sequences have a life and logic of their own. I would not want to see a sequel to the film, and at eighty-one minutes it isn't a second too short, but what it does, it does cheerfully, with great energy, and very well.

Running Free ★ ½

G, 82 m., 2000

Chase Moore (Young Richard), Jan Decleir (Boss Man), Maria Geelbooi (Nyka), Arie Verveen (Adult Richard), Graham Clarke (Mine Supervisor), Patrick Lyster (Officer). Directed by Sergei Bodrov and produced by Jean-Jacques Annaud. Screenplay by Jeanne Rosenberg, based on a story by Annaud and Rosenberg.

Running Free tells the life story of a horse in its own words. We do not find out much about horses in this process, alas, because the horse thinks and talks exactly like a young boy. The movie is another example, like Disney's *Dinosaur*, of a failure of nerve: Instead of challenging the audience to empathize with real animals, both movies supply them with the minds, vocabularies, and values of humans. What's the point?

As the film opens, the horse, later to be named Lucky, is born in the hold of a ship bound for German Southwest Africa, today's Namibia. It is 1911, and horses are needed to

work in the mines. Lucky has to swim ashore while still a nursing colt. He glimpses daylight for the first time, and tells us, "I didn't see anything green in this desert land." Hello? Lucky has never seen anything green at all in his entire life.

But the movie keeps making that same mistake, breaking the logic of the point of view. Adopted by a young orphan stable boy named Richard (Chase Moore), Lucky finds himself in a stable of purebreds ruled by a stallion named Caesar. Lucky wants to make friends with the stallion's daughter, Beauty, but, "I was only the stable boy's horse. I wasn't good enough to play with his daughter." And when Lucky's long-missing mother turns up, Caesar attacks her, apparently in a fit of class prejudice, although you'd think a stallion would be intrigued by a new girl in town, despite her family connections.

Will the mother die from the attack? "I stayed with her all night, praying that she would survive," Lucky tells us. Praying? I wanted the movie to forget the story and explore this breakthrough in horse theology. I am weary of debates about whether our pets will be with us in heaven, and am eager to learn if trainers will be allowed into horse heaven.

The human characters in the movie are one-dimensional cartoons, including a town boss who speaks English with an Afrikaans accent, not likely in a German colony. His son is a little Fauntleroy with a telescope, which he uses to spy on Richard and Lucky. Soon all the Europeans evacuate the town after a bombing raid, which raises the curtain on World War I. The horses are left behind, and Lucky escapes to the mountains, where he finds a hidden lake. Returning to the town, he leads the other horses there, where at last they realize their birthright and Run Free.

Uh-huh. But there is not a twig of living vegetation in their desert hideout, and although I am assured by the movie's press materials that there are wild horses in Namibia to this day, I doubt they could forage for long in the barren wasteland shown in this film. What do they eat?

I ask because it is my responsibility: Of all the film critics reviewing this movie, I will arguably be the only one who has actually visited Swakopmund and Walvis Bay, on the Diamond

Coast of the Namib Desert, and even ridden on the very train tracks to the capital, Windhoek, that the movie shows us. I am therefore acutely aware that race relations in the area in 1911 (and more recently) would scarcely have supported the friendship between Richard and Nyka (Maria Geelbooi), who plays the bushman girl who treats Lucky's snakebite. But then a movie that fudges about which side is which in World War I is unlikely to pause for such niceties.

I seem to be developing a rule about talking animals: They can talk if they're cartoons or Muppets, but not if they're real. This movie might have been more persuasive if the boy had told the story of the horse, instead of the horse telling the story of the boy. It's perfectly possible to make a good movie about an animal that does not speak, as Jean-Jacques Annaud, the producer of this film, proved with his 1989 film *The Bear*.

I also recall *The Black Stallion* (1979) and *White Fang* (1991). Since both of those splendid movies were cowritten by Jeanne Rosenberg, the author of *Running Free*, I can only guess that the talking horse was pressed upon her by executives who have no faith in the intelligence of today's audiences. Perhaps *Running Free* would appeal to younger children who really like horses, but see my review of *The Color of Paradise*, a film in release at the same time, for a glimpse of a truly inspired film for family audiences.

Rush Hour ★ ★ ★
PG-13, 94 m., 1998

Jackie Chan (Detective Lee), Chris Tucker (James Carter), Tom Wilkinson (Thomas Griffin), Elizabeth Pena (Tania Johnson), Tzi Ma (Consul Han), Julia Hsu (Soo Yung), Philip Baker Hall (Chief). Directed by Brett Ratner and produced by Roger Birnbaum, Arthur Sarkissian, and Jonathan Glickman. Screenplay by Jim Kouf and Ross Lamanna.

Rush Hour is our reliable friend, the Wunza Movie, pairing two opposites: Wunza legendary detective from Hong Kong, and wunza Los Angeles cop. And wunza Chinese guy, and wunza black guy. And wunza martial arts expert and wunza wisecracking showboat. Neither wunza original casting idea, but together, they make an entertaining team.

The movie teams up Jackie Chan, king of lighthearted action comedy, and Chris Tucker, who crosses Eddie Murphy with Chris Rock and comes up with a guy that, if you saw him a block away, you'd immediately start wondering how he was going to con you. There are comic possibilities even in their personal patterns. Chan is not known for his effortless command of English, and Tucker is a motormouth. Chan's persona is modest and self-effacing, and Tucker plays a shameless self-promoter.

The story: During the last days of Hong Kong's status as a British colony, supercop Chan busts up a smuggling ring, but the masterminds escape to the United States. There they kidnap the daughter of the Chinese consul, who tells the FBI he wants Chan, a family friend, flown in to help with the investigation. The feds want nothing to do with a cop from overseas, and they also don't want the LAPD involved. So they get the idea of pairing up the Chinese guy and the L.A. cop, so they can keep each other out of the way.

At L.A. police headquarters, this idea is well received after the chief (the redoubtable Philip Baker Hall) realizes it's a way to get his most troublesome detective out of his hair. That would be Carter, played by Chris Tucker as the kind of loose cannon who roars around the streets in a vintage Corvette and works undercover in dangerous situations.

Neither cop likes teamwork. Both work best alone. But Chan doesn't know his way around L.A., and Tucker needs to earn points with his chief. That's enough to fuel the lightweight screenplay by Jim Kouf and Ross Lamanna, which contains a lot of genuinely funny lines and even a reference to Roscoe's Chicken and Waffles, of *Jackie Brown* fame.

Chan is, of course, noted for his stunts, which he performs himself, without doubles. *Rush Hour* has a neat little example of his wall-climbing ability, and a breathtaking sequence in which he leaps from a double-decker bus to an overhead traffic sign to a truck. And there's a scene in a high atrium where he falls from a beam and slides to safety down a silk streamer. (It's useful to point out, I suppose, that although Chan does his own stunts, they are indeed stunts and not death-defying risks;

509

he does what a stunt man would do, but with the same safeguards and deceptive camera angles. He is brave, agile, and inventive, but not foolish.)

I like the way the plot handles Soo Yung (Julia Hsu), the consul's young daughter. Instead of being treated like a helpless pawn, she's portrayed as one of Jackie's little martial arts students in Hong Kong ("Have you been practicing your eye gouges?"), and when the kidnappers try to carry her off, she causes them no end of trouble. I also liked the way Chris Tucker (who was funny in *Money Talks*) talks his way into and out of situations, using a distracting stream of dialogue while he figures out what to do next. *Rush Hour* is lightweight and made out of familiar elements, but they're handled with humor and invention, and the Wunza formula can seem fresh if the characters are Botha couple of engaging performers.

Footnote: All Jackie Chan movies end with outtakes, which usually show him missing on stunts and breaking bones, etc. This time the emphasis is mostly on bloopers, where he and Tucker blow their lines. I like the missed stunts better. It's not that I enjoy seeing Jackie waving bravely from the stretcher as they wheel him into the ambulance, but that there's a tradition involved. To be sure, with the two major stunts in this movie, any mistakes could have been his last.

Rushmore ★ ★ ½
R, 93 m., 1999

Jason Schwartzman (Max Fischer), Bill Murray (Mr. Blume), Olivia Williams (Miss Cross), Brian Cox (Dr. Guggenheim), Seymour Cassel (Bert Fischer), Mason Gamble (Dirk Calloway), Sara Tanaka (Margaret Yang), Stephen McCole (Magnus Buchan). Directed by Wes Anderson and produced by Barry Mendel and Paul Schiff. Screenplay by Anderson and Owen Wilson.

Max Fischer, the hero of *Rushmore,* is an activity jock, one of those kids too bright and restless to color inside the lines. Although he's a lousy student, that doesn't stop him from organizing a movement to keep Latin on the curriculum of his exclusive prep school. His grades are so bad he's on "sudden death pro-

bation," but in his spare time he edits the school magazine and runs the fencing club, the bee-keeping club, the karate team, the French club, and the Max Fischer Players. With his bushy eyebrows and black horn-rims, he looks a little like a young Benjamin Braddock from *The Graduate.*

Max, played by Jason Schwartzman, has a secret. He's in the exclusive Rushmore Academy on a scholarship; his dad is a barber. Always dressed in a tie and snappy blazer (unless in costume for one of his activities), he speaks with an unnerving maturity, and is barely able to conceal his feelings of superiority for the headmaster (Brian Cox) and other adults, who enforce their stuffy rules because they are not, and never were, able to play without a net the way Max can.

Then Max encounters a problem even he cannot outflank. Reading a book in the school library, he finds a quote by Jacques Cousteau written in the margin. The book was recently checked out, he discovers, by Miss Cross (Olivia Williams), a first-grade teacher at Rushmore. She is, he finds, incredibly beautiful, and he falls instantly in love, devising a scheme to attract her attention by running a campaign for a school aquarium. Among the potential donors is a steel tycoon named Blume (Bill Murray). Murray has kids in Rushmore, but hates them. Soon he, too, is in love with Miss Cross.

Up until this point, even a little further, *Rushmore* has a kind of effortless grace. Max Fischer emerges as not just a brainy comic character, but as a kid who could do anything if he weren't always trying to do everything. It's ingenious the way he uses his political and organizing abilities to get his way with people, how he enlists a younger student (Mason Gamble) as his gofer, how he reasons patiently with the headmaster and thinks he can talk Miss Cross into being his girlfriend ("Max, has it ever occurred to you that you're far too young for me?").

Blume is played by Bill Murray with the right note to counter Max's strategies. He is, essentially, a kid himself—immature, vindictive, love-struck, self-centered, physically awkward, but with years more experience in getting his way. (Still, he winds up hiding from life at the bottom of a swimming pool, just like Benjamin.) The movie turns into a strategic duel between Max and Blume, and that could be funny, too, except that it gets a little mean when Max spills the beans to Blume's wife, and it feels too contrived. When plotting replaces stage-setting and character development, the air goes out of the movie.

Rushmore was directed by Wes Anderson and written by Anderson and his college friend, Owen Wilson. It's their second film, after the slight but engaging *Bottle Rocket* (1996). The legend of that film is well known, and suggests that Anderson and Wilson may have a little of Max Fischer in their own personalities—the film may have elements of self-portraiture.

They were friends at the University of Texas who made a short film, pitched it to screenwriter L. M. (Kit) Carson, got his encouragement, took it to the Sundance Film Festival, and cornered famous director James L. Brooks *(As Good As It Gets),* who liked it enough to help them get financing for a feature from Columbia. I am writing this review during the Sundance festival, where I have met a lot of kids trying to pitch their short films and get production deals, and having a good film is

not enough: You also need the relentless chutzpah of a Max Fischer.

Bill Murray has a way of turning up in perfect smaller roles; he stars in his own films, but since *Tootsie,* he has made supporting roles into a sort of parallel career. His Blume admires and hates Max for the same reason: Because he is reminded of himself. There are times when Blume is frustrated in his desire to win Miss Cross for himself, but from an objective viewpoint he can't resist admiring Max's strategy.

Anderson and Wilson are good offbeat filmmakers. They fill the corners of their story with nice touches, like the details of Max's wildly overambitious stage production of *Serpico.* But their film seems torn between conflicting possibilities: It's structured like a comedy, but there are undertows of darker themes, and I almost wish they'd allowed the plot to lead them into those shadows. The Max Fischer they give us is going to grow up into Benjamin Braddock. But there is an unrealized Max who would have become Charles Foster Kane.

S

Safe Men ★
R, 89 m., 1998

Sam Rockwell (Sam), Steve Zahn (Eddie), Paul Giamatti (Veal Chop), Michael Schmidt (Bernie Jr.), Michael Lerner (Big Fat Bernie Gayle), Harvey Fierstein (Goodstuff Leo), Mark Ruffalo (Frank), Christina Kirk (Hannah). Directed by John Hamburg and produced by Andrew Hauptman, Ellen Bronfman, Jeffrey Clifford, and Jonathan Cohen. Screenplay by Hamburg.

Safe Men whirls wildly from one bright idea to the next, trying to find a combo that will hold the movie together. No luck. This is one of those movies where you picture the author at his keyboard, chortling so loudly that he drowns out his own thoughts.

The movie takes place in Providence, Rhode Island, where Sam (Sam Rockwell) and Eddie (Steve Zahn) are the two dismally untalented members of a pathetic lounge act. (They're dismal; the lounge is pathetic—the scene looks like it was shot in somebody's rec room.) After their gig, they go to a bar where they're approached by a stranger with a weird story about a rich old man who has forgotten all about the oodles of cash in his safe.

The safe is ripe for cracking, the stranger says, but the guy can't do it himself; he's a male nurse with "Lawrence Nightingale Syndrome." Florence, Lawrence—they sound alike, but it's the kind of gag that only works in print, and that's the problem with a lot of the movie's dialogue.

Anyway, the whole con is a setup by a local Mafia boss who is convinced that Sam and Eddie are actually a couple of famous safecrackers. They're not, but they find themselves just as involved as if they were, as a bitter competition breaks out between the two powerful Jewish gangsters: Big Fat Bernie Gayle (Michael Lerner) and Goodstuff Leo (Harvey Fierstein). At stake is a valuable cup that one of them has in his safe and the other wants to present at his son's bar mitzvah. To name the cup would reveal the joke, although it's not much of a joke.

Sam and Eddie find themselves actually cracking safes, sometimes simultaneously with the two *real* safecrackers, leading to a series of coincidences in which it seems like they know what they're doing even though they don't. There is also some weak humor depending on the possibility that the tough mobsters (also including Paul Giamatti as a henchman) will hurt them badly if they don't go along.

There are isolated flashes of wit, especially in the satirically exaggerated bar mitzvah scene. And there's a certain amount of pleasure to be had from watching Lerner and Fierstein try to out-Mafia one another. And a small subplot when Sam gets a crush on Leo's daughter (Christina Kirk). But this is basically the kind of freshman project that should go straight to cable or video, clearing the way for its young writer-director, John Hamburg, to get on with his career.

Saving Private Ryan ★ ★ ★ ★
R, 170 m., 1998

Tom Hanks (Captain Miller), Tom Sizemore (Sergeant Horvath), Edward Burns (Private Reiben), Barry Pepper (Private Jackson), Adam Goldberg (Private Mellish), Vin Diesel (Private Caparzo), Giovanni Ribisi (T/4 Medic Wade), Jeremy Davies (Corporal Upham), Harve Presnell (General George Marshall), Matt Damon (Private Ryan). Directed by Steven Spielberg and produced by Spielberg, Ian Bryce, Mark Gordon, and Gary Levinsohn. Screenplay by Robert Rodat.

The soldiers assigned to find Private Ryan and bring him home can do the math for themselves. The army chief of staff has ordered them on the mission for propaganda purposes: Ryan's return will boost morale on the home front and put a human face on the carnage at Omaha Beach. His mother, who has already lost three sons in the war, will not have to add another telegram to the collection. But the eight men on the mission also have parents—and besides, they've been trained to kill Germans, not to risk their lives for publicity stunts. "This Ryan better be worth it," one of the men grumbles.

In Hollywood mythology, great battles wheel and turn on the actions of individual heroes.

In Steven Spielberg's *Saving Private Ryan*, thousands of terrified and seasick men, most of them new to combat, are thrown into the face of withering German fire. The landing on Omaha Beach was not about saving Private Ryan. It was about saving your ass.

The movie's opening sequence is as graphic as any war footage I've ever seen. In fierce dread and energy it's on a par with Oliver Stone's *Platoon*, and in scope surpasses it—because in the bloody early stages the landing forces and the enemy never meet eye to eye, but are simply faceless masses of men who have been ordered to shoot at one another until one side is destroyed.

Spielberg's camera makes no sense of the action. That is the purpose of his style. For the individual soldier on the beach, the landing was a chaos of noise, mud, blood, vomit, and death. The scene is filled with countless unrelated pieces of time, as when a soldier has his arm blown off. He staggers, confused, standing exposed to further fire, not sure what to do next, and then he bends over and picks up his arm, as if he will need it later.

This landing sequence is necessary in order to establish the distance between those who give the order that Private Ryan be saved, and those who are ordered to do the saving. For Captain Miller (Tom Hanks) and his men, the landing at Omaha has been a crucible of fire. For Army Chief George C. Marshall (Harve Presnell), in his Washington office, war seems more remote and statesmanlike; he treasures a letter Abraham Lincoln wrote consoling Mrs. Bixby of Boston about her sons who died in the Civil War. His advisers question the wisdom and indeed the possibility of a mission to save Ryan, but he barks, "If the boy's alive we are gonna send somebody to find him—and we are gonna get him the hell out of there."

That sets up the second act of the film, in which Miller and his men penetrate into French terrain still actively disputed by the Germans, while harboring mutinous thoughts about the wisdom of the mission. All of Miller's men have served with him before—except for Corporal Upham (Jeremy Davies), the translator, who speaks excellent German and French but has never fired a rifle in anger and is terrified almost to the point of incontinence. (I identified with Upham, and I suspect many honest viewers will agree with me: The war was fought by civilians just like him, whose lives had not prepared them for the reality of battle.)

The turning point in the film comes, I think, when the squadron happens upon a German machine-gun nest protecting a radar installation. It would be possible to go around it and avoid a confrontation. Indeed, that would be following orders. But they decide to attack the emplacement, and that is a form of protest: At risk to their lives, they are doing what they came to France to do, instead of what the top brass wants them to do.

Everything points to the third act, when Private Ryan is found and the soldiers decide what to do next. Spielberg and his screenwriter, Robert Rodat, have done a subtle and rather beautiful thing: They have made a philosophical film about war almost entirely in terms of action. *Saving Private Ryan* says things about war that are as complex and difficult as any essayist could possibly express, and does it with broad, strong images, with violence, with profanity, with action, with camaraderie. It is possible to express even the most thoughtful ideas in the simplest words and actions, and that's what Spielberg does. The film is doubly effective because he communicates his ideas in feelings, not words. I was reminded of *All Quiet on the Western Front*.

Steven Spielberg is as technically proficient as any filmmaker alive, and because of his great success he has access to every resource he requires. Both of those facts are important to the impact of *Saving Private Ryan*. He knows how to convey his feelings about men in combat, and he has the tools, the money, and the collaborators to make it possible.

His cinematographer, Janusz Kaminski, who also shot *Schindler's List*, brings a newsreel feel to a lot of the footage, but that's relatively easy compared to his most important achievement, which is to make everything visually intelligible. After the deliberate chaos of the landing scenes, Kaminski handles the attack on the machine-gun nest, and a prolonged sequence involving the defense of a bridge, in a way that keeps us oriented. It's not just men shooting at one another. We understand the plan of the action, the ebb and flow, the improvisation, the relative positions of the soldiers.

Then there is the human element. Hanks is

a good choice as Captain Miller, an English teacher who has survived experiences so unspeakable that he wonders if his wife will even recognize him. His hands tremble, he is on the brink of breakdown, but he does his best because that is his duty. All of the actors playing the men under him are effective, partly because Spielberg resists the temptation to make them zany "characters" in the tradition of World War II movies, and makes them deliberately ordinary. Matt Damon, as Private Ryan, exudes a different energy because he has not been through the landing at Omaha Beach; as a paratrooper, he landed inland, and although he has seen action, he has not gazed into the inferno.

They are all strong presences, but for me the key performance in the movie is by Jeremy Davies, as the frightened little interpreter. He is our entry into the reality because he sees the war clearly as a vast system designed to humiliate and destroy him. And so it is. His survival depends on his doing the very best he can, yes, but even more on chance. Eventually he arrives at his personal turning point, and his action writes the closing words of Spielberg's unspoken philosophical argument.

Saving Private Ryan is a powerful experience. I'm sure a lot of people will weep during it. Spielberg knows how to make audiences weep better than any director since Chaplin in *City Lights*. But weeping is an incomplete response, letting the audience off the hook. This film embodies ideas. After the immediate experience begins to fade, the implications remain, and grow.

Savior ★ ★ ★ ½
R, 103 m., 1998

Dennis Quaid (Guy), Natasa Ninkovic (Vera), Nastassja Kinski (Maria), Stellan Skarsgard (Dominic), Sergej Trifunovic (Goran), Neboisa Glogovac (Vera's Brother), Vesna Trivalic (Woman on Bus). Directed by Peter Antonijevic and produced by Oliver Stone and Janet Yang. Screenplay by Robert Orr.

Savior is a brutally honest war film that looks unblinkingly at how hate and prejudice can pose as patriotism. It stars Dennis Quaid as an American named Guy, whose wife and child are killed by a Muslim terrorist bomb in Paris. He walks into the nearest mosque, murders men at prayer, and then disappears into the French Foreign Legion. Six years later he is in Bosnia as a mercenary fighting for the Serbs against the Bosnians.

"We fight for no country, no faith, no political cause," he is told on the day he's sworn into the legion. "We fight for honor." One would like to think that honor might involve country, faith, or politics, but only the legion deserves the loyalty of a legionnaire, and it's this kind of macho, death-intoxicated craziness that Guy encounters in Bosnia. The Bosnians and Serbs have religious differences, but the film argues that much of the blood-hate on both sides involves psychotic male societies in which women are chattel—to be raped if they're not yours, and killed if they're yours and have been raped.

Guy buys into this ethic in the early scenes of the movie, blaming all Muslims for his family's murder by a lunatic fringe. Later, he is forced to focus on individual people, and finds it is not so easy to hate when you know someone. Empathy is the enemy of tribalism.

In Bosnia, he and his best friend Dominic (Stellan Skarsgard) kill for hire, and sometimes discuss what they do. Guy: "You've done nothing wrong here." Dominic: "It feels like I did." We see Guy use a sniperscope to take aim on an innocent young boy looking for his goat. Guy kills him. A flashback shows how Guy's friend was killed by a young girl concealing a grenade. An eye for an eye.

A truce is declared. Guy and his Serbian comrade Goran (Sergej Trifunovic) take custody of a very pregnant Serbian woman. Goran knows the woman's family. In a tunnel, he drags the woman out of the car and starts kicking her in the stomach. Her crime: being pregnant with a Muslim child. "She was raped," Guy protests. This is a meaningless concept to Goran. She has been defiled, and if she were a decent woman, then of course she would already have killed herself. No blame attaches to her rapists, and we assume Goran himself has enthusiastically raped as many Bosnian women as convenient, trusting them to kill themselves or be killed by their fathers, brothers, or helpful male neighbors.

Guy, who has spent years killing for hire, who

himself has killed in revenge, now finds he can stomach no more. He kills Goran and finds himself in possession of the woman, named Vera (Natasa Ninkovic), and her child. All of this is prologue to the film's central sections, in which Guy undergoes a change of heart because circumstances force him to empathize with these people instead of objectifying them as targets. His situation is complicated because Vera buys into the poisoned macho logic, and refuses to nurse or care for the baby. The story arrives at a point where her own father hands her a gun and expects her to shoot herself.

Truffaut once wondered if it was really possible to make an antiwar movie, since war films were inherently exciting and we tend to identify with one side or the other. Here is an antiwar film. It helps, I suppose, that we see it from outside: Most American audiences view the civil wars in Yugoslavia as insane. While one side or the other might seem to make a better ideological case, the fighting is based on ancient blood hatred, and the hatred is founded not on religion but on tribalism: If you are not like me, then I hate you. The primitive attitudes toward women make it easier to see how many fighters on both sides are killing for reasons more pathological than patriotic.

Quaid is an actor who is innately likable. Here we don't ever see the famous grin, the easy charm. He plays Guy as a man who essentially shares the values of the men on both sides of the war he finds himself in, until responsibility for an infant forces him back in touch with more civilized values.

Savior is not subtle. Directed by Peter Antonijevic, a Serbian who is evenhanded in his treatment of both sides, it was produced by Oliver Stone and his longtime colleague Janet Yang from a screenplay they purchased from Robert Orr, who was inspired by a true story. The symbolism is heavy-handed and the movie pounds its insights home with big, bold strokes. But Quaid and Ninkovic find the right tone for their relationship; it doesn't get soppy or turn into phony romance, but remains hardened by war. And the end of the story is cathartic but not "happy" in a contrived way. Too bad the music is allowed to swell into an inappropriate chorus, when the single woman's voice that began the song would have been a more effective closing note.

A movie like *Savior* is a reminder that human nature does not inevitably take us upward to higher moral ground, but sometimes drags us down to our dog-eat-dog beginnings. It is so easy to blame a group for the actions of a few of its members—to make them seem less than human, to justify our hatred for them. Of course, movies that demonstrate that are not as much fun as the other kind, in which those bastards get what they have coming to them.

The School of Flesh ★ ★ ★
R, 102 m., 1999

Isabelle Huppert (Dominique), Vincent Martinez (Quentin), Vincent Lindon (Chris), Marthe Keller (Madame Thorpe), Francois Berleand (Soukaz), Daniele Dubroux (Dominique's Friend), Bernard Le Coq (Cordier), Roxane Mesquida (Marine). Directed by Benoit Jacquot and produced by Fabienne Vonier. Screenplay by Jacques Fieschi, based on the novel by Yukio Mishima.

We look at French films about love like schoolchildren with our noses pressed against a window. We are so direct about love in North America. We date, we have relationships, we fall in love—as if a natural, unconscious process is taking place. In France, love is more like a discussion, a debate. One has to be right or wrong about it. Not about the other person—about the idea of love itself.

"I don't think you'll go the distance," the older woman says to the younger man in Benoit Jacquot's *The School of Flesh*. Later in the film, he tells her, "One day I decided to live without feelings." The first time she takes him out to dinner, he uses his fingers to pick up the fish on his plate. "Put it down," she says. "Why?" Her face betrays absolutely no expression: "You're with me."

One guesses that in another restaurant, with another woman, he would have used his fork for the fish. He is not without some sophistication; she found him as a bartender in a gay club. Using his fingers was a way of testing her; her response was the answer to an exam question. The exam involved the matter of class differences. They are not concerned that he is working class and she is a professional; what

515

matters is the tug-of-war and who will win as their styles clash.

It's a good question whether romance is involved at all in *The School of Flesh*, which is based on a Japanese novel by Yukio Mishima, who also wrote of class and power. Love is mentioned at various times, but is it a fact or a concept? How much is sex involved, for that matter? The man and woman have sex together, yes, but it doesn't seem as important to them as the battle of wills they engage in. The first time they see each other, they issue a mutual challenge with their eyes. The look they exchange isn't about lust, but power.

That first meeting is in a bar with a primarily gay clientele. Dominique (Isabelle Huppert), who works in the fashion business, sees Quentin (Vincent Martinez) behind the bar. He's a boxer, is twenty years younger, looks tough, has cold eyes—but not colder than Dominique's. Huppert, who is famous for impassivity in her movie roles, has rarely revealed less than here (Stephen Holden wrote that her tears appear "to emanate from a realm somewhere beyond feeling"). Their eyes lock, they size each other up, she leaves and she is back the next night.

She knows from a transvestite in the bar that Quentin is bisexual. Doesn't matter. She is in the grip of the kind of erotomania that must have what it must have. He realizes this and plays with it; there's a scene where he plays a video game in an arcade while she shifts impatiently on her feet, asks that they leave, leaves alone, turns around, comes back—and only then does he acknowledge her. The twist in the movie comes when he starts to become as obsessed with her as she is with him. And when she finds out his secrets—not the ones she thought she knew, but others.

I cannot imagine a Hollywood movie like this. Audiences would be baffled. Imagine two fairly tough stars—a younger guy like Vincent Gallo, say, and an alluring older woman like Susan Sarandon. I can imagine their sex scenes (indeed, I've seen them, between Sarandon and James Spader in *White Palace*). I can imagine conversations in cafés and arguments in bedrooms. What I cannot imagine is the holding back, the restraint, the intellectual side, as the two characters engage in a debate about the proper form of an affair. Ever hear the one about the three guys who see a couple through a window? "What are they doing?" asks the Englishman. "Making love," says the American. "Very badly," says the Frenchman.

Scream 3 ★ ★

R, 116 m., 2000

Neve Campbell (Sidney Prescott), Courteney Cox Arquette (Gale Weathers), David Arquette (Dewey Riley), Parker Posey (Jennifer Jolie), Scott Foley (Roman Bridge), Deon Richmond (Tyson Fox), Patrick Dempsey (Detective Kincaid), Lance Henriksen (John Milton), Liev Schreiber (Cotton Weary), Jenny McCarthy (Sarah Darling), Patrick Warburton (Guard). Directed by Wes Craven and produced by Cathy Konrad, Kevin Williamson, and Marianne Maddalena. Screenplay by Ehren Kruger.

The difference between a trilogy and a sequel, we're told in *Scream 3*, is that sequels go on and on, while a trilogy has a beginning, a middle, and an end: "In a trilogy, nobody's safe. Even the hero can die in the final chapter." So explains one of the movie buffs in the third of this self-aware slasher series in which the characters know all the horror clichés and get trapped in them anyway.

The action this time moves the key surviving actors from the previous *Screams* to Hollywood, where a horror film named *Stab 3* is under way. There is a death, and then another: The killer is slashing the actors in the same order they die in the screenplay. But the third victim may be hard to predict: "There were three different versions of the script," an executive explains, "to keep the ending off the Internet. I don't know which version the killer read." No matter; the fax machine rings, and it's a call from the killer, transmitting revised script pages.

That problem of spoilers on the Net could inspire a slasher movie of its own (serial killer, under delusion he is Freddy Krueger, kills to prove a Web rumor site is wrong). In an attempt to keep Websites from revealing the movie's secrets, Miramax's Dimension division delayed screenings until the last possible moment, and even then banned many Web-based critics from attending (although the lads from Playboy.com were hunkered down happily in the row in front of me).

Anyone who would reveal the identity of the killer in *Scream 3* would in any event be the lowest form of life, since the secret is absolutely unguessable. Why? Because the identity is absolutely arbitrary. It could be anyone in the movie or (this would be a neat twist) none of the above. The characters are so thin they're transparent. They function primarily to scream, split up when they should stick together, go alone into basements and dark rooms, and make ironic references to horror clichés and earlier movies in the series. The director, Wes Craven, covered the self-aware horror genre splendidly in *Wes Craven's New Nightmare* (1994), and this is the lite version.

Some of it is fun. You can play spot-the-cameo with visiting celebs like Roger Corman, Kevin Smith, and Carrie Fisher (she's a studio archivist who explains, "I was up for Princess Leia, but you know who gets it—the one who sleeps with George Lucas"). And you can appreciate the logic behind Parker Posey's reasoning. She plays the actress hired to portray TV journalist Gale Weathers (Courteney Cox Arquette), and tells her, "Everywhere you go, I'm gonna follow you, so if he wants to kill you, you'll be there to be killed, and he won't need to kill me."

Scream 3 is essentially an interlacing of irony and gotcha! scenes. The monster in his (or her) fright mask can be anywhere at any time and jump into the frame at any moment. All we know for sure is that two or three scares will be false. (When will the characters in these movies learn that when victims are being "cut up into fish sticks," it is *not funny* to sneak up behind friends to scare them?)

Neve Campbell is back as the key character, a woman so traumatized she has changed her name, moved to Monterey, and works for a crisis hot line. The camera loves her. She could become a really big star and giggle at clips from this film at her AFI tribute. Also starring are David Arquette as a former deputy, now a would-be security guard who's still in love with Gale Weathers; Scott Foley as the *Stab 3* director; Deon Richmond as a guy who knows all the movie conventions; Liev Schreiber as an ex-con talk show host; Patrick Dempsey as a cop; Lance Henriksen as a demented horror film director with old secrets; and Jenny McCarthy as an actress who does or does not get killed, but certainly wears a dress we will see again in *Playboy*'s annual "Sex in the Cinema" feature. Patrick Warburton, a rising action star, has a funny bit as a "professional celebrity guard" whose clients have "included Julia Roberts and Salman Rushdie."

My own feeling is relief that the series is at last ended. If *Scream* (1996) was like a funny joke, *Scream 2* (1997) was like somebody telling you, "Here's how I heard that joke," and *Scream 3* is like somebody who won't believe you've already heard it. What I will remember from the movie is that everyone uses cell phones constantly, which is convenient for the screenplay, since the characters can be anywhere and still call for help or threaten one another. Remember the 1980 horror movie named *Don't Answer the Phone*? If the *Scream 3* gang had taken that advice, there would have been no movie, just a lot of lonely characters scattered all over California, waiting for calls.

See the Sea and A Summer Dress
★ ★ ★
NO MPAA RATING, 52 m. and 15 m., 1999

Sasha Hails (Sasha), Marina de Van (Tatiana). Directed by Francois Ozon and produced by Oliver Delbosc and Marc Missonnier. Screenplay by Ozon.

Hitchcock believed that suspense came not in action, but in anticipation: not the bomb exploding, but the bomb under the table, waiting to explode. From the first shots of Francois Ozon's *See the Sea*, we sense impending disaster, but we're not sure what form it will take. There is a simple situation, involving two women and a baby at an isolated beach cottage, and yet the possibilities are many, and we speculate about first one outcome, then another.

Sasha (Sasha Hails), an Englishwoman, is living in a cottage in France with her ten-month-old daughter. Her husband is expected to join them, but seems distant and unreachable. A backpacker knocks at the door. This is

Tatiana (Marina de Van), a sullen, expressionless young woman who wants to pitch her tent in the yard. She doesn't ask so much as demand. Sasha's reply is curious: "It's my husband's property. I'd have to ask him." Eventually, maybe because she is lonely or intrigued, Sasha lets Tatiana stay.

What will the outcome be? Ozon creates the atmosphere of hot, drowsy summer moral laxity; we are reminded a little of Laura Dern's erotic boredom in *Smooth Talk*. There is the possibility of sex between the women, reinforced by scenes of casual nudity, but we somehow know that's not the point: Something sinister will happen. And then we're worried about that baby.

Sasha is a loving mother, billing and cooing, but a shockingly irresponsible one. She leaves the infant alone in the bath. Later, she leaves it on the beach while she wanders into a nearby wood, a gay cruising area where one of the anonymous men among the trees supplies what she abruptly indicates she desires. One day Sasha goes into town, and asks Tatiana to baby-sit.

This is not a woman you would choose for a baby-sitter. She is dirty and deliberately ill-mannered, bolting her food and then lifting up her plate to lick it clean. She asks questions in a challenging manner, and her face conceals what she thinks of the answers. We have seen her play a particularly nasty little secret trick on Sasha. In her aimlessness she resembles the heroine of Agnes Varda's *Vagabond,* but that woman was a victim, and Tatiana is not a victim.

The outcome is a surprise, and yet in a way we were waiting for it. The movie is about the waiting. It is fifty-two minutes long, and that's about the right length. Longer, and the plot would have had to add unnecessary details to the spare, clean, ominous style.

On the same program is a fifteen-minute short subject, also by Ozon, named *A Summer Dress*, which is lighter in tone. Apparently filmed on the same beach, it also uses the forest area where men cruise for sex, and also places a heterosexual encounter there, with watching eyes. The film follows a young man, who is perhaps gay, as he goes to the beach for a swim and is boldly invited into the woods by a woman who says she is his age (she looks older). He accompanies her, and what he discovers provides the film's payoff.

Both films are notable for the way they quietly slip into the hidden sexual spaces of their characters. Hollywood movies seem determined these days to present sex as an activity not unrelated to calisthenics. What Ozon knows about sex is like what Hitchcock knows about suspense: not the explosion, but the waiting for the bomb to go off.

A Self-Made Hero ★ ★ ★
NO MPAA RATING, 105 m., 1998

Mathieu Kassovitz (Albert Dehousse), Anouk Grinberg (Servane), Sandrine Kiberlain (Yvette), Albert Dupontel (Dionnet), Nadia Barentin (Mme Louvier/Mme Revuz/General's Wife). Directed by Jacques Audiard and produced by Patrick Godeau. Screenplay by Alain Le Henry and Jacques Audiard, based on the novel by Jean-Francois Deniau.

"The past only drags you down," the Captain advises Albert, who is a beggar at the time. Albert takes him at his word and reinvents himself as a hero of the French Resistance—so successfully that men who really were heroes have tears in their eyes when they think of his bravery. *A Self-Made Hero* is inspired by the way that some French belatedly recalled that they were always against the Nazis in World War II, but it is not simply an attack on hypocrisy. In a larger sense, it's about our human weakness for inventing stories about ourselves and telling them so often that we believe them.

Albert Dehousse (Mathieu Kassovitz) is schooled in deception at his mother's breast. From her he learns that his father was a hero in the first war: Doesn't she have his veteran's pension to prove it? From nasty local urchins Albert learns the more likely story, that his father was a drunk who died of liver failure, and his mother made the whole thing up.

Albert himself is an idle daydreamer, a blank slate on which various versions of a life story can be sketched. He reads romantic novels, and then tells a girl he is a novelist. She believes him and marries him, but her family so mistrusts him that it is only after the war he discovers they were in the Resistance, and sheltered Allied pilots who were shot down.

Albert spends the war as a salesman, having evaded the draft. From his father-in-law he learns that to make a sale, you must determine what a customer wants to believe, and confirm it. Fleeing his first marriage after the liberation, he is penniless in Paris when he meets the Captain (Albert Dupontel), a heroic Resistance parachutist who assumed so many fake identities during the war that he perhaps lost touch with himself and identified only with his deceptions. He bluntly counsels Albert to invent a new past.

This process comes easily to Albert because he has no present. Like Chance, the hero of *Being There*, he is such a cipher that other people see what they want. Albert studies papers on the Resistance, memorizes lists, even inserts himself into old newsreel footage. Some of his skills he learns during a period as private secretary to the enigmatic Mr. Jo, who survived the war by supplying both the Nazis and the Resistance with what they wanted. Albert, indeed, has a gift for finding those who can tutor him in deception: He even learns about the artifices of love from a prostitute.

A Self-Made Hero is not an angry exposé, but a bemused, cynical examination of human weakness. Not a week goes past without another story of an ambassador who invents wartime heroism, an executive who awards himself fictitious degrees, a government official who borrows someone else's childhood trauma and calls it his own. I myself have told stories so often they seem real to me, and can no longer be sure whether my friend McHugh really slapped King Constantine on the back in that hotel bar in Rome. All children tell you with great solemnity about adventures that never happened. Some children don't stop when they grow up.

As it must to all men, some degree of maturity eventually comes to Albert, and with it an uneasiness about what he has done. Even deception has its responsibilities, as when fate requires Albert to decide the fates of six Frenchmen who served in the German army. And then there is a woman he begins to love; he is seized by a great need to tell her the truth.

Albert is played by Mathieu Kassovitz, whose own films as a director *(Cafe au Lait, Hate)* skate along the cutting edge of France's racial tension. In those films he can seem brash,

quick, violent. Here he's more of a wraith, and the parallel with Chance is appropriate. Resistance heroes embrace him because his experience enhances their own; the real reason anyone listens to your story is so that you will have to listen to theirs.

Jacques Audiard, who directed the film and cowrote it (the screenplay won an award at Cannes), is of course aware of the way many French collaborationists suddenly discovered Resistance pasts after the war. But that process is too well known to need repeating. His film is more subtle and wide reaching, the story of a man for whom everything is equally unreal, who distrusts his own substance so deeply that he must be somebody else to be anybody at all.

Senseless ★ ★ ½
R, 88 m., 1998

Marlon Wayans (Darryl Witherspoon), David Spade (Scott Thorpe), Matthew Lillard (Tim LaFlour), Rip Torn (Randall Tyson), Tamara Taylor (Janice), Brad Dourif (Dr. Wheedon), Kenya Moore (Lorraine). Directed by Penelope Spheeris and produced by David Hoberman. Screenplay by Greg Erb and Craig Mazin.

Senseless is a Jim Carrey movie fighting to be a Penelope Spheeris movie, and losing. In this corner is Marlon Wayans, another of the large and talented Wayans family, playing a college student who becomes the pawn of a mad scientific experiment. And in the other corner, Spheeris *(The Decline of Western Civilization, Wayne's World, Black Sheep)*.

Wayans does Jim Carrey–style berserk physical comedy, and does it pretty well. Spheeris fills the crannies of the film with Gen-X counterculture stuff, including Wayans's college roommate, who is so deeply into body piercing that he not only wears studs in his eyebrows, tongue, and lower lip, but wears a gold chain linking those two parts of the anatomy which any prudent man would most hope to keep unbound.

Wayans plays Darryl Witherspoon, who is being dunned for past-due tuition, and in desperation seeks out Dr. Wheedon (Brad Dourif), an owlish scientist whose experimental potion enhances the five senses beyond belief.

Darryl hires on as a guinea pig, and the movie's gags involve what he does with his super-senses.

This is a promising idea, and *Senseless* has some fun with it. The slightest sound drives Darryl mad, and side effects make him too itchy to sit through an exam. But soon he's able to see, hear, taste, smell, and feel better than anyone else. That makes him a star on the hockey team, and a virtuoso in other areas too. (He's been raising money by donating blood and sperm, and now asks the sperm bank for a quote on two gallons.)

The film's villain is the supercilious Scott (David Spade), who maneuvers to keep Darryl out of his fraternity. That's important because an important alum of the fraternity (Rip Torn) might help a bright economics major get a job with a Wall Street firm. Darryl and Scott are finalists when tragedy strikes: Darryl incautiously takes a double dose of the magic potion and finds that his senses are cycling out of control. He can count on only four of the five at any given moment, and when Torn takes him to a Knicks game, his hearing cuts out during the national anthem and his eyesight fails as he sits next to an unamused Patrick Ewing.

This is not great comedy, and Wayans doesn't find ways to build and improvise, as Carrey does. But he's talented and has unbounded energy, a plastic face, and a rubber body. I liked him. And I liked his flirtation with Janice (Tamara Taylor), a co-ed who accepts his bizarre misadventures. I was not so fond of a subplot involving Lorraine (Kenya Moore), Janice's buxom sorority sister, who seems written in to supply an awkward and pointless seduction scene.

Penelope Spheeris, whose *Wayne's World* remains one of the funniest of recent movies, never finds a consistent tone here. The broad physical humor of the main plot contrasts weirdly with the character of the roommate (Matthew Lillard), who doesn't seem to vibrate in the same universe. His character could be funny in a different movie, but he seems at right angles to this one.

Set Me Free ★ ★ ★
NO MPAA RATING, 94 m., 2000

Karine Vanasse (Hanna), Alexandre Merineau (Paul), Pascale Bussieres (The Mother), Mike Manojlovic (The Father), Charlotte Christeler (Laura), Nancy Huston (The Teacher), Monique Mercure (The Grandmother), Anne-Marie Cadieux (The Prostitute). Directed by Lea Pool and produced by Lorraine Richard. Screenplay by Pool.

It is not reassuring when your father tells you, "Books are our only true friends." Where does that leave you—or your mom, or your brother? And yet what he says may be worth hearing. Hanna, the heroine of *Set Me Free*, is a thirteen-year-old growing up in 1963 in Montreal. Her father is distant, disturbed, incapable of supporting his family, and blames everyone but himself. Her mother is meek and suicidal. It's up to Hanna to find her own way in life, and that's what she does, at the movies.

Art can be a great consolation when you are a lonely teenager. It speaks directly to you. You find the right movie, the right song, the right book, and you are not alone. Books and movies are not our only friends, but they help us find true friends, and tell them apart from the crowd.

One day in the rain, Hanna (Karine Vanasse) sneaks into a theater and sees Jean-Luc Godard's *My Life to Live* (1962), where even the title is significant. It stars Anna Karina as an independent woman in Paris who leaves her husband and works as a prostitute to support herself. She keeps a distance from her clients; cigarettes form a wall between her and the world, and there is a famous shot where, as a man embraces her, she sullenly blows out smoke.

Not the character you would choose as a role model for a thirteen-year-old girl. But Hanna is unhappy and confused. She has just had her first period and does not quite understand it. Her father is cold to her mother, her brother, and herself, but then turns on the charm. There is no money in the household; her father (Mike Manojlovic) calls himself a writer but has published nothing, her mother (Pascale Bussieres) works as a seamstress, and the pawnbroker knows the kids by name. In this confusion, Hanna finds encouragement in the independent woman of the movie, who holds herself aloof, who is self-contained, who lets no man hurt her.

In her life there is some happiness. She idolizes her schoolteacher (Nancy Huston), who looks a little like Anna Karina. She makes a close school friend named Laura, and they share their first kiss together. Does this mean they will grow up to be lesbians? Maybe, but probably not; what it probably means is that they are so young that kissing is a mysterious activity not yet directly wired to sex and gender, and Laura offers tenderness Hanna desperately requires.

In school, like all the students, she is called upon to stand up and give her life details. This leads to her admission that her parents are not married. Religion? "My father is Jewish, my mother is Catholic," she says. And which is she? "Judaism passes the religion through the mother, which would make me Catholic, but Catholicism passes through the father, which would make me Jewish," she says. "Myself, I don't care."

Her father is a refugee from the Holocaust, an intellectual. Their apartment is filled with books. Her mother fell for him the first time she saw him, and got pregnant at sixteen with Paul, her brother. When her father found this out two years later, he decided to care for them, and soon Hanna was born. In a moment of revelation, Hanna's father tells her that he was married in Europe, and that although his wife may have died in the camps, he has no proof, and refuses to think of her as dead. Her mother also confides in Hanna. Despite their troubles, she will never leave her husband: "I need him."

Set Me Free is set in 1963, when the films of the French New Wave would have been influential in French-speaking Quebec. In some of its details, it resembles François Truffaut's *The 400 Blows*, which is about a young boy whose parents are unhappy, and who keeps a shrine to Balzac in his bedroom. Hanna's Balzac is Karina in *My Life to Live*. Leaning against a wall, smoking insolently, not giving a damn, Karina provides not a role model but a strategy. It is not only possible to stand aside from the pain of your life, it can even become a personal style.

The movie gets a little confused toward the end, I think, as its writer and director, Lea Pool, tries to settle things that could have been left unresolved. Hanna's tentative walk on the wild side is awkwardly handled. You walk out not quite satisfied. Later, when the movie settles in your mind, its central theme becomes clear. We grow by choosing those we admire, and pulling ourselves up on the hand they extend. For Hanna, the hands come from her teacher, from her friend, and from the woman in the movie she sees over and over. "I am responsible," says Karina in the movie. "I am responsible," says Hanna to herself. It is her life to live.

Shadrach ★ ★
PG-13, 88 m., 1998

Harvey Keitel (Vernon Dabney), Andie MacDowell (Trixie Dabney), Scott Terra (Paul Whitehurst), Monica Bugajeski (Ebonia Dabney), John Franklin Sawyer (Shadrach), Daniel Treat (Little Mole Dabney), Darrell Larson (Mr. Whitehurst), Deborah Hedwall (Mrs. Whitehurst). Directed by Susanna Styron and produced by Boaz Davidson, Bridget Terry, and John Thompson. Screenplay by Susanna Styron and Terry, based on a story by William Styron.

It is a strange coincidence that leads me to review *Shadrach,* based on a story by William Styron, on the same day as *Beloved,* based on a story by Toni Morrison. Both are about the aftermath of slavery. In *Shadrach,* a 101-year-old former slave completes a long trek in order to return to the plantation where he was born and wants to be buried. In *Beloved,* a mother kills her children rather than have them returned to the plantation she has escaped from.

It might seem like there are easy points to be scored here against Styron, a white southern novelist, but they wouldn't be fair. He has amply demonstrated, in *The Confessions of Nat Turner,* his own understanding of the horror of slavery.

And he is not arguing that the ancient Shadrach wants to be buried on "Dabney land" out of nostalgia for plantation days under the slave-owning Dabneys. The old man never really explains his motivation, but we sense it is made of nostalgia for his childhood on the plantation, and a feeling that since he worked this land it is more his own than any other land anywhere else.

Still, *Shadrach* is another one of those well-meaning films, like *Amistad*, in which slaves are the supporting characters in their own stories. *Beloved* brings its characters front and center and focuses on how slavery impacted their lives. It doesn't have much screen time for white people, good or bad. It is inescapable that none of the white characters in *Shadrach* have the slightest inkling of the reality of the experience that Shadrach and the characters in *Beloved* endured.

The movie takes place in 1935, in a Virginia deep in the Depression. We meet Paul Whitehurst (Scott Terra), a young boy whose affluent parents are setting out for a funeral. It is a long trip—maybe too long for a young boy. Paul is friendly with some of the children of the Dabney family, poor whites who no longer live in the mansion on the family plantation, but in a sharecropper's cabin. The Dabneys ask Paul to stay with them, and he's delighted at the chance to play with his best friend, Little Mole Dabney (Daniel Treat), and his cheerful sister Ebonia (Monica Bugajeski).

The Dabney parents, who are the best-drawn characters in the story, are Trixie (Andie MacDowell) and Vernon (Harvey Keitel). Vernon is a moonshiner, Trixie has a good heart but swigs too much beer, and the Dabney children are raising themselves to be strangers to soap.

Old Shadrach (John Franklin Sawyer) materializes one day. He is so ancient and feeble it hardly seems possible he walked to "Dabney land," but he did, and now he sits down and tells the Dabneys he wants to be buried there. When he dies, that sets in motion a subplot about the laws against human burial on private ground, and complications involving the segregated cemeteries in Virginia. The Dabneys solve these problems with a subterfuge that edges perilously close to slapstick, considering the issues being considered here.

Shadrach is a well-meaning film, directed by Susanna Styron from her father's autobiographical story. But without diminishing Shadrach's own determination and dignity (evoked in a minimalist, whispering performance by first-time actor Sawyer), it indulges in a certain sentimentality that is hard to accept in the dark weather stirred up by *Beloved*.

The movie even has Vernon Dabney wonder if the slaves weren't better off back when they had an assured place in the social order, and got their meals on time; the movie does not adopt this view as its own, and quietly corrects him, but I was left with a vision of Vernon trying to expound his theories to Sethe, the heroine of *Beloved*, who would rather have a child dead in freedom than alive in slavery.

Shaft ★ ★ ½
R, 98 m., 2000

Samuel L. Jackson (John Shaft), Vanessa Williams (Carmen), Jeffrey Wright (Peoples Hernandez), Christian Bale (Walter Wade), Busta Rhymes (Rasaan), Dan Hedaya (Jack Roselli), Toni Collette (Diane Palmieri), Richard Roundtree (Uncle John), Lee Tergesen (Luger). Directed by John Singleton and produced by Singleton and Scott Rudin. Screenplay by Singleton, Richard Price, and Shane Salerno.

John Singleton's *Shaft* is a blaxploitation film with a modern urban drama trapped inside. Or maybe it's the other way around. On the one hand, we have John Shaft telling a pickup, "It's my duty to please your booty." On the other hand, we have a scene between a rich kid and a drug dealer that's so well written and acted it's chilling.

At the center of the tug-of-war, pulled both ways and enjoying it, is Samuel L. Jackson, as a tough cop who throws his badge back at a judge (literally) and becomes a freelance vigilante. The story's broad outlines are familiar not only from early 1970s black exploitation movies, but also from the early *Dirty Harry* pictures, and when a top cop orders Shaft to get out of his precinct, it's like he's reciting dialogue from the classics.

The movie has the obligatory elements of black exploitation (big cars, drugs, cigars, guns, sleazy nightclubs, gold chains, racism, babes, black leather coats, expensive booze, crooked white cops). But a newer sensibility sneaks in, probably thanks to a screenplay primarily by Richard Price, who wrote *Clockers* and specializes in dialogue that allows the characters some poetry; I like lines like "It's Giuliani time!"

On top of reports that Singleton and Jackson had many disagreements on the set, there were stories that neither of them much liked the Price screenplay, maybe because it nailed the small moments but missed the broader Shaftian strokes. Whatever compromises were made, the result is a movie more interesting than it might have been: not just a retread of the old movie, but Shaft as more complicated than before, and with well-observed supporting characters.

Jackson is at the center of the action, "too black for the uniform, too blue for the brothers," wearing a wicked goatee that looks like it was designed by a comic book artist. He's a cop made angry when a rich man's son (Christian Bale) murders a black youth, gets an easy bail, and skips to Switzerland. As one of the first on the crime scene, Shaft believes that a waitress (Toni Collette) saw more than she admits. Two years pass, the rich kid returns to the country, Shaft nabs him, and then the plot involves his partner (Busta Rhymes), the drug kingpin (Jeffrey Wright), the sexy narcotics cop (Vanessa Williams), the larcenous cop (Dan Hedaya), and his partner Luger (Lee Tergesen). Always look twice at a cop named Luger.

The casting here makes for some interesting echoes. Hedaya, of course, played the crooked cop in *The Hurricane,* and Christian Bale had the title role in *American Psycho.* Toni Collette, who was the mother in *The Sixth Sense,* is a good choice for the waitress; there's always something a little edgy about her. There's another echo in Bale's hairstyle, which evokes uncanny memories of JFK Jr.

One modern thing about the movie is its low sexual quotient. Blaxploitation came along at a time when American movies were sexy, with lots of nudity and bedroom time. Modern action pictures seem prudish by comparison; like *Gone in 60 Seconds* and *Mission: Impossible 2,* this one prefers action to sex. Can it be that Hollywood's Friday night specials, which were aimed at teenage boys, have now lowered their sights to include a demographic group so young it thinks girls are creepy?

The most intriguing relationship in the movie is between Bale and Wright, as the rich kid and the drug dealer. There's a scene where Bale comes to Wright, hoping to pay for a hit.

Wright is not much into murder for hire, but wants the kid's connections as a way to develop a more affluent clientele for his drugs. The way they talk to each other, the words they choose, the attitudes they strike, the changes they go through, are as subtly menacing as scenes in a film by Lee or Scorsese. The movie doesn't give us stereotypes in these two familiar roles, but closely examined originals.

The John Shaft character is more mainstream, but Jackson has a way of bringing weight to his roles. He always looks like he means it. But there's a disconnect between the realism of the murder case and the fantasy of Shaft's career as an unleashed vigilante who leaves countless dead bodies behind him. Different scenes seem to occupy different levels of reality. Of course the movie ends with a gunfight and a chase scene. That goes without saying.

Is this a good movie? Not exactly; too much of it is on automatic pilot, as it must be, to satisfy the fans of the original *Shaft.* Is it better than I expected? Yes. There are flashes here of the talent that John Singleton has possessed ever since *Boyz N the Hood,* and strong acting, and efficient action. Jackson makes a commanding Shaft (and a supporting role by Richard Roundtree, the original Shaft, serves to pass the mantle). The movie is what it is, but more than it needs to be.

Shakespeare in Love ★ ★ ★ ★
R, 120 m., 1998

Gwyneth Paltrow (Viola De Lesseps), Joseph Fiennes (Will Shakespeare), Geoffrey Rush (Philip Henslowe), Colin Firth (Lord Wessex), Ben Affleck (Ned Alleyn), Judi Dench (Queen Elizabeth), Simon Callow (Tilney, Master of the Revels), Rupert Everett (Christopher Marlowe), Martin Clunes (Richard Burbage), Tom Wilkinson (Fennyman), Imelda Staunton (Nurse), Anthony Sher (Dr. Moth). Directed by John Madden and produced by David Parfitt, Donna Gigliotti, Harvey Weinstein, Edward Zwick, and Marc Norman. Screenplay by Norman and Tom Stoppard.

There is a boatman in *Shakespeare in Love* who ferries Shakespeare across the Thames while bragging, "I had Christopher Marlowe in my boat once." As Shakespeare steps ashore, the boatman tries to give him a script to read. The contemporary feel of the humor (like Shakespeare's coffee mug, inscribed "Souvenir of Stratford-upon-Avon") makes the movie play like a contest between *Masterpiece Theater* and Mel Brooks. Then the movie stirs in a sweet love story, juicy court intrigue, backstage politics, and some lovely moments from *Romeo and Juliet* (Shakespeare's working title: *Romeo and Ethel, the Pirate's Daughter*).

Is this a movie or an anthology? I didn't care. I was carried along by the wit, the energy, and a surprising sweetness. The movie serves as a reminder that Will Shakespeare was once a young playwright on the make, that theater in all times is as much business as show, and that *Romeo and Juliet* must have been written by a man in intimate communication with his libido. The screenplay is by Marc Norman and Tom Stoppard, whose play *Rosencrantz and Guildenstern are Dead* approached *Hamlet* from the points of view of two minor characters.

Shakespeare in Love is set in late Elizabethan England (the queen, played as a young woman by Cate Blanchett in *Elizabeth,* is played as an old one here by Judi Dench). Theater in London is booming—when the theaters aren't closed, that is, by plague warnings or bad debts. Shakespeare (Joseph Fiennes) is not as successful as the popular Marlowe (Rupert Everett), but he's a rising star, in demand by the impecunious impresario Henslowe (Geoffrey Rush), whose Rose Theater is in hock to a money lender, and Richard Burbage (Martin Clunes), whose Curtain Theater has Marlowe and would like to sign Shakespeare.

The film's opening scenes provide a cheerful survey of the business of theater—the buildings, the budgets, the script deadlines, the casting process. Shakespeare meanwhile struggles against deadlines and complains in therapy that his quill has broken (his therapist raises a Freudian eyebrow). What does it take to renew his energy? A sight of the beautiful Viola De Lesseps (Gwyneth Paltrow), a rich man's daughter with the taste to prefer Shakespeare to Marlowe, and the daring to put on men's clothes and audition for a role in Will's new play.

Players in drag were, of course, standard on the Elizabethan stage ("Stage love will never be true love," the dialogue complains, "while the law of the land has our beauties played by pip-squeak boys"). It was conventional not to notice the gender disguises, and *Shakespeare in Love* asks us to grant the same leeway as Viola first plays a woman auditioning to play a man, and later plays a man playing a woman. As the young man auditioning to play Romeo, Viola wears a mustache and trousers, and yet somehow inspires stirrings in Will's breeches; later, at a dance, he sees her as a woman and falls instantly in love.

Alas, Viola is to be married in two weeks to the odious Lord Wessex (Colin Firth), who will trade his title for her father's cash. Shakespeare nevertheless presses his case, in what turns out to be a real-life rehearsal for Romeo and Juliet's balcony scene, and when it is discovered that he violated Viola's bedchamber, he thinks fast and identifies himself as Marlowe. (This suggests an explanation for Marlowe's mysterious stabbing death at Deptford.) The threads of the story come together nicely on Viola's wedding day, which ends with her stepping into a role she could not possibly have foreseen.

The film has been directed by John Madden, who made *Mrs. Brown* (1997), about the affection between Queen Victoria and her horse trainer. Here again he finds a romance that leaps across barriers of wealth, titles, and class. The story is ingeniously Shakespearean in its dimensions, including high and low comedy, coincidences, masquerades, jokes about itself, topical references, and entrances with screwball timing. At the same time we get a good sense of how the audience was deployed in the theaters, where they stood or sat, and what their view was like—and also information about costuming, props, and stagecraft.

But all of that is handled lightly, as background, while intrigues fill the foreground, and the love story between Shakespeare and Viola slyly takes form. By the closing scene, where Viola breaks the law against women on the stage, we're surprised how much of Shakespeare's original power still resides in lines that now have two or even three additional meanings. There's a quiet realism in the development of the romance, which grows in the shadow of Viola's approaching nuptials: "This is not life, Will," she tells him. "It is a stolen season." And Judi Dench has a wicked scene as

Elizabeth, informing Wessex of his bride-to-be, "You're a lordly fool; she's been plucked since I saw her last, and not by you. It takes a woman to know it."

Fiennes and Paltrow make a fine romantic couple, high-spirited and fine-featured, and Ben Affleck prances through the center of the film as Ned Alleyn, the cocky actor. I also enjoyed the seasoned Shakespeareans who swelled the progress of a scene or two: Simon Callow as the Master of the Revels; Tom Wilkinson as Fennyman, the usurer; Imelda Staunton as Viola's nurse; Anthony Sher as Dr. Moth, the therapist.

A movie like this is a reminder of the long thread that connects Shakespeare to the kids opening tonight in a storefront on Lincoln Avenue: You get a theater, you learn the lines, you strut your stuff, you hope there's an audience, you fall in love with another member of the cast, and if sooner or later your revels must be ended, well, at least you reveled.

Shanghai Noon ★ ★ ★
PG-13, 110 m., 2000

Jackie Chan (Chon Wang), Owen Wilson (Roy O'Bannon), Lucy Liu (Princess Pei Pei), Brandon Merrill (Indian Wife), Roger Yuan (Lo Fong), Xander Berkeley (Van Cleef), Walton Goggins (Wallace), P. Adrien Dorval (Blue). Directed by Tom Dey and produced by Roger Birnbaum, Gary Barber, and Jonathan Glickman. Screenplay by Alfred Gough and Miles Millar.

The best way to criticize a movie, Jean-Luc Godard once said, is to make another movie. In that spirit, Shanghai Noon is the answer to Wild Wild West, although I am not sure these are the kinds of movies Godard had in mind. Jackie Chan's new action comedy is a wink at Westerns, martial arts, and buddy movies—enriched by a goofy performance by Owen Wilson, who would steal the movie if Chan were not so clever at sharing it with him.

The plot in a paragraph: China, the Forbidden City, 1881. The princess (Lucy Liu) resents her fate and hates her chosen fiancé. Her teacher offers to help her escape to America. She is kidnapped and held for ransom in Nevada. The three best Imperial Guards are selected to

rescue her. Jackie Chan goes along as a bag carrier for his uncle, who is their interpreter. In Nevada, Jackie teams up with a train robber named Roy O'Bannon (Wilson), and they rescue the princess with much help from an Indian maiden (Brandon Merrill).

The plot, of course, is only a clothesline for Jackie's martial arts sequences, Wilson's funny verbal riffs, and a lot of low humor. Material like this can be very bad. Here it is sort of wonderful, because of a light touch by director Tom Dey, who finds room both for Chan's effortless charm and for a droll performance by Owen Wilson, who, if this were a musical, would be a Beach Boy.

Wilson has been edging up on us. Most moviegoers don't know who he is. If you see everything, you'll remember him from Bottle Rocket, where he was engaging, and Minus Man, where he was profoundly disturbing. This movie will make him a star. He is too smart and versatile to be packaged within a narrow range (his career also includes writing credits on Bottle Rocket and Rushmore), but if he could do only what he does in Shanghai Noon, he could support himself with Adam Sandler roles.

His train robber is hard to describe; the character is funny because of his tone, not his dialogue or actions. He's a modern, laid-back, self-centered southern California dude with a Stetson and six-guns. Flirting with a passenger on the train he is robbing, he gets competitive: "I kinda like to do the talking." His comic timing is precise, as in a scene where he and Jackie Chan get into a weird drinking contest while sharing adjacent bathtubs in a bordello, and play a funny and utterly inexplicable word game.

Chan's character is named Chon Wang (say it out loud). As in his 1998 hit Rush Hour, he plays a man of limited vocabulary and much action; Chris Tucker in that film and Owen Wilson in this one are motormouths who cover for Chan's shaky English, which is no problem because his martial arts scenes are poetic. He's famous for using the props that come to hand in every fight, and here there is a sequence involving several things we didn't know could be done with evergreen trees.

Lucy Liu, as the princess, is not a damsel in distress, but brave and plucky, and stirred by the plight of her Chinese countrymen, who have been made indentured servants in a Nevada gold town. She doesn't want to return to China, but to stay in America—as a social worker or union organizer, I guess. Not so boldly portrayed is Brandon Merrill's Indian woman, who is married to Jackie in a ceremony that nobody seems to take seriously and that the movie itself has clearly forgotten all about by the time the last shot comes around.

Her pairing with Jackie Chan does, however, create a funny echo of *A Man Called Horse,* and on the way out of the theater I was challenged by my fellow critic Sergio Mims to name all the other movie references. He claimed to have spotted, I think, twenty-four. My mind boggled.

What *Shanghai Noon* proves—and here's how it's a criticism of *Wild Wild West*—is that no matter how much effort is put into production values and special effects, a movie like this finally depends on dialogue and characters. *Wild Wild West,* which came out almost exactly one year earlier, had a top-drawer cast (Will Smith, Kevin Kline, Kenneth Branagh), but what were they given to do? Plow through dim-witted dialogue between ungainly f/x scenes. Here Wilson angles on-screen and starts riffing, and we laugh. And Jackie Chan, who does his own stunts, creates moments of physical comedy so pure it's no wonder he has been compared with Buster Keaton. If you see only one martial arts Western this year (and there is probably an excellent chance of that), this is the one.

Shattered Image ★ ½
NO MPAA RATING, 103 m., 1999

William Baldwin (Brian), Anne Parillaud (Jessie), Graham Greene (Detective), Billy Wilmott (Lamond), Lisanne Falk (Paula/Laura), Bulle Ogier (Mrs. Ford). Directed by Raul Ruiz and produced by Barbet Schroeder, Lloyd Silverman, and Abby Stone. Screenplay by Duane Poole.

Shattered Image is a film so confoundedly and deliberately difficult to view, I felt like the laboratory mouse that fought its way through the maze and was rewarded with nothing more than a chlorophyll gumball. I sat in the dark,

earnestly scribbling notes and trying to make mental connections, until it occurred to me that I was being toyed with. Without giving away the ending, I can say that the plot exists at the level of a child's story that ends, "and then I woke up, and it was all a dream!"

Ah, if that only *did* give away the ending! Raul Ruiz, the director, is fond of stories in which the viewer is kept in the dark about the true nature of the characters' reality. In *Shattered Image* he outdoes himself, with the story of a woman named Jessie (Anne Parillaud, of *La Femme Nikita*) who is either a hit woman who dreams she is a rape victim, or a newly-wed who dreams she is a hit woman. Each character wakes up from dreams of the other, and as for Brian (William Baldwin)—who is he, really? Her new husband, or what?

Raul Ruiz is a Chilean-born director who has been involved in nearly eighty films since 1970, has shot in several European languages, and moves into English with *Shattered Image.* His interest in narrative game-playing can be seen to better effect in *Three Lives and Only One Death* (1997), the last film starring Marcello Mastroianni, who plays three roles—or maybe only one—in stories that occupy interlocking time lines.

In that film we quickly understand the underlying principle, and it's absorbing to see the time- and space-shifting that goes on. There are rules, even if they are only dimly understood principles of (take your choice) psychology, hallucination, imagination, or magic. In *Shattered Image* all is arbitrary until the end, and then it gets *really* arbitrary.

Faithful readers will know that I am not hostile to stories that conceal their reality. That was the strategy underlying *Dark City,* my choice as the best film of 1998. But in that film (and in *Three Lives*), the director is the audience's coconspirator, allowing glimpses or guesses of the solution.

Shattered Image, which is set alternately in the Caribbean and the Pacific Northwest, keeps the book of its secrets slammed shut. All is mystery until the "answer," which is singularly unsatisfying. And then there is another problem too. In *Three Lives,* we could always be interested in the actual events as they unfolded. In *Shattered Image,* the events seem more like arbitrary behavior designed to give Jessie something to do when loud noises and other triggers jerk her back and forth between dreams and reality (or reality and dreams, or dreams and dreams).

Apart from the narrative gimmick, the story is not intrinsically interesting. So we're like the mouse, negotiating the maze. There's not much of interest along the way, and when we get to the end and the titles roll up the screen, we have a good idea for a song they could play over the credits: Peggy Lee singing "Is That All There Is?"

She's All That ★ ★ ½
PG-13, 97 m., 1999

Freddie Prinze Jr. (Zack Siler), Rachael Leigh Cook (Laney Boggs), Matthew Lillard (Brock Hudson), Paul Walker (Dean Sampson), Jodi Lyn O'Keefe (Taylor Vaughan), Kevin Pollak (Wayne Boggs), Anna Paquin (Mackenzie Siler), Kieran Culkin (Simon Boggs). Directed by Robert Iscove and produced by Peter Abrams, Robert L. Levy, and Richard Gladstein. Screenplay by R. Lee Fleming Jr.

Sometimes while you're watching a movie, you can sense the presence of a wicked intelligence slipping zingers into a formula plot. I had that feeling all during *She's All That,* which is not based on a blindingly original idea (*Pygmalion* and *My Fair Lady* got there first). It's about how the most popular guy in the senior class makes a bet that he can take a dorky girl and turn her into a prom queen.

There's fun in the plot, but there's more fun around the edges. The movie stars Freddie Prinze Jr. as Zack, who has the third best grade point average in his class, and is also the captain of the soccer team and dates the beautiful class sexpot Taylor (Jodi Lyn O'Keefe). But Taylor breaks up with him after going to Daytona Beach and meeting Brock Hudson, star of a cable show in which real kids are cast more or less as themselves (MTV's *The Real World* is the model). I only got a quick glimpse, but I think Brock has a tattoo of himself on his right arm.

Taylor is sure she'll be prom queen. Zack's buddies bet him he can't take another girl and make her the queen. He accepts, and chooses Laney (Rachael Leigh Cook), a mousy wall-

flower who paints down in her basement. In this affluent southern California community, it doesn't help that her dad is "Dr. Pool" (Kevin Pollak), owner of a pool-cleaning service.

Will Laney undergo a startling transformation? What do you think? I wanted to applaud when Zack unleashed the classic line, "Do you always wear those glasses?" Of course, it is an unbreakable rule of this formula that the ugly duckling is a swan in disguise: Rachael Leigh Cook is in fact quite beautiful, as was Audrey Hepburn, you will recall, in *My Fair Lady.* Just once I'd like to see the *Pygmalion* formula applied to a woman who was truly unattractive.

To give the movie credit, it's as bored with the underlying plot as we are. Even the prom queen election is only a backdrop for more interesting material, as *She's All That* explores differences in class and style, and peppers its screenplay with very funny little moments.

Consider, for example, the scene where Zack seeks Laney in the fast-food joint where she works. McDonald's would be too much of a cliché. This is a Middle Eastern franchise: "Would you like to supersize those falafel balls?" Consider a scene that plays in the foreground while Laney's dad is watching *Jeopardy!* in the background and shouting out the answers. (To a question about the printer of the most famous Bible in history, he shouts out "Hewlett-Packard." I couldn't quite catch the question for which his answer is "Lou Rawls" and the correct answer is "the pope.")

Moments like that are almost better than the movie deserves. So is the way the movie treats Taylor, the villainess, who tries to seduce the vain Brock while he's watching himself on TV, and is told to stop getting spit on his chest. And although it's obligatory to have a party scene at which the bad girl humiliates the good girl by pouring something down her dress, I liked the way Taylor told Laney she was "a waste of perfectly good yearbook space."

High school movies never seem that convincing to me, maybe because all the students seem to be in their twenties and don't have zits. Freddie Prinze Jr., I learn, is twenty-three, and Rachael Leigh Cook is twenty. Still, they have a charm in their roles, muted somewhat in Cook's case because the plot requires her to be sullen much of the time. She lurks in the basement painting large dark canvases, and at first Zack doesn't realize he's really falling in love with her.

But of course he is. And although she resists his advances ("What is this, some kind of a dork outreach program?"), nothing can stand in the way of the happy ending. Watching the movie, I was grateful to the director, Robert Iscove, and the writer, Lee Fleming, for taking this weary material and doing what they could with it. There's so little wit in the movies today. Too many characters speak in big, clunky declarative sentences that serve only to push the plot ahead of them, like people trying to shove their cars out of the snow. *She's All That* is not a great movie, but it has its moments.

Shiloh 2: Shiloh Season ★ ★ ★
PG, 96 m., 1999

Michael Moriarty (Ray Preston), Scott Wilson (Judd Travers), Zachary Browne (Marty Preston), Rod Steiger (Doc Wallace), Ann Dowd (Louise Preston), Bonnie Bartlett (Mrs. Wallace), Rachel David (Becky), Joe Pichler (David Howard), Marissa Leigh (Samantha). Directed by Sandy Tung and produced by Dale Rosenbloom and Carl Borack. Screenplay by Rosenbloom, based on novels by Phyllis Reynolds Naylor.

Shiloh 2: Shiloh Season recycles the same characters and, in a way, the same problems as the wonderful original film, but carries the message a little further. The first film was about a boy who is adopted by a dog, loves it, and wants to protect it from its cruel owner—even if that means lying to his parents. This sequel is about how people get to be cruel in the first place, and what you might be able to do to help them.

What's unique about both films, which are based on novels by Phyllis Reynolds Naylor, is that they're about hard ethical issues that kids can identify with. A boy's dog inspires fierce love and protectiveness, and if he thinks adults (even his parents) might be a threat to the dog, he will instinctively do what he can to protect it. Even lie.

Who is to say he is wrong? Yes, "lying" is wrong—but what if it's the only weapon at your disposal to protect a dog that depends on you? I don't think I'd be pleased if a son of mine betrayed his dog. On the other hand, I don't think I'd let him know that. I'd let him find out in other ways. Sometimes parents and children have to enact these passion plays to learn lessons that are deeper than words.

Shiloh 2 takes place once again in an isolated rural area populated only by the Prestons, their alcoholic neighbor Judd Travers, and the friendly folks at the general store. At one point it occurred to me that the lives of the entire Preston family—father, mother, son, daughters, and dog—were completely dominated by Travers, who is their only visitor and the subject of most of their conversations. But there's a kind of purity to the way the story narrows down to the key players.

Marty Preston (Zachary Browne), now on the edge of adolescence, has been able to buy the dog Shiloh from Travers (Scott Wilson). That pleases his dad and mom (Michael Moriarty and Ann Dowd), and also watchful old Doc Wallace (Rod Steiger), who runs the store with his wife and their granddaughter, who is about Marty's age. But now Travers is drinking heavily, hunting out of season, and trespassing on Preston land. And someone is picking on him—scratching his car, knocking over his mailbox, freeing his remaining dogs.

Who is it? There's a line of dialogue that gives us a good idea, but Travers thinks it's Marty. This leads to several charged confrontations between the hunter and Marty's dad (played by Moriarty with solemn authority). Then there are a couple of emergencies—one serious, one a false alarm—and Shiloh plays a role both times.

Scott Wilson once again brings a humanity to the tricky role of Judd Travers, who is a pathetic being. Yes, he kicks dogs. But he was kicked himself as a child, and is a lonely man, living in poverty. (He claims to support himself by hunting, but his only success during this movie comes when he sits on his front porch and picks off one squirrel.) Doc Wallace knows something about the Travers family, and what he tells Marty leads to the ending, in which a life is redeemed—maybe. (I liked the frankness with which Marty prays, after Travers is injured, that the man get better, "but maybe don't let his legs get good enough to go hunting.")

Families do not often attend "family movies" in theaters, unless they're Disney cartoons or

TV spin-offs, but the original *Shiloh* was such a success on video that it justified a sequel. Both films demand to be discussed afterward by parents and their children. Neither is about the kind of dumb, empty-headed stuff that passes for children's entertainment. Kids are not stupid, and they wonder about issues like this. They may also suspect, as the movie observes, that "you have to be taught to be kind."

Show Me Love ★ ★ ★
NO MPAA RATING, 89 m., 2000

Alexandra Dahlstrom (Elin), Rebecca Liljeberg (Agnes), Erica Carlson (Jessica), Mathias Rust (Johan Hult), Stefan Horberg (Markus), Ralph Carlsson (Father Olof), Maria Hedborg (Mother Karin), Axel Widegren (Little Brother Oskar). Directed by Lukas Moodysson and produced by Lars Jonsson. Screenplay by Moodysson.

This is all I ask of a movie about teenagers: That they be as smart, as confused, as good-hearted, and as insecure as the kids I went to high school with. Such characters are so rare that when you encounter them in a movie like *Show Me Love,* they belong to a different species than the creatures in the weekly Hollywood teenager picture.

Show Me Love is set in Sweden, but could be set in any American small town where kids believe they are desperate outcasts in a cultural backwater. Elin (Alexandra Dahlstrom), one of the girls in the film, pages through a teen magazine and despairs when she finds that raves are "out." Her town is so behind the times that stuff is out before it even gets there. She is bored, bored, bored. She wants to be a model, but is even bored with that.

The movie is also about Agnes (Rebecca Liljeberg), who moved to the town more than a year ago but still has few friends; she's an outsider at school because students whisper she's a lesbian. They have no reason to think that, but they're right. She has a crush on Elin, and locks herself in her room to write her love letters on her computer. One day at a party, a girlfriend bets Elin she won't kiss Agnes, and she does, sending the wrong message to Agnes, who doesn't know about the bet.

This sounds, I know, like the setup for a sex-com, or maybe one of those Swedish romps of long ago (*Therese and Isabelle* comes to mind). What I haven't conveyed is the sweetness, tenderness, and naïveté of all of these scenes, in which both girls are essentially wandering cluelessly through half-understood life choices. What they find at the end of the film is not romance so much as self-knowledge and fortitude, and a disdain for "popularity."

The movie (which outgrossed *Titanic* to become the most successful film in Swedish history) is not a story of heroines and villains. Everyone in it is more or less on the same moral plane. It is not about distant and block-headed parents (the parents express love and understanding, as best they can, and we sympathize with their attempts to make sense of adolescent despair). It isn't about any of the standard characters (the stupid principal, the class nerd, the social snob) who wander through most Hollywood teenage movies on autopilot. It's about these specific people and their lives.

The movie is funny, gentle, and true. It knows how teenagers can be cruel, and how sharply they can regret it. Early in the film, Agnes's mother throws her a birthday party (she doesn't want one), and it looks like only one guest is going to turn up—her best friend, who is in a wheelchair. Mad at her parents, mad at herself, Agnes lashes out at her friend ("I don't want to be friends with a palsied cripple who listens to the Back Street Boys!") and mocks her gift of perfume. Later, she apologizes. The friend in the wheelchair is not all that deeply upset about the insult, because she has read it, correctly, as more about Agnes than about herself. In most American teenage movies, there's not depth enough for such subtlety: An insult is an insult, without nuance.

The film is refreshing in the way it handles "sex," and I put the word in quotes because there is hardly any sex in the film. While American teenage films cheerfully supply shower scenes, T&A, and four-letter words, this one is released without an MPAA rating, no doubt because its honesty would upset audiences accustomed to a cinema of dirty jokes. Two of the truest moments in the movie occur when the two girls confess they have no sexual experience. The "lesbian" reveals that the kiss on a bet was the first time she has kissed a girl, and Elin, who has a reputation for promiscuity, confides she is a virgin.

Show Me Love is not really about sexuality. It's more about vegetating in a town that makes the girls feel trapped. And it sees that the fault is not in the town, but in the girls: Maybe their boredom is a pose. Maybe all teenagers, in every town, feel like nothing is happening in their lives, and they will never find love or be understood or do thrilling things. Maybe that's just human nature. In its quiet, intelligent, understated way, this film loves teenagers; most teen movies just use them.

The Siege ★ ★ ½
R, 110 m., 1998

Denzel Washington (Anthony Hubbard), Annette Bening (Elise/Sharon), Bruce Willis (General Devereaux), Tony Shalhoub (Frank Haddad), Sami Bouajila (Samir Nazhde), Ahmed Ben Larby (Sheik Ahmed Bin Talal), Mosley Mohamed (Muezzin), Liana Pai (Tina Osu). Directed by Edward Zwick and produced by Lynda Obst and Zwick. Screenplay by Lawrence Wright, Menno Meyjes, and Zwick.

"What if they were black people? What if they were Italian?" These words are spoken by an unseen character in *The Siege*, but they get at the heart of the film, which is about a roundup of Arab Americans after terrorist bombs strike New York City. Okay, what if they *were* black or Italian? What if the movie was a fantasy about the army running rampant over the civil liberties of American Irish, Poles, Koreans? Wouldn't that be the same thing as rounding up the Arab Americans?

Not really, because the same feelings are not at stake. Of all our ethnic groups, only Arabs come from nations that are currently in a state of indefinitely suspended war with the United States. The vast majority of Arab-Americans are patriotic citizens who are happy to plunge into the melting pot with the rest of us (a point the movie does make), but a minority have been much in the news, especially after the World Trade Center bombing.

Many Americans do not draw those distinctions, and could not check off on a list those Arab countries we consider hostile, neutral, or friendly. There is a tendency to lump together "towelheads" (a term used in the movie). Arab-Americans feel vulnerable right now to

the kinds of things that happen in this movie, and that's why it's not the same thing as targeting other ethnic groups. (By way of illustration, it is unlikely, even unimaginable, after recent history, that a fantasy like *The Siege* would be made about the internment of Japanese- or Jewish-Americans.)

Oh, the movie tries to temper its material. "They love this country as much as we do," one American says in the film, unaware of the irony in the "they" and "we." The hero, an African-American played by Denzel Washington, has an Arab-American partner (Tony Shalhoub) who is angered when his own son is mistreated. The heroine, a U.S. spy played by Annette Bening, grew up in Lebanon and has an Arab-American lover (although it's a little more complicated than that). But the bottom line is that Arab terrorists blow up New York buses, a packed Broadway theater, and FBI headquarters.

Martial law is declared, the army moves in, and Arabs are detained without any rights. There's cat-and-mouse stuff involving the tracking of Arab bad guys, the usual computer and satellite gimmicks, and suspenseful stand-offs and shoot-outs. The dramatic outdoor mob, action, and army scenes are well handled by director Ed Zwick.

I'm not arguing that *The Siege* is a deliberately offensive movie. It's not that brainy. In its clumsy way it throws in comments now and then to show it knows the difference between Arab terrorists and American citizens. But the prejudicial attitudes embodied in the film are insidious, like the anti-Semitism that infected fiction and journalism in the 1930s—not just in Germany, but in Britain and America.

Watching the film, I felt uneasy. Events like those in the film are familiar. The World Trade Center was blown up in real life, not in a thriller. We've recently fired missiles at suspected terrorist centers. *The Siege* opens with actual footage of President Clinton commenting on television about those missiles, and the film implies that he is the president during the events in the story. Given how vulnerable our cities are to terrorism, and how vulnerable Arab-Americans are to defamation, was this movie really necessary?

The movie awkwardly tries to switch villains in the third act, adding an Orwellian twist. Its final thrust is against a military mind-set that runs rampant over civil liberties. The FBI and its allies have a face-off with an American general (Bruce Willis) who becomes military commander of New York under martial law and has disdain for the Constitution. Denzel Washington has a good speech where he observes that the enemy doesn't have to destroy our liberties if we do it for ourselves.

By the end of the movie the filmmakers can truthfully say they tried to balance out the villains. But most audiences won't give it that much thought. They'll leave the theater thinking of Arabs (who are handled as an undifferentiated group), not of dangers to the Constitution—which can be dismissed as the fevers of one man (Willis), who is handled like a traditional megalomaniac. ("This is the land of opportunity," he tells Arab-Americans. "The opportunity to turn yourself in.")

Most people will not be watching a political movie, but a popcorn movie. They may even be a little restless during the speechmaking toward the end. They'll be comfortable with the Arab villains because that's what they've been taught on the news. True, at the present moment most of America's enemies in the world are Arab. But at one time or another, this country has been at war with the home nations of most of the major ethnic groups in America. And it was "we" who were at war—all of us. Japanese-Americans who fought in American uniform in World War II will not have to have the buried message of *The Siege* explained to them.

Simon Birch ★ ★ ★
PG, 110 m., 1998

Ian Michael Smith (Simon Birch), Joseph Mazzello (Joe Wenteworth), Ashley Judd (Rebecca Wenteworth), Oliver Platt (Ben Goodrich), David Strathairn (Reverend Russell), Dana Ivey (Grandmother Wenteworth), Beatrice Winde (Hildie Grove), Jan Hooks (Miss Leavey), Jim Carrey (Adult Joe). Directed by Mark Steven Johnson and produced by Laurence Mark and Roger Birnbaum. Screenplay by Johnson.

Simon Birch is an unabashedly sentimental tearjerker. Either you stand back and resist it,

or you plunge in. There was something about its innocence and spunk that got to me, and I caved in. A lot of that had to do with how likable some of the characters are. We go to the movies for a lot of reasons, and one of them is to seek good company.

The movie takes place in 1964, in a New Hampshire town that obviously had Grandma Moses as its city planner. It's about a friendship between two boys, one a gawky preadolescent named Joe, the other a dwarf named Simon who believes God has chosen him for a mission in life. The opening narration reveals that two of the characters will die during the course of the movie; that softens the shock when they do, and lets the entire movie play as bittersweet nostalgia. It's all framed in a flashback, as an adult Joe (Jim Carrey) revisits the scenes of his childhood.

Joe is your average kid. Simon Birch is not. Played by Ian Michael Smith with remarkable cockiness, he's the smartest person in Sunday school and possibly in town. He is very short and very cute, and very wise about the fact of his dwarfism. When Joe tells him a local girl finds him cute, he sniffs, "She means cute like a baby turtle is cute. Girls don't kiss baby turtles." How do you know? asks Joe. "I just know. If you were me you'd know too."

Joe and Simon are drawn together because they're both misfits. Joe (Joseph Mazzello) is a boy without a father; his mother, Rebecca (Ashley Judd), steadfastly refuses to name names. "I don't understand why she doesn't just tell you," Simon says. "You're already a bastard; might as well be an enlightened one." Rebecca is a sunny, loving mother whose one lapse has, if anything, improved her character.

The other key characters could all be from Norman Rockwell paintings. They include Simon's loutish parents, who don't like him; Rev. Russell (David Strathairn), the local minister; Grandma Wenteworth (Dana Ivey), Rebecca's mother; Miss Leavey (Jan Hooks), the Sunday school teacher who endures Simon's theological insights; and Ben (Oliver Platt), a man Rebecca meets on the train and brings home for supper. (The last time Rebecca met someone on the Boston & Maine, her mother recalls, she came home pregnant.)

Simon and Joe occupy a world of their own, swimming and boating and slipping invisibly around town. Simon's dwarfism doesn't prevent him from going everywhere and doing everything, and even taking his turn at bat in a Little League game; when he finally does get a hit, there are tragic consequences. Simon uses his size as a license to say exactly what he thinks on all occasions, loudly and clearly, as when Rev. Russell is asking God's help for a fund-raiser and Simon stands up on his pew to announce: "I doubt if God is interested in our church activities. If God has made the bake sale a priority, we're all in a lot of trouble."

All of this is a scene-raiser for the melodramatic climax, in which it appears that God has perhaps indeed made Simon a priority. There are people who will find Simon's big scene contrived and cornball but, as I said, it all depends on the state of mind you assign to the picture. I've been seeing a lot of silent films lately, in which incredibly melodramatic developments are a way of life: What matters is not that they're unlikely or sentimental, but that the movie presents them with sincerity, and finds the right tone.

The movie's a directorial debut for Mark Steven Johnson, author of the *Grumpy Old Men* movies. He seems to know his way around small towns and broad emotions. His story was "suggested" by the novel *A Prayer for Owen Meany,* by John Irving, unread by me, although no doubt much more complex and ambiguous; Johnson goes for a purity of tone that children may identify with as much as adults.

Many of the scenes depend on the screen presence of Ian Michael Smith, making his movie debut with a refreshing brashness. Working with the more experienced Joseph Mazzello *(Radio Flyer, Jurassic Park),* he projects the confidence of a very bright small boy who has been the center of attention for a long time, and has learned to deal with it. By surrounding the boys with very nice people (the Ashley Judd and Oliver Platt characters) and not so nice people (the minister, the teacher), Johnson creates a film so direct and engaging that cynicism wilts in its sunny spirit.

Simpatico ★ ½
R, 106 m., 2000

Nick Nolte (Vinnie), Jeff Bridges (Carter), Sharon Stone (Rosie), Catherine Keener (Cecilia), Albert Finney (Simms), Shawn Hatosy (Young Vinnie), Kimberly Williams (Young Rosie), Liam Waite (Young Carter). Directed by Matthew Warchus and produced by Dan Lupovitz, Timm Oberwelland, and Jean-Francois Fonlupt. Screenplay by Warchus and David Nicholls, based on a play by Sam Shepard.

Simpatico is a long slog through perplexities and complexities that disguise what this really is: The kind of B-movie plot that used to clock in at seventy-five minutes on the bottom half of a double bill. It's based on a Sam Shepard play, unseen by me. Since Shepard is a good playwright, we're left with two possibilities: (1) It has been awkwardly adapted, or (2) it should have stayed in Shepard's desk drawer.

The plot involves a kind of exchange of personalities between Carter (Jeff Bridges), a rich Kentucky racehorse breeder, and Vinnie (Nick Nolte), a shabby layabout who has been blackmailing him for years. They were once friends, long ago when they were young, and involved in a scheme to cheat at the track by switching horses. Vinnie has some photos that Carter would not want anyone to see, and that gives him leverage. This time, he interrupts Carter in the middle of negotiations to sell an expensive horse named Simpatico, demanding that he fly to California to get him out of a fix. Seems a supermarket cashier named Cecilia (Catherine Keener) is accusing him of sexual misconduct.

Oh, but it's a lot more complicated than that, and neither Cecilia nor her relationship with Vinnie is quite as described. Two other figures from the past also enter: Rosie (Sharon Stone), now Carter's boozy but colorful wife, and Simms (Albert Finney), once a racing commissioner, now a tracer of bloodlines. Students of *noir* will know that the contemporary story will stir up old ghosts.

Those who are not *noir* lovers won't be in the dark for long, since director Matthew Warchus and his cowriter, David Nicholls, supply flashbacks that incriminate some of the characters (although not, in this day and age, seriously enough to inspire the vast heavings of this leviathan plot). Nolte and Bridges are portrayed as young men by Shawn Hatosy and Liam Waite, a casting decision that adds to the murkiness, since Hatosy, who is supposed to be young Nolte, looks more like young Bridges, and Waite, who is supposed to be young Bridges, looks like nobody else in the movie. This theme is developed further, I suppose, as Nolte and Bridges subtly start to resemble each other.

It happens that I've just revisited a complicated *noir*, Roman Polanski's *Chinatown*, which also involves sexual misconduct in the past and blackmail in the present. One reason it works so well is that the characters seem to drive the plot: Things turn out the way they do because the characters are who they are. The plot of *Simpatico* is like a clockwork mechanism that would tick whether or not anyone cared what time it was.

A Simple Plan ★ ★ ★ ★
R, 123 m., 1998

Bill Paxton (Hank Mitchell), Billy Bob Thornton (Jacob Mitchell), Bridget Fonda (Sarah Mitchell), Brent Briscoe (Lou), Gary Cole (Baxter), Becky Ann Baker (Nancy), Chelcie Ross (Carl), Jack Walsh (Mr. Pederson). Directed by Sam Raimi and produced by James Jacks and Adam Schroeder. Screenplay by Scott B. Smith, based on his novel.

"You work for the American Dream—you don't steal it." So says a Minnesota family man early in *A Simple Plan*, but he is only repeating an untested theory. Confronted with the actual presence of $4 million in cash, he finds his values bending, and eventually he's trapped in a horror story of greed, guilt, and murder.

The materials of Sam Raimi's *A Simple Plan* are not unfamiliar, but rarely is a film this skillful at drawing us, step by step, into the consequences of criminal action. The central character is Hank Mitchell (Bill Paxton), who in a narration at the beginning gives us his father's formula for happiness: "A wife he loves. A decent job. Friends and neighbors that like and respect him."

His older brother, Jacob (Billy Bob Thornton), trapped in a lifetime of dim loneliness, would like to go out with a girl who really likes him, and someday farm the place they grew up on. Jacob's best friend, Lou (Brent Briscoe), basically wants to get by, get drunk, and hang out. Hank's pregnant wife, Sarah (Bridget Fonda), would like enough money so she could plan the week's dinners without checking the coupons in the grocery ads.

All of these dreams seem within reach when the three men stumble across an airplane that has crashed in a nature preserve. On board they find the body of the pilot, and a cache of $4 million in bills. "You want to keep it?" Hank asks incredulously. The others do. Soon he does too. It should be a simple plan to hide the money, wait until spring, and divide it among themselves. It's probably drug money anyway, they tell themselves. Who will know? Who can complain?

Hank is the smartest of the three, a college graduate. Jacob, bucktoothed and nearsighted, has never been very bright. Lou is a loose cannon. Can Hank keep them all under control? Some of the film's most harrowing moments show Hank watching in agonized frustration as the others make big, dumb blunders. Right after they find the money, for example, a law officer happens by, and what does Jacob do but blurt out to Hank: "Did you tell him about the plane? It sure sounded like a plane."

At home, Hank's wife, Sarah, at first agrees it would be wrong to keep the money, but she turns that moral judgment around in a snap, and is soon making smart suggestions: "You have to return some of the money, so it looks like no one has been there." All three men begin to dream of what they could do with the money. Then circumstances inspire one impulsive, reckless act after another—acts I will not reveal, because the strength of this film is in the way it leads its characters into doing things they could never have contemplated.

A Simple Plan is one of the year's best films for a lot of reasons, including its ability to involve the audience almost breathlessly in a story of mounting tragedy. Like the reprehensible *Very Bad Things*, it is about friends stumbling into crime and then stumbling into bigger crimes in an attempt to conceal their guilt. One difference between the two films is that *A Simple Plan* faces its moral implications instead of mocking them. We are not allowed to stand outside the story and feel superior to it; we are drawn along, step by step, as the characters make compromises that lead to unimaginable consequences.

The performances can only be described as

flawless: I could not see a single error of tone or feeling. Paxton, Thornton, Fonda, and Briscoe don't reach, don't strain and don't signal. They simply embody their characters in performances based on a clear emotional logic that carries us along from the beginning to the end. Like Richard Brooks's *In Cold Blood* (1968), this is a film about ordinary people capable of monstrous deeds.

Thornton and Fonda have big scenes that, in other hands, might have led to grandstanding. They perform them so directly and simply that we are moved almost to tears—we identify with their feelings even while shuddering at their deeds.

Thornton's character, Jacob, has never been very bright, and has watched as Hank went to college and achieved what passes for success. At a crucial moment, when his brotherhood is appealed to, he looks at his friend Lou and his brother Hank and says, "We don't have one thing in common, me and him, except maybe our last name." He has another heartbreaking scene as they talk about women. Hank remembers the name of a girl Jacob dated years ago in high school. Jacob reveals that the girl's friends bet her $100 she wouldn't go steady with him for a month. As for Fonda, her best moment is a speech about facing a lifetime of struggling to make ends meet.

The characters are rich, full, and plausible. Raimi's direction and the screenplay by Scott Smith are meticulous in forming and building the characters, and placing them within a film that also functions as a thriller. There is the danger that the theft will be discovered. The deepening hole of crime they dig for themselves. Suspense over the source of the money. Mystery over the true identity of some characters. And two confrontations in the woods—one suspenseful, one heartbreaking.

All of this is seen against a backdrop of Minnesota in the winter (Raimi's friends the Coen brothers, who made *Fargo*, gave advice about shooting and lighting in the snow). The blanket of snow muffles voices, gives a soft edge to things, underlines the way the characters are isolated indoors, each in their own warm refuge. Outdoors, in the woods, foxes kill chickens and men kill each other. Angry black birds scramble to eat dead bodies. "Those things are always waiting for something to die

so they can eat it," Jacob says. "What a weird job."

Simply Irresistible ★ ★ ★
PG-13, 95 m., 1999

Sarah Michelle Gellar (Amanda Shelton), Sean Patrick Flanery (Tom Bartlett), Betty Buckley (Stella), Patricia Clarkson (Lois McNally), Dylan Baker (Jonathan Bendel), Christopher Durang (Gene O'Reilly), Larry Gilliard Jr. (Nolan Traynor). Directed by Mark Tarlov and produced by John Fiedler, Jon Amiel, and Joe Caracciolo Jr. Screenplay by Judith Roberts.

Simply Irresistible begins with one of the more unlikely Meet Cutes in movie history: Sarah Michelle Gellar chases a runaway crab up the trouser leg of the man she is destined to love. She owns one of those restaurants where all the customers know each other, like in a sitcom. I was settling down for a slow ride when somehow the movie caught hold and turned into an enchanting romantic comedy about people who float to the ceiling when they kiss. It's *Like Water for Chocolate* meets *Everyone Says I Love You*.

Gellar plays Amanda Shelton, whose restaurant in New York's SoHo is failing fast. No wonder. She's not such a good cook. Then one day a mysterious stranger appears in her vicinity and brings a magical crab. Yes, a magical crab. And the beady-eyed little crustacean sets itself up in her kitchen and somehow casts a spell. She becomes a great cook. An inspired cook. A cook so good that when the guy with the trousers tastes one of her desserts, he falls in love. "We kissed in a vanilla cloud," he tells his secretary. "This fog—it was warm, and it was wet, and it was like you could see what we were feeling."

The movie is as light as a soufflé, as fleeting as a breath of pumpkin pie on the wind from a widow's window. It is about almost nothing at all, except for a love story, the joy of eating, and a final sequence in a room that looks blessed by Astaire and Rogers.

Sarah Michelle Gellar is the star of TV's *Buffy the Vampire Slayer* and was in the original *I Know What You Did Last Summer*, where she was slashed by the Groton's Fisherman look-alike—a wise career move, freeing her from the sequel so she could make this movie. She plays Amanda Shelton perfectly straight, as a woman who is depressed by how she used to be a bad cook and now she is a great one. (I am reminded of the story about Lawrence Olivier, who moaned after a great performance as Othello, "Yes, but I don't know how I did it!")

Her new love is Sean Patrick Flanery, as Tom Bartlett, the manager of a new gourmet restaurant in the Henri Bendel store. (The second-string romance is between the grandson of Henri Bendel and Tom's secretary. They kiss after eating one of Amanda's eclairs.) Gellar is lovable, but this isn't a movie where the ground shakes, maybe because most of the love scenes take place while the couples are in midair. Nor are there any sex scenes per se. It's all soft, gauzy romance—a Valentine in which the *idea* of great love is disembodied from the old rumpy-pumpy.

When Tom recruits Amanda to cook for the premiere of his new restaurant, the movie generates a scene of simple, pure delight. It's a tough crowd (food critics, sniffy socialites), but after the appetizer, they're weeping with joy. After the entrée, transfixed in ecstatic meditation. Then dessert is served. If there is a heaven, this is its menu.

Simply Irresistible is old-fashioned and obvious, yes, like a featherweight comedy from the 1950s. But that's the charm. I love movies that cut loose from the moorings of the possible, and dance among their fancies. When Woody Allen waltzed with Goldie Hawn on the banks of the Seine and she floated in the air and just stayed up there, my heart danced too. And the closing scenes of *Simply Irresistible* are like that. It's not a great movie. But it's a charmer.

Six Days, Seven Nights ★ ★ ½
PG-13, 101 m., 1998

Harrison Ford (Quinn Harris), Anne Heche (Robin Monroe), David Schwimmer (Frank Martin), Jacqueline Obradors (Angelica), Temuera Morrison (Jager), Allison Janney (Marjorie), Douglas Westoh (Phillippe), Cliff Curtis (Kip). Directed by Ivan Reitman and produced by Reitman, Wallis Nicita, and Roger Birnbaum. Screenplay by Michael Browning.

Whenever pirates turn up in a romance set more recently than 1843, you figure the filmmakers ran out of ideas. *Six Days, Seven Nights* illustrates that principle. It's the kind of movie that provides diversion for the idle channel-surfer but isn't worth a trip to the theater. A lot of it seems cobbled together out of spare parts.

Harrison Ford and Anne Heche costar in an Opposites Attract formula that strands them on a South Pacific island. He once owned his own business, but simplified his life by moving to paradise as a charter pilot. She's a high-powered New York magazine editor (the third this month; Tina Brown should collect royalties). Heche and her would-be fiancé (David Schwimmer) arrive on the tropical isle, he proposes marriage, she accepts—and then hires Ford to fly her over to Tahiti for an emergency photo shoot.

When their plane crash-lands on an uninhabited island in a thunderstorm, Ford and Heche are thrown together in a fight for survival. (I would like to know what Ford's thoughts were in the scene where he dresses up in palm fronds to hunt birds). Back on the resort island, Schwimmer and Ford's friendly masseuse, an island seductress played by Jacqueline Obradors, mourn their missing lovers and seek consolation, or something, in each other's arms.

The screenplay by Michael Browning has little interest in the characters—certainly not enough to provide them with a movie's worth of conversation. It's devised along standard formula lines, and so desperate for a crisis that pirates conveniently materialize on two occasions simply to give the movie something to be about. If you want to see a movie that knows what to do with a man, a woman, and an island, see John Huston's *Heaven Knows, Mr. Allison*, in which Robert Mitchum and Deborah Kerr create atmosphere where Ford and Heche create only weather.

Not that they aren't pleasant enough to watch. Ford has a nice early drunk scene where he avoids the usual clichés and gives us a man who gets thoughtful and analytical in a sloshed sort of way. Heche is plucky and has unforced charm, and does a great job of looking searchingly into Ford's eyes while he talks to her. Meanwhile, Schwimmer and Obradors provide counterpoint, mirroring in low comedy what the stars are doing at a more elevated level.

Harrison Ford has an easy appeal in movies like this, and never pushes too hard. Anne Heche plays a nice duet with him. But their adventures on the island are like the greatest hits from other movies *(Butch Cassidy, Flight of the Phoenix)*, and when they have a couple of well-written dialogue scenes toward the end, you wonder why two intelligent people like these need pirates in their movie.

The Sixth Sense ★ ★ ★
PG-13, 106 m., 1999

Bruce Willis (Malcolm Crowe), Haley Joel Osment (Cole Sear), Toni Collette (Lynn Sear), Olivia Williams (Anna Crowe), Trevor Morgan (Tommy Tammisimo), Donnie Wahlberg (Vincent Gray), Peter Tambakis (Darren), Jeffrey Zubernis (Bobby), Bruce Norris (Stanley Cunningham). Directed by M. Night Shyamalan and produced by Frank Marshall, Kathleen Kennedy, and Barry Mendel. Screenplay by Shyamalan.

The Sixth Sense isn't a thriller in the modern sense, but more of a ghost story of the sort that flourished years ago, when ordinary people glimpsed hidden dimensions. It has long been believed that children are better than adults at seeing ghosts; the barriers of skepticism and disbelief are not yet in place. In this film, a small boy solemnly tells his psychologist: "I see dead people. They want me to do things for them." He seems to be correct.

The psychologist is Malcolm Crowe (Bruce Willis), who is shot by an intruder one night in his home—a man who had been his patient years earlier and believes he was wrongly treated. The man then turns the gun on himself. "The next fall," as the subtitles tell us, we see Crowe mended in body but perhaps not in spirit, as he takes on a new case, a boy named Cole Sear (Haley Joel Osment) who exhibits some of the same problems as the patient who shot at him. Maybe this time he can get it right.

The film shows us things adults do not see. When Cole's mother (Toni Collette) leaves the kitchen for just a second and comes back in the room, all of the doors and drawers are open. At school, he tells his teacher, "They used to hang people here." When the teacher wonders how Cole could possibly know things like that, he helpfully tells him, "When you were a boy they called you Stuttering Stanley."

It is Crowe's task to reach this boy and heal him, if healing is indeed what he needs. Perhaps he is calling for help; he knows the Latin for, "From out of the depths I cry unto you, oh Lord!" Crowe doesn't necessarily believe the boy's stories, but Crowe himself is suffering, in part because his wife, once so close, now seems to be drifting into an affair and doesn't seem to hear him when he talks to her. The boy tells him, "Talk to her when she's asleep. That's when she'll hear you."

Using an "as if" approach to therapy, Crowe asks Cole, "What do you think the dead people are trying to tell you?" This is an excellent question, seldom asked in ghost stories, where the heroes are usually so egocentric they think the ghosts have gone to all the trouble of appearing simply so the heroes can see them. Cole has some ideas. Crowe wonders whether the ideas aren't sound even if there aren't really ghosts.

Bruce Willis often finds himself in fantasies and science-fiction films. Perhaps he fits easily into them because he is so down-to-earth. He rarely seems ridiculous, even when everything else on the screen is absurd (see *Armageddon*), because he never overreaches; he usually plays his characters flat and matter-of-fact. Here there is a poignancy in his bewilderment. The film opened with the mayor presenting him with a citation, and that moment precisely marks the beginning of his professional decline. He goes down with a sort of doomed dignity.

Haley Joel Osment, his young costar, is a very good actor in a film where his character possibly has more lines than anyone else. He's in most of the scenes, and he has to *act* in them—this isn't a role for a cute kid who can stand there and look solemn in reaction shots. There are fairly involved dialogue passages between Willis and Osment that require good timing, reactions, and the ability to listen. Osment is more than equal to them. And although the tendency is to notice how good he is, not every adult actor can play heavy dramatic scenes with a kid and not seem to condescend (or, even worse, to be subtly coaching and leading him). Willis can. Those scenes give the movie its weight and make it as convincing as, under the circumstances, it can possibly be.

I have to admit I was blindsided by the ending. The solution to many of the film's puzzlements is right there in plain view, and the movie hasn't cheated, but the very boldness of the storytelling carried me right past the crucial hints and right through to the end of the film, where everything takes on an intriguing new dimension. The film was written and directed by M. Night Shyamalan, whose previous film, *Wide Awake,* was also about a little boy with a supernatural touch; he mourned his dead grandfather and demanded an explanation from God. I didn't think that one worked. *The Sixth Sense* has a kind of calm, sneaky self-confidence that allows it to take us down a strange path intriguingly.   ☞

The Skulls ★

PG-13, 107 m., 2000

Joshua Jackson (Luke McNamara), Paul Walker (Caleb Mandrake), Hill Harper (Will Beckford), Leslie Bibb (Chloe), Christopher McDonald (Martin Lombard), Steve Harris (Detective Sparrow), William Petersen (Ames Levritt), Craig T. Nelson (Litten Mandrake). Directed by Rob Cohen and produced by Neal H. Moritz and John Pogue. Screenplay by Pogue.

I would give a great deal to be able to see *The Skulls* on opening night in New Haven in a movie theater full of Yale students, with gales of laughter rolling at the screen. It isn't a comedy, but that won't stop anyone. *The Skulls* is one of the great howlers, a film that bears comparison, yes, with *The Greek Tycoon* or even *The Scarlet Letter.* It's so ludicrous in so many different ways it achieves a kind of forlorn grandeur. It's in a category by itself.

The movie claims to rip the lid off a secret campus society named the Skulls, which is obviously inspired by the Yale society known as Skull and Bones. The real Skull and Bones has existed for two centuries, and has counted presidents, tycoons, and CIA founders among its alumni. Membership was an honor—until now. After seeing this movie, members are likely to sneak out of the theater through the lavatory windows.

The story: Luke McNamara (Joshua Jackson) attends a university that is never mentioned by name (clues: It is in New Haven and has a lot of big Y's painted on its walls.). He is a townie, rides a bike, lost his father when he was one, is poor, works in the cafeteria. Yet he's tapped for membership in the Skulls because he is a star on the varsity rowing crew.

Luke's best friends are a black student journalist named Will Beckford (Hill Harper) and a rich girl named Chloe (Leslie Bibb). Luke secretly loves Chloe but keeps it a secret because "Chloe's parents own a private jet, and I've never even been in a jet." Another of Luke's friends is Caleb Mandrake (Paul Walker), whose father, Litten (Craig T. Nelson), is a Supreme Court candidate. With soap opera names like Caleb and Litten Mandrake (and Senator Ames Levritt), the film contains an enormous mystery, which is, why doesn't Chloe have a last name? I suggest Worsthorne-Waugh.

Luke is tapped for the Skulls. This involves racing around campus to answer lots of ringing pay phones, after which he and the other new pledges are drugged, pass out, and awaken in coffins, ready to be reborn in their new lives. They go through "revealing ceremonies" inside the Skulls' campus clubhouse, a Gothic monument so filled with vistas and arches and caverns and halls and pools and verandas that Dracula would have something along these lines if he could afford it.

Mel Brooks said it's good to be the king. It's better to be a Skull. Luke and his fellow tappees find $10,000 in their ATM accounts (later they get $100,000 checks). Beautiful women are supplied after an induction ceremony. They all get new sports cars. The Skulls insignia is branded on their wrists with a red-hot iron, but they get shiny new wristwatches to cover the scar. I'm thinking, how secret is a society when hookers are hired for the pledge class? Do they wear those watches in the shower? In this litigious age, is it safe to drug undergraduates into unconsciousness?

Each Skull is given a key to the clubhouse and a rule book. "There's a rule for all possible situations," they're told. I want that book. Rule One: Don't lose the rule book. Will, the journalist, steals Caleb's key and rule book and sneaks inside the clubhouse, and (I am now revealing certain plot secrets) is later found to have hanged himself. But was it really suicide? Luke thinks Caleb might know, and can ask him, because the Skulls have a bonding ceremony in which new members are assigned soul mates. You are locked in an iron cage with your soul mate and lowered into a pit in the floor, at which time you can ask him anything you want, and he has to answer truthfully, while the other Skulls listen to the words echoing through the crypt.

Many powerful adult men still take the Skulls very seriously. Not only Judge Litten Mandrake but Senator Ames Levritt (William Petersen), who are involved in a power struggle of their own. They put pressure on Luke to end his curiosity about Will's death. The following dialogue occurs, which will have the New Haven audience baying with joy:

"This is your preacceptance to the law school of your choice."

"I haven't even applied yet."

"Imagine that!"

Chloe is enlisted as Luke's sidekick for some Hardy Boys capers, but soon Luke is subjected to a forcible psychiatric examination at the campus health clinic (no laughter here), and bundled off to a mental hospital where, so far-reaching is the influence of the Skulls, he is kept in a zombie state with drugs while the senator and the judge struggle over his future. Oh, and there's a car chase scene. Oh, and a duel, in broad daylight, with all the Skulls watching, in an outdoor pavilion on the Skulls' lawn that includes a marble platform apparently designed specifically for duels.

The real Skull and Bones numbers among its alumni the two George Bushes. Of course, there's no connection between Skull and Bones and the fictional Skulls. Still, the next time George W. has a press conference, a reporter should ask to see under his wristwatch. Only kidding.

Slam ★ ★ ½
R, 100 m., 1998

Saul Williams (Raymond Joshua), Sonja Sohn (Lauren Bell), Bonz Malone (Hopha), Beau Sia (Jimmy Huang), Marion Barry (Judge). Directed by Marc Levin and produced by Levin, Richard Stratton, and Henri Kessler. Screenplay by Levin, Stratton, and Sonja Sohn.

Slam is a fable disguised as a slice of life, and cobbled together out of too many pieces that don't fit smoothly together. It's moving, but not as effective as it could have been. Inspired in part by the documentary *SlamNation*, it's the story of Ray, a Washington, D.C., prisoner whose life is transformed by poetry. And it also provides a glimpse of the world of competitive poetry slams, although Ray's story and the slam material don't seem to occupy the same level of intensity. Some scenes play like drama, others feel like they were grabbed documentary-style.

The movie stars Saul Williams, an effective actor, as Raymond Joshua, a young black man who is stopped by police who find four ounces of marijuana. He's innocent, he says, but he's advised by his public defender to cop a plea. That way he could get two to three years instead of up to ten. We can see he's stuck on the conveyor belt to prison, and a stern judge (played by former Washington mayor Marion Barry) gives him a weary lecture.

In prison, Ray's life is changed when he starts writing poetry and recites it one day in the prison yard, where the other inmates are (somewhat unconvincingly) transfixed. He attends a prison writing class, where Lauren, the teacher (Sonja Sohn), announces it's her last day: "They've cut this program." She is impressed by his writing and encourages him, and after he gets back on the street he finds her again, and enters her world of poetry slams. At one of them, she introduces him from the stage, and his poem is well received.

It's at about this point that the film loses its focus. Ray's arrest, conviction, and imprisonment were all filmed with realism. But the romance with Lauren seems out of another movie, and the scenes at poetry slams are awkwardly integrated: Either they weren't staged for this film, or the assistant director didn't have his extras under control.

Sometimes it works when characters are plugged into real events, but not this time. And having heard truly emotional, heartbreaking performances from slammers, I was underwhelmed by some of the material in this movie (the audiences, notoriously hard to please, are of course pushovers here).

The movie was made for about $1 million, but its shortcomings aren't because of the budget; they're because the director, Marc Levin, didn't decide clearly what level of reality to go for and stick to it. Better, maybe, to make a drama all the way through, and not unwind the tension with the semidoc poetry readings.

That approach would also have kept the focus on the relationship between Ray and Lauren, who are both well acted, and who are in an interesting dilemma: She's had hard times in her own past life, and while she wants to help an ex-con, she doesn't want to link her unfolding future to his problems. That Ray is a gifted poet doesn't make him an ideal mate.

There are issues lurking just out of sight here, but well known in the black community, about the shortage of eligible males and the reluctance of professional women to date beneath their economic level, but the movie doesn't really engage them. Lauren has some speeches that hint at what she's thinking, but then the movie dances away as if everything was simply a matter of the heart. We sense that Ray and Lauren are shaped more by the thousands of other relationship movies than by the specifics of their characters and their world. We sense their dialogue falling into the he-and-she patterns of screenplay formula—into the familiar rhythm in which attraction is followed by retreat and then by reluctant return and final acceptance.

To give the movie its due, there is an open ending, which is probably the right one; nothing is settled in Ray's life, and the movie doesn't try to squeeze a solution into 100 minutes. There is a lot of good material here, but unshaped and not sufficiently grappled with.

SlamNation ★ ★ ★
NO MPAA RATING, 91 m., 1998

A documentary directed and produced by Paul Devlin. Featuring Saul Williams, Jessica Care Moore, Beau Sia, Marc Smith, Mums the Schemer, Patricia Smith, Taylor Mali, and Daniel Ferri.

Poetry slams are a muscular verbal sport founded some twelve years ago in Chicago when a construction worker named Marc Smith got the idea of having poets read before a saloon audience. Their performances are graded from 1 to 10, like Olympic divers. The Green Mill, a tavern near Broadway and Law-rence in Uptown, is the birthplace of the slams, standing in relation to the sport roughly as Shakespeare's Globe does to drama.

Paul Devlin's SlamNation is a documentary about the 1996 National Poetry Slam, held in Portland, Oregon, with twenty-seven teams in the competition. The rules are simple: Four members to a team, every member must be a writer as well as a performer, no music, no props, no animal acts. There is a penalty for any poem that goes longer than three minutes. The judges are chosen from the audience. The performers are mostly dressed as if they're about to fix a leak in the basement.

Slams are nothing if not democratic. They are the only sport I'm aware of where the teams from Berwyn and San Francisco compete on the same field. (In 1996, Berwyn actually placed in the final four, led by its star, a slammer named Daniel Ferri, whose poem fiercely defends his baldness.) The documentary follows the New York team that eventually won the trophy (bronzed boxing gloves on a stack of books), and fielded four first-timers, including Saul Williams, who also stars in the fiction film Slam.

In evaluating the poetic content of the slams, one is tempted to take easy shots (poetry slams are to poetry as military music is to music?). Most of the material exists halfway between rap and Vachel Lindsay. Slams are essentially performance art, not literary art, and there is a shot of a New York book editor, sighing at his stack of slam manuscripts and observing that sometimes the poems don't translate well to the printed page.

Maybe that's because SlamNation, covering three semifinal rounds and the finals, inevitably focuses on the competition rather than the work.

I have had one personal experience of slam-style poetry, and it was unforgettable. In April 1998, at the annual meeting of the American Society of Newspaper Editors in Washington, D.C., the luncheon speaker was Secretary of State Madeleine Albright, who rattled off her speech as quickly as she could and hurried from the dais. Then the society's chairman called on a young woman to "give us one of your poems."

This was Patricia Smith, a friend of mine from her Chicago days, then a columnist for the *Boston Globe*. She performed a poem about a visit to a grade school class at which she asked, "How many of you know some dead people?" Almost every hand went up, she said, because all of these inner-city children knew dead people—many of them dead from drugs and gunshots. At the end a little girl thanked her for saying it was all right to know dead people. The girl was speaking of her own murdered mother.

This summary fails to capture the impact of Smith's poem, which surprised me to tears. I looked around the room and thought I had rarely seen so few words have such a strong impact.

Pat Smith, of course, was soon to get publicity of a different sort, when her paper accepted her resignation after she confirmed that some details of her columns had been made up. Making things up is not what a journalist is supposed to do, but it is what a poet is supposed to do. Seeing Smith again in *Slam-Nation*, as a member of the Boston team, I was reminded of the power of her words. She can see life and touch readers as few writers can. That is her vocation. Fiction and poetry exist to reach a different kind of truth. Maybe she had no business dealing with facts in the first place.

As for the other performers, I am prepared to believe that in context, uncut, seen as they should be, some of them have the same power. Others are basically soapbox orators with a new forum. In the cheerful anarchy of poetry slams, there is room for many styles. As a slammer named Jack McCarthy from Boston says: "You have to write one poem that everyone agrees is a poem. That qualifies you for your poetic license. After that, if you say it's a poem, it's a poem."

Slappy and the Stinkers ★ ★
PG, 78 m., 1998

B. D. Wong (Morgan Brinway), Bronson Pinchot (Roy), Jennifer Coolidge (Harriet), Joseph Ashton (Sonny), Gary LeRoi Gray (Domino), Carl Michael Lindner (Witz), Scarlett Pomers (Lucy), Travis Tedford (Loaf), Sam McMurray (Boccoli). Directed by Barnet Kellman and produced by Sid, Bill, and Jon

Sheinberg. Screenplay by Bob Wolterstorff and Mike Scott.

The opening moments of *Slappy and the Stinkers* filled me with shreds of hope: Was it possible that this movie, about five kids who kidnap a sea lion, would not be without wit? The story opens in music class, where the teacher (B. D. Wong) slogs through Gilbert and Sullivan while the kids in the chorus giggle at lines like "my bosom swells with pride."

A nice touch. And I liked the way the kids waved their hands desperately for permission to go to the washroom. That rang a bell. And the irritation of the teacher ("My big number is coming up!"). But the movie is not, alas, interested in continuing such social observation. It's really a retread of the *Little Rascals* or *Our Gang* comedies, in which lovable scamps—freckled, towheaded, and gap-toothed—get up to mischief.

The setup: The stinkers, so named because they're always in trouble, are poor kids on scholarship at a posh private academy. Everything they touch turns to trouble. In a long and spectacularly unfunny opening sequence, they attach a leaf blower to a hang glider and the headmaster's desk chair in an attempt to "go where no kid has ever gone before." The contraption of course goes exactly where the screenplay requires it to go for a long time after we have lost interest in whether it goes anywhere.

Then the kids sneak away for a visit to the aquarium. There they get involved with Slappy, a sea lion who passes a lot of gas and provides the kids with an excuse to say "fart," which, I recall from my own grade school days, is a word kids adore so much they are rarely happier than when saying it. The kids, who have seen *Free Willy*, decide Slappy should be stolen from the aquarium and returned to the sea, although they have some second thoughts: "There's Willy!" they say, seeing a familiar whale tail on the horizon. "Hey, don't killer whales eat sea lions?"

The spectacle of Willy making a meal of Slappy right in front of the horrified kids will have to wait, unfortunately, for the Leslie Nielsen version of this picture. The best horror *Slappy and the Stinkers* can come up with is an evil sea lion–napper named Boccoli (Sam McMurray), who dreams of Slappy starring in a circus act. Boccoli (who with just a little more trouble could have been called Broccoli) is an unshaven chain-smoker with a broken-down van, and a lot of stuff falls on him, and he falls on a lot of stuff. His function is to take a lickin' and keep on kidnappin'.

We actually see a snippet of the sea lion's circus act, in which Slappy jumps through a ring of fire. If you can visualize a sea lion, you might ask yourself, how easy would it be for one to jump through such a ring? The same thought occurred to me, and I studied the stunt closely. My best guess is that what we are actually witnessing is an arrangement between a catapult and a large black Hefty garbage bag.

Along with hilarities involving a cattle prod, and scenes in which it appears that Slappy has learned to understand, if not to speak, English, there are a lot of sight gags in the film involving the teacher getting slushy drinks in his face, and the kids getting peanut butter and jelly sandwiches on theirs, and many close-ups of the little tykes shrieking and trying manfully to get their tongues around the big words in the dialogue.

Yeah, but will kids like it? I dunno. I never much liked the Our Gang and Little Rascals movies. The kids seemed too doggone cute. The Bad News Bears were a lot more fun, but, mister, I've seen The Bad News Bears, and these ain't them.

SLC Punk! ★ ★ ★
R, 97 m., 1999

Matthew Lillard (Stevo), Michael Goorjian (Bob), Annabeth Gish (Trish), Jennifer Lien (Sandy), Christopher McDonald (Father), Devon Sawa (Sean), Jason Segel (Mike), Summer Phoenix (Brandy). Directed by James Merendino and produced by Sam Maydew and Peter Ward. Screenplay by Merendino.

When people adopt a fearful and aggressive personal style, we forget that somewhere inside, hidden by the punk look, the haircuts, the body piercing, the chains, the tattoos, or the gang regalia, is a person who basically just wants to be loved and understood. Telling the world to go to hell is often the response of people who believe the world has told them to go to hell.

James Merendino's SLC Punk! knows that, and the essential sweetness of its hero is what makes the movie more than just an attempt to shock. It's a memory of Salt Lake City in 1985, the high Reagan era, when Stevo and Heroin Bob are, as far as they know, the only two punks in town. They embrace the anarchism embodied in Sex Pistols songs (and there is a hilarious stoned explanation of chaos theory), but the depth of their rebellion can be gauged by the fact that Heroin Bob (Michael Goorjian) has never taken heroin, and has an irrational fear of needles.

Stevo (Matthew Lillard) narrates the film, which is a nostalgic tour of his world, done in much the same tone as Ray Liotta's voice-overs in Scorsese's GoodFellas. He explains, he theorizes, he addresses the camera directly, he identifies the various characters and cliques. His approach is anthropological. The Stevo character simultaneously stands inside and outside his world; he keeps an ironic angle on his rebellion, but can't see himself living the life of his father, a former "activist," who now explains, "I didn't sell out. I bought in."

Stevo is stuck in a limbo of parties, music, hanging out, long discussions, recreational mind-altering, and uncertainty. His dad wants him to go to Harvard ("If you want to rebel there, you can do it"). Stevo wants to go to the University of Utah, "and get a 4.0 in Damage." He stays in Salt Lake City and there's a flashback to explain how he got to his current punk state: We see a young Stevo in the basement, playing with Dungeons & Dragons figures, and the future Heroin Bob comes in with a tape, tells him D&D sucks, "listen to this," and leads him out of dweebdom.

Stevo's college career passes, more or less, in the movie's fractured memory style, and Bob's girlfriend Trish (Annabeth Gish) introduces him to Brandy (Summer Phoenix), who asks him, "Wouldn't it be more rebellious if you didn't spend so much time buying blue hair dye and going out to get punky clothes?" There are also details about Stevo's home life (his parents have divorced, his dad having traded in the old wife on a new Porsche), and about the improvisational style of days spent seeing what turns up next.

The film could have taken a lot of cheap shots at the Mormon culture of Salt Lake City, but most of its local details are more in the way of reporting than of satire. Stevo laments, for example, the problems involved in such a basic act as buying a six-pack of beer in a state where only low-alcohol 3.2 beer is sold, and the clerks in the state-owned liquor stores are all cops and phone in tips if you even look like you're thinking of doing anything illegal. There is also a debate with customers in a convenience store about the "curse on the land" and the imminent arrival of Satan. Here we witness something I have long suspected, that the exaggerated fascination with Satan in some religious quarters is the flip side of the heavy metal/Goth/satanic thing. Whether you worship Satan or oppose him, he stars in your fantasies.

Matthew Lillard is an actor easy to dislike, and no wonder, since he often plays supercilious twits. Here his performance dominates the film, and he does a subtle, tricky job of being both an obnoxious punk and a kid in search of his direction in life. He's very good.

In this season of blaming everything on the movies, a film like *SLC Punk!* will no doubt inspire knee-jerk moralists to deplore its depiction of an anarcho-punk lifestyle. But remember: A movie isn't about what it's about, but about how it's about it. What *SLC Punk!* is *really* about is Stevo's ironic distance on his lifestyle—about the way he lives it and analyzes it at the same time. The message isn't "live this way," but "look at the way you live." There's a little something there for all of us.

Sleepy Hollow ★ ★ ★ ½
R, 100 m., 1999

Johnny Depp (Ichabod Crane), Christina Ricci (Katrina Van Tassel), Miranda Richardson (Lady Van Tassel), Michael Gambon (Baltus Van Tassel), Casper Van Dien (Brom Van Brunt), Ian McDiarmid (Dr. Lancaster), Michael Gough (James Hardenbrook), Jeffrey Jones (Steenwyck), Richard Griffiths (Phillipse). Directed by Tim Burton and produced by Scott Rudin and Adam Schroeder. Screenplay by Andrew Kevin Walker and Kevin Yagher; based on Washington Irving's story "The Legend of Sleepy Hollow."

Tim Burton's *Sleepy Hollow* begins with a story that would not have distinguished one of the lesser Hammer horror films, and elevates it by sheer style and acting into something entertaining and sometimes rather elegant. It is one thing to see a frightened constable being taken for a ride in a carriage by a driver who has lost his head along the way. It is another to see the carriage bouncing down roads that have been modeled on paintings from the Hudson River School. This is the best-looking horror film since Coppola's *Bram Stoker's Dracula*.

It is not, however, titled *Washington Irving's Sleepy Hollow,* perhaps because the story has been altered out of all recognition from the Irving classic. Perhaps not. No power on Earth could persuade me to reread the original and find out. What it depends upon is Burton's gift for bizarre and eccentric special effects, and a superb performance by Johnny Depp, who discards everything we may ever have learned or thought about Ichabod Crane, and starts from scratch.

Depp plays Crane at the "dawn of a new century," he says, as 1799 rolls over to 1800. It is time to discard the barbaric torture of the past, he believes, and bring the legal system up-to-date, with improved methods of investigation and justice. He sees himself as a detective of the new order, and a New York judge, impatient with his constant interruptions, banishes him to the upstate hamlet of Sleepy Hollow, where there has been an outbreak of decapitations. Let him practice forensics there.

As Crane journeys north, the movie casts its visual spell. This is, among other things, an absolutely lovely film, with production design, art direction, and cinematography that create a distinctive place for the imagination. Not a real place—hardly a shot looks realistic, and some look cheerfully contrived—but a place in the mind. I loved the shot where mist extinguishes the torches that have been lighted by the night watch.

Burton's Sleepy Hollow is a dour place, the houses leaning together for support, the shutters slammed against newcomers. There is never a sunny day here. The faces of the village fathers are permanently frozen into disapproval. And the body count is mounting, while the head count stays at zero. The Horseman, it appears, not only decapitates his victims, but takes their skulls with him. "The heads were not found by the bodies?" exclaims Ichabod after his briefing on arrival. "The heads were not found—at all!" says a village elder. Snarls another: "Taken! By the Headless Horseman! Taken—back to hell!"

We meet some of the locals. Old Baltus Van Tassel (Michael Gambon), richest of the burghers. His comely daughter, Katrina (Christina Ricci), and her shapely stepmother, Lady Van Tassel (Miranda Richardson). And other local citizens, including one played by Jeffrey Jones, who always seems to be regarding us dubiously from above, at an oblique angle. The magistrate (Richard Griffiths) seems to know a good deal, at one point whispering to Crane that there are "four graves—but five victims!"

Crane dismisses it all as a case of superstition. He comes equipped with cases full of bizarre instruments of his own invention, including a set of eyepieces that make him look like the optometrist from hell. It becomes clear fairly quickly, however, that Ichabod is stronger on theory than practice, and has not much stomach for disinterring bodies, performing autopsies, or examining wounds. One head was "cut off—and the wound cauterized!" he exclaims, looking a little sick to his stomach. The locals explain that the Horseman's sword was forged in the fires below.

Johnny Depp is an actor able to disappear into characters, never more readily than in one of Burton's films. Together they created Edward Scissorhands and Ed Wood, and now here is an Ichabod Crane who is all posture and carefully learned mannerism, attitude, and fastidiousness. It's as if the Horseman gallops ahead in a traditional horror film, and Depp and Burton gallop right behind him in a satire. There's a lot of gore (the movie deserves its R rating), but it's not *mean* gore, if you know what I mean; it's gore dictated by the sad fate of the Headless Horseman.

The ending is perhaps too traditional. We know that the requirements of the genre absolutely insist on a struggle between Crane and the Horseman, followed by an explanation for his strange rides and harsh justice for those who deserve it. Burton at least does not linger over these episodes, or exploit them; he's too much in love with his moody setup to ruin the fun with final overkill. The most astonishing thing for me about the movie wasn't the Horseman anyway, but the fact that I actually found myself drawn into this old Classics Illustrated material—enthralled by a time and place so well evoked that the Horseman almost seemed natural there. ☞

Note: No power on Earth could drag from me the identity of the unbilled actor who plays the Horseman when he has a head. But you will agree he is the only logical choice.

Sliding Doors ★ ★
PG-13, 105 m., 1998

Gwyneth Paltrow (Helen), John Hannah (James), John Lynch (Gerry), Jeanne Tripplehorn (Lydia), Zara Turner (Anna), Douglas McFerran (Russell), Paul Brightwell (Clive), Nina Young (Claudia). Directed by Peter Howitt and produced by Sydney Pollack, Philippa Braithwaite, and William Horberg. Screenplay by Howitt.

Sliding Doors uses parallel time lines to explore the different paths that a woman's life might take after she does, and doesn't, find her lover in bed with another woman. I submit that there is a simple test to determine whether this plot can work: Is either time line interesting in itself? If not, then no amount of shifting back and forth between them can help. And I fear they are not.

The movie stars Gwyneth Paltrow as Helen, a London publicity executive who is fired for no good reason, and stalks out of her office in midmorning to take the underground train back home. In one scenario, she catches the train. In the other, she misses it because she's delayed, and the doors slide shut in her face. To save confusion, we will call these Scenarios A and B.

In A, Helen arrives home unexpectedly and finds her lover, Gerry (John Lynch), in the sack with his mistress, Lydia (Jeanne Tripplehorn). She confronts them, walks out, goes to a bar to get drunk, and runs into James (John Hannah).

James recognizes her, because earlier he chatted her up on the train. Over the course of the next few days, Helen A is comforted by her best friend, gets her long hair cut and dyed blond, and begins to fall in love with James.

In Scenario B, Helen misses the train, and by the time she arrives home Lydia is already off the scene. But she begins to suspect things when she realizes two brandy glasses were on the dresser. Eventually Helen B finds out about Lydia, who is the kind of woman who gets a sadistic satisfaction out of popping up unexpectedly and threatening to blow Gerry's cover.

The film cuts backs and forth between A and B. It is clear that Gerry is a creep, Lydia is a Fatal Attraction, and James is a thoroughly nice bloke, although of course the requirements of Screenwriting 101 force the movie into a manufactured crisis in which it appears that James may have been lying to Helen A. There's even one of those scenes that madden me, in which James goes to Helen A's best friend's house, is informed of the misunderstanding, could say two or three words to clear it all up—but doesn't, because he is a puppet of the plot.

Gwyneth Paltrow is engaging as the two Helens, and I have no complaints about her performance. Pity about the screenplay. It requires her to appear to be unobservant, gullible, and absentminded as the faithless Gerry hems and haws through absurdly contrived emergencies. The worst moment comes when he opens the kitchen blinds and Lydia is standing right outside them, staring at him, and he slams them shut and tries to pretend nothing happened. What we have here is a particularly annoying movie gimmick in which the other person (Lydia, in this case) knows exactly when and where to position herself to create the shock effect. We aren't allowed to wonder how many hours, or days, she was posted outside, maybe in the rain, waiting for him to open the blinds.

I am grateful that the movie provides Helen A and Helen B with different haircuts, which helps tell the story lines apart (a bandage is used in the early scenes). But as we switched relentlessly back and forth between A and B, I found that I wasn't looking forward to either story. True, James is played by Hannah with warmth and charm, but to what effect? Is he interesting as a person? Does he, or anyone in

the film, have much to say that's not at the service of the plot? I would have preferred Hypothetical Scenario C, in which Gwyneth Paltrow meets neither James nor Gerry, and stars in a smarter movie.

Slums of Beverly Hills ★ ★ ★
R, 91 m., 1998

Natasha Lyonne (Vivian), Alan Arkin (Murray), Marisa Tomei (Rita), Kevin Corrigan (Eliot), Eli Marienthal (Rickey), David Krumholtz (Ben), Jessica Walter (Doris), Carl Reiner(Mickey), Rita Moreno (Belle). Directed by Tamara Jenkins and produced by Michael Nozik and Stan Wlodkowski. Screenplay by Jenkins.

Slums of Beverly Hills was born to inspire a sitcom, and probably a pretty good one too. It's about a poor Jewish family that moves by night from one sleazy apartment to another, jumping the rent but always staying within Beverly Hills to take advantage of the educational system. Every move brings them into range of a fresh supply of wacky supporting characters.

The story's told through the eyes of Vivian (Natasha Lyonne), who will be a freshman in the fall, and is alarmed that her breasts have, in the words of her father, "sprouted overnight." Also sprouting is her sexual curiosity, which is enthusiastically encouraged by Eliot (Kevin Corrigan), the kid who lives across the hall of the latest pastel flea trap they've moved into. "I dropped out of school because I wanted to join the workforce," he tells her. "Doing what?" "Selling pot."

Dad is Murray Abramovitz, a sixty-five-year-old car salesman played by Alan Arkin as a man who seems to believe that if he had to have kids when he was fifty, he deserves everything he got. There are two boys in the family: Vivian's older brother Ben (David Krumholtz) and younger brother Rickey (Eli Marienthal), and they're all accustomed to being awakened at three in the morning and told to pack their stuff because the rent is due and, besides, Murray has found a "much nicer place that doesn't rob you blind."

Vivian thinks she hates her breasts. Her dad is always shouting at her to wear a bra, and the movie's best single shot is possibly the expression on her face when, under his orders, she puts on a bra under a skimpy halter top, creating a result more kinky than modest. "You've been blessed," the saleslady at the bra counter tells her. "Breasts are wonderful. You'll see."

She doesn't. But then life changes radically for the Abramovitzes when Rita (Marisa Tomei), the troubled daughter of Murray's rich brother, comes to stay with them. She's just gone over the wall of a rehab center, she's pregnant, and she enlists Vivian to help her deal with the rat who got her pregnant—an actor who does "Man of La Mancha" as a one-man show.

You can see the sitcom possibilities. The film, written and directed by Tamara Jenkins, is pitched pretty firmly at that level of ambition: broadly drawn characters, quick one-liners, squabbling family members, lots of sex. Yet it also has a certain sweetness, a good-hearted feeling for this family, which stays together and plugs away.

Alan Arkin is the key to the good feelings. He is a poor provider but a good father, who may skip out on the rent and be a lousy car salesman, but insists that his kids do their homework. One senses that his kids will grow up to be all right. Then there's his rich brother Mickey (Carl Reiner), who starts paying the rent in return for Murray taking his troublesome daughter off his hands. Mickey makes lots of money but has no class, and there's a painful scene in an airport restaurant where he blurts out crass insults, and Murray—who has been taking his handouts all his life—decides he's had enough.

Natasha Lyonne has the film's most important role, and is the key to the comedy. She does a good job of looking incredulous, and there's a lot in her life to be incredulous about. She also has a nice pragmatic approach to sexuality, as in a scene where she consults a plastic surgeon about on-the-spot breast reduction.

There are a couple of scenes that simply don't work, and the worst involves some tentative fooling around between Murray and Rita. I didn't believe it, I didn't like the way it played, and I think it should have been cut from the movie. It spoils the tone and introduces material that has no place in a story like this. The movie also grinds to a halt when Murray calls a black waiter "Jackson." Not funny, and not likely. But basically I enjoyed *Slums of Beverly Hills*—for the wisecracking, for the family squabbles, for the notion of squatters who stake a claim in a Beverly Hills where money, after all, is not the only currency.

Small Soldiers ★ ★ ½
PG-13, 110 m., 1998

David Cross (Irwin Wayfair), Jay Mohr (Larry Benson), Alexandra Wilson (Ms. Kegel), Denis Leary (Gil Mars), Gregory Smith (Alan Abernathy), Gregory Itzin (Mr. Florens), Dick Miller (Joe), Kirsten Dunst (Christy Fimple). Directed by Joe Dante and produced by Michael Finnell and Colin Wilson. Screenplay by Gavin Scott, Adam Rifkin, Ted Elliott, and Terry Rossio.

Small Soldiers is a family picture on the outside, and a mean, violent action picture on the inside. Since most of the violence happens to toys, I guess we're supposed to give it a pass, but I dunno: The toys are presented as individuals who can think for themselves, and there are believable heroes and villains among them. For smaller children, this could be a terrifying experience.

It's rated PG-13, but if the characters were human the movie would be a hard "R," just for the scene where characters get run over and chewed up by a lawn mower. I was a little amazed, indeed, by the whole concluding sequence, in which fireballs are lobbed, toy helicopters attack, and there's a struggle high in the air between killer toys and the movie's young hero, who are trying to electrocute each other. This is not a sequence a lot of grade-schoolers are ready for.

The movie's premise is intriguing. A toy company is purchased by a defense manufacturer, and the tough-skinned new owner (Denis Leary) orders his people to make "toys that actually do what they do in the commercials." Toys with batteries that don't run down, and minds of their own. His designers take him at his word and develop lines of toys using the company's X-1000 computer chip, which is also the brains of smart bombs and other military technology.

When these toys get into the marketplace, it's war. The toy characters are divided into two camps, the peaceful and zany Gorgonites and the professional killers of the Commando

Elite. The problem is with the commandos, who are humorless martinets that strut through the movie looking like mercenaries and making threats like pro wrestlers. They are truly evil, and they throw off the movie's moral balance.

A lot of the other stuff in the movie is funny and entertaining, and, to be fair, all of the special effects are top drawer, seamlessly combining live action, models, and animation. (Industrial Light and Magic supplied some of them, and the figures were designed by Stan Winston.)

The Gorgonites are led by a pensive, thoughtful Yoda-figure named Archer (voice of Frank Langella). They include little guys who kind of grow on you, including Ocula, who is basically an eyeball with three limbs. The Commando Elite have names like Chip Hazard and Butch Meathook. One of the inside jokes is that many of their voices were supplied by veterans of the *Dirty Dozen*, while the Gorgonites are voiced by actors from *This Is Spinal Tap*.

The movie's human hero is Alan (Gregory Smith), a kid who inadvertently sets off the toy wars. His new girlfriend is Christy (Kirsten Dunst), who gets a shock when she sees Barbie-type dolls being fitted with X-1000 chips so that they can join the battle too. Among the adults are Alan's parents, who are taken out of action after the commandos use a mousetrap as a catapult to drop sleeping pills into their drinks.

Part of the inspiration for *Small Soldiers* may have come from *Toy Story*, where toy soldiers were among the characters. But too much of it may have come from Sid, the human kid in that movie who lived next door, and entertained himself by taking his toys apart and reassembling them in grotesque ways. In *Small Soldiers*, toys have unspeakable things happen to them, and many of them end up looking like horror props. Chip Hazard meets an especially gruesome end.

What bothered me most about *Small Soldiers* is that it didn't tell me where to stand—what attitude to adopt. In movies for adults, I like that quality. But here is a movie being sold to kids, with a lot of toy tie-ins and ads on the children's TV channels. Below a certain age, they like to know what they can count on. When Barbie clones are being sliced and diced

by a lawn mower, are they going to understand the satirical purpose?

Roy Rogers's death earlier this year reminded me of how gentle and innocent his movies were. Sure, we called them "shoot-'em-ups," but Roy spent more time singing than shooting. Kids didn't leave the theater in a state of shock. Now they go to a kiddie movie, and there are scenes where toy characters are disemboweled and vivisected, and body parts crawl around in the street, separated from each other. Then there are other scenes that are perfectly innocent. We get two movies for the price of one. The nice movie would have been enough.

Small Time Crooks ★ ★ ★
PG, 95 m., 2000

Woody Allen (Ray Winkler), Tracey Ullman (Frenchy), Hugh Grant (David), Michael Rapaport (Denny), Tony Darrow (Tommy), Elaine May (May), Jon Lovitz (Benny), Elaine Stritch (Chi Chi Potter). Directed by Woody Allen and produced by Jean Doumanian.

Small Time Crooks is a flat-out comedy from Woody Allen, enhanced by a couple of plot U-turns that keep us from guessing where the plot is headed. Allen often plays two types of characters, intellectuals and dumbos, and this time he's at the freezing end of the IQ spectrum, as an ex-con and dishwasher with a plan to rob a bank. His wife, Frenchy (Tracey Ullman), is incredulous as he explains his scheme to rent a storefront and tunnel into the bank vault two stores down.

This looks a lot like the master plan in the Italian comedy *Big Deal on Madonna Street*, but in *Small Time Crooks* it's more of a false alarm. Ray and Frenchy open up a cookie store as a front for the heist, the cookies take off big-time, the heist is hopelessly bungled, and then Frenchy's cousin May (Elaine May) blabs to a cop about the tunneling in the basement. This leads indirectly to a franchise operation, and within a year Ray and Frenchy are rich beyond his, if not her, wildest dreams.

The first act of the movie has a lot of fun with Ray and his low-life criminal friends, including Jon Lovitz as a guy who has put his kids through college by torching buildings, and Michael Rapaport as a tunnel digger who wears his miner's cap backward, baseball cap style, so the light points behind him. If this heist idea had been spun out to feature length, however, it might have grown old and felt like other caper movies. Allen has a twist up his sleeve.

As millionaires, the Winklers put the nouveau in riche. Frenchy lavishes a fortune on their new luxury apartment, where Ray rattles around unhappily (he refuses to look at one abstract painting because it depresses him). At a housewarming, Frenchy offers her guests crudites (pronounced "CRUDE-ites") and adds, "They say I have a flair for decoration. This rug lights up." Ray follows behind miserably: "Show them your collection of leather pigs."

Then David (Hugh Grant) enters their lives. He's a British art expert, suave, a flatterer, and Frenchy wants to hire him to train them in culture. He quickly sees that Frenchy has "outgrown" Ray, and might be ripe for the plucking. He whisks her off on a whirl of gallery shows, opening nights, charity benefits, and chic restaurants, while Ray miserably seeks consolation in the simpler things: Knicks games, junk food, and the comforting company of May.

I've heard Woody Allen accused of making the same movie over and over, which is simply not fair. His recent films include an enchanting musical *(Everyone Says I Love You)*, a Felliniesque black-and-white social satire *(Celebrity)*, and the goofiness of Sean Penn's second-best jazz guitarist in the world, in *Sweet and Lowdown*. Now comes this straight comedy, with its malaprop dialogue ("I require your agreeance on this") and its sneaky way of edging from an honest bank job to sins like flattery, pride, and embezzlement.

Allen plays a blue-collar version of his basic persona, and has bracketed himself between two of the funniest women in America, Tracey Ullman, who is seen too rarely, and Elaine May, who is hardly seen in movies at all. The supporting cast is written more sharply than is often the case in comedies (where the star gets all the good lines), and there's a lesson lurking somewhere, about how money can't buy you happiness and may even cost you extra by losing it. Dumb as they (allegedly) are, the characters in *Small Time Crooks* are smarter, edgier,

and more original than the dreary crowd in so many new comedies. The movie opened on the same day as *Road Trip*. Now there's a choice.

Smoke Signals ★ ★ ★
PG-13, 89 m., 1998

Adam Beach (Victor Joseph), Evan Adams (Thomas Builds-the-Fire), Irene Bedard (Suzy Song), Gary Farmer (Arnold Joseph), Tantoo Cardinal (Arlene Joseph), Cody Lightning (Young Victor), Simon Baker (Young Thomas). Directed by Chris Eyre and produced by Scott Rosenfelt and Larry Estes. Screenplay by Sherman Alexie, based on his book *The Lone Ranger and Tonto Fistfight in Heaven*.

"It's a good day to be indigenous!" the reservation radio DJ tells his American Indian listeners as *Smoke Signals* opens. We cut to the station's traffic reporter, who scrutinizes an intersection that rarely seems to be used. "A big truck just went by," he announces. Later in the film, we will hear several choruses of a song about John Wayne's false teeth.

Smoke Signals comes billed as the first feature written, directed, coproduced, and acted by American Indians. It hardly seems necessary to even announce that: The film is so relaxed about its characters, so much at home in their world, that we sense it's an inside job. Most films about Native Americans have had points to make and scores to settle, like all those earnest 1950s white films about blacks. Blaxploitation broke the ice and liberated unrehearsed black voices, and now here are two young Indians who speak freshly, humorously, and for themselves.

The film opens in Idaho on a significant day: the Fourth of July, 1976. It's significant not only for America but for the infant Thomas Builds-the-Fire, who is saved by being thrown from an upper window when his house burns down at 3 A.M. He was caught in the arms of Arnold Joseph (Gary Farmer), a neighbor with a drinking problem, who is eventually kicked out by his wife (Tantoo Cardinal) and goes to live in Phoenix. He leaves behind his son Victor Joseph (Adam Beach).

And then, twenty years later, word comes that Arnold has died. Victor has a deep resentment against his father, but thinks he should go to Phoenix and pick up his ashes. He has no money for the journey, but Thomas Builds-the-Fire (Evan Adams) does—and offers to buy the bus tickets if Victor will take him along on the trip. That would be a big concession for Victor, who is tall and silent and has never much liked the skinny, talkative Thomas. But he has no choice. And as the movie settles into the rhythms of a road picture, the two characters talk, and the dialogue becomes the heart of the movie.

Smoke Signals was written by Sherman Alexie, based on his book *The Lone Ranger and Tonto Fistfight in Heaven.* He has a good ear for speech, and he allows his characters to refer to the real world, to TV and pop culture and the movies (the reserved Victor, impatient with Thomas's chatter, accuses him of having learned most of what he knows about Indians by watching *Dances With Wolves,* and advises him to spend more time "looking stoic").

There are references to General Custer and the U.S. Cavalry, to John Wayne and to U.S. policies toward Indians over the years, but *Smoke Signals* is free of the oppressive weight of victim culture; these characters don't live in the past and define themselves by the crimes committed against their people. They are the next generation; I'd assign them to Generation X if that didn't limit them too much.

If they are the future, Arnold, the Gary Farmer character, is the past. Victor nurses a resentment against him, but Thomas is understandably more open-minded, since the man did, after all, save his life. There are a few flashbacks to help explain the older man, and although they're brief, they're strong and well done: We see that Arnold is more complicated than his son imagines, and able to inspire the respect of the woman he was living with in Phoenix (Irene Bedard).

Smoke Signals is, in a way, a continuation of a 1989 movie named *Powwow Highway,* which starred this same Gary Farmer as a huge, gentle, insightful man, and A Martinez as more "modern." It, too, was a road movie, and it lived through its conversations. To see the two movies side-by-side is to observe how Native Americans, like all Americans, are not exempt from the melting pot—for better and worse.

The director, Chris Eyre, takes advantage of the road movie genre, which requires only a goal and then permits great freedom in the events along the way. The two men will eventually obtain the ashes, we expect, and also some wisdom. Meanwhile, we can watch them discover one another: the taciturn, inward man who was abused as a child, and the orphan who, it's true, seems to have gotten his worldview at secondhand through the media.

There's a particular satisfaction in listening to people talk about what they know well and care about. The subject isn't as important as the feeling. Listen to them discuss the ins and outs of an Indian specialty known as "fry bread," and you will sense what they know about the world.

Snake Eyes ★
R, 99 m., 1998

Nicolas Cage (Rick Santoro), Gary Sinise (Kevin Dunne), Carla Gugino (Julia Costello), John Heard (Gilbert Powell), Stan Shaw (Lincoln Tyler), Kevin Dunn (Lou Logan), Michael Rispoli (Jimmy George), David Anthony Higgins (Ned Campbell). Directed and produced by Brian De Palma. Screenplay by David Koepp.

If Brian De Palma were as good at rewriting as he is at visual style, *Snake Eyes* might have been a heck of a movie. He isn't, and it isn't. It's the worst kind of bad film: The kind that gets you all worked up and then lets you down, instead of just being lousy from the first shot.

Now about that first shot. It's wonderful. It's a Steadicam take that runs on and on, seemingly forever. Nicolas Cage is on-screen for almost every second of it, as a corrupt Atlantic City cop who scuttles backstage and ringside at a heavyweight championship. He shakes down a creep, he places a bet, he has a chitchat with his old friend who is in charge of security, he talks on the phone with his wife and kid, he shmoozes with a sexy blonde who sits down next to him, and he's sitting right in front of the secretary of defense when the man is assassinated.

I'd have to look at the film very carefully to be sure how long this uninterrupted single shot is; it's possible that De Palma has hidden a couple of cuts in the middle of swish-pans. No matter; he steals the crown here from the famous long takes by Scorsese in *GoodFellas* and Anderson in *Boogie Nights*, and it's virtuoso work, as the camera follows Cage up and down stairs and he never quits talking. Cage is wonderful, all the extras and supporting actors hit their marks right on time, the camerawork (by Stephen H. Burum) is perfectly coordinated, the energy level is high, there's great excitement, and I'm scribbling "terrific opening!" in my notes.

Alas, slowly at first and then with stunning rapidity, the movie falls apart. It has the elements for a good thriller, and De Palma still has some surprises up his sleeve, but it's a downhill slog.

The other key characters are played by Gary Sinise, as a navy officer who has taken over command of the security at the prizefight; Carla Gugino, as a woman with secret information she wants to deliver to the secretary of defense; and Stan Shaw as the defending champion.

A small cast, in a story using a structure De Palma has had fun with in the past, in films like *Blow Out* (1981). He shows an action and then repeats it from various points of view, adding information until a jigsaw of information falls into place. Occasionally we'll see a moment that doesn't seem to fit and then it will be explained later, and eventually the outlines of a conspiracy become clear.

There are nice ideas here, as when the Gugino character loses her glasses and has to flee from the bad guys without being able to see anything other than a blur. And moments when De Palma brutally rips up everything we thought we knew, and makes us start all over again. But there are also moments of dreadful implausibility. How likely is it, for example, inside a coliseum crawling with law enforcement, where thousands of fans have been forcibly detained, that no one would notice the heavyweight champ beating up a cop?

De Palma supplies one more fine shot, looking straight down through the ceilings of a series of hotel rooms until he finds the one he's looking for. But he's not on guard against lame dialogue, and at one point the desperate Gugino, looking for a place to hide and trying to convince a guy to take her upstairs to his room, actually says, "If you don't . . . I'll bet . . . somebody else will!"

Then comes an ending so improbable it seems to have been fashioned as a film school exercise: Find the Mistakes in This Scene. I can't describe it in detail without giving away too much of the plot, but imagine a grand climax in which a hurricane strikes Atlantic City and all of the key players find themselves standing outdoors in the middle of it, on live TV.

David Koepp, the writer, has been associated with some successful movies (*The Paper*, *Jurassic Park*, De Palma's *Carlito's Way*, and *Mission: Impossible*). What happened while he was writing this one? I would genuinely be curious to know how a professional screenwriter and an important director could both agree that *Snake Eyes* has a last act they're willing to sign their names to.

Snow Day ★ ½
PG, 90 m., 2000

Mark Webber (Hal Brandston), Zena Grey (Natalie Brandston), Schuyler Fisk (Lane Leonard), Emmanuelle Chriqui (Claire Bonner), David Paetkau (Chuck Wheeler), Chevy Chase (Tom Brandston), Chris Elliott (Snowplow Man), Jean Smart (Laura Brandston), Pam Grier (Tina). Directed by Chris Koch and produced by Julia Pistor and Albie Hecht. Screenplay by Will McRobb and Chris Viscardi.

Snow Day involves a very, very busy day in the life of an upstate New York teenager named Hal (Mark Webber), who is hopelessly in love with the unavailable school dreamboat, Claire (Emmanuelle Chriqui). He is, he believes, invisible to her, but that changes when a record snowfall forces the schools to close for a day, and gives him an opportunity to demonstrate what a unique and wonderful person he is—potentially, anyway.

The movie surrounds Hal with a large cast of supporting characters—too many probably for a two-hour movie, let alone this one that clocks at ninety minutes including end titles. There's his dad (Chevy Chase), a weatherman who resents having to wear silly costumes; and his mom (Jean Smart), a woman whose career keeps her so busy that she doesn't stop to smell the coffee, or enjoy the snow.

And, let's see, his kid sister, Natalie (Zena Grey), and his best female friend, Lane (Schuyler Fisk), and, of course Snowplow Man (Chris Elliott), whose hated plow clears the streets and thus makes it possible to go to school—not that these kids don't wander all over town on the snow day. In a film top-heavy with plot and character, Snowplow Man should have been the first to go; played by Elliott as a clone of a Texas Chainsaw gang member, he is rumored to have made the snow chains for his tires out of the braces of the kids he's run down.

The arc of the movie is familiar. Hal yearns for Claire and is advised on his campaign by Lane, the loyal gal pal who perhaps represents true love right there under his very nose, were he not too blind, of course, to see it. He has to struggle against a school wiseguy on a high-powered snowmobile, who claims Claire for his own, while his weatherman dad has to wear hula skirts on the air in a fight for ratings with the top-rated local weather jerk. There's also a hated school principal and a square DJ at the ice rink (he likes Al Martino) and the programming executive (Pam Grier) who makes Chevy wear the silly costumes.

One of the inspirations for *Snow Day* is the 1983 classic *A Christmas Story*, also narrated by the hero, also with a kooky dad, also with a dream (a BB gun rather than a girl). But that was a real story, a memory that went somewhere and evoked rich nostalgia. *Snow Day* is an uninspired assembly of characters and story lines that interrupt one another, until the battle against Snowplow Man takes over just when we're hoping he will disappear from the movie and set free the teenage romance trapped inside it.

Acting Observation: Chris Elliott comes from a rich comic heritage (his father is Bob of Bob and Ray), but where his dad treasured droll understatement, Chris froths with overacting. There's a scene toward the end where he's tied to a children-crossing sign and laughs maniacally, like a madman, for absolutely no reason. Why is this funny? He has gone mad? Always was mad? It is funny to hear him laugh? We look curiously at the screen, regarding behavior without purpose.

Observation Two: Chevy Chase has been in what can charitably be called more than his share of bad movies, but at least he knows how to deliver a laugh when he's given one.

(When his career-driven wife makes a rare appearance at dinner, he asks his son to "call security.") After the screening of *Snow Day*, I overheard another critic saying she couldn't believe she wished there had been more Chevy Chase, and I knew how she felt.

Third Observation: Through a coincidence in bookings, *Snow Day* and *Holy Smoke*, opened on the same day, and both contain Pam Grier roles that inspire only the thought, what's Pam Grier doing in such a lousy role? A year ago, she was in another lousy teenage movie, *Jawbreaker*. Is this the payoff for her wonderful performance in *Jackie Brown* (1997)? What a thoughtless place is Hollywood, and what talent it must feel free to waste.

Snow Falling on Cedars ★ ★ ★ ½
PG-13, 130 m., 2000

Ethan Hawke (Ishmael Chambers), Youki Kudoh Hatsue Miyamoto), Anne Suzuki (Young Hatsue Imada), Rick Yune (Kazuo Miyamoto), Max Von Sydow (Nels Gudmundsson), James Rebhorn (Alvin Hooks), Sam Shepard (Ishmael's Father), James Cromwell (Judge Fielding), Richard Jenkins (Sheriff Art Moran). Directed by Scott Hicks and produced by Harry J. Ufland, Ron Bass, Kathleen Kennedy, and Frank Marshall. Screenplay by Bass and Hicks, based on the novel by David Guterson.

Snow Falling on Cedars is a rich, many-layered film about a high school romance and a murder trial a decade later. The young lovers are Ishmael Chambers (Ethan Hawke), son of the local newspaper editor in a small Pacific Northwest town, and Hatsue Miyamoto (Youki Kudoh), daughter of Japanese-Americans. They meet at the time of Pearl Harbor, when feeling runs high against local Asians. Ishmael's father (Sam Shepard) runs editorials thundering, "These people are our neighbors," but then the U.S. government seizes their property and trucks them off to internment camps, in a shameful chapter of American history. Ten years later, Ishmael is editor of the paper, covering a murder trial. The defendant is the man Hatsue married in the camp.

Told this way, the story seems like crime and romance, but *Snow Falling on Cedars* reveals itself with the complexity of a novel, holding its themes up to the light so that first one and then another aspect can be seen. The style is crucial to the subject. The story unfolds in flashbacks, overlapping dialogue, half-understood events, flashes of memory, all seen in a variety of visual styles: color, desaturated color, black and white, even a little grainy 16mm. The look and sound of the film are not just easy flashiness, but match the story, which depends on the many different ways that the same events can be seen.

Above all there is a sense of place. Director Scott Hicks and his cinematographer, Robert Richardson, use a wide-screen canvas to envelop the story in trees and snow, rain and lowering skies, wetness and shadows. Rarely has a place been so evoked as part of a narrative. We sense that these people *are* neighbors partly because the forest crowds them together.

In this community the Japanese-Americans work as fishermen and shepherds, farmers and small-business holders, and their teenagers dance to the same pop tunes as everybody else. Yes, the races keep to themselves: Ishmael's mother disapproves of her son's friendship with Hatsue, whose own mother warns her against white boys. But boys with girls in love will fall, as e. e. cummings so simply put it, and Ishmael and Hatsue have a hidey-hole, a green cavern in the roots of a big cedar tree, where they meet to feel happy with one another. He asks her to marry him, and perhaps, if it had not been for the overwhelming fact of the war, this would have been a high school romance with a happy ending.

It is not, and in the early 1950s Ishmael covers a trial at which Kazuo Miyamoto (Rick Yune) is tried for the murder of a local fisherman whose body was found in some nets. He seems to have been bashed with a fish hook. There was bad blood between Kazuo and the victim; they fought a week before the death, and there is old bitterness involving the title to some land that was confiscated during the internment. The courtroom scenes pit a duty-bound prosecutor (James Rebhorn) against a tall, Lincolnesque defense attorney (Max Von Sydow), foreign-born, American to the core.

The movie slowly reveals its connections and motivations, which take on greater importance because the trial may result in all the relationships shifting again. If the husband is guilty, perhaps the teenage lovers can be reunited. Ishmael wants that, but does Hatsue? His resentment at being rejected even colors his coverage of the trial and his thinking about the accused man. We know Hatsue married Kazuo in the camps under pressure from her parents; does she love him? Is he guilty?

The only weakness in the film is its treatment of Kazuo, who is not seen in three dimensions but primarily through Ishmael's eyes. He is the man, after all, who has shared his life with Hatsue, and if they were married in the camps, well, people Ishmael's color put them there. Imagine the same triangle involving Jews and Nazis and see how it feels. We sympathize with Ishmael. Would we sympathize with a Nazi?

Because the movie is centered on Ishmael's point of view, Kazou is the interloper, the thief of love, and now probably a killer as well. From Kazou's point of view, which we can only infer, his society has put him behind barbed wire, discriminated against him, and now is rushing to a prejudiced judgment, while its representative stands ready to snatch away his bride. The movie never really sees him clearly. It places him over there at the defense table, or in long shot, objectively. It doesn't need him as a fully fleshed person, because he functions as a symbol and obstacle.

This may, however, be a weakness the film has to accept in order to get where it is going, because we need fears and confusions to make it more than just a courtroom drama. If we knew Kazou better, we might have a better notion of whether he could kill someone, and that would not help the story. In most movie trials we make fairly good guesses about guilt and innocence, but here there is real doubt, which plays against the bittersweetness of lost love.

And then there is the care given to the opposing attorneys, who are seen as quite particular people, especially Von Sydow, as Nels Gudmundsson, whose hands shake and whose voice sometimes trembles with anger as he defends the principles that drew him to immigrate to this land. The summation to the jury is a set piece in countless movies; rarely have I seen one better acted.

Snow Falling on Cedars is Scott Hicks's first film since *Shine,* the 1996 story of the pianist seized with paralyzing doubts. In both films he sees his stories as a whole, circling to their centers instead of starting at the beginning and trekking through. This film, written by Ron Bass and Hicks from the novel by David Guterson, is unusually satisfying in the way it unfolds. We don't feel the time structure is a gimmick; we learn what we need to know for each scene.

Some of them are of particular power, as when the Japanese-Americans are ordered from their homes by local authorities, told to take no more than will fit in a suitcase, and driven away to the internment "centers." We have seen scenes like this in stories about the Holocaust, and in parables of the future in which America has become a totalitarian state. Not everyone in the audience will have known it actually happened here.

A Soldier's Daughter Never Cries
★ ★ ★ ½
R, 124 m., 1998

Kris Kristofferson (Bill Willis), Barbara Hershey (Marcella Willis), Leelee Sobieski (Channe Willis), Jane Birkin (Mrs. Fortescue), Dominique Blanc (Candida), Jesse Bradford (Billy Willis), Virginie Ledoyen (Billy's Mother), Anthony Roth Costanzo (Francis Fortescue). Directed by James Ivory and produced by Ismail Merchant. Screenplay by Ivory and Ruth Prawer Jhabvala, based on a novel by Kaylie Jones.

You can sense the love of a daughter for her parents in every frame of *A Soldier's Daughter Never Cries*. It's brought into the foreground in only a couple of scenes, but it courses beneath the whole film, an underground river of gratitude for parents who were difficult and flawed, but prepared their kids for almost anything.

The movie is told through the eyes of Channe, a young girl whose father is a famous American novelist. In the 1960s, the family lives in Paris on the Ile St. Louis in the Seine. Bill Willis (Kris Kristofferson) and his wife, Marcella (Barbara Hershey), move in expatriate circles ("We're Euro-trash"), and the kids go to a school where the students come from wildly different backgrounds. At home, Dad writes, but doesn't tyrannize the family with the importance of his work, which he treats as a job ("Typing is the one thing I learned in high school of any use to me"). There is a younger brother, Billy, who was adopted under quasi-legal circumstances, and a nanny, Candida, who turns down a marriage proposal to stay with the family.

All of this is somewhat inspired, I gather, by fact. The movie is based on an autobiographical novel by Kaylie Jones, whose father, James Jones, was the author of *From Here to Eternity*, *The Thin Red Line*, and *Whistle*. Many of the parallels are obvious: Jones lived in Paris, drank a lot, and had heart problems. Other embellishments are no doubt fiction, but what cannot be concealed is that Kaylie was sometimes almost stunned by the way both parents treated her with respect as an individual, instead of patronizing her as a child.

The overarching plot line is simple: The children become teenagers, the father's health causes concerns, the family eventually decides to move back home to North Carolina. The film's appeal is in the details. It re-creates a childhood of wonderfully strange friends, eccentric visitors, a Paris which was more home for the children than for the parents, and a homecoming which was fraught for them all. The Willises are like a family sailing in a small boat from one comfortable but uncertain port after another.

The movie was directed by James Ivory and produced by Ismail Merchant, from a screenplay by their longtime collaborator, the novelist Ruth Prawer Jhabvala. She also knows about living in other people's countries, and indeed many of Ivory's films have been about expatriates and exiles (most recently another American in France, in *Jefferson in Paris*). There is a delight in the way they introduce new characters and weave them into the family's bohemian existence. This is one of their best films.

Channe and young Billy are played as teenagers by Leelee Sobieski and Jesse Bradford. We learn some of the circumstances of Billy's adoption, and there is a journal, kept by his mother at the age of fifteen, which he eventually has to decide whether to read or not. He has some anger and resentment, which his parents deal with tactfully; apart from anything else, the film is useful in the way it deals with the challenge of adoption.

Channe, at school, becomes close friends with the irrepressible Francis Fortescue (Anthony Roth Costanzo), who is the kind of one-off original the movie makes us grateful for. He is flamboyant and uninhibited, an opera fan whose clear, high voice has not yet broken, and who exuberantly serenades the night with his favorite arias. We suspect that perhaps he might grow up to discover he is gay, but the friendship takes place at a time when such possibilities are not yet relevant, and Channe and Francis become soul mates, enjoying the kind of art-besotted existence Channe's parents no doubt sought for themselves in Paris.

The film opens with a portrait of the Willises on the Paris cocktail party circuit, but North Carolina is a different story, with a big frame house and all the moods and customs of home. The kids hate it. They're called "frogs" at school. Channe responds by starting to drink and becoming promiscuous, and Billy vegetates in front of the TV set. Two of the best scenes involve a talk between father and daughter about girls who are too loose, and another, after Channe and a classmate really do fall in love, where Bill asks them if they're having sex. When he gets his answer, he suggests, sincerely, that they use the girl's bedroom: "They're gonna do it anyway; let them do it right."

A Soldier's Daughter Never Cries is not a textbook for every family. It is a story about this one. If a parent is remembered by his children only for what he did, then he spent too much time at work. What is better is to be valued for who you really were. If the parallels between this story and the growing up of Kaylie Jones are true ones, then James Jones was not just a good writer but a good man.

Sonatine ★ ★ ★ ½
R, 89 m., 1998

Beat Kitano (Murakama), Tetsu Watanabe (Uechi), Aya Kikumai (Miyuki), Masanobu Katsumura (Ryoji), Susumu Terashima (Ken), Ren Ohsugi (Katagiri), Tonbo Zushi (Kitajima), Kenichi Yajima (Takahashi). Directed by Takeshi Kitano and produced by Masayuki Mori, Hisao Nabeshima, and Takeo Yoshida. Screenplay by Kitano.

"Maybe you're too rich for this business," a friend tells Murakama, the stone-faced gangster hero of *Sonatine*. Murakama, who rarely says anything, has let it slip that he is tired. Very tired. When he is not actually engaged in the business of being a yakuza, he simply stops moving at all and sits, staring into space, sometimes with a cigarette, sometimes not.

He is tired of living, but not scared of dying, because death, he explains, would at least put an end to his fear of death, which is making his life not worth living. When he explains this perfectly logical reasoning, you look to see if he is smiling, but he isn't. He has it all worked out.

Sonatine is the latest film to be released in this country by Takeshi Kitano, who wrote, directed, and edited it—and stars in it under his acting name, Beat Kitano. It arrives here only a month after *Fireworks*, his 1997 Venice Film Festival winner, but was made in 1993, the fourth of his seven films. He is the biggest star in Japan right now, and as a filmmaker one of the most intriguing.

This film is even better than *Fireworks*. It shows how violent gangster movies need not be filled with stupid dialogue, nonstop action, and gratuitous gore. *Sonatine* is pure, minimal, and clean in its lines; I was reminded of Jean-Pierre Melville's *Le Samourai* (1967), another film about a professional killer who is all but paralyzed by existential dread.

Neither movie depends on extended action scenes because neither hero finds them fun. There is the sense in a lot of American action movies that Bruce Willis or Arnold Schwarzenegger enjoy the action in the way, say, that they might enjoy a football game. Murakama and the French samurai (Alain Delon) do jobs—jobs they have lost the heart for, jobs that have extinguished in them the enjoyment of life.

As the film opens, Murakama and his crew are being assigned by a yakuza overlord to travel to Okinawa as soldiers on loan to an ally who is facing gang warfare. They sense that something is phony about the assignment. "The last time you sent us out," Murakama tells his boss, "I lost three men. I didn't enjoy that." Murakama is correct in his suspicions: The district he controls has become so lucrative that the boss wants to move in and take over.

These yakuza live by a code so deep it even regulates their fury. Murakama administers a brutal beating to the boss's lieutenant, but they remain on speaking terms. Later, one yakuza stabs another in the stomach. Yet they sit side by side on a bus in Okinawa. "Ice cream?" says the guy who had the knife. "You stabbed me in the belly and it still hurts," the other replies, and we are not quite sure if he is rejecting the ice cream out of anger, or because he doesn't think it will stay down.

In Takeshi's universe, violence is as transient as a lightning bolt. It happens and is over. It means nothing. We sense that in a scene where three men play "paper, rock, scissors" to see who will get to point a pistol at his head and pull the trigger to see if there is a round in the chamber. We see it again in a chilling sequence where a gambler, who didn't want to pay protection, is dunked into the sea; Murakama gets into a conversation and almost forgets to notice how long the guy has been under. And we see it in the climactic battle scene, which is played entirely as flashes of lights against the windows of an apartment: Who else would have the wit, or the sadness, to leave the carnage offscreen?

Kitano was in a motorcycle accident a few years ago that paralyzed half his face. This film was made before the accident, but there's little difference between the way he appears here and in *Fireworks*. If ever there was an actor who could dispense with facial expression, he's the one.

The less he gives, the less he reveals, the less he says and does, the more his presence grows, until he becomes the cold, dangerous center of the story. And in his willingness to let characters languish in real time, to do nothing in between the moments of action, he forces us to look into their eyes and try to figure them out. Films that explain nothing often make everything clear. Films that explain everything often have nothing to explain.

Sour Grapes no stars

R, 92 m., 1998

Steven Weber (Evan), Craig Bierko (Richie), Jennifer Leigh Warren (Millie), Karen Sillas (Joan), Jack Burns (Eulogist), Viola Harris (Selma), Scott Erik (Teenage Richie), Michael Resnick (Teenage Evan). Directed by Larry David and produced by Laurie Lennard. Screenplay by David.

Sour Grapes is a comedy about things that aren't funny. It reminded me of *Crash*, an erotic thriller about things no one finds erotic. The big difference is that David Cronenberg, who made *Crash*, knew that people were not turned on by auto accidents. Larry David, who wrote and directed *Sour Grapes*, apparently thinks people are amused by cancer, accidental castration, racial stereotypes, and bitter family feuds.

Oh, I have no doubt that all of those subjects could be incorporated into a great comedy. It's all in the style and the timing. *Sour Grapes* is tone-deaf comedy; the material, the dialogue, the delivery, and even the sound track are labored and leaden. How to account for the fact that Larry David is one of the creators of *Seinfeld*? Maybe he works well with others.

I can't easily remember a film I've enjoyed less. *North*, a comedy I hated, was at least able to inflame me with dislike. *Sour Grapes* is a movie that deserves its title: It's puckered, deflated, and vinegary. It's a dead zone.

The story. Two cousins (Steven Weber and Craig Bierko) go to Atlantic City. One is a designer who wins a slot jackpot of more than $436,000. He was playing with quarters given him by the other guy. The other cousin, a surgeon, not unreasonably thinks he should get some of the winnings. If not half, then maybe a third. The winner offers him 3 percent.

This sets off several scenes of debate about what would be right or wrong in such a situation. Even a limo driver, hearing the winner's story, throws him out of the car: "You were playing with his money!" The losing doctor nevertheless gives his cousin a blue warm-up suit for his birthday, only to discover that the louse has given the suit away to an African-American street person.

So far all we have is a comic premise that doesn't deliver laughs. Now the movie heads for cringe-inducing material. We learn about the winner's ability to perform oral sex while alone. He's alone a lot because his wife is mad at him, but that's an opening for stereotyped Jewish mother scenes. The feud heats up until the enraged doctor lies to the winner: "You have terminal cancer. It's time to set your house in order." Ho, ho.

The winner wants to spare his mother the misery of watching her son die. So he gives her house key to the black bum in the warm-up suit and tells him to make himself at home. His plan: His mother will be scared to death by the sight of the black home invader. After she screams, we see the bum running down the street in Steppin' Fetchit style. Was there no one to hint to David that this was gratuitous and offensive?

Further material involves the surgeon getting so upset in the operating room that he reverses an X-ray film and removes the wrong testicle from a TV star—who then, of course, has to be told that they still had to go ahead and remove the remaining testicle. The star develops a castrato voice. Ho, ho.

This material is impossible to begin with. What makes it worse is the lack of lightness from the performers, who slog glumly through their dialogue as if they know what an aromatic turkey they're stuck in. Scene after scene clangs dead to the floor, starting with the funeral service that opens the film. The more I think of it, the more *Sour Grapes* really does resemble *Crash* (except that *Crash* was not a bad film). Both movies are like watching automobile accidents. Only one intended to be.

South ★ ★ ★

NO MPAA RATING, 80 m., 1915 (rereleased 2000)

A documentary featuring Ernest Shackleton, Captain Frank Worsley, Captain Frank Wild, Captain L. Hussey, Lieutenant J. Shenbouse, Frank Hurley, and Tom Crean. Directed by Hurley.

The most astonishing fact about *South* is that it exists at all. This is a documentary filmed in 1915 of Sir Ernest Shackleton's doomed expedition to the South Pole—a venture ending with his ship, *Endurance,* trapped in ice that eventually destroyed it, while he and five men made an 800-mile journey through frigid seas (and then scaled a glacier!) to bring help. That the expedition was filmed and that the film survived the shipwreck is astonishing.

South, which has now been restored, is essentially a home movie shot very far from home. The cinematographer, Frank Hurley, was a crew member whose approach is essentially to point his camera and trust to the subtitles to explain what we see. "Sir Ernest Shackleton, Leader of the Expedition," we read, while Shackleton poses self-consciously for posterity. Another title explains that a sick dog is being given medicine while the others look on enviously, thinking it's being fed. We see the crew member Tom Crean with a litter of puppies born onboard. Later, "Sulky, the black leader dog, trains the pups in harness."

Watching these images, we are absorbed, as we often are with silent film, in a reverie that is a collaboration with the images. We note how surprisingly small the *Endurance* is. How its crew of less than thirty become anonymous figures, bundled beyond recognition in cloth and fur, as they trudge across limitless snow. How the ship seems to be the only thing of human manufacture in the ice world. How later it is joined by another, as Shackleton tests a "motor sledge" which he thought might take the place of dog teams, but which had the unfortunate drawback of needing to be pushed by men or pulled by dogs. (And what dogs! There are breathtaking shots of them pulling a sled through snow powder almost over their heads.)

Some of Hurley's shots speak for themselves. It becomes clear that the worst Antarctic winter ever recorded will prevent the ship from reaching the point where Shackleton wants to drop off men, dogs, and supplies. Hurley and his camera hang from the prow of the *Endurance* as the ship opens up sudden, jagged cracks in the quickly forming ice. We see countless crab seals migrating north, as a title tells us a dismal season is on the way. We see the men building ice pylons to lead back to the ship because, in the storms of the Antarctic night, it is possible to become lost forever just a few yards from safety. And we see an astonishing sight:

The *Endurance* photographed in the middle of the polar night with the use of eighteen lightbulbs, which reflect off the ice on every line and mast to make it glitter like a ghost ship.

After the *Endurance* is locked in ice, the men use two-handed logger's saws to try to cut through. When the ship then backs up and tries to ram itself free, Hurley and his camera are positioned on the ice, dangerously close to the front of it, and we imagine them disappearing into a sudden fissure—but the ice holds, eventually breaking the rudder and then caving in the sides of the ship. The dogs are evacuated, skidding nervously to safety down a canvas chute. The camera watches as the *Endurance* tilts and dies, its masts toppling over.

There is, of course, no footage of the 800-mile journey in a small lifeboat that Shackleton completed to bring rescue (not a single man was lost from the expedition). But Hurley does show us the glacier they had to scale on South Georgia Island, in order to reach the inhabited far shore. And an albatross like the one that provided their first meal on land. They encountered "quaint birds and beasts," a subtitle tells us, and "these pictures were obtained with a good deal of time and effort"—an understatement.

There is probably too much natural history toward the end of the film; we see elephant seals while the fate of the stranded crew members hangs in abeyance. Finally all are united and cheered as they return to safety. The *Endurance* did not get anywhere near the South Pole, but the expedition did sail into legend—like Robert Falcon Scott's attempt in 1911–12, where he lost a race to the Pole to the Norwegian Roald Amundsen and died on the return, but far overshadowed the Norwegian's fame. Ironic, that the two most famous British South Pole explorers either failed to begin or died on the way back. (Kevin McCorry, a writer on polar expeditions, quotes Amundsen's laconic commentary, "Never underestimate the British habit of dying. The glory of self-sacrifice, the blessing of failure.")

The overwhelming impression left by *South*, however, is of the bravery of everyone who ventured to the Pole. These men did not have cargo planes to drop supplies, satellites to tell them their position, solar panels for heating and electricity, or even adequate clothing. But they had pluck, and Frank Hurley with his hand-cranked camera recorded them, still to be seen, specks of life and hope in an ice wilderness.

South Park: Bigger, Longer and Uncut ★ ★ ½
R, 80 m., 1999

An animated film with the voices of Trey Parker, Matthew Stone, Isaac Hayes, George Clooney, Minnie Driver, Mike Judge, and Eric Idle. Directed by Trey Parker and produced by Parker and Matt Stone. Screenplay by Parker, Stone, and Pam Brady.

The national debate about violence and obscenity in the movies has arrived in South Park. The "little redneck mountain town," where adult cynicism is found in the mouths of babes, is the setting for vicious social satire in *South Park: Bigger, Longer and Uncut*. The most slashing political commentary of the year is not in the new film by Oliver Stone, David Lynch, or John Sayles, but in an animated musical comedy about obscenity. Wait until you see the bedroom scenes between Satan and Saddam Hussein.

Waves of four-letter words roll out over the audience, which laughs with incredulity: People can't believe what they're hearing. The film has an R rating instead of NC-17 only because it's a cartoon, I suspect; even so, the MPAA has a lot of 'splaining to do. Not since Andrew Dice Clay passed into obscurity have sentences been constructed so completely out of the unspeakable.

I laughed. I did not always feel proud of myself while I was laughing, however. The movie is like a depraved extension of *Kids Say the Darnedest Things*, in which little children repeat what they've heard, and we cringe because we know what the words really mean. No target is too low, no attitude too mean or hurtful, no image too unthinkable. After making *South Park: Bigger, Longer and Uncut*, its creators, Trey Parker and Matt Stone, had better move on. They've taken *South Park* as far as it can go, and beyond.

If you've never seen the original Comedy Central TV show and somehow find yourself in the theater, you'll be jolted by the distance between the images and the content. The animation is deliberately crude, like elements cut out of construction paper. Characters are made of simple arrangements of basic geometrical shapes and solid colors. When they talk, their lips don't move; their entire heads tilt open in synch with the words. The effect is of sophisticated children slamming stuff around on the project table in first grade.

The story: A new R-rated movie has come to town, starring the Canadian stars Terrence and Phillip. It's titled *Asses of Fire*. (That's the mildest vulgarity in the movie, and the most extreme I can print in the paper.) The South Park kids bribe a homeless man to be their "adult guardian," attend the movie, drink in its nonstop, wall-to-wall language, and startle their class at school with streams of four-letter words.

One of their moms, deeply offended, founds the Mothers Against Canada (its acronym no doubt targeted at the cosmetics company). The neighbor to the north is blamed for all of the ills in U.S. society, Terrence and Phillip are arrested and condemned to death, and in retaliation the Canadian Air Force bombs the home of the Baldwin brothers in Hollywood. War is declared, leading to scenes your eyes will register but your mind will not believe, such as a USO show involving Winona Ryder doing unspeakable things with Ping-Pong balls.

The other plot strand begins after little Kenny is killed. (This is not a spoiler; little Kenny is killed in each and every episode of the TV series, always with the line, "Oh, my God! They've killed Kenny!") He goes to hell (we see Hitler and George Burns drifting past) and finds that Saddam Hussein, recently deceased, is having an affair with Satan. Saddam wants sex, Satan wants a meaningful relationship, and they inspire a book titled *Saddam Is from Mars, Satan Is from Venus*.

Key plot point: The deaths of Terrence and Phillip would be the seventh biblical sign of the apocalypse, triggering Armageddon. It's up to the South Park kids to save the world. All of this unfolds against an unending stream of satirical abuse, ethnic stereotyping, sexual vulgarity, and pointed political commentary that alternates common sense with the truly and hurtfully offensive.

I laughed, as I have reported. Sometimes the laughter was liberating, as good laughter can be, and sometimes it was simply disbe-

lieving: How could they get away with this? This is a season when the movies are hurtling themselves over the precipice of good taste. Every week brings its new surprises. I watch as Austin Powers drinks coffee that contains excrement, and two weeks later I go to *American Pie* and watch a character drink beer that contains the most famous bodily fluid from *There's Something About Mary*. In *Big Daddy*, I see an adult role model instruct a five-year-old on how to trip in-line skaters, urinate in public, and spill the french fries of complete strangers in McDonald's.

Now this—a cartoon, but it goes far beyond anything in any of those live-action movies. All it lacks is a point to its message. What is it saying? That movies have gone too far, or that protests against movies have gone too far? It is a sign of our times that I cannot tell. Perhaps it's simply anarchistic, and feels that if it throws enough shocking material at the wall, some of it will stick. A lot of the movie offended me. Some of it amazed me. It is too long and runs out of steam, but it serves as a signpost for our troubled times. Just for the information it contains about the way we live now, maybe thoughtful and concerned people should see it. After all, everyone else will. ☞

Note: Reading this again, I think it's more of a three-star review. The movie is unsettling, but that's a good thing; my doubts are a tribute to it.

The Spanish Prisoner ★ ★ ★ ½
PG, 112 m., 1998

Campbell Scott (Joe Ross), Rebecca Pidgeon (Susan Ricci), Steve Martin (Jimmy Dell), Ben Gazzara (Klein), Ricky Jay (George Lang), Felicity Huffman (McCune), Richard L. Freidman (Businessman). Directed by David Mamet and produced by Jean Doumanian. Screenplay by Mamet.

There are really only two screenwriters working at the moment whose words you can recognize as soon as you hear them: Quentin Tarantino and David Mamet. All of the others, however clever, deal in the ordinary rhythms of daily speech.

Tarantino we recognize because of the way his dialogue, like Mark Twain's, unfurls down the corridors of long inventive progressions, collecting proper names and trademarks along the way, to arrive at preposterous generalizations—delivered flatly, as if they were the simple truth.

Mamet is even easier to recognize. His characters often speak as if they're wary of the world, afraid of being misquoted, reluctant to say what's on their minds: As a protective shield, they fall into precise legalisms, invoking old sayings as if they're magic charms. Often they punctuate their dialogue with four-letter words, but in *The Spanish Prisoner* there is not a single obscenity, and we picture Mamet with a proud grin on his face, collecting his very first PG rating.

The movie does not take place in Spain and has no prisoners. The title refers to a classic con game. Mamet, whose favorite game is poker, loves films where the characters negotiate a thicket of lies. *The Spanish Prisoner* resembles Hitchcock in the way that everything takes place in full view, on sunny beaches and in brightly lighted rooms, with attractive people smilingly pulling the rug out from under the hero and revealing the abyss.

The hero is Joe Ross (Campbell Scott), who has invented a process that will make money for his company—so much money that when he writes the figure on a blackboard, we don't even see it, only the shining eyes of executives looking at it. ("The Process," he says. Pause. "And, by means of the Process, to control the world market." The missing words are replaced by greed.)

He works for Mr. Klein (Ben Gazzara), who has convened a meeting in the Caribbean to discuss the Process. Also on hand is George, a company lawyer played by Ricky Jay—a professional magician and expert in charlatans, who is Mamet's friend and collaborator. And there is Susan (Rebecca Pidgeon, Mamet's wife), whose heart is all aflutter for Joe Ross, and who is very smart and likes to prove it by saying smart things that end on a triumphant note, as if she expects a gold star on her report card. ("I'm a problem solver, and I have a heart of gold.")

To the Caribbean island comes a man named Jimmy Dell (Steve Martin), who may or may not have arrived by seaplane. We see how Mamet creates uncertainty: Joe thinks the man ar-

rived by seaplane, but Susan thinks he didn't and provides photographic proof (which, as far as we can see, proves nothing), and in the end it doesn't matter if he arrives by seaplane or not; the whole episode is used simply to introduce the idea that Jimmy Dell may not be what he seems.

He seems to be a rich, friendly New Yorker, who is trying to conceal an affair with a partner's wife. He says he has a sister in New York, and gives Joe a book to deliver to her ("Might I ask you a service?"). Joe has thus accepted a wrapped package from a stranger, which he plans to take on board a plane; you see how our minds start working, spotting conspiracies everywhere. But at this point the plot summary must end, before the surprises begin. I can only say that anything as valuable as the Process would be a target for industrial espionage, and that when enough millions of dollars are involved, few people are above temptation.

The Spanish Prisoner is delightful in the way a great card manipulator is delightful. It rolls its sleeves to above its elbows to show it has no hidden cards, and then produces them out of thin air. It has the buried structure of a card manipulator's spiel, in which a "story" is told about the cards, and they are given personalities and motives, even though they are only cards. Our attention is misdirected—we are human and invest our interest in the human motives attributed to the cards, and forget to watch closely to see where they are going and how they are being handled. Same thing with the characters in *The Spanish Prisoner*. They are all given motives—romance, greed, pride, friendship, curiosity—and all of these motives are inventions and misdirections; the magician cuts the deck, and the joker wins.

There is, I think, a hole in the end of the story big enough to drive a ferry boat through, but then again there's another way of looking at the whole thing that would account for that, if the con were exactly the reverse of what we're left believing. Not that it matters. The end of a magic trick is never the most interesting part; the setup is more fun, because we can test ourselves against the magician, who will certainly fool us. We like to be fooled. It's like being tickled. We say, "Stop! Stop!" and don't mean it.

Sphere ★ ½
PG-13, 120 m., 1998

Dustin Hoffman (Dr. Norman Goodman), Sharon Stone (Beth Halperin), Samuel L. Jackson (Harry Adams), Peter Coyote (Barnes), Liev Schreiber (Ted Fielding), Queen Latifah (Fletcher). Directed by Barry Levinson and produced by Levinson, Michael Crichton, and Andrew Wald. Screenplay by Stephen Hauser and Paul Attanasio, based on the novel by Crichton.

Michael Crichton is the science-fiction author people read if they think they're too good for "regular" science fiction. Too bad. What they get in *Sphere,* now filmed by Barry Levinson, is a watered-down version of the sci-fi classic *Solaris,* by Stanislaw Lem, which was made into an immeasurably better film by Andrei Tarkovsky.

The underlying idea is the same: Humans come into contact with an extraterrestrial presence that allows their minds to make their thoughts seem real. The earlier novel and film challenged our ideas about human consciousness. *Sphere* functions more like a whodunit in which the plot's hot potato is tossed from character to character.

As the movie opens, an expert team is brought to the middle of the Pacific, where an amazing thing has been found on the ocean floor: a giant spacecraft, apparently buried for nearly 300 years, that still emits a distant hum— suggesting it is intact and may harbor life. The members of the team: a psychologist (Dustin Hoffman), a mathematician (Samuel L. Jackson), a biochemist (Sharon Stone), and an astrophysicist (Liev Schreiber). In command of a navy "habitat" on the ocean floor next to the ship is Peter Coyote. The habitat's small crew includes radio operator Queen Latifah, from *Set It Off,* who is on hand to illustrate Hollywood's immutable law that the first character to die is always the African-American.

The descent to the ocean floor, accompanied by much talk about depressurization, will be a disappointment to anyone who remembers the suspense in similar scenes in James Cameron's *Abyss.* And the introduction of the spacecraft is also a disappointment:

Instead of the awe-inspiring first glimpses we remember from *Close Encounters* or even *Independence Day,* it's a throwaway. No wonder. The ocean-floor special effects are less than sensational, and the exteriors of the descent craft and the spacecraft are all too obviously models.

No matter, if the story holds our attention. At first it does. As long as we're in suspense, we're involved, because we anticipate great things. But *Sphere* is one of those movies where the end titles should be Peggy Lee singing "Is That All There Is?" The more the plot reveals, the more we realize how little there is to reveal, until finally the movie disintegrates into flaccid scenes where the surviving characters sit around talking about their puzzlements.

I have been careful to protect most of the film's secrets. I can be excused, I suppose, for revealing that what they find inside the spacecraft is, yes, a sphere. Where does this sphere come from? Who or what made it? How does it function? I am content to let it remain a mystery, so long as it entertains me, but after a promising start (it generates a *2001*-style hurtle through space and time), it just sits there, glowing and glowering, while the humans deal with the dangers of undersea life.

Hoffman, Jackson, Stone: These are good actors. How good is illustrated by how much they do with the flat, unyielding material. The last twenty minutes of the film are a slog through circular explanations and speculations that would have capsized lesser actors. They give it a good try, with dialogue that sounds either like characters analyzing the situation, or actors trying to figure out the plot.

Sphere feels rushed. The screenplay uses lots of talk to conceal the fact that the story has never been grappled with. The effects and the sets are pitched at the level of made-for-TV. The only excellence is in the acting, and even then the screenplay puts the characters through so many U-turns that dramatic momentum is impossible.

There are ideas sloshing around somewhere in the rising waters aboard the undersea habitat. The best one is an old science-fiction standby: Are humans mature enough to handle the secrets of the universe? Or are we but an infant species, whose fears and phobias prevent us from embracing the big picture? The last scenes are supposed to be a solemn confrontation of these questions, but they're punctuated by a special effects shot so puny and underwhelming that the spell is broken. That's all, folks. Put your hands together for Miss Peggy Lee.

Spice World ½★

PG, 93 m., 1998

Spice Girls (Themselves), Richard E. Grant (Clifford, the Manager), Claire Rushbrook (Deborah, the Assistant), Alan Cumming (Piers Cutherton-Smyth), Roger Moore (The Chief), George Wendt (Martin Barnfield), Meat Loaf (Dennis), Naoko Mori (Nicola). Cameos: Stephen Fry, Bob Hoskins, Elvis Costello, the Dream Boys, Bob Geldof, Elton John, Jonathan Ross. Directed by Bob Spiers and produced by Uri Fruchtmann and Barnaby Thompson. Screenplay by Kim Fuller.

The Spice Girls are easier to tell apart than the Mutant Ninja Turtles, but that is small consolation: What can you say about five women whose principal distinguishing characteristic is that they have different names?

They occupy *Spice World* as if they were watching it: They're so detached they can't even successfully lip-synch their own songs. During a rehearsal scene, their director tells them, with such truth that we may be hearing a secret message from the screenwriter, "That was absolutely perfect—without being actually any good."

Spice World is obviously intended as a ripoff of *A Hard Day's Night* (1964), which gave the Beatles to the movies. They should have ripped off more—everything they could get their hands on. The movie is a day in the life of a musical group that has become an overnight success, and we see them rehearse, perform, hang out together, and deal with such desperately contrived supporting characters as a trash newspaper editor, a paparazzo, and a manipulative manager.

All of these elements are inspired in one way or another by *A Hard Day's Night*. The huge difference, of course, is that the Beatles were talented—while, let's face it, the Spice Girls could be duplicated by any five women

under the age of thirty standing in line at Dunkin' Donuts.

The Beatles film played off the personalities of the Beatles. The Spice Girls have no personalities; their bodies are carriers for inane chatter. The Beatles film had such great music that every song in it is beloved all over the world. The Spice Girls' music is so bad that even *Spice World* avoids using any more of it than absolutely necessary.

The film's linking device is a big double-decker bus, painted like a Union Jack, which ferries the Girls past London landmarks (so many landmarks I suspect the filmmakers were desperately trying to stretch the running time). This bus is of ordinary size on the outside but three times too wide on the inside; it is fitted with all the conveniences of Spice Girlhood, except, apparently, toilet facilities, leading to the unusual sight of the Girls jumping off for a quick pee in the woods. (They do everything together.)

So lacking in human characteristics are the Girls that when the screenplay falls back on the last resort of the bankrupt filmmaking imagination—a live childbirth scene—they have to import one of their friends to have the baby. She at least had the wit to get pregnant, something beyond the Girls since it would involve a relationship, and thus an attention span. Words fail me as I try to describe my thoughts at the prospect of the five Spice Girls shouting "push!"

Star Kid ★ ★ ★

PG, 101 m., 1998

Joseph Mazzello (Spencer Griffith), Joey Simmrin (Turbo Bruntley), Alex Daniels (Cyborsuit), Arthur Burghardt (Cyborsuit Voice), Brian Simpson (Broodwarrior), Richard Gilliland (Roland [Dad]), Corinne Bohrer (Janet Holloway), Ashlee Levitch (Stacey [Sister]), Lauren Eckstrom (Michelle). Directed by Manny Coto and produced by Jennie Lew Tugend. Screenplay by Coto.

How would you like to climb inside a glistening metallic superhero suit and be partners with the intelligent cyborg that controls it? If you were a shy twelve-year-old boy, picked on by bullies and your brat of a sister, you'd love it.

Star Kid develops that fantasy in a lively action movie that young boys may especially enjoy—if their innocence hasn't already been hammered down by too much R-rated violence.

The movie stars Joseph Mazzello *(Jurassic Park, The River Wild)* as Spencer, a bright student whose imagination is centered on the adventures of a comic book hero named Midnight Warrior. He's got a hopeless crush on a girl at school named Michelle (Lauren Eckstrom), who also likes Midnight Warrior, and who would probably be his friend if he weren't paralyzed by shyness every time he tries to talk to her. At home, he has a preoccupied dad (Richard Gilliland) and a mean older sister (Ashlee Levitch) who gets resentful when she's required to baby-sit "the little scab juice."

One night everything changes for Spencer, when he sees a rocket land in a nearby junkyard. He scampers inside and finds the ship, still steaming, as it opens up to reveal a tall, glistening robotic cyborg inside. This creature, who looks like a detailed version of the visitor in *The Day the Earth Stood Still,* is inhabited by an intelligence that is quickly able to communicate with Spencer, inviting him to step inside and occupy his body.

We've already learned the back story. The creature was built by a race named the Trelkans, who look like Yoda with eczema, and are engaged in a struggle with the evil Broodwarriors. Spencer, once inside the suit, communicates face to face with a holographic image representing the cyborg's intelligence, and before long he's calling him Cy.

The movie's appeal is obvious: Inside the suit, Spencer becomes unbelievably strong and can do all kinds of neat stuff, like give the school bullies their comeuppance, impress Michelle, and let his sister see he's not a little scab juice anymore. There are comic scenes as Spencer awkwardly learns to control the suit, and then a climax when a Broodwarrior arrives on Earth for a final showdown.

Spencer is essentially living inside a comic book. A lot of action comics originate from the same premise—an ordinary guy like Clark Kent or Peter Parker is transformed into a paragon of strength and power. Adolescent readers like that; it suits their fantasies. *Star Kid,* written and directed by Manny Coto, has a sweet heart and a lot of sly wit, and the symbiosis between boy and cyborg is handled cleverly. For kids of a certain age, it pushes the right buttons.

Star Trek: Insurrection ★ ★
PG, 103 m., 1998

Patrick Stewart (Picard), Jonathan Frakes (Riker), Brent Spiner (Data), LeVar Burton (LaForge), Michael Dorn (Worf), Gates McFadden (Crusher), Marina Sirtis (Troi), F. Murray Abraham (Ru'afo), Donna Murphy (Anij), Anthony Zerbe (Admiral Dougherty). Directed by Jonathan Frakes and produced by Rick Berman. Screenplay by Berman and Michael Piller.

A funny thing happened to me on the way to writing this review of *Star Trek: Insurrection.* I discovered that several of the key filmmakers disagree with the film's plot premise. Maybe that's why this ninth *Star Trek* saga seems inert and unconvincing.

Here's the premise: In a region of space known as the Briar Patch, an idyllic planet is home to a race known as the Ba'ku. They are members of a placid agricultural commune, tilling the neat rows of their fields, and then returning to a city whose neo-Greco-Roman architecture looks uncannily like the shopping mall at Caesars Palace. The Ba'ku are a blissful people, and no wonder: They have the secret of immortality. The "metaphasic radiation" generated by the planet's rings acts like a fountain of youth on their planet.

The planet and the Ba'ku are currently the subject of a cultural survey team, which looks down on them from something like a stadium press box, but remains invisible. Then Data (Brent Spinner), the android, goes berserk and makes hostages of the survey team. The *Enterprise* speeds to the scene, so that Captain Picard (Patrick Stewart) can deal with the crisis. The plot thickens when it is revealed that the Son'a race, which is also part of the Federation, was once allied with the Ba'ku. But the Son'a chose a different path and are now dying out—most visibly in the scrofulous countenance of their leader, Ru'afo (F. Murray Abraham).

The Son'a want the Ba'ku kidnapped and forcibly ejected from their planet. There are, after all, only 600 of them. Why should their little nature preserve be more important than the health and longevity of the Son'a and billions of other Federation citizens? Picard counters with the Federation's Prime Directive, which instructs that the natural development of any civilization must not be interfered with.

The plot of *Star Trek: Insurrection* deals with the conflict between the desperate Son'a and the blissful Ba'ku, and is further complicated when Picard falls in love with the beautiful Ba'ku woman Anij (Donna Murphy). "You explore the universe," she tells him, "but have you ever explored a single moment in time?" (Picard is so lovestruck he forgets that his answer would be, "Yes!") Further complications result when the metaphasic radiation leaks into the *Enterprise* and inspires Riker (Jonathan Frakes) and Troi (Marina Sirtis) to start acting like horny teenagers.

As the best minds in the Federation wrestled with the ethical questions involved, I was also asking questions. Such as, aren't the Ba'ku basically just living in a gated community? Since this Eden-like planet has only 600 inhabitants, why couldn't others use the planet as a spa, circling inside those metaphasic rings and bathing in the radiation, which is probably faster acting in space than down on the surface? After all, we're not talking *magic* here, are we?

Above these practical questions looms a larger philosophical one. Wouldn't it be *right* to sacrifice the lifestyles of 600 Ba'ku in order to save billions? "I think maybe I would," said Jonathan Frakes when I asked him that question after the movie's press screening. Frakes plays Riker and directed the film. "You've got to be flexible," said Stewart, who plays Picard. "If it had been left in the hands of Picard, some solution could have been found." "Absolutely!" said Spiner, who plays Data. "I think I raised that question more than once." "I had to be very narrow-minded to serve the character," confessed Murphy, who plays Anij.

I agree. Our own civilization routinely kills legions of people in wars large and small, for reasons of ideology, territory, religion, or geography. Would we contemplate removing 600 people from their native environment in order to grant immortality to everyone alive? In a flash. It would be difficult, indeed, to fashion a philosophical objection to such a move,

which would result in the greatest good for the greatest number of people. But what about the rights of the Ba'ku? Hey, shouldn't they *volunteer* to help us all out? Especially since they need not die themselves?

The plot of *Star Trek: Insurrection* grinds through the usual conversations and crises, as the evil Ru'afo and his men carry forward their insidious plans, and Picard discovers that the Federation itself may be willing to play fast and loose with the Prime Directive. That's not exactly new; in the previous eight movies, there have in fact been many shots fired in anger at members of races who perhaps should have been left alone to "develop naturally"—presumably even if such development involves aggression and hostility. The overriding principle, let's face it, has been the Federation's own survival and best interests. So why not allow the Son'a the same ethnocentric behavior?

The movie is a work of fantasy, and these questions are not important unless they influence the film's entertainment value. Unfortunately, they do. There is a certain lackluster feeling to the way the key characters debate the issues, and perhaps that reflects the suspicion of the filmmakers that they have hitched their wagon to the wrong cause. The movie is shorter than the usual *Star Trek* saga, at 103 minutes, as if the central issue could not bear scrutiny at the usual length. Think how much more interesting it would have been if the Ba'ku had joined an interracial experiment to share immortality. What would happen if everyone in the Federation could live forever? Think how many more sequels there'd be.

Star Wars Episode I: The Phantom Menace ★ ★ ★ ½
PG, 133 m., 1999

Liam Neeson (Qui-Gon Jinn), Ewan McGregor (Obi-Wan Kenobi), Natalie Portman (Queen Amidala), Jake Lloyd (Anakin Skywalker), Pernilla August (Shmi Skywalker), Frank Oz (Yoda), Ian McDiarmid (Senator Palpatine), Oliver Ford Davies (Sio Bibble), Hugh Quarshie (Captain Panaka), Ahmed Best (Jar Jar Binks), Samuel L. Jackson (Mace Windu), Ray Park (Darth Maul), Peter Serafinowicz (Voice of Darth Maul), Ralph Brown (Ric Olie), Terence

Stamp (Chancellor Valorum). Directed by George Lucas and produced by Rick McCallum. Screenplay by Lucas.

If it were the first *Star Wars* movie, *The Phantom Menace* would be hailed as a visionary breakthrough. But this is the fourth movie in the famous series, and we think we know the territory; many of the early reviews have been blasé, paying lip service to the visuals and wondering why the characters aren't better developed. How quickly do we grow accustomed to wonders. I am reminded of the Asimov story *Nightfall,* about the planet where the stars were visible only once in a thousand years. So awesome was the sight that it drove men mad. We who can see the stars every night glance up casually at the cosmos and then quickly down again, searching for a Dairy Queen.

Star Wars Episode I: The Phantom Menace, to cite its full title, is an astonishing achievement in imaginative filmmaking. If some of the characters are less than compelling, perhaps that's inevitable: This is the first story in the chronology, and has to set up characters who (we already know) will become more interesting with the passage of time. Here we first see Obi-Wan Kenobi, Anakin Skywalker, Yoda, and prototypes of R2D2 and C3PO. Anakin is only a fresh-faced kid in Episode I; in IV, V, and VI he has become Darth Vader.

At the risk of offending devotees of the Force, I will say that the stories in the *Star Wars* movies have always been space operas, and that the importance of the movies comes from their energy, their sense of fun, their colorful inventions, and their state-of-the-art special effects. I do not attend expecting to gain insights into human behavior. Unlike many movies, these are made to be looked at more than listened to, and George Lucas and his collaborators have filled *Phantom Menace* with wonderful visuals.

There are new places here—new *kinds* of places. Consider the underwater cities, floating in their transparent membranes. The Senate chamber, a vast sphere with senators arrayed along the inside walls and speakers floating on pods in the center. And other places: The cityscape with the waterfall that has a dizzying descent through space. And other cities—one city Venetian, with canals, another looking like a hothouse version of imperial Rome, and a

third that seems to have grown out of desert sands.

Set against awesome backdrops, the characters in *Phantom Menace* inhabit a plot that is little more complex than the stories I grew up on in science-fiction magazines. The whole series sometimes feels like a cover from *Thrilling Wonder Stories* come to life. The dialogue is pretty flat and straightforward, although seasoned with a little quasi-classical formality, as if the characters had read but not retained *Julius Caesar.* I wish the *Star Wars* characters spoke with more elegance and wit (as Gore Vidal's Greeks and Romans do), but dialogue isn't the point anyway: These movies are about new things to look at.

The plot details (embargoes, blockades) tend to diminish the size of the movie's universe, anyway—to shrink it to the scale of a nineteenth-century trade dispute. The stars themselves are little more than pinpoints on a black curtain, and *Star Wars* has not drawn inspiration from the color photographs being captured by the Hubble telescope. The series is essentially human mythology, set in space but not occupying it. If Kubrick gave us man humbled by the universe, Lucas gives us the universe domesticated by man. His aliens are really just humans in odd skins. Consider Jar Jar Binks, a fully realized, computer-animated alien character whose physical movements seem based on afterthoughts. And Jabba the Hutt (who presides over the Pod race) has always seemed positively Dickensian to me.

Yet within the rules he has established, Lucas tells a good story. The key development in *Phantom* is the first meeting between the Jedi knight Qui-Gon Jinn (Liam Neeson) and the young boy Anakin Skywalker (Jake Lloyd)—who is, the Jedi immediately senses, fated for great things. Qui-Gon meets Anakin in a store where he's seeking replacement parts for his crippled ship. He soon finds himself backing the young slave in a high-speed Pod race—betting his ship itself against the cost of the replacement parts. The race is one of the film's high points, as the entrants rush between high cliff walls in a refinement of a similar race through metal canyons on a spaceship in *Star Wars.*

Why is Qui-Gon so confident that Anakin can win? Because he senses an unusual concentration of the Force—and perhaps because, like

John the Baptist, he instinctively recognizes the one whose way he is destined to prepare. The film's shakiness on the psychological level is evident, however, in the scene where young Anakin is told he must leave his mother (Pernilla August) and follow this tall Jedi stranger. Their mutual resignation to the parting seems awfully restrained. I expected a tearful scene of parting between mother and child, but the best we get is when Anakin asks if his mother can come along, and she replies, "Son, my place is here." As a slave?

The discovery and testing of Anakin supplies the film's most important action, but in a sense all the action is equally important, because it provides platforms for special-effects sequences. Sometimes our common sense undermines a sequence (as Jar Jar's people and the good guys fight a 'droid army, it becomes obvious that the 'droids are such bad fighters they should be returned for a refund). But mostly I was happy to drink in the sights on the screen, in the same spirit that I might enjoy *Metropolis, Forbidden Planet, 2001, Dark City,* or *The Matrix.* The difference is that Lucas's visuals are more fanciful and the energy level of his film more cheerful; he doesn't share the prevailing view that the future is a dark and lonely place.

What he does have, in abundance, is exhilaration. There is a sense of discovery in scene after scene of *Phantom Menace,* as he tries out new effects and ideas, and seamlessly integrates real characters and digital ones, real landscapes and imaginary places. We are standing at the threshold of a new age of epic cinema, I think, in which digital techniques mean that budgets will no longer limit the scope of scenes; filmmakers will be able to show us just about anything they can conceive of.

As surely as Anakin Skywalker points the way into the future of *Star Wars,* so does *The Phantom Menace* raise the curtain on this new freedom for filmmakers. And it's a lot of fun. The film has correctly been given the PG rating; it's suitable for younger viewers, and doesn't depend on violence for its effects. As for the bad rap about the characters—hey, I've seen space operas that put their emphasis on human personalities and relationships. They're called *Star Trek* movies. Give me membranous un-derwater cities and vast, hollow senatorial spheres any day. ☞

Steam: The Turkish Bath ★ ★
NO MPAA RATING, 96 m., 1999

Alessandro Gassman (Francesco), Francesca d'Aloja (Marta), Halil Ergun (Osman), Serif Sezer (Perran), Mehmet Gunsur (Mehmet), Basak Koklukaya (Fusun), Alberto Molinari (Paolo), Carlo Cecchi (Oscar), Zozo Toledo (Zozo). Directed by Ferzan Ozpetek and produced by Paolo Buzzi and Ozan Ergun. Screenplay by Stefano Tummolini and Ozpetek.

One of the peculiarities of *Steam: The Turkish Bath* is that it's about the sexual passions of two actors who don't seem very passionate. As the movie opens, they're married. Both are tall, thin, dark, solemn, and secretive. He seems like a well-meaning wimp. She seems like the kind of woman who would close her eyes during sex and fantasize about tomorrow's entries in her Day Timer.

The film opens in Rome, where their marriage seems shaky. They find fault with each other, but in vague terms that don't give us useful insights. Then the man, named Francesco (Alessandro Gassman), flies to Istanbul, where he has been left some property by an aunt.

The building turns out to be a Turkish bath, closed but still fondly remembered in the neighborhood. Francesco makes friends with the family of Osman, the man who used to manage the bath. Osman lives next door with his wife, comely daughter and comelier son. In his home Francesco finds a warmth and cheer that was missing from his sterile existence in Rome, and soon he's languishing in the arms of the son, named Mehmet (Mehmet Gunsur). He extends his stay and begins to renovate the Turkish bath, planning to reopen it.

No one suspects a thing—not even Osman (Halil Ergun), who in the nature of things must have learned a little something about what can go on in the steam. The film is reserved about sex and shy about nudity, employing its greatest passion for travelogue scenes of Istanbul, a city of great beauty and character.

Then Marta (Francesca d'Aloja), Francesco's

wife, arrives suddenly from Rome. The story tensions explode at a family dinner, although not quite in the way we expect (what Marta blurts out didn't surprise me, but I was amazed that this cool and well-mannered woman would make such an ugly scene). After moments of truth and revelation, there is a surprise ending that I found particularly unsatisfying.

Afterward, I found myself asking what exactly the point of the movie was. It is not a sex film; it's almost prudish in the reserve of its sex scenes. If it's a coming-out film, so what? Francesco's homosexuality is not a surprise to the audience or even, really, to his wife. If it is about how a man escapes from the fast lane in Rome and discovers the feeling of community in Istanbul—well, good for him.

Perhaps I would have cared more if the leads had been warmer, but both Gassman (son of Vittorio Gassman) and d'Aloja come across as cool and reserved. The Turks are much more fun: Gunsur, as the lover, is friendly and boyish, and Ergun, as the former custodian, is a cheerful man. Serif Sezer, as Ergun's wife and Gunsur's mother, is one of those beauties of a certain age who has lips that make you forget everything else except what it would be like to nibble them.

Stepmom ★ ★
PG-13, 124 m., 1998

Julia Roberts (Isabel Kelly), Susan Sarandon (Jackie Harrison), Ed Harris (Luke Harrison), Jena Malone (Anna Harrison), Liam Aiken (Ben Harrison), Lynn Whitfield (Dr. Sweikert), Darrell Larson (Duncan Samuels), Mary Louise Wilson (School Counselor). Directed by Chris Columbus and produced by Wendy Finerman, Mark Radcliffe, Michael Barnathan, and Columbus. Screenplay by Gigi Levangie, Jessie Nelson, Steven Rogers, Karen Leigh Hopkins, and Ron Bass.

Sometimes all you have to do is look at the casting and you can guess where a movie will take you. If a movie named *Stepmom* costars Susan Sarandon and Julia Roberts, you know it's a tearjerker. (With Jennifer Jason Leigh and Neve Campbell, you know it's drenched in sex; with Jamie Lee Curtis and Drew Barry-more, in blood.) The current iconography of Sarandon and Roberts falls somewhere between feminist heroism and sainthood; if Roberts is the stepmom, you know she's not going to have fangs and talons.

Still, the art of a movie like this is to conceal the obvious. When the levers and the pulleys of the plot are concealed by good writing and acting, we get great entertainments like *Terms of Endearment*. When they're fairly well masked, we get sincere films like *One True Thing*. When every prop and device is displayed in the lobby on our way into the theater, we get Chris Columbus's *Stepmom*.

The movie begins one year after a fashion photographer named Isabel (Julia Roberts) has started dating a businessman named Luke (Ed Harris). She thinks it's time she can be trusted to take care of his two kids for the weekend. He has his doubts, maybe because she's "not used to kids," maybe because he still sees his ex-wife, Jackie (Susan Sarandon), as the perfect mother. It's a question of trust. Jackie doesn't trust Isabel (or like her). Luke likes her but is unsure. The kids have been tutored by their mother to resent this new woman in their dad's life.

The children are Anna (Jena Malone) and Ben (Liam Aiken). She's just starting to date. He's in the lower grades, and afraid of losing his mommy because of this new woman ("Mommy, if you want me to hate her, I will"). Isabel really loves Luke and would like to love the kids, if they would let her. But every time she's late with a school pickup, Jackie turns up like an avenging angel with sarcastic criticisms. One day Isabel takes the children to Central Park, where she's doing a photo shoot, and Ben wanders away. By the time he's found safely, Jackie is issuing ultimatums: "That woman is to have nothing else to do with my children."

That's act one. Act two, of course, is the gradual weakening of the emotional walls, as Isabel earns the trust of the children and Jackie learns to let go. (Spoiler warning.) The upbeat TV ads don't contain a hint of this, but, yes, just like Debra Winger in *Terms of Endearment* and Meryl Streep in *One True Thing*, the Sarandon character doesn't have long to live. When she gets bad news from her doctor, she realizes that Isabel will inevitably one day be taking care of her kids, and that she'd better ease the transition. Act three is the Kleenex stuff, including separate farewells between the mother and each child.

The problem with the movie is the way it jumps up and down on first, second, and third before sliding into home. The movie hasn't been written so much as constructed by its five screenwriters, and although Gigi Levangie and Ron Bass, credited first and last, no doubt elevated the sophistication of the dialogue, these are people whose lives are gripped in the mighty vise of plotting. The skill of the actors, who invest their characters with small touches of humanity, is useful in distracting us from the emotional manipulations, but it's like they're brightening separate rooms of a haunted house.

The movie is really about the Sarandon character. Harris is absent for much of the second half, until he turns up for a family photo. Sarandon can create characters of astonishing conviction (Sister Helen Prejean in *Dead Man Walking*). Here she has to be unreasonable for half the movie and courageous for the rest; there's not a rest period where she just gets to be this woman. Every scene has a purpose; we're reminded of the value of those brief pillow scenes in which directors like Ozu take a beat and let us see their characters simply being.

To be sure, *Stepmom* has a certain tact. It wants us to cry, but it doesn't hold a gun on us, like *Patch Adams,* and enforce its emotions with sentimental terrorism. Roberts and Sarandon are immensely likable people, and Harris here seems caring and reasonable in a thankless role. We would have enjoyed spending time with them, if they'd been able to pull themselves away from the plot.

Stigmata ★ ★
R, 102 m., 1999

Patricia Arquette (Frankie Paige), Gabriel Byrne (Father Andrew Kiernan), Jonathan Pryce (Cardinal Houseman), Nia Long (Donna Chadway), Thomas Kopache (Father Durning), Rade Sherbedgia (Marion Petrocelli), Enrico Colantoni (Father Darius), Dick Latessa (Father Gianni Delmonico). Directed by Rupert Wainwright and produced by Frank Mancuso Jr. Screenplay by Tom Lazarus and Rick Ramage.

Stigmata is possibly the funniest movie ever made about Catholicism—from a theological point of view. Mainstream audiences will view it as a lurid horror movie, an *Exorcist* wannabe, but for students of the teachings of the church, it offers endless goofiness. It confuses the phenomenon of stigmata with satanic possession, thinks stigmata can be transmitted by relics, and portrays the Vatican as a conspiracy against miracles.

The story: In Brazil, a holy priest has come into possession of a lost gospel "told in the words of Jesus himself." In the priest's church is a bleeding statue of the Virgin Mary. The Vatican dispatches a miracle-buster, Father Andrew (Gabriel Byrne), to investigate. "The blood is warm and human," he tells his superiors. He wants to crate up the statue and ship it to the Vatican for investigation, but is prevented. (One pictures a vast Vatican storehouse of screen windows and refrigerator doors bearing miraculous images.)

The old priest has died, and in the marketplace an American tourist buys his rosary and mails it as a souvenir to her daughter, Frankie (Patricia Arquette), who is a hairdresser in Pittsburgh. Soon after receiving the rosary, Frankie begins to exhibit the signs of the stigmata—bleeding wounds on the wrists, head, and ankles, where Christ was pierced on the cross. Father Andrew is again dispatched to investigate, reminding me of Illeana Douglas's priceless advice to her haunted brother-in-law in *Stir of Echoes:* "Find one of those young priests with smoldering good looks to sort of guide you through this."

The priest decides Frankie cannot have the stigmata because she is not a believer: "It happens only to deeply religious people." Psychiatrists quiz her, to no avail ("Is there any stress in your life?" "I cut hair."). But alarming manifestations continue; Frankie bleeds, glass shatters, there are rumbles on the sound track, she has terrifying visions, and at one point she speaks to the priest in a deeply masculine voice, reminding us of nothing so much as Linda Blair in *The Exorcist.*

Now there's the problem. Linda Blair was

possessed by an evil spirit. Frankie has been entered by the Holy Spirit. Instead of freaking out in nightclubs and getting blood all over her bathroom, she should be in some sort of religious ecstasy, like Lili Taylor in *Household Saints*. It is not a dark and fearsome thing to be bathed in the blood of the Lamb.

It is also not possible, according to the very best church authorities, to catch the stigmata from a rosary. It is not a germ or a virus. It comes from within. If it didn't, you could cut up Padre Pio's bath towels and start your own blood drive. *Stigmata* does not know, or care, about the theology involved, and thus becomes peculiarly heretical by confusing the effects of being possessed by Jesus and by Beelzebub.

Meanwhile, back at the Vatican, the emotionally constipated Cardinal Houseman (Jonathan Pryce) rigidly opposes any notion that either the statue or Frankie actually bleeds. It's all a conspiracy, we learn, to suppress the gospel written in the actual words of Christ. The film, a storehouse of absurd theology, has the gall to end with one of those "factual" title cards, in which we learn that the "Gospel of St. Thomas," said to be in Christ's words, was denounced by the Vatican in 1945 as a "heresy." That doesn't mean it wouldn't be out in paperback if there was a market for it. It does mean the filmmakers have a shaky understanding of the difference between a heresy and a fake.

Does the film have redeeming moments? A few. Arquette is vulnerable and touching in an impossible role. I liked the idea of placing her character within a working-class world; there's a scene where one of the customers in the beauty shop resists having her hair treated by a woman with bleeding wrists. And Nia Long has fun with the role of Frankie's best friend; when your pal starts bleeding and hallucinating, it's obviously time for her to get out of the house and hit the clubs.

Stigmata has generated outrage in some Catholic circles. I don't know why. It provides a valuable recruiting service by suggesting to the masses that the church is the place to go for real miracles and supernatural manifestations. It is difficult to imagine this story involving a Unitarian. First get them in the door. Then start them on the catechism.   ☞

Still Crazy ★ ★ ★
R, 96 m., 1999

Stephen Rea (Tony), Billy Connolly (Hughie), Jimmy Nail (Les), Timothy Spall (Beano), Bill Nighy (Ray), Juliet Aubrey (Karen), Helene Bergstrom (Astrid), Bruce Robinson (Brian). Directed by Brian Gibson and produced by Amanda Marmot. Screenplay by Dick Clement and Ian La Frenais.

Still Crazy is a kinder, gentler version of *This Is Spinal Tap*, telling the story of a 1970s rock band that tries for a reunion twenty years after its last disastrous concert. Two decades have not been kind to the surviving members of Strange Fruit: One is a roofing contractor, one lives in a trailer in his mother's garden and hides from the tax man, one services condom machines in Ibiza, and even the one who held onto his money hasn't held onto enough of it. Two other members are dead.

None of the survivors remember the old days with much affection. There was jealousy, anger, and betrayal among band members, and the drugs and lifestyle didn't help. "God got tired of all that seventies excess," one observes. "That's why he invented the Sex Pistols." The band members have drifted out of touch, and like it that way.

But one day the keyboard man, Tony (Stephen Rea), is recognized in a restaurant by the son of the man who produced the disastrous 1977 concert at which Strange Fruit disintegrated. He suggests a reunion. Tony, who services the condom machines, still believes a little in the dream of rock 'n' roll (he wears Jimmy Hendrix's tooth around his neck). Besides, he needs the money, so he tracks down Karen (Juliet Aubrey), who was the group's secretary and gofer.

Together they go looking for the others, and find them: Ray Simms (Bill Nighy) is a cadaverous poseur living in a Victorian mansion with his bossy Swedish wife (Helena Bergstrom). He keeps his gold records in the crypt. Les Wickes (Jimmy Nail) is a roofer, tracked down by Tony on top of a church. Beano Baggot (Timothy Spall) works in a nursery, lives in a trailer, and fears a jail term from the tax authorities. Hughie (Billy Connolly) is the lead roadie. Brian (Bruce Robinson), the lead guitarist, disappeared long ago and is thought by everyone to be dead.

Not so reluctantly, the Fruit agree to do a "test tour" of Holland as a preliminary to a big seventies revival concert. They need the money. But they are all much decayed since their glory days, and only by not shaving and letting their hair grow rank are they able to conceal how bad they look—by looking worse.

Ray is a particularly dodgy case. Nagged by his wife, who micromanages every moment of his life, he's a recovering addict who is terrified of a fatal lapse back into drugs or booze. He stutters a little, makes profound statements that nobody else can quite understand, and cannot cope with the challenges of an ordinary day. His speech at a wedding reminds me of Rowan Atkinson's inept Mr. Bean.

The filmmakers must have personal experience with neurotic rock stars past their sell-by dates. The director, Brian Gibson, made the Tina Turner biopic *What's Love Got to Do With It,* and the writers are Dick Clement and Ian La Frenais, who wrote *The Commitments,* about an Irish group that would have been a garage band if they'd had a garage. They succeed in making Strange Fruit look and sound like a real band (the music was written and performed by various veterans of Foreigner, Spandau Ballet, Squeeze, and ELO), and there is an authenticity to the backstage desperation, as old wounds are reopened.

There are times when the film edges close to *Spinal Tap* territory, as when young fans are quick to boo the aging and uncertain group. In a way, the spirit of *Spinal Tap* hovers over the entire film, since its deadly aim has forever marked middle-aged rockers as targets of satire. But *Still Crazy* pays attention to the personalities of its heroes, and finds enough humor in reality, as when Ray slams his fiftieth birthday cake against the wall.

Some of the faces, especially Rea and Spall, are familiar from other recent British movies. But it's Bill Nighy who makes the most memorable impression. He conveys fear so well, especially that central kind of fear that forms when you can no longer trust yourself to do the right thing. There is a scene where he unwisely ventured onto some ice that cracks, and the way he handles it is unexpected, and right.

There aren't a lot of plot surprises in *Still Crazy* (the biggest surprise is telegraphed early on), and the ending is more or less as expected—indeed, as decreed by the comeback genre. But the characters are sharply defined and well written, and we come to like them. Twenty years ago they may have seemed like unapproachable rock gods, but now we see them as touching and vulnerable: Once they could do something fairly well, and now they have arrived at the stage in life where they can do it better—if they can do it at all.

Stir of Echoes ★ ★ ★
R, 110 m., 1999

Kevin Bacon (Tom), Kathryn Erbe (Maggie), Illeana Douglas (Lisa), Kevin Dunn (Frank), Conor O'Farrell (Harry), Zachary David Cope (Jake), Eddie Bo Smith Jr. (Neil [Cop]), Lusia Strus (Sheila). Directed by David Koepp and produced by Gavin Polone and Judy Hofflund. Screenplay by Koepp.

Stir of Echoes is a supernatural thriller firmly rooted in a blue-collar Chicago neighborhood, where everyone on the block knows each other—although not as well as they think. Kevin Bacon stars in one of his best performances, as a telephone lineman named Tom Witzky, who plays in a band, wants to break out of the routine of his life, and succeeds all too successfully. "I never wanted to be famous," he tells his wife. "I just never expected to be so ordinary."

But he has an extraordinary gift he doesn't know about: He's a receiver, able to see spirits. This gift is unlocked one boozy night at a beer party, when his sister-in-law Lisa (Illeana Douglas) talks about hypnosis. Tom claims he can't be hypnotized. Lisa tries. She evokes an empty theater and sends Tom drifting toward the screen; he spirals deeply into a trance, and awakens after a terrifying vision of violent but indistinct events in his own house.

The haunting visitations do not go away. They're linked, perhaps, to events on the street, where the neighbors are salt-of-the-earth types who are into buying old houses and fixing them up. Tom's nights are prowled by nightmares, and his lovemaking is interrupted by hallucinations of severed body parts (that will certainly do the trick). He starts calling in sick, and his wife, Maggie (Kathryn Erbe), is worried: Is he getting goofy? After the movies about satanic manifestations in Manhattan skyscrapers, it's nice to see weird things happening to people who hang out in the corner saloon, go to high school football games, and walk down the block to church. In a Manhattan movie, Tom's wife would have sent him to a shrink. In this Chicago version, she tells her sister: "He's used up all his sick days. They're gonna start docking him."

Only his son Jake (Zachary David Cope) understands. Early in the film he asks an unseen presence, "Does it hurt to be dead?" After a vision of a ghostly young woman named Samantha appears to Tom on his living room sofa, Jake reaches out and touches his hand: "Don't be afraid of it, Daddy." We learn that several months ago a mentally retarded girl disappeared in the neighborhood. Her sister baby-sits Jake, who somehow knows the name of the missing girl; Samantha told him.

Then Samantha tells Tom to "dig." So he digs. He digs up the backyard. Then he starts on the cellar. Eventually he brings in a pneumatic drill. This is the movie's weakest section; the writer-director, David Koepp, makes him dig more than is necessary to make the point. The movie's about ghosts, not digging, and I was reminded of Spielberg's *Close Encounters of the Third Kind*, in which Richard Dreyfuss, receiving impulses from aliens, sculpts his mashed potatoes. The director's cut toned down the mashed potatoes, and Koepp might one day consider similar repairs.

Tom's wife, Maggie, meanwhile comes into contact with a Chicago cop (Eddie Bo Smith Jr.) who is also a receiver, and there's an intriguing scene where she stumbles across a meeting of other people who can see supernatural dimensions. I would have liked more of that subplot, which isn't developed, but never mind: Koepp's screenplay dovetails the supernatural stuff with developments among the neighbors which are, wisely, more sad and tragic than sensational.

Kevin Bacon is sometimes able to suggest characters who are being driven mad by themselves. Here he implodes, in a role where that's the right choice; another actor might have reached too far. Kathryn Erbe is not merely

worried but also exasperated by her husband, which is the right realistic touch, and Illeana Douglas plays the kind of sister-in-law who takes what you like in your wife and carries it too far. (Asked for advice after nudging these events into motion, she unhelpfully suggests, "Find one of those young priests with smoldering good looks to sort of guide you through this.")

Fred Murphy's photography places these people in the real world, and there is one shot that's a stunner, starting with the lineman up on a pole making a call, and then pulling back and back until we see a vast Chicago River vista and no less than three L trains at the same time. That doesn't have anything to do with ghosts, I know, but it sure is a neat shot.

The Story of Us ★

R, 92 m., 1999

Bruce Willis (Ben Jordan), Michelle Pfeiffer (Katie Jordan), Colleen Rennison (Erin), Jake Sandvig (Josh), Rita Wilson (Rachel), Julie Hagerty (Liza), Paul Reiser (Dave), Tim Matheson (Marty), Red Buttons (Arnie), Jayne Meadows (Dot), Tom Poston (Harry). Directed by Rob Reiner and produced by Reiner, Jessie Nelson, and Alan Zweibel. Screenplay by Zweibel and Nelson.

Rob Reiner's *The Story of Us* is a sad-sack movie about the misery of a married couple (Bruce Willis and Michelle Pfeiffer) who fight most of the time. Watching it is like taking a long trip in a small car with the Bickersons. I leave it to you to guess whether the movie has a happy ending, but what if it does? A movie like this is about what we endure while we're watching it, not about where it finally arrives.

Meet the Jordans, Ben and Katie. He's a TV comedy writer; she composes crossword puzzles. They have two kids, Erin and Josh. Their marriage is a war zone: "Argument has become the condition for conversation," he observes. They fake happiness for the kids. How did they arrive at such pain? It is hard to say; the movie consists of flashbacks to their fights, but their problems are so generic we can't put a finger on anything.

Gene Siskel used to ask if a movie was as good as a documentary of the same actors having lunch. Watching *The Story of Us,* I imagined a documentary of the marriage of, say, Bruce Willis and Demi Moore. I do not say that to score a cheap point, but because Moore and Willis are spirited and intelligent people who no doubt had interesting fights about real issues, and not insipid fights about sitcom issues.

Example. The movie wants to illustrate poor communication. It shows Pfeiffer at home, where the washing machine is spewing suds all over the room and the kids are fighting. Willis calls her from outside their old apartment building, which is being torn down. He tells her the wrecking ball has just taken out their bedroom. She doesn't pay attention. His feelings are hurt.

The marriage counselor is in: She should shout, "The washer just exploded!" And he should say, "Catch you later!" Another marriage saved. Oh, and if I were her I'd turn off the power to the washing machine.

The movie is filled with lame and contrived "colorful" dialogue. Reiner, who plays a friend of the husband, gives him a long explanation of why appearances deceive. "We do not possess butts," he says, "but merely fleshy parts at the top of our legs." Whoa! Later there is a restaurant scene in which Willis screams angrily in a unsuccessful (indeed, melancholy) attempt to rip off Meg Ryan's famous restaurant orgasm in Reiner's *When Harry Met Sally.* At the end of his tirade, Willis jumps up and tells Reiner what he can "shove up the tops of your legs!"

Doesn't work, because (a) he's too angry to think up or stop for a punch line, (b) the line isn't funny, and (c) the setup wasn't funny either, because the concept isn't funny. Oh, and the scene ends with Reiner doing a double take directly into the camera. How many ways can one scene be mishandled?

Who thought this movie would be entertaining? The same person who thinks we need more dialogue about why guys do the wrong thing with rolls of toilet paper. And who thinks the misery of this film can be repaired by a showboat monologue at the end that's well delivered by Pfeiffer, but reads like an audition scene.

There is a famous short story about an unhappy couple, and about what happens when it comes time to tell their children they're getting a divorce. It is called "Separating," by John Updike. Read it to understand how much *The Story of Us* does not reach for or even guess.

The Straight Story ★ ★ ★ ★
G, 111 m., 1999

Richard Farnsworth (Alvin Straight), Sissy Spacek (Rose), Jane Heitz (Dorothy), James Cada (Danny Riordan), Everett McGill (Tom the Dealer), Jennifer Edwards (Brenda), Barbara E. Robertson (Deer Woman), John Farley (Thorvald), John Lordan (Priest), Harry Dean Stanton (Lyle). Directed by David Lynch and produced by Alain Sarde and Mary Sweeney. Screenplay by Sweeney and John Roach.

The first time I saw *The Straight Story,* I focused on the foreground and liked it. The second time I focused on the background, too, and loved it. The movie isn't just about Alvin Straight's odyssey through the small towns and rural districts of the Midwest, but about the people he finds to listen to and care for him. You'd think it was a fantasy, this kindness of strangers, if the movie weren't based on a true story.

Straight (Richard Farnsworth) is a seventy-three-year-old man from Laurens, Iowa, who learns that his brother is dying, and wants to see him one last time. His eyes are too bad to allow him to drive. He lives with his daughter Rose (Sissy Spacek), who is somewhat retarded and no good behind the wheel. Nor do they have a car. But they have a tractor-style lawn mower, and the moment Alvin's eyes light on it, he knows how he can drive the three hundred miles to Zion, Wisconsin. The first mower konks out, but he gets another one, a John Deere, hitches a little wagon to it, and stubbornly sets off down the road.

Along the way we will learn a lot about Alvin, including a painful secret he has kept ever since the war. He is not a sophisticated man, but when he speaks the words come out like the bricks of a wall built to last. Like Hemingway's dialogue, the screenplay by John Roach and Mary Sweeney finds poetry and truth in the exact choice of the right everyday words. Richard Farnsworth, who was seventy-nine when he made the film, speaks the lines with perfect repose and conviction.

Because the film was directed by David Lynch, who usually deals in the bizarre *(Wild at Heart, Twin Peaks)*, we keep waiting for the other shoe to drop—for Alvin's odyssey to intersect with the Twilight Zone. But it never does. Even when he encounters a potential weirdo, like the distraught woman whose car has killed fourteen deer in one week on the same stretch of highway (". . . and I *have* to take this road!"), she's not a sideshow exhibit and we think, yeah, you can hit a lot of deer on those country roads.

Alvin's journey to his brother is a journey into his past. He remembers when they were young and filled with wonder. He tells a stranger, "I want to sit with him and look up at the stars, like we used to, so long ago." He remembers his courtship and marriage. His army service as a sniper whose aim, one day, was too good. And about years lost to drinking and nastiness. He has emerged from the forge of his imperfections as a better man, purified, simple, and people along the way seem to sense that.

My favorite, of all of his stops, comes in a small town where he's almost killed when he loses a drive belt and speeds out of control down a hill. He comes to rest where some people in lawn chairs are watching the local firemen practicing putting out a fire.

In the town are twin brothers who squabble all the time, even while charging him by the hour to repair the mower, and a retired John Deere employee named Danny Riordan (James Cada), who lets Alvin camp for a while in his backyard (Alvin won't enter the house, even to use the phone). Danny is a rare man of instinctive sweetness and tact, who sees what the situation requires, and supplies it without display. He embodies all of our own feelings about this lovable old—yes, fool. He gently offers advice, but Alvin is firm: "You're a kind man talking to a stubborn man."

If Riordan and the deer lady and the dueling twins (and a forlorn young girl) are the background I was talking about, so are the locations themselves. The cinematographer, Freddie Francis, who once made the vastness of Utah a backdrop for *The Executioner's Song*,

knows how to evoke a landscape without making it too comforting. There are fields of waving corn and grain here, and rivers and woods and little red barns, but on the sound track the wind whispering in the trees plays a sad and lonely song, and we are reminded not of the fields we drive past on our way to picnics, but on our way to funerals, on autumn days when the roads are empty.

The faces in this movie are among its treasures. Farnsworth himself has a face like an old wrinkled billfold that he paid good money for and expects to see him out. There is another old man who sits next to him on a bar stool near the end of the movie, whose face is like the witness to time. And look and listen to the actor who plays the bartender in that same late scene, the one who serves the Miller Lite. I can't find his name in the credits, but he finds the right note: He knows how all good bartenders can seem like a friend bringing a present to a sickroom.

The last notes are also just right. Who will this dying brother be, and what will he say? Will the screenplay say too much or reach for easy sentimentality? Not at all. Just because you have to see someone doesn't mean you have a lot to gab about. No matter how far you've come. ☞

Note: I later discovered the actor who plays the bartender is Russell Reed.

Stuart Little ★ ★
PG, 92 m., 1999

Geena Davis (Mrs. Little), Hugh Laurie (Mr. Little), Jonathan Lipnicki (George Little). Voices of: Michael J. Fox (Stuart Little), Nathan Lane (Snowbell), Chazz Palminteri (Snowbell), Steve Zahn (Monty), Jim Doughan (Lucky). Directed by Rob Minkoff and produced by Douglas Wick. Screenplay by M. Night Shyamalan and Greg Brooker, based on the book by E. B. White.

Any other consideration about *Stuart Little* must take second place to the fact that it is about a nice family that adopts a mouse. Yes, a mouse, in all dimensions and particulars, albeit a mouse with a cute little sports coat and an earnest way of expressing himself in piping

English. Stuart is about two inches long, maybe a little longer. Early in the film Snowbell, the family cat, tries to eat him, but is forced to spit him up, damp but no worse for wear.

I once read the book by E. B. White on which this story is founded. The peculiar thing about the book is that Stuart, in the imagination of the reader, swells until he occupies as much psychic space as any of the other characters. He is a mouse, but his dialogue runs from margin to margin just like the words of the humans, and his needs and fears are as great. Our intelligence tells us Stuart is a mouse, but our imagination makes him into a full-size literary character.

In the book, Stuart works just fine as a character. But movies are an unforgivably literal medium, and the fact is, no live-action movie about Stuart Little can possibly work, *because he is so much smaller than everyone else!*

Stuart is definitely a mouse. He is very, very small. There is something pathetic about a scene where his new parents (Geena Davis and Hugh Laurie) tuck him in at bedtime. It doesn't matter how much they love him or how happy he is to be in this new home; all we can think about is how he hardly needs even the hem of his blanket. All through the movie I kept cringing at the terrible things that could happen to the family's miniature son. It didn't help that a few days earlier I'd seen another movie in which an equally cute and lovable mouse was stamped on by a sadist, and squished.

The movie of course puts Stuart through many adventures, and confronts him with tragic misunderstandings. He is provided with a new wardrobe and a tiny red convertible sportster to race around in, and is chased through Central Park by hungry cats. That sort of thing.

My mind reeled back to the grotesque family "comedy" named *Jack Frost*. That was the film in which a family's father dies and is reincarnated as a snowman. Now that is an amazing thing. If your dad came back as a snowman after being dead for a year, what would you ask him? Perhaps, is there an afterlife? Or, what is heaven like? Or—why a snowman? But no sooner does the snowman in *Jack Frost* appear than it is harnessed to a desperately banal plot about snowball fights at the high school.

Stuart Little is not anywhere near as bad as *Jack Frost* (it is twice as good—two stars instead of one). But it has the same problem: The *fact* of its hero upstages anything the plot can possibly come up with. A two-inch talking humanoid mouse upstages roadsters, cats, little brothers, everything. I tried imagining a movie that would deal seriously and curiously with an intelligent and polite child that looked like a mouse. Such a movie would have to be codirected by Tim Burton and David Lynch.

I am reminded of the old man who finds a frog in the road. "Kiss me," says the frog, "and I will turn into a beautiful princess." The man puts the frog in his pocket. "Didn't you hear my offer?" asks the frog in a muffled voice. "I heard it," the old man says, "but frankly, at my age, I'd rather have a talking frog." My guess is that the makers of *Stuart Little* might not understand the point of this story.

Such a Long Journey ★ ★ ★ ½
NO MPAA RATING, 113 m., 2000

Roshan Seth (Gustad Noble), Soni Razdan (Dilnavaz Noble), Om Puri (Ghulam), Naseeruddin Shah (Major Jimmy Bilimoria), Ranjit Chowdhry (Pavement Artist), Sam Dastor (Dinshawji), Kurush Deboo (Tehmul), Vrajesh Hirjee (Sohrab Noble). Directed by Sturla Gunnarsson and produced by Paul Stephens and Simon MacCorkindale. Screenplay by Sooni Taraporevala, based on the novel by Rohinton Mistry.

India is the closest we can come in today's world to the London of Dickens, with its poverty and wealth side by side, in a society teeming with benevolence and intrigue, eccentrics and thieves, the suspect and the saintly. *Such a Long Journey,* filmed on location in Bombay, is a film so rich in atmosphere it makes Western films look pale and underpopulated. It combines politics, religion, illness, and scheming in the story of one family in upheaval, and is very serious, and always amusing.

The story, set in 1971 at the time of the war between India and Pakistan, is based on the novel of the same name by Rohinton Mistry, an Indian now living in Toronto. I haven't read it, but I have read his latest novel, the magnificent *A Fine Balance,* which has the same ability to see how political issues impact the lives of the ordinary and the obscure. Mistry's novels have the droll irony of Dickens, as when a legless beggar and a beggarmaster turn out to be brothers, and the beggarmaster is so moved that he purchases the beggar a better cart to push himself around on.

Such a Long Journey takes place mostly in and around a large apartment complex, its courtyard, and the street, which the municipal authorities want to widen so that even more choking diesel fumes can cloud the air. We meet the hero, Gustad (Roshan Seth), in the process of defending the old concrete wall that protects his courtyard from the street, and later he strikes a bargain with an itinerant artist (Ranjit Chowdhry), who covers the wall with paintings from every conceivable religious tradition, with the thought that all of the groups represented will join in defending the wall.

A greater struggle is in store for Gustad. A Parsi whose family has fallen on hard times, he works in a bank and is asked by Major Jimmy (Naseeruddin Shah), a friend from long ago, to hide and launder some money. The go-between (Om Puri) implies these are official Indian government funds being secretly transferred to finance the war against Pakistan in Bangladesh. (The movie doesn't require us to know much about modern history in the subcontinent, since the story works entirely in terms of the personal lives of its characters.)

Gustad is a good and earnest man, who has adopted the local idiot as a kind of surrogate son, who is the unofficial mayor of his building, who is always on call to help his neighbors, who dotes on his little daughter, and bursts with pride that his son, Sohrab (Vrajesh Hirjee), has been accepted by the Indian Institute of Technology. Alas, Sohrad doesn't want to go to IIT; he hates engineering and wants to be an artist, and Gustad implores him to reconsider.

Gustad's relationship with his wife has elements of an Indian *Honeymooners*. The kitchen is her turf, where she defiantly spends long hours in consultation with a neighbor woman whom Gustad considers to be a witch (i.e., she has a different set of superstitions than his own). Their marriage is strong when it needs to be, as when their daughter falls ill with malaria.

All of these stories are told against the backdrop of the others who live in the apartment complex, the street vendors outside, and those who are understood to have claims to portions of the courtyard or sidewalk. There is great poverty in India, but because it is so common it's more of a condition of life than a particular shame, and Gustad is on easy terms with the people who live in, as well as on, his street.

Roshan Seth is not a name well known in the West, but his face is familiar; he played Nehru in *Gandhi*, the heroine's father in *Mississippi Masala*, the father again in *My Beautiful Laundrette*, and it is only poetic justice that he starred in the film of Dickens's *Little Dorrit*. In this role (which won him a Canadian Genie as the year's best actor), he plays an everyman, an earnest, worried, funny character always skirting on the edge of disaster, exuberantly immersed in his life. The way he masterminds the defense of the precious wall is brilliant, but the way he deals with its fate is even more touching, because it is simply human.

The director, Sturla Gunnarsson, is Icelandic, suggesting the universality of this story; the writer, Sooni Taraporevala, also wrote *Mississippi Masala* and *Salaam Bombay*. Their film is interesting not simply in terms of its plot (the politics, the money), but because of the medium it moves through—the streets of Bombay. It suggests a society that has more poverty than ours, but is not necessarily poorer, because it has a richer texture of daily life. *American Beauty* could not be an Indian story; it would be too hard to imagine Indian city dwellers with that much time to brood and isolate. ☞

Sugar Town ★ ★ ★
R, 93 m., 1999

Jade Gordon (Gwen), Ally Sheedy (Liz), Larry Klein (Burt), Rosanna Arquette (Eva), John Taylor (Clive), Michael Des Barres (Nick), Martin Kemp (Jonesy), Beverly D'Angelo (Jane), Vincent Berry (Nirvana), Lucinda Jenney (Kate). Directed by Allison Anders and Kurt Voss and produced by Daniel Hassid. Screenplay by Anders and Voss.

Sugar Town knows its characters. It inhabits two overlapping worlds in Los Angeles: The world of people who were famous once, and those who will never be famous but dream of nothing else. "We were all in seminal bands in the seventies and eighties," a middle-aged rock musician observes, sadly and defiantly, at a meeting to discuss forming a new band. The problem with being seminal is that you end up in the shadow of your offspring.

These has-beens have money. Not a lot, in some cases, but enough. The movie slides easily in and out of their homes, comfortable untidy structures in the Hollywood Hills, strong on the "features" Realtors brag about, but looking knocked together out of spare parts of better houses. Their clothes and hair reflect the way they looked when they were famous; their images are made from last year's merchandise.

The movie's insider atmosphere is honestly come by. The codirectors, Allison Anders and Kurt Voss, live in this world themselves, many of the actors are their friends, the houses are where some of these people actually live, and the movie was shot in three weeks. If it were a documentary, it would be a good one.

The problem with being fortyish is that you're still young enough to want to do dangerous things, but too old to ignore the dangers. Drugs are not free from the shadow of rehab. Sex is a need but not a drive; you want it, but it's so much trouble to go out and get it. Always at your back you hear time's winged chariot drawing near. It's bad enough to be asked to play Christina Ricci's mother, as a former slasher movie queen (Rosanna Arquette) observes, but worse because "*She's* not an ingenue anymore."

The movie cuts between a rich assortment of characters; it's like a low-rent, on-the-fly version of Robert Altman's *The Player* or *Short Cuts*. We meet a production designer (Ally Sheedy) who is so paralyzed by self-help mantras that she has no social life. "Your genital area is completely blocked," says her "openness counselor," offering a massage, which we suspect could unblock it using the most traditional of approaches. Her house is a mess. She hires a housekeeper (Jade Gordon), a showbiz wanna-be we see badgering a drugged-out composer for the "three hit songs" she has paid him to write. When Sheedy finally gets a date (with a music agent), the housekeeper sabotages the date by advising against a sexy black dress and in favor of a painting smock that's "more you," then gets a ride home from the agent and descends directly to openness counseling.

Arquette's former slasher queen lives with an eighties rock hero (John Taylor of Duran Duran). One of his former lovers dumps a kid at his door—his kid, she says—and disappears. The kid (Vincent Berry) hates his name, which is Nirvana. He's about eleven, wears earrings and black eye makeup, and is very angry. "I *said*—call me *nerve!*" he snaps at her. "You want some hot chocolate?" she asks. He softens up considerably when he realizes she is the star of his favorite slasher videos.

Other characters include the pregnant wife (Lucinda Jenney) of a studio musician, her drug-damaged brother-in-law, and the Latino musician who wants to seduce her husband. Jenney's performance is the most touching in the movie, especially in the way she handles the brother-in-law. The rock agent, named Burt (Larry Klein) strikes gold. He discovers a rich widow (Beverly D'Angelo) who will provide backing for an album if she can sleep with a former glam-rock star (Michael Des Barres). Their scene together is the movie's funniest; he painstakingly reproduces his famous image with makeup and clothes, only to have her size up his bare-chested leopard leotard and ask, "Did you pull this out of mothballs just for me?"

One thing you notice in Los Angeles is that everyone seems to be connected to "the business" in one way or another, if only in their plans. Sheedy meets a wheatgrass machine operator at the health food store, who turns out, of course, to have a screenplay and newly taken publicity stills. There's a certain double-reverse poignancy in observing that some of the cast members (Michael Des Barres, John Taylor, Martin Kemp) are indeed rock legends, and some, like Des Barres and Ally Sheedy, are in the midst of actual career comebacks like the others dream of.

The movie is not profound or tightly plotted or a "statement," nor should it be. It captures day-to-day drifting in a city without seasons, where most business meetings are so circular and unfocused it's hard to notice when they stop resulting in deals and simply exist for their own sake. You can make enough money in a brief season of fame that if you are halfway prudent with it, you can live forever like this, making plans and reminding people who you are, or were, or will be.

Summer of Sam ★ ★ ★ ½
R, 136 m., 1999

John Leguizamo (Vinny), Adrien Brody (Ritchie), Mira Sorvino (Dionna), Jennifer Esposito (Ruby), Michael Rispoli (Joey T), Saverio Guerra (Woodstock), Brian Tarantino (Bobby Del Fiore), Al Palagonia (Anthony), Ben Gazzara (Luigi), Bebe Neuwirth (Gloria). Directed by Spike Lee and produced by Lee and Jon Kilik. Screenplay by Lee, Victor Colicchio, and Michael Imperioli.

Spike Lee's *Summer of Sam* is his first film with no major African-American characters, but it has a theme familiar to blacks and other minorities: scapegoating. In the summer of 1977, when New York City is gripped by paranoid fear of the serial killer who calls himself the Son of Sam, the residents of an Italian-American neighborhood in the Bronx are looking for a suspect. Anyone who stands out from the crowd is a candidate.

Lee's best films thrum with a wound-up energy, and *Summer of Sam* vibrates with fear, guilt, and lust. It's not about the killer, but about his victims—not those he murdered, but those whose overheated imaginations bloomed into a lynch mob mentality. There is a sequence near the end of the film that shows a side of human nature as ugly as it is familiar: the fever to find someone to blame, and the need to blame someone who is different.

We see the Son of Sam from time to time in the film, often as a shadowy presence, but his appearances are more like punctuation than drama. The story centers on several characters in a tightly knit neighborhood—one of those neighborhoods so insular that everyone suspects the killer may be someone they know. That's not because they think a killer must live among them, but because it's hard to imagine anyone living anywhere else.

The key characters are two couples. Vinny (John Leguizamo) is a hairdresser with a rov-

ing eye, married none too faithfully to Dionna (Mira Sorvino), who is a waitress in her father's restaurant. Ritchie (Adrien Brody) is a local kid who has mysteriously developed a punk haircut and a British accent. He dates the sexy Ruby (Jennifer Esposito), but leads a double life as a dancer in a gay club. The movie doesn't involve them in plot mechanics so much as follow them for human atmosphere; we get to know them and their friends and neighbors, and then watch them change as the pall of murder settles over the city.

Lee is a city kid himself, from Brooklyn, and makes the city's background noise into a sort of parallel sound track. There's the voice of Phil Rizzuto doing play-by-play as Reggie Jackson slams the Yankees into the World Series. The hit songs of the summer, disco and otherwise. The almost sexual quality of gossip; people are turned on by spreading rumors, and feed off each other's excitement. The tone is set by the opening shot of columnist Jimmy Breslin, introducing the film. It was to Breslin that the killer wrote the first of his famous notes to the papers, identifying himself as the monster, and saying he would kill again.

The *Summer of Sam* screenplay, written by Lee with Victor Colicchio and Michael Imperioli, isn't the inside, autobiographical job of a Scorsese film, but more of an analytical outsider's view. We learn things. There is a certain conviction in a scene where the police turn to a local Mafia boss (Ben Gazzara) for help from his troops in finding the killer; he has power in the neighborhood, this is known to everyone, and the cops put it to pragmatic use.

We watch Vinny, the Leguizamo character, as he cheats on his wife, notably with Gloria (Bebe Neuwirth), the sexpot at the beauty salon where he works. We watch as he stumbles on two of Sam's victims and returns home, chastened, believing God spared him, and vowing to start treating his wife better. In this neighborhood, it's personal; if you have a near brush with Sam, it's a sign. And Lee shows us Dionna wearing a blond wig on a date with her husband, because the killer seems to single out brunettes. She does it for safety's sake, but there's a sexual undercurrent: Wearing the wig and risking the wrath of Sam is kind of a turn-on.

The summer of 1977 was at the height of the so-called sexual revolution; Plato's Retreat was famous and AIDS unheard-of, and both of the principal couples are caught up in the fever. Vinny and Dionna experiment at a sex club, and Ritchie gets involved in gay porno films. In a confused way he believes his career as a sex worker is connected to his (mostly imaginary) career as a punk rock star. For him, all forms of show business feel more or less the same.

In the neighborhood, people hang around talking, speculating, killing time, often where the street dead-ends into the water. One of the regulars has a theory that Son of Sam is in fact Reggie Jackson (the killer uses a .44 handgun; Jackson's number is 44). The local priest is also a suspect; after all, he lives alone and can come and go as he wants. And then, slowly, frighteningly, attention becomes focused on Ritchie, the neighborhood kid who has chosen to flaunt his weird lifestyle.

Lee has a wealth of material here, and the film tumbles through it with exuberance. He likes the energy, the street-level culture, the music, the way that when conversation fails, sex can take over the burden of entertainment. And there is a deeper theme, too: the theme of how scapegoats are chosen. What's interesting is not that misfits are singled out as suspects; it's that the ringleaders require validation for their suspicions. At the end of the film, everyone's looking for Vinny. They need him to agree with their choice of victim—to validate their fever. It's as if they know they're wrong, but if Vinny says they're right, then they can't be blamed.

Summer of Sam is like a companion piece to Lee's *Do the Right Thing* (1989). In a different neighborhood, in a different summer, the same process takes place: The neighborhood feels threatened and needs to project its fear on an outsider. It is often lamented that in modern city neighborhoods, people don't get to know their neighbors. That may be a blessing in disguise.

Sunshine ★ ★ ★
R, 180 m., 2000

Ralph Fiennes (Ignatz, Adam, Ivan), Rosemary Harris (Valerie [Older]), Rachel Weisz (Greta), Jennifer Ehle (Valerie [Younger]), Molly Parker (Hannah), Deborah Unger (Carola), William Hurt (Andor Knorr), James Frain (Gustave [Younger]), John Neville (Gustave [Older]). Directed by Istvan Szabo and produced by Robert Lantos, Jonathan Debin, Andras Hamori, and Rainer Koelmel. Screenplay by Szabo and Israel Horovitz.

"One gang was as bad as another," says an old woman at the end of Istvan Szabo's *Sunshine*. In her long lifetime in Hungary she has lived under the emperor, the Nazis, and the Communists. And she watched as the West betrayed the 1956 uprising. She has seen some members of her Jewish family spend the century trying to accommodate themselves to the shifting winds of politics and society, and failing. She has seen other members fight against the prevailing tyrannies, only to find them replaced by new ones.

And she has witnessed the Holocaust bearing down over three generations—not as an aberration, a contagion spread by Hitler, but as the inexorable result of long years of anti-Semitism. We are reminded of the 1999 documentary *Last Days*, also about Holocaust victims in Hungary, which observes that the persecution of the Jews there began fairly late in the war, at a time when Hitler's thinly stretched resources were needed for tasks other than genocide.

But the Nazis had help. "Nice, ordinary Hungarian people did the dirty work," we learn, and there is even the possibility that some members of the Sonnenschein family, which the movie follows over three generations, would have helped had they not been Jewish and therefore ineligible. The movie shows family members determined to think of themselves as good Hungarians. The family name is changed to Sors to make it "more Hungarian," and Adam Sors, in the middle generation, converts to Catholicism, joins an officers' club, and wins a gold medal for fencing in the Olympics.

But assimilation is not the answer, as he learns when he remains too long in Hungary, believing a national hero like himself immune to anti-Semitism. There is a heartbreaking scene in a Nazi death camp where he tells an officer that he is a loyal Hungarian army officer, too—and a gold medalist. "Strip," the officer tells him, and soon his naked body has been crucified and sprayed with water until it forms a grotesque ice sculpture.

Szabo's epic tells the story of one family in one country, but it will do as a millennial record of a century in which one bright political idea after another promised to bring happiness and only enforced misery. The Sonnenschein family fortune is founded on "Sunshine," an invigorating tonic with a secret recipe. The film does not need to underline the symbolism that the formula for the tonic is lost as the century unfolds.

Ralph Fiennes plays the father, son, and grandson, each one rebuffed or repelled by a Hungary in agony. Ignatz Sonnenschein, whose story begins the film (with some flashbacks about his father), is a successful businessman who presides over a comfortable bourgeoisie home and thinks of standing for parliament. His brother Gustave (James Frain, and later John Neville) is disgusted he would support a corrupt regime, and Ignatz speaks hopefully of progressive elements in the regime and the emperor's openness to reform.

After the war, a Communist government gets in briefly, and Gustave joins it. Then the rise of the right ends that chapter, and he is placed under house arrest before fleeing to France. Meanwhile, Fiennes now plays Adam Sors, whose attention is focused on fencing; since the best fencers are in the officers' club, he takes lessons and converts to Catholicism so he can join it too. He doesn't take religion seriously; it's just a ticket you punch in order to fence.

His son Ivan (Fiennes again—uncanny in his ability to suggest the three different personalities) emerges after the war as a police officer under the new Communist regime. Ivan grows close to an idealist named Knorr (William Hurt), who believes in communism and wants to do a good job, and therefore is a threat to the government. This sequence, showing a weary Hungary being betrayed once again by a corrupt regime, is the most effective, because it pounds the message home: The people running the Communist government are more of the nice, ordinary Hungarians who helped with the Holocaust. The point

isn't that Hungarians are any worse than anyone else—but that, alas, human nature is much the same everywhere, and more generous with lackeys than heroes.

At three hours *Sunshine* made some audience members restless when it premiered at the Toronto Film Festival, but this is a movie of substance and thrilling historical sweep, and its three hours allow Szabo to show the family's destiny forming and shifting under pressure. At every moment there is a choice between ethics and expediency; at no moment is the choice clear or easy. Many Holocaust stories (like *Jakob the Liar*) dramatize the tragedy as a simple case of good and evil. And so it was, but that lesson is obvious. The buried message of *Sunshine* is more complex.

It suggests, first, that some Jews were slow to scent the danger because they were seduced into thinking their personal status gave them immunity (so do we all). Second, that those who felt communism was the answer to fascism did not understand how all "isms" distrust democracy and appeal to bullies. Third, that the Holocaust is being mirrored today all over the world, as groups hate and murder each other on the basis of religion, color, and nationality. The Sonnenschein family learned these lessons generation after generation during the century. So did we all. Not that human nature seems to have learned much as a result. Is there any reason to think fewer people will die in the twenty-first century than died in the twentieth, because they belong to a different tribe?

Superstar ★
PG-13, 82 m., 1999

Molly Shannon (Mary Katherine Gallagher), Will Ferrell (Sky), Elaine Hendrix (Evian), Harland Williams (Slater), Mark McKinney (Father Ritley), Glynis Johns (Grandma), Emmy Laybourne (Helen). Directed by Bruce McCulloch and produced by Lorne Michaels. Screenplay by Steven Wayne Koren.

I wouldn't be surprised to learn that newcomers to the *Saturday Night Live* cast are given two immediate assignments: Find someone you can imitate, and create a goony character. The second assignment has a better payoff. Chevy Chase can no doubt still do a pratfall like Gerald Ford, but who wants him to? But if Martin Short ever resurrects Ed Grimley, I'd buy a ticket. Maybe that's why so many of the *SNL* recurring characters get to star in movie spin-offs. Was *Blues Brothers* the first? How far we have fallen.

Most of the *SNL* goonies are, alas, not as funny as the Brothers, *Wayne's World*, or Ed Grimley—a truth abundantly demonstrated by *Superstar*, a feature-length spin-off based on Molly Shannon's character, Mary Katherine Gallagher. Here is a portrait of a character so sad and hapless, so hard to like, so impossible to empathize with, that watching it feels like an act of unkindness. The film is only eighty-two minutes long, including the generous closing credits, and yet long before it's over it runs out of any reason for existing.

Mary Catherine Gallagher, you may know, is plain and hostile, a homely little bundle of resentment with a supercharged fantasy life. In *Superstar*, she attends a Catholic school and dreams of sharing a wet kiss with Sky Corrigan (Will Ferrell), a football hero. That's all she wants—that, and to become a superstar. She confides these fantasies to a tree. Yes, a tree on the lawn in front of the school, which she French-kisses while whispering lurid scenarios.

I am prepared to concede there could be something funny about French-kissing a tree. To read about it, as you just have, may have inspired a smile. What you do not want to see is a girl actually kissing a tree—licking the bark, rubbing her knee against it, and . . . but I can't go on. The fact destroys the humor. The movie becomes a documentary. We are looking at an actress licking a tree. As Divine demonstrated in his notorious poop scene in *Pink Flamingos*, there are some scenes during which, however willing, we are unable to suspend our disbelief.

There's another problem. Mary Katherine isn't simply an "unpopular" girl—she's creepy and not very nice. She's one of those people who inspires in you the inexplicable desire to be hurtful and cruel. You don't meet people like that very often, but when you meet them, you know who they are. And you want to get away from them before you do something that would undermine your self-image as a nice person.

The plot involves lots of Catholic jokes. A few are funny, including a priceless moment involving twittering nuns, which captures some kind of truth—not about nuns, but about twittering. Others are lame or forced ("Catholic Cheerleaders against VD," Jesus explaining himself as a by-product of REM sleep, Mary Katherine doing a reading from *Sybil* in the confessional). Too bad the Catholic League is so busy attacking good films, like *Dogma*, that it can't spare the time to picket bad ones. I'm not in favor of protesting films on the basis of theology, but to picket them because they're boring could be an act of mercy.

Sweet and Lowdown ★ ★ ★ ½
PG-13, 95 m., 1999

Sean Penn (Emmet Ray), Samantha Morton (Hattie), Uma Thurman (Blanche), Anthony LaPaglia (Al Torrio), Brian Markinson (Bill Shields), Gretchen Mol (Ellie), James Urbaniak (Harry), John Waters (Mr. Hayes). Directed by Woody Allen and produced by Jean Doumanian. Screenplay by Allen.

Emmet Ray is like a man with a very large dog on a leash. The dog is his talent, and it drags him where it wants to go. There are times in *Sweet and Lowdown* when Ray, "the second-best jazz guitarist in the world," seems almost like a bystander as his fingers and his instinct create heavenly jazz. When the music stops he's helpless: He doesn't have a clue when it comes to personal relationships, he has little idea how the world works, and the only way he can recognize true love is by losing it.

Emmet Ray is a fictional character, but so convincing in Woody Allen's *Sweet and Lowdown* that he seems like a real chapter of jazz history we somehow overlooked. Sean Penn, whose performances are master classes in the art of character development, makes him into an exasperating misfit whose sins are all forgiven once he begins to play. With his goofy little mustache and a wardrobe that seems patterned on secondhand guesses about what a gypsy jazzman in Paris might wear, Emmet Ray looks like a square peg lacking even the round hole.

Here is a man who, when we first meet him, is already considered peerless among American jazz guitarists, yet is running a string of hookers as a sideline. Who drinks so much that only sheer good luck spares him, night after night, from getting himself killed. Who is forgiven by his colleagues, most of the time because when he plays there is magic happening right there on the stage.

Here is a man so lonely that he doesn't even know the concept. "Your feelings are locked away so deeply you don't even know where to find them," he's told. He's wounded: "You say that like it's a bad thing." One day on the boardwalk at Atlantic City, he meets the woman who would be the love of his life if he were sufficiently self-aware to understand that. Her name is Hattie (Samantha Morton), and she is a mute, although Emmet is so self-absorbed that it takes him quite a while to realize she never says anything.

Morton plays Hattie like one of the great silent film heroines. Before dialogue, before the Method, before sound, actors were hired because they embodied roles. You could be a carpenter or a secretary one day and be pushed before the camera on the next. Mabel Normand's *The Extra Girl* (1923) tells such a story. Morton is an accomplished British actress, but here she is not used as an actress so much as a presence, as in the silent days, with eyes that drink in Emmet, a body that yearns toward him, and a heart that's a pool of unconditional love and admiration. Her love is all the more remarkable because she can hear, which allows her not only to understand his music, but to endure his inept and often crude stabs at conversation.

Emmet, of course, is too unhinged to understand what a treasure she is. You don't know what you've got till it's gone. Vain, with an inferiority complex, a pushover for flattery, he is swept away by a society floozy named Blanche (Uma Thurman), who catches him stealing a knickknack at a party. She doesn't care; she's a little fascinated that a man she believes to be a genius would still harbor the instincts of a petty thief. "You have genuine crudeness," she tells him, as if she were saying he had nice eyes.

Sweet and Lowdown is structured by Allen as a docudrama; we hear Allen's own voice explaining passages in Ray's life, and we see jazz experts like Nat Hentoff who comment on aspects of Ray's career. Jazz history often seems constructed out of barroom stories improved upon over the years, and Emmet Ray's life unfolds like lovingly polished anecdotes; there are even alternate endings to some of the legendary episodes.

Looming over everything is Ray's awe of Django Reinhardt, the Spanish gypsy who ruled the Hot Club of Paris from the 1930s to the 1950s; despite having lost fingers in a childhood accident, he played the guitar as nobody has before or since. Again and again, Ray ruefully observes that he is indeed the best—except for that gypsy in France. A moment when he finally encounters Django provides one of the movie's best laughs.

The guitar playing in the movie is actually by Howard Alden. You will want to own the sound track. Alden taught Sean Penn to play the guitar, in lessons so successful that Allen's camera never has to cheat: We hear Emmet Ray and we see Emmet Ray's fingers, and there is never reason to doubt that Penn is actually playing the guitar.

Emmet Ray is the least Woody-like character I can remember at the center of an Allen movie. He embodies Allen's love of jazz, but few of his other famous characteristics, save perhaps for attracting worshipful women. Much has been made in some psychobabble reviews of the fact that Hattie is mute, as if that represents Allen's ideal woman; perhaps it's inevitable that a director whose films have been so autobiographical would attract speculation like that, but Allen's real-life partners, from Louise Lasser through Diane Keaton and Mia Farrow to the Soon-Yi Previn seen in the 1998 documentary *Wild Man Blues,* have all been assertive and verbal. I think Hattie is seen as Emmet's ideal woman, not Woody's, and it's interesting that Allen, who has gradually stopped casting himself as the lead in his films, now seems happy to make the leads into characters other than versions of himself.

I have made Emmet Ray sound like a doofus and a cold emotional monster, and those are elements in his character, but *Sweet and Lowdown* doesn't leave it at that. There is also a sweetness and innocence in the character, and his eyes warm when he's playing. You sense that this is a man who was equipped by life with few of the skills and insights needed for happiness, and that music transports him to a place he otherwise can hardly remember. If Emmet Ray's talent is indeed like a large dog, pulling him around, then I am reminded of a pet cemetery marker in Errol Morris's *Gates of Heaven,* which reads: "I knew love. I knew this dog."

Swept From the Sea ★ ★
PG-13, 114 m., 1998

Rachel Weisz (Amy Foster), Vincent Perez (Yanko), Ian McKellen (Dr. James Kennedy), Kathy Bates (Miss Swaffer), Joss Ackland (Mr. Swaffer), Tony Haygarth (Mr. Smith), Fiona Victory (Mrs. Smith), Tom Bell (Isaac Foster). Directed by Beeban Kidron and produced by Polly Tapson, Charles Steel, and Kidron. Screenplay by Tim Willocks.

Swept From the Sea is a plodding retelling of *Amy Foster,* not one of Joseph Conrad's best short stories. It follows the original more or less faithfully, except for the addition of a subtle element of homosexuality—which, if it had been less subtle, might have made the movie more intriguing.

The story involves a doomed love affair between a simple country girl and a Russian peasant who is swept onto the Cornish shore in 1888, after his emigrant ship sinks on its way to America. The peasant, whose hair, beard, and rags make him look like a wild man, speaks no English. He is feared by the locals—except for Amy Foster (Rachel Weisz), a local girl born in scandal and working for the Swaffers, a farm family. Amy is thought to be retarded, but it is more complicated than that; she was a student at the parish school for years, we learn, without making the slightest effort to read and write. Then she read and wrote for a month, to prove a point, and then stopped again.

Amy and the castaway, whose name is Yanko (Vincent Perez), fall in love, court, are married, and have a child. These events are closely monitored by James Kennedy (Ian McKellen), the local doctor, who shares the general feeling that Yanko is simpleminded until the Rus-

sian whips him at chess. With quiet hints and lingering looks, the film makes it clear that the doctor becomes attracted to the well-built Yanko, and resentful of Amy Foster for possessing his time and love.

Conrad's original story was narrated by Dr. Kennedy, who is not shy in describing Yanko's physical beauty, so the filmmakers are not unjustified in making his feelings more overt. Conrad has Kennedy speaking to the author of the tale, so that we got a narration within a narration. In the film, the doctor tells it instead to the bedridden Miss Swaffer, creating an unnecessary question: Why does he need to tell her things she already knows at firsthand? Better to simply eliminate the narrator and the flashbacks, and just tell the story from beginning to end.

The director is Beeban Kidron, whose films *(Antonia & Jane, To Wong Foo, Thanks for Everything, Julie Newman)* have been miles away from this sort of overwrought historical melodrama. She enters into the spirit of the enterprise with one of the most remarkable opening shots I have seen, as the camera sweeps over miles of ocean before rising to the top of a cliff and to the lonely figures of a mother and a child. There are also effective storm scenes, and the landscape is evoked as Conrad described it, as low and flat, a depressing setting for a population devoted enthusiastically to the hatred of outsiders.

This drabness is relieved by Amy's secret grotto, where she keeps treasures given to her by the ocean, and where she takes Yanko, also a gift of the sea; when they make love in the grotto's waters, however, I couldn't help wondering about the source of the shimmering underwater illumination.

I suppose the film can be excused for casting the slender and beautiful Rachel Weisz as Amy, described by Conrad as squat and dull-faced. The story is about two outsiders who find one another, and the movie remains faithful to that idea while adding another outsider, the doctor, who is never quite said to be homosexual but goes out of his way to be as near to Yanko as he can, as often as possible, and whose dislike of Amy extends to rudeness. At the end of the film, after the doctor has told Miss Swaffer (Kathy Bates) all that he knows about the histories of the two unfortunate people, she asks, "Did your own love blind you to hers?"

Kidron and her screenwriter, Tim Willocks, are not reaching in making Kennedy homosexual (certain lines in the story point in that direction). But why make his sexuality so understated many viewers will miss it? For fear of offending an audience that has turned up for a conventional period romance?

McKellen plays the character subtly and with restraint, even deliberate repression; there is the possibility the doctor has not acknowledged his sexuality and is responding only to unexamined feelings. But at the end, when the sad story has played out, there is a moment in which Dr. Kennedy lashes out, and the moment would play better and provide more of a dramatic shock if the movie had been clearer about the nature of the feelings he is expressing. As it is, *Swept From the Sea* is a disappointment, a film in which good and evil dutifully go through their paces, while the character who could have added complexity and intrigue remains, unfortunately, unrealized.

The Swindle ★ ★ ★
NO MPAA RATING, 105 m., 1999

Isabelle Huppert (Betty), Michel Serrault (Victor), Francois Cluzet (Maurice), Jean-Francois Balmer (Monsieur K), Jackie Berroyer (Chatillon), Jean Benguigui (Guadeloupe Gangster), Mony Dalmes (Signora Trotti). Directed by Claude Chabrol and produced by Marin Karmitz. Screenplay by Chabrol.

While their comrades in the French New Wave are either dead (Truffaut, Malle) or work rarely (Godard, Resnais, Rivette), Claude Chabrol and Eric Rohmer soldier on, prolific and creative. Other directors give difficult birth to each new project, but they've created worlds that easily produce new stories—Rohmer the world of minutely observed romance, Chabrol the world of crime and depravity.

The Swindle is Chabrol's fiftieth film, made with the practiced ease of a master. It's typical of his droll confidence that a man sprawls asleep in a chair during a key scene involving death threats and the breaking of fingers—and typical of Chabrol's restraint that he never cuts to the sleeping man for a quick laugh, but only subtly reveals him on the edges of the screen.

The movie stars Isabelle Huppert and Michel Serrault as Betty and Victor (if those are indeed their real names). She's fortyish, he's seventyish, they're con artists, and it's impossible to say what their personal relationship is: Friends? Lovers? Relatives? Even a hint at the end is left ambiguous. (It's a tribute to the actors, and to Chabrol, that in any given scene they could convincingly have any one of those three relationships.)

The movie starts with a warm-up con game. Betty poses as an available woman in a casino, and reels in a wealthy hardware dealer. She spikes his drink, he passes out in his room, and she and Victor relieve him of some, but not all, of his money—so that when he comes to, he won't remember his wagers well enough to be sure he was robbed.

That caper establishes the working partnership. Then the film ventures into a more complicated con—so complicated we're never quite sure if Betty and Victor are even conning one another. Betty has latched onto a financial courier for a crime syndicate, and has her eyes on the millions of Swiss francs in his locked briefcase. "Swissss! Swisssss!" Victor hisses cheerfully, relishing the superiority of Swiss to French francs.

The courier, Maurice (Francois Cluzet), is a polished man about Betty's age, and there's the hint of a romance between them. Or is that only in Victor's jealous eyes? Or is he really jealous? And is Betty planning to steal the money from Maurice and Victor? Or only from Maurice? Or is Victor planning to steal it from Betty? And what about the powerful criminals who consider the money, after all, to be their property?

The plot unfolds as an understated comedy. Serrault, who has made more than 150 films, seems to twinkle as he schemes. Huppert is, of course, famous for her impassivity (see her in *The School of Flesh*), but here she adds a kind of crazy flair, suddenly exaggerating a word or a gesture, as if amusing herself while going through the steps of a confidence charade. The movie adds sneaky little running jokes, like the way Serrault is forever being mistaken for an employee of whatever establishment he's in. Or the way a meal is lovingly ordered (there's great food in almost all of Chabrol's films).

Chabrol has always been an admirer of Hitchcock, and here he displays a Hitchcockian touch from time to time, almost deliberately. Consider the scene where the three principals observe a dance performance at a winter resort: Betty says she is too warm and leaves, followed first by one man and then the other; as they walk down the aisle all eyes are upon them. It's a reminder of how Hitchcock liked to put characters at a public event where escape meant breaking the rules.

By the end of the film we may still be murky about just what Betty and Victor were planning, and about their true relationship. That's part of the fun. Magicians don't reveal their secrets lightly ("The trick is told when the trick is sold"), and neither do con men. The con man this time, of course, is Chabrol, who has conned us into enjoying the entire film without giving away his own secrets.

T

The Talented Mr. Ripley ★ ★ ★ ★
R, 140 m., 1999

Matt Damon (Tom Ripley), Gwyneth Paltrow (Marge Sherwood), Jude Law (Dickie Greenleaf), Cate Blanchett (Meredith Logue), Philip Seymour Hoffman (Freddie Miles), Jack Davenport (Peter Smith-Kingsley), James Rebhorn (Herbert Greenleaf), Sergio Rubini (Inspector Roverini), Philip Baker Hall (Alvin MacCarron). Directed by Anthony Minghella and produced by William Horberg and Tom Sternberg. Screenplay by Minghella, based on the novel by Patricia Highsmith.

Villains usually last through only one crime novel, while heroes are good for a whole series. That's a great inconvenience for their authors, because villains are usually more colorful than heroes. Patricia Highsmith's novels about Tom Ripley are the exception, a series of books about a man who is irredeemably bad, and yet charming, intelligent, and thoughtful about the price he pays for his amoral lifestyle.

The Talented Mr. Ripley, her first Ripley novel, published in 1955, shows Ripley in the process of inventing himself and finding his life's work. He was a poor man who wanted to be a rich man, an unknown man who wanted not to be famous but simply to be *someone else.* Some men are envious of other men's cars, or wives, or fortunes. Ripley coveted their identities.

The novel shows him annexing the life and identity of a man named Greenleaf. It was filmed in 1960 by Rene Clement as *Purple Noon,* with Alain Delon as Ripley, and now it has been filmed again by Anthony Minghella *(The English Patient),* with Matt Damon in the title role. One of the pleasures of the two adaptations is that the plots are sufficiently different that you can watch one without knowing how the other turns out—or even what happens along the way. That despite the fact that they both revolve around Ripley's decision that he can be Greenleaf as well as, or better than, Greenleaf can be himself.

Purple Noon begins with the two men already friends. *The Talented Mr. Ripley,* adapted by Minghella, has a better idea: Ripley is an opportunist who stumbles onto an opening into Greenleaf's life and takes it. He borrows a Princeton blazer to play the piano at a rooftop party in Manhattan, and a rich couple assume he must have known their son Dickie at Princeton. He agrees.

The Greenleafs are concerned about Dickie (Jude Law), who has decamped to the decadence of Europe and shows no sign of coming home. They offer Tom Ripley a deal: They'll finance his own trip to Europe and pay him $1,000 if he returns with their son. Cut to a beach in Italy, where Dickie suns with Marge Sherwood (Gwyneth Paltrow), and the original deception turns evil.

Remember that Ripley is already impersonating someone—Dickie's old Princeton friend. That works with Dickie ("I've completely forgotten him," he tells Marge), but eventually he wonders if anything Tom tells him is the truth. Ripley, at this point still developing the skills that will carry him through several more adventures, instinctively knows that the best way to lie is to admit to lying, and to tell the truth whenever convenient. When Dickie asks him what his talents are, he replies, "Forging signatures, telling lies, and impersonating almost anyone." Quite true. And then he does a chilling impersonation of Mr. Greenleaf asking him to bring Dickie back to America. "I feel like he's here," Dickie says, as Tom does his father's voice.

By confessing his mission, Tom disarms Dickie, and is soon accepted into his circle, which also includes an epicurean friend named Freddie Miles (Philip Seymour Hoffman). Also moving through Europe at about the same time is a rich girl named Meredith Logue (Cate Blanchett), who believes things about Tom that Dickie must not be allowed to know. But I am growing vague, and must grow vaguer, because the whole point of the movie is to show Tom Ripley learning to use subterfuge, improvisation, and lightning-fast thinking under pressure to become Dickie Greenleaf.

Highsmith wrote *The Talented Mr. Ripley* five years after writing *Strangers on a Train,* which Hitchcock made into a film he sometimes called his favorite. The two stories are similar. *Strangers* is about a man who meets another man and offers to trade crimes with him: I'll kill the person you hate, and you kill the person I hate, and since neither one of us has any connection with our victim or any motive for killing him, we'll never be caught. *Talented* has Dickie blamed for the drowning death of a local woman, and Ripley "trading" that death as a cover-up for another.

Hitchcock's film subtly suggested a homosexual feeling in the instigator, and Tom Ripley also seems to have feelings for Dickie Greenleaf—although narcissism and sexuality are so mixed up in his mind that Ripley almost seems to want to became Greenleaf so that he can love himself (both Ripley movies have a scene of Ripley dressed in Dickie's clothes and posing in a mirror). This undercurrent is wisely never brought up to the level of conscious action, because so many of Tom Ripley's complicated needs and desires are deeply buried; he finds out what he wants to do by doing it.

Matt Damon is bland and ordinary as Ripley, and then takes on the vivid coloration of others—even a jazz singer. Jude Law makes Dickie almost deserving of his fate, because of the way he adopts new friends and then discards them. Gwyneth Paltrow's role is tricky: Yes, Dickie is her boyfriend, but he's cold and treats her badly, and there are times when she would intuit the dread secret if she weren't so distracted by the way she already resents Dickie.

The movie is as intelligent a thriller as you'll see this year. It is also insidious in the way it leads us to identify with Tom Ripley. He is the protagonist, we see everything through his eyes, and Dickie is not especially lovable; that means we are a coconspirator in situations where it seems inconceivable that his deception will not be discovered. He's a monster, but we want him to get away with it. There is one sequence in the film, involving an apartment, a landlady, the police, and a friend who knows the real Dickie, that depends on such meticulous timing and improvisation that if you made it speedier, you'd have the Marx brothers.

Tango ★ ★ ★ ½
PG-13, 112 m., 1999

Miguel Angel Sola (Mario Suarez), Cecilia Narova (Laura Fuentes), Mia Maestro (Elena Flores), Juan Carlos Copes (Carlos Nebbia), Julio Bocca (Himself), Juan Luis Galiardo (Angelo Larroca). Directed by Carlos Saura and produced by Luis A. Scalella, Carlos Mentasti, and Juan Carlos Codazzi. Screenplay by Saura.

The tango is based on suspicion, sex, and insincerity. It is not a dance for virgins. It is for the wounded and the wary. The opening shots of Carlos Saura's *Tango*, after a slow pan across Buenos Aires, are of a man who has given his life to the dance, and has a bad leg and a walking stick as his reward. This is the weary, graceful Mario (Miguel Angel Sola), who is preparing a new show based on the tango.

At the same time, perhaps Mario also represents Carlos Saura. The movie, one of 1999's Oscar nominees, has many layers: It is a film about the making of a film, and also a film about the making of a stage production. We are never quite sure what is intended as real and what is part of the stage production. That's especially true of some of the dance visuals, which use mirrors, special effects, trick lighting, and silhouettes so that we can't tell if we're looking at the real dancers or their reflections. A special set was constructed to shoot the film in this way, and the photography, by the great three-time Oscar winner Vittorio Storaro, is like a celebration of his gift.

If the film is visually beautiful, it is also ravishing as a musical—which is really what it is, with its passionate music and angry dance sequences. It is said the musical is dead, but it lives here, and Saura of course has made several films where music is crucial to the weave of the story; his credits include *Blood Wedding, Carmen,* and *Flamenco.*

Early in the film, Mario visits a club run by the sinister Angelo Larroca (Juan Luis Galiardo), who asks him a favor: an audition for his girlfriend, Elena (Mia Maestro). Mario can hardly refuse, because Angelo owns 50 percent of the show. Mario watches Elena dance, and realizes she is very good. He begins to fall in love with her, which is dangerous; when he makes a guarded proposal at dinner, she says, "Come off it—you know who I'm living with!"

Yes, he does. So does his estranged wife, Laura (Cecilia Narova), who warns him off the girl. But Mario and Elena draw closer, until finally they are sleeping with each other even though Angelo has threatened to punish cheating with death. What adds an additional element to their romance is Mario's essential sadness; he is like a man who has given up hope of being happy, and at one point he calls himself "A solitary animal—one of those old lions who roam the African savanna."

Of course, there is always the question of how much of this story is real, and how much of it is actually the story of the stage production. Saura allows us to see his cameras at times, suggesting that what we see is being filmed—for this film? Back and forth flow the lines of possibility and reality.

There are several dance sequences of special power. One is an almost vicious duet between Elena and Laura. Another uses dancers as soldiers, and suggests the time in Argentina's history when many people disappeared forever. That time is also evoked by images of startling simplicity: Torture, for example, is suggested by light on a single chair. And there is also a sequence, showing mostly just feet and legs, that suggests the arrival of immigrants to Argentina. You see in *Tango* that there are still things to be discovered about how dancing can be shown on the screen.

Recently, for one reason or another, I've seen a lot of tango. A stage performance in Paris, for example, and the 1997 British movie *The Tango Lesson*. Apart from the larger dimensions of the dance, there is the bottom line of technical skill. The legs of the dancers move so swiftly and so close to one another that only long practice and perfect timing prevents falls—even injuries. With the tango you never get the feeling the dancers have just met. They have a long history together, and not necessarily a happy one; they dance as a challenge, a boast, a taunt, a sexual put-down. It is the one dance where the woman gives as good as she gets, and the sexes are equal.

The romantic stories in *Tango* reflect that kind of dynamic. Mario and his estranged wife talk the way tango dancers dance. The early stages of Mario's seduction of Elena are like an emotional duel. The role of Angelo, the tough guy, is like a stage tango performance when a stranger arrives and tries to take command. It isn't real. It is real. It's all rehearsed, but they really mean it. It's only a show, but it reflects what's going on in the dancers' lives. It's only a dance. Yes, but life is only a dance.

Tarzan ★ ★ ★ ★
G, 88 m., 1999

With the voices of: Brian Blessed (Clayton), Glenn Close (Kala), Minnie Driver (Jane), Tony Goldwyn (Tarzan), Nigel Hawthorne (Professor Porter), Lance Henriksen (Kerchak), Wayne Knight (Tantor), Alex D. Linz (Young Tarzan), Rosie O'Donnell (Terk). Directed by Kevin Lima and Chris Buck and produced by Bonnie Arnold. Screenplay by Tab Murphy, Bob Tzudiker, and Noni White, based on the story "Tarzan of the Apes" by Edgar Rice Burroughs.

Something deep within the Tarzan myth speaks to us, and Disney's new animated *Tarzan* captures it. Maybe it's the notion that we can all inhabit this planet together, man and beast, and get along. The surface of the movie is adventure, comedy, and movement—there are sequences here as exciting as the ballroom scene in *Beauty and the Beast*—but underneath is something of substance. The most durable movie character in history emerges this time as a man who asks the question, "Why are you threatened by anyone different than you?"

This is not the confident Tarzan of so many Edgar Rice Burroughs novels and Johnny Weissmuller movies, discovering cities of gold. It is a Tarzan who knows from the day he compares his hand with the hand of Kala, the ape who has adopted him, that he is different. A Tarzan who is still different even after he meets other humans—because his experience is not the same. The movie doesn't insist on this thread of meaning, but it gives the movie weight. Like all the best Disney animated films, this one is about something other than cute characters and cheerful songs. It speaks even to the youngest members of the audience, who, like Tarzan, must have days when they feel surrounded by tall, rumbling, autocratic bipeds.

The movie is also a lot of fun. It has scenes that move through space with a freedom undreamed of in older animated films, and unreachable by any live-action process. Disney uses a process called Deep Canvas, a computer-assisted animation tool that handles the details during swoops through three dimensions. There's a sequence where Tarzan helps Jane escape from a band of monkeys, and as they hurtle through the treetops and loop-the-loop on byways of vines, it's like a roller-coaster ride.

The origin of Tarzan is one of the great masterstrokes of twentieth-century fiction. Burroughs, who never visited Africa, imagined it in much the same way that a child might, peering into a picture book of gorillas and elephants. The opening sequence of *Tarzan* encapsulates the story of how the young British baby and his parents were shipwrecked on the coast of Africa, built a treehouse, and lived in it. In the film, the infant is discovered by the curious gorilla Kala, after Sabor the leopard has killed his parents (offscreen, mercifully, although of course almost all Disney movies are about orphans in one way or another). She names the baby Tarzan, and brings it home to the family, where her mate, Kerchak, growls, "He can stay—but that doesn't make him my son!"

The look of the African forest is one of the great beauties of the film. There is such a depth to some scenes, and a feeling of great space in shots like the one where a waterfall tumbles off a mountain wall, while tiny birds make their way through the sky. Against this primeval wilderness, the Disney animators strike a sort of compromise with the laws of the jungle. Some animals (the leopard, for example) are true to their natures and are predators. Others, like the humanoid apes, are sentimentalized; Kala, voiced by Glenn Close, sounds like a suburban mom, and Terk, the wacky sidekick, sounds like—well, Rosie O'Donnell.

The leader of the pack, Kerchak (Lance Henrikson), is rumbling and distant, but there's an elephant who talks like a twelve-stepper ("I've had it with you and your emotional constipation"). Oddly, the animals have normal English dialogue when they are heard by one another, but are reduced to soft gutturals in the presence of outside humans. (Tarzan, who

has been chatting with Kala for years, is reduced to talking in little coos after Jane turns up, and we are denied what would no doubt have been an invaluable scene in which Kala tells him the facts of life.)

Jane is voiced by Minnie Driver, as a peppy British girl with lots of moxie. She's come with her father, the walrus-faced Professor Porter (Nigel Hawthorne), to study the gorillas; their guide is Clayton (Brian Blessed), with the graying sideburns of Stewart Granger and the sneers of a Victorian villain. The human plot, as you can guess, includes Clayton's nefarious plans for the gorillas and Tarzan's defense of them. The more interesting plot involves the tug-of-war after Tarzan and Jane fall in love ("I'm in a tree with a man who talks with gorillas!"). Will he return to London with her, or will she stay in the jungle? Burroughs had one answer; Disney has another.

There are, of course, no Africans in this movie. (The opening song promises us a paradise unspoiled by man.) This may be just as well. The Tarzan myth doesn't take place in Africa so much as in a kind of archetypal wilderness occupied only by its own characters. Burroughs used some Africans in his books, but that was after Tarzan got involved in politics (fighting the Germans in South West Africa, for example). At the stage of the story where this film is set, the presence of any additional characters would be disastrous, because they would bring in the real world, and this story has to close out reality to work at all. (*The Lion King*, of course, didn't even have room for Tarzan.)

Tarzan, like *The Hunchback of Notre Dame*, represents another attempt by Disney to push the envelope of animation. Taking a page from the Japanese, where animation is an accepted art form for serious films, *Tarzan* isn't a kiddie cartoon but a movie that works on one level for children (who will like the "Trashin' the Camp" production number), and another for adults (who may stir at scenes like the one where the gorillas reveal themselves to their visitors). The Disney animators also borrow a technique that has been useful to the Japanese, of exaggerating the size of eyes and mouths to make emotions clearer.

I saw *Tarzan* once, and went to see it again. This kind of bright, colorful, hyperkinetic animation is a visual exhilaration. Animation cuts loose from what we can actually see, and shows us what we might ideally see. Like *Mulan* and *A Bug's Life,* this is a film where grown-ups do not need to be accompanied by a non-adult guardian.   ☞

The Taste of Cherry ★
NO MPAA RATING, 95 m., 1998

Homayon Ershadi (Mr. Badii), Abdolrahman Bagheri (Taxidermist), Afshin Khorshid Bakhtiari (Soldier), Safar Ali Moradi (Soldier), Mir Hossein Noori (Seminarian). Directed and produced by Abbas Kiarostami. Screenplay by Kiarostami.

There was great drama at Cannes in 1997 when the Iranian director Abbas Kiarostami was allowed, at the last moment, to leave his country and attend the festival premiere of his new film, *The Taste of Cherry.* He received a standing ovation as he entered the theater, and another at the end of his film (although this time mixed with boos), and the jury eventually made the film cowinner of the Palme d'Or.

Back at the Hotel Splendid, standing in the lobby, I found myself in lively disagreement with two critics I respect, Jonathan Rosenbaum of the *Chicago Reader* and Dave Kehr of the *New York Daily News.* Both believed they had seen a masterpiece. I thought I had seen an emperor without any clothes.

A case can be made for the movie, but it would involve transforming the experience of viewing the film (which is excruciatingly boring) into something more interesting, a fable about life and death. Just as a bad novel can be made into a good movie, so can a boring movie be made into a fascinating movie review.

The story: A man in a Range Rover drives through the wastelands outside Tehran, crisscrossing a barren industrial landscape of construction sites and shantytowns, populated by young men looking for work. The driver picks up a young serviceman, asking him, at length, if he's looking for a job: "If you've got money problems, I can help." Is this a homosexual pickup? Kiarostami deliberately allows us to draw that inference for a time, before gradually revealing the true nature of the job.

The man, Mr. Badii (Homayon Ershadi),

wants to commit suicide. He has dug a hole in the ground. He plans to climb into it and take pills. He wants to pay the other man to come around at 6 A.M. and call down to him. "If I answer, pull me out. If I don't, throw in twenty shovels of earth to bury me."

The serviceman runs away. Badii resumes his employment quest, first asking a seminarian, who turns him down because suicide is forbidden by the Koran, and then an elderly taxidermist. The older man agrees because he needs money to help his son, but argues against suicide. He makes a speech on Mother Earth and her provisions, and asks Badii, "Can you do without the taste of cherries?"

That, essentially, is the story (I will not reveal if Badii gets his wish). Kiarostami tells it in a monotone. Conversations are very long, elusive, and enigmatic. Intentions are misunderstood. The car is seen driving for long periods in the wasteland, or parked overlooking desolation, while Badii smokes a cigarette. Any two characters are rarely seen in the same shot, reportedly because Kiarostami shot the movie himself, first sitting in the driver's seat, then in the passenger's seat.

Defenders of the film, and there are many, speak of Kiarostami's willingness to accept silence, passivity, a slow pace, deliberation, inactivity. Viewers who have short attention spans will grow restless, we learn, but if we allow ourselves to accept Kiarostami's time sense, if we open ourselves to the existential dilemma of the main character, then we will sense the film's greatness.

But will we? I have abundant patience with long, slow films, if they engage me. I fondly recall *Taiga,* the eight-hour documentary about the yurt-dwelling nomads of Outer Mongolia. I understand intellectually what Kiarostami is doing. I am not impatiently asking for action or incident. What I do feel, however, is that Kiarostami's style here is an affectation; the subject matter does not make it necessary, and is not benefited by it.

If we're to feel sympathy for Badii, wouldn't it help to know more about him? To know, in fact, *anything at all* about him? What purpose does it serve to suggest at first he may be a homosexual? (Not what purpose for the audience—what purpose for Badii himself? Surely he must be aware his intentions are being misinterpreted.) And why must we see Kiarostami's camera crew—a tiresome distancing strategy to remind us we are seeing a movie? If there is one thing *The Taste of Cherry* does not lack, it is such a reminder: The film is such a lifeless drone that we experience it *only* as a movie.

Yes, there is a humanistic feeling underlying the action. Yes, an Iranian director making a film on the forbidden subject of suicide must have courage. Yes, we applaud the stirrings of artistic independence in the strict Islamic republic. But is *The Taste of Cherry* a worthwhile viewing experience? I say it is not.

Teaching Mrs. Tingle ★ ½
PG-13, 94 m., 1999

Helen Mirren (Mrs. Tingle), Katie Holmes (Leigh Ann Watson), Jeffrey Tambor (Coach Wenchell), Barry Watson (Luke Churner), Marisa Coughlan (Jo Lynn Jordan), Liz Stauber (Trudie Tucker), Michael McKean (Principal Potter), Molly Ringwald (Miss Banks), Vivica A. Fox (Mrs. Gold). Directed by Kevin Williamson and produced by Cathy Konrad. Screenplay by Williamson.

Helen Mirren is a very good actress. All too good for *Teaching Mrs. Tingle,* where she creates a character so hateful and venomous that the same energy, more usefully directed, could have generated a great Lady Macbeth. She is correct to believe that comic characters are best when played straight. They depend on the situation to make them funny. There is nothing funny about the situation in *Teaching Mrs. Tingle.*

The movie resembles *Election* in its attempt to deal with the dog-eat-dog world of ambitious high school students, where grade points can make an enormous difference. But it lacks that movie's sly observations about human nature, and bludgeons the audience with broad, crude, creepy developments. Here is a movie that leaves us without anyone to like very much, and no one to care about. It was written and directed by Kevin Williamson, whose screenplays for the *Scream* pictures depend on comic slasher situations for their appeal; here, required to create more believable characters, he finds the wrong ones for this kind of story.

Katie Holmes stars as Leigh Ann Watson, an honor student only a few percentage points shy of becoming class valedictorian. Much depends on the grade she gets in history, a class that Mrs. Tingle (Mirren) rules with an iron fist and cruel sarcasm. She seems to take an almost erotic delight in humiliating her students in public, and singles out Leigh Ann for special ridicule, maybe just because she's smart and pretty.

Also in the picture: Jo Lynn Jordan (Marisa Coughlan), Leigh Ann's best friend; their classmate and friend Luke Churner (Barry Watson), who combines the better qualities of slobs and oafs; and Trudie Tucker (Liz Stauber), who is Leigh Ann's bitter rival for valedictorian. Oh, and there's Michael McKean as the high school principal; Mrs. Tingle knows he's in AA and threatens to blackmail him for secret drinking. And Coach Wenchell (Jeffrey Tambor), whose relationship with Mrs. Tingle is reflected in his nickname, Spanky (in this case it is best spelled Spankee).

Leigh Ann turns in a history project in the form of a journal that might have been kept by a pilgrim woman; it's leather-bound, with meticulous calligraphy and decorations, and would make the judges of the History Book Club weep with gratitude. Mrs. Tingle scornfully mocks it after only glancing at the front page. Later, she pounces on the three friends in the gym. Luke has stolen a copy of Mrs. Tingle's final exam and stuffs it into Leigh Ann's backpack, where Mrs. Tingle finds it. Now Leigh Ann faces expulsion.

All of this serves as setup to the heart of the movie, which is spent with Mrs. Tingle tied to her bed while the three students desperately try to figure out what to do next. If this were a serious hostage or kidnapping movie, some of the resulting material might seem appropriate. Mirren approaches Mrs. Tingle like a prisoner of war in a serious film, playing mind games with her captors. There are scenes that are intended as farce (unexpected arrivals and phone calls), but they're flat and lifeless. We have no sympathy for Mrs. Tingle, but at least she has life, while the three students are simply constructions—walking, talking containers for the plot.

Is it possible that some high school students hate their teachers so much that they'll play along with *Teaching Mrs. Tingle*? I doubt it, because Mrs. Tingle isn't hateful in an entertaining way. She belongs in one of those anguished South American movies about political prisoners and their captors facing ethical dilemmas. And the kids belong in *Scream 3.* 🖝

Tea with Mussolini ★ ★ ½
PG, 117 m., 1999

Cher (Elsa), Judi Dench (Arabella), Joan Plowright (Mary), Maggie Smith (Lady Hester), Lily Tomlin (Georgie), Baird Wallace (Luca), Charlie Lucas (Luca [child]), Massimo Ghini (Paolo). Directed by Franco Zeffirelli and produced by Riccardo Tozzi, Giovannella Zannoni, and Clive Parsons. Screenplay by John Mortimer and Zeffirelli, based on Zeffirelli's autobiography.

How accurate *Tea with Mussolini* is I cannot say, but it is based on the autobiography of the film director Franco Zeffirelli, who directed it, so we can be sure it is true to what he remembers, or wants to remember. The film tells of a boy named Luca, born out of wedlock to a clothing manufacturer in Florence. His mother is dead, his father's wife visits him at school to hiss that he is a bastard, and his best friend is an old expatriate Brit named Mary (Joan Plowright), who has been hired to turn him into a perfect English gentleman.

As the film opens in the early 1930s, we are told, the Italians and the British have a mutual love affair. We see it reflected in the daily lives of a gaggle of eccentric British ladies of more than a certain age, who gather in Doney's Tea Rooms and the galleries of the Uffizi to gossip—about each other, mostly. After Luca's father orders Mary to return him to the orphanage, she finds she cares for him too much, and takes him instead to live with her at the Pensione Shelley. And thus young Luca is plunged into the intrigues and artistic passions of the "Scorpioni," which is the nickname for the ladies with their stinging wit.

These ladies are played by a cast as eclectic as it is engaging. The grand dame of the Scorpioni is Lady Hester (Maggie Smith), the widow of the former British ambassador. The artistic soul of the group is Arabella (Judi Dench), who informs young Luca, "I have warmed both hands before the fires of Michelangelo and Botticelli." The most visible eccentric, in a congregation of flamboyance, is Georgie (Lily Tomlin), an archaeologist who works among the ruins in pants and overalls that match her cheerfully lesbian inclinations. Mary seems almost average in this company, a sweet lady who supports herself by typing florid Italian into sensible English.

And then there is Elsa Morganthal (Cher), an outlandish American who swoops in and out of Florence like a summer squall. She's an art collector, whose purchases are financed by a rich and absent husband (who is "too cheap to slip a poor girl a little Picasso"). Resembling Peggy Guggenheim, who made her headquarters in Venice, Elsa is loud, flamboyant, and unwise enough to fall in love with her chauffeur, a cad with patent-leather hair who sells fake art to her, steals her money, and when the time comes, betrays her to the fascists.

The character of Luca is a little overwhelmed by all of these outsize personalities, and indeed the movie might actually have been better without him. Yes, Luca is supposed to be Zeffirelli, and the director is telling his own story—but he seems to inhabit it mostly as an observer. The two actors engaged to play Luca aren't given much to say, and although as a young man Luca joins the Resistance, that activity consists mostly of lurking behind trees and appearing when he is required by the plot. Zeffirelli may look out through Luca's eyes, but not into a mirror.

The ladies supply quite enough entertainment all on their own. Lady Hester charges off to Rome for tea with Mussolini, who assures her that she and her British friends have nothing to worry about, and then poses for photos that will be useful propaganda (ambassador's wife has tea with dictator, finds him a nice chap). Soon, however, the brownshirts are breaking the windows of the tearoom, and the ladies are put under custody and shipped off to a beautiful mountaintop village.

The movie is heavier with events than with plot. Things are always happening, but it's hard to see the connections, and the material involving Elsa's love affair, Lady Hester's draft-dodging male relative, and Arabella's dog all coexists uneasily. (The draft dodger hides from the fascists by dressing in drag, only to finally

589

snap, run into the street, cry out "I'm a man!" strip off his dress, and join the Resistance.) Elsa, the Cher character, meanwhile ignores the dangers for a Jew in Italy, and makes unwise statements such as, "Musso? I think his butt's too big to push around the dance floor."

I enjoyed the movie in a certain way, as a kind of sub–Merchant-Ivory combination of eccentric ladies and enchanting scenery. I liked the performances of the women (including Cher; people keep forgetting what a good actress she can be). I wanted to see more of Tomlin's bracingly frank archaeologist (why do movie lesbians have to recite so much dialogue that keys off their sexuality?). But the movie seemed the stuff of anecdote, not drama, and as the alleged protagonist, Luca/Franco is too young much of the time to play more than a bystander's role. Zeffirelli, of course, grew up to direct better movies *(Romeo and Juliet,* the Burton-Taylor *Taming of the Shrew,* the Mel Gibson *Hamlet)* and opera, and to speak flawless English.

10 Things I Hate About You ★ ★ ½
PG-13, 94 m., 1999

Heath Ledger (Patrick Verona), Julia Stiles (Katarina Stratford), Joseph Gordon-Levitt (Cameron James), Larisa Oleynik (Bianca Stratford), David Krumholtz (Michael Eckman), Larry Miller (Mr. Stratford), Andrew Keegan (Joey Donner), Susan May Pratt (Mandella), Gabrielle Union (Chastity), Allison Janney (Counselor), Daryl "Chill" Mitchell (English Teacher). Directed by Gil Junger and produced by Andrew Lazar. Screenplay by Karen McCullah Lutz and Kirsten Smith.

I'm trying to remember the last movie I saw that didn't end with a high school prom. *Ravenous,* maybe. Even the *next* film I've seen, *Never Been Kissed,* ends with a prom. The high school romance genre has become so popular that it's running out of new ideas, and has taken to recycling classic literature.

My colleague James Berardinelli made a list recently: *Clueless* was based on *Emma, She's All That* was inspired by *Pygmalion,* and *Cruel Intentions* was recycled from *Les Liaisons Dangereuses* (prompting Stanley Kauffmann to observe that it was better back in the days

when high school students were allowed to take over the city government for a day, instead of remaking French novels). To this list we might also add the update of *Great Expectations,* Cinderella's true story in *Ever After,* and *William Shakespeare's Romeo and Juliet,* which was anything but. There's even *Rage: Carrie 2*—a retread of *Carrie,* a work that ranks in my opinion right up there with the best of Austen, Shaw, and Shakespeare.

10 Things I Hate About You is inspired, in a sortuva kinduva way, by Shakespeare's *The Taming of the Shrew,* in the same sense that *Starship Troopers* was inspired by *Titus Andronicus.* It doesn't remake Shakespeare so much as evoke him as a talisman by setting its story at Padua High School, naming its characters Stratford and Verona, making one of the heroines a shrew, etc. There is even a scene where the shrew is assigned to rewrite a Shakespeare sonnet.

And yet . . . gee, the movie is charming, even despite its exhausted wheeze of an ancient recycled plot idea (boy takes bribe to ask girl to prom, then discovers that he really likes her— but then she finds out about the bribe and hates him). I haven't seen that idea in almost two months, since *She's All That* (boy makes bet he can turn plain wallflower into prom queen and does, but falls in love with her, after which she discovers, etc., etc.).

The story this time involves two Seattle sisters. Bianca Stratford (Larisa Oleynik) is popular and wears a lot of red dresses. Her shrewish older sister Katarina (Julia Stiles) is unpopular, never dates, and is the class brain. (When the English teacher asks his class for reactions to a Hemingway novel, she snaps, "Hemingway was an alcoholic who hung around Picasso hoping to nail his leftovers.")

Two guys want to take Bianca to the prom. One is shy and likable. The other is a blowhard. But Bianca's father (Larry Miller) has forbidden her to date until her older sister Katarina starts going out. So a plot is hatched to convince Patrick (Heath Ledger), the school outlaw, to ask her to the prom. He takes a $300 bribe, but then realizes that Kat is actually quite lovely, etc., and really falls in love with her, after which, etc.

I think we simply have to dump the entire plot and appreciate the performances and some of the jolliest scenes. I liked, to begin with, the spirit of the high school teachers. Allison Janney is the sex-mad counselor, and Daryl "Chill" Mitchell is the English teacher who performs Shakespeare's sonnets as if they were rap lyrics. (I've got news for you: They work pretty well as rap, and I expect the album any day.)

I also liked the sweet, tentative feeling between Ledger and Stiles. He has a scene that brings the whole movie to an enjoyable halt. Trying to win her heart, he waits until she's on the athletic field, and then sings "I Love You Baby" over the P.A. system, having bribed the marching band to accompany him. Those scenes are worth the price of admission—almost. But then other scenes are a drag.

All teenage movies have at least one boring and endless party scene, in which everyone is wildly dressed, drunk, and relentlessly colorful (in *Never Been Kissed,* some of the kids come as the Village People). These scenes inevitably involve (a) a fight, (b) barfing, and (c) a tearful romantic breakup In Front of Everybody. That scene was tedious, and so was a scene where the would-be lovers throw paint balloons at each other. I know there has to be a scene of carefree, colorful frolic, but as I watched them rubbing paint in each other's hair I began to yearn for that old standby, the obligatory Tilt-a-Whirl ride.

I liked the movie's spirit, and the actors, and some of the scenes. The music, much of it by a band named Letters to Cleo, is subtle and inventive while still cheerful. The movie almost but not quite achieves liftoff against the gravitational pull of the tired story formula. Sometimes it's a mistake to have acting this charming; the characters become so engaging and spontaneous we notice how they're trapped in the plot.

The Terrorist ★ ★ ★ ½
NO MPAA RATING, 95 m., 2000

Ayesha Dharkar (Malli), Parmeshwaran (Vasu), Vishnu Vardhan (Thyagu), Bhanu Prakash (Perumal), Vinshwa (Lotus). Directed by Santosh Sivan and produced by Jit Joshi and A. Sreekar Prasad. Screenplay by Sivan, Ravi Deshpande, and Vijay Deveshwar. In Tamil with English subtitles.

She is nineteen years old and a soldier in a revolutionary movement. Her brother has died for the cause, and she has killed for it. A volunteer is needed for a suicide mission. She steps forward, fiercely and silently, and is accepted. She will become a "thinking bomb," and after she places a garland of flowers around a politician's neck, she will blow them both to pieces.

The Terrorist does not name its time or place, or the politician, but it seems broadly inspired by the 1991 assassination of India's Rajiv Gandhi. It is not a political film, but a personal one. If you have ever wondered what kind of person volunteers to become a human bomb, and what they think about in the days before their death, this film wonders too.

And its director, Santosh Sivan, does something filmmakers find almost impossible. It follows this young woman without identifying with her mission. We do not want her to succeed. Films are such a first-person medium—they identify so strongly with their protagonists—that they generate sympathy even for evil: Did we want Hannibal Lecter to escape? Of course we did. And at the end of *The Day of the Jackal* (1973) we instinctively wanted the assassin to succeed, simply because we had been following him for two hours. Of course we think murder is wrong, but fiction tends to argue for its heroes. Consider *Crime and Punishment.*

In *The Terrorist,* we do not want the young girl, named Malli, to succeed. That's despite the way the movie paints her loyalty to her cause, and the possibility that her cause is right. The movie is quiet and persuasive as it shows Malli learning more about her life in what may be her last days than she ever knew before.

Played by Ayesha Dharkar, a young actress with expressive eyes and a beauty that is innate, not cosmetic, Malli doesn't talk much, and we sense that she has deep wounds; her brother's death in the same cause suggests a painful background. After she volunteers for the mission, she is passed along an underground network of conspirators to the farm where she will spend her final days. One of her guides is a boy of thirteen or fourteen named Lotus (Vinshwa), who leads her down the center of a shallow river and shows her where to step to avoid land mines and booby traps. He has guided many others this way, he says; they have all later been killed. When a truck blows up, he weeps: "There will be blood everywhere." No more than a child, he is traumatized by his life.

Also on the journey she meets a young soldier who is mortally wounded. In a scene of great delicacy, she cradles him on the forest floor, and he whispers that he has never been so close to a woman in his life. Nor, we sense, has she ever been so close to a man. Just as Sivan makes a movie that does not identify with its violent mission, so he creates a love scene that is not about sex, but communication, surcease, healing.

Eventually Malli arrives at a farm and is given a room of her own. We meet the farmer Vasu (Parmeshwaran) and his helper. These are characters to remind us of the gentle humor of the great Indian novelist R. K. Narayan. Their philosophy and religion is a part of their lives, and the farmer tells Malli: "A flower is the earth smiling." He always sets an extra place at dinner for his wife, who is in a coma and has not stirred for seven years. Malli sees the woman in the room next to her own, staring sightlessly at nothing.

Malli's terrorist contact and his sidekick rehearse her carefully, and select clothing that will conceal the bomb strapped around her middle. They are narrow functionaries, telling her that news of her action will go out to all the world. It is unclear if the farmer knows of her mission (I think he doesn't). He argues for life, not in words so much as in how he conducts his own life.

Malli says little in the film. Sometimes the sound track uses the sound of quiet breathing, which places us inside her head. She regards herself in the mirror, and we intuit what she's thinking. Conversations she has with the farmer put her action in a new light, with new consequences. All leads up to an ending that is the right ending for this film, although few members of the audience will anticipate it.

There is no shortage of those prepared to sacrifice their lives to kill others and advance their cause. If we disagree with them, they are fanatics. If we agree, they are heroes. At least they are personally involved and prepared to pay with their lives, which in a sense is more ethical than killing by remote control at long distance and calling it "modern warfare."

But what do they think? How do they feel?

I've often wondered what goes through the mind of a condemned prisoner, who knows the exact hour of his death. How much stranger it must seem to be your own willing executioner: to die voluntarily because an idea is bigger than yourself. In my mind, the self is the biggest of all ideas; without it, there are no ideas. Does Malli arrive at this conclusion?

That's the Way I Like It ★ ★ ★
PG-13, 95 m., 1999

Adrian Pang (Ah Hock), Madeline Tan (Ah Mei), Pierre Png (Richard), Anna Belle Francis (Julie), Steven Lim (Boon), Westley Wong (Bobby), Caleb Goh (Leslie/Ah Bend). Directed by Glen Goei and produced by Goei, Jeffrey Chiang, and Tan Chih Chong. Screenplay by Goei.

That's the Way I Like It is a lighthearted disco kung-fu musical—a Singapore retread of *Saturday Night Fever* crossed with a little Bruce Lee. It's not a satire, but another pass through the same material, right down to the Galaxy 2000 Disco, the ear-boxing at the dinner table, and the famous white suit. John Travolta must be smiling.

Singapore, 1977. Adrian Pang plays Ah Hock, a guy who works in a supermarket, dreams of owning a new Triumph motorcycle, and has been many times to see *Forever Fever,* which is the Singapore title for the Travolta film. When a local disco announces a dance contest with a prize big enough to buy the Triumph, he signs up for dance lessons at the Bonnie and Clyde Dance Studio.

Meanwhile, at home, Ah Hock gets no respect. In the original movie, the family doted on the older brother, who was a priest. In this film, it's the younger brother, who is studying to be a doctor. Ah Hock is seen as the family goof-up, and in a scene that will resonate for lovers of the Travolta film, his father slaps him alongside the head, and Ah Hock bursts out in Singapore English: "Why you have to hit my hair?" True to the tradition of the Hollywood movie, the other brother makes a stunning announcement at the dinner table; Travolta's brother revealed he was leaving the priesthood, while Ah Hock's brother has changed his name from Ah Bend to Leslie, and further revelations follow.

Saturday Night Fever has Travolta abandoning his sweet neighborhood girlfriend in order to choose a lovelier girl as his contest partner. Same thing here; good, loyal Ah Mei (Madeline Tan) gets replaced by slinky Julie (Anna Belle Francis), angering her own boyfriend, a rat. The contest of course ends with Ah Hock doing a solo, the disco ball painting the room in light as the sound track reprises familiar songs (the movie has a lot of the same music, covered by Singapore soundalikes).

Two imaginary advisers inspire Ah Hock on his way to the big contest: Bruce Lee, whose motto from *Enter the Dragon* ("Don't think—feel") becomes his credo, and John Travolta himself, who appears in fantasy sequences and gives him advice about life. (Well, not really Travolta, but a look-alike seen in shadow and profile, like Humphrey Bogart in *Play It Again, Sam*.) Inspired, Ah Hock finds a locally tailored knock-off of Travolta's famous white suit.

Adrian Pang makes a likable hero, not without humor about his own predicaments, filled with passion and energy as he battles with his boss at the supermarket, and conquers a last-minute trap set by the bad guy. *Saturday Night Fever* this movie isn't, but it's not supposed to be: It's a funny homage, a nod to the way some movies are universal in their appeal. I said Travolta must be smiling. Gene Siskel, who bought the original white disco suit at a charity auction and treasured it as much as Ah Hock cherishes his, must be grinning too.

The Theory of Flight ★ ★ ½
R, 100 m., 1999

Helena Bonham Carter (Jane), Kenneth Branagh (Richard), Gemma Jones (Anne), Holly Aird (Julie). Directed by Peter Greengrass and produced by Ruth Caleb, Anant Singh, Helena Spring, and David Thompson. Screenplay by Richard Hawkins.

Godard said that the best way to criticize a movie is to make another movie. That has already been done in the case of *The Theory of Flight*, a British film about a young woman in a wheelchair who desperately desires to have sex. The movie that eclipses this one is *Dance Me to My Song*, an Australian film that played in 1998 at the Cannes Film Festival and silenced the audience with its stark courage. (It still lacks American distribution.)

The Theory of Flight stars Helena Bonham Carter as Jane, the young woman in the chair, who suffers from ALS and uses a voice synthesizer to help her communicate. It is a good performance—but just that, a performance. What is astonishing about *Dance Me to My Song* is that it was written by a young woman named Heather Rose, who has cerebral palsy, lives in a chair, communicates with a machine—and actually plays Julia, the heroine of her movie.

To compare Jane and Julia is not fair, since neither film could have known about the other and both are good-hearted. But I will do it anyway. Jane, the Bonham-Carter character, has had bad luck with her helpers, until she draws the quirky Richard (Kenneth Branagh), an artist who has been assigned to her after being sentenced to community service for having caused a lot of trouble when he jumped off a building with homemade wings.

Compare that idealized situation with the plight of Julia, in the Australian movie. Her disease is so advanced she can barely move, and she has been assigned a series of empty-headed and cruel companions who steal her money and let her lie in her own messes while they chatter on the phone.

Jane wants sex, and informs Richard by playing a little speech that she has programmed into her synthesizer. "Help me lose my virginity," she says. "I know realistically I'll never get the whole deal. But that doesn't mean I shouldn't get as much as I can."

For Julia it is not that easy (not that it is easy for Jane). She is a virtual captive of her apartment, has no way to meet other people, and in an astonishing sequence takes things into her own hands. Using her battery-powered chair, she escapes from her house and onto the sidewalk, where she accosts a young man and begins, in her own way, to seduce him. Consider that Heather Rose plays all of these scenes herself, without doubles, and is cruelly handicapped in speech and movement, and you will begin to guess how powerful it all becomes.

Both young women are frank in their speech. They like four-letter words, which growl out of their synthesizers like Stephen Hawking on a bad day. Both of their targets are at first disbelieving, then reluctant. And so on. Enough of the plots.

Recently I have been getting a lot of flak from readers who object to my review of *Patch Adams*, the Robin Williams film. How can I dislike this film, they ask, when its message is so heartwarming? The movie argues that doctors must care more for their patients, they inform me, and that laughter is the best medicine. Some of the letters are from people whose loved ones are critically ill, and have either endured impersonal medical treatment, or benefited from doctors and nurses who do care.

I agree with these correspondents that laughter is the best medicine. I agree that the personal touch is invaluable in the healing professions. But they have confused the message with the movie. Who could disagree with the sentiments in *Patch Adams*? And what do they have to do with the film's shameless and manipulative cynicism? I write back: "Remember, it's not what the movie is about—it's *how* it's about it!"

I wish I could rent a theater and show these good people a double feature of *The Theory of Flight* and *Dance Me to My Song*. Here are two movies that are essentially about the same thing. The British film uses big stars and cutes everything up (much of the plot involves whether Branagh can build a flying machine, and whether he and the young woman can overcome their personal versions of fear of flying). The Australian film is an act of the will by a cerebral palsy sufferer whose own achievement is even greater than her heroine's. (As anyone in Hollywood can tell you, it is a lot easier to get someone to sleep with you than to get a screenplay produced.)

The Theory of Flight is actually fairly enjoyable. At least it doesn't drown its message in syrup and cornball sentiment like *Patch Adams*. It has a lot of refreshing humor. But then, when you see the real thing, when you see *Dance Me to My Song*, you're struck by the difference. Two movies. Same story. Same objective. Similar characters. Similar situation. One is an entertainment. The other is a thunderbolt.

There's Something About Mary ★ ★ ★
R, 119 m., 1998

Ben Stiller (Ted), Cameron Diaz (Mary), Matt Dillon (Healy), Chris Elliott (Dom), W. Earl Brown (Warren), Lee Evans (Tucker), Lin Shaye (Magda), Jeffrey Tambor (Sully). Directed by Peter Farrelly and Bobby Farrelly and produced by Bradley Thomas, Charles Wessler, Frank Beddor, Michael Steinberg, and Mark S. Fischer. Screenplay by Ed Decter, John J. Strauss, and the Farrellys.

What a blessed relief is laughter. It flies in the face of manners, values, political correctness, and decorum. It exposes us for what we are, the only animal with a sense of humor. *There's Something About Mary* is an unalloyed exercise in bad taste, and contains five or six explosively funny sequences. Okay, five explosive, one moderate.

I love it when a movie takes control, sweeps away my doubts and objections, and compels me to laugh. I'm having a physical reaction, not an intellectual one. There's such freedom in laughing so loudly. I feel cleansed.

There's Something About Mary is the latest work by Peter and Bobby Farrelly, brothers whose earlier credits include *Dumb and Dumber* and *Kingpin*. Good taste is not their strong suit. *Dumb and Dumber* included a scene where a blind boy realizes his parakeet's head is held on with Scotch tape. *Kingpin* includes a scene where a bowler's artificial hand gets stuck in the ball and rolls down the alley, flop-flop-flop.

Now here is a movie about a woman who is beautiful, sunny, good, and pure, and inspires a remarkable array of creeps to fall into love with her. There's . . . just something about her. Mary is played by Cameron Diaz as a high school knockout who amazes the geeky Ted (Ben Stiller) by asking him to the prom even though he has pounds of braces on his teeth. ("I have a thing about braces," she muses, long after.)

Ted turns up proudly for the date, only to set off the first of the movie's uproariously funny sequences when he asks to use the toilet and then somehow catches in his zipper that part of the male anatomy one least wants to think about in connection with zippers. ("Is it the frank or the beans?" asks Mary's solicitous stepfather.)

In a lesser film, that would be that: The directors would expect us to laugh at his misfortune and the plot would roll on. Not the Farrelly brothers. When they get something going, they keep on building, daring themselves to top each outrage. I won't reveal how the scene develops, apart from noting the perfect timing involved with the unexpected close-up.

Thirteen years pass. Ted is still in love with Mary. He hires a sleazy investigator named Healy (Matt Dillon) to track her down. Healy, wearing one of those mustaches that shout "Distrust me!" finds her in Miami, discovers she is an unbelievable babe who is still single, and decides to grab her for himself. He tells Ted she weighs 250 pounds, has four children by three fathers, and has just shipped out for Japan as a mail-order bride.

Healy's trick is to eavesdrop on Mary's conversations, so he'll know just what she wants to hear. Among the things most important to her is her retarded brother Warren (W. Earl Brown), who doesn't like to have his ears touched. Healy poses as the person of her dreams (an architect with a condo in Nepal, who loves to work with retarded people), but he raises the suspicions of another of her suitors, Tucker (Lee Evans), who is an architect who uses crutches. Maybe.

Further plot description would be pointless. The plot exists, like all screwball plots, simply to steer us from one gag to the next. In the TV ads you may already have seen the moment when the dog of Mary's deeply tanned neighbor needs to have its heart restarted. That's because the dog has been tranquilized. There is also a scene where the dog is on speed, and his human target does things with walls and furniture not seen since Donald O'Connor's "Make 'em Laugh" sequence in *Singin' in the Rain.*

Then there are the peculiar and intimate preparations Ted goes through in anticipation of his first date with Mary. I have paused here at the keyboard for many minutes, trying to decide how to describe them (a) in a family newspaper, and (b) without spoiling the fun. I cannot. I will simply observe in admiration

that after the scene explodes in disbelieving, prolonged laughter, the Farrellys find a way to blindside us with a completely unanticipated consequence that sets us off all over again.

Among the other characters in the movie are Chris Elliott, as Dom, a friend of Ted's, who has a nervous eczema condition ("Do you know what it feels like to have a whitehead on your eyeball?"), and Magda (Lin Shaye), the neighbor whose tan makes her look like she's been put through the same process that produces Slim Jims. Magda is funny in a bizarre, over-the-top way, but Dom is more creepy than funny, or is it just that we're afraid we'll catch his skin rash?

Stanley Kauffmann, the great film critic of the *New Republic,* was on Charlie Rose's show the other night, sharing the discoveries of forty years as a film critic. What he has noticed over the years, he said, is that we are getting more good dramatic films than in the old days—but fewer good entertainments. It is easier to excel at drama than at comedy. I have no idea if Kauffmann will like *There's Something About Mary,* but his point applies for me: After months and months of comedies that did not make me laugh, here at last is one that did.

The Thief ★ ★ ★
R, 97 m., 1998

Vladimir Mashkov (Tolyan), Ekatarina Rednikova (Katia), Misha Philipchuk (Sanya). Directed by Pavel Chukhrai and produced by Igor Tolstunov. Screenplay by Chukhrai.

It is clear fairly early in *The Thief* that the title character represents Stalin, and it's one of the strengths of the film that the symbolism never gets in the way of a convincing, heartbreaking story. The movie, one of the 1998 Oscar nominees for Best Foreign Film, never pushes too hard to make its point, but what's clear in every frame is the sense of hopelessness and betrayal in the years after World War II.

The movie is told through the eyes of Sanya, who is born on the roadside to a homeless mother in 1946, the first year of the Cold War. He is six when he and his mother are approached on a train by a man named Tolyan, who is dressed as an army officer and may once have been one—or perhaps not. Nothing about him is trustworthy, a lesson the mother and boy learn through many hard lessons.

"Uncle" Tolyan is a charming, mustachioed man, tall and robust in a land where many citizens seem weak, ill, and hungry. It takes money to be healthy, and Tolyan is a thief—not only of money and possessions, but also of hearts. The mother, Katia (Ekatarina Rednikova), falls for him almost on sight, but of course her situation is desperate and there are sound Darwinian reasons for choosing a healthy, strong mate when you are unable to provide for yourself and your child. He looks like shelter from the poverty and hopelessness of 1952.

For the boy (Misha Philipchuk), it is a little more complicated. He often has visions of his real father, who died before he was born but speaks to him and promises to return soon. Yet all little boys are impressed by soldiers, and when Tolyan (Vladimir Mashkov) asks Sanya to look after his revolver, the boy's eyes grow as wide as saucers. Soon the three are living together as a family, and the boy enters into an uneasy mixture of fear, respect, and love for the man.

Tolyan, it is true, is a charmer. He is popular in the series of boardinghouses where they take a room, or part of a flat, and meals are often communal affairs fueled by vodka. He likes to propose toasts to Stalin, and encourage the others to get drunk, and then steal into their apartments. It is not unknown for the mother and boy to get urgent messages to meet him, immediately, at the train station, and they live a nomadic existence. The army uniform and Tolyan's ability to bluff are protections against identity checks and police questions. So are his "wife" and "son."

The movie proceeds in two fronts. We gradually learn more about the real nature of Tolyan and his criminal activities, and at the same time the relationships among the three people deepen and grow more complicated. Sanya in particular is conflicted. He indulges the fantasy that his real father will return. He resents Tolyan for being a fake, a thief, and a philanderer. And yet he admires him, too, and feels both shame and pride when the man uses him to squeeze through a small window and open a flat to be burgled.

Behind, beneath, around everything is the everyday reality of life in Stalin's Russia. The most touching sequence in the movie shows a transfer of prisoners from a district prison to transport that will take them to Siberia. Their friends and relatives wait in the snow for a glimpse of them. The prisoners are released from jail and sent running down a gauntlet of men and dogs, as their loved ones shout out desperate messages.

Did ordinary Russians think of Stalin the way Sanya thinks of Tolyan? As a big, bluff provider who would protect them—as a liar and a thief, but not without charm? That is the implication lurking in every frame of *The Thief*, but the movie works because it doesn't insist on the parallels. And the final sequence, of disillusionment and betrayal, is the saddest, because in it Tolyan is finally reduced to telling the truth.

The Thin Red Line ★ ★ ★
R, 170 m., 1999

Sean Penn (First Sergeant Welsh), Adrien Brody (Corporal Fife), Nick Nolte (Lieutenant Colonel Tall), Jim Caviezel (Private Witt), John Cusack (Captain Gaff), George Clooney (Captain Bosche), Ben Chaplin (Private Bell), Woody Harrelson (Sergeant Keck), Elias Koteas (Captain Staros), John Travolta (Brigadier General Quintard). Directed by Terrence Malick and produced by Robert Michael Geisler, John Roberdeau, and Grant Hill. Screenplay by Malick, based on the novel by James Jones.

The actors in *The Thin Red Line* are making one movie, and the director is making another. This leads to an almost hallucinatory sense of displacement, as the actors struggle for realism, and the movie's point of view hovers above them like a high school kid all filled with big questions. My guess is that any veteran of the actual battle of Guadalcanal would describe this movie with an eight-letter word much beloved in the army.

The movie's schizophrenia keeps it from greatness (this film has no firm idea of what it is about), but doesn't make it bad. It is, in fact, sort of fascinating: a film in the act of becoming, a field trial, an experiment in which a dreamy poet meditates on stark reality. It's like horror seen through the detachment of drugs or dementia. The sound track allows us to hear the thoughts of the characters, but there is no conviction that these characters would have these thoughts. They all seem to be musing in the same voice, the voice of a man who is older, more educated, more poetic and less worldly than any of these characters seem likely to be. The voice of the director.

Terrence Malick is the director of two of the best films I have ever seen, *Badlands* (1973) and *Days of Heaven* (1978). *The Thin Red Line* feels like an extension of the second film, in which a narrator muses on the underlying tragedy that is sometimes shown on the screen, sometimes implied. Both films are founded on a transcendental sense that all natural things share their underlying reality in the mind of God. The film opens with a question: "Why does nature contend with itself?" It shows a crocodile, a killing machine. Later, as men prove more deadly than crocodiles, it shows a bird, its wing shattered by gunfire, pulling itself along the ground. In a way the film is not about war at all, but simply about the way in which all living beings are founded on the necessity of killing one another (and eating one another, either literally or figuratively).

The film opens with an idyll on a Pacific island. Two soldiers have gone AWOL and live blissfully with tribal people who exist in a prelapsarian state, eating the fruit that falls from the trees and the fish that leap from the seas, and smiling contentedly at the bounty of Eden. This is, the movie implies, a society that reflects man's best nature. But reality interrupts when the two soldiers are captured and returned to their army company for the assault on a crucial hill on Guadalcanal.

During the battle scenes, there will be flashbacks to the island idyll—and other flashbacks as a solider remembers his love for his wife. Against these simple pleasures is stacked the ideology of war, as expressed by a colonel (Nick Nolte) who read Homer at West Point ("in Greek") and is intoxicated to be in battle at last after having studied it so long. The plot of the second act of the film involves the taking of a well-defended hill, and the colonel prefers that it be attacked in a frontal assault; a captain (Elias Koteas) resists this plan as sui-

cidal, and is right from a strategic point of view but wrong when viewed through the colonel's blood lust: "You are not gonna take your men around in the jungle to avoid a goddamn fight."

The soldiers are not well developed as individual characters. Covered in grime and blood, they look much alike, and we strain to hear their names, barked out mostly in one syllable (Welsh, Fife, Tall, Witt, Gaff, Bosche, Bell, Keck, Staros). Sometimes during an action we are not sure who we are watching, and have to piece it together afterward. I am sure battle is like that, but I'm not sure that was Malick's point: I think he was just not much interested in the destinies and personalities of individual characters.

It was not this way in the novel by James Jones, which inspired the screenplay. Jones drew his characters sharply, and indicated the ways in which each acted according to his ability and personality; his novel could have been filmed by Spielberg in the style of *Saving Private Ryan*. Malick's movie sees it more as a crapshoot. For defying his superior officers, the captain is offered first a court-martial, later a Silver Star, and then a Purple Heart. It is all the same. He is also transferred stateside by the colonel, and instead of insisting on staying with his men, he confesses he is rather happy to be going. This is not a movie of conventional war clichés.

The battle scenes themselves are masterful in creating a sense of the geography of a particular hill, the way it is defended by Japanese bunkers, the ways in which the American soldiers attempt to take it. The camera crouches low in the grass, and as Malick focuses on locusts or blades of grass, we are reminded that a battle like this must have taken place with the soldiers' eyes inches from the ground. The Japanese throughout are totally depersonalized (in one crucial scene, their language is not even translated with subtitles); they aren't seen as enemies, so much as necessary antagonists— an expression of nature's compulsion to "contend with itself." (One wonders what murky philosophical voice-over questions were floating above the Japanese soldiers in *The Thin Red Line*. Were they also dreaming about nature, immortality, humanity, and death?)

Actors like Sean Penn, John Cusack, Jim

Caviezel, and Ben Chaplin find the perfect tone for scenes of a few seconds or a minute, and then are dropped before a rhythm can be established. We get the sense that we are re-joining characters in the middle of interrupted actions. Koteas and Nolte come the closest to creating rounded performances, and Woody Harrelson has a good death scene; actors like John Travolta and George Clooney are on screen so briefly they don't have time to seem like anything other than guest stars.

The central intelligence in the film doesn't belong to any of the characters, or even to their voice-over philosophies. It belongs to Malick, whose ideas about war are heartfelt but not profound; the questions he asks are inescapable, but one wonders if soldiers in combat ever ask them (one guesses they ask themselves what they should do next, and how in the hell they can keep themselves from being shot). It's as if the film, long in prepro-duction, drifted away from the Jones novel (which was based on Jones's personal combat experience) and into a meditation not so much on war, as on film. Aren't most of the voice-over observations really not about war, but about war films? About their materials and ra-tionales, about why one would make them, and what one would hope to say?

Any film that can inspire thoughts like these is worth seeing. But the audience has to finish the work: Malick isn't sure where he's going or what he's saying. That may be a good thing. If a question has no answer, it is not useful to be supplied with one. Still, one leaves the theater bemused by what seems to be a universal law: While most war films are "antiwar," they are always antiwar from the point of view of the winning side. They say, "War is hell, and we won." Shouldn't antiwar films be told from the point of view of the losers? War was hell, and they lost.

The Third Miracle ★ ★ ★

R, 119 m., 2000

Ed Harris (Father Frank Shore), Anne Heche (Roxanne), Armin Mueller-Stahl (Archbishop Werner), Barbara Sukowa (Helen O'Regan), Ken James (Father Paul Panak), James Gallanders (Brother Gregory), Caterina Scorsone (Maria Witkowski), Michael Rispoli (John Leone). Directed by Agnieszka Holland and produced by Fred Fuchs, Steven Haft, and Elie Samaha. Screenplay by John Romano and Richard Vetere, based on the novel by Vetere.

Here is a rarity, a film about religion that is neither pious nor sensational, simply curious. No satanic possessions, no angelic choirs, no evil spirits, no lovers joined beyond the grave. Just a man doing his job. The man is Father Frank Shore, and he is a postulator—a priest assigned to investigate the possibility that some-one was a saint. If he is convinced, he goes be-fore a church tribunal and argues the case against another priest whose job is popularly known as "the devil's advocate."

Ed Harris plays Frank Shore as a man with many doubts of his own. After deflating one popular candidate for sainthood, he became known as "the miracle killer," and in his dark moments he broods that he "destroyed the faith of an entire community." Now perhaps he will have to do it again. It is 1979, in a devout Chicago ethnic community, and a statue weeps blood every November. That is the month of the death of a woman named Helen O'Regan (Barbara Sukowa), who is credited with heal-ing young Maria Witkowski, dying of lupus.

Was Helen indeed a saint? Is the statue weep-ing real blood? What blood type? Father Shore is far from an ideal priest. We first see him work-ing in a soup kitchen, having left more main-stream duties in a crisis of faith. Maybe he doesn't believe in much of anything anymore—except that the case of Helen O'Regan deserves a clear and unprejudiced investigation.

Many a saint has made it onto holy cards with somewhat dubious credentials (Did Pat-rick really drive the snakes from Ireland? Did Christopher really carry Jesus on his shoul-ders?). But in recent centuries the church has become rigorous in recognizing miracles and canonizing saints—so rigorous that the Ameri-can church has produced only three saints. In an age when many churches scorn science and ask members to simply believe, the Catholic Church retains the rather brave notion that religion really exists in the physical world, that miracles really happen and can be logically in-vestigated.

The Third Miracle, directed by Agnieszka Holland, has been written by John Romano and Richard Vetere, and based on Vetere's novel. It has no scenes of Arnold Schwarzenegger trying to prevent Satan from impregnating a virgin with the Antichrist. Instead, it is about church politics, and about a priest who doubts himself more than his faith.

His life only grows more complicated when he meets Roxanne O'Regan (Anne Heche), the daughter of the dead candidate for sainthood. There is a delicate scene at her mother's grave, where she and the priest have joined over a bottle of vodka to celebrate Helen's birthday. Their dialogue does that dance two people perform when they seem to be talking objectively but are really flirting. Finally Roxanne asks Frank if he believes all the church stuff. He asks her why she wants to know. "Because I can tell you like this," she says, on exactly the right note of teasing and invitation.

Ah, but the infallible church is made of fallible men. Frank can harbor doubts and lusts and nevertheless think his job is worth doing. Up against him is the fleshy, contemptuous Archbishop Werner (Armin Mueller-Stahl), the devil's advocate, who thinks three saints are quite enough for America. And then there is the problem of Maria Witkowski (Caterina Scorsone), who may have been cured of lupus but now is on life support after drug abuse and prostitution. "God wasted a miracle!" her mother cries.

Agnieszka Holland is a director whose films embody a grave intelligence; her credits include *Europa, Europa,* about a Jewish boy who conceals his religion to survive the Holocaust; *The Secret Garden,* based on the classic about a girl adrift in a house full of family secrets; and *Washington Square,* Henry James's novel about an heiress who is courted for her money. She pays close attention to the emotional weather of her characters, and is helped here by Ed Harris, whose priest talks as if he has finally decided to say something he's been thinking about for a long time, and Anne Heche, whose Roxanne approaches sexuality like a loaded gun.

In *The Third Miracle* Holland is not much interested in getting us to believe in miracles, or in whether Father Frank is true to his vow of chastity. She is concerned more with the way institutions interact with the emotions of their members. People *need* to believe in mir-

acles, which is why, paradoxically, they resent those who investigate them. Believers aren't interested in proof one way or the other: They want validation. The fact that the church has refused to recognize the appearances of the Virgin at Medjugorje has done nothing to discourage the crowds of faithful tourists. There is a temptation (literally) for the church to go along with popular fancy and endorse the enthusiasms of the faithful. But to applaud bogus saints would be an insult to the real ones.

As Father Shore and Archbishop Werner face each other across a table in a board room, they are like antagonists in any global corporation. They would like to introduce a miraculous new product, but must be sure it will not damage the stock of the company. By seeing the church as an earthly institution and its priests as men doing their best to remain logical in the face of popular ecstasy, *The Third Miracle* puts Hollywood's pop spirituality to shame. ☞

The 13th Warrior ★ ½
R, 103 m., 1999

Antonio Banderas (Ahmed Ibn Fahdlan), Diane Venora (Queen Weilew), Dennis Storhoi (Herger [Joyous]), Vladimir Kulich (Buliwyf), Omar Sharif (Melchisidek), Anders T. Andersen (Wigliff [King's Son]), Richard Bremmer (Skeld [Superstitious]), Tony Curran (Weath [Musician]). Directed by John McTiernan and produced by McTiernan, Michael Crichton, and Ned Dowd. Screenplay by William Wisher and Warren Lewis, based on *Eaters of the Dead* by Crichton.

Released more than a year after it was completed, *The 13th Warrior* shows every sign of a production run amok. With a budget said to be over $100 million, it displays a lot of cash on the screen, but little thought. To extract the story from the endless scenes of action and carnage is more effort than it's worth. The film seems to have been conceived from the special effects on down. Instead of beginning with a good story and then adding f/x as needed, it apparently began with f/x and then the story was shoehorned into the pauses in the action.

It could have been different. This could, indeed, have been a fascinating tale. Based on *Eaters of the Dead,* a 1974 novel by Michael

Crichton, the story combines two intriguing sources. One is the real-life adventure of Ahmed Ibn Fahdlan, an Arab poet who traveled north to the Viking lands in the tenth century. The other is the Old English epic poem *Beowulf*. At some point early in the production, it was apparently determined that endless scenes of longhaired Vikings in sword fights would be more interesting than the telling of these stories.

Antonio Banderas, perhaps hoping for another swashbuckling success like *The Mask of Zorro*, stars as Ahmed, a poet who has the misfortune to fall in love with the wife of a powerful friend of the Sultan. Threatened with dire consequences, Ahmed joins a veteran courtier (Omar Sharif in a cameo) in traveling north as an ambassador to the Vikings, where he is seen as a curiosity and a challenge. The Norsemen cheerfully insult him, confident he doesn't understand them, but a montage shows him learning the language and startling them with his reply. Soon he's called upon to recite a poem at a funeral, a scene that develops inadvertently into a hilarious version of history's first poetry slam.

Times are not good for the Vikings. A mysterious tribe of enemies who believe they possess the spirits of bears presents a flesh-eating threat. They have returned, as I recall, from ancient times. Thirteen warriors must be chosen to fight the evil. Ahmed is, of course, destined to be the thirteenth. He's a poet, not a fighter, but quickly learns to wield a scimitar.

And that's about it, except for miles and miles of carnage. (It's a little unsettling to sit through nonstop slaughter and then witness a pious conclusion that celebrates "a useful servant of God.") The movie's director of record is John McTiernan (*Die Hard, The Last Action Hero*), although after an earlier version of the film performed badly in sneak previews, new scenes were reportedly shot under the direction of Michael Crichton. It's all to no avail: *The 13th Warrior* is another example of f/x run wild, lumbering from one expensive set-piece to the next without taking the time to tell a story that might make us care.

This Is My Father ★ ★ ★
R, 120 m., 1999

Aidan Quinn (Kieran O'Day), Moya Farrelly (Fiona Flynn), James Caan (Kieran Johnson), Gina Moxley (Mary Flynn), Colm Meaney (Seamus), Moira Deady (Mrs. Kearney), Stephen Rea (Father Quinn), John Cusack (Eddie Sharp, the Pilot), Brendan Gleeson (Officer Jim). Directed by Paul Quinn and produced by Nicolas Clermont and Philip King.

On my first trip to Ireland, in 1967, I was taken to a party after the pubs closed. There were bottles of whiskey and Guinness stout, someone had a concertina, and there was a singsong. In the bedroom, a couple was making out. Eventually they emerged to join the party, and I noticed that, to my young eyes, they were "old"—in their forties.

On the way home, I asked my friend McHugh about that, and he explained that they had been engaged for fifteen years, that they were putting off marriage until the man made more money, and until "family matters" got sorted out. Necking at parties was undoubtedly the extent of their sex lives, since intercourse before marriage was a mortal sin. I said I thought it was sad that two middle-aged people, who had loved each other since they were young, had put their lives on hold. "Welcome to Ireland," he said.

It is not like that anymore in Ireland, where some of the old customs have died with startling speed. But that is the Ireland remembered in *This Is My Father*, a film about lives ruled by guilt, fear, prejudice, and dour family pride. For every cheerful Irish comedy about free spirits with quick wits, there is a story like this one, about characters sitting in dark rooms, ruminating on old grudges and fresh resentments, and using the rules of the church, when convenient, as justification for their own spites and dreads.

The movie is said to be based on a true family story and has been made by Chicago's Quinn brothers. Aidan Quinn stars as an orphaned tenant farmer who falls in love with the daughter of the woman who owns the land he works. Paul Quinn directs. Declan Quinn, the cinematographer, is known for such work as *Leaving Las Vegas*. It is so much a family project that there is even a role for a friend, John Cusack, who drops in out of the sky in a small plane, lands on the beach, and figures in a scene as charming as it is irrelevant.

The heart of the story involves Kieran O'Day (Aidan Quinn) and Fiona Flynn (Moya Farrelly), who fall passionately in love in 1939. He is an orphan, being raised by a tenant couple named the Maneys (Donal Donnelly and Maria Mc-Dermottroe) on land owned by Fiona's mother, Mary (Gina Moxley). The mother has fierce pride, not improved by a drinking problem, and looks down on her neighbors. Of course she opposes a liaison between her daughter and a tenant.

This story is told in flashback. In the present day, we meet a sad, tired high school teacher (James Caan) whose mother is dying and whose life is going nowhere. He determines to go back to Ireland and search for his roots. In the village where his mother came from, he finds an old gypsy woman (Moira Deady) who remembers with perfect clarity everything that happened in 1939, and triggers the flashbacks. The modern story is almost not essential (we forget Caan in the midst of the flashback), but it does trigger a happy ending in which much is explained.

The key element in the romance between Kieran and Fiona, and the one that reminded me of my first visit to Ireland, is the way their sex lives are ruled by others, whose own real motives are masked under the cover of church law. Mrs. Flynn is spiteful, mean, and bitter, or she would find a way for her daughter to be happy. Kieran's love is all the more poignant because he sincerely believes himself to be an occasion of sin for Fiona, and castigates himself for endangering her immortal soul.

Fiona's mother pays lip service to the church, but her real motives are fueled by class prejudice and social climbing, and there is a cruel moment when she accuses Kieran of molesting her daughter. She also threatens the Maneys, who have raised him, with the loss of their land and livelihood. One scene which rings true to life is the way the village policemen, negotiating a tricky path between the laws of this world and the next, give Kieran broad hints about their plans for eventually arresting him—should he still be in the vicinity, of course. Sensibly, he is not, but the cost of his

freedom is his happiness, and that price is underlined by a message which the Caan character discovers, and delivers several decades too late.

I believe *This Is My Father* is indeed based on true family stories (or legends, which are the same thing), because it insists on details that are more important to the narrator than to the listener. The entire construction of the Caan character, for example, is explained no doubt by a relative's visit back to the old country. The story might have been simpler, sadder, and sweeter if it had taken place entirely in 1939—but like all stories, it belongs to the teller, not the subject.

The Thomas Crown Affair ★ ★ ½
R, 114 m., 1999

Pierce Brosnan (Thomas Crown), Rene Russo (Catherine Banning), Denis Leary (Michael McCann), Ben Gazzara (Andrew Wallace), Frankie Faison (Paretti), Fritz Weaver (John Reynolds), Charles Keating (Golchan), Mark Margolis (Knutzhorn), Faye Dunaway (Psychiatrist). Directed by John McTiernan and produced by Pierce Brosnan and Beau St. Clair. Screenplay by Leslie Dixon and Kurt Wimmer, based on a story by Alan R. Trustman.

The Thomas Crown Affair uses a $100 million art theft as foreplay between two people who, unfortunately, are both more interested in the theft than in each other. Pierce Brosnan stars in the title role, as a man who has everything money can buy, and has moved on to what money can't buy—a $100 million Monet, which he steals in broad daylight from the Metropolitan Museum of Art. Then he becomes interested in something money might be able to buy: an insurance investigator named Catherine Banning (Rene Russo).

His theft has been so clever it might never be possible for her to prove he took the painting. So he more or less *tells* her he was the thief, a conclusion she has arrived at on her own. Her problem is that without the painting or any other evidence, she doesn't have a case. For that matter, she's not a cop and isn't interested in a conviction so much as in saving her company from having to write a $100 million check.

601

The movie is a retread of Norman Jewison's 1968 film, which starred Steve McQueen as a bank robber opposite Faye Dunaway, and had a lot of split-screen photography that quickly wore out its welcome. This movie has a superior caper but less chemistry. The way Thomas Crown gets the painting out of the Met, and what happens to it subsequently, is really very cleverly devised. But while McQueen and Dunaway seemed barely able to keep their hands off of one another, Brosnan and Russo play elegant mind games that sometimes seem almost designed to postpone the rumpy-pumpy.

The movie has been directed by John McTiernan (*Die Hard, The Hunt for Red October*) with less steam and more suavity than his usual credits; it's the kind of sophisticated caper that Cary Grant used to walk through without getting his suit wrinkled. The caper and investigation are the backdrops for an elaborate seduction in which Crown essentially asks the woman's permission to steal the painting. He seems to think he deserves points for having masterminded the theft as a challenge rather than a job: If a man doesn't need $100 million, I gather, he isn't as much to blame for stealing it.

Teasing Banning with hints and scraps of clues, he flies her off to his villa in the Caribbean, takes her on a glider flight, buys her dinners, and gives her presents, including a painting she makes the mistake of admiring. He also suggests that the life of an insurance investigator is not nearly as interesting as the life of his mistress—which may be true, but is undermined somewhat by her suspicion that he already has a mistress and is just stringing her along.

The movie has a low-key, luxurious feeling to it. It's languorous and comfortable. Brosnan and Russo seem to massage their words before saying them. But it all feels like an exercise. We don't sense that they're really important to one another: The game is more important for both of them than the prize. Faye Dunaway, who has a role here as Crown's (unnecessary) psychiatrist, had more electricity in 1968 and still does than Rene Russo, who was exciting opposite Clint Eastwood in *In the Line of Fire*, but now matches Brosnan's dreamy detachment. There's much more tension between Sean Connery and Catherine Zeta-Jones in the somewhat similar *Entrapment*.

I dunno. It's not a bad movie. It might be fun to see on an airplane or to rent on video. But despite the cleverness of the caper and the beauty of the lush locations, the wit in the dialogue and the neat twists and turns, it never seems to risk anything. There's something odd about a caper romance where you never believe anyone is really ever going to go to jail or bed.　☞

Three Kings ★ ★ ★
R, 115 m., 1999

George Clooney (Sergeant Major Archie Gates), Mark Wahlberg (Sergeant Troy Barlow), Ice Cube (Chief), Spike Jonze (Conrad Vig), Nora Dunn (Adriana Cruz), Mykelti Williamson (Colonel Horn), Jamie Kennedy (Walter), Cliff Curtis (Amir). Directed by David O. Russell and produced by Charles Roven, Paul Junger Witt, and Edward L. McDonnell. Screenplay by Russell, based on a story by John Ridley.

Three Kings is some kind of weird masterpiece, a screw-loose war picture that sends action and humor crashing head-on into one another and spinning off into political anger. It has the freedom and recklessness of Oliver Stone or Robert Altman in their mad-dog days, and a visual style that hungers for impact. A lot of movies show bodies being hit by bullets. This one sends the camera inside to show a bullet cavity filling up with bile.

David O. Russell, who wrote and directed, announces his arrival as a major player. Like the best films of Scorsese, Stone, Altman, and Tarantino, this one sings with the exhiliration of pure filmmaking, and embodies ideas in its action and characters. Most movies doze in a haze of calculation and formula; *Three Kings* is awake and hyper.

The movie takes place at the end of the Gulf War of 1991 ("Operation Desert Storm," according to the Pentagon publicists). The first words set the tone: "Are we shooting?" The truce is so new that soldiers are not sure, and a guy waving a white flag gets his head shot off in a misunderstanding. Shame. Three U.S. soldiers find an Iraqi with a piece of paper stuck where the sun don't shine. An officer issues a rubber glove and tells a private to pull it out. The guy wants two gloves, but he'll do it with one, he's told: "That's how the chain of command works."

The map shows the location of gold bullion looted from Kuwait by Saddam's troops and buried in secret bunkers. ("Bullion? Is that a little cube you put in hot water?") The three soldiers are Sergeant Troy Barlow (Mark Wahlberg), Chief Elgin (Ice Cube), and Private Conrad Vig (Spike Jonze). They attract the attention of Sergeant Major Archie Gates (George Clooney), a Special Forces veteran who decides on the spot to lead them on an unauthorized mission to steal the treasure. This involves dumping the cable news reporter he's been assigned to escort. She's Adriana Cruz, played by Nora Dunn as a Christiane Amanpour clone so driven by journalistic zeal that she is heedless of her own safety or anything else but a story. The gold, of course, would be a story.

The movie unreels with breakneck energy; it's one of those experiences like *Natural Born Killers*, where death and violence are a drumbeat in the background of every plot point. Russell's screenplay illustrates the difference between a great action picture and the others: The action grows out of the story, instead of the story being about the action. The Clooney character commandeers a Humvee and leads his men on a loony ride through the desert, where their target practice with footballs somehow reminded me of the water-skiing sequence in *Apocalypse Now*.

A political undercurrent bubbles all through the film. A truce has been declared, and Saddam's men have stopped shooting at Americans and fallen back to the secondary assignment of taming unhappy Iraqis who were expecting him to be overthrown. ("Bush told the people to rise up against Saddam. They thought they'd have our support. They didn't. Now they're being slaughtered.") Strange, the irony in Iraqis killing Iraqis while American gold thieves benefit from the confusion.

Most Hollywood movies stereotype their Arab characters. *Three Kings* is startling in the way it shows how the world is shrinking and cultures are mixing and sharing values. Clooney and his men see a woman shot dead by Saddam's men, and later meet her husband and children. Is this man a tearful anonymous desert simpleton, grateful to his brave saviors? Not at all. "I'm a B-school graduate from Bowling Green," he tells them. "Your planes blew up all my cafés."

It's a small world, made smaller by the culture of war. The TV journalist stands calmly in the middle of danger, accepted by both sides because they think it's natural they should be on television. When the Mark Wahlberg character is captured and locked in a room, he finds it filled with the loot of war, including a lot of cell phones. When he tries to call his wife in America to give her the coordinates of his position, he has to deal with obtuse telephone operators.

Three Kings has plot structure as traditional as anything in *Gunga Din* or an *Indiana Jones* picture, and links it to a fierce political viewpoint, intelligent characters, and sudden bursts of comedy. It renews clichés. We've seen the wounded buddy who has to be dragged along through the action. But we haven't seen one with a lung wound, and a valve hammered into his chest to relieve the built-up air pressure. We've seen desert warfare before, but usually it looks scenic. Russell's cameraman, Newton Thomas Sigel, uses a grainy, bleached style that makes the movie look like it was left out in a sandstorm.

Like many natural action stars, Clooney can do what needs to be done with absolute conviction; we believe him as a leader. Wahlberg and Ice Cube seem caught up in the action, Wahlberg as a natural target, the Cube as a National Guardsman who believes he stands inside a ring of Jesus' grace. Spike Jonze, himself a director (*Being John Malkovich*), is the obligatory hillbilly, needed for the ethnic mix we always get in war movies. It's interesting how Nora Dunn's cable journalist isn't turned into a cheap parody of Amanpour, but focuses on the obsessiveness that possesses any good war correspondent.

This is David O. Russell's third picture, after *Spanking the Monkey* (liked by many, unseen by me) and the inventive, unhinged comedy *Flirting With Disaster* (1997). Like that one, *Three Kings* bounces lots of distinct characters against one another and isn't afraid to punctuate the laughs with moments of true observation and emotion. This is his first movie with a studio budget, and it shows not only enthusiasm, but the control to aim that enthusiasm where he wants it to go. *Three Kings* is one of the best movies of 1999, even if I kept wondering why it wasn't named *Four Kings*. ☞

Three Seasons ★ ★ ★
PG-13, 113 m., 1999

Don Duong (Hai [Cyclo Driver]), Nguyen Ngoc Hiep (Kien An), Tran Manh Cuong (Teacher Dao), Harvey Keitel (James Hager), Zoe Bui (Lan), Nguyen Huu Duoc (Woody [Peddler]), Minh Ngoc (Truck Driver), Hoang Phat Trieu (Huy). Directed by Tony Bui and produced by Jason Kliot, Joana Vicente, and Tony Bui. Screenplay by Tony Bui, based on a story by Tony Bui and Timothy Linh Bui.

We require Asia to be ancient, traditional, and mysterious. It fills a need. We don't want to know that Hong Kong is a trade capital and Japan is an economic giant. We're looking for Shangri-La, for the sentimental fantasies of generations of Western writers who fell for the romantic idea of the East—and centuries of Eastern writers who did too.

Three Seasons, filmed in Ho Chi Minh City by Tony Bui, a twenty-six-year-old American born in Vietnam, allows us to enjoy fantasies which, in America, would be politically incorrect. Like the best-selling *Memoirs of a Geisha,* it romanticizes prostitution, makes poverty picturesque, transforms hardship into fable. We do not approve of small boys working as street peddlers, of young women organized to sell flowers for a cult, of hookers servicing rich businessmen and snubbing their own people. But because *Three Seasons* is so languorously beautiful, because it has the sentiment of a Chaplin film, because exotic customs and settings are so seductive, we change the rules. What is wrong in Chicago becomes colorful, even enchanting, in the former Saigon.

I say all this as a disclaimer, because I'm certainly not above the pleasures of a film like *Three Seasons.* Taken as reporting, it shows deplorable conditions. Taken as a fable, it's enchanting. Art often offers us such bargains; it is better to attend *La Bohème* than to freeze in a garret. No wonder *Three Seasons* won everything in sight at Sundance: Grand Jury Prize, Audience Award, and Best Cinematography.

The movie takes place in a modern Vietnam that, at first, looks like the past. Beautiful young women in tiny flat-bottomed boats paddle in shallow waters among flower pads. As they pick white lotus blossoms, they sing. The scene is overshadowed by a dark temple that looks abandoned. "It is the Teacher's house," one of the new girls is told. "He has not left it for years. None of us have ever seen him."

The newcomer, named Kien An (Nguyen Ngoc Hiep), is trucked with the others into the city to sell their flowers. We meet some of the others who live there. Woody (Nguyen Huu Duoc) is a boy of nine or ten who sells gum and cigarettes from a box that hangs from a strap around his neck. Hai (Don Duong) drives a cyclo (a bicycle rickshaw) and hangs out with his buddies near the luxury hotels, where the towels must be perfumed because "everyone we drive from there has a fresh smell." Lan (Zoe Bui) is a prostitute who works the big hotels; she runs from a shop, leaps into Hai's cyclo, and asks him to step on it.

Then there's James Hager (Harvey Keitel), the mysterious American who has spent weeks sitting in an aluminum chair on a sidewalk, smoking and staring into space. His story is more modern. He left a daughter behind in Vietnam, and has come back to find her, and "maybe make some kind of peace with this place." (Keitel is the film's executive producer, once again lending his presence to a director's first film; no actor has put himself more on the line in support of young filmmakers.)

The interlocking stories of these characters remind us not only of Chaplinesque sentimentality, but also of the poor street people of Italian neorealist films like *Bicycle Thief* and *Shoeshine,* and of the languorous beauty of recent Asian films like *The Scent of Green Papaya* and *Raise the Red Lantern.* Lisa Rinzler's cinematography makes the city and surrounding countryside look poor but breathtakingly beautiful, and even sad shots, like the little peddler standing in the rain, have a kind of poetic grace.

Of the stories, the one I responded to most deeply involved the hooker and the cyclo driver, who loves and respects her. One day she says her dream is to spend the whole night in an air-conditioned room. He asks her price ($50), wins that much in a race for cyclo drivers, and treats her to her dream. She is grateful, but resists his further advances: She somehow feels she is not entitled to ordinary human emotion.

There are touching, somewhat contrived, revelations involving the unseen Teacher, whose teaching seems far in the past. The song of the new young girl reminds him of the songs of the floating market in his childhood, "the only time I was pure and whole." And she discovers his secrets. The outcome of the story involving the American G.I. is less effective, because we've seen such material before.

Three Seasons is extravagantly beautiful, especially in scenes where artifice is permitted, as when an unlikely shower of spring blossoms floats down from the sky. It's a remarkably ambitious work by the twenty-six-year-old Bui, who financed it on a shoestring but makes it look expensive. It arrives billed as the first American fiction film shot entirely in postwar Vietnam; although Bui acknowledges his script had to win government approval, he was allowed to portray prostitution and poverty— perhaps because the city is seen not in a documentary way, but through the lens of fable. The result may not reflect the Vietnam of reality, but it's as close to life as most romantic melodramas, which is probably the point. And it's a lot more interesting.

Three to Tango ★
PG-13, 98 m., 1999

Matthew Perry (Oscar Novak), Neve Campbell (Amy Post), Dylan McDermott (Charles Newman), Oliver Platt (Peter Steinberg), Cylk Cozart (Kevin Cartwright), John C. McGinley (Strauss), Bob Balaban (Decker), Deborah Rush (Lenore). Directed by Damon Santostefano and produced by Bobby Newmyer, Jeffrey Silver, and Bettina Sofia Viviano. Screenplay by Rodney Vaccaro and Aline Brosh McKenna.

Neve Campbell is amazingly cute. I have admired her in other movies, but now, in *Three to Tango*, which gave me nothing else to think about, I was free to observe her intently. She has wide, intelligent eyes, kissable lips, and a face both sweet and carnal, like Doris Day's. I support her decision to never wear any garment that comes within a foot of her neck.

In *Three to Tango* she is mired in a plot of such stupidity that there is only one thing to do, and that is to look at her. In her more erotic moments she twinkles with enjoyment at her own naughtiness; consider a scene where she slithers in a bubble bath and describes a lesbian flirtation with her Brazilian roommate in college. She's having as much fun with this dialogue as we are.

She's telling the story to a character named Oscar (Matthew Perry), who she thinks is gay. It's all a misunderstanding. Oscar and his business partner Peter (Oliver Platt), who *is* gay, are architects who desperately need a $90 million commission from a rich Chicago builder (Dylan McDermott). The builder is a married man and the Neve Campbell character, named Amy, is his mistress. He assigns Oscar to "keep an eye" on Amy, assuming that Oscar is safe because he's gay.

Why does everyone think Oscar is gay? Because this is an Idiot Plot, in which no one ever says what obviously must be said to clear up the confusion. That's because they want that commission. We see a model for their $90 million project, which resembles Chicago's Lincoln Park Conservatory in the eighth month of its pregnancy.

Of course, Oscar and Amy fall in love. And what a Meet Cute they have! On their first evening together, they go out, their taxi explodes (yes, explodes), and they run in the rain and wade in the mud and find a restaurant where they eat tuna melts that make them sick, and they run outside and hurl. This is the Meet Cute as Meet Puke. And on the same date she manages to cause Oscar incredible pain with a sharp door handle to his netherlands. No movie like this is complete without male pattern bruising.

Only about a week after first being considered gay, Oscar is named Gay Man of the Year. It's like they're waiting outside the closet with his trophy. He can't decline the honor because he wants the commission. But then, at the awards banquet, a door in the back opens and Amy walks in. (This is the old Dramatic Late-Arriving Person Who Means Everything to the Speaker Ploy.) Looking into her wide, intelligent eyes, cunningly placed eighteen inches above her wide, intelligent breasts, Oscar blurts out the truth: "I am not gay!" Then we hear the Slowly Gathering Ovation (one brave man stands up and starts to clap slowly, others follow, applause builds to crescendo).

I was wondering how easily the Gay Man of the Year could get a standing ovation for announcing at the awards banquet that he was not gay, but my question was answered in the end credits. Although skyline shots and one early scene create the impression that the movie was made in Chicago, it was actually shot in Toronto. Those Canadians are just so doggone supportive.

This review would not be complete without mention of a scene where Oscar grows distraught and runs through the streets of Chinatown. As he approaches the camera, several Peking ducks, or maybe they are only chickens, are thrown at him from offscreen. Why? Why, indeed. Why, oh why.   ☞

Time Code ★ ★ ★

R, 93 m., 2000

Stellan Skarsgard (Alex Green), Saffron Burrows (Emma), Salma Hayek (Rose), Jeanne Tripplehorn (Lauren Hathaway), Glenne Headly (Therapist), Holly Hunter (Executive), Danny Huston (Randy), Kyle MacLachlan (Bunny Drysdale). Directed by Mike Figgis and produced by Figgis and Annie Stewart. Screenplay by Figgis.

I remember the gleam in Mike Figgis's eyes when he talked of filming *Leaving Las Vegas* in cheaper, faster 16mm instead of the standard 35mm. "We didn't have to get a permit from the city or rope off the streets," he said. "We just jumped out of the car, set up the camera, and started shooting." Yes, and made the best film of 1995. Now he's directed a production where they didn't even have to set up the camera.

Time Code was shot entirely with digital cameras, handheld, in real time. The screen is split into four segments, and each one is a single take about ninety-three minutes long. The stories are interrelated, and sometimes the characters in separate quadrants cross paths and are seen by more than one camera. This is not as confusing as it sounds, because Figgis increases the volume of the dialogue for the picture he wants us to focus on, and dials down on the other three.

What is the purpose of the experiment? Above all, to show it can be done. With *Leaving Las Vegas,* the camera strategy came second to the story, and was simply the best way to get it on the screen. In *Time Code,* the story is upstaged by the method, sometimes more, sometimes less, and a viewer not interested in the method is likely to be underwhelmed.

What Figgis demonstrates is that a theatrical film can be made with inexpensive, lightweight digital cameras, and that the picture quality is easily strong enough to transfer to 35mm. He also experiments with the notion of filming in real time, which has long fascinated directors. Hitchcock orchestrated *Rope* (1948) so that it appeared to be all one shot, and Godard famously said that the truth came at twenty-four frames per second, and every cut was a lie.

Apart from proving it can be done, however, what is the purpose of Figgis's experiment? The first films ever made were shot in one take. Just about everybody agrees that the introduction of editing was an improvement. To paraphrase Wilde's Lady Bracknell: To make a film in one unbroken shot may be regarded as a misfortune; to make it in four looks like carelessness. Figgis has put style and technique in the foreground, and it upstages the performances in what is, after all, a perfunctory story.

When I go to an experimental film, I am in one mind-set. When I go to a mainstream feature, I am in another. If the film works, it carries me along with it. I lose track of the extraneous and am absorbed by the story. Anything that breaks this concentration is risky, and Figgis, with a four-way screen, breaks it deliberately. The film never happens to us. We are always conscious of watching it. The style isn't as annoying as it might sound, but it does no favors to the story.

Cinema semiologists speak of the "disjoined signifier," and by that they refer to the separation of the viewer from the signified—in this case, from the story. So there I've done it. Used the words "semiologists" and "disjoined signifier" in a review. My students will be proud of me. Most readers will have bailed out. My defense is that *Time Code* is not likely to attract anyone who doesn't know what semiology is—or, if it attracts them, will not satisfy them.

The story involves interlocking adulteries, told in four parallel stories that begin at 3 P.M. on November 19, 1999, on Sunset Boulevard in or near Book Soup and the office building on the corner. We meet a limousine lesbian, Lauren (Jeanne Tripplehorn), a cokehead who is in love with Rose (Salma Hayek) and eavesdrops on her with a paging device as she has quick and meaningless sex with an alcoholic film executive (Stellan Skarsgard). Other characters include the executive's wife (Saffron Burrows), an ad executive (Holly Hunter), a shrink (Glenne Headly), and others in and around the entertainment industry. There is pointed satire during a "creative meeting" (an oxymoron), and at the end passion bursts out. The action is interrupted by no less than three earthquakes, which must have required fancy timing in coordinating the cameras and actors.

There may be a story buried here somewhere, and even splendid performances. We could try to extract them on a second or third viewing, but why use a style that obscures them? If *Time Code* demonstrates that four unbroken stories can be told at the same time, it also demonstrates that the experiment need not be repeated.

Still, I recommend the film. Mike Figgis is a man who lives and breathes the cinema (see his 1999 film *The Loss of Sexual Innocence* for an altogether more breathtaking and, yes, daring experiment in storytelling). While most filmmakers are content to plod their dreary way from one foregone conclusion to another, Figgis is out there on the edge, joyously pulling off cockamamie stunts like this one. I'm glad I saw the film. It challenged me. The actors were the coproducers and joined in the spirit of the enterprise, testing their own limits. *Time Code* has a place in the history of the movies. But now I want to see Figgis cut back to one camera (digital if he must), resume editing, and conduct experiments that are more likely to arouse my sense of awe than my sense of timing.

Titan A.E. ★ ★ ★ ½
PG, 92 m., 2000

With the voices of: Matt Damon (Cale), Bill Pullman (Korso), John Leguizamo (Gune), Nathan Lane (Preed), Janeane Garofalo (Stith), Drew Barrymore (Akima), Ron Perlman (Professor Sam Tucker), Alex D. Linz (Young Cale). Directed by Don Bluth and Gary Goldman and produced by David Kirschner, Goldman, and Bluth. Screenplay by Ben Edlund, John August, and Joss Whedon, based on a story by Hans Bauer and Randall McCormick.

Here's the animated space adventure I've been hoping for—a film that uses the freedom of animation to visualize the strangeness of the universe in ways live action cannot duplicate, and then joins its vision to a rousing story. Don Bluth and Gary Goldman's *Titan A.E.* creates the kinds of feelings I had as a teenager, paging eagerly through Asimov and Heinlein. There are moments when it even stirs a little awe.

The movie is pure slam-bam space opera. Its stills could be transferred intact to the covers of old issues of *Amazing Stories*. Yet it has the largeness of spirit that good SF can generate: It isn't just action and warfare, but also a play of ideas. Some of its galactic visuals are beautiful in the same way photos by the Hubble Space Telescope are beautiful: They show a careless hand casting colors and energy across unimaginable expanses of space, using stars and planets as its paintbox.

As the film opens, in A.D. 3028, Earth has been destroyed by the evil race of Drej, who fear the intelligence of humans. Survivors flee on spaceships, one of them the gigantic *Titan*, which carries crucial information on board. That ship was designed by the hero's father, who apparently disappears along with the *Titan*.

When we first meet Cale (voice by Matt Damon), he's a "colony bum," working in a space dump floating between the stars, where conditions are harsh ("I wish they'd kill my food before they give it to me"). He's bitter and indifferent because he believes he has been abandoned by his father. Yet he holds the key to the future of Earth and mankind in the palm of his hand—literally, in the form of a genetically coded map that reveals the hiding place of *Titan*. Soon he's on a mission to find *Titan*, with partners including a beautiful girl named Akima (Drew Barrymore), who treasures Earth's heritage and collects artifacts of its past, like baseballs. The captain of their expedition is the grave, responsible Korso (Bill Pullman); Gune (John Leguizamo) is the navigator.

The main story involves their journey to find *Titan* before the Drej can capture or destroy it. This quest involves high and low comedy, an exciting chase scene, and then one of the most involving hunt sequences I've seen in any movie, animated or not—a cat-and-mouse game played out in the Ice Rings of Tigrin. These are massive structures of interstellar ice, which form a ring like a miniature galaxy. They offer some protection from the sensing devices of the Drej, but can tear a spaceship to pieces with their huge, jagged masses.

The Ice Rings sequence is a perfect example of what animation can do and live action cannot. The vast, frozen shards of ice are clear and ominous, with a convincing presence, and the sound track does a masterful job of adding a dimension. We know sound does not travel in space, but do not care, because the groanings and creakings of the ancient ice masses are like cries of despair, and somewhere within the frozen maze lies *Titan* with its precious cargo.

The movie is rambunctious in its action scenes, which owe more than a little to *Star Wars* (just as *Star Wars* owes more than a little to old pulp SF and Saturday serials). But it's not simpleminded. I liked a scene where the heroes are trying to sneak past a hostile and suspicious guard. They've constructed counterfeit uniforms. The guard leads them on, pretends to be fooled, and then laughs in their faces, telling them their uniforms are obviously constructed from bedspreads. "An intelligent guard!" says one of the good guys. "Didn't see that one coming."

The movie adds small details that evoke the wonder of the universe. At one point in the journey, the ship is followed by space sprites—energy beings that follow space vessels and mean good luck, as dolphins do at sea. We get a sense of space not merely as a fearsome void, but as a place big enough to include even whimsy. And *Star Wars* is evoked again with the tradition that the human heroes have car-

toonish sidekicks. Preed (voice by Nathan Lane) is a first mate who seems to have a genetic similarity to Jar Jar Binks in *The Phantom Menace*. Stith (Janeane Garofalo) is the weapons master who looks like an extremely callipygian kangaroo. The evil Drej are seen as crackling white-blue force fields, seemingly at one with their ships.

One test for any movie is when you forget it's a movie and simply surf along on the narrative. That can happen as easily with animation as live action, and it happens here.

I argue for animation because I believe it provides an additional dimension for film art; it frees filmmakers from the anchor of realism that's built into every live-action film, and allows them to visualize their imaginations. Animation need not be limited to family films and cheerful fantasies. The Japanese have known that for years, and *Titan A.E.* owes as large a debt to Japanese anime as to *Star Wars*.

The movie works as adventure, as the *Star Wars* pictures do (and as live-action SF films like *Starship Troopers* do not). It tells a story cleverly designed to explain more or less reasonably why Cale, in the words of the ancient SF cliché, "has the future of Earth in his hands!" There is a sense of wonder here.

Titus ★ ★ ★ ½
R, 165 m., 2000

Anthony Hopkins (Titus), Jessica Lange (Tamora), Alan Cumming (Saturninus), Harry Lennix (Aaron), Jonathan Rhys Meyers (Chiron), Angus Macfadyen (Lucius), Matthew Rhys (Demetrius), Colm Feore (Marcus), James Frain (Bassianus), Laura Fraser (Lavinia). Directed by Julie Taymor and produced by Jody Patton, Conchita Airoldi, and Taymor. Screenplay by Taymor, adapted from William Shakespeare's *Titus Andronicus*.

So bloodthirsty is Shakespeare's *Titus Andronicus* that critics like Harold Bloom believe it must be a parody—perhaps Shakespeare's attempt to settle the hash of Christopher Marlowe, whose plays were soaked in violence. Other readers, like the sainted Mark Van Doren, dismiss it out of hand. Inhuman and unfeeling, he called it, and "no tragedy at all if pity and terror are essential to the tragic experience." Certainly most agree it is the least of Shakespeare's tragedies, as well as the first.

But consider young Shakespeare near the beginning of his career, trying to upstage the star dramatists and attract attention to himself. Imagine him sitting down to write the equivalent of today's horror films. Just as Kevin Williamson's screenplays for *Scream* and *I Know What You Did Last Summer* use special effects and wild coincidence to mow down their casts, so does *Titus Andronicus* heap up the gore, and then wink to show the playwright is in on the joke.

Titus as *Scream 1593*? Bloom cites the scene where Titus is promised the return of his sons if he will send Saturninus his hand—only to find the hand returned with only the heads of his sons. Grief-stricken, Titus assigns tasks. He, with his remaining hand, will carry one of the heads. He asks his brother to take the other. That leaves the severed hand. At this point in the play his daughter, Lavinia, has no hands (or tongue) after being raped and mutilated by the emperor's sons, and so he instructs her, "Bear thou my hand, sweet wench, between thy teeth." Bloom invites scholars to read that line aloud without smiling, and says Shakespeare knew the play "was a howler, and expected the more discerning to wallow in it self-consciously."

That is exactly what Julie Taymor has done, in a brilliant and absurd film of *Titus Andronicus* that goes over the top, doubles back, and goes over the top again. The film is imperfect, but how can you make a perfect film of a play that flaunts its flaws so joyfully? Some critics have sniffed at its excesses and visual inventions—many of them the same dour enforcers who didn't like the biblical surprise in *Magnolia*. I have had enough good taste and restraint for a lifetime, and love it when a director has the courage to go for broke. God forbid we should ever get a devout and tasteful production of *Titus Andronicus*.

It cannot be a coincidence that the title role is played by Anthony Hopkins. Not when by Act 5 he is serving Tamora (Jessica Lange) meat pies made out of her sons, and smacking his lips in precisely the same way that Hannibal Lecter drooled over fava beans. *Titus Andronicus* was no doubt Lecter's favorite Shakespeare play, opening as it does with Titus returning to Rome with the corpses of twenty-one of his sons and their four surviving brothers, and pausing in his victory speech only long enough to condemn the eldest son of Tamora, vanquished queen of the Goths, to be hacked limb from limb and the pieces thrown on a fire.

Titus is not the hero of the film because it has no hero. He is as vicious as the others, and when he notes that "Rome is a wilderness of tigers," he should have included himself. Hopkins plays him, like Hannibal Lecter, as a man pitiable, intelligent, and depraved, as he strides through a revenge story so gory that there seems a good chance no one will be left alive at the end.

Some of the contrivance is outrageous. Consider the scene where a hole in the forest floor gradually fills up with corpses, as Aaron the Moor (Harry Lennix), the play's grand schemer, unfolds a devious plan to defeat both Titus and Saturninus and seduce Tamora. This hole, of course, would be convenient on the stage, where it could be represented by a trap door, but in the woods, as Saturninus (Alan Cumming) apprehensively peers over the side, it takes on all the credibility of an Abbott and Costello setup. Or consider the scene late in the play where Titus breaks the neck of his own long-suffering daughter, as if losing her tongue and arms were not bad luck enough, and then pities the fates that made him do it.

Taymor is the director of the Broadway musical *The Lion King*, which is one of the most exhilarating experiences I have ever had in a theater. In her first film she again shows a command of costumes and staging, ritual and procession, archetypes and comic relief. She makes it clear in her opening shot (a modern boy waging a food fight with his plastic action figures) that she sees the connection between *Titus Andronicus* and the modern culture of violence in children's entertainment. *Titus* would make a video game, with the tattooed Tamora as Lara Croft.

Taymor's period is basically a fanciful version of ancient Rome, but in the mix she includes modern cars and tanks, loud speakers and popemobiles, newspapers and radio speeches. Like Richard Loncraine and Ian McKellen's *Richard III* (1995), she sees the possibilities in fascist trappings as Saturninus seizes control of Rome and marries Tamora. There's a jazzy wedding orgy, crypto-Nazi costuming, and a scene staged in front of a vast modern structure made of arches, a reminder of the joke that fascist architecture looked like Mussolini ordered it over the phone.

She lavishes great energy on staging and photography. Like the makers of a cartoon, Taymor and her cinematographer, Luciano Tovoli, sometimes move the camera in time with music or sound effects; as the picture swoops or pulls away, so does Elliot Goldenthal's score. There are scenes of rigid choreography, as in the entry into Rome, where Titus's army marches like the little green soldiers in *Toy Story*. And other scenes where the movements are so voluptuous we are reminded of *Fellini Satyricon*.

Mark Van Doren was correct. There is no lesson to be learned from *Titus Andronicus*. It is a tragedy without a hero, without values, without a point, and therefore as modern as a horror exploitation film or a video game. It is not a catharsis, but a killing gallery where the characters speak in poetry. Freed of pious meaning, the actors bury themselves in technique and the opportunity of stylized melodrama. Anyone who doesn't enjoy this film for what it is must explain: How could it be other? This is the film Shakespeare's play deserves, and perhaps even a little more. ☞

Topsy-Turvy ★ ★ ★ ★
R, 160 m., 2000

Allan Corduner (Arthur Sullivan), Jim Broadbent (William Schwenck Gilbert), Lesley Manville (Lucy Gilbert ["Kitty"]), Ron Cook (Richard D'Oyly Carte), Timothy Spall (Richard Temple), Wendy Nottingham (Helen Lenoir), Kevin McKidd (Durward Lely), Martin Savage (George Grossmith), Shirley Henderson (Leonora Braham), Alison Steadman (Madame Leon). Directed by Mike Leigh and produced by Simon Channing-Williams. Screenplay by Leigh.

Mike Leigh's *Topsy-Turvy* is the work of a man helplessly in love with the theater. In a gloriously entertaining period piece, he tells the story of the genesis, preparation, and presentation of a comic opera—Gilbert and Sullivan's *The Mikado*—celebrating all the dreaming and hard work, personality conflict and team spirit, inspiration and mundane detail of every theatrical presentation, however inspired or inept. Every production is completely different, and they are all exactly like this.

As the movie opens, Arthur Sullivan and William Schwenck Gilbert rule the London stage. Their comic operettas, produced by the famed impresario Richard D'Oyly Carte, have even paid for the construction of the Savoy Theater—where, alas, their latest collaboration, *Princess Ida,* has flopped so badly that even Gilbert's dentist tells him it went on too long.

Sullivan, the composer, has had enough. Newly knighted by the queen, he decides it is time to compose serious operas: "This work with Gilbert is quite simply killing me." He flees to Paris and a bordello, where D'Oyly Carte tracks him down and learns that there may never be another collaboration between Gilbert (Jim Broadbent) and Sullivan (Allan Corduner). When Sullivan returns to London, he has a meeting with Gilbert, tense and studiously polite, and rejects Gilbert's latest scenario, which is as silly as all of the others: "Oh, Gilbert! You and your world of Topsy-Turvy-dom!"

The two men are quite different. Sullivan is a womanizer and dandy, Gilbert a businessman with an eagle eye for theatrical detail. One day in the middle of the impasse, his wife, Kitty (Lesley Manville), drags him to London's newly opened Japan exhibition, where he observes a Kabuki performance, sips green tea, and buys a sword that his butler nails up over the door. Not long after, as he paces his study, the sword falls down, and inspiration strikes: Gilbert races to his desk to begin writing *The Mikado*.

The world of Gilbert and Sullivan is one of whimsical goofiness, presented with rigorous attention to detail. The fun is in the tension between absurd contrivance and meticulous delivery; consider the song "I Am the Very Model of a Modern Major-General" from *The Pirates of Penzance*, which is delivered with the discipline of a metronome, but at breakneck pace. The form itself is a poke in the eye for Victorian values: The plots and songs uphold the conventional while making it seem clearly mad.

Mike Leigh might seem to be the last of

modern British directors to be attracted to the world of the Savoy operas. His films, which do not begin with finished screenplays but are "devised" by the director in collaboration with his actors, have always been about modern Britain—often about inarticulate, alienated, shy, hostile types, who are as psychologically awkward in his comedies as in his hard-edged work. His credits include *Life Is Sweet, Naked,* and *Secrets and Lies,* and nothing remotely in the same cosmos as Gilbert and Sullivan.

But think again. Leigh has worked as much in the theater as for film, and his films depend more than most on the theatrical disciplines of improvisation and rehearsal. In London his productions have often been in vest-pocket theaters where even details like printing the tickets and hiring the stagehands may not have escaped his attention. He is a man of the theater in every atom of his being, and that is why there is a direct connection between his work and Gilbert and Sullivan.

The earlier reaches of *Topsy-Turvy* resemble in broad outline other films about theater: a flop, a crisis, a vow to never work again, a sudden inspiration, a new start. All well done, but the film begins to glow when the decision is made to go ahead with *The Mikado.* This is not merely a film that goes backstage, but also one that goes into accounting ledgers, hiring practices, costume design, personnel problems, casting decisions, sex lives, and the endless detail work of rehearsal: Hours of work are needed to manufacture and perfect even a silly throwaway moment, so that it is thrown away with style and wit, instead of merely being misplaced.

My favorite scene is one in which Gilbert rehearses his actors in line readings. The actor George Grossmith (Martin Savage) expresses insufficient alarm, and Gilbert reminds him that his character is under sentence of death, "by something lingering. By either boiling oil or melted lead. Kindly bear that in mind." There is also much travail over the correct pronunciation of "corroborative."

Many of the cast members are veterans of earlier Leigh films, including the pear-shaped, pouty-lipped Timothy Spall, whose character blinks back tears as his big song seems doomed in dress rehearsal. Jim Broadbent makes a precise Gilbert, bluff and incisive, and Allan Cor-

duner's Sullivan is a study in the partner who cannot admit that his greatness lies always in collaboration. Leigh's construction is canny as he follows big musical numbers like "Three Little Maids" from rehearsal through opening night, and the costumes and sets faithfully recreate the classic D'Oyly Carte Co. productions.

Not everyone is familiar with Gilbert and Sullivan. Do they need to be to enjoy *Topsy-Turvy*? No more, I suspect, than one needs to know all about Shakespeare to enjoy *Shakespeare in Love*—although with both films, the more you do know, the more you enjoy. The two films have been compared because both are British, both are about theatrical geniuses, both deal with theatrical lore. The difference is that *Shakespeare in Love* centers on a love story, and *Topsy-Turvy* is about love of the theater. Romantic love ages and matures. Love of the theater, it reminds us, is somehow always adolescent—heedless, passionate, guilty.

Toy Story 2 ★ ★ ★ ½
G, 85 m., 1999

Tom Hanks (Woody), Tim Allen (Buzz Lightyear), Don Rickles (Mr. Potato Head), Jim Varney (Slinky Dog), Wallace Shawn (Rex), John Ratzenberger (Hamm), Annie Potts (Bo Peep), Joan Cusack (Jessie the Cowgirl), R. Lee Ermey (Sergeant), Kelsey Grammer (Prospector), Jodi Benson (Barbie), Estelle Harris (Mrs. Potato Head), Wayne Knight (Toy Collector), Laurie Metcalf (Mrs. Davis), John Morris (Andy), David Ogden Stiers (Bullseye). Directed by John Lasseter and produced by Helene Plotkin and Karen Robert Jackson. Screenplay by Andrew Stanton, Rita Hsiao, Doug Chamberlain, and Chris Webb.

I forgot something about toys a long time ago, and *Toy Story 2* reminded me. It involves the love, pity, and guilt that a child feels for a favorite toy. A doll or an action figure (or a Pokémon) is *yours* in the same way a pet is. It depends on you. It misses you. It can't do anything by itself. It needs you and is troubled when you're not there.

Toy Story 2 knows this, and for smaller viewers that knowledge may be the most important thing about it—more important than the story or the skill of the animation. This is a movie about what you hope your toys do when you're not around—and what you fear. They have lives of their own, but you are the sun in the sky of their universe, and when you treat them badly their feelings are wounded.

The story begins with Andy, the little boy who owns the *Toy Story* toys, going off to camp. Woody, the cowboy, is in bad shape with a torn arm, and gets left behind. This is crushing to Woody, but worse is to come, when he gets scooped up by Big Al the toy collector, repaired, mended, and repainted—and scheduled for sale to a toy museum in Japan.

At first this adventure is kind of fun for Woody, who finds out for the first time that he is part of a set of toys, the Roundup Gang, that also includes a cowgirl named Jessie, a horse named Bullseye, and a prospector named Stinky Pete. Woody is blown away to discover he even starred in a black-and-white TV puppet show in the fifties, and begins to think that since Andy might eventually abandon him, he might enjoy retiring as the star attraction in a toy museum.

Meanwhile, Buzz Lightyear and the other toys return from camp, discover what has happened, and lead a dangerous cross-town mission to rescue Woody. And we begin to get insights into the private lives of toys. Stinky Pete, for example, is bitter because no kid ever bought him, and he's still in his original box. Jessie is spunky and liberated, but this cowgirl does get the blues; she sings the winsome "When She Loved Me" about her former owner Emily, who tossed her under the bed and forgot her. "You never forget kids, but they forget you," Buzz sighs, but he argues for the position that it is better to be loved for the length of a childhood than admired forever behind glass in a museum.

The movie once again features the enchanting three-dimensional feel of computer-generated animation by Pixar, and has been directed by John Lasseter, the creator of the 1995 *Toy Story*. The tale of this film is almost as thrilling as Woody's fate: It was originally intended as a lowly direct-to-video release, but then the early scenes played so well that Pixar retrenched and started over again with a theatrical feature. In other words, this isn't a made-for-video that they decided to put into theaters, but a version intended from the first to be theatrical.

That's important, because it means more detail and complexity went into the animation.

The stars of the voice track certainly seem to remember how they once identified with toys. Many of the actors from the first movie are back again, including Tom Hanks as Woody, Tim Allen as Buzz, Don Rickles as Mr. Potato Head, and Jim Varney as Slinky Dog. The key newcomer is Joan Cusack as Jessie the cowgirl, and she brings new life to the cast by confronting the others with a female character who's a little less domestic than Mrs. Potato Head.

Hanks is responsible for what's probably the movie's high point; he sings "You've Got a Friend in Me," and seems to speak for all toys everywhere. His Woody has, indeed, grown into quite a philosopher. His thoughts about life, love, and belonging to someone are kind of profound. The screenplay by Andrew Stanton, Rita Hsiao, Doug Chamberlain, and Chris Webb isn't just a series of adventures (although there are plenty of those), but a kind of inside job in which we discover that all toys think the way every kid knows his toys think. ☞

Trekkies ★ ★ ★
PG, 86 m., 1999

A documentary directed by Roger Nygard and produced by Keith Border. Narrated by Denise Crosby and featuring LeVar Burton, Frank D'Amico, John de Lancie, James Doohan, Michael Dorn, Jonathan Frakes, DeForest Kelly, Walter Koenig, Kate Mulgrew, Anne Murphy, Nichelle Nichols, Leonard Nimoy, William Shatner, Brent Spiner, and George Takei.

When Barbara Adams of Little Rock, Arkansas, was called to serve as a Whitewater juror, she arrived dressed appropriately, in her opinion. She was in a lieutenant commander's uniform as commanding officer of the USS *Artemis*, the Little Rock unit of the Federation Alliance. In other words, she was a *Star Trek* fan.

When the judge demurred at her costume and she made national news, she refused to back down: "If the president himself were on trial," she said, "I would still wear the uniform. I am an officer in the Federation universe twenty-four hours a day." Plus, she was setting a good example: "I don't want my officers to ever be ashamed to wear their uniforms."

As Adams is making these statements in *Trekkies*, a new documentary, I was looking closely for any sign of a smile. She was dead serious. *Star Trek* is her life. Old soldiers get their dress uniforms out of mothballs to prove the point that "formal wear" can mean either a tuxedo or a military uniform. And Lieutenant Commander Adams honors her uniform in the same spirit.

Not everyone in *Trekkies* is as serious about the long-running series of TV programs and movies. But most of them are as obsessed. Consider Denis Bourguinon, a dentist in Orlando whose Star Base Dental is an office completely designed around a *Star Trek* motif. Even his aides and hygienists are in uniform. One says she held out for a year before putting on the outfit. What convinced her? "He told me I had to."

Then there is the Canadian man who has designed a motorized life-support chair like one seen in the series, and drives around town in it, only his head visible above what looks like a steam cabinet. Or the father-and-son team whose pickup looks like a lunar lander and might someday be able to "shoot a 1,000-foot beam." And consider the *Star Trek* auction where someone bid $40 for a half-filled water glass used by a cast member with a virus. The lucky bidder drank the rest of the water so he could have the virus too.

I've been vaguely aware of the further shores of *Star Trek* fandom through my mail and contact with audiences at screenings. And I've sensed a certain tone of awe about it in the voices of many cast members I've interviewed, from Leonard Nimoy and William Shatner on down, or up. It's not so much a hobby, more a way of life. "Somewhere in the world," Denise (Tasha Yar) Crosby, the film's narrator, informs us, "there is a *Star Trek* event every weekend." We meet Richard Arnold, a *Star Trek* consultant, who has visited 360 of them.

Trekkies and Trekkers evolved out of the older and broader-based science-fiction fandom, which began with mimeographed magazines in the 1940s and went on to sponsor gigantic WorldCons and influence the tone and jargon of the Web (many Web pages are mutated fanzines). Fandom began the tradition of dressing in the costumes of science-fiction characters, and *Star Trek* fandom is intensely involved in that side of things—to such a degree that the dentist and his wife cheerfully hint that many different species play roles in their fantasy lives.

To some degree, dressing up and role-playing in a *Star Trek* context may be a cover for cross-dressing impulses in general. To a much larger degree, it is probably just good fun. I was going to say "good, clean fun," but was reminded of an attractive black woman in the movie who, as Mistress Janeway, pens popular S&M fantasies with a *Star Trek* theme, in which aliens do things to one another that humans can hardly hope to appreciate.

Sinclair Lewis, who I believe invented the term "boosterism," would appreciate a uniquely American strain in Trekdom, which feels compelled, like so many popular movements, to cloak its fun in do-gooderism. Trekkies talk at length about how the world would be a saner and more peaceful place if the *Star Trek* philosophy ruled our lives. No doubt it would be a lot more entertaining, too, especially during root canals.

The Trial ★ ★ ★

NO MPAA RATING, 118 m., 1963 (rereleased 2000)

Anthony Perkins (Joseph K), Jeanne Moreau (Miss Burstner), Orson Welles (Advocate), Madeline Robinson (Mrs. Brubach), Elsa Martinelli (Hilda), Suzanne Flon (Miss Pittl), Akim Tamiroff (Bloch), Romy Schneider (Leni). Directed by Orson Welles and produced by Alexander Salkind. Screenplay by Welles, based on the novel by Franz Kafka.

I was once involved in a project to convince Orson Welles to record a commentary track for *Citizen Kane*. Seemed like a good idea, but not to the great one, who rumbled that he had made a great many films other than *Kane* and was tired of talking about it.

One he might have talked about was *The Trial* (1963), his version of the Kafka story about a man accused of—something, he knows not what. It starred Anthony Perkins in his squirmy post-*Psycho* mode, it had a baroque visual style, and it was one of the few times, after *Kane*, when Welles was able to get his vision onto the screen intact. For years the negative of the film was thought to be lost, but then it was rediscovered and restored.

The world of the movie is like a nightmare, with its hero popping from one surrealistic situation to another. Water towers open into file rooms, a woman does laundry while through the door a trial is under way, and huge trunks are dragged across empty landscapes and then back again. The black-and-white photography shows Welles's love of shadows, extreme camera angles, and spectacular sets. He shot it mostly inside the Gare d'Orsay in Paris, which, after it closed as a train station and before it was reborn as a museum, offered vast spaces; the office where Perkins's character works consists of rows of desks and typists extending almost to infinity, like a similar scene in the silent film *The Crowd*.

Franz Kafka published his novel in Prague in 1925; it reflected his own paranoia, but it was prophetic, foreseeing Stalin's Gulag and Hitler's Holocaust, in which innocent people wake up one morning to discover they are guilty of being themselves. It is a tribute to his vision that the word "Kafkesque" has, like "catch-22," moved beyond the work to describe things we all see in the world.

Anthony Perkins is a good choice to play Joseph K, the bureaucrat who awakens to find strange men in his room, men who treat him as a suspect and yet give him no information. Perkins could turn in an instant from ingratiating smarminess to anger, from supplication to indignation, his voice barking out ultimatums and then suddenly going high-pitched and stuttery. And watch his body language as he goes into his confiding mode, hitching closer to other characters, buddy-style, looking forward to neat secrets.

The film follows his attempts to discover what he is charged with, and how he can defend himself. Every Freudian slip is used against him (he refers to a "pornograph player," and a man in a black suit carefully notes that down). He finds himself in a courtroom where the audience is cued by secret signs from the judge. He petitions the court's official portrait painter, who claims he can fix cases and obtain a "provisional acquittal." And in the longest sequence, he visits the cavernous home of the Advocate, played by Welles as an ominous sybarite who

spends much of his time in bed, smoking cigars and being tended by his mistress (Romy Schneider).

The Advocate has obscure powers in matters such as Joseph K is charged with, whatever they are. He has had a pathetic little man living in his maid's room for a long time, hoping for news on his case, kissing the Advocate's hand, falling to his knees. He would like Joseph to behave in the same way. The Advocate's home reaches out in all directions, like a loft, factory, and junk shop, illuminated by hundreds of guttering candles, decorated by portraits of judges, littered with so many bales of old legal papers that one shot looks like the closing scene in *Citizen Kane*. But neither here nor elsewhere can Joseph come to grips with his dilemma.

Perkins was one of those actors everyone thought was gay. He kept his sexuality private, and used his nervous style of speech and movement to suggest inner disconnects. From an article by Edward Guthmann in the *San Francisco Chronicle*, I learn that Welles confided to his friend Henry Jaglom that he knew Perkins was a homosexual, "and used that quality in Perkins to suggest another texture in Joseph K, a fear of exposure."

"The whole homosexuality thing—using Perkins that way—was incredible for that time," Jaglom told Guthmann. "It was intentional on Orson's part: He had these three gorgeous women (Jeanne Moreau, Romy Schneider, Elsa Martinelli) trying to seduce this guy, who was completely repressed and incapable of responding." That provides an additional key to the film, which could be interpreted as a nightmare in which women make demands Joseph is uninterested in meeting, while bureaucrats in black coats follow him everywhere with obscure threats of legal disaster.

But there is also another way of looking at *The Trial*, and that is to see it as autobiographical. After *Citizen Kane* (1941) and *The Magnificent Ambersons* (1942, a masterpiece with its ending hacked to pieces by the studio), Welles seldom found the freedom to make films when and how he desired. His life became a wandering from one place to another. Beautiful women rotated through his beds. He was reduced to a supplicant who begged financing from wealthy but maddening men. He was never able to find out exactly what crime he had committed that made him "unbankable" in Hollywood. Because Welles plays the Advocate, there is a tendency to think the character is inspired by him, but I can think of another suspect: Alexander Salkind, producer of *The Trial* and much later of the *Superman* movies, who like the Advocate, liked people to beg for money and power which, in fact, he did not always have.

Seen in this restored version (available on video from Milestone), *The Trial* is above all a visual achievement, an exuberant use of camera placement and movement and inventive lighting. Study the scene where the screaming girls chase Joseph K up the stairs to the painter's studio and peer at him through the slats of the walls, and you will see what Richard Lester saw before he filmed the screaming girls in *A Hard Day's Night* and had them peer at the Beatles through the slats of a railway luggage car.

The ending is problematical. Mushroom clouds are not Kafkaesque because they represent a final conclusion, and in Kafka's world nothing ever concludes. But then comes another ending: the voice of Orson Welles, speaking the end credits, placing his own claim on every frame of the film, and we wonder, is this his way of telling us *The Trial* is more than ordinarily personal? He was a man who made the greatest film ever made, and was never forgiven for it.

Trick ★ ★
R, 90 m., 1999

Christian Campbell (Gabriel), John Paul Pitoc (Mark), Tori Spelling (Katherine), Steve Hayes (Perry), Brad Beyer (Rich), Lorri Bagley (Judy), Kevin Chamberlin (Perry's Ex), Clinton Leupp (Miss Coco Peru). Directed by Jim Fall and produced by Eric d'Arbeloff, Fall, and Ross Katz. Screenplay by Jason Schafer.

There's an e-mail making the rounds that urges gay moviegoers to "support" gay-themed films by being sure to attend on the crucial opening weekend. It cites a similar effort to encourage blacks to support black films from the outset. I myself have urged readers to support various films that might be overlooked, but it's all a futile enterprise: No one in the history of the

movies has purchased a ticket to "support" a film. People go only because they really want to.

Besides, what message would it send to "support" a gay film like *Trick*? The message, I suppose, would be that gays should have romantic comedies just as dim and dumb as the straight versions—although I cannot offhand remember many recent straight films this witless. The movie imposes a Doris Day story line on material that wants to be more sexual; it's about a character whose quasi-virginity is preserved through an improbable series of mishaps and coincidences.

The Doris Day character this time is Gabriel (Christian Campbell, Neve's brother), an office worker who dreams of writing musical comedies, even though he admits to his best pal Katherine (Tori Spelling) that his kind of song is dead. He's right. She sings an audition piece to deadening effect, and in the dark I scribbled: "She's singing the *whole song!*" The movie confuses a comic moment with a musical number.

Disconsolate, Gabriel drifts into a gay bar, where his groin thrums at the sight of Mark (John Paul Pitoc), a go-go boy whose nickname is not "Beer Can" because of his drinking habits. Of course Mark would forever be out of reach of the shy Gabriel—or so he thinks, until they run into each other on the subway, make eye contact, and end up trying to find a place where they can be alone together.

This is where the Doris Day plot difficulties kick in. Spelling won't vacate Gabe's apartment because she has to print 500 copies of her résumé, and later his macho roommate and ditzy girlfriend claim the turf for their own. Gabe and Mark drift through the night to drag clubs and diners, increasingly discouraged. Why, oh why, is there no place where they can have sex?

There's a problem with the character of Mark, played by Pitoc with an occasional sour look, as if he's unsure whether to smolder or leave. He follows Gabe around faithfully, but never really seems to *want* to sleep with him: He's like a man waiting to collect an overdue car payment. Gabe, meanwhile, actually brags to people that his new friend is a go-go boy; he's like a deejay on a date with a porn actress.

Another problem is that the director, Jim Fall, treats too many of the supporting actors as if he owes them favors. It's as if he promised them big scenes if they worked cheap. We get full-length renditions in piano bars, Spelling's protracted audition, and so on. It's as if the screenplay wants to keep moving but the camera can't drag itself away from whatever it's watching.

Would this same movie be entertaining with heterosexual characters? In today's world, it would hardly be thinkable. The premise is so hackneyed that any characters in this plot would come across as dopes. I guess the Mark character would be the boy in the straight version, which makes his sullen passivity all the stranger: It's like he's allowing himself to be dragged around by a partner much keener on the whole idea than he is.

Trippin' ★ ★ ½
R, 92 m., 1999

Deon Richmond (Gregory Reed), Donald Adeosun Faison (June), Maia Campbell (Cinny Hawkins), Guy Torry (Fish), Aloma Wright (Louis Reed), Harold Sylvester (Willie Reed), Cleavon McClendon (Jamal), Bill Henderson (Gramps), Michael Warren (Shapik). Directed by David Hubbard (as David Raynr) and produced by Marc Abraham and Caitlin Scanlon. Screenplay by Gary Hardwick.

To judge by a lot of the movies I've been seeing, the most pressing issue of our time (indeed, the *only* issue in most movies about teenagers) is who to take to the senior prom. Faithful readers will know that this question has been raised in at least six movies already this year, and I'm not even counting the one about who Carrie II will kill at the prom.

Trippin' transports this issue to the African-American community, in a high-spirited comedy about a likable senior named Gregory Reed (Deon Richmond), who puts off everything until the last possible moment. When he approaches his parents with a request for "funds to finance my senior prom activities," they laugh at him: He hasn't even sent in his college applications yet, his dad points out. First things first.

Gregory's problem is that he lives in a world of daydreams. The movie opens with one—an island fantasy, shot in the style of a music video, with Gregory basking in the admiration of a brace of Hawaiian Tropics girls. A friend of

his, who wears leg braces, inspires a daydream in which he becomes the Terminator crossed with RoboCop. And a visit to an army recruiting office triggers a fantasy in which Gregory receives the Medal of Honor—plus, the president tells him, "unreleased CDs from Tupac and Notorious B.I.G."

Gregory has fallen in love with Cinny Hawkins (the beautiful Maia Campbell), and would like to ask her to the prom—but lacks the funds and the courage. His friends advise him to impress her with his bright future, so he lies and says he's been given a full scholarship to UCLA. There's a sweet scene where they wander through a dock area, dreaming of the voyages they could take—on the sea and in life.

There seems to be, alas, a requirement that almost every movie about black teenagers include drugs somewhere in the plot. *Trippin'* supplies a no-good drug dealer who at one point has Gregory's friend hanging upside down from a crane, and the scenes involving this villain don't really seem necessary. I guess the crime stuff is there to provide the plot with prefab suspense, but it might have been more fun to develop Cinny's character more fully, since there's a lot more to her than simply beauty.

Trippin' does have some amiable scenes involving Gregory's family, including his strict dad (Harold Sylvester), his sympathetic mother (Aloma Wright), and Gramps (Bill Henderson), who has no truck with attempts to improve his nutrition, and bangs on the table while demanding pork sausage. And there's a no-nonsense teacher (Michael Warren) who tries to jolt Gregory out of his mind-trips and into some kind of organized approach to the rest of his life.

The movie is sweet, but predictable, and we get about three more daydreams than we really require. Deon Richmond and Maia Campbell both possess radiant smiles, which is important in a movie where a character's appearance supplies at least half of the character development. Whether Richmond and Campbell will someday be getting the kind of roles that go to Denzel Washington and Halle Berry is impossible to predict, but on the basis of their work here, it's not implausible.

Did I like the movie? Not enough to recommend it, except to someone who really wants to see another senior prom cliffhanger. Still, there are so many grim and gritty urban violence movies that it's good to see nice African-American kids in a comedy, even if it's so lacking in imagination that it finds it necessary to hang them upside down.

True Crime ★ ★ ★
R, 127 m., 1999

Clint Eastwood (Steve Everett), Isaiah Washington (Frank Beachum), Denis Leary (Bob Findley), Lisa Gay Hamilton (Frank's Wife), James Woods (Alan Mann), Diane Venora (Barbara). Directed by Clint Eastwood and produced by Eastwood, Richard D. Zanuck, and Lili Fini Zanuck. Screenplay by Larry Gross, Paul Brickman, and Stephen Schiff, based on the novel by Andrew Klavan.

Clint Eastwood's *True Crime* follows the rhythm of a newspaperman's day. For those who cover breaking news, many days are about the same. When they begin, time seems to stretch out generously toward the deadline. There's leisure for coffee and phone calls, jokes and arguments. Then a blip appears on the radar screen: an assignment. Seemingly a simple assignment. Then the assignment reveals itself as more complicated. The reporter makes some calls.

If there's anything to the story at all, a moment arrives when it becomes, to the reporter, the most important story in the world. His mind shapes the form it should take. He badgers sources for the missing pieces. The deadline approaches, his attention focuses, the finish line is the only thing visible, and then facts, story, deadline, and satisfaction come all at the same time. A deadline reporter's day, in other words, is a lot like sex.

Eastwood uses this rhythm to make *True Crime* into a wickedly effective thriller. He plays Steve Everett, a reporter for the *Oakland Tribune*. Steve used to work out east, but got fired for "screwing the owner's underage daughter." The movie's Web page says he worked for the *New York Times,* but this detail has been dropped from the movie, no doubt when the information about the owner's daughter was added. Now he's having an affair with the wife of Findlay, his city editor (Denis Leary).

Everett's personal life is a mess. His wife, Barbara (Diane Venora), knew he cheated when she married him, but thought it was only with her. Now they have a young daughter, but Everett seems too busy to be a good dad (there's a scene where he pushes her stroller through the zoo at a dead run). Everett's also a little shaky; he was a drunk until two months ago, when he graduated to recovering alcoholic.

He's assigned to write a routine story about the last hours of a man on death row: Frank Beachum (Isaiah Washington), convicted of the shooting death of a pregnant clerk in a convenience store. Both the city editor and the editor-in-chief (James Woods) know Everett is a hotshot with a habit of turning routine stories into federal cases, and they warn him against trying to save Beachum at the eleventh hour. But it's in Everett's blood to sniff out the story behind the story. He becomes convinced the wrong man is going to be executed. "When my nose tells me something stinks—I gotta have faith in it," he tells Beachum.

This is Eastwood's twenty-first film as a director, and experience has given him patience. He knows that even in a deadline story like this, not all scenes have to have the same breakneck pace. He doesn't direct like a child of MTV, for whom every moment has to vibrate to the same beat. Eastwood knows about story arc, and as a jazz fan he also knows about improvising a little before returning to the main theme.

True Crime has a nice rhythm to it, intercutting the character's problems at home, his interviews with the prisoner, his lunch with a witness, his unsettling encounter with the grandmother of another witness. And then, as the midnight hour of execution draws closer, Eastwood tightens the noose of inexorably mounting tension. There are scenes involving an obnoxious prison chaplain, and a basically gentle warden, and the mechanical details of execution. Cuts to the governor who can stay the execution. Tests of the telephone hot lines. Battles with his editors. Last-minute revelations. Like a good pitcher, he gives the movie a nice slow curve, and a fast break.

Many recent thrillers are so concerned with technology that the human characters are almost in the way. We get gun battles and car chases that we don't care about, because we don't know the people firing the guns or driving the cars. I liked the way Eastwood and his writers (Larry Gross, Paul Brickman, and Stephen Schiff) lovingly added the small details. For example, the relationships that both the reporter and the condemned man have with their daughters. And a problem when the prisoner's little girl can't find the right color crayon for her drawing of green pastures.

In England twenty-five years ago, traditional beer was being pushed off the market by a pasteurized product that had been pumped full of carbonation (in other words, by American beer). A man named Richard Boston started the Real Beer Campaign. Maybe it's time for a movement in favor of real movies. Movies with tempo and character details and style, instead of actionfests with Attention Deficit Disorder. Clint Eastwood could be honorary chairman.

The Truman Show ★ ★ ★ ★
PG, 104 m., 1998

Jim Carrey (Truman Burbank), Laura Linney (Meryl), Noah Emmerich (Marlon), Natascha McElhone (Lauren/Sylvia), Holland Taylor (Mother), Ed Harris (Christof), Brian Delate (Kirk), Paul Giamatti (Simeon). Directed by Peter Weir and produced by Scott Rudin, Andrew Niccol, Edward S. Feldman, and Adam Schroeder. Screenplay by Niccol.

The Truman Show is founded on an enormous secret, which all of the studio's advertising has been determined to reveal. I didn't know the secret when I saw the film, and was able to enjoy the little doubts and wonderings that the filmmakers so carefully planted. If by some good chance you do not know the secret, read no further.

Those fortunate audience members (I trust they have all left the room?) will be able to appreciate the meticulous way director Peter Weir and writer Andrew Niccol have constructed a jigsaw plot around their central character, who doesn't suspect that he's living his entire life on live television. Yes, he lives in an improbably ideal world, but I fell for that: I assumed the movie was taking a sitcom view of life, in which neighbors greet each other over white picket fences, and Ozzie and Harriet are real people.

Actually, it's Seaside, a planned community on the Gulf Coast near Panama City. Called Seahaven in the movie, it looks like a nice place to live. Certainly Truman Burbank (Jim Carrey) doesn't know anything else. You accept the world you're given, the filmmakers suggest; more thoughtful viewers will get the buried message, which is that we accept almost everything in our lives without examining it very closely. When was the last time you reflected on how really odd a tree looks?

Truman works as a sales executive at an insurance company, is happily married to Meryl (Laura Linney), and doesn't find it suspicious that she describes household products in the language of TV commercials. He is happy, in a way, but an uneasiness gnaws away at him. Something is missing, and he thinks perhaps he might find it in Fiji, where Lauren (Natascha McElhone), the only woman he really loved, has allegedly moved with her family.

Why did she leave so quickly? Perhaps because she was not a safe bet for Truman's world: The actress who played her (named Sylvia) developed real feeling and pity for Truman, and felt he should know the truth about his existence. Meryl, on the other hand, is a reliable pro (which raises the question, unanswered, of their sex life).

Truman's world is controlled by a TV producer named Christof (Ed Harris), whose control room is high in the artificial dome that provides the sky and horizon of Seahaven. He discusses his programming on talk shows, and dismisses the protests of those (including Sylvia) who believe Truman is the victim of a cruel deception. Meanwhile, the whole world watches Truman's every move, and some viewers even leave the TV on all night as he sleeps.

The trajectory of the screenplay is more or less inevitable: Truman must gradually realize the truth of his environment and try to escape from it. It's clever the way he's kept on his island by implanted traumas about travel and water. As the story unfolds, however, we're not simply expected to follow it; we're invited to think about the implications. About a world in which modern communications make celebrity possible, and inhuman.

Until fairly recently, the only way you could become really famous was to be royalty, or a writer, actor, preacher, or politician—and even then, most people had knowledge of you only through words or printed pictures. Television, with its insatiable hunger for material, has made celebrities into "content," devouring their lives and secrets. If you think *The Truman Show* is an exaggeration, reflect that Princess Diana lived under similar conditions from the day she became engaged to Charles.

Carrey is a surprisingly good choice to play Truman. We catch glimpses of his manic comic persona, just to make us comfortable with his presence in the character, but this is a well-planned performance; Carrey is on the right note as a guy raised to be liked and likable, who decides his life requires more risk and hardship. Like the angels in *City of Angels*, he'd like to take his chances.

Ed Harris finds the right notes as Christof, the TV Svengali. He uses the technospeak by which we distance ourselves from the real meanings of our words. (If TV producers ever spoke frankly about what they were really doing, they'd come across like Bulworth.) For Harris, the demands of the show take precedence over any other values, and if you think that's an exaggeration, tell it to the TV news people who broadcast that Los Angeles suicide.

I enjoyed *The Truman Show* on its levels of comedy and drama; I *liked* Truman in the same way I liked Forrest Gump—because he was a good man, honest and easy to sympathize with. But the underlying ideas made the movie more than just an entertainment. Like *Gattaca*, the previous film written by Niccol, it brings into focus the new values that technology is forcing on humanity. Because we can engineer genetics, because we can telecast real lives—of course we must, right? But are these good things to do? The irony is, the people who will finally answer that question will be the very ones produced by the process.

Tumbleweeds ★ ★ ★
PG-13, 100 m., 1999

Janet McTeer (Mary Jo Walker), Kimberly J. Brown (Ava Walker), Jay O. Sanders (Dan), Gavin O'Connor (Jack Ranson), Michael J. Pollard (Mr. Cummings), Laurel Holloman (Laurie Pendleton), Lois Smith (Ginger). Directed by Gavin O'Connor and produced by Gregory O'Connor. Screenplay by Gavin O'Connor and Angela Shelton.

American movies have a deep faith that if you hit the road and point west, at the end of the journey you will find—well, whatever you're looking for. Romance, fame, truth, understanding, all dreamed of as you look out over the sea. Those who go west are often poor, or unlucky in love, or have been roughly treated by life. Those who go east, on the other hand, are usually smart, aggressive, and ambitious. Has there ever been a movie in which a couple of losers from the Dust Bowl, down on their luck, head east and arrive in triumph at Coney Island?

We also have a faith in the wisdom of youth, and in the ability of parents to be redeemed by children. (We have an equal faith in the ability of children to be redeemed by parents, but fewer adults than teenagers buy movie tickets, so fewer of those movies are made.) *Tumbleweeds*, like *Anywhere But Here*, which opened only a month earlier, is about a troubled mother and her wise daughter, who share a road journey to California while both deal with the mother's immaturity and untidy sex life.

Is there a rule that we must prefer one of these films to the other? I don't know why there should be. I liked them about equally well, and certainly *Tumbleweeds*, which premiered in January 1999 at Sundance, cannot be blamed because its distributor couldn't get it into theaters before its twin.

Tumbleweeds is a little grittier than *Anywhere But Here*; it lacks the gloss of the other film and is positioned a notch or two lower on the socioeconomic ladder. In *Anywhere*, the mother pins her hopes on romance with an orthodondist, while in *Tumbleweeds* it is a truck driver who looks like the Marlboro Man. Both movies make much of the daughters' school opportunities, reminding us that America is a classless society where the speedometer is set back to zero for every generation. Ava (Kimberly J. Brown) may find herself spending the night with her mother, Mary Jo (Janet McTeer), in a borrowed camper, but she is auditioning to play Juliet, and no child is wholly disadvantaged who has access to Shakespeare.

Mary Jo is a woman who depends on the kindness of strange men. She has a mental Rolodex of guys who once thrummed to her charms, and pilots an old car around the Southwest looking them up. Her memory improves on reality; a man recalled as a leading car dealer turns out to run a used parts lot. But the friendly Marlborian truck driver (played by Gavin O'Connor, the director and cowriter) seems at first to be promising. He fixes a leaking hose in her radiator, later finds himself in the same pool hall where she stops for a drink, and soon Mary Jo and Ava are moving in.

By now they are in San Diego, where Mary Jo seeks employment. One of her interviewers is Michael J. Pollard, who examines her résumé and observes that either she likes to move around a lot or she's a wanted woman. She gets a job as a phone slave at a guard company (she calls you when your alarm goes off). But then the Marlboro Man gets angry when she doesn't order what he recommends at a restaurant. "I know where this is going," she says, having much experience of men who believe their kind suggestions should be understood as orders.

Will they move towns again? Resume the quest for the right man, the right home, the right school for Ava? Ava thinks not. As played by Brown, she is a thoughtful, appealing young woman who knows her mother all too well. McTeer makes Mary Jo into a woman who has two basic problems: A fatal attraction to the wrong men, and an inability to stay put long enough to work herself up the job ladder.

There is a right man around. He is Dan (Jay O. Sanders), a coworker who lost his own wife and tells Ava about that in one of the movie's best scenes. Will they get together? Would that be the right thing for either one of them? Movies like *Tumbleweeds* exist in the details, not the outcome. Even a happy ending, we suspect, would be temporary. We don't mind, since the characters have been intriguing to know and easy to care about.

20 Dates ½★
R, 88 m., 1999

Myles Berkowitz (Himself), Richard Arlook (His Agent), Tia Carrere (Herself), Elisabeth Wagner (Elisabeth), Robert McKee (Himself). Directed by Myles Berkowitz and produced by Elie Samaha, Jason Villard, and Mark McGarry. Screenplay by Berkowitz.

20 Dates tells the story of Myles Berkowitz, a man who wants to make a film and to fall in love. These areas are his "two greatest failures, professional and personal," so he decides to make a film about going out on twenty dates. By the end of the film he has won the love of the lovely Elisabeth—maybe—but his professional life is obviously still a failure.

The film has the obnoxious tone of a boring home movie narrated by a guy shouting in your ear. We learn how he gets a $60,000 investment from a man named Elie Samaha and uses it to hire a cameraman and a soundman to follow him around on his dates. Elie is never seen on film, but is taped with an (allegedly) hidden recorder while he threatens Berkowitz, complains about the quality of the footage, and insists on sex, stars—and a scene with Tia Carrere.

Elie has a point. Even though $60,000 is a low budget, you can't exactly see the money up there on the screen. I've seen features shot for half as much that were more impressive. What's worse is that Berkowitz loses our trust early in the film and never regains it. I don't know how much of this film is real, if any of it is. Some scenes are admittedly staged, and others feel that way.

Even though Berkowitz presumably displays himself in his best light, I couldn't find a moment when he said anything of charm or interest to one of his dates. He's surprised when one woman is offended to learn she's being photographed with a hidden camera, and when another one delivers an (unseen) hand wound that requires twenty stitches. The movie's best dialogue is: "I could have sworn that Karen and I had fallen in love. And now, it's never to be, because I couldn't ever get close to her—at least not closer than ninety feet, which was specified in the restraining order."

One of his dates, Stephanie, is a Hollywood wardrobe mistress. He asks her for free costumes for his movie (if it's a documentary, why does it need costumes?). She leaves for the rest room, "and I never saw her again." Distraught, he consults Robert McKee, a writing teacher, and McKee gives him theories about screen romance, which are irrelevant, of course, to an allegedly true-life documentary.

And what about Elie? He sounds unpleasant, vulgar, and tasteless (although no more so than many Hollywood producers). But why are we shown the outside of the county jail during his last conversation? Is he inside? What for? He promises to supply Tia Carrere, who indeed turns up in the film, describing Elie as a "very good friend." She may want to change her number.

There's a 1996 film available on video named *Me and My Matchmaker,* by Mark Wexler, about a filmmaker who consults a matchmaker and goes on dates, which he films himself. It is incomparably more entertaining, funny, professional, absorbing, honest, revealing, surprising, and convincing than *20 Dates.* It works wonderfully to demonstrate just how incompetent and annoying *20 Dates* really is.

28 Days ★ ★ ★
PG-13, 103 m., 2000

Sandra Bullock (Gwen Cummings), Viggo Mortensen (Eddie Boone), Dominic West (Jasper), Elizabeth Perkins (Lily), Azura Skye (Andrea), Steve Buscemi (Cornell), Alan Tudyk (Gerhardt), Michael O'Malley (Oliver), Reni Santoni (Daniel). Directed by Betty Thomas and produced by Jenno Topping. Screenplay by Susannah Grant.

Every drunk considers himself a special case, unique, an exception to the rules. Odd, since for the practicing alcoholic, daily life is mostly unchanging, an attempt to negotiate daily responsibilities while drinking enough but not too much. When this attempt fails, as it often does, it results in events that the drunk thinks make him colorful. True variety comes only with sobriety. Plus, now he can remember it.

This is the lesson learned by Gwen Cummings, the character played by Sandra Bullock in *28 Days.* As the story opens, her life is either wild and crazy, or confused and sad, depending on where you stand. She parties all night with her boyfriend Jasper (Dominic West). After the clubs, the drinks, the designer drugs, they commence what may turn out to be sex,

if they can stay awake long enough. Then a candle starts a fire, which they extinguish with champagne. What a ball.

In the morning, Gwen's day begins with a pass at the refrigerator so smooth and practiced she hardly seems to even open it while extracting a cold beer. Gwen is an accident waiting to happen—to herself, or innocent bystanders. Her victim is her sister Lily (Elizabeth Perkins). "Gwen, you make it impossible to love you," Lily says when she arrives late at the church for Lily's wedding. At the reception, Gwen delivers an insulting toast, knocks over the cake while dancing, steals a limousine to go buy another cake, and crashes it into a house. Not a good day.

Cut to Serenity Glen, where Gwen has been sentenced to twenty-eight days of rehab in lieu of jail time. The PA system makes a running commentary out of *M*A*S*H*-style announcements. The patients do a lot of peppy group singing (too much, if you ask me). "I don't have a health problem," Gwen protests. "I play Ultimate Frisbee twice a week." The patients include the usual cuckoo's nest of colorful characters, although they're a little more plausible than in most inmate populations. We meet Daniel (Reni Santoni), a doctor who pumped his own stomach to control his drinking, and wound up giving himself an emergency tracheotomy. Gerhardt (Alan Tudyk), prissy and critical, a dancer and coke addict. And Andrea (Azura Skye), Gwen's teenage roommate.

Gwen's counselor is Cornell, played by Steve Buscemi, who inspires a grin when we see him in a movie, because he's usually good for strange scenes and dialogue. Not this time; he plays the role straight, revealing toughness and a certain weary experience, as if all of Gwen's cherished kookiness is for him a very, very old joke. There's a nice scene where she says exactly the wrong things to him before discovering he's her counselor.

Another fellow patient is Eddie Boone (Viggo Mortensen), a baseball pitcher with a substance abuse problem. Of course they begin a tentative, unstated courtship. Of course Jasper, on weekend visits, misunderstands ("Where are all the celebrities?" he asks on his first arrival, looking around for Elizabeth Taylor). Of course there is a fight. This subplot is predictable, but made perceptive because Gwen and Eddie illustrate the lifeboat mentality in which sailors on the ship of rehab have only each other to cling to.

The movie was written by Susannah Grant, who also wrote Julia Roberts's hit film *Erin Brockovich*. I differed with *Erin* for the same reason I like *28 Days*: The tone of the central character. I found that Roberts, enormously likable though she is, upstaged the material in *Erin Brockovich* by unwise costume choices and scenes that were too obviously intended as showcases. Bullock brings a kind of ground-level vulnerability to *28 Days* that doesn't make her into a victim but simply into one more suitable case for treatment. Bullock, like Roberts, is likable, but in *28 Days* at least that's not the point.

Note: 28 Days *is rated* PG-13 *and might be effective as a cautionary tale for teenagers.*

The 24-Hour Woman ★ ★ ★
R, 95 m., 1999

Rosie Perez (Grace Santos), Marianne Jean-Baptiste (Madeline Labelle), Patti LuPone (Joan Marshall), Karen Duffy (Margo Lynn), Diego Serrano (Eddie Diaz), Wendell Pierce (Roy Labelle), Melissa Leo (Dr. Suzanne Pincus). Directed by Nancy Savoca and produced by Richard Guay, Larry Meistrich, and Peter Newman. Screenplay by Savoca and Guay.

The look in Grace's eyes is hard to describe as she watches her daughter, Daisy, take her first steps, and no wonder: She's seeing it on video. She missed her daughter's first birthday and the first steps because she was arrested trying to jump over a subway turnstile with a birthday present. And she yelled at the cop because she was so frustrated after a crazy day at work and then the struggle to find the toy, one of those overnight sensations that inspires buying panics at Toys-R-Us.

Grace, played at top speed by Rosie Perez, is a TV producer just finishing her first year as a working mom. She's at the end of her rope. First came the surprise news that she was pregnant. Then her husband, the host of the show, announced her pregnancy on TV. Then the executive producer (Patti LuPone) found out she's expected to deliver in November: "During sweeps!" Then the show made her pregnancy a ratings-winner on cable, and it got picked up by a network. Meanwhile Grace has been running herself ragged, trying to keep up.

Her mom smiles at Grace's faith that she can be a mother and hold a full-time job: "I remember when you were born. I was gonna write my novel while you slept." But Grace tries to juggle both lives, although hiring a nanny is an alarming experience: "So far all we've met are Nazi nurses and emotionally disturbed women with no skills." To balance her experience, there's the case of her new assistant, Madeline (Marianne Jean-Baptiste), who is returning to the workforce after taking time out for a family, and whose husband (Wendell Pierce) is playing househusband, not without grumbles.

The 24-Hour Woman is a message picture wrapped inside a screwball comedy, with a touch of satire aimed at TV talk shows. It doesn't all work, but it happens so fast we don't get stuck in the awkward parts. Rosie Perez's Grace is the engine that pulls the story with so much energy she seems to vibrate. Some will see her character as exaggerated. Not me. She's half-Brooklynite and half–TV producer, and from what I've seen of both species, hyperactivity is built in.

The only person on the show more driven than Grace is the Patti LuPone character, who has true tunnel vision and cares only about ratings and programming gimmicks (one of her segment titles: "Romancing the Stone: How to Kick-Start Your Man's Love Machine"). The message of the movie is that new mothers who want to work are pretty much on their own. They get more lip service than real help from their husbands, and fellow females at work are running too hard to pause for sisterhood. "Take your baby and go home," Joan shouts at her at one point. "I got a show to do here."

The movie's not an idealized *Ms.* magazine vision of a working mom breast-feeding between conference calls. Its message is more Darwinian: Motherhood releases powerful drives in a woman, which are good for her children but bad for her career. No matter how hard Grace tries, she can't get rid of the guilt when she's not with her baby. And the other people in her life, who do not share these mother's instincts, simply do not care as much, or at all.

The movie was directed and cowritten by Nancy Savoca, who in three earlier films also considered social institutions through a woman's eyes. Her *True Love* (1989) was about a bride who suddenly understood that she was being sacrificed on the altar of her family's expectations. Her *Dogfight* (1991) was about a woman who discovers she has been asked out on a date as part of a contest—four guys on their way to Vietnam are trying to see who can pick up the homeliest girl. And *Household Saints* (1993) was about a grandmother who was a devout Catholic, a mother and a husband who had drifted into secular ways, and a granddaughter who literally wanted to be a saint. Behavior that would have seemed admirable to the grandmother seemed like insanity to the mother.

Now comes *The 24-Hour Woman*, which one imagines contains some of Savoca's own experiences. Her casting of Rosie Perez is a good one, because Perez is the most grounded of actors; you can't find the slightest hint of theory or conceit in her performances, which seem founded on total identification with the character. She isn't a "working woman" or a "Puerto Rican yuppie" but simply Grace Santos, with her marriage, her kid, and her job. She doesn't have time for abstractions. This isn't the kind of movie that would make a working woman think twice about having a child. It would make her think twice about having a job. And if that's reactionary, then tough luck: What's a mom going to do when little Lily starts crying and only one person can comfort her?

TwentyFourSeven ★ ★

R, 96 m., 1998

Bob Hoskins (Alan Darcy), Frank Harper (Ronnie Marsh), Pamela Cundell (Auntie Iris), Danny Nussbaum (Tim), James Hooton (Knighty), Darren O. Campbell (Daz), Justin Brady (Gadget), Jimmy Hynd (Meggy). Directed by Shane Meadows and produced by Imogen West. Screenplay by Meadows and Paul Fraser.

I've never been able to understand why boxing is so often recommended as a worthwhile pastime for idle lads in depressed areas. As a possible avenue to future employment, it ranks well below the chances of making it in the NBA, and has the added inconvenience that you get hit all the time. There is, in fact, almost no legitimate job that depends on boxing skills, unless it be nightclub bouncing.

And yet there's a whole body of films about earnest reformers who look around the neighborhood, see young men who are unemployed and aimless, and decide that what they need is a boxing club. Just this year we've had Jim Sheridan's *The Boxer*, with Daniel Day-Lewis as an ex-IRA man who starts a club in Belfast, and now Shane Meadows's *TwentyFourSeven*, with Bob Hoskins starting a club in the British Midlands.

Although both seem to feel that practicing the manly art will help their members develop self-confidence and personal goals, I'm more persuaded by the theory that if they spend all day beating up each other they'll be too tired in the evening to beat up civilians. Another motive, in *The Boxer*, is to run the club along nonsectarian lines, so that Catholics and Protestants can pound each other without regard for sect or creed.

TwentyFourSeven takes place in a desolate postindustrial wasteland in England, where the unemployed are warehoused in government housing and spend their days watching the telly, visiting the pub, and weighing the possibilities of petty crime. Their idea of amusement is to spit in a friend's chips when he isn't looking.

Into this bleak prospect comes Bob Hoskins, a former local lad who remembers when there was a boxing club and times were better. He determines to start the club again, and recruits the local louts, including one who's better off than the others because his dad is a gangster. The gangster is happy to see his son's days fruitfully occupied and helps underwrite the club, although in an excess of zeal (or bad timing) he manages to knock Hoskins unconscious against his car, and then complains about the blood on his paint job.

Hoskins, as he often does, brings a sweetness and conviction to his character. He conducts an inarticulate romantic campaign aimed at a local shop girl who is not interested, and in one of the film's best scenes he takes an aged aunt dancing. There's a certain humor in the boxing sequences (the first match turns into a brawl), and a good feeling for local color. But the personal tragedy of the Hoskins character evolves unconvincingly from the story of the boxing club, and I was left with the curious impression that the director would have rather made a documentary and not told a story at all.

Twice Upon a Yesterday ★ ½
R, 92 m., 1999

Lena Headey (Sylvia Weld), Douglas Henshall (Victor Bukowski), Penelope Cruz (Louise), Gustavo Salmeron (Rafael), Mark Strong (Dave Summers), Eusebio Lazaro (Don Miguel), Charlotte Coleman (Alison Hayes), Elizabeth McGovern (Diane). Directed by Maria Ripoll and produced by Juan Gordon. Screenplay by Rafa Russo.

Twice Upon a Yesterday has the kind of title that promises you'll hate the movie, and in this case the movie doesn't disappoint. It's a tedious contrivance about a messy drunk who is given a second chance in life, only to discover that life has a grudge against him both times. The story gives us a London actor named Victor (Douglas Henshall), who breaks up with his girlfriend, Sylvia (Lena Headey), telling her he loves someone else. Then his new love wears thin and he discovers he loves Sylvia after all—too late, because she's moved on with her life.

Enter a fairy godmother–type figure, a barmaid played by Elizabeth McGovern, who steers him toward a couple of trash collectors who are meant to remind us of Don Quixote and Sancho Panza. They show him, in a trash bin, all of the parts of his life he has thrown away, and give him another chance—reeling the thread of time backward so that he can retrieve his fatal mistake with Sylvia.

But hold on a second. Movies like this are always blinded by their concern for the hero and *his* all-important second chance. What about Sylvia? Breaking up with Victor was the best thing that's ever happened to her, we feel—after having spent more time with him than we really want to, even if it is his movie. When he says, "I don't know where I am in time," how can we be sure he's confused by the plot machinations and not merely sloshed?

Victor is a bore who's smashed most of the time, and if the great wheels of the universe revolve to give him a second chance, is there no hope for the Sylvias? Are women simply a plot convenience for the hero? I ask even though the film was directed by a woman, Maria Ripoll. She should have known better.

Movies come in cycles, governed by some occult law of synchronicity, and recently there have been several movies about alternatives in time, with the characters trying first one and then another set of decisions. Divergent time lines figured in *Groundhog Day*, with Bill Murray living the same day until he got it right. Gwyneth Paltrow, in *Sliding Doors*, was snared in alternate time lines, romance, and adultery. The new German film *Run Lola Run* plays the same twenty minutes three different ways. And now here's poor Victor, stumbling into the past to try to repair the wreckage of his life.

Much depends, in these films, on whether we care for the hero. If we like him, we wish him well. Victor is not likable. There is, however, a character we like quite a lot: Louise (Penelope Cruz), who mysteriously replaces McGovern as the barmaid, and whom Victor falls in love with. I must not reveal too much about the plot—including exactly when, and why, this romance takes place—but trust me, if we wanted Victor to find happiness, it would be a lot easier to forgive him for finding it again and again.

Twilight ★ ★
R, 104 m., 1998

Paul Newman (Harry Ross), Susan Sarandon (Catherine Ames), Gene Hackman (Jack Ames), Stockard Channing (Verna), Reese Witherspoon (Mel Ames), Giancarlo Esposito (Reuben), James Garner (Raymond Hope), Liev Schreiber (Jeff Willis), Margo Martindale (Gloria Lamar), John Spencer (Captain Phil Egan), M. Emmet Walsh (Lester Ivar). Directed by Robert Benton and produced by Arlene Donovan and Scott Rudin. Screenplay by Benton and Richard Russo.

Before a concert, the orchestra members warm up by playing snatches of difficult passages from familiar scores. *Twilight* is a movie that feels like that: The filmmakers, seasoned professionals, perform familiar scenes from the world of *film noir*. They do riffs, they noodle a little, they provide snatches from famous arias. But the curtain never goes up.

The reason to see the film is to observe how relaxed and serene Paul Newman is before the camera. How, at seventy-two, he has absorbed everything he needs to know about how to be a movie actor, so that at every moment he is at home in his skin and the skin of his character. It's sad to see all that assurance used in the service of a plot so worn and mechanical. Marcello Mastroianni, who in his humor, ease, and sex appeal resembled Newman, chose more challenging projects at a similar stage in his life.

The other veterans in the cast are Gene Hackman, Susan Sarandon, and James Garner. They know as much about acting as Newman does, although the film gives them fewer opportunities to display it. Garner, indeed, is the man to call if you need an actor who can slip beneath even Newman's level of comfortability. But the movie's story is too obvious in its message, and too absurd in its plotting.

The message: The characters are nearing the end of the line. They know the moves but are losing the daylight. "Your prostate started acting up yet?" Garner asks Newman. After Newman's character is shot in the groin, the rumor goes around that he's no longer a candidate for the full monty. What kind of a private eye doesn't have any privates? For all of the characters, this is the last hurrah, and that's especially true for Hackman's, who is dying of cancer.

The plot: Harry, the Newman character, is described as "cop, private investigator, drunk, husband, father." He has failed at all of those roles, and now, sober, broke, single, and retired, he lives on the estate of Jack and Catherine Ames (Hackman and Sarandon), movie stars who are old friends. One day Jack gives him a package to deliver. At the address he's sent to, he discovers Lester, a dying man (M. Emmet Walsh) whom someone has already shot. When he goes to the man's apartment, he finds newspaper clippings from twenty years ago, about the death of Catherine Ames's first husband.

Were Catherine or Jack involved in the murder? Who was paying for the investigation? Harry wants to know. His trail leads him to Raymond Hope (Garner), a guy he knew on the force, who has made a lot of money as a studio security chief, and lives very well. It also leads to Catherine's bedroom. He's had a crush on her for years, but no sooner is there a romantic breakthrough than the intercom rings: Jack is having an attack.

Jack discovers Catherine's infidelity through the kind of clue (she's wearing Harry's polo shirt) that seems left over from much older films. Harry knows Catherine was at the apartment where Lester died, because he smelled her perfume there. These are clues at the Perry Mason level, but the complete explanation, when it comes, doesn't depend on them. It's lowered into the film from the sky.

The screenplay, by director Robert Benton and his cowriter, Richard Russo, is bits and pieces. The movie appeals because we like the actors, not because we care about their characters. They're like living beings caught in a clockwork mechanism. Also caught are several characters who hang around the periphery without enough to do: Stockard Channing as a cop Harry's fooled around with in the past, and Giancarlo Esposito as a limo driver who turns up out of nowhere and becomes an inexplicable sidekick. Reese Witherspoon plays the sexpot Ames daughter.

Newman's previous film, *Nobody's Fool*, was also written and directed by Benton, based on a novel by Russo. It gave Newman one of his great roles, as an aging failure, still able to dream, hope, and repair the wreckage of a life. Here we have essentially the same character description, including the same roguish, unflagging sexuality, but the payoff isn't a rich human portrait, it's a contrived manipulation of arbitrary devices from old crime stories. Who cares?

Twin Falls Idaho ★ ★ ★ ★
R, 105 m., 1999

Mark Polish (Blake Falls), Michael Polish (Francis Falls), Michele Hicks (Penny), Lesley Ann Warren (Francine), Patrick Bauchau (Miles), Jon Gries (Jay), Garrett Morris (Jesus), William Katt (Surgeon). Directed by Michael Polish and produced by Marshall Persinger, Rena Ronson, and Steven J. Wolfe. Screenplay by Mark Polish and Michael Polish.

In a hotel like this, we feel, anything could happen. There is a certain kind of fleabag, with a barren lobby and a strange elevator operator, which has developed in the movies as a mythic backdrop for private eyes, addicts, crooks on the lam, would-be novelists—anyone who needs to hide out on a budget.

Twin Falls Idaho opens with a hooker being dropped off in front the Hotel Idaho and knocking on a room door, which is opened a crack to reveal a sad and solemn face. The room is occupied, we learn, by the Falls brothers, Blake and Francis, who are joined at the hip and share one leg. It is their birthday, and Francis has ordered her as a gift for his brother—and therefore possibly for himself, we speculate, our minds working out how many genitals might accompany three legs.

The hooker, whose name is Penny (Michele Hicks), flees when she understands the situation. She has to return because she has forgotten her purse, and this time she gets drawn into the world of Blake and Francis (played by identical twins Mark and Michael Polish). They aren't angry at her for leaving, just as they didn't seem much aroused by her arrival. Sex, we guess, may be something they have little experience of; this birthday present may have been more of a gesture, an act of defiance. Where did the twins come from? What is their story?

Penny has walked in on a scene making it clear that Francis is sick. She knows a doctor who will make a house call, she tells them, unless he wants his wife to find out about her. Miles (the urbane and yet somehow ominous actor Patrick Bauchau) arrives, and we learn that Francis has a weak heart. Blake's heart is keeping them both alive, but that may not last for long, and then they will both die—or Francis will, leaving Blake with a loneliness so profound, after the life they have led, that he can scarcely imagine it. (He tells Penny he has never been alone, except for the moment before he goes to sleep and the first moment after he wakes up.)

Twin Falls Idaho was written by the Polish brothers and directed by Michael. It is one of those films not much interested in plot but fascinated by what it is like to be somebody, or two somebodies. The movie doesn't depend on special effects to create a shared body (except for one shot that's not especially convinc-

ing), and instead uses the performances. Mark and Michael Polish seem constantly to be confiding in one another, and indeed when you spend your life within inches of another person's ear, you learn to murmur. We can imagine their lifetime of isolation from the normal things people do, and there is a heartbreaking dream shot toward the end of the film, just showing two boys riding bicycles.

Soon it is Halloween, and Penny (who is a prostitute by desperation, not through career choice) takes the brothers to a costume party. This could, of course, be the occasion for bad jokes, but it inspires her empathy: "Show some compassion. This is the one night of the entire year when they're both normal." Gradually we get glimpses of where they came from. We meet their enigmatic mother (Lesley Ann Warren). We hear a little of their story. We learn that they may have checked into the hotel to die. Hicks is gentle, tender, and sad with them, setting the film's tone (although there is also room for irony and even some laughter).

I have a special feeling for movies that want to forget about plot and conflict, and spend their time instead in regarding particular lives. Like π or *Happiness*, this film is a meditation on the situation of its characters. There's no payoff, no answer, no solution, no resolution, because how can there be? You are who you are, and life either goes on or it doesn't. The key bond in the film seems to be between the brothers, but then we realize their bond is given, not chosen, and so doesn't mean as much as the bond between the two of them and Penny. Her business is to minister to the lonely and the needy, and these two boys make her feel so helpless that her own solitude is exposed. In its quiet, dark, claustrophobic way, this is one of the best films of 1999.

Two Girls and a Guy ★ ★ ★
R, 92 m., 1998

Robert Downey Jr. (Blake), Natasha Gregson Wagner (Lou), Heather Graham (Carla). Directed by James Toback and produced by Edward R. Pressman and Chris Hanley. Screenplay by Toback.

Sometimes the story behind a movie can bring an angle to what's on the screen. Consider *Two*

Girls and a Guy, written and directed by James Toback, and starring Robert Downey Jr. The story involves a two-timing actor who returns to his Manhattan apartment to be confronted by both of his girlfriends, who've just found out about each other.

Here's the background:

—Toback and Downey worked together before, in *The Pick-Up Artist* (1987), where Downey played a compulsive womanizer who bounded through the streets of New York, fast-talking pretty girls. He was a cad and a liar, but likable; Pauline Kael wrote that "Downey, whose soul is floppy-eared, gives the movie a fairy-tale sunniness."

—James Toback himself is, or was, a notorious pickup artist. How notorious? The late *Spy* magazine once printed a double fold-out chart of his activity during just one month. With the names of his female targets running down the left-hand side of the page, the magazine used a grid to chronicle his various approaches, and how many of his favorite pickup lines ("I work closely with Warren Beatty") he used on each woman.

—When Downey was shown on television, being led to jail in handcuffs on drug charges, Toback was watching, and says he sat down immediately to write a screenplay for his old friend. "When I saw him in that orange jail jumpsuit, I knew he was ready to play this role," Toback told me at the 1997 Toronto Film Festival. Of course, perhaps Toback (whose screenplays include *The Gambler* and *Bugsy*) was also ready to write it; the film is confessional and contrite.

—*Two Girls and a Guy* was written in four days and filmed in just eleven, mostly inside a single apartment in SoHo. Not long after, Downey went back to court and eventually to jail, only to be released this month.

Downey is not floppy-eared or sunny in the new film, but he is resilient and unbowed. Confronted with both of his girlfriends (Heather Graham and Natasha Gregson Wagner), he talks and thinks quickly, saying he meant it when he told them both he had "never experienced real love" before.

"He decided consciously to start with both of us at the same time!" Lou (Wagner) says. And as they work it out, it appears he did meet them at about the same time. He saw each girl three nights of the week, excusing himself on the other nights because of the illness of his mother, whom neither one ever met.

The two women meet on his doorstep, break into his apartment, and are hiding there when he returns from a trip and leaves phone messages for them both. When he sees them, he's at a loss for words, but soon they come tumbling out; Toback in person is a torrential talker, and here Downey is as persuasive as a snake oil salesman and Wagner (Natalie Wood's daughter) fires out high-energy dialogue like Robin Williams.

What can be said, really? He's a cheating, lying SOB, and both women find even more colorful terms to describe him, both as a person and in terms of his various parts. The movie is essentially a filmed stage play, one of those idea-plays like Shaw liked to write, in which men and women ponder their differences and complexities. Is it true that men are polygamous by nature? It's much more complex than that, the movie suggests, especially after Lou suggests that her interest in Blake might expand to include Carla (Graham).

Downey, whatever his problems, is a fine actor, smart and in command of his presence, and he's persuasive here as he defends himself: "I'm an actor. And actors lie." There is a show-stopping scene when he looks at himself in a mirror and warns himself to get his act together. There are some notes in the movie that I could have done without, including an offstage gunshot and a tearjerker ending. But I enjoyed the ebb and flow of their time together.

What shows Toback has learned something since his days as a *Spy* cover boy is that the movie doesn't pretend any of these three people is *really* in love. They're playing at being in love, but essentially all three are soloists, looking out for themselves, and the women can sustain outrage only so long before they begin to seek additional amusements and possibilities. As for the man, well, he always told them his favorite song was "You Don't Know Me."

200 Cigarettes ½★

R, 97 m., 1999

Ben Affleck (Bartender), Casey Affleck (Tom), Janeane Garofalo (Ellie), Courtney Love (Lucy),

Gaby Hoffmann (Stephie), Kate Hudson (Cindy), Martha Plimpton (Monica), Paul Rudd (Kevin), Guillermo Diaz (Dave), Brian McCardie (Eric), Christina Ricci (Val), Jay Mohr (Jack), Angela Featherstone (Caitlyn). Directed by Risa Bramon Garcia and produced by Betsy Beers, David Gale, and Van Toffler. Screenplay by Shana Larsen.

All those cigarettes, and nobody knows how to smoke. Everybody in *200 Cigarettes* smokes nearly all the time, but none of them show any style or flair with their cigarettes. And the cinematographer doesn't know how to light smoke so it looks great.

He should have studied *Out of the Past* (1947), the greatest cigarette-smoking movie of all time. The trick, as demonstrated by Jacques Tourneur and his cameraman, Nicholas Musuraca, is to throw a lot of light into the empty space where the characters are going to exhale. When they do, they produce great white clouds of smoke, which express their moods, their personalities, and their energy levels. There were guns in *Out of the Past*, but the real hostility came when Robert Mitchum and Kirk Douglas smoked at each other.

The cast of *200 Cigarettes* reads like a roll call of hot talent. They're the kinds of young stars who are on lots of magazine covers and have Web pages devoted to them, and so they know they will live forever and are immune to the diseases of smoking. I wish them well. But if they must smoke in the movies, can't they at least be great smokers, like my mother was? When she was smoking you always knew exactly how she felt because of the way she used her cigarette and her hands and the smoke itself as a prop to help her express herself. She should have been good; she learned from Bette Davis movies.

The stars of *200 Cigarettes*, on the other hand, belong to the suck-and-blow school of smokeology. They inhale, not too deeply, and exhale, not too convincingly, and they squint in their close-ups while smoke curls up from below the screen. Their smoke emerges as small, pale, noxious gray clouds. When Robert Mitchum exhaled at a guy, the guy ducked out of the way.

I suppose there will be someone who counts the cigarettes in *200 Cigarettes* to see if there are actually 200. That will at least be something to do during the movie, which is a lame and labored conceit about an assortment of would-be colorful characters on their way to a New Year's Eve party in 1981. Onto the pyre of this dreadful film are thrown the talents of such as Ben Affleck, Casey Affleck, Janeane Garofalo, Courtney Love, Gaby Hoffmann, Kate Hudson, Martha Plimpton, Paul Rudd, Guillermo Diaz, Brian McCardie, Jay Mohr, Christina Ricci, Angela Featherstone, and others equally unlucky.

Ricci and Love have the kinds of self-contained personalities that hew out living space for their characters no matter where they find themselves, but the others are pretty much lost. The witless screenplay provides its characters with aimless dialogue and meaningless confrontations, and they are dressed not like people who might have been alive in 1981, but like people going to a costume party where 1981 is the theme. (There is not a single reason, by the way, why the plot requires the film to be set in 1981 or any other year.)

Seeing a film like this helps you to realize that actors are empty vessels waiting to be filled with characters and dialogue. As people, they are no doubt much smarter and funnier than the cretins in this film. I am reminded of Gene Siskel's bottom-line test for a film: "Is this movie more entertaining than a documentary of the same people having lunch?" Here they are contained by small ideas and arch dialogue, and lack the juice of life. Maybe another 200 cigarettes would have helped; coughing would be better than some of this dialogue.

Two Women ★ ★ ★ ½
NO MPAA RATING, 96 m., 2000

Niki Karimi (Fereshteh), Marila Zare'i (Roya), Mohammad Reza Forutan (The Stalker). Directed by Tahmineh Milani. Screenplay by Milani.

She is a brilliant student who seems to be leading her own life in the Tehran of the early 1980s. Then the madness of men reaches out and swats her down. Her story is told in *Two Women*, an angry and heartbreaking film, made in Iran by a woman, about a patriarchal society that puts cruel limits on the freedom of women to lead independent lives.

Fereshteh is from a provincial town, and it is to her father's credit that he allows her to attend university, since he believes her proper place is at home, married, giving him grandchildren. In Tehran she excels in a "man's" field, sciences, and loves the heady freedom of books, classrooms, campus life, and her friends.

Perhaps it is her very air of freedom that attracts the strange young man on the motorbike, who begins to stalk her. Fereshteh's spirit has not been broken, and that both attracts and appalls him. He is an erotomaniac able to think of nothing but this woman. He makes advances bordering on assault. He sees her frequently with a young man, her cousin, and thinks it is her boyfriend. One day, after she has rejected his advances, the man on the motorbike speeds up and throws acid at the cousin.

There is a court case, but it is almost beside the point. She has disgraced her family. How? By being involved in a scandal that calls attention to her status as an independent woman. There is almost the thought that it must have been her own fault, to so inflame a man that he would make an acid attack. Fereshteh's father pulls her out of school, makes her return to their small town, and forces an arranged marriage with a man in his forties who is no worse than most of the men of his age and class in the town—which is to say, a man totally incapable of understanding her needs and rights.

Two Women deals in the details of daily life in postrevolutionary Iran: in the unspoken ways that a woman's duties, her clothing, her behavior, who she speaks to, what she says, all express her servitude in a male-dominated society. Her husband is a pathetic creature whose self-esteem seems to depend largely on his ability to limit and control her. When she behaves with any independence, he feels like a cowboy who has been thrown by his horse: His duty, obviously, is to beat and train her until she becomes a docile beast.

The movie expresses powerful currents in Iranian society. It was directed by Tahmineh Milani, whose films have made her a symbol of hope among feminists in Iran—although, really, why would one need to be a feminist to believe women should be as free as men? Her film steps carefully. It makes no overt or specific criticisms of Iranian laws or politics; it focuses on Fereshteh's life and plight, and we are left to draw our own larger conclusions.

I met Milani and her husband, Mohammed, an architect, at the Calcutta Film Festival in November 1999, and was struck by how hopeful she seemed about the currents of change in her homeland, which until a generation ago was one of the more progressive societies in the Middle East. And indeed, recent election results show an overwhelming sentiment for modernizing Iran once again, and moderating the stern rule of the fundamentalist clerics.

At every film festival I attend, I hear that the new Iranian cinema is the most exciting in the world. Films like this are evidence of it. So is a new Iranian children's film named *The Color of Paradise*, about a small blind boy, very bright, who is taken out of school and apprenticed to a blind carpenter—because the boy's father, a widower, feels a blind son will be a liability in the marriage market. These films tell very specific human stories, but their buried message is clear: They swim through the waters of a rigid patriarchy that fears change and distrusts women. The extra beat of anger, throbbing beneath the surface, gives them a transforming energy.

U

U-571 ★ ★
PG-13, 115 m., 2000

Matthew McConaughey (Tyler), Bill Paxton (Dahlgren), Harvey Keitel (Chief), Jon Bon Jovi (Emmett), David Keith (Coonan), Thomas Kretschmann (Wassner), Jake Weber (Hirsch), Jack Noseworthy (Wentz). Directed by Jonathan Mostow and produced by Dino De Laurentiis and Martha De Laurentiis. Screenplay by Mostow, Sam Montgomery, and David Ayer.

U-571 is a clever windup toy of a movie, almost a trailer for a video game. Compared to *Das Boot* or *The Hunt for Red October,* it's thin soup. The characters are perfunctory, the action is recycled straight out of standard submarine formulas, and there is one shot where a man is supposed to be drowning and you can just about see he's standing on the bottom of the studio water tank.

To some degree movies like this always work, at least on a dumb action level. The German destroyer is overhead dropping depth charges, and the crew waits in hushed suspense while the underwater explosions grow nearer. We're all sweating along with them. But hold on a minute. We saw the Nazis rolling the depth charges overboard, and they were evenly spaced. As the first ones explode at a distance, there are several seconds between each one. Then they get closer. And when the charges are right on top of the sub, they explode one right after another, like a string of firecrackers— dozens of them, as leaks spring and water gushes in and lights blink and the surround sound rocks the theater.

At a moment like this, I shouldn't be thinking about the special effects. But I am. They call attention to themselves. They say the filmmakers have made a conscious decision to abandon plausibility and put on a show for the kids. And make no mistake: This is a movie for action-oriented kids. *Das Boot* and *The Hunt for Red October* were about military professionals whose personalities were crucial to the plot. The story of *U-571* is the flimsiest excuse for a fabricated action payoff. Submarine

service veterans in the audience are going to be laughing their heads off.

Matthew McConaughey stars as Tyler, an ambitious young man who thinks he's ready for his first command. Not so fast, says Captain Dahlgren (Bill Paxton). He didn't recommend his second-in-command because he thinks he's not ready yet: not prepared, for example, to sacrifice the lives of some men to save others, or the mission. This info is imparted at one of those obligatory movie dance parties at which all the navy guys look handsome in white dress uniform, just before they get an emergency call back to the boat.

The mission: A German U-boat is disabled in the mid-Atlantic. On board is the secret Enigma machine, used to cipher messages. The unbreakable Enigma code allows the Nazis to control the shipping lanes. The mission of Dahlgren, Tyler, and their men: Disguise their U.S. sub as a Nazi vessel, get to the other sub before the German rescuers can, impersonate Germans, capture the sub with a boarding party, grab Enigma, and sink the sub so the rescuers won't suspect what happened.

"But we're not marine fighting men," protests one of the sailors. "Neither is the other crew," says a marine on board, who has conveyed these instructions. "And I'll train your men." Uh-huh. In less than a week? There are no scenes of training, and I'm not sure what happened to the marine.

The details of the confrontation with the Nazi sub I will not reveal. Of course it goes without saying that Tyler gets a chance to take command and see if he has what it takes to sacrifice lives in order to save his men and his mission, etc. If you remember the vivid personalities of the sub crews in *Das Boot* and *Red October,* you're going to be keenly aware that no one in this movie seems like much of an individual. When they do have dialogue, it's functional, spare, and aimed at the plot. Even Harvey Keitel, as the Chief, is reduced to barking out declarative sentences.

The crew members seem awfully young, awfully green, awfully fearful, and so headstrong they border on mutiny. There's a scene where the (disguised) U.S. sub is checked out by a German reconnaissance plane, and a young sailor on the bridge panics. He's sure the plane is going to strafe them, and orders the man on the deck machine gun to fire at it. His superior officer orders the gunner to stand fast. The kid screams "Fire! Fire!" As the plane comes closer, the officer and the kid are both shouting their orders at the gunner. Without actually consulting navy regulations, my best guess is, that kid should be court-martialed.

You can enjoy *U-571* as a big, dumb war movie without a brain in its head. But that doesn't stop it from looking cheesy. Producers Dino and Martha De Laurentiis and director Jonathan Mostow *(Breakdown)* have counted on fast action to distract from the plausibility of most of the scenes at sea (especially shots of the raft boarding party). Inside the sub, they have the usual clichés: The sub dives to beyond its rated depth, metal plates creak, and bolt heads fire loose under the pressure.

U-571 can't be blamed for one story element that's standard in all sub movies: The subs can be hammered, battered, shelled, depth-bombed, and squeezed by pressure, and have leaks, fires, shattered gauges, ruptures, broken air hoses, weak batteries, and inoperable diesel engines—but in the heat of action, everything more or less somehow works. Better than the screenplay, anyway.

In case you're wondering, the German sub on display at the Museum of Science and Industry in Chicago is *U-505*, and it was boarded and captured not by submariners, but by sailors from the USS *Pillsbury*, part of the escort group of the carrier USS *Guadalcanal*. No Enigma machine was involved. That was in 1944. An Enigma machine was obtained on May 9, 1941, when HMS *Bulldog* captured *U-110*. On August 23, 1941, *U-570* was captured by HMS planes and ships, without Enigma. This fictional movie about a fictional U.S. submarine mission is followed by a mention in the end credits of those actual British missions. Oh, the British deciphered the Enigma code too. Come to think of it, they pretty much did everything in real life that the Americans do in this movie. ☞

Unmade Beds ★ ★ ½
NO MPAA RATING, 93 m., 1998

Brenda Monte (Brenda), Michael De Stefano (Michael), Aimee Copp (Aimee), Mikey Russo (Mikey). Directed by Nicholas Barker and produced by Steve Wax. Screenplay by Barker.

Brenda, sexy Italian, buxom, blond, 40s, seeks man to give her money and go away.

Michael, 40, 5-4, graying temples, seeks marriage, fears that "if I die a bachelor, all I will leave behind me is stuff."

Aimee, 28, 225 pounds, blond, wants husband, children; has job, health benefits.

Mikey, 50ish, screenwriter, doesn't date mutts: "I remember making love to three gorgeous women in 24 hours in 1974. One of those women would still be with me today if I was a faithful kind of a guy."

Those are the four protagonists in Nicholas Barker's *Unmade Beds*, a film that walks and talks like a documentary but is, I am assured, entirely scripted. Barker found his subjects by answering 400 personal ads in New York, and screening the advertisers until he had found four who projected humor, personality, and bleak desperation.

Early in the film he shows an Edward Hopper painting of empty urban windows, and the scenes of his film are separated by telephoto shots of New York apartment windows, some empty, others filled by people living their lives or simply looking out at the street below.

One of them is Brenda Monte, a tough-talking woman who has often been told she has a great body, "but now they add those three little words, 'for your age.'" Her problem: "My income is $2,000 a month. My expenses are $3,000." All she is to her teenage daughter "is a cash machine and a taxi." What she wants from a man is money.

Mikey Russo, the "screenwriter," has never sold a screenplay. His apartment, filled with erotic art, says one thing to women: They're there for sex. The medicine cabinet is stocked with all their needs, even toothbrushes. "I'm not cheap. They get Oral-Bs." We sense he doesn't have many visitors. He has himself paged to get out of buying dinner.

Aimee Copp has a nice smile and a warm laugh, but is overweight and desperate for a man. Her aunt recently called her and said she had checked with the whole family ("and I'm sure she did") and the family would be "okay" if she decided to have a child out of wedlock. In other words, they've given up any hope she will ever get married.

Michael De Stefano stands 5-4 and is sensitive about his height. He tells dates they can meet in a public place, and if they can't stand the sight of him, they can just walk away. He keeps talking about how everyone, even his parents, suspects he is gay.

All of these people use their real names in the movie. Whether we are seeing their real lives is a good question. This is not *cinema verité*; some scenes took ten takes. "The movie contains a lot of truth," Barker told a Toronto festival audience, "but precious little reality." A couple of the characters "tell major lies."

You know it's scripted anyway, because of two stylistic giveaways: The characters never stumble over words, and the camera continues unbroken dialogue passages while cutting from one angle to another. But, hey, Robert Flaherty scripted *Nanook of the North*. There's more than one path to truth.

The movie has moments that seem absolutely authentic, as when Aimee tells her friend she has always had a weight problem and will always have a weight problem, and she needs a man who is comfortable with that. There are other moments that feel scripted, as when Brenda says she shoplifts dog food because "they're God's creatures—I shouldn't have to pay for it."

Then again, maybe Brenda would say that. She's disarmingly direct, and the movie's best scene occurs when she conducts a guided critical tour of her body, dispassionately pointing out the parts that are holding up and the places that are starting to sag. I am not sure if I believe she really gets married to an immigrant for cash, but I believe every word of her description of her bridal trousseau, including the price she actually paid for her $400 dress.

At the end of the film, I concluded that Brenda will be okay, and the other three characters are single because getting married is the only thing that interests them. That can scare away a first date. It's a bad sign when a girl tells you she has her own health plan, and a guy

points out the fresh toothbrushes. You don't sense a lot of confidence there. We never meet the immigrant Brenda goes to marry, but I'll bet there'd be a movie in *his* story.

Up at the Villa ★ ★ ★
PG-13, 115 m., 2000

Kristin Scott Thomas (Mary Panton), Sean Penn (Rowley Flint), Anne Bancroft (Princess San Ferdinando), James Fox (Sir Edgar Swift), Jeremy Davies (Karl Richter), Derek Jacobi ("Lucky" Leadbetter), Massimo Ghini (Beppino Leopardi), Dudley Sutton (Harold Atkinson). Directed by Philip Haas and produced by Geoff Stier. Screenplay by Belinda Haas from the novella by W. Somerset Maugham.

Does anyone read Somerset Maugham anymore? From the 1920s to the 1950s he was the most respected "popular" novelist in the world, or the most popular "respected" novelist (the praise was always tempered with quotation marks). He traveled the world to the haunts of British expatriates; his stories, whether set in Singapore or Italy, often dealt with the choice between prudent and passionate romance. He knew his characters; he had a deep knowledge of shallow people.

Philip Haas's *Up at the Villa* is based on Maugham's novella about a group of British expats in Florence, enjoying their last days of mannered sloth before the outbreak of World War II. It is not the same story that Franco Zeffirelli told in his 1999 movie *Tea With Mussolini*, but his characters and these characters would have known each other by name.

The villa of the title is occupied by a temporary guest, Mary Panton (Kristin Scott Thomas), a pretty widow in her mid-thirties. Her husband drank up and gambled away their money and himself. Now she depends on the kindness of friends. An old friend named Sir Edgar Swift (James Fox) has just journeyed over from Cannes to propose marriage to her. He is tall, slender, will not see sixty again, and has manners that make you want to sit very still. Soon he will be named governor of Bengal; Mary would become the first lady of British society in Calcutta. Mary's adviser on this possibility is the Principessa San Ferdinando (Anne Bancroft), who has a town house, thanks to a rich

Italian husband, now dead, "so ugly he frightened the horses."

Sir Edgar's is an attractive offer to Mary. She asks time to think it over. She doesn't love Sir Edgar—but what, asks the princess, does love have to do with it? In a frank heart-to-heart, the princess explains that she married for security and took lovers for entertainment, although sex, she sighs, supplies you in old age with neither the fond memories nor the security of wealth. Once, says the princess (Bancroft delivering this confidence at the end of a virtuoso monologue as they walk in the garden), she made love recklessly for a single night with a risky young man, just for the fun of it.

At the princess's table in a restaurant that night, Mary is seated next to a brash, rich American named Rowley Flint (Sean Penn). He is married, separated, bold. He wants to spend the night with her. She likes him, but says no. He responds insolently, she slaps him and dumps him, and on the way home picks up a pathetic little unshaven violinist she saw in the restaurant. He is Karl Richter (Jeremy Davies), an Austrian refugee from Hitler. She takes pity on him and brings him into her bed, where, inspired by the princess's story, she gives him such a night to remember that she is still wearing her pearls in the morning.

Now the plot develops surprises. A hint or two: Mary turns to Rowley to help her out of a fix. The local Fascist Party chief (Massimo Ghini) threatens legal action against Rowley. Mary is prepared to betray a confidence of the princess to help Rowley. And then Sir Edgar returns for his answer. "I have some things I must tell you," she says, and the camera moves outside on the lawn and we see them through a window as they talk. In my notes I wrote: "She's got a lot of 'splaining to do."

This whole movie is about manners. There is sex and violence, but the movie is not about giving in to them; it's about carrying on as if they didn't exist—as if the part of you that was involved was a distant relation who will not be asked back again very soon. Kristin Scott Thomas is smashing, as Mary Panton would say. She is a woman with no financial means, who must decide between loveless security and insecure love. She has to jump fast; she will be thrown out of the villa and declared an enemy alien any day now. Yet . . .

Mary has character. The whole movie leads up to, and savors, exactly what she tells Sir Edgar, and exactly what he tells her, and then, after they both think about what they have been told, what they tell each other. It is an exquisite verbal minuet; modern psychobabble would shred their conversational elegance like a madman with a machete.

It is not necessary to have manners to appreciate them, but you must at least understand why other people would want to have them. That is the case with the wild card in the cast, "Lucky" Leadbetter (Derek Jacobi), an old queen with his hair and beard dyed ginger. He looks so uncannily like the satanic dancing man in the nightclub scene in *La Dolce Vita* that I'll bet Jacobi showed the movie to his barber. "Lucky" is not essential to the story but knows all the characters and where, and why, the skeletons are buried, and he will make all of this into a story someday. Like Maugham.

Urban Legend ★ ★
R, 98 m., 1998

Alicia Witt (Natalie), Jared Leto (Paul), Rebecca Gayheart (Brenda), Robert Englund (Professor Wexler), Natasha Gregson Wagner (Michelle), Michael Rosenbaum (Parker), Loretta Devine (Reese), Joshua Jackson (Damon), Tara Reid (Sasha), John Neville (Dean Adams). Directed by Jamie Blanks and produced by Neal H. Moritz, Gina Matthews, and Michael McDonnell. Screenplay by Silvio Horta.

I really wish I knew more about music. There must be a name for the kind of loud, sudden chord that slasher movies depend on. You know the effect. The foreground is filled with the heroine, carefully framed so that we can see nothing behind her. She turns around, there's a shock cut to a big close-up of another face, and on the sound track we get the "thwaaaaank!" of the chord. Then we realize—hey, it's only Natalie! Or Brenda! Or Michelle!

"Sorry—didn't mean to scare you," Natalie/Brenda/Michelle says, while the heroine grins foolishly and both parties laugh with relief. I've got a tip for Natalie/Brenda/Michelle. When the campus is in the grip of a mad slasher, the dead outnumber the living in the dorms, and security guards start sliding through pools of blood—it is seriously uncool to sneak up silently behind someone and grab them by the shoulder. If they're packing, you're dead meat.

Urban Legend makes heavy use of what we may as well name the Creep Chord. It's the movie's punctuation mark. There's a moment of relief, and then the buildup, and then "thwaaaank!" Just to keep things interesting, about every third time it's not Natalie/Brenda, etc., but a slasher with an ax.

The slasher prowls the campus wearing one of those L. L. Bean subzero Arctic parkas where the fur lining on the hood sticks out so far that you can't see the face inside. If I were dean of students, I'd ban all forms of head covering for the duration of the emergency. Of course, the dean of students may *be* the killer; this movie doesn't waste a single character—every single person in it is possibly the slasher.

Still, you have to wonder why a person in a conspicuous parka isn't noticed creeping around the campus and even into a heated swimming pool area (sorry—that one's a false alarm; the person in the parka is an innocent who just happens to like to wear a subzero parka in hot and humid environments). I am reminded of *I Know What You Did Last Summer* (1997), in which the slasher dressed at all times in a slicker and a rubber rain hat, like the Groton's Fisherman, and yet was never noticed in a coastal resort town in summer when it was not raining.

Urban Legend is in the *Scream* tradition, which means that its characters are allowed to be aware of the traditions of their genre. In this case, the killings are deliberately planned to reenact famous urban legends. I will only reveal the opening example, in which a woman grows frightened when the alarming goon who runs the gas pumps tries to lure her inside the station. She beans him, breaks a window, and escapes back to her car—too late for him to warn her there's an ax murderer hiding in the backseat.

My favorite urban legend, the phantom Doberman, is overlooked by the movie, but it hits a lot of the other bases, including the babysitter who traces a threatening call and discovers it's coming from . . . upstairs. These kinds of movies used to star the dregs of the B-

movie stables but the casts look a lot better these days; up-and-coming stars are assembled, and knocked off one by one. The real killer is the one person you would never, ever, not in a million years, even remotely suspect, unless your I.Q. is above 60.

The film is competently made, and the attractive cast emotes and screams energetically, and does a good job of unwisely grabbing each other by the shoulders. The gore is within reasonable bounds, as slasher movies go; oddly enough, today's truly violent movies are the comedies. The stars include Alicia Witt, Jared Leto, Natasha Gregson Wagner, Rebecca Gayheart, and Robert (Freddy Krueger) Englund, who is to slasher movies as the Quaker is to oatmeal.

Urban Legend is not art. But for its teenage audience, it serves the same purpose, which is to speed the meeting of like minds. Everybody knows how it works. The guy puts his arm casually around his date's shoulders. Natalie/Brenda/Michelle goes poking around in the abandoned campus building where the massacre took place years ago. The Creep Chord blasts out of the Dolby speakers, everyone jumps, and if in the confusion his hand slips south, well, who says cable will ever replace the theatrical experience?

U.S. Marshals ★ ★ ½
PG-13, 123 m., 1998

Tommy Lee Jones (Marshal Sam Gerard), Wesley Snipes (Sheridan), Robert Downey Jr. (John Royce), Joe Pantoliano (Deputy Marshal Cosmo Renfro), Kate Nelligan (U.S. Marshal Walsh), Irene Jacob (Marie), Daniel Roebuck (Biggs), Tom Wood (Newman). Directed by Stuart Baird and produced by Arnold Kopelson and Anne Kopelson. Screenplay by John Pogue, based on characters created by Roy Huggins.

I didn't expect *U.S. Marshals* to be the equal of *The Fugitive*, and it isn't. But I hoped it would approach the taut tension of the 1993 film, and it doesn't. It has extra scenes, needless characters, an aimless plot, and a solution that the hero seems to keep learning and then forgetting.

The hero is U.S. Deputy Marshal Sam Gerard, played by Tommy Lee Jones in a reprise of his costarring role in *The Fugitive*. The fact that they made this quasi-sequel without its original star (Harrison Ford) is a tribute to the strength of Jones's presence in the earlier film, where he had more dialogue than the lead. Jones made a big impression there, and won an Oscar. Here he hits the same marks with the same razor-edged delivery; everything's right about his performance except that it's in a rambling movie.

Take the opening sequence, where Jones disguises himself as a fast-food chicken to supervise a stakeout of a wanted man. There's a break-in, a fight, some violence, an arrest, TV interviews, a jailing, a tavern scene to celebrate, a reprimand by his superior (Kate Nelligan)—and all for what? So that the guy they caught can be put on a plane to a Missouri prison, and Sam Gerard can be put on the same flight—but not to guard the guy. No, Sam is flying on to Washington. The guy they caught and fought with is utterly unnecessary for the rest of the movie.

But also on that plane to Missouri is another character, played by Wesley Snipes. When we first see him he's a Chicago tow-truck driver. Another driver causes a crash, he's hospitalized, his prints are checked, and he's arrested and charged with the murders of two agents in New York. He protests that it's a case of mistaken identity. Is it?

Never mind that for a moment. Stop to consider. All you need for the movie to get rolling, is to establish the Snipes character and get him on that plane with Marshal Gerard. The marshal doesn't need a lot of establishing because (1) we know him from the earlier movie, and (2) Tommy Lee Jones can establish himself with three lines of dialogue, as he did in the first film.

By lingering over the chicken-suit raid, the movie has wasted time. More time is wasted by supplying a girlfriend for Snipes, played by Irene Jacob. This character is utterly superfluous. Example: She turns up at a cemetery in the middle of a shoot-out, flees with Snipes, can't make it over a wall, and is left behind. (That wall . . . hmmm. How can Snipes leap high enough to get atop the wall, but Jacob can't even jump high enough to reach his outstretched hand lowered to her?)

The movie gets rolling at around the twenty-five-minute mark, with a spectacular plane crash, reminding us of the train crash in *The Fugitive*. One prisoner escapes: Snipes. The marshal coordinates a manhunt that looks like it costs millions (helicopters, roadblocks for a twenty-mile radius, teams combing the woods, etc.). "We got a fugitive," he barks, in a line supplied as a convenience for the producers of the TV spots.

The State Department gets involved, revealing that Snipes is a bigger fish than anybody thought. And the marshal is supplied with a shadow: an agent named Royce (Robert Downey Jr.), who will follow him everywhere. They spar. "You sure you wanna get cute with me?" the marshal asks him. And, "I love that nickel-plated sissy pistol." Royce falls under the Law of Economy of Characters: A seemingly unnecessary sidekick will inevitably turn out to be—but you know how it goes.

The movie settles into a chase structure, with set pieces: a confrontation in a swamp, a cat-and-mouse game in a cemetery, and a chase through an old folks' home. It's there that the Snipes character commits the Fallacy of the Climbing Fugitive (fleeing man climbs stairs, tower, scaffold, etc., even though he can't possibly escape at the top unless he can fly). There is, however, a reason for him to climb—a spectacular escape that would have made Batman proud.

There is an explanation for all of this. We know or guess its outlines early in the film. The marshal figures it out, too ("This is a 'ruthless assassin' who keeps going out of his way to let people live"). He even discovers videotape evidence revealing the real story. And yet, in the cemetery, even when the evil Chinese agent tries to kill the fugitive, the marshal and his men still chase Snipes. It's like Gerard keeps absentmindedly overlooking what he's learned earlier in the film.

The result is unconvincing and disorganized. Yes, there are some spectacular stunts and slick special-effects sequences. Yes, Jones is right on the money, and Snipes makes a sympathetic fugitive. But it's the story that has to pull this train, and its derailment is about as definitive as the train crash in the earlier film.

V

Varsity Blues ★ ★
R, 100 m., 1999

James Van Der Beek (Mox), Jon Voight (Coach Kilmer), Paul Walker (Lance Harbor), Ron Lester (Billy Bob), Scott Caan (Tweeder), Richard Lineback (Joe Harbor), Tiffany C. Love (Collette Harbor), Amy Smart (Julie Harbor). Directed by Brian Robbins and produced by Tova Laiter, Mike Tollin, and Robbins. Screenplay by W. Peter Iliff.

Varsity Blues is not your average sports movie. It brings an outsider viewpoint to the material, which involves a Texas high school quarterback who would rather win an academic scholarship than play football. The character, named Mox and played by James Van Der Beek of TV's *Dawson's Creek*, is a good kid— so good that at one point he asks himself why he's always being so good—and although the movie contains *Animal House*–style gross-outs, it doesn't applaud them.

The central struggle is between Mox and Coach Kilmer (Jon Voight, in another of a group of striking recent performances). Kilmer is a close-cropped martinet who addresses pep rallies with a vaguely Hitlerian salute, and has won two state titles and twenty-two district championships in thirty years. Now he wants the twenty-third, at any cost.

The movie takes place in a west Texas town not unlike the setting of *The Last Picture Show*, although the kids get away with even more these days. (When one steals a squad car and drives around town with his buddies and their girlfriends, all naked, that merely inspires some "boys will be boys" talk at the local diner.) Some plot elements are hard to believe (could a high school teacher get away with stripping at a nearby topless club?), but others, including the way players are injected with painkillers before a big game, feel truthful.

The movie was directed by Brian Robbins, who made the high-spirited *Good Burger* (1997), and here again we see the impulses of a satirist winking from behind the constraints of a genre. I enjoyed, for example, the subplot involving Mox's kid brother, the religion-obsessed Kyle, who makes his first entrance with a crucifix strapped to his back and by the end of the film has founded a cult with his playmates. Maybe his spirituality is inherited; their father asks Mox, "Did you pray for more playing time?"

The arc of the movie involves one football season, during which Coach Kilmer will or will not win his twenty-third title. Of course it ends with a Big Game and a Big Play, with seconds on the clock, but this is a movie that doesn't buy into all the tenets of our national sports religion; the subtext is that winning *isn't* everything.

One of Mox's friends is the enormous Billy Bob (Ron Lester), whose breakfast consists of pancakes chased down with syrup swigged straight from the bottle. Without revealing what happens to him, I will express my gratitude to Robbins and his writer, W. Peter Iliff, for not marching lockstep down the well-traveled road of inevitable developments. I also enjoyed the relationship between Mox and Lance (Paul Walker), the starting quarterback; instead of making Lance into the obligatory jerk, the movie pays more attention. To the standard role of the town sexpot, Tiffany C. Love brings a certain poignancy; she always goes for the starting quarterback, but she's not a slut so much as a realist.

All of this sounds as if *Varsity Blues* is a good movie, and parts of it are, but the parts never quite come together. Scenes work, but they don't pile up and build momentum. Van Der Beek is convincing and likable, Voight's performance has a kind of doomed grandeur, and the characters are seen with quirky humor. (When Billy Bob gets knocked cold during a game, for example, and the trainer asks him how many fingers he's holding up, Mox explains, "With Billy Bob, you gotta go true or false. Billy Bob, is he holding up fingers? Yes or no?") The movie doesn't quite get over the top, but you sense that Brian Robbins has the right instincts, and is ready to break loose for a touchdown.

The Velocity of Gary ★ ★
R, 100 m., 1999

Thomas Jane (Gary), Vincent D'Onofrio (Valentino), Salma Hayek (Mary Carmen),

Olivia d'Abo (Veronica), Chad Lindberg (Kid Joey). Directed by Dan Ireland and produced by Dan Lupovitz. Screenplay by James Still.

The Velocity of Gary proves once again that it's less interesting to see unconventional people express traditional values than to see conventional people express untraditional values.

Movies about the sexual underground seem compelled to show their rebels bonding together into symbolic families; their characters may seen bizarre, but at heart they express profoundly conservative social values. I'm more intrigued by films like *Happiness* and *In the Company of Men*. It's more fun to see conventional characters break the rules than for outlaws to follow them.

The Velocity of Gary (subtitled *Not His Real Name*) chronicles the world of Times Square male hustlers, porno stars, drag queens, and doughnut shop waitresses. All of these people are, of course, touchingly good-hearted, smiling through bad times. Vincent D'Onofrio stars, as Valentino, a well-known porn actor whose worsening illness (never named) causes his two lovers to join in making them all a home. The lovers are the hustler Gary (Thomas Jane) and the waitress Mary Carmen (Salma Hayek), and also in the picture is the deaf drag queen Kid Joey (Chad Lindberg), who mimes to the songs of Patsy Cline—not easy when you can't hear them.

All of these characters are engaging in a conventional sort of way, although their behavior seems generated less by their lives than by the demands of the screenplay. Consider an early scene where Gary, bare to the waist, soaks himself at a fire hydrant and then stalks off into the city. Hydrants can be refreshing on a hot day, and this makes a great shot, but would a homeless man lightly contemplate hours in wet jeans and squelchy shoes? No matter; soon he's rescued Kid Joey from gay-bashers, carrying the Kid off in his arms like John Wayne with Natalie Wood in *The Searchers*.

The director is Dan Ireland, who also worked with D'Onofrio in *The Whole Wide World*, the 1997 film about pulp writer Robert E. Howard. That one, about a man who sat in his room in Texas and wrote about Conan the Barbarian, was quietly, sadly gripping. In *The Velocity of Gary*, there is never quite the feeling that these

people occupy a real world; their colorful exteriors are like costumes, and inside are simply actors following instructions.

Velvet Goldmine ★ ★
R, 127 m., 1998

Ewan McGregor (Curt Wild), Jonathan Rhys-Meyers (Brian Slade), Toni Collette (Mandy Slade), Christian Bale (Arthur Stuart), Eddie Izzard (Jerry Divine), Emily Woof (Shannon), Michael Feast (Cecil), Janet McTeer (Female Narrator). Directed by Todd Haynes and produced by Christine Vachon. Screenplay by James Lyons and Haynes.

Velvet Goldmine is a movie made up of beginnings, endings, and fresh starts. There isn't enough in between. It wants to be a movie in search of a truth, but it's more like a movie in search of itself. Not everyone who leaves the theater will be able to pass a quiz on exactly what happens.

Set in the 1970s, it's the story of the life, death, and resurrection of a glam-rock idol named Brian Slade, played by Jonathan Rhys-Meyers and probably inspired by David Bowie. After headlining a brief but dazzling era of glitter rock, he fakes his own death onstage. When the hoax is revealed, his cocaine use increases, his sales plummet, and he disappears from view. A decade later, in the fraught year of 1984, a journalist named Arthur Stuart (Christian Bale) is assigned to find out what really happened to Brian Slade.

Do we care? Not much. Slade is not made into a convincing character in *Velvet Goldmine*, although his stage appearances are entertaining enough. But a better reason for our disinterest is that the film bogs down in the apparatus of the search for Slade. Clumsily borrowing moments from *Citizen Kane*, it has its journalist interview Slade's ex-wife and business associates, and there is even a sequence of shots specifically mirroring *Kane*'s first interview with the mogul's former wife Susan.

Citizen Kane may have been voted the greatest of all American films (which it is), but how many people watching *Velvet Goldmine* will appreciate a scene where a former Slade partner is seen in a wheelchair, just like Joseph

Cotten? Many of them will still be puzzling out the opening of the film, which begins in Dublin with the birth of Oscar Wilde, who says at an early age, "I want to be a pop idol."

I guess this prologue is intended to establish a link between Wilde and the Bowie generation of cross-dressing performance artists who teased audiences with their apparent bisexuality. Brian Slade, in the movie, is married to an American catwoman named Mandy (Toni Collette), but has an affair with a rising rock star named Curt Wild (Ewan McGregor), who looks like Kurt Cobain, is heedless like Oscar Wilde, and is so original onstage that he upstages Slade, who complains, "I just wish it had been me. I wish I'd thought of it." (His wife, as wise as all the wives of brilliant men, tells him, "You will.")

The film evokes snatches of the 1970s rock scene (and another of its opening moments evokes early shots from the Beatles' *A Hard Day's Night*). But it doesn't settle for long enough on any one approach to become very interesting. It's not a career film, or a rags-to-riches film, or an exposé, or an attack, or a dirge, or a musical, but a little of all of those, chopped up and run through a confusing assortment of flashbacks and memories.

The lesson seems to be that Brian Slade was an ambitious, semitalented poseur who cheated his audience once too often, and then fooled them again in a way only the movie and its inquiring reporter fully understand. In the wreckage of his first incarnation are left his wife, lovers, managers, and fans. It is a little disconcerting that the last twenty minutes, if not more, consist of a series of scenes that all feel as if they could be the last scene in the movie: *Velvet Goldmine* keeps promising to quit, but doesn't make good.

David Bowie (if Slade is indeed meant to be Bowie) deserves better than this. He was more talented and smarter than Slade, reinvented himself in full view, and in the long run can only be said to have triumphed (if being married to Iman, pioneering a multimedia art project, and being the richest of all non-Beatle British rock stars is a triumph, and I submit that it is). Bowie is also more interesting than his fictional alter ego in *Velvet Goldmine*, and if glam rock was not great music at least it inaugurated the era of concerts as theatrical spectacles, and inspired its audiences to dress in something other than the hippie uniform.

Todd Haynes, the director and writer, is an American whose first two films (*Poison* and *Safe*) were tightly focused, spare, and bleak. *Safe* starred Julianne Moore as a woman allergic to very nearly everything—or was she only allergic to herself? These films were perceptive character studies. In *Velvet Goldmine*, there is the sense that the film's arms were spread too wide, gathered in all of the possible approaches to the material, and couldn't decide on just one.

Very Bad Things ★
R, 101 m., 1998

Christian Slater (Robert Boyd), Cameron Diaz (Laura Garrety), Daniel Stern (Adam Berkow), Jeanne Tripplehorn (Lois Berkow), Jon Favreau (Kyle Fisher), Jeremy Piven (Michael Berkow), Leland Orser (Charles Moore), Carla Scott (Tina), Russell B. McKenzie (Security Guard), Joey Zimmerman (Adam Berkow Jr.), Tyler Malinger (Timmy Berkow). Directed by Peter Berg and produced by Michael Schiffer, Diane Nabatoff, and Cindy Cowan. Screenplay by Berg.

Peter Berg's *Very Bad Things* isn't a bad movie, just a reprehensible one. It presents as comedy things that are not amusing. If you think this movie is funny, that tells me things about you that I don't want to know.

What bothers me most, after two viewings, is its confidence that an audience would be entertained by its sad, sick vision, tainted by racism. If this material had been presented straight, as a drama, the movie would have felt more honest and might have been more successful. Its cynicism is the most unattractive thing about it—the assumption that an audience has no moral limits, and will laugh at cruelty simply to feel hip. I know moral detachment is a key strategy of the ironic pose, but there is a point, once reached, which provides a test of your underlying values.

The film involves five friends who go on a bachelor party to Las Vegas. Kyle Fisher (Jon Favreau) is on the eve of marriage to the wedding-obsessed Laura (Cameron Diaz). His pals include a realty agent named Robert Boyd

(Christian Slater), the antagonistic Berkow brothers Adam (Daniel Stern) and Michael (Jeremy Piven), and a mechanic named Charles (Leland Orser), who doesn't talk much.

In Vegas, there's a montage showing them gambling, tossing back shots, and snorting cocaine. A stripper named Tina (Carla Scott) arrives, does lap dances, and is steered into the bathroom by Michael. He lurches drunkenly about the room with her until her head is accidentally impaled on a coat hook. She's dead. (When I saw the film at the Toronto festival, the audience laughed at a shot showing her feet hanging above the floor. Why?)

Some of the men want to dial 911, but Robert takes charge. How will it look that a hooker has turned up dead in their suite? "Take away the horror of the situation. Take away the tragedy of her death. Take away all the moral and ethical considerations you've had drummed into you since childhood, and what are you left with? A 105-pound problem."

His solution? Cut her up and bury her in the desert. He browbeats the others into agreement, but then a black security guard enters with a complaint about noise. The guard (Russell B. McKenzie) sees the dead body, and Robert stabs him with a corkscrew. Now there are two bodies to dispose of, and the guys stride through a hardware store like the Reservoir Dogs.

The movie makes it a point that some of the guys are Jewish, and uses that to get laughs as they bury the bodies. Jewish law, one argues, requires that the body parts be kept together— so they should dig up the dismembered pieces and sort them out. "She's Asian," says another. "Do they have Jews in Asia?" The answer is yes, although surely such a theory would apply to anyone. They start rearranging: "We'll start with black. Then we'll go to Asian."

My thoughts here are complex. The movie is not blatantly racist, and yet a note of some kind is being played when white men kill an Asian and a black. Why then make it a point that some of them are Jewish? What is the purpose, exactly? Please don't tell me it's humor. I'm not asking for political correctness; I'm simply observing the way the movie tries to show how hip it is by rubbing our noses in race.

The events described take about thirty minutes. There is not a single funny thing that happens once the men get to Vegas (Diaz has some funny early stuff about the wedding). Nor is the aftermath funny, as the men freak out with guilt and fear. Robert makes threats to hold them in line, but more deaths follow, and the last act of the film spins out a grisly, unfunny, screwball plot. By the time of the wedding, when potentially comic material crawls back in over the dead bodies, it's way too late to laugh; the movie's tone is too mean-spirited and sour.

Very Bad Things isn't bad on the technical and acting level, and Slater makes a convincing engine to drive the evil. Peter Berg shows that he can direct a good movie, even if he hasn't. If he'd dumped the irony and looked this material straight in the eye, it might have been a better experience. His screenplay has effective lines, as when Robert coldly reasons, "What we have here was not a good thing, but it was, under the circumstances, the smart play." Or when he uses self-help platitudes to rationalize murder ("Given the fact that we are alive and they are not, we chose life over death").

But the film wants it both ways. At a Jewish funeral, the sad song of the cantor is subtly mocked by upbeat jazz segueing into the next scene. Mourners fall onto the coffin in a scene that is embarrassing, not funny. When a widow (Jeanne Tripplehorn) struggles with Robert, she bites his groin, and as he fights back we hear female ululations on the sound track. What's that about? I won't even get into the bonus material about her handicapped child and three-legged dog.

Very Bad Things filled me with dismay. The material doesn't match the genre; it's an attempt to exploit black humor without the control of tone necessary to pull it off. I left the theater feeling sad and angry. On the movie's Website, you can download a stripper. I'm surprised you can't kill her.

The Virgin Suicides ★ ★ ★ ½
R, 97 m., 2000

James Woods (Mr. Lisbon), Kathleen Turner (Mrs. Lisbon), Kirsten Dunst (Lux Lisbon), Josh Harnett (Trip Fontaine), Hanna Hall (Cecilia Lisbon), Chelsea Swain (Bonnie Lisbon), A. J.

Cook (Mary Lisbon), Leslie Hayman (Therese Lisbon), Danny DeVito (Dr. Horniker). Directed by Sofia Coppola and produced by Francis Ford Coppola, Julie Costanzo, Dan Halsted, and Chris Hanley. Screenplay by Sofia Coppola, based on the novel by Jeffrey Eugenides.

It is not important how the Lisbon sisters looked. What is important is how the teenage boys in the neighborhood thought they looked. There is a time in the adolescent season of every boy when a particular girl seems to have materialized in his dreams with backlighting from heaven. Sofia Coppola's *The Virgin Suicides* is narrated by an adult who speaks for "we"—for all the boys in a Michigan suburban neighborhood twenty-five years ago, who loved and lusted after the Lisbon girls. We know from the title and the opening words that the girls killed themselves. Most of the reviews have focused on the girls. They miss the other subject—the gawky, insecure yearning of the boys.

The movie is as much about those guys, "we," as about the Lisbon girls. About how Trip Fontaine (Josh Harnett), the leader of the pack, loses his baby fat and shoots up into a junior stud who is blindsided by sex and beauty, and dazzled by Lux Lisbon (Kirsten Dunst), who of the perfect Lisbon girls is the most perfect. In every class there is one couple that has sex while the others are still talking about it, and Trip and Lux make love on the night of the big dance. But that is not the point. The point is that she wakes up the next morning, alone, in the middle of the football field. And the point is that Trip, as the adult narrator, remembers not only that "she was the still point of the turning world then" and "most people never taste that kind of love" but also, "I liked her a lot. But out there on the football field, it was different."

Yes, it was. It was the end of adolescence and the beginning of a lifetime of compromises, disenchantments, and real things. First sex is ideal only in legend. In life it attaches plumbing, fluids, gropings, fumblings, and pain to what was only an hour ago a platonic ideal. Trip left Lux not because he was a pig, but because he was a boy, and broken with grief at the loss of his—their—dream. And when the

Lisbon girls kill themselves, do not blame their deaths on their weird parents. Mourn for the passing of everyone you knew and everyone you were in the last summer before sex. Mourn for the idealism of inexperience.

The Virgin Suicides provides perfunctory reasons why the Lisbon girls might have been unhappy. Their mother (Kathleen Turner) is a hysteric so rattled by her daughters' blooming sexuality that she adds cloth to their prom dresses until they appear in "four identical sacks." Their father (James Woods) is the well-meaning but emasculated high school math teacher who ends up chatting about photosynthesis with his plants. These parents look gruesome to us. All parents look gruesome to kids, and all of their attempts at discipline seem unreasonable. The teenage years of the Lisbon girls are no better or worse than most teenage years. This is not the story of daughters driven to their deaths.

The story it most reminds me of, indeed, is *Picnic at Hanging Rock* (1975), about a party of young girls, not unlike the Lisbon sisters in appearance and sexual experience, who go for a school outing one day and disappear into the wilderness, never to be seen again. Were they captured? Killed in a fall? Trapped somehow? Bitten by snakes? Simply lost in the maze of nature? What happened to them is not the point. Their disappearance is the point. One moment they were smiling and bowing in their white dresses in the sun, and the next they were gone forever. The lack of any explanation is the whole point: For those left behind, they are preserved forever in the perfection they possessed when they were last seen.

The Virgin Suicides is Sofia Coppola's first film, based on the much-discussed novel by Jeffrey Eugenides. She has the courage to play it in a minor key. She doesn't hammer home ideas and interpretations. She is content with the air of mystery and loss that hangs in the air like bitter poignancy. Tolstoy said all happy families are the same. Yes, but he should have added, there are hardly any happy families.

To live in a family group with walls around it is unnatural for a species that evolved in tribes and villages. What would work itself out in the give-and-take of a community gets grotesque when allowed to fester in the hothouse of a single-family home. A mild-mannered teacher and a strong-willed woman turn into a paralyzed captive and a harridan. Their daughters see themselves as captives of these parents, who hysterically project their own failure upon the children. The worship the girls receive from the neighborhood boys confuses them: If they are perfect, why are they seen as such flawed and dangerous creatures? And then the reality of sex, too young, peels back the innocent idealism and reveals its secret engine, which is animal and brutal, lustful and contemptuous.

In a way, the Lisbon girls and the neighborhood boys never existed, except in their own adolescent imaginations. They were imaginary creatures, waiting for the dream to end through death or adulthood. "Cecilia was the first to go," the narrator tells us right at the beginning. We see her talking to a psychiatrist after she tries to slash her wrists. "You're not even old enough to know how hard life gets," he tells her. "Obviously, doctor," she says, "you've never been a thirteen-year-old girl." No, but his profession and every adult life is to some degree a search for the happiness she does not even know she has.

Virus ★
R, 96 m., 1999

Jamie Lee Curtis (Kit Foster), William Baldwin (Steve Baker), Donald Sutherland (Captain Everton), Joanna Pacula (Nadia), Marshall Bell (J. W. Woods Jr.), Julio Oscar Mechoso (Squeaky), Sherman Augustus (Richie), Cliff Curtis (Hiko). Directed by John Bruno and produced by Gale Anne Hurd. Written by Chuck Pfarrer and Dennis Feldman, based on the Dark Horse Comic Book Series *Virus* by Chuck Pfarrer.

Ever notice how movies come in twos? It's as if the same idea descends upon several Hollywood producers at once, perhaps because someone who hates movies is sticking pins in his dolls. *Virus* is more or less the same movie as *Deep Rising*, which opened a year earlier. Both begin with small boats in the Pacific. Both boats come upon giant floating ships that are seemingly deserted. Both giant ships are in-habited by a vicious monster. Both movies send the heroes racing around the ship trying to destroy the monster. Both movies also have lots of knee-deep water, fierce storms, Spielbergian visible flashlight beams cutting through the gloom, and red digital readouts.

Deep Rising was one of the worst movies of 1998. *Virus* is easily worse. It didn't help that the print I saw was so underlit that often I could see hardly anything on the screen. Was that because the movie was filmed that way, or because the projector bulb was dimmed to extend its life span? I don't know and in a way I don't care, because to see this movie more clearly would not be to like it better.

Virus opens with berserk tugboat captain Donald Sutherland and his crew towing a barge through a typhoon. The barge is sinking and the crew, led by Jamie Lee Curtis and William Baldwin, want to cut it loose. But the barge represents the skipper's net worth, and he'd rather go to the bottom with it. This sequence is necessary to set up the skipper's avarice.

In the eye of the storm, the tug comes upon a drifting Russian satellite communications ship. In the movie's opening credits, we have already seen what happened to the ship: A drifting space cloud enveloped the *Mir* space station and sent a bolt of energy down to the ship's satellite dish, and apparently the energy included a virus that takes over the onboard computers and represents a vast, if never clearly defined, threat to life on Earth.

Sutherland wants to claim the ship for salvage. The crew board it and soon are fighting the virus. "The ship's steering itself!" one character cries. The chilling answer: "Ships don't steer themselves." Uh, oh. The methods of the virus are strange. It creates robots, and uses them to grab crew members and turn them into strange creatures that are half-man, half–Radio Shack. It's up to Curtis, Baldwin, and their crewmates to outsmart the virus, which seems none too bright and spends most of its time clomping around and issuing threatening statements with a basso profundo voice synthesizer.

The movie's special effects are not exactly slick, and the creature itself is a distinct letdown. It looks like a very tall humanoid figure hammered together out of crushed auto parts, with several headlights for its eyes. It crunches through steel bulkheads and crushes all barriers to its progress, but is this an efficient way for a virus to behave? It could be cruising the Internet instead of doing a Robocop number.

The last half-hour of the movie is almost unseeable. In dark dimness, various human and other figures race around in a lot of water and flashlight beams, and there is much screaming. Occasionally an eye, a limb, or a bloody face emerges from the gloom. Many instructions are shouted. If you can explain to me the exact function of that rocket tube that turns up at the end, I will be sincerely grateful. If you can explain how anyone could survive that function, I will be amazed. The last shot is an homage to *The African Queen,* a movie I earnestly recommend instead of this one.

W

Wag the Dog ★ ★ ★ ★
R, 97 m., 1998

Dustin Hoffman (Stanley Motss), Robert De Niro (Conrad Brean), Anne Heche (Winifred Ames), Woody Harrelson (Sergeant William Schumann), Denis Leary (Fad King), Willie Nelson (Johnny Green), Andrea Martin (Liz Butsky), Kirsten Dunst (Tacy Lime). Directed by Barry Levinson and produced by Jane Rosenthal, Robert De Niro, and Levinson. Screenplay by David Mamet and Hilary Henkin, based on the book *American Hero* by Larry Beinhart.

So, why *did* we invade Grenada? A terrorist bomb killed all those Marines in Beirut, the White House was taking flak, and suddenly our Marines were landing on a Caribbean island few people had heard of, everybody was tying yellow ribbons 'round old oak trees, and Clint Eastwood was making the movie. The Grenadan invasion, I have read, produced more decorations than combatants. By the time it was over, the Reagan presidency had proven the republic could still flex its muscle—we could take out a Caribbean Marxist regime at will, Cuba notwithstanding.

Barry Levinson's *Wag the Dog* cites Grenada as an example of how easy it is to whip up patriotic frenzy, and how dubious the motives can sometimes be. The movie is a satire that contains just enough realistic ballast to be teasingly plausible; like *Dr. Strangelove*, it makes you laugh, and then it makes you wonder. Just today, I read a Strangelovian story in the paper revealing that some of Russia's nuclear missiles, still aimed at the United States, have gone unattended because their guards were denied their bonus rations of four pounds of sausage a month. It is getting harder and harder for satire to stay ahead of reality.

In the movie, a U.S. president is accused of luring an underage "Firefly Girl" into an anteroom of the Oval Office, and there presenting her with opportunities no Firefly Girl should anticipate from her commander in chief. A presidential election is weeks away, the opposition candidate starts using "Thank Heaven for Little Girls" in his TV ads, and White House aide Winifred Ames (Anne Heche) leads a spin doctor named Conrad Brean (Robert De Niro) into bunkers far beneath the White House for an emergency session.

Brean, a Mr. Fixit who has masterminded a lot of shady scenarios, has a motto: "To change the story, change the lead." To distract the press from the Firefly Girl scandal, he advises extending a presidential trip to Asia, while issuing official denials that the new B-3 bomber is being activated ahead of schedule. "But there *is* no B-3 bomber," he's told. "Perfect! Deny it even exists!"

Meanwhile, he cooks up a phony international crisis with Albania. Why Albania? Nobody is sure where it is, nobody cares, and you can't get any news out of it. Nobody can even think of any Albanians except—maybe the Belushi brothers? To produce the graphic look and feel of the war, Brean flies to Hollywood and enlists the services of a producer named Stanley Motss (Dustin Hoffman), who is hard to convince at first. He wants proof that Brean has a direct line to the White House. He gets it. As they watch a live briefing by a presidential spokesman, Brean dictates into a cell phone and the spokesman repeats, word for word, what he hears on his earpiece. (I was reminded of the line in *Broadcast News:* "Goes in here, comes out there.")

Motss assembles the pieces for a media blitz. As spokesmen warn of Albanian terrorists skulking south from Canada with "suitcase bombs," Motss supervises the design of a logo for use on the news channels, hires Willie Nelson to write the song that will become the conflict's "spontaneous" anthem, and fakes news footage of a hapless Albanian girl (Kirsten Dunst) fleeing from rapists with her kitten. (Dunst is an American actress, and the kitten, before it is created with special effects, is a bag of Tostitos.)

But what about a martyr? Motss cooks up "good old Shoe," Sergeant William Schumann (Woody Harrelson), who is allegedly rescued from the hands of the Albanians to be flown back for a hero's welcome. Shoe inspires a shtick, too: Kids start lobbing their old gym shoes over power lines, and throwing them onto the court during basketball games, as a spontaneous display of patriotism.

It's creepy how this material is absurd and convincing at the same time. Levinson, working from a smart, talky script by David Mamet and Hilary Henkin, based on the book *American Hero* by Larry Beinhart, deconstructs the media blitz that invariably accompanies any modern international crisis. Even when a conflict is real and necessary (the Gulf War, for example), the packaging of it is invariably shallow and unquestioning; like sportswriters, war correspondents abandon any pretense of objectivity and detachment, and cheerfully root for our side.

For Hoffman, this is the best performance in some time, inspired, it is said, by producer Robert Evans. (In power and influence, however, Motss seems more like Ray Stark.) Like a lot of Hollywood power brokers, Hoffman's Motss combines intelligence with insecurity and insincerity, and frets because he won't get "credit" for his secret manipulations. De Niro's Brean, on the other hand, is a creature born to live in shadow, and De Niro plays him with the poker-faced plausibility of real spin doctors, who tell lies as a professional specialty. Their conversations are crafted by Mamet as a verbal ballet between two men who love the jargon of their crafts.

"Why does a dog wag its tail?" Brean asks at one point. "Because the dog is smarter than the tail. If the tail was smarter, it would wag the dog." In the Breanian universe, the tail is smarter, and we, dear readers, are invited to be the dogs.

Waking Ned Devine ★ ★ ★
PG, 91 m., 1998

Ian Bannen (Jackie O'Shea), David Kelly (Michael O'Sullivan), Fionnula Flanagan (Annie O'Shea), Susan Lynch (Maggie), James Nesbitt (Pig Finn), Maura O'Malley (Mrs. Kennedy), Robert Hickey (Maurice), Brendan F. Dempsey (Jim Kelly), Dermot Kerrigan (Father Patrick), Eileen Dromey (Lizzy Quinn). Directed by Kirk Jones and produced by Glynis Murray and Richard Holmes. Screenplay by Jones.

Waking Ned Devine opens with the news that someone in the Irish hamlet of Tullymore (population fifty-three—uh, fifty-two) has won the National Lottery. Who could it be? The locals, who have lived in each other's pockets for years, snoop and gossip and seize upon the slightest deviation from habit as proof that someone expects a windfall. But there are no leads, and finally in desperation a chicken supper is held, at which the winner will perhaps be revealed. No luck. But one person doesn't attend the dinner: Ned Devine.

Jackie O'Shea (Ian Bannen) and Michael O'Sullivan (David Kelly) hasten to Ned's cottage to find him seated in front of the television set, clutching the winning ticket—and dead. The winnings, they are astounded to learn, are not several hundred thousand pounds, as they had assumed, but nearly 7 million pounds. A fortune! Alas, since Ned Devine is dead, the money will be recycled back into the kitty for next week's drawing.

Right? Not on your life. Jackie and Michael hatch a plan to fool the visiting official from Dublin, who after all has never laid eyes on Ned in his life (few have, outside of Tullymore). Michael will impersonate Ned. The whole town will of course have to be in on the scheme, and so Jackie and Michael draw up an agreement in which their friends and neighbors will join in the deception and share in the prize.

That's the premise of another one of those delightful village comedies that seem to spin out of the British isles at least annually. *Waking Ned Devine* can take its place with *Local Hero, The Snapper, The Full Monty, The Englishman Who Went Up a Hill and Came Down a Mountain, Brassed Off, Circle of Friends, Eat the Peach*, and many others. Why don't we have more small-town comedies like this from America? Why are small towns in the United Kingdom and Ireland seen as conspiracies of friends, while American small towns are so often depicted as filled with liars or wackos?

One of the joys of *Waking Ned Devine* is in the richness of the local eccentric population. There is, for example, the mean-spirited Lizzy Quinn (Eileen Dromey), who tools around on her battery-powered chair, scowling and spreading ill will. Contrast her with the hardworking Pig Finn (James Nesbitt), a handsome young pig farmer who loves Maggie (Susan Lynch). She loves him too, but not the way he smells. Either the pigs go or she does. And there is the substitute village priest (Dermot Kerrigan), filling in during the regular's vacation, who has solemn talks about theology with bright young Maurice (Robert Hickey), who says of a life devoted to the Lord: "I don't think I could work for someone I never met."

The treasure of the local population is Michael O'Sullivan, who is played by David Kelly in what can only be described as a performance arriving at the ultimate reaches of geezerdom. Kelly, with his twinkling eyes and turkey neck, is engaging, conspiratorial, and delighted by all things not too wicked. Stealing 6.8 million pounds from the lottery is, of course, not too wicked. Like Nigel Hawthorne in *The Madness of King George* or Simon Callow in *Four Weddings and a Funeral*, Kelly is one of those seasoned and expert actors who is well known in the United Kingdom (he was a character on *Fawlty Towers*), but will be a delightful discovery for North American audiences. There is a scene where he must get back to Ned Devine's cottage at breakneck speed to beat out the Lotto official from Dublin (Brendan F. Dempsey). Why he must dash down back lanes on a motorcycle while completely naked I will leave to you to discover; the sight inspires uproarious laughter.

That's one of the movie's big laughs. Another involves a telephone booth. Most of the time we're smiling more than laughing; we recognize the human nature involved in *Waking Ned Devine*, and we like the way Kirk Jones, the writer and director, throws up obstacles just to have fun leaping over them. One reason we like village comedies from Ireland and the United Kingdom is of course that they're funny. Another is to meet the characters and the actors, and enjoy the pleasure of their company. I have a feeling that an evening spent with David Kelly would be a merry one.

Waking the Dead ★ ★ ½
R, 105 m., 2000

Billy Crudup (Fielding Pierce), Jennifer Connelly (Sarah Williams), Janet McTeer (Caroline Pierce), Molly Parker (Juliet Beck), Sandra Oh (Kim), Hal Holbrook (Isaac Green), Lawrence Dane (Governor Kinosis), Paul Hipp (Danny Pierce). Directed by Keith Gordon and produced by Gordon, Stuart Kleinman, and Linda Reisman. Screenplay by Gordon and Robert Dillon, based on the novel by Scott Spencer.

There is a mystery in *Waking the Dead*, and at the end we are supplied with its answer, but I have seen the movie twice and do not know for sure what the answer is. There are two possibilities. Either would do. If it were a thriller or a ghost story, it wouldn't much matter, but the film has serious romantic and political themes, and in one way or another we really need to know, or it's all been a meaningless game.

The film begins in 1982, with a young politician named Fielding Pierce (Billy Crudup) who learns on the news that his friend Sarah Williams (Jennifer Connelly) has been killed by a car bomb attack in Minneapolis. She was working with a group of political activists opposed to U.S. actions in Chile. Fielding screams out in anguish, and we flash back to his first meeting with Sarah, in 1972, when she was his brother's secretary. The brother publishes a magazine very like *Rolling Stone*. Fielding is in the Coast Guard to avoid service in Vietnam. Sarah is self-confident, outspoken, political.

The film, based on the novel by Scott Spencer, is a tug-of-war between Fielding's desire to work within the system and Sarah's conviction that it's rotten to the core. As they grow closer romantically, they grow further apart politically, until finally their love is like a sacrifice thrown on the bonfire of their ambitions. There comes a time at a fund-raising benefit when Sarah tells off a fat-cat who has written a column supporting the military junta in Chile. That is not good for Fielding's career.

The film does a lot of flashing back and forth between 1972, when Fielding's life is simple and idealistic, and 1982, when he is in the hands of Chicago political fixers. Hal Holbrook is assigned once again to the Hal Holbrook Role, which he has won so often it should be retired: He has to sit in the shadows of a boardroom or a private club, smoke a cigar, drink a brandy, and pull strings behind the scenes. He is the go-between for Fielding and Governor Kinosis (Lawrence Dane), who offers Fielding a shot at a safe congressional seat.

Fielding wants it. Sarah sees it as the selling of his soul. As the two of them ride the L together, Jennifer Connelly has a strong and bitter scene in which she explains exactly what he is doing and why it is wrong. They're drifting apart, and Fielding resents the presence in her life of a gimlet-eyed radical priest. We see her meeting with Chilean refugees. She leaves for Chile to bring some more out. Then she dies in the car bombing.

Or does she? The film toys with us, and with Fielding, who begins to imagine he sees Sarah here and there—on the street, in a crowd. There is one almost subliminal shot in which her face flashes on a TV screen, just as he turns away. Did he see it? Or was it in his imagination? Or did he not see it? And in that case, since we saw it, was it the first shot of the next story on the news, or a subtle hint that this movie has something in common with *Ghost*?

To speculate would be to give away the ending—which I can't do anyway, since I'm not sure of it. What I do know is that *Waking the Dead* has a good heart and some fine performances, but is too muddled at the story level to involve us emotionally. It's a sweet film. The relationship between Sarah and Fielding is a little deeper and more affectionate than we expect in plot-driven melodramas.

There are fuzzy spots; we never find out anything specific about Sarah's political activism, we never see the Chicago pols actually trying to influence Fielding in an inappropriate way, and we never know exactly what role the Catholic Church plays, except to lend its cinematic images and locations. I was amused when another critic pointed out that, to save money perhaps, the moviemakers show Fielding savoring his political victory all alone by himself.

Oscar nominee Janet McTeer plays Fielding's sister, in the kind of role every actress hopes she can escape from by getting an Oscar nomination. Paul Hipp plays his Jann Wennerish brother, who falls in love with a Korean hooker (Sandra Oh) he meets in a massage parlor, and tries to convince Fielding to pull strings so she can get her green card. This entire subplot should have been excised swiftly and mercilessly. And at the end, we are left with—what? When we invest emotional capital, we deserve a payoff.

A Walk on the Moon ★ ★
R, 106 m., 1999

Diane Lane (Pearl Kantrowitz), Viggo Mortensen (Walker Jerome), Liev Schreiber (Marty Kantrowitz), Anna Paquin (Alison Kantrowitz), Tovah Feldshuh (Lilian Kantrowitz), Bobby Boriello (Daniel Kantrowitz). Directed by Tony Goldwyn and produced by Dustin Hoffman, Goldwyn, Jay Cohen, Neil Koenigsberg, Lee Gottsegen, and Murray Schisgal. Screenplay by Pamela Gray.

"Sometimes I just wish I was a whole other person," says Pearl Kantrowitz, who is the subject, if not precisely the heroine, of *A Walk on the Moon*. It is the summer of 1969, and Pearl and her husband, Marty, have taken a bungalow in a Catskills resort. Pearl spends the week with their teenage daughter, their younger son, and her mother-in-law. Marty drives up from the city on the weekends.

The summer of 1969 is, of course, the summer of Woodstock, which is being held nearby. And Pearl (Diane Lane), who was married at a very early age to the only man she ever slept with, feels trapped in the stodgy domesticity of the resort—where wives and families are aired while the man labors in town. She doesn't know it, but she's ripe for the Blouse Man (Viggo Mortensen).

The Blouse Man drives a truck from resort to resort. It opens out into a retail store, offering marked-down prices on blouses and accessories. Funny, but he doesn't look like a Blouse Man: With his long hair and chiseled features, he looks more like a cross between a hippie and the hero on the cover of a paperback romance. He senses quickly that Pearl is shopping for more than blouses, and offers her a free tie-dyed T-shirt and his phone number. The T-shirt is crucial, symbolizing a time when women of Pearl's age were in the throes of the Sexual Revolution. Soon Pearl is using the phone number. "I wonder," she asks the Blouse

Man, "if you had plans for watching the moon walk?"

A Walk on the Moon is one small step for the Blouse Man, a giant leap for Pearl Kantrowitz. In the arms of the Blouse Man, she experiences sexual passion and a taste of freedom, and soon they're skinny-dipping just like the hippies at Woodstock. The festival indeed exudes a siren call, and Pearl, like a teenage girl slipping out of the house for a concert, finally sneaks off to attend it with the Blouse Man. Marty (Liev Schreiber), meanwhile, is stuck in the Woodstock traffic jam. And their daughter, Alison (Anna Paquin), who has gotten her period and her first boyfriend more or less simultaneously, is at Woodstock, too—where she sees her mother.

The movie is a memory of a time and place now largely gone (these days Pearl and Marty would be more likely to take the family to Disney World or Hawaii). It evokes the heady feelings of 1969, when rock was mistaken for revolution. To be near Woodstock and in heat with a long-haired god, but not be able to go there, is a Dantean punishment. But the movie also has thoughts about the nature of freedom and responsibility. "Do you think you're the only one whose dreams didn't come true?" asks Marty, whose early marriage meant he became a TV repairman instead of a college graduate.

Watching the gathering clouds over the marriage, Pearl's mother-in-law, Lilian (Tovah Feldshuh), sees all and understands much. If Pearl is not an entirely sympathetic character, Lilian Kantrowitz is a saint. She calls her son to warn him of trouble, she watches silently as Pearl defiantly leaves the house, and perhaps she understands Pearl's fear of being trapped in a life lived as an accessory to a man.

So the underlying strength of the story is there. Unfortunately, the casting and some of the romantic scenes sabotage it. Liev Schreiber is a good actor and I have admired him in many movies, but put him beside Viggo Mortensen and the Blouse Man wins; you can hardly blame Pearl for surrendering. (I am reminded of a TV news interview about that movie where Demi Moore was offered $1 million to sleep with Robert Redford. "Would you sleep with Robert Redford for a million dollars?" a woman in a mall was asked. She replied: "I'd sleep with him for 50 cents.")

The movie's problem is that it loads the casting in a way that tilts the movie in the direction of a Harlequin romance. Mortensen looks like one of those long-haired, barechested, muscular buccaneers on the covers of the paperbacks; all he needs is a Gothic tower behind him, with one light in a window. The movie exhibits almost unseemly haste in speeding Pearl and the Blouse Man toward love-making, and then lingers over their sex scenes as if they were an end in themselves, and not a transgression in a larger story. As Pearl and the Blouse Man cavort naked under a waterfall, the movie forgets its ethical questions and becomes soft-core lust.

Then, alas, there is the reckoning. We know sooner or later there will be anger and recrimination, self-revelation and confession, acceptance and resolve, wasp attacks and rescues. We've enjoyed those sex scenes, and now, like Pearl, we have to pay. Somewhere in the midst of the dramaturgy is a fine performance by Anna Paquin (from *The Piano*) as a teenage girl struggling with new ideas and raging hormones. Everytime I saw her character on screen, I thought: There's the real story.

The War Zone ★ ★ ★ ★
NO MPAA RATING, 99 m., 2000

Ray Winstone (Dad), Tilda Swinton (Mum), Lara Belmont (Jessie), Freddie Cunliffe (Tom), Colin J. Farrell (Nick), Aisling O'Sullivan (Carol), Kate Ashfield (Lucy). Directed by Tim Roth and produced by Sarah Radclyffe and Dixie Linder. Screenplay by Alexander Stuart, based on his novel *The War Zone*.

It must have been something like this in medieval times, families living in isolation, cut off from neighbors, forced indoors by the weather, their animal and sexual functions not always shielded from view. Tim Roth's *The War Zone*, brilliant and heartbreaking, takes place in the present but is timeless; most particularly it is cut off from the fix-it culture of psychobabble, which defines all the politically correct ways to consider incest. The movie is not about incest as an issue, but about incest as a blow to the heart and the soul—a real event, here, now, in a family that seems close and happy. Not a topic on a talk show.

The movie takes place in winter in Devon, which is wet and gray, the sky squeezing joy out of the day. The family has moved from London "to make a fresh start," the mother says. They live in a comfortable cottage, warm and sheltered, life centering around the big kitchen table. Mom (Tilda Swinton) is very pregnant. Dad (Ray Winstone) is bluff and cheery, extroverted, a good guy. Tom (Freddie Cunliffe) is a fifteen-year-old, silent and sad because he misses his friends in London. Jessie (Lara Belmont) is eighteen years old, ripe with beauty. This looks like a cheerful story.

Roth tells it obliquely, sensitive to the ways families keep secrets even from themselves. Early in the film the mother's time comes and the whole family rushes to the hospital; there's a car crash, but a happy ending, as they gather in the maternity ward with the newcomer, all of them cut and bruised, but survivors. Back at home, there is a comfort with the physical side of life. Mom nurses her child in kitchen scenes like renaissance paintings. Tom is comfortable with his sister's casual nudity while they have a heart-to-heart talk. Mum helps wash her men at the kitchen sink, Jessie dries her brother's hair in the laundry room, the family seems comfortable with one another.

Then Tom glimpses a disturbing part of a moment between his father and his sister. He challenges Jessie. She says nothing happened. Something did happen, and more will happen, including a scene of graphic hurtfulness. But this isn't a case of Tom discovering incest in his family and blowing the whistle. It's much more complicated. How does he feel about his sister and about her relationship with her new boyfriend, Nick? What about his father's eerie split personality, able to deny his behavior and see Tom's interference as an assault on their happy family? What about the mother's willingness not to know? What about his sister's denial? Does it spring from shame, fear, or a desire to shield Tom and her mother from the knowledge?

And what about a curious episode when Jessie and Tom visit London, and Jessie almost seems to have set up Tom to sleep with one of her friends—as what? Consolation? A bribe? Revenge? The movie's refusal to declare exactly what the London episode means is admirable, because this is not a zero-sum accounting of good and evil, but a messy, elusive, painfully complex tragedy in which no one is driven by just one motive.

When Tom is accused of destroying the family and having a filthy mind, there is a sense in which he accepts this analysis. One critic of the film wrote that a "teenaged boy (from the big city, no less) would surely be more savvy—no matter how distraught—about the workings and potential resolutions of such a situation." Only in textbooks. When you're fifteen, what you learn in social studies and from talk shows is a lot different from how you confront your own family.

Incest is not unfamiliar as a subject for movies, but most incest stories are about characters simplified into monsters and victims. We know intellectually that most child abusers were abused children, but few films pause to reflect how that lifelong hurt reflects itself in real situations. The father here is both better and worse because of his own probably traumatic childhood. He must long ago have often promised himself that he would be different than his own father, that he would be a good dad—loving, kind, warm, cheerful—and so he is, all except for when he is not. When he's accused of evil, he explodes in anger—the anger of the father he is now and also the anger of the child he once was. For a moment his son is, in a sense, the abuser, making Dad feel guilty and shameful just as his own father must have, and tearing down all his efforts to be better, to be different.

Unsurprisingly, *The War Zone* affects viewers much more powerfully than a simple morality tale might. It is not simply about the evil of incest, but about its dynamic, about the way it plays upon guilt and shame and addresses old and secret wounds. The critic James Berardinelli says that when he saw the movie at the Toronto Film Festival, a viewer ran from the theater saying he couldn't take it anymore, and went looking to pull a fire alarm. Tim Roth was standing near the exit and intercepted him, becoming confessor for an emotional outpouring that the movie had inspired.

Roth is one of the best actors now working, and with this movie he reveals himself as a director of surprising gifts. I cannot imagine *The War Zone* being better directed by anyone else, even though Ingmar Bergman and Ken

Loach come to mind. Roth and his actors, and Stuart's screenplay, understand these people and their situation down to the final nuance, and are willing to let silence, timing, and visuals reveal what dialogue would cheapen. Not many movies bring you to a dead halt of sorrow and empathy. This one does.

The Waterboy ★
PG-13, 86 m., 1998

Adam Sandler (Bobby Boucher), Kathy Bates (Mama Boucher), Henry Winkler (Coach Klein), Fairuza Balk (Vicki Vallencourt), Jerry Reed (Red Beaulieu), Larry Gilliard Jr. (Derek Wallace), Blake Clark (Farmer Fran), Peter Dante (Gee Grenouille). Directed by Frank Coraci and produced by Robert Simonds and Jack Giarraputo. Screenplay by Tim Herlihy and Adam Sandler.

I believe in giving every movie the benefit of the doubt. I walked into *The Waterboy*, sat down, took a sip of my delicious medium roast coffee, and felt at peace with the world. How nice it would be, I thought, to give Adam Sandler a good review for a change. Good will and caffeine suffused my being, and as the lights went down I all but beamed at the screen.

Then Adam Sandler spoke and all was lost. His character's voice is made of a lisp, a whine, a nasal grating, and an accent that nobody in Louisiana actually has, although the movies pretend that they do. His character is a thirty-one-year-old man who, soon after the film opens, is fired as the waterboy of a championship football team. Then he talks himself into a job with a team of losers, led by the insecure Coach Klein (Henry Winkler).

Bobby Boucher, the waterboy, is one of those people who is so insufferable, in a passive-aggressive way, that you have to believe they know what they're doing. No one could be that annoying by accident. I am occasionally buttonholed by such specimens. They stand too close, they talk too loudly, they are not looking at me but at an invisible TelePrompTer somewhere over my shoulder. If I were a man of action, I would head-butt them and take my chances with the courts.

The Waterboy tries to force this character into the ancient movie mold of the misunderstood simple little guy with a heart of gold. By the end of the movie we are supposed to like him, I think, especially as the whole school turns up in a candlelight vigil outside the hospital where he waits at the bedside of his (not) dying mother. There is only one way I can see myself liking this character. That would be if *The Waterboy*, like *That Obscure Object of Desire* and *Lost Highway*, had two different actors play the same character, so that by the end Bobby Boucher was being portrayed by Tom Hanks.

Kathy Bates has the best scenes in the movie, as Bobby's mother, a possessive and manipulative creature who has kept her son tied to her apron strings in their bayou cabin, which looks like it was furnished by the same artist who draws "How Many Mistakes Can You Find in This Picture?" Mama Boucher and Bobby share space with large animals and junk-shop treasures, and she serves giant swamp snakes, coiled in a tasty brew of herbs and spices. Bates makes her character work as a comic creation, and knows the line between parody and wretched excess.

Henry Winkler is luckless as Coach Klein, because he is given little to do other than be a creature of the plot. And the plot is that exhausted wheeze of a sports-movie formula, in which the hero is scorned by everyone until he comes off the bench, shows remarkable talent, and (a) wins or (b) loses the big game. (I do not want to reveal the ending, so you will have to guess for yourself which it is. If you voted for (b), you are reading the wrong movie critic.)

Do I have something visceral against Adam Sandler? I hope not. I try to keep an open mind and approach every movie with high hopes. It would give me enormous satisfaction (and relief) to like him in a movie. But I suggest he is making a tactical error when he creates a character whose manner and voice have the effect of fingernails on a blackboard, and then expects us to hang in there for a whole movie.

The Wedding Singer ★
PG-13, 96 m., 1998

Adam Sandler (Robbie), Drew Barrymore (Julia), Christine Taylor (Holly), Allen Covert (Sammy), Matthew Glave (Glenn), Ellen

Albertini Dow (Rosie), Angela Featherstone (Linda), Alexis Arquette (George). Directed by Frank Coraci and produced by Robert Simonds and Jack Giarraputo. Screenplay by Tim Herlihy.

The Wedding Singer tells the story of, yes, a wedding singer from New Jersey, who is cloyingly sweet at some times and a cruel monster at others. The filmmakers are obviously unaware of his split personality; the screenplay reads like a collaboration between Jekyll and Hyde. Did anybody, at any stage, give the story the slightest thought?

The plot is so familiar the end credits should have issued a blanket thank-you to a century of Hollywood love-coms. Through a torturous series of contrived misunderstandings, the boy and girl avoid happiness for most of the movie, although not as successfully as we do. It's your basic off-the-shelf formula in which two people fall in love, but are kept apart because (a) they're engaged to creeps; (b) they say the wrong things at the wrong times; and (c) they get bad information. It's exhausting, seeing the characters work so hard at avoiding the obvious.

Of course, there's the obligatory scene where the good girl goes to the good boy's house to say she loves him, but the bad girl answers the door and lies to her. I spent the weekend looking at old Astaire and Rogers movies, which basically had the same plot: She thinks he's a married man, and almost gets married to the slimy bandleader before he finally figures everything out and declares his love at the eleventh hour.

The big differences between Astaire and Rogers in *Swing Time* and Adam Sandler and Drew Barrymore in *The Wedding Singer* is that (1) in 1936 they were more sophisticated than we are now, and *knew* the plot was inane, and had fun with that fact, and (2) they could dance. One of the sad by-products of the dumbing-down of America is that we're now forced to witness the goofy plots of the 1930s played sincerely, as if they were really deep.

Sandler is the wedding singer. He's engaged to a slut who stands him up at the altar because, sob, "the man I fell in love with six years ago was a rock singer who licked the microphone like David Lee Roth—and now you're only a . . . a . . . wedding singer!" Barrymore, meanwhile, is engaged to a macho monster who brags about how he's cheating on her. Sandler and Barrymore meet because she's a waitress at the weddings where he sings. We know immediately they are meant for each other. Why do we know this? Because we are conscious and sentient. It takes them a lot longer.

The basic miscalculation in Adam Sandler's career plan is to ever play the lead. He is not a lead. He is the best friend, or the creep, or the loser boyfriend. He doesn't have the voice to play a lead: Even at his most sincere, he sounds like he's doing stand-up—like he's mocking a character in a movie he saw last night. Barrymore, on the other hand, has the stuff to play a lead (I commend you once again to the underrated *Mad Love*). But what is she doing in this one—in a plot her grandfather would have found old-fashioned? At least when she gets a good line (she tries out the married name "Mrs. Julia Gulia") she knows how to handle it.

The best laughs in the film come right at the top, in an unbilled cameo by the invaluable Steve Buscemi, as a drunken best man who makes a shambles of a wedding toast. He has the timing, the presence, and the intelligence to go right to the edge. Sandler, on the other hand, always keeps something in reserve—his talent. It's like he's afraid of committing; he holds back so he can use the "only kidding" defense.

I could bore you with more plot details. About why he thinks she's happy and she thinks he's happy and they're both wrong and she flies to Vegas to marry the stinker, and he . . . but why bother? And why even mention that the movie is set in the mid-1980s and makes a lot of mid-1980s references that are supposed to be funny but sound exactly like lame dialogue? And what about the curious cameos by faded stars and inexplicably cast character actors? And why do they write the role of a Boy George clone for Alexis Arquette and then do nothing with the character except let him hang there on screen? And why does the tourist section of the plane have fewer seats than first class? And, and, and . . .

Welcome to Sarajevo ★ ★

R, 102 m., 1998

Stephen Dillane (Henderson), Woody
Harrelson (Flynn), Marisa Tomei (Nina),
Emira Nusevic (Emira), Kerry Fox (Jane
Carson), Goran Visnjic (Risto), James Nesbitt
(Gregg), Emily Lloyd (Annie McGee). Directed
by Michael Winterbottom and produced by
Graham Broadbent and Damian Jones.
Screenplay by Frank Cottrell Boyce, based
on the book *Natasha's Story* by Michael
Nicholson.

My confidence in *Welcome to Sarajevo* was undermined by the film's uncertain air of improvisation. Like Haskell Wexler's *Medium Cool*,
which plunged into the midst of the riots at
the 1968 Democratic Convention in Chicago,
it combines fact and fiction, real and fake
news footage, and actors side-by-side with
local people. Wexler pulled it off. Michael Winterbottom, who made this film about a 1992
Sarajevo where the smoke seems to be still rising from the latest shellings, doesn't quite.

The movie centers itself on a group of journalists who take harrowing risks to cover a
war that their editors and viewers back home
aren't very interested in. Stephen Dillane plays
Henderson, a British reporter who finds his
latest big story has been pushed off the front
page by the divorce of the Duchess of York.
And Woody Harrelson plays Flynn, a high-
profile news star on American TV, who walks
into the range of sniper fire to aid a wounded
altar boy—after first making sure, of course,
that the cameras are rolling. His reasoning:
"Well you know, oddly enough, back home no
one has ever heard of Sarajevo and everyone
has heard of me."

The story of Henderson forms the core of
the movie. He's in anguish over the fates of
children who are war victims, and narrates
footage of a big UN plane taking off: "Children are dying in the most dangerous corner
of the most dangerous city on earth—but this
plane is flying out of here empty." He eventually takes things into his own hands, smuggling a young girl orphan out of Sarajevo by
quasi-legal means, so that he and his wife can
adopt her. This story thread is based on fact—

British TV reporter Michael Nicholson and
his wife adopted an orphan, and he wrote a
book about it.

One can imagine a strong film about that
part of the story. One can also imagine a film
about war correspondents under fire and
frustrated by an indifferent world. The problem is that Winterbottom has imagined both
stories and several others, and tells them in a
style designed to feel as if reality has been
caught on the fly. What it more often feels like,
alas, is the venerable Second City formula for
improvisation—"Something wonderful right
away!"—and too often we sense that the actors are drifting and the story is at sea.

That's especially true of the Woody Harrelson scenes. He's an interesting, intense actor,
and a good choice for a character living recklessly under fire. But too often I got the feeling
that Winterbottom, having imported American stars (Marisa Tomei is also in the cast),
tried to plug them into spur-of-the-moment,
spontaneous situations that didn't fit with the
rest of the film. There's the feeling that the
central characters don't really know each other
as well as they should. The film arrives in fragments, without a sense of destination.

Films like this, of course, lament for the
children—for helpless orphans and altar boys
gunned down by partisan and sectarian snipers.
But the snipers were altar boys only a few
years ago, and altar boys grow up to become
snipers. The film decries "violence" but doesn't
name names: Much of the evil that has descended on this part of the world is caused by
tribalism and religious fanaticism (when one
group kills another in the name of their God,
that is fanaticism).

So often there is a style of reporting events
like the Bosnian tragedy in which words like
"partisans" are used instead of "religious fanatics," because although a man might kill others
for worshiping the wrong god, of course we
must not offend his religion. *Welcome to Sarajevo* tiptoes around that awkwardness with
easy pieties, in which an orphan is spared, a
man is a hero, cynicism masks bravery—and
the underlying issues are not addressed. A better and braver film about this part of the
world is Milcho Manchevsky's *Before the Rain*
(1995), which shows clearly how the circle of

killing goes around and around, fueled by the mindless passion that my God, my language, my ancestors, give me the right to kill you.

Western ★ ★
NO MPAA RATING, 121 m., 1999

Sergi Lopez (Paco), Sacha Bourdo (Nino), Elisabeth Vitali (Marinette), Marie Matheron (Nathalie), Basile Sieouka (Baptiste), Jean-Louis Dupont (Policeman), Olivier Herveet (Hospital Doctor). Directed by Manuel Poirier and produced by Maurice Bernart. Screenplay by Poirier and Jean Francois Goyet.

Western is a road movie about a friendship between two men and their search for the love of the right woman. The roads they travel are in western France, in the district of Brittany, which looks rough and dour but, on the evidence of this film, has the kindest and most accommodating women in the world.

The Meet Cute between the men occurs when Paco (Sergi Lopez), a shoe salesman from Spain, gives a lift to Nino (Sacha Bourdo), a Russian who lived in Italy before moving to France. Nino tricks Paco and steals his car, when the stranded Paco sees him on the street the next day, he chases him and beats him so badly Nino lands in the hospital. Paco visits him there, says he is sorry to have hit him so hard, and the men become friends. Since Paco has lost his job along with his car, they hit the road.

Road movies are the oldest genre known to man, and the most flexible, since anything can happen on the road and there's always a fresh supply of characters. Paco, who has always been a ladies' man, in fact has already found a woman: Marinette (Elisabeth Vitali), who befriended him after his car was stolen and even let him sleep overnight on her sofa bed. Soon they've kissed and think they may be in love, but Marinette wants a thirty-day cooling-off period, so the two men hitch around Brittany, depending on the kindness of strangers.

If Paco has always had luck with women, Nino has had none. He's a short, unprepossessing man with a defeatist attitude, and one day Paco stands next to him at the roadside, points to a nearby village, and says, "I'm sure that in that town, there has to be a woman for

you." "Really?" "Yes, there is a minimum of one woman in every town in France for you."

This belief leads them to conduct a phony door-to-door survey as a ruse for finding the right woman for Nino, and along the way they make a new friend, Baptiste (Basile Sieouka), an African from Senegal in a wheelchair. He teaches them the "bonjour" game, in which they get points every time a stranger returns their greeting. "Go back where you came from!" one man snarls at Baptiste, who laughs uproariously; all three of these men are strangers in a foreign land.

The emotional center of the story comes when Paco meets a woman named Nathalie (Marie Matheron), who invites them home for dinner, likes the way Nino cooks chicken, and unexpectedly goes for Nino rather than Paco. This woman's lifestyle seems unlikely (she is a male daydream of an earth mother), but she provides the excuse for the film's ending—which is intended as joyous, but seemed too pat and complacent to me.

Western, directed and cowritten by Manuel Poirier, won the Grand Jury Prize, or second place, in 1997 at Cannes; that's the same prize *Life Is Beautiful* won in 1998. Set in France, it absorbed a certain offhand flair. The same material, filmed in America, might seem thin and contrived; the adventures are arbitrary, the cuteness of the men grows wearing, and when Nino has an accident with a chainsaw, we can see contrivance shading off into desperation.

The movie is slow-going. Paco and Nino are the kinds of open-faced proletarian heroes found more often in fables than in life. Their luck as homeless men in finding a ready supply of trusting and hospitable women is uncanny, even unbelievable. The movie insists on their charm, instead of letting us find it for ourselves. And although the leading actresses are sunny and vital, they are fantasy women, not real ones (who would be smarter and warier).

One of the women in the film collects children fathered by an assortment of men who capture her fancy and then drift away, apparently with her blessings. The movie smiles on this practice, instead of wondering how she found so many men so indifferent to their own children. By the end of the film she has given birth to her own orphanage, and could hire the family out as a package to the casting director for *Oliver Twist*. The jury at Cannes loved this, but I squirmed, and speculated that the subtitles and the European cachet gives the film immunity. In English, with American actors, this story would be unbearable.

What Dreams May Come ★ ★ ★ ½
PG-13, 113 m., 1998

Robin Williams (Chris Nielsen), Cuba Gooding Jr. (Albert), Annabella Sciorra (Annie Nielsen), Max Von Sydow (The Tracker), Rosalind Chow (Leona), Jessica Brooks Grant (Marie Nielsen), Josh Paddock (Ian Nielsen). Directed by Vincent Ward and produced by Stephen Simon and Barnet Bain. Screenplay by Ron Bass, based on the novel by Richard Matheson.

Vincent Ward's *What Dreams May Come* is so breathtaking, so beautiful, so bold in its imagination, that it's a surprise at the end to find it doesn't finally deliver. It takes us to the emotional brink, but it doesn't push us over. It ends on a curiously unconvincing note—a conventional resolution in a movie that for most of its length has been daring and visionary.

So, yes, I have my disappointments with it. But I would not want them to discourage you from seeing it, because this is a film that even in its imperfect form shows how movies can imagine the unknown, can lead our imaginations into wonderful places. And it contains heartbreakingly effective performances by Robin Williams and Annabella Sciorra. The movie is so good it shows us how it could have been better: It seems headed for a great leap, we can sense it coming, and then it settles. If Hollywood is determined to shortchange us with an obligatory happy ending, then it shouldn't torment us with a movie that deserves better.

I hesitate to reveal too many secrets, but the film's setup was so thoroughly publicized that you probably already know certain key facts. Save the review until later if you don't.

The facts you know from the ads and the trailers are that Chris and Annie (Williams and Sciorra) have a Meet Cute when their boats collide on a Swiss lake. They marry. They have two children. They are happy. Then

both of the children are killed in an accident. Annie has a breakdown, Chris nurses her through, art works as therapy, they are somehow patching their lives back together—and then Chris is killed.

The film follows him into the next world, and creates it with visuals that seem borrowed from his own memories and imagination. In one sequence that is among the most visually exciting I have ever seen, he occupies a landscape that is a painting, and as he plucks a flower it turns to oil paint in his hand. Other parts of this world seem cheerfully assembled from the storage rooms of images we keep in our minds: Renaissance art, the pre-Raphaelites, greeting cards, angel kitsch (cherubs float past on plump clouds). Later, when Chris ventures into hell, the images are darker and more fearsome—Bosch crossed with Dali.

There is a guide in the next world named Albert (Cuba Gooding Jr.). Is he all that he seems? Now we have ventured beyond the information in the ads, and I will be more circumspect. The story, inspired by a novel by Richard Matheson, is founded on the assumption that heaven exists in a state of flux, that its inhabitants assume identities that please themselves, or us; that having been bound within one identity during life, we are set free. Heaven, in one sense, means becoming who you want to be.

And hell? "Hell is for those who don't know they're dead," says Albert. Or they know they're dead but don't know what the deal is. Or they won't go along with the deal. Many of those in hell are guilty of the greatest sin against God, which is despair: They believe they are beyond hope.

After the death of her children and husband, Annie has despaired and killed herself and gone to hell. Chris wants to find her: "I'm her soul mate." Albert says that's not possible: "Nothing will make her recognize you." But he acts as a guide and Chris ventures into hell, which, like heaven, has been realized with a visual intensity and originality that is astonishing. In this film the road to hell is paved, not with good intentions, but with the faces of the damned, bitter and complaining (the face and voice of Chris's father are played by the German director Werner Herzog).

What happens then, what happens throughout the film, is like nothing you have seen before. Vincent Ward is a New Zealand director whose works have not always reached a large audience, but have always dared for big ideas and bold visuals to express them. He made *The Navigator* (1988), about medieval Englishmen who tunnel to escape the plague—and emerge in the present. And then, in 1993, the great *Map of the Human Heart*, about the odyssey of an Eskimo boy from Alaska in the 1930s to London in the war, and from a great love affair to high adventure.

What Dreams May Come ends, like *The Navigator*, with the characters seeking their destiny in a cathedral—but this one, like many of the film's images, is like none you have seen before. It is upside down, the great vaulted ceilings providing a floor and a landscape. Since I have mentioned Herzog, I had might as well quote his belief that our century is "starving for great images." This film provides them, and also provides quiet moments of winsome human nature, as when a character played by Rosalind Chow explains why she appears to be an Asian flight attendant, and when another, played by Max Von Sydow, explains the rules of the game as he understands them.

Robin Williams somehow has a quality that makes him seem at home in imaginary universes. Remember him in *Popeye, The Adventures of Baron Munchausen, Toys, Jumanji,* and in his animated incarnation in *Aladdin.* There is a muscular reality about him, despite his mercurial wit, that anchors him and makes the fantastic images around him seem almost plausible. He is good, too, at emotion: He brings us along with him. In Annabella Sciorra he has a costar whose own character is deeply unhappy and yet touching; her sin of despair was committed, we believe, because she loved so much and was so happy she cannot exist in the absence of those feelings.

And yet, as I've suggested, the movie somehow gathers all these threads and its triumphant art direction and special effects, and then doesn't get across the finish line with them. I walked out of the theater sensing that I should have felt more, that an opportunity had been lost. *What Dreams May Come* takes us too far and risks too much to turn conventional at the end. It could have been better. It could perhaps

have been the best film of the year. Whatever its shortcomings, it is a film to treasure.

Whatever ★ ★ ★
R, 112 m., 1998

Liza Weil (Anna Stockard), Chad Morgan (Brenda Talbot), Frederic Forrest (Chaminski), Kathryn Rossetter (Carol Stockard), Marc Riffon (Martin), Dan Montano (Zak), John G. Connolly (Woods), Gary Wolf (Eddie). Directed by Susan Skoog and produced by Ellin Baumel, Michelle Yahn, Kevin Segalla, and Skoog. Screenplay by Skoog.

Whatever is a movie that knows how a lot of kids survive the teenage years through sheer blind luck. Others die or have their lives destroyed because their luck is bad. Most people, I imagine, keep teenage secrets that still make them cringe years later—memories of stupid chances they shouldn't have taken, and relief that they weren't caught.

Anna, the heroine of *Whatever,* is not a bad girl but she is an unhappy one, and she drifts into danger without even giving it much thought. Isn't it amazing how everything a girl has been taught all her life sometimes means nothing in the face of temptation by a boy who is reckless and stupid, but seems to offer freedom?

It's the early 1980s. Anna (Liza Weil) attends high school in New Jersey. Her best friend, Brenda (Chad Morgan), values herself so lightly that she has sex with guys just to get her hands on their jugs of wine. Anna is taking art classes and hopes to be accepted by Cooper Union, a good school in Manhattan. Her teacher (Frederic Forrest), an aging hippie in a time warp, urges her to do her thing. Anna lives with her mother (Kathryn Rossetter) and unpleasant younger brother; they often prepare their own meals while their mother is out on dates with a married man she hopes will pay their bills.

Anna is smart, but not a good student. She's not into booze and sex the way her friend Brenda is, but she figures, without giving it much thought, that these are areas where she might as well do some experimenting. She has a crush on a kid named Martin (Marc Riffon), who has been out of town but now returns from his self-styled wanderings with lessons about "the passion of one's existence." A lot of the time Anna spends doing nothing while listening to bad music.

The movie unfolds episodically. Brenda suggests cutting school and taking a trip to New York. Anna visits Cooper Union but doesn't really connect. They pick up a couple of twenty-five-year-olds in a bar. They pretend to be older than they are. Something embarrassing happens that will turn into a funny story many years from now, when the confusion and pain have been outgrown.

Back in New Jersey, there are a couple of guys hanging around who have already done time in a reformatory, and are low-level would-be drug dealers who suggest a trip to Florida. Brenda wants to go. Anna agrees passively. This trip could produce the turning point in her life; it could result in trouble that would last for years. The way it turns out, and the subtle way those scenes are written and acted, give us a glimpse inside the character of one of the guys—who has probably already taken the wrong turn himself, but still has his feelings.

The movie was written and directed by Susan Skoog, who accepts a difficult challenge by making Anna neither a rebel nor an endangered good girl, but simply an average person whose potential, if any, is still wrapped up inside adolescent confusion and resentment. She's at a stage. She doesn't express herself very well and often clams up, and the counselor at high school is exasperated because she seems to be drifting into trouble without much meaning to. She gets into trouble for smoking in the school restroom, and we sense she doesn't even care if she smokes or not—she just thinks she ought to.

Movies like this depend on observation. Yes, there's some plot, especially when Brenda seizes an occasion to strike back at the stepfather who has abused her. But it's significant that Brenda takes action, not Anna—who usually has no particular action in mind. She's along for the ride. Doesn't care how, doesn't know where. The suspense involves whether she'll avoid trouble long enough to grow out of the stage where she allows herself to drift into it. Seeing a movie like this could do a lot of kids some good. Parents, I suspect, would find it terrifying.

Whatever It Takes ★ ½
PG-13, 92 m., 2000

Shane West (Ryan Woodman), Jodi Lyn O'Keefe (Ashley Grant), Marla Sokoloff (Maggie Carter), James Franco (Chris Campbell), Julia Sweeney (Ryan's Mom). Directed by David Hubbard and produced by Paul Schiff. Screenplay by Mark Schwahn, loosely based on Edmund Rostand's play Cyrano de Bergerac.

Whatever It Takes is still another movie arguing that the American teenager's IQ level hovers in the low 90s. It involves teenagers who have never existed, doing things no teenager has ever done, for reasons no teenager would understand. Of course, it's aimed at the teenage market. Maybe it's intended as escapism.

The screenplay is "loosely based on *Cyrano de Bergerac*," according to the credits. My guess is, it's based on the Cliff's Notes for *Cyrano*, studied only long enough to rip off the scene where Cyrano hides in the bushes and whispers lines for his friend to repeat to the beautiful Roxanne.

Cyrano in this version is the wonderfully named Ryan Woodman (Shane West), whose house is next door to Maggie (Marla Sokoloff). So close, indeed, that the balconies of their bedrooms almost touch, and they are in constant communication, although "only good friends." Ryan has a crush on Ashley (Jodi Lyn O'Keefe), the school sexpot. His best pal Chris (James Franco) warns him Ashley is beyond his grasp, but Ryan can dream.

If you know *Cyrano*, or have seen such splendid adaptations as Fred Schepisi's *Roxanne* (1987) with Steve Martin and Daryl Hannah, you can guess the key scene. Ryan talks Chris into going out with Maggie and then hides behind the scenery of a school play while prompting him with lines he knows Maggie will fall for. With Maggie neutralized, Ryan goes out with Ashley—who is a conceited, arrogant snob, of course, and will get her comeuppance in one of those cruel scenes reserved for stuck-up high school sexpots.

The film contains a funny scene, but it doesn't involve any of the leads. It's by Ryan's mom (Julia Sweeney), also the school nurse, who lectures the student body on safe sex, using a six-foot male reproductive organ as a visual aid. She is not Mrs. Woodman for nothing. As a responsible reporter I will also note that the film contains a nude shower scene, which observes all of the rules about nudity almost but not quite being shown.

And, let's see, there is a scene where Ashley gets drunk and throws up on her date, and a scene set in an old folks' home that makes use of enough flatulence to score a brief concerto. And a scene ripped off from *It's a Wonderful Life*, as the high school gym floor opens up during a dance to dunk the students in the swimming pool beneath. Forget about the situation inspired by *Cyrano:* Is there *anything* in this movie that isn't borrowed?

What Planet Are You From? ★

R, 100 m., 2000

Garry Shandling (Harold Anderson), Annette Bening (Susan Hart), Greg Kinnear (Perry Gordon), Ben Kingsley (Graydon), Linda Fiorentino (Helen Gordon), John Goodman (Roland Jones), Caroline Aaron (Nadine Jones), Judy Greer (Rebecca). Directed by Mike Nichols and produced by Nichols, Garry Shandling, and Neil Machlis. Screenplay by Shandling, Michael Leeson, Ed Solomon, and Peter Tolan.

Here is the most uncomfortable movie of the new year, an exercise in feel-good smut. *What Planet Are You From?* starts out as a dirty comedy, but then abandons the comedy, followed by the dirt, and by the end is actually trying to be poignant. For that to work, we'd have to like the hero, and Garry Shandling makes that difficult. He begrudges every emotion, as if there's no more where that came from. That worked on TV's *Larry Sanders Show*—it's why his character was funny—but here he can't make the movie's U-turn into sentimentality.

He plays an alien from a distant planet, where the inhabitants have no emotions and no genitals. Possibly this goes hand in hand. He is outfitted with human reproductive equipment, given the name Harold Anderson, and sent to Earth to impregnate a human woman so that his race can conquer our planet. When Harold becomes aroused, a loud whirling noise emanates from his pants.

If I were a comedy writer I would deal with that alarming noise. I would assume that the other characters in the movie would find it extremely disturbing. I put it to my female readers: If you were on a date with a guy and every time he looked dreamy-eyed it sounded like an operating garbage disposal was secreted somewhere on his person, wouldn't you be thinking of ways to say you just wanted to be friends?

The lame joke in *What Planet Are You From?* is that women hear the noise, find it curious and ask about it, and Harold makes feeble attempts to explain it away, and of course the more aroused he becomes the louder it hums, and when his ardor cools the volume drops. You understand. If you find this even slightly funny, you'd better see this movie, since the device is never likely to be employed again.

On Earth, Harold gets a job in a bank with the lecherous Perry (Greg Kinnear), and soon he is romancing a woman named Susan (Annette Bening) and contemplating the possibility of sex with Perry's wife, Helen (Linda Fiorentino). Fiorentino, of course, starred in the most unforgettable sexual put-down in recent movie history (in *The Last Seduction*, where she calls the bluff of a barroom braggart). There is a scene here with the same setup: She's sitting next to Harold in a bar, there is a humming from the nether regions of his wardrobe, etc., and I was wondering, is it too much to ask that the movie provide a hilarious homage? It was. Think of the lost possibilities.

Harold and Susan fly off to Vegas, get married, and have a honeymoon that consists of days of uninterrupted sex ("I had so many orgasms," she says, "that some are still stacked up and waiting to land"). Then she discovers Harold's only interest in her is as a breeder. She is crushed and angry, and the movie turns to cheap emotion during her pregnancy and inevitable live childbirth scene, after which Harold finds to his amazement that he may have emotions after all.

The film was directed by Mike Nichols, whose uneven career makes you wonder. Half of his films are good to great (his previous credit is *Primary Colors*) and the other half you're at a loss to account for. What went into the theory that *What Planet Are You From?* was filmable? Even if the screenplay by Garry

Shandling and three other writers seemed promising on the page, why star Shandling in it? Why not an actor who projects joy of performance—why not Kinnear, for example?

Shandling's shtick is unavailability. His public persona is of a man unwilling to be in public. Words squeeze embarrassed from his lips as if he feels guilty to be talking. *Larry Sanders* used this presence brilliantly. But it depends on its limitations. If you're making a movie about a man who has a strange noise coming from his pants, you should cast an actor who looks different when it isn't.

Where the Heart Is ★ ★ ½
PG-13, 121 m., 2000

Natalie Portman (Novalee Nation), Ashley Judd (Lexie Coop), James Frain (Forney), Stockard Channing (Sister Husband), Joan Cusack (Ruth Meyers), Jim Beaver (Clawhammer), Rodger Boyce (Harry the Policeman), Dylan Bruno (Willy Jack Pickens), Keith David (Moses Whitecotton), Sally Field (Mama Lil), Richard Jones (Mr. Sprock). Directed by Matt Williams and produced by Susan Cartsonis. Screenplay by Lowell Ganz and Babaloo Mandel, based on the novel by Billie Letts.

Remember that game in school where the teacher would write the first sentence of a story and then pass it around the class? Everybody would write a sentence, but the paper was folded so you could read only the last sentence before yours. *Where the Heart Is* has a screenplay like that, zigging and zagging and wildly careening from one melodramatic development to the next. What halfway holds it together are the performances, which are convincing and deserve a story with a touch more sanity.

The movie is based on a popular novel by Billie Letts, about a seventeen-year-old unwed mother named Novalee Nation (Natalie Portman), who is abandoned by her no-good boyfriend in a Wal-Mart in Sequoia, Oklahoma, and lives secretly in the store until she gives birth to her child, little Americus. The baby is delivered by the town's substitute librarian, Forney (James Frain), who has been following her, moonstruck, and breaks through the store's plate-glass window as she goes into labor. She finds a home locally with Sister Husband (Stockard Channing) and her partner, Mr. Sprock (Richard Jones).

Novalee is lucky to have landed in a town populated exclusively by character actors. Everyone in Sequoia, and indeed everyone in her life, is a salt-of-the-earth, good ol' eccentric, and that surely includes her new best friend Lexie Coop (Ashley Judd) who is always going and getting herself pregnant. When Novalee names her new baby Americus, Lexie is impressed. She names her kids after snacks: Praline, Baby Ruth . . .

The people in the movie are lovable and sympathetic, and if they live in a world of folksy fantasy, at least it looks like a good place to live. For example, Novalee makes a friend of Moses Whitecotton (Keith David), a photographer in the Wal-Mart, and soon she's exhibiting talent as a gifted photographer. But the characters have to negotiate the plot like runners through a minefield, as one weird and improbable situation after another comes up. At one point Novalee is about to be sucked up into the funnel cloud of a tornado, and clings upside down to the steps of the storm shelter with the fingertips of one hand while snatching little Americus as the child is about to be blown past her. Uh-huh.

There are times when you wonder, how self-aware *are* these people? Sister Husband is wonderfully played by Channing, who brings humanity and warmth to the character, but what's with her blessing before meals: ". . . and we ask forgiveness, Lord, for the fornication that Mr. Sprock and I have committed again this morning right here on this very kitchen table." Does she know that's funny? Or is she being sincere?

God has to forgive a lot of fornicating in this movie. Lexie, the Judd character, is forever taking up with the wrong man. She seems to be the town nurse, but has an imperfect understanding of birth control, not to mention abysmal taste in men (until at last she meets Ernie the Exterminator). Novalee's own unorthodox delivery gets on the TV news and attracts the attention of devout folks from as far away as Midnight, Mississippi, who travel to Sequoia, kidnap Americus, and abandon the infant in the crib of the local nativity scene. (The symbolism of this act is elusive; it could as easily be sacrilegious as disapproving.)

Novalee's first boyfriend, the father of her child, is the no-good would-be country singer Willy Jack Pickens (Dylan Bruno). After he abandons her, he's arrested while in the company of a fourteen-year-old hitchhiking thief, and is sent off to prison. When Novalee has the "Wal-Mart baby" and becomes a TV star, that fetches her lying mother, Mama Lil (Sally Field) from New Orleans. Meanwhile, the story follows later developments in Willy Jack's case, as he signs with a hard-boiled talent agent (Joan Cusack).

By now I'm ducking down in my seat to keep out of the line of fire of the plot. This movie is so heavy on incident, contrivance, coincidence, improbability, sudden reversals, and dizzying flash-forwards (sometimes years at a time) that it seems a wonder the characters don't crash into each other in the confusion. Melodramatic elements are slapped on top of one another like a hurry-up plasterboarding job. The happy ending is so laboriously obvious that it's a little amazing, really, how Natalie Portman manages to find sweetness in it, for Novalee and for us.

Portman is quite an actress. I've been an admirer since her early work in *Beautiful Girls*. Here she's the calm eye of the storm, mightily aided by Ashley Judd, who brings a plausibility to Lexie that the character surely needs. James Frain, as the lonely librarian with a secret in his family, has to undergo a remarkable personality change, from skitterish neurotic to stable nice guy, but the movie is so busy he finds time to sneak off and do that. There is a core of truth to these three and their story, and real humanity in Channing's work as Sister Husband, but it would all mean a lot more if the screenplay had dialed down its manic inventions. And every time I looked at Portman or Judd, I was aware that whatever else Sequoia, Oklahoma, may lack, it obviously has makeup and hair facilities to rival Beverly Hills.

Where the Money Is ★ ★ ★
PG-13, 89 m., 2000

Paul Newman (Henry), Linda Fiorentino (Carol), Dermot Mulroney (Wayne), Susan Barnes (Mrs. Foster), Anne Pitoniak (Mrs. Tetlow), Bruce MacVittie (Karl), Irma St. Paul (Mrs. Galer), Michel Perron (Guard). Directed by Marek Kanievska and produced by Ridley Scott, Charles Weinstock, Chris Zarpas, and Christopher Dorr. Screenplay by E. Max Frye, Topper Lilien, and Carroll Cartwright.

Where the Money Is has a preposterous plot, but it's not about a plot; it's about acting. It's about how Paul Newman at seventy-five is still cool, sleek, and utterly self-confident, and about how Linda Fiorentino's low, calm voice sneaks in under his cover and challenges him in places he is glad to be reminded of. Watching these two working together is like watching a couple of thoroughbreds going around a track. You know they'll end up back where they started and you don't even have any money on the race, but look at that form.

Fiorentino plays a discontented nurse in a small town, married to the same guy (Dermot Mulroney) since high school. "We were king and queen of the prom, so it sort of made sense to get married," she tells Newman. "When did it stop making sense?" he asks. Newman can say a line like that to a woman and convince her it *never* made sense, even if she didn't know it until he asked the question.

I have given away a plot point by revealing that he speaks. In the opening scenes of the movie, he appears to be an old man paralyzed by a stroke. He can't move his body, he can't talk, he doesn't even look at anything. It's all an act: He's a veteran bank robber who has studied yoga in order to fake stroke symptoms, so he can be moved from prison to the retirement home, which he figures will be easier to escape from. Actually, it's not such a big point to reveal, since (a) we somehow intuit that Paul Newman wouldn't be starring in the movie if he didn't move or speak for ninety minutes, and (b) all the TV commercials and review clips show him moving and speaking.

The old crook, named Henry, is a good actor, and fools everybody except Carol, the nurse played by Fiorentino. She notices subtle clues, and tries to coax him out of his shell with a lap dance (she is dressed at the time, but in a nurse's uniform, which is always interesting). He resists. This is good yoga. She abandons sex for more direct methods, and he's forced to admit that he can indeed walk and talk. By later that night he's even dancing in the local tavern with Carol and her husband, Wayne.

Carol realizes that Henry is her ticket out of town. Either he still has a lot of money stashed away from all those bank jobs, or he can help her steal some more. Wayne finds this thinking seriously flawed, but eventually the three of them end up as partners in an armored car heist. The heist is as to the movie as Sinatra's cigarette and drink are to his song: superfluous, but it gives him something to do with his hands.

Newman you know all about. At his age he has such sex appeal that when the husband gets jealous, we believe it. He has that shucks, ma'am grin, and then you see in his eyes the look of a man who is still driving racing cars, and can find an opening at 160 mph. He counsels Wayne about an encounter with some dangerous men: "Be cool to these guys, right? Look them in the eye—but not like you're gonna remember their faces."

Fiorentino is a special case, an actress who in the wrong movie (*What Planet Are You From?*) seems clueless, and in the right one (*After Hours, The Last Seduction*) can make every scene be about what she's thinking she'd rather be doing. She is best employed playing a character who is the smartest person in the movie, which is the case this time.

As for the bank robber and his stroke: A lot of reviews are going to pair this movie with *Diamonds*, another 2000 movie involving a great movie star and a stroke. That one starred Kirk Douglas, who really did have a stroke, and has made a remarkable comeback. But the strokes in the two plots aren't the connection—after all, one is real and one is fake, and that's a big difference. The comparison should be between two aging but gifted stars looking for worthy projects.

Diamonds has a plot as dumb as a box of tofu. *Where the Money Is* has a plot marginally smarter, dialogue considerably smarter, and better opportunities for the human qualities of the actors to escape from the requirements of the story. After you see this movie, you want to see Paul Newman in another one. After you see *Diamonds*, you don't want to see another movie for a long time.

The Whole Nine Yards ★ ★ ★
R, 99 m., 2000

Bruce Willis (Jimmy Tudeski), Matthew Perry (Oz Oseransky), Rosanna Arquette (Sophie), Michael Clarke Duncan (Frankie Figs), Natasha Henstridge (Cynthi), Amanda Peet (Jill), Kevin Pollak (Yanni Gogolack), Harland Williams (Buffalo Steve). Directed by Jonathan Lynn and produced by David Willis and Allan Kaufman. Screenplay by Mitchell Kapner.

A subtle but unmistakable aura of jolliness sneaks from the screen during *The Whole Nine Yards,* and eventually we suspect that the actors are barely suppressing giggles. This is the kind of standard material everyone could do in lockstep, but you sense inner smiles, and you suspect the actors are enjoying themselves. George C. Scott said that a key element in any role was "the joy of performance"—the feeling that the actor is having a good time. This cast seems vastly amused.

Of course, I have no way of knowing if that was really the case. The actors may have hated one another and spent their evenings having anonymous pizzas delivered to each other's hotel rooms. All I can report is my subjective feeling. I know this is not the greatest comedy of all time, or even of the first seven weeks of the century, but I was entertained beyond all expectation.

One of the reasons for that is a perfect performance by Amanda Peet. I say it is perfect because it exactly matches what is required, and then adds a level of heedless glee. I do not write as a longtime fan: Amanda Peet has been in seventeen previous movies without inspiring any cartwheels, but this time, as an ambitious young woman named Jill who would like to kill people for a living, she is so disarmingly, infectiously funny that finally all she has to do is smile to get a laugh.

Jill's role model is Jimmy Tudeski (Bruce Willis), a professional hit man known as Jimmy the Tulip. As the film opens, he has moved in next door to a Montreal dentist named Oz Oseransky (Matthew Perry), whose French-Canadian wife, Sophie (Rosanna Arquette), smokes cigarettes and wishes he were dead. So insufferable is this woman that Jill, who is Oz's office receptionist, volunteers, "You'd be

659

doing the world a favor if you just had her whacked."

Everybody is having everybody whacked in *The Whole Nine Yards*. Jimmy the Tulip is being sought by Yanni Gogolak (Kevin Pollak), a Chicago gangster, who wants him whacked. Sophie wants Oz to go to Chicago and rat on the Tulip so they can collect the finder's fee. Oz does not much want to do this, but flies to Chicago and is taken under the muscular arms of Yanni's henchman Frankie Figs (Michael Clarke Duncan, the big guy from *The Green Mile*), and ushered into the Gogolak presence. Every actor in the movie has at least one juicy scene, and Pollak has fun with his, combining an impenetrable accent with key words that are spat out like hot oysters.

There is more to the plot, all of which you will have to discover for yourself. What I can describe is the amusement the actors exude. Bruce Willis has played countless hit men. This one simply has to stand there and suggest the potential for painful action. "It's not important how many people I kill," he explains to Perry; "what's important is how I get along with the people who are still alive." Willis glows as absurdities revolve around him. One of those absurdities is Matthew Perry's dentist, who is always running into things, like glass doors and Michael Clarke Duncan. He falls in love with the Tulip's wife, Cynthia (Natasha Henstridge), who is being held captive by Gogolak—but there I go with the plot again.

I think you have to be observant during this film. There are some moments that are likely to be funny no matter what, but others depend on a certain momentum that gets going if you tune in to the underlying good humor. Here is a cast full of actors required to be silly while keeping a straight face, and somehow they have developed a faith that the screenplay is funny, and, of course, their belief makes it funny, and there you are.

And it would be worth renting the video just to study Amanda Peet's face and listen to her voice during her early encounters with the Tulip. She makes it all look so easy we forget that what she accomplishes is just about impossible: She is funny because of her personality without resorting to a "funny personality." They don't teach that in acting school.

Why Do Fools Fall in Love ★ ★
R, 115 m., 1998

Halle Berry (Zola Taylor), Larenz Tate (Frankie Lymon), Vivica A. Fox (Elizabeth Waters), Lela Rochon (Emira Eagle), Paul Mazursky (Morris Levy). Directed by Gregory Nava and produced by Paul Hall and Stephen Nemeth. Written by Tina Andrews. Screenplay by Andrews.

Frankie Lymon was thirteen when he had his big hit record and twenty-five when he died. The record fell like a gift from the sky, hit the top of the charts, and can still be heard on the golden oldies stations. The rest of his life played like the flip side. *Why Do Fools Fall in Love* tells the story of how he married three women (at least according to them), got into trouble with drugs and the army, and self-destructed prematurely, leaving his ex-wives and/or widows squabbling in court over the estate.

There are several angles this material might have been approached from, and the director tries several without hitting on one that works. By the end of the film we're not even left with anyone to root for; we realize with a little astonishment, waiting for the court verdict, that we don't care who wins.

The movie is not really about Frankie Lymon (Larenz Tate), who remains an enigma. Nor does it have many insights into the three claimants to his estate: Zola Taylor (Halle Berry), a singer with the Platters, who was his first girl and his second wife; Elizabeth Waters (Vivica A. Fox), a shoplifter who loved him so much she became a hooker to pay for his drug rehab; and Emira Eagle (Lela Rochon), a churchgoing waitress who was there when he needed her after he was drafted into the army and sent to Georgia for training.

What made Frankie run? The movie clearly doesn't know. It sets the story against a convincing backdrop of the 1950s rock 'n' roll industry, provides some high-energy musical sequences, and finds moments of drama as Frankie is beaten by drug money collectors, steals a mink stole from one woman to give to another, and threatens to throw dogs out the window—all while somehow remaining a lovable madcap. Well, most of the time.

The usual generic conventions seem missing. There is no real sense of loss in Frankie's death, since his early promise, if genuine, was so quickly dissipated. There is no sense that he betrayed the three women: He loved them all, after his fashion, and was so needy he simply reached out to the closest one. An awkward courtroom scene at the end belatedly tries to pin some of the blame on a record producer (Paul Mazursky), who stole cowriting credit and perhaps a lot of Frankie's profits, but the producer, if guilty, was still not responsible for most of the events in the movie. Frankie was. His song should have been, "When I'm Not With the One I Love, I Love the One I'm With."

The movie's director is Gregory Nava, whose artistry in films like *El Norte, My Family,* and *Selena* seems missing this time: His films usually proceed from passion and commitment, and here the inspiration seems to be missing. It's as if someone read about Lymon's three wives in court and decided it would be a great story without ever deciding what the story was.

The four principal actors all provide the spectacle of talent without purpose: They do what they can with their characters and their scenes, but the screenplay doesn't provide them with an arc or a purpose. When their characters reappear, we haven't been waiting for them. When they're offscreen, we don't miss them. That's true even of Frankie, who is missing a fair amount of the time.

What approach might have worked? Hard to say. Maybe the whole thing should have been seen exclusively through Frankie's eyes, as a kid who has his fifteen minutes of fame at an early age and then dines out for the rest of his life on other people's memories. That would have meant jettisoning the whole court case and its flashbacks, but the court stuff doesn't work anyway. Maybe straight chronology would have been a better idea, allowing Frankie to be the focus, and allowing us to follow his moves more clearly from one woman to the next and back again. As it stands, *Why Do Fools Fall in Love* never convinces us its story is worth telling, and never finds a way to tell it, even if it is.

Wide Awake ★ ★
PG, 90 m., 1998

Joseph Cross (Joshua Beal), Timothy Reifsnyder (Dave O'Hara), Dana Delany (Mrs. Beal), Denis Leary (Mr. Beal), Robert Loggia (Grandpa Beal), Rosie O'Donnell (Sister Terry), Julia Stiles (Neena Beal). Directed by M. Night Shyamalan and produced by Cary Woods and Cathy Konrad. Screenplay by Shyamalan.

In an opening scene of *Wide Awake,* the fifth-grade kids in a Catholic school have a spirited discussion about whether the unbaptized can get into heaven. This rang a bell. Morning religion class in my grade school was much the same; the nuns tried to teach us principles, and we were always getting sidetracked on technicalities.

When *Wide Awake* observes moments like these in the classroom, it's an entertaining film. I liked, for example, Rosie O'Donnell's performance as Sister Terry, a Philadelphia Phillies fan, and was reminded of my own teacher, Sister Marie Donald, who was also our basketball coach. A film accurately remembering Catholic school in the pre–Vatican II era could be a charmer.

But the movie has higher and, I'm afraid, more contrived goals. Its hero is young Joshua (Joseph Cross), who has been depressed ever since his beloved grandfather (Robert Loggia) died of bone marrow cancer. He mopes about his granddad's room, he doesn't want to get up for school, he is the despair of his parents (Dana Delany and Denis Leary) and annoys his sister (Julia Stiles). Finally he announces to his best friend, Dave (Timothy Reifsnyder), that he's going on a mission to find out if his grandfather is okay.

Joshua's mission, which occupies much of the movie, involves his demand for a sign from heaven. Along the way, he also sneaks into a girls' school to cross-examine a cardinal and holds a photo of the pope hostage in the rain. Does he get his sign? The movie is rated PG, a tip-off that it does not end with Joshua taking a tough position in favor of existential nothingness. (It is clever how the movie hides the "sign" in plain view all along.)

I wonder who the movie was made for. Smaller kids, I'm afraid, will find it both slow and depressing, especially the parts about why God allows bad things to happen. The health problems of Dave, the best friend, may also come as an unsettling shock. Older kids, on the other hand, are likely to find it too cute, and adults are better advised to see the French film *Ponette*, a more intelligent treatment of a child asking hard questions about heaven.

The film does have some pleasures, however. One of them is Rosie O'Donnell's performance. Although I can relate to her cheerful energy on television, I've not been a fan of her work in movies—especially not in *Exit to Eden* (1994), where she played a dominatrix as if her whip didn't fit.

In *Wide Awake*, however, she finds a role that she seems comfortable in and creates a character I would have liked to see more of. Becoming a nun is sometimes seen as a renunciation of independence and freedom, but for some women it is liberating—a role they feel relaxed in, allowing them to express themselves. Movies give us priests and nuns who are tortured and neurotic, but O'Donnell's Sister Terry seems happy and fulfilled; her role suits her personality.

As for the rest of the movie: Well, Joseph Cross is an effective and convincing little performer, but I always felt I was looking at a movie, not the actions of a real little boy. At the end of his film, when he reads his essay to his class, I asked myself if fifth-graders really thought and wrote like that. No, I decided, they don't. But screenwriters do.

Wilde ★ ★ ★ ½
R, 116 m., 1998

Stephen Fry (Oscar Wilde), Jude Law (Lord Alfred Douglas), Vanessa Redgrave (Lady Speranza Wilde), Jennifer Ehle (Constance Wilde), Gemma Jones (Lady Queensberry), Judy Parfitt (Lady Mount-Temple), Michael Sheen (Robert Ross), Zoe Wanamaker (Ada Leverson), Tom Wilkinson (Marquis of Queensberry). Directed by Brian Gilbert and produced by Marc Samuelson and Peter Samuelson. Screenplay by Julian Mitchell, based on the book *Oscar Wilde* by Richard Ellmann.

"Wickedness," Oscar Wilde said, "is a myth invented by good people to account for the curious attractiveness of others." Wilde himself was considered in some quarters the most wicked man of his time, in others the most attractive—a gifted artist who was a martyr to convention.

At the very peak of his fame, after his play *The Importance of Being Earnest* opened to wild success in 1895, Wilde was convicted of "gross indecency," and spent his few remaining years in prison or decline. A century later his reputation, personal and professional, could not stand higher, and this new biopic joins two new stage productions in celebrating his rise, fall, and immortality. If he were alive today he would no doubt describe his homosexuality as a good career move.

Wilde's personal tragedy would be of little lasting interest were it not for the enduring popularity of his work, and the sensational nature of his fall. There were no doubt as many homosexuals in Wilde's day as there are now, but most of them either repressed their feelings or kept them secret. Homosexual behavior was, after all, against the law. It was Wilde's misfortune to fall in love with a reckless and vain young man who hated his pigheaded father, and wanted to use Wilde's fame as a taunt.

Worse luck that the father was the marquess of Queensbury, a famous figure in boxing and horse racing. Still worse luck that when the marquess left an insulting message at Wilde's club, Wilde unwisely sued him. And dashedly bad luck that the marquis's attorneys were able to produce in court "rent boys" from a male brothel, who testified that the marquis was correct in describing Wilde as a sodomite.

Consider that a century later gay men are being knighted, and you see what bad timing it was to be born in 1854. In another sense, Wilde's genius required a backdrop of Victorian stuffiness. Many of the people in his audiences understood what he was writing between the lines, but accepted it as funny and daring—as long as it stayed between the lines. ("Earnest," for example, was in Wilde's time a synonym for "gay.") Wilde was famous for his quips and one-liners, which survive because they almost always contain a center of truth.

With immense self-enjoyment, he punctured hypocrisy ("I never take any notice of what common people say, and I never interfere with what charming people do").

Brian Gilbert's *Wilde*, with a screenplay by Julian Mitchell, based on Richard Ellmann's famous biography, has the good fortune to star Stephen Fry, a British author, actor, and comedian who looks a lot like Wilde and has many of the same attributes: He is very tall, he is somewhat plump, he is gay, he is funny, he makes his conversation into an art. That he is also a fine actor is important, because the film requires him to show many conflicting aspects of Wilde's life: How he loved his wife and children, how his homosexuality was oriented not so much toward the physical as toward the idealistic, how he was so successful for so long in charming everyone in his life that he actually believed he could charm an English courtroom out of a sentence for sodomy.

Wilde was the dandy as superstar; in the years before mass media, he wrote best-sellers and long-running plays, and went on enormously popular lecture tours (the film opens with him down in a silver mine in Nevada, reading poetry to the miners and beaming upon their muscular torsos). He invented the type exploited by the later Elvis Presley: the peacock in full plumage, kidding himself.

Born in Dublin, he came out of Ireland more or less expecting to behave as a heterosexual, and was sincere in his marriage to Constance (Jennifer Ehle). He loved his children, and the movie uses one of his children's stories as a counterpoint. But when a young Canadian houseguest named Robbie (Michael Sheen) boldly approached him in the parlor late one night, Wilde responded. He might have settled into an existence of discreet bisexuality had it not been for his meeting, some years later, the beautiful young Lord Alfred Douglas (Jude Law), known as "Bosie"—who was, if Wilde had only realized it, more interested in his fame than his body.

Bosie liked to flirt and flaunt. There is a scene in a restaurant where the two men smoke, smile, and hold hands, while all of London seems to look on. Bosie did that to shock. Wilde did it because he was a genuinely sweet man who believed in expressing his feelings, and was naive about how much leeway he'd be given because of his fame. Bosie's physical interest in Wilde soon waned, and he took the playwright to a famous male brothel, which Wilde seems to have seen as an opportunity to expose handsome working-class lads to the possibilities of higher culture.

It is so sad how ripe Wilde was for destruction. We can see the beginning of the end in an extraordinary scene in a restaurant, where Wilde calmly charms the tough, angry marquess of Queensbury (Tom Wilkinson). The marquess is happy to exchange tips about fly-fishing, but warns Wilde to stay away from his son (ironic, since Wilde was the seduced, not the seducer). Soon it all comes down to a humiliating courtroom scene, despite the desperate advice of loyal Robbie to stay far away from the law. Those who know of Wilde at thirdhand may be under the impression that the marquess hauled him into court; actually, it was Wilde who sued the marquess for slander.

Stephen Fry brings a depth and gentleness to the role that says what can be said about Oscar Wilde: That he was a funny and gifted idealist in a society that valued hypocrisy above honesty. Because he could make people laugh, he thought they always would. Bosie lived on for years, boring generations of undergraduates with his fatuous egotism. He grew gross and ugly. Wilde once said that he could forgive a man for what he was, but not for what he became.

Wild Man Blues ★ ★ ★
PG, 104 m., 1998

A documentary film directed by Barbara Kopple and produced by Jean Doumanian. With Woody Allen, Soon-Yi Previn, Letty Aronson, Eddy Davis, and others.

Early in *Wild Man Blues*, as they arrive in Europe, a subtitle identifies one of the women with Woody Allen as "Letty Aronson, Woody Allen's sister," and the other simply as "Soon-Yi Previn." One can only speculate how long a subtitle it would have taken to explain *her* presence. "Theoretically, this should be fun for us," Allen observes at the start of a tour with his New Orleans jazz band. Theoretically, it should, but the greatest pleasure for Woody seems to be having his worst fears confirmed. An omelet in Spain seems "vulcanized." A gondola ride in Venice leads to seasickness. An audience in Rome is "anesthetized, like a jury." In Milan he worries that the hotel might bread their laundry.

Wild Man Blues, Barbara Kopple's documentary about the tour, could be retitled *The Innocents Abroad*—although Woody, sixtyish, not Soon-Yi, twenty-fiveish, is the innocent. What was I expecting from this scrutiny of Allen on tour with the adopted daughter of his former companion Mia Farrow? Perhaps something slightly scandalous—the aging rake flaunting his Asian girlfriend in continental hot spots. But it's not like that at all.

Woody and Soon-Yi, who was soon to become his wife, seem to have a stable and workable relationship, in which Allen plays his usual role as the dubious neurotic, and Miss Previn is calm and authoritative—a combination of wife, mother, and manager. She seems to be good for him. Whether he is good for her, of course, has been a matter of controversy, but this film supports what Allen said when their affair was first revealed: "The heart has its reasons."

Soon-Yi seems more like the adult in the partnership. At one point, she advises him to be more animated when he appears on stage with his band. "I'm not gonna bob my head or tap my feet," he says. "They want to see you bob a little," she says, and he gets defensive: "I'm appropriately animated for a human being in the context in which I appear." But at the next concert, he bobs a little.

Little romantic passion is revealed on-screen, perhaps because of mutual reticence. At one point, checking into another of the vast hotel suites they occupy, Woody looks around hopefully for a real king-size bed, instead of two twin beds pushed up against each other. No luck. He frets that he could fall into the crack between the two beds and get stuck. Here is an example of their morning conversation: She: "The shower was excellent, wasn't it?" He: "Yes, great pressure."

The ostensible purpose of the documentary is to showcase Allen's seven-piece band and its music. But the audiences come to see Woody more than to listen to the music, and so do we. The music is entertaining, and the crowds like

it (except for the stone-faced concertgoers in Rome, who look like they paid for their benefit tickets by donating blood). Eddy Davis, the banjo player and musical director, remembers that he first met Allen at Mister Kelly's in Chicago in the 1960s, and even then "he was a serious clarinetist."

Apparently terrified that he might say something funny and betray his serious calling as a musician, Allen introduces the numbers with the gravity of a heart surgeon announcing his next incision. Forced to attend a series of receptions before or after the concerts, he deals graciously with some fans, impatiently with others. When an official in black tie announces, "I present to you my wife," Allen nods and says, "This is the notorious Soon-Yi Previn."

Kopple made the Oscar-winning documentaries *Harlan County, USA* and *American Dream*, both about labor disputes. She might seem an unlikely choice for this material, but no doubt her track record gained Allen's trust. To his credit he hasn't exercised veto power over the results (if he had, he probably would have removed his observation that as a child Soon-Yi "was eating out of garbage pails").

In a closing sequence, Woody and Soon-Yi visit the director's elderly parents in New York. His father, examining various trophies presented to Woody on tour, seems more interested in the quality of the engraving than in the honors. His mother admits she would have preferred "a nice Jewish girl" to Soon-Yi, and wonders if her son might not, after all, have been more successful as a pharmacist.

Woody seems at times to be inviting his parents' comments with leading questions, and the reunion has been interpreted by some as illustrating his "Jewish self-hate," but that's a charge sometimes misused to punish anything other than perfect piety and filial regard. So Woody didn't like Hebrew school? I was bored during Catechism. A lot of Protestant kids would rather play baseball than go to Sunday school. That's not self-hate; it's human nature.

Wild Things ★ ★ ★
R, 113 m., 1998

Kevin Bacon (Ray Duquette), Matt Dillon (Sam Lombardo), Neve Campbell (Suzie Toller), Theresa Russell (Sandra Van Ryan), Denise Richards (Kelly Van Ryan), Daphne Rubin-Vega (Gloria Perez), Robert Wagner (Tom Baxter), Bill Murray (Ken Bowden), Carrie Snodgress (Ruby). Directed by John McNaughton and produced by Rodney Liber and Steven A. Jones. Screenplay by Stephen Peters.

Wild Things is lurid trash, with a plot so twisted they're still explaining it during the closing titles. It's like a three-way collision between a soft-core sex film, a soap opera, and a B-grade *noir*. I liked it. This being the latest example of Florida *noir* (hot on the high heels of *Palmetto*), it has a little of everything, including ominous shots of alligators looking like they know more than they're telling.

The movie solidifies Neve Campbell's position as the queen of slick exploitation, gives Matt Dillon and Kevin Bacon lots of chances to squint ominously, and has a sex scene with Denise Richards (of *Starship Troopers*) that is either gratuitous or indispensable, depending on your point of view. Plus it has Bill Murray as a storefront lawyer who delivers twenty minutes of hilarity, which at the time is the last thing we're expecting.

Movies like this either entertain or offend audiences; there's no neutral ground. Either you're a connoisseur of melodramatic comic vulgarity, or you're not. You know who you are. I don't want to get any postcards telling me this movie is in bad taste. I'm warning you: It *is* in bad taste. Bad taste elevated to the level of demented sleaze.

The plot: Matt Dillon plays Lombardo, a high school teacher who was "educator of the year" and has an engraved crystal goblet to prove it. As the movie opens, he writes SEX CRIMES on the board at a school assembly, and introduces speakers on the subject, including police officers Duquette (Bacon) and Perez (Daphne Rubin-Vega). In the back of the room, a student named Suzie (Neve Campbell) stalks out, suggesting which part of her anatomy one of the speakers can kiss. I wasn't sure if she was referring to Bacon or Dillon,

but this is the kind of plot where it works either way.

Then we meet Kelly Van Ryan (Denise Richards), the richest kid in the upscale Florida enclave of Blue Bay. She's got the hots for Mr. Lombardo. She follows him home, asks for rides, washes his Jeep, and turns up in his living room so thoroughly wetted-down she reminds us of the classic Hollywood line about Esther Williams: "Dry, she ain't much. Wet, she's a star!" Later, we see her leaving the teacher's humble bungalow, looking mad.

Why is she mad? I will tread carefully; a publicist was stationed at the door of the screening, handing out letters begging the press not to give away the ending. The problem is, the ending of this film begins at the forty-five-minute mark and is so complicated, I doubt if it *can* be given away. What sets up everything, in any event, is Kelly's testimony that she was raped by Mr. Lombardo—and the surprise testimony of Suzie that she was too.

Suzie lives in a trashy trailer out behind an alligator farm run by Carrie Snodgress. But Kelly lives on the right side of town, in manorial splendor, with her bikini-wearing, martini-drinking mom (Theresa Russell), who has had an affair with Lombardo. Hearing her daughter has been raped by him, Mom is enraged, and snarls, "That SOB must be insane to think he can do this to me!" That's the kind of dialogue that elevates ordinary trash into the kind that glows in the dark. Here's another line, after a murder: "My mother would kill me if she knew I took the Rover!"

Bill Murray lands in the middle of this pie like a plum from heaven. Wearing a neck brace as part of an insurance scam, Murray runs his shabby storefront law office like a big downtown spread; when he asks his secretary to "show Mr. Duquette his way out," all she needs to do is look up and say, "Good-bye," since the door is in arm's reach of everything else in the office.

Without giving away the ending, that's about all I can tell you. See the movie and you'll understand how very much I must leave unsaid. The director is John McNaughton, whose work includes two inspired films, *Henry: Portrait of a Serial Killer* and *Normal Life*. He likes to show audiences how wrong their expectations are by upsetting them. That worked in *Henry* as grim tragedy, and it works here as satire.

Don't leave when the end titles start to roll. Credit cookies (those little bonus scenes they stick in between Key Grip and Location Catering) are usually used for outtakes showing Matthau and Lemmon blowing their lines, or Jackie Chan breaking his legs. In *Wild Things,* McNaughton does something new: flashbacks, showing us stuff that was offscreen the first time around. The movie is still explaining itself as the curtains close, and then the audience explains it some more on its way out of the theater.

Wild Wild West ★

PG-13, 107 m., 1999

Will Smith (James T. West), Kevin Kline (Artemus Gordon), Kenneth Branagh (Dr. Arliss Loveless), Salma Hayek (Rita Escobar), Ted Levine (McGrath), Frederique Van Der Wal (Amazonia), Musetta Vander (Munitia), Sofia Eng (Miss Lippenreider), M. Emmet Walsh (Coleman). Directed by Barry Sonnenfeld and produced by Sonnenfeld and Jon Peters. Screenplay by S. S. Wilson, Brent Maddock, Jeffrey Price, and Peter S. Seaman, based on a story by Jim Thomas and John Thomas.

Wild Wild West is a comedy dead zone. You stare in disbelief as scenes flop and die. The movie is all concept and no content; the elaborate special effects are like watching money burn on the screen. You know something has gone wrong when a story is about two heroes in the Old West, and the last shot is of a mechanical spider riding off into the sunset.

Will Smith and Kevin Kline costar, as special federal agents who are assigned by President U. S. Grant to investigate the disappearance of lots of top scientists. They stumble over a plot to assassinate Grant by a megalomaniac who wants to give half the country back to Britain and Spain, and keep the rest in the hands of the villain. Salma Hayek teams up with them, as a woman who says her father was one of the kidnapped geniuses. The bad guy (Kenneth Branagh) is a mad inventor who makes giant steam-powered iron tarantulas and spiders, which are not very practical in Monument Valley, but who cares?

Certainly not anyone in the movie. Smith and Kline have so little chemistry they seem to be acting in front of rear-projections of each other. They go through the motions, but there's no eye contact. Imagine Bill Clinton and Kenneth Starr as partners in a celebrity golf tournament.

The Kline character is said to be a master of disguise, and first appears in drag as a dance hall girl, wearing a false plastic bosom so persuasive that when a siren turns up later in the movie, her décolletage looks unconvincing by comparison. That doesn't stop Smith from giving her cleavage a few jolly thumps, and then telling a white lynch mob he was simply following the example of his African ancestors, who communicated by pounding on drums— and bosoms, I guess. (In a movie where almost nothing is funny, the race references are painfully lame.)

One of the running gags is about how the Kline character can invent almost anything, right on the spot. He rigs a rail car so that it can shoot people into the air, have them fall through openings that appear in the roof, and land in a chair. The rig works in opposition to the first law of motion, but never mind: In a movie where anything can happen, does it matter that anything does?

Kenneth Branagh's character has no body from the waist down, but operates from a clever wheelchair and, later, with mechanical legs. He has weird facial hair and lots of bizarre plans, and an evil general on his payroll has a weird miniature ear trumpet permanently screwed into the side of his face. His gigantic artificial war machines look like they were recycled from *Star Wars,* right down to their command cockpits.

There are moments when all artifice fails and you realize you are regarding desperate actors, trapped on the screen, fully aware they've been left hanging out to dry. Consider an early scene where Will Smith and a sexy girl are embracing in a water tank when the evil General McGrath rides into town. Smith is made to look at McGrath out of a knothole, while continuing to make automatic midair smooching movements with his lips—as if he doesn't realize he's not still kissing the woman. Uh, huh.

Wild Wild West is so bad it violates not one but two rules from *Ebert's Bigger Little Movie*

Glossary. By casting M. Emmet Walsh as the train engineer, it invalidates the Stanton-Walsh Rule, which states that no movie starring Harry Dean Stanton or M. Emmet Walsh can be altogether bad. And by featuring Kevin Kline without facial hair, it violates the Kevin Kline Mustache Principle, which observes that Kline wears a mustache in comedies but is clean-shaven in serious roles. Of course, Kline can always appeal on the grounds that although he is clean-shaven in his principal role here, he sports facial hair in three other roles he plays in the movie—or perhaps he could use the defense that *Wild Wild West* is not a comedy.

William Shakespeare's A Midsummer Night's Dream ★ ★ ★
PG-13, 115 m., 1999

Kevin Kline (Nick Bottom), Michelle Pfeiffer (Titania), Rupert Everett (Oberon), Stanley Tucci (Puck [Robin]), Calista Flockhart (Helena), Anna Friel (Hermia), Christian Bale (Demetrius), Dominic West (Lysander), David Strathairn (Theseus), Sophie Marceau (Hippolyta). Directed by Michael Hoffman and produced by Leslie Urdang and Hoffman. Screenplay by Hoffman, based on the play by William Shakespeare.

"Reason and love keep little company together nowadays."

So says Bottom in Shakespeare's *A Midsummer Night's Dream,* and he could be describing the play he occupies. It is an enchanted folly, suggesting that romance is a matter of chance, since love is blind; at the right moment we are likely to fall in love with the first person our eyes light upon. Much of the play's fun comes during a long night in the forest, where a mischief-maker anoints the eyes of sleeping lovers with magic potions that cause them to adore the first person they see upon awakening.

This causes all sorts of confusions, not least when Titania, the Fairy Queen herself, falls in love with a weaver who has grown donkey's ears. The weaver is Bottom (Kevin Kline), and he and the mischievous Puck (Stanley Tucci) are the most important characters in the play, although it also involves dukes, kings, queens, and high-born lovers. Bottom has a good heart

and bumbles through, and Puck (also called Robin Goodfellow) spreads misunderstanding wherever he goes. The young lovers are pawns in a magic show: When they can't see the one they love, they love the one they see.

Michael Hoffman's new film of *William Shakespeare's A Midsummer Night's Dream* (who else's?) is updated to the nineteenth century, set in Italy, and furnished with bicycles and operatic interludes. But it is founded on Shakespeare's language and is faithful, by and large, to the original play. Harold Bloom complains in his wise best-seller *Shakespeare: The Invention of the Human* that the play's romantic capers have been twisted by modern adaptations into "the notion that sexual violence and bestiality are at the center of this humane and wise drama." He might approve of this version, which is gentle and lighthearted, and portrays Bottom not as a lustful animal but as a nice enough fellow who has had the misfortune to wake up with donkey's ears—"amiably innocent, and not very bawdy," as Bloom describes him.

Kevin Kline is, of course, the embodiment of amiability, as he bashfully parries the passionate advances of Titania (Michelle Pfeiffer). Her eyes have been anointed with magical ointment at the behest of her husband, Oberon, (Rupert Everett), who hopes to steal away the young boy they both dote on. When she opens them to regard Bottom, she is besotted with love and inspired to some of Shakespeare's most lyrical poetry:

I'll give thee fairies to attend on thee;
And they shall fetch thee jewels from
* the deep,*
And sing, while thou on pressed flowers
* dost sleep.*

Meanwhile, more magical potions, distributed carelessly by Puck, have hopelessly confused the relationships among four young people who were introduced at the beginning of the play. They are Helena (Calista Flockhart), Hermia (Anna Friel), Demetrius (Christian Bale), and Lysander (Dominic West). Now follow this closely. Hermia has been promised by her father to Demetrius, but she loves Lysander. Demetrius was Helena's lover, but now claims to prefers Hermia. Hermia is offered three cruel choices by the duke, Theseus (David Strathairn): marry according to her father's wishes, go into a convent, or die. Desperate, she flees to a nearby wood with Lysander, her true love. Helena, who loves Demetrius, tips him off to follow them; maybe if he sees his intended in the arms of another man, he will return to Helena's arms.

The wood grows crowded. Also turning up at the same moonlit rendezvous are Bottom and his friends, workmen from the village who plan to rehearse a play to be performed at the wedding of Theseus and *his* intended, Queen Hippolyta (Sophie Marceau). And flickering about the glen are Oberon, Titania, Puck, and assorted fairies. Only the most determined typecasting helps us tell them apart: As many times as I've been through this play in one form or another, I can't always distinguish the four young lovers, who seem interchangeable. They function mostly to be meddled with by Puck's potions.

Hoffman, whose wonderful *Restoration* recreated a time of fire and plague, here conducts with a playful touch. There are small gems of stagecraft for all of the actors, including Snout, the village tinker, who plays a wall in the performance for the duke, and makes a circle with his thumb and finger to represent a chink in it. It's wonderful to behold Pfeiffer's infatuation with the donkey-eared Bottom, whom she winds in her arms as "doth the woodbine the sweet honeysuckle gently twist"; her love is so real, we almost believe it. Kline's Bottom tactfully humors her mad infatuation, good-natured and accepting. And Tucci's Puck suggests sometimes that he has a darker side, but is not so much malicious as incompetent.

Midsummer Night's Dream is another entry in Shakespeare's recent renaissance on film. Consider *Much Ado About Nothing,* Ian McKellen's *Richard III,* Al Pacino's documentary *Looking for Richard,* Laurence Fishburne as *Othello,* Branagh's *Hamlet,* Helena Bonham Carter in *Twelfth Night,* Baz Luhrmann's modern street version of *Romeo and Juliet,* the Lear-inspired *A Thousand Acres,* the remake of *Taming of the Shrew* as *10 Things I Hate About You,* and the bard's celebration in *Shakespeare in Love, Hamlet* with Ethan Hawke, Branagh's *Love's Labour's Lost,* Mekhi Phifer as Othello in the modern urban drama *O,* and

Anthony Hopkins in *Titus,* based on the rarely staged Titus Andronicus ("All Rome's a wilderness of tigers").

Why is Shakespeare so popular with filmmakers when he contains so few car chases and explosions? Because he is the measuring stick by which actors and directors test themselves. His insights into human nature are so true that he has, as Bloom argues in his book, actually created our modern idea of the human personality. Before Hamlet asked, "To be, or not to be?" dramatic characters just were. Ever since, they have known and questioned themselves. Even in a comedy like *Midsummer,* there are quick flashes of brilliance that help us see ourselves. "What fools these mortals be," indeed.

Windhorse ★ ★

NO MPAA RATING, 97 m., 1999

Dadon (Dolkar), Name Withheld (Pema), Jampa Kelsang (Dorjee), Richard Chang (Duan-ping), Lu Yu (Mr. Du), Tenzin Pema (Young Dolkar), Deepak Tserin (Young Dorjee), Pasang Dolma (Young Pema). Directed and produced by Paul Wagner. Screenplay by Julia Elliot, Thupten Tsering, and Wagner.

Windhorse is a well-meaning but clunky film about a Tibetan family's life under Chinese occupation. Its heart is in the right place, and there's intrinsic interest in a film that was daringly shot partly on location in Tibet itself. But anyone interested enough in the cause of Tibet to attend the film is probably going to consider the story a simplistic melodrama.

The prologue begins in 1979, when children playing in the streets become witnesses to the killing of a relative by Chinese soldiers. We jump forward to 1998, and meet the children as grown-ups. Dolkar (Dadon) sings in a karaoke bar and dates a Chinese broadcast official named Duan-ping (Richard Chang). Her brother Dorjee (Jampa Kelsang), who hates the Chinese, spends most of his time drinking and playing pool. Their cousin Pema (played by a Tibetan actress whose name has been withheld) has become a nun.

Duan-ping, more of a dupe than a villain, realizes he can curry favor with his superiors by recruiting Dolkar to sing on the local TV station, which carries mostly propaganda. She rehearses songs in praise of Chairman Mao, and invites her boyfriend home for tea; her grandmother spits in it in the kitchen before coming in to serve.

Meanwhile, Pema's nunnery is ill-treated by Chinese officials, who forbid anyone to possess a picture of the Dalai Lama—or even think of him. One day in the market she grows so filled with emotion that she shouts anti-Chinese slogans and is arrested. Eventually she is delivered by the Chinese to the home of her cousins so badly beaten her life is in danger.

Under these circumstances, can Dolkar still go ahead with the TV show? Will Dorjee sober up and play a role? What will happen to Pema? These are all the matters of melodrama, and it's at this level that the movie chooses to work; change the name and the costumes, and it's as simplistic as any other propaganda film. Perhaps on video, in the right hands, in Tibet, it will play as a powerful statement. But judged for its film qualities rather than its politics, it's routine. The qualities that recommend it are the authentic locations and the conviction of the actors, who deserved a more challenging screenplay.

Footnote: The film's value as politics is underlined by a controversy at the 1998 Hawaii International Film Festival, where the Chinese protested its inclusion in competition for the main prize. Director Paul Wagner at first withdrew the film from the festival, then decided to allow it to show out of competition, on the reasonable grounds that he would rather have it seen than make a point.

Wing Commander ★
PG-13, 100 m., 1999

Freddie Prinze Jr. (Blair), Saffron Burrows (Deveraux), Matthew Lillard (Maniac), Tcheky Karyo (Paladin), Jurgen Prochnow (Gerald), David Suchet (Sansky), Ginny Holder (Rosie Forbes), David Warner (Tolwyn). Directed by Chris Roberts and produced by Todd Moyer. Screenplay by Roberts.

Jurgen Prochnow, who played the submarine captain in *Das Boot,* is one of the stars of *Wing Commander,* and no wonder: This is a sub movie exported to deep space, complete with the obligatory warning about the onboard oxygen running low. "Torpedoes incoming!" a watch officer shouts. "Brace yourself!" It's 500 years in the future. If the weapons developed by the race of evil Kilrathi only inspire you to "brace yourself," we might reasonably ask what the Kilrathi have been doing with their time.

Other marine notes: "Hard to port!" is a command at one point. Reasonable at sea, but in space, where a ship is not sailing on a horizontal surface, not so useful. "Quiet! There's a destroyer!" someone shouts, and then everyone on board holds their breath, as there are subtle sonar "pings" on the sound track, and we hear the rumble of a giant vessel overhead. Or underhead. Wherever. "In space," as *Alien* reminded us, "no one can hear you scream." There is an excellent reason for that: Vacuums do not conduct sound waves, not even those caused by giant destroyers.

Such logic is, of course, irrelevant to *Wing Commander,* a movie based on a video game and looking like one a lot of the time, as dashing pilots fly around blowing up enemy targets. Our side kills about a zillion Kilrathi for every one of our guys that buys it, but when heroes die, of course, they die in the order laid down by ancient movie clichés. The moment I saw that one of the pilots was an attractive black woman (Ginny Holder), I knew she'd go down, or up, in flames.

The plot involves war between the humans and the Kilrathi, who have refused all offers of peace and wish only to be targets in the crosshairs of video computer screens. Indeed, according to a Web page, they hope to "destroy the universe," which seems self-defeating. The Kilrathi are ugly turtleoid creatures with goatees, who talk like voice synthesizers cranked way down, heavy on the bass.

Against them stand the noble earthlings, although the film's hero, Blair (Freddie Prinze Jr.) is suspect in some circles because he is a half-breed. Yes, his mother was a Pilgrim. Who were the Pilgrims? Humans who were the original space voyagers and developed a gene useful for instinctively navigating in "space-time itself." (Just about all navigation is done in space-time itself, but never mind.) Pilgrims went too far and dared too much, so timid later men resented them—but if you need someone to skip across a Gravity Hole, a Pilgrim is your man.

There are actors on board capable of splendid performances. The commander of the fleet is played by David Warner, who brings utter believability to, alas, banal dialogue. Two of the other officers, played by Tcheky Karyo and Prochnow, are also fine; I'd like to see them in a real navy movie. Prinze shows again an easy grace and instant likability. Matthew Lillard, as a hotshot pilot named Maniac, gets into a daredevil competition with the Holder character, and I enjoyed their energy. And the perfectly named Saffron Burrows has a pleasing presence as the head of the pilot squadron, although having recently seen her in a real movie (Mike Figgis's *The Loss of Sexual Innocence,* at Sundance), I assume she took this role to pay the utility bills.

These actors, alas, are at the service of a submoronic script and special effects that look like a video game writ large. *Wing Commander* arrived at the end of a week that began with the death of the creator of *2001: A Space Odyssey.* Close the pod bay door, Hal. And turn off the lights.

The Winslow Boy ★ ★ ★ ½
G, 110 m., 1999

Nigel Hawthorne (Arthur Winslow), Jeremy Northam (Sir Robert Morton), Rebecca Pidgeon (Catherine Winslow), Gemma Jones (Grace Winslow), Guy Edwards (Ronnie Winslow), Matthew Pidgeon (Dickie Winslow), Colin Stinton (Desmond Curry), Aden Gillett (John Watherstone). Directed by David Mamet and produced by Sarah Green. Screenplay by Mamet, based on the play by Terence Rattigan.

The Winslow Boy, based on a play set in 1912, is said to be a strange choice for David Mamet, whose work usually involves lowlifes and con men, gamblers and thieves. Not really. This film, like many of his stories, is about whether an offscreen crime really took place. And it employs his knack for using the crime as a surface distraction while his real subject takes form at a buried level. *The Winslow Boy* seems to be about a young boy accused of theft. It is actually about a father prepared to ruin his family to prove that the boy's word (and by extension his own word) can be trusted. And about a woman who conducts two courtships in plain view while a third, the real one, takes place entirely between the lines.

The movie is based on a 1940s play by Terence Rattigan, inspired by a true story. It involves the Winslow family of South Kensington, London—the father a retired bank official, wife pleased with their life, adult daughter a suffragette, older son at Oxford, younger son a cadet at the Royal Naval Academy. One day the young cadet, named Ronnie, is found standing terrified in the garden. He has been expelled from school for stealing a five-shilling postal order.

In a scene that establishes the moral foundation for the entire story, his father, Arthur, calls him into the study after dinner and demands the truth, adding, "A lie between us cannot be hidden." Did he steal the money? "No, father, I didn't." The father is played by Nigel Hawthorne *(The Madness of King George),* who is stern, firm, and on the brink of old age. He believes his son and calls in the family solicitor to mount a defense. Soon one of the most famous attorneys in London has been hired: Sir Robert Morton (Jeremy Northam), who led the defense of Oscar Wilde. The father devotes his family's large but finite resources to the expensive legal battle, which eventually leads to the older son being brought home from Oxford, servants being dismissed, and possessions being sold. Arthur's wife, Grace (Gemma Jones), protests that justice is not worth the price being paid, but Arthur persists in his unwavering obsession.

The court case inspires newspaper headlines, popular songs, public demonstrations, and debates in Parliament. It proceeds on the surface level of the film. Underneath, hidden in a murk of emotional contradictions, is the buried life of the suffragette daughter, Catherine (Rebecca Pidgeon). She is engaged to the respectable, bloodless John Watherstone (Aden Gillett). She has known for years that Desmond, the family solicitor (Colin Stinton), is in love with her. As the case gains notoriety, John's ardor cools: He fears the name Winslow is becoming a laughingstock. And as John fades, Desmond's hopes grow. But the only interesting tension between Catherine and a man involves her disapproval of the great Sir Robert

Morton, who rejects her feelings about women's equality and indeed disagrees with more or less every idea she possesses.

It is an interesting law of romance that a truly strong woman will choose a strong man who disagrees with her over a weak one who goes along. Strength demands intelligence, intelligence demands stimulation, and weakness is boring. It is better to find a partner you can contend with for a lifetime than one who accommodates you because he doesn't really care. That is the psychological principle on which Mamet's hidden story is founded, and it all leads up to the famous closing line of Rattigan's play, "How little you know about men." A line innocuous in itself, but electrifying in context.

In a lesser film, we would be required to get involved in the defense of young Ronnie Winslow, and there would be a big courtroom scene and artificial suspense and an obligatory payoff. Mamet doesn't make films on automatic pilot, and Rattigan's play is not about who is right, but about how important it is to be right. There is a wonderful audacity in the way that the outcome of the case happens offscreen and is announced in an indirect manner. The real drama isn't about poor little Ronnie, but about the passions he has unleashed in his household—between his parents, and between his sister and her suitors, declared and undeclared.

A story like this, when done badly, is about plot. When done well, it is about character. All of the characters are well-bred, and brought up in a time when reticence was valued above all. Today's audiences have been raised in a climate of emotional promiscuity; confession and self-humiliation are leaking from the daytime talk shows into our personal styles. But there's no fun and no class in simply blurting out everything one feels. Mamet's characters are interesting precisely because of the reserve and detachment they bring to passion. Sixty seconds of wondering if someone +is about to kiss you is more entertaining than sixty minutes of kissing. By understanding that, Mamet is able to deliver a G-rated film that is largely about adult sexuality.

That brings us to the key performances by Jeremy Northam and Rebecca Pidgeon, as Sir Robert and the suffragette. Pidgeon's performance has been criticized in some circles (no doubt the fact that she is Mrs. Mamet was a warning flag). She is said to be too reticent, too mannered, too cold. Those adjectives describe her performance, but miss the point. What her critics seem to desire is a willingness to roll over and play friendly puppy to Sir Robert. But Pidgeon's character, Catherine, is not a people-pleaser; she is scarcely interested in knowing you unless you are clever enough to clear the hurdle of her defenses. Her public personality is a performance game, and Sir Robert knows it—because his is too. That's why their conversations are so erotic. Spill the beans, and the conversation is history. Speak in code, with wit and challenge, and the process of decryption is like foreplay.

The Winter Guest ★ ★ ½
R, 110 m., 1998

Phyllida Law (Elspeth), Emma Thompson (Frances), Gary Hollywood (Alex), Arlene Cockburn (Nita), Sheila Reid (Lily), Sandra Voe (Chloe), Douglas Murphy (Sam), Sean Biggerstaff (Tom). Directed by Alan Rickman and produced by Ken Lipper, Edward R. Pressman, and Steve Clark-Hall. Screenplay by Sharman Macdonald.

Winter in Scotland is as muted as a wake. So far north the sun is slow to rise and early to set, and a day can be blindingly bright or always seem like twilight. *The Winter Guest* follows four sets of characters through a day in a Scots village, and its purpose is not to draw a lesson or tell a story, but to evoke a mood. To see this film is like spending a day in a village near St Andrews, and with a shock I realized I had once lingered for an afternoon in this village, or one much like it—in August, when the days were long and the trees were green.

Everything is different in winter. The people disappear inside and count on one another. The film opens with a well-coifed woman in her sixties, in a long fur coat, making her way across a field in bitter cold. This is Elspeth (Phyllida Law), and she is on her way to the house of her daughter Frances (Emma Thompson). She fears losing her. Frances's husband has died, and she has retreated into an angry silence beyond mourning. Perhaps she will leave Scotland and move to Australia with her teenage son, Alex (Gary Hollywood).

Alex has an admirer. Her name is Nita (Arlene Cockburn), and she has a crush on him. Early on the day of the film she ambushes him with a snowball, and at first they scuffle but then they begin to talk, and by the end of the day they will be boyfriend and girlfriend, with all the uncertainty that that means at their age.

There are two boys walking by the frozen sea. It is a school day, but they have stayed away, and no one will look for them here. They are Sam (Douglas Murphy) and Tom (Sean Biggerstaff), and the emptiness of the town and the quiet of the weekday has made them a little more serious than they planned; they look about twelve or thirteen, and tentatively talk about more serious things than they would have six months ago.

Two old ladies wait for a bus. They are Lily (Sheila Reid) and Chloe (Sandra Voe), and they are connoisseurs of funerals. Like the girl in *Huckleberry Finn* who loved to mourn, they find something cheerful about the rituals of death. They scour the death notices and compare notes on funerals past; they are old enough and ordinary enough that no one ever questions them when they attend a funeral; they look like the relatives you are sure you have forgotten.

The Winter Guest, based on a play by Sharman Macdonald, follows these four couples and listens to them. There isn't a lot of interaction between them, although Alex does bring Nita home, and she does talk with Frances. Since there is no plot engine to drag them all to the same station, we're forced to decide why they find themselves in this film, and what connection they have. Is the Winter Guest death? Do these couples represent four stages of life? Childhood, courtship, parenthood, and old age?

The central strands involve Elspeth and Frances. Phyllida Law and Emma Thompson are mother and daughter in real life, and in the film they have the familiarity of a lifelong couple. They know each other's speech rhythms. They look alike. When Frances closes herself off and refuses to talk, the worry lines between Elspeth's eyes seem real—the stress of a mother who loves a daughter and cannot reach her. Frances at one point buries her ears in the bathwater to block out words she doesn't want to hear, but it's hard to ignore someone if you're also concerned about them—and Frances is worried that Elspeth is growing older and soon will not be able to take care of herself.

The other three couples have defined roles. They are sure who they are, and more or less clear on how they should be acting on this winter day. But Elspeth and Frances are unsprung. The death of Frances's husband has changed everything, redefined it, ended a stage of life. There is so much pain that talking about it is unbearable, and so the mother and daughter talk around it.

The Winter Guest is the directing debut of Alan Rickman, an actor who makes intelligent British films *(Truly, Madly, Deeply; Sense and Sensibility)* and makes big money as a villain in American films *(Die Hard)*. He has great command here of look and tone, and I felt I knew what it would be like to wander the streets of that village in Scotland. But the film left me feeling strangely hollow. Perhaps it was meant to. At the end there is an emptiness, like stepping into air, or like a play interrupted after the first act.

Without Limits ★ ★ ★
PG-13, 118 m., 1998

Billy Crudup (Steve Prefontaine), Donald Sutherland (Bill Bowerman), Monica Potter (Mary Marckx), Jeremy Sisto (Frank Shorter), Billy Burke (Kenny Moore), Matthew Lillard (Roscoe Devine), Dean Norris (Bill Dellinger), Gabe Olds (Don Kardong). Directed by Robert Towne and produced by Tom Cruise and Paula Wagner. Screenplay by Towne and Kenny Moore.

Without Limits is the second recent film about Steve Prefontaine, the legendary American runner who brought his sport into the headlines and helped topple the creaky amateur athletic establishment. Like *Prefontaine* (1997), it focuses on the star's abrasive personality and his refusal to pace himself; the only way he wanted to win was by "flat-out leading all the way." By the time he died in a road accident, he held most of the American distance records, and one of them still stands.

Why two movies about Steve Prefontaine?

Because two directors wanted to make them, and neither one backed down. *Prefontaine* was by Steve James *(Hoop Dreams)*, starred Jared Leto, and had former marine drill sergeant R. Lee Ermey as the legendary Oregon coach Bill Bowerman. *Without Limits* is by Robert Towne (screenwriter of *Chinatown*, writer-director of *Personal Best*), stars Billy Crudup, and has Donald Sutherland playing Bowerman.

The earlier film focuses more on Prefontaine's stubborn battle with the AAU and other amateur bodies that essentially dictated the terms under which Americans could run. It makes it clear that a late invitational meet in Oregon with Finnish athletes was held as a deliberate challenge to the amateur establishment. Towne's film is less quirky, more a conventional sports movie, but it benefits by giving more attention to the relationship between Pre and Bowerman.

And Sutherland's performance is the film's treasure. Watching the way he gently tries to direct his headstrong young star, we are seeing a version of Phil Jackson's zen and the art of coaching. "What do you think a track coach *does*, Pre?" he asks at one point, since Pre seems to think the coach's primary function is to frustrate him. Sutherland brings a deep patience to Bowerman, who understands that running is a matter of endurance and strategy as well as heart: "Men of Oregon, I invite you to become students of your events." Pre thinks heart is enough, and explains his success simply: "I can endure more pain than anyone you've ever met."

The film follows Pre from his early sports failures (he was no good at football) and into running, where he quickly drew attention. The earlier film points out that his legs were short for a runner, and of unequal length; this one sees him more as naturally gifted, but heedless with his talent. We follow his progress from record to record, and from girlfriend to girlfriend (Mary Marckx, played by Monica Potter, is the true love, but he shuts her out of his life for obscure reasons). Everything leads up to the 1972 Munich Olympics, marred by the terrorist attack on Israeli athletes.

But the point of the story is contained in the epilogue. Pre returns to Oregon as an amateur who is expected to work at menial jobs (he becomes a bartender) and live at the poverty line (he gets a mobile home) while training for the next Olympics. Other countries

support their athletes, and Pre leads a campaign to reform America's rules. He makes no attempts to win friends, and in *Prefontaine* he tells a press conference: "To hell with love of country; I'm looking out for me."

Without Limits is less interested in the politics and the crusade, and sees Pre more in personal, psychological terms. I prefer the earlier approach, which contains more information about why Pre is important even today. Robert Towne's affecting *Personal Best* (1982) told the story of a talented woman runner in terms of both her sport and her romantic involvement with another woman athlete; Prefontaine is more interesting as a public figure than a private one.

Wonder Boys ★ ★ ★
R, 112 m., 2000

Michael Douglas (Grady Tripp), Tobey Maguire (James Leer), Frances McDormand (Sara Gaskell), Robert Downey Jr. (Terry Crabtree), Katie Holmes (Hannah Green), Richard Thomas (Walter Gaskell), Rip Torn (Q). Directed by Curtis Hanson and produced by Scott Rudin and Hanson. Screenplay by Steve Kloves, based upon the novel by Michael Chabon.

My father was an electrician at the University of Illinois. He never taught me a thing about electricity. "Every time I walk through the English building," he said, "I see the professors in their offices with their feet up on the desk, reading books and smoking their pipes. Now that's the life for you."

I thought I would be an English professor. Then I got into this game. Sometimes I am overwhelmed with a sense of loss: I remember myself walking across the snowy campus at dusk, a book bag thrown over my shoulder, on the way to the seminar room to drink coffee and talk about Cather or Faulkner. And I remember the endless weekends, driving around town in somebody's oversize American car, following rumors of parties. And the emotional and romantic confusion that played out at those parties, where everyone was too smart and too high and filled with themselves.

Wonder Boys is the most accurate movie about campus life I can remember. It is accurate, not because it captures intellectual debate or campus politics, but because it knows two things: (1) students come and go but the faculty actually lives there, and (2) many faculty members stay stuck in graduate student mode for decades. Michael Douglas plays a character like that. It is his best performance in years, muted, gentle, and wondering. He is a boy wonder long past his sell-by date, a fiftyish English professor named Grady Tripp who wrote a good novel seven years ago and now, everyone believes, has writer's block.

Wonder Boys follows him around a Pittsburgh campus in winter during a literary festival, as characters drift in and out of focus on his emotional viewfinder. His wife (we never see her) has just left him. His boss is Walter Gaskell (Richard Thomas), the head of the English department. Walter's wife, Sara (Frances McDormand), is the chancellor. Grady is having an affair with Sara. His New York editor, Crabtree (Robert Downey Jr.), is in town for the festival, and wonders where the new manuscript is. The famous writer "Q" (Rip Torn) is a visiting speaker. Two of Grady's students occupy his attention: James Leer (Tobey Maguire), who has written a novel and is moody and difficult and a pathological liar; and Hannah Green (Katie Holmes), who rents a room in Grady's house and would probably share his bed, although it has not come to that.

Because Grady is tired, depressed, and continuously stoned on pot, these characters all have more or less equal importance. That is, when he's looking at them they represent problems, and when they're absent, he can forget about them.

The movie is an unsprung screwball comedy, slowed down to real-life speed. Mishaps trip over one another in their eagerness to mess with Grady's mind. One thing leads to another. He goes to a party at the Gaskells' house and Sara tells him she is pregnant. He steps outside for a reefer, sees James standing in the dark with a gun, invites him in, and sneaks him upstairs to show him a secret closet where Walter Gaskell keeps his treasure (the suit Marilyn Monroe wore on her wedding day). Then the Gaskells' blind dog bites him and James shoots the dog dead.

At a certain velocity, this would be wacky. One of the wise decisions of *Wonder Boys* is to avoid that velocity. Grady plods around town in a pink bathrobe, trying to repair damage,

tell the truth, give good advice, be a decent man, and keep his life from falling apart. The brilliance of the movie can be seen in its details: (1) Hannah is brought onstage as an obvious love interest, but is a decoy; (2) Crabtree picks up a transvestite on the airplane, but dumps him for James, who is not exactly straight or gay (neither is Crabtree); (3) when the transvestite needs a ride, Grady says, "I'm your man" but their drive results not in sex but in truth-telling; and (4) Sara is not hysterical about being pregnant and is understanding, actually, about Grady's chaotic lifestyle.

So all the obvious payoffs are short-circuited. No mechanical sex scenes. No amazing revelation that the transvestite is not a woman (everyone in the movie clocks him instantly). No emotional show-offs. And the sex in the movie, gay and straight, is handled sanely, as a calming pastime after long and nutty evenings. (Notice how comfortable the Downey character is with his weaknesses of the flesh.)

Let me give one more example of how the movie uses observation instead of wheezy clichés. When Q, the writer, is giving his speech, he pontificates about piloting the boat of inspiration to the shore of achievement. James utters a loud, high-pitched giggle. In a lesser movie James would have continued, making some kind of angry and rebellious statement. Not in *Wonder Boys*, where James thinks Q is ludicrous, laughs rudely once, and then shuts up.

And listen to the dialogue. Grady has been working on his second novel so long it now runs well over 2,000 single-spaced pages. Hannah suggests tactfully that by including the "genealogies of everyone's horses, and their dental records," Grady's work "reads as if you didn't make any choices." The right line in a movie that does make choices. She also wonders if the book would have more shape if he hadn't been stoned when he wrote it. Yes, his brilliant first book was written on reefer, but then a lot of first novels are written long before they're actually put down on paper.

Wonder Boys is the first movie by Curtis Hanson since his *L.A. Confidential.* In a very different way, it is as accomplished. The screenplay by Steve Kloves, based on a novel by Michael Chabon, is European in its preference for character over plot. This is a funny and touching story that contains dead dogs, Monroe memorabilia, a stolen car, sex, adultery, pregnancy, guns, dope, and cops, but it is not about any of those things. It is about people, and especially about trying to be a good teacher.

Could one weekend on a real campus possibly contain all of these events? Easily, given the tendency of writers to make themselves deliberately colorful. Grady knows exactly what he's doing. Of Hannah he observes: "She was a junkie for the printed word. Lucky for me, I manufactured her drug of choice." ☞

Woo ★ ½
R, 80 m., 1998

Jada Pinkett Smith (Woo), Tommy Davidson (Tim), Duane Martin (Frankie), Michael Ralph (Romaine), Darrel M. Heath (Hop), Dave Chappelle (Lenny), Paula Jai Parker (Claudette), LL Cool J (Darryl). Directed by Daisy V. S. Mayer and produced by Beth Hubbard and Michael Hubbard. Screenplay by David C. Johnson.

Woo is about a collision between black lifestyles when a sexpot looking for "someone impulsive and exciting" ends up with a middle-class professional, and puts him through a severe psychosexual test-drive. When the smoke clears, she's revealed as not quite as streetwise as she pretends, and he turns out to have a few personality secrets concealed behind that white collar. Along the way, the movie touches on subjects usually sidestepped in African-American films, including the discomfort of black professionals around "country" behavior.

Jada Pinkett Smith stars as Woo, a girl who likes to party and is looking for a man. Her transvestite psychic friend predicts that a dynamic Virgo is in her future, but she doubts it. That night, she drops in on her cousin Claudette (Paula Jai Parker) and her boyfriend, Lenny (Dave Chappelle), but they want to be alone together, so Lenny talks his friend Tim (Tommy Davidson of *In Living Color*) into taking her out. Tim is a law clerk, studying for the bar; Woo suspects a bore, but agrees to the date when she finds out he's a Virgo.

That's the setup for a movie constructed so loosely that I had the feeling some of the characters were introduced after we'd already met them. The film is a series of episodes in which

Woo and Tim demonstrate to each other's satisfaction (and certainly to ours) that they have no business being out on a date with one another—although, of course, after they survive assorted bizarre adventures a certain camaraderie grows up between them. As hostages of each other, they develop reciprocal Stockholm syndrome.

The running joke is that Tim doesn't know much about women or, for that matter, black culture. Fixed up on the blind date with Woo, he goes across the hall to get tips from his neighbor Darryl (LL Cool J), who supplies him with a kit containing various stimulants and preventives, and a cassette of absolutely guaranteed romantic music ("by the time you get to side B, you should be naked").

Woo is not in the mood to be wooed, however, and the evening breaks down into episodes like the one in an Italian restaurant, where polite Tim doesn't get very far with the waiter, but Woo (who turns out to speak Italian) does. Then she sees an old friend through the window, and their reunion essentially demolishes the restaurant.

Movies like this don't really establish their characters and draw much of the humor out of their personalities; they go for quick payoffs, easy slapstick and in-jokes based on insults and code words. It's harmless and sometimes entertaining, but compared to Tommy Davidson's previous film, *Booty Call* (1997), or for that matter Jada Pinkett Smith's work in *Set It Off* and *The Nutty Professor*, it's lightweight and disposable.

The Wood ★ ★ ★
R, 106 m., 1999

Sean Nelson (Young Mike), Trent Cameron (Young Roland), Duane Finley (Young Slim), Malinda Williams (Young Alicia), Taye Diggs (Roland), Omar Epps (Mike), Richard T. Jones (Slim), Elayn Taylor (Roland's Mother), De'Aundre Bonds (Young Stacey), Sanaa Lathan (Alicia), Lisa Raye (The Bride), Tamala Jones (Tanya). Directed by Rick Famuyiwa and produced by Albert Berger, Ron Yerxa, and David Gale. Screenplay by Famuyiwa.

The Wood is a sweet, lighthearted comedy about three friends who stick together from high school until a wedding day. Nothing unusual about that, but these are African-American characters, and Hollywood seems incapable of imagining young black men who are not into violence, drugs, and trouble. The black middle class, millions of Americans, is generally invisible to moviemakers, who retail negative images of life in the hood—often for the entertainment of suburban kids, white and black, whose own lives are completely different.

The movie's title provides a clue: the wood, not the hood. Apart from the obvious pun, it applies to Inglewood, California, where three friends meet in high school, date, have some narrow escapes from trouble, and come of age. The film opens on the wedding day of Roland (Taye Diggs), and we meet his best friends Slim (Richard T. Jones) and Mike (Omar Epps), who narrates directly to the camera.

The wedding cake has arrived, but Roland is missing, and his buddies track him down to the house of a former girlfriend. He's terrified of marriage, and as his friends try to give him courage and make him presentable (he's been drinking), we get flashbacks to their younger days.

The flashback scenes, set in the eighties, are the real heart of the movie. As young men, the characters are played by Sean Nelson (Mike), Trent Cameron (Roland), and Duane Finley (Slim). And they're black teenagers like we rarely see in the movies: not angry, not alienated, not inarticulate, not packing guns, not into trouble—but sharing values, hopes, and fears typical of any adolescent. Most black teenagers are like this, although you wouldn't guess it from the movies. They have a lot in common with the heroes of *American Pie,* although they're not nearly as sexually sophisticated. (That's accurate, I think. Few porno stars have as much self-assurance as the kids in *American Pie.* Amazing, that the *Pie* raunchfest and this, much more innocent coming-of-age movie, have the same R rating.)

We join the three friends in various rites of passage. We see Mike getting a crush on a girl. Working up the nerve to ask her to dance. Not knowing what to say. Being encouraged by the girl's friendship—and, yes, her sympathy. Getting in a playground fight with her brother. The girl Mike likes is Alicia (played as a teenager by the warm, supportive Malinda Williams),

and there's a funny sequence that is a lot more accurate about early sexual experiences, I think, than *American Pie* will ever know.

There's another sequence that powerfully shows how close kids can come to getting in real trouble. The three friends are in a convenience store when it is stuck up—by someone they know but do not like. They do not support him, but are more or less forced to join him and a buddy in a car, which is soon stopped by the cops. A bust at that point would have forever altered their lives, giving them rap sheets as accomplices to armed robbery. Lives can be destroyed by being in the wrong place at the wrong time.

Although the adult stars top-line the movie, the flashback structure feels piled on top of the real story. The writer-director, a USC film school graduate named Rick Famuyiwa, would have been wise to dump the 1990s stuff altogether and stick with the kids in the eighties, although that would have cost him the marquee value of Diggs and Epps. The movie feels a little uncertain, as if it's moving from present to past under the demands of a screenplay rather than because it really feels that way. But the growing-up stuff is kind of wonderful.

The World Is Not Enough ★ ★ ★ ½
PG-13, 128 m., 1999

Pierce Brosnan (James Bond), Sophie Marceau (Elektra), Robert Carlyle (Renard), Denise Richards (Christmas Jones), Robbie Coltrane (Valentin Zukovsky), Judi Dench (M), Desmond Llewelyn (Q), John Cleese (R), Maria Grazia Cucinotta (Cigar Girl). Directed by Michael Apted and produced by Michael G. Wilson and Barbara Broccoli. Screenplay by Neal Purvis, Robert Wade, and Bruce Feirstein.

If *The World Is Not Enough* is a splendid comic thriller, exciting and graceful, endlessly inventive, because it is also the nineteenth James Bond movie, it comes with so much history that one reviews it like wine, comparing it to earlier famous vintages; I guess that's part of the fun. This is a good one.

Instead of summarizing the plot, let's tick off the Bond trademarks and see how they measure up:

1. Bond himself. Pierce Brosnan. The best except for Sean Connery. He knows that even the most outrageous double entendres are pronounced with a straight face. He is proud that a generation has grown up knowing the term "double entendre" only because of Bond movies.

2. Regulars. There's real poignancy this time, because Q, the inventor of all of Bond's gizmos, is retiring. Desmond Llewelyn has played the character in almost every Bond film since *From Russia With Love* in 1963 (notable exception: *Live and Let Die* in 1973, when the producers dropped Q after an insane decision that the series needed fewer gimmicks). Llewelyn is now eighty-five, and after demonstrating a few nice touches on his latest inventions, he sinks from sight in an appropriate and, darn it, touching way.

3. Guest stars. Who could replace Q? John Cleese, of course. "Does this make you . . . R?" asks Bond, after Cleese demonstrates a BMW speedster with titanium armor "and six cup holders."

4. M16. Judi Dench is back for the third time as Bond's boss M, with the same regal self-confidence she displayed as Queens Elizabeth *(Shakespeare in Love)* and Victoria *(Mrs. Brown)*. She does not condescend to the role, but plays it fiercely, creating an intelligence chief who actually seems focused and serious, even in the uproar of a Bond plot.

5. Sex bombs. Usually two major ones, a good girl who seems bad, and a bad girl who seems good. Both first-rate this time. Sophie Marceau plays Elektra King, daughter of a tycoon behind an oil pipeline linking the old Soviet oil fields to Europe. Denise Richards plays Christmas Jones, a nuclear scientist whose knowledge can save or doom the world. I will not reveal who is bad/good or good/bad.

6. Chase sequences. Lots of them. By powerboat on the Thames (and across dry land, and back on the Thames), and then into a hot-air balloon. By skis down a mountain, pursued by hang-gliding, bomb-throwing parasailers whose devices convert into snowmobiles. By land, in the BMW. Under the sea, as Bond breaks into a submarine and later pursues a villain by popping outside the sub and then in again.

7. Megalomaniac villains. There is a terrific early appearance of the archterrorist Renard (Robert Carlyle). His oversized skull rises from the floor in a hologram, and then takes on flesh. M explains that a bullet in his brain is gradually robbing him of his senses, but that "he'll grow stronger every day until he dies." Bond walks around the hologram, and reaches inside Renard's head to trace the path of the bullet. Another villain is played by Robbie Coltrane, who gets mileage out of always seeming like he'd really prefer to be a nice guy.

8. Locations. Not simply the oil fields of Azerbaijan, but Frank Gehry's new art museum in Bilbao, Spain, which figures in a nifty opening sequence, and the Millennium Dome on the banks of the Thames, which becomes a landing pad after a balloon explodes. Also a Hindu holy place with flames that never die.

9. Weird ways to die. How about vivisection by helicopter-borne rotary tree-trimming blades? Or garroting in an antique torture chair?

10. Sensational escapes. There is nothing like a Bond picture to make you believe a man can safely bungee-jump from a tall building, after tying one end of a window shade cord to his belt and the other end to an unconscious body.

All of these elements are assembled by director Michael Apted and writers Neal Purvis, Robert Wade, and Bruce Feirstein into a Bond picture that for once doesn't seem like set pieces uneasily glued together, but proceeds in a more or less logical way to explain what the problem and solution might be. Bond's one-liners seem more part of his character this time, not wisecrack inserts, and Carlyle's villain emerges as more three-dimensional and motivated, less of a caricature, than the evildoers in some of the Bond films.

My favorite moment? A small one, almost a throwaway. The movie answers one question I've had for a long time: How do the bad guys always manage to find all their equipment spontaneously, on remote locations where they could not have planned ahead? After the snow chase sequence, a villain complains morosely that the parasails were rented, and "were supposed to be returned."

X

The X Files: Fight the Future ★ ★ ★
PG-13, 122 m., 1998

David Duchovny (Agent Fox Mulder), Gillian
Anderson (Agent Dana Scully), Martin Landau
(Kurtzweil), Armin Mueller-Stahl (Strughold),
Blythe Danner (Cassidy), Mitch Pileggi
(Director Skinner), William B. David (Cigarette-
Smoking Man), John Neville (Well-Manicured
Man). Directed by Rob Bowman and produced
by Chris Carter and Daniel Sackheim.
Screenplay by Carter.

As pure movie, *The X Files* more or less works.
As a story, it needs a sequel, a prequel, and
Cliffs Notes. I'm not sure even the filmmakers
can explain exactly what happens in the movie
and why. It doesn't make much difference if
you've seen every episode of the TV series or
none: The film is essentially self-contained,
and that includes its enigmas. X-philes will
probably be as puzzled at the end as an infrequent viewer like myself.

Puzzled, but not dissatisfied. Like *Mission:
Impossible*, this is a movie that depends on
surface, on mystery, on atmosphere, on vague
hints and murky warnings. Since the underlying plot is completely goofy, it's probably just
as well that it's not spelled out. If it were, this
would play more like a seminar on the works
of Whitley Strieber. Instead, producer-writer
Chris Carter, who conceived the TV series, reassembles his basic elements in a glossy extravaganza that ends, apparently, with humankind
facing precisely the same danger it did at the
beginning.

The story involves, of course, Mulder and
Scully, who call each other "Mulder!" and
"Scully!" so often they must be paid by the word.
FBI agents Fox Mulder (David Duchovny) and
Dana Scully (Gillian Anderson) have been in-
vestigating a cover-up of aliens among us.
Yanked off their X-files and assigned to an anti-
terrorism unit, they get involved in the explo-
sion of a Dallas high-rise.

The alien conspiracy theorist Kurtzweil
(Martin Landau) tells Mulder some of the
bombing victims were already dead, and the
blast was a plot to account for their bodies.
(There is a shot of the ruined building, its

front blasted away, that evokes disturbing memories of the Oklahoma City tragedy; that shot
could have been removed from the film with
absolutely no loss.)

We already know something about the
dead bodies. The film opens in "North Texas,
35,000 B.C." (a long time before it was north
Texas), with prehistoric men encountering violent, creepy, leaky beings in a cave. In "Present Day: North Texas," a kid falls into the same
cave, and sluglike beings slither into his nose
and eye sockets. What are these?

"The original inhabitant of this planet," we
eventually learn, and a mighty patient inhabitant, too, if it had to wait for us to evolve. The
alien creatures are a "virus," and yet they also
seem to have bodily form, unless they inhabit
hijacked bodies, which they can indeed do, although that begs the question of what they
were to begin with, who built the large object
we see in the final scenes, etc.

It's tricky work, not giving away the plot of
a movie you don't understand. The story is
less concerned with the aliens than with the
cover-up, and there are several scenes (maybe
one too many) of agents Scully and Mulder
being grilled by an FBI panel about their mis-
deeds. I can't fault the FBI here. If I were investigating unreliable field agents and they
told me they spent the weekend in Antarctica,
I'd want to know what they were smoking.

Speaking of smoking, the Cigarette-Smoking
Man (known on the Web as the Cancer Man)
is in the movie, of course. Has there ever been
a more thankless role? William B. David, who
plays him, has to inhale, exhale, or light up
every time we see him. The Well-Manicured
Man (John Neville) has more to do, as does
Director Skinner (Mitch Pileggi), but the best
supporting performance is by Landau, as a
desperate man who lurks in the back booths
of shady bars, passing info to the X-agents.

What does he know? What's being covered
up? Why are all the powerful men having the
secret meeting in London? If you watch the
show you will guess it has something to do
with covering up the Aliens Among Us. What
are they doing here? What are their hopes and
plans? There's dialogue in which we get the
answers to these questions, I guess, but they

didn't fit together for me. And when the large unnamed object appears at the end, I wanted to know where it came from, where it was going, what it was leaving behind, and why. I also wanted a better look at it (the special effects are too cloudy).

There is little real drama, as such, in *The X Files*. Mulder and Scully are in love with one another, but sublimate all their feelings into their work. Do they kiss? Would I tell you? Do their lips meet? Is that one question, or two? They spend much of their time gaining unchallenged entry into vast installations that should be better guarded. One of these installations involves corn and bees. Why? We are told, but I didn't believe it. Nor do I understand why humans cooperate with the aliens; what sort of Faustian bargain has been struck?

Much has been made of the fact that *The X Files* is not so much a film based on a TV series as a continuation of that series in film form. The movie feeds out of last season and into the next one. No final answers are therefore provided about anything; it's as if, at the end of *Casablanca,* the airplane circled around and landed again. But I liked the way the movie looked, and the unforced urgency of Mulder and Scully, and the way the plot was told through verbal puzzles and visual revelations, rather than through boring action scenes. And it was a relief to discover that the guys in the black helicopters are just as clueless as the rest of us.

Xiu Xiu: The Sent-Down Girl ★ ★ ★
R, 99 m., 1999

Lu Lu (Wen Xiu), Lopsang (Lao Jin), Gao Jie (Mother), Li Qianqian (Sister), Lu Yue (Father), Qiao Qian (Chen Li), Gao Qiang (Peddler), Qin Wenyuan (Motorcycle Man). Directed by Joan Chen and produced by Chen and Alice Chan. Screenplay by Chen and Yan Geling, based on Yan Geling's novella "Tian Yu."

"May you live in interesting times."
—Chinese curse, perhaps apocryphal

In a time of movies about sex and silly teenagers, here is a film that arrives with a jolt of hard reality, about a fifteen-year-old Chinese girl who was not lucky enough to be born into the consumer paradise of *American Pie*. To those who find savage satire in *South Park: Bigger, Longer and Uncut* (I am among them), here is a story about people who would weep with joy to have the problems *South Park* attacks.

Joan Chen's *Xiu Xiu: The Sent-Down Girl* is set in 1975, when the madness of the Cultural Revolution was still destroying the lives of millions of Chinese. A plague of fanaticism was upon the land. Wen Xiu (the title is her nickname) lives in the provincial city of Chengdu, goes to school, has a boyfriend, wears blouses sewn by her father, a tailor. Then she is selected to be "sent down" to a remote rural area, where as a city girl she can have her revolutionary values renewed by living with the proletariat. Countless others were also exiled from home, family, and friends by such directives.

The girl (Lu Lu) is sent to the high steppes near Tibet to live in the tent of a horse herder named Lao Jin (Lopsang). A wide river snakes through the territory, hardly seeming to flow. Lao Jin's tent, patched and leaky to the cold winds, is considered a safe haven because it is known in the district that he was castrated by "enemy soldiers" (their nationality unclear). Xiu Xiu is not a brave, independent heroine, a woman warrior; she is a kid, homesick and frightened, and not very sophisticated about her situation.

Life with Lao Jin is painted by Chen as essentially a lonely exile in a far place, where the man does most of the work and Xiu Xiu behaves much as a teenager might if she were sent to the farm for the summer. She is modest, undresses behind curtains, treats Lao Jin in an almost condescending fashion, does not see how much he cares for her, and about her. On the day when she has been away for six months, she puts on her nice sweater and a scarf, expecting officials to come and return her to her home.

They do not come. She has essentially been forgotten. (The ostensible purpose of her exile was to train horses for a women's cavalry that does not exist.) "Every place is the same," Lao Jin reassures her, a philosophy that is no consolation. One day a passing stranger tells her that there are ways a pretty girl can buy her way home. And soon, after an abrupt transition, she is having sex with him—and then with a series of men who all promise they can get her sent back to Chengdu, although why would they bother, when it is so pleasant to have her convenient to their needs?

Xiu Xiu is based on a screenplay and novel by Yan Geling, who teaches at Columbia College Chicago. It was shot on location in China, even in the forbidden zone near Tibet, by Chen, the Chinese-born actress from *Tai Pan, The Last Emperor,* and *Heaven and Earth.* Born in 1961, she was making her first movies at about the time this story is set. The film was made without the approval of the Chinese government, and since most of the scenes are set in remote isolation, there was no one to see— and, indeed, there are no overt political statements in the film, although it functions as a cry of regret and rage.

Other films have been set in this same period: *The Blue Kite; Farewell, My Concubine; To Live.* They were about the madness in the cities, where friends and neighbors denounced each other to save their own lives. This one is about evil on a larger scale (bureaucracies destroying lives because of policies no one seems responsible for) and a smaller one (the unspeakable cruelty of the man who rapes Xiu Xiu after giving her false hopes). Those other films were Chinese productions, although given limited release in China because of their politics (the Chinese government was, however, happy to earn foreign exchange by having them shown overseas). *Xiu Xiu* will not be seen in China, nor is Chen welcome to return there; it is the kind of film which in a simple parable indicts an entire nation and its sainted leader, Mao.

Because Lao Jin is an inarticulate peasant and Xiu Xiu is a naive and immature girl, there is little dialogue between them. This is not a movie about opposites attracting, but about two fellow prisoners who scarcely speak the same language. We are invited to interpret their looks, their silences, and their feelings— especially Lao Jin's passive sadness as Xiu Xiu is violated. The resolution of their stories, when it comes, is almost inevitable. During the film, a cadre of displaced young "revolutionaries" look at a propaganda film in which shiny-faced workers sing patriotic songs. I have a fantasy in which the characters in half a dozen American teenage sex comedies wander into the wrong room at the multiplex and see *Xiu Xiu.*

X-Men ★ ★ ½
PG-13, 96 m., 2000

Hugh Jackman (Logan/Wolverine), Patrick Stewart (Xavier), Ian McKellen (Magneto), Famke Janssen (Dr. Jean Grey), James Marsden (Cyclops), Halle Berry (Storm), Anna Paquin (Rogue), Tyler Mane (Sabretooth), Rebecca Romijn-Stamos (Mystique), Ray Park (Toad). Directed by Bryan Singer and produced by Lauren Shuler Donner and Ralph Winter. Screenplay by David Hayter, based on a story by Tom DeSanto and Singer.

The origin story is crucial to all superhero epics, from the gods of ancient Greece right down to Superman's parents. Next in importance is an explanation of superpowers: what they are, how they work. That's reasonable when there is one superhero, like Superman or the Crow, but in *X-Men,* with eight major characters and more in supporting roles, the movie gets top-heavy. At the halfway mark, it had just about finished introducing the characters.

That matches my experience of the *X-Men* comic books. The characters spent an inordinate amount of time accounting for themselves. Action spills across full pages as the heroes *splatt* and *kerrruuunch* each other, but the dialogue balloons are like little advertisements for themselves, as they describe their powers, limitations, and motivations.

Since the Marvel Comics empire hopes *X-Men* is the first entry in a franchise, it's understandable that the setups would play an important role in the first film. If only there were more to the payoff. The events that end the movie are sort of anticlimactic, and the special effects, while energetic, are not as persuasive as they might be (at one point an airplane clearly looks like a model, bouncing as it lands on water).

X-Men is at least not a manic editing frenzy for atrophied attention spans. It's restrained and introspective for a superhero epic, and fans of the comic books may like that. Graphic novels (as they sometimes deserve to be called) take themselves as seriously as the ones without pictures, and you can tell that here when the opening scene shows Jews being forced into death camps in Poland in 1944. One could argue that the Holocaust is not appropriate subject matter for an action movie based on a comic book, but having talked to some *X-Men* fans I believe that in their minds the medium is as deep and portentous as, say, *Sophie's Choice*.

The Holocaust scene introduces Magneto (Ian McKellen) as a child; his mental powers twist iron gates out of shape. The narrator informs us that "evolution takes thousands and thousands of years," which is putting it mildly, and that we live in an age of great evolutionary leaps forward. Some of the X-Men develop paranormal powers that cannot be accounted for by the strictly physical mutations that form the basis of Darwinian theory; I get restless when real science is evoked in the name of pseudoscience, but hey, that's just me.

Magneto's opponent in *X-Men* is Xavier (Patrick Stewart), another mutant of the same generation. They aren't enemies so much as ideological opposites. Magneto, having seen the Holocaust, has a deep pessimism about human nature. Xavier, who runs a school for mutants in Westchester County, where it doubtless seems no stranger than the other private schools, hopes these new powers can be used for good. Bruce Davison plays the McCarthy-like senator who waves a list of "known mutants" during a congressional hearing and wants them all registered—no doubt for dire purposes. Magneto wants to counter by using a device that can convert world leaders to mutants. (The world leaders are conveniently meeting on an island near Ellis Island, so the Statue of Liberty can be a prop.)

How a machine could create a desired mutation within a generation is not much explored by the movie, which also eludes the question of why you would want to invest your enemies with your powers. No matter; Xavier,

who can read minds, leads his good mutants in a battle to foil Magneto, and that's the plot, or most of it.

X-Men is arguably heavy on mutants; they have a way of coming onstage, doing their tricks, and disappearing. The leads are Wolverine (Hugh Jackman), whose fists sprout deadly blades; Cyclops (James Marsden), who wears a wraparound visor to control and aim his laserlike eyes; the prosaically named Dr. Jean Grey (Famke Janssen), who can move objects with her mind; Storm (Halle Berry in a platinum wig), who can control the weather; and Rogue (Anna Paquin), a teenager who is new to this stuff. I can't help wondering how a guy whose knuckles turn into switchblades gets to be the top-ranking superhero. If Storm can control, say, a tropical storm, she's obviously the most powerful, even if her feats here are limited to local climate control.

Magneto's team is not as colorful as the good guys, and includes Mystique (Rebecca Romijn-Stamos), who in the Japanese anime tradition can change her shape (as her costume tries to keep up), and Toad (Ray Park), who has a tongue that can whip out to great distances. Why is it that Xavier's team has impressive skills, while Magneto's team has specialties that would prove invaluable to a stripper?

I started out liking this movie, while waiting for something really interesting to happen. When nothing did, I still didn't dislike it; I assume the X-Men will further develop their personalities if there is a sequel, and maybe find time to get involved in a story. No doubt fans of the comics will understand subtle allusions and fine points of behavior; they should linger in the lobby after each screening to answer questions. ☞

Y

Your Friends and Neighbors ★ ★ ★ ★
R, 99 m., 1998

Jason Patric (Cary), Nastassja Kinski (Cheri), Ben Stiller (Jerry), Catherine Keener (Terri), Aaron Eckhart (Barry), Amy Brenneman (Mary). Directed by Neil LaBute and produced by Steve Golin and Jason Patric. Screenplay by LaBute.

Neil LaBute's *Your Friends and Neighbors* is a film about monstrous selfishness—about people whose minds are focused exclusively on their own needs. They use the language of sharing and caring when it suits them, but only to their own ends. Here is the most revealing exchange in the film:

"Are you, like, a good person?"

"Hey! I'm eating lunch!"

The movie looks at sexual behavior with a sharp, unforgiving cynicism. And yet it's not really about sex. It's about power, about enforcing your will on another, about having what you want when you want it. Sex is only the medium of exchange. LaBute is merciless. His previous film, *In the Company of Men,* was about two men who play a cruel trick on a woman. In this film, the trick is played on all the characters by the society that raised and surrounded them. They've been emotionally shortchanged and will never hear a lot of the notes on the human piano.

LaBute's *Your Friends and Neighbors* is to *In the Company of Men* as Tarantino's *Pulp Fiction* was to *Reservoir Dogs.* In both cases, the second film reveals the full scope of the talent, and the director, given greater resources, paints what he earlier sketched. In LaBute's world, the characters are deeply wounded and resentful, they are locked onto their own egos, they are like infants for which everything is either "me!" or "mine!" Sometimes this can be very funny—for the audience, not for them.

Of course they have fashionable exteriors. They live in good "spaces," they have good jobs, they eat in trendy restaurants, and are well-dressed. They look good. They know that. And yet there is some kind of a wall closing them off from one another. Early in the film, the character played by Aaron Eckhart frankly confesses that he is his own favorite sexual partner. A character played by Catherine Keener can't stand it when her husband (Ben Stiller) talks during sex, and later, after sex with Nastassja Kinski, when she's asked, "What did you like the best?" she replies, "I liked the silence best."

Ben Stiller and Keener are a couple; Eckhart and Amy Brenneman are a couple. In addition to Kinski, who works as an artist's assistant, there is another single character played by Jason Patric. During the course of the movie these people will cheat on and with one another in various ways.

A plot summary, describing who does what and with whom, would be pointless. The underlying truth is that no one cares for or about anybody else very much, and all of the fooling around is just an exercise in selfishness. The other day I spent a long time looking at the penguins in the Shedd Aquarium. Every once in a while two of them would square off into a squawking fit over which rock they were entitled to stand on. Big deal. Meanwhile, they're helpless captives inside a system that has cut them off from their full natures, and they don't even know it. Same thing in this movie.

LaBute, who writes and directs, is an intriguing new talent. His emphasis is on writing: As a director, he is functional, straightforward, and uncluttered. As a writer, he composes dialogue that can be funny, heartless, and satirical all at once. He doesn't insist on the funny moments, because they might distort the tone, but they're fine, as when the Keener character tells Kinski she's a writer—"if you read the sides of a tampon box." She writes ad copy, in other words. Later, in a store, Kinski reads the sides of a tampon box and asks, "Did you write this?" It's like she's picking up an author's latest volume in a bookstore, although in this case the medium is carefully chosen.

The Jason Patric character, too, makes his living off the physical expression of sex: He's possibly a gynecologist (that's hinted, but left vague). The Aaron Eckhart character, who pleasures himself as no other person can, is cheating on his wife with . . . himself, and likes the look of his lover. The Brenneman character is enraged to be treated like an object by her new lover, but of course is treated like one by Eckhart, her husband. And treats him like one. Only the Kinski character seems adrift, as if she wants to be nice and is a little puzzled that Keener can't seem to receive on that frequency.

LaBute deliberately isolates these characters from identification with any particular city, so we can't categorize them and distance ourselves with an easy statement like, "Look at how they behave in Los Angeles." They live in a generic, affluent America. There are no exteriors in the movie. The interiors are modern homes, restaurants, exercise clubs, offices, bedrooms, bookstores. These people are not someone else. In the immortal words of Pogo, "We has met the enemy, and it is us."

This is a movie with the impact of the original stage production of Albee's *Who's Afraid of Virginia Woolf*. It has a similar form, but is more cruel and unforgiving than *Carnal Knowledge*. Mamet has written some stuff like this. It contains hardly any nudity and no physical violence, but the MPAA at first slapped it with an NC-17 rating, perhaps in an oblique tribute to its power (on appeal, it got an R). It's the kind of date movie that makes you want to go home alone.

You've Got Mail ★ ★ ★
PG, 116 m., 1998

Tom Hanks (Joe Fox), Meg Ryan (Kathleen Kelly), Parker Posey (Patricia Eden), Jean Stapleton (Birdie), Steve Zahn (George Pappas), David Chappelle (Kevin Scanlon), Greg Kinnear (Frank Navasky). Directed by Nora Ephron and produced by Lauren Shuler Donner and Nora Ephron. Screenplay by Nora Ephron and Delia Ephron.

The appeal of *You've Got Mail* is as old as love and as new as the Web. It stars Tom Hanks and Meg Ryan as immensely lovable people whose purpose it is to display their lovability for two hours, while we desperately yearn for them to solve their problems, fall into one another's arms, and get down to the old rumpy-pumpy.

They meet in a chat room on AOL, and soon they're revealing deep secrets (but no personal facts) in daily and even hourly e-mail sessions. The movie's call to arms is the inane

chirp of the maddening "You've Got Mail!" voice (which prompts me to growl, "Yes, and I'm gonna stick it up your modem!"). But the e-mail is really just the MacGuffin—the device necessary to keep two people who fall in love on-line from finding out that they already know and hate each other in real life.

The plot surrounds Hanks and Ryan not only with e-mail lore, but with the Yuppie Urban Lifestyle. It's the kind of movie where the characters walk into Starbucks and we never for a moment think "product placement!" because, frankly, we can't imagine them anywhere else. Where the generations are so confused by modern mating appetites that Joe Fox (the Hanks character) can walk into a bookstore with two young children and introduce them as his brother and his aunt ("Matt is my father's son, and Annabel is my grandfather's daughter").

Kathleen, the Meg Ryan character, runs the children's bookshop she inherited from her mother. She and her loyal staff read all the books, know all the customers, and provide full service and love. Joe Fox is the third generation to run a chain of gigantic book megastores. When the new Fox Books opens around the corner from Kathleen's shop, it's only a matter of time until the little store is forced out of business. Kathleen turns for advice and solace to her anonymous on-line friend—who is, of course, Joe.

And yet this is not *quite* an Idiot Plot, so called because a word from either party would instantly end the confusion. It maintains the confusion only up to a point, and then does an interesting thing: allows Joe to find out Kathleen's real identity while still keeping her quite reasonably in the dark. And, oh, the poignant irony, as Joe has to stand there and be insulted by the woman he loves. "You're nothing but a suit!" she says. "That's my cue," he says. "Good night." And as he nobly conceals his pain, we are solaced only by the knowledge that sooner or later the scales will fall from her eyes.

The movie was directed by Nora Ephron, who first paired Hanks and Ryan in *Sleepless in Seattle* (1993) and has made an emotional, if not a literal, sequel. That earlier film was partly inspired by *An Affair to Remember*, and this one is inspired by *The Shop Around the Corner*, but both are really inspired by the appeal of

Ryan and Hanks, who have more winning smiles than most people have expressions.

Ephron and her cowriter, her sister Delia, have surrounded the characters with cultural references that we can congratulate ourselves on recognizing: Not only Jane Austen, but the love affair carried on by correspondence between George Bernard Shaw and Mrs. Patrick Campbell. Not only *The Godfather* (which "contains the answers to all of life's questions") but Anthony Powell and Generalissimo Franco. (It is one of the movie's quietly hilarious conceits that the little store's elderly bookkeeper, played by Jean Stapleton, was in love years ago with a man who couldn't marry her "because he had to run Spain.")

The plot I shall not describe, because it consists of nothing but itself, so any description would make it redundant. What you have are two people the audience desires to see together, and a lot of devices to keep them apart. There is the added complication that both Hanks and Ryan begin the movie with other partners (Parker Posey and Greg Kinnear—respectively, of course). The partners get dumped without much fuss, and then we're left with these two lonely single people, who have neat jobs but no one to rub toes with, and who are trapped by fate in a situation where he is destroying her dream, and she is turning to him (without knowing it is him) for consolation. Perfect.

The movie is sophisticated enough not to make the megastore into the villain. Say what you will, those giant stores are fun to spend time in, and there is a scene where Kathleen ventures anonymously into Joe's big store for the first time and looks around, at the magazine racks and the café and all the books—and then there's the heartbreaking moment when she overhears a question in the children's section, and she knows the answer but of course the clerk doesn't, and so she supplies the answer, but it makes her cry, and Joe overhears everything. Whoa.

Z

Zero Effect ★ ★ ★ ½
R, 115 m., 1998

Bill Pullman (Daryl Zero), Ben Stiller (Steve Arlo), Ryan O'Neal (Gregory Stark), Kim Dickens (Gloria Sullivan), Angela Featherstone (Jess), Hugh Ross (Bill), Sara Devincentis (Daisy), Matt O'Toole (Kragen Vincent). Directed by Jake Kasdan and produced by Lisa Henson, Janet Yang, and Kasdan. Screenplay by Kasdan.

Zero Effect opens with the key character off-screen. His name is Daryl Zero, he's the best private detective in the world, and he's a recluse who prefers to be represented in public by a hireling. Sounds like the setup for a comedy, but this is one of those movies that creeps up on you, insidiously gathering power. By the end, I was surprised how much I was involved.

The hireling, named Steve Arlo, is played by Ben Stiller as a dry, detached functionary. He represents Zero at a meeting with a millionaire named Stark (Ryan O'Neal), who wants to find some lost keys—one of them to a safe-deposit box. Stark is being blackmailed by someone who may have access to the secret of dark deeds in the past.

Arlo enjoys spinning amazing tales about Zero. He's the kind of guy who feels personally enhanced by his boss's qualities. "He has a deeply nuanced understanding of human nature," Arlo says of Zero, but when we see Zero he looks more like a case for treatment. He lives behind a steel door with six locks on it. He eats little except for tuna fish from a can. And he likes to bounce on the bed while singing very bad folk songs of his own composition.

Yet this man is indeed an investigative genius, and soon he's meeting a young woman named Gloria (Kim Dickens) and using his sense of smell to tell her she's a paramedic. Zero is strangely split: He's hopelessly incompetent in his personal life, but when he goes into P.I. mode he's cool, competent, suave, and self-confident. Using Arlo as his assistant, he begins to unravel a murder that took place more than two decades ago, and leads to a trail of hidden identities.

To describe the details of the case would be wrong. They lead to surprises and reversals that are among the movie's pleasures (the last scenes force us to rearrange almost everything we thought we knew about the plot). The movie was written and directed by Jake Kasdan, son of the writer-director Lawrence Kasdan, and it's an exercise in devious construction—like one of those Ross Macdonald novels in which the sins of the fathers are visited upon the children.

If the plot is ingenious, it's the personal stuff that makes the movie increasingly delightful. Daryl Zero is baffled and challenged by Gloria, who is one of the few people he's ever met whose mind he can't more or less read. She fools him. She's shielded. She intuitively understands him the way he understands other people. When he claims to be in town at an accountant's convention, she finds a way to check that: She asks him to do her income tax.

Midway through the movie, I was being nudged by echoes of another story, and then I realized that *Zero Effect* was probably inspired by the relationship between Sherlock Holmes and the faithful Watson—Holmes, who could sit in his study and use pure deduction to solve a crime. When Zero describes his methods, he sounds Holmesian: "Objectivity . . . and observation. The two obs."

If Zero is like Holmes, Gloria is certainly like Irene Adler, from *A Scandal in Bohemia*. She was the one woman for Holmes, the one who got under his skin and into his mind. And as Gloria begins to have that effect on Zero, a softening and humanizing takes place: He becomes less weird, less insistent on his peculiar rituals, more like a guy.

Zero Effect begins, as I said, like a comedy—one not a million miles away from the kind of private-eye parody David Spade or Mike Myers might make. The Bill Pullman character, the first time we see him, seems like a goofy, off-the-shelf weirdo. But Pullman, from *While You Were Sleeping* and *Independence Day*, can drop the facade and let you see the complications inside. He also costarred in *Sleepless in Seattle*, and it's uncanny, by the end of *Zero Effect*, how much this private-eye caper has started to touch some of the same notes.

2001 Revisited

When Stanley Kubrick's 2001: A Space Odyssey was first released, the year 2001 seemed unimaginably distant. Now it is here. How well did Kubrick predict the future? He was too optimistic with his ideas of lunar bases and space passenger vehicles (and much too optimistic in assuming that Pan Am would survive to run them), but, seen today, his film does not seem dated. It stands outside movie fashion, one of a kind, an epic that still has the power to astonish. Curiously, I've heard from some readers that they watched the movie and it didn't do much for them. In every case, they watched it on video. This is not really a movie for video. It must be seen on a big screen—ideally, in 70mm, although that is hard to do. Here is my re-review of the movie, first published in 1997 in the Great Movies Series, followed by my original review from 1968.

The genius is not in how much Stanley Kubrick does in *2001: A Space Odyssey*, but in how little. This is the work of an artist so sublimely confident that he doesn't include a single shot simply to keep our attention. He reduces each scene to its essence, and leaves it on-screen long enough for us to contemplate it, to inhabit it in our imaginations. Alone among science-fiction movies, *2001* is not concerned with thrilling us, but with inspiring our awe.

No little part of his effect comes from the music. Although Kubrick commissioned an original score from Alex North, he used classical recordings as a temporary track while editing the film, and they worked so well that he kept them. This was a crucial decision. North's score, which is available on a recording, is a good job of film composition but would have been wrong for *2001* because, like all scores, it attempts to underline the action—to give us emotional cues. The classical music chosen by Kubrick exists *outside* the action; it uplifts, it wants to be sublime, it brings a seriousness and transcendence to the visuals.

Consider two examples. The Johann Strauss waltz "Blue Danube," which accompanies the docking of the space shuttle and the space sta-

tion, is deliberately slow, and so is the action. Obviously such a docking process would have to take place with extreme caution (as we now know from experience), but other directors might have found the space ballet too slow, and punched it up with thrilling music, which would have been wrong.

We are asked in the scene to contemplate the process, to stand in space and watch. We know the music. It proceeds as it must. And so, through a peculiar logic, the space hardware moves slowly because it's keeping the tempo of the waltz. At the same time, there is an exaltation in the music that helps us feel the majesty of the process.

Now consider Kubrick's famous use of Richard Strauss's "Thus Spake Zarathustra." Inspired by the words of Nietzsche, its five bold opening notes embody the ascension of man into spheres reserved for the gods. It is cold, frightening, magnificent.

It is associated in the film with the first entry of man's consciousness into the universe—and with the eventual passage of that consciousness onto a new level, symbolized by the Star Child at the end of the film. When classical music is associated with popular entertainment, the result is usually to trivialize it (who can listen to the "William Tell Overture" without thinking of the Lone Ranger?). Kubrick's film is almost unique in *enhancing* the music by its association with his images.

I was present at the Los Angeles premiere of the film, in 1968, at the Pantages Theater. It is impossible to adequately describe the anticipation in the audience. Kubrick had been working on the film in secrecy for some years, in collaboration, the audience knew, with the author Arthur C. Clarke, the special-effects expert Douglas Trumbull, and consultants who advised him on the specific details of his imaginary future—everything from space station design to corporate logos. Fearing to fly and facing a deadline, Kubrick had sailed from England on the *Queen Elizabeth*, using an editing room on board, and had continued to edit the film during a cross-country train journey. Now it was finally ready to be seen.

To describe that first screening as a disaster would be wrong, for many of those who remained until the end knew they had seen one of the greatest films ever made. But not everyone remained. Rock Hudson stalked down the aisle, audibly complaining, "Will someone tell me what the hell this is about?" There were many other walkouts, and some restlessness at the film's slow pace (Kubrick immediately cut about seventeen minutes, including a pod sequence that essentially repeated another one). The film did not provide the clear narrative and easy entertainment cues the audience expected. The closing sequences, with the astronaut inexplicably finding himself in a bedroom somewhere beyond Jupiter, were baffling. The overnight Hollywood judgment was that Kubrick had become derailed, that in his obsession with effects and set pieces, he had failed to make a movie.

What he had actually done was make a philosophical statement about man's place in the universe, using images as those before him had used words, music, or prayer. And he had made it in a way that invited us to contemplate it—not to experience it vicariously as entertainment, as we might in a good conventional science-fiction film, but to stand outside it as a philosopher might, and think about it.

The film falls into several movements. In the first, prehistoric apes, confronted by a mysterious black monolith, teach themselves that bones can be used as weapons, and thus discover their first tools. I have always felt that the smooth artificial surfaces and right angles of the monolith, which was obviously *made* by intelligent beings, triggered the realization in an ape brain that intelligence could be used to shape the objects of the world.

The bone is thrown into the air, and dissolves into a space shuttle (this has been called the longest flash-forward in the history of the cinema). We meet Dr. Heywood Floyd (William Sylvester), en route to a space station and the Moon. This section is willfully antinarrative; there are no breathless dialogue passages to tell us of his mission, and instead Kubrick shows us the minutiae of the flight: The design of the cabin, the details of in-flight service, the effects of zero gravity.

Then comes the docking sequence, with its waltz, and for a time even the restless in the audience are silenced, I imagine, by the sheer wonder of the visuals. On board, we see familiar brand names, we participate in an enigmatic conference among the scientists of several nations, we see such gimmicks as a videophone and a zero-gravity toilet.

The sequence on the Moon (which looks as real as the actual video of the Moon-landing a year later) is a variation on the film's opening sequence. Man is confronted with a monolith, just as the apes were, and is drawn to a similar conclusion: *This must have been made.* And as the first monolith led to the discovery of tools, so the second leads to the employment of man's most elaborate tool: the space ship *Discovery*, employed by man in partnership with the artificial intelligence of the onboard computer, named HAL 9000.

Life on board the *Discovery* is presented as a long, eventless routine of exercise, maintenance checks, and chess games with HAL. Only when the astronauts fear that HAL's programming has failed does a level of suspense emerge; their challenge is to somehow get around HAL, which has been programmed to believe, "This mission is too important for me to allow you to jeopardize it." Their efforts lead to one of the great shots in the cinema, as the men attempt to have a private conversation in a space pod, and HAL reads their lips. The way Kubrick edits this scene so that we can discover what HAL is doing is masterful in its restraint: He makes it clear, but doesn't insist on it. He trusts our intelligence.

Later comes the famous "star gate" sequence, a sound and light journey in which the astronaut Dave Bowman (Keir Dullea) travels through what we might now call a wormhole, into another place, or dimension, that is unexplained. At journey's end is the comfortable bedroom suite in which he grows old, eating his meals quietly, napping, living the life (I imagine) of a zoo animal who has been placed in a familiar environment. And then the Star Child. There is never an explanation of the other race which presumably left the monoliths and provided the star gate and the bedroom. *2001* lore suggests Kubrick and Clarke tried and failed to create plausible aliens. It is just as well. The alien race exists more effectively in negative space: We react to its invisible presence more strongly than we possibly could to any actual representation.

2001: A Space Odyssey is in many respects a silent film. There are few conversations that could not be handled with title cards. Much of the dialogue exists only to *show* people talking to one another, without much regard to content (this is true of the conference on the space station). Ironically, the dialogue containing the most feeling comes from HAL, as it pleads for its "life" and sings *Daisy.*

The film creates its effects essentially out of visuals and music. It is meditative. It does not cater to us, but wants to inspire us, enlarge us. Nearly thirty years after it was made, it has not dated in any important detail, and although special effects have become more versatile in the computer age, Trumbull's work remains completely convincing—more convincing, perhaps, than more sophisticated effects in later films, because it looks more plausible, more like documentary footage than like elements in a story.

Only a few films are transcendent, and work upon our minds and imaginations like music or prayer or a vast belittling landscape. Most movies are about characters with a goal in mind, who obtain it after difficulties either comic or dramatic. *2001: A Space Odyssey* is not about a goal but about a quest, a need. It does not hook its effects on specific plot points, nor does it ask us to identify with Dave Bowman or any other character. It says to us: We became men when we learned to think. Our minds have given us the tools to understand where we live and who we are. Now it is time to move on to the next step, to know that we live not on a planet but among the stars, and that we are not flesh but intelligence.

2001: A Space Odyssey ★ ★ ★ ★
G, 139 m., 1968

Keir Dullea (David Bowman), Gary Lockwood (Frank Poole), William Sylvester (Heywood Floyd), Daniel Richter (Moonwatcher), Leonard Rossiter (Smyslov), Margaret Tyzack (Elena). MGM presents a film directed by Stanley Kubrick and produced by Kubrick and Victor Lyndon. Screenplay by Arthur C. Clarke and Kubrick, based on Clarke's story *The Sentinel.* Photographed by John Alcott and Geoffrey Unsworth. Special effects by Douglas Trumbull. Music by Aram Khachaturyan, Gyorgy Ligeti, Johann Strauss, and Richard Strauss. Edited by Ray Lovejoy. Production design by Ernest Archer, Harry Lange, and Anthony Masters.

It was e. e. cummings, the poet, who said he'd rather learn from one bird how to sing than teach 10,000 stars how not to dance. I imagine cummings would not have enjoyed Stanley Kubrick's *2001: A Space Odyssey,* in which stars dance but birds do not sing. The fascinating thing about this film is that it fails on the human level but succeeds magnificently on a cosmic scale.

Kubrick's universe, and the spaceships he constructed to explore it, are simply out of scale with human concerns. The ships are perfect, impersonal machines that venture from one planet to another, and if men are tucked away somewhere inside them, then they get there too. But the achievement belongs to the machine. And Kubrick's actors seem to sense this; they are lifelike but without emotion, like figures in a wax museum. Yet the machines are necessary because man himself is so helpless in the face of the universe.

Kubrick begins his film with a sequence in which one tribe of apes discovers how splendid it is to be able to hit the members of another tribe over the head. Thus do man's ancestors become tool-using animals. At the same time, a strange monolith appears on Earth. Until this moment in the film, we have seen only natural shapes: earth and sky and arms and legs. The shock of the monolith's straight edges and square corners among the weathered rocks is one of the most effective moments in the film. Here, you see, is perfection. The apes circle it warily, reaching out to touch, then jerking away. In a million years, man will reach for the stars with the same tentative motion.

Who put the monolith there? Kubrick never answers, for which I suppose we must be thankful. The action advances to the year 2001, when explorers on the Moon find another of the monoliths. This one beams signals toward Jupiter.

And man, confident of his machines, brashly follows the trail.

Only at this point does a plot develop. The ship is manned by two pilots, Keir Dullea and Gary Lockwood. Three scientists are put on board in suspended animation to conserve supplies. The pilots grow suspicious of the computer, HAL, which runs the ship. But they behave so strangely—talking in monotones like characters from *Dragnet*—that we're hardly interested.

There is hardly any character development in the plot, then, and as a result little suspense. What remains fascinating is the fanatic care with which Kubrick has built his machines and achieved his special effects. There is not a single moment, in this long film, when the audience can see through the props. The stars look like stars and outer space is bold and bleak.

Some of Kubrick's effects have been criticized as tedious. Perhaps they are, but I can understand his motives. If his space vehicles move with agonizing precision, wouldn't we have laughed if they'd zipped around like props on *Captain Video*? This is how it would really be, you find yourself believing.

In any event, all the machines and computers are forgotten in the astonishing last half-hour of this film, and man somehow comes back into his own. Another monolith is found beyond Jupiter, pointing to the stars. It apparently draws the spaceship into a universe where time and space are twisted.

What Kubrick is saying, in the final sequence, apparently, is that man will eventually outgrow his machines, or be drawn beyond them by some cosmic awareness. He will then become a child again, but a child of an infinitely more advanced, more ancient race, just as apes once became, to their own dismay, the infant stage of man.

And the monoliths? Just road markers, I suppose, each one pointing to a destination so awesome that the traveler cannot imagine it without being transfigured. Or as cummings wrote on another occasion, "Listen—there's a hell of a good universe next door; let's go."

The Best Films of 1999

1. *Being John Malkovich*

The Telluride and Toronto Festivals had already started lobbing in great new films, and by the time I saw *Being John Malkovich* and *Three Kings* early in October, it was clear that Hollywood's hounds of creativity had been set loose and were running free. The last four months of 1999 were a rich and exciting time for moviegoers—there were so many wonderful films that for the first time in a long time, it was hard to keep up.

Being John Malkovich was the year's best, a film so endlessly inventive that I started grinning at the way it kept devising new ways to surprise me. Most movies top load their bright ideas in the first half-hour; this first feature from music video vet Spike Jonze, with screenplay by Charlie Kaufman, is a continuing cascade. And unlike many MTV refugees, Jonze doesn't crank up the volume and the visual overkill; his film unfolds slyly, with delight, like a magician showing you the trick is far from over.

John Cusack stars, as a man who gets a job on floor 7½ of a very strange building (the visuals inspire sustained laughter). Behind a filing case, he finds a hole in the wall that is a portal directly into the brain of the actor John Malkovich (playing himself). First Cusack and then a series of paying customers line up to take their trip inside Malkovich, and in one dizzying scene Malkovich even enters his own brain, which is like turning your consciousness inside-out. The movie is funny and very smart, metaphysical in a way, and so bountiful you feel not just admiration but gratitude.

2. *Magnolia*

Another film that seems set free from convention. It begins with a Ricky Jay narration about strange coincidences, and we think that's a setup for coincidences in this film, but actually it's a different kind of tip-off. Writer-director Paul Thomas Anderson *(Boogie Nights)* intercuts several stories about people in or near the L.A. entertainment industry, in a series of scenes about fathers and sons, about impending death, about people on the edge. You can feel the joy of the actors, sinking their teeth into showboat roles, and Tom Cruise takes a role that could be parody (a professional stud who teaches seminars on picking up women) and U-turns it into a surprising examination of the stud's painful past.

3. *Three Kings*

Another dazzling display of directorial virtuosity, by David O. Russell. On one level, it's an adventure tale about soldiers in the Gulf War who capture a map to Saddam's horde of stolen gold. On another level, it's a catch-22 examination of the insanity of war, where every morning you find out who you are, or aren't, shooting at today. The world seems to shrink while we're watching, as a prisoner places a cellular call to his wife and a cable news reporter stands in the middle of the action. The violence and arbitrary nature of war is captured in startling photography (wounds have never seemed so real), and the movie is somehow cocky, satiric, and moving all at once. Remarkable that this war-action comedy could also be praised by President Clinton for its politics.

4. *Boys Don't Cry*

Two of the year's best performances, by Hilary Swank and Chloe Sevigny, in the story of a girl named Teena Brandon who declared herself a boy named Brandon Teena. Not a hip excursion along the gender divide, but a small-town story of a girl (Swank) who acted according to a nature she only murkily understood, and another girl (Sevigny) who may have suspected there was something strange about Brandon, but found "he" was infinitely preferable to the town's violent and brain-blinkered louts. Kimberly Peirce's movie helps us understand the motives behind gay-bashing and murder, crimes that feed on ignorance and low self-esteem, often fueled by drugs and booze.

5. *Bringing Out the Dead*

A harrowing, exhilarating ride on the wild side from Martin Scorsese, who stars Nicolas Cage as a paramedic in an emergency response vehicle in New York's Hell's Kitchen. Scorsese's kinetic camera and Paul Schrader's passionate script give the movie a headlong energy; the Cage character ventures out every night into a sea of suffering, with little hope he can really make much of a difference: "I came to realize that my work was less about saving lives than about bearing witness." In an age of irony, Scorsese and Schrader refuse to stand back from their existential themes, but plunge in without compromise.

6. *Princess Mononoke*

Hayao Miyazaki is the greatest living animator, and this is his best work, set at the dawn of the Iron Age, when some men still lived in harmony with nature and others were trying to tame and defeat it. It is not a simplistic tale of good and evil, but the story of how humans, forest animals, and nature gods all fight for their share of the new emerging order. One of the most visually inventive films I have ever seen, it's proof that animation is suited not only for family films, but also provides the freedom to tell stories that would otherwise be impossible to visualize.

7. *The War Zone*

Tim Roth, a great actor, here proves he is a great director as well. A seemingly happy family from London has relocated to a bleak landscape in Devon, in winter. The mother is having another baby; a boy realizes his sister is being abused by their father. The film is not simply about incest (it is not simply about anything), but about how families can be built on lies and maintained by emotional blackmail. As subtle, complex, and harrowing as a film by Bergman.

8. *American Beauty*

The last year in the life of a man who is unloved by his wife, not respected by his daughter, and not needed at work. At the end of the year his life is a shambles, but in a strange way he has found happiness. Kevin Spacey's performance is one of the year's best, with Annette Bening and Thora Birch making family dinnertime a species of hell; the family next door has problems of its own, in a suburbia that seems to hum with hate, fear, resentment, and lust. Sam Mendes's direction shows a world glossy on the surface, disturbing just beneath.

9. *Topsy-Turvy*

One of the best films ever made about life in the theater. Mike Leigh's story is about a crisis in the most famous of London theatrical partnerships, when Sullivan tells Gilbert he doesn't want to write any more silly operettas. Then Gilbert concocts the plot of *The Mikado*, and they're off in a frenzy of contracts, theater leases, salaries, personnel problems, casting, rehearsals, costumes, and backstage romance. A sustained rehearsal scene, with Jim Broadbent as Gilbert, shows how performances are built bit by bit and detail by detail. Lots of great music too.

10. *The Insider*

The story of a tobacco industry scientist (Russell Crowe) who is gingerly coaxed into telling his secrets by a patient producer for *60 Minutes* (Al Pacino). Two backstage stories, one about big tobacco's cover-up of damaging facts, the other about the problems that reporter Mike Wallace (Christopher Plummer) and executive producer Don Hewitt (Philip Baker Hall) have getting CBS to air the segment. A brilliant story of journalism fueled by anger, as it becomes clear the tobacco industry knew its product was deadly, and lied about it.

Special Jury Prize

At major film festivals around the world, something called the Special Jury Prize is awarded to a film the jurors love, but which didn't quite win first place. In recent years I've chosen five titles, named alphabetically, for such an award. Call it a tie for eleventh place.

Eric Rohmer's *An Autumn Tale* was a sunny story of a forty-fiveish French woman who owns a vineyard but (her friend thinks) needs a husband. Her daughter's girlfriend thinks the same thing, and their intersecting schemes lead to high and warm humor at someone else's wedding.

Robert Altman's *Cookie's Fortune* takes place in a small Mississippi town where a death is mistaken for a murder, leading to strange alliances and the discovery of old family skeletons. Rich comic performances by Glenn Close, Julianne Moore, Charles S. Dutton, and a colorful supporting cast.

Norman Jewison's *The Hurricane* stars Denzel Washington in a performance of astonishing power, as Ruben "Hurricane" Carter, a boxer framed for murder and given three life sentences. The film's emotional wallop develops after a young boy buys his first book, a used one, for a quarter. It is Carter's autobiography, and it inspires the boy and his foster family to mount a seemingly doomed appeal for the boxer's freedom.

Patricia Rozema's *Mansfield Park* was an uncommonly intelligent story made from Jane Austen's novel and journals, showing a young woman (Frances O'Connor) whose matrimonial future seems to offer limited choices—until she boldly takes her life into her own hands.

Anthony Minghella's *The Talented Mr. Ripley* stars Matt Damon as a poor man who wants to steal, not a rich man's wealth, but his identity. Sent under false pretenses to bring a playboy (Jude Law) back from Europe, he weaves a tissue of lies and impersonations, improvising brilliantly when on the edge of being exposed. Gwyneth Paltrow plays the rich kid's girlfriend, who isn't as suspicious as she should be, because he's so unreliable anyway.

The Chuck Jones Award

Named for the beloved author of so many of the finest moments of Bugs and Daffy, this category honors the best work in animation. In addition to *Princess Mononoke,* which is in my top ten, the award goes alphabetically to:

Fantasia 2000, a new demonstration of Walt Disney's 1940 brainstorm: Why not set classical music to animated fantasies, both realistic and abstract? Seen on the big IMAX screen, it's a wondrous sound and light trip.

The Iron Giant tells an enchanting story about a boy who makes friends with a robot from outer space at the height of the Sputnik era. The Giant was designed as a weapon, but, with echoes of *E.T.,* becomes the boy's friend and learns he is not doomed to kill because "you are what you choose to be."

South Park. On this one I was, and still am, conflicted. It is incredibly raunchy, testing the limits of R and the possibilities of nausea, yet at the same time bold in its social satire and fear-less in the way it exposes hypocrisy. One balances between admiration and disbelief. I guess that's a compliment.

Tarzan was inspired not so much by the countless B movies as by the original Edgar Rice Burroughs book, transformed here into a story that embodies notions of animal rights. The Disney animation is liberating, especially in sequences where Tarzan carries Jane on a dizzying flight through the treetops.

Toy Story 2. There's a crisis when a battered Woody, left behind by his owner, seems destined to be shipped forever to a toy museum in Japan. What's better? Immortality as an exhibit, or a short life as a child's most beloved toy? Comedy, action, brilliant computer animation—and philosophy.

Documents from Life

A good documentary can create a fascination beyond any fiction, because what we see really counts for the people it is happening to. This year was especially rich in documentaries; these are my favorites, alphabetically.

American Movie, by Chris Smith, charts the long, strange trip of Mark Borchardt, a Wisconsin man who *must* make movies—and makes his disordered life a mission to that end, enlisting aged uncles, unwilling friends, and a long-suffering mother. He's convinced a short horror film will finance his long-dreamed-of major work, and we watch with laughter and sometimes disbelief as he marches heedlessly toward his dream.

Genghis Blues is another strange odyssey. A blind San Francisco bluesman named Paul Pena hears haunting music on his shortwave radio, learns it is "throat singing" from the (then) Soviet Republic of Tuva, learns how to do it himself, and journeys to Tuva for the annual competition. One of those films where every scene seems as unlikely as it is persuasive.

Julia Sweeney's *God Said, 'Ha!'* is a monologue about a year in her life when her brother's cancer led to the brother and both of her parents moving in with her, with results both sad and comic ("Julia," says her mom, "I found a bulb—but I didn't know if there was some special way to screw it in"). The film has a special meaning, and offers comic catharsis for families touched by cancer.

Doug Block's *Home Page* was a film for the

century's end: Filmed with a handheld digital camera, it told the story of Justin Hall, whose all-revealing journal helped set the tone for the early months of the emerging Web. After a Sundance premiere, it was marketed in an appropriate way, with free screenings on the Web (www.ifilm.com) to promote a New York theatrical opening and a simultaneous video release.

The Last Days, part of Steven Spielberg's Holocaust project, preserved testimony from survivors of the death camps in Hungary. Stories both heartbreaking and horrifying lead up to an ending that has a theme (and power) similar to *Schindler's List:* U.S. Representative Tom Lantos and his wife, who lost all of their family members, are surrounded by a lawnful of grandchildren.

Mr. Death is the latest from Errol Morris, the gifted artist whose films become meditations on man's struggle against death and nature. His subject this time: A man whose limited expertise (designing killing machines for death rows) leads him into an ill-advised alliance with Holocaust deniers. Why does he cherish their embrace? The hangman always needs friends.

On the Ropes is as powerful, in its way, as *Hoop Dreams,* telling the stories of three boxers who hope to use the sport to escape from poverty. Most heartbreaking is the experience of Tyrene Manson, a Golden Gloves candidate who is railroaded on an unlikely drug charge by an uncaring court and inattentive attorneys (both prosecuting and defense). The film makes you so angry you want to shout at the screen.

Honorable Mention

Hirokazu Kore-eda's *After Life,* the Japanese fable of a heavenly way station; *Blair Witch,* by Eduardo Sanchez and Daniel Myrick, which won huge audiences with its story of low-rent filmmakers lost in the woods; Goran Paskaljevic's powerful *Cabaret Balkan,* with its cynical view of endless rounds of ethnic hate and terror; Majid Majidi's wonderful film from Iran, *Children of Heaven,* which told the story of a poor boy's desperation to replace his sister's lost shoes; Erick Zonca's *The Dreamlife of Angels,* the shaky friendship of two working-class girls in France; Milos Forman's *Man on the Moon,* with its uncanny performance by Jim Carrey as the tunnel-visioned comic Andy Kaufman; Lawrence Kasdan's gentle *Mumford,* about people curing themselves by learning to listen a little better; Francois Girard's *Red Violin,* many stories, much romance and intrigue, one violin; Tim Burton's *Sleepy Hollow,* one of the best-looking, most atmospheric films of the year; David Lynch's *The Straight Story,* with its luminous performance by Richard Farnsworth; and Michael Polish's *Twin Falls Idaho,* written by and starring Michael and his brother Mark as conjoined twins—lonely, yet never alone.

And I also valued: *All About My Mother, Bowfinger, Civil Action, Dick, Dogma, Election, Eyes Wide Shut, Felicia's Journey, General, The Green Mile, Guinevere, Last Night, Liberty Heights, Limbo, The Loss of Sexual Innocence, My Name Is Joe, My Son the Fanatic, October Sky, The Phantom Menace, Private Confessions, Summer of Sam, Sweet and Lowdown, Tango, The Winslow Boy, sw* and *The World Is Not Enough.*

The Best Films of the 1990s

When I asked the director Martin Scorsese to join me on TV to select the ten best films of the 1990s, I wasn't surprised when only three titles turned up on both our lists. There is no science involved. It is all opinion—subjective, stubborn, sometimes defiant, as we defend the movies that spoke most urgently to us.

Nothing illustrates that more than the top title on Scorsese's list, a Chinese film actually made in 1986. He defends his choice on the grounds that it wasn't widely seen here until 1990—and more to the point, he loved it and passionately wanted to talk about it. My own first choice is a documentary, even though fictional films are probably expected on such lists. But no other film in the 1990s reached me like *Hoop Dreams* did.

Here is Scorsese's list: 1. *Horse Thief* (Zhuangzhuang Tian); 2. *The Thin Red Line* (Terrence Malick); 3. *A Borrowed Life* (Nien-Jen Wu);

4. *Eyes Wide Shut* (Stanley Kubrick); 5. *Bad Lieutenant* (Abel Ferrara); 6. *Breaking the Waves* (Lars von Trier); 7. *Bottle Rocket* (Wes Anderson); 8. *Crash* (David Cronenberg); 9. *Fargo* (Ethan and Joel Coen); 10. (tie) *Malcolm X* (Spike Lee) and *Heat* (Michael Mann). His comments are available at www.ebert-roeper-movies.com.

My List:

1. *Hoop Dreams*

Sheer chance plays a role in the success of any film, and rarely has it produced more moving results than in this documentary about two Chicago grade-school kids who dream of pro basketball stardom. The film follows Arthur Agee and William Gates through high school. Both are recruited by a suburban powerhouse; one ends up back at his neighborhood school. One makes it to the state tournament, the other watches from the stands. A perceptive social document, yes, but because the camera is there at the right time and events turn out as they do, a film where the real-life drama outreaches any fiction film of the decade. Made by Steve James, Frederick Marx, and Peter Gilbert.

2. *Pulp Fiction*

Quentin Tarantino's 1994 film was certainly the most influential of the 1990s, inspiring dozens of Sundance wanna-bes to experiment with circular plot lines and pop-topical dialogue references. But what made the film great was its vivid characters and a story that cycled through humor, irony, stylistic invention, and sudden violence. QT used generic conventions, but broke free of their payoffs; we thought we knew where we stood, but we didn't. And just before moments of violence he cut away to perfectly timed reaction shots, redeeming laughter from what in lesser hands would have been gore. Inventive, fresh, endlessly entertaining.

3. *GoodFellas*

Martin Scorsese's 1990 movie starred Ray Liotta in the based-on-fact story of Henry Hill, a mid-level mobster who talked to the feds and disappeared into witness protection. The film follows Hill's progress through the mob, from starstruck kid to flashy spender to coke-addled paranoid. Robert De Niro, Joe Pesci, Lorraine Bracco, and Paul Sorvino have key roles in a film where the logic of the mob code produces both humor and moments of heart-stopping violence (Pesci's instantaneous recognition of his own inevitable death is a supreme film event). As the feds' net tightens around Henry Hill in the closing scenes, Scorsese subtly increases the tempo, until we seem to be running right along with him.

4. *Fargo*

The decade's supreme human comedy, starring Frances McDormand as the police chief of Brainerd, Minnesota, who trudges through deep snows, comforts her hubby, and plunders hotel buffets while unraveling the foolish schemes of a car salesman (William H. Macy). He only wants to get some money out of his father-in-law, but sets in motion a kidnapping and a bloodbath. Ethan and Joel Coen's dialogue gently kids Minnesota speech patterns while lovingly showing ordinary folks in extraordinary situations. Macy's desperate attempts at damage control are doomed and hilarious; McDormand creates one of the screen's unforgettable characters. The snowbound landscape sets an atmosphere both beautiful and forbidding.

5. *Three Colors: Blue, White and Red*

The late Polish director Krzysztof Kieslowski flowered during the decade. After ending the 1980s with *The Decalogue*, ten hour-long films whose modern stories mirrored the Ten Commandments, he entered the 1990s with *The Double Life of Veronique* and then made *Blue* (1993), *White*, and *Red* (both 1994). Inspired by the French goals of liberty, equality, and fraternity, they dealt boldly with coincidence, synchronicity, and unexpected connections between people seemingly not destined to meet. Like Tarantino, Kieslowski allowed his plots to circle and loop; his leading performances by Juliette Binoche, Julie Delpy, and Irene Jacob were masterful portraits of intelligent women trying to puzzle their way through the contradictions of fate.

6. *Schindler's List*

Steven Spielberg's Holocaust epic affirmed the worth of ethical conduct even in seemingly hopeless circumstances. Liam Neeson starred as Oskar Schindler, a German gentile who opened a munitions factory in Nazi-occupied Poland

and employed Jews at starvation wages. His ostensible goal was to become rich. By the end of the war he had saved the lives of hundreds of Jews and defrauded the Nazis with a factory that never produced a single usable shell. Those he saved were a small number compared to the millions who died, but his act affirmed humanity in the midst of evil. Spielberg's film shows the Holocaust in vivid and terrible detail, extracts a small story of hope from it, and ends with the overwhelming emotional impact of those who survived because of Schindler, and their descendants, visiting his grave.

7. *Breaking the Waves*

Lars von Trier's *Breaking the Waves* (1996) hammers at conventional morality with the belief that God not only sees all, but understands and forgives a great deal more than we give him credit for. Emily Watson and Stellan Skarsgard, newcomers at the time, star in the story of a romance between a rough oil-rig worker and a simple village girl who is transfixed, and transformed, by love. When an accident brings the man near death, her own faith comes into conflict with the stern teachings of her church elders, and then, in a moment of great symbolic force, her fierce convictions are affirmed by heaven itself.

8. *Leaving Las Vegas*

I admire films that go for broke, that push the emotional boundaries, that are not timid in their exploration of human extremes. Mike Figgis's *Leaving Las Vegas* (1995) centers on a Nicolas Cage performance that shows a man drowning in an alcoholic crack-up. An early scene, in which he tries to appear jocular while his brain seems about to fly apart, creates tension that the film never releases. He goes to Vegas to drink himself to death, encounters a call girl (Elisabeth Shue) who is touched by his suffering, and finds a kind of redemption even as his life spirals away. Shooting quickly in 16mm, Figgis was able to capture fragile human emotions on the run.

9. *Malcolm X*

Spike Lee's 1992 biography of the Black Muslim leader was a continuation, in a way, of the choice presented at the end of his *Do the Right Thing* (1989) between the nonviolence of Martin Luther King and Malcolm's starker vision. Denzel Washington's performance was strong but also supple, showing the way life and experience changed and shaped Malcolm on his journey from a street kid to a leader whose philosophy was broadening even at the moment of his assassination. Like so many of Lee's films, an exercise in empathy, in which we are not simply confronted by Malcolm, but allowed to identify with him.

10. *JFK*

Not a factual film about the Kennedy assassination, but truthful and accurate in the way it depicts how millions of Americans *feel* about his death. We are sure the whole truth has not been told, that dark conspiracies played out, that the guilty remained unidentified. And Oliver Stone's 1991 film plays on that paranoia with its brilliant mixture of styles and tones, starring Kevin Costner as a district attorney who is convinced he knows the answer to the mystery. Breathtakingly paced, filmed with dead-on period accuracy, capturing the whole hidden world of the Rubys and Shaws and others exposed to the glare of JFK conspiracy-hunters.

The Most Influential Films of the Century

The motion picture was invented before 1900, but "the movies" as we know them are entirely a twentieth-century phenomenon, shaping our times and sharing these 100 years with us. This was the first century recorded for the eyes and ears of the future; think what we would give to see even the most trivial film from the year 1000, and consider what a gift we leave.

This list of the ten most influential films of the century is not to be confused with a selection of the century's best, although a few titles would be on both lists. As film grew into an art form, these were the milestones along the way.

1. The early Chaplin shorts

In 1913, there were no Charlie Chaplin movies. In 1914, he made no less than thirty-five, in an astonishing outpouring of energy and creativity that made Chaplin the first great star. Stardom was to become so inseparable from the movies that it is startling to realize that many early films had unbilled performers. In the earliest days just the moving picture was enough; audiences were astonished by moving trains and gunshots. Then Chaplin and his contemporaries demonstrated how completely the movies could capture a unique personality.

2. *Birth of a Nation*

D. W. Griffith's 1915 film is a tarnished masterpiece, a breakthrough in art and craft, linked to a story so racist it is almost unwatchable. This was the film that defined the film language, that taught audiences and filmmakers all over the world the emerging grammar of the shot, the montage, and the camera. At 159 minutes, it tilted Hollywood's balance away from shorts and toward the more evolved features that would become the backbone of the new art form. What a shame that it also glorified the Ku Klux Klan.

3. *Battleship Potemkin*

Sergei Eisenstein's 1925 film about a revolutionary uprising of Russian sailors was considered so dangerous that it was still banned decades later in some countries, including its native Soviet Union. It demonstrated Eisenstein's influential theory of montage—of the way images took on new meanings because of the way they were juxtaposed. It also demonstrated the power of film as politics, polemic, and propaganda—power that many regimes, not least the Nazis, would use to alter world history.

4. *The Jazz Singer*

"You ain't heard nothin' yet!" Al Jolson promised, and movies were never the same. The first talkie was released in 1927 (actually, it was a silent with sound passages tacked on), and although silent film survived through 1928 ("the greatest single year in the history of the movies," argues Peter Bogdanovich), the talkies were the future. Purists argued that sound destroyed the pure art of silent film; others said the movies were a hybrid from the beginning, borrowing whatever they could from every possible art and science.

5. *Snow White and the Seven Dwarfs*

Eisenstein himself called Disney's 1937 animated feature the greatest film in history. Excessive praise, but world audiences were enthralled by the first full-length cartoon. Animation was as old as the movies (the underlying principle was much older), but Disney was the first to take it seriously as a worthy style for complex characters and themes. Disney's annual features continue to win enormous audiences and have grown in artistry and sophistication; audiences, alas, seem resistant to animation by anyone else, despite some recent success by the geniuses of Japanese "anime."

6. *Citizen Kane*

If *Birth of a Nation* assembled all the breakthroughs prior to 1915, Orson Welles's 1941 masterpiece was the harvest of the emerging art form. It was not the first to use deep-focus photography, or overlapping dialogue, or interlocking flashbacks, or rotating points of view, or trick photography, or a teasing combination of fact and fiction, or a sampling of genres (newsreel, comedy, drama, musical, biopic), or a charismatic director who was what the French later defined as an "auteur." But in the way it assembled the pieces, it dazzled audiences and other filmmakers and so fully exploited its resources that *Kane* is often voted the greatest of all films.

7. *Shadows*

John Cassavetes's 1960 film was a salvo that shook Hollywood to its foundations. Renting a 16mm camera and working with friends on a poverty budget, he made a film totally outside the studio system. That had been done before, of course, but *Shadows* was the symbolic standard-bearer of the emerging New American Cinema movement, which gave birth to underground films and to today's booming indies. Cassavetes demonstrated that it was not necessary to have studio backing and tons of expensive equipment to make a theatrical film.

8. *Star Wars*

There had been blockbusters before, from *Birth of a Nation* to *GWTW* to *Lawrence of Arabia*. But George Lucas's 1977 space opera changed all the rules. It defined the summer as the prime releasing season, placed a new emphasis on young audiences, used special effects, animation, computers, and exhilarating action to speed up the pacing, and grossed so much money that many of the best young directors gave up their quest for the Great American Film and aimed for the box-office crown instead. Now most of the top-grossers every year follow in *Star Wars'* footsteps, from *Armageddon* to *The Matrix* to *Titanic*.

9. *Toy Story*

This delightful 1995 computer-animated feature may have been the first film of the twenty-first-century. It was the first feature made entirely on computers, which allowed more realistic movement of the elements and the point of view, and characters that were more three-dimensional in appearance. Someday, computer-animated movies may be able to re-create "real" human actors and settings. Whether that is desirable or not, *Toy Story* demonstrated that it was on the horizon. If films immigrate from celluloid and flesh and blood to the digital domain, this film will be seen as the turning point.

10. *The Blair Witch Project*

Important not for its entertainment value, which was considerable, but for what it represented in technical terms. It was the first indie blockbuster, a film made for about $24,000 and shot entirely on inexpensive, handheld cameras (one film, one video), which grossed more than $150 million. The message was inescapable: In the next century, technology will place the capacity for feature filmmaking into the hands of anyone who is sufficiently motivated, and audiences will not demand traditional "production values" before parting with their money.

* * *

There is not one conclusion, but two. Films are getting bigger and smaller, cheaper and more expensive, both at once. While mass-marketed blockbusters dominate the market, independent directors have the ability to make their own films almost by hand. Digital techniques are crucial to both trends. Will the future belong to *Star Wars* clones made with *Toy Story* techniques? Or to films made in the tradition of the early Chaplin quickies (some shot in a day), the Cassavetes-inspired independents, and the *Blair Witch* technology? It belongs to both, I think. Which will be interesting.

Interviews

Woody Allen

May 18, 2000—In his new movie *Small Time Crooks*, Woody Allen plays an ex-con who dreams up a bank heist. It involves tunneling into a vault from a basement down the street, and he installs his wife (Tracey Ullman) to run a cookie store as a cover. The cookies make them millionaires, the money goes to her head, and she hires a British art expert (Hugh Grant) to tutor her on culture, while her husband misses his old pals and their card games.

Allen rarely travels to promote his movies. But this time he agreed to some campus appearances, including a Q&A session at the University of Chicago. Before he headed down to the campus in Hyde Park, we talked in his hotel room, and here are some of the things I learned:

—"I did stand-up here for five or six years in the mid-1960s, and cut my first two albums in Chicago. That's when I met Jean and John Doumanian; she's produced a lot of my films. We used to hang out at O'Connell's, diagonally across from Mr. Kelly's. It was an all-night coffee shop. We liked to sit in the window and watch Rush Street. I was the opening night celebrity at Franksville, the hot dog place up from O'Connell's. I declared it open. I was the best they could do. We'd attend Cubs games and eat ribs at the Black Angus, and go to Hefner's place frequently."

—"I've made about one movie a year for thirty-five years. I've been productive, but it's not as big a deal as one thinks because I've had factors that enabled this to happen. Right from the start I have the mechanics in place, so when I pull the thing out of the typewriter, I hand it to the production manager and they're budgeting, casting, and going. With some other person, Scorsese or a director of that quality, he's gotta get the money for it. He says, 'Well, I need $58 million to make this movie,' and he's gotta interest Leonardo DiCaprio now or Sharon Stone or somebody. I don't have that problem. As soon as the script is over it's like hitting the ground running. When *Small Time Crooks* was finished, and I

don't mean this to sound facetious (it will, but it's not), I gave it to DreamWorks—and then what do I do with my life? I'm home, I play with the baby, I go for a walk with my wife, I practice the clarinet, I watch a Knicks game, I see a movie. That's easy for a couple of days or a week. Then I don't know what to do with my life. So I start writing again. And if you're a writer, how long does it take to write a script?"

—"I'm accused of sameness. I have a feeling that in some way that's not perceptible to me, people think my films are like Chinese food. There are 800 different dishes, but in the end it's all Chinese food. When I ask people, 'Why don't you come to my movies?' they say, 'Gee, I saw *Everyone Says I Love You*, I saw *Broadway Danny Rose*, I saw one of the others on television, and I just loved it.' And I wonder, why didn't they see it when it was out? I guess they thought it was one of those Woody Allen pictures. What if I was the Marx Brothers? I'd be very happy to see a Marx Brothers film every year. I don't know; for some reason I've never been able to really maintain a big audience."

—"Basically, I'm a wit. That's even with an out-and-out comedy like *Small Time Crooks*. I think DreamWorks was taken aback by the wit of it. Wit is scary to people. They said, 'What kind of film are you doing?' I said, 'It'll be a film I know you guys will like, because it's a comedy about a group of people who try and rob a bank.' But soon the witty part of the idea came in, that it was really the cookie business that took off, and that's how they suddenly got rich, and how the wealth affected them, and the executives started to sense it was *about* something, in some small way, and began to expect smaller box-office returns."

—"I think a story has to *go* somewhere. It can't just be the same idea from beginning to end. When I did *Purple Rose of Cairo*, I put it away half-written and was not gonna come back to it, because when the actor steps off the screen, that's a great idea, but then what? He steps down off the screen and I have half a movie. But six months later when it was still in the drawer, I happened to think, what if the real actor in Hollywood comes to the town, and both the actor and his screen image are in love with the girl, and she's gotta choose between them? Now the thing became worth doing."

—"With the plot of *Small Time Crooks,* people ask, 'Do you think that money changes people?' It doesn't change people. What it does is liberate them to be who they really are. In this movie, Ray thinks he needs a big score to be happy. He really needs maybe a couple of bucks, but that's all. He doesn't need to rob a bank. That's too big a score because all he wants to do is eat stone crabs and turkey meatballs, and watch television and shoot a little pool. But suddenly he finds he's eating game birds on a bed of lettuce with some kind of sauce, and it's not what he wants in life."

—"I'm sandwiched in the picture between two female comic geniuses, Tracey Ullman and Elaine May. I gotta pull my weight. Tracey is amazing. Sam Cohn, my agent years ago, said, 'You gotta see this other client of mine.' And I said I had six million things on my mind. 'Play this tape! Play this tape!' I kept the tape in my house for months and then one day I played it and I couldn't believe how hilarious she was. Elaine May I've known for thirty-five years, in New York, and she's always been elusive and hilarious. I wanted her for *Take the Money and Run* years ago and she said, 'You wouldn't wanna lay eyes on me. I'm wearing a neck brace.' She wasn't wearing a neck brace; she was just hard to get for movies. This time I sent her the script and she wanted to do it. And Hugh Grant, it just so happened I hit him between films. He had finished one and was not gonna do another one for a little while, so . . ."

—"I get wonderful casts for my movies, if they're between jobs. Nobody is going to turn down $10 million to do a Spielberg film to be in my film for the fun of being in it. But if they're not doing anything else and I send them the material and they like it . . . well, often they *do* like it, because my films concentrate on eccentric or exotic characters, and they like that. Whereas, they may get $10 million to do a picture where they're forced to do special effects and car chases that are not very stimulating. We have a top for everybody of $50,000. It's $5,000 a week for ten weeks and that's whether you're Julia Roberts or whoever. That's all we can afford, so they have to want to do it. Some want their price no matter what. They will not consider working for a cheaper price. I went to George C. Scott and couldn't even get him to read the script, because unless the money was settled first, he was not interested."

—"Soon Yi bought me this sweater. It's been great for me. Now we have a little child. If anyone had told me I would wind up married to a much younger Asian woman, with no interest in show business, I'd have told them they were crazy. All I would go out with were little blond actresses, or women who did something in show business. Suddenly, I find myself with a woman whose interest in life is teaching learning-disabled children, who is not interested in show business, who is much my junior and doesn't know many of the references from my life experience. She's a wonderful person and makes me very, very happy. It's interesting how little you know about yourself as you go through life. I think, my God, why didn't I meet her sooner? I would have had so many more years of happiness."

At the Movies with President Clinton

Washington, D.C., February 3, 2000—He was an only child until he was ten, and both his parents worked. But you could go to the movies for a dime, he remembers, and he went to a lot of them.

"I saw every movie that came my way when I was a child," President Clinton says, "and they fired my imagination—they inspired me. I think it's interesting that I'm fifty-three years old and my favorite movie is *High Noon,* a movie I saw when I was six."

It is one thing to describe yourself as a movie buff. It is another thing to belong to that small club whose members consider the movies a necessity of life. Clinton has often said the best perk in his job is the White House screening room. My guess is, if there wasn't one, he'd sneak out to the multiplex.

In December 1999, I had the opportunity to talk at length with the president about the movies. I expected him to mention *High Noon* and *Casablanca,* and he did—but what about his strongly held opinions about *Fight Club, American Beauty,* and *Three Kings*? Or his favorite recent film, *The Harmonists,* about a German singing group during the rise of the Third Reich? It's a wonderful film, but would you expect the president to have heard of it? This is a man who could talk about the movies for a living.

He'll be fifty-four when he leaves office, and looking for work. There's speculation in Hollywood that he might succeed Jack Valenti as head of the Motion Picture Association of America. He sidestepped my question about that ("I don't know. . . . I'd enjoy doing anything that allowed me to see every new movie that came along . . . but I've never given it any thought"). Still, his proposal for an overhauled movie and TV ratings system, given in his State of the Union address, indicates he may have given it *some* thought, and Clinton is sound on the key international issue facing the MPAA: charges that Hollywood is swamping local film markets. He echoes the Valenti line: "I don't think they should deprive their people of making the choice of coming to American movies."

Of the films he's seen recently, David O. Russell's *Three Kings* is a favorite, perhaps not least because it obliquely criticizes the Gulf War policies of President George Bush. It stars George Clooney, Mark Wahlberg, and Ice Cube in the story of three soldiers who take advantage of a cease-fire to try to steal Saddam Hussein's horde of stolen Kuwaiti gold.

"I loved it," Clinton said, "because it accomplished all these different things. It's a great cheap-thrills movie. Clooney's unbelievable—the screen loves him, and all the other guys are good. It's a tragedy as well as a comedy. And then they do all that high-tech stuff—showing you how bullet wounds affect the body."

He's referring to a special-effects scene where the camera seems to follow a bullet right into a body.

"And," he added, "they tell the very sad story that our country has to come to terms with—of how we falsely raised the hopes of Shiites in the south of Iraq. And what has been done to them since then. Draining those swamps, changing their lives after thousands

of years. It's an atrocity, what Saddam Hussein did to them."

The moviegoer turns into the politician halfway through that analysis. But, of course, *Three Kings* was that rarity, an action comedy with a political conscience.

Clinton also found David Fincher's *Fight Club,* last summer's anticonsumerism movie with Brad Pitt and Edward Norton, "quite good." The film began with an attack on prosperity, which its heroes found so empty that they founded secret clubs where they could seek meaning in their lives by beating each other up.

"Norton and Pitt played their roles really well," Clinton said. "And Helena Bonham Carter was a very compelling figure in it." But it was "a little too nihilist" for him, he said. "It's simply not true that the material advances we've had are inherently bad or empty. They give you the power to define your life more. And I don't mean just for rich people, I mean people that have a decent, middle-class life. It's not all there is to life, but it creates the possibility of fashioning a life that has integrity and meaning."

I wonder, I said, why suburbia is always such a punching bag in the movies. I mentioned *American Beauty,* a front-runner for Oscar nominations.

"I think in a funny way it's like *Fight Club,*" the president said. "It's like, there's got to be more to life than this. Okay, so we've got this nice little neat, suburban lifestyle and we're comfortable—and now what? It was also a disturbing movie, but I thought it was an amazing film. Kevin Spacey was amazing, Annette Bening was great, the kids were just great."

I asked him what movie had affected him deeply, either recently or in his whole lifetime.

"That's hard for me to say because I'm such an ardent moviegoer. I try to see everything. But . . . the story of the five German singers and the piano player."

The Harmonists.

"I loved that movie. It was profoundly moving to me. The idea that these three Jews and three Catholics in pre-Nazi Germany had this jazz group with this very tightly written harmony. That they model it off of an American group they hear, they became the rage of Europe, they come to the United States, and they have to decide whether to stay together. The Nazis say they can't sing anymore, because they can't allow Jews and Catholics to sing together. God, it was a moving thing. The sort of earnestness and almost naive joy of what they did, as against the darkness of the systematic evil that ran up against them."

Our time was about up. As Clinton stood, he mentioned that *Life Is Beautiful* was another of his recent favorites. Then he smiled, remembering an encounter with the irrepressible Roberto Benigni in Italy last year.

"He ran across the room and hurled himself into my arms," the president said.

"What did the Secret Service do?"

He grinned. "They didn't know what to do. What could they do? It was Benigni, you know?"

* * *

The presidential moviegoer on:

—Films that should have been on the AFI's list of 100 great American movies: "*L.A. Confidential.* And at least one of Mel Brooks's movies, either *The Producers* or *Blazing Saddles.* And *The Ten Commandments.* Yul Brynner's obsessive Rameses was just great."

—*Casablanca:* "It's a story about love and honor and courage—the stuff that people care about. Bogart is fabulous in it, and Bergman brings tears to your eyes. I mean, I still can't watch the movie without saying, 'God, I wish I'd known that woman.' She's just riveting on the screen."

—Bogart: "He was magic. He was great in the dramas, he was a great comedian, he was really funny in the funny roles, and in the movies where he played a bad guy he was a compelling bad guy, but it didn't destroy his box-office appeal. He could get away with anything on the screen because he was so authentic. He was gangbusters."

—Meryl Streep: "One of the two or three greatest female actresses ever on the screen. How did she develop the accent for *Sophie's Choice*? And she's also the best actress when she's *not* talking. I remember in *The Deer Hunter,* which is my favorite Vietnam War movie, there's a long period of time where she doesn't say a word; it's one of the most effective scenes I've ever seen in the movies."

—Robert De Niro: "Look at all the different roles De Niro's been in. He's in sixteenth-century south Brazil and he's Jake LaMotta and he's great in all those Italian mobster movies. He's got a real range. Tom Hanks has that kind of range too. He's sort of tactile. He's skinny for *Philadelphia* and he puts on weight for *The Green Mile.*"

—Oscar prediction: "I just saw *The Hurricane* the other night. Denzel Washington had to lose all this weight and become a middleweight boxer for it. It's an inherently compelling story. I think it will be taken very seriously."

—Why the movies are important: "The biggest problem we have in human society now is the oldest, most primitive problem—which is our tribalism, our tendency to go beyond a natural pride in our group, whether it's a racial or an ethnic or religious group or whatever, to fear and distrust and dehumanization and violence against the other. What we've got to learn to do is not just to tolerate each other, but to actually celebrate our differences. The only way you can do that is to be secure in the knowledge that your common humanity is more important than your most significant differences. And movies can help do that. It's really, really important."

Roy Disney

December 28, 1999—One of the side effects of being Walt Disney's nephew is that you are constantly being asked for the name of your favorite Disney movie.

"God knows I've been asked a lot," Roy Disney was telling me. "I always say *Fantasia.* I put *Snow White* second because I think it's another kind of a miracle. But *Fantasia* to me was like a box of chocolates, if you'll forgive the Gump analogy. There's a lot of flavors in there and you can kinda pick and choose."

That was both the glory and the problem with *Fantasia,* which was a flop on its first box-office release in 1940. Audiences who had cheered Disney's first two feature-length cartoons, *Snow White and the Seven Dwarfs* and *Pinocchio,* were dubious about a selection of classical standards matched up to animation that ranged from Mickey Mouse to near-abstraction.

Walt originally thought of *Fantasia* as a work in progress, Roy said; the original plan was that from time to time new music would be added and older segments put in storage. One day Roy's father, Walt's brother Roy, even came home from work with the latest bright idea: "Walt's gonna do the *Flight of the Bumblebee*, and he's gonna fly the bee all the way around the room in stereo."

With the 1940 box-office disappointment, all such plans were put on hold—even after the 1957 rerelease finally put the movie in the black, an achievement that greatly cheered Disney, who died in 1966. The movie was rereleased again in 1968, Roy said, "and then we restored the film pretty thoroughly at the end of the 1980s and released it theatrically, and then on video in 1991. The 1968 release was the famous psychedelic one. For *Fantasia* and *2001*, everybody had to go sit in the front row and smoke a joint, and it was—wow, what were they smoking when they made that movie?"

Now Roy, the kingpin of Disney animation, has dusted off the old vision and produced *Fantasia 2000*, which is entirely new except for everyone's favorite segment from the original, Mickey Mouse in *The Sorcerer's Apprentice*.

The movie's premiere screenings in North America were all in the giant-screen IMAX process, with its banks of surround-sound speakers. That would have pleased Walt, whose original film pioneered movie stereo: "There was this enormous stereo system named Fantasound," Roy said, "that he insisted be installed in the theaters, with speakers everywhere, very expensive, and only good for this one movie. A lot of theater owners said they'd never ever install it, and Walt wouldn't let 'em run it if they didn't."

Disney was visiting Chicago for the opening night of another studio endeavor, the rock opera *Aïda*, by Elton John and Tim Rice, which was in a pre-Broadway run at the Cadillac Palace. We had coffee in his suite at the Four Seasons. In person he looks a lot like his Uncle Walt, right down to the mustache, and his speaking style is folksy and direct. He sounds more like your own uncle than a high-powered Hollywood executive.

He said he was as surprised as anyone that *Fantasia 2000* has turned out to be a film for the changing of the millennium.

"When we started this thing pretty near ten years ago, we had no idea it would all come to-gether for the year 2000. The idea for a new *Fantasia* became viable when the video came out in 1991 and it sold 20 million copies around the world. I went back to Michael Eisner and said, hey, you know, we can actually afford to make the new one now, off the profits on the video. The first notion I had was to carry out Walt's original vision—take the old film, stick in some new pieces, and call it a semi-new movie. But as we started making new stuff, we began to realize that the pieces didn't always go together. The sixty-year-old film has a pace that's more leisurely than we would use in a film made today, and the technology of the new pieces looked and sounded a lot better. Gradually we realized we had to make a new movie. We kept *The Sorcerer's Apprentice*, partly as a homage to the original and partly just because it's still as much fun as when it was new."

Of course Mickey's sequence was originally shot for 35mm and had to be blown up for IMAX, which offers a much higher resolution. "IMAX has a thing they call defocusing, degraining," he said, "where they actually throw it a little bit out of focus and it sort of makes the grain dissolve a little bit so it looks better. It's amazing how the music sounds, too, since it's been through God knows how many iterations with how many restorers. It swoops around the room on you a few times with that weird stereo they did, but it's amazingly good."

You had the whole world of classical music to choose from in making *Fantasia 2000*, I said. Who decided what to use?

"I was certainly the instigator, and I added right from the beginning the 'Pines of Rome' and the Shostakovich piano concerto. Joe Grant, who worked on the original *Fantasia* and was still with us in 1992, brought both the 'Carnival of the Animals' piece and the idea of the flamingo turning into a yo-yo. Michael Eisner called one day after attending the graduation of one of his kids, and said 'Pomp and Circumstance' was a must."

And, of course, who in the Disney stable has more pomp than Donald Duck?

"It's kind of a compliment to Mickey in the *Sorcerer's Apprentice* to let Donald Duck into this film," Roy smiled. "And this is really the old Donald, the guy that loses his cool. It's great when that elephant tromps on him. So that was a lot of fun.

"Our hardest music search probably was for a finale that had the same emotional impact as the original film's combination of 'Night on Bald Mountain' and 'Ave Maria.' We considered Beethoven's 'Ninth' and the 'Hallelujah Chorus,' and finally we settled on Stravinsky's 'Firebird.' I had an idea for the images. I'd driven by Mount St. Helen's not too long after the eruption up there, and I carried that image with me for a long time. And I thought, if I could put a camera up here for the next thousand years and watch what happens to this place, and time-lapse it in five minutes—and that was our finale."

Richard Farnsworth

October 10, 1999—I wonder if Richard Farnsworth would mind if I called him a geezer. Maybe not, if I provided my definition of a geezer: anyone who can sing "I'm an Old Cowhand" and make you believe it. He wears jeans and a cowboy hat like working clothes, and although he's appeared in hundreds of movies and even been nominated for an Oscar, he describes himself as a rancher. You talk to him and sense he'd choke before he told a fib or uttered a four-letter word.

We're having lunch in the Floradora Saloon on Main Street in Telluride, Colorado. He's joined by his fiancée, Jewel Van Valin, whose hair and clothes make her look like a pretty schoolmarm in an old Western—not just for today, she says, but because that's how she always dresses. Farnsworth's new movie, *The Straight Story,* played the night before in the Telluride Film Festival. Now everybody wants his autograph and tells him he'll be nominated for an Oscar. This all happened before, in 1978, when he was nominated for his supporting performance (as an old cowhand) in *Comes a Horseman,* and in 1982, when he starred in *The Grey Fox* as a stagecoach robber who gets out of jail after thirty-three years and switches to robbing trains.

When he made those pictures, he was around sixty, looking older. Now he's seventy-nine, looking exactly the same age. *The Straight Story* is based on the true story of Alvin Straight, an Iowa man who wanted to pay one last visit to his dying brother in Wisconsin. His eyes weren't good enough to get a driver's license, so he hitched up a wagon to a lawn tractor and putt-putted all the way there, depending along the way on the kindness of strangers.

This is a good-hearted G-rated picture by David Lynch, who usually makes bizarre R-rated extravaganzas *(Wild at Heart, Twin Peaks, Blue Velvet).* Why such a sweet movie from the master of the weird? Maybe because the screenplay is by Mary Sweeney, Lynch's partner, who, like everyone else, fell in love with the notion of the geezer on his tractor, defying everybody.

It was an easy role for him to identify with, Farnsworth told me after we settled in at the Floradora.

"I've been around a lot. I've been a farmer, drove a tractor. I identified with him in quite a few things. I liked it because the dialogue weren't so smooth; nothing was hard, you know. Some scripts, you know, you wanna change the dialogue so you can pronounce it. It just reads peculiar.

"But all the same I was gonna turn it down because I had to have a hip replacement. But Dave assured me that he'd make a special seat on the tractor that would mold to me and wouldn't hurt me. The seat was designed by Jack Fisk. That's Sissy Spacek's husband. He was the production designer. Dave told me, 'Jack has come up with a seat that's got silicone in it and it moves to the body, takes the shock off.' So I said, okay. I'm so glad I did. I'd hate to have got out there and not be able to finish it."

That was purely you on the tractor, in all of those shots?

"I did it, mile after mile after mile. Day after day. Dave's awful patient, though. You know, he could tell I was gettin' tired and he'd say, 'That's it for today.' And he'd probably gone much farther with somebody else."

Our drinks arrived. Farnsworth's was a martini.

"Well, here's to you," he said, raising his glass. He sipped. "I have one before lunch. At the ranch I'll make one for myself. It just gives me a little more appetite. But I don't drink any more than that. This'll be it for me."

Most people are happy to get one role of a lifetime, and you've had three, I said. How do you figure that?

He smiled and his face crinkled.

"Well, it's not because I pursued it, you know. I've always been a rancher. I was a stuntman for thirty-five years before I did *Comes a Horseman*. They wanted an old guy that could rope and ride. I'd done that plenty as a stunt man. But I don't know why they thought about me as an actor because I had never acted in the movies. So when they called me over they showed me the script, God, there was so much in it that I didn't think I could handle. Alan Pakula, who was directing it, said, 'You'll have ten weeks to shoot it. We don't shoot these in one day, you know. You might go for days and not even work.' So I took the script and practiced. It seemed to go pretty good. I went back and I read a few lines with Jane Fonda, and Pakula says, 'You do it just like that. You got the job.'"

Working as a stuntman, you had a chance to watch a lot of actors working.

"I was as close as you can get to Hank Fonda. He was kind of a loner but I doubled Hank by size. I did some work with him and Joel Mc-Crea. I really admired their style."

Farnsworth's cheeseburger arrived and he spread ketchup on it as if caulking a leak. I asked him how he got into the stunt business in the first place.

"I roped and rodeoed, and in 1937 Paramount put an ad in the paper that they wanted 200 riders for *Marco Polo*. It was $7 a day to ride, and the wrangling was about $12 a day. I'd been working at a barn for $5 a week. I worked on it for five weeks and made enough money to buy a car, and that's it. I stayed and did *Gunga Din* the next year. That got me started. I did *A Day at the Races* with the Marx Brothers. I was a steeplechase rider."

One thing I like about *The Straight Story*, I said, is the simplicity of the story and the performance. You decide exactly what you have to do. Your brother is dying, your daughter (Sissy Spacek) can't drive either, and so you just use logic and get on the lawn tractor.

"I got to meet Alvin Straight's family. That was a way of getting to know him. He was independent. He was legally blind, and he had both hips were bad, and he was gonna drive himself. He didn't want any help. He drove himself across the country in his new John Deere mower and he was really like that. People we met that put him up said, 'Boy, we had a heck of a time even gettin' him to come into the house.' He wanted to stay out in his little trailer and eat his hot dogs."

I was thinking John Ford could have directed this picture.

"He could have. I worked with John a lot as a stuntman but I never worked as an actor because he'd get a little bit hostile with actors."

He was supposed to be cantankerous.

"He was opinionated, I'll say that. But they all loved him. I couldn't stand somebody shoutin'."

Would Ford even be tough to people like John Wayne and Henry Fonda?

"He could say anything he wanted to Wayne. He got Wayne his first break, you know, and with the Duke it was 'Mr. Ford' to the day the man died."

You knew all the movie cowboys?

"TV too. I worked on them all. *Gunsmoke* was probably the best. I did a few *Rawhides* with Clint Eastwood. I told somebody—'You know, I don't believe he can make it. His expression don't change.' Well, how wrong could you be? I've worked with Clint a lot as a director and as an actor."

Some people are saying you might get another Oscar nomination for *The Straight Story*.

"Wouldn't that be something. Of course, there's lots of competition. I'm a member of the Academy, and we got sent 110 tapes last year. That was a lot of film. I sent 'em all to my daughter. Oh, we watched a few of 'em, the better ones, so people said."

You're only getting films that *somebody* thinks are pretty good.

Farnsworth grinned.

"Some of 'em were pretty bad. I can't believe that they take the time to even make videos of some of 'em."

He mopped up the last of his ketchup with a french fry.

"But you know, I've almost been out of this business for fifteen years. Just ranching. The last film I did was pretty rowdy. It was called *The Getaway*. I come in at the last. But I didn't have to use any four-letter words. I've never had to curse in a movie and I'm not about to start in now."

Tyrene Manson

March 9, 2000—One grain of rice.

The jury that sent Tyrene Manson to jail for drug possession was never told the amount she allegedly possessed.

"Take one grain of rice off your plate," she told me. "That's the size that they found. But they never let the people on the jury know what size it was. I guess they kinda thought it was a whole heap."

And on the basis of that tiny amount, found in a room used by several adults, including a cocaine-addicted uncle, Tyrene Manson missed her Golden Gloves fight, was sent to prison, is in the third year of her sentence, and may not be able to attend the Academy Awards on March 26.

Yes, she's been invited to the Oscars, because *On the Ropes,* a film about her and two other young boxers, has been nominated for Best Documentary.

"A grain of rice," I said. "That could just fall out of somebody's clothes."

"That's how," she said.

In the film, we learn that Tyrene shared the room with four others, including the two cousins she was raising as a mother. It also doubled as an upstairs living room, and was open to anyone who came into the house, including associates of her Uncle Randy, a drug user.

Tyrene says she has never used drugs. At the time of her arrest, the police were searching for evidence against Randy, who had been arrested for selling drugs to undercover police. She was in training for the Golden Gloves, where she was considered a contender.

She spent the day of her scheduled fight in a courtroom, and went directly to jail. The film indicates that her defense attorney was incompetent, and that the judge was on autopilot. It is a measure of their attitudes that they allowed themselves to be filmed as part of an assembly-line process that sends poor defendants to jail with only a cursory nod in the direction of due process.

Tyrene Manson is still serving her sentence, but she has been moved from prison to a correctional facility, "sort of a halfway house," and is on a work-release program that allows her to work nine to five as a secretary at the Leviticus Church of God in Christ, in Jamaica, Queens. That's where I telephoned her the other morning.

She has been invited to attend the Academy Awards, she said, but "they're saying 'no' because the only time you're allowed to go out of state is for a death in your immediate family."

Have you thought about appealing to the governor?

"That's what we're working on now. Governor Pataki is who we would have to appeal to. He doesn't know of me right now, but we're trying to get people involved, like city councilmen."

It would be poetic justice if Denzel Washington won as Best Actor for his portrayal of Hurricane Carter, a boxer framed for murder, on the same night that *On the Ropes* won as Best Documentary for the story of another young black boxer behind bars.

There is, however, some good news for Tyrene Manson these days. *On the Ropes* has been optioned by Warner Bros. as the source for a fictional film to be directed by Brad Silberling *(City of Angels).*

The documentary tells three stories about young boxers in training at the same gym: Manson's, and those of George Walton, who seems to have pro potential, and Noel Santiago. In the film, George eventually signs with professional promoters, to the deep disappointment of Harry Keitt, a middle-aged trainer who started the gym as a way of rehabilitating himself after a murder charge.

The Hollywood treatment will combine Manson's character with Walton's story, "and that's not all the good that came out of this," she told me, "because George and I are engaged now."

What about some of the others in the movie? Your Uncle Randy?

"God has to bring me through right now," she said, "because I just got the word yesterday that my uncle passed away. While I was at church they called me and they told me to pass the news on to his daughters that I was raising."

She was raising two sisters, Equana and Ebony Tile, and "the oldest one, Equana, she's about to be twenty-one, she's getting ready to have a baby in April. When I got put in prison, she was still a virgin and then she lost her virginity and she's pregnant and we have to deal with that also."

She said it was possible her uncle died of an overdose: "My aunt passed away from AIDS, and her birthday was on Friday, so I believe that he probably got extra high to get over that, you know. They say he just dropped dead as he was going to open up the door."

Manson's next hearing for a reduction in sentence is in October, "but that's an early board, and my regular board is in October 2001." She continues to train as a boxer, she said, although the correctional facility doesn't have proper equipment like the prison did. She has a Golden Gloves match scheduled, but still hasn't received permission to participate in it.

Her last appeal was rejected in January 1999. "And then I just said I'm not even gonna fight it anymore. I'm tired."

"I've met, like, good-hearted people that want to help out—so many people tell me that attorneys are looking at the film and they wanna help me, but you know, no one has ever stepped up to do pro bono. I'm not even appealing at this point, just asking for the sentence to be cut to time served, because it's almost three years now."

For evidence the size of a grain of rice, and good reason to suppose its source was a convicted drug dealer who lived in the same house.

"I just want this society to say, like, how much more do I owe them?"

Note: Manson's parole board gave her permission to attend the Oscars.

Hayao Miyazaki

October 24, 1999—Most movie interviews are a job of work for the journalist, but sometimes you find yourself in the presence of a genius, and then you grow still and attentive, trying to remember everything. So it was when I interviewed Bergman, Hitchcock, and Fellini, and so it was again in September 1999, when I interviewed Hayao Miyazaki in Toronto.

The name is not familiar to you. That is because although you love movies, you have not yet discovered that you would love his movies. He and his Studio Ghibli collaborator Isao Takahata *(Grave of the Fireflies)* are arguably the greatest directors of animation in the world. John Lasseter, who directed *Toy Story,* says when he's stuck for inspiration, he watches a Miyazaki film and the logjam breaks. Miyazaki's most recent film, *Princess Mononoke,* broke every record at the Japanese box office, passing even *E.T.,* before finally being dethroned by *Titanic.*

Yet few people in North America know his name, because when we think of animation (which the Japanese call "anime"), we think of Disney. And although we spend a quarter of a billion dollars on each new Disney cartoon, we are shy of work by anyone else. So let me point out that Miyazaki's lifework has been purchased for this continent by Disney itself, and when *Princess Mononoke* opened, it was released by Disney's Miramax. Since it comes with the Disney seal, just pretend it's the next title after *The Lion King* or *Tarzan.*

Actually, it is much more than that—a visionary epic set at the dawn of the Iron Age, based on Japanese myths about a time when men could still speak with the spirits of animals and nature. It is not a "children's movie," although any child old enough to have an intelligent conversation about a film will probably love it. It is a real movie, using animation instead of live action, but expressing the vision of its maker, a man whose work has given me some of my best moments as a moviegoer.

He is standing in the room with me now, giving a little half-bow like a businessman, smiling, indicating his translator with an apologetic hand. He is known as a taskmaster, a workaholic who personally approves every one of the tens of thousands of drawings that go into his films. I expect someone exacting, like Bergman, or forbidding, like Hitchcock, and here is a man who clearly seems pleased as punch to be at the Toronto Film Festival.

Ebert: I think that *Princess Mononoke* should be nominated for Best Picture.

Miyazaki (little bow): Thank you.

E: Why do you choose to make animation instead of live action?

M: Because I had my heart stolen by animated features.

E: When you were a little boy?

M: When I was ten and when I was twenty-three.

E: Do you remember the titles?

M: *White Serpent Story.* It was the first Japanese animated feature ever made. And when I was twenty-three, there was a Soviet film called *The Snow Queen.* I loved the Disney films, but they never moved me to make this my life's work. They didn't have that effect on me. Technically, obviously, *White Serpent Story* was far below anything that Disney was creating. I could understand and sympathize with the hearts of the people who were portrayed on the screen. I think that's why they stole my heart.

E: In this country animation's for family pictures, but in Japan it's considered to be equal with live action. Is that true?

M: It's actually not true that anime is perceived as always fitting for adults. Unfortunately, of the many films in the anime genre, there are very few that I could actually recommend to you wholeheartedly. There's a lot of sexual exploitation of women, and explicit and graphic violence for its own sake. And of course with anime TV series, the budget is so low there's no room to maneuver or play.

E: I was told that Miyazaki-san personally drew around 80,000 of the frames in *Princess Mononoke*. Is that . . .

M: I've never actually counted how many I physically drew myself, but I'm deeply involved in checking and redrawing and touching up all the artwork that comes from the animators. So that's maybe where that legend comes from.

E: What was your plan when you made your first film?

M: I thought I'd take a first step, calmly measuring that step without thinking about the long, long road ahead.

E: In *Princess Mononoke* there is a marvelous monster, a boar monster with flesh of snakes, and it's one of the most amazing sights I've ever seen in a film. It couldn't be done with "realistic" special effects—it would look like a mess. Only animation could make it clear.

M: You're absolutely right. We tried to let the computer handle it, but it didn't work out at all, so we all joined forces and created the monster.

E: I didn't even mean special effects with animation, but special effects in a live-action picture. If you tried to make a live-action picture with that monster, it wouldn't show up; you couldn't see the individual snakes. It seems that animation can make things more clear than reality itself.

M: That's what I was striving for! I'm a very emotional person and when I get enraged or furious I feel like black insects crawl out of my pores. My staff are more peaceful, so it was difficult for them to imagine what it feels like to be taken over by uncontrollable rage.

E: So the boar monster is based on the artist himself? On you?

M: Perhaps. I believe that rage and violent aggression are essential parts of us as human beings, and I think it's absolutely impossible to eliminate that impulse. The issue we con-

front as human beings is how to control and manage that impulse. I know that small children will watch this film, but I intentionally chose not to shield them from that very obvious and apparent reality.

E: So you think it should have a G rating? (It has been rated PG-13.)

M: In Japan we don't have that kind of rating system. We have adult films, but that's the only category we have. When I began making this film I thought I didn't want it to be seen by young children. But the closer I came to completion, the more I began to believe that younger children would be able to intuitively understand the message. What my producer decided, for the TV advertising in Japan, was to show the most shocking scenes. Of course, that works as a marketing technique, but also we really wanted parents to know what they were getting into, so there wouldn't be any nasty surprises and they could make an intelligent decision.

E: I'm frustrated that in North America people automatically go to the new Disney picture, but it's very hard to get them to go to any other animation. For example, *The Iron Giant* didn't do too well recently. What are you doing to spread the word that *Princess Mononoke* is the film to see, even if it doesn't have the little Disney logo?

M (smiles): You see me here. That's what I'm here for.

E: Every video store in North America has an anime section with hundreds of tapes. Yet these films rarely play in theaters. Who is watching these tapes? There must be millions of fans hidden away somewhere because even in the small towns they have Japanese anime. It must be an audience that has discovered them without any media push.

M: The situation isn't that different in Japan. If you play anime in the theaters not all that many people come to see it, even if there are tremendous video sales of the same product. So maybe in their own minds they've created a delineation between those movies you see in a theater and those you enjoy at home.

E: But *Princess Mononoke* was the biggest hit in Japan, until *Titanic*.

M: Frankly, that left me baffled. I have no idea why that happened. None of our films at Ghibli Studio up to *Totoro* were able to make

back their budgets simply from theatrical releases. We got into the black from secondary
rights. The first time we went into the black
from theatrical was with *Kiki's Delivery Service.* So it's not like we started in Japan with
some ready-made, brilliant, active theater-
going audience for anime.

E: You had to develop your audience . . .

M: Not exactly. At Ghibli the direction we've
always intentionally taken is that every time
the audience develops an expectation of what
we're going to deliver, we immediately betray
it with the next film.

E: In your drawings you often exaggerate
the mouth and eyes to convey extreme emotion; in Disney's new *Tarzan* picture, baby
Tarzan seems to look exactly like a Miyazaki
character, as if the Americans have been studying his work.

M (chuckles): Actually, our work depends
on how much we can appropriate from other
people's work! Painting, music, films, literature . . . it's all grist for the mill. We think of
our work not as individual creativity but like a
lifelong baton relay. Your work passes through
your body and your life; you transform it into
something, and then you pass it on to the next
generation.

E: Is *Princess Mononoke* based upon Japanese myths?

M: So much of what I've absorbed as myth
is now a part of myself that it's difficult for me
to delineate what's original, what's myth, what's
history, what's me, what belongs to the past.
But I think that many of the elements in the
film were commonsense intuitive understanding for Japanese people of my generation. The
fact that there were Japanese people at that
time working in the woods, felling trees in
order to have the fire to make forged steel and
iron, that is historical fact. Fortunately, Japan
is blessed with abundant rainfall so we could
keep on felling trees without losing the forest,
and the forest myths.

E: Someone told me that Miyazaki-san is
not going to make another film. Surely that is
not true.

M: I always make every film believing that
it will be my last. But the truth is at my age
(fifty-eight) I can no longer afford the kind of
intensive labor that I spent on the last one. If
my staff will agree to my participating as a di-

rector without quite the intensity of labor,
then there are many more films that I would
like to do.

E: But you have this staff, so you tell them
to?

M (smiles): Not that easy.

E: They must love you, though, and want to
work with you.

M: I'm always a dictator.

E: One last question. My wife and I were
in Japan and we were able to meet two men
who had been appointed Living National
Treasures—a man who makes pots and a man
who makes kimonos. You must be a national
treasure too.

M: Don't make me a Living National Treasure, please! Because I want to be able to always have the possibility of making outrageous
films.

Susan Sarandon

November 7, 1999—"When people close to me
looked at this screenplay," Susan Sarandon was
saying, "they were like, 'This is crazy.'" Her character in *Anywhere But Here,* was not exactly a
charmer: "She's a hateful person, she's unsym-
pathetic, and nothing happens. That was the
general feeling, anyway."

Sarandon saw it differently. She was intrigued by the story of a mother who feels
trapped in a small Wisconsin town, and decides one day to buy a used Mercedes and haul
her teenage daughter cross-country to Beverly
Hills. The master plan is that the mother will
get a job in the school system, and the daughter will go to auditions and become a star.

There are two ways to consider this mother,
whose name is Adele. One is that she is borderline manic. The other is that she's dramatic
and obsessive, yes, but she's right when she
tells her daughter her fate is not to be "a nothing girl in a nothing factory in a nothing town."

The daughter's name is Ann. She's played
by Natalie Portman, who became famous playing Queen Amidala in *The Phantom Menace,*
but was being taken very seriously two or
three years earlier because of her good work in
movies like *Beautiful Girls.* She plays the stable
half of their relationship, the one who tries to
calm and guide her mother and maintain
their mutual sanity.

As for Adele: "This woman's enormous

strength is her undeniable power of denial," Sarandon told me, analyzing her character like a case study. "She's bigger than life and she has dreams that are bigger than where she is, and she reads *People* magazine, and in her mind where's the logical place to go? Beverly Hills.

"I know she probably has one of those personality disorders where you go first and think it through later. So did our forefathers. This entire country was based on a bunch of eccentrics who came here without a prayer—well, with *just* a prayer—and no money and no sense of what they were getting into. That's what Adele does. She heads for Hollywood in her desperate love for this girl. Remember, Adele is doing it for Ann. She wants all the wrong things for all the right reasons, and God bless her."

Sarandon and I were talking a day or two after the premiere of *Anywhere But Here* at the Toronto Film Festival. She is one of the most intelligent of actors and one of the most analytical, discussing her characters as if she'd seen them in a movie instead of playing them herself. She is known for taking chances, and often they pay off—as when she and her partner, Tim Robbins, made *Dead Man Walking* (1995) and she won the Best Actress Award for her performance as Sister Helen Prejean, a woman who has an extraordinary spiritual confrontation with a condemned man (Sean Penn).

That's the kind of chance it makes sense to take, however. The movie's dark subject matter might not attract huge audiences (although this time it did), but the role was substantial and had meaning. It may actually take more nerve to sign up for a character like Adele—who is, as Sarandon notes, not very likable, and who shares the screen with a rising star who is very likable indeed. You get the impression that Sarandon doesn't much ponder such questions. She has had such longevity in Hollywood, ever since she played a hippie chick in *Joe* in 1970, because she goes for the interesting character and not the favorable image.

"You can almost imagine the reviews," Sarandon grinned. "'While Susan Sarandon chews up the scenery, Natalie Portman gives the film its heart and reality.' But really my job was to be completely over the top. You're out there, you know. You're not a reactive character. The other night was only the second time I've seen the movie, and I went, 'Oh, my God, how is anyone gonna take this person? She's so in your face.' Some people just wanna struggle, struggle, struggle, you know. So you try to find a way to still have an audience accept her. I think of her as the female counterpart to Nicholson in *As Good as It Gets,* saying insulting things."

Do you like your character less than I do? I asked.

"No, I love her. But . . ."

You seem to be pretty critical of her.

"One of the reasons I liked her is that she's the antithesis of the mothers I played in *Lorenzo's Oil* or *Stepmom.* The first big mistake you make as a parent is you forget who you are in an attempt to be a good parent. You go into some kind of trance and reproduce your own parents. You forget how to have fun. I love the fact that she has a sense of wonder about things, and playfulness. She forgets to pay the bills every now and then, and that's not admirable, but when she wants to watch the sun come up, that's just so great."

I think when this girl Ann grows up, I said, maybe she becomes a writer and writes a book about her mother, and discovers she has a lot of love and appreciation for her, having probably gone through her whole twenties being mad at her.

Sarandon smiled. "Gore Vidal told me something great once," she said. "I went to stay with him when I had my daughter. We were talking about being parents and he said, 'You know, you're gonna be a great parent, but what you have to understand, Susan, is that every parent gives their child neuroses. You just have to hope they're productive ones.' I'm of the school that I'd rather nurture than mold. When kids take different directions you don't have to take it personally. I've never striven for normalcy in the raising of my children."

Her children are shared with the actor and director Tim Robbins, whom she met just before they costarred in *Bull Durham* (1988). In addition to *Dead Man Walking,* they've worked together in Robert Altman's *The Player,* and on two films Robbins also directed: *Bob Roberts* (1992) and *The Cradle Will Rock.* Together and apart, they're ready to take interesting projects with shaky financial prospects, if they believe in them.

"You follow your heart. I got some award in Hollywood recently. One of these things where everybody was in the room, all the producers and writers, and I said, you know, everyone in this room has one story that you absolutely have to tell. What a difference it would make to the season of films that's coming out if you had made it."

You and Tim must really be kind of inspirations for each other, I said, because you're both kind of . . .

"Thoughtful?"

Well, thoughtful, but also out there with idealistic projects more often than not. You kind of test each other.

"In the end, for all of the difficulties we have with each other, and the bumpiness that anybody has in a relationship between two strong, opinionated people, I think what's allowed us to survive is mutual respect and a moral bottom line and a standard of things that we're interested in. That helps us calm down about whether the toilet seat's up, or . . . you know, the cohabitational problems and the parenting problems."

Mentioning *Bull Durham,* I said—which, of course, also has Kevin Costner in it—you know, I just reviewed his new baseball movie, *For Love of the Game,* which I guess he hates. The studio cut it to get a PG-13. I wonder what it would have been like with the R-rated original cut.

"It's a shame," she said. "Here again you've got a studio motivated by greed rather than trying to make the best movie possible. They say, 'Let's get rid of this and get rid of that because then it'll get a rating that allows us to appeal to the largest audience.' But by not making it the best movie possible—it doesn't."

Martin Scorsese

October 21, 1999—Martin Scorsese's new movie, *Bringing Out the Dead,* is one of his best. That means a lot when you are arguably the greatest active American director. It stars Nicolas Cage as a paramedic whose runs through Hell's Kitchen are like a bus route through Dante's Inferno.

I telephoned Scorsese earlier this week,

plunging once again into his rapid-fire Walter Winchell dialogue. To deconstruct his verbal riffs into the form of a traditional interview would lose the music. Here are some of the notes he hit:

1. The first things I thought of, when I read Joe Connelly's book, were Nick Cage's face and his eyes. His uncle Francis (Coppola) had us meet a few years ago. You know, you meet some people sometimes, you don't wanna spend five months with them on the set, you know what I'm saying? Well, this guy seemed to be polite. He was a nice guy to be around and then Brian DePalma told me he was great to work with. I know his films over the years. He's inventive and he goes from an expressive style, almost like silent film, like Lon Chaney whom he adores, to something extremely internal. So I thought immediately of Nick for this.

2. Some people keep asking, "Gee, New York looks a little different now." And I say, "But you're looking at the surface. This is not about New York. This is about suffering; it's about humanity. It's about what our part is in life." This whole thing about how New York is changing, getting better. It goes in cycles. Some people are saying, "The movie is representative of New York in the *early* 1990s. It's different now." I say it's not so. We were there; we were shooting in that area. They were out; they were there. Those people. And if some of them aren't on the streets, believe me, they gotta be someplace. I saw some of the places where they are. You don't wanna know. It's like underneath the city in a hole. Under the railroads. It's the end of life. It's the dregs. It's down. You can't get any lower.

3. The Nick Cage character has three copilots, a different partner every night. John Goodman is probably in the best shape. Goodman basically worries about where he's gonna eat, takes a few minutes off, takes a nap. Ving Rhames, he gets religion. But the thing about Ving's character is that you can't make him work more than two nights or he gets overexcited. And then, of course, the Tom Sizemore character, he's a paramilitary, he's in there. He knows what to do when he gets there, but he freaks out from time to time.

4. The people they're carrying in their ambulance, I saw it like that in the Bowery. I saw

it happening to some of the people in my old neighborhood. I grew up with them, in a way. Some of them when they weren't drinking were kinda nice. They worked for people in the grocery store. But when they got drunk, there was no dealing with them. And people would just become frustrated and hit them. I saw it happen all the time.

5. That title, *Bringing Out the Dead*—Joe Connelly chose that title with a sense of humor. It's based on a reference to *Monty Python and the Holy Grail*. You remember? "Bring out your dead," John Cleese tells them. He takes out one person and the guy says, "I'm not dead yet." He says, "Don't be a baby. Come on." Remember, he puts him on the cart? He says, "He's very ill. He's gonna die any second."

6. When I read the galleys of the book, I told (producer) Scott Rudin, who gave me the book, "The only man who could write a script of this is Paul Schrader." (Schrader also wrote Scorsese's *Taxi Driver, Raging Bull,* and *The Last Temptation of Christ.*) The last scene that Paul wrote, it's not that way in the book. Nick says, "Rose, forgive me. Forgive me, Rose." And she says, "Nobody told you to suffer. It was your idea." And when Schrader wrote that, I said, "Oh—of course." And that's the connection between us. We never really discuss it, but over the years we've had this similarity to each other. I said to him, "It's so beautiful. And you're right because you can't forgive yourself. You want everybody else to forgive you." We're tied to each other with this sort of thing.

7. When you bring somebody back to life, you feel like God, you are God. But one has to get past the idea of the ego and the pride. Hey, the job isn't about bringing people back to life; it's about being there, it's about compassion for the suffering, suffering with them.

8. Right after we finished shooting, another guy fell on a fence in New York. This happens all the time. Every few months there's an impaling like that. We shot the emergency room in Bellevue on the ground floor; we built the set down there. A few stories above, one of the doctors had a section of the fence they took out of the man, as a showpiece in his office. That was the incident that inspired the scene in the movie.

9. Helen (Morris, his wife, a book editor) told me last night there was a big deal on the Web about the *New York Times* walking out of the movie. But it wasn't a critic. It was Bernie Weinraub, their Hollywood columnist. And I said, well, Bernie, I know him a little bit. He liked *Casino.* He hurt us very badly on *Age of Innocence* in an article he wrote in the *Times* where he complained about us having a big budget on *Age of Innocence,* and he hit Daniel Day-Lewis and Michelle Pfeiffer for not taking less than their usual fee. By the way, they did take less. I don't know how much but they did. We were compared unfavorably to *Remains of the Day* and pictures like that because they're made for a good price and we were wasting money. And that was it. They gave us $32 million; we went a little bit over but not a lot, and $32 million was the average amount for a film being made at that time. If somebody wanted to give us $30 million, and somebody else wanted to give us $32 million, I'd take the 32.

10. I'm still going to make *Dino,* the Dean Martin picture, with Tom Hanks. We're gonna hopefully do it right after *Gangs of New York,* which I've been trying for years to get done. Jay Cocks and I have been rewriting the script since January. We got Leonardo DiCaprio, we may have Bob De Niro to play the archvillain, hero-villain, whatever. It's taken ten months to make the deal, mainly because it's a lot of money in the film and you gotta be careful and you have to get the right amount of star power in it. It's only become real since Monday of this week. We're ready to go. And then deal with *Dino* right after, I hope. Tom Hanks and I were speaking about it only a couple of weeks ago.

Lars von Trier

Cannes, France, May 22, 2000—We gather silently on a hillside above the sea, with a view of the mountains in the far mist. It is like a hospital waiting room. Farther down the hillside, we can see Lars von Trier sitting in the shade of a cabana, giving an interview. He is famously phobic—worried about elevators, closed spaces, upper floors, crowds. Here at the Hotel du Cap d'Antibes, he is surrounded by light and air.

Von Trier preoccupied the Cannes Film Festival this year. His film, *Dancer in the Dark,* inspired the most passion, pro and con, and a few days later would win both the Palme d'Or, or top prize, and the Best Actress Award (page 775). His style is distinct and, for some, difficult. He plunges into the action with a handheld video camera, and for musical numbers he employed 100 video cameras at once, finding the choreography in the editing process. His Dogma 95 movement, a cinematic vow of chastity, has had an influence with its ban on most of the strategies of the traditionally well-made film.

If von Trier is phobic, he has been upstaged by his star, the Icelandic pop singer Bjork. She did come to Cannes, and was embraced by von Trier, lifted off the ground and spun around, during the ovation after the official screening of the film. But then she refused to attend the press conference, refused all interviews, skulked, and disappeared—only to surface, radiant, at the awards ceremony, where she was an unexpected but popular winner.

The Danish director has not learned the art of spin control, and said bluntly during his press conference that working with her was "like being around a dying person all the time." She is not an actor, he said, but someone who felt her character's experiences were literally real. Since she is condemned to death in the film, "It was extremely awkward, because I was like her executioner."

In the film, Bjork plays a punch-press operator in Washington State in the early 1960s, who is going blind and wants money for an operation for her son, who faces the same fate. She is not good at protecting herself, and her behavior after being charged with murder is a study in wrong things said and right ones left unsaid. It's an odd quality of this film and *Breaking the Waves* (1996), which won the Cannes Jury Prize, that the heroines are apparently mentally retarded, and yet no one (in the film or even in the reviews) ever seems to mention that—as if their childlike simplicity is a trait and not a symptom.

As for von Trier himself, when I descend to the cabana, it is a surprise. I expect a menacing, dogmatic, unyielding, angry man—the man who was so unhappy to win the jury prize and not the Palme d'Or that in his acceptance speech he gave "no thanks to the evil dwarf," a reference to jury president Roman Polanski. Here before me was a slight, informal, friendly person, wearing a T-shirt and sitting in the shade with a bottle of mineral water.

He has not read any of the reviews of his film, he said. That would include the *Variety* review, which was brutal ("auteurist self-importance that's artistically bankrupt on almost every level").

"I've heard from some journalists that there are some Americans who don't like it because they think it is an unfair image of America, which I am sure it is, since I have never been to America," he says. Because he will not fly, he found locations in Sweden that looked like Washington, and rented lots of old American cars. "It was by chance that we found these old machines, so we could build our factory."

Bjork's costar in the film is Catherine Deneuve, certainly the most beautiful punch-press operator in movie history. I asked if her presence was distracting for this story.

"That's a problem with all stars, isn't it? Actually, she was very good at the punch press. I have a sink back home that she did." As for reality, "I just want things to be possible. Anyway, possible enough that the audience will believe that it could happen in this film."

I mentioned his difficulties with Bjork.

"I never said it was difficult. To make her deliver what she has delivered on the screen was extremely easy. She is the ideal of an actor. She believed everything that was happening in the story. What was not so easy was that it was extremely painful for her."

She treated you like her executioner?

"Yes, and that is not very nice. I don't think I would like to be an executioner. The way she worked, she couldn't look at me in any other way than as the man who wanted her to go through all this suffering. It's hard enough being a director and a producer who stupidly enough has got into a project where he could lose not only his company but his home, where his children live, and his entire fortune."

That was a reference to Bjork's attempts to escape from the film, a $20 million production that would have collapsed without her.

The film began with von Trier's desire to make a musical. He hired Bjork after seeing her in music videos. He loved the old Gene Kelly musicals from Hollywood, but wanted a different look, which he has certainly achieved; one musical number is staged on a railroad bridge with a real train rumbling past inches from the actors. Others are on the shop floor and in prison.

His plot, about a woman betrayed by a weak cop, is straight out of silent melodrama, or opera. "After I wrote the whole script, I saw a little cartoon with a blind girl. I thought wow, that's fantastic! So then she became blind all of a sudden, just by chance."

As the principal author of the Dogma 95 statement, von Trier is now a leader of a movement, a small one, with Danish allies like Thomas Vinterberg *(Celebration)* and one American disciple, Harmony Korine *(julien donkey-boy)*.

"I must shamefully admit I haven't seen the film that he did," he said, "but I talked a lot with Harmony. He is a very nice young man, very strange. Of course the Dogma rules were meant for me. I would like somebody to come to me and say I was not allowed to do this or that. I had spent so much time on a crane, on planning a camera movement, on working with the color, on trying to make interesting sound afterward, on putting in music. . . . I made a full list, and thought it would be extremely interesting for me to do a film that banned all of these things. These limitations give us a new freedom and a new lust for film."

Much of the film is shot with a handheld camera, and its rapid movement caused some people in the front rows to feel vertigo.

"I know. It was the same for *Breaking the Waves.* I handle the camera myself. I am well-situated to work with the actors. It's a pity to make actors leave the room while the cameraman sets up the shot. I feel so much in contact with the actors. I'm not framing. Dogma is not about framing, but pointing. I pointed the camera toward what I wanted, or what I knew Bjork could give. In some of the close-ups you can feel that I am physically very close to her. I think her performance benefits from this."

You are not the kind of person I expected, I said. From your fearsome reputation, I came expecting Peckinpah, but you are more like Truffaut.

He smiled. "If people want to talk to me, I am happy. But if you come and yell at me, then I have an attitude. I accept that people like or dislike, but when they hate me and want to hit me, then I can show another side. Not that I want a fight. As you see, I am very small. In the schoolyard I invented techniques of fleeing that you wouldn't believe."

Essays

AFI's 100 Funniest Films

The Answer Man queries himself on the list of the 100 Funniest American Movies, as revealed by the American Film Institute:

Q: Now that you've seen the list, what's your immediate impression?

A: It contains a lot of good video rental ideas. I've seen 96 of the 100 films, and liked or loved almost all of them.

Q: What significance does the list have?

A: None. Comedy, like other forms of art, cannot be measured, only appreciated.

Q: What is the purpose of the list?

A: To raise money for the American Film Institute, which is a worthy cause. Like the AFI's equally meaningless lists of 100 Greatest American Movies and 100 Greatest Stars, this list exists to generate a television special and video store tie-ins, which will produce funds for the AFI.

Q: Are any lists like this meaningful?

A: Lists of box-office winners have a certain concrete undeniability. The poll taken every ten years by *Sight & Sound*, the British film magazine, is useful as a gauge of shifting critical winds over time. Individual lists provide insights into those who make them; when Martin Scorsese lists his ten favorite films from the 1990s, that's interesting. But to rank movies from 1 to 100 after a vote of hundreds of "leaders from across the film community" is an exercise in statistics, not criticism.

Q: Now get off your high horse and say what you liked about the list.

A: *Some Like It Hot* is a worthy title to be in first place. They were right to pick *Duck Soup* as the best of the Marx Brothers films. I'm glad Mel Brooks placed three titles in the top fifteen, although *The Producers* is a funnier film than *Blazing Saddles*. They remembered the silent geniuses Keaton and Chaplin, and even mentioned Keaton first—yet, while *The General* is indeed his best film, it is not his funniest. Where are the other silent clowns? The Three Stooges? Jim Carrey?

Q: The best titles least known to most moviegoers?

A: *The Lady Eve, The Palm Beach Story, Lost in America, The Navigator.*

Q: Titles that shouldn't be on the list?

A. I have never shared the general enthusiasm for the Coen Brothers' *Raising Arizona,* but am assured at least weekly I am wrong. Placing it at No. 31 and their *Fargo* down at No. 93 seems screwy. I am glad, though, that *Fargo* was seen as a comedy—a human comedy with dark undertones—and not just as a crime picture. If I had my way, it could trade places with *It Happened One Night* at No. 8.

Q: Titles that should be on the list?

A: *Kingpin.* And what about *Roger & Me*? Were documentaries not allowed? If *Fargo* qualifies, why not *Pulp Fiction*? Was *Being John Malkovich* too recent to swim into focus?

Q: Cary Grant is in eight of the 100 films. Does that make him America's funniest actor?

A: The whole point was that he was not funny, at least not visibly. He always kept his cool. You could never spot him going for a laugh. Keaton was the same way. On the other hand, the Marx Brothers and Woody Allen both star in five of the titles, and they *do* try to be funny. Whatever works.

Q: What is the funniest movie on the list?

A: *The Producers.* Thank you. Thank you very much. You've been a wonderful audience. No, really.

Buying Marilyn and *Kane*

November 15, 1999—The only Oscar associated with Orson Welles's *Citizen Kane* will be auctioned on Wednesday in Hollywood. Some speculate it will break the $1,267,500 record set October 27 by the dress worn by Marilyn Monroe when she sang "Happy Birthday" to President John F. Kennedy in Madison Square Garden. After all, Monroe wore a lot of dresses, but only one Oscar was ever given to *Citizen Kane,* which is routinely voted the greatest film of all time. My guess, though, is that it will bring considerably less.

Bidders for memorabilia are symbolically

buying the famous people associated with them. How else to explain the $10,000 paid for an old Elvis Presley credit card? *Kane* may be the greatest film, but Welles ranks below the canonized supercelebrities Marilyn and JFK. Besides, the dress buyer got a twofer: Marilyn not only wore the dress while singing "Happy Birthday," but JFK perhaps unwrapped his present later that evening.

Back to *Citizen Kane*. I think its Oscar will bring less than the record $550,000 paid in 1996 for Clark Gable's Oscar for "It Happened One Night." That's because buyers would rather "own" Gable. The *Kane* statuette was awarded to the screenplay, and shared by Orson Welles and Herman Mankiewicz, who each got copies. Welles's would be worth more, but is mired in litigation. Frank Mankiewicz, Herman's son, explained why his family is selling the Oscar: "We had it a long time and thought it ought to get more public display. I'm hoping whoever buys it will put it in a museum or something." Just once, it would be refreshing to read, "The family talked it over, and would rather have the money than the Oscar. Our father always used it as a doorstop anyway."

Are such treasures good investments? It's a truism that when a man can afford any car he wants, he buys the car he dreamed of owning when he got his first driver's license. That's why a nice 1957 Chevy Bel Air could cost you more than $100,000, while a genuine classic like the Model T would cost a lot less. The Monroe dress was purchased as an investment by Gotta Have It! collectibles, which automatically enhanced the shelf value of its entire stock. It will probably be sold to someone with much sentiment about Marilyn, JFK, and '57 Chevys. A century from now, Monroe and JFK may be as dated as Mae West and Teddy Roosevelt, but *Citizen Kane* will still be a great film. Still . . . I wouldn't want the Oscar. I own the movie on laser disc and DVD. That's better.

My favorite dialogue in *Kane* is when Mr. Bernstein tells the reporter: "A fellow will remember a lot of things you wouldn't think he'd remember. You take me. One day, back in 1896, I was crossing over to Jersey on the ferry, and as we pulled out, there was another ferry pulling in, and on it there was a girl waiting to get off. A white dress she had on. She was carrying a

white parasol. I only saw her for one second. She didn't see me at all, but I'll bet a month hasn't gone by since that I haven't thought of that girl."

Would I want to own that white parasol? It's not for sale, because it existed only in the imaginations of Mankiewicz and Welles. Besides, I own it anyway. Not a month goes by when I don't think of it.

Celluloid vs. Digital: The War for the Soul of the Cinema

I have seen the future of the cinema, and it is not digital. No matter what you've read, the movie theater of the future will not use digital video projectors, and it will not beam the signal down from satellites. It will use film, and the film will be right there in the theater with you. How can this be? How can a technology that is a century old possibly be preferable to new digital gizmos? This is a story of the limitations of video projection, and the hidden resources of light-through-celluloid. Please read carefully. The future of traditional cinema is at stake.

In recent months the *Wall Street Journal, New York Times,* and *Los Angeles Times* have carried breathless reports that Hollywood is on the brink of a digital revolution. Even *Wired* magazine, usually informed on technical matters, printed the howler that digital projection is "far better" than film. George Lucas and Texas Instruments have teamed up to showcase *The Phantom Menace* with digital projection in theaters on both coasts. Disney is now preparing digital theatrical demos; its *Bicentennial Man* will open in digital on Friday in a few theaters.

These custom installations, we are told, are the first wave of a technological revolution that will overtake movie theaters. No longer will an underpaid projectionist struggle in the booth with ungainly cans of film. New movies will zip down from space and be projected onto the screen with startling clarity. Digital video projection (jargon watch: "dijection") is being embraced by Hollywood, we read, because it will save the studios the cost of manufacturing and shipping prints all over the world.

But how good is digital projection? I saw it demonstrated at the Cannes Film Festival in 1999 and 2000, and have read reports of those who've attended the custom *Phantom Menace* installations. A system offered by Hughes is not very persuasive, the witnesses say, but the Texas Instruments system is better; reviews range from "85 percent as good as a real movie" to "about as good." The special effects in *Phantom Menace* looked especially sharp, viewers said, and there's a reason: They were computer-generated in the first place, and so arrived at the screen without stepping down a generation to film. And because they depicted imaginary places, it was impossible to judge them on the basis of how we know the real world looks.

"Dijection" offers a wonderful new prospect, if it's for real. But it's not the only possible future. Far from the boardrooms of Texas Instruments, which has unlimited financial resources and wants to grab the world movie distribution market, there is an alternative film-based projection system that is much cheaper than digital, uses existing technology, and (hold onto your hats) is not "about as good" as existing film, but, its inventors claim, 500 *percent better*. That is not a misprint.

This system is called MaxiVision48. I have seen it demonstrated. It produces a picture so breathtakingly clear it is like 3-D in reverse: Like looking through an open window into the real world. Motion is shown without the jumpiness and blurring of existing film projection, details are sharper, and our eyes are bathed in visual persuasion.

The inventor of MaxiVision is a Hollywood film editor named Dean Goodhill (he shared an Oscar nomination for *The Fugitive*). One of his partners is a manufacturer named Ty Safreno, whose company, Trust Automation Inc., of San Luis Obispo, California, builds digital robotics systems for tasks that must be vibration free, like the manufacture of Pentium chips. Another associate is Optical Research of Pasadena; they make Panavision lenses, and have designed the MaxiVision lenses.

Without getting into labyrinthine technical explanations, here is how MaxiVision48 works:

—It can project film at forty-eight frames per second (fps), twice the existing twenty-four fps rate. That provides a picture of startling clarity. At forty-eight frames, it uses 50 percent more film than at present. But MV48 also has an "economy mode" that offers low-budget filmmakers savings of up to 25 percent on film.

—The MV48 projector can switch on the fly between twenty-four and forty-eight fps formats in the same movie, allowing extra clarity for scenes that can use it. And it can handle any existing 35mm film format—unlike digital projection, which would obsolete a century of old prints.

—MV48 uses a new system to pull the film past the projector bulb without any jitter or bounce. Goodhill says he can't go into detail while his patent is pending, but explains in general terms that MV48 completely eliminates the jiggle that all current films experience as they dance past the projector bulb. Watching it, I was startled to see how rock solid the picture was, and how that added to clarity.

—The result: "We figure it's 500 percent better than existing film or the Texas Instruments video projection system, take your choice," Goodhill told me.

It is also a lot cheaper, because it retrofits existing projectors, uses the original lamp housings, and doesn't involve installing high-tech computer equipment. MaxiVision's business plan calls for leasing the projectors at $280 a month, but if you wanted to buy one, it would cost you around $10,000. Estimates for the Texas Instruments digital projector, on the other hand, range from $110,000 to $150,000 per screen.

The contrast between the two systems is not limited to costs. Here are additional reasons why the death of film has been much exaggerated:

—The TI systems in the demo theaters bear no relationship to the real world. They're custom installations that do not address the problem of how a real film would get to a real theater. The source of their signal is an array of twenty prerecorded eighteen-gigabyte hard drives, trucked to each theater. This array costs an additional $75,000, apart from the cost of trucking and installation.

—Even so, a movie is so memory-intensive that these arrays must compress the digital signal by a ratio of four-to-one. At a recent seminar at the Directors' Guild in Los Angeles, however, digital projection spokesmen said that in the real world, satellite downlinked movies would require forty-to-one data compression. This level of compression in movie delivery has never been demonstrated publicly, by TI or anyone else.

—The TI picture on the screen would *not be as good* as the HDTV television sets now on sale in consumer electronics outlets! TI's MDD chip has specs of 1280 by 1024, while HDTV clocks at 1920 by 1080. For the first time in history, consumers could see a better picture at home than in a movie theater. A higher-quality digital picture would involve even more cost, compression, and transmission challenges.

—One advantage of a film print is that the director and cinematographer can "time" the print to be sure the colors and visual elements are right. In a digital theater, the projectionist would be free to adjust the color, tint, and contrast according to his whims. Since many projectionists do not even know how to properly frame a picture or set the correct lamp brightness, this is a frightening prospect.

—How much would the digital projection specialist be paid? The technicians operating the TI demo installations are paid more than the managers of most theaters. Hollywood is happy to save money, but are exhibitors happy to spend it?

—What about piracy? Movies will be downloaded just once, then stored in each theater. Thieves could try two approaches. They could grab the signal from the satellite and try to break the encryption (as DVD encryption has just been broken). But there is a more obvious security gap: At some point before it reaches the projector, the encrypted signal has to be decoded. Pirates could bribe a projectionist to let them intercept the decoded signal. Result: A perfect digital copy of the new movie. When the next *Star Wars* movie opens in 4,000 theaters, how many armed guards will 20th Century-Fox have to assign to the projection booths?

—Film is harder to pirate than digital video, because a physical film print must be stolen and copied. An MV 48 print would be even harder to pirate than current films; it would not fit the equipment in any pirate lab. Those fly-by-night operations, which use ancient equipment cannibalized over the decades, would have to find expensive new machines.

All of these are practical questions. They set aside the aesthetic advantage that MaxiVision48 has over digital. Once you've seen the system, you just can't get it out of your mind.

You have to actually go to San Luis Obispo, south of San Francisco, to see MaxiVision48 demonstrated. That's where the prototype projector resides, in Ty Safreno's facility. Not many Hollywood studio honchos have made that trek.

On the day I visited, I was joined by Todd McCarthy, the chief film critic of *Variety,* and two leading cinematographers, Allen Daviau (*E.T., Bugsy*) and Dean Cundey (*Jurassic Park, Apollo 13*).

We saw a scene that had been shot for Goodhill by another cameraman who likes the system, Steven Poster, vice president of the American Society of Cinematographers. Poster deliberately assembled a scene filled with technical pitfalls for traditional film and video systems:

We see actor Peter Billingsley walking toward the camera, wearing a patterned shirt. He is passed by another guy, wearing a T-shirt with something written on it. The camera tilts down as Billingsley picks up a hose to water a lawn. The camera continues to move past a white picket fence. In the background, a truck drives out of a parking lot.

Not great art, but great headaches for cinematographers, who know that picket fences will seem to "flutter" if panned too quickly, that water droplets will blur, and that the sign on the side of a moving truck cannot be read. All true in the old systems. With MV48, we could read the writing on the shirt, see every picket in the fence, see the drops of water as if in real life, and read the side of the truck. Case closed.

McCarthy and the cinematographers praised what they saw. I was blown away. I've seen other high-quality film projection systems, such as 70mm, IMAX, and Douglas Trumbull's Showscan process. All are very good, but they involve wide film gauges, unwieldy print sizes, and special projectors. MV48 uses projectors and prints that look a lot like the current specs, with costs in the same ballpark.

Why, then, do we read so much about digital projection and so little about MaxiVision48? One obvious reason is that Texas Instruments has deep pockets to promote its system, plus the backing of propellor-head George Lucas, who dreams of making movies entirely on computers and essentially wants to show them on theater-size monitors.

Another reason is that many Hollywood executives are, frankly, not much interested in technical matters. Their attention is occupied by projects, stories, casting, advertising, and box office, as it should be. When they hear the magical term "digital" and are told their movies will whiz to theaters via satellite, they assume it's all part of the computer revolution and don't ask more questions.

Hollywood has not spent a dime, for example, to research the intriguing question, do film and digital create different brain states? Some theoreticians believe that film creates reverie, video creates hypnosis; wouldn't it be ironic if digital audiences found they were missing an ineffable part of the moviegoing experience?

Now that a decision is on the horizon, Goodhill's process deserves attention. One of the ironies of MaxiVision48 is that it's so logical and inexpensive—such a brilliant example of lateral thinking—that a couple of guys *could* build it in a lab in San Luis Obispo. If it were more expensive, it might attract more attention.

The big film companies like Kodak and Fuji should like the system, since it will help them sell more film. The directors who love celluloid, like Spielberg and Scorsese, should know about MV48. And there are other applications. Retail outlets use "video walls" to create atmosphere. Rain Forest cafes could put you in the jungle. NikeTown could put you on the court with Michael Jordan. No more million-dollar walls of video screens, but a $10,000 projector and a wall-size picture.

But the industry has to listen. At the end of its first century, it shouldn't be so cheerful about throwing out everything that "film" means. And it should get over its infatuation with the "digital" buzzword.

When I told Dean Goodhill I was working on this article, he e-mailed me:

"I'll make a special offer. We're leasing MV48 for $280 a month, but for $2,800 a month, which is closer to the per-screen cost of the digital system, we'll throw in a little chrome plate that says 'digital' on it."

The Summer of Raunch

What used to be called "good taste" is no longer a factor in Hollywood's screenplay decisions. Vulgarity is embraced, obscenity is cherished, scatology is cheerfully showcased. Semen is found everywhere except where nature intended. That brown object in the coffee pot is not a bran muffin. If you've seen one penis in a mass-audience movie, you've seen half a dozen. Public urination and masturbation inspire punch lines, not arrests. The characters with the raunchiest language are not stevedores, but preschoolers from the little Colorado town of South Park.

I make these observations not as a moralist but as a reporter. I go to all the movies, and I observe that ordinary characters in movies made for ordinary people are talking and acting completely without inhibition. The four-letter words aren't always even intended to shock; they're often just part of the verbal furniture. Most of this behavior comes from teenage characters in movies aimed at the teenage market.

Hit movies don't lead society, they reflect it. Movies that are ahead of the curve usually flop at the box office. But a movie that does well (like *There's Something About Mary, Big Daddy, South Park,* or *American Pie*) is accurately reflecting popular taste. Having seen most of these movies with general audiences in real movie theaters, I know that people like them. They laugh the loudest at the raunchiest parts. So do I, sometimes.

What's odd is that this collapse of Hollywood inhibition has not been matched by an increase in frankness about sexual subjects. The movies are less grown-up, not more. As vulgarity increases, it pushes sensuality and sexuality off the screen. There is less actual nudity today than twenty years ago (apart from the penises, of course, which inevitably inspire jokes based on size and pain). Long, slow, sexy love scenes were big in the 1970s, but today's movies don't want to slow down for them. Sexual action advances at a cartoon pace and is more like wrestling than ballet.

The Summer of Raunch no doubt has many sources, but one, I think, is the hypocrisy of the MPAA rating system. Because the NC-17 rating (and its predecessor, the X) are hardly ever used for theatrical movies, America has become a nation where you can show anything on the screen—as long as it isn't truly adult content. Teenagers can attend movies with four-letter jokes about condoms, sperm, pubic hair, urine, penis size, and unorthodox masturbatory techniques, but a tender scene between two nude people who love each other and are expressing it in the conventional physical way? Gee, that would be too dirty.

In the absence of a workable adult rating, all content has to be crammed down into the R category, which has become a catchall. R-rated movies thrive on double entendres, euphemisms, implications, and the secondhand detritus of sex. They nudge, wink, and imply, but they don't deal with mature sexual values. They're stuck at the level of a dirty joke.

Thirty years without a workable, practical adults-only movie rating has created a society with few movies about what one should do, and lots of movies about what you can get away with. In the name of a hypocritical morality, the MPAA is promoting smarminess at the cost of grown-up values.

It is time for an A rating, to be positioned between the R and the NC-17. The NC-17 would return to the useful X, which everybody understands, and would apply to hard-core porn. The new A would be for nonporno movies that are not intended for *anyone* under seventeen. The roughest third of the R-rated movies would properly belong in that category.

With the A rating, America would no longer be the only major movie-producing nation with no practical category for adult films. Kids under seventeen would have a fair chance of seeing movies that were not hammering down the door of good taste. Viewers over seventeen would have a fair chance of seeing movies where sexuality is not limited to the level of junior high school locker-room legends.

In the middle of the Summer of Raunch, my wish for Hollywood, the MPAA, and the yukking audiences of America is: Oh, grow up!

The Grinch That Stole the Oscars

March 13, 2000—The *Wall Street Journal* wants to be the Grinch That Stole the Oscars.

If the *Journal* has its way, we'll be able to read the names of this year's Oscar winners in its weekend edition for March 17, nine days before the Academy Awards ceremony. *WSJ* staffers are reportedly involved in a project to contact all of the 5,000-plus Academy members and ask them who they're planning to vote for.

This is a spectacularly bad idea, and has only two possible outcomes:

1. If the *Journal* is correct, it will have spoiled the fun of millions of people who enjoy watching the Oscarcast and sharing the suspense when the names are read and the winners are announced.

2. If the *Journal* is wrong, it will be a laughing-stock.

As a reporter who has covered the Oscars since the days when Bob Hope was the emcee, I cheerfully agree that the ceremony is silly and staged mostly to publicize the American film industry. Everybody knows that.

But it's fun too. When I'm in the pressroom and a favorite wins or a dark horse scores an upset, a cheer goes up. And it goes up all over the world, where people hold Oscar parties, gather in bars and restaurants, listen to short-wave radios, watch satellite TV, even cluster around the radio room on cruise ships. The Oscars are a global ritual during which the most famous stars in the world win or lose, and the world watches—in suspense, until now.

As interested as we are in the outcome, it has no deep meaning in the real world, except to the financial fortunes of the films and the careers of the winners. Not only does the best film often lose, it's frequently not even nominated. The Oscar ceremony is spectacle, not science. It makes no difference if we know on Friday who will win on Sunday. We don't want to know. We want to tune in and find out for ourselves. That's if the *Journal* is right. If it's wrong, it's *really* been wasting our time.

But what if the Journal poll is *almost* right? Say it correctly calls the first four major categories. What happens then? Do viewers decide they already know the final outcome and go to bed? Do the Academy's Nielsen ratings suffer? The Academy uses income from the Oscarcast to finance its library, screening, preservation, and educational programs. It's a worthy cause. Can it sue the *Journal* for wrongful loss of income?

On its other pages, the *Journal* reports on money. Perhaps its resources would be better used by telephoning major mutual fund managers and asking them what stocks they plan to buy next week. Now that I'd like to know. As for who wins the Oscars—well, my predictions will be in Sunday's paper. Maybe I'll guess right, and maybe I'll guess wrong. See, that's where the fun comes in.

Footnote: Both the Journal *and I scored 80 percent.*

In Memoriam

Robert Bresson

Robert Bresson, the lonely giant of the French cinema, is dead.

The director, whose austere masterpieces evoked praise but little imitation, died December 22, 1999, in Paris at ninety-eight, after a long illness that inspired retrospectives and tributes at the Film Center of the Art Institute of Chicago and in Toronto, London, Edinburgh, and Tokyo. In Chicago, all of the screenings sold out, even though Bresson's films were often ignored by audiences on first release.

Bresson was one of a handful of directors whose very frames identified their author. Like Fellini, Hitchcock, and Ozu, he had such a distinctive way of seeing that his films resembled no others. What you noticed was the extreme restraint of his actors (he preferred to call them "models"), and the way the action centered on what his characters saw, rather than what they did. "The thing that matters," he said, "is not what they show me but what they hide from me and, above all, *what they do not suspect is in them.*"

His actors had no difficulty conveying that state, because Bresson never discussed characters, plot, or motivation with them, only instructing them minutely on how to move and what to say. He shunned displays of emotions in his work, rehearsing and shooting a scene over and over, until the actors seemed to be going through the motions without thought. Oddly, this style created films of great passion: Because the actors didn't act out the emotions, the audience could internalize them.

Bresson's best-known film was probably *The Trial of Joan of Arc* (1963), in which Joan was seen entirely as a spiritual creature; not for him the gaudy excess of the battle scenes in the recent French extravaganza *The Messenger: The Story of Joan of Arc*. He advised against music in movies, avoided all special effects, and when he did show a medieval battle scene, as in *Lancelot of the Lake* (1974), it was typical that he shot his characters from the neck down, dressed in armor, focusing on physical agony rather than personalities.

In *Pickpocket* (1959), he studied on the exact physical methods of his hero, leaving us to guess at his motivations, which were not theft so much as a cry of loneliness from a man cut off from the world. In *A Man Escaped* (1956), he shows a jailbreak based not on cunning or trickery but on infinite patience and the minute observation of the habits of others. In *Mouchette* (1966), one of his most touching films, a young girl is cruelly treated by her village, and kills herself; the death is a moment of freedom and ecstasy. *Au Hasard Balthazar* (1966) was about the suffering of a mule. *The Diary of a Country Priest* (1950) was about a young priest whose true spirituality baffles those who seek the comfort of superficial religion. It was cited as an influence by the Russian Andrei Tarkovsky, another director whose films resembled prayer. His final film, *L'Argent* (1983), tells the story of a young man who unwittingly passes a counterfeit note, setting into motion a strange chain of moral circumstances.

Newcomers to his work were often baffled. Those who looked more closely became fascinated. I taught a class on his work a few years ago, and watched the students begin with doubt and end in admiration. Through his discipline there beat a passion that made flashier, showier directors seem shabby.

"To see his films is to marvel that other directors have had the ingenuity to evolve such elaborate styles and yet restrict them to superficial messages," wrote the critic David Thomson. Quite so; the second entry in Bresson's *Notes on the Cinematographer* reads: "The facility of using my resources well diminishes when their number grows." What did he think of movies that assault us with blasts of sound and special effects? His notes are like psalms, with such entries as: "If the eye is entirely won, give nothing or almost nothing to the ear. One cannot be at the same time all eye and all ear."

Producers were not daring enough, and audiences not curious enough, to easily support the kind of art to which he devoted his career. His movies were few and far between—thirteen in forty years. For lovers of film, they are like the stations of the cross.

Walter Matthau

Walter Matthau, who claimed that "Foghorn" was his middle name, is dead at seventy-nine. The beloved actor, whose face was mapped with laugh lines, died of a heart attack early Saturday morning, July 1, 2000. He was brought into a Santa Monica hospital in cardiac arrest, and pronounced dead at 1:41 A.M. PDT.

It was the kind of end he had long anticipated; he joked about his heart problems, once telephoning his doctor in the middle of an interview to ask, "Is coffee a vaso-dilator or a vaso-constrictor? Check it out, will ya? You have the book right on your desk."

"He walks like a windup toy," his favorite costar Jack Lemmon once said. His face was hangdog until it lit up in a smile, and then the sun came out. He always said he didn't look like an actor but like a guy you were in the Army with. He never really looked young. Like Robert Mitchum, he seemed born middle-aged, and if you look at some of his early films, like *A Face in the Crowd* (1957), he already had the creases and the slouch of a racetrack tout.

After service in World War II, he did a decade on the stage before beginning to get character roles in the movies. He was friends in those days with Tony Curtis, "who had the good looks," went to Hollywood in 1949, and returned a year later as a star. "He was waiting in Shubert Alley when I came out of a stage door," Matthau told me, "jumping up and down and shouting about how he had made it with Yvonne DeCarlo." Matthau didn't have the looks for a young leading man, but as he grew into his face and ungainly frame, he became a character star. Even in his first film, *The Kentuckian* (1955), he was a hard-bitten saloonkeeper.

Matthau appeared in some fifty-six films, and won the Academy Award for Best Supporting Actor in 1966 for *The Fortune Cookie* ("I'd just had a heart attack," he told me, "and they wanted to give me their little award before I went to my great reward"). He was nominated as Best Actor for *Kotch* (1971), where, at forty-eight, he was able to play a convincing old-timer, and *The Sunshine Boys* (1975), where he stepped in after Jack Benny's death and made the role of an old vaudevillian his own. He starred opposite George Burns, and the two of them went on tour together to promote it, doing an ad lib routine that turned their interviews into a double act.

In comedy he never tried to be funny, and in tragedy he never tried to be sad. He was just this big (six feet, three inches), shambling, sardonic guy whose dialogue had the ease and persuasion of overheard truth. He was ideal as a foil for quick-talkers like Jack Lemmon, and together they made nine movies. The first was *The Fortune Cookie*. True stardom came with *The Odd Couple* (1968), where he, of course, was the unkempt sportswriter Oscar Madison to Lemmon's persnickety photographer Felix Unger. In addition to *The Odd Couple*, they also costarred in *Kotch*, which Lemmon directed; the classic Chicago newspaper comedy *The Front Page* (1974); *Buddy Buddy* (1981); *JFK* (1991); *Grumpy Old Men* (1993); *Grumpier Old Men* (1996); and *The Grass Harp* (1996), directed by his son Charlie.

In *JFK*, he played Louisiana Senator Russell Long, and had a scene on an airplane where all of the other passengers, he claimed, were speech teachers. He assumed the young man in the seat next to him was an extra, "and I asked him pleasantly, 'Do you live in New Orleans?'" It was Kevin Costner.

Matthau was a favorite actor of two giants of American comedy, director Billy Wilder and playwright Neil Simon. He made three films with Wilder, and starred in the screen versions of five Simon comedies. He recalled meeting Simon for the first time at a New York party. Their conversation, he said, consisted of Simon saying, "You ought to be in my next play," and Matthau replying, "Who are you?"

Later, he said, when they were preparing the film, "I told Simon, 'I don't want to play Oscar. I want to play Felix because Oscar is too easy. He gets all the laughs. Felix is a hard part; that's the part I want to play.' And Simon tells me, 'Walter, do me a favor. Act on your own time.'"

Matthau was known as an inveterate gambler, and had a groove worn into one thumb by the nail of the opposite hand during the tension of horse races and basketball games. He told me in 1994 he had lost $50 million in betting over the years. Years earlier, visiting him on the set of Wilder's *Buddy Buddy*, I had asked him if he still gambled.

"Hardly at all. For big stakes, that is. Of course I gamble, to make the games interesting. But five hundred dollars a game, tops. Or sometimes a thousand. No heart attack bets."

Do you follow basketball pretty closely?

"Pretty closely."

How many games did Indiana lose during the regular season?

"Nine. What scores do you want to know?"

Matthau had the timing of a stand-up comic, but didn't go for punch lines, expressing his humor instead in anecdotes. He and Lemmon had a long-standing shtick about whether or not Matthau had saved Lemmon's life when Jack allegedly choked on a horehound drop in Utah. Their conflicting versions of the story developed over the years into bizarre recitations in which Lemmon recalled turning blue and dropping to his knees while Matthau ignored him, and Matthau recalled performing the Heimlich maneuver at great pain to himself since he had just had open-heart surgery, "and had a chest that looked like a Christmas turkey." Matthau blamed Lemmon's failure to remember this feat on a lack of oxygen to the brain.

Studio publicists despaired of writing an accurate biography of Matthau, who made up different facts every time he was asked. He once claimed his father was a priest thrown out of the Eastern Orthodox Church in czarist Russia for preaching the infallibility of the pope. Actually, his father was a peddler who left home when Walter was three, and young Walter Matuschanskavasky, born in 1920 in New York, the son of Russian-Jewish immigrants, grew up in poverty on the Lower East Side.

He seemed destined for the theater almost from birth. He was reading Shakespeare at seven and appearing onstage at eight. He played children in plays in the Yiddish theater district along Second Avenue, went into summer stock in 1946, and got his first Broadway job in 1948. Not surprisingly, he played Nathan Detroit in the 1955 production of *Guys and Dolls*.

In the movies, he had a key early role as the sheriff pursuing Kirk Douglas in *Lonely Are the Brave* (1962). Even then he was unimpressed by Hollywood royalty, and told me years later: "The only guy that was ever affected by climatic conditions in his acting was Kirk Douglas. He did a superb job in *Lonely Are the Brave* because we were shooting that picture up at about

twelve thousand feet and the rarefied atmosphere sapped him of any energy or strength that he had. That was his best performance."

He played a thief in *Charade* (1963), costarred with Barbra Streisand in *Hello, Dolly!* (1969), was hilarious as a bankrupt millionaire in Elaine May's *A New Leaf* (1971), survived *Earthquake* (1974), made two thrillers the same year (*The Laughing Policeman* and *The Taking of Pelham One Two Three*), had a surprise success as a Little League coach in *The Bad News Bears* (1976), played a widowed doctor who simultaneously woos and flees Glenda Jackson in *House Calls* (1978), was perfectly cast as the next-door neighbor Mr. Wilson in *Dennis the Menace* (1993), and played a surprisingly convincing Albert Einstein in *I.Q.* (1994).

He and Lemmon were amazed by the success of their *Grumpy Old Men* pictures, which in some ways were a spin-off of *The Odd Couple*; oddly, *The Odd Couple II* was a misfire. Matthau's most recent film was *Hanging Up*, released in February. He played a veteran comedy writer, now bedridden, whose final illness was a catalyst for the troubled relationships of his three daughters, played by Meg Ryan, Diane Keaton, and Lisa Kudrow.

Matthau was married first to Grace Geraldine Johnson, by whom he had two children, Jennie and David. His second wife was the actress Carol Marcus, whom he wed in 1959. They had a son, Charlie. Carol, formerly wed twice to playwright William Saroyan, is a character in her own right. In our 1994 interview, he explained their marital happiness: "I think the secret is to get rid of all your money so you have to keep on working, which my wife and I do very well. We simply get rid of the money. She collects objects. She has 18,427,000 objects in the house. I, on the other hand, give all the money to the bookies."

George C. Scott

George C. Scott is dead at seventy-one. He was a powerful screen and stage presence whose enormous range was illustrated by his two famous military roles: General Buck Turgidson in *Dr. Strangelove* and General George S. Patton in *Patton*.

Scott won an Academy Award as Best Actor for *Patton*, but refused it, saying the Oscars were a "meat market—barbaric and innately corrupt." He not only stayed home on the night he was nominated, but didn't even watch the show on television: He had a hockey game on.

Scott had been in uncertain health in recent years, and was found dead September 22, 1999, at his home in Westlake Village, near Los Angeles. No cause of death was given. He continued working almost to the end, winning an Emmy (also rejected) for his made-for-TV work in *12 Angry Men* last year, and appearing in May in a TV remake of *Inherit the Wind*.

From the moment Otto Preminger cast him as a slick out-of-town lawyer in *Anatomy of a Murder* (1959), opposite Jimmy Stewart, Scott reigned as one of the most charismatic and engaging of American movie actors. He won an Oscar nomination for that role, and also for his unforgettable work as the hateful sports promoter Bert in Robert Rossen's *The Hustler* (1961), a performance Pauline Kael called satanic, and for his driven doctor in *The Hospital* (1971).

Five years after *Anatomy*, Scott played Buck Turgidson in Stanley Kubrick's *Dr. Strangelove*, sounding some of the funniest notes in that eerie comedy. As global annihilation is discussed in the "war room," he proudly boasts to the U.S. president about the pilot of a runaway bomber headed for Russia: "He can barrel in that baby so low!" He swoops his arms like wings, joyfully, until he remembers he is celebrating nuclear doom.

In that role, Scott took pleasure in pushing Turgidson to the limit, as a gum-chewing, womanizing hambone who approaches war as a boy's game. His other famous general, in Franklin Schaffner's *Patton* (1970), was flamboyant yet secretive—a man filled with a vision of his own destiny, yet not without a certain wry humor. The film's opening shot, as Scott in dress uniform appears before an American flag and delivers his philosophy of war, is one of the most effective curtain-raisers in movie history.

When Scott was nominated for that role, he asked the academy to withdraw his name. It did not, and he won, but he did no showboating. The other famous Oscar refusenik, Marlon Brando, followed Scott's lead two years later and refused to attend the ceremony, but sent an "Indian princess" named Sasheen Littlefeather to accept in his place. Scott just stayed away and went on with his work. He didn't think actors should compete with each other for awards.

The 1960s and 1970s were Scott's great decades as a movie actor, and *The Hustler, Dr. Strangelove*, and *Patton* were joined by other great performances. In Richard Lester's *Petulia* (1968), he was a divorced doctor enraptured by an eccentric (Julie Christie). In Arthur Hiller's *The Hospital*, he was a doctor again, mired in an inhuman bureaucracy. He was enjoyable in Stanley Kramer's *Oklahoma Crude* (1973), as a drifter hired by Faye Dunaway to protect her oil fields against big business. In 1977, he played a character created (and inspired) by Ernest Hemingway, in Shaffner's *Islands in the Stream*.

Scott's gift for comedy was displayed in Stanley Donen's *Movie Movie* (1978), two hour-long stories put together into a "double feature." He played a grizzled fight promoter and a Broadway impresario, and was great fun in both roles. A year later, in 1979, he gave his last great film performance, in Paul Schrader's *Hardcore*, playing a fundamentalist father from Grand Rapids who follows his runaway daughter into the sexual and drug underworld of the West Coast.

Scott worked steadily in films in the '80s and '90s, but made no important ones. His best work during those years was on the stage, which he said he preferred anyway: "I have to work in the theater to stay sane." He won four Tony Awards for work on Broadway, in *Comes a Day* (1958), *The Andersonville Trial* (1959), *Uncle Vanya* (1974), and *Death of a Salesman*, which he also directed, in 1975.

Scott's early acting years were spent on the road, in stock companies. A heavy drinker, he went through two marriages and five broken noses during that period, and later was married three more times, twice to Colleen Dewhurst, finally in 1972 to Trish Van Devere.

His big break came at the age of thirty, when he was selected by Joseph Papp for his New York Shakespeare Festival. I would have loved to have seen his 1957 performance in the title role of *Richard III*; the role must have been a good fit for his fire, his hard-edged humor, his decisive physical details, and his stagecraft.

Scott was born in a small mining town, Wise, Virginia, on October 18, 1927. He enlisted in the marines in 1945, and spent four years assigned to Arlington National Cemetery on a ceremonial burial detail. He traced his drinking to that period, and told the Associated Press: "You can't look at that many widows in veils and hear that many 'Taps' without taking to drink." After a short stint as a journalism student at the University of Missouri ("I realized acting paid a lot better"), he went on the stage. He had six children, including the actor Campbell Scott.

Arthur Hiller once said that Scott would have preferred not to be a movie star—he would have been happier as a character actor. But character actors often have to disappear into roles and Scott was always visible. He was not a recessive or subtle actor, but one who attacked his roles with zeal and a distinctive personal style.

Asked once by Gene Siskel what a critic should look for in a performance, Scott provided three rules. First, the actor must be correctly cast, or all is lost. Second, what choices does the actor make in the role's key emotional moments? Third, is there a joy in performance? Without the third, he added, all else is irrelevant: You have to sense that the actor, the material, and the role have come together in happy agreement. Watch George C. Scott in *Dr. Strangelove* or *Patton,* and what you sense is beyond craft or even art. It is joy.

Film Festivals

Telluride Film Festival
Oscar Season Starts Today!

Telluride, Colorado—The autumn movie season begins for me on the night when the curtain goes up on the first screening at the Telluride Film Festival. After a long summer of special effects, explosions, stabbings, shootings, gross-out comedies, supernatural mystifications, horror stories, and movies about the alarmingly sophisticated sex lives of teenagers, September brings relief.

Of course, some of the summer movies are very good. But autumn brings a back-to-school feeling, and going to Telluride is like buying a new three-ring binder and a book bag to carry it in. You have the feeling you'll make new friends and wonderful discoveries, and maybe even learn something.

The Telluride Festival, held every Labor Day weekend, celebrated its twenty-fifth anniversary last year. It's small, expensive, and hard to get to, but it's one of the best experiences a film lover can have. The selection process includes only films the organizers think are really good (most festivals show lots of films they don't necessarily even like). The town itself is so small that you run into the filmmakers without even trying, and this is one of the few festivals that industry professionals attend even if they don't have business to do.

Part of the mystique of Telluride is the secrecy over its schedule. In early years that was inspired by a real uncertainty about what films would actually turn up. Now it's part of the cachet. Cofounders Bill and Stella Pence and Tom Luddy are essentially asking us to trust them. Also, they want people to attend the festival as a whole, not be lured by famous names. And frequently they have "unofficial" screenings of films that allegedly aren't scheduled to be premiered for weeks or months.

Sometimes the name of a title or guest can leak out. This year, I hear that the sublime French actress Catherine Deneuve will attend and receive the Telluride Medal, and the festival will premiere her new film, *Place Vendome*, about the troubled widow of a very complicated diamond dealer.

Also promised this year is the much-anticipated U.S. premiere of *Princess Mononoke*, the new film by Japan's master of anime, Hayao Miyazaki. The movie was Japan's all-time box-office champ until it was passed by *Titanic*, and Miramax grabbed the distribution rights away from its parent, Disney, claiming that its specialized distribution strategies will find a crossover animation market. Miyazaki, whose credits include the wonderful animated films *My Neighbor Totoro* and *Kiki's Delivery Service*, was set to attend the festival but has had to cancel.

The opening night film will be *The Straight Story*, by David Lynch, whose *Blue Velvet* caused a sensation at Telluride in 1986. No two films could be less similar. *The Straight Story*, which premiered at Cannes, stars seventy-nine-year-old Richard Farnsworth as an Iowa farmer who determines to have one last visit with his brother in Wisconsin. The old man doesn't have a driver's license, however—and so he drives there on a lawn tractor.

Also said to be on the schedule is *Black and White*, the new movie by James Toback, about white teenagers who venture into the Harlem hip-hop scene. Robert Downey Jr., who starred in Toback's *Two Girls and a Guy* (1997), is back in this one. Also on tap, according to *Variety*: Dennis Hopper, Holly Hunter, Billy Crudup, and Dennis Leary are in *Jesus' Son*, by Alison MacLean, about addiction and recovery.

Following Telluride comes Toronto, September 9–19, after Cannes the second-largest film festival in the world. Between them, they preview many of the films we'll be talking about in the months to come. Lots of Oscar nominees will be among them.

But the best thing about Telluride isn't really the new films, which will open in theaters. It's the sidebar programs, which fill up about half the slots. There'll be a new restoration of a silent film, with a live sound track by the Alloy Orchestra. A special series by the guest programmer (still secret; last year it was Peter Bogdanovich, showing five titles from 1928, "the greatest year in movie history"). Tributes to legendary actors, directors, and craftspeople. A panel discussion and free lunch at the top of the ski lift.

And talk. Lots of talk. In the bracing mountain air, late at night in the moonlight, on the way from the Sheridan Opera House to the Mason's Hall, to stop in the middle of the street and talk about great movies is consolation, somehow, for the dreck you've processed all summer long.

Chuck Jones and Catherine Deneuve and David Lynch

September 3, 1999—It's a combination of a film festival and a ski weekend, greatly improved by the absence of snow. Moviegoers at this year's twenty-sixth Telluride Film Festival can take the ski lift to the top of the mountain, but what they find there is a little unexpected: the Chuck Jones Cinema, named for the animator who brought Bugs Bunny and Wile E. Coyote to life.

The new mountaintop cinema was inaugurated here Friday with screenings of comedy shorts by Jones, Chaplin, Keaton, and Laurel and Hardy. The silent films were accompanied by live musical scores performed by the Alloy Orchestra, also a Telluride tradition.

And we were off and running for a weekend extravaganza at which old, new, foreign, and domestic films play in some of the strangest places: at the century-old Sheridan Opera House, the Mason's Hall, the temporary Max Cinema constructed every year inside the high school gym, the Nugget theater on Main Street, and under the stars at the Abel Gance Open-Air Cinema, where the tickets are free but the forecast was for rain.

The festival starts even before you get here. At the airport I ran into David Lynch, who is one of the winners of the Telluride Medal this year. He's here with Mary Sweeney, who wrote his new film *The Straight Story,* starring Richard Farnsworth as an old man who goes to visit his dying brother by driving a lawn tractor from Iowa to Nebraska. It was at Telluride that Lynch's *Blue Velvet* premiered to great controversy.

Also at the airport, I talked with Rick Schmidlin, who will unveil at Telluride his 250-minute

restoration of Erich von Stroheim's legendary *Greed*—which was butchered before its release by Hollywood philistines and will never be fully restored; using von Stroheim's shooting script and hundreds of stills, Schmidlin has come as close as possible to re-creating the original experience.

Friday morning began with a brunch at the Skyline Ranch above the town, where I ran into repertory film expert Gary Meyer. "Where else but at Telluride," he asked, "can you witness Peter Sellars, Werner Herzog, David Lynch, and Ken Burns singing 'Puff, the Magic Dragon' with Peter Yarrow?"

Sellars is this year's guest director. Known for his unorthodox stage and opera productions, he has focused his selections on avant-garde video work, including a tribute to video artist Bill Viola, for this first year when Telluride has had video projection facilities.

Catherine Deneuve, the French screen goddess, received the Telluride Medal at the opening night tribute; Lynch's tribute will be Saturday, and the third of the annual medals will go to composer Philip Glass, who is here with his new score for the 1931 version of *Dracula.*

Deneuve sat through a retrospective of some of her most famous roles, including the all-singing *Umbrellas of Cherbourg;* two Luis Buñuel films about the strange shores of sexuality *(Belle de Jour* and *Tristana);* her famous lesbian scene with Susan Sarandon in *The Hunger;* and her Oscar-nominated performance as a French colonial woman in *Indochine.* The audience was charmed by a scene from the little-known *Don't Touch the White Woman,* a 1976 comedy by Marco Ferreri that costarred her longtime love Marcello Mastroianni as General George Armstrong Custer. Knocking on his bedroom door and obviously hoping for love, she tells him, "I have brought you . . . a club sandwich."

Deneuve said she never really planned to become an actress, but was recruited by her older sister Francoise Dorleac for small roles; it was Jacques Demy's *Cherbourg* that made her a star, and she has worked ever since, often for new directors or in offbeat roles. She wondered if she could have had such a rich career in Hollywood, where there is a greater penalty for failure. She did work in Hollywood (Robert Aldrich's *Hustle,* with Burt Reynolds, was one of the clips), but wondered if she could live there "for much more than four months at a time."

Most of this year's Telluride films remain to be screened. Of those I have seen, Deneuve's *Place Vendome* is a standout. Directed by Nicole Garcia, it stars Deneuve as the alcoholic wife of a famous Paris diamond dealer, whose unexpected death leaves her in the middle of his unfinished and possibly dangerous business. Deneuve's performance ranges from icy calculation to drunken pathos; the story's thriller elements are given an extra dimension by her character's personal struggle to pull her life back together. Deneuve also stars in another festival selection, Raul Ruiz's *Time Regained*, an adaptation of the novel by Proust.

East Is East, by Philip Kadelbach, is another wonderful discovery. It's the story of George and Ella Khan and their seven children. He's an immigrant from Pakistan, his wife is British, and their kids are a mystery to both of them. Adrienne Shelley's *I'll Take You There* could be described as an antirelationship comedy, starring Reg Rogers as a Realtor who falls into an abysm of depression after his wife leaves him. His sister arranges a blind date with an unkempt and disorganized friend (Ally Sheedy), who forces him to drive her to the bedside of her dying grandmother (Alice Drummond, in a scene-stealing combination of tough love and wiggy humor).

Chosen as the first feature at the Chuck Jones was *My Best Fiend*, a harrowing documentary about the love-hate relationship between director Werner Herzog and his favorite actor, the tempestuous and neurotic Klaus Kinski. At one point they have their hands around each other's throats—not entirely in fun. Herzog has been a friend of Telluride since its earliest years, when he organized an annual directors' softball game; to open the Jones Cinema with a Herzog film was a symbolic linkage between two directors whose very different kinds of films are linked by a love for the sudden and unexpected.

Chuck Jones himself was not able to be present. The eighty-seven-year-old animator wanted to come, according to festival cofounder Bill Pence, "but couldn't find a doctor willing to give him permission." Jones's definition of this festival high in the Rockies: "The most fun you can have without breathing."

Princess Mononoke's American Premiere

September 4, 1999—The day began with one of the most wondrous films I ever hope to see. *The Princess Mononoke*, by the Japanese master of animation Hayao Miyazaki, is a symphony of action and images, a thrilling epic of warriors and monsters, forest creatures and magical spells, with an underlying allegory about the relationship of man and nature. Not a children's film, it is a film for all ages that demonstrates why, for some stories, the special-effects wizards are only spinning their wheels, because some images cannot be visualized unless they are drawn.

How appropriate it was that the Telluride Film Festival screening was held in the new Chuck Jones Cinema, at the top of the ski lift. Jones, whose Warner Bros. cartoons are treasures, specialized in shape-shifting, in characters and objects that were infinitely plastic. At eighty-seven he was warned by the doctors not to test his heart against the thin Telluride air, but how much he would have enjoyed the spellbinding opening scene of *The Princess Mononoke*, in which a watchtower is attacked by a fearsome many-legged beast whose body seems made of writhing snakes.

An image like that simply cannot be made with special effects; it would emerge too complex and murky. It takes the clarity of drawing to bring it fully alive. Miyazaki has resisted computer animation, and less than 10 percent of this film uses it; most of it is drawn by hand, the traditional way, and the master personally did 80,000 of the 144,000 hand drawings. The result is an endlessly enchanting film, visually original and astonishing, about a mythical society poised on the edge of the Iron Age, when beasts and men can still speak to one another, unless the forest spirit is destroyed.

The Princess Mononoke was the top-grossing film in Japanese history until it was dethroned by *Titanic*. It was preceded in the American market by two of Miyazaki's magical family-oriented films, *My Neighbor Totoro* and *Kiki's Delivery Service*. This one transcends everything else he has done, and is being given a major push by Miramax. If the Motion Picture Academy truly does seek out the five best features of the year, then it is hard to see how it can fail to nominate this one.

Richard Farnsworth

September 4, 1999—Richard Farnsworth seems to make a habit of coming to Telluride with the roles of a lifetime. In 1982, he was here with *The Grey Fox*, about an aging train robber. Now he's back in David Lynch's *The Straight Story*, about an old man who drives a lawn tractor from Iowa to Wisconsin to visit his dying brother. Both films seem uniquely suited to his bedrock-solid acting style, which projects absolute, no-nonsense believability.

Farnsworth himself, at seventy-nine still active as a rancher, is a walking repository of Hollywood lore. He spent his early years as a stunt man, working for John Ford and the other greats, and he drops memories like jewels: He was a steeplechase rider in the Marx Brothers' *A Day at the Races*, and a soldier in *Gone With the Wind*, and "ran around in a tunic all day" on *Gunga Din*, and worked for Cecil B. DeMille on *The Ten Commandments*, and is glad he wasn't an actor for Ford "because he was hard on his actors."

He came to speaking roles late, at forty-six, and got an Oscar nomination in 1978 for *Comes a Horseman*, as an old cowboy. "I can't do Philadelphia lawyers or nuclear physicists," he smiles, "and I'm pretty choosy about my roles." At lunch with his fiancée, Jewel Van Valin, he said they were on the way to a vacation in Tahiti when his agent begged him to have another look at the script of *The Straight Story*. He said he didn't know if he was up to the role: "I was scheduled for hip replacement, and riding on that tractor looked painful." But Lynch promised a custom-made silicone cushion on the seat, and Farnsworth took the role that got him a six-minute standing ovation at Cannes.

"I'm solvent," he said, "and I don't have to act for a living. I only want to make decent family pictures. I've never said a four-letter word on the screen and it's too late to start now." Ironic but appropriate that he stars in the first G-rated film by Lynch, whose credits include *Blue Velvet*, *Twin Peaks*, and *Wild at Heart*.

James Toback

September 4, 1999—James Toback, mercurial director and polemicist, was here for the premiere of *Black and White*, his high-energy crazy quilt of stories about the intersecting worlds of blacks and whites in America, especially at the teenage level. The rap group Wu-Tang Clan and Mike Tyson share scenes with such as Brooke Shields (who is making a video documentary about why white kids admire and emulate black lifestyles). Ben Stiller plays a crooked gambler turned crooked cop; Claudia Schiffer is an anthropology student who betrays her black athlete boyfriend; and Robert Downey Jr. has a hilarious role as Shields's husband ("everyone but you knows I'm gay!").

Outside the theater, Toback was outraged about the prison sentence just handed out to Downey, who also starred in his films *The Pickup Artist* and *Two Girls and a Guy*.

"He has the bad luck to come up against the most vindictive judge in California," Toback said. "He made Robert Downey the first actor sent to jail for using drugs since Robert Mitchum, fifty years ago. How about all the other actors who use drugs? Here is a man who has an illness. He is not a criminal."

Toback said he advised Downey, "If you have to use, I have one word for you: Amsterdam. Get on a plane, go over there, do whatever you have to do, come back."

He recalled Downey's amazing statement after sentencing: "I feel like a man who has a gun pointed into his mouth, and I like the taste of the metal."

"Right there, you can see this is a man who is battling a terrible compulsion," Toback said. "When he used again, he *knew* he would get caught, because he knew they were testing him regularly. So it wasn't a 100-to-1 shot, or 50-to-1, but a dead certainty. He was asking to go to jail. Why couldn't the judge see the tragedy of the man standing in front of him?"

* * *

The secret sneak preview late Saturday night was the first public screening of *Sweet and Low-Down*, Woody Allen's new film, with still another one of those performances where Sean Penn seems to reinvent himself. He plays Emmet Ray, described as a jazz guitarist who emerged in the 1930s as "the best in the world, except for Django Reinhardt." So much is he in awe of Reinhardt, indeed, that he faints when he sees him.

The movie alternates fictional flashbacks with testimony by experts remembering the legendary figure, including jazz historian Nat Hentoff and Allen himself. What Penn creates is a goofy, self-centered genius—monstrous but likable—whose whole being seems transformed when he plays. (Penn does amazingly convincing fingering on the guitar.) He falls in love with a mute girl he meets on the Boardwalk at Atlantic City, and her sweet smile and expressive face remind you of a Chaplin heroine. But he warns her not to fall in love: As a genius, he explains, he has to walk alone.

Discoveries Every Two Hours

September 6, 1999—There are times when I wonder why I even go to the new movies at Telluride, since the special programs and retrospectives are so valuable. Yesterday I saw a surprise screening of the latest Werner Herzog documentary and then attended his birthday party on the lawn of the Mason's Hall. And an hour later I was watching a beautifully restored print of the 1931 Bela Lugosi *Dracula,* with a new score composed by Philip Glass, who conducted a live performance of it with the Kronos Quartet.

Then again, I also saw three wonderful new features. I might have seen four, but at midnight I was just too tired to drag myself to *Wisconsin Death Trap.* The new films were *Me Myself I,* a gentle comedy about a woman's life choices; *The Girl on the Bridge,* an enchanted love story; and Carlos Diegues's *Orfeu,* a retelling of the same myth that inspired the 1959 Oscar winner *Black Orpheus.*

Me Myself I is an Australian film that has the kind of breakthrough potential of *Shine;* it was directed by Pip Karmel, who edited that film. It stars the intelligent, expressive Rachel Griffiths as a journalist who yearns in her thirties for the right man, and sometimes wonders why she didn't marry her first love. Through a supernatural transformation scene, she is inserted into that alternate lifeline, and finds herself married and with three high-spirited children.

It's one thing to dream about sleeping with the man you loved thirteen years ago. It's another thing to find yourself in bed with him at a troubled time in the marriage. It's one thing to wonder if you should have had children. It's another thing to be asked by the youngest to wipe his butt. This is the kind of sweet, thoughtful comedy that could be enormously appealing to women, because it combines high-flying romantic notions with the nitty-gritty of actually being a working mother.

Patrice Leconte is the inventive director of three of the best films of the decade: *Monsieur Hire,* based on a Simenon story about a voyeur who turns into a killer; *The Hairdresser's Husband,* about a fetishist who falls hopelessly in love with the woman cutting his hair; and *Ridicule,* about a rural architect who visits the decadent court of Louis XVI, finds that verbal irony is valued there, and develops a latent skill at insult.

Now comes *The Girl on the Bridge,* an unclassifiable love story about a circus knife-thrower who is haunted by the eyes of a woman about to throw herself from a bridge. He recruits her for his act; if she is willing to die, why not take a chance with his knives? The story takes them aboard a cruise ship (it's risky to throw knives in a storm) and to Istanbul, whose Turkish music exerts some kind of fascination for Leconte, whose hairdresser's husband sometimes did weird Middle Eastern dances right there in the salon.

Orfeu is by Carlos Diegues, whose *Xica* and *Bye Bye Brazil* were triumphs of the Brazilian New Wave. The new film returns to the materials of Marcel Camus's 1959 *Black Orpheus,* telling the tragic story of Orfeu, a man who leads a Carnival dance troupe, and falls in love with Euridice, a girl from a rural area who comes to visit her aunt. The story has been updated to involve tension between the police and Rio's hill dwellers, whose ghetto is poor but overflowing with life and energy.

The film incorporates the light and music of Carnival with the daily lives of the slum dwellers, and magic realism with flamboyant passion. It succeeds in taking its mythical characters, who are larger than life, and telling their stories in a way that includes hard realism about drugs and corruption.

Werner Herzog's birthday is September 5, and the great German director celebrates it most years at Telluride. He was here this year for the screening of *My Best Fiend,* his documentary about the wild-man actor Klaus Kinski, but a surprise screening was arranged on Sunday afternoon of *Wings of Hope,* his newest film, and then a big birthday cake was served outside the hall.

Wings of Hope follows *Little Dieter Needs to Fly* (1998) in a series Herzog calls "Voyages to Hell." It tells the story of a Peruvian aircraft that crashed in the rain forest on Christmas Eve of

1970. All were presumed dead, but more than a week later a teenage girl named Juliana Koepcke walked alive out of the jungle.

Herzog has a special interest in that flight; he was booked on it, to travel to his locations for *Aguirre, the Wrath of God,* and was bumped off—saving his life and all of his subsequent films. He finds the young survivor, now a middle-aged woman who still works as a naturalist in the jungle, and retraces her walk back to civilization. It is easy to see her natural spunk as she crawls inside a hollow tree to study the nocturnal habits of bats.

The film is filled with stark images: a child's coin purse, found on the forest floor; parts of the fuselage and control panels; the heel from a woman's shoe. The woman wonders if she was saved by being strapped into one chair of a row of three, which spiraled down like a maple leaf, its descent broken by vines. She describes her wounds, her strategy of following jungle streams, her lucky knowledge that crocodiles wouldn't harm her but stingrays would. It is an amazing film.

And then to *Dracula,* which must have as many famous lines as any movie ever made ("I never drink . . . wine"). The movie was made at the dawn of the sound era and lacked a musical score; Philip Glass has matched his new composition with Tod Browning's eerie images, and he conducted the Kronos Quartet in a performance that underlined the experience without upstaging it.

This is my final Telluride report; I'm off to the picnic in the city park, and then it's on to the Toronto festival. At the end of a summer with too many moronic action pictures, Telluride and Toronto are reminders of how the movies can sometimes be wonderful, even noble.

Toronto Film Festival
The Annual Oscar Preview

Toronto, Canada—The 1999 Toronto Film Festival, eleven days and 319 films long, opens Thursday with a quarter of a million moviegoers looking for next year's top Oscar winners—or maybe trying to avoid them. The films come from fifty-two countries, and 171 of them will be world or North American premieres. People plan their vacations around this festival; last year at a Vietnamese musical I sat next to Barbara Strange, who told me she planned to see 45 movies and "exist on bottled water, dried apricots, and mixed nuts."

This is the largest public film festival in the world (as opposed to Cannes, which is more of a trade fair). It comes at a time when autumn is just beginning to bring a chill to the Ontario nights, and to add a tang to the coffee and bran muffin you bolt down on your way to the earliest morning press screening. After a summer of action films made for (and possibly by) teenage boys, this is the beginning of the fall good-movie season. Last year the North American premiere of *Shakespeare in Love* was held here. And *Life Is Beautiful.* And *Happiness.* And *Waking Ned Devine.*

The program lands with a thud. It is as big as an auto parts catalog. From years of experience

I know it divides films into several categories. The nightly Galas are devoted to films of broad audience appeal. The Masters Series spotlights new works by great directors (Greenaway, Kaige, Kitano, Saura, Paul Cox). Special Presentations fall somewhere in between. There is also attention paid to new European cinema, to discoveries from Asia, to gay films, to midnight cult movies. A movie doesn't need to develop a consensus to get into the festival; nine different programmers select the films, each one standing up for his or her own choices.

Will next year's Oscar-winning best picture be shown in the next eleven days? Some early viewers are saying Sam Mendes's *American Beauty,* with Kevin Spacey weathering a midlife crisis, is the best film of the year. The buzz is also strong for Wayne Wang's *Anywhere But Here,* with Susan Sarandon as a mother who drags her daughter (Natalie Portman) to Beverly Hills. Lawrence Kasdan's *Mumford* stars Loren Dean as a psychologist (he says) who has a way of solving everyone's problems. *Snow Falling on Cedars* by Scott Hicks (his first movie since *Shine*) stars Ethan Hawke and Youki Kudoh in an adaptation of the best-seller about a romantic aftermath of World War II.

The big indee distributors like Miramax,

Sony Classics, Fox Searchlight, and *Blair Witch* beneficiary Artisan all make Toronto their roll-out platform. This year Miramax has a big push behind *Princess Mononoke,* the wondrous Japanese animated feature that I saw a few days ago at Telluride. The Sony titles include *Black and White,* James Toback's already controversial movie about white kids who dig black culture. Artisan picked up Jim Jarmusch's *Ghost Dog* at Cannes and will showcase it here; it stars Forest Whittaker as a gentle, self-styled samurai who goes to work for the mob.

There will be heated discussions after *Dogma,* Kevin Smith's much-anticipated comedy about Catholicism; some church groups oppose it, others find worthiness under the satire. Reportedly trimmed (for pacing, not content) after its Cannes showing last May, it's one of the scarce tickets. Another big draw is the hot Japanese director Takeshi Kitano, whose films combine action with Zen. He's coming with *Kikujiro,* said to be a comic change of pace.

Rachel Griffiths had a triumph here last year in *Hilary and Jackie,* playing the sister of a doomed cellist; the role won her an Oscar nomination. She's back with perhaps the most popular film from Telluride, *Me Myself I,* about a journalist in her thirties who wonders what it would have been like to have a family with the man she really loved—and gets the chance to find out. Toronto doesn't have a jury, but it does ask patrons to vote for their favorite film, and this may be the front-runner.

Errol Morris is the brilliant, offbeat documentarian who examines the strange corners of the human mind. Last winter at Sundance, he screened a work in progress, *Mr. Death: The Rise and Fall of Fred A. Leuchter Jr.* It told the story of a man who had success designing killing machines for death rows, before unwisely getting involved with neo-Nazis who wanted him to help them deny the Holocaust. The movie was riveting and yet at the same time curiously vague in its intent; Morris said it needed more work and disappeared into his editing room, to re-emerge with a revised print for Toronto.

The names of other directors in the festival suggest flavors and tones; experienced moviegoers have instant associations when they learn Toronto will have films by Manhattan's Woody Allen, China's Chen Kaige, Mexico's Arturo Ripstein, Spain's Carlos Saura, and the cheerfully dour Finn Aki Kaurismaki. Paul Schrader, who had a triumph with *Affliction,* is back with *Forever Mine,* starring Joseph Fiennes, Ray Liotta, and Gretchen Mol in a story of romantic obsession. And Bill Forsyth, the Scottish director who created so much delight in the 1980s, is back after a furlough with *Gregory's Two Girls.*

The major theaters involved in the Toronto fest are all located near the subway lines, and you can shuttle from one to another in a few minutes. I meet people who see five or six movies a day. Then there are the parties every night. The press conferences. The lunches, the dinners, the seminars. And standing in line, which with zealous, note-comparing festivalgoers has a joy of its own. Toronto never tires of reminding you it has "the highest per capita movie attendance in North America." The average goes up a notch during festival week.

The Opening Weekend

September 13, 1999—You hurry between theaters, barely enough time between curtains, and one gift after another comes from the screen. Your only regret is that for every good film you see, the people next to you are describing three you missed. This is the payoff after a slow summer at the movies, when it sometimes seemed directors were no longer swinging for the fences, but just happy to get on base.

Over the opening weekend of the twenty-forth Toronto Film Festival, these have been some of the high-profile treasures: *American Beauty, Felicia's Journey, Mumford, Snow Falling on Cedars, Gregory's Two Girls,* and *Dogma.* The weekend, of course, is top-loaded with bigger films, and the week to come will see more indie and imported titles, but the mood here is kind of euphoric. Here are some musings:

• *American Beauty* is a film expected to win Oscar nominations, and Kevin Spacey is walking on eggshells, aware that he's given a strong performance as a white-collar drudge whose wife and teenage daughter hate him, whose daughter's classmate inspires his lust, and who quits his job, blackmails his boss, and starts pumping iron.

This is an actor's picture. Look at Annette Bening as his wife, a Realtor who makes shabby properties look like dream homes and tries the same thing with her marriage. Thora Birch as their daughter, contemptuous of parents she can see right through. A newcomer named Wes Bentley as the boy next door, who understands that his father, a retired colonel, is pathologically sick, but tries to keep his head low and deal with it. And Chris Cooper as the father, who beats his son "for your own good."

Will the academy find this material too dark for nominations? Oscar likes to put on a happy face for Best Picture, but there should be acting nominations, and a mention for first-time director Sam Mendes, a Royal Shakespeare Company veteran.

• Kevin Smith's *Dogma* has stirred people up in Toronto, as it did at Cannes. It's a comedy about Catholicism, denounced by some church groups, although I've talked to Catholics who've seen it and liked it, maybe because they understand the references. No comedy has ever been more drenched in theology; Smith, who says he goes to Mass every Sunday, seems to have downloaded his catechism into his screenplay. Since I wrote about the movie from Cannes, it's been sold by controversy-shy Miramax to Lion's Gate, which plans a fall release.

Strange how a film like this, which takes religion seriously (even if as a comic premise), attracts more heat than junk like *Stigmata*. As I reflected when conservative Catholic groups attacked Scorsese's *The Last Temptation of Christ*, at least they have taste; they target only the good pictures. Dozens of pictures open every month that mock ethical behavior and are ignored; but make a smart movie with a point, and it's in trouble. I guess the theory is that people dumb enough to see slasher movies don't know they're about values.

• *Mumford*, by Lawrence Kasdan, is a real charmer. It's a comedy set in the bucolic midwestern town of Mumford, where private lives are seething with lust, disappointment, and disappointed lust. To this town comes a mysterious young psychologist (Loren Dean), whose name is coincidentally also Mumford—if that is a coincidence, or, for that matter, if that is his name. Patients seek him out because he has a healing gift. Hope Davis plays a woman who seems to be dying of hopelessness; Jason Lee plays a Bill Gates–style zillionaire who has no one to share with; and Pruitt Taylor Vince, the dirty phone-caller from *Happiness*, is still inflamed by those trashy magazines.

Some doubt the new doctor's goodness. Martin Short is a busybody spoilsport, who churns up the local shrinks; they seem to wonder how anyone this good could be on the level. *Mumford* is like the other side of the *American Beauty* coin; the characters are just as messed up, but with light at the end of the tunnel.

• It's rare to see a film as visually inventive and ambitious as Scott Hicks's *Snow Falling on Cedars*. Previous films by the same cinematographer, Robert Richardson, such as the Oliver Stone movies *JFK* and *Natural Born Killers*, exercised the same freedom to move between color and black and white, to use different kinds of exposures, to use not only 35mm but also 16mm and Super8. In those films he was showing degrees of reality, however, and in *Snow Falling on Cedars*, his craft is at the service of a story made of impressions and fragmented memories.

Hicks (whose previous film was *Shine*) worked with Ron Bass on a screenplay of David Guterson's best-selling novel, and along with editor Hank Corwin they construct a many-layered story in which the past and present are brought together in a murder trial. Ethan Hawke and Youki Kudoh *(Picture Bride)* star, as teenagers in the Pacific Northwest, he white, she Japanese-American, who are friends as children and then fall in love, keeping the romance a secret from her disapproving parents. When the Japanese-American population is shipped out to concentration camps, she breaks with him—and all the strands of the story come together five years later, when her husband is charged with murder.

The movie could have been a straightforward crime story—setup, crime, courtroom scenes. Hicks and his collaborators are more ambitious. They evoke the feeling of the time and place, the sadness, the unfairness, and racism that lie beneath the trial. This is an impressionistic film; it doesn't tell, it leads us to feelings.

• *Felicia's Journey*, which opened the festival, is Atom Egoyan's first film since the great *The Sweet Hereafter*. It's a meticulous character study, with one of Bob Hoskins's best performances, as Hilditch, a lonely man who takes pride in running the lunchroom at a factory. At home, he cooks gourmet meals and follows a strict regime. We also meet Felicia (Elaine Cassidy), a runaway from Ireland, looking for a boyfriend who has abandoned her. Hilditch offers Felicia a ride, befriends her, and gradually we understand the horror beneath the banal surface.

The movie is based on a novel by William Trevor, one of the greatest living writers, good at building up emotional effects out of the precise observation of detail. Egoyan's wife, Arsinee Khanjian, plays a French chef whose videotape cooking instructions give Hilditch inspiration; as the connection between the chef and the man grows clear, the plight of the girl becomes doubly tragic.

• It's been nearly twenty years since a Scotsman named Bill Forsyth made a goofy, lovable film named *Gregory's Girl*. It starred the gawky, almost birdlike John Gordon Sinclair as an adolescent schoolboy hopelessly confused by girls. Forsyth's sweet comedies *(Local Hero, Comfort and Joy)* won him large audiences, but after the disappointment of *Being Human* (1993), he disappeared for a few years. Now he's back with *Gregory's Two Girls*, not a sequel but a fresh visit to the same character, still played by Sinclair, now a teacher in the school where he was once a pupil.

The two girls of the title are a dancing-eyed student (new discovery Carly McKinnon) and the older music teacher (Maria Doyle Kennedy) who is his friend and therefore not his lover. He harbors strong feelings for the student—indeed, he seems about the same emotional age as her—in a story that dances on the edge of scandal but stays on this side with good humor and silliness. The story unexpectedly evokes the radical philosopher Noam Chomsky in its plot about a local factory that may be making instruments of torture.

These are a few of the films I have seen. More are coming. If a movie critic's life was always like this, I would go mad with delight, or perhaps just with exhaustion.

Just Listen to The Dude

September 13, 1999—The Dude is standing in the middle of the press office at the Toronto Film Festival. I have been out of my hotel room for four minutes and he has found me.

"This one you gotta see," he tells me.

He hands me two Xeroxed sheets stapled together. They advertise a movie named *Goat on Fire and Smiling Fish*. With a certainty that bor-

ders on helpless acceptance, I know that although 317 movies are playing at the festival and I will not see at least 280 of them, I will be seeing *Goat on Fire and Smiling Fish*.

"What's it about?" I ask.

"This is Kevin Jordan," The Dude says, indicating a tall, dark-haired, intense young man. "He directed it."

I shake hands with Kevin Jordan. We are strangers and yet our fates are entwined. It's as if we are both passengers in The Dude's small aircraft.

"Here," says The Dude, turning back the first of the two sheets, so that I can see he has reproduced a page from the festival catalog, describing the film. "This is so good, we had to pay Michelle Maheux $10 to write it."

I know Michelle Maheux and know that although she has doubtless been offered inducements far in excess of $10 over the years, she has never compromised her ferocious vision as a programmer of the Discovery section of the Toronto festival. I know The Dude and know that his idealism is so profound that he probably thinks $10 is a plausible size for a bribe—even in Canadian dollars, which works out to about $6.80 American.

The Dude's name is Jeff Dowd. He is tall and large and has a lot of unruly curly hair and a big mustache. If you saw the Coen brothers' movie named *The Big Lebowski*, Jeff Bridges was playing a character based on him, although The Dude is a great deal more abstentious than the Bridges' character. If he were not, the movie would have been called *The Late Lebowski*. The Coens and Dowd go back a long way, to 1984, when he was telling me, "You gotta see this one. It's called *Blood Simple*. These are the Coen brothers."

Dowd wears so many hats it is difficult to assign him a title. Today he is playing the role of "rep." Whether distributor's rep, producer's rep, director's rep, or another species of rep is impossible to say. He is "repping" the film, that is for sure.

"Marty Scorsese liked this so much he decided to present it," Dowd is saying. I peer at the top Xerox sheet again. Sure enough, it says "MARTIN SCORSESE" in big black letters, and beneath them, in a smaller typeface, "cordially invites you to the premiere screening."

Did Scorsese produce the movie? No. Is he

distributing it? No. Does he have a piece of it? No. Does he hope to work with Kevin Jordan in the future? No, Scorsese directs his own films. The long and the short of it is, Martin Scorsese cordially invited me to attend the premiere screening. Why does Scorsese extend this invitation? My instinct is that there is one degree of separation between Kevin Jordan, Martin Scorsese, and The Dude.

But no, I would be wrong. Scorsese found Kevin Jordan on his own. "He saw one of my short films," Jordan told me. "He took me out to lunch, and started a Martin Scorsese scholarship that paid for my senior year at NYU. Then I was an assistant to him on *Kundun* in Morocco. My family owns a lobster house in Brooklyn. He loves lobster. When I finished my film, I sent it to him hot off the Avid, and he gave me some suggestions, what to tighten up, some ideas about music . . ."

How did you find the film? I asked Dowd.

"I didn't," he said. "It found me. I've only been repping this film for about fifteen days."

"I saw him on a panel at the L.A. Independent Filmmakers Festival," Jordan said. "He seemed like the coolest dude on the panel."

The Dude beamed.

"We were planning on coming up here and just wild-posting the movie," Jordan said. That means sticking posters up all over town. "Jeff said he would help us. We haven't even signed a contract yet."

People like The Dude are one of the ways good movies find audiences in a world where bad movies are promoted with $40 million advertising budgets. He doesn't have that kind of money, but he's good at getting out the word. He has repped titles like *The Black Stallion, Chariots of Fire, Hoosiers, The Stunt Man,* and, of course, *Blair Witch.*

"How I got started," he said, "I was a political activist in the 1960s. Civil rights, Vietnam. I saw a movie named *Hearts and Minds,* about the war. I had a friend in Seattle named Randy Finley, who had a little 100-seat theater named the Movie House. We were both so moved by this film. He wanted to show it. But the studio gave it to the only hardtop of this drive-in company.

"I asked Randy, would you be willing to take out a little two-inch ad telling people to go see this movie in your competitor's theater? He did. Then I got front-page play on the story."

The Dude beamed.

"The movie wound up running seventeen weeks and setting a house record!"

But in your competitor's theater, I pointed out.

He shrugged. "Just so people see them," he said. "I'd walk up and down the lines for hit movies, handing out brochures for what we were showing. The way I figure it is, who goes to movies? People who go to movies, that's who. They may or may not read *Premiere* magazine. They may or may not watch TV. But they go to movies. So if Warner Bros. spends $40 million to promote a movie and they're standing in line to see it, why not tell them about my movie?"

The Dude said *Goat on Fire and Smiling Fish* would be playing next Thursday, Friday, and Saturday. I said I would be sure to see it.

"A lot of the movies I rep," he said, "they're not what they seem to be. You take *The Black Stallion.* The studio said it would never appeal to children because the first eighteen minutes were without dialogue. I hold a test screening. A little girl, five years old, is in front of me. She tells her mommy she has to pee. She gets up and stands in the aisle, still watching the screen, and she stands there for the next ten minutes. Her knees are knocking together she has to pee so bad, but she can't stop watching."

The Dude beamed.

"The whole history of *The Black Stallion* was changed right then and there."

A Star for Lou Jacobi

September 4, 1999—"These two newlyweds are driving down to Miami on their honeymoon," Lou Jacobi is telling me. "The guy puts his hand on his wife's leg. 'Why don't you go farther?' she asks him. So he goes to Fort Lauderdale."

This is in the Movenpick restaurant on Yorkville, where we are having lunch before Lou is scheduled to dedicate his star on Canada's Walk of Fame. Every time I see Lou, he tells me new jokes. I call him on the phone, he tells me jokes. We go to dinner, he does ten minutes of stand-up for the people at the next table. Lou Jacobi is not happy unless everyone around him is smiling.

Lou is the only man I know who can be introduced just like Jack Benny: star of stage, screen, radio, TV, records, and the violin. He made his stage debut at the age of twelve, playing a violin prodigy in *The Priest and the Rabbi,* a Toronto stage play where it turned out (I'm not entirely clear about this) that he was the son of the priest, or of the rabbi, or they were brothers. "I was off after the first act," he said, so maybe he never got to stay around for the end of the play.

You may remember him from Woody Allen's *Everything You Ever Wanted to Know About Sex*, where he played a dinner guest who excused himself, went upstairs, raided the hostess's closet, put on a dress, was almost caught, escaped out a window, and was arrested by a cop who wanted to know why a man was wearing a dress and a mustache.

He was also in Barry Levinson's *Avalon*, as the Jewish uncle who drove out to the suburbs from the old city neighborhood, arrived late, stood in the doorway and said disbelievingly, "You cut the turkey without me?" And he was the bartender in Billy Wilder's *Irma la Douce*, and a lot of other films, and did a lot of TV (he was a regular on the Dean Martin program). On Broadway, he starred in Neil Simon's first play, *Come Blow Your Horn*, in *The Diary of Anne Frank*, in Simon's *The Sunshine Boys*, and in *Don't Drink the Water*, a play Woody Allen wrote for him.

I am writing down these credits partly because it is Lou Jacobi's day. But mostly I am writing them because I love Lou and his wife, Ruth, whom he didn't marry until he was forty-three, his sister told me today, "because finally he knew he'd found the right girl."

I met Lou at Dusty and Joan Cohl's annual Chinese dinner at the Toronto Film Festival twenty years ago. He offered the toast at my wedding. I've reviewed a few of his film performances, but at eight-five Lou is mostly retired now. What inspires me is the way Lou and Ruth have preserved their zest for living. They attack every moment like a thrilling opportunity.

Tuesday, halfway through this year's film festival, Lou and Ruth were at lunch with their friends Dusty and Joan. Bill Marshall, who founded the festival with Dusty, was also at the table, along with film critic Kathleen Carroll and man-about-town Billy Ballard.

"On our first date in 1947, Dusty took me to a benefit at a club, and Lou was the entertainment," Joan told me. "He was wearing a dress and a blond wig and was sprawled on a piano, singing about a naughty lady named Sadie."

In those days Lou played the Canadian borscht belt, nightclubs, weddings, and stag parties. ("Oooooh, I told the dirtiest jokes!" he twinkled.) Only later did he become a stage star, first in London, then on Broadway. Even after he became admired as a serious actor, he still went for laughs; his record albums have titles like "Tijuana Al and his Jewish Brass," and "The Yiddish Are Coming! The Yiddish Are Coming!"

As you make your way through life, sometimes you happen upon people who know how to be happy. I look at Lou and I'm not afraid to be eighty-five like Lou is, if I can get there in Lou's style.

At lunch on Tuesday, Lou had a new joke. He had to stand up to tell it.

"An old guy is walking down the street with two big watermelons in his hands," Lou said. "A guy asks him, 'How do I get to CBS?'"

Lou pantomimes an old man with arthritis.

First he leans over and puts down one watermelon.

Then he leans over and puts down the other watermelon.

Then he puts up his hands and shrugs.

Girls, Boys, and Cheerleaders

September 14, 1999—What strange connections take place in your mind when you see *Boys Don't Cry* and *But I'm a Cheerleader* within a few hours of one another. Premiering at the Toronto Film Festival, here are two sides of the gay-hating coin, one tragic, one funny. What did the man say in the play? We laugh, that we may not cry.

Boys Don't Cry struck me so powerfully on first viewing that it wasn't until hours later that I realized how *really* good it is. The immediate emotional impact forced aside thoughts of direction, writing, and performance, and I was simply there, inside the story of a girl named Teena Brandon who decided to become a boy named Brandon Teena, and fell in love, and was murdered.

This true story from 1993 has already inspired a documentary (this year's *The Brandon Teena Story*), and TV coverage ranging from the news magazines to Jerry Springer. You might guess that the story of a twenty-one-year-old Nebraskan can't support all that attention, but you'd be wrong: Like *Romeo and Juliet*, this tragedy of deception and love can support any number of interpretations, and seems destined to become part of our folklore, a death that holds up a mirror to society.

But I'm a Cheerleader, on the other hand, is a raucous comedy that exists halfway between the Friday night teenage sex romp and the midnight cult movie. It stars refugees from both genres: not only Natasha Lyonne, but RuPaul Charles and Mink Stole. The movie, written by Brian Wayne Peterson and directed by Jamie Babbit, tells the story of a high school cheerleader named Megan (Lyonne), whose parents become convinced she is a lesbian. (There are several warning signals: She likes tofu, has Melissa Etheridge posters, sleeps on sheets inspired by Georgia O'Keeffe's petal paintings.)

After an "intervention" by friends and family, she's shipped off to rehab at True Directions, a camp run by Cathy Moriarty to reprogram homosexual teenagers. She's subjected to a recovery program with five steps, but balks at the first one ("We admitted we were homosexual . . ."). With the glee of John Waters crossed with *Animal House,* the movie introduces characters like Rock, Moriarty's son, who discos with a weed cutter, and two nearby gay men, middle-aged and tubby, who use their van to help the kids make midnight escapes from imprisonment. Lyonne, whose adorable lower lip is in a perpetual pout at this treatment, stubbornly insists she isn't a lesbian, although the idea of kissing a woman becomes more interesting to her than swapping spit with her boyfriend, who uses his tongue like a Roto Rooter.

The lighthearted humor of *But I'm a Cheerleader* is a universe away from the world of Brandon Teena (Hilary Swank), who as a teenage girl from Lincoln, Nebraska, gets in trouble for stealing things and running away. She doesn't think of herself as a lesbian but as a boy, and at about the age of twenty she gets a short haircut, stuffs a sock in her jeans and a Marlboro in her mouth, and walks into a bar to see what will happen.

Moving to a small town an hour or two away from Lincoln, she—now he—falls in with a crowd of redneck pool players and their girls, and is soon dating Lana (Chloe Sevigny), a girl about her age. They live in the violent world of drinking and drugging macho bullies, who at

first accept Brandon ("you sure have little hands") and then eventually discover the secret.

The film was directed by Kimberley Peirce, who cowrote it with Andy Bienen. They avoid all the pitfalls of symbolism and polemics and simply allow their story to emerge from these lives. Hilary Swank achieves a convincing compromise between female and male, and embodies Brandon's uncomplicated desires with a kind of enthusiastic purity. This is not a person who recites clichés about being "a man trapped in a woman's body," but a good-looking kid who wants to have a good time, to party, and fall in love. When Brandon whispers to a cop, late in the film, about a "sexual identity crisis," you sense these are words that have been heard but not understood.

Brandon's gender might not fool anyone in a Toronto bar, but what she's doing is so alien to the worldview of the people she lives with that, frankly, they just can't imagine it. Neither can Lana, at first. Then, in crucial, delicate scenes that make the movie plausible and moving, they kiss and neck and do obscure sexual fumbling. And we understand that at some point Lana knows, and yet she doesn't know. That in some deep place she realizes Brandon is not a boy, but she never puts a name to what is happening, and shies away from the implications, so that her realization is a deep and secret treasure. Later, when the truth is clear to everyone, one of the things she mourns is the loss of her own gentle self-deception.

In the documentary I saw earlier this year, made by Susan Muska and Greta Olafsdottir, we met some of the women who dated the real Brandon Teena. They all remember him warmly: "He knew how to treat a woman." In *Boys Don't Cry,* we meet men who do not—troubled, disturbed, ignorant men who beat and rape and then ask, "You all right?" The law officers who interview Brandon are equally clueless. And Brandon has little personal information about gender confusion; the film has an innocence in the way Brandon concentrates on practice, not theory.

When you see movies like these at film festivals, it's always a mystery how they'll do at the box office. *But I'm a Cheerleader* inspired waves of laughter at its first public screening, and is likely to draw big comedy audiences if the subject matter doesn't ghettoize it. *Boys Don't Cry* is a more interesting challenge. This is, flat out, a compelling and absorbing film for general audiences, the kind of movie like *Midnight Cowboy, Philadelphia,* or *The Crying Game* that can reach and touch anyone. It's not sociological, it's not ideological, it's simply the sad and beautiful story of two star-crossed lovers: *Romeo and Juliet* in a trailer park.

Movie studios believe some films belong in art houses and others belong in malls. *Boys Don't Cry* is one of the best films of the year. But its story is so touching and compelling, so convincingly and simply told, that it would absorb any mall audience given the chance to see it. Just as Teena Brandon always insisted she was not lesbian but simply a boy, so this is not a "lesbian movie," but simply the story of two lovers in a world without pity.

Robin, Om, and Sigourney

September 15, 1999—Hanging around after the screenings:

There was a nasty article recently in *Salon,* the on-line magazine, complaining that Robin Williams has given up on making people laugh and is building a new image as a noble everyman. After such elevating projects as *What Dreams May Come, Patch Adams,* and the new *Jakob the Liar,* the article wondered whatever happened to the jolly side of Williams's persona.

Jakob the Liar, premiering here, is indeed a dark and uplifting story, with Williams as one of many Jewish prisoners in a Polish ghetto, its exits blocked by walls and Nazi machine guns. He overhears a radio story that gives reason to hope that the war may be going against Germany, tells his fellow captives, and sees how it cheers them. So he begins to fabricate more radio bulletins, allegedly heard on his secret radio.

"It's not a question of choosing a comedy or choosing a serious film," Williams told me Wednesday. "I choose on the basis of the project."

So . . . is a comedy on the horizon?

"What I know that I must do now," he said, "is just go back to the clubs and do six months of stand-up. I need to clear the decks. Open the windows. Back to basics."

What is it about stand-up? I asked. All you stand-up guys seem to invest it with an aura, as

if it exists above, or below, everything else you do.

At this impenetrable question, Williams raised an eyebrow, but responded gamely: "You're working without a net. Just you and the mike and the audience. If you fail, it's not the fault of the director or the screenplay. It's your fault. There's a kind of . . . purity to it."

* * *

Om Puri is in the peculiar position of being famous in the West for films that have never played in India, and being famous in India for films that have never played in the West. He makes one film a year in England, and several films a year in India, and he's on a shuttle between two lives.

You may not know his name, but the face might stir memories, from *Gandhi* and *City of Joy.* His newest British film is a lovely human comedy named *East Is East.* He plays an immigrant from Pakistan who has seven children with his English wife. They run a fish-and-chips shop together, working long hours. He wants to raise his children in the ways of the old country, but they are assimilating at a blinding pace, and his wife is no comfort, with her British ideas and her long-suffering ways.

The movie is a comedy with social insights, based around marriages both arranged and unarranged, and Puri is a solid rock at its center—not a bad man or even a rigid one, but simply a man who fears losing what he values most.

Puri's other forthcoming movie is *My Son the Fanatic,* an edgy story about a taxi driver in a Midlands town who works nights for the extra money, and is startled and unsettled to discover that he and a hooker he drives (Rachel Griffiths) seem to be falling in love. At home is a wife with whom he no longer has anything in common, and a son who has turned to what the father considers religious fanaticism—even moving his guru into the house.

"Neither of these films is likely to be seen in India or Pakistan," Puri was telling me. The sexual and religious content "would not disturb most people, you understand, but there is always that 10 percent who cause trouble."

Working mostly in the Bombay film industry, Puri made many 1970s films during the boom of the New Indian Cinema, even working with the great Satyajit Ray, "but eventually one looks at the empty pocketbook and begins to reflect about the realities of old age," he sighed, and so in recent years he has starred in more commercial films, some of them enormous hits.

The mass-market Indian films I've seen, I said, seemed to have a little of everything: drama, romance, music, action, dancing.

His face brightened. "Yes. For one ticket, you get everything. And they shoot them like crazy. Some actors may be making six films at a time. Never a dull moment. Sometimes I work on one film in the morning and one in the afternoon."

How do you transfer your thinking from one character to another?

He paused as if trying to find a gentle way to describe the films. "Some of the films are . . . rather broad in their styles," he said. "Sometimes there is not all that much difference between the characters."

The sad thing about modern Bombay films, he said, "is that they just throw the songs in whenever they feel like it. In the old days, the songs made a comment on the story. Now it is just, let's have a song!"

I have admired the immense subtlety Om Puri brings to his Western roles; there are nuances in *My Son the Fanatic* that are crucial in allowing the romance to work at all, and moments between Puri and Griffiths that are based on deep, quiet observation. Yet at home he plays in broad melodramas? How does he shift gears?

He spread his palms. "You concentrate on the job at hand."

* * *

One of the festival's best films is *A Map of the World*, by first-time director Scott Elliott, with a performance by Sigourney Weaver that creates an absolutely new and original character in a role that might, in other hands, have fallen into easy observation. What's astonishing about the film is how awake it is, how it doesn't fall into predictable story routines.

Weaver's character, a Wisconsin farm wife, mother, and school nurse named Alice, has a series of disasters befall her, and although these events could be handled in soppy docudrama fashion, they are not: Weaver and her collaborators surprise us again and again by the way the character responds not according to the require-

ments of genre fiction, but according to the rhythms of her stubborn and proud personality.

She is, I observed, an actress of unusual range. She was once described by *Variety* as "the only actress who can open an action picture," which means her name on the marquee of an *Alien* film guarantees a huge weekend. She is also known for quiet, quirky, difficult roles in movies like *The Ice Storm* or *Death and the Maiden*. It's a fair distance between *A Map of the World* and battling matriarchal alien spiders.

"I've often thought it would be fun to work in repertory," she said. "Different roles on a rotating basis. Comedies, dramas, the classics, experimental. It keeps you on your toes."

For *A Map of the Heart*, she said, one of the most difficult experiences was preparing for scenes where she is in the city jail.

"I went through the whole process of being booked in. Fingerprinting, mug shots, everything. They couldn't get my fingerprints to register, and they kept working at it, and it was so—dehumanizing. And then the reality inside, where the sentence itself is like a kind of torture. No privacy. The lights. Always being watched. A guard told me, 'Well, you can always watch TV.' But of course, the TV is *always*. The problem is, you can't not watch it."

Sex vs. Eroticism

September 16, 1999—*Romance,* from France, and *Lies,* from Korea, are the two most sexually explicit films in this year's Toronto Film Festival, providing details even a gynecologist would find educational. Both are pitiless in their scrutiny of the obsessions of their characters.

I viewed them one right after the other, and found myself listening to the laughter in the audience. Mostly it seemed to be the women who were laughing—disbelievingly during the Korean film, with recognition during the French one. The men sat in silence, not amused as the heroines reduced their partners to mindless service providers. If pornography is about the objectification of the sex object, here is revenge for movies that treat women that way.

It is said that women are less concerned with outward physical beauty then men, and more concerned with the ability of their partners to provide security and stability. Both of these films (one directed by a man, both told from the female point of view) show us women who view their partners as a source of precisely what they want in bed. Physical appeal is beside the point. The men in the French film are a foppish male model, a middle-aged businessman, and a guy who gets to tag along when his awesome equipment is required on a date. The hero of the Korean film is a scrawny thirty-eight-year-old college professor who looks vaguely like John Lennon.

The heroines of both films are attractive, although the Korean film is indifferent to its schoolgirl heroine's beauty. We only rarely get a good look at her face, which is never lingered upon in appreciation. The French film does take care to portray its heroine as beautiful an desirable. Can you guess which was directed by a man? Maybe.

The titles could be reversed. *Romance* contains only lies, and *Lies* is the story of a romance in which the lovers are brutally honest. Both are narrated by one of the characters; both narrations are flat and factual, like descriptions of a traffic accident by a dazed survivor. *Romance,* by Catherine Breillat (whose *36 Fillette* was about a young girl whose large breasts led her prematurely into sexuality), is about a woman who finds no satisfaction from her abstentious boyfriend, or from anybody else, seek as she does, until she encounters a polite, attentive, middle-aged expert in bondage. *Lies,* by Jang Sun Woo, is about an eighteen-year-old schoolgirl and a thirty-eight-year-old professor who are drawn into an escalating spiral of sadomasochism.

Neither of these films is erotic in any conventional way. There is not a single scene that seems intended to be arousing, except perhaps to specialized tastes. The directors seem more fascinated by the pathology of the characters than by their libidos. *Romance* at least sets its story in the conventional French world of apartments, cafés, and meeting places, and its characters talk about their desires and problems. *Lies* is about two people who have nothing in common except their overwhelming need to beat each other, and be beaten. There is some doubt whether the girl enjoys the pain ("I like it because you like it," she tells the professor). There is no doubt that he does. The French woman (Caroline Ducey) seems bemused by her own behavior, which she analyzes like an outsider. She doesn't connect easily with anyone, and perhaps has chosen her boyfriend because of his passivity. She likes the bondage enthusiast because "he ties me up but doesn't tie me down." After sessions, they chat over caviar and vodka, and at last we see pleasure reflected on her face.

There is graphic detail in the film, including a scene where she is examined first by the gynecologist, then by several interns, each one slipping on his sanitary glove when he's next in line. She sort of enjoys that, and also a fantasy in which her body is stuck through a hole in a wall; on one side, she is vulnerable to the patrons in a brothel, while on the other she is giving birth. (Don't worry if you can't picture this; it's the idea that counts—perhaps, I fear, as a metaphor of woman's lot.) In one quick edit, Breillat cuts from sperm to the ointment used before an ultrasound picture of the womb—the slickest flash-forward since *Citizen Kane* cut from "Merry Christmas" to "Happy New Year."

The heroine in *Romance* is seen basically in a social setting, as a modern woman with needs and feelings that not many men can understand. Even her bondage friend is valued more for the care he takes than for the results he gets. In *Lies,* on the other hand, we get an almost documentary look at two people so single-minded that a walk in the woods is just an opportunity to search for promising switches. Late in the film, homeless and wandering from one cheap love hotel to another, they pass a construction site and experimentally heft some of the boards. "Take the one with the nail in it," the man says. He is not joking.

Lies is not pornographic because it does not seek to arouse, but it shares the directness of the porno film; the characters exist primarily in terms of their sexual identity, there are few conversations of note, and even the director seems slightly impatient during the interludes between sex. I was reminded of the late Brendan Gill's perceptive definition of a porno film: any film in which we grow restless because of the time the characters are taking to get in and out of cars and walk in and out of rooms.

Watching these two films with packed houses of Toronto Film Festival patrons added a curious overlay to the experience. The moviegoers were the usual cross section of ages and backgrounds; some, no doubt, were not even at their first choice of film, and got their tickets as second prize in the festival lottery system.

739

There were some walkouts, but not many. Scenes of the most striking brutality, of close-up explicitness, were witnessed by audiences that seemed interested, if not fascinated. The MPAA of course would slap both of these films with an instant and horrified NC-17 if they were ever submitted (they will go out unrated). But the audiences I joined took them in stride. These are simply stories of people seeking happiness in their own desperate ways. In the French film, the heroine thinks she will find it, which makes it a comedy. In the Korean film, the heroine thinks she will lose it, which makes it a tragedy.

The Dude Delivers

September 17, 1999—The Dude was right.

Faithful readers will recall that within four minutes of my arrival in the press office on the opening day of the Toronto Film Festival last week, I was ambushed by The Dude, who said, "This one you gotta see!" and warmly pressed into my hands a flier for a movie named *Goat on Fire and Smiling Fish.*

Thursday night I attended the world premiere of the goat and fish movie, and bathed once again in the kind of joy mixed with relief that an audience feels when it senses it has discovered something. There was a standing ovation for a remarkable supporting performance, and then one of those situations where no one wants to leave the theater.

The Dude, you may remember, is named Jeff Dowd, and is a producer's rep so colorful that he inspired his friends the Coen brothers, to base *The Big Lebowski* on his untamed personality. He turns up at film festivals like a race track tout. At Sundance this year, he cornered me at the luggage carousel at Salt Lake City airport, before I had even retrieved my bags, and was whispering *Blair Witch Project* into my ear. He was not even repping *Blair Witch.* Like all good touts, he likes to share a sure thing even if he doesn't have money on it himself.

In the case of *Goat on Fire and Smiling Fish,* he was repping a movie that was made for around $40,000 in a shooting schedule of twelve days by three pals. The movie was directed by an NYU graduate named Kevin Jordan, stars his best friends Derick and Steven Martini, and was cowritten by Kevin and Derick. Kevin and Derick are twenty-five; Steven is twenty-three.

The movie is about the romantic adventures of two brothers in Los Angeles, and it's sweet, goofy, and funny. The standing ovation was for a supporting performance by Bill Henderson, a singer and actor *(City Slickers)* who plays a ninety-year-old veteran of the black movie industry. "You're certainly not ninety, are you?" I asked him. "Not as yet," he replied.

I experienced déjà vu, remembering the 1995 Sundance premiere of *The Brothers McMullen,* another low-budget brothers movie that warmed audience hearts. There was even the same sort of reunion; Jordan's parents and various friends and relatives were in the audience, and we got the obligatory line, "Look, ma! I'm a filmmaker!" for his mother Eileen. Jordan's dad was there, too—Bill, the lobsterman from Brooklyn.

Standing around afterward were buyers for some of the indie distribution companies—figures who are expert at melting into the shadows after unsuccessful screenings. "Do you own this film?" I asked Jeff Lipski of Goldwyn, and he replied with the two words that filmmakers dream of, "Not yet."

The movie's title, we learn, comes from nicknames given to the two brothers by their grandmother, who was half Italian and half Native American and named them in their cradles: *Goat on Fire* for the older, dour brother Chris (Derick Martini), and "Smiling Fish" for the younger, cheerful Tony (Steven Martini). Their parents met as tourists on the Universal Studio Tour. They were orphaned "due to an unfortunate traffic accident on the 105 Freeway," and are sharing a house in a lower-income Los Angeles neighborhood.

Chris works as an accountant. Tony vaguely moves on the fringes of the movie industry, like every third person in L.A. They both make romantic moves during the film. Chris, whose girlfriend cries during sex, meets a beautiful Italian girl named Anna (Rosemarie Addeo), who is an animal wrangler and turns up for one date with a chicken named Bob. Tony falls in love with the woman who delivers his mail (Christa Miller); she is from Wyoming but is in L.A. so her daughter can audition for a role on a sitcom.

These love stories may put you in mind of the romantic difficulties of *The Brothers McMullen,* but *Goat on Fire and Smiling Fish* doesn't have the darker undertones (even though it does contain the obligatory unanticipated pregnancy). The film is lighter and sweeter, more effervescent.

And it contains the unforgettable character of Clive, the elderly uncle of the man Chris works for. "Pick up my uncle at the home where he lives and bring him in to work," the boss tells him, and Chris comes to treasure his daily encounters with Clive, who was a soundman on "race pictures" made in the 1930s and 1940s by and for African-Americans. He tells stories of Paul Robeson and the other greats, and explains his theory that when a man and a woman really have chemistry, it makes something crackle in the sound of their dialogue.

Clive is blunt and to the point at all times. "What are you going to do at the office?" Chris asks him. "Bull—— and busywork," he replies. He is assigned a cubicle like all the other workers, but immediately builds a tent over it, moves in a decorator lamp, and furnishes it like a cozy little room. Inside, behind the tent flap, he tells Chris stories of the great love of his life. It is not only a wonderful performance, but a key one, since he is the screenplay's conduit for a romantic worldview that helps the goat on fire understand his own life.

Friday morning, not too early, I debriefed The Dude on what was happening on the rep front.

"There's a lot of interest," he said. "I can't name names, but a lot of people are talking to us about the picture. What you gotta understand is, this isn't about the highest bid; it's about a marriage. This is the kind of movie where the distributor has to understand it's about reviews and word of mouth. The way things are today, with films moving out of the theaters so quickly, you can't open a picture like this on 1,000 screens. The filmmakers have to visit the key cities, do a couple of days of publicity, get the word out, and then the audience will find it."

Are you weighing offers?

"The way this will work is, more people will see the movie at the industry screening on Friday. Then at the Uptown on Saturday. But a lot of people pulled out of town by midweek. They'll have to see it. This isn't the kind of movie you describe to your partners over the phone. They gotta see it. We'll have screenings on Tuesday and Wednesday in New York and L.A."

The print shown here, he said, was out of the lab less than twenty-four hours. Jordan and his actors saw it for the first time Thursday. "A $40,000 picture like this," The Dude said, "after it's picked up, they'll spend at least that much on postproduction. Tweaking, getting the balance right, cleaning up the sound track, just like they did with *Blair Witch* and *Brothers McMullen.*"

I'd just typed those words when the phone rang. The Dude again, still repping.

"I was just thinking," he said, "in a competitive marketplace, the key to this picture is, it's a date movie. If I'm a twenty-five-year-old guy and I took someone to the movie, that could be the start of a special evening. Or two girlfriends, going out to the movies together, ideas about dating and life. Even if I was two guys, it would hit home."

Although I can just about picture The Dude as two guys, I sense that repping is beginning to segue into spinning. Which is, of course, the next step.

Memories of Toronto

September 20, 1999—Waiting in the lobby of the Elgin theater Friday night, I talked to a guy who had seen forty-five films in this year's Toronto Film Festival: "Yesterday I saw a $60 million movie I can hardly remember, and a $40,000 film I'll never forget."

Festivals impose a Darwinian selection process; the good ones elbow the others out of your memory. Here's a selection, by no means complete, of titles I've especially admired.

• *Princess Mononoke* is a wondrous experience by the Japanese master Hayao Miyazaki, an animated epic adventure from the mists of the Iron Age, when men and beasts talked with one another. Using ancient myths and the Japanese fascination with shape-shifting, he tells of strange lands, a forest god, and a fearsome tribe of bear-men. This is not a children's film (some images are intense) but a flesh-and-blood movie, that uses animation to create powerful images: a loathsome boar-monster, for example, with flesh of writhing snakes. This is one of the year's best films.

• Tom Gilroy's *Spring Forward* is like cool water and fresh wind, a film so pure-hearted that cynicism falls before it. It stars Ned Beatty and Liev Schreiber as workers for a small town's landscaping department. The older man is near retirement, the younger one is clinging to his first job after prison. They share the cab of a truck and the secrets of their lives, in conversations where they feel free to say what they really think. How hopeful and poetic they both are—how philosophical, once they find themselves free of that gruff reticence that many men use as a barrier.

• Patricia Rozema's *Mansfield Park* identifies with Jane Austen's intelligence rather than her atmosphere; among recent adaptations, it's closer to *Persuasion* than *Sense and Sensibility*. The story of a poor girl brought by an aunt to live in a great country house, it shows her determined to marry the man of her choice; she tells herself stories that help her see the patterns in her life. Frances O'Connor is the spirited heroine, and Embeth Davidtz has a remarkable scene in which she explains the whole situation in precisely the wrong way. Of the films I saw at Toronto this year, *Mansfield Park* has the best shot at a Best Picture nomination.

• What a specific and quirky performance Sigourney Weaver gives in Scott Elliott's *Map of the World*. She plays the kind of woman who marches to her own drummer and says exactly what she must say, damn the consequences. She's a farm wife and school nurse with legal difficulties that are not her fault—although she's no help with her stubborn attitude. It's rare for a movie to keep us in genuine, not contrived, suspense because a character is so real that we sense she's floating free of all the conventions of stories of this type.

• *Sunshine,* by Hungary's Istvan Szabo, considers the Holocaust like a train bearing down over three generations upon a Jewish family from Budapest. Acted in English by a gifted cast (with Ralph Fiennes in a triple role), it shows the Holocaust not as an aberration, a contagion spread by Hitler, but as the inexorable result of long years of anti-Semitism. The Sonnenschein family thinks of itself as good Hungarians; the father in the middle generation changes his name, converts to Catholicism, and wins a gold medal for fencing in the Olympics. But assimilation is not the answer.

The film has a thrilling historical sweep, as its characters are buffeted by political winds. First they live under the "liberal" emperor, then under wartime fascism, finally under the Communist regime. At every moment there is a choice between ethics and expediency; at no moment is the choice clear or easy. This is an awesomely thoughtful film. Its three hours allow Szabo to show the family destiny forming and shifting under pressure. Too long? No good movie is too long, just as no bad movie is short enough.

• Chris Smith's *American Movie* is a rich comic treasure, a documentary about the unconquerable compulsion some people have to make a movie. Its hero is Mark Borchardt, a lanky-haired visionary from a blue-collar Milwaukee suburb, who mercilessly drives his family and friends in service to his vision, while draining his Uncle Bill's life savings to make a short horror film named *Coven*. Borchardt is no less gifted (or not much) than any other first-time filmmaker with no resources, no money, an incompetent crew, spaced-out actors, and a script that depends largely on circumstances. For every first-time filmmaker who gets a film into the Toronto festival, there are 500 who do not. This is the story of one of them.

• *Mr. Death: The Rise and Fall of Fred A. Leuchter Jr.* is the new documentary by Errol Morris, about a man who has success designing killing machines for death rows, and then is swept up by neo-Nazis intent on proving that there were no gas chambers at Auschwitz. Pathetic, clueless Fred visits the site of the death camp and collects brick samples like a high school kid working on a project. He finds no gas residue; legitimate scientists in the film patiently explain that his methods could not possibly test for gas or anything else—except for the presence of bricks.

All of Morris's films are labyrinthine in their strategies. This one is not really about Holocaust deniers, but about the dynamic that draws them together—a need to belong and find friendship, bathed in the comforting poison of a shared hatred. By the end of the film we realize Leuchter is not an anti-Semite so much as a pathetic creature who has found acceptance from neo-Nazis, and enjoys their picnics and get-togethers.

• Soren Kragh-Jacobsen's *Mifune* comes wrapped in the flag of the Dogma movement, that Danish declaration of rigorous filmmaking principles, but the film itself is a goofy romantic comedy about a man who returns home to care for the shabby family farm and his retarded brother, and falls in love with the housekeeper. What it proves is that a good film's ideology emerges from the material, and cannot be imposed; this film might have been essentially the same if the Dogma statement had never been written.

• Meryl Streep must be weary of talk about her mastery of accents, but listen to her closely in Wes Craven's *Music of the Heart*. She plays a divorced navy wife who wants to resurrect a career as a music teacher, and starts a violin program at a grammar school in East Harlem. The story is constructed out of conventional pleasures (no less pleasurable for being conventional), and there is a warm glow at the end. But Streep's technique is extraordinary.

Because she talks here like an "average American," it is easy to think she has no accent at all. But she has never before in any film talked remotely like the way she speaks as the violin teacher Roberta Guaspari. There is a subtle kind of artlessness in her voice, a lack of final polish, a working without a net—the sound of a woman who grew up near a shrill, uneducated grandmother. The look and the body language are also new and specific. It is easier for an actress to play a completely different sort of character, I think, than to make an ordinary one new.

• Godard said the way to criticize a movie is to make another movie. I was not among the fans of *Sliding Doors*, the film about a woman moving between alternative lifelines, and now Pip Karmel has made *Me Myself I* to demonstrate a better approach to the device. This is one of the most charming films of the year, with a wonderful performance by Rachel Griffiths as a thirtyish journalist named Pamela who wonders what might have happened if she'd married that guy she was really in love with and had kids.

A flash of movie magic, and it happens. With all of her memories intact, she finds herself inside an alternative Pamela who is married and has three kids. She has to fake the skills of motherhood, and (speaking of faking) have sex for the first time with a man who has been sleeping with her for twelve years. *Sliding Doors* was about the paradoxes of the time-line gimmick, but *Me Myself I* is about the character—about what she feels and discovers.

• Coky Giedroyc's *Women Talking Dirty* is a daffy little comedy about two best friends in Edinburgh, played by Helena Bonham Carter and Gina McKee, who are betrayed in a particularly hurtful way by a man in their lives. McKee was the woman in the wheelchair in *Notting Hill*'s boozy dinner party, and this film also has a menagerie of colorful friends who gather for wine and truth. Its appeal grows from the specific qualities of McKee and Bonham Carter, who are infectious; there is a second when Bonham Carter wants her friend to let her in the house, is refused, then accepted, and vibrates with intense joy and relief. Such moments may only last for a blink, but they are what characters are made of.

• The last film I saw on the festival's tenth day was Michael Apted's documentary *Me and Isaac Newton*, which circles through the stories of several great scientists, who meditate on how they got started, what inspired them, and what they're looking for. Among the remarkable subjects: theoretical physicist Michio Kaku, who asked his mother if he could build a particle accelerator in the garage ("sure!"), and Patricia Wright, who walked out of a rock concert, bought a monkey in a pet store, and ended up as a famous primatologist who has created a rain forest preserve in Madagascar.

Apted is a successful feature filmmaker (*Coal Miner's Daughter, Gorillas in the Mist*, the new James Bond film) who alone among his colleagues regularly returns to the documentary form. His *42 Up*, continuing a long-running series of docs revisiting the same people every seven years, opens in November; this project is one of the most interesting uses of film I have ever encountered.

There were many other good films at the festival. Some of them, like *Limey; Ghost Dog; Happy, Texas; Black and White*; and *L'Humanite* I wrote about from Sundance, Cannes, or Telluride. The best single film I saw this year? How can you choose between a heartbreaking drama like Kimberley Peirce's *Boys Don't Cry*, which I wrote about last week, and an animated fantasy like Miyazaki's *Princess Mononoke*? You can't. You don't.

Toronto 2000: The Winners

September 20, 1999—*American Beauty*, which opens in theaters on Friday, strengthened its position as an Oscar candidate by winning the Air Canada People's Choice Award here Sunday, on the closing day of the Toronto Film Festival.

The festival has no official jury, but presents several independently administered awards. The Air Canada prize, the most coveted, is voted on by filmgoers as they leave theaters; a statistical formula balances the scores of films in large and small houses.

American Beauty stars Kevin Spacey and Annette Bening as discontented suburbanites whose daughter hates them. It's a dark comedy by first-time director Sam Mendes, with strong supporting performances by Thora Birch as the daughter, and Wes Bentley as the battered boy next door. When Spacey breaks loose from his malaise, it is by admitting his lust for a fellow member of his daughter's cheerleading team.

That the movie won a popular ballot at this festival with 250,000 admissions helps quiet the fears of its distributor, DreamWorks, that it may be too dark to appeal to Motion Picture Academy voters.

The Benson & Hedges Film Discovery Award, voted on by some 775 journalists covering the festival, went to Kevin Jordan's *Goat on Fire and Smiling Fish*, the story of two brothers in Los Angeles, their struggles with romance, and their unclassifiable friendships. It was also a first film, shot in twelve days on a $40,000 budget, and with some of the same buzz as previous sleepers like *The Brothers McMullen*. The award was a closing-day triumph for The Dude (film rep Jeff Dowd), whose adventures in promoting it were chronicled in some of my Toronto reports.

The FIPRESCI Award is given at this and many other festivals by a jury selected by an international federation of film critics. It went to *Shower*, by Zhang Yang of China, a comedy that contrasts old and new through characters who gather in an old-fashioned bathhouse.

The CityTV Award, given to the best first Canadian feature, went to Catherine Annau for *Just Watch Me: Trudeau and the '70s Generation*, about the charismatic prime minister who held the country together during tumultuous times. The Toronto City Award for best Canadian film went to Jeremy Podeswa for *The Five Senses*, about a group of characters who each lose one of their senses.

Calcutta Film Festival
A Festival without Miramax

Calcutta, India—I have been here at the Calcutta Film Festival for five days without once hearing the word "Miramax." No one has discussed a deal. There has been no speculation about a film's box-office prospects. I have not seen a single star. I have been plunged into a world of passionate debate about film—nonstop talking about theory, politics, and art. For the visiting American, dazed and sedated by the weekly mumbo-jumbo about the weekend's top ten grossers, this is like a wake-up plunge into cold water.

Festival films are showing all over Calcutta, and every house for every film, no matter how obscure, is sold out. The focus is at Nandan, the West Bengal Film Centre, where movies screen in vast auditoriums and small rooms tucked obscurely away under the eaves. Panel discussions run nonstop at the same time.

Still blurry with jet lag, I am on a panel titled "Film-Telefilm-Films: A Spielberg Phenome-non." The six panelists spend much of their time trying to worry out the meaning of this subject. The Indian director Ashoke Viswanathan goes right back to the beginning, explaining why still photos projected at twenty-four frames a second seem to be moving. The Australian director Paul Cox, inspired by a question about the greatest living directors, announces, "The greatest living directors are all dead." Just as I am clearing my throat to begin by own profound remarks, Ansu Sur, the head of the festival, announces a break, and we all repair to a room next door to sip tea and eat cookies, and gaze on an exhibit of still photos from the works of Hitchcock.

Calcutta is said to be the intellectual center of India. Bombay is the film center, and "Bollywood" produces more films every year than Hollywood. But Calcutta was the home of Satyajit Ray, the greatest Indian director and patron saint of Bengali film lovers. "In Bombay it is all business, in Delhi it is all politics, in Calcutta it is all philosophy," I was told by a young man behind me in line at the Pepsi stand.

The grounds of Nandan are chockablock with dozens of little private refreshment stands, offering Pepsi, coffee, tea, snacks, and Indian fast food, vegetarian or nonvegetarian. There is also an open-air book bazaar, a dozen or so dealers with their wares displayed on tables. There are more books about Ingmar Bergman than anyone else. There are no books about Austin Powers.

The grounds of Nandan are filled with conversation. On the grass, students in threes and fours sit in the sun with the festival program, discussing the films they have seen. On railings and benches, older people nod in earnest debate. Nobody asks me about Tom Cruise but I am closely examined on *Battleship Potemkin.* I was told to expect beggar children in Calcutta, hanging on my sleeve, but there are none here. Instead, every time I show my face outside a screening, I am urgently required to lend my presence to a discussion forum, immediately. "But I have to go to another movie," I tell the man from the Association of Film Societies. "If only for a moment or two," he says, obviously gauging how long it will take me to download my best insights.

Every evening we official delegates gather at dinner parties in the Calcutta Club, the Bengal Club, the Cricket Club. I find myself seeking out Tahmineh Milani, the feminist heroine of the new Iranian cinema, whose *Two Women* is about a woman of genius who feels trapped and discouraged by her country's cultural revolution. She and her architect husband talk not about agents and deals, but about making films under a regime that imposes religious restrictions, but seems to be growing more flexible.

I meet Mitra Sen, from Toronto, an Indian born in London and raised in Nashville. Her short film is *Just a Little Red Dot,* about a Sri Lankan girl who is new to a grade school class. She wears the "bindi," or red dot, in the center of her forehead, and this is the subject of great curiosity among the other students. Soon they all want one. But an older student taunts the red-dot wearers. The kids name the bindis "Cool Dots," and form a club to distribute them. They come to symbolize cultural diversity. Mitra Sen tells me the Cool Dot Clubs are spreading across Canada.

It is my turn to express ignorance. I have seen a million red dots in my life, and never quite known what they mean. Are they religious? Do they symbolize something? An older Indian woman overhears my question and fills me in: "For me, it's just cosmetic. If I don't have my dot, my forehead feels naked. Years ago, it meant that a woman was married, or a widow. Today, we wear them because we like the way they look." I decide I like the way they look too.

I go downtown to the Lighthouse, a gigantic cinema that is also participating in the festival, and meet John Mantosh, whose family has owned it for generations. "I am half and half," he beams. "Half Indian, half Swiss." We drink Cokes in the theater's cavernous Art Deco restaurant. "For years this was a dance hall," he says. "During the Second World War, every British soldier in Calcutta must have passed through here."

A waiter brings a plate of cashews with fresh coriander sprinkled on top. John dispatches his young son Rafael upstairs to bring down the theater's guest book. We examine the signatures: James Stewart, Shirley MacLaine, Dame Sybil Thorndyke, Lord Montbatten. Alfred Hitchcock has drawn in his famous self-caricature. His signature is large and bold. His wife, Alma, has signed in a tiny hand beneath it.

"Right now we are showing *Phantom Menace,*" John tells me. "It is doing pretty well."

"What is your all-time most successful film?" I ask.

"That is an easy one to answer. *Baby's Day Out.*"

I recall the film. It was shot in Chicago by John Hughes, and is about a baby who wanders safely past appalling dangers. The film costars Joe Mantegna; the baby succeeds at one point in setting his crotch afire. *Baby's Day Out* was a colossal critical and commercial failure for Hughes, or so I thought.

"It ran and ran and ran," John Mantosh told me. "Seventeen weeks at least, filling every seat in our largest auditorium, 1,400 seats. Let me tell you, business would be better if every film were that good."

I return to the Delegates' Room at Nandan. Tea and cookies are served every ten minutes. I recognize Subrata Mitra, who was Satyajit Ray's cinematographer. I was on a jury with him once at the Hawaii Film Festival. Together, he and Ray began with the films of the *Apu Trilogy,* and he remembered at Hawaii that the first day of filming was the first day Ray had worked as a director and Mitra had worked as a cinematographer.

"I remember when you won the Eastman Kodak Award at Hawaii," I tell him. "In your speech you thanked your camera and your film."

"Yes, I remember that night all too well," he said. "In your speech you called the *Apu* films among the ten greatest films of all time. But when the man from Eastman Kodak spoke, he only placed them among the top 100 films of all time. They gave me my award. I took it up to my room and looked for a citation. Not a word. No engraving of my name. Nothing. Just a plastic clock such as one could buy in the trophy shop. I brought it home and have never taken it out of the box."

Everything falls into place. In Calcutta they take this stuff seriously. In Bombay, they would have been happy to get the clock.

A Moviegoer in Calcutta

November 17, 1999—This is the story of one afternoon at the Calcutta Film Festival.

I meet my driver outside the hotel. Everyone in Calcutta who has a car has a driver. This is not because they are too lazy to drive themselves. It is because they are too frightened. Driving in Calcutta traffic is like living inside a dangerous and violent video game.

I clamber into the backseat of my Sumo Tata, a Jeepish vehicle that looks capable of scaling the Himalayas. Half the front windshield is obscured by a large sheet of paper identifying me as an official guest of the government of West Bengal. We roar into the street at full speed without the slightest glance to see if there is any approaching traffic. That is their problem. You try to avoid running into anything in front of you, and everybody behind you tries to avoid running into you.

There are no white lines on the streets in Calcutta. They would be a waste of good paint. Cars drive wherever there is an opening. In general, you stay on your side of the street, unless an opportunity opens up on the other side. Every square inch of the pavement, from curb to curb, is occupied by cars, buses, taxis, people, and the occasional horse. In America we squander half our streets with empty space between vehicles.

All drivers honk their horns constantly. There is a kind of code. Some honks mean, "Pedestrian, jump out of the way quickly as I am not going to stop." Others mean, "I am now cutting you off." Little toots mean, "Don't get any ideas about slowing down because I am maintaining a constant speed and am 1½ inches from your rear bumper." Long, angry blasts mean, "You are heading directly toward me in my lane." Then there is a happy little tap that simply means, "I exist."

A bus drives at right angles in front of four lanes of traffic. We stop suddenly. This is unusual, because Calcutta drivers hardly ever stop except, occasionally, at their destinations. We do not stop quite soon enough and crash into the taxi in front of us. My driver and the taxi driver exchange many observations and much advice to each other in Hindi. They do not, however, get out of their cars to inspect the damage, perhaps because anyone foolish enough to get out of a car in the middle of this traffic might just as well go ahead and throw themselves under the wheels of a speeding truck in the same smooth motion.

We arrive at the Lighthouse Cinema in downtown Calcutta. This is a vast old movie palace originally built by the J. Arthur Rank organization in the days of the British Raj. The street outside is a riot of joyous capitalism. There are luggage stores, motor scooter repairmen, clothing merchants, a used-book stand, a sari shop, and countless fast-food vendors cooking bread and savories over small stoves in the open air. That's just in the street. The sidewalks are also jammed. There are no American chains here, perhaps because opportunists would open fast-food stands right there inside McDonald's to supply snacks to the people waiting in line.

I am greeted at the door of the Lighthouse by John Mantosh, the owner of the theater. We go up in an elevator that contains framed photographs of Shirley MacLaine and David Niven. In John's office, I meet his wife, Susie. I have been told she is the granddaughter of the king of Nepal. She reminds me of Rosie O'Donnell.

She takes my photo. "With Susie it is nothing but click-click-click all the day long," John tells me. "We just took the children to Disney World in Orlando. Susie exposed 500 rolls of film. We have every second of the trip recorded on film. She started with a picture of us opening the door to leave the house. Then a picture of us walking through the door. Then a picture of us closing the door. Then a picture of the closed door."

Susie bubbles with good cheer and offers everyone tea.

"If I lived in Calcutta, you would be my good friend," I tell her. "Are you hungry?" she says. "You look a little hungry. Let me get you something."

"I just ate," I tell her, and change the subject: "Are you really the granddaughter of the king of Nepal?" This is a rather personal question, but with Susie I sense that one does not stand on ceremony.

"My family were the powers behind the throne," she says. "My grandfather was the man who ran everything for the king of Nepal. Here he is right here." She plunges into her handbag and extracts a six-inch stack of snapshots, many of which show her children standing beneath an oil portrait of a distinguished man in a turban.

"It is time for the screening to begin," says John.

We are going to see *Two Women,* a film from Iran by Tahmineh Milani. I have met the director and her husband, the architect Mohammed Nikbin, at several festival dinners and they have become good friends. They arrive and we all file into the balcony of the theater. Paul Cox, the director from Australia, is along too. We settle down. Advertisements on the screen advise us that the theater brought us sound in the 1930s and now brings us stereo. Other ads tell us where to purchase the best belts, and ask us not to spit. The movie starts.

"The sound is too shrill!" says Tahmineh Milani. She gets up to find the projectionist, which is not going to be easy, because you have to go outside and up some stairs and through an office to find the projectors, which beam the picture through a wall into the theater.

It is a powerful film. It tells the story of a woman who is a brilliant math student in Tehran, whose life is destroyed by a stalker who follows her everywhere. The stalker throws acid at her cousin, and then chases her on his motor scooter, and her car crashes into some children. She doesn't kill anyone, but his scooter does claim a life. The stalker is given thirteen years in jail and vows to kill her when he is released. But the woman's father is outraged because she has brought disgrace on the family in the first place by attracting the attentions of the stalker. She is

pulled out of university and returned to a small town, where her family makes her marry a wet-eyed, middle-aged man who is pathologically jealous and keeps the telephone locked in a cabinet.

Two Women is not only well acted and directed, but subtly persuasive. Without making a single overt statement about the male-dominated fundamentalist regime in Iran, it makes a strong argument about women's rights. I am so absorbed I hardly notice that the sound has been adjusted and now sounds fine.

The story arrives at a crisis. The heroine's father has locked her in a room. The lights go up, and a card saying "Interval" flashes on the screen. Ushers appear with trays of Cokes and potato chips. We stand up and discuss the movie so far. Susie reappears.

"You look hungry," she says. "Let me get you something."

"I am having some potato chips," I say.

"Your mouth says you're not hungry, but your eyes tell another story," says Susie.

The movie starts again. I am astonished that Tahmineh Milani has been able to make *Two Women* in Iran. Obviously there is more freedom there than we have been led to believe. Once again I am wrapped up in the story. There is a tap on my shoulder. It is Susie. She has brought me a pizza and a cup of coffee.

Reader, what could I do? I ate the pizza. It was one of the best pizzas I have ever eaten. And as I sat in the balcony of the Lighthouse Cinema in Calcutta and ate Susie's pizza while watching a brave film from Iran, I felt something, and it was happiness.

Going to the Movies in India

Hyderabad, India, November 23, 1999—After the Calcutta Film Festival, I stop for a few days in Hyderabad, the pearl capital of central India, where they are holding their fourteenth annual Golden Elephant Children's Film Festival. Headquarters is the Holiday Inn Krishna, where a papier-mâché elephant dominates the lobby. After Calcutta's bump-'em traffic, Hyderabad is a relief; the drivers here are as laid-back as the typical Manhattan cabbie.

I plan to catch some children's films. My friend Uma da Cunha, a Bombay casting director and production consultant, tells me I should also see a typical Hindi blockbuster in a typical theater with a typical audience. This is a great idea. India has the largest film industry in the world; its studios in Bombay (or "Bollywood") churn out as many as 600 titles a year, heavy on melodrama, romance, action, and song and dance—all in the same movie.

The kiddie matinee begins at two in a cavernous neighborhood cinema. Squadrons of kids are lined up outside, sorted according to age, gender, and school uniform. Delegates and journalists are admitted early, and we grab aisle seats near the back. The seats are hard but not unforgiving: They recline, so that we can gaze up blissfully at the screen, like in a planetarium.

The kids charge in. These are happy kids. They shout and scream and whistle, skipping down the aisles two by two, holding hands buddy-system. Their teachers brandish wooden rulers, the scepters of their trade, and shout dire warnings. Fifty girls in blue-and-white uniforms romp into the seats in front of me, but then a teacher whacks a seat with her ruler and they all leap up again and are replaced by fifty boys in shorts, white shirts, and ties.

The movie is *Malli*, an award-winner about a poor village girl who admires the veterinarian and spies on his work. She meets a rich deaf girl who is visiting from the city. They sneak off together to play. A village elder tells Malli about a precious eyestone that was lost long ago and has magical powers. A peacock god manifests himself to her; in his tail is the same design as the eyestone. Men dressed in khaki walk through the forest with rifles, and one of them wounds the little doe that has become Malli's friend. She rips her brand-new green skirt to bind the wound, and deposits the little deer on the vet's doorstop. This good deed is rewarded: She finds the magic stone.

The kids appreciate this film with an intensity approaching ecstasy. When Malli succeeds, they cheer. When she fails, they groan. When the evil men with rifles appear, they hoot and whistle. When there is a song, they clap along. When Malli runs through the forest, the audience makes a sound that is kind of a ululating affirmation, as if they are running with her.

I have never heard louder appreciation from any audience, but no matter—the sound is turned up to rock-concert volume. Every theater I have visited in India advertises stereo and air conditioning, and is at pains to demonstrate

that it has both. The sound thunders from the speakers, and blasts of arctic air roar from the ventilation system. This is a warm climate but I have learned to bring a jacket to every screening.

There is an intermission, so that vendors can sell popcorn and potato chips. I go into the lobby and find a counter that offers the flat, crispy pastries known as "elephant ears." I order one and it tastes exactly the same as the identical pastry at the Swedish Bakery in Harbert, Michigan, where I am a leading consumer of elephant ears.

That evening we are sitting in the buffet area of the Holiday Inn Krisha, making plans to attend the Bollywood production. It is eight P.M.

"We will stop on the way and get a bite to eat," says an actress who is on the festival jury.

"But...you said the theater was half an hour away, and the show starts at nine," I said. "Won't we be late?"

She makes that distinctive Indian head movement that is not a shake or a nod, but a sort of circular combination of both. I have learned that it means, "Yes, probably, but one never knows."

"Piffle," she says. "We'll get there late. Nobody comes on time."

Uma da Cunha adds: "And sometimes they don't stay for the whole film, either. These films are always at least two and a half hours long."

We are given a lift by B. Narsing Rao, a tall and friendly man Uma describes as a director, painter, poet, and playwright. We arrive at a vast and towering cinema. Neon signs reach for the sky. Enormous billboards advertise the film.

"The stars are so famous they don't even put their names on the posters," Uma tells me. "Those names are for the director and the musical director."

We go into a lobby that stretches in every direction as far as marble can reach. We climb a wide inclined ramp. The first level is for ten rupee seats. Next are the twenty rupee seats. Higher and higher we climb, looking ruefully at a disabled escalator, until we reach heaven—seats that cost thirty rupees, or about seventy-five cents.

The movie is under way. It's in Hindi, although the characters occasionally switch to English, which is the only language spoken in every part of India. Uma translates for me: "This is a rich family. There is a dispute over land. The son has come home from America. The father is that man with the very deep voice. His name is Amrish Puri. He is Mr. Villain of Indian cinema. Fans love his voice."

The son from America wears blue jeans, a baseball cap, and a backpack. He stands on a mountaintop and breathes the air of home, and then leaps off and slides halfway down the mountain, just out of joy. When he arrives home, his father can barely be bothered to look up from the *Economic Times* newspaper. His mother, who has hair like an American rockabilly star, wants him to get married.

The hero wanders around and sees the most beautiful woman in the world. I am not exaggerating. The actress is Aishwaria Rai, and she was voted Miss Universe. She is one of the two or three most gorgeous women I have ever seen in a movie. Totally unaware that the hero is watching her, she sings a song for—well, for nobody in particular, I guess, since she is unaware. This is just how she passes the time. Two other beautiful women join her in a choreographed dance, and then twenty-four whirling dervishes with baggy silk pantaloons join in.

"She is a poor girl," Uma tells me. Not too poor to have backup singers and a chorus line when she sings to herself, I reflect. The boy is smitten. He tries to catch her eye. She refuses to return his smile. She looks studiously indifferent. The boy is intrigued. So am I. In an American movie we would already be into the condom jokes.

Back home, the family sits outside on lawn chairs, all facing the camera, while the father reads *Fortune* magazine. The boy wanders up to a high mountain pasture, loses his footing, and falls off. He grabs a tree. The girl, who happens to find herself in the same high pasture, throws him a rope, and she and her two friends and a few of the guys in pantaloons pull the guy up to where he can grasp her hand, just like Cary Grant and Eva Marie Saint in *North by Northwest*.

"Ah!" says Uma. "They are holding hands!"

"She is saving him," I say.

"Yes, that is the excuse," she says. "It is not right to touch the bride before marriage."

So thrilled is the hero to have his hand held that he inadvertently pulls the heroine over with him, and both of them dangle at the end of the rope before being hauled up by the pantaloon squad. Soon after, she sings another song, while he watches, unobserved.

I have to admit: This is fun. There is an innocence in this pure entertainment that Hollywood has somehow lost. I pull my sport coat up over my head, to shield myself from the ferocious blasts of air conditioning, and reflect that Doris Day stories are alive and well in India.

Now comes a scene of such peculiar eroticism that you will have to take my word for it— it was sexy. At a reception, the heroine scratches her chin. The hero, across the room, scratches his chin. The heroine touches her nose. The hero touches his nose. She brushes back her hair. He brushes back his hair. What fills him with maddening desire is that *she does not reveal by even a flicker of an eyelid that she notices him doing this*. She is a good girl and will not make eye contact, even though they have held hands.

Trays of soft drinks are brought around. She takes a bottle of Coke and sips through a straw. He takes a Coke and sips through a straw. "Coca-Cola is sponsoring this movie," Uma explains. Product placement is up-front in India.

The hero removes the straw and *drinks from the bottle with his lips*. The woman does not seem to notice. He puts the bottle *back* on the tray, and tells the waiter to take the tray to where the heroine is standing with her girlfriends. The waiter offers her the tray. *Will her lips touch the same Coke bottle as his?* Or will she choose Thums Up cola (without the "b"), the other leading Indian brand? The suspense is unbearable. She rejects the tray. But then—this is cinema at its best!—her girlfriend reaches for the same bottle, and the heroine snatches it away. *She did notice! She was looking all the time!*

Now the heroine is holding the Coke bottle herself. Does she drink from it? I would like to tell you, I really would, but this is a family newspaper.

Sundance Film Festival
Opening Night at Sundance

Park City, Utah—Beverly Hills slicksters and Manhattan indie distributors are packing their goose-down coats and Elmer Fudd hats and gearing up for the Sundance Film Festival, which is held every January here in this Utah ski resort, often in the middle of a snowstorm.

The Y2K edition opens today with the opening night premiere of *What's Cooking* by Gurinder Chadha, and Indian-American whose story follows four Los Angeles families (African-American, Jewish, Latino, and Vietnamese) through their Thanksgiving celebrations. That screening will be in Salt Lake City's big Abravanel Hall, and then it's up the hill in the 4WD SUVs to brave Park City's jampacked nine days of screenings.

I remember this festival when it was small and humble. "The U.S. Film Festival in Park City," it was called in the early 1980s, and it all fit into the local Holiday Inn, with screenings across the parking lot in the triplex. Now it is the most important single festival in America, a showcase for new work by independent filmmakers, plus all kinds of sidebars including world cinema and documentaries. All the big specialized distributors are here, looking for product they can release in the next twelve months.

Guessing right can be baffling. Last year's festival included sales for titles like *American Movie, Happy, Texas,* and *Tumbleweeds,* but its biggest hit—the greatest box office success in festival history—came right out of left field.

Like all the other critics, I'd studied the program, trying to choose among hundreds of films I'd never heard of, and faxed in my advance ticket requests. Now I was standing in the baggage claim area at the Salt Lake City airport and Jeff Dowd, a distributor's rep known as The Dude, was whispering in my ear, "Three words: *Blair Witch Project.*" This unheralded zilch-budget handheld horror film was the one to see, he assured me, and he was right: The movie went on to gross something like $150 million at the box office.

Could anyone have predicted that success? Not a chance. The big boys like Miramax and Sony Classics passed on the film, and an upstart named Artisan bought it. Maybe the buzz was a hint. Sundance festival director Geoff Gilmore

had to keep adding extra screenings to handle the demand, and by week's end if you hadn't seen *Blair Witch* you were out of the loop.

This year's *Blair Witch,* if any, is by definition still a mystery. The festival's selections were chosen from an awesome field; *Variety's* Todd McCarthy reports that 1,650 features were submitted, including 849 for the sixteen slots in the offical dramatic competition. I could tell you the ones I have tickets for, but that would be spinning my wheels: I don't have a clue what the big discoveries will be, and maybe even The Dude doesn't, either.

I can predict, however, the festival's dominant topic of discussion: The rise of digital. This may be the first year in which more of the Sundance features were shot on digital video than film, and the festival has installed lots of digital projection equipment. The movie industry seems poised to switch over from a century of film projection to the new digital projectors, but now great controversy has swirled up around the topic, led by advocates (like myself) of the competing MaxiVision48 film system that offers a picture 500 percent better than current film or video.

At a panel discussion at New York's Museum of Modern Art a week ago, observers were startled by the audience's opposition to "dijection" and its support of traditional film projection. A Sundance panel discussion on Sunday will renew the debate. Certainly shooting on digital is a godsend to new filmmakers with low budgets, but for mainstream commercial films the industry has always boasted of the best possible picture; will excellence in theatrical projection be a victim of cost-cutting? Sundance will be wondering.

A New Millennium for American Independent Filmmaking

January 22, 2000—About half of the films at the Sundance Film Festival this year have been shot the low-cost digital way, and 26 percent of them were directed by women. Those two statistics, possibly related, point the way into the new millennium for American independent filmmaking.

Digital production means lower costs. When anyone with a $1,500 handheld camera can theoretically make a "real movie" that's snapped up by distributors and plays in theaters, the bar has been lowered a notch for directors trying to break into the film world. That makes it easier for women and minorities. And when those films or their previews can be distributed on the Web, even the definition of "distributor" has changed.

An example from the festival's opening night. The premiere film was *What's Cooking?*, a comedy with its serious side, about four Los Angeles families gathering for Thanksgiving dinner. One family is Vietnamese. One is African-American. One is Latino. One is Jewish. After the movie, I met its director, whose name is Gurinder Chadha. She was born in India, raised in London, and now lives in Los Angeles. "We made our own United Nations," she said, smiling.

Her picture was shot the traditional way, on film, and now, as she stood in the lobby of the vast Abravanel Hall, cameras crowded around her. A few were from local TV stations. The rest were Webcams. Smashcuts.com and HollywoodOnSet.com wanted to talk to her. Leonard Klady of Reporter.com was hovering. All over the world, at least in theory, movie fans were sharing her triumph; relatives in England and India could glimpse her bring interviewed—probably in shaky stamp-sized windows with jerky sound and warnings of "buffering," but glimpse her all the same.

I see a familiar face waving from over her shoulder. It's the kid. Exactly one year ago tonight, I was accosted by Stuart Acher, a twenty-two-year-old Boston film school grad who wanted me to look at his video, *Bobby Loves Mangos*. Uh, huh. I explained that there were 156 movies in the festival for me to see, that I didn't have a VHS machine in my room, that I was running as fast as I could, etc., but the kid didn't give up.

A few days later, as I was grabbing a coffee in the bar of the Yarrow Hotel, he bribed the bartender to show his movie on the big-screen TV. How could I refuse to watch it? And you know what? It was good. I wrote about the kid, he got an agent, he made a deal, he's in preproduction.

But wait. You haven't heard this year's update. At the car rental counter in Salt Lake City that afternoon, I'd met a guy named Mika Salmi. "We're working with the kid," he said. He pressed his card into my hands. He's CEO and founder of Atomfilms.com. I know his

site. It offers streaming video of short films—kind of a worldwide audition.

"We bought Stuart's film for our site," Salmi said. "He's at this festival working with us. Nobody should have to go through what he went through to get somebody to see his film. So what we're doing is, Atomfilms will have a Winnebago camper here that's sort of a screening room on wheels. We'll drive around town and park outside the theaters and parties. Filmmakers can bring us their shorts and show them to us. If we like them, we'll put them on the Web. Stuart is helping us run the operation."

Last year, bribing bartenders. This year, your own Winnebago. The mind boggles at what the future may hold.

I push through the crowd to the kid. "I know all about your Winnebago deal," I say.

"I can't wait to show you my new film," he says.

Psycho at Sundance

January 24, 2000—*American Psycho* was the most anticipated film at this year's Sundance Film Festival, and now it gains another distinction, as the most loathed. As a film critic I am a target for anyone who wants to supply an opinion of a movie, and ever since Friday night people have been hurling themselves at me, foaming with rage at this film about a cold-hearted yuppie psychopath. My best guess: People who threw up here last year during *The Blair Witch Project* would gladly go back and throw up again rather than see *American Psycho* a second time.

The film stars Christian Bale in what is, actually, an accomplished and skillful performance as Patrick Bateman, the subject of Bret Easton Ellis's praised and reviled best-seller. The more you hate Bateman, and you do, the more you have to hand it to Bale for his courage in creating this monster. Credit goes also to director Mary Harron *(I Shot Andy Warhol)* for going all the way with her material, for uncompromising fidelity to Ellis's portrait of a man who admits nobody is at home in his soul—a man whose values are expressed in brand names and status symbols, and who spends his secret hours horribly killing and mutilating his victims.

Imagine a *GQ* cover boy crossed with Jeffrey Dahmer. Give him a big job on Wall Street.

That's Patrick Bateman. The Sundance audience hated the film. The hate seemed to reach right across the spectrum, from Salt Lake City Mormons who found it evil ("a crime against humanity," one woman told me) to hip Sundance indee film types who, uncomfortable with moral outrage, spoke sadly in hushed voices about its chances at the box office.

American Psycho is cold. Very cold. From its antiseptic interiors to the stony face of its hero and the frosted screams of his victim's heads in his refrigerator, it's as icy a film as I've seen. There is absolutely no attempt to make Batemen into anything other than the most hateful character within the power of the filmmakers to create.

No doubt there is a case to be made for the film. It is well made—the better to disgust us with, to be sure. It is an attack on the yuppie values of the Me Decade. It shows materialism and selfishness taken to their ultimate extremes. As an object lesson, it can even be seen as ultimately serving a moral purpose. It is not a bad film. But it is an agonizing experience.

* * *

Now clear your mind. Come with me to the good-hearted *Compensation*, as far removed from *American Psycho* as it is possible to go and still remain within the same civilization. This is a film that stars the same two actors in two matched romances. Both take place in Chicago: one circa 1910, the other in the present day. In both stories, the woman is deaf and the man can hear, and tries to learn sign language. The backdrop is the changing nature of African-American lives during the century.

The director is Zeinabu irene Davis (she likes the small "i" on her middle name), formerly a professor at Northwestern, now living in San Diego. Her husband, Marc A. Chery, a onetime librarian for the Chicago Public Library, is the screenwriter and producer. The stars are Michelle A. Banks, who is deaf, and John Earl Jelks.

Davis's inspiration is silent film, and particularly the many films produced by and for blacks at a time when movie theaters were segregated. The earlier story is told as a silent film, and the modern story uses similar techniques; in it, we can hear the dialogue, but it is all subtitled anyway, for deaf audience members.

Both stories are dreamy, atmospheric reveries, rich in humor and social observation. The early story deals with the blow to the heroine's life when the only Chicago school for the deaf is segregated in 1910. Her boyfriend, newly arrived from Mississippi, is illiterate, and so she teaches him reading and writing and American Sign Language all at once. In the modern story, the fiancé takes ASL classes, but in both stories there is opposition to the romance from those who tell the heroine that a hearing man will never truly be able to understand her needs.

This is a small, quiet, enchanting film about characters who endure and prevail and trust themselves. The style is perfectly suited to the material. It makes you feel good. Strap the American Psycho to a chair and make him watch *Compensation,* and his head would explode.

* * *

I've seen ten films so far at Sundance, some of them, I fear, destined to play nowhere else. I'll comment on some of them in later articles, but here's one more for today: Stanley Tucci's *Joe Gould's Secret,* about the strange and strained long-term friendship between *New Yorker* staff writer Joseph Mitchell (Tucci) and a brilliant, charming bum named Joe Gould (Ian Holm).

Gould was New York's favorite bohemian in the 1930s and 1940s. He supported himself by demanding contributions to the "Joe Gould fund," and claimed to be writing an epic "oral history of New York"—wandering the streets and writing down everything of interest that he heard. Mitchell writes an article about Gould, and then another. Gould and Mitchell develop a love-hate relationship, in which it is often the homeless bum who takes the moral high ground.

The film has more secrets than the one referred to in the title. You will have to see it to understand what I mean, but one of the secrets is that it is really about Joseph Mitchell, and Joe Gould operates in a way as a mirror turned to his soul.

Digital Ups and Downs and Outs

January 24, 2000—For a century, movies have been projected onto a big screen by a bright light shining through a moving strip of celluloid. If the prophets of the coming digital age are correct, film will disappear from that equation at some point in the next decade, and movies will be recorded and projected by digital means. Already the comfortable old word "photography" is being replaced by "image capture."

This year's Sundance Film Festival is besotted by digital. Sony has a big exhibit space outside the Prospector Square screening room to show off its newest professional cameras. Apple has rented a storefront on Main Street. Live Web cams are roaming the lobbies. Digital projectors have been installed in a lot of theaters. And Bernard Rose is ecstatic.

"My new film cost nothing!" cried the British director *(Candyman, Immortal Beloved)* at a digital panel on Saturday. "I used the digital camera myself. No cinematographer. My stars were my producers. We had a nine-man team. No electricians and no grips, because we didn't use lights. Just available light. The biggest expense was feeding everyone at restaurants."

He showed a trailer for the film, named *Ivansxtc* (say it aloud), which looked as professional as a big-ticket production. Rose usually works the traditional Hollywood studio way, and had the audience laughing with his complaints about too many crew members and the expense of catering their meals.

"The only thing that's worth anything in this new digital world," he declared, "is intellectual property."

Many of the independent filmmakers here would agree. The next day, I was on another digital panel with the actor Ethan Hawke, who has just finished directing his first film—on digital. He talked about the freedom of being able to film an intimate conversation between two actors, using three cameras, because the cost was negligible. As an actor, he said, he often feels at the mercy of a big production and its expensive costs, as the time clock keeps ticking. Digital frees him to concentrate on the work.

"I used to wish I'd been alive at the time of the French New Wave," Hawke said. "Now I feel like I am." He said Thomas Vinterberg's *The Celebration* (1998), a film shot on digital with available light, "was the most exciting thing to happen to actors since Marlon Brando." Vinterberg, Lars von Trier, and other advocates of the influential Dogma 95 movement have called for films shot on digital, handheld, with no special effects or music, and no artificial lighting.

Famed cinematographer John Bailey *(In the Line of Fire, Groundhog Day)*, on the same panel, loves to work with film but also enjoyed the

freedom of digital on the new film he directed and photographed, *Via Dolorosa*, a David Hare performance piece. He observed, however, that the look of *The Celebration* was possible not simply because it was entirely shot on digital, but because an experienced cinematographer was using the camera. "The problem with digital," he said, "is that you can shoot forever on three cameras and it costs nothing—but you don't get a single good shot."

No one was predicting the death of film. But shooting on digital video was embraced as a cheaper, faster way to make films free of the typical $60 million Hollywood budgets. "It places the means of production in the hands of the workers," I said, not originally.

Digital projection, on the other hand, is still very debatable. Although many industryites believe the day will come when movies are beamed from satellites directly to theaters, and projected as video, not film, others were not convinced the picture quality was up to par. Larry Thorpe, the Sony guru who has done as much as anyone to pursue what he calls "the Holy Grail of film quality on video," showed three versions of the same shot—one shot on 35mm film but projected on 16mm film, the other two shot with high-definition television. The audience actually booed the video images, which were noticeably inferior to 16mm film, let alone 35mm. But then, of course, came the disclaimer that the video projector being used was not state-of-the-art.

I got in a plug for MaxiVision48, the film-based projection system that costs 10 percent as much as current video projectors and is claimed to be five times better. The argument against it is that studios want to save the cost of manufacturing and distributing prints; digital will allow them to transmit movies by satellite. I argued that moviegoers don't care how much the studio saves; they just want the best possible picture. Studios are not known for fiscal prudence; why should they start cost-cutting by giving ticket buyers an inferior picture?

One amusing development during the panel: Although digital cameras can easily shoot at the equivalent of twenty-four, thirty, forty-eight, or sixty frames per second, Hollywood has been demanding that the traditional twenty-four fps rate be duplicated by the new professional-model video cameras. Sony's newest model, a

$100,000 model unveiled at Sundance, can shoot at the frame rate of your choice, but "24p" is preferred by the studios. Panel member Jason Kliot, producer of last year's Sundance winner *Three Seasons,* argued that there is something about twenty-four fps that is "just right"—a fit between the eye and the mind. He observed that George Lucas actually altered the look of his digital version of *The Phantom Menace* to reproduce the twenty-four-frame flicker effect, which disappears at higher frame rates.

Strange, that millions are being lavished to reproduce by digital what already exists on film, warts and all. But many film people believe there's something tawdry about the video look. Reviewing the side-by-side film and video comparison, one audience member sniffed that the video "had the visual look of soap opera."

The bottom line seems to be: Shooting in digital is fine, but projecting with digital is still a swampland of unanswered questions. For low-budget filmmakers, digital is a godsend. But audiences still enjoy the lush image quality of celluloid projection. I think they would enjoy MaxiVision48 even more. But will they ever get the chance to see it, as Hollywood (and "Indeewood") pursue the digital bandwagon?

Tammy Faye Comes to Sundance

January 24, 2000—"When she was born," her aunt recalls, "she had perfectly manicured fingernails." She still does. She also has eyelashes so firmly attached that she never removes them: "They have to sort of wear out. When one falls off, I replace it." Tammy Faye, once the evangelizing queen of a global satellite network, now "living in virtual exile in a gated community in Palm Springs," came to the Sundance Film Festival over the weekend and won the hearts of the heathens.

The Eyes of Tammy Faye, a new documentary by Fenton Bailey and Randy Barbato, got a standing ovation here after its first screening on Friday, and Tammy Faye had to get out her Kleenex and dab at the tears before answering questions from the audience. Afterward, she was mobbed by autograph seekers, at a festival where Christian Bale and Jodie Foster can walk through a crowd in peace.

Her saga is well known. She and first husband Jim Bakker began as traveling evangelists, parlayed a puppet show into TV stardom, created

three TV networks, were the first Christian broadcasters with their own satellite, and built the multimillion-dollar theme park Heritage USA near Charlotte, North Carolina—while Jim, according to the courts, was defrauding his viewers of millions. He went to prison, is now on parole and remarried. After their divorce ("we're still friends"), Tammy married Roe Messner, who oversaw construction on Heritage USA. Alas, he was convicted of bankruptcy fraud, spent two years in prison, was released in early 1999, and was at Sundance to stand by his woman.

All movies about women like this are required by law to contain the words "she's a survivor." But Jim J. Bullock, the gay cohost of her most recent talk show, *Jim J. and Tammy Faye,* puts a new spin on it: "She's a survivor. After the holocaust, there will be roaches, Tammy Faye, and Cher."

When Jim Bakker and Tammy Faye were on the air in the 1980s, I confess to watching them, not because I was saved, but because I was fascinated. They were like two little puppets themselves—Howdy Doody and Betty Boop made flesh. Tammy Faye cried on nearly every show, and sang with the force of a Brenda Lee, and when she'd do her famous version of "We're Blest," yes, dear reader, I would sing along with her.

The documentary reveals that she was a bundle of nerves in those days, as Jim withdrew into an obsession with Heritage USA empire-building (and brooded, no doubt, over his infamous one-night stand with Jessica Hahn). Tammy became addicted to pills, and her attention sometimes seemed to drift; directors Bailey and Barbato plundered the video archives to find moments like the one where Jim says, "Now Tammy's going to sing for us," and Tammy is discovered wandering at the back of the set, gazing at a prop and saying, "I'm looking at this boat."

But she did have chemistry and a natural TV presence, and narrator Ru Paul Charles points out that she'd do two or three shows in a row, entirely ad-lib, completely comfortable without a script.

Ru Paul? Yes, the famous drag queen is the film's narrator, and a subtext of *The Eyes of Tammy Faye* is that unlike most Christian televangelists (especially her nemesis Jerry Falwell), she has always been friendly with gays. Old videotape shows her commiserating with an HIV-positive preacher, at a time when mainstream shows still shunned the topic of AIDS, and she chose the gay Bullock as the cohost on her comeback attempt. (One segment shows him pulling a brassiere out of her purse and waving it over his head, claiming it's his.)

Codirectors Bailey and Barbato are also openly gay, and there was a hint in some of their Sundance remarks that they got into this project because they saw Tammy Faye as a camp icon. So she is, as in a sequence where she explains the amazing contents of her makeup kit ("I don't know what this is," she confesses about one product). But she is also, we sense, a woman of great generosity of spirit, and a TV natural: The star she most reminds me of is Lucille Ball.

Was she in on the scams? She was never charged, never brought to trial. In the doc, she walks through the ruins of Heritage USA, which has been padlocked for ten years ("I'd love to give this place a good coat of paint"), and the Palm Springs home she and Jim shared at the end. She lived in comfort and still does. But the movie tacitly implies she didn't do anything criminal, that what you saw on TV was the real Tammy Faye, all of her, with no hidden edges or secrets. In terms of broadcast hours, she lived more of her life on live TV than perhaps anyone else in history. And as she wiped away her tears before the Sundance audience, I realized she was, in a sense, on live TV right then and there. Always is. Like Jim Carrey in *The Truman Show*, only in on the secret.

The Halfway Mark

January 25, 2000—At the midpoint of this year's Sundance Film Festival, no great blinding vision has dazzled audiences. The festival seems mostly midrange, skewed toward safe, quirky comedies, and lacking the exciting discoveries of years past like *In the Company of Men* or *American Movie.*

Of course, I haven't seen most of the 156 or so entries, buzz cannot be trusted, and there are many movies to go. But since my last report only two movies have really reached me: A modern-dress version of *Hamlet,* and a delightful comedy named *The Cup,* said to be the first film from Bhutan.

Where is Bhutan? you may be asking. That's the same question I was asked by some kids with a video camera as I sat in the Egyptian theater waiting for the film to begin. The Sundance Institute has invited students from Bhutan and Latin America to attend this year's festival.

"Near India and Pakistan?" I asked.

"Right," the kid said. "Is it an independent country?"

"I think it might be an Indian state," I said.

"Okay," said the kid.

"Is it?"

"I don't know. I'm from Latin America."

We were still debating the question when the film began. It's a wonderful comedy that has a good chance of breaking through to wide American audiences with its good humor and a remarkable performance by Orgyen Tobgyal, an irrepressible fourteen-year-old.

The movie is set in a Tibetan Buddhist monastery in exile in India, where older monks watch over a class of kids who may wear robes and have shaved heads, but are otherwise just like schoolkids the world over, passing notes during worship services and reading football magazines.

Young Orgyen is a soccer fan who desperately wants to see the World Cup finals between France and Brazil, since "France is the only country that supports Tibet." He has to mastermind a scheme to get a TV, a satellite dish, and (most difficult) the approval of the abbot. As he schemes, *The Cup* provides a portrait of daily monastery life that is refreshingly different from the usual solemn profundities; the abbot looks out his window at the kids playing soccer with a Coke can, and sighs.

The film was directed by Khyentse Norbu, who for the maker of such a jolly movie seemed more solemn than most festival filmmakers when I took his picture. No wonder: I later learned from the program notes that "he was recognized at age six as the incarnation of the nineteenth-century Tibetan saint Jamyang Khyentse Wangpo."

* * *

Michael Almereyda's *Hamlet* is yet one more new approach to the most challenging of all dramas, using Shakespeare's own language (much trimmed from the original) in a story set in today's Manhattan, where the goal is not to be king of Denmark but CEO of the Denmark Corp. (the front page of *USA Today* trumpets Fortinbras's takeover bid).

Ethan Hawke stars as Hamlet, Kyle MacLachlan is the usurper who killed his father, Liev

Schreiber is Laertes, and Bill Murray makes an engaging Polonius. Hamlet's room is a den of video and computer equipment, and some of his soliloquies are in concert with his own taped images. "To be or not to be" is delivered with wicked irony in the "Action" section of a video store.

The film demonstrates what has been proven time and again: Shakespeare really has no country or period. His dramas are universal, and indeed the idea of modern corporate infighting is a good fit for Denmark's palace intrigues.

Show Me the Alien—Please!

January 25, 2000—There is not simply Sundance, but the sidebar festival Slamdance, held at a local inn and with no connection to the big fest. And Slamdance has begat still smaller hangers-on, like Slumdance, Lodance (for films shot on video), and Lapdance (erotic films). Park City's Main Street is awash with fliers, posters, and screening notices, and some filmmakers will do anything to get their movies noticed.

I wrote a year ago of Stuart Acher, a kid who bribed a motel bartender to play his film on the big-screen TV that I happened to be standing beside. This year the art of bringing the film to the audience has reached a new peak with the street guerrilla tactics of director Devon Crowley and cameraman Kirk Davis, who accosted me at the Independent Film Channel party.

Crowley was carrying two stereo speakers. Davis held a portable TV monitor in his hands. They had battery packs strapped to their backs. "Here's your chance to see our new movie *Show Me the Alien!*" Crowley cried, holding the speakers on either side of my head to produce stereo effect.

I watched a minute or two of the film while they shoved fliers into my pockets that described it as "*Spinal Tap* meets *E.T.* and gets shagged!"

The next day I was standing in front of the Egyptian theater when a large alien approached me.

"Are you one of the guys I met last night?"

"Uh-huh," said a muffled voice.

Just then a couple of security guards appeared out of nowhere and wrestled the alien to the ground. Another alien appeared, and a fight broke out. Then the aliens hypnotized the guards

and bystanders, and led them marching down Main Street, chanting "Show me the alien!"

One of the onlookers was Kaleo Quenzar, who said he had to admire the enterprise of the alien guys. Quenzar was holding a hand-lettered cardboard sign that said, "Will work for distribution."

The Filth and the Fury

January 26, 2000—"It's the weirdest thing," Julien Temple was saying. "You look at that old TV news footage of the Sex Pistols today, and they look normal. It's the newscasters who look like freaks."

Temple is the director of *The Filth and the Fury*, a new documentary about the Sex Pistols, which was the most notorious if not the most successful of the pioneering punk rock groups. We were standing in the lobby at the Sundance Film Festival, awaiting the arrival of John Lydon, still better known as Johnny Rotten, who along with the doomed Sid Vicious fronted the group. Steve Jones, the group's bass guitarist, had come in with Temple but was hard for Pistols fans to recognize, since he's settled into middle age with the look of a retired middleweight.

"I'm knackered," Jones observed. "I'd rather go back to the room and get some sleep."

"Odd, isn't it?" Temple said. "Me making two documentaries on the same group." His *The Great Rock 'n' Roll Swindle* (1980) was also about the Pistols, but it was told primarily from the self-aggrandizing point of view of Malcolm McLaren, the group's manager. *The Filth and the Fury*, he said, is from the band's point of view.

Johnny Rotten arrived in a blaze of flashbulbs, still with the spiky blond hair and the bad-boy smirk. He was wearing some kind of quasireligious costume that made him look like a satanic functionary. A crew from VH-1 followed him in, shooting a documentary. We had met before, in the late 1970s, when McLaren hired me to write the screenplay for an ill-fated Russ Meyer film, *Who Killed Bambi?* that was to star the Pistols.

"My last memory of you," I said, "was, we were in Meyer's car outside an all-night store in London and you were complaining that McLaren was making thousands and had you on a salary of £12 a week, and you wanted a loan from Russ to buy some baked beans and a six-pack."

"We were sailing," he said, "on the Ship of Fools."

The movie re-creates the extraordinary impact the Sex Pistols made with performances that were not so much music as cries of rage against the British establishment. The band became so notorious that they were banned in many cities, once toured under an assumed name, and inspired a London city councilor to say, "They would be much improved by being dead." Most of the narration is by Rotten and Jones, although McLaren is seen, sort of, talking through a rubber bondage mask.

What's clear is that the Pistols then and now had two hated targets: McLaren, always referred to as "the Manager," and Nancy Spungen, described by Rotten as "Sid Vicious's heroin dealer-slash-girlfriend." After she started supplying Vicious with drugs, the band began a downhill slide that ended with a disastrous American tour. Nancy was found stabbed to death in a New York hotel, and Sid, suspected of the crime, died soon after of an overdose. "My best friend. I couldn't help him," says Rotten, beginning a diatribe against heroin as the worst enemy of creativity.

But...."what we fought for, you're benefiting from today!" Rotten shouted from the stage after the screening. He added that it was still too dangerous for him to return to England.

Bad Boys

January 26, 2000—It was bad boys night at Sundance. Earlier the same evening, Emilio Estevez and his brother Charlie Sheen arrived for the premiere of *Rated X,* the new movie directed by Estevez and starring the brothers as Jim and Artie Mitchell, the San Francisco pioneers of porn whose *Behind the Green Door* grossed $40 million (although most of that, they were dismayed to learn, was raked in by the mob, with pirated prints).

Like the Sex Pistols movie, *Rated X* is a cautionary tragedy about drugs. Both Artie and Jim vacuum up so much cocaine that their lives are reduced to snorting, nosebleeds, insanity, and despair. Artie at one point wanders the streets of San Francisco like a madman and is barred by his brother from the theater they operated.

Jim cleans up, cold turkey, and tries to get Artie into rehab, but his brother steers into drug psychosis instead, and finally it is Jim who snaps and shoots his brother dead. The obligatory final title cards inform us that Jim did less than three years of a six-year sentence for voluntary manslaughter, and today still manages the sex theater in San Francisco.

The film sees sex as strictly business for the Mitchells, whose *Green Door* benefited from waves of publicity when its star, Marilyn Chambers, was spotted as the model on the Ivory Snow box. Artie was the wild concept guy, Jim was the dependable follow-through man, and their mother and father beamed proudly through the premieres of their films. Briefly, at the beginning, there was some feeling that their films could be artistic (Peter Bogdanovich plays their disapproving cinema professor at San Francisco State). By the end, they were simply a byproduct of cocaine abuse.

Two Great Docs

January 27, 2000—Two documentaries about wounded families, one angry, the other healing, have caused a stir during the closing days of the Sundance Film Festival. *Just, Melvin* is the lacerating portrait of a monster who molested almost everyone in two families, and seems to have gotten away with murder. *Legacy* is the story of how a family from a Chicago housing project, devastated by the murder of a fourteen-year-old relative, was able to break the cycle of welfare and make a new beginning.

Five years ago the Chicago media gave great attention to the death of Terrell Collins, a fourteen-year-old honor student who was senselessly killed by another child with a gun. Terrell had been chosen by documentarian Tod S. Lending as the subject of a film about a young man from the tough Harry Horner housing project who was headed to a private school on a scholarship. "I did the first filming one morning," Lending recalls, "and two hours later I got a call that Terrell had been shot."

He filmed the funeral, and then kept on filming, focusing on Terrell's extended family. His narrator became Nicole Collins, about Terrell's age, and in the film she introduces us to her grandmother, Dorothy, her mother, Alaissa, and her aunt Wanda, who was Terrell's mother. Theirs was a three-generation welfare family, with Dorothy as the rock of support. Wanda, a drug addict, had six children out of wedlock and Alaissa had five. No fathers were still in the picture.

In a strange sense, Nicole tells us, the death of Terrell acted as a catalyst. He was the family's great hope, the straight-A student who was their shining light. When he died, the family decided, in some deep, unspoken way, to try to pull itself together and get off welfare. It is not easy. In a catch-22, Alaissa loses a job because she can't attend training sessions without leaving her children untended; welfare won't provide child care until she gets the job. But by the end of five years, Nicole, a student at Northern Illinois University, is able to report that her mother is teaching kindergarten, her aunt is clean and sober, her grandmother has bought her own home—and the hated Harry Horner project has been torn down. It is an inspiring story and a very moving film.

Just, Melvin, in contrast, is a portrait of a family that still has open wounds and deep psychic scars after decades of abuse. The title refers to Melvin Just, who as a husband, father, stepfather, and grandfather committed incest and abuse against almost everyone in his family, repeatedly. Two of his stepdaughters were witnesses when he strangled a visiting nurse, a crime for which he was never tried. The survivors to this day are in a state of shock, which the camera plainly shows: Some live in campers or vans, and alcoholism and prostitution are symptoms.

The film was made by James Ronald Whitney, one of Melvin's grandsons, with the support of his mother, Ann Marie. It is not the first documentary about family abuse, but it is probably the most painful. It isn't uncommon to hear abuse or incest victims share their memories, but *Just, Melvin* does the unimaginable and shows the evil old man being confronted by the accusations, first in an extraordinary meeting with James, later in a family visit to his hospital room.

Whitney said after the screening that he had escaped the long-term fate of other family members because of the strength of his mother, a woman who once tried to shoot Melvin, and who, strong and intelligent, steered Whitney away from drugs and trouble and into show business (we see him as a winning dancer on *Star Search*). His film is not only devastating but subtle in its artistry, with great attention to a sound track that suggests the echoes of long-ago words of hate and current painful memories. Nothing in the film quite prepares us for the closing scenes at a burial service, where a pastor reads futile words of comfort while drunken family members alternate between grief and rage.

Being at the Right Movie

January 28, 2000—I spend a lot of my time at the Sundance Film Festival being told I am at the wrong movie. Think how I felt when *Saving Grace*, a comedy set in Cornwall and starring Brenda *(Secrets and Lies)* Blethyn, made this year's top distribution deal of $4 million, and a local TV station asked me what I thought about it. "Saving who?" I asked.

You pick your movies according to buzz and instinct. I was planning to see *Love and Basketball* on Wednesday night and *Just, Melvin* on Thursday morning, but then I heard I shouldn't miss *Girlfight*, which was also screening Thursday morning. Okay: *Just, Melvin* was also screening Wednesday night, at the same time as *Love and Basketball*. Since *Just, Melvin* had been touted (accurately) as one of the best docs of the year, I skipped *L&B*, only to be told at *Girlfight* that it was terrific. So it goes.

Girlfight was terrific too. It's the story of an eighteen-year-old Hispanic woman who wants to be a prizefighter. She has a hot temper and gets in fights at school—and now convinces a trainer to give her lessons. A sweet, uncertain romance develops between her and a guy who looks like a pro contender, and what would you say the odds are the two of them end up in the ring together? The film stars Michelle Rodriguez as the inward, sometimes brooding girl fighter, and was directed by Karyn Kusama, who handles the story not as another boxing movie but as a character drama in the ring.

Here are some other movies I saw and told people they should have:

• *Panic* stars William H. Macy, that master of barely concealed alarm, as a man who was raised from childhood by his father (Donald Sutherland) to be a professional hit man. Now he's in his forties and unhappy, and goes to see a psychiatrist (John Ritter). In the waiting room, he meets a strong-minded twenty-three-year-old (Neve Campbell) and falls instantly in love, although their eventual relationship is based more on psychological sparring than on sex.

Is his love wrong? Will he ever be free of his father's control? Can he pull the trigger on his latest assignment? It sounds like a comedy, and indeed there are many laughs, both funny and wry. But *Panic,* written and directed by Henry Bromell, has undertones more serious than the hit-man story line may suggest.

• A lot of movies contain philosophical speeches, but few of them really mean anything. In *The Big Kahuna,* the payoff is surprisingly thoughtful. Three sales executives (Kevin Spacey, Danny DeVito, and Peter Facinelli) spend a long night in a hotel hospitality suite in Wichita, arguing over machine lubricants, cheese balls, Jesus Christ, and career paths. Spacey and DeVito, longtime friends, have worked for years in the marketing department. At the convention, they're hoping to snare a big kahuna who might place a large order. Facinelli, new to the company, doesn't even know who the kahuna is, but talks to him all evening about Jesus.

When he finds this out, Spacey is enraged: They've lost a sale, and the kid shouldn't be practicing his religion on company time. DeVito sees more deeply and delivers a long monologue about the difference between a conviction and a sales pitch. The movie, directed by John Swanbeck from a play and screenplay by Roger Rueff, doesn't try to "open up" the stage version, but zeros in on it with sudden, sharp humor and surprising insight.

• Mark Gibson's *Lush* is one of the festival's sleepers, the story of a former pro golfer (Campbell Scott) who gets out of prison and lands in a New Orleans fleabag hotel. He meets a lawyer (Jared Harris) who drinks even more than he does, and gets involved in a Raymond Chandleresque world of rapacious divorces, country club lizards, and Bourbon Street lowlifes. Then the story makes a U-turn into peculiar developments that illustrate the principle that if you drink enough, anything is capable of happening to you—or you'll think it did.

• *Two Family House,* written and directed by Raymond DeFelitta, is the story of a man who is lured outside the rigid rules of his Staten Island Italian-American neighborhood by love and a stubborn integrity. Michael Rispoli stars as an unhappily married factory worker who dreams of opening his own tavern. He buys a house he wants to convert, and finds he has a tenant: a brutal drunk with a vulnerable young wife, who eventually has a child whose color does not match the husband's.

The husband disappears, and the would-be tavern owner feels an instinctive sympathy with the young woman (Kelly MacDonald), even though everyone he knows despises her for having a black child out of wedlock. The story's not about love or sex or even owning your own bar, so much as it's about how some people can't help doing the right thing, even when they think they don't want to.

• If *Short Cuts* begat *Magnolia,* then *Magnolia* in a way leads into *Things You Can Tell Just by Looking at Her,* written and directed by Rodrigo Garcia. Like the other two films, it tells a group of stories set in the San Fernando Valley and involving people whose lives connect in unexpected ways. All of the stories are about relationships that may be good or bad but are all unlikely. Glenn Close is a doctor, Holly Hunter has an unwanted pregnancy, Cameron Diaz is blind and likes to fantasize about cases worked on by her detective sister (Amy Brenneman), and Kathy Baker is astonished to find herself so strongly attracted to the dwarf who has moved in across the street. The film cares about its characters— it's almost protective, as they blunder toward, or away from, what makes them happy.

Sundance 2000: The Winners

January 31, 2000—*Girlfight,* Karyn Kusama's story of a tough Brooklyn girl who wants to be a boxer, and *You Can Count on Me,* Kenneth Lonergan's story of an orphaned brother and sister who uneasily get to know each other as adults, shared the grand jury prize for best dramatic film here Saturday at the Sundance Film Festival. In addition, Lonergan won the Waldo Salt screenwriting award, and Kusama was picked as the best director.

The grand jury prize for best documentary went to *Long Night's Journey into Day,* a documentary by Frances Reid and Deborah Hoffmann about the Truth and Reconciliation Commission in South Africa.

The Ballad of Ramblin' Jack, a doc about footloose troubadour Ramblin' Jack Elliott, won the special jury prize for artistic achievement. It was directed by Aiyana Elliott; Ramblin' Jack, a National Medal of Arts winner, sang at a Park City party after the premiere.

Almost as important as the Sundance jury

prizes are the audience awards, voted on by filmgoers as they leave the theaters. This year's audience favorite among dramatic films was Raymond DeFelitta's *Two Family House*, starring Michael Rispoli as a Staten Island man in the 1960s who feels protective toward an abandoned woman with an out-of-wedlock baby.

The audience award for documentary film went to *Dark Days*, by Marc Singer, the story of homeless people who would rather live underground in Amtrak tunnels than brave the drug-ridden world of city shelters. In the world cinema category, the audience award went to Nigel Cole's *Saving Grace*, starring Brenda Blethyn as a newly widowed Cornish woman who discovers her husband was a rake and spent all the money. Her groundskeeper has an idea for raising funds: They can grow pot.

Dark Days picked up two other major awards. It won the Freedom of Expression Award, given by the Playboy Foundation, and split the cinematography prize with Andrew Young's *Americanos: Latino Life in the United States*.

Also in the documentary category, the prize for writing went to Daniel McCabe, Paul Stekler, and Steve Fayer for *George Wallace: Settin' the Woods on Fire*, about the rise and fall of the Georgia governor. And the documentary directing award went to Rob Epstein and Jeffrey Friedman for *Paragraph 175*, about homosexuals who survived the Holocaust.

In the dramatic competition, the jury honored the entire cast of *SongCatcher* for their ensemble performance. Headed by Janet McTeer as a musicologist who ventures into Appalachia in the early 1900s, the cast also includes Aidan Quinn, Pat Carroll, Jane Adams, Gregory Cook, and Iris Dement.

For outstanding individual performance the jury honored Donal Logue, in *The Tao of Steve*, the story of a heavyset deep thinker who tries to seduce women with the power of his intellect. The award for best cinematography in a dramatic film went to Tom Krueger for *Committed*, a film about a marriage where the husband (Casey Affleck) runs away to find himself, and his wife (Heather Graham) follows along to be sure he doesn't get lost.

The Latin American jury split its top prize between Luis Estrada's *Herod's Law*, about an idealistic politician who turns into a tyrant, and Arturo Ripstein's *No One Writes to the Colonel*, based on the novel by Gabriel Garcia Marquez.

This was a year when the often-overlooked short films got a lot of attention; their suitability to Webcasting drew many dot-coms to Sundance to bid for hot shorts, and the hottest, winning the jury prize for short filmmaking, was *Five Feet High and Rising*, directed by Peter Sollett.

Several of the winners have already been purchased for distribution and will open later in the year—some of them not until Oscar season opens in the fall, if previous years are any guide. *Saving Grace* was purchased by Fine Line for $4 million, the fest's top sale. *Girlfight* went to Sony Screen Gems for $1.5 million, and Lions Gate bought *Two Family House*, but wouldn't reveal the amount.

Floating Film Festival
Floating with Studs

Oranjestad, Aruba, February 7, 2000—I am talking with Studs Terkel about his years of interviewing people, and I am thinking, some people get lucky in life. While most of us bend slowly under the inexorable burden of age, a guy like Studs, at eighty-seven, is still cracking wise, playing roles, doing accents, performing snatches of song, having a couple of martinis before dinner, and a big Monte Cristo cigar afterward.

I did a Q&A session with Studs on this sixth Floating Film Festival, on board the Holland-America cruise ship *Maasdam*, en route to the Panama Canal. This is the only film festival with shuffleboard, bingo, and a karaoke night. Studs and I are discussing *The Spectator*, his new book of interviews with stars of stage, screen, and television—everyone from Lillian Gish to Arnold Schwarzenegger.

This is how his mind works. I ask him about Jimmy Cagney. He starts telling the story of the Cagney scene where he shoves the grapefruit in the woman's face. "That was Mae . . ." starts Studs. "Marsh," I supply helpfully. "No, Mae Clarke," Studs says firmly. He's right. Mae Clarke. He remembers every name, every line of dialogue, every lyric.

"Cagney said the script told him to throw

some scrambled eggs at her. Naw, that was too messy. So there was a grapefruit there and he just picked that up."

Studs says he started going to the movies early. His mother ran the Wells-Grand Hotel in Chicago, a haven for advance men who came to town to promote new shows and movies. They'd give him free tickets. He remembers seeing silent classics like *The Cabinet of Dr. Caligari* and *The Last Laugh* free, and falling in love with the movies.

Studs seems so contemporary, you forget sometimes how long he's been around. I refer to *Cradle Will Rock,* a recent Tim Robbins movie about an agitprop depression musical that was barred from its own theater. Producers Orson Welles and John Houseman and composer Marc Blitzstein led the audience in a parade down Broadway to another theater.

"Did you see it?" I ask Studs.

"See it?" he says. "I was in it."

He performed in the Chicago production at a time when Chicago was a center of network radio, and he got lots of work on soap operas and dramas, mostly playing gangsters. In 1950, his *Studs' Place* was one of the three cornerstones of the Chicago School of TV, along with Dave Garroway's original *Today* show and *Kukla, Fran and Ollie.* Then Studs was blacklisted, his show was dropped, and he landed in the mid-1950s on WFMT, beginning a forty-five-year run as an interviewer. His tapes of conversations became best-selling books like *Division Street America, Working, Hard Times,* and *The Good War.*

Now he's working on a new one. In late December, Studs lost Ida, his wife of sixty-two years. In mourning, he began to talk to people about "that country from which no traveler returns"—death. On board the Floating Film Festival, he's seeking subjects, and you see them over in the corner of a lounge, heads bent low over the tape recorder, Studs asking, "So whaddya think happens next?"

* * *

The programmers for the FFF include Richard Corliss of *Time;* his wife, Mary, who is curator of film prints for the Museum of Modern Art; Jim Emerson of Reel.com; Kathleen Carroll of Film Scouts.com, who runs an upstate New York film festival; George Anthony, head of entertainment programming for the Canadian Broadcasting Corp.; Hannah Fisher, a programmer for the Calcutta festival; and Harry Knowles, proprietor of the Ain't It Cool Website. The festival began in 1991 and is run biannually by Dusty Cohl, who cofounded the Toronto Film Festival, now North America's largest.

Twice or three times a day, we gather in the ship's theater to see new movies. Among the highlights so far: *Shower,* by Zhang Yang of China, about the passing of an ancient bathhouse and the way of life it represented; *Goat on Fire and Smiling Fish,* by Kevin Jordan of the United States, about the girlfriend problems of two orphaned brothers; *East Is East,* by Damien O'Donnell of the United Kingdom, starring Om Puri as a Pakistani whose London family doesn't seem interested in his old-country ways; *In Full Gallop,* by Poland's Krzysztof Zanussi, about a ten-year-old caught in the web of his aunt's intrigues; *New Waterford Girl,* by Allan Moyle, starring Liane Balaban as a fifteen-year-old girl who feels trapped in her remote Canadian town; and Raymond DeFelitta's *Two Family House,* winner of the Audience Award at Sundance this year, about a Staten Island man who risks rejection by everyone he knows when he befriends a white woman whose black baby was born out of wedlock.

Coming up: Eight more movies, a shot-by-shot analysis of *Citizen Kane,* and the Panama Canal, which is not a movie but may be able to lure a few of the FFF Floaters out of the dark and onto the deck.

The Psycho at Sea

Panama Canal, February 10, 2000—Okay, what is it? A parable, a fantasy, a cop-out, or porno chic? *American Psycho* played Wednesday aboard the Floating Film Festival, and there was an uproar afterward as the audience duked it out.

"It doesn't matter if there are really killings or not," cried Jim Emerson of Reel.com. "It certainly does!" shouted Judge Harvey Brownstone of Toronto. "I like the classic perfection of well-made films better than these exercises in style," mourned Jeff (The Dude) Dowd, whose list of favorites *(Some Like It Hot...)* was drowned out in the tumult. "A real disappointment," said red-bearded Harry Knowles of Ain't It Cool News. "Has redeeming features on a psychological level," said gray-bearded Richard Corliss of *Time.*

Festival founder Dusty Cohl announced that

Eddie Greenspan, Canada's best-known trial attorney, had walked out of the film and declared that the psycho killer "is innocent and deserves an expensive defense."

American Psycho stirred up similar controversy two weeks ago when it premiered at the Sundance Film Festival. The showing aboard the Holland-America *Maasdam* was its second public screening, and the two festival audiences may be the only ones to see it in its original NC-17-rated version. The MPAA slapped the dreaded adults-only tag on the movie not for its ax murder, its chainsaw massacre, its stabbings during sex, its bodies hanging in a closet, or its heads stored in the refrigerator, but for a three-way sexual event that is so cold and abstract it seems like an argument against sex in any form.

Unless Lions Gate, the distributor, trims the scene, the movie will be one of the rare wide releases with an NC-17 barrier at the box office. I hope the scene is left in, so that audiences can witness with their own eyes how seriously twisted the MPAA standards are.

The movie, which stars Christian Bale in a courageous and queasily effective performance, was directed by Mary Herron from the Bret Easton Ellis best-seller about a materialistic yuppie in the "Me Decade" who becomes a serial killer—or does he? Do the events in the film really happen, or are they delusions? (It is impossible to give away the answer to this question, because the movie does not supply one.)

The novel was turned down by one publisher before being picked up by another. The movie has also had a tumultuous history. Herron was originally scheduled to direct Christian Bale in the project. Then Leonardo Di Caprio became "attached" to it, the budget multiplied, and at one point Oliver Stone was mentioned as the director. Finally, all settled down, the project returned to Herron *(I Shot Andy Warhol)*, and Bale was back in the lead.

He is effective, and so is the film—but to what end? A full review must wait until the movie opens, and I welcome that time to ponder the mystery of a wonderfully made film about—well, what?

Floating 2000 Winners

San Juan, Costa Rica, February 14, 2000—Consider now these two films: *Two Family House* and *The Color of Paradise.* One from Staten Island. One from Iran. One the winner of the popular vote on board the sixth Floating Film Festival. The other the winner of the Critic's Prize. What does it mean that the critics and the others did not agree?

The Floating Festival is not high on anybody's list of the most important and influential film-fests in the world, although it may indeed be the most fun. But it does involve the screening of some thirty films for an audience of filmgoers crazy enough to attend it. (How many people do you know who get on a cruise ship so they can watch three movies a day?)

Every film was followed by a discussion, sometimes a passionate one; when Jim Emerson of Reel.com got up after *American Psycho* and told the audience it was "pretty obvious" what the film was about, he found out forty-five loud minutes later that it was neither obvious nor pretty. The festgoers were a cross section of movie fans, ranging from insiders (producers, directors, Billy Zane's parents) to outsiders (a judge, a political campaign consultant, a mathematician). When the smoke had settled and the films had been screened, their overall verdict was loud and clear: Next time, please, not so many subtitles.

Yes, they enjoyed the subtitled *Shower,* from China, which placed second in both the popular and critic's votes with its story of the closing of a bathhouse and the end of the traditional culture it represented. Yes, they admired one of my selections, *The Terrorist,* the heartrending story of a seventeen-year-old girl who volunteers to become a human bomb. Yes, they applauded Patrice Leconte's *The Girl on the Bridge,* the French film about a circus knife-thrower who approaches a girl about to throw herself from a bridge, and argues that if she is willing to die, she should join his act (he throws the knives aboard a cruise ship—not easy in high seas).

Yes, they enjoyed all of those films. But—too many subtitles! they sniffed. And the film they voted for was in English, was accessible, was entertaining, was moving, was not an art film but a human story movingly told. Raymond DeFelitta's *Two Family House,* which also won the Audience Award two weeks earlier at Sundance, stars Michael Rispoli as Buddy, a Staten

Island man in the 1960s who dreams of opening a bar. The building he buys has a couple living upstairs, and when the woman has a baby obviously not fathered by her drunken white husband, Buddy empathizes with her—to the disapproval of his wife.

What about the film voted first by the eight movie critics on board? Majid Majidi's *The Color of Paradise* is the new work by the Iranian director whose *The Children of Heaven* was an Oscar nominee last year (I've invited both *Heaven* and *The Terrorist* to my Overlooked Film Festival in Champaign-Urbana, Illinois, in April). *Paradise* was chosen by fest programmer Mary Corliss, curator of film stills for the Museum of Modern Art, whose introduction noted that many consider the new Iranian cinema the most exciting in the world today. It tells the story of a bright, lovable blind boy whose mother has died and whose father wants to get rid of him—because a blind child will hurt his own remarriage hopes. The boy is uncannily well adjusted to the world. After his father yanks him out of a school for the blind, he begs to be allowed to go to the local school—where, using Braille, he shows himself more competent than the other students. But the father has no interest, and apprentices him to a blind carpenter.

The new Iranian films *are* exciting, not least because they represent, in a veiled way, criticism of Iran's patriarchal traditional leadership. I am reminded of *Two Women,* an Iranian film by Tahmineh Milani, which I saw in November at the Calcutta festival. It is about a bright woman university student singled out by a stalker. He throws acid at her cousin and is jailed—but the attention brought upon the blameless woman disgraces her, and her father pulls her out of school, brings her home, and forces her to marry a middle-aged dope who will accept such damaged goods. Both of these films say people must be valued for themselves and not simply categorized according to their worth in moribund tradition.

Which of the two films is better—the American or the Iranian? I would not be willing to say, because they reflect such different values, styles, and reasons for being made that comparison is pointless. I enjoyed *Two Family House* immensely, and will give it an enthusiastic review when it opens in the autumn. It shows one ordinary man, heir to all the prejudices and opinions of his time and place, who steps outside of them because he sees that a woman needs help—and because he loves her.

I also valued *The Color of Paradise* enormously, not least because Majidi's mastery of style is put at the service of a story so simple and touching it is like a parable—like *The Bicycle Thief* or *Il Postino*. And what also attracted me was its window into another culture. I know little about Iran. I want to know more. I drank in the streets, the landscapes, the interiors, the clothes, the personal styles. I am curious about the world and this film fed my hunger.

Yes, it has subtitles. Subtitles are the price you pay for not being provincial in your filmgoing. It is easy enough to choose from countless films in English. Most of them will not enrich you or tell you anything you don't know—indeed, the pleasure we get from a lot of them is how they flatter our sense of recognition. But when we stop being curious and stop reaching out beyond the familiar, we start to die. Films with subtitles are the ones most likely to enlarge our ideas. That's all the more true because we can easily see all the English-language films, but it takes an extraordinary foreign-language film to even get distribution in North America.

So the critics picked the subtitled film from Iran, and the public picked the American film. Oh, but I almost forgot: *Two Family House* placed third in the critic's poll, after *Shower*. So critics know how to have a good time too. It's just that they have, perhaps, more curiosity about what constitutes a good time.

Overlooked Film Festival

For two years now I've been programming my Overlooked Film Festival at the University of Illinois at Urbana. This is my introduction to the 2000 festival.

* * *

Urbana, Illinois—Good films are an endangered species. Unless a movie opens on 3,000 screens with a multimillion-dollar advertising campaign, it may not be able to attract the attention of its potential audience. Moviegoers have to be attentive and curious to know that a small film in a perhaps obscure venue may be the best film playing in town. Too often they cave in to the publicity and go to the latest Hollywood no-brainer. The purpose of the Overlooked Film Festival is to provide a second chance for wonderful but overlooked films and genres, and to bring to Urbana-Champaign and downstate Illinois some of the most creative artists in the world of cinema.

Of course the definition "overlooked" can be defined in many ways. After I selected *Children of Heaven*, Miramax's Cynthia Swartz reminded me it was an Oscar nominee and did well at the box office. Yes, I replied, but subtitled films themselves are overlooked, as well as Iranian films and serious films by and for families. We are scheduling *Children of Heaven* as the free family screening because I believe kids who can read are old enough for subtitles; it's never too early to introduce them to the best of world cinema.

Oklahoma! too is hardly overlooked—not when the whole audience knows most of the score by heart. But its format is overlooked; we will be presenting it in thirty-frame-per-second Todd AO Vision. It may be the first Todd-AO thirty fps to ever play south of Chicago in Illinois, and it will startle audiences with its clarity. Once again the ace technical team of James Bond and Steve Krause, who first worked with us on the *2001* screening at Cyberfest and made such a contribution at the first Overlooked, will supply the rare projector and the expertise. Tim Zinnemann, a film producer and son of *Oklahoma*'s great director Fred Zinnemann, will be here in person for a screening that honors the late director's birthday.

The Last Laugh and *Un Chein Andalu* are two of the most famous films ever made, in some circles. But a silent film and a Surrealist film are not ordinary fare, and we will also present live musical scores by Concrete, the band from St. Joe–Benton Harbor, Michigan, who had such a triumph last year with *Potemkin*. This year we also present a modern silent film, Charles Lane's enchanting and moving *Sidewalk Stories*, made with great courage in 1990, which was well into the talkie era. Lane will be here in person.

Dark City did get a national rollout, but not the kind of marketing I thought it deserved. I picked it as the best film of the year, and thought it was superior to the more successful *The Matrix*, which had a similar buried theme. Science-fiction and special-effects pictures are themselves overlooked by people who don't, or think they don't, like the genre. This film may surprise them.

Documentaries are often overlooked, even though they are the most immediate and vibrant of film forms, and this year we have two great ones. *Legacy* tells the story of a Chicago family that regrouped and transformed itself after a family tragedy, and its narrator, Nicole Collins, will be our guest after the screening, along with director Tod S. Lending.

American Movie, which won at Sundance a year ago, is the funny and perceptive story of Mark Borchardt, a truly independent filmmaker whose handmade horror movies are American folk art. After the screening, we will show *Coven*, the film Borchardt is seen making in *American Movie*, and I'm sure he would agree it is overlooked. Director Chris Smith and producer Sarah Price will join Mark on the Virginia stage (and *Coven* will be for sale in the lobby).

Animation is not overlooked if it is from Disney, DreamWorks, or Warner Bros. But in Japan, anime is a major art form; it hardly ever plays on big screens in America. We will present *Grave of the Fireflies*, which has been called the most emotionally powerful animated film ever made. If all goes well, the great animator Isao Takakata will fly from Japan to join us,

From Australia, two very different films. I first saw Paul Cox's *A Woman's Tale* in 1992, and have been haunted by it ever since. Sheila Florance, who won the Australian Oscar for her work, is brave and true, and her performance is a fitting successor to the powerful work of Heather Rose in last year's *Dance Me to My Song*. Cox himself is one of the most original and gifted of all directors, and this screening will inspire you, I hope, to seek out some of his other films. I have had good times with Cox in Cannes, Montreal, Toronto, Honolulu, Chicago, and Calcutta, and now at last in Urbana-Champaign.

Also from Australia: *The Castle,* which I saw on the 1998 Floating Film Festival. (The Floating's founder, Dusty Cohl, is an Overlooked guest this year, so ask the bearded guy in the cowboy hat all about it.) The audience roared with laughter, but the film curiously failed to have much of a success in America. I expect the Overlooked audience to agree with me that it's a weird, inspired, and lovable comedy. Director Rob Sitch will be here in person.

The Terrorist is exactly the kind of film you should hear about, but don't. John Malkovich saw it when he was on the jury of the Cairo Film Festival, and was so impressed he set up a screening in Chicago, and arranged to present it in America. It is currently in release, although unless you care about good films and are paying attention, you might not realize that. When I saw it, I was stunned. *The Terrorist* provides a portrait of a young woman who volunteers to become a human bomb, following her for the last few days before the planned assassination. It is from India, where I saw *Malli,* the new work by the same director, Santosh Sivan, when I was at the Calcutta and Hyderabad film festivals in November. I am pleased its star, Ayesha Dharkar, will be with us, along with producer Mark Burton.

Last but very far from least is an old friend, Henry Jaglom, whose *Deja Vu,* made with and starring Victoria Holt, is an astonishingly moving story of love and fate. Jaglom has been a major presence among independent American filmmakers for three decades, making films in his own time, in his own way, often with friends and family. For those who related to the grown-up love story of Eric Rohmer's *An Autumn Tale* last year, here is another intelligent, emotional experience. Jaglom and Holt will be here.

It is hard to choose the films for the Overlooked every year; there are so many deserving candidates. Movie critics despair sometimes because they know of so many good films that are overlooked, and so many bad ones that are not. For a few days in April, at the Virginia Theater, the balance tilts the other way.

Cannes Film Festival
Eyes Wide Open, Then Shut

Cannes, France—I am sure that the opening of this year's Cannes Film Festival will be a night to remember, but I will not remember it because I have already RSVPed in the negative. I will not attend the inaugural projection of Roland Joffe's *Vatel,* even though it does star Gérard Depardieu and Uma Thurman, and even though I am invited to the party afterward. I especially do not want to attend the party.

After many years at the festival, there is one thing I know for sure about the opening night film: I will sleep through it. After the all-night flight to London, after the flight to Nice, after the taxi driver who wants to pay for his Mercedes with just the one trip to Cannes, after being greeted by Madame Cagnet at the Hotel Splendid and feasting on the gigantic strawberries that are her welcome gift, I will fall immediately into a profound slumber.

Three or four hours later, I will awaken. The opening night audience in their tuxedos will be marching up the red carpet of the Palais des Festivals, but my wife and I will be marching in the opposite direction—down to La Pizza, by the old yacht harbor.

This is an old tradition, meeting your friends at La Pizza on the opening night. It was started by a legendary publicist named Renee Furst, who would bombard you with faxes for days in advance about her fabulous party at La Pizza, and then arrange for you to sit next to the directors of the great but obscure films she was repping. Now the critics call the opening night gathering the Renee Furst Memorial Dinner, but it is so informal that nobody reserves a table, or even knows when it begins.

Sleep comes like a thief and steals your reason in the first few days of the festival. Morning screenings are fine. Toward evening the step slows and the mind crawls. A documentary about the midnight parties after the evening screenings could be titled *Night of the Living Dead.*

* * *

Quelle scandale at the festival this year. Gilles Jacob, the festival director, is embroiled in a messy lawsuit brought by Oliver Barrot, the man who seemed destined (at least to himself) to be Jacob's successor. As an old French proverb goes, there is many a slip between the successor and the succession.

For as long as I can remember, the quiet, diplomatic, and iron-willed M. Jacob has been the director of the festival, and the quiet, diplomatic, and diplomatically quiet Pierre Viot has been the president. Jacob chooses all the films in the official competition, appoints the chairman of the jury, oversees its deliberations, hosts official dinners, and has the last word on everything.

Earlier this year M. Viot announced that he would be retiring. It was then announced (this is a little murky) that after a transitional year, Jacob would become president and Oliver Barrot, a TV journalist, would, or might, or could possibly, become director, although not this year, or perhaps ever. In the meantime, Barrot was given a one-year appointment as something or other.

Then, in April, as he was blissfully luxuriating at the movies (where else?), Barrot was told he no longer had the job. Only three months had passed since his appointment. What had he done wrong? It was a "psychological phenomenon" on Jacob's part, Barrot told *Variety*'s Alison James. He did not explain this diagnosis, but I will: Jacob was constitutionally incapable of envisioning Barrot in the job Jacob had held for so long.

One of the changes Barrot is said to have suggested was moving the festival from May, when the Hollywood studios offer mostly dim-witted summer thrillers, to September, the opening of the good movie season. This change would be fraught with hazard, since the Toronto and Venice festivals already own the autumn, and it is likely that if push came to shove, Toronto would be king of the hill.

* * *

This year the official competition offers such usually interesting directors as Joffe, the Coen brothers (*O Brother, Where Art Thou?*), James Ivory (*The Golden Bowl*), Neil Labute (*Nurse Betty*), Ken Loach (*Bread & Roses*), Nagisa Oshima (*Tabou*), Liv Ullmann (*The Faithless*), Lars von Trier (*Dancer in the Dark*), and Wong Kar-wai, whose film is titled *In the Mood for Love*.

The jury is headed by the French director Luc Besson, most recently responsible for *The Messenger: The Story of Joan of Arc.* The festival is still shell-shocked after the 1999 jury, headed by the Canadian David Cronenberg, honored a selection of winners that were as uncommercial as they were honorable and indeed worthy; a *little* attention to the box office, on the part of the jury, is not entirely frowned upon.

This year's jurors include the Indian novelist Arundhati Roy; the actresses Aitana Sanchez-Gijon (Spain), Kristin Scott Thomas (Great Britain), Nicole Garcia (France), and Barbara Sukowa (Germany); the British actor Jeremy Irons; the directors Jonathan Demme (United States) and Mario Martone (Italy); and the French writer Patrick Modiano.

Waiting for Lars

May 11, 2000—The world of cinema has gathered here at the fifty-third Cannes Film Festival, all except for the Danish genius Lars von Trier, who is making his way overland by camper from Copenhagen. "I am receiving daily reports on his progress," said Mark Ordesky of Fine Line Features, who is releasing *Dancing in the Dark*, von Trier's official festival entry. "He is driving here while listening to horrifying Danish rock music and stopping to eat fast food."

Von Trier is one of the authors of *Dogma 95*, the cinematic vow of chastity that has influenced several of this year's entries. It calls for location shooting, no outside musical scores, handheld cameras, no lighting except from the sun or sources within the scene, and the traditional 1:1.33 screen ratio. Dogma is to modern cinema as the Amish are to automobiles.

"Does Dogma prohibit the use of airplanes?" I asked.

"No," said Ordesky, "but he is phobic about flying."

Von Trier's movie plays later in the week, but Ordesky was sitting in the row in front of me for the screening of *The King Is Alive*, another Dogma signatory, which is in the festival sideboard known as Un Certain Regard. That means the festival holds the film in a certain regard, which at Cannes is an honor, even though it looks a lot like the second team.

So influential is Dogma that even the fire curtain at the festival's giant auditorium is a large white rectangle in the ratio of 1:1.33, or four feet wide to every three feet high—the ratio of all movies until widescreen was introduced in the early 1950s. For most screenings it is a false alarm; the 1:1.33 oblong rises out of sight, to reveal a conventional wide screen.

But not for *The King Is Alive,* a harrowing multinational film by Kristian Levring about a group of travelers in Africa who continue their journey by bus after their plane is grounded. A broken compass strands them 200 miles from the nearest village, at an abandoned pipeline station. Their most capable member gives them five rules for desert survival and then treks off for help, while those left behind wither in the sun while engaging in adulteries and rehearsing a production of *King Lear.* Yes, *King Lear.* One of the group is an actor who knows it by heart and writes out all the roles, The movie stars Janet McTeer, Jennifer Jason Leigh, Bruce Davison, and others, and not many movies about people dying in the desert have had more distinguished dialogue.

I've seen seven films so far, and my favorite is *Innocence,* a touching work by the Australian master Paul Cox, about a couple who were each other's first true loves, and meet again after fifty years. Julia Blake and Charles Tingwell, actors who are both seventyish, bring a passion and risk to their renewed love affair that is heartstopping. This is not a formula film with phony setbacks and a happy ending, but a truthful, philosophical film about what love means, what time means, and how time can steal love or deepen it. Most movie romances are about the desire of producers to team up two highly paid stars. Cox's film is about how you may only get one true romance in life, and it's never too late to admit it.

Another of my early favorites is the official entry *Nurse Betty,* by Neil LaBute, whose first two works were the harrowing white-collar dramas *In the Company of Men* and *Your Friends and Neighbors.* This one is a comedy with a nicely off-center flywheel, starring Renee Zellweger as a simple Kansas waitress whose fantasy life centers around a doctor (Greg Kinnear) on a soap opera. When two drug dealers (Morgan Freeman and Chris Rock) kill her husband (Aaron Eckhart), she loses all contact with reality and sets out to Los Angeles to find her "former fiancé," the doctor.

Drugs, murders, and cross-country chases are the stuff of countless routine movies, but LaBute sidesteps clichés like a broken-field runner, and there is a fascinating development when Kinnear and his producer don't realize Zellweger *really* thinks she's Nurse Betty, and think she's a method actress auditioning for a role.

The official entry *Bread and Roses* is the first American film by Ken Loach, the left-wing British director who specializes in working-class subjects. His story involves a janitor's strike in Los Angeles, and his heroine is an undocumented Mexican who falls in love with the Jewish union organizer. The performances and characters are appealing, and the movie makes a strong case against nonunion cleaning services that pay cleaners less today than they were paid in 1982, but the movie is didactic and the politics are by the numbers.

What the movie did provide, for me, was background to the recent strike of Chicago suburban janitors, who are paid half as much as unionized city workers. Every working person deserves a living wage, and building managers who victimize the poorest of their employees should be ashamed.

Blackboards, an Iranian film, provided my most difficult experience so far. Iran has produced some of the best films I've seen recently *(Two Women, Children of Heaven, Color of Paradise),* but this is from the Iranian school of dusty minimalism and the endless repetition of monosyllables. It's about itinerant schoolteachers who trek the mountains with their blackboards strapped to their backs, and how one teacher marries a woman with a small child. You can see how this material could be human and memorable, but the style is so limiting it makes Dogma 95 look like a license to party.

In my first dispatch I said I would be skipping the opening night film, Roland Joffe's *Vatel,* because I had learned through long experience that after an all-night flight to Europe I am invariably too sleepy for the opener. I caught up with *Vatel* as my fourth screening late on my first full day here, and slept through it anyway. I can't blame that on the film, since I dozed off during the opening titles. I awoke only occasionally, to see Gérard Depardieu as the faithful steward of a count desperate to impress Louis XIV with a feast beyond a monarch's dreams. If ever there was an actor born to play an impresario of excess, that actor is Depardieu; in his last film he was compared to a Yugo, and although on principle I am opposed to witticisms based on weight, truth in criticism requires me to report he is approaching SUV status.

To Go to the Hotel du Cap, or Not to Go

May 15, 2000—The big stars don't like to stay in town. It's more prestigious for them, and no doubt more comfortable, to stay forty-five minutes away at the Hotel du Cap d'Antibes, which is the kind of hotel where it is not an affectation but a necessity to pull out a big roll of bills of high denomination, because the Hotel du Cap accepts no checks or credit cards—only cash. Cash for everything. Cash for rooms, cash for drinks, cash for a towel in the beach cabana.

Why only cash? In America one would assume they were laundering money or evading taxes, but, of course, such a grand hotel in France would never do such a thing, so it must simply be to inconvenience their clients. The big stars, of course, never handle cash themselves, and so their minions skulk about with both hands clasped uneasily on bulging briefcases. Meanwhile, the stars grant interviews to the worshipful press, or at least those willing to sacrifice half a day in Cannes to make the trip.

On Monday, for example, one could catch a special bus outside the Carlton Hotel at 10:45 A.M. in order to participate, from 12 to 1 P.M., in "print roundtables" for the stars of *O Brother! Where Art Thou?* the official festival entry by the Coen brothers. For several minutes apiece, George Clooney, John Turturro, Tim Blake Nelson, and the Coen brothers will visit your table to answer your questions and those of a dozen other journalists. These sound bites can then be massaged into customized rewrites of the press kit.

I will not be making the trek to the Cap. It would mean missing the press screenings of three other official entries, which is a lot to ask, don't you think? For that matter, I also did not go out to the Cap for the official Sunday night dinner after the screening of the Merchant-Ivory production *The Golden Bowl.* Buses for that journey were to leave at 9:30 P.M., returning well after midnight. Unless the critic exercises vigilance, the Cannes Film Festival could turn into a commute to Cap d'Antibes.

After many years of thought, I have concluded that what is happening in town is likely to be more interesting, and certainly closer to sea level. By the time a star has decided that tens of thousands of dollars must be spent and dozens of journalists required to sacrifice half a day for an hour of "round robins," that star is too big to say anything of interest at such an event. His publicist will have advised him to save it for *Vanity Fair, Talk,* or Barbara Walters, and not squander it on the likes of journalists who have been reduced to the pathetic necessity of spending two and a half hours on a bus for fifteen minutes apiece with revolving table-hoppers.

Saturday I saw three official entries in the Palais des Festival—three more like those I would have had to miss to take the bus. Then I strolled ten minutes down the beachfront to the Directors' Fortnight and chatted with Michelle Rodriguez and Santiago Douglas, the stars of *Girlfight,* an American indie film that is a sensation among those critics lucky enough not to be on the bus during its screenings. They were both actually happy to be in town! Yes! "Me! At Cannes!" said Rodriguez. "Think of it!"

The movie was directed by Karyn Kusama, who won the director's prize at Sundance this year; her film shared the top prize. It's about an eighteen-year-old Hispanic woman (Rodriguez) who convinces a trainer to give her boxing lessons, turns out to be good, and ends up in the ring fighting her boyfriend (Douglas).

This was Michelle's first role. What inspired her to become an actor? "My brother told me to get a job," she said. Rodriguez still gives real answers to questions. "First I worked as an extra. That was going nowhere. I saw an ad in *Backstage* for open auditions for this movie. I tried out, and it worked out."

Yes, it did, because she was sensational, and now she's a rising star.

"When you really got hit in a scene," I said, "and it hurt, did that make you mad?"

"In the last fight," she said, "Santiago hit me by mistake. It was a blooper: Hey! Don't start with me! I got mad and I jumped at him—so I had to leave the ring and just compose myself, just breathe. I didn't take it overboard."

She says, he says.

"When I hit Michelle," said Santiago Douglas, "here was why. In the movie so far she had won all of her fights. I realized by then she had no fear in her eyes. She was overconfident. So I really hit her. It was to help the movie."

Michelle's eyes narrowed.

"You did that on purpose?"

"I did," he said.

"You hit me on purpose!?!"

She did not know this before. She playfully socked him on the arm, but like one of those playground punches that are less playful than they look, you know, and he was smiling, but she . . . well, you can stay right in town and find out stuff that helps you see a movie in a whole new light.

This Rodriguez, she's something. She's smart, good-looking, and tough.

"After the movie I stopped doing the boxing, because your ego flies all over the place," she said, "and I started to welcome the challenge of someone in the street stepping up to me. You know?"

I think I know.

Running the Cannes Marathon

May 15, 2000—Since my last dispatch I have seen nine films, four of them more than three hours long, bringing my Cannes total to sixteen movies in six days. I feel like the hero of *A Clockwork Orange*, who had his eyelids propped open with toothpicks while cinema was force-fed into his brain. Most of them involve adultery, although there have been four weddings, a woman boxer, a vampire, motion sickness, and a lot of bluegrass music.

Yes, I explain to a correspondent from a dot-com, I always see the movies again back in Chicago before reviewing them. That is not because I want to study them more deeply. It is because I fear confusing them.

Woman on Top, for example, was about a woman with motion sickness (that explains the title), while the Chinese film *Devils on the Doorstep created* motion sickness with its swooshing, handheld camera on the giant screen. I am fairly sure that the bluegrass music is not in Ingmar Bergman's screenplay about adultery, but did we actually see the two weddings in *The Golden Bowl*, or were they offscreen? Certainly *Yi yi*, from Taiwan, started at a wedding, and *The Wedding*, from Russia, took place entirely at a wedding. (In my notes on the Russian film, I wrote: "One of the danger signals of alcoholism is when you tell someone there is a crate of vodka under your bed.")

The best two films I have seen in the last three days are *Faithless*, directed by Liv Ullmann from the Bergman screenplay, and *Girlfight*, by Karyn Kusama, which I wrote about yesterday. The Ullmann film was a poignant reminder of what movies were like in the 1970s, when they were as serious about big issues as today's movies are about little ones. It is a long, deep, lacerating examination of adultery, beginning with the observation that not even death can cause as much pain as a divorce. When we consider that Bergman himself was married five times and that he had a daughter by Ullmann, who did not marry him, we can only assume the screenplay is well informed.

Erland Josephson plays "Bergman," a movie director who has apparently hired an actress (Lena Endre) to improvise scenes with him as he writes a screenplay about a woman's relationships with two men. It is possible that the actress is more, or less, than she seems, and at the end of the film there is enough ambiguity to make us wonder if, perhaps, she even represents the daughter of the person she portrays. Whatever her exact definition, she is played by Endre in a performance so exact and harrowing that she is probably the front-runner for the Best Actress prize.

The weekend was dominated by two big studio films, *The Golden Bowl*, a Henry James adaptation by James Ivory, and *O Brother, Where Art Thou?* by the Coen brothers. Both have substantial qualities, neither is entirely successful, and I will wait for second viewings before making final decisions. *The Golden Bowl* got off to a shaky start with giant letters on the screening identifying the Nick Nolte character as "America's First Billionaire." Since this information is manifestly unnecessary about a man who lives in one castle, rents another, and buys more statues than Citizen Kane, it signals the filmmaker's lack of faith in the intelligence of the audience—always an alarming portent.

The James novel, his last, tells of the billionaire (Nick Nolte) and his daughter (Kate Beckinsale), who both marry—she an impecunious Italian prince (Jeremy Northam), he the daughter's impecunious childhood friend (Uma Thurman). What the viewer knows but the father and daughter do not is that the prince and the friend knew each other (much better than they ought to have) before they married the daughter and her father. James settles this situation without the four characters ever once openly discussing it among themselves, and Ivory's version is true to that discipline, which sets him a tricky challenge.

The Coen brothers' film is about three escapees from a southern chain gang, who jingle about the South chained to one another, eventually free themselves, and become, among other things, the composers of a bluegrass hit. George Clooney, John Turturro, and Tim Blake Nelson play the leads. Whether the film is a folly, a fancy, or simply a conceit, I am not quite sure. I liked it more than I should have and less than I wanted to.

Fast Food Fast Women is a sub–Woody Allen New York story, written and directed by Amos Kollek, and enormously entertaining in its parts, which never become a whole. It is about lonely people who never quite connect. Louise Lasser gives the best performance of her career, as a widow who has to cast a shy widower (Robert Modica) out of his shell; Anna Thompson plays a waitress who falls for a taxi driver but plays him wrong. I liked the movie, but maybe it needed one more run through the rewrite car wash.

As for the films from Taiwan, Russia, and China, and *Shadow of the Vampire,* in which it turns out that Max Shreck, the star of the silent classic *Nosferatu,* really *was* a vampire . . . I'll get back to you. Have to rush off to that new Japanese film by Oshima. It's only 100 minutes long, although his films often feature castrations, which, paradoxically, can add amazingly to their subjective length.

May I Have the Check PLEASE

May 16, 2000—My editor was impressed that I had seen sixteen movies in five days. "I could easily double that," I told her, "if I could get anyone to bring me a check."

What is it with the French reluctance to present *l'addition* after a meal? They have a horror of taking your money. Your typical dining experience in a French restaurant consists of:

• Nine minutes: You are ignored while standing hopefully in doorway, while waiters and owners rush past you with their eyes sharply averted, as if you are a flasher.

• Seventeen minutes. You wait for the presentation of the *la carte.* This is a publication

the size of a bedspread, and hidden within its folds is *le menu,* which translates as "Blue Plate Special."

• Twelve minutes. You peer at the food items and try to remember your high school French. Your choices are limited to chicken and lamb, because *poulet* and *agneau* are the only words you can recall. (You also know the words for "french fries" and "ice cream," because those are the only two things they serve in a French restaurant that you really want to eat.)

• Four minutes. You note that *le menu* is a three-course meal half as expensive as anything else. You ask the waiter to translate it for you. Today's special commences with a soup of gruel of the barnacle. The main course is tripe corkscrews marinated in brine, gratinee. For dessert, *le chef recommendez* a pie made from mustard greens, pine nuts, and raisins, asleep on its bed of rhubarb.

• Thirty-eight minutes. You wait for your order to be served. The waiter arrives at your table bearing two dishes, and says, *Vousnous-pretdecider?* as fast as he can. This translates as, "Which has which?" You and your wife look at the two dishes he holds. She has ordered fish. You have ordered chicken or lamb, you forget. It is impossible to tell which of the dishes might be fish or, for that matter, might not be fish. Both dishes consist of brown stuff piled in the middle of the plate on a bed of more brown stuff, mounted by a sculpture made from greens that when you were a kid your old man told you not to come in from the yard until they were all yanked out by the roots.

• Nine minutes. You dine.

• Two hours and seventeeen minutes. You wait for the check. The first hour of this time passes with the waiters rushing past your table on obscure missions involving standing outside the restaurant smoking cigarettes. The second hour is taken up with assurances that the bill will be presented momentarily. At the beginning of the third hour, you experiment with the possibility that the waiter is not French, and ask for *l'addition* in several other languages, including Italian, in which the correct word would sound very rude if it were English, which however it isn't, not that the waiter speaks it anyway.

• Forty-five minutes. The waiter waves a check cheerfully at your table from across the room, and presents it to the proprietor's grandmother. This is a formidable old lady dressed in deep mourning, who sits on a high stool behind an elevated podium and is the master of an adding machine with a crank on it that she wields as if smashing walnuts. She adjusts her bifocals, which are chained to her neck by a jeweled cord, and double-checks the addition seventeen times. She simultaneously prepares the bills of sale for three real-estate transactions, says *oui!* countless times into a telephone, and leans over to talk tenderly to what is apparently a living creature residing under her podium—a dog, possibly, or her husband.

• Four minutes. The bill is presented. You slam down your Visa card, but the waiter is too fast, and has hopped across the room before he can see it.

• Two minutes. Another waiter, whom you have never seen before and will never see again, arrives at your table with a battery-powered device into which he inserts the card. This device, the size of an electric razor, telephones the home office in Omaha, confirms the transaction, and prints out a receipt, which you must sign. You are impressed by this technology until you return home, receive your bill, and discover that the device believes there are $6 to the franc and not the other way around.

On your way into the restaurant, you saw a new McDonald's across the street, and lamented this despicable invasion of French culture by crass American materialism. Now all you can think of is their french fries. You deserve a break today.

Boos and/or Cheers

May 17, 2000—Films are booed at Cannes for two reasons: because they are bad, or because they are infuriating. Those in the second category are likely to be quite good, although they make you so mad you have to step back and cool off in order to appreciate their qualities.

Consider *Dancer in the Dark,* the new film by the Danish rebel Lars von Trier. It is the most debated film at Cannes this year, and it was roundly booed at its first screening Wednesday morning. Does that make it bad? No. Will it drive you nuts? Without question.

The film is set in America and filmed in English, on locations suggesting a southern factory town in the 1950s. But two of the leading characters are Europeans; the rock singer Bjork plays

the lead, a young mother who operates a punch press even though she is going blind. Catherine Deneuve, usually seen in elegant roles, plays her best friend in the factory, and is quite effective, albeit as the most beautiful punch-press operator in movie history.

Von Trier is one of the authors of Dogma 95, the cinematic vow of chastity, and true to its tenets, *Dancer in the Dark* includes vertiginous photography with a handheld camera that swishes back and forth from one actor to another like a home movie of a birthday party. Then the drab video look is replaced on several occasions by a more saturated film look, as the movie bursts into song with musical numbers set on a railroad bridge, the factory floor, and even death row.

Yes, the Bjork character goes to prison, in a plot that seems lifted directly from the broadest silent melodrama. She saves money to pay for an operation that will prevent her son from also going blind, and after many complications there is the first trial sequence I have ever seen in which the defense attorney says not one word.

There is scarcely a moment in the movie that is believable on a realistic level, but it contains great emotional truth. There is scarcely a shot that does not distract from its content, and yet somehow the content gathers force. The style is maddening, and yet a conventional, "well made" movie could not have anything like the same effect. I wanted to applaud and boo at the same time. That is a compliment.

Von Trier, who is phobic about flying, has arrived on the Riviera in the camper he drove from Denmark, and is reported to be headquartering at the Hotel du Cap d'Antibes, where he has parked next to the Ferraris and Benzes in the hotel driveway. I'll go out there Friday to interview him (see page 711). I forgive him for staying at the Cap because he is there not out of snobbery but fear.

It is a compliment to his film, a very sincere one, that *Dancer in the Dark* kept me awake every single second, since I had attended the 12:30 A.M. screening of Darren Aronofsky's *Requiem for a Dream*, got to sleep at 3 A.M., and had to get up again at 7 to attend the von Trier. The festival is a sleep-deprivation marathon that turns into a requiem for everyone's dreams.

The Aronofsky film is a favorite of the midnight-screening crowd, although I found it less challenging than his brilliant first work, π. It stars Jared Leto, Jennifer Connelly, and Marlon Wayans as young heroin addicts, and has one of the best performances in the festival by Ellen Burstyn, as Leto's mother, who gets hooked on diet pills. The downward spiral into addiction has been seen before, but the style of the movie is riveting, as Aronofsky finds visual equivalents for being high, confused, deranged, and in withdrawal, and ends his film with a harrowing montage.

Willem Dafoe creates another of the festival's most memorable performances in *Shadow of a Vampire*, a film by E. Elias Merhige about the making of F. W. Murnau's silent classic *Nosferatu*. That was the film that essentially gave birth to the vampire film genre, and was centered on a haunting and profoundly creepy performance by Max Schreck, as the vampire. He was uncannily convincing, and in the new film, we learn that Schreck was not a method actor but, in fact, actually a vampire. Dafoe disappears into the character of the nosferatu, eerie, lonely, and frightening.

Tabou, by the Japanese master Nagisa Oshima, is set in 1865, inside the camp of a samurai militia unit that is thrown into upheaval by the recruitment of an extraordinarily beautiful boy as one of the new warriors. The samurai chief of staff (played by the Japanese director Takeshi Kitano under his acting name of Beat Takeshi), observes that even his superior is stirred by the boy's appearance, and muses, "He does not lean that way." Many of the samurai do, but this is not a "gay film." Instead, it's a gradually unfolding mystery with suspense and dry wit. (The festival joke is that the American title should be *Not to Ask, Not to Tell*.)

Gregory Peck was honored at an official dinner Tuesday night, hosted by fest director Gilles Jacob and president Pierre Viot. He's the subject of *A Conversation with Gregory Peck*, directed by Oscar winner Barbara Kopple (*Harlan County, USA*). At Peck's side was his French-born wife, Dominique; Viot noted in his speech that she came to interview Peck in Paris in 1955, "and the interview is still going on."

Beanie Goes to Nebraska

May 18, 2000—The festival is a wilderness of pitches. Everyone here has an idea for a movie, or a treatment, or a book to be adapted, or rights to buy, or a screenplay to sell, or a video they want you to look at. I avoid pitches with a cunning based on experience. People don't want to talk to you. They want to sell you. Soon you're mired in an endless description of their idea for a movie. I've heard them all.

Beanie Barnes did not have a pitch. She and her friends were looking for nothing more than a seat at McDonald's. It was all so strange. I realized I was pitching her—with her own idea. I was telling her she was sitting on the first foolproof idea for a movie I'd heard all year.

It happened like this.

I was running on eight hours of sleep in two nights. I wanted to grab something to eat, fast, and get a nap. I went to McDonald's. There are days when you don't have the patience, the strength, or the energy to enjoy a French meal.

There are little metal tables outside McDonald's here, overlooking the old yacht port and the sea. I sat down at one. Three American college women, clutching their Happy Meals, wandered past and asked me that most basic question, "Seen any good movies?" I had. Soon we were trading titles, and I asked them if they would join me. They would.

They were all interns at the American Pavilion of the festival. They had scholarships from Kodak. They wanted to maybe work in the movie business some day. Two said they were from "USC."

"But not the USC you're thinking of," they said. "The University of South Carolina."

"Where are you from?" I asked the third, whose name was Beanie Barnes.

"I'm from Los Angeles," she said, "but I go to school in the Midwest."

"Where in the Midwest?"

"Nebraska."

"What are you studying?"

"I'm a senior in broadcasting."

"Beanie has written a novel," one of her friends said.

"What's it called?"

"*Mirror of the Stranger*," she said.

"What's it about?"

"It's a Forest Gump–type thing. Sort of *Pulp Fiction*esque. It was at Doubleday for seven months, but the editor who liked it left. Now, I don't know."

"How did you start out in Los Angeles and end up at Nebraska?" I asked Beanie Barnes.

"I had a sports scholarship."

"Basketball?" I asked, if only because basketball was the first women's sport that came to mind.

"No," she said. "Football."

"Football? They have women's football at Nebraska?"

"I'm on the men's team."

"You mean," I said, "the *real* team?" I know that is the question of a male chauvinist pig, but you understand my confusion. Beanie Barnes did not look like a member of the University of Nebraska's men's football varsity.

"Yep," she said. "I'm a specialist. A kicker. A punter."

"Have you . . . played in games?"

"I've only been in one game. But I really am on the team."

"How tall are you? How much do you weigh?"

"I'm five-four, and my basic weight is 120, but I'm at 140 now for spring ball, and I'm trying to get up to 150 so I can be considered as a receiver."

It was refreshing to hear a woman talk about her efforts to gain weight. "But I'm only 10.5 percent body fat," she added, in what sounded not like vanity but like a simple statement of fact.

I looked at her while an idea was born in my imagination.

"This is a movie!" I said. "You're sitting on a great pitch! A five-four African-American woman from Los Angeles goes to the University of Nebraska and joins the men's football team."

"You think so?" she said dubiously.

"Of course! It's a natural. Did the guys resent you?" I was already thinking of clichés.

"Not at all. They were very friendly and supportive. They block like crazy to protect me."

"That's even better!" I said. "Have you written a treatment? Do you have a screenplay?"

"I never even thought about it," she said.

"I'm going to write a piece about this," I said. "This is the first time in all the years I've been coming to Cannes that I've ever heard a pitch that I *knew* could be made into a movie."

"I dunno . . ." she said.

"Can I write about this? Can I take your picture?"

I could, and I did, and I have.

I don't want the usual 10 percent. Just a line in the credits will be fine. For the title, I'm thinking, *Beanie Goes to Nebraska.*

Be honest. You want to see this movie.

Partying with Liz and Harvey

May 19, 2000—I am a little dizzy. I have just returned from a $2,500-a-ticket dinner auction that followed a fashion show of Victoria's Secret swimwear and included Kenneth Branagh and James Caan stripping to the waist to be massaged by supermodel Heidi Klum on top of a piano later to be played by Elton John, while Harvey Weinstein auctioned off lunch with Nelson Mandela for $100,000.

The annual AMFAR Cinema against AIDS Benefit at the Cannes Film Festival, now in its tenth year, is for a worthy cause. This year it raised more than $2.5 million for AIDS research. But it is growing more surrealistic by leaps and bounds. This year the event was held at the Palm Beach Casino at Cannes, and a giant tent was erected next door for the fashion show. Hollywood moguls, directors, supermodels, and billionaire arms dealer Adnan Khashoggi mingled with Prince Albert of Monaco, Sean Penn, Gregory Peck, and Naomi Campbell, and the star of the evening was Elizabeth Taylor, fresh from being made a dame of the British Empire.

After her welcoming speech she sat in the front row of the Paris-style runway show and watched as some of the most famous models in the world modeled items from the Victoria's Secret collection, including one swimsuit that seemed slightly impractical since it included angel's wings. These costumes are to swimming as Fred Astaire's tuxedos are to headwaiting.

After the show was over, I asked Dame Elizabeth how she felt about it.

"I feel like a swim," she said.

A silent auction offered luxury items like a week on the private Italian island (yacht included) that once belonged to Rudolph Nureyev. Or a vacation at three top Thai spas. Or a week in a French chateau for you and a dozen friends—staff, chef, and chauffeur included.

The private auction and the fashion show were followed by dinner and a public auction masterminded by Miramax chief Harvey Weinstein, who this year not only offered a massage by Heidi Klum, but persuaded Branagh and Caan to take off their shirts and act as subjects for a demonstration of her skills. The massage went for $33,000. "Karl Marx is dead," observed the director James Gray.

Also auctioned off was a dance with Prince Albert, purchased for $28,000 by a man who did not much want to dance with the prince (who seemed eager not to dance with him); they negotiated an on-the-spot deal to trade the prince for model Karen Mulder. Another $100,000 was bid by Weinstein to persuade Elton John to play and sing one (1) song. Meanwhile, waiters staggered under trays laden with dinner prepared by Chef Roger Verge of the Moulin de Moulins, the famous hillside restaurant above Cannes. The AMFAR auction has always been held at the Moulin, but this year, Chef Verge told me sadly, "We could not find the room for the Victoria's Secret show, you know, as it is a small village."

After Dame Elizabeth's welcoming speech was interrupted by someone's cell phone, I fell into conversation with Anant Singh, who is the most important movie producer in South Africa, and who arranged the $100,000 lunch with Nelson Mandela.

"Cell phones have been ringing all through every screening I've been going to," I said. "It's driving me crazy."

"In our theaters in South Africa," he said, "we are installing a jamming device that prevents people from receiving calls while they're in the theater."

"That is a brilliant idea," I said. "Why don't they do that at Cannes?"

"Why do you think?" he asked.

I was about to speculate that the people here would rather take phone calls than watch movies, but we were interrupted. Harvey was auctioning off a concert of "The Girl from Ipanema," as performed for you by five Brazilian supermodels.

The Best for Last

May 22, 2000—Why did they save the best for last? *Songs from the Second Floor* and *In the Mood for Love,* two brilliant final entries in this year's Cannes Film Festival, played on Saturday as the hotels were emptying and the traffic jams clearing. By Sunday, when the awards are given out, hardly anyone is left except for the journalists and the winners. But they were both winners.

The two films could not have been more different. *Songs from the Second Floor,* by Roy Andersson of Sweden, is the most daring and provocative of this year's films, and also the funniest, in a bleak and mordant way. It shared the jury prize. *In the Mood for Love,* by Wong Kar-wai of Hong Kong, is a sad love story about two neighbors who discover that their spouses are having an affair. They also fall in love, but are reluctant to act on their feelings because that would make them no better than their partners. It won for best actor, and for its editing and cinematography.

The Swedish film is audacious, offensive, original, surrealistic. It is a series of vignettes in a lonely city gripped by psychic meltdown. A man collapses in a corridor and clings to his boss's leg when he is fired. A magician makes a horrible mistake while sawing a man in half. Gridlock stops all of the city's traffic. In a strange ceremony witnessed by clerics and dignitaries, a blindfolded little girl is made to walk the plank and fall into a deep pit full of broken stones. A bankrupt businessman empties a truck full of crucifixes at the town dump and moans that he invested in a loser.

Some of the scenes are sacrilegious. Some are pathetic, as when a drunken woman tries to pull herself back up onto a bar stool while a man in a tuxedo vomits. Some are just plain funny, as when a businessman tries to explain a suspicious fire to insurance investigators, while through the window a parade of flagellants goes past. I scribbled names into my notes: Beckett, Buñuel, Tati, Kafka—but Andersson has created his own world.

Wong Kar-wai is famous for films that end in a bittersweet minor key, and *In the Mood for Love* points to its ending the whole way. Maggie Cheung and Tony Leung, two of the biggest stars in Asia, would seem destined to star as lovers, but the film provides no easy payoff. Visually, it isolates the characters; they're in a city so overcrowded that despite good jobs they must rent rooms in the apartments of others. They always seem to be in empty spaces, at night, often in the rain—or in diners where they occupy booths like the subjects of an Edward Hopper painting. Like the British classic *Brief Encounters,* this is a film about a love that cannot be consummated without destroying itself.

Of the other films I've seen in the last few days, the most interesting was *Eureka,* from Japan, by Aoyama Shinji. It begins with six dead after an armed man takes a bus hostage, and then follows several lives, including the driver and two schoolchildren. Deliberately looking away from the violence itself, the film focuses on the lingering despair of the survivors. At 3¼ hours long and in black and white, it is not destined for mass-market release, but it is a haunting achievement.

Olivier Assayas's French film *Sentimental Destinies* is three hours long (this is the year of the endless film), but likely to be more commercial. It follows the family that controlled the Limoges china firm through good times and bad, world wars, death, and marriage. Emmanuelle Béart plays the second wife of the Protestant cleric (Charles Berling) who leaves his pulpit to run the firm, in a film about how the responsibilities of business can challenge the soul.

Bernard Rose's *Ivansxtc* (say it aloud) stars Danny Huston as a Hollywood executive who implodes with cocaine. The drug abuse story is not new, although Huston's performance is touching and observant. What is important about the film (shown outside the official competition) is that it was shot on video with the cast members doubling as crew; it shows that movies of a professional caliber and polished production look can be made for next to nothing.

I've seen twenty of the twenty-three official entries this year. In my first story from Cannes, nine days ago, I said the best film I'd seen so far was *Innocence*, by Paul Cox, which was not an official selection. Now I have seen everything and that statement is still true. "It's too sentimental for the official competition," a Cannes insider confided. But its sentiment is contained in fearless honesty and truth; it tells the story of a man and woman in their late sixties who find that the passion they felt for each other as teenagers has survived fifty years and marriages to others.

It is said that films about older people don't work at the box office. Maybe not, but great love stories do. The official entries have paraded through the Palais day after day, some brilliant, some not, but Cox's is the only film at this festival that people have described with an intense warmth and affection, and that has made many of them cry—not in sorrow, but in admiration and recognition. *Innocence* and *Songs from the Second Floor* occupy opposite ends of the emotional and stylistic spectrum, but they are both works by directors who know exactly what they want to do, and how, and why.

Cannes 2000: The Winners!

May 22, 2000—A Danish film set in America but filmed in Sweden with stars from Iceland, France, and the United States won the coveted Palme d'Or here Sunday night, at the fifty-third Cannes Film Festival. Lars von Trier's *Dancer in the Dark* picked up the top prize even though it got the most negative review in the recent history of *Variety*, the show-biz bible. And its star, the Icelandic pop singer Bjork, won as best actress even though von Trier insists she is not an actress at all.

The movie stars Bjork as a mentally retarded punch-press operator who is going blind. Catherine Deneuve, who presented the best film award, costars. Von Trier is the author of the Dogma 95 statement, which calls for films to be shot on video with available light and sound, and this is the first Dogma film to win the top prize.

In interviews all week Von Trier said Bjork was not an actress but played her character as if the story were the literal truth. In his acceptance speech, he said, "I know she doesn't believe it when I say it, but if you see Bjork, tell her I love her." This statement was even more odd since she arrived at the awards on his arm.

The best actor award went to the Hong Kong actor Tony Leung, for the bittersweet *In the Mood for Love*, by Wong Kar-wai, about neighbors who discover their spouses are having an affair, and then fall in love themselves.

The Grand Jury Prize, or second place, went to *Devils on the Doorstep*, a long Chinese film about villagers who are given two Japanese soldiers to keep as prisoners. The Jury Prize, which is more or less third prize, although Cannes does not describe it that way, was shared by *Blackboard*, about itinerent teachers, by the twenty-year-old Iranian woman director Samira Makhmalbaf, and *Songs from the Second Floor*, a surrealistic black comedy by Sweden's Roy Andersson.

Best director was Taiwan's Edward Yang, for *Yi yi*, also known as *A One, A Two*, a story of a failing marriage. The technical prize, for editing and cinematography, went to *In the Mood for Love*, and a special honorary ensemble acting award went to the cast of *La Noce*, a Russian film about a marriage.

The Iranian cinema, considered one of the most productive in the world right now, not only shared the Jury Prize, but saw two of its films tie for the Camera d'Or, given for the best first film. They were *A Time of Drunken Horses*, by Bahman Ghobadi, and *Djomeh*, by Hassan Yektapanah.

There are three major prizes at Cannes given by separate juries. The Critics' Prize was won by the Mexican film *Love Is a Bitch*. The Un Certain Regard section, a sidebar of the official competition, was won by the American film *Things You Can Tell Just by Looking at Her*. And the International Critics' Prize went to the Japanese film *Eureka*.

The awards were presented in a star-spangled ceremony that lasted just a fourth as long as the Oscars, and included actor James Caan, a presenter, thanking the festival for naming itself after him.

Questions for the Movie Answer Man

Actors

Q. Now that Jodie Foster has dropped out of *Hannibal*, the sequel to *Silence of the Lambs*, why couldn't Thandie Newton or another black actress play Clarice? Effectively, a black actress like Newton could introduce the dilemma of racism (on top of the sexism Starling already is victim of in *Hannibal*), better motivating her ambivalence in the Lector vs. the FBI scenario.

—Andrew Ritchie, London, England

A. Interesting idea. There is a theory that Clarice was black in early drafts of Thomas Harris's novel, which would more fully explain her alienation from the FBI culture. Although the sequel needs Anthony Hopkins as Lector (and has him), a different FBI agent would not be out of the question. Newton would be a good choice. Another possibility: Kasi Lemmons, who played Clarice's friend Ardelia Mapp in the original.

Q. Now that *Shaft* is coming out, reports have surfaced about differences between its star, Samuel L. Jackson, and its director, John Singleton. A story on Salon.com says Jackson is "wary of directors who, like Singleton, try to con him into doing the scene their way." His quote: "I refuse. I'm the one who's up there on the screen, so I'll only do it my way because I'm the one who ends up taking the blame for their silly choices." Who is right? The director or the star?

—Susan Lake, Urbana, Illinois

A. There are certainly two schools of thought. Alfred Hitchcock, accused of saying that actors were cattle, said, "I never said that. I only said they should be *treated* like cattle." But here is what Bette Davis told writer-director Joseph Mankiewicz while they were filming *All About Eve*:

"You do not appear upon the screen, forty feet high and thirty feet wide. Me, I'm an actress and I do appear upon that screen, that big. What I say and do, and how I look, is what millions of people see and listen to. If I make a horse's ass of myself on that screen, it is I—me—Bette Davis—who is the forty-by-thirty-foot horse's ass as far as they're concerned. Not the writer, the director, the producer, or the studio gate-man—nobody but me. I am up there as the representative horse's ass for all concerned."

AFI Lists

Q. The film that most shocked me with its absence from the AFI 100 Funniest List was *Ferris Beuller's Day Off*, which I consider the pinnacle of the 1980s teen-comedy boom, and one of my top 10 of all time. *Beverly Hills Cop*? *Mrs. Doubtfire*? *City Slickers*? I'd swap *Ferris* for one of those.

—Greg Dean Schmitz, creator, Upcomingmovies.com

A. Your letter is one of countless communications I received asking why various titles were or were not on the list. The important thing to remember is: This list is completely meaningless. The same voters, polled today, would probably list several different titles. How much thought can the average voter give while ticking off titles from a list of 400 finalists? I'd love a statistician to compare the titles with the frequency of the first letters in the names of a cross section of movies, to see if (as I suspect) films toward the top of the alphabetical list had an advantage. The list is useful for video rental ideas, and to raise money for the AFI, and that's about it. Still, I have been impressed over recent years by how many people have told me *Ferris Bueller* is one of their favorite films. It is gaining a cult following.

After Life

Q. Just read your review of *After Life* and while I am intrigued by the premise I have to say that the contemplation of spending eternity with a single memory, however delightful, is truly frightening. Even the best memory would lose its appeal after repeated "viewings." From a more metaphysical point of view, what is a soul if not the culmination of one's life experiences? Being left with but one piece of your life means losing who you are. Can anyone name a single event that defines them wholly? I can't. Hirokazu Kore-eda's vision of heaven seems hellish to me.

—Jason Fortun, Minneapolis, Minnesota

A. I think Kore-eda intends you to spend eternity *within* the memory, not just remembering it. In any event, the premise is not so much a literal idea of the afterlife as a way to show people trying to decide what truly made them happy—why their life was worth living. *After Life* is a wonderful film.

American Beauty

Q. Thora Birch is under eighteen. Was that a stand-in for her topless scene in *American Beauty*? Isn't it illegal for minors to be shown nude in films?

—Buddy Hurlock, Hockessin, Delaware

A. A spokesperson for the Jinks/Cohen Company, the producers, says: "It is not illegal to have people under eighteen nude or partially nude on film. The California Child Labor Board approved the scene, and its representative was on the set when it was filmed, as were Thora's parents."

Q. In the credits of *American Beauty* one of the thank-yous is to "Dr. Bill and Alice." I'm convinced that this is no coincidence, but a reference to the characters in Kubrick's *Eyes Wide Shut*. The couples in both movies have been asleep throughout their marriages and each movie chronicles events that may or may not cause each partner to wake up. Then again, maybe I didn't escape grad school in time to not overanalyze everything?

—Nicole Cody, Memphis, Tennessee

A. You got out in time. A DreamWorks spokesperson says: "Yes, it is an homage to Tom Cruise and Nicole Kidman, who are good friends with *American Beauty* director Sam Mendes. Sam directed Nicole on Broadway in *The Blue Room*."

American Film Theater

Q. Will the films included in the American Film Theater project of the early 1970s ever be rereleased? I remember Gene Wilder and Zero Mostel in *Rhinoceros*, Alan Bates in *Butley*, a great production of *A Long Day's Journey into Night*, etc., and I would love to see them again. I thought there was a twenty-five-year embargo, but we are past that now.

—John Keenum, Worcester, Massachusetts

A. There's good news, according to Tina Landau, a director and playwright at Chicago's Steppenwolf theater. She is the daughter of Edie and the late Ely Landau, who produced the AFT. It offered new films of great plays, one a month, shown on a hard-ticket basis. There was no *Long Day's Journey* (Landau produced that in 1962), but the series did include *The Iceman Cometh* (Lee Marvin, Robert Ryan), *In Celebration* (Bates), *Galileo* (Topol, John Gielgud), *Lost in the Stars* (Brock Peters), *Luther* (Stacy Keach), *A Delicate Balance* (Katharine Hepburn), and *Man in the Glass Booth* (Maximilian Schell). After a stay in copyright limbo, she tells me, the films will be available on video in the foreseeable future.

American Pie

Q. I went to *American Pie* today, and left the theater depressed for two reasons. 1) The preview for the 3-D IMAX film *Encounter in the Third Dimension* looked interesting and I had a slight urge to see it, which was killed after I noticed those responsible for making the trailer had written *Encounter in the Thrid Dimension*. 2) When Jim, the lead character in *American Pie*, finds the note written by his mom, in regard to the pie she just baked, it reads "Jim—Apple! You're favorite!" You are favorite indeed.

—Leigh Emshey, Innisfail, Alberta

A. Yeah, but you're *American Pie* had some great-looking grils in it.

Animation and Anime

Q. How do Pinocchio's nose holes grow? 1. They grow bigger. 2. They do not grow and end up in the tip of the nose. 3. They do not grow and stay where they are, in the end of the nose. 4. Pinocchio has no nose holes at all. This looks like a very stupid question, but for over a week it has been the main topic of a lot of biology students in Holland during lunch break.

—Maarten van Haaren, Lierderholthuis, Netherlands

A. Pinocchio has no nostrils at all. However, when his nose grows long it does gain branches, leaves, and a bird's nest.

Q. I was watching a Looney Tunes cartoon, and something struck me as strange. Whenever something heavy falls on a character, it's an anvil. Why an anvil? Anvils aren't exactly common anymore, yet they've been a cartoon staple for ages. Do you know what was the first cartoon to feature a falling anvil, who came up with it, and why?

—Evan Talbott, Baltimore, Maryland

A. My friend Leonard Maltin knows all about such matters and is the author of *Of Mice and Men: A History of American Animated Cartoons.* He tells me: "I don't think there's any way of determining the first anvil to fall in a cartoon! As to *why* an anvil, it's just part of the cartoon lexicon; everything has to have a quick, identifiable visual symbol, and an anvil says 'heavy' in no uncertain terms. Tex Avery especially liked them and it wouldn't surprise me if he was the first to use one. He even figured out how few frames it would take to come out of nowhere and still be visible as more than just a blur; I think the answer was five frames, or about one fifth of a second!"

Q. Re your Answer Man item about the student whose teacher equated all Japanese anime with *Rape Man. Rape Man* is not animated, but a Japanese live-action series. The *Japanese Cinema Encyclopedia* by Thomas Weisser and Yuko Mihara Weisser describes it. I've never seen it but I understand that it played more as a comedy.

—Mike Duncan, St. Louis, Missouri

A. I heard from dozens of people about *Rape Man.* Kris Gallimore of Thunder Bay, Ontario, says it was mentioned as a comic book on a recent episode of the TV series *The Practice.* Ken Chan of the CompuServe Showbiz Forum writes: "Perhaps the teacher in question is watching too much television:

a few weeks ago, on the NBC series *Law & Order: Special Victims Unit,* there was a short courtroom scene involving a Japanese adult comic book (manga) called *Rape Man.*" Ed Slota of the same forum says the name was appropriated by Steve Albini, formerly of Big Black, for a new band name. And Cindy Mullens of Fairmont, West Virginia, writes: "It was a comic book first. The targets of *Rape Man* were Japanese women who were adopting the lifestyles of Western women— career women besting men in the workplace, getting promotions, and refusing to stay at home, cook, and have lots of babies." My point remains: For the teacher to equate the wonders of Japanese anime with the obscure *Rape Man* is blatantly unfair.

Anna and the King

Q. As a member of the Thai culture, I find your review of the movie *Anna and the King* objectionable. Certainly a critic may give a scathing review to a bad movie. However, in this case, you ventured into abuse and insult of another culture. The Thai king Mongkut is known for his initiative well over a century ago to prohibit men from selling their wives and parents from coercing children to marry, as well as for laying groundwork for the abolition of slavery to be accomplished in the subsequent reign of his son, but perhaps the dramatized version of this king was so far from actuality that you compared him to Hitler and Hannibal Lector! What's more, you reminded the readers of a more modern aspect of Thailand in your punch line about Bangkok being a "world center of sex tourism" (a tradition ostensibly established by the king, you said). Are we as readers supposed to find some parallel in an exotic, bad movie and an exotic, immoral country? You described the British attitude toward Siam and the Thai king during Anna's time as "racist and jingoistic." Can you claim your own attitude is much better?

—Ekachai Sombunlcharoen, Bangkok, Thailand

A. Yes, I can. Surely one can be critical of a country without being considered racist if its inhabitants are not the same race as oneself? What I found amusing was the attempt by the end credits to paint the bright future Mongkut steered his country toward, a vision perhaps not yet perfectly realized, if indeed sex tourism and even child prostitution are facts of life, as is widely reported. I wrote of Mongkut, "Yes, he is charming; Hitler is said to have been charming, and so, of course, was Hannibal Lector." This was witty but uncalled-for, and indeed my whole review is a mite overwrought. I am tired of the endless versions of this schmaltzy love story, but should not have taken it out on an innocent bystander like Thailand. The film has been banned there, by the way, which ranks somewhere between outrageous censorship and good film criticism.

The Astronaut's Wife

Q. In your discussion of *The Astronaut's Wife*, you suggested that some women might value the experience of being pregnant with an alien child. This is not only true, but they might not mind giving birth on the Internet.

—Michael Jones, Chicago, Illinois

A. A brilliant screenplay idea. With few exceptions, Hollywood assumes aliens are hostile and must be destroyed. I'm reminded, however, by George Bacon of Cedaredge, Colorado, of John Carpenter's *Starman* (1984)—with Jeff Bridges as a gentle alien who leaves behind a pregnant Karen Allen when he returns home. The kid would be in high school now.

Aunt Fritzie

Q. Has it come to your attention that Nancy's Aunt Fritzie is now employed as a music critic?

—Ronnie Barzell, Los Angeles, California

A. It has. Over the decades I have had many theories about Aunt Fritzie's employment, some of them fueled by her tight dresses, shiny nylons, and high heels. This explains everything. If Sluggo becomes a movie critic, that's where I draw the line.

Austin Powers: The Spy Who Shagged Me

Q. AAAaarrrrgghh! Roger Ebert *come back*. Dr. Idiotevil clearly has a shill behind the reviewer's desk! How can you possibly justify giving such a favorable review to such a nasty little boy flick like *Austin Powers: The Spy Who Shagged Me*? Isn't anyone going to be responsible enough to question taste and good judgment in entertainment ever again? This movie is nauseating garbage that is not fit for children or other humans to see. Where are the responsible humans who footed the bill for this ode to the potty? Mike Myers, you should be ashamed of yourself.

—Linda Hart, San Mateo, California

A. Your response is based on my *negative* but somewhat affectionate 2.5 star review. If I'd given it 3 stars, we might have lost you. Little boy movies seem to be just what America wants right now: the movie set a three-day record of $54.7 million, and Mike Myers, to paraphrase Liberace, is laughing all the way to the potty.

Being John Malkovich

Q. Have heard a lot about this new movie *Being John Malkovich*, in which John Cusack finds a portal into the brain of John Malkovich, who plays himself. Why did Malkovich agree to do this?

—Baxter Wolfe, Arlington Heights, Illinois

A. Maybe because it was a brilliant screenplay. Or maybe because they said if he turned it down, they could always make it *Being Sean Penn*.

Q. Far be it from me to criticize a movie as outstanding as *Being John Malkovich*. However, I did notice one unmined comic possibility. In the film, John Cusack's character, says that he can't remember any movies that Malkovich has been in. He should have been able to remember at least one: *Con Air*. After all, Cusack was in that movie too.

—Mark Dayton, Costa Mesa, California

A. True, and funny—but while Malkovich plays Malkovich in the movie, Cusack does not play Cusack.

Q. In *Being John Malkovich*, the character played by John Malkovich is listed in the credits as "John Horatio Malkovich." Is that his real name?

—Casey Anderson, Schaumberg, Illinois

A. No. His real name is John Gavin Malkovich. Wonder why they changed it.

Q. Regarding the 7½ floor in *Being John Malkovich:* The 7½ floor couldn't have been unique in the movie's building. Here's why. If a 7½ floor is created between the 7th and 8th floors, then the 7th floor must also have been half-size, which means there would have been two half-size floors in that building. I promise I'll get a life now.

—Joni Abrams, Chicago, Illinois

A. Although your logic is persuasive at first glance, a moment's thought reveals that just because floor 7½ is half-size does not mean floor 7 has to be half-size also. The architect can make it any height he pleases. This is a subset of the rule in which many buildings have no 13th floor.

Birth of a Nation

Q. I really have to take exception to your inclusion of *Birth of a Nation* as a milestone in filmmaking. Just as you wouldn't consider reviewing a snuff film, regardless of the level of expertise utilized in creating it, I can't understand why you would take the time to even consider this as anything other than early racist propaganda. The only thing that this film furthered was the stereotyping of African-Americans and racial hatred.

—Paul C. Wright

A. Influence and values are two different things. In my choice of the ten "most influential films of the century," I described D. W. Griffith's *Birth of a Nation* as "a masterpiece, a breakthrough in art and craft, linked to a story so racist, it is almost unwatchable." All quite true. This was a list of *influential* films. No film was more influential in establishing the international language of cinema than *Birth of a Nation*. In making a list of Germany's most influential books, should we leave off *Mein Kampf*? Griffith wrote a heartfelt letter to *Sight & Sound* magazine in the 1950s defending himself against charges that he was a racist. Yet certainly he made a racist movie. Perhaps he was too naive or thoughtless to realize it. So different was the climate in those days that the president, the liberal

Woodrow Wilson, praised *Birth of a Nation* as "history written by lightning." Griffith also made *Intolerance*, which is against racism, and *Broken Blossoms*, which may have been the first Hollywood movie about an interracial love affair.

Black and White

Q. I've read with great interest your comments concerning the benefits of black-and-white films, and I couldn't agree more. In fact, I have actually taken several videos, turned the color off on my TV, and watched them! It's amazing how many poor or average movies are improved somehow by having them in black and white. It gives the film more depth, more surrealism—an almost *film noir* edge and mystery. This isn't to say that the latest Pauly Shore movie is improved, of course, but you know what I mean. What do you think of my practice?

—Bob Sassone, video columnist, *Boston Herald*

A. Although I am opposed to colorizing black-and-white movies, I must confess that I have occasionally decolorized color movies, and find that they frequently play better that way, especially if the color is either garish or faded. Recently I found that *The Barefoot Contessa* made the transition especially well.

The Blair Witch Project

Q. Just saw *The Blair Witch Project*. Here's some food for thought. Mary Brown spoke of seeing a creature that was hairy like a man/beast and had a weird-looking face. She herself seemed to be a man dressed like a woman. She had a weird face, and we could not see if her body was hairy. She was referred to as "Crazy Mary." Could this be the witch? Mary knew about the documentary, saw their equipment, and could have followed them into the woods, using witchcraft to torment them.

—Vincent Santino, Phoenix, Arizona

A. Like *2001* and *Pulp Fiction*, *The Blair Witch Project* seems destined to inspire endless interpretations. My own best guess is that *something* was there in the woods (how else to explain the twigs and slime?) but that the movie ends without a solution.

Q. Shame on you for adding to the hype of *The Blair Witch Project.* This film was a major disappointment, in part because of your glowing review, and also because I was motion-sick from about thirty minutes into the film. My wife and I were looking forward to a low-tech, well-executed, honest scary movie; we left the theater feeling robbed and nauseous given the camera twitch overkill. Your credibility and value to moviegoers has been damaged.

—Klaus Esser, Downingtown, Pennsylvania

A. Several people have told me the movie's handheld camera style made them motion-sick. Might be because you were sitting too close to the screen. Must have made it difficult for you to judge the film on its other merits, however.

Q. I'm irritated by the hypocrisy of film criticism. Most critics hail *The Blair Witch Project* as genius. The style, acting, and film-making of the movie *is* genius, but the effect of the movie remains in question. It is creepy in a residual-thought sort of way, but not too scary. Why? Because implied horror can only go so far. Visuals are necessary to a certain degree. Here's where the hypocrisy comes into play. *The Sixth Sense* is a movie that takes a good script and good moviemaking, and turns it into a very effective horror film. The entire audience seemed to cringe at what was waiting outside the frame. There was a legitimate feeling of horror. The director showed just enough to keep the audience extremely afraid. The ending blew me away. But *Sixth Sense* will take a backseat to *Blair Witch* because it isn't as innovative. I truly feel that most of the critics know *Sixth Sense* is a better film, but refuse to admit it. Do you?

—Vincent Santino, Phoenix, Arizona

A. I admired both films, *Blair Witch* more. Audiences for *Blair Witch* are sharply divided between those who admire it and those who don't. Its defenders like the fake-doc style, and, yes, do believe the ending is scary. But it has other qualities, not least the effectiveness and humor of the performances in the first hour, which are so convincing they are almost transparent. Whatever audiences eventually decide, *Blair Witch* will become the most profitable film of all time in relation to its cost ($22,000, before studio postproduction) and its projected box-office take (some say $150 million).

Q. What do you think about *The Blair Witch Project* having a sound track despite not having any songs in the movie? In most Hollywood films, the filmmakers or studios stick popular songs into the movies, even if they don't fit, just so they can have a hip sound track. But now Artisan has proven that even a movie with no songs can still have a sound track. What is a sound track if not songs that are in the movie? Songs with titles that make them sound like they *could* have been in the movie? Songs by artists who *wish* they were associated with the movie? I personally find this practice appalling.

—Rhys Southan, Austin, Texas

A. The sound track CD allegedly contains songs that were found on a tape in Josh's car after he and his fellow characters disappeared. Titles include "Gloomy Sunday" by Lydia Lunch, "Don't Go to Sleep without Me" by the Creatures, and "The Cellar" by Antonio Cora. Surely only purists would complain that some of the songs were recorded after the date in 1994 when Josh allegedly died. My opinion? If you like the music on its own merits, then what's the harm? It's less of a scam than movie sound tracks which, because of the high cost of rights, fail to contain songs that actually were in a movie.

Q. No matter how supposedly great *Blair Witch Project* may be, I will not see it in the theater. I can't see paying admission to a theater with state-of-the-art surround sound and quality projection to view a film that doesn't fully utilize the available technology. I will do without the audience reaction and wait to view this film (that cost less than $100,000 to make) when it's released on video—in the theater I call my basement.

—T. R. Munson, Smithtown, New York

A. It's going to look even cheaper down there.

Q. I'm confused and hope you might help me. A few months ago, I saw a digital film in

Orlando entitled *The Last Broadcast,* the plot of which is nearly identical to *The Blair Witch Project* scheduled for release this week. With all the talk about *Blair Witch,* I haven't heard *The Last Broadcast* mentioned at all. What gives?

—Glenn Mobley, Orlando, Florida

A. *The Last Broadcast* is described as the story of an investigation of the Jersey Devil by two cable TV hosts and two fans, who go into the wild to film a documentary. One of them is eventually charged with murder. Without having seen it, I can't say how close it is to *Blair Witch,* but of course it's common for similar movies to be made simultaneously. By the time it was aired in March 1998, *Blair Witch* was already in the can. *Last Broadcast* got some good reviews, and may get a new lease on life if *Blair Witch* does as well as expected.

Q. It really bugs me when people complain about the shaky camera in *Blair Witch.* "I hated it!" they say. "The camera movement made me sick!" I'm willing to accept this from a moviegoer who may not know any better, but what's sickening is when a newspaper pans it for the same reason. I expect them to know better, or are they so stupid that they just don't get it?

—Bruce Maiman, Monterey, California

A. *The Blair Witch Project* hasn't received the respect it deserves because many viewers confuse its style with its construction. Yes, it was shot with cheap handheld cameras. But the structure of the film is subtle and effective, and that's why it works. Stand back from the visuals and notice how suspense is built in a counterpoint of humor, realism, and character, and you're looking at a well-made film. It didn't just happen by giving the actors cameras and having them run around in the woods.

Casablanca

Q. I've been watching the new restored DVD edition of *Casablanca,* and thought I heard Peter Lorre tell Humphrey Bogart that the famous letters of transit were signed by "General de Gaulle." Surely the signature of the leader of the Free French would be useless in Nazi-controlled Morocco. What gives?

—Greg Nelson, Chicago, Illinois

A. By happy chance I have just finished exploring *Casablanca* during my annual ten-hour stop-action film analysis at the Conference on World Affairs at the University of Colorado. We played Lorre's speech again and again. It sounded like "de Gaulle" to me, but others said he was actually saying "General Weygand." Somebody suggested we look at the DVD's subtitles. The English subtitles are quite clear: "de Gaulle." Somebody asked what the French subtitles said. They were quite clear, too: "Weygand."

Celluloid vs. Digital

Q. I recently saw the "digital" projection of *Phantom Menace* (at the Burbank fourteen theaters—the Texas Instruments version). While it's hard to gauge the full effects of a new technology on a film one has already seen, nonetheless I found the experience seriously lacking. To tell you the truth, I felt like I was watching a giant TV screen. My friend (who can't wait until DVD is the norm, simply based on the fact that videotape loses its sharpness over time) loved it. Afterward, when I expressed my displeasure about the new format, he basically said I had been "brainwashed" into not liking it by your comments. Honestly though, I think I would have had the same reaction regardless of what you said. There's simply something "different" about film and this digital stuff.

—Jeff Taplin, United Talent, Los Angeles, California

A. I support DVD, films shot on digital, and digital special effects, but I believe that digital projection in theaters is, at this point, a case of the emperor not having any clothes. The digital demo I saw at Cannes was just simply not as good as film. But here is another opinion:

Q. I went to all three theaters playing *The Phantom Menace* with digital in L.A. this weekend and was unimpressed with the Hughes/JVC equipment (which was at two of the three screens), but stunned and amazed by the near perfection of the Texas Instruments projector. It was, amazingly enough, better than film. I know you hate to read that, but it was. Not that I have closed my mind to your preferred system. I really would love to know more about it and hopefully, end up seeing it.

—David Poland, TNT Rough Cut
Website columnist, Los Angeles, California

A. I have not yet seen *Phantom Menace* in digital, and I want to. But what you saw is not quite the same as what millions of moviegoers would see, any more than the crystal-clear film screenings in Westwood are the same as those in cheapo theaters that turn down the wattage to extend the life of their projector bulbs. You saw a custom-built installation with squads of TI acolytes hovering in the booth. As yet no foolproof system for delivering a digital film to thousands of theaters exists, and one likely candidate—satellite—would involve compression and compromised picture quality. Digital projection is also likely to create nightmares for moviegoers, since few theaters will want to replace their underpaid projectionists with an expensive trained computer systems specialist. How would you like it if the movie went down as often as the computers at your bank? Meanwhile, the film-based MaxiVision48 is cheaper, uses existing film technology, and is more than twice as good as the best digital projection. The danger is that digital mania will seduce the movie industry into throwing out a century of experience in favor of a problematic system that is not even cheaper, once you factor in the $150,000 per-screen installation and the high costs of in-booth maintenance. That would be a tragedy.

Q. Do you think there is any way to stop or at least slow the digital behemoth? I've read in your column about MaxiVision48 and visited their website (www.maxivision48.com). What troubles me is that I've heard next to nothing about this system in the mainstream media, which seem to consider digital projection inevitable in theaters. They compare it to the coming of sound and color.

—Sean Blake, Lawrence, Kansas

A. The crucial difference is that sound and color were perceived as improvements by the audience. Digital projection at best is seen as only "almost as good" or "about as good" as film. It is expensive, tricky, and if

adopted will be perceived as no better than the high-def home TV in the consumer pipeline. Theaters have traditionally offered *better* pictures than TV, not the same. MaxiVision, on the other hand, uses existing film technology at forty-eight frames per second, plus a vibration-free projector, to project a picture estimated at 260 percent better than existing film or digital projection. It is much cheaper, and uses tested technology. Unlike 70mm (which it is superior to) it does not require wider film stock or expensive projectors. Common sense is entirely on the side of MaxiVision and against Texas Instruments' digital projection systems. The problem is that some of the top execs in Hollywood have little understanding of technology (they focus on production) and have jumped on the digital bandwagon because they mistakenly think anything "digital" must be better than film. A grassroots movement against digital and in favor of film is growing; Matthew Eggers and Mathew Jones document it on their Website, www.cinemanifesto.org.

Q. Please keep up the crusade for film-on-film projection. I just heard from a friend who saw a digital projection of *Bicentennial Man,* and he said he saw tons of artifacts, including "mosaicing" on lateral movement. No surprise there, but how come we get industry "experts" coming out of exhibitor showings claiming that it's just like film? The only people who can really judge are the cinematographers, no? Apart from us fans, I mean!

—David Bordwell, professor of film,
University of Wisconsin, Madison, Wisconson

A. I'm at the Sundance Film Festival, where a side-by-side comparison between digital projection and 16mm film (not even 35) inspired actual boos for digital. We're told Hollywood needs to dump film and go to digital projection in order to save costs on prints and shipping. But Cynthia Swartz, a vice president at Miramax, tells me that prints and shipping represent only 2 to 3 percent of a typical Hollywood film's budget (marketing and ads can cost 25 percent). If Hollywood indeed plans to take film away from us and replace it with video to save money, here's an interesting question: Will they pass the savings on to us in the form of lower ticket prices? (Sound of uncontrollable laughter.)

Chill Factor

Q. In your review of *Chill Factor*, you write that David Paymer's character has dialogue "seemingly cowritten by Carl Sagan and Mephistopheles." You cite his lamentation: "I am become Death—the destroyer of worlds." This is precisely what J. Robert Oppenheimer is reported to have said on witnessing the first test of an atomic bomb at Alamogordo, and he was quoting from the Bhagavad-Gita.

—Bruce Reznick, Urbana, Illinois

A. As well he might.

Cocaine

Q. This is something I've always wondered about. How do actors and directors fake cocaine snorting in films? So many movies feature gratuitous shots of characters sniffing up large amounts of white powder, but how is it faked? Are they really snorting something up their noses? What do they use?

—Jason Gubbels, Appleton, Wisconsin

A. I turned for an answer to director Darren Aronofsky (π), whose recent Cannes entry *Requiem for a Dream* told a harrowing story of drug addiction. He replied: "I'm sorry to report that I can't be an expert on this question. Because our snorting scenes were extreme close-ups the actors weren't even on set. We used a miniature vacuum cleaner attached to a rolled-up dollar bill. Our vacuum cleaner could snort anything from lye to bleach for all eternity. Personally, I too have always been curious how actors snort line after line. If it was a film from the seventies the answer may be method acting."

Q. The Answer Man column was asked how actors can be shown in close-up snorting cocaine. Your response only explained how a director used a small vacuum cleaner to get a close-up. Interviewed about his drug film, *Bright Lights, Big City*, Michael J. Fox

said a special type of sugar was used. What he wasn't told is, the sugar melts and later that night he discovered the less-than-glamorous side of acting when the syrup flowed freely from his nose.

—Ted Miller, producer, WBAY.com

A. Quite right. Howard Jackson of Kent, Ohio, also writes me to note that on the *Easy Rider* DVD it's explained (or claimed) that Peter Fonda is snorting powdered sugar.

Cradle Will Rock

Q. The John Carpenter who portrays William Randolph Hearst in *Cradle Will Rock* is *not* the same individual who directed *Halloween,* but rather the acclaimed stage actor of the same name. He is linked incorrectly at the IMDB.

—Jeffrey Castel de Oro, Los Angeles, California

A. Thank you for steering me to his bio under *Cradle Will Rock* at Yahoo Movies, where he has a long list of credits. I trusted the Internet Movie Database, which is usually right, but was wrong this time.

Critics

Q. *Entertainment Weekly* magazine recently dumped one of its Critical Mass film critics, the *L.A. Weekly*'s Manohla Dargis, because her reviews were considered too harsh. She's a tough critic and gave lower grades to movies like *Phantom Menace*, which got an F. Should she have been allowed to continue to bring down the *EW* curve? Was her taste too highbrow for a rating system based on grading mainstream studio movies?

—Anne Thompson, New York City, New York

A. Her perspective added a nice balance to *EW*'s mix, and exposed the magazine's readers to the possibility that not everybody was on the same wavelength. Editors once looked for tough critics. Now too many of them look for critics who will reflect reader tastes, instead of leading them. *EW*'s own critics have strong tastes; my guess is Dargis's grades were not a problem in the magazine so much as on the magazine's TV show. Television likes happytalk and consensus; dissent is confusing for viewers.

Q. I read the film critic in a political magazine my father gets. It seems like every time I read his review of a film I thought was great, he hated it. He always backs up his criticism with obscure scholarly comparison, quoting from sophisticated books and citing old movies. I can't help wondering, when I walk out of a theater having completely enjoyed a movie that he didn't, am I somehow too young to have good taste? Or is it that film critics have become too jaded and have lost their compassion and love for film?

—Dan Gilbert, Vestal, New York

A. Let's start by assuming the magazine didn't choose its critic to appeal to the sons of its readers. You are not too young to have good taste, but there's still room to develop that taste. The fact that you ask such questions is a very good sign. Are critics jaded? In most cases, they love film more than the average moviegoer, which is why they hold it to a high standard. And shouldn't they have more compassion for moviegoers than for movies?

Q. No interview with Sandra Bullock seems complete nowadays without her bringing up her disgust with herself for agreeing to star in *Speed 2*. She begs our forgiveness. You gave three stars to the movie, going against the critical consensus. Do you think she is truly contrite, or is she trying to curry favor with the critics after the film's critical savaging?

—Lloyd A. White, Rockville, Maryland

A. The dissing of *Speed 2* has become a popular folk ritual, and Ms. Bullock has cravenly joined in. She would have performed more of a service by warning us against *Forces of Nature*. I am grateful to movies that show me what I haven't seen before, and *Speed 2* had a cruise ship plowing right up the main street of a Caribbean village.

Q. I saw a news item that must have you plenty discouraged. Here is a partial quote: "Do movie critics' reviews matter to the success or failure of a movie's box-office success? According to a study released today by Copernicus, a global marketing strategy and research firm, the answer is a resounding no.

'What critics think about a movie,' according to Dr. Kevin J. Clancy, CEO of Copernicus, 'is surprisingly unrelated to domestic box-office sales . . . what critics think is bad may have tremendous upside potential.'" Your response?

—Greg Nelson, Chicago, Illinois

A. Duh! I wonder how much it cost to produce results that have been common knowledge for as long as there have been movie critics. Our job is to suggest, however imperfectly, that the best movie in town may not always be the most successful. If Dr. Clancy automatically attends the top-grossing film, I recommend my reviews to him, urgently. On the other hand, anyone who uses the phrase "upside potential" may be beyond help.

Cult Movies

Q. What is the definition of a "cult movie"?

—Alexei Tolkachev, Irvine, California

A. A movie my friends and I love even though the world says we're crazy.

Cybermovies

Q. I live in the dorms here at University of Colorado and we have very fast ethernet connections and can download extremely large files in minutes. Because of this, everyone on my floor seems to be getting newly released films on their computers every day, sometimes even before the movie is out. What do you think the impact on Hollywood will be when millions of Americans are downloading these illegal, pirated movies from the Internet?

—Chris Justus, Boulder, Colorado

A. Hollywood will try to stop it, with encryption, tracing, and legal punishments. It is theft, after all. My best guess is that a student is ten times more likely to steal a movie via the Net than to sneak into a movie without paying. Somehow the Net makes it a techno-victory instead of just gate-crashing.

Dancer in the Dark

Q. After reading your report about *Dancer in the Dark* being roundly booed at its Cannes screening, I read the following Reuters report: "Danish director Lars von Trier won a wild standing ovation at the Cannes Film Festival on Wednesday for his weepy melodrama *Dancer in the Dark*, emerging as the favorite for the Golden Palm that has eluded him twice." How do you figure a movie goes from being booed by one crowd to receiving a tearful standing ovation from another? Is there that much of a split among Cannes attendees?

—Ron Spiegelhalter, Manchester, New Hampshire

A. It was booed at the press screening, cheered by the black-tie evening crowd in the presence of von Trier and Bjork. The morning crowd consists of critics, film festival programmers, cinematheque operators, cineastes, etc. The evening crowd is buyers and sellers, studio executives, local dignitaries, freebie tickets from distributors, people with clout, hotel executives, real-estate developers, arms dealers, etc., including a sizable number of ticket holders who are guests of the film's distribution company. No surprise that the reactions were different; every evening screening is cheered.

Directing

Q. I'm a film and video grad student who was recently told by a professor that taking a painting class was a waste of time to someone studying film, and that I should be concentrating on taking computer courses like motion graphics if I expect to get a job. I believe very strongly that other mediums like painting and photography contribute a great deal to the development of a successful filmmaker. What is your opinion on this?

—Dana Duffy, Savannah, Georgia

A. The professor is correct if he intends you to become a technician rather than an artist. He sounds to me like he should be teaching in a trade school.

Q. That "kid" you wrote about from Sundance a couple of years ago—the one who ambushed you in a coffee shop by bribing the bartender to put his video on the big screen—whatever happened to him?

—Pet Danforth, Oak Park, Illinois

A. The kid was named Stuart Acher. He got an agent, has made some deals, says he's on the brink of big things. Meanwhile, *Bobby Loves Mangos*, the film he showed to me, is playing at www.ifilm.com. It is, as I wrote at the time, surprisingly good. (While you're at ifilm, also check out *405* by Bruce Branit and Jeremy Hunt. Take my word for it.)

Disney Villains

Q. I saw *Dinosaur* this weekend and the ending struck me as a case of déjà vu. Like many Disney movies of the last ten years, the villain dies by falling. Is this because Disney wants its heroes to remain unstained by the act of murder (even in self-defense)?

—Tony Gray, Cary, North Carolina

A. I think you're on to something. It would look bad for the hero to be a killer, and awkward for the villain to be disposed of by a minor character. Here's the official Disney position, from a studio spokesperson: "Each of our films is created by a distinct group of filmmakers who bring their own sensibilities and storytelling talents to the project. It is true that several Disney villains have met their demise by falling but that is usually relevant and specific to the story. Each film is unique unto itself and there are no rules or guidelines for disposing of villains here at the studio."

Documentaries

Q. I note that the Motion Picture Academy has again revised the rules for how documentaries are nominated for the Oscars. After myriad complaints, not least from *Siskel & Ebert* in the infamous *Hoop Dreams* scandal, the new system begins with fifty documentarians who are Academy members, dividing up the sixty or seventy eligible films, so that the same small group of volunteers isn't required to see all of them. After they trim the list to twelve, the semifinalists will be screened in Los Angeles, New York, and San Francisco. All Academy members in those areas will then vote for the five nominees, if they qualify by attending most of the screenings. Do you think this will work?

—Susan Lake, Urbana, Illinois

A. Yes, I do. I think it is a fair and practical way around the previous problem of finding volunteers willing to sit through seventy films. (Under that process, audience members would shine their flashlights when they grew impatient; such films as *Hoop Dreams* and *Roger & Me* were not even seen in their entirety.) My only suggestion would be that the screenings of the finalists should be open to the public (with Academy members admitted free). That would create an instant festival showcase of good documentaries, provide advance buzz for the finalists, and generate revenue, which could underwrite the process and be shared with the filmmakers.

Q. Several of the best-reviewed documentaries of 1999, including *American Movie* and *Mr. Death*, were not nominated for Oscars. Given your outrage in the past over such omissions as *Hoop Dreams* and *Roger & Me*, how do you feel?

—Susan Lake, Urbana, Illinois

A. This year's finalists were chosen in a reformed process that used documentarians as prescreeners. I haven't seen two of the five nominees, so can't fairly say how good a job they did. But when it comes to documentaries, the Academy seems reluctant to nominate two kinds: (1) any film that was funny, successful, and got rave reviews; and (2) any film directed by Errol Morris. Whether that would account for the absence of those two titles, I sayeth not.

Q. In his speech accepting the Oscar for Best Documentary for *One Day in September*, its producer, Arthur Cohn, made a big deal out of the fact that the Academy was willing to honor it even though it hadn't yet had a theatrical release. Now I hear grumblings that that's *why* it won. Your analysis?

—Susan Lake, Urbana, Illinois

A. It works like this. The documentary and foreign film bylaws require that you have to have seen all five nominated films in order to qualify to vote. Therefore, if you can get your unreleased film nominated, you hold "Academy screenings," and make a concerted effort to recruit friendly audiences. By definition, the only voters who have seen all five films are the ones who have seen yours. Wim Wenders, director of the supposed frontrunner, *The Buena Vista Social Club*, is

reportedly plenty honked off over losing. Nanette Burstein and Brett Morgen, who made *On the Ropes*, another contender, feel it would be inappropriate for them to comment. But Joe Berliner, director of the great docs *Brother's Keeper* and *Paradise Lost*, is fed up and isn't going to take it any more. He tells me, "The entire Oscar nominating history for docs turns my stomach. The long list of snubbed films (as well as the long list of undeserved winners) confirms for me that this award in this category has little meaning other than the skill to manipulate the system. (Of course there are always exceptions— deserving films that actually get recognized.) Until there is a documentary branch of the Academy that treats docs like any other film in any other category, nothing will change, despite the recent Band-Aid attempt to improve the situation."

Q. I am writing about the Best Documentary Oscar given this year to *Last Day in September*. There have been complaints that its producer, Arthur Cohn, took unfair advantage of the "reforms" in the category to tilt the pool of eligible voters toward his film. Under Academy rules, voters must see all five nominated documentaries in order to cast ballots. Cohn's critics say that once his film made the shortlist, he held only a few screenings, and particularly invited his friends. Since only those who had seen his film were eligible to vote, his strategy was to show it to as few people as possible. Your opinion?

—Greg Nelson, Chicago, Illinois

A. At Cannes this year I encountered Wendy Lidell, vice president of Winstar Cinema, whose doc *On the Ropes* was another of the year's nominees. Although other losers in the category, such as the heavily favored Wim Wenders (*The Buena Vista Social Club*) declined to comment on the controversy, Lidell agreed to go on the record.

She writes the AM: "Here is my analysis of the flaws in the Academy Award documentary voting procedure. The system was revised following the *Hoop Dreams* flap some years ago, but the job was only done halfway. The prenomination process was taken out of the hands of a voluntary committee and given over to a qualified panel of documentary experts, and this did result in a vastly improved pool of eligible films on a prenominated shortlist. But at that point, the old rules kicked in, and only those Academy members who viewed *all* of the shortlisted films could vote for nominees, and only those members who viewed *all* nominees could vote for the winner.

"This procedure strongly favors Academy insiders. Anyone who is well connected can control the voting pool by limiting access to his or her film. That is why it is so often a film that has not been theatrically released that wins the award. The Academy rules state that a documentary may qualify by playing one week in a theater in L.A. County or Manhattan. That exhibition must be advertised in the local press, but it may be a daily matinee, and often, few if any people attend because it is not reviewed or otherwise publicized. That means that the producer with the most friends in the Academy who are willing to sit through five nominated films has the advantage. Moreover, members may sign an affidavit that they have seen any film that is in general release, but cannot do so for films that have not been released. This again, limits the voting pool in favor of the unreleased films.

"It may well be that *One Day in September,* which I have been told qualified by playing one week in Encino, is the best of the five nominees, but we don't know since none of us outside Encino and the Academy have been able to see it. Wouldn't it be better for a film to compete after its theatrical release?

"If the Academy wants to promote the theatrical distribution of documentary features, it does no good to have the award given every year to a film that nobody has heard of. This only serves to perpetuate the notion that documentaries are not important. If bona fide theatrically released films were consistently nominated and awarded, people might begin to think of documentaries as 'real movies' and go see them in the theaters. And that would be good for everyone."

I sent Lidell's statement to Arthur Cohn, who replies: "It would appear to be advisable that you contact the Academy of Motion Picture Arts and Sciences in this regard for any queries you may have. Allow me to as-

sure you in the meantime that we have been very careful to strictly follow all Academy rules and regulations."

Dogma

Q. *Dogma*—good or bad? Kevin Smith claims to be a devout Catholic and says his film is pro-faith. I am a Catholic and I wasn't upset by anything in the script, but then again I know it is only a movie and shouldn't be seen as more. Smith himself has said that the Catholic League is more mad at Disney for originally owning the picture than they are at the movie itself—that their protest is more about Disney, and the movie is just a means.

—James Coffey, Escondido, California

A. The Catholic League, a small but noisy organization run by William Donohue with no official sanction by the church, is currently gathering signatures on a petition asking Disney to dump its Miramax subsidiary. Since Miramax had already decided not to distribute *Dogma* as long ago as May, one would think the League would direct its protests against the film's current distributor. Surely its proper concern is the content of the film, not a company's business decisions? Why the obsession with Disney? Perhaps because there is more publicity to be gained by attacking a larger target.

Q. I just saw *Dogma*. If it is blasphemous, it is Catholic blasphemy and God is not angry. Kevin Smith makes (perhaps unintentionally) four important points about God: God is incomprehensible, absent, strange, and love. Very sound theology. Also, Catholic theology does work—or at least do the stories on which it is based.

—Fr. Andrew Greeley, Chicago, Illinois

A. Not all films with Catholic themes are so knowledgable. I just saw *End of Days*, in which Arnold Schwarzenegger does combat with Satan. The theology is not sound, but the plot is certainly incomprehensible, absent, and strange.

Double Jeopardy

Q. I saw *Double Jeopardy* last night. Not to be gross, but when Ashley Judd was inside the coffin do you think there would be gases from the corpse that might ignite when she used the cigarette lighter?

—Bob Ludwig, Scarborough, Maine

A. Apparently not. And if there were, she should have a long talk with her agent.

Q. Regarding *Double Jeopardy,* I thought I'd point out what is ignored by virtually every movie on the subject. Double jeopardy protects a person from multiple prosecutions for the *same* crime.

—Mike Ruskai, Sayreville, New Jersey

A. Absolutely correct. Just because Ashley Judd's character was convicted of killing her husband on the boat doesn't mean she's free to kill him in Times Square. The ending of the movie neatly sidesteps the issue, of course.

Dubbing

Q. What is your opinion about dubbing foreign films? Miramax is rereleasing *Life Is Beautiful,* this time dubbed into English. I hate dubbing and consider it to be a marring of the original product. Even if one can't understand the original language, one *does* get a significant flavor of the performance. Having lived in Europe for several years, I have ample experience comparing the original dialogue and performances in American films with the dubbed version. The dubbed performances are, in most cases, awful. How can one expect a subpar actor to duplicate, say, Robert De Niro's performance in *Raging Bull,* or Woody Allen's performances in any of his films? My great fear is that we will lose the choice of seeing wonderful foreign films in their original version in order to cater to filmgoers who don't care as much about this issue.

—Carlo Dallapiccola, College Park, Maryland

A. That's unlikely, since most people who wouldn't go to a subtitled film wouldn't go to a foreign film at all. Although most nations routinely dub all films into the local language (often badly), U.S. audiences are adamant in demanding subtitles, and a dubbed release like this is a rarity—justified, Miramax hopes, by the film's popularity and its crossover appeal to mass audiences.

DVD and VHS

Q. I have and continue to build a nice library of VHS videos and am not really interested in DVD. Will I eventually be forced to go that route and invest in the equipment because I will find no one to repair my VCR, and VHS tapes will no longer be produced, etc.? I fear technology/the economy-machine is driving our choices and don't like it. Does one really have a good choice in this matter?

—Donald J. Nevin, St. Paul, Minnesota

A. VHS tapes will continue to prosper for the forseeable future. The only immediate casualty of DVD is the laser disc. But eventually DVD home recording machines will become available, and when they become affordable, VHS will fade away, because DVD picture quality is so much better.

End of Days

Q. In your review of *End of Days,* you wrote: "Let's see. Rome is seven hours ahead of New York. In other words, those clever monks said, 'The baby will be conceived between six and seven A.M. on January 1, Rome time, but that will be between eleven P.M. and twelve A.M. in a city that does not yet exist, on a continent we have no knowledge of, assuming the world is round, and there are different times in different places as it revolves around the Sun, which of course it would be a heresy to suggest.' With headaches like this, no wonder they invented Gregorian chants to take the load off."

Not that I expected the movie to have any of this right, but (1) the Gregorian calendar was instituted during the papacy of Gregory 13, in 1582—when America was well known, although New York wasn't around yet; (2) Gregorian chant originated during the papacy of Gregory 1 (590–604); (3) scholars have known the world was round since the time of Aristotle if not earlier; (4) different times at different places on Earth have nothing to do with its revolution around the Sun, but rather its rotation on its axis—but you'll get the same effect if the Sun goes around Earth every day, so it doesn't depend on your solar system model. Varying local time would have been well known to scholars by the 1580s, since this was well after circumnavigation of the globe; (5) Copernicanism was not declared heretical by the Catholic Church until 1616.

—Richard Rees, Westfield, Massachusetts

A. For my penance, I will see *End of Days* again.

Q. Why did Arnold go through all that trouble to keep the Devil from impregnating Robin Tunney in *End of Days* when all he had to do was impregnate her first? Now that would be a movie.

—Patrick Franklin, Norman, Oklahoma

A. It would also be the world's greatest pickup line: "Quick—let me impregnate you before the Devil does!"

Entrapment

Q. In *Entrapment,* a main part of the plot is that the two main characters will gain ten seconds off the clock by "stealing" a tenth of a second every minute for one hour. But wait—just add that up. Pull off your shoes if you have to. Okay now, do you see the problem? That adds up to *six* seconds! What rule of Movie Math am I overlooking?

—Dave Walsh, Bloomington, Illinois

A. You're forgetting that nobody in a movie theater is willing to pull off their shoes. Have you ever taken a good look at the floor?

Erin Brockovich

Q. In your review of *Erin Brockovich,* you found fault with Julia Roberts's costuming, and felt it undermined the film's credibility. I work in Westlake Village, in an office that leases space from Mary & Vititoe. I see Ms. Brockovich regularly. She is an intelligent and thoroughly admirable lady. She dresses to this day in the same striking manner portrayed in the film. I think the costume designer worked very hard to capture the precise nuances of Ms. Brockovich's sartorial choices. For me, and for anyone familiar with Erin Brockovich, Julia Roberts's costuming enhanced the film's credibility.

—Cinthea Stahl, Los Angeles, California

A. I know the real Erin Brockovich dresses like that, but when Julia Roberts, the glamorous movie star, dresses so boldly, a different message is being sent. Accuracy is not a defense in drama. Only effectiveness is.

Q. In *Erin Brockovich,* Julia Roberts is filmed in a continuous shot taking a ticket off her windshield, stepping into her car, and driving off into an intersection where she gets hit by a BMW at a high speed. I doubt director Steven Soderbergh would put Julia Roberts in such peril. How did he do it?

—David Bischkem, Milwaukee, Wisconsin

A. Universal spokesman Brad Mendelson replies: "Director Steven Soderbergh and cinematographer Ed Lachman worked with the visual-effects supervisor, Tom Smith of Cinesite Hollywood, to create the car accident scene. It is composed of three different elements. The first is a shot of Julia Roberts getting into the car and pulling away. The second is a shot of a stunt driver hitting a radio-controlled car with a mannequin in the driver's seat. The third is a "clean pass," in which the motion-controlled move was repeated without the car to give the compositors material to cut, paste, and blend. The negative was then converted to digital format and the first two elements were grafted onto a single seamless shot."

Eyes Wide Shut

Q. I read in *Mr. Showbiz:* "Once again, Europeans prove more amenable to sex and nudity than their American counterparts. British cinemagoers will be treated to sixty-five more seconds of orgiastic sex in the explicit Tom Cruise–Nicole Kidman *Eyes Wide Shut* than will Stateside audiences. So much for Stanley Kubrick and so much for Tom Cruise's vow that the film wouldn't be cut." Your feelings?

—Paul Idol, Ft. Lee, New Jersey

A. The sixty-five seconds are still in the American version, but with digitally produced figures standing in front of crucial parts of the screen to block the sight of sexual activity. Both Britain and Canada have workable categories for adult films. America is the only major moviegoing nation in which, for all practical purposes, no studio film can be adults-only. The NC-17 rating, like the X before it, has been surrendered to pornography. Obviously there should be an A rating between the R and the NC-17, to accommodate just such films as *Eyes Wide Shut*. Canadians, meanwhile, are in an uproar that they have to see the American version even through they have a category perfectly able to accept Kubrick's preferred cut. Cultural imperialism marches on.

Q. Thank you for speaking out about the travesty that Warner Bros. is perpetuating with *Eyes Wide Shut*. I originally read about the digitally altered sixty-five seconds in Richard Schickel's *Time* magazine article. This is truly a sad day for film enthusiasts. I believe that it is time for someone to step in and deal with the MPAA's perversion of their power. There seems to be no rhyme or reason to their decisions. For example, the original tagline of the *South Park* movie, *All Hell Breaks Loose*, was rejected due to the use of the word "hell." The MPAA claims the rating system is only to inform potential viewers about objectionable subject matter, but it is farcical for them to act as if their rulings have no effect on a film's box-office potential, especially the stigmatized NC-17. I will still see *Eyes Wide Shut*, because I love Stanley Kubrick's work and consider him a true artist. That does not change the fact that I am extremely disappointed in Warner Bros. Although they are in business to make money, it would be nice to see them strive to support those filmmakers who have an artistic vision, rather than solely support mind-numbing dreck such as *Wild, Wild West*.

—Jeremy Slate, Tallahassee, Florida

A. America sleeps better at night knowing that the offensive *All Hell Breaks Loose* was not part of the campaign for *South Park: Bigger, Longer and Uncut*, a title the MPAA did not object to. The MPAA serves a useful purpose as a guide for parents. But as an unintended side effect, it prevents adults from seeing films as their directors intended them to be seen.

Still, it's not fair to single out Warner Bros. as a villain. True, the studio digitally altered the film; reportedly that was also Kubrick's desire, to get the R rating. But Warner deserves credit for showing both versions to critics at the Los Angeles premieres. Movies

are silently cut all the time to qualify for the R rating; we learn about it only after the fact, when the video "director's cut" shows what was left out of the theatrical release. By screening *ESW* pre- and postdigital, the studio was at least able to demonstrate that digital masking was better than cuts that would have disrupted the flow of Kubrick's mesmerizing cinematography.

Q. My question concerns the backwards speech read over the speakers in the initial (pre–rumpy-pumpy) gathering at the masquerade ball in *Eyes Wide Shut*. It is obvious that something is being said backwards, but I don't particularly want to bring recording equipment into the theater to find out what it is.

—Matt Thiesen, Maple Grove, Minnesota

A. The orgy master is saying, "Paul is dead." Just joking. Actually, I believe that's a foreign language and not backwards speech at all. I'd appreciate hearing from anyone who argues otherwise.

Q. *Eyes Wide Shut* is being shown here in Japan without any digital manipulating. The film is rated R-18, which means no one under eighteen gets in. Usually, the sight of pubic hair is censored by pixelating or blurring (this even happens in porn films), but *Eyes Wide Shut* wasn't touched at all. I don't understand all the fuss.

—Jason Chau, Niigata, Japan

A. Japan's censors have a long tradition of obscuring pubic hair; that the Kubrick film was shown unaltered suggests, perhaps, that they respect his stature as an artist. Of course it is showing as "adults only," a choice impossible under the MPAA's broken-down rating system. That's why we need the A rating between R and the discredited NC-17.

Q. Just finished reading *Tinker, Tailor, Soldier, Spy*, by John LeCarre. On page 97: "The Dutch set him a honey trap, my dear, and he barged in with his eyes wide shut." Do you know the origin of the expression?

—Michael Marren, Chicago, Illinois

A. In *Eyes Wide Open*, his memoir about writing the screenplay with Kubrick, Frederic Raphael writes: "Can he really consider *Eyes*

Wide Shut a poetic title? Perhaps its charm is that it is undoubtedly of his own composition." Perhaps, too, Kubrick read the LeCarre novel and the phrase stuck in his memory.

Q. I was horrified to learn that after all the controversy over the censored American version of Stanley Kubrick's *Eyes Wide Shut,* Warner Bros. is releasing only the censored version on DVD! I thought DVD was a format for film buffs, people who would seriously be interested in seeing Stanley Kubrick's original cut of the film.

—Danny Stuyck, Houston, Texas

A. Kubrick's original version showed the Tom Cruise character wandering through an orgy, which included long shots, fairly indistinct, of couples involved in sex. After the MPAA socked this version with the unacceptable NC-17 rating, the studio created bizarre digitally animated figures who "stood" between the audience and the offending action, blocking it. Both versions were shown to the press at the world premiere, and then Kubrick's associate producer, Jan Harlan, defended the censored version while (and this is crucial) agreeing that Kubrick would have preferred the original version. Of course Kubrick fans assumed that the original version would be released as a "director's cut" on DVD and tape. It will not be, at least in North America, and the studio has received a firestorm of protest.

I contacted Pamela Godfrey, vice president of Worldwide Publicity for Warner Bros. Home Video, who said: "There was a misconception that there were two versions of *Eyes Wide Shut.* The film distributed internationally is exactly the same in length and content as the U.S. version. The only difference is the 'digital amendment' that was required for the U.S. version was removed for the international distribution. The DVD that is being released will follow the pattern of the theatrical releases: the DVD released in the United States will have the 'digital amendment'; the DVD released outside the United States will not. Added on the DVD release are interviews with Tom Cruise, Nicole Kidman, and Steven Spielberg which were conducted after Stanley Kubrick's death."

Of course, a film is not "exactly the same"

in content if the content has been digitally altered. To argue otherwise is Orwellian. Although the studio has argued that Kubrick "wanted" this altered R-rated version to be released on the DVD, in that case why is his original cut being released outside the United States? Is that against his wishes? The entire episode illustrates the poisonous influence that the unworkable NC-17 rating exerts over the American film industry. Jack Valenti defends the ratings system with the zeal of George Armstrong Custer. Sooner or later it must be amended to permit American adults to make and view adult films.

Q. Thank you for calling Warner Bros. on the carpet over their upcoming censored release of *Eyes Wide Shut.* The independently owned video stores that I deal with want the uncut version, and are angered by Warner's decision. There is a feeling that Warner has capitulated to Blockbuster, which won't stock NC-17, and is trying to keep competitors from stocking versions they don't carry.

—Ed Slota, Providence, Rhode Island

A. Blockbuster's inability to tell the difference between hard-core pornography and serious adult films has made the NC-17 rating the kiss of death. While it cheerfully retails sleazy "unrated" t&a, its hypocrisy makes the release of Stanley Kubrick's original cut commercially impossible. Warners says it is following Kubrick's "wishes" in releasing the digitally censored version, and yet the original uncensored cut is being released elsewhere in the world. Did Stanley have different wishes for different marketing territories?

Q. The DVD version of Stanley Kubrick's *Eyes Wide Shut* is indeed the censored U.S. theatrical print, but the injustice to this underrated film doesn't stop there. Warner Bros., as per Kubrick's wishes, will not be releasing the film in wide-screen format. This is the same practice used on the director's previous two films, *The Shining* and *Full Metal Jacket.* All three films were shot in a 1.33:1 aspect ratio, the top and bottom of the film frame being "masked" for theatrical exhibition. When released to TV and video, the full frame of the film is visible, meaning the full width of the film is present, with a hair more information at the top and bottom than could be seen in theaters. All well and good, some might say, but the original theatrical composition is forever lost. Can anyone explain why a filmmaker as meticulous as Kubrick would not only allow but prefer such questionable video treatments of his films?

—Louis Gutenberger, Reno, Nevada

A. Kubrick preferred his films to fill the video screen, and so he shot them with an eye to compositions that would look good both in theatrical wide screen and on the TV screen, where extra head and footroom is visible. "The framing on the full-screen presentation looks perfectly balanced in every shot," says the hard-to-please Douglas Pratt in his *DVD-LaserDisc Newsletter*. The irony is that when wide-screen HDTV arrives, Warner will have to decide how to interpret Kubrick's wishes: Did he intend for the 1.33:1 composition to be centered in the wider screen?

Q. I checked out the *Eyes Wide Shut* DVD to see if the flub I noticed in the movie had been fixed. It had! I'm referring to the appearance of a crew member (or maybe Kubrick himself) reflected in one of the stainless steel shower stall posts in Ziegler's bathroom. This occurs at the end of Dr. Harford's examination of the overdosed woman . . . just as Ziegler says something about "this being between just you and me." On the DVD, where once there was a reflection there is now a blank white space. It makes me wonder if on the next DVD of Kubrick's *Spartacus*, those soldiers with wristwatches will no longer know the time of day.

—David Kodeski, Chicago, Illinois

A. See, that's the thing about digital. Nothing stays put. Meddlers can go in and fiddle. First they add the digital *Austin Powers* cutouts standing around at the orgy scene. Then they take out the reflection in the bathroom, which home video fanatics were really looking forward to spotting for themselves. Kubrick was a perfectionist who edited his own films. My guess: He saw the reflection, but disregarded it, because the shot worked

the way he wanted it to. A "mistake" like that is a wink from the filmmaker.

Q. In discussing the controversy about *Eyes Wide Shut*, you frequently point out the digital *Austin Powers* cutouts. In addition to this concession, did Stanley Kubrick do any other editing, such as taking *out* any shots? The reason I ask is because when I saw the film here in Los Angeles on opening day, there was a very brief shot of Cruise and Kidman which, in the video, is missing. It came just after the two-shot sequence of them kissing in front of the mirror and it consisted of an extreme close-up of the actors in an embrace. This was followed by a loud *pop* in the sound track (which seemed to mark the end of the reel), a jumpy cut, and then the fade in to the elevator opening at Dr. Hartford's office the next day. Has anyone else reported seeing this shot?

—Matthew Yium, Los Angeles, California

A. Pamela Godfrey of Warner Bros. says she checked with the technicians who mastered the DVD, and they told her: "We checked picture continuity for the feature and confirm that the two-shot of Cruise and Kidman kissing in front of the mirror ends with a slow fade to black. The next shot is the elevator door opening at Cruise's office. There is no missing shot in the video master. This is the original cut of this scene; it has not been altered in any way from the original cut which was finalized and approved. Note that the elevator sequence is the first cut to the head of reel 1B which may account for the pop if seen theatrically. The pop does not appear in the video master."

Fight Club

Q. My friends and I recently attended a sneak preview of *Fight Club*. During the first twenty minutes of the film, many of us noticed split-second images of a person standing next to Edward Norton in his scenes. Any idea what it was we saw?

—John Kane, Richmond, Virginia

A. Director David Fincher confirms there are several subliminal images early in *Fight Club*, but says identifying them would reveal too much about the film.

Q. Since you gave a negative review to *Fight Club,* do you agree with members of Congress who believe movies like this inspire violence in our society?

—Casey Anderson, Schaumberg, Illinois

A. There is little convincing evidence of direct linkage between violent images and violent actions. Violent people sometimes cite media images, but they may be annexing images that match their inarticulate pre-existing drives and feelings. A new book by Richard Rhodes, *Why They Kill: The Discoveries of a Maverick Criminologist,* cites studies indicating that criminals must pass through four clearly defined stages before they act out violently, and those stages are defined within the family, not by the media. Brutal families produce brutal children. The spectacle of congressmen fulminating against violent movies in the week after they voted down the Test Ban Treaty would be funny if it were not sad.

Q. How can you berate a masterpiece like *Fight Club,* not recognizing any of the *Clockwork Orange* aspects of it relating to modern society, and praise *Bringing Out the Dead*? I agree *BOTD* is a solid film but by no means on the genius level of *FC*. Fincher's work doesn't say it is fun to get hit or that men are men because we fight. I believe he's using this as a metaphor for the lack of a struggle we as young men have today. There are no world wars to engage in, no social revolutions to define us. We as a group are internally battling with our identities and how to function within this mind-numbing, product-oriented life. I wish you would reevaluate this film and look at it through less literal eyes. By accusing it of being pornography and violently inciteful, clearly begging for it to be censored, haven't you become what you so fervently preached against this summer regarding the MPAA and *Eyes Wide Shut*?

—Jason T. Howell, Tallahassee , Florida

A. If this movie takes the place of war in your attempt to define yourself, I don't think its message is getting through. Paul Schrader, who wrote *Bringing Out the Dead,* talks of two kinds of characters—those who elucidate, and those who remain mysterious.

He prefers the latter, and so do I. He also says he prefers the existential mode to the ironic mode. Me too. *BOTD* is mysterious and existential; *FC* is ironic and elucidating. Take your pick.

I did describe *FC* as "macho porn," which I think is fair enough. (Not one single woman has written me in defense of the movie; dozens of men have.) I wrote, "a lot more people will leave this movie and get in fights than will leave it discussing Tyler Durden's moral philosophy." That wording may have been careless. I didn't mean to imply the movie is an incitement to violence, but that it's not an incitement to thought.

Q. My theory about *Fight Club:* The main characters live on Paper Street. It's also the name of their soap company. The narrator identifies with a character out of a magazine whose name is Jack ("I am Jack's diminishing self-worth"). Together, this makes Jack Paper. Jackie Paper, you'll recall, is the name of the main character's alter-ego in "Puff the Magic Dragon," a free-spirited, ocean mist–frolicking type of kid.

—Sandor Weisz, Chicago, Illinois

A. You are inciting me to thought.

The F-Word

Q. Now that it supplies roughly 5 percent of all the dialogue in R-rated movies, can you tell me when the f-word was first heard from the screen?

—Ronnie Barzell, Los Angeles, California

A. The last time a reader asked that, neither the MPAA Code and Ratings Administration nor the Motion Picture Academy was able to supply the answer. Now we know. According to *The F-Word,* a new British reference edited by Jesse Sheidlower, the first movie to utter the word was Robert Altman's *M*A*S*H,* released on January 25, 1970. Second place: Michael Sarne's *Myra Breckenridge,* from June 1970. Both were rated R.

Final Destination

Q. James Wong's *Final Destination* featured characters named after directors of suspense or horror films. Joe Dante used a similar tribute in *The Howling,* naming characters for directors of werewolf movies. Are there other films that have used this in-joke?

—Ed Fik, Canyon Country, California

A. In-jokes involving character's names are more common than we know, since some of the names are not famous. Here's a list of the horror-related last names in *Final Destination*: Browning, Rivers, Horton, Lewton, Weine, Schreck, Hitchcock, Chaney.

Flintstones in Viva Rock Vegas

Q. You have long mentioned that you pride yourself on asking, "what did this movie set out to accomplish, and how well does it meet its stated goal?" However, you mercilessly trashed the new Flintstones movie, because . . . I dunno . . . it was not witty or classy? *The Flintstones in Viva Rock Vegas* was a silly kids' movie based on a silly kids' show—it was sweet and harmless. It seems like you temporarily abandoned one of your most laudable critical qualities.

—Ed Vaira, San Diego, California

A. Yeah, but . . . over the weekend at my Overlooked Film Festival at the University of Illinois, I showed the Oscar-nominated Iranian family film *Children of Heaven* to an audience of hundreds of children. You could have heard a pin drop. They loved it, learned from it, cheered it, were better for having seen it, accepted the subtitles, and asked intelligent questions afterward. Childhood is short and precious and I am not sure it's enough that a movie is harmless. Indeed, to the degree that the Flintstones sequel trains kids to expect nothing substantial at the movies, it is not harmless at all.

42 Up

Q. Last night, TV Ontario aired the 1999 installment of Michael Apted's *7-Up* series, *42 Up*. Have I missed something, or has there *not* ever been a discussion of the sex-role distinctions that are glaringly apparent? I realize that an unspoken hope of the project was to document the end of the British class system. However, I continue to be amazed at how many careers the young men have succeeded at, and how complacent and circumscribed

the young women's lives seem to be, almost as if they are still waiting for something to happen, at age forty-two.

—Patricia Nolan, Toronto, Ontario

A. The participants analyze their own lives, and the women apparently do not draw the same conclusions that you do. Apted says if he had the series to do over again, he would have chosen more women. Now a new *7-Up* series has been started, which will visit a fresh group of British subjects every seven years. The women in this group, growing up in the twenty-first century, may have quite different stories.

Frequency

Q. My husband and I saw *Frequency* tonight. We thought it was an excellent movie. But one thing bugged us immensely. In the police station, the father sets off one fire sprinkler, and then *all* the sprinklers in the station go off. *This does not happen.* Sprinklers are activated by heat, when the fire melts a link in the specific sprinkler. If all the sprinklers in the building went off, the water pressure would drop too low to put out the fire. I know this because I was a fire protection engineer for an insurance company. I have seen this happen over and over in movies, and it drives me nuts.

—Robbi Joy Eklow, Grayslake, Illinois

A. Me too. But maybe it explains why whenever any character goes outside at night, the streets are wet.

The General

Q. Last night I finally saw John Boorman's great film, *The General*. Since it premiered last year at Cannes the reviews have all touted the film's black-and-white cinematography; however, the copy I rented had a washed-out but distinct color scheme: reds, blues, yellows, the works. Is this in fact the film that appeared in theaters, or did somebody slip in some colorization for the video release?

—Craig Simpson, Reynoldsburg, Ohio

A. The VHS version is in color, and is also panned-and-scanned. The DVD version has color on one side of the disc and black and white on the other, and both sides are letterboxed. My source at Sony says Boorman preferred the film in black and white, but shot it in "desaturated color" with an eye to the VHS and television markets. DVD users are assumed to prefer the real thing. My advice to VHS users: Turn down the color. This film's soul is black and white.

The General's Daughter

Q. In your review of *The General's Daughter* you mentioned that the seediness of the movie was hard to take. I want to give you my view, which is that this was an antirape film, and the violence, sexual seediness, and promiscuity was the whole point of the story. My husband had a similar view to yours; he didn't think it was "necessary" to show the rape—it could have been implied. He thought it was horrible to watch. But did anyone say Spielberg should have just "implied" the violence in *Saving Private Ryan*? *No!* That's what made it a great antiwar film. I thought *The General's Daughter* was a powerful, beautifully done film that really depicted the horror of rape and what it does to the victim psychologically.
—Judy Carr, Tucson, Arizona

A. *Saving Private Ryan* was, in my opinion, a prowar film, about a war that most people feel it was necessary for us to fight. Movies generally tend to argue in favor of what they show, no matter what they say about it. Of course *The General's Daughter* was against rape, but by lingering in the scenes in which the victim is staked to the ground, strangled, etc., it assured that those are the images that linger in the mind.

Ghost Dog

Q. You mention in your *Ghost Dog* review a killing in which Forest Whitaker fires a gun up through a drain, killing a man in the bathroom. This may well draw its inspiration from the fabled death of one of Japan's greatest samurai, Uesugi Kenshin, who revived the practice of single combat between respected samurai opponents during the sixteenth century. Officially he died of an apoplectic fit in the lavatory, but there is a tradition that a ninja had hidden himself in the cesspit and killed Kenshin with an upward thrust of his spear. Think there might be something to it?
—Bryan Hodges, Memphis, Tennessee

A. Yes, but thanks to advances in plumbing, Ghost Dog only had to stand in the basement.

Q. The Answer Man fielded a question about a shooting in *Ghost Dog*, where Forest Whitaker fires a gun up a drain and kills someone in the bathroom above. This sounds exactly like one of the killings in Suzuki's *Branded to Kill* (1967). Jarmusch could well have seen it before making *Ghost Dog*. Not knocking him, you understand— I adore him—just speculating.
—Michael Schlesinger, Sony Classics, Culver City, California

A. You guessed right. Says Reid Rosefelt, the unit publicist on the film: "I believe the scene is an homage to the cult Japanese action film *Branded to Kill*, where the hitman hero performs a hit in a similar fashion. While I never questioned Jim Jarmusch about this scene, Jim has said on many occasions that *Branded to Kill* was an inspiration for *Ghost Dog*."

Gladiator

Q. In *Gladiator*, when the crowd wants to spare the life of Maximus, they give the "thumbs-up" sign. Isn't this historically inaccurate?
—Joseph Rogers, Chicago, Illinois

A. Quite so, as I pointed out in my review of the movie. Here is what the invaluable *Brewer's Dictionary of Phrase and Fable* has to say on the subject: "In the ancient Roman combats, when a gladiator was vanquished it rested with the spectators to decide whether he should be slain or not. If they wished him to live, they shut up their thumbs in their fists; if to be slain they turned out their thumbs."

Q. Now that *Gladiator* has emerged as the new box-office champ, do you have any remorse over your review that said it was "muddy, fuzzy, and indistinct"?
—Ronnie Barzell, Los Angeles, California

A. Not at all. I was astonished by how few critics and viewers picked up on the shabby visual look of *Gladiator*. Corners were cut, especially in the decision to go with low-resolution digital effects. Contrast it with *Titus*, which is set in an imaginary combination of ancient and contemporary Rome. It has a visual look that shames *Gladiator*. I wonder sometimes if some audience members really *look* at the movies they see. There are exit surveys claiming audiences believe digital projection is "as good as" film, when anyone can see it is not. In the case of *Gladiator*, weren't people bothered by the unfocused, hazy look of the Coliseum? Just because f/x are created by computers doesn't mean they can't be lousy. In *Battlefield Earth*, consider the unconvincing computer-generated shots of Denver in the year 3000. Compare them with the old-fashioned but much more convincing shots of a city in ruins in John Carpenter's *Escape from New York* (1981). The "digital" buzzword inspires knee-jerk reactions; high tech doesn't automatically mean high quality.

Q. Just a note to say that the undefeated champion in *Gladiator* is not named Titus. The first time I saw it, I thought the announcer was saying Tigros, but a check of the credits reveals that the character's name is Tiger, obviously to match the animals he fights with. Wonder how his career would've been different if his parents had named him Bunny, Lamb, or Puppy?
—Greg Dean Schmitz, creator, Upcomingmovies.com

A. For that matter, do you think we would have liked the emperor Commodus better with a less Kubrickian name?

Q. As a 3-D animator by profession, I can tell you that the dark and cheap Colisseum scenes in *Gladiator* are as you described them in your review. There is a technique that blurs and darkens the image of computer-generated animation in order to hide unrealistic detail and the fake look of much computer-generated content. I could even see the patterns of movement on the crowd in the overhead shots. I guess it went cheap out of the lab.
—Santiago Batiz-Benet, Seattle, Washington

A. Ah, but to be fair, there is much discussion about whether the movie's quality differs from theater to theater. One of the industry's most respected experts on image quality originally wrote me that he saw "Two and a half hours of out of focus film . . . half resolution (2K) digital work . . . it gives me a headache . . . mighty murky indeed." He later went back and saw it in another theater, and had a much more favorable impression. While at Cannes, I asked two independent observers (producers of our TV show) to recheck the screen where I saw the film and another screen. Their verdict: "It looked exactly the same: Dark, grayish, grimy. In both theaters we remarked what we'd noticed the first time around: that often in interior close-ups the side of a face away from the camera is totally in shadow, with virtually no glints from the eye or highlights on the cheekbone, etc. Hard to know if that was deliberate or the result of inadequate light in the projector."

High Fidelity

Q. Is it me or is John Cusack the most underrated actor in American movies right now? He has never received an Academy Award nomination, nor has he starred in any blockbusters (he did have a supporting role in the Nicholas Cage vehicle *Con Air*), but he seems to lend quality to everything in which he appears. Why do you suppose he fails to capture the recognition he deserves?
—Tim Tremain, Vancouver, British Columbia

A. Right now Cusack's *High Fidelity* is getting enormous recognition, and he was the key to *Being John Malkovich*, last year's best film. In many ways, including even his appearance, he reminds me of my favorite actor, Robert Mitchum—a superb professional and a gifted artist who fit into his roles so effortlessly that he didn't attract the kind of attention given to actors who sweat and strain.

Q. I'm a loyal Howard Stern listener, but wanted to tell you that you are right and he is dead wrong about *High Fidelity*. I loved this movie! In the John Cusack character I saw just about every guy I've ever dated—telling himself (and his buddies) one thing and acting in a totally unrelated manner.

—Bonnie Cameron, Memphis, Tennessee

A. Stern raked me over the coals during a recent visit to his show because I liked *High Fidelity*. This from the man who loved *Outside Providence*. Nuff said.

Hometowns

Q. I know of at least two movies that mention my hometown of Ash Fork, Arizona: *The Baltimore Bullet* and *Universal Soldier*. Do any other movies mention the town? Or where could I find the info for myself?

—Timothy Roeder, Mebane, North Carolina

A. You can search under locations and keywords at the Internet Movie Database (www.imdb.com), but it's far from complete. You will, however, be fascinated to learn that my hometown, Urbana, Illinois, is mentioned in better movies than yours: *Some Like It Hot* and *2001: A Space Odyssey*.

The Hurricane

Q. I read that *New York Daily News* film critic Jack Mathews has deleted *The Hurricane* from his 1999 Top 10 list. His reasoning? According to the story, he "objects to the film's claim that three Canadians were responsible for digging up the information that eventually cleared Carter, insisting that the real heroes in the case were in fact Carter's lawyers." There are two reasons I am baffled by Mathews's comments. First, I read the exact opposite information in the *Calgary Sun*. That article claims that *Hurricane* actually downplayed the roles of the Canadians, while pushing the Americans into the limelight. Second, although some of the facts of the story may have been altered, the story was still realistic and the movie was wonderful. What's the deal?

—Leigh Emshey, Innisfail, Alberta

A. A biopic is the last place to go for factual information about a person. Movies, even those "based on fact," are parables that

alter and simplify stories for greater dramatic impact. Would we enjoy the story of Carter's pro bono lawyers more than the story of a fifteen-year-old kid whose life is redeemed after he reads Carter's book? Not likely. *The Hurricane* reportedly failed to get more Oscar nominations because of negative publicity about how it dealt with the facts. But if factual accuracy is involved, the Academy might also reconsider its recognition this year of *The Insider* (Mike Wallace feels misrepresented), *Straight Story* (I hear Alvin Straight was really one mean SOB), *Music of the Heart* (Roberta Guaspari's story has been charged with wholesale revisionism), *Boys Don't Cry* (one woman named in the film is suing), and *Being John Malkovich* (John Malkovich's real middle name is Gavin, not Horatio).

The Insider

Q. After attending *The Insider* I was given a card asking me to call and participate in a survey about the movie. Curious, I called. Without identifying who was sponsoring the survey, which was automated, I was asked for my opinion of how the movie portrayed the Brown and Williamson tobacco company. Of course the movie only reinforced my negative feelings about tobacco companies in general, but the red flag went up, and I did not want to give them anything they could use against the moviemaker. The whole thing was a little chilling. What do you think about this and a theater that would allow it?

—Ann Fallen, Surfaced, Florida

A. The survey was sponsored by Brown and Williamson, according to *Bloomberg News*, which says the company will use the results in trying to decide whether to sue for libel. The story adds: "A spokesman for the tobacco company said that it did not disclose its name in order to prevent the results from becoming skewed." A Touchstone Pictures spokesman told me, "There is nothing statistically valid about this kind of telephone survey. In fact, it is set up so that it can be skewed by Brown and Williamson and others in the tobacco industry to generate the desired outcome by having employees and members repeatedly call the number." If I had been asked by the survey, this would have been my answer: The movie strengthened my preexisting conviction that they are selling a deadly product, know it, and lied about it.

Left Breasts

Q. It seems that whenever only one breast of a female is shown it is the left one. Is there some class in movie director school where this is taught? I don't get it. Do you have any explanation?

—Bill Brescia, Bloomington, Indiana

A. Of course. If the woman is facing the camera, the left breast is invariably closer to the "strong axis," or harmonious balancing point, just to the right of center, as suggested by discoveries about visual composition by the painters of the Renaissance.

Q. I read with great interest the Answer Man's theory about why when only one female breast is shown in a movie, it is usually the left one. I was interested in your response referring to the "strong axis" or harmonious balancing point, etc. I have a question for you. I am left-handed, and I notice how many times TV ads that depict someone eating show the person eating with their left hand. Us lefties are in a minority, so why are lefties so often shown in eating commercials? My only conclusion is that we are a mirror image for the "righties" and therefore it is visually more "balanced" to show what most people would see if they looked at themselves in the mirror.

—Karin Fulcher, Tsawwassen, British Columbia

A. Your guess is correct. Watching the TV screen, we all (lefties and righties) identify more easily with the hand on the right side of the screen (which would be the left hand). Rules involving the "strong axis" and the harmonious balancing point apply, since the left hand of a person facing the camera is on the strong axis (just to the right of center). Of course these rules apply only to the impractical American custom of using the fork in the right hand, putting it down, switching it, etc. In the rest of the world, where the fork usually remains in the left hand during most of the meal, right-handed eaters would be used on TV commercials.

License Plates

Q. I've noticed in several movies the California license plate 2GAT123, usually on the star's car. Is there something special about that license plate?

—Kevin M. Evans, Boston, Massachusetts

A. Those plates are the equivalent of the nonexistent "555" prefix on movie telephone numbers. But what do they *mean*? At Leon Pool's Vanity Plates site (www.chaos.umd.edu/misc/origplates), I found out more than I wanted to know. Theory one, from Randal L. Shwartz: "2G = 2 G (2000) [RPM]. AT = at. 123 = 123 [MPH]. In other words, it's simply coasting at lo-revs at that speed." Theory two, from Arthur Bagiski: "G stands for acceleration equal to earth gravity (9.8 m/sec2). So, the plate reads: Two times the acceleration of 9.8 at 1(first), 2(second), and at 3(third) gear."

Locations

Q. I just saw *The Thirteenth Floor,* and I noticed in one of the scenes in the forties world that there was a grand swimming pool. Wasn't this the same pool that was in *Cruel Intentions*? Both are Sony movies, and were probably produced at the same time. Since when have studios recycled sets? Did Reese Witherspoon and Craig Bierko bump into each other unexpectedly?

—Eric Knopp, San Francisco, California

A. A Sony Pictures rep says the pool of the Biltmore Hotel in downtown Los Angeles was used for both films.

Loving Movies

Q. I lost my passion and love for movies. How do I get it back?

—Romolo Perriello, New York City, New York

A. Start all over again at the beginning. First Buster Keaton, then Chaplin, then you might be feeling good enough for the Marx Brothers. They made a movie with Marilyn Monroe . . . and by now, you're back in the swing.

Man on the Moon

Q. In Bob Zmuda's new book about Andy Kaufman, he mentions how he worked for a famous screenwriter, whom he would only call "Mr. X." He tells us of the wildly eccentric things Mr. X would do and how the tales he would tell led to his and Andy's collaboration, and how these stories led to Andy's form of "comedy." Do you know who this bizarre screenwriter is? With Jim Carrey playing Kaufman in *Man on the Moon*, soon to be released, it might help give an insight on what drove Andy to his particular brand of humor.

—Scott Boudet, Tallahassee, Florida

A. I referred your question to Bill Zehme, author of the just published *Lost in the Funhouse: The Life and Mind of Andy Kaufman.* He replies: "Before he came into Andy's life (May 1974, a full year later than claimed), Zmuda worked odd jobs for the renegade screenwriter Norman Wexler *(Serpico, Joe, Saturday Night Fever)* who died this year. Wexler, as I point out in my book, was a legendary kook 'whose supposed eccentric furies and quixotic adventures had makings of further inspiration for [Kaufman's fictional lounge lizard character] Tony Clifton.' Andy's creation of Clifton predated Zmuda, but Zmuda's stories about Wexler's sociopathic and oblivious behavior certainly thrilled Andy. Clifton's abrasive demeanor was largely based on that of comedian Richard Belzer, well known for heckling an audience before it had a chance to heckle him."

The Matrix

Q. A recent Answer Man column noted how the street names in *The Matrix* were also streets in Chicago. There's obviously a bug in *The Matrix*: the Chicago street names are combined with the landmarks and company logos of Sydney, Australia. And for some strange reason, all the streets in this strange city are "one way," and it's difficult to see into the interiors of cars for all the reflections. Does this have anything to do with the fact that Australians drive on the other side of the road?

—Murray Chapman, Internet Movie Database

A. Inspired by your e-mail address, I went to www.imdb.com, the most invaluable single movie site on the Web, and discovered that *The Matrix* locations were indeed in Sydney, Australia.

Q. If the machines in *The Matrix* were so smart, why didn't they use docile cows as their energy source instead of feisty humans? Not only would they have substantially reduced the risk of mutiny, but the upkeep on the Matrix would have been practically nil. An endless field of grass ought to do it for a cow. Granted, they have the box-office draw of Keanu Reeves and that babe in black leather.

—A. L. McLean, Chicago, Illinois

A. I don't follow your reasoning. Doesn't Elsie wear black leather?

Me, Myself & Irene

Q. A group is protesting *Me, Myself & Irene* because in their opinion it reinforces negative stereotypes about schizophrenia. The group claims it wants to educate people on this issue. So why can't they do it and allow the general public to decide for itself whether to see the movie? I have an uncle who is schizophrenic. It is a sad disease, and it handicaps people and impairs them on many levels. But it wouldn't stop him from recognizing comic ideas and wit. What's wrong with people? There simply isn't a bone of wit or irony left in anyone's body.

—Paul West, Seattle, Washington

A. I am reminded of the protests about Mr. Magoo's nearsightedness. I believe audiences are smart enough to know the difference between comedy and real life.

Mission Impossible 2

Q. Is it just me, or did *Mission: Impossible 2* seem a bit derivative of Hitchcock's *Notorious* (one of your Great Movies)? Even the race track scenes seemed familiar. Was Robert Towne's script just paying homage to a great film?

—Adam M. Davis, Bend, Oregon

A. More than a bit derivative, right down to the key idea of the new lover who is ordered by the spymaster to ask his girl to seduce her former lover. (In *Notorious,* Cary Grant orders Ingrid Bergman into Claude Rains's arms; here Tom Cruise asks Thandie Newton to return to Dougray Scott.) But the plot is just a laundry line for the action sequences, which director John Woo handles with mastery. In a way, *MI2* is James Bond reinvented for the twenty-first century. I liked it a lot.

Mission to Mars

Q. In *Mission to Mars,* I was upset at the *rotating* double helix made from M&M's by an astronaut in space. I mean, what were they rotating around? Maybe in the future they have electromagnetically attractive candy?

—Sean O'Brien, Baltimore, Maryland

A. You refer to the M&M's that float in midair to represent a DNA strand. In zero gravity, according to Newton, they would either stay at rest or move in the direction they were propelled, but would not instinctively find the double helix formation. This scene brings new meaning to the concept of product placement.

Q. In *Mission to Mars,* Gary Sinise says, "That DNA looks human!" A cursory look at twenty-three chromosome pairs will tell the observer nothing about from which species it originates, since there are billions of base pairs inclusive. The makers of many science-fiction movies do not do any research concerning their subject. Is it because they are made for unsophisticated teenage audiences? Would a simple phone call or question entail too much effort?

—Edward M. Connell, Albany, New York

A. You know, until I got your message, I thought it not only looked human but actually resembled M&M's. Then I remembered that in the movie another character points out that you can't tell if it's human just by looking.

MPAA Ratings

Q. I've been following your arguments for an A rating to be placed between the R and the NC-17. Another problem is theater owners who become a ratings board all on their own, effectively overruling the MPAA when

they see fit. When I saw *The Wood,* the theater was packed with young teenagers. I guess that about 50 percent of the audience was between the ages of twelve and seventeen. Funny, considering the same theater would not allow those teenagers to purchase a ticket for *Eyes Wide Shut,* despite the fact that they are both rated R. So the theater decided that some R-rated films are worse than others.

—Jason Ihle, East Northport, New York

A. The problem is that the R category has been stretched to the bursting point because there is no other place for a movie to go. Some theater owners sensibly decide on their own which films are truly for older audiences, and which ones got the R only on technicalities. R is so bloated because NC-17 is identified with porn, and is not a practical, workable choice for a film in mass distribution. My point is that the A should *not* replace the NC-17, but come between the R and NC-17, creating a clear category for films that are intended for adults but do not cross the line into hard-core pornography. Jack Valenti and I had a spirited airing of our views in columns in *Variety,* and I was encouraged that Peter Bart, *Variety's* editor, wrote an open letter to Valenti arguing that there was something to be said for the A rating.

Valenti keeps talking about the rights of parents and teenagers. The R category addresses those rights. Now it is time for adults to have the right to see movies as their directors prefer them to be seen.

Q. If I ever meet Jack Valenti, I want to tell him of my experience seeing *Eyes Wide Shut.* There were about one hundred people in the theater, exactly one of whom looked under eighteen. That one was a boy of about 10 who was there with a man of about forty, presumably his father. (I'll withhold my opinion of a father who would take his young son to *Eyes Wide Shut* when *Tarzan* was playing in the same multiplex.) The boy sat right in front of me, so I couldn't help but notice his restlessness. During the sex scenes he seemed embarrassed to be with his father; during the rest of the film he seemed bored. So if we had the A rating that you propose, ninety-nine of the one hundred people in the theater would have been able to see Kubrick's film the way it was intended (rather than the *Austin Powers* version) and the ten-year-old would have been sent to *Tarzan*. I know Mr. Valenti would object to this, but I'm not sure why.

—Michael David Smith, Urbana, Illinois

A. Could it be that Valenti and his bosses, the theater owners, oppose *any* category that would actually prevent them from selling tickets? Is this a question of artistic freedom, or retailing?

Q. I am a twelve-year-old movie lover who feels gypped by adults who try to regulate my movie watching habits. Why do parents feel it is fine for children to watch profanity *(Cop Land, Blue Thunder)* and movies with excessive gore and violence *(Natural Born Killers, Scream)*, but clam up when a movie includes sexually explicit content? I have been prohibited from seeing such powerful films such as *American Beauty* and *Leaving Las Vegas* solely because of the sexual aspect. What do you think is more damaging to a young person, seeing a girl hanging dead from a tree, or Gwyneth Paltrow's breasts?

—Pat Gustini, Washington, D.C.

A. The MPAA Code and Ratings Administration has consistently ruled over the years against Gwyneth Paltrow's breasts. However, you little dickens, I should point out that all of the titles you mention are R-rated, so not everyone thinks it is fine for you to see them.

Q. Here in Australia we have a workable adult rating, the R rating; nobody under eighteen can be admitted. This rating is completely noncontroversial: films that get it are shown in the multiplexes, advertised in newspapers, etc. From the point of view of more serious and artistic films this works fine. However, Australian censors are more tolerant of sex and less tolerant of violence than is the case in the United States. Often, the ratings board gives R to violent films for which male teenagers are a large part of the intended audience. Therefore, such films are often cut to get a different rating before being released in Australia. Often we are not told about this. You may argue that in many cases the loss of a few seconds of violence is no great loss, but it rather annoys me that I

am unable to see a film the way the filmmakers intended, whatever the film is.

—Michael Jennings, Sydney, Australia

A. Many Americans believe the MPAA is too strict on sex, too lenient on violence. But we could argue about standards all day. What is needed in the United States is a rating like yours, that allows American studios to release films as their directors intended them, without the informal boycott now triggered by NC-17.

Q. There was an article in *Entertainment Weekly* about your feud with Jack Valenti over the MPAA rating system. Discussing your call for a new A rating, Valenti said if a film got rated NC-17 under your system, the producer could sue for punitive damages. He added: "If Mr. Ebert's employers would legally indemnify the ratings system, then I'd seriously consider the A rating in a week." Any comment?

—Casey Anderson, Schaumberg, Illinois

A. Now I understand. Valenti agrees with me that the A rating is worthy of serious consideration, but is prevented from acting because he fears pornographers would sue him if the MPAA said their movies were dirty. Valenti's argument is pure horsefeathers because porn movies are never submitted for ratings, and the A rating would cover all adult movies that were not hard-core pornography.

Q. While attending *Sleepy Hollow* this weekend, I saw a trailer for the upcoming film *Next Friday,* the sequel to *Friday* starring Ice Cube. I was shocked when I heard the f-word in the trailer not once, but several times. Now, I'm no prude (I saw both *South Park* and *American Pie* twice each), but I was offended that a major studio had so little confidence in their product that they thought the only way they could attract my attention was to spout obscenities at me. Has any other film to your knowledge used the f-word in a trailer before?

—Brian Lundmark, Norman, Oklahoma

A. According to Richard L. Taylor, vice president for public affairs of the MPAA, the deciding factor is the rating of the film the trailer is being shown with. *Next Friday* has two trailers, one rated R, the other for "all audiences." Since *Sleepy Hollow* was an R-rated film, you got the R trailer (the f-word is not exactly in the spirit of the Headless Horseman fable, but what the heck). Taylor says there have been other instances in which R-rated trailers contained rough or explicit language.

Q. The highly anticipated film *American Psycho* was recently slapped with an NC-17, not because of the gruesome murders, but because of one scene containing a threesome. A similar fate befell *Black and White*. Why is it that sex is considered more dangerous to minors than violence? It seems that the message being sent is that violence is more acceptable than lovemaking. And why is there an NC-17? Doesn't this rating imply that the MPAA knows better than a legal guardian what is appropriate for their child?

—Clarke Speicher, Seaford, Delaware

A. No, it implies that the movie industry would rather self-apply the rating than be at the mercy of countless local censor boards. The problem with NC-17, as I never tire of explaining, is that the rating has been rendered anathema because of its association with porno. I just saw *American Psycho* at Sundance, and it is indeed an adult film (for the sex and the violence). What is needed is an A rating, between R and NC-17, categorizing it as adult but not hard-core. That would protect minors while avoiding the stigma of porn.

Q. When I saw Larry Clark's *Another Day in Paradise* in the theater I felt it was a good movie with great acting, but Natasha Gregson Wagner's character was underdeveloped. At the time I blamed the filmmakers. Now I've seen the director's cut on DVD and found that a key scene with Wagner's character had been cut out, thanks to the MPAA. Times like that make me wonder why I don't just wait for DVDs and skip the theater completely, except that I love seeing movies in theaters. On the commentary track, director Larry Clark says this film was reviewed at the same time that the MPAA found *Saving*

Private Ryan's violence suitable for an R, suggesting some filmmakers get favorable treatment. Judging by the scenes that were cut compared with the intense pummeling I experienced when I saw *Saving Private Ryan*, I must agree. I realize the MPAA system will always be too subjective to ever be consistent and fair, but perhaps they should review films without knowing who the filmmakers are?

—Robert Mason

A. Hollywood gossip is such that they usually know who the filmmakers are even without looking at the titles, but your suggestion is intriguing, since the chances of Larry Clark and Steven Spielberg getting the same treatment at the hands of the MPAA are zilch.

Q. There has been considerable uproar over the slicing and dicing of *American Psycho* and I don't mean on the screen. As I live in a remote northern Canadian town I thought I would not get the opportunity to see this film before the studio was forced to make edits to satisfy the MPAA. But it turns out the Canadian release of the film will be intact. Each province in Canada looks after its own film ratings and our most populous province, Ontario, has already rated the film R as it presently exists. How, in the era of free trade, can the MPAA justify an edited version showing in Detroit, Michigan, while across the river in Windsor, Ontario, the original cut is freely available? Do you think the MPAA would respond to pressure from studios or theater owners if Americans along the U.S./Canada border boycotted the American release in favor of the original version showing in Canada?

—Frank McCallum, Fort Vermilion, Alberta

A. I doubt it. The two versions are too similar. I have seen the uncut version of *American Psycho*. The MPAA rated the film R only after cuts were made in a sex scene that would strike most people as tame in the first place. All the gore and slaughter remain. It's as if the MPAA was making a symbolic trim to get off the hook of having misapplied the NC-17 in the first place.

Music

Q. What's this? The music on the trailers for Hitchcock's *Rear Window* seems to come from Ed Wood's *Plan 9 from Outer Space*. One reason may be because the Hitchcock picture never had much of a score to begin with. The sounds and images dominate.
—Paul West, Seattle, Washington

A. I queried Robert Harris, who with James Katz restored the superb print now in rerelease around the country. He replies: "I have the trailer and just checked out the DVD of *Plan 9*, but can't locate the exact piece of music. It certainly does sound like the same type of music, if not exactly the same."

And David Bondelevitch, who teaches film music at USC, writes: "I'm not a *Plan 9* expert, so can neither confirm nor deny. However, if it is the same piece, it is certainly not the original recording. It was nicely mixed in Dolby Digital 5.1 when I saw the trailer (and I wondered what the music was, since Hitch made a big point out of not using any score music in the film itself). If memory serves, the music in *Plan 9* was not original either. It was all from an existing music library."

In other words, Hitchcock and Wood both went shopping in the same library, and bought the same music? Or maybe Wood just said, "I'll have whatever he's having."

Q. Re the Answer Man for February 27: As an old *Plan 9 from Outer Space* fan from way back, I can confirm that the music in the *Rear Window* trailer is indeed the main title music from Ed Wood's epic, although it's certainly not in *Rear Window* itself. This is not unprecedented: Back in 1988 when I reissued *The Manchurian Candidate*, the malletheads in MGM/UA's marketing department simply took the original trailer, wiped the sound track, and laid in stock music—which was instantly recognizable from the original *Night of the Living Dead!*
—Michael Schlesinger, Sony Classics, Culver City, California

A. You're lucky they didn't look at the title, decide it was a political campaign film, and lay in *Happy Days Are Here Again.*

Q. How should Oscar-nominated songs be judged? Should it be based on the song standing on its own as a song, or should the scene it accompanies be taken into account? I bring this up because I came close to crying while watching the "When She Loved Me" piece in *Toy Story 2.* I've never made up my mind if it was the song, the images accompanying it, or the combination of the two that caused that reaction.
—Mark Reichert, St. Louis, Missouri

A. My guess is that songs that reinforce the emotional content of scenes have a better chance, because voters are more likely to remember them. My own choice would also be Randy Newman's "When She Loved Me."

Music of the Heart

Q. Your review of *Music of the Heart* talks about how "real" this film is. My brother is the real-life character played by Aidan Quinn, and I grew up in Roberta's hometown, so I know this story is false. The Central Park East School is not at all as the film portrays it, and the school is so upset about the unfairness and unreality of this film that a note to that effect has been sent home to the parents. Roberta sent her own sons there. It is a progressive, safe, integrated school. The other music teacher was portrayed so inaccurately that I understand he is considering suing for defamation of character. His choruses and yearly opera performances are the equal of the violin program, and my brother speaks of him as an exemplary teacher. The film portrays Central Park East as a sinkhole and Roberta as a heroine who sweeps in and saves it. This is not true. She has an excellent program, but so does the other music teacher and so do the other teachers in the school. If the film chose to use the school's real name, then the film should also have portrayed the real nature of the school.
—Linda Esposito, Rome, New York

A. The notion of truth in films "based on real life" is filled with pitfalls. It is an ancient Hollywood tendency to skew every story toward the character played by the star, and to punch up the drama, fabricating scenes if necessary. When I see a film "based on a true story," I assume it will be about as fictional as most films. (The Coen brothers made a wry nod in this direction when their completely fictional *Fargo* began by claiming to be true.) Regarding *Music of the Heart*, articles by the AP and the *New York Times* have suggested that many of the facts are not as portrayed. The other music teacher, played by Josh Pais, is such a negative caricature that even while watching the film I had my doubts. I asked Miramax for a response to your letter, and was referred by a spokesperson to this disclaimer in the end titles: "While this picture is based upon a true story, certain characters' names have been changed, some main characters have been composited or invented, and a number of incidents fictionalized."

National Board of Review

Q. In a recent Answer Man column, you said you had never met anybody from the National Board of Review, that mysterious organization that's first with a list of the year's best movies. Did that item inspire any board members to contact you?
—Casey Anderson, Schaumberg, Illinois

A. No, but last weekend at the Telluride Film Festival, a woman stood in front of me and announced that (a) she existed, and (b) she was a director of the National Board of Review. Her name was Lois Ballon, and it was a relief to meet her because now I can tell Robert Stack to call off his Unsolved Mysteries investigation.

The Next Best Thing

Q. In *The Next Best Thing*, the plot hinges on the fact that characters played by Madonna and Rupert Everett sleep drunkenly with each other, and she gets pregnant. Where is the condom? These people have lost their best friend to AIDS, yet they have unprotected sex. I am stunned that Madonna and Everett would allow this transgression, and that not one critic has mentioned it.
—Robin Murray, San Francisco, California

A. An excellent point. On the other hand, there would be no movie if they had used a condom. (I know there is a plot secret involved here, but it doesn't affect this point.)

The Ninth Gate

Q. Did you notice the figure in the window of the castle during the final shot of *The Ninth Gate*, as Johnny Depp walks toward the light? I'm guessing the obvious—Satan.
—John Silver, Greensboro, North Carolina

A. Either that, or the hanging man in *The Wizard of Oz*, who later turned up, of course, as a ghost behind the curtains in *Three Men and a Baby*.

Omelets

Q. I had the pleasure last night of watching *Big Night* on video. Your review mentions the unbroken closing shot of Secondo preparing the omelet. I thought this was one of the most brilliant scenes I have come across. We don't know what happens after the Big Night but we know that Secondo will continue to take care of things and that Primo accepts his younger brother's caregiving. I would appreciate hearing any more thoughts that you may have on the scene. It has really taken hold of me.
—Chris Wilkinson, Toronto, Ontario

A. Godard said that every edit is a lie. Cooking that omelet in a montage would have been a TV commercial. Cooking it in one unbroken shot was a performance. Even audience members not consciously aware that there were no edits would understand in a deeper way that Secondo loved to cook.

On the Ropes

Q. I wanted to update you on the current status of Tyrene Manson, the main character of *On the Ropes*, which has just been nominated for an Oscar as Best Documentary. Tyrene was transferred from Beacon Correctional Facility during September 1999 with the understanding that she would only serve thirty days at the Bayview Correctional Facility in New York City. After she reached Bayview she was informed that she would not be eligible for parole until October of 2000. Evidently, some of the women at this facility ended up breaking their probation soon after leaving Bayview. Therefore, the rules changed at this facility for all incarcerated females. Tyrene is a dynamic, hardworking, intelligent, focused Christian woman who has endured many difficult and unfair situations. Although she has been an exemplary prisoner from the time she reached Albion Correctional Facility to the present, she is still incarcerated. Since the film was nominated for an Academy Award, Tyrene was asked to meet with the press in Los Angeles to discuss the film. She was not allowed to attend this press conference, nor is she allowed to have television interviews or to pursue her love of boxing.

—Diane Mellen, Park City, Utah

A. When we talked at this year's Sundance Film Festival, you told me that *On the Ropes* moved you so deeply you got involved in Manson's defense efforts. My hope is that the film's nomination will create even more outrage over the apparently unjust way in which she was tried and convicted. If Denzel Washington wins an Oscar as Best Actor for portraying Hurricane Carter, another black boxer who was framed into a prison sentence, I hope his acceptance speech ends with "Free Tyrene Manson!"

Oscarcast

Q. During the Oscar presentation for Best Live Action Short, my sister and I heard a man's voice speaking over the music and titles. During the first nominee, the voice said, "That's not it," then during the third, "Not it either," and finally, after the nominee, the voice said, "That's the one." Oddly enough, it was. We have no idea where the voice came from. Jude Law was presenting, but he shouldn't have known.

—Rebekah Askeland, Bolingbrook, Illinois

A. Ric Robertson, executive administrator of the Academy, replies: "Before Jude Law announced the name of the nominees, he said, 'One of the films has the most interesting title of the nominees this year.' As his copresenter said the title of the first nominee, he said, 'That's not it.' He kept saying that till the title of the last nominee came up, *My Mother Dreams the Satan's Disciples in New York,* and then he said, 'That's the one.' Coincidentally, that's the film that won the award."

Q. Why didn't they mention Stanley Kubrick in the Oscars segment remembering movie people who passed away last year?

—David Crucy, Yonkers, New York

A. Kubrick was included in last year's tribute. An actor they did forget this year, however, was DeForest Kelley, the beloved "Bones" of *Star Trek.*

Q. Why does everyone who mentions Warren Beatty's Thalberg award keep talking about Beatty being the only individual nominated for best picture, actor, director, and screenplay for the same film? I thought Orson Welles did this with *Citizen Kane,* and Woody Allen with *Annie Hall.* Are my record books wrong?

—Stephen Moulds, Nashville, Tennessee

A. Jack Nicholson got a little carried away in his introduction.

Q. It really angers me that Curly of the Three Stooges is often shown in those "We love the movies" film-clip-with-music segments shown at the Academy Awards, yet the Stooges were never even considered for a lifetime-achievement Oscar. Those insecure and pretentious Hollywood snots should remember what they actually enjoyed on film rather than accept whatever the self-named elitists tell them to like.

—Greg Brown, Chicago, Illinois

A. A posthumous honorary Oscar for the Three Stooges would unleash a standing ovation the likes of which has never been witnessed in Academy history. But it will never happen.

Q. What in heaven's name can be done to bring the Oscars in at under four hours, and make the show less of a snore-fest?

—Greg Nelson, Chicago, Illinois

A. Your question languished in my in-box for weeks, because I was helpless to answer it. Nothing can be done, I would have said, and eventually the Oscarcast will run all night, like a talk show. But then the mail from London brought the *Spectator,* and in it I found a brilliant suggestion by Mark Steyn, the magazine's film critic: *Why not forbid winners to thank anyone?* He asks: "Why can't the Academy, just tell these butt-numbing yawn-mongers that all the people they want to thank will be listed on the official Website but that they will have to use their 45 seconds on TV to say something else?" This is an inspired idea. Among its other virtues, it would provide a test of whether the winners *have* forty-five seconds' worth of anything to say.

The Patriot

Q. Just saw *The Patriot* with a packed house. There were young children in the audience. I find that unbelievably annoying, and I wonder what in hell the parents are thinking? I guess they're not.
—Jeff Joseph, Lancaster, California

A. The movie, rated R, had an extended scene in which Mel Gibson's young sons ambush and kill British soldiers and one of them shouts, "I'm glad I killed them!" Of course the R rating is hardly observed by theaters with a movie like this, and is useful only so the MPAA can say they told us so after stunned parents stagger out with shell-shocked kids.

The Perfect Storm

Q. My wife and I recently saw *The Perfect Storm*. While we both enjoyed the movie, my wife wondered how the writers of the movie (and the author of the book) knew what happened to the crew of the boat. I mean, how did they know that the ice machine broke (among other things)? I know this is not a documentary, but I couldn't help wondering.
—Doug Crooks, San Diego, California

A. Beyond a certain point, they didn't know, and used conjecture, hypothesis, logic, and the experience of other fishing crews.

Playing Jesus

Q. I've heard rumors that Robert Powell, the incredibly dead-on actor who portrayed Jesus in Franco Zeffirelli's *Jesus of Nazareth*, was so influenced by the part of Christ that it affected him for years. In fact, some have suggested that he virtually dropped out of films and then out of sight, being so moved by the role and its influences. Whatever happened to Powell?
—James Merolla, Barrington, Rhode Island

A. The Internet Movie Database lists twenty-four credits for Powell since he played Jesus in 1977. One of his roles: Dr. Victor Frankenstein.

Popcorn

Q. There was a big stink a couple of years ago about killer popcorn in the nation's theaters. Apparently one bag had more saturated fat than a zillion Quarter Pounders. Then there was publicity about how theaters were switching to healthier recipes. Is the popcorn now safe to eat?
—Susan Lake, Urbana, Illinois

A. There has been much backsliding at the popcorn counter. Michael Jacobson of the Center for Science in the Public Interest tells me: "It's turning out that the trans fat in the hydrogenated shortening in which many theaters pop their popcorn is extremely conducive to heart disease—probably substantially worse than butter." The original CSPI study showed that a large bag of theater popcorn contains eighty grams of fat, fifty-three of them saturated. That's for popcorn without *any* topping. On the McDonald's scale, it works out to six Big Macs. Unless a theater advertises that it uses a healthy oil like canola, I think it's prudent to avoid popcorn unless you don't care how the movie ends.

Princess Mononoke

Q. You wrote from the Telluride festival that *Princess Mononoke* deserves an Oscar nomination as one of the best films of the year. Does an animated film seriously have a chance?
—Pet Danforth, Oak Park, Illinois

A. Animation, yes (*Beauty and the Beast* was nominated in 1991). But *Princess Mononoke*, no. Cynthia Swartz of Miramax tells me: "Unfortunately, in one of those silly Academy twists, it is not eligible for anything because it was the Japanese entry in the foreign language category two years ago."

Q. Thanks for your enthusiasm over *Princess Mononoke*. I recently defended Japanese animation in my film class, but was shot down viciously by the teacher and others who claimed anime was only "targeted at horny twelve-year-old boys." The teacher seemed convinced that the only Japanese cartoon out there was something he called *Rape Man,* which, apparently, "everyone over there loves." No one wanted to hear a word I said.

—Sean Molloy, Rochester, New York

A. Your teacher would not be able to make such statements if he had the slightest knowledge about anime. I have never heard of *Rape Man,* and could not find it listed in the Internet Movie Database. How remarkable it is the only title that has captured his attention. Show him *Grave of the Fireflies* and ask him what he thinks.

Q. What's your opinion on taking children to see *Princess Mononoke*? I have three boys, the youngest just eleven. He is mature for his age and has seen a fair number of movies with violence in them. (The scene of Luke Skywalker getting his hand cut off comes to mind.) He has never had nightmares from anything he has seen and I am sure he would enjoy the story line of *Princess Mononoke* immensely. I get so desperate trying to find good movies to take him to that I am pretty sure it would be worth the risk to take him to this one but I wanted to hear what you have to say.

—David Fallon, Cleveland, Ohio

A. *Mononoke* would be okay for an eleven-year-old. It is not excessively gory or gruesome—not a horror or violence film— just intense adventure. The story may be too complicated for smaller kids.

Product Placement

Q. What's up with all the bright yellow Kodak bags in *Galaxy Quest*? They are quite prominent in the convention scenes. I'm sure it was product placement but it looked so odd it was funny. Does anyone need that much film?

—Corrina Frigon, Solvay, New York

A. Hint to product placers: Products look more convincing when they are being used, not being held up to the camera.

Quick Cutting

Q. I want to recommend *The Rise of the Image the Fall of the Word* by Mitchell

Stephens. The book deals with the new editing style of "quick cutting"—the extremely rapid change from one shot to another with very little time spent on any one shot. This style is becoming common in action movies (*Armageddon, Gone in 60 Seconds, Shaft)* but not in *Mission: Impossible 2.* My wife and I have found that this technique separates us from what we are seeing on the screen and prevents us from becoming involved. It makes the suspension of disbelief difficult or impossible. Much as I have always hated the French style of lingering over a scene long after it should end, it is preferable to quick-cut sequences that leave me totally unsatisfied. *Shaft* left us devoid of any feeling other than boredom.

—Professor Richard J. Gaylord,
University of Illinois, Urbana, Illinois

A. Quick-cutting is often associated with an action film that either has no real story or no confidence in it. The relative failure of *Gone in 60 Seconds* indicates some moviegoers may be getting fed up. There is little time for involved dialogue, and thus for characterization; the heroes of the movies are more like action figures than traditional movie characters. Sometimes quick-cutting works as part of an overall strategy (as in Oliver Stone's *Natural Born Killers*) but more often it is an attempt to supply with style what is missing in content.

Quotes

Q. You made it clear that you didn't think *Austin Powers: The Spy Who Shagged Me* was very good, but I saw a commercial for the movie recently where they were rattling off positive quotes, and I was shocked to see that you were quoted as saying "Big laughs!" I assume that you did say this, but it was clearly taken out of context. Don't you think that it is a little unethical?

—Chad M. Roberts, Seattle, Washington

A. A little, but I did say it, and so they're playing by the rules. And hey, *Austin Powers* does have some monster laughs. (Let's see how long that takes to get into print!)

Q. Do you get miffed when you see a phrase from one of your reviews get misused by studios? I keep seeing and hearing ads that say: "Roger Ebert says *Rules of Engagement* works splendidly . . ." But they leave out the obvious sarcasm that followed.

—Robert F. Burnier, Chicago, Illinois

A. Here is the complete sentence: *Rules of Engagement* works splendidly as a courtroom thriller about military values, as long as you don't expect it to seriously consider those values."

The Red Violin

Q. I loved *The Red Violin,* but was left with one thing that bugged me. Isn't Morritz, the character played by Samuel L. Jackson, short a violin at the end? He replaced the real one with the copy that he had borrowed. What is he going to give that collector or museum back as a replacement?

—Marian Moore, Harvey, Louisiana

A. Beth English, publicity director for Lions Gate Films, replies, "Morritz is not short a violin at the end of the film. He replaced the real one with a copy that he had not borrowed, as you suggest in your question, but purchased from a private collector in London. This copy of a Bussotti violin was made at about the same time as the Red Violin."

Remakes

Q. Just heard that Mike Nichols is planning to do a remake of *Kind Hearts and Coronets,* starring Robin Williams and Will Smith. Nichols is quoted as saying he plans to "change the main theme from class struggle to race relations, and change the ending." How, then, is this a remake?

—Ken Bearden, Wyandotte, Michigan

A. I am reminded of Jack L. Warner's decision to make a film on the Lindbergh kidnapping: "Only we have to change the name, of course. And it can't be about kidnapping, because that's against the Production Code. Also, the kid's father shouldn't fly."

Rings on Their Fingers

Q. I have noticed many actors and actresses wearing bands or diamond rings on the fourth finger of their right hands while portraying single characters. Is this meant to acknowl-

edge real-life marriages and engagements or just a sign that they love jewelry? This phenomenon puzzles me to no end.

—Anne Naismith, Baltimore, Maryland

A. I referred your question to the director Allison Anders, whose *Sugar Town* is a movie about Hollywood actors and musicians. She says it's just a fashion choice and doesn't symbolize anything. She added a postscript about a married TV personality she once had an affair with, who sometimes did not wear his wedding ring on TV, but I don't think that applies to your question.

Romance

Q. I realize the art vs. pornography debate has been going on since the beginning of time, but doesn't the new French film *Romance* cross some kind of line? I mean, if the lead actress is actually having sex with the male actors, and one of them is an established porn star, isn't *Romance* a porn film?

—Cindy L. Cup Choy, Honolulu, Hawaii

A. Sex is an activity. Pornography is an attitude toward that activity. *Romance* does not have that attitude.

Rosebud

Q. In a literature course that I am taking we recently read an excerpt from a thirteenth-century French allegorical poem called "Romance of the Rose." In it, the character suffers many heartaches for the love of a rosebud. I was wondering if you knew whether or not this inspired the "rosebud" in *Citizen Kane.*

—John Kinard, Columbia, South Carolina

A. Apparently not. The screenplay was cowritten by Welles and Herman J. Mankiewicz, and was inspired in part by Mankiewicz's experiences as a regular guest at William Randolph Hearst's legendary castle, San Simeon. He was friendly with Hearst's mistress, Marion Davies, and Hollywood lore has long held that from her he learned that "rosebud" was Hearst's pet name for that most precious region of her anatomy.

Rumpy-Pumpy

Q. I saw *The Thomas Crown Affair* and decided to check your review. After reading it, I have only one question: "Rumpy-pumpy?"
—Tom Ballew, Kansas City, Missouri

A. A splendid expression, which you will find in the *New Shorter Oxford English Dictionary,* listed as being of mid-twentieth-century origin. I first encountered it in *A Clockwork Orange.* I have no idea what it means.

Running Times

Q. Why is it that whenever a film tops the two- or three-hour mark, critics and the public can't handle it? Personally, when I am watching a picture that is fresh and alive, with characters that command my attention and interest, it seems natural for me to *want* to see more, not less. From my work in retail at a video store, I have observed that people would rather rent two bad two-hour films rather than watch a good three-hour picture. What's the deal here?
—Paul West, Seattle, Washington

A. My rule: No good movie is too long. No bad movie is short enough. Since theaters don't increase ticket prices for longer movies, I think of them as the cinematic equivalent of the shampoo bottles with "30 percent more!"

Q. I recently read in the new *Guinness Book of Records* about the longest movie ever, the eight-five-hour *Cure for Insomnia.* It sounded very strange—a 40,080-page poem, sex scenes, and rock bands. Have you heard of it or seen it? Where can it be found?
—Jamie Matwin, Thunder Bay, Ontario

A. Harry Knowles of the Ain't it Cool Web Site is an expert on cult films. He replies: "The only thing I could get out of all my sources for this rare-as-can-be film is that 'I once heard that someone in Indiana had the only known 35mm print.' Another said with absolute certainty, 'it has never been available on video, laser disc, or DVD.' To which I replied, 'duh!'"

If the film ever surfaces, it sounds like a candidate for Knowles's famous all-night Butt-numb-a-thons.

Scary Movie

Q. I would like to know why your review of the movie *Scary Movie* didn't warn parents that there was going to be so much sexuality in the movie. I went to see this movie based on your review. Not once did you mention the fact that it was not appropriate for children. This movie should have been rated NC-17.
—Collette Taylor, Chicago, Illinois

A. And might have been, if the NC-17 rating were workable, which it is not, as I have been tirelessly informing the MPAA for years. My review did carry the following warning in the credits information: "Classified R (for strong, crude sexual humor, language, drug use, and violence)."

Q. Last night I saw *Scary Movie.* As a fan of gross-out comedy, I thought the movie to be above par. However, as I sat in the theater I couldn't help but notice how many children were in the theater. Not teenagers, but children twelve and under. This is how little the R rating really means. Because this movie looked like a funny horror movie, these parents had completely ignored the R, thinking it would be on the same level as *Scream*'s R. It clearly wasn't and as an avid moviegoer, I was truly embarrassed for the six-year-old girl in front of me who, judging by her reaction, had never seen a male up close and personal. How do we protect against this?
—Jennifer Cordero, Memphis, Tennessee

A. By establishing a workable A rating for films that are not pornographic but are intended for adults and not suitable for children. The MPAA and its masters, the theater owners, oppose this rating because it might cost them ticket sales.

Scorsese

Q. Martin Scorsese is regarded as one of the great directors of our time. He was ranked as the fifth best director in the AFI's list of greatest directors. However, Scorsese has not been able to win a Best Director Oscar. Do you believe that he should have been awarded for *GoodFellas* and do you believe that he still has a chance of gaining this award in the next few years?
—Matthew Pippia, Bundaberg, Queensland

A. Yes, he should have won for *GoodFellas*—and for *Raging Bull* and *Taxi Driver* too. Some say the California-centric Academy has a prejudice against New York–based directors. Another theory is that the Academy is seized by a fit of public-spirited humbuggery at Oscar time and likes to reward more uplifting films.

Short Actors

Q. My father, who is six-foot-four, insists that today's movies are populated by dwarves. The sight of Tom Cruise or Dustin Hoffman sets him into apoplexy. He says—I'm not exaggerating—that tall actors are discriminated against because of some sort of Hollywood conspiracy. I try to tell him that there are plenty of tall actors and that the proportion of tall, short, and average height is probably no different among movie stars than in the rest of the country. He tells me I'm not paying attention.

—Mike Holtzclaw, *Daily Press*, Newport News, Virginia

A. You are basically correct; actors come in many shapes and sizes. Close-ups are a great equalizing device (consider what an amazing impact Danny DeVito has in anything he does). Actresses who are taller than average (Sigourney Weaver, Saffron Burrows) sometimes have trouble getting cast opposite insecure stars, but it says something for Tom Cruise (who is not short but of average height) that he loves to work with his taller wife. Here's a theory to try out on your dad: Stars of both sexes tend to have larger heads, in relationship to body size, than the average person. That allows them to dominate in closer shots.

The Sixth Sense

Q. After seeing *The Sixth Sense*, my friends and I had a question. Donnie Wahlberg's character, Vincent, has a birthmark (white spot) in his hair, right behind his right ear, and so did Haley Joel Osment's character, Cole. Is there are any relation to be made here?

—Derek Jennings, Raleigh, North Carolina

A. Jose Rodriguez, assistant to director N. Night Shyamalan, says: "During research for the story, the director found that people who experience extreme trauma sometimes lost pigment in their hair. The relation between Cole and Vincent is that they both experienced extreme trauma and lost pigment in their hair."

Q. In your review of *The Sixth Sense*, you say that the ending "doesn't cheat." However, you criticized *Arlington Road* for its surprise conclusion, saying the ending is "so implausible that we stop caring and scratch our heads". Do you find that a logical analysis of *The Sixth Sense* proves its ending more plausible than that of *Arlington Road*?

—Ron Porto, Palisades Park, New Jersey

A. Sure, the ending of *The Sixth Sense* is a stretcher—but perfectly logical within the terms of the story. If the film had ended with everything depending on the exact timing and outcome of a high-speed traffic accident, then *that* would have been implausible.

Q. Did you know that Bruce Willis is playing a Jewish psychiatrist in *The Sixth Sense*? In fact, he is a dybbuk. When I found out the kid was seeing ghosts I remembered learning about dybbuks from my grandparents. I went back a second time to see if there were any inconsistencies with the dybbuk theory, and didn't see any. I went back a third time just to watch the phenomenal performance of the kid. I hope he gets an Oscar for it.

—Richard J. Gaylord, University of Illinois, Urbana, Illinois

A. Director N. Night Shyamalan prefers not to comment because the answer might give away the secret of the film. As for the young actor, Haley Joel Osment, he is inspired in a difficult and complex performance, and may get a supporting nod. I hope the Academy doesn't overlook Bruce Willis, however, who is not only strong in the lead, but no doubt contributed to Osment's work. As Robert Mitchum observed after working with the two children in *Night of the Hunter*, adult actors are sometimes as involved in the direction of children in movies as the director is.

Sleepy Hollow

Q. In your review of *Sleepy Hollow*, you refused to reveal the actor who plays the Hessian Horseman, but the billboards for the film boldly display the unmistakable (name deleted) alongside Johnny Depp. Do you think knowing too much about a movie ruins the film for the audience? I recently saw *Being John Malkovich*, having read the script on the Internet, and I was pleasantly surprised that the ending was different in the film. I am going to try harder to allow a film to work its magic on me without me being tainted by too much information.
—Raul Borja, Los Angeles, California

A. Tim Burton, the director, obviously thought it should be a small delight for the audience when it finally sees the Headless One's head. But the posters, TV ads, and preview trailers all make his identity pretty obvious. Why are such spoilers so frequent? Because advertising and marketing people focus on their own job, which is to sell tickets, and will gladly give away the surprises, the ending, or the whole store to lure more people into the theater.

Q. In *Sleepy Hollow*, we see the manic Hessian's sharpened teeth and are told why he has them. Later, when we see his skull, it sports a normal and near-perfect set of choppers. The sharpened dentures don't come back until the H.H. is totally refleshed. Is this a glaring continuity error in a film that otherwise devoted lavish attention to almost every detail?
—James Fineran, Salisbury, Maryland

A. Yes. Unless . . . (creepy music) . . . that was not really the Horseman's skull . . .

Song of the South

Q. One of your colleagues on a recent TV show suggested that the Disney film *Song of the South* be rereleased on home video, based on its artistic value. When you accurately pointed out the racist elements of the work, he suggested that the film would foster useful discussions about intolerance. In his view, the hateful elements in *Song of the South* were not worth keeping it off the video shelves.

As a black man and father I must say that no movie, no matter how groundbreaking, that contains the poisonous symbols of hatred should be encouraged for widespread distribution. If one wants to study those film innovations, let it be done in film school. If you are black in America, and you attempt to find films that depict the spectrum of black culture, you are hard-pressed. If you are looking for something positive you end up with an even shorter list. I cannot easily explain away racism to my six-year-old son. Is your colleague going to be available to undo the damage that would be done to my kid by images contained in *Song of the South*? How about damage control for a world of kids? Believe me, there are enough racist movies available at video stores already. We don't need any more.
—Truth Thomas

A. I am against censorship and believe that no films or books should be burned or banned, but film school study is one thing and a general release is another. Any new Disney film immediately becomes part of the consciousness of almost every child in America, and I would not want to be a black child going to school in the weeks after *Song of the South* was first seen by my classmates. Peter Schneider, chairman of the Disney Studios, tells me that the studio has decided to continue to hold the film out of release.

South Park

Q. In remarks made recently on TV, you seemed to be changing your mind about *South Park*. Yes or no?
—Emerson Thorne, Chicago, Illinois

A. I gave *South Park* a marginal thumbs down (2.5 stars) because of what I called the movie's mean spirit, but I did like its intelligence and energy, and as the smoke clears from the summer of 1999 it's clear to me that this was a movie that took chances and made scathing criticisms of the broken-down MPAA rating system. I got carried away by my immediate reaction, but at least I was right when I called it "the most slashing political commentary of the year."

Q. I understand the writers of the Oscar-nominated Best Song "Blame Canada," Trey

Parker and Marc Shaimin, have rejected a request that they tone down the song's lyrics for the Oscarcast. An impasse?

—Ronnie Barzell, Los Angeles, California

A. Sort of. They said the song was nominated as written, and should be performed as written—and the Academy can simply bleep the offensive words if it doesn't like them. The whole dustup dramatizes the gulf between common usage and media standards; one of the words in the song, referring to bodily vapors, is in common use in grade school but cannot be mentioned on the Oscarcast.

Q. Here's an idea for the Oscar show presentation of "Blame Canada" that I only hope the Zanucks will attempt to realize. It could be the best "song" number since Isaac Hayes performed "Shaft!" It should begin with a solo by Anne Murray, who is joined, as the song builds, by other Canadian warblers, one by one: Bryan Adams, Celine Dion, Gordon Lightfoot, and so on, until it reaches a Canadian crescendo.

—Jim Emerson, Seattle, Washington

A. A brilliant idea. Alas, *Entertainment Weekly* reports that Anne Murray can't appear as she has a golf tournament that day. And we all know that a golf tournament is way more important and lots more fun than the Oscars. Here's my backup plan: John McDermott, the Irish Canadian tenor from Toronto, should recruit his Three Irish Tenors stablemates and give the song the performance it deserves.

Star Wars Episode I: The Phantom Menace

Q. How do you feel about the attacks on *The Phantom Menace*, which insinuate that George Lucas is racist in his depiction of the alien characters, who are said to mimic ethnic stereotypes? I feel this notion is ridiculous.

—Tommy Sigmon, Chicago, Illinois

A. Any movie of blockbuster proportions lures part-time critics out of the woodwork, to practice their punditry where it is not always appropriate. *Phantom Menace* is a visually superb extravaganza aimed at about a twelve-year-old IQ. Jar-Jar Binks is a goofy

and likable alien with some amusing moves; the actor and dancer Ahmed Best brings offbeat originality to the body language. That's it. People who think the character is racist are barking up the wrong stereotype. I get so tired of the PC police.

Here's another insight, from reader Steven Bailey, of Jacksonville Beach, Florida: "I don't know why everyone's so down on Jar Jar; I found him pretty amusing myself. I thought the scene where Jar Jar dodges the blue globes was a direct homage to Buster Keaton's famous boulder-dodging scene in *Seven Chances*, and I thought it was just as funny. Nobody else in America has even mentioned this."

Q. Regarding the "pink zone" that the laser-sword fencers pass through in *Phantom Menace*, you quote George Lucas as saying, "That's one of those areas I'll probably fix in the Special Edition." What? Has Lucasfilm become the Microsoft of moviemaking—releasing an inadequately quality-controlled product, and planning to fix the bugs later? Lucas's explanation doesn't answer your reader's question: What *is* that pink zone? Yes, it's a set of force fields designed to separate and delay the people running through it. But why would anyone build such a thing? Is Naboo some kind of puzzle-crazed society where the engineers drop huge, elaborate, clever, energy-wasting contraptions in the middle of utility catwalks, just for fun? I suspect that when the hard-core *Star Wars* fans analyze this film frame by frame, they'll look at the wall switch that Darth Maul hits to activate the pink zone, see a label written in the *Star Wars* alphabet, get out their secret *Star Wars* code books, and decipher its real name: "Plot Device."

—Chris Rowland, Plainsboro, New Jersey

A. Reminds me that the pipes labeled GNDN in the *Star Trek* movies stand for "Goes Nowhere, Does Nothing." My guess is that the pink zone was a bright idea that didn't pay off, and Lucas is frank enough to admit it.

Q. Like some of the people who recently differed with you, I originally believed the *Star Wars* saga was set in the past ("A long time ago . . ."). But now I'm certain it's set in the future, for one reason: Jar Jar Binks uses the phrase "Exsqueeze me?"—a phrase coined in 1992 by Mike Myers in *Wayne's World.* Watch for "I'm not worthy" when Jar Jar appears in Episode Two. Not!

—Ryan Hopak, Hollywood, California

A. Even more proof *Star Wars* is set in the future: Don't they use the word "hello"? It wasn't coined until the invention of the telephone.

Stigmata

Q. *Stigmata* is not as silly as you say. My friends and I left the theater having experienced a dazzling and powerful film. You talked about demonic possession. The spirit (not the demon) that possessed Frankie was a Catholic priest angry at the church because it would not publish what he believed to be the gospel Jesus himself wrote. We don't have a demon who wants to ravage the world and kill people, as silly horror movies portray. We have a priest who wants to be heard, and his only way to get this word out to the world is through possessing the atheist, Frankie. Nor does *Stigmata* imply that the stigmata itself comes through the rosary. It comes due to the possession by the spirit of Father Almeida. At the end of your review you talk about Catholics and the outrage that this film has caused. A Catholic friend watched it with us and thought it was incredible. He even agreed with the corruption of the Catholic Church that was illustrated in the film.

—Nathan Miller, Castleton, Vermont

A. You assume that the opinion of a Catholic friend who went to the movie with you is naturally more valid than that of any church spokesman. Churches don't work that way. But you make some interesting points. Here's my take. Father Almeida has the stigmata, meaning he is filled with the spirit of Jesus. His rosary is mailed to America, Frankie touches it, and afterwards exhibits the stigmata, which has apparently been transmitted through the rosary. She is therefore not filled with Almeida's spirit, but Christ's. Impossible, since one must have deep faith to exhibit the stigmata. It's not a secondary symptom of possession by a third party. If it were only Almeida possessing her,

there should be no stigmata. If the deep masculine voice is Almeida's, then Christ is Almeida's spokesman, which has things the wrong way around; that's like preferring the opinion of your friend to that of the church.

The Straight Story

Q. Did you note that Chris Farley's actual brothers played the twins in *The Straight Story?*

—Tom Kennedy, Denver, Colorado

A. John and Kevin Farley played Thorvald and Rat, the twins who wrangle over repairs to the old man's John Deere tractor. Their performances do remind me of Chris Farley's gift for characters who were cheerful despite internal tension.

In my review I mentioned another performance: "Look and listen to the actor who plays the bartender . . . the one who serves the Miller Lite. I can't find his name in the credits, but he finds the right note: He knows how all good bartenders can seem like a friend bringing a present to a sickroom." Pat Wier of Chicago writes that the actor is her next-door neighbor Russell Reed, who also does the voice for one of the Keebler elves.

Strange but True

Q. While I was picking out a video last night, two guys came in with a case of beer each (no Canadian jokes please). They were looking through the Action section. For some reason, *Dead Man Walking* was filed under Action.

Guy 1: What about this one?

Guy 2: Nope. Saw it. There's nothing but acting in it.

—Mike Spearns, St. John's, Newfoundland

A. If you see Guy 2 again, tell him I thought his criticism was perceptive and accurate.

Such a Long Journey

Q. I haven't seen the movie *Such a Long Journey,* but I believe that Gustad's son Sohrab gets an admission call from the Indian Institute of Technology, not the Illinois Institute of Technology as you say in your review. This is important to the plot because the Indian Institute of Technology is the premier institute for engineering in India, and it is almost every Indian parent's dream that their child is accepted at IIT. Being an Indian and having gone through that stage myself, I can understand how Gustad must have felt.

—Swaminathan Anantha, Chicago, Illinois

A. You are quite right. I heard "IIT" and as a Chicago chauvinist assumed "Illinois Institute of Technology."

Talking in Movies

Q. We just returned from attempting to watch the film *Double Jeopardy*. I say attempting because there was a person behind us who talked in a regular voice throughout the entire film. After about an hour of this my girlfriend told the person to shut up. The other person shouted, "I can talk as much as I want!" As I was involved in the film and didn't want the movie totally ruined, I said, "Stop it. Don't be an ass," or words to that effect. Ten minutes later we were both escorted out by the police, charged with disorderly conduct, and told we were banned from the theater for sixty days. The other person told the police we used obscene language in her presence, which we didn't. It is an interesting point as the movie was liberally laced with the f-word. I am in my middle fifties and not given to scream obscenities at people in a movie theater.

—Hal G. Scheie, LaCrosse, Wisconsin

A. People who talk during movies may have rabies and should be approached cautiously. Since the link between their eyes and tongue bypasses the brain, it is effective to simply stand up, blocking their view of the screen. Deprived of inspiration for their running commentary, they fall silent or revert to soft animal snuffling noises as they root in their popcorn.

Tarzan

Q. I just saw *Tarzan* and loved the movie. My question is: Were my eyes deceiving me, or did Mrs. Potts and Chip from *The Little Mermaid* make cameo, albeit nonspeaking, appearances during the *Trashin' the Camp* scenes? Of course many teapots and teacups

(with chips) look alike so it may be my mind creating a link that is simply not there.

—Jim Tsai, Philadelphia, Pennsylvania

A. Thomas Schumacher, president of Walt Disney Feature Animation and Theatrical Production, replies: "Yes indeed, good catch. That was in fact Mrs. Potts. Her cameo seemed a fitting tribute and you'll be comforted to know she is one of the few items not 'trashed' in that sequence."

Teaching Mrs. Tingle

Q. Kevin Williamson's *Dawson's Creek* has a teacher in the show named *Mrs. Tingle*. As you know, Williamson also has a film coming out titled, *Teaching Mrs. Tingle*. What is his fascination with this name? Is this a reference to a real teacher that Kevin disliked when he was in high school?

—Chris Regina, Princeton, New Jersey

A. That's a pretty good guess. Williamson told Howard Rosenberg in a Movieline interview about a high school English teacher he called "Mrs. Tingle," who cut him off in the middle of a short-story reading in front of her class: "She then proceeded to predict that he'd never amount to anything as a writer, and ordered him to go sit down because he had a voice that shouldn't be heard."

I wonder if Mrs. Tingle has seen the movies Williamson has written, *Scream* and *I Know What You Did Last Summer*. No, on second thought, I don't.

Technicalities

Q. Why doesn't Hollywood realize that the view through binoculars is not two circles fused together, but just one circular field of view?

—John Koenig, Waconia, Minnesota

A. Hollywood knows that, but the convention of two linked circles provides convenient visual shorthand. One circle on the screen would be confused with an iris shot, and be more distracting than the traditional approach, which has grown comfortable.

Q. Your observation that exhibitors in 1940 refused to install Walt Disney's Fantasound system for *Fantasia* is probably accurate, but the "real" reason it was never heard outside of New York was that the government forbade RCA to manufacture Fantasound, because of the probability of retooling the company for war technology in the near future (according to Marc Eliot in *Walt Disney: Hollywood's Dark Prince*). Of course, exhibitors once again rejected stereo sound as part of the CinemaScope process a decade later, giving us a clue as to how esoteric stereo must have seemed, so no doubt they were also a big obstacle in 1940.

—Robert Armstrong, Chicago, Illinois

A. I have a certain sympathy with the exhibitors. The disaster movie *Earthquake* featured something named "Sensurround Sound," which essentially consisted of subwoofers the size of refrigerator cartons, cranked up as high as they would go. When the system was unveiled at the late United Artists theater in Chicago, chunks of plaster started falling from the ceiling.

Q. In both *Dumb and Dumber* and *There's Something About Mary*, the Farrelly brothers have used the name Mary as the main female character. Seeing that they have only made three major movies, and "Mary" is in two, is this a coincidence, or do they really like someone named Mary?

—Jack O'Brien, Rocky Hill, Connecticut

A. Peter Farrelly tells me: "No. Our mother is named Marion, but that's not the same." So it's just one of those strange unsolved mysteries.

Q. I was watching *Inside the Actor's Studio* on TV the other day and heard Billy Crystal talk about how some actors have a "tip" or a "catch" that they use in each of their movies (Tom Cruise's wide smile, Keanu Reeve's annoying "whoa!"). What is your favorite "catch" used by a star? One of mine would be Samuel L. Jackson's expression when he is really mad. The same in every movie, but always effective.

—Mikhel Burgland, Fort Wayne, Indiana

A. I like the way William H. Macy frowns earnestly as if he really, really wants to understand, but you're not making it easy for him.

Q. In the movie *To Have and Have Not*, why does Lauren Bacall's character call Humphry Bogart "Steve" when his character's name is Harry Morgan?

—Tsuneaki Miyazawa, Ajax, New York

A. According to Tim Dirks (whose Website, www.filmsite.org, is a trove of information about classic movies), Bogart and Bacall call each other "Slim" and "Steve," which in real life were the pet names of the director, Howard Hawks, and his own wife.

Q. What is it with Tom Hanks going to the bathroom in so many of his films? In *A League of Their Own*, an early scene shows Hanks's character with a hangover, relieving himself in the former men's locker room, currently occupied by the girl's baseball team. In *Forrest Gump* he tells JFK that he has to pee. And in *The Green Mile*, the first hour of the movie is all about his character's urinary tract problems. One of the trademarks of Stanley Kubrick films is that all of his movies had at least one scene set in a bathroom. It's a shame he never directed Tom Hanks, because one can only imagine what they could have accomplished together.

—Arthur Allen, Kent, Washington

A. There is still time for Hanks to work with John Landis, who includes the dialogue "See you next Wednesday" in every one of his films, after first hearing it in Kubrick's *2001*. One can imagine the line being used, for example, just before the long-suffering Hanks disappears into the bathroom.

Q. I just saw *Eyes Wide Shut* on video. Kubrick is my favorite filmmaker but I won't bore you with my enthusiastic adoration of this masterpiece. What puzzled me was an exterior dolly shot in which the main character is walking down the street, and he passes a jewelry shop. And on the awning of this shop is the name of the jeweler—and their phone number with the "555" prefix that always spoils my suspension of disbelief. Since the phone number has no significance to the story whatsoever, I find it incredible that someone would go to the effort of building a fake awning and putting a phone number on it that screams out, "This is just a movie!"

—Steven Dahlman, Minneapolis, Minnesota

A. Like many moviegoers, you know that there is no "555" prefix and so movies employ it to avoid using a real number. Kubrick was known for his sly sense of humor, and my best guess is that he did it simply to amuse himself.

Theology

Q. I was just wondering why the devil and vampires are only always battled by Catholics? Where are the movies about Lutheran pastors vs. the devil? Or a Baptist destroying vampires by blessing an entire river? I mean, sure, Catholics have cool rituals and provide romantic tension with that whole celibacy thing, but the Greek Orthodox have cool rituals as well. I want to see a rabbi face the devil. I want Buddhist monks and Mormons. I am sick of only Catholics getting to kick Satanic butt for the Lord.

—Cort Jensen, Missoula, Montana

A. I referred your question to my friend Father Andrew Greeley, who is not only a priest but the author of many best-selling novels that are about conflict with evil. He replies: "Because of its sacramental imagination, which sees goodness and evil lurking everywhere, Catholicism often seems a more mysterious religion and hence one more open to wonder and surprise and perhaps horror. Or to put it another way, where there are vigil lights anything can happen."

The Third Miracle

Q. Given that Ed Harris spends much of *The Third Miracle* looking for the titular third miracle, a remarkable feat that would guarantee Helen O'Regan sainthood, I find it extraordinary that he overlooks what seems to me to be her most amazing accomplishment: Having herself videotaped at a first-communion party in 1970, long before the advent of camcorders.

—Tim Carvell, Los Angeles, California

A. Miraculous doesn't begin to describe this.

The Thomas Crown Affair

Q. In *The Thomas Crown Affair*, Brosnan and Russo are having dinner and he refers to her hometown of Lima, Ohio. He pronounces

it "Leema." She does not correct him by telling him it's pronounced "Liema." I thought this might be part of the plot—that he was testing her and that this would be proof that she was someone other than who she said she was. Finally I realized it was just a gaffe. Aren't there dialogue coaches in movies anymore that catch these things?

—Teresa Ash, Rock Island, Illinois

A. Maybe they were focusing on the pronunciation of "Monet."

3-D

Q. Why hasn't the 3-D concept taken off and become acceptable? Theme parks have been using 3-D images for years to great effect. Why have films relegated 3-D to cheesy schlock? When we go to the movies we demand realistic surround sound, but when it comes to the picture we refuse to let it be anything but 2-D!

—Micah Haddad, Memphis, Tennessee

A. The 3-D effect at IMAX and Omnimax theaters is impressive, using expensive custom glasses. But 3-D as it has been presented in ordinary theatrical films has always looked crappy; it's not more realistic but less—a distraction.

Three Kings

Q. I have heard that at least one special effect in *Three Kings* was filmed by inflicting damage to a cadaver. Is this so? Were arrangements made with the deceased prior to death, along the lines of donating one's body to science? What do you think are the ethical considerations here? I'd love to see the movie, but I feel this is going too far.

—Patrick Logan, Portland, Oregon

A. You are referring to shots that seem to take place inside human bodies. Director David O. Russell tells me he jokingly told an interviewer that he used real corpses for those shots. Not true. "It was a prosthesis," he said. "Was it too hard to control the lighting inside a real corpse?" I asked. "Yeah."

Q. Went to *Three Kings*, which I liked, but I found the audience response at one point disturbing. A cow accidentally stepped on a land mine. The audience broke out in uproarious laughter, the loudest of the whole show. To my mind the director didn't play this scene for humor. I suddenly felt I was in an auditorium full of vicious cretins. But then, it's Colorado. Do you have a take on this?

—Timothy E. Klay, Boulder, Colorado

A. Not a real cow. After seeing hundreds of cows playing every imaginable role on the boulevards of Chicago all summer as part of our wonderful Cow Art project, the exploding cow seemed like just another show-off.

Q. On the *Howard Stern* show you said *Three Kings* uses the cliché of a truck explosion being shown from several different angles. Actually, it was quite the opposite. The truck set off a mine that flipped it into the air, then hit the ground—and landed on another mine! This is why the truck blasted *back* into the air.

—Tim Tori, Glendale, California

A. You are correct. Apologies to director David O. Russell, who told me he deliberately planned the scene to avoid the cliché.

Q. Your review of *Three Kings* incorrectly identified George Clooney's character as a "sgt. major" (which is a noncommissioned officer). He was actually a "major" (a commissioned officer). This is important as it is the officer, who is supposed to know better, that leads the group of NCOs into harm's way.

—Aaron Lipple, Allen , Texas

A. Much confusion here. The movie's press kit names Clooney as a sergeant major, but later refers to him as a captain. Bob Yates of Warrensburg, Missouri, was so frustrated he did some research: The movie's Website, he says, lists Clooney as a major, but the *New York Times* and *USA Today* say he is a captain, *Le Press* from Montreal makes him *le capitaine*. The *Boston Globe* plays it safe with "an officer," and *Time* makes no mention of rank. The *New York Post* got it right. A major he is.

Three to Tango

Q. In your recent review of *Three to Tango*, you mentioned that Neve Campbell had "intelligent breasts," which obviously made

me wonder, what would classify as ignorant breasts?

—Michael McDuff, Sydney, Australia

A. Those that don't encourage your best thinking.

Titles

Q. How should we understand the title of the Hitchcock movie *North by Northwest*? The hero is not traveling North via Northwest; neither does he fly Northwest Airlines (unless it was that short moment when I dozed off). I will be perfectly satisfied with an answer such as "Hitchcock wanted to intrigue the viewer with a title as ambiguous before watching the movie as it is afterward; and obviously he succeeded in your case." However, if you have any explanation that is more precise or insightful, I would appreciate it.

—Alexei Tolkachev, Moscow, Russia

A. Hitchcock wanted to intrigue the viewer with a title as ambiguous before watching the movie as it is afterward; and obviously he succeeded in your case. According to some sources, the title comes from Shakespeare, although that doesn't help explain it:

> I am but mad north-north-west:
> When the wind is southerly I know a hawk
> from a handsaw.
> (*Hamlet*, Act 2, Scene 2)

Q. The Answer Man discussed the meaning of the title *North by Northwest*. Hint: The story begins in New York City, and ends at Mount Rushmore in South Dakota. What direction is that journey?

—Steve Dhuey, Madison, Wisconsin

A. West by Northwest.

Q. I have been watching quite a few older Westerns such as Clint Eastwood's *The Good, the Bad, and the Ugly* and am fuzzy on the term "spaghetti Western." Can you explain how movies attain this status?

—Brian Nichols, Saginaw, Michigan

A. The term was coined to describe Westerns supposedly made in Italy by Clint Eastwood and Sergio Leone, even though they were in fact filmed in Spain, were inspired by samurai movies, and would more accurately have been called "sushi Westerns." For fun, watch these four movies in a row: *Yojimbo, A Fistful of Dollars, Sanjuro,* and *For a Few Dollars More.*

Titus

Q. In your review of *Titus,* you quote Harold Bloom, who says he is sure that Shakespeare intended his play to be parody. Bloom cites the scene where Titus asks his daughter Lavinia, who has had both her hands cut off, to carry his own severed hand in her teeth. Stanley Wells, editing Shakespeare for the Oxford University Press, could not believe his hero Shakespeare could write such a line. His edition prefers "Bear thou my hand, sweet wench, between thine arms."
—Susan Lake, Urbana, Illinois

A. That has the advantage of leaving her teeth free to carry one of her brothers' heads.

Toy Story 2

Q. I recently saw *Toy Story 2* with my kids. Think of the toy as symbols for parents. In the early years of childhood, we are everything to children, and they go nowhere without us. As they get older, we become less important in their everyday life. As parents, we know that will happen, but like Woody observes at the end of the movie, we wouldn't miss a single day of that period of a child's life. Were the filmmakers thinking along the same line, or am I an overly sentimental, self-absorbed parent?
—Mark Waring, Omaha, Nebraska

A. You may have put your finger on the curious strength of the film's appeal to adults.

Trailers

Q. What's with trailers these days? According to what I read, *Flawless* is about a man suffering from a stroke and becoming a better person through speech lessons with a transvestite. And *The Talented Mr. Ripley* is a dark film about a man who murders a friend to take his place. Those sound like two films I would like to see. But the trailers present them as, respectively, a wacky action film and a sex-drenched comedy similar to *Cruel*

Intentions. Don't movie companies want people who actually appreciate film to come see their movies?
—Terrence Newton, Victoria, British Columbia

A. They figure they get them anyway. Marketing people want *all* movies to be wacky action, sex-drenched comedy, or both. So they advertise them that way. Robert De Niro made *Flawless* so he could play a character whose speech was affected by a stroke, but the studio publicity department has not allowed you to hear him saying one single word.

U-571

Q. The previews for *U-571* show the captured German submarine captain telling the Americans, "When they realize what you've discovered, they'll send every ship in the navy to destroy you." Actually the characters say several times in the movie that if the Germans realize the *Enigma* has been captured, all the Germans have to do is change their codes.
—Bennett Haselton, Seattle, Washington

A. Yeah, the whole point of sinking the German sub is to conceal the fact that its *Enigma* machine had been snatched. But that line sure sounds great in the ads.

Video Store Ratings

Q. I saw your review recommending *King of Masks* (a Chinese film with subtitles) as a family film. But when I went to Blockbuster to rent it, it was rated YRV. The clerk said this rating is even more restrictive than an R. Did I misunderstand? Or could the rating be mislabeled? What would make this movie worse than an R? FYI, my children are aged nine, thirteen, and sixteen and there are some things that we just don't allow them to see.
—Paul Sherbo

A. The clerk did not understand Blockbuster's YRV rating, which has no connection to the MPAA ratings, but is applied by Blockbuster itself to videos the MPAA has not rated. YRV means "youth-restricted viewing," and means Blockbuster will not rent them to those under seventeen. Since Blockbuster does not evaluate individual videos but simply slaps YRV on anything "unrated," the ironic result is that family films like *King of Masks* get lumped right in with soft-core sex and swimsuit videos. In my review of *King of Masks,* I noted it was "suitable for all but younger children," and it is.

Q. I recently rented a copy of *Fight Club* at my local Blockbuster. I know that as a family-oriented video store they refuse to handle NC-17 rated movies. They also put Youth-Restricted Viewing stickers on any and all movies without a rating, regardless (it seems) whether or not the movie might be appropriate for children. *Fight Club* was released in the theaters with an R rating, but I recall several scenes in the film release that I noticed were edited from the video. There is a scene where Myra tells Tyler Durden, "I want to have your abortion." Also another scene where we see Brad Pitt's character editing pornographic material into children's videos. As it is narrated we are given a quick glimpse of male genitalia while the narrator makes a graphic comment. The narration was still there, but the visual was gone.

—Joel Murray, Golden, Colorado

A. Steven Feldstein of Fox says the studio did no editing of the film: "The film that was in the theaters is the film they transferred to the video." You are mistaken in your memory of the "abortion" speech, which was cut from the film before release, but is included among the extras on the DVD.

Liz Green, public relations director for Blockbuster, says the company will carry the DVD of *Fight Club,* including its unrated material. This illustrates the company's illogical approach to ratings. It will not carry films with the NC-17 rating, but will carry "director's cuts" that include material that in some cases was deleted in order to avoid the NC-17. Regarding Blockbuster's Youth-Restricted Viewing, this is a rating that means only one thing: The film has not been rated at all, by anyone. Unfortunately, many ill-informed Blockbuster employees believe it means the film is not appropriate for children. Blockbuster's use of this rating is so careless that it has been applied to such excellent children's films as *King of Masks.* Why are some chil-

dren's films not rated? Because the MPAA charges a fee for the rating, and the distributors of films in limited release often cannot afford it.

Viewing Conditions

Q. This is in response to the person who felt shortchanged because movie employees would come in during the ending credits banging trash cans and brooms. You have to understand that most large theaters carry more than one major movie at a time. So, while *The Phantom Menace* is getting out in one theater, *Big Daddy* is getting out five minutes later in another. In order to clean all the theaters in time sometimes they have to clean while the credits are still rolling.

—Jacob Galvez, Phoenix, Arizona

A. Try this Movie Math: If they let the credits roll, the movies would still end at the same times, relative to one another. So early banging solves nothing.

Q. The Answer Man recently wrote, "The credits and the end music are included in the admission price; demand a refund if you're shortchanged." What do you say about previews? I attended a late showing of the godawful Adam Sandler starrer, *The Waterboy,* which started fifteen minutes late. To compensate, I presume, the movie started up immediately without one preview (which I have come to enjoy as part of my moviegoing experience). Should I have asked for my money back?

—Joshua Rafofsky, Los Angeles, California

A. Absolutely! One refund for the trailers you didn't see, and another for the movie you did see.

Q. I appreciate how you regularly inform your readers about how some sleazy theater owners run their projectors on "low" lamp intensity in order to save money. I have another annoyance. Many movie theaters, even in big cities, do not allow the entire movie credits to roll before they start: 1) closing the screen curtains; 2) turning up the lights; and 3) noisily bringing in the brooms and garbage bags to clean up. Some movie companies have caught onto this and have deliberately added a scene or two to the very end of the movie so that you *have* to sit through the credits.

—Bob Makarowski, New York City, New York

A. Credit cookies are an effective way to keep the audience seated, but only if the audience knows they're coming. Half the audience I joined for *Austin Powers: The Spy Who Shagged Me* was on its feet before the first cookie appeared. I agree with you that the credits and the end music are included in the admission price; demand a refund if you're shortchanged.

Q. A cell phone story. While I was watching *Frequency,* a lady one row back took a call and conducted a conversation—unnerving, evoking comments all around her—but at least it was during a lighthearted scene in the movie. Still, "cinema rage" must have coiled up inside me. And it struck during the double showdown. I was confused enough by the plot. Then came another electronic warble. Immediately all my unspoken protests from the first incident spring to the surface: The lady does *not* have her phone on vibrate. She's *not* by an aisle seat, so she *can't* duck out of the room quickly. She's *not* switching the phone off, but engaging in conversation. This resulted in me saying, "Hang up!" And, about three seconds later, louder, "Hang it *up!*" I didn't hear any more out of her, but I had residual adrenalin pumping through my body and, for about the next two minutes, could not concentrate. So at the climax of the movie, someone's phone went off and, I guess, so did I.

—Jim Carey, Glen Ellyn, Illinois

A. I like the approach they take to cell phones at the Telluride Film Festival. The first time your phone rings during a screening, they issue a warning. The second time, they confiscate the phone. That she left the phone turned on *after* the first call shows she was not merely pea-brained but deliberately rude. If she ever receives a ham radio message from a parent who has been dead for thirty years, I hope a cell phone starts ringing so loudly she can't hear a word.

Q. I saw the movie *Gossip* at my nearby multiplex. The picture was very dim and some of the indoor scenes were barely visible. After the movie, I complained to the manager. He said that I should have complained earlier. Since I was in a distant auditorium, I would have missed a significant part of the movie. I said that it appeared the projection bulb was set to a low setting to extend its life. He said that there is no such thing. I informed him that you have written about it. He said that Roger Ebert is wrong; they only have one setting.

—John Keating, Chicago, Illinois

A. The manager is mistaken. Many theater chains routinely order projectionists to turn down the bulb intensity in the mistaken belief that it will extend the life of the expensive bulbs. As a result, films look darker than their makers intended. The Answer Man quoted Carl Donath of Kodak in February 1999: "A dirty secret is that movies are under-lit in most theaters. Films are produced with the intent that they be projected at the brightness of 16 foot-lamberts. Field research by Kodak found that they are often shown at between 8 and 10 foot-lamberts, well under the SMPTE standard for brightness. To get theaters up to this and other standards, Kodak is introducing the Screencheck Experience program." Ironically, testing shows that bulbs burn just about as long at full power, so theater chains are not only cheap, but stupid. Clip this item, laminate it, and have it ready to show theater managers at a moment's notice.

Why Don't They . . . ?

Q. I am a big fan of Patrick O'Brian's Aubrey/Maurtin series of novels and have wondered why they have never been made into a movie. They would seem to have it all: Action, romance, intrigue, the historical angle. Do you know if anyone owns the rights or if anyone has every tried to get a movie deal?

—Eric Killian, Vancouver, Washington

A. These swashbuckling, seafaring novels with lots of nineteenth-century sailing minutiae have an enormous following, but not in the demographic group of sixteen-to-twenty-five-year-old males whose support is needed if a picture is to open strongly. I've listened to

Master and Commander and *H.M.S. Surprise* on audiobooks, however, and recommend them, especially for Robert Hardy's great gusto in the reading. (You didn't ask, but the single greatest performance in the history of audiobooks is Sean Barrett's reading of *Perfume*, by Patrick Suskind.)

Wisconsin

Q. Harvey Karten, one of my favorite on-line critics, recently wrote: "The state of Wisconsin has not fared well in the movies lately. Ralph Farnsworth gets laughed at for being from 'Wisconsin: the Party State,' in *The Straight Story*. Susan Sarandon can't wait to get away from Bay City in *Anywhere But Here*. Matt Damon as a fallen angel is exiled to the Dairy State in *Dogma*. And in *Wisconsin Death Trip*, James Marsh exposes multiple cases of murder, madness, and mayhem in the Black River Falls, Wisconsin, of the 1890s. Now, in Scott Elliott's *A Map of the World*, the townsfolk in a rural Wisconsin burg misinterpret the words and gestures of one of its outspoken residents, as Sigourney Weaver, the urban transplant to a farm near Racine, makes a painful transition from alien to outcast."

Why do you suppose Wisconsin is suddenly movie shorthand for hell?
—Harris Allsworth, Chicago, Illinois

A. Search me. Karten could also have cited *American Movie*, Chris Smith's wonderful new documentary about Mark Borchardt, a never-say-die horror auteur from Menomonee Falls. I've always thought of Wisconsin as one of our more enlightened states. To be sure, it gave the world Senator Joseph McCarthy and Ed Gein (the inspiration for Norman Bates), but it also gave us Houdini, Orson Welles, Frank Lloyd Wright, and Liberace. Not to mention "On, Wisconsin!" the greatest of all fight songs.

Wonder Boys

Q. I read that Tobey Maguire's character in *Wonder Boys* mistakenly lists Alan Ladd's death as a suicide, that Paramount has apologized to the Ladd family and will remove the line from the video release. Does this mean that if a person is important enough he can

have lines removed from films if he doesn't like them? The line is also in Michael Chabon's novel. Should Villard Books also remove it from the text?
—Jason Ihle, New London, Connecticut

A. Alan Ladd Sr. was not a suicide. Chabon might have been trying to make a point by having the character get it wrong, but it is a big mistake for a small payoff. You would not have to be "important" to get a line like that changed, but in Hollywood Alan Ladd Jr. certainly is—and well liked too.

Q. I read on Harry Knowles's Website that Paramount is planning a rerelease of *Wonder Boys* in October. I have seen studios rerelease films after they get nominated for Academy awards *(Insider, L.A. Confidential)* but I have never seen a film get rereleased in the same year. I am assuming that the studio thinks it may have an Oscar contender on its shelf and that the marketing of the film got screwed up. Most people I have talked to didn't even know about the film at all. Have you ever seen anything like this before, and how do you think *Wonder Boys* will do the second time around?
—Richard Duke, Jonesboro, Arkansas

A. I think *Wonder Boys* was one of the best films of the year, with probably Michael Douglas's best performance, as an English professor and writer on the skids. The film did less than $19 million in its February release, despite great reviews. In today's box-office climate, movies are forced to do or die in their first weekends, and a movie like *Wonder Boys*, which appeals to moviegoers with more experience of life, is not allowed to gradually build an audience. Paramount does indeed intuit it has an Oscar contender, and the rerelease is a gamble that the film has earned.

X-Men

Q. I came across an article on the Dark Horizons Website that said the original running time of *X-Men* was 135 minutes "but around 45 minutes was removed to make it faster and pacier. A lot of slower, nonaction, character development scenes were chopped." I'm discouraged. I am not an X-Men or even a comic book fan, but I was psyched to see the film version. But why? The best parts about a comic book, or any story, are the characters. If you take out the character development, subplots and their history, what do you have left? Eye candy! Forty-five minutes out of 135? That's a third of the film! The length of a film doesn't make it any better or worse, but the story should never be compromised.

—J. Nino, New York

A. That may help explain a problem I had with the film, which is that it was too much setup and not enough payoff. By the time the characters were introduced and their superpowers demonstrated, we were already at the halfway mark.

Glossary Entries

(These are contributions to my glossary project. Hundreds of entries were collected in *Ebert's Bigger Little Movie Glossary,* published in 1999. Contributions are always welcome.

* * *

Bad Nick Rule. If a movie character is named "Nick," odds are that he is either a bad guy or has a serious character flaw.
　　　　　—Nick Lang, Arlington, Virginia

BBC Universal Service Rule. Unless it's George Burns, the voice of God in a movie is always deep, resonant, well modulated, and invariably slightly British.
　　　　　—Ann Whitworth-Unemori, Savannah, Georgia

Bond Bounce. In action pictures, when explosions hurl stuntmen into the air, it is always obvious that they have just jumped on a trampoline (see any *007* movie).
　　　　　—Robert Musial, Grosse Pointe Woods, Michigan

Carmen Coincidence. Whenever a movie shows a scene from an opera, it must have some creepy resonance within the film's own plot.
　　　　　—Ian Waldron-Mantgani, Liverpool, England

Elastic Briefcase Rule. In any movie with a ransom or payoff, the briefcase is always full of cash regardless of the amount of money involved.
　　　　　—Joe Duchene, Urbana, Illinois

Exit Poll Syndrome. When TV ads consist of the "spontaneous" comments of viewers exiting the movie theater, the film is invariably a stinker.
　　　　　—David Hoffman, Hanover, Pennsylvania

Frank Lloyd Sandcastle Syndrome. All sandcastles in movies, especially those built by children, look as if they were constructed by a dedicated team of architects, designers, and crafts- men, working for weeks.
　　　　　—R.E.

Friendless Orphan Rule. No character who lacks parents may have friends or extended family. Holidays must be spent alone, preferably talking to a cat.
　　　　　—Mary Riley, Chicago, Illinois

I'm Not a Ferocious Warrior but I Play One in the Movies. The frightened villagers *(The Three Amigos),* ants *(A Bug's Life),* or aliens *(Galaxy Quest)* hire some muscle to save themselves from treacherous villains. But as luck would have it, they have hired actors!
　　　　　—Henrik Hansen, London, England

Inevitable Exit Line. Whenever a movie character says he is definitely, absolutely, irrevocably *not going*—the next shot shows him going.
　　　　　—R.E.

Keystone Kop-Out. Speeded-up sequences in any movie not actually starring the Keystone Kops are a warning sign of directorial desperation.
　　　　　—R.E.

Late in Life Syndrome. Movie parents are often older than most real-life parents. Most teenagers have fortyish parents, but in the movies the parents seem closer to their midfifties, probably because most directors are uncomfortable with the notion of parents younger than they are.
　　　　　—R.E.

Nightmare Position. Never in cinematic history has anyone ever awakened from a nightmare while sleeping on their stomachs. Every nightmare victim lunges into a seated position after sleeping on their back.
　　　　　—John Moore, Denver, Colorado

Oh Yeah? Rule. In all ads for horror movies, a character will shout out the one thing that turns out to be very mistaken: "Bats do *not* kill people!" "There are no such things as ghosts!" "He can't still be alive!" "The campus is perfectly safe." "Nothing could escape from that tomb." "An alien virus cannot survive for long on earth."

"Don't worry; I'll be fine." "No lizard that large has walked the earth in a million years."

—Jess Chia, Richmond, British Columbia

Roll Over Beethoven, etc., Obligatory Reveal. When one character is romantically obsessed with another and calls them at home in the middle of the night, and they answer the phone while propped up on one elbow, when they flop back down the shot will inevitably reveal they are not alone in bed.

—R.E.

Run, Leica, Run. In thrillers, the mysterious man who takes photographs of the hero is always chased. With a few exceptions like π, he is never caught.

—Jaime N. Christley, Oak Harbor, Washington

SNL Grandma Rule. In a surprising number of films featuring ex-cast members of *Saturday Night Live,* the main plot device involves saving Grandma or another older person from losing her house, livelihood, etc. See *The Blues Brothers, Happy Gilmore, Dirty Work,* etc.

—Pat McDonald, Chicago, Illinois

Stay Put, Don't Do Anything Rule. When during an action movie an adult asks the smaller person to hide and not move and not do *anything,* the smaller person will invariably not stay there and will either get into trouble or inadvertently save the day.

—David Taylor, Oak Park, Illinois

"This Just Keeps Getting Better and Better" Rule. Line uttered for no reason other than that it makes a great button for the trailer *(Men in Black, EDtv, The Mummy).*

—Michael Schlesinger, Culver City, California

Toupee Effect. If a special effect is so obvious that the audience thinks, "Wow! What a great special effect!" it is by definition a terrible special effect. This reaction is similar to pointing to someone's head and saying, "Wow! Now that is one natural-looking toupee!"

—Andy Ihnatko, Westwood, Massachusetts

Treetop Exclusionary Crash Rule. No airplane that disappears out of sight over a hill, treetops, or buildings ever lands safely; instead, a fireball explodes behind the foreground object.

—R.E.

Unimportant Terrorist. Whenever a terrorist or kidnapper is asked by the authorities, "What is your name?" he invariably answers, "My name is not important." This is frequently followed by, "What *is* important is . . ."

—Richard Leung, Toronto, Ontario

Urban Cowboy Rule. Characters in any city, no matter how large, are never more than twenty minutes from a smoke-filled country and western bar with line dancing, cowboy boots, ten-gallon hats, and people who speak with a Texas drawl.

—Matthew Dean, Chicago, Illinois

What Sort of Oysters? Rule. In any comedy set in a rural or exotic locale, the hero will sample a native dish, find it delicious, and then be informed it was either an insect or was prepared from the genitalia or excrement of a native animal.

—Andrew Milner, Bryn Mawr, Pennsylvania

Whirlybird Gets the Worm Rule. All helicopters piloted by bad guys blow up.

—Steve Lalanne, Toronto, Ontario

Whistle-Stop Rule. Whenever a football practice is shown in a film, the coach's whistle blows within two seconds after the beginning of the scene, so that the characters can continue or start a discussion.

—Gerardo Valero, Mexico City, Mexico

Reviews Appearing in Previous Editions
of the *Video Companion/Movie Yearbook*

A

About Last Night . . . , 1986, R, ★★★★ — 1998
Above the Law, 1988, R, ★★★ — 1995
Above the Rim, 1994, R, ★★★ — 1995
Absence of Malice, 1981, PG, ★★★ — 1998
Absolute Power, 1997, R, ★★★½ — 1998
Accidental Tourist, The,
 1988, PG, ★★★★ — 1998
Accompanist, The, 1994, PG, ★★★½ — 1998
Accused, The, 1988, R, ★★★ — 1998
Ace Ventura: Pet Detective,
 1994, PG-13, ★ — 1998
Ace Ventura: When Nature Calls,
 1995, PG-13, ★½ — 1998
Addams Family, The, 1991, PG-13, ★★ — 1997
Addams Family Values,
 1993, PG-13, ★★★ — 1998
Addicted to Love, 1997, R, ★★ — 1998
Addiction, The, 1995, NR, ★★½ — 1997
Adjuster, The, 1992, R, ★★★ — 1998
Adventures of Baron Munchausen, The,
 1989, PG, ★★★ — 1998
Adventures of Ford Fairlane, The,
 1990, R, ★ — 1992
Adventures of Huck Finn, The,
 1993, PG, ★★★ — 1998
Adventures of Priscilla, Queen of the
 Desert, The, 1994, R, ★★½ — 1998
After Hours, 1985, R, ★★★★ — 1998
After the Rehearsal, 1984, R, ★★★★ — 1998
Against All Odds, 1984, R, ★★★ — 1998
Age of Innocence, The,
 1993, PG, ★★★★ — 1998
Agnes of God, 1985, PG-13, ★ — 1989
Air Bud, 1997, PG, ★★★ — 2000
Air Force One, 1997, R, ★★½ — 2000
Airplane!, 1980, PG, ★★★ — 1998
Airport, 1970, G, ★★ — 1996
Airport 1975, 1974, PG, ★★½ — 1996
Aladdin, 1992, G, ★★★ — 1998
Alaska, 1996, PG, ★★★ — 1999
Albino Alligator, 1997, R, ★★ — 2000
Alex in Wonderland, 1971, R, ★★★★ — 1998
Alice, 1990, PG-13, ★★★ — 1998
Alice Doesn't Live Here Anymore,
 1974, PG, ★★★★ — 1998

Alien Nation, 1988, R, ★★ — 1994
Alien Resurrection, 1997, R, ★½ — 2000
Aliens, 1986, R, ★★★½ — 1998
Alien³, 1992, R, ★½ — 1997
Alive, 1993, R, ★★½ — 1997
All Dogs Go to Heaven, 1989, G, ★★★ — 1998
Allegro Non Tropo, 1977, NR, ★★★½ — 1995
Alligator, 1980, R, ★ — 1990
All Night Long, 1981, R, ★★ — 1986
All of Me, 1984, PG, ★★★½ — 1998
. . . All the Marbles, 1981, R, ★★ — 1986
All the President's Men, 1976, PG, ★★★½ — 1998
All the Right Moves, 1983, R, ★★★ — 1998
All the Vermeers in New York,
 1992, NR, ★★★ — 1998
Almost an Angel, 1990, PG, ★★½ — 1995
Altered States, 1980, R, ★★★½ — 1998
Always, 1989, PG, ★★ — 1997
Amadeus, 1984, PG, ★★★★ — 1998
Amarcord, 1974, R, ★★★★ — 1998
Amateur, 1995, R, ★★½ — 1996
American Buffalo, 1996, R, ★★½ — 1999
American Dream, 1992, NR, ★★★★ — 1998
American Flyers, 1985, PG-13, ★★½ — 1995
American Gigolo, 1980, R, ★★★½ — 1998
American Graffiti, 1973, PG, ★★★★ — 1998
American in Paris, An, 1952, G, ★★★½ — 1997
American Me, 1992, R, ★★★½ — 1998
American President, The,
 1995, PG-13, ★★★★ — 1998
American Tail: Fievel Goes West, An,
 1991, G, ★★½ — 1998
American Werewolf in London, An,
 1981, R, ★★ — 1998
American Werewolf in Paris, An,
 1997, R, ★ — 2000
Amistad, 1997, R, ★★★ — 2000
Amityville II: The Possession,
 1982, R, ★★ — 1988
Amos & Andrew, 1993, PG-13, ★★½ — 1995
Anaconda, 1997, PG-13, ★★★½ — 1998
Anastasia, 1997, G, ★★★½ — 2000
Angel at My Table, An, 1991, R, ★★★★ — 1998
Angel Baby, 1997, NR, ★★★ — 2000
Angel Heart, 1987, R, ★★★½ — 1998

Title	Ed.
Beautiful Girls, 1996, R, ★★★½	1999
Beautiful Thing, 1996, R, ★★★	1999
Beauty and the Beast, 1991, G, ★★★★	1998
Beavis and Butt-Head Do America, 1996, PG-13, ★★★	1999
Bed of Roses, 1996, PG-13, ★★	1999
Beethoven, 1992, PG, ★★½	1993
Beethoven's 2nd, 1993, PG, ★★	1995
Beetlejuice, 1988, PG, ★★	1998
Before Sunrise, 1995, R, ★★★	1998
Before the Rain, 1995, NR, ★★★★	1998
Being There, 1980, PG, ★★★★	1998
Belle de Jour, 1967, R, ★★★★	1997
Belle Epoque, 1993, NR, ★★★½	1998
Benny and Joon, 1993, PG, ★★★	1998
Bent, 1997, NC-17, ★★	2000
Best Boy, 1980, NR, ★★★★	1998
Best Little Whorehouse in Texas, The, 1982, R, ★★	1991
Betrayal, 1983, R, ★★★★	1998
Betrayed, 1988, R, ★★	1993
Betsy's Wedding, 1990, R, ★★	1993
Beverly Hillbillies, The, 1993, PG, ½★	1995
Beverly Hills Cop, 1984, R, ★★½	1998
Beverly Hills Cop II, 1987, R, ★	1995
Beyond Rangoon, 1995, R, ★★★	1998
Beyond the Limit, 1983, R, ★★½	1989
Beyond Therapy, 1987, R, ★	1988
Beyond the Valley of the Dolls, 1970, NC-17, Stars N/A	1997
Big, 1988, PG, ★★★	1998
Big Bang, The, 1990, R, ★★★	1995
Big Brawl, The, 1980, R, ★½	1986
Big Business, 1988, PG, ★★	1993
Big Chill, The, 1983, R, ★★½	1998
Big Easy, The, 1987, R, ★★★★	1998
Big Foot, 1971, PG, ½★	1990
Big Red One, The, 1980, PG, ★★★	1996
Big Squeeze, The, 1996, R, ★	1999
Big Town, The, 1987, R, ★★★½	1998
Bill & Ted's Bogus Journey, 1991, PG-13, ★★★	1998
Billy Bathgate, 1991, R, ★★	1993
Billy Jack, 1971, PG, ★★½	1993
Bird, 1988, R, ★★★½	1998
Birdcage, The, 1995, R, ★★★	1999
Bird on a Wire, 1990, PG-13, ★★½	1993
Birdy, 1985, R, ★★★★	1998
Bitter Moon, 1994, R, ★★★	1998
Black Cauldron, The, 1985, PG, ★★★½	1987
Black Marble, The, 1980, PG, ★★★½	1998

Title	Ed.
Black Rain (Michael Douglas), 1989, R, ★★	1993
Black Rain (Japan), 1990, NR, ★★★½	1998
Black Robe, 1991, R, ★★½	1994
Black Stallion, The, 1980, G, ★★★★	1998
Black Stallion Returns, The, 1983, PG, ★★½	1986
Black Widow, 1987, R, ★★½	1991
Blade Runner, 1982, R, ★★★	1998
Blade Runner: The Director's Cut, 1992, R, ★★★	1997
Blame It on Rio, 1984, R, ★	1987
Blaze, 1989, R, ★★★½	1998
Blind Date, 1987, PG-13, ★★½	1988
Blink, 1994, R, ★★★½	1998
Bliss, 1997, R, ★★★½	1998
Blood and Wine, 1997, R, ★★★½	1998
Blood Simple, 1985, R, ★★★★	1998
Blown Away, 1994, R, ★★	1996
Blow Out, 1981, R, ★★★★	1998
Blue, 1994, R, ★★★½	1998
Blue Chips, 1994, PG-13, ★★★	1998
Blue Collar, 1978, R, ★★★★	1998
Blue Kite, The, 1994, NR, ★★★★	1998
Blue Lagoon, The, 1980, R, ½★	1991
Blues Brothers, The, 1980, R, ★★★	1998
Blue Sky, 1994, PG-13, ★★★	1998
Blue Steel, 1990, R, ★★★	1998
Blue Velvet, 1986, R, ★	1998
Blume in Love, 1973, R, ★★★★	1998
Blush, 1996, NR, ★★½	1999
Bob Roberts, 1992, R, ★★★	1998
Bodies, Rest and Motion, 1993, R, ★★	1994
Body Double, 1984, R, ★★★½	1998
Bodyguard, The, 1992, R, ★★★	1998
Body of Evidence, 1993, R, ½★	1994
Body Snatchers, 1994, R, ★★★★	1998
Bogus, 1996, PG, ★★★	1999
Bolero, 1984, NR, ½★	1993
Bonfire of the Vanities, The, 1990, R, ★★½	1998
Boogie Nights, 1997, R, ★★★★	2000
Boomerang, 1992, R, ★★★	1998
Boost, The, 1988, R, ★★★½	1998
Booty Call, 1997, R, ★★★	1998
Bopha!, 1993, PG-13, ★★★½	1998
Born on the Fourth of July, 1989, R, ★★★★	1998
Born Yesterday, 1993, PG, ★	1994
Bostonians, The, 1984, PG, ★★★	1998
Bound, 1996, R, ★★★★	1999

Bound by Honor, 1993, R, ★★	1994	Bull Durham, 1988, R, ★★★½	1998
Bounty, The, 1984, PG, ★★★★	1998	Bulletproof, 1996, R, ★★	1999
Box of Moonlight, 1997, R, ★★★	2000	Bulletproof Heart, 1995, R, ★★★	1998
Boyfriends and Girlfriends,		Bullets Over Broadway, 1994, R, ★★★½	1998
1988, PG, ★★★	1998	'Burbs, The, 1989, PG, ★★	1992
Boys, 1996, PG-13, ★★	1999	Burden of Dreams, 1982, NR, ★★★★	1998
Boys on the Side, 1995, R, ★★★½	1998	Burglar, 1987, R, ★	1989
Boy Who Could Fly, The,		Buster, 1988, R, ★★★	1998
1986, PG, ★★★	1996	Buster and Billie, 1974, R, ★★★	1995
Boyz N the Hood, 1991, R, ★★★★	1998	Butcher's Wife, The, 1991, PG-13, ★★½	1997
Brady Bunch Movie, The,		Butley, 1974, NR, ★★★★	1987
1995, PG-13, ★★	1997	Butterfly Kiss, 1996, R, ★★	1999
Brainscan, 1994, R, ★★	1995	Bye Bye Brazil, 1979, NR, ★★★★	1996
Brainstorm, 1983, PG, ★★	1986	Bye Bye, Love, 1995, PG-13, ★★	1996
Bram Stoker's Dracula, 1992, R, ★★★	1998		
Brassed Off, 1997, R, ★★★	1998	# C	
Braveheart, 1995, R, ★★★½	1998	Cabaret, 1972, PG, ★★★½	1998
Brazil, 1985, R, ★★	1998	Cable Guy, The, 1996, PG-13, ★★	1999
Breakdown, 1997, R, ★★★	1998	Cactus, 1987, NR, ★★★	1998
Breakfast Club, The, 1985, R, ★★★	1998	Caddyshack, 1980, R, ★★½	1998
Breaking Away, 1979, PG, ★★★★	1998	Cadillac Man, 1990, R, ★★	1994
Breaking In, 1989, R, ★★★	1995	California Split, 1974, R, ★★★★	1998
Breaking the Waves, 1996, R, ★★★★	1999	Caligula, 1980, NR, no stars	1990
Breakin' 2—Electric Boogaloo,		Camille Claudel, 1989, R, ★★★½	1998
1984, PG, ★★★	1995	Candyman, 1992, R, ★★★	1998
Breathless, 1983, R, ★★½	1989	Candyman: Farewell to the Flesh,	
Brewster's Millions, 1985, PG, ★	1988	1995, R, ★★	1996
Bridges of Madison County, The,		Cannery Row, 1982, PG, ★★½	1987
1995, PG-13, ★★★½	1998	Cannonball Run, The, 1981, PG, ½★	1991
Brief History of Time, A, 1992, NR, ★★½	1994	Cannonball Run II, 1984, PG, ½★	1988
Bright Angel, 1991, R, ★★★½	1998	Cape Fear, 1991, R, ★★★	1998
Bright Lights, Big City, 1988, R, ★★★½	1998	Career Girls, 1997, R, ★★★	2000
Brighton Beach Memoirs,		Carlito's Way, 1993, R, ★★★½	1998
1986, PG-13, ★★	1989	Carmen, 1984, PG, ★★★★	1998
Bring Me the Head of Alfredo Garcia,		Carmen (dance), 1983, R, ★★★★	1995
1974, R, ★★★★	1998	Carnival of Souls, 1962, NR, ★★★	1997
Broadcast News, 1987, R, ★★★★	1998	Carrie, 1976, R, ★★★½	1998
Broadway Danny Rose, 1984, PG, ★★★½	1998	Carried Away, 1996, R, ★★★	1999
Broken Arrow, 1996, R, ★★	1999	Carrington, 1995, R, ★★★★	1998
Broken English, 1997, NR, ★★★	2000	Car Wash, 1976, PG, ★★★½	1995
Bronx Tale, A, 1993, R, ★★★★	1998	Casablanca, 1942, NR, ★★★★	1997
Brother from Another Planet, The,		Casino, 1995, R, ★★★★	1998
1984, PG, ★★★½	1998	Casper, 1995, PG, ★★★	1998
Brother's Keeper, 1993, NR, ★★★★	1998	Casualties of War, 1989, R, ★★★	1998
Brother's Kiss, A, 1997, R, ★★★	2000	Cat People, 1982, R, ★★★½	1998
Brothers McMullen, The, 1995, R, ★★★	1998	Cats Don't Dance, 1997, G, ★★★	2000
Brubaker, 1980, R, ★★½	1991	Cat's Eye, 1985, PG-13, ★★★	1986
Buddy, 1997, PG, ★★	2000	Caught, 1996, R, ★★★	1999
Buddy Holly Story, The,		Caveman, 1981, PG, ★½	1986
1978, PG, ★★★½	1998	Celestial Clockwork, 1996, NR, ★★★	1999
Bugsy, 1991, R, ★★★★	1998	Celluloid Closet, The,	
Bugsy Malone, 1976, G, ★★★½	1998	1995, NR, ★★★½	1999

Celtic Pride, 1996, PG-13, ★★	1999
Cement Garden, The, 1994, NR, ★★★	1998
Cemetery Club, The, 1992, PG-13, ★★★	1998
Chain Reaction, 1996, PG-13, ★★½	1999
Chamber, The, 1996, R, ★★	1999
Chances Are, 1989, PG, ★★★½	1998
Chaplin, 1993, PG-13, ★★	1994
Chapter Two, 1980, PG, ★★	1992
Chariots of Fire, 1981, PG, ★★★★	1998
Chase, The, 1994, PG-13, ★★½	1995
Chasing Amy, 1997, R, ★★★½	1998
Chattahoochee, 1990, R, ★★½	1992
Chef in Love, A, 1997, PG-13, ★★★	2000
Children of the Revolution, 1997, R, ★★	2000
Child's Play, 1988, R, ★★★	1998
China Moon, 1994, R, ★★★½	1998
China Syndrome, The, 1979, PG, ★★★★	1998
Chinatown, 1974, R, ★★★★	1998
Chocolat, 1989, PG-13, ★★★★	1998
Choose Me, 1984, R, ★★★½	1998
Chorus Line, A, 1985, PG-13, ★★★½	1998
Christiane F., 1981, R, ★★★½	1998
Christine, 1983, R, ★★★	1998
Christmas Story, A, 1983, PG, ★★★	1998
Christopher Columbus: The Discovery, 1992, PG-13, ★	1994
Chuck Berry Hail! Hail! Rock 'n' Roll, 1987, PG, ★★★★	1998
Chungking Express, 1996, PG-13, ★★★	1999
Cinderella, 1950, G, ★★★	1997
Cinema Paradiso, 1989, NR, ★★★½	1998
Circle of Friends, 1995, PG-13, ★★★½	1998
Citizen Kane, 1941, NR, ★★★★	1998
Citizen Ruth, 1997, R, ★★★	2000
City Hall, 1996, R, ★★½	1999
City Heat, 1984, PG, ½★	1991
City of Hope, 1991, R, ★★★★	1998
City of Industry, 1997, R, ★½	2000
City of Joy, 1992, PG-13, ★★★	1995
City of Lost Children, 1995, R, ★★★	1998
City of Women, 1981, R, ★★½	1991
City Slickers, 1991, PG-13, ★★★½	1998
City Slickers II: The Legend of Curly's Gold, 1994, PG-13, ★★	1995
Claire's Knee, 1971, PG, ★★★★	1998
Clan of the Cave Bear, 1985, R, ★½	1989
Clash of the Titans, 1981, PG, ★★★½	1998
Class Action, 1991, R, ★★★	1995
Class of 1984, The, 1982, R, ★★★½	1995
Class of 1999, 1990, R, ★★	1992
Clean and Sober, 1988, R, ★★★½	1998
Clean, Shaven, 1995, NR, ★★★½	1998
Clerks, 1994, R, ★★★	1998
Client, The, 1994, PG-13, ★★½	1998
Cliffhanger, 1993, R, ★★★	1998
Clifford, 1994, PG, ½★	1995
Clockers, 1995, R, ★★★½	1998
Close Encounters of the Third Kind: The Special Edition, 1980, PG, ★★★★	1998
Close to Eden, 1992, NR, ★★★	1998
Clueless, 1995, PG-13, ★★★½	1998
Coal Miner's Daughter, 1980, PG, ★★★	1998
Cobb, 1994, R, ★★	1996
Coca-Cola Kid, The, 1985, NR, ★★★	1987
Cocktail, 1988, R, ★★	1993
Cocoon, 1985, PG-13, ★★★	1998
Cocoon: The Return, 1988, PG, ★★½	1997
Code of Silence, 1985, R, ★★★½	1998
Cold Comfort Farm, 1995, PG, ★★★	1999
Cold Fever, 1996, NR, ★★★	1999
Color of Money, The, 1986, R, ★★½	1998
Color of Night, 1994, R, ★½	1996
Color Purple, The, 1985, PG-13, ★★★★	1998
Colors, 1988, R, ★★★	1998
Coma, 1978, PG, ★★★	1995
Come Back to the 5 & Dime, Jimmy Dean, Jimmy Dean, 1982, PG, ★★★	1998
Come See the Paradise, 1991, R, ★★★	1998
Comfort of Strangers, The, 1991, R, ★★½	1994
Coming Home, 1978, R, ★★★★	1998
Commandments, 1997, R, ★★	2000
Commitments, The, 1991, R, ★★★	1998
Company of Wolves, The, 1985, R, ★★★	1987
Competition, The, 1981, PG, ★★★	1995
Compromising Positions, 1985, R, ★★	1987
Con Air, 1997, R, ★★★	1998
Conan the Barbarian, 1982, R, ★★★	1998
Conan the Destroyer, 1984, PG, ★★★	1998
Coneheads, 1993, PG, ★½	1995
Congo, 1995, PG-13, ★★★	1998
Conspiracy Theory, 1997, R, ★★½	2000
Contact, 1997, PG, ★★★½	1998
Contempt, 1997, NR, ★★★	2000
Continental Divide, 1981, PG, ★★★	1998
Conversation, The, 1974, PG, ★★★★	1998
Cookie, 1989, R, ★★	1992
Cook, the Thief, His Wife and Her Lover, The, 1990, NR, ★★★★	1998
Cool Runnings, 1993, PG, ★★½	1995
Cop, 1988, R, ★★★	1998
Cop and a Half, 1993, PG, ★★★	1995
Cop Land, 1997, R, ★★	2000
Cops and Robbersons, 1994, PG, ★★	1995

D

Dennis the Menace, 1993, PG, ★★½ — 1995
Desert Hearts, 1985, R, ★★½ — 1988
Designated Mourner, The, 1997, R, ★★★ — 2000
Desperado, 1995, R, ★★ — 1997
Desperate Hours, 1990, R, ★★ — 1992
Desperately Seeking Susan,
  1985, PG-13, ★★★ — 1998
Devil in a Blue Dress, 1995, R, ★★★ — 1998
Devil's Advocate, 1997, R, ★★½ — 2000
Devil's Own, The, 1997, R, ★★½ — 1998
Diabolique, 1955, NR, ★★★½ — 1999
Diabolique, 1995, R, ★★ — 1997
Diamonds Are Forever, 1971, PG, ★★★ — 1998
Diary of a Mad Housewife,
  1970, R, ★★★ — 1996
Dice Rules, 1991, NC-17, no stars — 1992
Dick Tracy, 1990, PG, ★★★★ — 1998
Die Hard, 1988, R, ★★ — 1998
Die Hard 2: Die Harder, 1990, R, ★★★½ — 1998
Die Hard With a Vengeance,
  1995, R, ★★★ — 1998
Different for Girls, 1997, R, ★★★ — 2000
Dim Sum, 1985, PG, ★★★ — 1998
Diner, 1982, R, ★★★½ — 1998
Dirty Dancing, 1987, PG-13, ★ — 1995
Dirty Harry, 1971, R, ★★★ — 1998
Dirty Rotten Scoundrels,
  1988, PG, ★★★ — 1998
Disappearance of Garcia Lorca, The,
  1997, R, ★★★ — 2000
Disclosure, 1994, R, ★★ — 1996
Discreet Charm of the Bourgeoisie, The,
  1972, PG, ★★★★ — 1998
Distinguished Gentleman, The,
  1992, R, ★★ — 1994
Diva, 1981, R, ★★★★ — 1998
Divine Madness, 1980, R, ★★★½ — 1998
D.O.A., 1988, R, ★★★ — 1998
Doc Hollywood, 1991, PG-13, ★★★ — 1998
Doctor, The, 1991, PG-13, ★★★½ — 1998
Doctor Zhivago, 1965, PG-13, ★★★ — 1997
Dog Day Afternoon, 1975, R, ★★★½ — 1998
Dogfight, 1991, R, ★★★ — 1998
Dogs of War, The, 1981, R, ★★★ — 1988
Dolores Claiborne, 1995, R, ★★★ — 1998
Dominick and Eugene,
  1988, PG-13, ★★★½ — 1998
Don Juan DeMarco, 1995, PG-13, ★★ — 1996
Donnie Brasco, 1997, R, ★★★½ — 1998
Doom Generation, The,
  1995, NR, no stars — 1997
Doors, The, 1991, R, ★★½ — 1998

Do the Right Thing, 1989, R, ★★★★ — 1998
Double Life of Veronique, The,
  1991, NR, ★★★½ — 1998
Double Team, 1997, R, ★★ — 2000
Down and Out in Beverly Hills,
  1986, R, ★★★★ — 1998
Down by Law, 1986, R, ★★★ — 1998
Down Periscope, 1996, PG-13, ★★★ — 1999
Dragnet, 1987, PG-13, ★★★ — 1998
Dragonheart, 1995, PG-13, ★★★ — 1999
Dragonslayer, 1981, PG, ★★★ — 1989
Dragon: The Bruce Lee Story,
  1993, PG-13, ★★½ — 1995
Draughtsman's Contract, The,
  1983, R, ★★★★ — 1998
Dreamchild, 1985, PG, ★★★ — 1998
Dream Lover, 1994, R, ★★★ — 1998
Dreamscape, 1984, PG-13, ★★★ — 1989
Dream Team, The, 1989, PG-13, ★★ — 1993
Dream With the Fishes, 1997, R, ★★★ — 1998
Dressed to Kill, 1980, R, ★★★ — 1998
Dresser, The, 1984, PG, ★★★★ — 1998
Drive, He Said, 1971, R, ★★★ — 1998
Driving Miss Daisy, 1989, PG, ★★★★ — 1998
Drop Zone, 1994, R, ★★½ — 1997
Drowning by Numbers, 1991, NR, ★★ — 1995
Dr. Strangelove, 1964, PG, ★★★★ — 1997
Drugstore Cowboy, 1989, R, ★★★★ — 1998
Dry White Season, A, 1989, R, ★★★★ — 1998
D3: The Mighty Ducks, 1996, PG, ★ — 1999
Dumb and Dumber, 1994, PG-13, ★★ — 1998
Dune, 1984, PG-13, ★ — 1988
Dutch, 1991, PG-13, ★½ — 1993
Dying Young, 1991, R, ★★ — 1994

E

Earth Girls Are Easy, 1989, PG, ★★★ — 1998
Easy Money, 1983, R, ★★½ — 1994
Easy Rider, 1969, R, ★★★★ — 1997
Eating Raoul, 1983, R, ★★ — 1995
Eddie, 1996, PG-13, ★½ — 1999
Eddie and the Cruisers, 1983, PG, ★★ — 1987
Edge, The, 1997, R, ★★★ — 2000
Ed's Next Move, 1996, R, ★★★ — 1999
Educating Rita, 1983, PG, ★★ — 1995
Edward Scissorhands, 1990, PG-13, ★★ — 1997
Ed Wood, 1994, R, ★★★½ — 1998
Efficiency Expert, The, 1992, PG, ★★★ — 1998
Eighth Day, The, 1997, NR, ★★★ — 2000
8 Heads in a Duffel Bag, 1997, R, ★★ — 2000
Eight Men Out, 1988, PG, ★★ — 1993
Eight Seconds, 1994, PG-13, ★★ — 1995

Few Good Men, A, 1992, R, ★★½	1997
Field, The, 1991, PG-13, ★	1993
Field of Dreams, 1989, PG, ★★★★	1998
Fiendish Plot of Dr. Fu Manchu, The, 1980, PG, ★	1986
Fierce Creatures, 1997, PG-13, ★★½	2000
Fifth Element, The, 1997, PG-13, ★★★	2000
52 Pick-Up, 1986, R, ★★★½	1997
Final Analysis, 1992, R, ★★½	1995
Final Conflict, The (Omen III), 1981, R, ★★	1987
Final Countdown, The, 1980, PG, ★★	1988
Fire, 1997, NR, ★★★	2000
Firefox, 1982, PG, ★★★½	1998
Fire in the Sky, 1993, PG-13, ★★½	1994
Firestarter, 1984, R, ★★	1987
Firm, The, 1993, R, ★★★	1998
First Blood, 1982, R, ★★★	1998
Firstborn, 1984, PG, ★★	1987
First Deadly Sin, The, 1980, R, ★★★	1986
First Knight, 1995, PG-13, ★★	1997
First Wives Club, The, 1996, PG, ★★	1999
Fish Called Wanda, A, 1988, R, ★★★★	1998
Fisher King, The, 1991, R, ★★	1994
Fitzcarraldo, 1982, PG, ★★★★	1998
Five Easy Pieces, 1970, R, ★★★★	1998
Five Heartbeats, The, 1991, R, ★★★	1998
Flamingo Kid, The, 1984, PG-13, ★★★½	1998
Flashback, 1990, R, ★★★	1998
Flashdance, 1983, R, ★½	1994
Flash Gordon, 1980, PG, ★★½	1988
Flash of Green, A, 1985, NR, ★★★	1987
Flatliners, 1990, R, ★★★	1998
Fled, 1996, R, ★★	1999
Flesh and Bone, 1993, R, ★★	1995
Fletch, 1985, PG, ★★½	1995
Fletch Lives, 1989, PG, ★½	1995
Flintstones, The, 1994, PG, ★★½	1997
Flipper, 1995, PG, ★★	1999
Flirt, 1996, NR, ★★	1999
Flirting, 1992, NR, ★★★★	1998
Flower of My Secret, The, 1996, R, ★½	1999
Flubber, 1997, PG, ★	2000
Fly Away Home, 1996, PG, ★★★½	1999
Fog, The, 1980, R, ★★	1988
Fool for Love, 1985, R, ★★★	1998
Fools Rush In, 1997, PG-13, ★★★	1998
Footloose, 1984, PG, ★½	1995
Forever Young, 1992, PG, ★★½	1994
Forget Paris, 1995, PG-13, ★★★½	1998
For Keeps, 1988, PG-13, ★★★	1998
For Love or Money, 1993, PG, ★★	1995

Formula, The, 1980, R, ★★	1987
For Queen and Country, 1989, R, ★★	1992
Forrest Gump, 1994, PG-13, ★★★★	1998
For Richer or Poorer, 1997, PG-13, ★★	2000
For Roseanna, 1997, PG-13, ★★★	2000
Fort Apache, the Bronx, 1981, R, ★★	1987
For the Boys, 1991, R, ★★	1993
48 HRS, 1982, R, ★★★½	1998
For Your Eyes Only, 1981, PG, ★★	1998
Four Friends, 1981, R, ★★★★	1998
4 Little Girls, 1997, NR, ★★★★	2000
Four Rooms, 1995, R, ★★	1998
1492: Conquest of Paradise, 1992, PG-13, ★★★	1996
Fourth Protocol, The, 1987, R, ★★★½	1998
Fourth War, The, 1990, R, ★★★	1998
Four Weddings and a Funeral, 1994, R, ★★★½	1998
Fox and the Hound, The, 1981, G, ★★★	1998
Foxes, 1980, R, ★★★	1998
Frances, 1983, R, ★★★½	1998
Frankie and Johnny, 1991, R, ★★½	1995
Frankie Starlight, 1995, R, ★★★½	1998
Frantic, 1988, R, ★★★	1998
Fraternity Vacation, 1985, R, ★	1990
Freeway, 1997, R, ★★★½	1998
Free Willy, 1993, PG, ★★★½	1998
Free Willy 3: The Rescue, 1997, PG, ★★★	2000
French Kiss, 1995, PG-13, ★★	1997
French Lieutenant's Woman, The, 1981, R, ★★★½	1998
Frenzy, 1972, R, ★★★★	1998
Fresh, 1994, R, ★★★★	1998
Freshman, The, 1990, PG, ★★★½	1998
Friday the 13th, Part II, 1981, R, ½★	1993
Fried Green Tomatoes, 1992, PG-13, ★★★	1998
Friends of Eddie Coyle, The, 1973, R, ★★★★	1998
Frighteners, The, 1996, R, ★	1999
Fright Night, 1985, R, ★★★	1996
Fringe Dwellers, The, 1987, PG-13, ★★★½	1996
From Dusk Till Dawn, 1996, R, ★★★	1999
From the Journals of Jean Seberg, 1996, NR, ★★★½	1999
Frozen Assets, 1992, PG-13, no stars	1994
Fugitive, The, 1993, PG-13, ★★★★	1998
Full Metal Jacket, 1987, R, ★★½	1998
Full Monty, The, 1997, R, ★★★	2000
Full Moon on Blue Water, 1988, R, ★★	1992

Groundhog Day, 1993, PG, ★★★ — 1998
Grumpier Old Men, 1995, PG-13, ★★ — 1997
Grumpy Old Men, 1993, PG-13, ★★ — 1997
Guantanamera, 1997, NR, ★★★ — 2000
Guardian, The, 1990, R, ★ — 1992
Guarding Tess, 1994, PG-13, ★★★½ — 1998
Guelwaar, 1994, NR, ★★★★ — 1998
Guilty as Sin, 1993, R, ★★★ — 1996
Guilty by Suspicion,
   1991, PG-13, ★★★½ — 1998
Guimba the Tyrant, 1996, NR, ★★★ — 1999
Gunmen, 1994, R, ★½ — 1995

H

Habit, 1997, NR, ★★★ — 1998
Hackers, 1995, PG-13, ★★★ — 1998
Hair, 1979, R, ★★★★ — 1998
Hairspray, 1988, PG, ★★★ — 1998
Half Moon Street, 1986, R, ★★★ — 1998
Halloween, 1978, R, ★★★★ — 1998
Halloween II, 1981, R, ★★ — 1993
Halloween III, 1982, R, ★½ — 1993
Hamlet, 1990, PG, ★★★½ — 1998
Hamlet, 1997, PG-13, ★★★★ — 1998
Handmaid's Tale, The, 1990, R, ★★ — 1995
Hangin' With the Homeboys,
   1991, R, ★★★ — 1998
Hannah and Her Sisters,
   1985, PG-13, ★★★★ — 1998
Hans Christian Andersen's Thumbelina,
   1994, G, ★★ — 1995
Happy Gilmore, 1996, PG-13, ★½ — 1999
Hard Choices, 1986, NR, ★★★½ — 1998
Hardcore, 1979, R, ★★★★ — 1998
Hard Eight, 1997, R, ★★★½ — 1998
Hardly Working, 1981, R, no stars — 1986
Hard Way, The, 1991, R, ★★★½ — 1998
Harlan County, U.S.A.,
   1976, PG, ★★★★ — 1998
Harlem Nights, 1989, R, ★★ — 1993
Harold and Maude, 1971, PG, ★½ — 1991
Harriet the Spy, 1996, PG, ★★ — 1999
Harry & Son, 1984, PG, ★ — 1986
Harry and the Hendersons,
   1987, PG, ★★ — 1993
Harry and Tonto, 1974, PG, ★★★★ — 1998
Hate (La Haine), 1995, NR, ★★★ — 1999
Havana, 1990, R, ★★★ — 1998
Hear My Song, 1992, R, ★★★½ — 1998
Hearse, The, 1980, PG, ½★ — 1986
Heart Beat, 1980, R, ★★½ — 1991

Heartbreakers, 1985, R, ★★★½ — 1998
Heartbreak Hotel, 1988, PG-13, ★ — 1994
Heartbreak Kid, The, 1972, PG, ★★★½ — 1998
Heartbreak Ridge, 1986, R, ★★★ — 1998
Heartburn, 1986, R, ★★ — 1993
Heartland, 1981, PG, ★★★★ — 1998
Heart of Midnight, 1989, R, ★★½ — 1993
Hearts of Darkness, 1991, NR, ★★★½ — 1998
Heat, 1987, R, ★★ — 1988
Heat, 1995, R, ★★★½ — 1998
Heat and Dust, 1983, R, ★★★ — 1998
Heathers, 1989, R, ★★½ — 1994
Heaven, 1987, PG-13, ★★ — 1990
Heaven and Earth, 1993, R, ★★★½ — 1998
Heaven Help Us, 1985, R, ★★½ — 1989
Heavenly Creatures, 1994, R, ★★★½ — 1998
Heavenly Kid, The, 1985, PG-13, ★ — 1987
Heaven's Gate, 1981, R, ½★ — 1994
Heaven's Prisoners, 1995, R, ★★ — 1999
Heavy, 1996, NR, ★★★½ — 1999
Heidi Fleiss, Hollywood Madam,
   1995, NR, ★★★★ — 1999
Hellbound: Hellraiser II, 1988, R, ½★ — 1990
Hell Night, 1981, R, ★ — 1986
Henry and June, 1990, NC-17, ★★★ — 1998
Henry V, 1989, NR, ★★★½ — 1998
Henry: Portrait of a Serial Killer,
   1986, NR, ★★★½ — 1998
Her Alibi, 1989, PG, ½★ — 1993
Hercules, 1997, G, ★★★½ — 1998
Hero, 1992, PG-13, ★★ — 1994
Hero and the Terror, 1987, R, ★★ — 1991
Hidden, The, 1987, R, ★★★ — 1996
Hidden Agenda, 1990, R, ★★★ — 1998
Hidden Fortress, The,
   1958, NR, ★★★★ — 1997
Hideaway, 1995, R, ★★★ — 1998
High Anxiety, 1978, PG, ★★½ — 1995
Higher Learning, 1995, R, ★★★ — 1998
High Hopes, 1989, NR, ★★★★ — 1998
Highlander 2: The Quickening,
   1991, R, ½★ — 1993
High Road to China, 1983, PG, ★★ — 1987
High School High, 1996, PG-13, ★½ — 1999
High Season, 1988, R, ★★★ — 1998
History of the World—Part I,
   1981, R, ★★ — 1995
Hitcher, The, 1985, R, no stars — 1990
Hocus Pocus, 1993, PG, ★ — 1995
Hoffa, 1992, R, ★★★½ — 1998
Hollywood Shuffle, 1987, R, ★★★ — 1998

Homage, 1996, R, ★★½ — 1999
Home Alone, 1990, PG, ★★½ — 1998
Home Alone 2: Lost in New York,
 1992, PG, ★★ — 1995
Home Alone 3, 1997, PG, ★★★ — 2000
Home and the World, The,
 1986, NR, ★★★ — 1987
Home of Our Own, A, 1993, PG, ★★★ — 1998
Home of the Brave, 1986, NR, ★★★½ — 1998
Homeward Bound: The Incredible
 Journey, 1993, G, ★★★ — 1998
Homeward Bound II: Lost in San
 Francisco, 1996, G, ★★ — 1999
Homicide, 1991, R, ★★★★ — 1998
Honey, I Blew Up the Kid, 1992, PG, ★½ — 1994
Honey, I Shrunk the Kids, 1989, PG, ★★ — 1995
Honeymoon in Vegas,
 1992, PG-13, ★★★½ — 1998
Honkytonk Man, 1982, PG, ★★★ — 1998
Hoodlum, 1997, R, ★★★ — 2000
Hook, 1991, PG, ★★ — 1994
Hoop Dreams, 1994, PG-13, ★★★★ — 1998
Hoosiers, 1987, PG, ★★★★ — 1998
Hope and Glory, 1987, PG-13, ★★★ — 1998
Horseman on the Roof, The,
 1995, R, ★★★ — 1999
Hotel de Love, 1997, R, ★★½ — 2000
Hotel Terminus, 1988, NR, ★★★ — 1996
Hot Shots, Part Deux, 1993, PG-13, ★★★ — 1998
Hot Spot, The, 1990, R, ★★★ — 1996
House Arrest, 1996, PG, ★ — 1999
Household Saints, 1993, R, ★★★★ — 1998
Housekeeping, 1988, PG, ★★★★ — 1998
House of Games, 1987, R, ★★★★ — 1998
House of the Spirits, The, 1994, R, ★★ — 1995
House of Yes, The, 1997, R, ★★½ — 2000
House on Carroll Street, The,
 1988, PG, ★★★ — 1998
House Party, 1990, R, ★★★ — 1998
House Party 2, 1991, R, ★★ — 1993
Housesitter, 1992, PG, ★★★ — 1998
Howards End, 1992, PG, ★★★★ — 1998
Howling, The, 1981, R, ★★ — 1992
Howling II, 1986, R, ★ — 1987
How to Make an American Quilt,
 1995, PG-13, ★★ — 1997
Hudsucker Proxy, The, 1994, PG, ★★ — 1997
Hugh Hefner: Once Upon a Time,
 1992, NR, ★★★ — 1996
Hunchback of Notre Dame, The,
 1995, G, ★★★★ — 1999
Hunger, The, 1983, R, ★½ — 1991

Hunt for Red October, The,
 1990, PG, ★★★½ — 1998
Husbands and Wives, 1992, R, ★★★½ — 1998
Hype!, 1997, NR, ★★★ — 1998

I

Iceman, 1984, PG, ★★★★ — 1998
Ice Storm, The, 1997, R, ★★★★ — 2000
Idolmaker, The, 1980, PG, ★★★ — 1998
If Looks Could Kill, 1991, PG-13, ★★★ — 1995
If Lucy Fell, 1996, R, ★ — 1999
I Know What You Did Last Summer,
 1997, R, ★ — 2000
I Like It Like That, 1994, R, ★★★ — 1998
Il Ladro di Bambini, 1993, NR, ★★★★ — 1998
I'll Do Anything, 1994, PG-13, ★★★ — 1998
I Love You to Death, 1990, R, ★★★ — 1998
I, Madman, 1989, R, ★★★ — 1996
Imaginary Crimes, 1994, PG, ★★★½ — 1998
Imagine: John Lennon, 1988, R, ★★★ — 1997
Immediate Family, 1989, PG-13, ★★ — 1992
Immortal Beloved, 1995, R, ★★★½ — 1998
I'm Not Rappaport, 1997, PG-13, ★★½ — 1998
Impromptu, 1991, PG-13, ★★½ — 1994
Impulse, 1990, R, ★★★ — 1998
In and Out, 1997, PG-13, ★★★ — 2000
In Country, 1989, R, ★★★ — 1998
Incredible Shrinking Woman, The,
 1981, PG, ★★½ — 1991
Incredibly True Adventure of Two Girls
 in Love, The, 1995, R, ★★★ — 1998
Indecent Proposal, 1993, R, ★★★ — 1998
Independence Day, 1996, PG-13, ★★½ — 1999
Indiana Jones and the Last Crusade,
 1989, PG-13, ★★★½ — 1998
Indiana Jones and the Temple of Doom,
 1984, PG, ★★★★ — 1998
Indian in the Cupboard, 1995, PG, ★★ — 1997
Indian Runner, The, 1991, R, ★★★ — 1996
Indian Summer, 1993, PG-13, ★★★ — 1998
Indochine, 1993, PG-13, ★★½ — 1994
I Never Promised You a Rose Garden,
 1977, R, ★★★ — 1996
I Never Sang for My Father,
 1971, PG, ★★★★ — 1998
Infinity, 1996, PG, ★★★ — 1999
Infra-Man, 1976, PG, ★★½ — 1996
Inkwell, The, 1994, R, ★★★ — 1995
In Love and War, 1997, PG-13, ★★ — 2000
Inner Circle, The, 1992, PG-13, ★★★ — 1996
Innerspace, 1987, PG, ★★★ — 1996
Innocent, The, 1995, R, ★★★ — 1998

Innocent Blood, 1992, R, ★★	1994
Innocent Man, An, 1989, R, ★¹/₂	1993
Insignificance, 1985, R, ★★★	1996
Interiors, 1978, PG, ★★★★	1998
Intersection, 1994, R, ★	1995
Interview With the Vampire,	
1994, R, ★★★	1998
Intervista, 1993, NR, ★★¹/₂	1995
In the Company of Men, 1997, R,	
★★★★	2000
In the Line of Fire, 1993, R, ★★★¹/₂	1998
In the Mood, 1987, PG-13, ★★★	1995
In the Mouth of Madness, 1995, R, ★★	1996
In the Name of the Father, 1994, R, ★★★	1998
Intimate Relations, 1997, R, ★★	2000
Into the Night, 1985, R, ★	1987
Into the West, 1993, PG, ★★★¹/₂	1998
Invasion USA, 1985, R, ¹/₂★	1987
Inventing the Abbotts, 1997, R, ★★	1998
I.Q., 1994, PG, ★★★¹/₂	1998
Ironweed, 1988, R, ★★★	1998
Iron Will, 1994, PG, ★★	1995
Irreconcilable Differences,	
1984, PG, ★★★¹/₂	1995
Ishtar, 1987, PG-13, ¹/₂★	1994
I Shot Andy Warhol, 1995, NR, ★★★¹/₂	1999
I Spit on Your Grave, 1980, R, no stars	1990
It Could Happen to You,	
1994, PG, ★★★¹/₂	1998
It's All True, 1993, G, ★★★	1997
It's a Wonderful Life, 1946, NR, ★★★★	1997
It's My Party, 1995, R, ★★★	1999
It Takes Two, 1995, PG, ★★	1997
I've Heard the Mermaids Singing,	
1987, NR, ★★★¹/₂	1998
I Wanna Hold Your Hand,	
1978, PG, ★★¹/₂	1994

J

Jack, 1996, PG-13, ★¹/₂	1999
Jackal, The, 1997, R, ★¹/₂	2000
Jack and Sarah, 1996, R, ★★★	1999
Jackie Brown, 1997, R, ★★★★	2000
Jackie Chan's First Strike,	
1997, PG-13, ★★★	1998
Jacknife, 1989, R, ★★★	1996
Jack's Back, 1988, R, ★★★	1996
Jack the Bear, 1993, PG-13, ★★★	1996
Jacob's Ladder, 1990, R, ★★★¹/₂	1998
Jacquot, 1993, NR, ★★★¹/₂	1996
Jade, 1995, R, ★★	1997
Jagged Edge, 1985, R, ★★★¹/₂	1998

James and the Giant Peach,	
1995, PG, ★★★	1999
Jamon Jamon, 1994, NR, ★★★¹/₂	1998
Jane Eyre, 1995, PG, ★★★¹/₂	1999
Jason's Lyric, 1994, R, ★★★	1998
Jaws, 1975, PG, ★★★★	1998
Jaws the Revenge, 1987, PG-13, no stars	1993
Jazz Singer, The, 1980, PG, ★	1987
Jean de Florette, 1987, PG, ★★★¹/₂	1998
Jefferson in Paris, 1995, PG-13, ★★	1997
Jeremiah Johnson, 1972, PG, ★★★	1998
Jerry Maguire, 1996, R, ★★★	1999
Jesus of Montreal, 1990, R, ★★★¹/₂	1998
Jewel of the Nile, The, 1985, PG, ★★★	1998
JFK, 1991, R, ★★★★	1998
Jimmy Hollywood, 1994, R, ★★¹/₂	1997
Jingle All the Way, 1996, PG, ★★¹/₂	1999
Joe Vs. the Volcano, 1990, PG, ★★★¹/₂	1998
Johnny Dangerously, 1984, PG-13, ★★	1993
Johnny Got His Gun, 1971, R, ★★★★	1998
Johnny Handsome, 1989, R, ★★★¹/₂	1998
Johnny Mnemonic, 1995, R, ★★	1996
johns, 1997, R, ★★★	1998
Jo Jo Dancer, Your Life Is Calling,	
1986, R, ★★★	1998
Josh and S.A.M., 1993, PG-13, ★★	1995
Journey of August King, The,	
1996, PG-13, ★¹/₂	1999
Journey of Hope, 1990, NR, ★★¹/₂	1995
Journey of Natty Gann, The,	
1985, PG, ★★★	1998
Joy Luck Club, The, 1993, R, ★★★★	1998
Jude, 1996, R, ★★★	1999
Judge Dredd, 1995, R, ★★	1996
Ju Dou, 1991, NR, ★★★¹/₂	1998
Juice, 1992, R, ★★★	1998
Julia, 1977, PG, ★★¹/₂	1988
Julia and Julia, 1988, R, ★★★	1998
Jumanji, 1995, PG, ★¹/₂	1998
Jumpin' Jack Flash, 1986, PG-13, ★★	1990
Jungle Fever, 1991, R, ★★★¹/₂	1998
Jungle 2 Jungle, 1997, PG, ★	1998
Junior, 1994, PG-13, ★★★¹/₂	1998
Jurassic Park, 1993, PG-13, ★★★	1998
Juror, The, 1996, R, ★★	1999
Just Between Friends, 1985, PG-13, ★¹/₂	1987
Just Cause, 1995, R, ★★	1997

K

Kafka, 1992, PG-13, ★★	1994
Kagemusha, 1980, PG, ★★★★	1998
Kalifornia, 1993, R, ★★★★	1998

Kama Sutra, 1997, NR, ★★	1998
Kansas City, 1996, R, ★★★	1999
Karate Kid, The, 1984, PG, ★★★★	1998
Karate Kid Part III, The, 1989, PG, ★¹/₂	1993
Kazaam, 1996, PG, ★¹/₂	1999
Kerouac, 1985, NR, ★★¹/₂	1987
Kicked in the Head, 1997, R, ★¹/₂	2000
Kicking and Screaming, 1995, R, ★★★	1998
Kids, 1995, NR, ★★★¹/₂	1998
Kids in the Hall: Brain Candy, 1996, R, ★	1999
Killer: A Journal of Murder, 1996, R, ★★	1999
Killing Fields, The, 1984, R, ★★★★	1998
Killing Zoe, 1994, R, ★★¹/₂	1996
Kindergarten Cop, 1990, PG-13, ★★★	1998
King David, 1985, PG-13, ★	1987
King Lear, 1972, PG, ★★★	1998
King of Comedy, The, 1983, PG, ★★★	1998
King of Marvin Gardens, The, 1972, R, ★★★	1998
King of New York, 1990, R, ★★	1993
King of the Gypsies, 1978, R, ★★★	1998
King of the Hill, 1993, PG-13, ★★★★	1998
Kinjite: Forbidden Subjects, 1989, R, ★	1993
Kiss Before Dying, A, 1991, R, ★★★	1998
Kissed, 1997, NR, ★★★	1998
Kiss Me, Guido, 1997, R, ★★	2000
Kiss of Death, 1995, R, ★★	1996
Kiss of the Spider Woman, 1985, R, ★★★¹/₂	1998
Kiss or Kill, 1997, R, ★★★	2000
Kiss the Girls, 1997, R, ★★★¹/₂	2000
Klute, 1971, R, ★★★¹/₂	1998
K-9, 1989, PG, ★★	1993
Kolya, 1997, PG-13, ★★★¹/₂	1998
Koyaanisqatsi, 1983, NR, ★★★	1998
Krays, The, 1990, R, ★★★¹/₂	1998
K2, 1992, R, ★★	1994
Kung Fu Master, 1989, R, ★★★	1998

L

La Bamba, 1987, PG-13, ★★★	1998
La Belle Noiseuse, 1992, NR, ★★★★	1998
La Cage aux Folles, 1979, R, ★★★★	1998
La Ceremonie, 1997, NR, ★★★	2000
L.A. Confidential, 1997, R, ★★★★	2000
Ladybird, Ladybird, 1995, NR, ★★★★	1998
Lady in White, 1988, PG-13, ★★★	1995
Lady Sings the Blues, 1972, R, ★★★	1998
La Femme Nikita, 1991, R, ★★★	1998
Lair of the White Worm, The, 1988, R, ★★	1991
La Lectrice, 1989, R, ★★★★	1998

Land and Freedom, 1995, NR, ★★★	1999
Land Before Time, The, 1988, G, ★★★	1996
Larger Than Life, 1996, PG, ★¹/₂	1999
Lassiter, 1984, R, ★★★	1995
Last Action Hero, The, 1993, PG-13, ★★¹/₂	1995
Last Boy Scout, The, 1991, R, ★★★	1996
Last Dance, 1995, R, ★★¹/₂	1999
Last Days of Chez Nous, The, 1993, R, ★★★¹/₂	1998
Last Detail, The, 1974, R, ★★★★	1998
Last Dragon, The, 1985, PG-13, ★★¹/₂	1991
Last Emperor, The, 1987, PG-13, ★★★★	1998
Last Exit to Brooklyn, 1990, R, ★★★¹/₂	1998
Last Flight of Noah's Ark, The, 1980, G, ¹/₂★	1986
Last House on the Left, 1972, R, ★★★¹/₂	1998
Last Man Standing, 1996, R, ★	1999
Last Metro, The, 1980, NR, ★★★	1998
Last of the Dogmen, 1995, PG, ★★★	1998
Last of the Mohicans, The, 1992, R, ★★★	1998
L.A. Story, 1991, PG-13, ★★★★	1998
Last Picture Show, The, 1971, R, ★★★★	1998
La Strada, 1954, NR, ★★★¹/₂	1997
Last Seduction, The, 1994, NR, ★★★★	1998
Last Starfighter, The, 1984, PG, ★★¹/₂	1991
Last Supper, The, 1995, R, ★★★	1999
Last Tango in Paris, 1972, X, ★★★★	1998
Last Temptation of Christ, The, 1988, R, ★★★★	1998
Late for Dinner, 1991, PG, ★★¹/₂	1993
Late Show, The, 1977, PG, ★★★★	1998
Lawrence of Arabia, 1962, PG, ★★★★	1997
Laws of Gravity, 1992, R, ★★★	1996
League of Their Own, A, 1992, PG, ★★★	1998
Lean on Me, 1989, PG-13, ★★¹/₂	1993
Leap of Faith, 1992, PG-13, ★★★	1998
Leave It to Beaver, 1997, PG, ★★★	2000
Leaving Las Vegas, 1995, R, ★★★★	1998
Leaving Normal, 1992, R, ★★¹/₂	1994
Legend, 1986, PG, ★★	1989
Legend of Hell House, The, 1973, PG, ★★★¹/₂	1995
Legends of the Fall, 1995, R, ★★★	1998
Léolo, 1993, NR, ★★★★	1998
Less Than Zero, 1987, R, ★★★★	1998
Les Voleurs (The Thieves), 1996, R, ★★★¹/₂	1999
Lethal Weapon, 1987, R, ★★★★	1998
Lethal Weapon 2, 1989, R, ★★★¹/₂	1998
Lethal Weapon 3, 1992, R, ★★★	1998
Let Him Have It, 1992, R, ★★★¹/₂	1998

Let's Spend the Night Together, 1983, PG, ★★½	1994
Lianna, 1983, R, ★★★½	1998
Liar Liar, 1997, PG-13, ★★★	1998
Licence to Kill, 1989, PG-13, ★★★½	1998
Life Is Sweet, 1991, NR, ★★★★	1998
Life Less Ordinary, A, 1997, R, ★★	2000
Life Stinks, 1991, PG-13, ★★★	1998
Life With Mikey, 1993, PG, ★★	1995
Lightning Jack, 1994, PG-13, ★★	1995
Light of Day, 1987, PG-13, ★★★½	1998
Light Sleeper, 1992, R, ★★★★	1998
Like Father, Like Son, 1987, PG-13, ★	1991
Like Water for Chocolate, 1993, R, ★★★★	1998
Lion King, The, 1994, G, ★★★½	1998
Listen Up: The Lives of Quincy Jones, 1990, PG-13, ★★★½	1998
Little Big League, 1994, PG, ★★★½	1998
Little Big Man, 1971, PG, ★★★★	1998
Little Buddha, 1994, PG, ★★	1995
Little Darlings, 1980, R, ★★	1987
Little Dorrit, 1988, G, ★★★★	1998
Little Drummer Girl, 1984, R, ★★	1991
Little Indian Big City, 1995, PG, no stars	1999
Little Man Tate, 1991, PG, ★★★½	1998
Little Mermaid, The, 1989, G, ★★★★	1998
Little Nikita, 1988, PG, ★½	1991
Little Odessa, 1995, R, ★★	1996
Little Princess, A, 1995, G, ★★★½	1998
Little Vera, 1989, R, ★★★	1996
Little Women, 1994, PG, ★★★½	1998
Living Daylights, The, 1987, PG, ★★	1994
Local Hero, 1983, PG, ★★★★	1998
Locusts, The, 1997, R, ★★½	2000
Lonely Guy, The, 1984, R, ★½	1995
Lonely Lady, The, 1983, R, ½★	1988
Lonely Passion of Judith Hearne, The, 1988, R, ★★★	1998
Lone Star, 1996, R, ★★★★	1999
Lone Wolf McQuade, 1983, PG, ★★★½	1995
Long Goodbye, The, 1973, R, ★★★	1996
Long Good Friday, The, 1982, R, ★★★★	1998
Long Kiss Goodnight, The, 1996, R, ★★½	1999
Longtime Companion, 1990, R, ★★★½	1998
Long Walk Home, The, 1991, PG, ★★★½	1998
Looking for Mr. Goodbar, 1977, R, ★★★	1998
Look Who's Talking, 1989, PG-13, ★★★	1998
Look Who's Talking Now, 1993, PG-13, ★	1995
Loose Cannons, 1990, R, ★	1992
Lord of Illusions, 1995, R, ★★★	1998

Lords of Discipline, 1983, R, ★★	1991
Lorenzo's Oil, 1993, PG-13, ★★★★	1998
Losing Isaiah, 1995, R, ★★½	1997
Lost Angels, 1989, R, ★★½	1992
Lost Boys, The, 1987, R, ★★½	1993
Lost Highway, 1997, R, ★★	1998
Lost in America, 1985, R, ★★★★	1998
Lost in Yonkers, 1993, PG, ★★★	1998
Lost World: Jurassic Park, The, 1997, PG-13, ★★	1998
Louie Bluie, 1985, NR, ★★★½	1996
Love Affair, 1994, PG-13, ★★★	1998
Love Always, 1997, R, ½★	2000
Love and Human Remains, 1995, NR, ★★½	1997
Love and Other Catastrophes, 1997, R, ★★	2000
Love Field, 1993, PG-13, ★★½	1997
love jones, 1997, R, ★★★	1998
Love Letters, 1984, R, ★★★½	1998
Lover, The, 1992, R, ★★	1996
Love Serenade, 1997, R, ★★★	2000
Lovesick, 1983, PG, ★★★	1989
Love Story, 1970, PG, ★★★★	1998
Love Streams, 1984, PG-13, ★★★★	1998
Love! Valour! Compassion!, 1997, R, ★★★	1998
Lucas, 1985, PG-13, ★★★★	1998
Lumiere & Company, 1996, NR, ★★★	1999
Lust in the Dust, 1985, R, ★★	1990

M

Maborosi, 1997, NR, ★★★★	1998
Mac, 1993, R, ★★★½	1998
Macbeth, 1972, R, ★★★★	1998
Madame Bovary, 1991, NR, ★★★	1998
Madame Butterfly, 1996, NR, ★★★	1999
Madame Sousatzka, 1988, PG-13, ★★★★	1998
Mad City, 1997, PG-13, ★★½	2000
Mad Dog and Glory, 1993, R, ★★★½	1998
Mad Dog Time, 1996, R, no stars	1999
Made in America, 1993, PG-13, ★★★	1998
Mad Love, 1995, PG-13, ★★★	1998
Mad Max Beyond Thunderdome, 1985, R, ★★★★	1998
Madness of King George, The, 1995, NR, ★★★★	1998
Major Payne, 1995, PG-13, ★★★	1998
Making Love, 1982, R, ★★	1988
Making Mr. Right, 1987, PG-13, ★★★½	1998
Malcolm X, 1992, PG-13, ★★★★	1998

Malice, 1993, R, ★★	1995
Mambo Kings, The, 1992, R, ★★★½	1998
Manchurian Candidate, The,	
1962, PG-13, ★★★★	1997
Mandela, 1997, NR, ★★★	2000
Manhattan, 1979, R, ★★★½	1998
Manhattan Murder Mystery,	
1993, PG, ★★★	1998
Manhattan Project, The,	
1986, PG-13, ★★★★	1998
Man in the Moon, The,	
1991, PG-13, ★★★★	1998
Mannequin, 1987, PG, ½★	1990
Manny and Lo, 1996, R, ★★★½	1999
Man of Iron, 1980, NR, ★★★★	1998
Manon of the Spring, 1987, PG, ★★★★	1998
Man Who Knew Too Little, The, 1997,	
PG, ★	2000
Man Who Loved Women, The,	
1983, R, ★★	1988
Man Who Would Be King, The,	
1975, PG, ★★★★	1998
Man Without a Face, The,	
1993, PG-13, ★★★	1998
Man With Two Brains, The, 1983, R, ★★	1995
Map of the Human Heart,	
1993, R, ★★★★	1998
Margaret's Museum, 1997, R, ★★★½	1998
Marie, 1985, PG-13, ★★★	1987
Marriage of Maria Braun, The,	
1979, R, ★★★★	1998
Marrying Man, The, 1991, R, ★★★	1995
Mars Attacks!, 1996, PG-13, ★★	1999
Marvin's Room, 1997, PG-13, ★★★½	1998
Mary Reilly, 1996, R, ★★★	1998
Mary Shelley's Frankenstein,	
1994, R, ★★½	1997
M*A*S*H, 1970, R, ★★★★	1998
Mask, 1985, PG-13, ★★★½	1998
Mask, The, 1994, PG-13, ★★★	1998
Masquerade, 1988, R, ★★★	1998
Masterminds, 1997, PG-13, ½★	2000
Matchmaker, The, 1997, R, ★★★	2000
Matilda, 1996, PG, ★★★	1999
Matinee, 1993, PG, ★★★½	1998
Maurice, 1987, R, ★★★	1998
Maverick, 1994, PG, ★★★	1998
Max Dugan Returns, 1983, PG, ★★½	1986
Maxie, 1985, PG, 1/2★	1987
Maybe . . . Maybe Not, 1996, R, ★★★	1999
May Fools, 1990, R, ★★★	1998

M. Butterfly, 1993, R, ★★½	1995
McCabe and Mrs. Miller,	
1971, R, ★★★★	1998
Me and My Matchmaker,	
1996, NR, ★★★	1999
Mean Streets, 1974, R, ★★★★	1998
Medicine Man, The, 1992, PG-13, ★½	1994
Meeting Venus, 1991, PG-13, ★★★	1995
Melvin and Howard, 1980, R, ★★★½	1998
Memoirs of an Invisible Man,	
1992, PG-13, ★★½	1994
Memories of Me, 1988, PG-13, ★★★½	1998
Memphis Belle, 1990, PG-13, ★★★	1998
Menace II Society, 1993, R, ★★★★	1998
Men Don't Leave, 1990, PG-13, ★★	1991
Men in Black, 1997, PG-13, ★★★	1998
Men of Respect, 1991, R, ★	1992
Mephisto, 1981, NR, ★★★★	1998
Mermaids, 1990, PG-13, ★★★	1998
Merry Christmas, Mr. Lawrence,	
1983, R, ★★½	1991
Meteor Man, The, 1993, PG, ★★½	1995
Metro, 1997, R, ★★★	1998
Metropolis, 1926, NR, ★★★★	1997
Metropolitan, 1990, PG-13, ★★★½	1998
Miami Blues, 1990, R, ★★	1993
Miami Rhapsody, 1995, PG-13, ★★★	1998
Michael, 1996, PG, ★★★	1999
Michael Collins, 1996, R, ★★★	1999
Micki & Maude, 1984, PG-13, ★★★★	1998
Microcosmos, 1997, G, ★★★★	1998
Midnight Clear, A, 1992, R, ★★★	1998
Midnight Cowboy, 1969, R, ★★★	1997
Midnight in the Garden of Good	
and Evil, 1997, R, ★★½	2000
Midnight Run, 1988, R, ★★★½	1998
Midsummer Night's Sex Comedy, A,	
1982, PG, ★★	1997
Mighty Aphrodite, 1995, R, ★★★½	1998
Mighty Ducks, The, 1992, PG, ★★	1994
Mighty Morphin Power Rangers™:	
The Movie, 1995, PG, ½★	1997
Mighty Quinn, The, 1989, R, ★★★★	1998
Milagro Beanfield War, The,	
1988, R, ★★½	1993
Miles From Home, 1988, R, ★★★	1998
Milk Money, 1994, PG-13, ★	1996
Miller's Crossing, 1990, R, ★★★	1998
Mimic, 1997, R, ★★★½	2000
Miracle Mile, 1989, R, ★★★	1998
Miracle on 34th Street, 1994, PG, ★★★	1998

Mirror Has Two Faces, The,	
1996, PG-13, ★★★	1999
Misery, 1990, R, ★★★	1998
Mishima, 1985, R, ★★★★	1998
Miss Firecracker, 1989, PG, ★★★½	1998
Missing, 1982, R, ★★★	1998
Mission, The, 1986, PG, ★★½	1993
Mission Impossible, 1996, PG-13, ★★★	1999
Mississippi Burning, 1988, R, ★★★★	1998
Mississippi Masala, 1992, R, ★★★½	1998
Mo' Better Blues, 1990, R, ★★★	1998
Moderns, The, 1988, NR, ★★★	1998
Mommie Dearest, 1981, PG, ★	1998
Mona Lisa, 1986, R, ★★★★	1998
Money Pit, The, 1986, PG-13, ★	1991
Money Talks, 1997, R, ★★★	2000
Money Train, 1995, R, ★½	1997
Monkey Trouble, 1994, PG, ★★★	1998
Monsieur Hire, 1990, PG-13, ★★★★	1998
Monsignor, 1982, R, ★	1987
Month by the Lake, A, 1995, PG, ★★★½	1998
Monty Python's Meaning of Life,	
1983, R, ★★½	1995
Moonlighting, 1982, PG, ★★★★	1998
Moon Over Parador, 1988, PG-13, ★★	1993
Moonstruck, 1987, PG, ★★★★	1998
Morning After, The, 1986, R, ★★★	1996
Mortal Thoughts, 1991, R, ★★★	1998
Moscow on the Hudson,	
1984, R, ★★★★	1998
Mosquito Coast, The, 1986, PG, ★★	1993
Motel Hell, 1980, R, ★★★	1996
Mother, 1997, PG-13, ★★★½	1998
Mother Night, 1996, R, ★★½	1999
Mother's Day, 1980, R, no stars	1991
Mountains of the Moon,	
1990, R, ★★★½	1998
Mouse Hunt, 1997, PG, ★★	2000
Mr. and Mrs. Bridge,	
1991, PG-13, ★★★★	1998
Mr. Baseball, 1992, PG-13, ★★★	1998
Mr. Destiny, 1990, PG-13, ★★	1992
Mr. Holland's Opus, 1996, PG, ★★★½	1999
Mister Johnson, 1991, PG-13, ★★★	1998
Mr. Jones, 1993, R, ★★★	1998
Mr. Magoo, 1997, PG, ½★	2000
Mr. Mom, 1983, PG, ★★	1987
Mr. Saturday Night, 1992, R, ★★★	1995
Mr. Wonderful, 1993, PG-13, ★½	1995
Mrs. Brown, 1997, PG, ★★★½	2000
Mrs. Doubtfire, 1993, PG-13, ★★½	1998
Mrs. Parker and the Vicious Circle,	
1994, R, ★★★½	1998
Mrs. Winterbourne, 1996, PG-13, ★★½	1999
Much Ado About Nothing,	
1993, PG-13, ★★★	1998
Mulholland Falls, 1996, R, ★★★½	1999
Multiplicity, 1996, PG-13, ★★½	1999
Muppet Christmas Carol, The,	
1992, G, ★★★	1998
Muppet Movie, The, 1979, G, ★★★½	1998
Muppets Take Manhattan, The,	
1984, G, ★★★	1998
Muppet Treasure Island, 1996, G, ★★½	1999
Murder at 1600, 1997, R, ★★½	1998
Murder in the First, 1995, R, ★★	1996
Murder on the Orient Express,	
1974, PG, ★★★	1998
Muriel's Wedding, 1995, R, ★★★½	1998
Murphy's Romance, 1985, PG-13, ★★★	1998
Music Box, 1990, PG-13, ★★	1993
Music Lovers, The, 1971, R, ★★	1993
Music of Chance, The, 1993, NR, ★★★	1998
My Beautiful Laundrette, 1986, R, ★★★	1998
My Best Friend's Wedding,	
1997, PG-13, ★★★	1998
My Bodyguard, 1980, PG, ★★★½	1998
My Brilliant Career, 1980, NR, ★★★½	1998
My Cousin Vinny, 1992, R, ★★½	1998
My Dinner with André,	
1981, NR, ★★★★	1998
My Fair Lady, 1964, G, ★★★★	1997
My Family, 1995, R, ★★★★	1998
My Father's Glory, 1991, G, ★★★★	1998
My Father the Hero, 1994, PG, ★★	1995
My Favorite Season, 1995, NR, ★★★	1999
My Favorite Year, 1982, PG, ★★★½	1998
My Fellow Americans, 1996, PG-13, ★★½	1999
My Girl, 1991, PG, ★★★½	1998
My Girl 2, 1994, PG, ★★	1995
My Heroes Have Always Been Cowboys,	
1991, PG, ★★	1992
My Left Foot, 1989, R, ★★★★	1998
My Life, 1993, PG-13, ★★½	1995
My Mother's Castle, 1991, PG, ★★★★	1998
My Own Private Idaho, 1991, R, ★★★½	1998
My Stepmother Is an Alien,	
1988, PG-13, ★★	1993
Mystery Science Theater 3000:	
The Movie, 1996, PG-13, ★★★	1999
Mystery Train, 1990, R, ★★★½	1998
Mystic Pizza, 1988, R, ★★★½	1998

Myth of Fingerprints, The, 1997, R, ★¹/₂ — 2000

My Tutor, 1983, R, ★★★ — 1986

N

Nadine, 1987, PG, ★★¹/₂ — 1993

Naked, 1994, NR, ★★★★ — 1998

Naked Gun, The, 1988, PG-13, ★★★¹/₂ — 1998

Naked Gun 2¹/₂: The Smell of Fear, The, 1991, PG-13, ★★★ — 1998

Naked Gun 33¹/₃: The Final Insult, 1994, PG-13, ★★★ — 1998

Naked in New York, 1994, R, ★★★ — 1998

Naked Lunch, 1992, R, ★★¹/₂ — 1994

Name of the Rose, The, 1986, R, ★★¹/₂ — 1995

Narrow Margin, 1990, R, ★¹/₂ — 1992

Nashville, 1975, R, ★★★★ — 1998

Nasty Girl, The, 1991, PG-13, ★★¹/₂ — 1993

National Lampoon's Animal House, 1978, R, ★★★★ — 1998

National Lampoon's Christmas Vacation, 1989, PG-13, ★★ — 1995

National Lampoon's Loaded Weapon I, 1993, PG-13, ★ — 1994

Natural, The, 1984, PG, ★★ — 1995

Natural Born Killers, 1994, R, ★★★★ — 1998

Navy Seals, 1990, R, ★¹/₂ — 1992

Necessary Roughness, 1991, PG-13, ★★★ — 1996

Needful Things, 1993, R, ★¹/₂ — 1995

Neighbors, 1981, R, ★★★ — 1996

Nell, 1994, PG-13, ★★★ — 1998

Nelly and Monsieur Arnaud, 1996, NR, ★★★¹/₂ — 1999

Nenette et Boni, 1997, NR, ★★★ — 2000

Net, The, 1995, PG-13, ★★★ — 1998

Network, 1976, R, ★★★★ — 1998

Neverending Story, The, 1984, PG, ★★★ — 1998

Never Say Never Again, 1983, PG, ★★★¹/₂ — 1998

New Age, The, 1994, R, ★★★¹/₂ — 1998

New Jack City, 1991, R, ★★★¹/₂ — 1998

New Jersey Drive, 1995, R, ★★★ — 1998

Newsies, 1992, PG, ★¹/₂ — 1993

New York, New York, 1977, PG, ★★★ — 1998

New York Stories, 1989, PG, 1998
    Life Lessons, ★★★¹/₂
    Life Without Zoe, ★¹/₂
    Oedipus Wrecks, ★★ — 2000

Nick and Jane, 1997, R, ¹/₂★ — 2000

Nico Icon, 1996, NR, ★★★ — 1999

Night and the City, 1992, R, ★★ — 1994

Night Falls on Manhattan, 1997, R, ★★★ — 2000

Nightmare on Elm Street 3, A: Dream Warriors, 1987, R, ★¹/₂ — 1990

Night of the Living Dead, 1990, R, ★ — 1992

Night on Earth, 1992, R, ★★★ — 1998

Nina Takes a Lover, 1995, R, ★★ — 1997

9¹/₂ Weeks, 1985, R, ★★★¹/₂ — 1998

Nine Months, 1995, PG-13, ★★ — 1998

1984, 1984, R, ★★★¹/₂ — 1998

Nine to Five, 1980, PG, ★★★ — 1998

Nixon, 1995, R, ★★★★ — 1998

Nobody's Fool, 1986, PG-13, ★★ — 1991

Nobody's Fool, 1995, R, ★★★¹/₂ — 1998

No Escape, 1994, R, ★★ — 1995

Nomads, 1985, R, ★¹/₂ — 1987

No Man's Land, 1987, R, ★★★ — 1998

No Mercy, 1986, R, ★★★ — 1996

Normal Life, 1996, R, ★★★¹/₂ — 1999

Norma Rae, 1979, PG, ★★★ — 1998

North, 1994, PG, no stars — 1997

North Dallas Forty, 1979, R, ★★★¹/₂ — 1998

Nosferatu, 1979, R, ★★★★ — 1998

Nothing But a Man, 1964, NR, ★★★¹/₂ — 1997

Nothing in Common, 1986, PG, ★★¹/₂ — 1988

Nothing to Lose, 1997, R, ★★ — 2000

Not Without My Daughter, 1990, PG-13, ★★★ — 1998

No Way Out, 1987, R, ★★★★ — 1998

Nuns on the Run, 1990, PG-13, ★ — 1993

Nuts, 1987, R, ★★ — 1993

Nutty Professor, The, 1996, PG-13, ★★★ — 1999

O

Object of Beauty, The, 1991, R, ★★★¹/₂ — 1998

Off Beat, 1986, PG, ★★★¹/₂ — 1995

Officer and a Gentleman, An, 1982, R, ★★★★ — 1998

Of Mice and Men, 1992, PG-13, ★★★¹/₂ — 1998

Oh, God!, 1977, PG, ★★★¹/₂ — 1998

Oh, God! Book II, 1980, PG, ★★ — 1995

Oh, God! You Devil, 1984, PG, ★★★¹/₂ — 1998

Old Gringo, 1989, R, ★★ — 1993

Oleanna, 1994, NR, ★★ — 1997

Oliver & Co., 1988, G, ★★★ — 1998

Once Around, 1990, R, ★★★¹/₂ — 1998

Once Upon a Forest, 1993, G, ★★¹/₂ — 1995

Once Upon a Time in America, 1984, R,
    ★—short version
    ★★★★—original version — 1998

Once Upon a Time . . . When We Were Colored, 1996, PG, ★★★★ — 1999

Once Were Warriors, 1995, R, ★★★¹⁄₂	1998	Paradise Road, 1997, R, ★★	1998
One False Move, 1992, R, ★★★★	1998	Parenthood, 1989, PG-13, ★★★★	1998
One Fine Day, 1996, PG, ★★	1999	Parents, 1989, R, ★★	1993
One Flew Over the Cuckoo's Nest,		Paris Is Burning, 1991, NR, ★★★	1996
1975, R, ★★★	1998	Paris, Texas, 1984, R, ★★★★	1998
One from the Heart, 1982, PG, ★★	1995	Pascali's Island, 1988, PG-13, ★★★	1998
One Good Cop, 1991, R, ★★	1994	Passage to Indi: A, 1984, PG, ★★★★	1998
187, 1997, R, ★★	2000	Passenger 57, 1992, R, ★★★	1998
101 Dalmatians, 1961, G, ★★★	1998	Passion Fish, 1993, R, ★★★★	1998
101 Dalmatians, 1996, G, ★★¹⁄₂	1999	Paternity, 1981, PG, ★★	1986
One Magic Christmas, 1985, G, ★★	1987	Patriot Games, 1992, R, ★★¹⁄₂	1995
$1,000,000 Duck, 1971, G, ★	1987	Patton, 1970, PG, ★★★★	1998
One Night Stand, 1997, R, ★★★	2000	Patty Hearst, 1988, R, ★★★	1998
1,000 Pieces of Gold, 1991, NR, ★★★	1996	PCU, 1994, PG-13, ★★	1995
One-Trick Pony, 1980, R, ★★★¹⁄₂	1998	Peacemaker, The, 1997, R, ★★¹⁄₂	2000
On Golden Pond, 1981, PG, ★★★★	1998	Peeping Tom, 1960, NR, ★★★¹⁄₂	1997
Onion Field, The, 1979, R, ★★★★	1998	Peggy Sue Got Married,	
Only When I Laugh, 1981, R, ★	1987	1986, PG-13, ★★★★	1998
Only You, 1994, PG, ★★★¹⁄₂	1998	Pelican Brief, The, 1993, PG-13, ★★★	1998
On the Edge, 1986, PG-13, ★★★¹⁄₂	1989	Pelle the Conqueror, 1988, NR, ★★★¹⁄₂	1998
On the Right Track, 1981, PG, ★★¹⁄₂	1986	Pennies from Heaven, 1981, R, ★★	1986
On the Road Again, 1980, PG, ★★★	1998	People vs. Larry Flynt, The,	
Opening Night, 1978, PG-13, ★★★	1998	1996, R, ★★★★	1999
Operation Condor, 1997, PG-13, ★★★	1998	Perez Family, The, 1995, R, ★★★	1998
Ordinary People, 1980, R, ★★★★	1998	Perfect, 1985, R, ★¹⁄₂	1987
Orlando, 1993, PG-13, ★★★¹⁄₂	1998	Perfect Candidate, A, 1996, NR, ★★★	1999
Orphans, 1987, R, ★★¹⁄₂	1993	Perfect World, A, 1993, PG-13, ★★★★	1998
Othello, 1952, NR, ★★★	1997	Performance, 1970, R, ★★¹⁄₂	1993
Othello, 1995, R, ★★	1998	Permanent Record, 1988, PG-13, ★★★★	1998
Other People's Money,		Personal Best, 1982, R, ★★★★	1998
1991, PG-13, ★★★¹⁄₂	1998	Personal Services, 1987, R, ★★★¹⁄₂	1998
Outbreak, 1995, R, ★★★¹⁄₂	1998	Persuasion, 1995, PG, ★★★¹⁄₂	1998
Outlaw Josey Wales, The, 1976, PG, ★★★	1998	Peter's Friends, 1992, R, ★★★¹⁄₂	1998
Out of Africa, 1985, PG, ★★★★	1998	Phantom, The, 1996, PG, ★★★¹⁄₂	1999
Out of the Blue, 1982, R, ★★★¹⁄₂	1998	Phantom of Liberty, The,	
Outrageous Fortune, 1987, R, ★★	1993	1974, R, ★★★★	1998
Out to Sea, 1997, PG-13, ★★★	1998	Phenomenon, 1996, PG, ★★★	1999
Overboard, 1987, PG, ★★★	1995	Philadelphia, 1994, PG-13, ★★★¹⁄₂	1998
		Physical Evidence, 1989, R, ★★	1992
P		Piano, The, 1993, R, ★★★★	1998
Pacific Heights, 1990, R, ★★	1993	Picnic, 1996, PG, ★★	1999
Package, The, 1989, R, ★★★	1998	Picnic at Hanging Rock,	
Pale Rider, 1985, R, ★★★	1998	1980, PG, ★★★¹⁄₂	1998
Pallbearer, The, 1996, PG-13, ★★★	1999	Picture Bride, 1995, PG-13, ★★★	1998
Palookaville, 1996, R, ★★★	1999	Picture Perfect, 1997, PG-13, ★★	2000
Panther, 1995, R, ★★¹⁄₂	1996	Pillow Book, The, 1997, NR, ★★★¹⁄₂	1998
Paper, The, 1994, R, ★★★¹⁄₂	1998	Pink Cadillac, 1989, PG-13, ★	1992
Paperback Romance, 1997, R, ★★★	2000	Pink Flamingos, 1997, NC-17, no stars	1998
Paper Chase, The, 1973, PG, ★★★★	1998	Pink Flamingos (reissue), 1997, NC-17,	
Paperhouse, 1989, PG-13, ★★★★	1998	not relevant	2000
Paradise, 1991, PG-13, ★★	1993	Pinocchio, 1940, G, ★★★★	1997

Rage in Harlem, A, 1991, R, ★★★	1998
Raggedy Man, 1981, PG, ★★★½	1995
Raging Bull, 1980, R, ★★★★	1998
Ragtime, 1981, PG, ★★★½	1998
Raiders of the Lost Ark, 1981, PG, ★★★★	1998
Rainbow, The, 1989, R, ★★★	1998
Raining Stones, 1994, NR, ★★★½	1998
Rainmaker, The, 1997, PG-13, ★★★	2000
Rain Man, 1988, R, ★★★½	1998
Raise the Red Lantern, 1992, PG, ★★★★	1998
Raise the Titanic, 1980, PG, ★★½	1986
Raising Arizona, 1987, PG-13, ★½	1995
Rambling Rose, 1991, R, ★★★	1998
Rambo: First Blood Part II,	
1985, R, ★★★	1996
Ran, 1985, R, ★★★★	1998
Ransom, 1996, R, ★★★	1999
Rapa Nui, 1994, R, ★★	1997
Rapture, The, 1991, R, ★★★★	1998
Razor's Edge, The, 1984, PG-13, ★★½	1988
Ready to Wear, 1994, R, ★★½	1997
Real Genius, 1985, PG-13, ★★★½	1998
Reality Bites, 1994, PG-13, ★★	1995
Real McCoy, The, 1993, PG-13, ★★	1995
Re-Animator, 1985, NR, ★★★	1998
Red, 1994, R, ★★★★	1998
Red Corner, 1997, R, ★★	2000
Red Heat, 1988, R, ★★★	1998
Red Rock West, 1994, R, ★★★½	1998
Reds, 1981, PG, ★★★½	1998
Red Sonja, 1985, PG-13, ★½	1987
Ref, The, 1994, R, ★★★	1998
Regarding Henry, 1991, PG-13, ★★	1994
Relic, The, 1997, R, ★★★	1998
Remains of the Day, 1993, PG, ★★★½	1998
Renaissance Man, 1994, PG-13, ★½	1995
Rendevous in Paris, 1996, NR, ★★★½	1999
Repo Man, 1984, R, ★★★	1998
Rescuers Down Under, The,	
1990, G, ★★★	1998
Reservoir Dogs, 1992, R, ★★½	1998
Restoration, 1996, R, ★★★½	1999
Return of the Jedi (Special Edition),	
1997, PG, ★★★★	1998
Return of the Living Dead, 1985, R, ★★★	1987
Return of the Secaucus Seven,	
1981, NR, ★★★	1998
Return to Oz, 1985, PG, ★★	1987
Revenge, 1990, R, ★★½	1993
Revenge of the Nerds II, 1987, PG-13, ★½	1990
Revenge of the Pink Panther,	
1978, PG, ★★★	1995

Reversal of Fortune, 1990, R, ★★★★	1998
Rhapsody in August, 1992, PG, ★★★	1998
Rhinestone, 1984, PG, ★	1987
Rich and Famous, 1981, R, ★★½	1987
Richard Pryor Here and Now,	
1983, R, ★★★★	1996
Richard Pryor Live on the Sunset Strip,	
1982, R, ★★★★	1996
Richard III, 1996, R, ★★★½	1999
Richie Rich, 1994, PG, ★★★	1998
Rich in Love, 1993, PG-13, ★★★	1998
Rich Man's Wife, The, 1996, R, ★★½	1999
Ridicule, 1996, R, ★★★½	1999
Right Stuff, The, 1983, PG, ★★★★	1998
Rising Sun, 1993, R, ★★	1995
Risky Business, 1983, R, ★★★★	1998
Rita, Sue and Bob Too, 1987, R, ★★★	1996
River, The, 1985, PG-13, ★★	1991
River Runs Through It, A,	
1992, PG, ★★★½	1998
River's Edge, 1987, R, ★★★½	1998
River Wild, The, 1994, PG-13, ★★	1997
Road House, 1989, R, ★★½	1993
Road Warrior, The, 1982, R, ★★★½	1998
Robin Hood: Prince of Thieves,	
1991, PG-13, ★★	1997
RoboCop, 1987, R, ★★★	1998
RoboCop II, 1990, R, ★★	1995
RoboCop 3, 1993, PG-13, ★½	1995
Rob Roy, 1995, R, ★★★½	1998
Rock, The, 1996, R, ★★★½	1999
Rocketeer, The, 1991, PG-13, ★★★	1998
Rocket Man, 1997, PG, ★★★	2000
Rocky, 1976, PG, ★★★★	1998
Rocky II, 1979, PG, ★★★	1998
Rocky IV, 1986, PG, ★★	1993
Rocky V, 1990, PG-13, ★★	1993
Rocky Horror Picture Show, The,	
1975, R, ★★½	1998
Roger & Me, 1989, R, ★★★★	1998
Romancing the Stone, 1984, PG, ★★★	1998
Romeo Is Bleeding, 1994, R, ★★	1995
Romy and Michele's High School Reunion,	
1997, R, ★★★	1998
Rookie of the Year, 1993, PG, ★★★	1996
Room with a View, A,	
1985, PG-13, ★★★★	1998
Rosalie Goes Shopping, 1990, PG, ★★★	1998
Rose, The, 1979, R, ★★★	1998
Rosewood, 1997, R, ★★★½	1998
Rough Magic, 1997, PG-13, ★★	1998
Roujin-Z, 1996, PG-13, ★★★	1999

She's Out of Control, 1989, PG, no stars	1992
She's So Lovely, 1997, R, ★★★	2000
She's the One, 1996, R, ★★	1999
Shiloh, 1997, PG, ★★★½	2000
Shine, 1996, PG-13, ★★★★	1999
Shining Through, 1992, R, ★★	1994
Shirley Valentine, 1989, R, ★	1993
Shoah, 1986, NR, ★★★★	1998
Shock to the System, A, 1990, R, ★★★	1996
Shooting Party, The, 1985, NR, ★★★	1987
Shootist, The, 1976, PG, ★★★½	1998
Shoot the Moon, 1982, R, ★★★½	1998
Shoot to Kill, 1988, R, ★★★	1996
Short Cuts, 1993, R, ★★★★	1998
Showgirls, 1995, NC-17, ★★½	1997
Shy People, 1988, R, ★★★★	1998
Sick: The Life & Death of Bob Flanagan,	
Supermasochist, 1997, NR, ★★★½	2000
Sid & Nancy, 1986, R, ★★★★	1998
Sidewalk Stories, 1989, R, ★★★½	1998
Silence of the Lambs, The,	
1991, R, ★★★½	1998
Silent Movie, 1976, PG, ★★★★	1998
Silent Running, 1972, G, ★★★★	1998
Silkwood, 1983, R, ★★★★	1998
Silverado, 1985, PG-13, ★★★½	1998
Simple Men, 1992, R, ★★	1995
Simple Wish, A, 1997, PG, ★½	2000
Sing, 1989, PG-13, ★★★	1996
Singin' in the Rain, 1952, G, ★★★★	1997
Singles, 1992, PG-13, ★★★	1998
Single White Female, 1992, R, ★★★	1996
Sirens, 1994, R, ★★★½	1998
Sister Act, 1992, PG, ★★½	1996
Sister Act 2: Back in the Habit,	
1993, PG, ★★	1995
Sisters, 1973, R, ★★★	1998
Sixteen Candles, 1984, PG, ★★★	1998
Sixth Man, The, 1997, PG-13, ★½	2000
Skin Deep, 1989, R, ★★★	1998
Slacker, 1991, R, ★★★	1998
Slaves of New York, 1989, R, ½★	1993
Sleeper, 1973, PG, ★★★½	1998
Sleeping with the Enemy, 1991, R, ★½	1994
Sleepless in Seattle, 1993, PG, ★★★	1998
Sleuth, 1972, PG, ★★★★	1998
Sling Blade, 1996, R, ★★★½	1999
Slugger's Wife, The, 1985, PG-13, ★★	1986
Small Change, 1976, PG, ★★★★	1998
Smash Palace, 1982, R, ★★★★	1998
Smilla's Sense of Snow, 1997, R, ★★★	1998
Smoke, 1995, R, ★★★	1998

Smokey and the Bandit II, 1980, PG, ★	1986
Smooth Talk, 1986, PG-13, ★★★½	1998
Snapper, The, 1993, R, ★★★½	1998
Sneakers, 1992, PG-13, ★★½	1994
Sniper, 1993, R, ★★★	1996
Soapdish, 1991, PG-13, ★★★½	1998
So I Married an Axe Murderer,	
1993, PG-13, ★★½	1995
Soldier of Orange, 1980, PG, ★★★½	1986
Soldier's Story, A, 1984, PG, ★★½	1993
Some Kind of Wonderful,	
1987, PG-13, ★★★	1998
Some Mother's Son, 1996, R, ★★★	1999
Someone to Watch Over Me, 1987, R, ★★	1992
Something to Talk About,	
1995, R, ★★★½	1998
Something Wild, 1986, R, ★★★½	1998
Sometimes a Great Notion,	
1971, PG, ★★★	1998
Somewhere in Time, 1980, PG, ★★	1988
Sommersby, 1993, PG-13, ★★	1994
Songwriter, 1985, R, ★★★½	1996
Son-in-Law, 1993, PG-13, ★★	1995
Sophie's Choice, 1982, R, ★★★★	1998
Soul Food, 1997, R, ★★★½	2000
Soul Man, 1986, PG-13, ★	1989
Sounder, 1972, G, ★★★★	1998
South Central, 1992, R, ★★★	1996
Southern Comfort, 1981, R, ★★★	1996
Spaceballs, 1987, PG, ★★½	1991
Space Jam, 1996, PG, ★★★½	1999
Spartacus, 1960, PG-13, ★★★	1997
Spawn, 1997, PG-13, ★★★½	2000
Special Effects Documentary,	
1996, NR, ★★★	1999
Species, 1995, R, ★★	1997
Speechless, 1994, PG-13, ★★	1996
Speed, 1994, R, ★★★★	1997
Speed 2: Cruise Control, 1997, PG-13,	
★★★½	2000
Spider's Stratagem, The, 1973, PG, ★★★	1998
Spike of Bensonhurst, 1988, R, ★★★	1998
Spitfire Grill, The, 1996, PG-13, ★★	1999
Splash, 1984, PG, ★½	1993
Spring Break, 1983, R, ★	1988
Sprung, 1997, R, ★½	2000
Spy Who Loved Me, The,	
1977, PG, ★★★½	1998
Stairway to Heaven, 1946, PG, ★★★★	1997
Stakeout, 1987, R, ★★★	1996
Stand and Deliver, 1988, PG-13, ★★½	1994
Stanley & Iris, 1990, PG-13, ★★½	1993

Stardust Memories, 1980, PG, ★★	1997
STAR 80, 1983, R, ★★★★	1998
Stargate, 1994, PG-13, ★	1997
Star Is Born, A, 1954 (1983), PG, ★★★★	1997
Starmaker, The, 1996, R, ★★★	1999
Starman, 1984, PG, ★★★	1998
Star Maps, 1997, R, ★★	2000
Stars Fell on Henrietta, The,	
1995, PG, ★★	1997
Starship Troopers, 1997, R, ★★	2000
Star Trek: First Contact,	
1996, PG-13, ★★★½	1999
Star Trek: Generations, 1994, PG, ★★	1997
Star Trek: The Motion Picture,	
1979, G, ★★★	1998
Star Trek II: The Wrath of Khan,	
1982, PG, ★★★	1998
Star Trek III: The Search for Spock,	
1984, PG, ★★★	1998
Star Trek IV: The Voyage Home,	
1986, PG, ★★★½	1998
Star Trek V: The Final Frontier,	
1989, PG, ★★	1997
Star Trek VI: The Undiscovered Country,	
1991, PG, ★★★	1998
Star Wars, 1977, PG, ★★★★	1997
Star Wars (Special Edition), PG,	
1997, ★★★★	1998
State of Grace, 1990, R, ★★★½	1998
Stay Hungry, 1976, R, ★★★	1996
Staying Alive, 1983, PG, ★	1994
Staying Together, 1989, R, ★★	1993
Stealing Beauty, 1996, R, ★★	1999
Steel Magnolias, 1989, PG, ★★★	1998
Stella, 1990, PG-13, ★★★½	1998
Stepfather, The, 1987, R, ★★½	1994
Stephen King's Silver Bullet,	
1985, R, ★★★	1988
Stepping Out, 1991, PG, ★★	1994
Stevie, 1981, NR, ★★★★	1998
Sting II, The, 1983, PG, ★★	1986
Stir Crazy, 1980, R, ★★	1987
Stonewall, 1996, NR, ★★½	1999
Stop Making Sense, 1984, NR, ★★★½	1998
Stop! Or My Mom Will Shoot,	
1992, PG-13, ½★	1994
Stormy Monday, 1988, R, ★★★½	1998
Story of Qiu Ju, The, 1993, NR, ★★★½	1997
Story of Women, 1990, R, ★★½	1993
Storyville, 1992, R, ★★★½	1998
Straight Out of Brooklyn, 1991, R, ★★★	1998
Straight Talk, 1992, PG, ★★	1994
Straight Time, 1978, R, ★★★½	1998
Strange Days, 1995, R, ★★★★	1998
Stranger Among Us, A, 1992, PG-13, ★½	1994
Stranger than Paradise, 1984, R, ★★★★	1998
Strapless, 1990, R, ★★★	1998
Strawberry and Chocolate,	
1995, R, ★★★½	1998
Streamers, 1984, R, ★★★★	1998
Streetcar Named Desire, A,	
1951, PG, ★★★★	1997
Street Smart, 1987, R, ★★★	1998
Streets of Fire, 1984, PG, ★★★	1988
Streetwise, 1985, R, ★★★★	1998
Strictly Ballroom, 1993, PG, ★★★	1998
Strictly Business, 1991, PG-13, ★★½	1993
Striking Distance, 1993, R, ★½	1995
Stripes, 1981, R, ★★★½	1998
Stripper, 1986, R, ★★★	1987
Striptease, 1996, R, ★★	1999
Stroker Ace, 1983, PG, ★½	1986
Stroszek, 1978, NR, ★★★★	1998
Stuart Saves His Family,	
1995, PG-13, ★★★	1998
Stuff, The, 1985, R, ★½	1987
Stunt Man, The, 1980, R, ★★	1988
Substance of Fire, The, 1997, R, ★★★	2000
Substitute, The, 1996, R, ★	1999
Suburban Commando, 1991, PG, ★	1993
subUrbia, 1997, R, ★★★½	1998
Sudden Death, 1995, R, ★★½	1998
Sudden Impact, 1983, R, ★★★	1998
Sugar Hill, 1994, R, ★★★★	1998
Summer House, The, 1993, NR, ★★★	1998
Summer of '42, 1971, R, ★★½	1987
Sunday, 1997, NR, ★★★	2000
Sunday Bloody Sunday, 1971, R, ★★★★	1998
Sunset Park, 1996, R, ★★	1999
Super, The, 1991, R, ★★	1995
Supergirl, 1984, PG, ★★	1988
Superman, 1978, PG, ★★★★	1998
Superman II, 1981, PG, ★★★★	1998
Superman III, 1983, PG, ★★½	1998
Superstar: The Life and Times of	
Andy Warhol, 1991, NR, ★★★	1997
Sure Thing, The, 1985, PG-13, ★★★½	1998
Surrender, 1987, PG, ★★	1989
Survivors, The, 1983, R, ★½	1991
Suspect, 1987, R, ★★½	1993
Swamp Thing, 1982, R, ★★★	1998
Swann in Love, 1984, R, ★★★	1996

Three Lives and Only One Death, 1997,
  NR, ★★★   2000
Three Men and a Baby, 1987, PG, ★★★   1998
Three Men and a Little Lady,
  1990, PG, ★★   1994
Three Musketeers, The, 1993, PG, ★★   1995
3 Ninjas Kick Back, 1994, PG, ★★½   1995
Three of Hearts, 1993, R, ★★★   1996
Threesome, 1994, R, ★★★   1996
3 Women, 1977, PG, ★★★★   1998
Throw Momma from the Train,
  1987, PG-13, ★★   1993
Thunderheart, 1992, R, ★★★½   1998
THX 1138, 1971, PG, ★★★   1998
Ticket to Heaven, 1981, R, ★★★½   1998
Tie Me Up! Tie Me Down!, 1990, NR, ★★   1993
Tiger's Tale, A, 1988, R, ★★   1989
Tightrope, 1984, R, ★★★½   1998
'Til There Was You, 1997, PG-13, ½★   1998
Tim Burton's Nightmare Before
  Christmas, 1993, PG, ★★★½   1998
Time Bandits, 1981, PG, ★★★   1998
Timecop, 1994, R, ★★   1997
Time of Destiny, A, 1988, PG-13, ★★★½   1998
Times of Harvey Milk, The,
  1985, NR, ★★★½   1997
Tin Cup, 1996, R, ★★★   1999
Tin Drum, The, 1980, R, ★★   1988
Tin Men, 1987, R, ★★★   1998
Titanic, 1997, PG-13, ★★★★   2000
To Be or Not To Be, 1983, R, ★★★   1998
To Die For, 1995, R, ★★★½   1998
To Gillian on Her 37th Birthday,
  1996, PG-13, ★★   1999
Tokyo Story, 1953, G, ★★★★   1997
To Live, 1994, NR, ★★★½   1998
To Live and Die in L.A., 1985, R, ★★★★   1998
Tom and Viv, 1995, PG-13, ★★½   1996
Tommy, 1975, PG, ★★★   1998
Tomorrow Never Dies, 1997, PG-13,
  ★★★   2000
Too Beautiful for You, 1990, R, ★★★½   1998
Tootsie, 1982, PG, ★★★★   1998
Topaz, 1970, PG, ★★★½   1998
Top Gun, 1986, PG, ★★½   1998
Top Secret!, 1984, R, ★★★½   1998
Torch Song Trilogy, 1988, R, ★★★½   1998
To Sleep With Anger, 1990, PG, ★★½   1993
Total Recall, 1990, R, ★★★½   1998
Toto le Heros, 1992, NR, ★★½   1994
Touch, 1997, R, ★★½   2000

Tough Enough, 1983, PG, ★★★   1986
Tough Guys Don't Dance, 1987, R, ★★½   1993
To Wong Foo, Thanks for Everything!
  Julie Newmar, 1995, PG-13, ★★½   1997
Toys, 1992, PG-13, ★★½   1994
Toy Story, 1995, G, ★★★½   1998
Track 29, 1988, R, ★★★   1996
Trading Places, 1983, R, ★★★½   1998
Trainspotting, 1996, R, ★★★   1998
Traveller, 1997, R, ★★★   2000
Trees Lounge, 1996, R, ★★★½   1999
Trespass, 1992, R, ★★½   1994
Trial, The, 1994, NR, ★★½   1996
Trial and Error, 1997, PG-13, ★★★   1998
Tribute, 1981, PG, ★★★   1996
Trip to Bountiful, The, 1985, PG, ★★★½   1998
Tron, 1982, PG, ★★★★   1998
Troop Beverly Hills, 1989, PG, ★★   1994
Trouble in Mind, 1985, R, ★★★★   1998
Troublesome Creek: A Midwestern, 1997,
  NR, ★★★   2000
True Believer, 1989, R, ★★★   1996
True Colors, 1991, R, ★★   1994
True Confessions, 1981, R, ★★★   1996
True Lies, 1994, R, ★★★   1998
True Love, 1989, R, ★★★   1996
True Romance, 1993, R, ★★★   1998
True Stories, 1986, PG-13, ★★★½   1998
Truly, Madly, Deeply, 1991, NR, ★★★   1998
Trust, 1991, R, ★★   1994
Truth About Cats and Dogs, The,
  1996, PG-13, ★★★½   1999
Truth or Dare, 1991, R, ★★★½   1998
Tucker: The Man and His Dream,
  1988, PG, ★★½   1993
Tune in Tomorrow . . . ,
  1990, PG-13, ★★½   1993
Turbulence, 1997, R, ★   1998
Turk 182!, 1985, PG-13, ★   1987
Turning Point, The, 1977, PG, ★★★½   1998
Turtle Diary, 1985, PG-13, ★★★½   1998
Twelfth Night, 1996, PG, ★★★½   1999
12 Monkeys, 1996, R, ★★★   1999
Twenty Bucks, 1994, R, ★★★   1996
28 Up, 1985, NR, ★★★★   1998
29th Street, 1991, R, ★★★   1996
Twice in a Lifetime, 1985, R, ★★★½   1998
Twilight Zone—the Movie,
  1983, PG, ★★★½   1998
Twins, 1988, PG, ★★★   1998
Twin Town, 1997, NR, ★★   2000

Twister, 1995, PG-13, ★★	1999
Two Bits, 1996, PG-13, ★½	1999
Two Deaths, 1996, R, ★	1999
Two English Girls, 1972, R, ★★★★	1998
Two Jakes, The, 1990, R, ★★★½	1998
Two Much, 1996, PG-13, ★½	1999
Two of a Kind, 1983, PG, ½★	1986
2001: A Space Odyssey, 1968, G, ★★★★	1997
2010, 1984, PG, ★★★	1996

U

Uforia, 1985, PG, ★★★★	1998
Ulee's Gold, 1997, R, ★★★½	1998
Ulysses' Gaze, 1997, NR, ★	2000
Umbrellas of Cherbourg, The, 1996, NR, ★★★½	1999
Unbearable Lightness of Being, The, 1988, R, ★★★★	1998
Uncle Buck, 1989, PG, ★½	1993
Un Coeur en Hiver, 1993, NR, ★★★½	1998
Under Fire, 1983, R, ★★★½	1998
Under Siege, 1992, R, ★★★	1996
Under the Volcano, 1984, R, ★★★★	1998
Unforgiven, 1992, R, ★★★★	1998
Unhook the Stars, 1997, R, ★★★	1998
Universal Soldier, 1992, R, ★★	1994
Unlawful Entry, 1992, R, ★★★	1996
Unmarried Woman, An, 1978, R, ★★★★	1998
Unstrung Heroes, 1995, PG, ★★★½	1998
Untamed Heart, 1993, PG-13, ★★★	1996
Until September, 1984, R, ½★	1987
Until the End of the World, 1992, R, ★★	1994
Untouchables, The, 1987, R, ★★½	1994
Unzipped, 1995, PG-13, ★★★	1998
Up Close and Personal, 1996, PG-13, ★★★	1999
Up the Creek, 1984, R, ★★★	1989
Up the Sandbox, 1973, R, ★★★	1996
Used Cars, 1980, R, ★★	1994
Used People, 1992, PG-13, ★★	1994
Usual Suspects, The, 1995, R, ★½	1997
U-Turn, 1997, R, ★½	2000

V

Vagabond, 1986, NR, ★★★★	1998
Valley Girl, 1983, R, ★★★	1998
Valmont, 1989, R, ★★★½	1998
Van, The, 1997, R, ★★★	2000
Vanishing, The, 1991, NR, ★★★½	1998
Vanishing, The, 1993, R, ★	1994

Vanya on 42nd Street, 1994, PG, ★★★½	1998
Verdict, The, 1982, R, ★★★★	1998
Very Brady Sequel, A, 1996, PG-13, ★★½	1999
Vice Versa, 1988, PG, ★★★½	1998
Victor/Victoria, 1982, R, ★★★	1998
Videodrome, 1983, R, ★½	1988
Vincent, 1989, NR, ★★★★	1998
Vincent & Theo, 1990, PG-13, ★★★½	1998
Violets Are Blue, 1986, PG-13, ★★★	1987
Virtuosity, 1995, R, ★★★	1998
Vision Quest, 1985, R, ★★★½	1998
Visions of Eight, 1973, NR, ★★★	1998
Visions of Light: The Art of Cinematography, 1993, NR, ★★★½	1998
Visitors, The, 1996, R, ★★	1999
Vixen, 1969, X, ★★★	1996
Volcano, 1997, PG-13, ★½	1998

W

Waco: The Rules of Engagement, 1997, NR, ★★★½	2000
Wages of Fear, The, 1953, NR, ★★★★	1997
Waiting for Guffman, 1997, R, ★★★	1998
Waiting to Exhale, 1995, R, ★★★	1998
Walkabout, 1971, PG, ★★★★	1998
Walk in the Clouds, A, 1995, PG-13, ★★★★	1998
Wall Street, 1987, R, ★★★½	1998
WarGames, 1983, PG, ★★★★	1998
War of the Roses, The, 1989, R, ★★★	1998
War Party, 1989, R, ★	1991
Warriors of Virtue, 1997, PG, ★★	2000
War Room, The, 1994, NR, ★★★½	1998
Washington Square, 1997, PG, ★★★	2000
Watcher in the Woods, The, 1981, PG, ★★	1986
Waterdance, The, 1992, R, ★★★½	1998
Waterworld, 1995, PG-13, ★★½	1997
Wayne's World, 1992, PG-13, ★★★	1998
Wayne's World 2, 1993, PG-13, ★★★	1998
Weavers: Wasn't That a Time!, The, 1982, PG, ★★★★	1998
Wedding, A, 1978, PG, ★★★½	1998
Wedding Banquet, The, 1993, NR, ★★★	1998
Weeds, 1987, R, ★★★	1996
Weekend at Bernie's, 1989, PG-13, ★	1992
Week's Vacation, A, 1980, NR, ★★★½	1998
Weird Science, 1985, PG-13, ★★★½	1998
Welcome Home, 1989, R, ★★	1992

X, Y, Z

Xanadu, 1980, PG, ★★	1988
Year of Living Dangerously, The,	
1983, PG, ★★★★	1998
Year of the Gun, 1991, R, ★★★	1996
Year of the Horse, 1997, R, ★	2000
Year of the Quiet Sun,	
1986, PG, ★★★★	1987
Yentl, 1983, PG, ★★★½	1998
Youngblood, 1985, PG-13, ★★	1987
Young Doctors in Love, 1982, R, ★★	1991

Young Einstein, 1989, PG, ★	1992
Young Frankenstein, 1974, PG, ★★★★	1998
Young Poisoner's Handbook, The,	
1996, NR, ★★★½	1999
Young Sherlock Holmes,	
1985, PG-13, ★★★	1998
Zabriskie Point, 1970, R, ★★	1991
Zelig, 1983, PG, ★★★	1998
Zentropa, 1992, R, ★★★	1996
Zorro, the Gay Blade, 1981, PG, ★★	1991

Note: The right-hand column is the year in which the review last appeared in *Roger Ebert's Video Companion* or *Roger Ebert's Movie Yearbook*.

Index

A

Simon Birch, 531; *Truman Show, The*, 618
Carriero, Antonio: *Edge of 17*, 162
Carroll, Rocky: *Best Laid Plans*, 49
Carroll, Willard: dir., *Playing by Heart*, 458
Carson, L. M. Kit: *Hurricane Streets*, 267
Carter, Helena Bonham: *Fight Club*, 193; *Merry War, A*, 367; *Theory of Flight, The*, 593
Carter, Jim: *Merry War, A*, 367
Cartlidge, Katrin: *Claire Dolan*, 107
Casar, Amira: *Marie Baie des Anges*, 355
Casella, Max: *Analyze This*, 18; *Dinosaur*, 143
Cash, June Carter: *Apostle, The*, 27
Cassavetes, Nick: *Astronaut's Wife, The*, 32
Cassel, Seymour: *Rushmore*, 510
Cassel, Vincent: *Elizabeth*, 171; *Messenger: The Story of Joan of Arc, The*, 369
Cassidy, Elaine: *Felicia's Journey*, 191
Castejon, Jesus: *Butterfly*, 90
Castellano, Richard S.: *Analyze This*, 18
Castle, The, 93
Cates, Georgina: *Clay Pigeons*, 108
Catillon, Brigitte: *Artemisia*, 31
Caton, Michael: *Castle, The*, 93
Cattrall, Kim: *Baby Geniuses*, 39
Caught Up, 94
Caulfield, Maxwell: *Real Blonde, The*, 486
Cavanaugh, Christine: *Rugrats*, 504
Caviezel, James: *Frequency*, 205; *Ride With the Devil*, 494; *Thin Red Line, The*, 596
Cecchi, Carlo: *Red Violin, The*, 487; *Steam: The Turkish Bath*, 564
Celebration, The, 95
Celebrity, 96
Center Stage, 97
Central Station, 97
Cervi, Valentina: *Artemisia*, 31
Chabert, Lacey: *Lost in Space*, 334
Chabrol, Claude: dir., *Swindle, The*, 581
Chadwick, June: *Diamonds*, 141
Chaffin, Aimee: *Pariah*, 441

Chahine, Youssef: *Destiny*, 138
Chamberlin, Kevin: *Trick*, 615
Chambers, Emma: *Notting Hill*, 418
Chan, Jackie: *Mr. Nice Guy*, 389; *Rush Hour*, 509; *Shanghai Noon*, 525
Chan, Kim: *Corruptor, The*, 114
Chang, Richard: *Windhorse*, 668
Chang, Sylvia: *Red Violin, The*, 487
Channing, Stockard: *Grease*, 230; *Isn't She Great?*, 282; *Practical Magic*, 466; *Twilight*, 624; *Where the Heart Is*, 657
Chaplin, Ben: *Thin Red Line, The*, 596
Chaplin, Geraldine: *Cousin Bette*, 116
Chapman, Brenda: dir., *Prince of Egypt, The*, 471
Chapman, Lonny: *Nightwatch*, 413
Chappelle, Dave: *Blue Streak*, 70; *Woo*, 675; *You've Got Mail*, 683
Chappelle, Joe: dir., *Phantoms*, 453
Character, 98
Charendoff, Tara: *Rugrats*, 504
Chartoff, Melanie: *Rugrats*, 504
Chase, Cheryl: *Rugrats*, 504
Chase, Chevy: *Snow Day*, 549
Chatman, Glenndon: *Love & Basketball*, 335
Chaykin, Maury: *Enemy of the State*, 177; *Love . nd Death on Long Island*, 336; *Mystery, Alaska*, 404
Chaynne: *Dance With Me*, 124
Cheadle, Don: *Bulworth*, 87; *Mission to Mars*, 380; *Out of Sight*, 433
Che-Kirk Wong: dir., *Big Hit, The*, 56
Chelsom, Peter: dir., *Mighty, The*, 375
Chen, Joan: dir., *Xiu Xiu: The Sent-Down Girl*, 679
Cheng Ping: *Mighty Peking Man*, 377
Chen Wanlei: *Fallen Angels*, 187
Cher: *Tea with Mussolini*, 589
Chereau, Patrice: *Lucie Aubrac*, 343
Cherot, Christopher Scott: *Hav Plenty*, 246; dir., *Hav Plenty*, 246
Cherry, Maj. Fred: *Return With Honor*, 493

Chesnais, Patrick: *Post Coitum, Animal Triste*, 465
Chevrier, Arno: *Agnes Browne*, 6
Chicago Cab, 99
Chicken Run, 100
Children of Heaven, 101
Chill Factor, 102
Chiume, Connie: *I Dreamed of Africa*, 272
Chokling, Neten: *Cup, The*, 122
Cholodenko, Lisa: dir., *High Art*, 251
Chonjor, Lama: *Cup, The*, 122
Choudhury, Sarita: *Perfect Murder, A*, 450
Chow, China: *Big Hit, The*, 56
Chow, Rosalind: *What Dreams May Come*, 653
Chowdhry, Ranjit: *Such a Long Journey*, 572
Chow Yun-Fat: *Anna and the King*, 21; *Corruptor, The*, 114; *Replacement Killers, The*, 500
Chriqui, Emmanuelle: *Snow Day*, 549
Christ, Chad: *Jawbreaker*, 288
Christeler, Charlotte: *Set Me Free*, 520
Christian, Roger: dir., *Battlefield Earth*, 42
Christie, Julie: *Afterglow*, 4
Chrystall, Belle: *Edge of the World, The*, 163
Chukhrai, Pavel: dir., *Thief, The*, 595
Chyna: *Beyond the Mat*, 52
Cider House Rules, The, 103
City of Angels, 104
Civil Action, A, 105
Claire Dolan, 107
Clapp, Gordon: *Rage: Carrie 2, The*, 481
Clark, Blake: *Waterboy, The*, 649
Clark, Bob: dir., *Baby Geniuses*, 39
Clark, Candy: *Niagara, Niagara*, 411
Clark, Larry: dir., *Another Day in Paradise*, 22
Clark, Spencer Treat: *Arlington Road*, 29
Clarke, Graham: *Running Free*, 508
Clarkson, Patricia: *Green Mile, The*, 232; *High Art*, 251; *Playing by Heart*, 458; *Simply Irresistible*, 534
Clash, Kevin: *Muppets from Space*, 394